D1072107

Studies in Victorian Life and Literature

ALSO BY RICHARD D. ALTICK

THE
PRESENCE
OF THE
PRESENT

*Topics of the Day in the
Victorian Novel*

RICHARD D. ALTICK

OHIO STATE UNIVERSITY PRESS

Columbus

The publisher gratefully acknowledges support for this book by the
National Endowment for the Humanities, an independent federal agency.

Library of Congress Cataloging-in-Publication Data

Altick, Richard Daniel, 1915–
    The presence of the present : topics of the day in the Victorian
novel / Richard D. Altick.
        p.   cm. — (Studies in Victorian life and literature)
    Includes bibliographical references.
    ISBN 0–8142–0518–6 (alk. paper)
    1. English fiction—19th century—History and criticism.
2. Realism in literature.   3. History in literature.   I. Title.
II. Series.
    PR878.R4A48   1990   90–34806
823′.80912—dc20   CIP

The paper in this book meets the guidelines for permanence and durability of
the Committee on Production Guidelines for Book Longevity of the Council on
Library Resources.

Printed in the U.S.A.

9 8 7 6 5 4 3 2 1

CONTENTS

PREFACE

LOOKING BACK, I realize that the idea of this book originated many years ago, when I first discovered the pleasures of reading Victorian literature, especially fiction, alongside contemporary documents of Victorian life and the steadily increasing number of works by modern social historians of the period. In the ensuing decades, during which I published a handful of essays on particular aspects of topicality in Carlyle and Dickens, the prospect of a large-scale study of the numerous strands of immediate interest that bound a Victorian novel to readers in its own time still hung low on the horizon, if indeed it was visible at all; but it now appears that I was heading inexorably toward it. The point of no return was passed in October 1985, when I delivered the annual series of Alexander Lectures at the University of Toronto, an occasion that afforded me a timely opportunity to review and organize what I had so far learned. The fact that a noticeable number of my auditors came back day after day, coupled with the interest expressed by my gracious hosts, emboldened me to go on to explore more intensively, and I hope with added understanding, the terrain sketched out in my talks.

At that time, I was well into my fourth year of retirement from the faculty of the Ohio State University. The encouragement I received at Toronto now was echoed on my home grounds. Oblivious of, or wantonly disregarding, the widespread assumption that once an emeritus-hood is conferred, an academic institution ceases to be concerned with its recipient's scholarly pursuits—off the payroll, out of mind—several executives at the university continued to support my research as they and their predecessors in office had done throughout my tenured years. Dean G. Micheal Riley of the College of Humanities generously subsidized the word processing of my typescript. In the post-production stage, as it would have been called had the product been a film or a sound recording, Murray Beja, chair of the Department of English, provided the services of Colleen Hammers, whose indefatigable attention to detail in checking references and quotations, doing other footwork, and finally preparing the index proved her to be the sort of assistant whom every scholar dreams of having by his side. And Peter John Givler, director of the Ohio State University Press, not only suggested but virtually insisted that the book should have many illustrations, the bill to be sent to the press. Anyone who proceeds beyond the Introduction will appreciate how much the text is enhanced by the presence of so many contemporary pictures, which enable us to recreate more confidently and vividly than would otherwise be possible the images of persons, places, and events that a novel's words evoked in the minds of its first readers.

To this friendly consortium, as well as everyone at the press who had a hand in converting the formidable printout into the comeliness of traditional print, go my warmest thanks.

R. D. A.

INTRODUCTION

ON THE VERY FIRST PAGE of the very first issue of *Punch*, dated 17 July 1841, its editors announced the policy that was to govern every word and picture in their weekly paper: "*Punch* . . . makes the most of the present, regardless of the past or future." As things turned out, this purpose reached far beyond the precincts of comic journalism; it was the spirit that dominated Victorian fiction as well. Novelists, too, sought to make the most of the present.

This book explores the effect which that single aspect of realistic technique had upon the Victorian novel, from *Pickwick Papers* to Trollope's last novels and *The Mayor of Casterbridge*. The experiences of everyday life in a rapidly changing world and a sprinkling of large events provided novelists with the materials that would most satisfy their readers' insatiable interest in the contemporary scene and at the same time authenticate a novel's characters and settings, ensuring the ready imaginative assent on the part of readers that every writer of fiction, whether a romancer, a fantasist, or a naturalist, aspires to achieve.

The historical approach to this great body of literature is, of course, not new. The topicality of Dickens's novels, in particular, has been impressively revealed by a succession of scholars inspired by the pioneer work, a generation ago, of Humphry House, Kathleen Tillotson, and John Butt. My own approach to the works of the Victorian novelists at large owes much to their example. In addition, many books have been written about the novelists' handling of broad subjects that were peculiarly characteristic of the times. There have been full-length studies of the presence in Victorian fiction of such social and cultural themes as religion, with special attention to the Oxford Movement, Evangelicalism, and Dissent, of philanthropy, love and marriage, school and university life, and the impact of the industrial revolution. Still other books have been written about individual classes of fictional characters, from Jews and working people to captains of industry and speculative financiers. Even before the feminist movement turned literary criticism in a new direction, there were books about Victorian novelists' treatment of women as heroines, wives, governesses, and even maiden aunts. And alongside Mario Praz's lengthy demonstration of "the eclipse of the hero" one finds books about Victorian dandies and nondandiacal gentlemen.

All such studies are, in effect, attempts to analyze, in the interest of literary understanding, aspects of Victorian social life and culture as they were exemplified in classes or movements or were personified in character types. To adopt a term current in present-day historiography, they show how the Victorian *mentalité*—the common fund of information, opinions, assumptions, and idea- and value-structures—was manifested in the product the novelists set before their public. My aim is somewhat similar, except that instead of tracing sustained themes through a selected expanse of Victorian fiction I have concentrated on the small timely particulars that found their way into the novels' texts—details that are overlooked by, and indeed do not belong in, books that take a broader view of the way the contemporary "real world" was introduced into the fictional fabric.

There is no concise, ready-made term that exactly fits the materials from which novelists create the effect of contemporaneity. The phrase used by a critic of Thackeray in 1856, "minute and characteristic indicia of the times,"[1] is too fancy for everyday use, and, like "temporal details," it can embrace the period color of a past age as well as the present. I have therefore chosen "topicalities," which has the incidental advantage of being one word instead of two, and in doing so have drastically enlarged its scope. Topicalities in the strict sense are references to people, events, or places that were present in the public consciousness, usually but not always as news items at the time a novel was published or within recent memory. The word as I use it also includes what might be called physical topicalities—objects and scenes that were new presences in the contemporary view, the visible results of change.[†] It covers, therefore, all the details of everyday life and knowledge that were characteristic of the Victorian scene. Admittedly, bankruptcy and elections, the subjects of three late chapters, were hardly novelties then. But both figured much more prominently in contemporary life than they had earlier, and their special flavor, including their significance to bystanders (and sometimes participants), was quite different from the one each had possessed in the preceding century.

[†] It is true that people who were too young to remember when railways, for instance, did not exist would not have regarded them as novelties. I have circumvented this difficulty by treating such (relatively) new presences simply as tokens of modernity—things that distinguished the scene a thirty-year-old reader knew in 1860 from the one his grandfather had known at the same age.

Taken all together, these events and objects comprised what can most conveniently be called time-specific details, which are identifiably associated with a given time, in contrast to time-neutral details, which belong to no such specific time. Thus, details of setting and accessories of everyday living, still familiar in Victorian days, that might just as easily have been found in Fielding's novels, belong to the latter category and do not constitute materials that are distinctively Victorian, as time-specific ones do.

Among such details are many that call for explanatory footnotes in edited texts of the novels, glosses that become increasingly necessary and numerous as the Victorian *mentalité* recedes further and further from our ready understanding, and what was once an allusive vocabulary freely shared by writers and readers becomes a private language the key to which has been misplaced. But terse, austerely informative footnotes are dry and drained of any imaginative suggestion, and the fact that they must be printed in isolation from the text, either at the bottom of the page or, more remotely, at the back of the book, inevitably implies that the elucidation they offer is, at best, only peripheral to what the author is saying. Here I have set out to breathe new life into such factual material and to relate it to the texts from which it was artificially detached through the modern exigencies of editing and printing.

Most of the topical subjects explored in these chapters, however, have never figured in the explicatory apparatus of any edition, and rarely in critical interpretations, although they always had lively pertinence to a novel's early readers: the half-legendary figures of Stultz the fashionable tailor and Robins the magniloquent auctioneer, the grievous decay of Vauxhall Gardens as a place of outdoor London entertainment, the messages conveyed by cigar smoking and the wearing of gloves, the social standing of brewers vis-à-vis that of physicians, London neighborhoods and bus riding as silent social discriminants, the trauma of bankruptcy and the consequent selling up of homes, the changing attitudes toward red-haired women and the euphemistic use of the word *auburn* in that connection, the jokey career of the crinoline, the recurrence of catch phrases like "Have not I a right to do what I will with my own?", the humors and corrupt practices of parliamentary elections . . . These and many more topical subjects turn up time and again in Victorian fiction; and though I cite many occurrences in specific novels, I have allowed numerous others to go unnoticed, so that the present-day reader of a Victorian novel may have the pleasure of encountering, recognizing, and interpreting them on his own.

Restoring the historical context requires us to establish what the words in question—for our purposes, the words embodying topicalities—meant to a novel's first readers. While textual editors are interested chiefly in establishing what an author actually *wrote*, a critic on historical principles is concerned with what he *meant* when he drew on the topical vocabulary he shared with his readers. We witness the familiar process by which language constantly presses beyond the confines of the barest, most literal meaning to convey a little more from author to reader than is contained in the arbitrary denotation—the dictionary definition—of the words. Like metaphors and symbols, topical allusions have their own aura of suggestion. To re-create an aura that has faded with the passage of years requires, as it were, a psychocultural leap backward, guided by scholarship and imagination working in harmony, until, so far as our distance in time, place, and social circumstances permits, we see with the initial readers' eyes and react with their minds. In doing so, we follow Ruskin's dictum that we can neither interpret nor criticize works of art—he was writing here specifically of buildings—"until we can fully place ourselves in the position of those to whom their expression was originally addressed, and until we are certain that we understand every symbol" (including, I hope he would have added, topical allusions) "and are capable of being touched by every association which its builders employed as letters of their language."[2]

After many years of criticism that has plumbed the labyrinthine depths of a selected few Victorian novels, it is refreshing and advantageous to return to the surface, to a vantage point from which one can observe the play of topicalities in the most accessible layer of meaning. The topical is often misconceived to be the ephemeral, and Victorian novelists were sometimes chided for their fondness for topical details which not only, as George Henry Lewes maintained, missed the point of serious literary art but conferred on a novel a built-in obsolescence. But when they introduced those topicalities, the possibility of diminished timeliness was furthest from the writers' minds; uppermost was the usefulness of topical references in strengthening a sense of community between themselves and the readers of their own day, not a scarcely envisioned posterity.

The very quality that leads some modern readers to reject Victorian novels as irretrievably dated can be turned into an asset when the texts are newly illuminated by an informed exercise of the historical imagination. It is not quite a paradox to say that, in fact, ephemerality is part of a Victorian novel's permanent worth. An awareness of the topicalities that its first readers discovered and responded to enables us to read, with greater understanding than is otherwise possible, the living book of Victorian fiction.

1
The Glare of the Present

1

TWO REMARKS by Victorian writers of fiction, uttered thirty-eight
years apart, handily bracket the span of time in which the novel came to
be dominated, as was *Punch*, by the resolution to "make the most of the
present." The first is by Harriet Martineau, at that moment (1832) the
successful author of a series of didactic tales illustrating the "truths" of
political economy. Praising the late Sir Walter Scott's demonstration of
"the power of fiction as an agent of morals and philosophy" in his many
romances set in times past, she observed, "The same passions still sway
human hearts; but they must be shown to be intensified or repressed by
the new impulses which a new state of things affords."[1] Much later
(1870), Anthony Trollope, Martineau's junior by only thirteen years but
a member of a wholly new generation of novelists, told an Edinburgh
audience in the course of a lecture "On Prose Fiction as a Rational
Amusement," "The novelist is bound to adapt himself to his age; and is
almost forced to be ephemeral."[2]

The distance in import between the two statements measures what
had happened to the English novel between 1832 and 1870. Martineau
wrote when the Enlightenment concept of universal, essentially change-
less, human nature remained influential, but Scott's practice in his novels, his lavish particularization of the superficialities of dress, scene, and
the accessories of daily living peculiar to their time, challenged its applicability to fictional technique. To recall Dr. Johnson's celebrated metaphor, perhaps there was something to be said, after all, for numbering
the streaks of the tulip. Trollope spoke when the realism which this implies had become established as the de facto, if not necessarily the critically de jure, mode of English fiction, not least the contemporary realism
of his own forty-seven novels.

Timeliness in the midst of timelessness, even at the possible cost of
ephemerality: this was what Victorian readers expected as the genre of

5

fiction was rising in critical and popular esteem, from the marginally respectable level of popular entertainment that its sibling, the drama, had occupied in Shakespeare's time to one on which it overtook poetry as the most widely read kind of current literature. Fictional narrative given credibility by borrowing the topical matter of journalism: this was the quality of the Victorian novel as it was produced for an audience steadily expanding to a totally unprecedented size, thousands of titles every year, millions upon millions of copies bought or borrowed. The variety of this flood of fictional narrative is so great that one ventures any generalization at one's peril. But if any comprehensive characterization can be made with assurance, it is the one bracketed by Martineau's and Trollope's dicta. In the span of years between 1832 and 1870—a span extended in the present book to the time of Trollope's death a dozen years later—novelists attentive to their audiences were increasingly conscious of their obligation to write primarily of the Here and Now.

It was a demand imposed by what was, and remains, one of the most deep-seated qualities of human nature, coequal with the other ineluctable ones Scott revealed in the socially distributed casts of the Waverley novels, from swineherds to barons. No testimony from cultural anthropology is necessary to remind us that the normal mental condition of man is to live in the present that, for better or for worse, surrounds us. This very moment, the pinpoint of time in which these words are written, and the later one in which they are read, is the temporal dimension that rules the little envelope of space in which we live. Most of our waking hours are spent contemplating, or reacting to, the circumstances of this moment. We may call up the past as a refuge from abrasive actuality or the site of emotions recollected, perhaps in tranquillity, perhaps not; and we may thrust our imaginations forward into the future, with hope or apprehension, as the prospect seems to require. But it is only in the present that reasonably sane people keep their home address.

This was true of the earliest man, living perilously and intent only on self-preservation, and it is equally true of human beings today. The scope and acuteness of this abiding sense of the present, however, have varied with the conditions of social life in any given place and time. The popularity of the fictions of Defoe, Richardson, Fielding, Smollett, and Sterne, set as they were in contemporary life, is witness enough to the impact that the sense of the present had on writers and their readers in the eighteenth century. But never had it been as strong as it was to be in Victorian England, as an accompaniment to and symptom of what today's psychological jargon impels us to call an identity crisis. A 440-page paperback anthology published two decades ago (George Levine's *The*

Emergence of Victorian Consciousness: The Spirit of the Age [1967]) collects a
body of contemporary comment from the years 1824–37 alone, a sign
that the process of social self-examination was well under way before
Victoria came to the throne. The phrase "spirit of the age," though it
had often been used by continental writers, notably Montesquieu and
Voltaire, in the two preceding centuries, entered the English vocabulary
only about 1820.[3] Four years later, William Hazlitt adopted it as the title
of a volume of essays.

Writing in the *Examiner* on 9 January 1831, John Stuart Mill described, as succinctly as anyone, the sharpened self-awareness, the sense
of uniqueness, that was part of the intensifying effort contemporary English society was making to define itself and fix its bearings in an increasingly complex and baffling world:

> Before men begin to think much and long on the peculiarities of their own
> times, they must have begun to think that those times are, or are destined
> to be, distinguished in a very remarkable manner from the times which
> preceded them. . . . [M]ankind are now conscious of their new position.
> The conviction is already not far from being universal, that the times are
> pregnant with change; and that the nineteenth century will be known to
> posterity as the era of one of the greatest revolutions of which history has
> preserved the remembrance, in the human mind, and in the whole consti-
> tution of human society.

In December 1831, less than a year after Mill's essay appeared in the
Examiner, Thomas Carlyle wrote in the *Edinburgh Review*, "Never since
the beginning of Time, was there, that we hear or read of, so intensely
self-conscious a Society. Our whole relations to the Universe and to our
fellow man have become an Inquiry, a Doubt: nothing will go on of its
own accord, and do its function quietly; but all things must be probed
into, the whole working of man's world be anatomically studied."

Reading the signs of the times—pondering the social entrails, interpreting the political zodiac—was an exercise that embraced both the
present and the future. The "change" Mill spoke of infused the whole
developing sense of the portentous pregnancy of the moment. The effects of the French Revolution, still reverberating through the first decades of the century; the increasingly conspicuous presence, physical as
well as social and economic, of the industrial revolution; the Romantic
poets' new perspective on the natural world and human life—all converged to make these years the scene of change that struck some as bewilderingly swift (as compared with previous human experience, though
not when measured against many aspects of life in our own time). "The
world," says Mr. Deane in George Eliot's *The Mill on the Floss*, "goes on at

a smarter pace now than it did when I was a young fellow. Why, sir, forty
years ago, . . . a man expected to pull between the shafts the best part of
his life, before he got the whip in his hand. The looms went slowish, and
fashions didn't alter quite so fast: I'd a best suit that lasted me six years.
Everything was on a lower scale" (6.5:345)[†]—and he might have said
"slower," too, or so it seemed as people looked back. Disorientation was
a price one had to pay for living in this world of inexorable change. In
Dickens's *Dombey and Son*, Sol Gills, the nautical instrument maker, says
to Walter Gay as he points to the carved figure of a little midshipman
that is the sign of his old-fashioned business, "When that uniform was
worn, then indeed, fortunes were to be made, and were made. But competition, competition—new invention, new invention—alteration, alteration—the world's gone past me. I hardly know where I am myself;
much less where my customers are" (4:93).

The existing ideologies and institutions of English society were largely
unprepared to deal with these unanticipated fundamental changes and
new directions, which pointed to a future that seemed, according to
one's temperament, either roseate or gray shading into black. Commenting on Sir Henry Holland's italicized observation in 1858 that "we
are living in *an age of transition*"—the idea had by then become a commonplace—Walter Houghton said, "It is peculiarly Victorian. For although all ages are ages of transition, never before had men thought of
their own time as an era of change *from* the past *to* the future."[4] Exac-
erbating this keener awareness was a troubling sense of crisis. The political drama of the early 1830s, in particular, sometimes expressed itself
in terms of idealistic expectations (millennialism) or the opposite, profound fear (apocalypticism), depending on whether one viewed electoral
reform as the high macadam-paved road to Utopia or the quickest way
to a social hell.

Significantly, the Victorian period was the first in English history to
be christened while it was still in progress. The adjective was first used
as early as 1839, when a writer in the *Athenaeum* remarked, "Perhaps the
Annean authors, though inferior to the Elizabethans, are, on a general
summation of merits, no less superior to the latter-day Georgian and
Victorian."[‡]

[†] In these citations, the first part refers to the chapter (and sometimes, as in the case of
The Mill on the Floss, the book or volume) in most if not all editions; the second, at the right
of the colon, to the (volume and) page(s) in the edition used, as listed on pages 807–11
below.

[‡] This citation, in the new supplement to the *Oxford English Dictionary*, antedates by
eleven years the first given in the parent work, E. P. Hood's statement in 1850 that "The
Victorian Commonwealth is the most wonderful picture on the face of the earth."

The age thus became one of communal narcissism, peering ever more closely at itself and becoming equally fascinated and disturbed, and (less often) puzzled by what it saw. The activity was so widespread that self-consciousness eventually became part of the age's image of itself: it was conscious of *being* self-conscious.

In 1829 Carlyle issued one of his earliest proclamations, a call to social stocktaking: "[W]e ... admit that the present is an important time—as all present time necessarily is. ... We were wise indeed, could we discern truly the signs of our own time; and, by knowledge of its wants and advantages, wisely adjust our own position in it. Let us then, instead of gazing idly into the obscure distance, look calmly around us, for a little, on the perplexed scene where we stand."[5] Writers who responded to Carlyle's summons came to constitute a new breed of literary men. Some of the keenest minds of the century devoted themselves to anatomizing the society of their day and refining their conceptions of an ideally healthy, vigorous national community. In the aggregate their works might have borne the comprehensive title preempted by Edward Bulwer for his panoramic 1833 survey, *England and the English*. Their reference was always to the present, the momentarily fixed point against which social change must be measured. The Victorian sages and prophets asked, Where do we stand *now*, in relation to past experience and our vision of a possible future?

Most readers of Victorian fiction were beyond the reach of the sages who sought to shape a philosophical definition of the age they lived in. Unlike Matthew Arnold, they did not have a deep sense of angst, of being overwhelmed by change, or of being oppressed, Wordsworth-like, by a world that was too much with them. But their consciousness was firmly attached to the familiar social environment circumscribed by the present moment, where there was room for neither a past nor a future but only an inferential clock face representing Today. In Podsnap's Weltanschauung, in *Our Mutual Friend*,

> the world got up at eight, shaved close at a quarter-past, breakfasted at nine, went to the City at ten, came home at half-past five, and dined at seven. Mr. Podsnap's notions of the Arts in their integrity might have been stated thus. Literature; large print, respectfully descriptive of getting up at eight, shaving close at a quarter past, breakfasting at nine, going to the City at ten, coming home at half-past five, and dining at seven. Painting and Sculpture; models and portraits representing Professors of getting up at eight, shaving close at a quarter past, breakfasting at nine, going to the City at ten, coming home at half-past five, and dining at seven. Music; a respectable performance (without variations) on stringed and wind instruments, sedately expressive of getting up at eight, shaving close at a quarter past,

breakfasting at nine, going to the City at ten, coming home at half-past five, and dining at seven. Nothing else to be permitted to those same vagrants the Arts, on pain of excommunication. (1.11 : 174–75)

This, according to Dickens, was the constricted frame in which the mid-Victorian bourgeois mind operated. Allowing for his penchant for hyperbole, it was, as far as it went, a reasonably faithful portrait. The kind of literature that was most in demand was the kind that somehow reflected, as newspapers did, the world—including the domestic realm delineated by Podsnap's daily routine—its readers knew best. In the image provided by fiction they learned about themselves. As a magazine contributor commented in 1871, "The education of novel-reading is the only kind of education that many even of the higher and middle-classes can be said to have."[6]

To live comfortably in a present vibrant with change, as the Victorians sought to do, implied a desire to be au courant, thus distancing themselves from the past (even in a period when the various popular styles of public and domestic architecture strove for visual evocations of the past). Thomas Love Peacock, as we shall shortly see, singled out as a characteristic sign of Regency times the popular appetite for fashion, the "lust for novelty," as Neil McKendrick calls it in his description of the birth of the English consumer society.[7] Originally a concern only of the blue-blooded and wealthy—it was no accident that "the fashion" came to designate a particular social class—this fetish of up-to-dateness, embracing costume, furniture, and other consumer goods as well as literature, filtered down to lower social strata. With the greater use of advertising, in newspapers and by other means, to stimulate the demand for the new and the development of the means of mass producing cheaper goods to satisfy it, a wider economic base was created for this conspicuous-consumption market. To this extent, the widespread popular Victorian craving for novelty can be traced to a foible in upper-class life, where most fashion continued to originate.

No one hit off the vogue to be voguish more acerbly than Dickens in *Bleak House*, when he described the array of tradesmen who both shaped and served the whims expressed by the Lady Dedlocks of the "little world" of rank and wealth:

Is a new dress, a new custom, a new singer, a new dancer, a new form of jewellery, a new dwarf or giant, a new chapel, a new anything, to be set up? There are deferential people, in a dozen callings, whom my Lady Dedlock suspects of nothing but prostration before her . . . "If you want to address our people, sir," say Blaze and Sparkle the jewellers—meaning by our people, Lady Dedlock and the rest—"you must remember that you are not dealing with the general public; you must hit our people in their weakest place, and their weakest place is such a place." "To make this article go down, gentlemen," say Sheen and Gloss the mercers, to their friends the manufacturers, "you must come to us, because we know where to have the fashionable people, and we can make it fashionable." "If you want to get this print [i.e., book] upon the tables of my high connexion, sir," says Mr. Sladdery the librarian, "or if you want to get this dwarf or giant into the houses of my high connexion, sir, or if you want to secure to this entertainment the patronage of my high connexion, sir, you must leave it, if you please, to me. . . ." (2 : 59–60)

In an ironic reprise of the theme near the end of the novel, the latest fashionable novelty is news of Lady Dedlock's flight into the snowstorm and the scandalous rumors it has inevitably bred, "for several hours the topic of the age, the feature of the century." Said Mr. Sladdery the librarian, whom we may interpret as representing Charles Edward Mudie, proprietor of Mudie's Select Circulating Library, to a visitor, who may well have been a novelist who specialized in topical subjects:

"Why yes, sir, there certainly *are* reports concerning Lady Dedlock, very current indeed among my high connexion, sir. You see, my high connexion must talk about something, sir; and it's only to get a subject into vogue with one or two ladies I could name, to make it go down with the whole. Just what I should have done with those ladies, sir, in the case of any novelty you had left to me to bring in, they have done of themselves in the case through knowing Lady Dedlock, and being perhaps a little innocently jealous of her too, sir. You'll find, sir, that this topic will be very popular among my high connexion. If it had been a speculation, sir, it would have brought money." (58 : 842–43)

Novelty was a precious commodity in the publishing and circulating-library world, a fact of Victorian life that underlies the whole argument of the present book.

Under the circumstances I have described, the words *new* and *modern* shone like coins fresh from the Royal Mint. As a label of recommendation, *modern* seems, Dwight Culler suggests, "to have entered the language in the first third of the nineteenth-century, probably about the same time that *spirit of the age* became popular"[8]—and, one may add, that *fashionable* acquired a judgmental quality. Descriptively, it had a wide chronological application in nineteenth-century usage, ranging from the original one—"anything not classical or antique," thus embracing virtually the entire Christian era—through the middle ground of "anything from the time after the Middle Ages," to the most restricted sense, "anything associated with very recent times, including the present day." As the years passed, the word usually had this last application, even though the oldest still persisted, as in Arnold's lectures on "The Modern Element in Literature," which began with Augustan Rome. In the titles of novels and in critical discussions of fiction, it is hard to tell the exact weight the ambiguous word was meant to bear. How "modern," in any particular case, *was* "modern"? Post-1800? Post-1850 in a novel published in 1860?

Sometimes both *modern* and *new* were used meretriciously, as language often is in commercial contexts. And they were two-sided, like coins, in another respect: although their conspicuous presence in the marketplace implied that the rage for novelty to which "new" and "modern" products catered was an admirable development, in some quarters there was a revulsion against the euphoric insistence that all that was new was, by that very fact, good. "New men are carrying out new measures, and carting away the useless rubbish of past centuries!"; the words of the Reverend Obadiah Slope as he instructed Mr. Harding on the hard actualities of modern life in his inaugural sermon chilled Trollope's heart as he wrote in *Barchester Towers*:

> What cruel words these had been; and how often are they now used with all the heartless cruelty of a Slope! A man is sufficiently condemned if it can only be shown that either in politics or religion he does not belong to some new school established within the last score of years. He may then regard himself as rubbish and expect to be carted away. A man is nothing now unless he has within him a full appreciation of the new era; an era in which it would seem that neither honesty nor truth is very desirable, but in which success is the only touchstone of merit. . . . We must talk, think, and live up to the spirit of the times, and write up to it too, if that cacoethes be upon us, or else we are nought. New men and new measures, long credit and few scruples, great success or wonderful ruin, such are now the tastes of Englishmen who know how to live. (13:231)

And there was obvious, some would say laborious, irony in Dickens's harping on *new* in *Our Mutual Friend*:

> Mr. and Mrs. Veneering were bran-new people in a bran-new house in a bran-new quarter of London. Everything about the Veneerings was spick and span new. All their furniture was new, all their friends were new, all their servants were new, their plate was new, their carriage was new, their harness was new, their horses were new, their pictures were new, they themselves were new, they were as newly married as was lawfully compatible with their having a bran-new baby. . . . (1.1:48)

A word that had a golden glint in some Victorian contexts was pure brass, as in this one. But however it was used, its ubiquity in connections ranging from consumer vanity products to literary works indicates the way the idea of novelty, and therefore of presentness, permeated everyday thought and hovered near the top of the popular scale of values.

2.

In the first third of the century, books apart, most of the ongoing commentary and debate over current social, political, and economic questions took place in the magisterial quarterly journals of opinion, the *Quarterly*, *Edinburgh*, and *Westminster* reviews, which were addressed to a select, well-educated audience. In Victorian times their initially strong influence was transferred to less ponderous monthly and weekly symposiums on the issues of the day, such as the *Spectator*, the *Saturday Review*, and the *Fortnightly Review*, which appealed to a somewhat larger readership composed of both highbrows and an emerging class of higher middlebrows. The name modern historians have given to this new cluster of thoughtful and often contentious periodicals, "the higher journalism," is most apposite. In them, topicalities—particular cases in point, drawn from the trends and events of the moment—were invoked not only in discussions of current problems but in canvasses of broader and deeper subjects. Applications and illustrations drawn from the news of the day, the materials of the (comparatively) lower journalism, leavened and seasoned the loaf of general principles.

The transition from the old-style intellectual quarterlies to the more brisk, up-to-the-moment weeklies and monthlies reflected a larger, more momentous shift in the very way people thought and read, a change in which newspapers also played a part. As early as 1785 George Crabbe had written, in a poem called "The News-Paper":

> Sing, drooping Muse, the cause of thy decline,
> Why reign no more the once triumphant Nine.—
> Alas! new charms the wavering many gain,
> And rival sheets the reader's eye detain;
> A daily swarm, that banish every Muse,
> Come flying forth, and mortals call them NEWS:
> For these unread the noblest volumes lie,
> For these in sheets unsoil'd the Muses die;
> Unbought, unblest, the virgin copies wait
> In vain for fame, and sink unseen to fate.[9]

Thus, as the eighteenth century neared its end, readers were habitually adding information acquired through newspapers to the traditional body of "literary" (cultural) knowledge an educated man was expected

Benjamin Robert Haydon's *Waiting for The Times, the Morning After the Debate on Reform, 8 October 1831* reflects the unprecedented importance the daily press acquired in those turbulent years as a mouthpiece and molder of public opinion. Painted between 11 October and 4 November and immediately followed by a second version, this picture is an unusual example of instant journalism in the fine arts. It foreshadowed the similar promptness with which novelists were to seize upon topicalities in the years to come.

to possess. But this infiltration of current news into the communal mind then occurred only on a miniature scale. Eighteenth- and early nineteenth-century London and provincial papers had limited circulations. Facilities for news gathering were still primitive, and most papers had less domestic and foreign "intelligence" than advertisements and nontopical editorial matter. Political controversy was carried on more extensively in books and pamphlets—and swarms of satirical prints—than in newspaper columns.

Nevertheless, the incessant excitements of the French Revolution and the ensuing Napoleonic Wars sharpened the demand for news and magnified the importance of the press far out of proportion to its as yet modest size. In 1807 Robert Southey asserted that there were a quarter of a million people in England, out of a total population of some nine million, "who read the news every day and converse upon it." [10] Where he got that figure we cannot tell—it may have been out of thin air—but

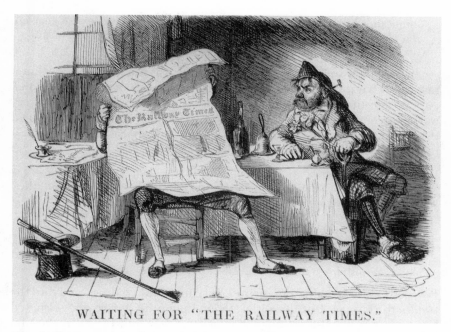

WAITING FOR "THE RAILWAY TIMES."

The "railway mania" of the mid-1840s (see pages 604–6 and 643–45) made
newspapers freshly indispensable, both for financial and political information
that affected hundreds of thousands of middle-class investors and for the promise of full employment for construction workers ("navvies"). This clever echo of
Haydon's painting appeared in *Punch*, 11 October 1845.

his point was that newspapers had begun to play a heightened role in
the nation's thinking. The tumultuous agitation that culminated in the
passage of the First Reform Bill in 1832 made newspapers an absolute
necessity to the amorphous social body that was emerging as the locale
of the new, powerful force of public opinion. John Stuart Mill wrote four
years later:

> A more powerful, though not so ostensible, instrument of combination than
> any of these [he had been discussing "associations" of various kinds, includ-
> ing trade unions], has but lately become universally accessible—the newspa-
> per. The newspaper carries the voice of the many home to every individual
> among them; by the newspaper, each learns that all others are feeling
> as he feels, and that if he is ready, he will find them also prepared to act
> upon what they feel. The newspaper is the telegraph which carries the sig-
> nal throughout the country, and the flag round which it rallies. Hundreds
> of newspapers, speaking in the same voice at once, and the rapidity of com-

munication afforded by improved means of locomotion, were what enabled the whole country to combine in that simultaneous, energetic demonstration of determined will which carried the Reform Act.[11]

But the new social role of the newspaper was not confined to what it said and what it impelled its readers to believe—or not to believe. Newspapers, and the periodical press in general, were seen to affect the very way people thought—indeed, the whole restless climate and pace of their minds. In 1818, in an unfinished "Essay on Fashionable Literature," Thomas Love Peacock commented,

> though all fashionable people read (gentlemen who have been at college excepted), yet as the soul of fashion is novelty, the books and the dress of the season go out of date together; and to be amused this year by that which amused others twelve months ago would be to plead guilty to the heinous charge of having lived out of the world. . . . The newspaper of the day, the favorite magazine of the month, the review of the quarter, the tour, the novel, and the poem which are most recent in date and most fashionable in name, furnish forth the morning table of the literary dilettante.[12]

Peacock's essay remained in manuscript, unpublished, until well into the twentieth century. But the social phenomenon he described was noted by others whose observations did find their way into print. In the first volume of the *Athenaeum*, a pioneer and long-lived cultural weekly (1828–1921), a contributor ("Theodore Elbert, a young Swede") wrote with concern of the current state of the English periodical press and its impact on readers:

> Truth and science are things of trimestrial [i.e., quarterly] immortality; the noblest subjects "which the gods love," "die young" in monthly magazines; and the mind of the nation is amused and kept awake by a succession of little excitements, a constant buzz, and a petty titillation. Great libraries sleep amid their dust, while newspapers are worn to bits by the successive fingers of a hundred readers. These flying sheets, the true pinions of rumour, are borne upon the breeze to every corner and outskirt of society; and myriads who have never dreamed of any principles to which to refer facts, and by which to interpret them, are saturated and overwhelmed with details, and opinions, and thoughts, not born of reason, and feelings which are fancies, the produce and stock-in-trade of the present hour. We live not in the duration of time, but amid a succession of moments. There is no continuous movement, but a repetition of ephemeral impulses: and England has become a mighty stockbroker, to whom ages past and future are nothing, and whose sole purpose and taste is to watch the news.[13]

Anyone who has spent much time in the contemporary records of nineteenth-century English life and thought recognizes that the "young

Swede" exaggerated. Still, there was a kernel of incisive observation at the center of his hyperbole, as subsequent developments proved. Writing almost thirty years later (1855–56, though the book, *The New Zealander*, would not be published until 1972), Trollope made the same comparison and expressed the same complaint, and by that time had much more reason for doing so:

> We have got to think that nothing is worth our notice that cannot be produced, enjoyed, and disposed of with the utmost imaginable despatch. Some short half century since, when our two great quarterly reviews were first established, the literary world conceived that such productions, appearing as they did at every three months' interval, and discoursing as they did on every subject incident to literature, gave sufficient evidence of rapidity of performance. But how is the world changed now! We were amused the other day by a description [in the *Times* for 19 October 1855] of the heavy Edinburgh and its awful period of three months' gyration [gestation?]. What value can be attached to an opinion for the maturing of which a quarter of a year has been found necessary? The world and the world's way of thinking will have changed between the time when the author dipped his pen in the ink, and the far distant day on which his lucubrations see the open air. A quarterly indeed! Are not monthlies stale before they appear, unless indeed they can forerun their own dates? Is not a weekly newspaper so heavy an affair that its present use is confined to ladies in distant counties?
>
> Now-a-days a daily newspaper is the only pabulum sufficiently new, and sufficiently exciting for the over-strained public mind. That too will soon fail to satisfy the craving of the British public for news. It is positively a fact that the London morning newspapers are becoming antiquated. The Times, if it intend to hold its own, must publish itself at least three times a day, and each time with new matter. At every meal we must have our literature reeking wet from the steam press. The tidings of each morning will soon be utterly obsolete and forgotten before the sound of the dinner bell shall have greeted our ears.[14]

In the interim, much had happened. The impatience the *Athenaeum* writer had described in 1828 had become an addiction fed by the incomparably greater supply of news that had become available. The repressive taxes on newspapers as such, along with related ones on advertisements and paper, had kept their prices high and limited their circulation. Looking back from the vantage point of 1859–60 in his novel *Plain or Ringlets?*, Robert Smith Surtees recalled that forty years earlier, a four-page London paper had cost sevenpence; there were then "No family breakfast table-cloth-like sheets, with information from all parts of the globe," transmitted and assembled by the latest technical

With every passing year, the newspaper press was more visible, its offices, delivery carts, and newsboys, a new kind of street sellers, becoming familiar adjuncts to the city scene. As this picture from the *Illustrated London News* for 4 January 1862 shows, the steady growth of the press was a topicality in itself.

devices. Now the crippling newspaper tax had been repealed (1855—the paper tax would follow six years later), and in quick response the newly established *Daily Telegraph* reduced its price from twopence to an unprecedented penny. In the same year that Surtees wrote (1859), an anonymous contributor to the *British Quarterly Review* took particular note of this development:

> Any person who has observed the extraordinary consumption of the *Telegraph*, *Standard*, *Star*, and *Morning News* at railroad stations, on board the Thames steamboats, and in all the leading thoroughfares and public places, must be aware that the circulation of newspapers has undergone not a

Just as the world globe in the background of Phiz's title page for the Library Edition of *Dombey and Son* (1859) symbolizes the far-flung interests of Mr. Dombey's exporting firm, so his absorption in the newspaper, a characteristic Victorian habit, is a token of his indifference to his beautiful and passionate wife.

change, but a revolution. It has not only spread beyond its former limits, but it has created, or absorbed, a wholly new class of readers. The penny journal, containing an ample supply of the usual current news, excellent and reliable foreign correspondence, literary criticisms, often distinguished by greater independence than those of journals of higher pretensions, and leading articles of more than average ability, and, to its honour, we may add, conducted generally with moderation and good taste, has penetrated to thousands of obscure and populous recesses, in which the luxury of a daily paper was unknown before. . . . The population of 1829 may be taken in round numbers at upwards of 16,000,000, and the present population at about 23,000,000. Thus, while the population has increased by less than one half, the circle of newspaper readers has been expanded to more than ten times its former dimensions.[15]

3.

It is particularly noteworthy that this summary appeared in an article on popular fiction, which was now seen as sharing a common readership with the new mass circulation press. The constituency of this readership was very different from the old, which in the eighteenth and early nineteenth centuries had comprised the restricted audience for serious discussions of all kinds of cultural subjects, including essays, poetry, and the leading examples of fiction (the very word *novel* fortuitously suggested the comparatively recent emergence of this literary form).[†] The new audience was composed of men and women, indifferently schooled for the most part, who were developing an appetite for print despite their lack of an education based on the supremacy of Greek and Latin and, outside the curriculum, on the inherited body of "polite literature." The new common denominator was not an ingrained sense of a golden and remote past such as immersion in classical texts, supplemented by an acquaintance with relatively modern belles lettres, especially English and French, would provide to the ideally educated reader. Instead, the whole set of mind among this steadily expanding audience was predominantly topical, deriving its substance from newspapers and other periodicals with a timely cast. In a speech at Manchester in 1850, Richard Cobden remarked, "I believe it has been said that one copy of *The Times* contains more useful information than the whole of the historical works of Thucydides."[16] (Note the limiting word *useful*.) Newspaper reading became a domestic ritual, a daily one in the upper portion of the market, a more or less weekly one in the lower, where leisure for private reading ordinarily was available only on Sunday (though from the days of the *Spectator* and *Tatler* in the age of Queen Anne newspapers were common reading matter at taverns, where in the troubled times a century later, following the Napoleonic Wars, their contents could trigger political arguments any night of the week).

[†] If once active semantic associations that have long since vanished from the vocabulary are still preserved in some obscure warehouse of the communal memory, an explorer will discover that in the seventeenth and early eighteenth centuries *novel* actually meant "news" and *novelist*, a "news-monger" as well as "an innovator, an introducer of something new; a favourer of novelty." (*O.E.D.*)

The proliferation of newspapers in Victorian days bonded readers, now a mass rather than a small, select audience, by providing them with a common base of information, a shared vocabulary centering on topicalities that novelists, among other writers, could rely on as they chose their allusions. They lived—and read whatever they read—in what Francis Palgrave called in 1888 "the glare of the present."[17] They responded most readily, spontaneously, and knowledgeably to intimations of the present moment. Indeed, it was exclusive concentration on topics of the day that made *Punch* and the *Illustrated London News*, whose first issues appeared within a year of each other (17 July 1841 and 14 May 1842), the most characteristic periodicals of their time.

Events described in the fiction of the 1850s and 1860s demonstrate how familiar an appurtenance to daily life newspapers had become by then. They repeatedly furnished novelists with credible plot pivots. The action of Trollope's *The Warden*, for example, was set in motion by Tom Towers's exposé in the daily *Jupiter* of Mr. Harding's sinecure at Hiram's Hospital, the fictional equivalent of the hard-hitting editorializing that often enlivened the pages of the *Times*. As Alfred Austin pointed out in a perceptive article on the sensational school of novelists in the sixties, the daily newspaper was their "invaluable modern ally" as they sought to authenticate their plots, which often strained credulity. "In it," he said, "may be inserted false announcements of births, false announcements of deaths, and false announcements of marriages; and the well-known 'agony column' is the sensational novel in embryo."[18] Thus the plots of both *Lady Audley's Secret* and *Aurora Floyd*, Mary Elizabeth Braddon's two biggest hits, hinged on false press reports—in the former, the incorrect news of the death of Mrs. George Talboys (later Lady Audley), and in the latter, the equally mistaken announcement of the death of the scoundrelly jockey and horse trainer Conyers, whose concealed marriage to Aurora Floyd is the "secret" of that novel. In Mrs. Henry Wood's *East Lynne*, the papers printed a false report of Lady Isabel Vane's death in a railway wreck in France, thus enabling her to assume a new identity behind her scars and blue spectacles. But the news dispatches did not have to be erroneous or the advertisements fraudulent. All four of the newspaper items that periodically recharged the plot of Wilkie Collins's *Armadale* (1864–66)—two in the agony columns appealing for information about a lost person, one an employment advertisement, and the fourth a news story ("disaster at sea")—were genuine in their fictional context. One might think that Collins relied too heavily on the newspaper as a realistic device, but Dickens outdid him at that very moment. The central plot of *Our Mutual Friend* is based on a newspaper sensation that Dickens invented for the occasion. The story Mortimer Lightwood tells over the wine at the Veneerings' dinner table in the novel's opening chapter purports to be a widely discussed subject of the day. "[L]ike the tides on which it had been borne to the knowledge of men, the Harmon Murder—as it came to be popularly called—went up and down, and ebbed and flowed, now in the town, now in the country, now among palaces, now among hovels, now among lords and ladies and gentlefolks, now among labourers and hammerers and ballast-heavers . . ." (1.3:74). It was the news stuff of which novels were made. In *Our Mutual Friend*, not only were the ensuing sensational incidents themselves reported in the press but the newspapers were a frequent means of communication among the characters. They played one role or another on no fewer than nine occasions in the course of the novel.

Since it was widely assumed that most Victorian novel readers were women,[†] the question arises, How well equipped were they to comprehend and respond to the topicalities they encountered? Or did novelists, in this regard, have primarily in mind the men in their audience, who, like Twemlow over his dry toast and weak tea in his stable-flat and in his Pall Mall club, and Podsnap at his place of business (both in *Our Mutual Friend*), were habitual newspaper readers? The popular stereotype of the middle-class Victorian woman as a sheltered, sensitive creature, protected from the chill winds of the day's events outside the home except as they directly affected the domestic fireside, would suggest that women did not read newspapers much. There was Miss Thorne in *Barchester Towers*, for instance, who not only "would not open a modern quarterly [and] did not choose to see a magazine in her drawing-room" but "would not have polluted her fingers with a shred of the 'Times' for any consideration" (22:302); but Trollope makes clear that this aversion was one of her old-maidenly idiosyncrasies. We would not be surprised to find a similar avoidance common among the spinsters of Elizabeth Gaskell's backwater Cranford, who lived by preference a full century in the past, as Miss Thorne did with her devotion to Addison and Steele, Defoe ("the best known novelist of his country"), and Fielding ("a young but meritorious novice in the fields of romance"). It is quite likely that women in the country, and in certain walks of life such as lower-middle-class Dis-

---

[†] No figures seem to exist that would prove or disprove this assumption. On the related question of what proportion of the approximately "7,100 Victorians who could legitimately title themselves 'novelist'"(*Stanford Companion to Victorian Fiction*, ed. John Sutherland [Stanford, Calif., 1989], p. 1) were women, there is more evidence. Of the 878 novelists receiving entries in the *Stanford Companion*, 312, or 36 percent, were women. My own rough analysis of the entries in the relevant sections of the *New Cambridge Bibliography of English Literature* and Michael Sadleir's *Nineteenth Century Fiction* (Cambridge, 1951) arrives at similar percentages, 31 and 35, respectively. So male novelists would seem to have outnumbered females two to one.

sent, had less interest in the day's news than their more urban and worldly sisters. In Margaret Oliphant's *Salem Chapel* (1862–63) Mrs. Tufton, the wife of the retired minister of the chapel, says, "You young men always like the 'Times;' but they never put in anything that is interesting to me in the 'Times'" (41:2.322). If such women read newspapers, it was not the national dailies but their local papers, with their reports of happenings nearby and among people they knew.

Younger women in families with aspirations toward a gentility they did not possess seemingly were not encouraged to read newspapers, an avoidance that may have matured into a lifelong abstinence. When the newly married Bella Wilfer Rokesmith did so in *Our Mutual Friend*, "so that she might be close up with John on general topics when John came home, . . . incidentally mentioning the commodities that were looking up in the markets, and how much gold had been taken to the Bank" (4.5:750), Dickens made of it a "charming" deviation from what was expected of such a young person. She should read *The Complete British Family Housewife*, certainly; but scarcely the *Times*'s financial columns. One could not envision Georgiana Podsnap getting anywhere near a copy of the morning's *Daily Telegraph*.

But in fiction there is much countervailing evidence of women's reading newspapers. As early as 1826, in T. H. Lister's three-decker novel *Granby*, "old Mrs. Printley reads the Morning Post[†] through every day— quite through—every advertisement—stamp-mark and all. It exactly occupies her time from the breakfast hour till three o'clock" (3.13:3.198). Unlike Mrs. Tufton in *Salem Chapel*, the heroine Beatrice, in Julia Kavanagh's novel of that name (1864), "was very fond of the *Times*. It was to her the great world from which she was virtually shut out. She would not weary of its close-printed columns, full of information so complete and so varied. She read the long debates, the prolix accounts of trials, the police reports, the daily news domestic and foreign; and she felt like one who hears far inland the wild roar of the ocean."[19] This must have been a common incentive among women of a certain temperament—a daily-except-Sunday vicarious escape from the doll's house of suppressive domestic life.

By this time, if not earlier, novelists portrayed women reading newspapers for other purposes. Some frankly avowed their delight in reading detailed accounts of murders and the ensuing trials (see Chapter 13 be-

---

[†]Except for the *Times*, no other paper is referred to as often in Victorian novels as the venerable *Morning Post*. From the beginning of the century to the end, it was society's "newspaper of record," which could be depended upon to furnish the most detailed coverage of the activities of the fashionable world. Its presence in the hands of a man or woman in fiction was a favorite initial stroke of characterization, instantly proclaiming where his or her interests were centered.

Two characters in Dickens's fiction illustrate the increase in the number of women newspaper readers: David Copperfield's Aunt Betsey, a representative of the leisured middle class (above); and Miss Abbey Potterson, landlady of the Six Jolly Fellowship Porters dockland public house, in *Our Mutual Friend* (opposite).

low). Others pursued more intellectual interests in the daily papers and the weekly journals of opinion. In Wilkie Collins's *The New Magdalen* (1873) Lady Janet Roy, an elderly independent-minded person, is seen reading the newspaper, and a number of similar characters in Trollope's novels, including the outspokenly reactionary Miss Jemima Stanbury in *He Knew He Was Right*, must have acquired at least some of their armory of strong biases from their reading of topical periodicals. Middle-class women were by no means wholly ignorant of current affairs.

4.

The effect of the common Victorian enthusiasm for reading about the present was felt in every literary genre, most abundantly in fiction but

also in poetry, reaching from the works of the contemporary masters to the popular level of comic verse and theatrical entertainment. This was not a new development. Responding to the incessant religious, political, and literary controversies of the Restoration and the earlier eighteenth century, poems like Butler's *Hudibras*, Dryden's *Absalom and Achitophel* and *MacFlecknoe*, and Pope's *Dunciad* had of course been heavy with topicality, although such works appealed only to the small, sophisticated audience which alone cared about those inner-circle squabbles and was equipped to understand and relish the satirical allusions. Even fewer people, virtually none at all, had access to, let alone comprehended, the intricate and arcane allegorical allusiveness of William Blake, although the ultimate factual sources of his commentary on the revolutions in America and France, the Napoleonic Wars, and the present state of "Albion"—its colonial expansion, its domestic politics—were the newspapers of the day.

The high Romantic ideal of poetry as it developed in the first decades of the new century held that poetry should be concerned with timeless subjects, as befitted a literary form that sought to wrest philosophy from the philosophers and religion from the divines and to give voice to the deepest insights into the nature of man, society, and the universe of which an inspired poet, a *vates*, was capable. But critical doctrine was often quietly set aside when the aftermath of the French Revolution and the ensuing Napoleonic Wars thrust England into a protracted domestic crisis. No major poet of the time was unaffected, and several, notably Shelley and Byron, wrote in response to particular events poems that were both topical in content and propagandist in intention. Most were written in behalf of the liberal-radical cause, but Wordsworth, once a youthful Jacobin and now the only survivor of the Big Five (or Six, if Blake is included), joined the opposite side, inveighing, for example, against the First Reform Bill, as the much younger Tennyson was doing at the same moment. From this point onward, Wordsworth frequently deviated from his practice of memorializing only private occasions in his verse. Among his sonnets were ones on "Steamboats, Viaducts, and Railways" and "On the Projected Kendal and Windermere Railway," both warning of the threatened desecration of nature, specifically the Lake District. Others took strong positions, for or against, on the proposed copyright law to extend protection of authors' literary properties, a short-lived campaign to eliminate the death penalty, the radicals' proposal to institute the secret ballot, the proliferation of "Illustrated Books and Newspapers," which he regarded as a sign of the relentless decline of literary culture in a democratized society, and even the Commonwealth of Pennsylvania's notorious default of its bonds in 1845.

But the Romantic poet who most often drew upon topicalities to—in this case—entertain his readers, rather than persuade them, was Byron. Both "English Bards and Scotch Reviewers" and *Don Juan* are replete with swipes at various literary figures of the day, and the immediate timeliness of the latter poem was enhanced by allusions to new inventions and commodities (Rowland's Macassar Oil, Congreve's rockets for use in sea rescues, Davy's mining lantern, gas lighting, panoramas) and celebrities ranging from the false prophetess Joanna Southcote and a recent swimmer of the Hellespont to Mrs. Elizabeth Fry, the Quaker prison reformer, and the antislavery crusader William Wilberforce.

Poets of the next generation were caught in a bind between the Romantic insistence that their art should be dedicated to philosophical and visionary subjects and the developing Victorian view that they should also instruct, admonish, and exhort the common man or woman, inferentially following Wordsworth's doctrine in his preface to *Lyrical Ballads*, in language they would have no trouble understanding. Tennyson's creative imagination drew most of its sustenance from the past and from old poetry, but as G. M. Young once remarked, his literary character included "a well-marked strain of journalistic adaptability." [20] In the earliest years of his practice, he alluded to such events as the Reform Bill agitation, Chartism, and the Corn Law controversy of the mid-1840s. In *The Princess* (1847) he satirized the women's education movement, and in *Maud* (1855), written against the background of the Crimean War, he introduced a whole string of topicalities to illustrate what he deemed to be the moral degeneration of mid-Victorian society, a vein to which he returned at the end of his life in the utterly despairing "Locksley Hall Sixty Years After." The terms of the poet laureateship required him to be topical on certain occasions, and in his official capacity he produced numerous pieces celebrating national or royal events ("Ode on the Death of the Duke of Wellington," "A Welcome to Alexandra"). Unofficially, he wrote "The Charge of the Light Brigade," commemorating both the criminal ineptitude of military commanders and the wasted heroism of Crimean foot soldiers. In 1852 he wrote a handful of poems on the rough patch in Anglo-French relations that had led to the formation of volunteer rifle brigades to repel the expected invaders.

As a devotee of science and an initial believer in progress in the Victorian style, Tennyson welcomed the most conspicuous example of the new engineering technology, the railway, though the early poem "Mechanophilus" (ca. 1833), in which it is acclaimed along with other such feats, was not published until 1892. It is remarkable for the swaggering imperiousness of the lines

> Dash back that ocean with a pier,
> Strow yonder mountain flat,
> A railway there, a tunnel here,
> Mix me this Zone with that!

—lines which are outdone in the Tennyson canon only by several in a rejected version of "The Gardener's Daughter":

> . . . on the bustling quay
> At eve, when, new-arrived, the packet stilled
> Her splashing paddle wheels, and overhead
> The snoring funnel whizzed with silver steam. [21]

Steeped as Browning was in the obscure records of the past (a quite different one from the past of which Tennyson dreamed), he seldom introduced the English present into his poems until the middle of his career. *Pippa Passes* (1841), however, contains several topical references; the Luigi scene, for example, reflects an early stage of the Italian resistance to Austrian rule, a cause that would never be absent from the Victorian liberal conscience for the next thirty years. "The Italian in England" (1845) is a monologue spoken by another revolutionist, exiled, like Mazzini, in England. Its companion poem, "The Englishman in Italy," ends with a sudden burst of vehement topicality, when the speaker, who had been improvising verses to allay a little girl's fright of the sirocco, invokes another hot wind, of English origin—the agitation, then nearing its climax, to repeal the Corn Laws:

> —"Such trifles!" you say?
> Fortù, in my England at home,
> Men meet gravely to-day
> And debate, if abolishing Corn-laws
> Be righteous and wise
> —If 't were proper, Scirocco should vanish
> In black from the skies!
>
> (lines 286–92)

"The Lost Leader" (1845) deplored Wordsworth's acceptance of a Civil List pension in October 1842 and his appointment as poet laureate in April of the following year. "Bishop Blougram's Apology" (1855), one of the very few poems in which Browning directly commented on the contemporary English scene, contained a number of more or less timely allusions. Blougram's alter ego is Cardinal Wiseman, and in the course of his intellectually adroit "apology" while being interviewed by a brash Fleet Street journalist, he refers to the late but well-remembered society figure Count D'Orsay, Strauss's *Leben Jesu*, Verdi's opera *Macbeth*, the new collected edition of Balzac, "this war" (the Crimean), "our novel hierarchy" (the new Roman Catholic organizational structure in England), and his interviewer's own

> . . . lively lightsome article we took
> Almost for the true Dickens,—what's its name?
> "The Slum and Cellar, or Whitechapel life
> Limned after dark!"
>
> (lines 949–52)[22]

To the extent that "Bishop Blougram's Apology" was an oblique commentary on mid-nineteenth-century religious developments, it was kin to Browning's several major religious poems, "Saul," "An Epistle of Karshish," "Cleon," and "A Death in the Desert," in which real or imaginary characters in biblical times were placed in situations, and given speeches, that anticipated the plight of would-be Christian believers in an age of encroaching doubt. The rebellious ruminations of Browning's Caliban in "Caliban upon Setebos; or, Natural Theology in the Island" bore upon no situation prevailing in the time of Shakespeare, creator of the anthropoid beast in *The Tempest*, but upon a modernity troubled by the rationalistic implications of natural theology. The reflections of a late-seventeenth-century pope especially, in *The Ring and the Book*, were actually directed to the troubled Victorian mind. Browning in fact sometimes admitted his analogical intention. When he sent "The Bishop Orders His Tomb at St. Praxed's Church," set in sixteenth-century Rome, to *Hood's Magazine* in 1845, he called it "a pet of mine, and just the thing for the time—what with the Oxford business, and Camden [ecclesiastical-architectural and -antiquarian] society and other embroilments."[23]

In 1864, Browning took up another topical subject, the current rage for spiritualism, in "Mr. Sludge, 'the Medium'," an ad hominem attack on the momentarily celebrated American adept at the mystery, Daniel Dunglass Home. His deepest immersion in topical subjects then followed, with *Prince Hohenstiel Schwangau, Saviour of Society* (1871), a poem that is largely incomprehensible without a good knowledge of the inflamed state of opinion concerning Napoleon III at that time; *Red Cotton Night-Cap Country* (1873), a rendering of a true-life story of French crime, so close to the facts that Browning had to change the names of all the people involved to avoid a libel suit; and *The Inn Album* (1877), the most densely topical of all Browning's poems and, it may well be, of all poems by major Victorian poets.[24] It was based on an old scandal, the De Ros court case of 1837 (see pages 536–37 below), and in the course of its three thousand-odd lines Browning alluded to subjects as diverse as recent operatic productions in London (*Don Giovanni, Lohengrin*), roller skating, a newly discovered asteroid, Derby winners, the politicians Gladstone and "Dizzy," the Colenso religious controversy, the departure of two Arctic expeditions, a pair of new, widely advertised perfumes, and Apollinaris water, a recently introduced consumer product whose proprietor was George Smith, the publisher, investing the profits he had made from the novels of the Brontës and Thackeray and the *Cornhill Magazine*.

Viewed against the magnitude of both Tennyson's and Browning's oeuvres, however, the incidence of poems with topical subjects or incidental topical allusions is extremely small. Tennyson was faithful to the classics-fed, rurally centered English poetic tradition, and Browning's innovations, much as they affected his contemporary critical reputation, were not notably in the direction of intensified topicality. In the very middle of the century, the result in part of the PreRaphaelite doctrine that painters, liberated from the outworn formulism of the Old Masters, should pay more attention to the modern subject, there was a small effort to steer poets in the same direction, particularly toward the neglected but increasingly conspicuous subject of the city.[25] In *Alton Locke* (1850), Charles Kingsley's Scotsman mouthpiece Sandy Mackaye laid down the principle that "True poetry, like true charity, . . . begins at hame" (8 : 80), and two writers in the PreRaphaelite-oriented *Germ* in the same year, F. G. Stephens and J. L. Tupper, affirmed the same doctrine as applied to both poetry and painting ("the poetry of the things about us; our railways, factories, mines, roaring cities, steam vessels, and the endless novelties and wonders produced every day").

The notion had become something of a commonplace by the time Elizabeth Barrett Browning wrote in her verse novel *Aurora Leigh* (1857):

> Nay, if there's room for poets in this world
> A little overgrown (I think there is)
> Their sole work is to represent the age,
> Their age, not Charlemagne's,—this live, throbbing age
> That brawls, cheats, maddens, calculates, aspires,
> And spends more passion, more heroic heat,
> Betwixt the mirrors of its drawing-rooms,
> Than Roland with his knights at Roncesvalles.[26]

But, with such conspicuous exceptions as Swinburne's rhapsodies on political themes from Mazzini and Gerard Manley Hopkins's poem inspired by a news event in December 1875, the wreck of the steamer *Deutschland*, the new generation of poets eschewed topicalities—which, indeed, may have been one reason why the book-reading audience turned to fiction instead. "Serious" poetry was not concerned with current happenings or the novelties of the physical scene. Instead, the chief locus of topicality in verse remained where it had been since the first years of the century, in comic journalism and its theatrical counterpart. It is possible, indeed, that serious poets avoided topicalities as assiduously as they ordinarily did because such allusions were tarred with the brush of popular entertainment. When Tennyson and Browning momentarily lapsed into timeliness they seemed, outside political contexts, to be doffing their vatic mantle and invading, with unsuitable cap and bells, the turf of the licensed jester. The result was seldom happy, as witness Tennyson's uncertainty of touch when he treated topicalities in the comic spirit, in *The Princess*. The descent from Parnassus to the jocose realm of *Punch* and the pantomime was too steep, the landing too abrupt, to recommend it.

The foremost comic poet of the Regency and earliest Victorian years was Thomas Hood, whose canon, apart from such "romantic" pieces as "The Plea of the Midsummer Fairies," the grim "Eugene Aram," and that early classic of social protest, "The Song of the Shirt," is composed of a staggering collection of topical facetiae, lengthy or short jeux d'esprit reeking with puns and studded with exclamation points. Hood, to make a precarious living, turned himself into a kind of humor machine, programmed to produce the maximum number of easy laughs in any given number of lines. With the exception of numerous treatments of public issues of the day in the form of "addresses" to their respective proponents, Hood's kind of topicalities did not relate primarily to news events. Instead, they took the form of witty improvisations on the trivia of everyday life, "manners" as we would call them. From the perspective of a century and a half, they are closer to the weekly contents of *Punch* than to Byronic comedy. Buried in them are uncountable "in-jokes" from which posterity is excluded. Only Hood's contemporaries would have recognized them and welcomed their humor for whatever it was worth. They are often a comic rendering of situations in common life— petty annoyances, anxieties, prejudices, vanities, fatuities—that were real enough in their time, however pointless they have since become. But they helped establish topicality as an essential ingredient in the Victorian comic tradition.

So did the light verse that Winthrop Mackworth Praed (1802–39) contributed to newspapers, magazines, and some of the coffee-table "annuals" that had a vogue from the 1820s almost to the middle of the century. Much of Praed's verse was reminiscent of the Byron of *Don Juan*, hence accommodated numerous topical allusions; and "The Bridal of Belmont," anticipating Browning's "The Flight of the Duchess," set off its pseudo-medieval trappings with modern touches such as "When Lady Mary sings Rossini, / Or stares at spectral Paganini," "the slang that falls / From dukes and dupes at Tattersall's" (horse auction room), and "a mystery quite as murky / As galvanism to Owyhee [Hawaii], / Or annual Parliaments [one of the six demands of the "People's Charter"] to Turkey."[27]

William Edmonstoune Aytoun and Theodore Martin's *Book of Ballads* "edited by Bon Gaultier" (1845—originally published in *Blackwood's Magazine* and *Tait's Edinburgh Magazine* between 1841 and 1845) was devoted to literary pastiches which often had topical content.[28] "The Lay of the Lovelorn," a parody of "Locksley Hall," referred glancingly to "the injured Daniel Good," a celebrated murderer of the moment, the notorious London magistrate Sir Peter Laurie (see page 603 below), and the evidently wealthy widow of George Shillibeer, the pioneer of London bus transport. Speculation on who would succeed Southey in the laureateship (1843) inspired a series of comic poems in the same volume, recalling both Byron's "English Bards and Scotch Reviewers" and *Rejected Addresses*, a popular collection of parodies of contemporary authors by James and Horace Smith (1812). Prefaced by a poem supposedly by "the great poet who now wears the bays," a Wordsworthian sonnet on himself as laureate—a hit at the venerable poet's reputed egotism—the poems "forwarded to the Home Secretary, by the unsuccessful competitors" included "The Laureates' Tourney" by the Honorable T—— B—— M'A——, "The Laureate" by A—— T—— and "A Midnight Meditation" by Sir E—— B—— L——.

From the verse of Hood and Praed the comic tradition in print flowed to, and through, *Punch* (1841) and its rivals established in the sixties, *Fun* (1861) and *Judy* (1867). In *Fun* appeared William Schwenck Gilbert's *Bab Ballads*, which during their intermittent nine-year run (1862–71) found laughs in such subjects as recent railway accidents, a pan-Anglican synod of British, American, and Colonial bishops at Lambeth (the incongruity of gaitered bishops presiding over savage sees was appreciable), an order from the Chief Commissioner of Metropolitan Police permitting policemen to wear beards as from 3 April 1869, and such toys and entertainments as the Zoetrope, a relative of the kaleidoscope, and Professor Pepper, who was famous for his ghost effects onstage at the Royal Polytechnic Institute and elsewhere.[29]

Meanwhile, there was a parallel tradition in the popular theatre (it is significant that several hard-working comic journalists moonlighted there as scriptwriters). As early as the eighteenth century, the English pantomime had added to its indispensable staples of Harlequin, Pantaloon, Columbine, Clown, and climactic transformation scenes a substantial measure of topicality, taking up, in the words of the modern historian of the genre, "the curiosities and novelties of the day . . . as backgrounds for knockabout humor or as subjects for temperate satire." During the reign (1806–36) of the great Grimaldi, he continues, the pantomime became "an unofficial and informal chronicle of the age. It is possible to see these thirty years . . . recorded in often comically satiric terms which illuminate events and attitudes, technical achievements and artistic movements, major political and social crises, and everyday trivia."[30] From season to season, the writers of pantomime librettos inserted into the sacrosanct framework of the genre current political issues, including the perennially vexed problem of the Corn Laws, late developments in wars and empire-building, and domestic novelties like gas lighting, steamboats, railways, and ballooning. The tone ranged from satire (of the malfunctioning New Poor Law) to compassion (the trials of poverty, as revealed by various humanitarians in and out of government).

From the mid-1820s, two pantomime-derived entertainments, burlesques and extravaganzas, owed much of their popularity to scripts featuring Hood's stock in trade, witty rhymes and puns and topical references. After 1841, they might justly have been called stage adaptations of recent numbers of *Punch*. Together, they flooded the Victorian theatre, particularly at Christmas and Easter, with humorous treatments of news events and the novelties and fads of everyday life. And in a much lower locale of nightly entertainment, taverns and nightclubs, some reasonably decorous and some not, featured, in addition to songs by the assembled drinkers, solo acts that foreshadowed the late Victorian music hall. In *Bleak House*, when the bizarre death of old Krook electrifies the Cook's Court neighborhood, "The Sol [Sol's Arms] skilfully carries a vein of the prevailing interest through the Harmonic nights. Little Swills, in what are professionally known as 'patter' allusions to the subject, is received with loud applause . . ." (39:614–15).

Patter songs reached their apotheosis in the Gilbert and Sullivan operettas, in which major elements of the burlesque, extravaganza, and music hall converged. There were topicalities in all, ranging from dominant themes, as in *Patience*'s satire of the aesthetic movement, to casual but pointed allusions, as when, in the second act of *Iolanthe* (1882), the chorus sang the praises of "Captain Shaw" and the Fairy Queen added, in an aside, "Oh, Captain Shaw / Type of true love kept under! / Could thy Brigade / With cold cascade / Quench my great love, I wonder?" This was a compliment to Captain Eyre Massey Shaw, chief of the London Fire Brigade, who was a regular first-nighter (hence he was addressed in person across the footlights at the first performance) and, more significantly, a well-known man-about-town. Six years later, the song would become extra timely when he was one of the several co-respondents in the sensational Lord Colin Campbell divorce case.[31] In the Savoy operas, as in Victorian popular music at large, the audience's appreciation of the quips and fanciful elaboration of the day's lighter topics, sometimes grafted onto a mythological or fairy story or a plot no more believable than that of an Italian opera, was fed by their acquaintance with newspapers—or, as with Captain Shaw, the latest gossip sheets.

5.

It was in fiction, however, the literary form preferred by the largest number of nineteenth-century readers—"the common people—the people of ordinary comprehension and everyday sympathies," who, said Margaret Oliphant in 1855, comprised "the novelist's true audience"[32]—that

Victorian writers most copiously obliged the demand for modernity of subject. In 1824, Sir Walter Scott had defined a novel as a "fictitious narrative [in which] the events are accommodated to the ordinary train of human events, and the modern state of society."[33] George Moir, in his article on "Modern Romance and Novel" in the *Encyclopaedia Britannica* (1842), declared that the eighteenth century had witnessed a transfer of interest from an old genre to a newer one: "The novel aspired . . . to perform for a reading and refined age, what the drama had done for a ruder and more excitable period; to embody the spirit of the times in pictures at once amusing and accurate, and in the form best calculated to awaken attention and interest in those to whom they are addressed."[34] As the *Prospective Review* summarized the point in 1850, the novel was "the vital offspring of modern wants and tendencies."[35]

This affinity between the novel and the audience's sense of the present was already evident in the best remembered fiction of Richardson, Fielding, and Smollett, as well as in Fanny Burney's light comedies of London social life, *Evelina* (1778) and *Cecilia* (1782). Indeed, to the novelist Clara Reeve, in her early attempt at writing literary history, *The Progress of Romance* (1785), the affinity constituted the very definition of the genre. A novel, she said, was "a picture of real life and manners, and of the times in which it is written."[36] As the eighteenth century neared its end, interspersed with titles appealing to contemporary readers' other strong taste, for Gothic chillers à la Ann Radcliffe, such titles as these could be seen on the shelves of bookshops and circulating libraries:

> *The Recess, or a Tale of the Times* (1783–85)
> *The Two Mentors: A Modern Story* (1783) [Clara Reeve]
> *The New Sylph, or, Guardian Angel* (1788)
> *Slavery; or, The Times* (1792)
> *Susanna; or, Traits of a Modern Miss* (1792)
> *Elinor; or, The World as It Is* (1798)
> *Rosella, or Modern Occurrences* (1798)
> *A Tale of the Times* (1799)

In the years around the turn of the century there was a brief spate of pamphleteering novels. Robert Bage (*Man As He Is* [1792] and *Hermsprong; or Man As He Is Not* [1796]) and William Godwin (*Things As They Are; or the Adventures of Caleb Williams* [1794]) used fictional frameworks to propagandize for the radical political views that the French Revolution had nurtured on British soil. Several women novelists, headed by Maria Edgeworth, turned out didactic tales. In both cases fiction received a strong tincture of contemporary relevance. This quality of timeliness was maintained and heightened as a new subgenre of fiction, the so-called fashionable novel, emerged.[37] Soon abandoning whatever slight pretense of ideology or edification it had borrowed from those other forms, it devoted itself to the presentation of glittering life in high society, a kind of fictionized gossip-column or jet-set journalism. "The fashionable materials for novel-writing," said Charles R. Maturin in the preface to his own novel *The Wild Irish Boy* (1808), "I know to be a lounge in Bond-street, a phaeton-tour in the Park, a masquerade with appropriate scenery, and a birthday or birthnight, with dresses and decorations, accurately copied from the newspapers. He who writes with a hope of being read must write something like this." George Meredith succinctly described fashionable fiction many years later (*Diana of the Crossways* [1884], 17:195) as "rich scandal of the aristocracy, diversified by stinging epigrams to the address of discernible personages." The alternative, somewhat disrespectful name by which it came to be known was launched by William Hazlitt in 1827. Of the work of one practitioner, Theodore Hook, he wrote: "[He] . . . informs you that the quality eat fish with silver forks. This is all he knows about the matter: is this all they feel? The fact is new to him: it is old to them. It is so new to him and he is so delighted with it, that provided a few select persons eat fish with silver forks, he considers it a circumstance of no consequence if a whole country starves: but these privileged persons are not surely thinking all the time and every day of their lives of that which Mr. Theodore Hook has never forgotten since he first witnessed it, viz. that *they eat their fish with a silver fork.*"[38]

The silver fork novel remained in vogue well into the 1840s, when its decline was symptomatized and perhaps hastened by Samuel Warren's broad satire in his interminable novel *Ten Thousand a Year* (1839–41), Catherine Gore's in her own later novels, which are sometimes read as genuine examples of the genre, and Thackeray's parody of her style in "Lords and Liveries," one of his "Punch's Prize Novelists" (*Punch*, 12–26 June 1847). During its heyday the silver fork novel set out, as Michael Sadleir once wrote in the course of a brilliant description of this literary curiosity, "to portray the ordinary lives of contemporary aristocrats; and the greater the detail in which the gilded leisure, foreign travel, the informal talk, the houses, rooms, carriages, clothes and aspirations of these enviable folks were set forth, the more acceptable the 'tale' to a public greedy for just such luxurious precision."[39] This public consisted of readers drawn from the class depicted, who wanted to gaze upon themselves reflected in the novelist's mirror and could afford to buy the books at the high price for which they were sold, and those who rented them from a circulating library for the sake of the presumably knowledgeable descriptions of life in an exotic sphere of society to which they could never reasonably aspire.

Theoretically, silver fork novels could be set in past "fashionable"

backgrounds, the court of Louis XIV, for instance, or that of Charles II,
as some of them were. But the great majority were distinguished by their
contemporaneity, and a fashionable novel could never be mistaken for
an example of the historical romance which flourished at the same time.
The contrast between the two was apparent from the moment the romance, in the masterly hands of Sir Walter Scott, began to appeal to a
far wider audience than ever took up a fashionable novel. In the first
chapter of *Waverley* (1814), Scott explained why he chose the subtitle
" 'Tis Sixty Years Since":

> . . . if my Waverley had been entitled, "A Tale of the Times," wouldst thou
> not, gentle reader, have demanded from me a dashing sketch of the fash-
> ionable world, a few anecdotes of private scandal thinly veiled, and if lus-
> ciously painted so much the better; a heroine from Grosvenor Square, and
> a hero from the Barouche Club or the Four-in-Hand, with a set of subordi-
> nate characters from the elegantes of Queen Anne Street East, or the dash-
> ing heroes of the Bow-Street Office? . . . By fixing then the date of my story
> Sixty Years before this present 1st November, 1805 [when he began to write
> the novel], I would have my readers understand that they will meet in the
> following pages neither a romance of chivalry, nor a tale of modern man-
> ners; that my hero will neither have iron on his shoulders, as of yore, nor
> on the heels of his boots, as is the present fashion of Bond Street; and that
> my damsels will neither be clothed "in purple and in pall," like the Lady
> Alice of an old ballad, nor reduced to the primitive nakedness of a modern
> fashionable at a rout.

A sampling of the lists of novels published in the first third of the
century shows how shrewdly the novelists, or their publishers, devised
titles to meet the rising demand for fiction of "today." (It is noticeable
that some of the titles are hybrids, suggesting at the same time other
types of popular fiction, the Gothic tale and the historical romance.
Their producers were bent on obliging more than one kind of taste inside the covers of a single novel.)

The Orphans of Llangloed. A Modern Tale (1802)
A Modern Instance in Domestic Life (1803)
The World We Live In (1804)
The Modern Griselda: A Tale (1805)
Fleetwood; or, The New Man of Feeling (1805) [Godwin]
Life As It Is; or, A Peep into Fashionable Parties (1807)
The Age We Live In (1809)
The Beau Monde; or, Scenes in Fashionable Life (1809)
Osrick; or, Modern Horrors. A Romance (1809)
The Modern Villa and the Ancient Castle (1810)
Sir Ralph Bigod. A Romance of the Nineteenth Century (1811)

Self Indulgence: A Tale of the Nineteenth Century (1812)
The Modern Kate; or, A Husband Perplexed (1812)
Old Times and New; or, Sir Lionel and His Protégée (1812)
Good Men of Modern Date: A Satirical Tale (1812)
Amabel; or, Memoirs of a Woman of Fashion (1813)
The Modern Calypso; or, Widow's Captivation (1813)
Patience and Perseverance: or the Modern Griselda (1813)
Jane Dunstanville, or Characters as They Are (1813)
The Son of the Viscount and the Daughters of an Earl:
    A Novel Depicting Recent Scenes in Fashionable Life (1813)
The Hypocrite; or, The Modern Janus (1814)
The Prison-House; or, The World We Live In (1814)
Modern Times, or The Age We Live In (1814)
Paired—Not Matched; or, Matrimony in the Nineteenth Century (1815)
The Lairds of Glenfern; or, Highlanders of the Nineteenth Century (1816)
Frankenstein: or the Modern Prometheus (1818) [Mrs. Shelley]
The Maid of Killarney, or Albion and Flora: A Modern Tale (1818)
    [The Rev. Patrick Brontë]
Anastatius: or Memoirs of a Modern Greek (1819)
Ernestus Berchtold, or The Modern Oedipus: A Tale (1819)
Matilda: A Tale of the Day (1826)
Whitehall: or The Days of George IV (1827)†
The Anglo-Irish of the Nineteenth Century: A Novel (1828)
Yes and No: A Tale of the Day (1828)
Women as They Are, or The Manners of the Day (1830)
Mothers and Daughters: A Tale of the Year 1830 (1831)
The New Road to Ruin (1833)
Gale Middleton: A Story of the Present Day (1833)

By this time, critics generally agreed that the novel was the form of literature best suited to the yeasty new day. As Bulwer put it in 1838, "Unquestionably, there is far more food for the philosophy of fiction in the stir and ferment, the luxuriant ideas and conflicting hopes, the working reason, the excited imagination that belong to this era of rapid and visible transition, than in the times of 'belted knights and barons bold,' when the wisest sage had fewer thoughts than a very ordinary mortal can boast of now."[40] Modern life was spinning out materials for fiction at a prodigious clip, and the term "modern tale" was by now familiar in the criticism, literary commentary, and publishers' advertising of the period, as if it were an established category coequal with, and contrasted with, the historical romance. As an umbrella genre, it embraced not only

---

†A particularly ingenious subtitle, suggesting a conventional historical romance—but George IV's reign still had three years to go.

fashionable novels and the Newgate novels (fictionalized lives of criminals) that enjoyed a brief, controversial vogue alongside them, but religious novels (starred in the following lists), Irish tales, tales of the supernatural in contemporary settings, and sensation novels, a class that
turned up here and there in the forties but was given a specific name
and a separate identity only in the early sixties. The titles of representative early Victorian novels, some by authors remembered today, attest to
the ascendancy of the "tale of the times."

> Modern Society . . . The Conclusion of Modern Accomplishments (1837)
> *The Converts: A Tale of the Nineteenth Century, or Romanism and Protestantism
>   Brought to Bear in Their True Light Against One Another (1837)
> The Dowager: or The New School for Scandal (1840)
> Modern Flirtations; or A Month at Harrowgate (1841)
> *St. Antholin's, or, Old Churches and New. A Tale for the Times (1841)
> *Charles Lever; or, The Man of the Nineteenth Century (1841)
> *Bernard Leslie, or, A Tale of the Last Ten Years (1842)
> Jessie Phillips: A Tale of the Present Day (1843) [Frances Trollope]
> Modern Chivalry, or A New Orlando Furioso (1843)
> Coningsby; or The New Generation (1844) [Disraeli]
> *Mary Spencer: A Tale for the Times (1844)
> *Sir Roland Ashton: A Tale of the Times (1844)
> *Hawkstone: A Tale of and for England in 184– (1845)
> *Ridley Seldon, or The Way to Keep Lent. A Tale for the Times (1845)
> Strathern: or Life at Home and Abroad; a Story of the Present Day (1845)
> Tancred: or The New Crusade (1847) [Disraeli]
> *The Modern Unbeliever (1847)
> *Trevor; or, The New St. Francis, a Tale for the Times (1847)
> *Clarendon: A Tale of Recent Times (1848)

By the middle of the century, a novel was virtually assumed to be a
story of the present day. Echoing Clara Reeve's dictum at the distance
of three-quarters of a century, a contributor to *Sharpe's London Magazine* (1861) remarked, "[M]ost of our modern school of critics would accept . . . that the only proper subject matter for the novel was the *manners* of the time in which it was written," thus excluding any novel set in
the past.[41] In 1858 Trollope took the manuscript of *The Three Clerks* to
the publishing firm of Hurst and Blackett. "I hope it's not historical,
Mr. Trollope?" said the firm's manager. "Whatever you do, don't be historical; your historical novel is not worth a damn." Trollope was so taken
with the remark that he used it twice in his novels, besides repeating it
in his *Autobiography*.[42] In *Castle Richmond* (1862) the variant on the manager's statement ran, "It depends very much on the subject, upon the
name, sir, and the subject;—daily life, sir; that's what suits us; daily

English life. Now, your historical novel, sir, is not worth the paper it's written on." And in *The Way We Live Now* (1874–75) Mr. Loiter, the publisher, receives Lady Carbury's proposal to write a novel for him: "Whatever you do, Lady Carbury, don't be historical. Your historical novel, Lady Carbury, isn't worth a ———" (89:717). (In deference to the proprieties, he completed the sentence with "straw".) [†]

The year after Trollope's instructive experience at Hurst and Black-ett's, Thackeray was diverted from writing more historical fiction—*The Virginians*, the sequel to *The History of Henry Esmond*, was nearing the end of its run in monthly parts—when, in signing a contract with Smith, Elder and Company to edit the new *Cornhill Magazine*, he also agreed to write "two novels the scenes of which are to be descriptive of contemporary English life[,] society and manners." [43] His publishers knew as well as Hurst and Blackett's man what would sell in the present market, a judgment that continued to be reflected in the titles of novels:

  Stuart of Dunleath: A Story of Modern Times (1851) [Caroline Norton]
 *Alfred Lennox; or, Puseyism Unveiled, a Tale for the Times (1851)
  Basil: A Story of Modern Life (1852) [Wilkie Collins]
  The Dean's Daughter; or, The Days We Live In (1853) [Mrs. Gore]
  Hard Times, For These Times (1854) [Dickens]
 *Experience; or, The Young Church-Woman, A Tale of the Times (1854)
  Aspen Court: A Story of Our Own Time (1855)
  Two Years Ago (1857) [Charles Kingsley]
  Held in Bondage, or Granville de Vigne: A Tale of the Day (1863) ["Ouida"]
 *Lucretia; or, The Heroine of the Nineteenth Century (1868)
 *Vivia, a Modern Story (1870)
  A Terrible Temptation: A Story of the Day (1871) [Charles Reade]
  Lord Kilgobbin: A Tale of Ireland in Our Own Time (1872)
  The New Magdalen (1873) [Collins]
  A Simpleton: A Story of the Day (1873) [Reade]
  Innocent: A Tale of Modern Life (1874)
  Clytie: A Tale of Modern Life (1874)
  The Way We Live Now (1875) [Trollope]
 *The Wyndham Family, A Story of Modern Life (1876)
  The Haunted Hotel: A Mystery of Modern Venice (1879) [Collins]

 [†] Lady Carbury was no Charlotte Brontë, but it is interesting to note that the latter felt herself incapable of adapting to the public demand. "I cannot," she told her own publisher, George Smith, in 1852, "write books handling the topics of the day; it is of no use trying." (*The Brontës: Their Lives, Friendships and Correspondences*, Vol. 2 [The Shakespeare Head Brontë, Oxford, 1932], 13:14.) But *Villette*, published the next year, and *The Professor* (1857) had contemporary settings.

A Laodicean: A Story of Today (1881) [Hardy]
A Romance of the Nineteenth Century (1881) [W. H. Mallock]
Heart and Science: A Story of the Present Time (1882) [Collins]
Hester: A Story of Contemporary Life (1883)
A Modern Lover (1883) [George Moore]

6.

If there were such a Platonic construct as a typical Victorian novel, its perfect epigraph would be the one Dickens had intended for *Martin Chuzzlewit* but decided not to use: "Your homes the scene, yourselves the actors, here!"—"you" being the novelist's audience at large, mostly middle-class and thoroughly domestic in its everyday way of life. This wide embrace contrasted sharply with the narrow scope of the fashionable novel, which, while it purported to be a faithful picture of contemporary manners, was restricted to portraying life in a small, unrepresentative portion of society, the haut monde. Another, somewhat older subgenre that retained some popularity at the time, the Gothic romance in vulgarized form, had no greater relevance to the everyday interests and experiences of the common reader. That was why Jane Austen's unpretentious but wonderfully observant novels of domestic life were so refreshing to readers like Sir Walter Scott. In his review of *Emma*, published in 1815, he wrote:

> . . . a style of novel has arisen, within the last fifteen or twenty years, dif-
> fering from [the Gothic romance] in the points upon which the interest
> hinges; neither alarming our credulity nor amusing our imagination by
> wild variety of incident, or by those pictures of romantic affection and sen-
> sibility, which were formerly as certain attributes of fictitious characters as
> they are of rare occurrence among those who actually live and die. The
> substitute for these excitements, which had lost much of their poignancy by
> the repeated and injudicious use of them, was the art of copying from na-
> ture as she really exists in the common walks of life, and presenting to the
> reader, instead of the splendid scenes of an imaginary world, a correct and
> striking representation of that which is daily taking place around him. . . .
> We . . . bestow no mean compliment upon the author of Emma, when we
> say that, keeping close to common incidents, and to such characters as oc-
> cupy the ordinary walks of life, she has produced sketches of such spirit
> and originality, that we never miss the excitation which depends upon a
> narrative of uncommon events, arising from the consideration of minds,
> manners, and sentiments, greatly above our own. In this class she stands
> almost alone; for the scenes of Miss Edgeworth are laid in higher life, var-
> ied by more romantic incident, and by her remarkable power of embodying
> and illustrating national [i.e., Irish] character.[+] But the author of Emma

confines herself chiefly to the middling classes of society. . . . The narrative of all her novels is composed of such common occurrences as may have fallen under the observation of most folks; and her dramatis personae conduct themselves upon the motives and principles which the readers may recognize as ruling their own and that of most of their acquaintances.[44]

Jane Austen's death in 1817, said a writer in the *Athenaeum* in 1831, "made a chasm in our light literature, the domestic novel with its home-born incidents, its 'familiar matter of to-day,' its slight array of names and great cognizance of people and things, its confinement to country life, and total oblivion of costume, manners, the great world, and 'the mirror of fashion.' . . . [T]he revival of the domestic novel would make a pleasant interlude to the showy, sketchy, novels of high life."[45] But relief from the silver fork view of the contemporary world as seen through a quizzing-glass first arrived, not in the form of a post-Austenian revival of domestic fiction, but from the unexpected quarter of a young London journalist whose first book was titled *Sketches by Boz Illustrative of Every-Day Life and Every-Day People.*

This collection of Dickens's earliest newspaper and magazine articles was not fiction except insofar as it included some narrative pieces and a large and variegated gallery of character sketches, but its genesis was inseparable from that of *Pickwick Papers* (*Sketches*, first series, appeared on 8 February 1836, and the first number of *Pickwick*, dated April, on 31 March). The enthusiasm both books aroused testified to the rich lode of interest Dickens had opened: he had done for common city life what Jane Austen had done for life on a higher social plane in the country. He was praised for "bringing out the meaning and interest of objects which would altogether escape the observation of ordinary minds" (the *Examiner*), "the romance, as it were, of real life" (the *Spectator*).[46] Writing in long retrospect, John Forster, Dickens's friend and biographer, stressed the exhilarating novelty of this depiction of the contemporary urban scene: "Things are painted literally as they are; and, whatever the picture, whether of every-day vulgar, shabby genteel, or downright low, with neither the condescending air which is affectation, nor the too familiar one which is slang"—a thrust at the comic distortion of London materials in Pierce Egan's *Life in London*, a chronicle of the adventures by day and night of a pair of rakes about town named Tom and Jerry.

---

†Four years earlier, in a review of Maturin's Gothic novel, *The Fatal Revenge* (*Quarterly Review*, May 1810), Scott had praised "Miss Edgeworth, whose true and vivid pictures of modern life contain the only sketches reminding us of the human beings, whom, secluded as we are, we have actually seen and conversed with in various parts of this great metropolis."

"It was a picture," Forster continued, "of every-day London at its best and worst, in its humours and enjoyments as well as its sufferings and sins, pervaded everywhere . . . with that subtle sense and mastery of feeling which gives to the reader's sympathies invariably right direction, and awakens consideration, tenderness and kindness precisely for those who most need such help."[47] The popularity of both *Sketches by Boz* and *Pickwick Papers*, each in its own degree, revealed how strong was the common reader's craving to read about people he was sure existed, because they were all around him.

Although the nineteenth century had no monopoly on "everyday life"—the life actually led by people in any age was "everyday," and stories with a domestic tilt laid in ancient Rome or Savonarola's Florence might equally well have borne titles with such a suggestion—the use of the phrase had a strong implication of modernity: "*our* everyday life." By 1860 a writer in *Fraser's Magazine* could declare without fear of contradiction that "the novel of daily real life is that of which we are least apt to weary,"[48] a consideration that governed the subtitling of novels like Mrs. Gaskell's *Wives and Daughters* (1864–66): *An Every-Day Story*. To some critics, the presence in a novel of a whole cast of believable Victorian men and women was its highest recommendation. Theodore Martin's praise of Thackeray typified the judgment, eventually a critical cliché, that was also applied to George Eliot and Trollope, though decreasingly, as time passed, to Dickens:

> To place before us the men and women who compose the sum of that life in the midst of which we are moving,—to show them to us in such situations as we might see them in any day of our lives,—to probe the principles upon which the framework of society in the nineteenth century is based . . . in a word, to paint life as it is, coloured as little as may be with the hues of the imagination, and to teach wholesome truths for every-day necessities, was the higher task to which Mr. Thackeray [began to address himself in *Vanity Fair*].[49]

The virtual identification of "everyday" with "today" had the desired effect of seeming to guarantee the truth to life of fictional narratives. The same result was sought by the use of words like *fact* and *real life*, which, beginning in the late eighteenth century, came to be seen as often on the title pages of novels as they were heard many years later in the Coketown schoolroom:

> *The Indian Adventure; or, The History of Mr. Vanneck, a Novel,*
>   *Founded on Facts* (1780)
> *Female Sensibility; or, The History of Emma Pomfret. A Novel,*
>   *Founded on Facts* (1783)

Ela: or The Delusions of the Heart. A Tale, Founded on Facts (1788)
Charlotte, or A Tale of Truth (1791)
Louisa Forrester; or, Characters Drawn from Real Life (1799)
*Castle Rackrent. An Hibernian Tale, Taken from Facts and from the Manners
    of the Irish Squires Before the Year 1782* (1800) [Maria Edgeworth]
Tales of Truth (1800)
The Mysterious Visit: A Novel Founded on Facts (1802)
The World As It Goes (1802)
A Picture from Life (1804)
The Cottage of Merlin Vale: A History Founded on Facts (1809)
*Characteristic Incidents Drawn from Real Life; or, The History
    of the Rockinhams* (1810)
Brighton in an Uproar: A Novel Founded on Facts (1811)
Crim.con; a Novel Founded on Facts (1812)
Friends Unmasked; or, Scenes in Real Life Founded on Facts (1812)
Tales of Real Life (1813)
Madelina: A Tale Founded on Facts (1814)
The Cumberland Cottage. A Story, Founded on Facts (1818)
Sophia; or, The Dangerous Indiscretion: A Tale Founded upon Facts (1818)
No Fiction: A Narrative Founded on Recent and Interesting Facts (1819)
Hauberk Hall: A Series of Facts (1823)
*Scotch Novel Reading, or Modern Quackery: A Novel Really Founded on Facts,
    by a Cockney* (1824)
Beatrice: A Tale Founded on Facts (1829)
Romances of Real Life (1829) [Mrs. Gore]
Dramatic Scenes from Real Life (1833)
The Romance of Real Life (1833)
Marmaduke Herbert; or, The Fatal Error: A Novel Founded on Fact (1847)
    [Lady Blessington]
Margaret Graham: A Tale Founded on Facts (1848)
The Steward: A Romance of Real Life (1850)
Willy Reilly and His Dear Colleen Bawn: A Tale Founded upon Fact (1855)
Rachel Gray: A Tale Founded on Fact (1856)

Such asseverations of "truth" in fictional literature were, of course, nothing new; they had always been employed to neutralize the scrupled suspicion with which the puritanical regarded all works of the imagination. Now they occurred in a new literary milieu, but they still were intended in part to quell doubts on the part of readers affected by the Evangelical aversion to fiction. And to the broader minded, they still served to underscore the novelist's realistic intention. As late as 1862–63, Mary Elizabeth Braddon found it advisable to assure readers of her sensation novel *Aurora Floyd* that "my story is a true one,—not only true in a general sense, but strictly true as to the leading facts which I am about to relate" (1:14).

The presence of such assurances (often not substantiated beyond the title page) was always intended to distinguish a novel, which was "true," from a romance, which made no pretense of being so. In early attempts to devise a simple taxonomy of fictional narrative, the romance was regularly considered to be the antithesis of the novel. The dramatist William Congreve, in the preface to his short novel *Incognita: or, Love and Duty* (1692), wrote:

> Romances are generally composed of the Constant Loves and invincible Courages of Hero's, Heroins, Kings and Queens, Mortals of the first Rank, and so forth; where lofty Language, miraculous Contingencies and impossible Performances, elevate and surprize the Reader into a giddy Delight. . . . Novels are of a more familiar nature; Come near us, and represent to us Intrigues in practice, delight us with Accidents and odd Events, but not such as are wholly unusual or unpresidented [*sic*], such which not being so distant from our Belief bring also the pleasure nearer us. Romances give more of Wonder, Novels more Delight.

Subsequent writers boiled down Congreve's definition to its bare bones. (Clara Reeve: "The Romance in lofty language, describes what never happened nor is likely to happen." Scott: "A fictitious narrative in prose or verse; the interest of which turns upon marvellous and uncommon incidents.")

In the cool Enlightenment climate of eighteenth-century England, the romance had been reduced to the status of an entertainment based on despised superstition and of little legitimate interest to a discriminating reader steeped in the classic tradition. When the adjective "historical" was linked with it early in the nineteenth century, however, the word regained much of its old glamour, especially because it was the term regularly used to categorize Sir Walter Scott's fiction. In his novels, there might be—and were—more than a few "marvellous and uncommon incidents," but on the whole Scott's magic made the characters and most of their actions psychologically credible and the historical setting seemingly authentic. So, in that regard, historical romance was a respectable genre in early nineteenth-century England.

Nevertheless, the primary meaning of "romance" persisted, and when, as often happened, it was modified by "Gothic," it suffered another kind of degradation. The true Gothic romance, laden with servings of marvelous and uncommon incidents in the manner of Horace Walpole, Clara Reeve, Ann Radcliffe, and Matthew Gregory ("Monk") Lewis, was debased in the early Victorian form of the penny dreadfuls and shilling shockers that were the common reading fare of errand boys and workingmen: romance for the barely literate underclass. It was against this background of degeneration that a reviewer of a novel by Frances Trollope revived the old distinction, with the romance coming out decidedly second best:

> A romance . . . strives to paint man as a being of passion alone; its view of life is taken by the flare of torches; artificial lights and abrupt shadows— dazzling brilliancy and fathomless gloom—such are the laws of its chiaroscuro, such the effects it loves to produce. Everything it presents is rendered wildly picturesque, mysteriously indefined, by the flickering glare which is thrown over the picture. In short, the Novel . . . appeals to the observant and reasoning faculties . . . ;—the Romance, on the contrary, addresses itself to the imagination alone, and, most often, requires for its full enjoyment an absolute torpor of both observation and reason.[50]

Given the utilitarian, no-nonsense atmosphere of the time, whose cultural heroes included Bacon and Newton, in any such comparison there was bound to be a marked bias against the romance. It was not mere coy depreciation but a shrewd awareness of the prevailing wind of popular taste that led Charlotte Brontë to assure the first readers of *Shirley* (1849) that "something real, cool, and solid lies before you; something *unromantic* as Monday morning" (1:7; italics mine).

The debasement of the word *romance*, however, was by no means complete. To many readers, it still had a powerful residual appeal even though they may have had little taste for the extreme literary attributes it connoted. Despite the seeming oxymoron, the concept of a romantic story of everyday life began to develop as novelists and publishers sought to have the best of both worlds. The word was domesticated to describe incidents and settings in an otherwise sedate novel which removed it, without sacrificing credibility, from the dull predictability of everyday life. In his *Encyclopaedia Britannica* article (1842), George Moir wrote, as if foreseeing the publication of *Wuthering Heights* five years later, "There are many works which we might call novels, in as much as the scene is laid in modern times, and the general course of the incidents is that of every-day life, but in which the even tenor of the story is occasionally broken by scenes of powerful passion, or incidents of a mysterious and terrible character, elevating the composition for the time into the sphere of the romantic."[51] Moir proposed, as a resolution of the inconvenient dichotomy, "the word tale, as a middle term between the others," and this had, in fact, often been used in the titles of novels as a synonym for "story," without the increasingly strong suggestion of contemporaneity that "novel" conveyed.

Dickens in particular sought to redeem *romance* from its disparaging shades of meaning. His often-quoted assertion in the preface to *Bleak House*, that in that novel "I have purposely dwelt upon the romantic side of familiar things," epitomized his lifelong penchant, first evident in *Sketches by Boz*, for justifying the ways of the imagination as enriching, or providing a short-term escape from, humdrum existence.[†] The most "romantic" episode in *Bleak House* was Krook's greasy liquidation by spontaneous combustion, and Dickens's strenuous but unconvincing attempt to prove that this episode had scientific warrant shows how anxious Victorian novelists (except, say, for Bulwer-Lytton on occasion, and Sheridan Le Fanu, who specialized in the supernatural) were to distance themselves from Congreve's "miraculous Contingencies and impossible Performances." Yet although writers of middle-class domestic fiction sought to root their narratives in common experience, from time to time they did as Dickens did, removing the story line from the constraints of everyday life and infusing it with a tincture of unlikelihood, converting "romance" into melodrama, in the manner of such producers of pavement literature as G. W. M. Reynolds.

The practice reached its apogee—or nadir, depending on one's point of view—in the sensation fiction of the 1860s, which specialized in contriving unexpected excitements in a modern setting. In this context, the word *romance* in a title could reasonably be construed as the promise of sensational happenings which were not unnatural but merely exceptional. Thus the much-enduring word was adapted to a new commercial-literary use, and the title of James Payn's popular mystery novel *Lost Sir Massingberd: A Romance of Real Life* (1864) could hardly have been improved upon as far as reader appeal was concerned. It was no wonder that Charles Reade applied the rubber-stamp subtitle "A Matter-of-Fact Romance" to no fewer than three of his novels (*Jack of All Trades* [1857–58], *The Wandering Heir* [1875], and *Single Heart and Double Face* [1882]).

Implicit in the foregoing collage of critical definitions and opinions respecting the advantages of contemporary settings, truth to life, and

---

[†] Wilkie Collins had closely anticipated Dickens's idea, though he did not use the word *romance*, in his "Letter of Dedication" prefixed to *Basil* (1852): "I have not thought it either politic or necessary, while adhering to realities, to adhere to every-day realities only. In other words, I have not stooped so low as to assure myself of the reader's belief in the probability of my story by never once calling on him for the exercise of his faith. Those extraordinary accidents and events which happen to few men seemed to me to be as legitimate materials for fiction to work with—when there was a good object in using them—as the ordinary accidents and events which may, and do, happen to us all."

the representation of "everyday" people and events was the emerging issue of realism, which began to assert its claim to attention alongside such older matters of craft as organic unity, structure, and the handling and disposition of incidents. In its earliest stages, the heart of the problem was the means by which novelists could achieve the highest goal of their art: the portrayal of men's and women's "souls" as, according to current belief, they are, have been, and always will be—in short, truth to the permanent principles of psychological, or "moral," life. Subordinate to such questions was this one: How much detail, and what kinds, should be chosen to create for the ordinary reader the same "truth to life" he was accustomed to find in his daily newspaper or, for that matter, in his everyday experience? The question dated from the beginning of the century, and it originally related to the historical romance: in stories laid in the past, how admissible were circumstantial particulars of costume and setting that fixed them in a certain time and place and not in another? In his "Dedicatory Epistle to The Rev. Doctor Dryasdust" in *Ivanhoe* (1819), which Harriet Martineau may well have had in mind when she made the remark quoted at the beginning of this chapter, Scott made two points. One was that "the great proportion" of details "both of language and manners" that the writer of historical romance had at his disposal was "as proper to the present time as to those in which he has laid his time of action." Time-neutral rather than time-specific, they contributed their due share to the realistic effect. The second observation followed from the first: a writer, like a landscape painter, could achieve that effect by a sparing use of detail, so long as what he did use was faithful to nature. "[I]t is not required," Scott said (anticipating the critics of PreRaphaelite painting half a century later), "that he should descend to copy all her more minute features, or represent with absolute exactness the very herbs, flowers, and trees with which the spot is decorated." Realism, whether in portraying nature or the haunts of men, could be accomplished by small means, but of course the writer must avoid all that were "inconsistent with the manners of the age" or, in a word, anachronistic.

In practice, Scott gave a long leash to his descriptive powers, whose scope included many details "peculiar" to the historical period and society in which he located his plots. Not the least of the attractions his novels had for his multitudes of readers was their pictorial detail, which reminded many of Dutch painting. Some critics applauded this prodigality of visual effect; but even when they questioned the artistic justification of "such matters of mere detail as the description of costume, of equipments, or of furniture," as did T. H. Lister in 1832, in an *Edinburgh*

Review article on the Waverley novels, details served a moderately useful purpose. "Many of these," he wrote, "if we try them on a question of taste, will be admitted to be tedious; but we must view them in another light, and accept them as affording information which we could not have obtained, but at an expense of trouble and research, for which their real value would scarcely compensate."[52]

Other critics, however, refused to advance even this extenuation. The consensus in the 1830s—expressed also by a reviewer of a batch of recent romances in the *Edinburgh Review*[53] and by Edward Bulwer, a practicing novelist, a year later in his essay "On the Art of Fiction"[54]— was most succinctly stated by Carlyle in his review of Lockhart's life of Scott: "Not by slashed breeches, steeple-hats, buff-belts, or antiquated speech, can romance heroes continue to interest us; but simply and solely, in the long run, by being men. Buff-belts and all manner of jerkins and costumes are transitory; man alone is perennial."[55]

From the historical romance, the critical issue leapt to "the novel of today." Silver fork fiction was notorious in its time for its item-by-item inventories of costume which turned their characters into elegantly talkative clotheshorses, and for the recital of viands served at dinner parties which turned some pages into elaborate, French-flecked menu cards. Here, Lister's half-hearted defense of detail on instructional grounds might still apply to readers who were as remote from contemporary fashionable society as they were from the sixteenth-century society of *Kenilworth.* Elsewhere, the educational argument was irrelevant. Nothing was more familiar to Victorian readers than the immediate world in which they themselves lived, in all its commonplace particulars. Novelists were under no obligation to describe for them what they already knew and took for granted. London readers, at least, did not have to be told that the central streets of the metropolis were jammed with horse-drawn vehicles, and few readers anywhere needed to have a drawing room in a middle-class home described for them—they only had to raise their eyes from the pages of the novel they were reading, fresh from Mudie's library. Despite the generous space allowance Victorian novelists enjoyed, for them to have specified what their readers already knew would have been an act of supererogation.

So might have run the argument from common sense, which did not figure noticeably in the debate as critical orthodoxy was applied to the novel, now increasingly held accountable before the bar of received aesthetic theory. The touchstone of acceptable fictional art remained the same: it must concern itself with the essential and permanent, not the superficial and transitory. Particularity of description inevitably inhibited the free exercise of imagination on the part of both author and reader.

Still, the public taste ran strongly toward realistic specification. Whether it was Carlyle's steeple hats and buff belts or the time-specific articles of costume worn by Dickens's shabby genteel or working-class characters, the principle—and the appeal—was the same. The critical orthodoxy of the moment was overwhelmed by the empirical evidence of each year's harvest of new novels, as the following chapters will show.

2

The Topical Novelists

꿎

THE REALISTIC MODE that the novel assumed throughout most of the Victorian years was due largely to the affinity it had acquired with both journalism and its reformist cousin, pamphleteering. Fiction ceased to be the "mere" entertainment it had been in the eighteenth century, when Sir Anthony Absolute denounced the circulating library, whose main stock consisted of novels, as "an evergreen tree of diabolical knowledge," the more diabolical because the books were so readable. Taken more seriously with the passage of every nineteenth-century year, fiction was not only a faithful mirror of everyday life but, on some occasions, a critic of society and its fallible institutions. "Unless he writes with a purpose," wrote the "eminent dramatist" Brown to the "eminent novelist" Snooks in Thackeray's "A Plan for a Prize Novel" (*Punch*, 22 February 1851), "a novelist in our days is good for nothing. This one writes with a Socialist purpose; that with a Conservative purpose: this author or authoress with the most delicate skill insinuates Catholicism into you, and you find yourself all but a Papist in the third volume: another doctors you with low church remedies to work inwardly upon you, and which you swallow down unsuspiciously as children do calomel in jelly."

Thackeray overstated the case, as he meant to do. But beneath the hyperbole there was a core of truth. A thin scattering of novels with some sort of purpose had appeared in the first decades of the century, when the handful of radical "philosophical" novels by Bage, Godwin, and others, which appeared in the 1790s, were succeeded after an interval by the short stories of Harriet Martineau, who sought to popularize a very different strain of political and economic thought: nine volumes under the series title *Illustrations of Political Economy* (1832–34) and four more collected as *Poor Laws and Paupers Illustrated* (1833–34). Their doctrinaire intention conspicuously outweighed simple entertainment, and their success encouraged other writers to set forth their pet theories in fictional guise. This trend seems to have reached its peak about the middle of the century. Eight years after Thackeray called attention to it, David Masson declared, in his survey of British fiction (1859):

> . . . it is in accordance with what has been said concerning the state of Britain and of Europe during the last ten years, that the proportion of Novels of such a kind—Novels made in the service not of "contemporary fun," merely, but also of contemporary earnest—should have been on the increase. Such, at all events, has been the fact; and so, in addition to the increase and extension of a persevering spirit of realism, we have to report, as characteristic of British novel-writing recently and at present, a great development of the Novel of Purpose.
>
> Not only, for example, have we had novels representing duly, as interesting phenomena of the time, Chartism, Socialism, etc., in the sphere of secular politics, and Anglo-Catholicism, Evangelicism [*sic*], Broad Church, etc., in the sphere of ecclesiastical opinion; we have also had novels in which the doctrines distinguished by these, or by other names, have been either inculcated, or satirized and reprobated, separately or jointly—Roman Catholic novels, Anglo-Catholic novels, Evangelical novels, Broad-Church novels, Christian Socialist novels, Temperance novels, Woman's Rights novels, etc. Hardly a question or doctrine of the last ten years can be pointed out that has not had a novel framed in its interest, positively or negatively. To a great extent, tales and novels now serve the purpose of pamphlets.[1]

It is noteworthy that in both Thackeray's and Masson's comments, religious novels are particularly prominent. (Note the number starred in the lists in the preceding chapter.) They were more numerous than any other kind of fiction devoted to a single close group of themes. The genre, as Margaret Maison has written, had many mansions: "'theological romances', 'Oxford Movement tales', novels of religious propaganda designed to disseminate a variety of forms of Christian belief, and assorted spiritual biographies in fiction, including converts' confessions of all kinds, from the apologies of ardent agnostics to the testimonies of Catholic 'perverts'."[2] Some of these novels were homiletic, some cautionary-exemplary, some propagandist-polemical. By no means all dealt with, or were even tinged by, doctrinal issues; many were concerned with the church in its various relations with society, including charity, education, domestic habits and morals, and public morality. Most were located in the present, and even when they were not (a fair number were set in the first Christian centuries), their popularity was due to their supposed pertinence to contemporary affairs.

Masson's breakdown of mid-Victorian fiction into so many categories reflects the most impressive evidence we have of the way novelists responded to contemporary religious, political, and social movements, remaking the literary genre into a truly "public" art. (Eleven years later, Trollope, in his lecture "On Prose Fiction as a Rational Amusement," offered a simpler, and in some respects different, taxonomy: "All the habits and ways of our domestic and public lives are portrayed to us in novels. We have political novels, social-science novels, law-life novels, civil-service novels, commercial novels, fashionable novels—and I am told that novels even of clerical life have been written.") [3]

Never before had the novel been so tightly and extensively involved in the events of the day. It was not simply a matter of a new didacticism appearing to replace the one that had languished, Harriet Martineau's excepted, after the first years of the century. Though it is hard to tell which came first—the profusion of fiction or the multiplication of its categories—there was a positive connection between the two. When ideological concerns of various sorts increasingly animated the public mind, the art of fiction was prepared to express and debate them in imaginative frameworks. Fiction, in short, met the social needs of the hour.

The overtly partisan novels that Thackeray and Masson had in mind represented the marriage of fiction and topicality in its purest form; their very raison d'être stemmed from the concerns of the moment. But nearly all have sunk without a trace, disappearing as their respective subjects lost their timeliness and controversial pertinence and leaving no more than a handful of works by major Victorian authors that can be called either novels of purpose or, more specifically, novels of protest. And to categorize even these is to risk overstating the presence of the argumentative content. Disraeli's *Sybil*, Gaskell's *Mary Barton*, Dickens's *Hard Times* and *Bleak House*, for example—the products of a single decade—are much more than enlarged pamphlets; perhaps the only novels with any claim to remembrance that can be so described are Kingsley's *Yeast* and *Alton Locke*. More typically, the social theme of a novel, its topical center, appears only intermittently, as part of a larger pattern.

On the whole, Dickens was as topical, using the word in its broadest application, as any other novelist of his day. He was, in fact, the first prominent member of his profession after the silver fork school to fully realize the commercial worth of subjects that appealed to the newspaper- and novel-reading public's appetite for contemporaneity. He was also typical, insofar as the specifically argumentative strain in his novels bore the same proportion to its overall topical content as it did in Victorian fiction at large. By temperament he was primarily a journalist, and a reformer only sporadically.[†] But by merging the two roles or, more pre-

---

[†]The most judicious summary of the issue remains Humphry House's: "He seemed topical to thousands: he was not too topical for them to see the point, nor too advanced to

cisely, assimilating the second into the first, Dickens did more than any-one else in his time to establish realism as the dominant mode of fiction. From his beginnings as a newspaperman whose usual beats enabled him to observe several large aspects of contemporary life, including the de-bates in the first reformed Parliament, then (briefly) as the editor of *Bentley's Miscellany* and the newly founded *Daily News*, and between 1850 and 1870 editor of two popular weekly papers, *Household Words* and *All the Year Round*, to which he frequently contributed, from professional necessity he had to keep his finger on the pulse of the moment.

Another powerful impulse toward topical realism came from Thack-eray, whose attachment to the present moment, or to a kindred social scene in the well-remembered past, was fixed by the circumstances of his career. Like Dickens, he had begun as a journalist (after a false start as a painter), but as a literary and art critic, not a roving reporter. Most important, he was a prolific contributor to *Punch*, which was dedicated to providing a weekly rundown of current events, foibles, and person-alities seen from a facetious, or sometimes an incisively serious, angle. Any member of the *Punch* circle was, by definition, a professional ob-server of the passing scene. It was scarcely accidental that Thackeray's best series of *Punch* pieces, "The Snobs of England, by one of them-selves" (28 February 1846–27 February 1847, collected in volume form the next year) was to *Vanity Fair*, his first full-scale novel, whose first numbers in January and February 1847 they overlapped, what *Sketches by Boz* had been to *Pickwick Papers*. Both "Snobs" and *Sketches* were in-tensely topical, much more so than reading them in collected form re-veals, because Thackeray excised some parts of the *Punch* text of "Snobs" just as Dickens had sweepingly revised his newspaper feature articles before they were gathered as *Sketches by Boz*. [‡]

Even before Dickens and Thackeray began their careers as novelists, two other authors, politicians in this case, were emerging from their ap-prenticeship as writers of society fiction to steer the early Victorian novel

---

have the public conscience on his side. Detached now from his time he may seem more original and adventurous than he was; for then he was only giving wider publicity in 'in-imitable' form to a number of social facts and social abuses which had already been rec-ognized if not explored before him. He shared a great deal of common experience with his public, so that it could gratefully and proudly say, 'How true!'; he so exploited his knowledge that the public recognized its master in knowing; but he also shared with it an attitude to what they both knew, and caught exactly the tone which clarified and reinforced the public's sense of right and wrong, and flattered its moral feelings" (*The Dickens World*, pp. 41–42).

[‡] In future citations, the issue of *Punch* in which the relevant piece appeared will be followed by a reference to its location in John Sutherland's well-annotated edition of *The Book of Snobs* (its book-form title, abbreviated as *BS*).

in the same direction, toward a firmer connection with current affairs and the world beyond elite society. Edward Bulwer's *Pelham* (1828) and *Paul Clifford* (1830) had timely elements, and Benjamin Disraeli's trilogy of political novels (*Coningsby* [1844], *Sybil* [1845], and *Tancred* [1847]), although most of their characters and some of their settings were indigenous to the fashionable novel, were also novels of ideas, in which the exposition of political and social issues from the viewpoint of the Young England movement was carried on partly through Disraeli's authorial voice and partly through guided conversation. The presumably judicious aristocrats and politicians who engaged in this always civilized discourse were as up-to-date in their opinions as the editorial writers on the daily and weekly newspapers. These novels were not as strictly confined to the drawing rooms of Mayfair mansions and country estates as their late Regency precursors had been; in *Sybil*, Disraeli introduced his readers to the smoky and otherwise malodorous atmosphere of Wodgate (Willenhall, near Wolverhampton), as "realistic" a setting as a novelist could find.[†]

Meanwhile, Bulwer had been alternating between historical romances and fiction set in the present day, notably *Ernest Maltravers* (1837) and its sequel, *Alice, or The Mysteries* (1838), pretentious novels of ideas in which the leading characters discoursed interminably on moral systems, metaphysics, and aesthetics derived from German idealistic philosophy. This kind of windy, nebulous fiction pleased neither reviewers nor public, and to recoup his critical and popular fortune Bulwer-Lytton (as he was called after 1843) was impelled to resuscitate other novels he had been working on years before and had then abandoned. The results were *The Caxtons*, published in 1848–49, *My Novel* (1850–53), and *What Will He Do With It?* (1857–59). Here Bulwer-Lytton sought to win his audience back by freely inserting topicalities into stories of domestic life.

During these same early and mid-Victorian years—his first book of fiction, *Jorrocks' Jaunts and Jollities*, was serialized in the *New Sporting Magazine* in 1831–34 and thus predated *Pickwick Papers* (1836–37), and his last, *Mr. Facey Romford's Hounds*, was published in 1864–65, simultaneously with Dickens's last completed novel, *Our Mutual Friend*—Robert Smith Surtees was making a far less appreciated contribution to the widening stream of realistic fiction. None of his novels were best-sellers,

---

[†]At the end of his life Disraeli wrote what amounted to an amber-colored reprise of his political trilogy. In *Endymion* (1880), he adopted the same system of chronological precision, noting dates, as the narrative progressed, from the Reform Bill agitation of 1830–32 down to the Crimean War. Once again he recreated the conversations of political leaders on subjects of then current interest; how far they also expressed Disraeli's thinking as of 1880 is another matter.

and Surtees never received a tithe of the critical attention that came the way of his fellow novelists with more serious aims. But in sheer quantity of time-specific details the total body of his fiction surpasses its better known rivals. While primarily "sporting novels," a dismissive critical label that accounts for their relative obscurity in their own time, books like *Hillingdon Hall* (1843–44), *Ask Mamma* (1857–58), and *Plain or Ringlets?* (1859–60) have matchless value as brightly colored and particularized depictions of the immediately contemporary social scene, not the hunting field alone.[4]

Although Surtees took a satirical view of his slice of middle-class life, mainly in the country, as a fox-hunting squire in County Durham he felt no reformist impulse, and in that respect there was a gulf between him and two authors of protest novels at mid-century, Elizabeth Gaskell and Charles Kingsley. Gaskell, the wife of a Unitarian minister in Manchester, was only beginning her writing career, but she already had a seasoned novelist's awareness of the commercial value of topical subjects, even though she was of two minds about her own employment of them in her novel of labor-management conflict, *Mary Barton*. A few days before the Chartist populist-radical movement reached its climactic show of strength on 10 April 1848, she revealed to her publisher the same eagerness to cash in on the subject of the day that had led Browning three years earlier to recommend "The Bishop Orders His Tomb at St. Praxed's" to his own publisher. "I hope," she wrote Edward Chapman, "you will not think me impatient in expressing my natural wish to learn when you are going to press, as I think the present state of public events may be not unfavourable to a tale, founded in some measure on the present relations between Masters and their work-people." But in July, writing again to Chapman, she tried to evade the suspicion of opportunism. "I hardly know what you mean by an 'explanatory preface,'" she said, apparently in response to his suggestion that she take that means of specifically relating her novel to the burning issue of that tense year. "The only thing I should like to make clear is that it is no catchpenny run up since the [subsequent] events on the Continent have directed public attention to the consideration of the state of affairs between the Employers, & their work-people."[5]

At the same moment that *Mary Barton* appeared in book form (it was not serialized), a portion of Charles Kingsley's *Yeast* ran in the monthly numbers of *Fraser's Magazine*. In that novel and *Alton Locke* (1850), Kingsley resumed the exposé of working and living conditions in the wage-earning portion of the population that Disraeli had helped to begin in *Sybil*, taking one of the two halves into which Disraeli had divided the nation and subdividing it into the rural poor (*Yeast*) and the urban

Birket Foster's drawing (*Illustrated London News*, 4 March 1848) captures the excitement with which Britain awaited the latest news of the revolutionary events in France at a time when the native working-class radicals, the Chartists, were preparing their much-feared march on Parliament. This was the climate in which, a month later (2 April), Elizabeth Gaskell alerted her publisher to the fortunate topicality of her novel, *Mary Barton*.

poor (*Alton Locke*). In *Two Years Ago* (1857), Kingsley wrapped up a whole package of contemporary themes: the urgent need for sanitary reform—a particular hobbyhorse of his—as dramatized by a cholera epidemic in a West Country fishing village, the Crimean War, American abolitionism, the latest stage of the Oxford movement, the nascent art for art's sake doctrine, and London literary life with its penchant for lionizing popular authors.

While social problems preoccupied Gaskell and Kingsley, an obscure newcomer to authorship sought to capitalize on another issue of the day, the perennial Irish question. Anthony Trollope's first attempts at fiction, *The Macdermotts of Ballycoran* (1847) and *The Kellys and O'Kellys, or Landlords and Tenants: A Tale of Irish Life* (1848), marked the virtually unnoticed debut of a novelist who was to become the most comprehensive portrayer of contemporary middle- and upper-class life. He was the only major novelist to set his scenes almost entirely in the immediate present. Only one of his forty-seven novels (*La Vendée*) had a historical setting, in revolutionary France. Two others were slightly distanced from the present, *Lady Anna* (England in the 1830s) and *The Bertrams* (published 1859, set in the 1840s).

After Dickens died in 1870, Trollope had only two rivals as a novelist specializing in realistic narratives laid in the present day. (Mary Elizabeth Braddon and Margaret Oliphant were at least as prolific, but although they shared Trollope's audience they do not, for good reason, share his late-twentieth-century fame.) Wilkie Collins and Charles Reade were known chiefly as novelists who traded on the public's appetite for stories featuring suspenseful plots, exciting incidents, crime or sin in respectable society, and always, by preference, with a present-day English setting. Collins had an acute sense of the size and expectations of the readership that awaited such products; his article on "The Unknown Public" in *Household Words* (21 August 1858) is a locus classicus on the subject. Like Bulwer-Lytton, he found it in his interest to jettison the historical romance—his *Antonina, or The Fall of Rome* (1850), had been a critical though not a commercial success—in favor of a "tale of the times." "Many subjects in Modern History," he explained in the original dedication to *Basil* two years later, "I knew were open to me. . . . But, on this occasion, the temptation of trying if I could not successfully address myself, at once, to the readiest sympathies and the largest number of readers, by writing a story of our own times, was too much for me. So I wrote this book."[6] Whether or not he fully shared Dickens's reformist zeal, Collins saw the commercial value of combining a contemporary realistic setting with a social theme that lent itself to melodramatic treatment. "What brought good Wilkie's genius nigh perdition?" asked

Swinburne in an often repeated couplet, and answered, "Some demon whispered—'Wilkie: have a mission!'"[7]

Collins's reputation suffered in the latter years of his working life, partly because he was too obviously writing potboilers and partly because, as with Dickens, an influential element of critical opinion held that a work of fiction was no place for propaganda. Reade, by contrast, had no great literary reputation to lose. Even more than Collins, he was regarded as a producer of fiction that was more journalism than art. This was Reade's own choice. Catering to the mass public's perverse and insatiable desire to know the worst about the world they lived in was, to him, the only road, albeit a low one, that a writer-for-profit could take:

> I write for the public, . . . and the public don't care about the dead. They are more interested in the living, and in the great tragi-comedy of humanity that is around and about them and environs them in every street, at every crossing, in every hole and corner. An aristocratic divorce suit, the last great social scandal, a sensational suicide from Waterloo Bridge, a woman murdered in Seven Dials, or a baby found strangled in a bonnet-box at Piccadilly Circus, interests them much more than Margaret's piety or Gerard's journey to Rome. For one reader who has read "The Cloister and the Hearth," a thousand have read "It Is Never Too Late to Mend." The paying public prefers a live ass to a dead lion.[8]

No other well-known novelist of his time harbored so irresistible an urge to pamphleteer; the contumacious Reade built whole long novels around selected flagrant reproaches to Victorian smugness. Concluding *Put Yourself in His Place*, he wrote: ". . . I have drawn my pen against cowardly assassination and sordid tyranny: I have taken a few undeniable truths, out of many, and have labored to make my readers realize those appalling facts of the day, which most men know, but not one in a thousand comprehends, and not one in a hundred thousand *realizes*, until fiction—which, whatever you may have been told to the contrary, is the highest, widest, noblest, and greatest of all the arts—comes to his aid, studies, penetrates, digests, the hard facts of chronicles and blue-books, and makes their dry bones live" (11.2:161). Too often, however, his reformist impulses and his bent for sensationalism got in each other's way—or collaborated—and if some discriminating readers were affronted by the clumsiness of his plotting and the slapdash coarseness of his prose, others were put off by his messages, delivered bluntly and at intolerable length. Nevertheless, no Victorian novels were more closely "of the moment" than some of Reade's productions.

3
Forms and Sources

1.

MUCH NEWLY PUBLISHED FICTION was tied to the moment by more than the allusive text. Fully two-thirds of the novels represented in this book appeared first as serials, either in separately published monthly (less often, weekly) numbers or in magazines, which meant that each installment was displayed on the same newsagents' counters that held the latest newspapers. Such fiction gained topicality by osmosis, as it were. The physical juxtaposition was a familiar token of the fact that fiction readers were also readers of newspapers and magazines whose minds were filled with the happenings and issues of the day. The current segment of a novel, moreover, was, by very virtue of the way it appeared, "timely." Serialization made the progressing fiction a recurrent event in time, and therefore a topicality in itself, presenting new matter from week to week or month to month—a current event in the root meaning of the adjective, as contrasted with book publication, which was a single event at one moment of time. Timeliness, in this sense, was built into serialized fiction and guaranteed for the length of the run. No Victorian consumer product was fresher than a just-issued number of a novel.

What a boon this was to novelists who valued topicalities as a means of enhancing the air of modernity that they sought to create! It enabled them to get a reference to an item of current interest into print at the earliest possible moment, rather than embedding it in a text which, if first given to the public in completed book form, might not be read for many months, perhaps years, after composition had begun—an interval during which a topicality might well have lost its initial interest. The existence of the part-issue practice, indeed, may well have rendered topicalities more attractive to novelists than they would otherwise have been.

On 24 February 1848, the deposed French "citizen king," Louis Philippe, fled from revolutionary Paris in that most bourgeois of vehicles, a hansom cab—a touch of farcical relief that tickled onlookers on the English side of the Channel and for a moment took their minds off the looming Chartist menace at home. Among the vicarious spectators by way of the newspapers was Thackeray, who, writing the April number of *Vanity Fair*, said of the abdication of Becky Sharp's maid after her mistress and Lord Steyne had been surprised by Rawdon Crawley, "Fifine went off in a cab, as we have known more exalted persons of her nation to do under similar circumstances" (55:527). (In this instance, Thackeray had a visitation of prophetic topicality. No sooner was this number in the hands of readers than cabs-for-hire again figured [10 April] in a home-produced anticlimax, when the Chartist leaders, their great protest march having collapsed, delivered their bulky petition to Parliament in a procession of such vehicles.)†

In February 1861, inmates at the Chatham Convict Prison, dissatisfied with their treatment, erupted in a bloody riot. Dickens was then writing *Great Expectations*, and in the installment that appeared in *All the Year Round* on 13 April, Pip, the narrator, with whom Dickens shared his aversion to the mollycoddling of jailbirds, described his visit to Newgate with Wemmick: "At that time [many years in the past], jails were much neglected, and the period of exaggerated reaction consequent on all public wrong-doing—and which is always its heaviest and longest punishment—was still far off. So, felons were not lodged and fed better than soldiers (to say nothing of paupers), and seldom set fire to their prisons with the excusable object of improving the flavour of their soup" (32:280). At the end of that same year (14 December), the Prince Consort died at Windsor, and in the installment of *Aurora Floyd* that appeared in the next number of *Temple Bar* (January 1862), Mary Elizabeth Braddon wrote of "that great sorrow at Windsor" in "the dull light of the December day," "when rough omnibus-drivers forgot to blaspheme at each other, and tied decent scraps of crape upon their whips . . ." (5:51).

The fact that preliminary publication in installments kept the text fluid before it could harden in the form of a complete book enabled novelists to adjust their stock of topicalities as circumstances suggested. Most timely references in the original part-issue were retained in the subsequent bound volume(s), and some, not appearing in the serializa-

---

†On a later occasion, Thackeray went a step further, breaking out of the chronological framework of *The Newcomes* for a moment in order to involve one of his characters in a recent topicality. In part 12 (September 1854), set in the early 1840s, he reported that "Lady Ann Newcome . . . signed the address to Mrs. Stowe, the other day, along with thousands more virtuous British matrons" (38:1.300). This was an address of welcome from the Committee of the Anti-Slavery Society, presented at a soirée at Willis's Rooms on 25 May 1853. "By far the greatest number of guests present," said the *Times* next day, "were ladies," one of whom, if she followed up her signature with her presence, every reader of *The Newcomes* would have recognized.

tion, were added then. Others that had lost their immediate interest were deleted. Unless the two texts of a given novel are systematically compared—an operation still to be performed for most novelists, including Trollope, Wilkie Collins, Reade, and Surtees—there is no way of knowing how often either of these kinds of textual alteration occurred. A collation of the *New Monthly Magazine* version of Surtees's *Mr. Sponge's Sporting Tour* (January 1849–April 1851) with the first book edition (1853) reveals that while most of the topicalities in the original text survived, a few were subjected to Surtees's revising pen.[†] Two were related to the "railway mania" that had lately convulsed the English financial scene with its accompanying fraudulence (see pages 604–11 and 643–48 below). Originally, Surtees wrote at one place, "As our friend Jawleyford was stamping about his study anathematising a letter he had received from the solicitors to the Doembrown and Sinkall Railway, calling upon him for 'another thousand' . . . ." In the book, he brought the fortunes of that enterprise up to date by substituting the melancholy words, "informing him that they were going to indulge in the winding-up act" (25:155). Earlier in the serialized narrative had appeared another, even more direct reference to the scandal: "with such utter disregard of method and regularity that it would puzzle even those eminent accountants, Messrs. Jay, Quilter, Crosby, & Co., to comb them out into anything like shape, as much as the celebrated Eastern Counties Railway accounts did after they had been 'cooked' at Albert Gate." Surtees's readers would have instantly recognized the allusion: the high-flying, ledger-adjusting railway financier George Hudson lived in an ostentatious mansion in that fashionable neighborhood. In volume form, however (14:71), Surtees condensed the passage, omitting the allusions to the Eastern Counties Railway accounts and to Albert Gate; Hudson's paper empire had collapsed in the interim, and he no longer lived at that address.

At still another place, Surtees simply substituted a fresher example. In the magazine version (July 1849) the horse fancier Jawleyford reads a volume of Macaulay's history of England, hot from the press. But in the book version, he reads Disraeli's *Life of George Bentinck*, an even more recent publication (1852) and one much better suited to his interests, because Bentinck, who had died four years earlier, was a leading figure in racing circles and the owner of a famous stud.[‡]

[†] In this case, there was an intervening edition—thirteen monthly parts, illustrated by John Leech (1852–53)—which complicated the textual history. In the present book, unless otherwise stated, all topicalities are cited from a novel's text as it appeared in volume form.

[‡] The same revisionary process can be studied in the case of at least two of Surtees's other novels. *Jorrocks' Jaunts and Jollities* in its volume form (1838) contained timely references that were not—could not have been—present in the serialized version of 1831–34.

The sustained currency of a serialized novel was often singled out by critics as a distinctive part of its appeal, strengthening as it did the author's prized rapport with his readers. As the *Illustrated London News*'s obituary of Dickens in 1870 put it:

> It was just as if we received a letter or a visit, at regular intervals, from a kindly observant gossip, who was in the habit of watching the domestic life of the Nicklebys or the Chuzzlewits, and who would let us know from time to time how they were going on. There was no assumption, in general, of having a complete and finished history to deliver; he came at fixed periods merely to report what he had perceived since his last budget was opened for us. The course of his narrative seemed to run on, somehow, almost simultaneously with the real progress of events; only keeping a little behind, so that he might have time to write down whatever happened, and to tell us.

The completion of *The Newcomes* in the summer of 1855 elicited several such appreciations. "It is a proud privilege," wrote Whitwell Elwin in the September *Quarterly Review*, "to have been able, month by month, for nearly two years, to interweave [Thackeray's] fictions into the daily existence of his readers, and bring his mimic characters into competition with the living world, till forgetting they were shadows, we have followed their fortunes, and discussed their destinies and conduct as though they had been breathing flesh and blood."[1]

This form of publication also increased the suspense with which a Dickens or a Thackeray imbued his plots. In book form, a reader was kept guessing (in extreme cases, on tenterhooks) only as long as it took him to speed from the first page to the last. In a serial that appeared at measured intervals, he had no choice but to wait. Another reviewer of *The Newcomes*, in the *Spectator*, stressed the intensity of the reader's involvement as the story unfolded:

> What can we say that has not been said over hundreds of dining-tables, in countless drawingrooms, students' chambers, under-graduates' rooms? Has not London for months been in consternation lest Ethel should waste her fair youth and noble heart in fruitless repentance, and that benevolent auntism we all respect so much, owe so much to, but so shudder at as a fate

---

A remark on an early page, "this was in the old Poor Law time" (3:47), referred to the passage of the so-called new law in 1834, and "the late reign," mentioned in connection with a steamboat named the *Royal Adelaide* (7:108), became "late" only in 1837, when William IV died and Queen Adelaide was made a widow. When *Handley Cross*, first published as *Gin-and-Water Hunt* in the *New Sporting Magazine* from March 1838 to August 1839, was reissued in monthly parts from March 1853 to October 1854, the text was updated with allusions to such topics as "Mr. Dickens's household words," the periodical founded in 1850 (11:85), Bloomerism (1851: see pages 308–11 below) (62:438), and *Uncle Tom's Cabin*, 1852 ("Vy you'll be vot they call a man of 'all vork,' a wite nigger—a wite Uncle Tom in fact!") (15:110).

for our favourites in life and books? Was there not even a moment when a single hint about the importance of "baptismal regeneration" made the profane throw the number violently to the other end of the room, as a vision rose of Venus-Diana with shorn tresses and close white cap, her bow straitened to a ferule, her cestus cut up for the personal adornment of her Anglican director, and all her little loves, all the bevy of nymphs, turned into smugfaced choristers and demure village schoolmistresses? Has not the failure of the Bundelcund Bank hung over town with a prescient gloom, only lightened by the consciousness that Colonel Newcome's nobility of heart and mind could never be insolvent, come what run upon it there might? Has not Rosey Mackenzie's removal, by childbirth or any natural cause, and, that wanting, by poison administered so as to save Clive's neck and reputation, been almost prayed for in the churches? Were we not all present at the case of "Newcome, Bart. v. Lord Highgate," and did we not clap our inward hands with keen applause as the defendant's counsel painted, as only that distinguished mover of juries can paint, the character and brutal conduct of the injured husband?[2]

The timeliness of part-issue was further enhanced when a novelist correlated his progressing narrative with the seasons. Beginning with the sixth part of *Pickwick Papers*, Dickens gave his readers what purported to be a veracious account of the Pickwickians' activities in the month just past. The shooting scene appeared in the October 1836 number, the description of Christmas at Dingley Dell in the January 1837 number, and, in that for March, Sam Weller's laborious effort to compose a valentine for his Mary, along with—ironic juxtaposition!—the trial of the widow Bardell's suit against Pickwick for breach of promise. The chronology was even coordinated with the annual sequence of law terms. Thus *Pickwick Papers*, whose explosive success in serialized form was chiefly responsible for widespread adoption of the practice in the ensuing years, had the effect of a fictionized newspaper, a retrospect of recent occurrences in an imaginary world.[3] Once in a while, other novelists worked appropriate seasonal allusions into their serialized text, as did Surtees in the December 1850 installment of *Mr. Sponge's Sporting Tour*: "Mr. Sponge thought over the horrors of Christmas. . . . Why, the very idea of the bills—many, doubtless, headed, 'To bill delivered for 1849,' if not, indeed, 'for 1848–9'—would be enough to drive hilarity miles and miles away in the distance. And yet to that dread season, dear reader, we are all rapidly approaching! The thought of its horrors caused Mr. Sponge to stick spurs into the chestnut, and hurry the horse home to Puddingpote Bower" (59:461).†

---

† In his edition, John Sutherland has pointed out the close coordination of the seasons in the serialization of "The Snobs of England," a practice that spilled over, of course, from the other timely textual and pictorial contents of *Punch*. "Illustrations show characters

The newspaperlike quality of part-issue fiction was maintained in still another way, one that connected the imagined world with the real world of the consumer. Dickens's publishers, Chapman and Hall, at once realized the value of the *Pickwick* numbers as an advertising medium. Like other nineteenth-century publishers, they customarily added at the end of their books a few pages advertising other titles on their list, and they inserted such house advertisements in *Pickwick*, beginning with the first part. The true innovation occurred when, in an early number, paid advertisements for other products, including those of rival publishers, began to appear. The advertising leaves were continued, their number varying from eight to thirty-two pages, in all of Dickens's subsequent part-issued novels.[4]

Among the first products to be promoted in the *Pickwick Advertiser*, as the added pages were called, were the already celebrated ones of a firm named Rowlands, their Macassar Oil for the hair and Kalydor for the skin. Rowlands remained among the most faithful buyers of space in the supplements of part-issue fiction. Like Dickens, they saw the advantage of tying in their texts with the monthly date of publication. During the London season Macassar Oil was recommended to all who "court the GAY AND FESTIVE SCENES especially during the Dance or the heated atmosphere of crowded assemblies." When the party moved outdoors and "the RIDE, and DRIVE and the recurrence of the summer solstice invite[d] the full display of FEMALE BEAUTY," it was Kalydor that would be indispensable for "neutralizing the effects produced by temporary exposure to solar heat upon the neck, arms, and face." At the seaside, however, Macassar Oil had to be resorted to once again, to counteract the "dryness of the hair" and its "tendency to FALL OFF."

Another heavy advertiser, in the monthly numbers of fiction as well as in other media, was the cheap-clothing firm of E. (for Elias) Moses and Sons (see pages 237–39 below). Bound into four issues of *Martin Chuzzlewit* were small booklets recommending Moses garments, and Moses regularly bought either the inside front or back wrapper of succeeding Dickens novels, the headlines being followed by substantial blocks of promotional prose or, more arrestingly, a stanza or two of doggerel verse. Sometimes Moses' copy, like Rowlands', was keyed to the season: "March Gales," "April Showers," "May Flower," "Spring

skating in winter, gardening in autumn. Public events like the Royal Academy Exhibition, Whitsun excursions, and pantomimes are appropriately introduced. Universities and the law are discussed in term time. Politics are absent from the work while Parliament is in recess and very prominent while it is sitting. Social season is, like parliamentary session, reflected as it happens. And when the season finishes the snob makes the traditional trip to France in September, and then goes into the country" ([209]).

ESTABLISHED 1814.

By the time this advertisement appeared, in the *Our Mutual Friend Advertiser* for August 1864, Rowlands' line of cosmetic preparations had been energetically promoted for half a century. Their respective qualities were especially familiar to the readers of the monthly numbers of Dickens's and Thackeray's novels.

and Summer Dress," "Christmas." Some attention-grabbing captions referred to topical events, as in the *Bleak House* numbers: "New Empire" (part 5, July 1852: clothes for emigrants); "What a Stir" (part 7, September: on the approaching general election); and "Table-Moving" (part 17, July 1853: the craze for spiritualism and table rapping, a new import from America).[†] Still other Moses captions attempted tie-ins with the

---

[†]Table rapping and other forms of spiritualism are alluded to several times in Victorian fiction. In *Two Years Ago* (1857) Kingsley says of the heroine, Grace Harvey, "Happy for her that she was in Protestant and common-sense England, and in a country parish, where mesmerism and spirit-rapping were unknown. Had she been an American, she

novel's text, as if they had an informant in the printer's office who gave them advance information about the contents of the next number: "Anti-Bleak House" (part 1, March 1852: clothes that protected against foul weather, such as Dickens described in the memorable opening pages of the number); "A Suit in Chancery and a Suit out of Chancery" (part 4, June: as the punning title suggests, a lumbering jeu d'esprit, seeking to divide clothes into two categories).

Other advertisers in the *Bleak House* numbers promoted goods especially appropriate to the novel. In parts 11 and 15 (January and May 1853, Partridge and Cozens, law stationers at 127–28 Chancery Lane, presented a long price list of their stock of "Solicitors' Office Papers" and supplies, including wax, red tape, "Writing Parchments" (Indentures, ruled by machine; Bills and Answers; Memorial Skins, "various sizes kept ruled"; "Plain Parchment," various sizes, unruled), steel pens, and so forth. This inventory coincided with the one Dickens had described in the beginning of chapter 10 (part 3, May 1852) as the stock in trade of Mr. Snagsby, whose shop in Cook's (actually Took's) Court, Cursitor Street, was only a few hundred feet away from the real-life Partridge and Cozens'. The Reverend Mr. Chadband's oiliness, to which Dickens called special attention in part 6 (August), may have been due in part to his use of either Rowlands' Macassar Oil or Milton's Hair Lubricant, both of which had already appeared in the advertising leaves. And in part 2 (April), Thomas Harrison and Son's Chrystal Spectacles, which promised to alleviate "the many painful sensations in the eyes frequently complained of by ladies when at Needlework, Music, &c," had particular pertinence to the large number of characters in the novel who wore spectacles, monocles, or quizzing glasses, or flourished lorgnettes: not, oddly enough, the woman who one would think needed glasses most, Mrs. Jellyby, bent over her copious domestic and foreign correspondence relative to Christianizing the natives in far-off Borrioboola-Gha, nor even her ink-stained amanuensis daughter Caddy, but certainly Tulkinghorn, Conversation Kenge, Mrs. Quale, Mrs. Rouncewell, Mrs.

---

might have become one of the most lucrative 'mediums;' had she been born in a Romish country, she would have probably become an even more famous personage" (10:166–67). John Mellish, in Braddon's *Aurora Floyd* (1862–63), "was not a spiritualist; and unless one of the tables at Mellish could have given him 'a tip' for the 'Sellinger' or great Ebot [two racing fixtures], he would have cared very little if every inch of walnut and rosewood in his house had grown oracular" (13:121). And in *Great Expectations* (1860–61), Pip says of himself, upon Uncle Pumblechook's finding tar water in the brandy bottle, "I moved the table, like a Medium of the present day" (4:60)—probably referring to Daniel Dunglass Home, the flamboyant spiritualist whom Browning excoriated in "Mr. Sludge, 'the Medium.'"

Pardiggle, Mr. Jellyby, Inspector Bucket in disguise, Sir Leicester Dedlock, his cousin Volumnia, and Mr. Turveydrop—an impressive list, for
a single novel, of sufferers from myopia or astigmatism.[†]

<h1 style="text-align:center">2.</h1>

In the minds of a novel's first readers, no topical allusion stood in
absolute isolation. Each was subtly affected by its place in each reader's
accumulated store of information and its penumbra of associations, and
how it got there. Daily newspapers, popular weeklies, middlebrow
magazines, highbrow quarterly reviews, books on topics of the moment,
controversial pamphlets: whichever particular ones were the source of a
given novelist's knowledge, a certain number of his readers knew a few
or many, and whatever pertinent knowledge they possessed would have
imperceptibly governed the impact a particular allusion had. To recreate
what it precisely meant in an individual case would be beyond the powers of the most formidable research, even though the raw materials
abound in the printed sources that would have animated, perhaps clarified or enlarged, the reader's response.

Speculation, however, can be a bit more firmly grounded when its
scope is limited. It is axiomatic (or should be, now that so-called intertex-
tuality is among the leading concerns of critics) that to appreciate the
full flavor and contemporary meaning of any novel serialized in a magazine one must read the surrounding contents, in order to duplicate, so
far as possible at the distance of more than a century, the way in which
the physically proximate content of nonfiction affected the first readers'
response to the fiction. All fiction serialized in magazines inescapably
took on coloration from the pages that adjoined it, issue after issue. Even
before magazine serialization became as common as it was in the mid-
Victorian period, quasi-fictional sketches and topical satires underwent
the same process. Reading Thackeray's "Jeames's Diary" (*Punch*, 2 August 1845–7 February 1846) and "The Snobs of England" (*Punch*, 28
February 1846–27 February 1847) in volume form, one is deprived of
much of the meaning each had for those who followed it week by week.
As Thackeray wrote each installment, he knew it would appear in a paper whose specialty was timeliness, usually with a humorous slant; from
one viewpoint it might be said that his contributions offered a running
commentary on, and illustration of, some of each issue's adjoining con-

---

[†]Though not unknown in earlier centuries—Shakespeare alludes to them several
times—spectacles had never been as common as they became in Victorian times. Their
very profusion made them something of a novelty.

tents. Thus those two serials acquired extra meaning from their original matrix, including the drawings; their original essential spirit was that of the paper in which they appeared.

The fact that "The Snobs of England" overlapped the publication in monthly numbers of *Dombey and Son*, which ran from October 1846 to April 1848, encourages us to believe that the men and women who simultaneously read both had a liberal education in snobbism in its many varieties and ramifications. Thackeray more than once anticipated Dickens's characters and themes, as in his more than usually excoriating portrait of the "military snob" typified by Lieutenant-General the Honourable Sir Granby Tufto, K.C.B., K.T.S., K.H., K.S.W., &c., &c. (*Punch*, 2 May 1846; *BS*, 39–40). Meeting the apoplectic-complexioned Major Joey Bagstock a few months later in *Dombey and Son* (part 2, November 1846), readers could hardly have helped comparing the two. Thackeray's Tufto was unquestionably the more repulsive, the more immoral: alongside him, explosive Old Joey was almost innocuous, despite his marriage-market machinations in behalf of Dombey. This is one response readers could have had; on the other hand, carried-over memories of Tufto might well have darkened Dickens's portrait of Bagstock. Similarly, when people read of the disastrous dinner party at the Dombeys', they would have been tempted to add details from Thackeray's description of like events in his chapters on "Dining Out Snobs" and "Dinner-Giving Snobs Further Considered" (*Punch*, 29 August and 5 September 1846; *BS*, 98–105). In effect the *Punch* series prepared readers for those passages in *Dombey and Son* in which Dickens did his own anatomizing of the snob mentality as Thackeray broadly defined it.

Most periodicals that survived beyond their first few years acquired steady nuclei of readers who became attuned to their individual atmosphere—the spectrum of their interests, biases, perspectives—and thus brought an already conditioned mind to the reading of new serials in their pages. Dickens's *Household Words* served as a running commentary on topical themes found in the novels he published between 1850 and 1859. The truly intent reader in the 1850s would have been obliged to buy the paper every week if he wished to receive Dickens's full topical message. Sometimes the relevant articles appeared before the echoing passage in a novel, sometimes afterward. In the March 1850 number of *David Copperfield*, published a month before the first issue of the paper, Dickens devoted several pages to deficiencies in that venerable but now degenerate institution, Doctors' Commons. In *Household Words* for the following 23 September, he ran an article by himself and his subeditor, W. H. Wills, documenting the charges he had made in the fictional context.

In similar fashion, regular buyers of *Household Words* were prepared in advance for the appearance of *Hard Times* in its pages from 1 April to 12 August 1854. Large-scale strikes had been in the news for several years, and in the issue for 11 January 1851, for instance, Dickens had published an earnest admonition to striking railwaymen. This wave of labor unrest was climaxed by the biggest strike of all, that of the Preston weavers, between September 1853 and April 1854. Dickens printed at least two articles dealing specifically with the Preston situation, one of which was his own exercise in on-the-spot reporting ("On Strike," 11 February 1854). Such pieces, along with articles in other periodicals, prepared readers for the imminent novel, which not only acquired coloration from the other contents of *Household Words* but depended on those contents to make points, or elaborate on them, as Dickens was disinclined to do in the novel itself.

Hard Times therefore represented a special blend of fiction and journalism. Joseph Butwin has written:

> Each installment seems to enjoy both the status of a leading article and the special identity of a signed novel inserted into the journal. The reader who meets the novel in the journal comes away with a quite different impression of the meaning of the fiction than the reader of the hard-cover volume called *Hard Times for These Times*. In *Household Words* it is simply *Hard Times*. The reader of the journal did not need the expanded title. Every article appeared under the sign of novelty; all was news, all was timely. Having read the installment, the reader continues into other reports, equally timely. . . . Other novels that invoke the facts of historical or contemporary life do not necessarily encourage verification. *Hard Times*, by virtue of its format, does. The fiction leads the reader to the threshold of fact; the threshold is easily crossed within the same journal.[5]

A number of *Household Words* articles, by Dickens and others, on jobbery, red tape, speculation, and the current disorganized state of politics, prepared readers for *Little Dorrit* or supplied background color and commentary during its serial run from December 1855 to June 1857. Among these was a series of three Arabian Nights pastiches by Dickens himself, "The Thousand and One Humbugs" (21 April–5 May 1855), in which, with less than his usual felicity, he expostulated on the defects of such institutions and persons as the Howsa Kummauns, the Grand Vizier Parmarstoon, Scarli Tapa and the Forty Thieves, the Penshunlist, and Jobbiana. In the issue for 30 April 1856, just as part 6 of *Little Dorrit* was appearing, he inveighed against the "inability of the commissions [of inquiry] to attach blame for the Crimean disasters"—a whitewashing of the governmental agencies he was pillorying collectively in the form of the Circumlocution Office. When, after a quarrel with his publishers,

Dickens replaced *Household Words* with *All the Year Round* in 1859, he continued to relate what he wrote in his novels to what he printed in his paper. While *Our Mutual Friend* was appearing in monthly parts (May 1864–November 1865), he was running a series of articles by M. R. Mason on the feverish speculation that could make an investor a plutocrat one day and a pauper the next.[6]

But while Dickens's periodicals provided the closest links between his fiction and actuality through the accident that the editor was simply the novelist wearing another hat, they were, of course, not the only current publications that documented his, or anyone else's, fiction. The satire of the Court of Chancery, present from the first chapter of *Bleak House* almost to the last, drew its factual basis from a variety of printed sources. Some readers would have remembered articles that had appeared two years earlier (1850) in the *Westminster Review* as well as *Household Words* itself, and the lawyers among them would have seen an article on "Chancery Abuses and Reforms" in the *Law Magazine* for August 1850; a follow-up article, with special pertinence to the hopeless situation of Gridley, one of Chancery's many victims, appeared in August 1852, coincidentally with the sixth number of *Bleak House*.[7]

The *Times* and several other London dailies gave readers much greater detailed information on current topics that popular weeklies like Dickens's provided only sporadically and in simplified form. In a ground-breaking exercise of the kind, John Butt and Kathleen Tillotson examined the files of the *Times* for 1850–51 and concluded, "Of the five subjects to which *The Times* kept recurring during the months immediately preceding the inception of *Bleak House*, three [Chancery, the chaotic political situation, and London sanitation, or lack of it] take a prominent part in the novel, and one of the remaining two [Puseyism] is memorably represented." (The one not referred to is the Crystal Palace exhibition.)[8] Again, to read in the *Times* files the same articles that Dickens read as he was writing *Little Dorrit*, for instance, with its mirroring of the current outcropping of the Sabbatarian crusade in the person of the grim sabbath-keeping Mrs. Clennam, is to gain a stronger grasp of the state of informed opinion on such matters, and of Dickens's mind as, on behalf of his wide audience, he transformed fact into fiction.[9]

This is also true of an equally well-known paper some distance removed from the *Times* in both tone and point of view. As Philip Collins has shown, Dickens and *Punch* shared many opinions on current topics.[10] They joined in deploring "the New Poor Law, the Corn Laws, nostalgia for 'the good old times', Tite-Barnaclism [in the Circumlocution Office], the Pope and 'papal aggression' in Britain, Puseyites, spiritualists, the English Sunday, Young England, Disraeli, the Pre-Raphaelites,

FARADAY GIVING HIS CARD TO FATHER THAMES;
And we hope the Dirty Fellow will consult the learned Professor.

Although most *Punch* readers would have been aware of the topical occasion of this cartoon (21 July 1855), only those who were also readers of the *Times* would have appreciated its immediate point. A fortnight earlier (9 July) the paper had published a letter from the noted scientist Michael Faraday complaining of the "feculence" and stench of the polluted Thames (see pages 417–19).

Constance (literary). "HAVE YOU READ THIS ACCOUNT OF 'THE MILL ON THE FLOSS,' DEAR?"
Edith (literal). "NO, INDEED, I HAVE NOT; AND I WONDER THAT YOU CAN FIND ANYTHING TO INTEREST YOU IN THE DESCRIPTION OF A DISGUSTING PRIZE-FIGHT!"

Sometimes a new novel by a popular author inspired *Punch* jokes. George Eliot's *The Mill on the Floss* was published on 4 April 1860; on 17 April occurred the famous Sayers-Heenan "mill" (Victorian slang for prizefight). In its issue for 28 April, *Punch* combined these two topics of the day, as shown here.

and the Tooting baby-farming scandal."[†] Most of these topics, treated in *Punch* with its characteristic satirical or indignant edge, turned up simultaneously or soon after in Dickens's fiction. It would be possible, indeed, to produce a modern edition of *Bleak House*, among his other novels, interspersed with relevant prose, verse, and cartoons from the

[†]This last was a scandal of 1849, in which a hundred and fifty infants and children at a squalid baby farm at Tooting—an entry-level counterpart of Squeers' Yorkshire academy—died of cholera, to which starvation, lack of sanitation and medical care, gross overcrowding, and brutal treatment had made them especially vulnerable. Snagsby's pathetic, epileptic maidservant, Guster, in *Bleak House*, was a refugee from such an asylum. Another, more recent scandal was even more pertinent. This was the case of a young servant girl, Jane Wilbred, whose mistress, a Mrs. Sloane, took her from the West Union

! AWFUL APPARITION !

Wilkie Collins's *The Woman in White* concluded its serialization in *All the Year Round* in August 1860, and in its immediately following bound-volume form it gained new throngs of readers who, like the nocturnal one shown in *Punch* (6 April 1861), took fearful pleasure in having their nerves set on edge. *"Mrs. T. (to T., who has been reading the popular novel):* 'Pray, Mr. Tomkins, are you never coming upstairs? How much longer are you going to sit up with that "Woman in White?" ' "

Punch of those years. They would constitute a highly illuminating commentary on the text.

A final way in which a newly published novel reached outside its covers into everyday life was its becoming embedded in the public consciousness in its own right, the consequence of an extraordinary degree of popularity. The prize exhibit here, it need hardly be said, is *Pickwick*

Workhouse and deliberately starved her, forcing her to eat offal, scraps, and her own excrement. Mrs. Snagsby, Guster's mistress, had her failings, but compared with Mrs. Sloane she must have been an angel of compassion, as Dickens's readers would have realized. Details of these two cases of child abuse are in A. W. C. Brice and K. J. Fielding, "Dickens and the Tooting Disaster," *Victorian Studies* 12 (1968): 227–44, and Trevor Blount, "*Bleak House* and the Sloane Scandal of 1850 Again," *Dickens Studies* 3 (1967): 63–67, respectively.

Papers. "[I]n less than six months from the appearance of the first number . . . ," wrote Abraham Hayward (?) in the *Quarterly Review* for October 1837, "the whole reading public were talking about them—the
names of Winkle, Wardell, Weller, Snodgrass, Dodson and Fogg, had
become familiar in our mouths as household terms; and Mr. Dickens
was the grand object of interest to the whole tribe of 'Leo-hunters,' male
and female, of the metropolis. Nay, Pickwick chintzes figured in linen-
drapers' windows, and Weller corduroys in breeches-makers' advertisements; Boz cabs might be seen rattling through the streets, and the portrait of the author of 'Pelham' [Bulwer-Lytton] or 'Crichton' [W. H.
Ainsworth] was scraped down or pasted over to make room for that of
the new popular favourite in the omnibusses." Favorite Pickwick characters were depicted in Staffordshire figurines, sold to be displayed on a
mantel or a bric-à-brac shelf, and in the various outlets for the printed
word were offered numerous unauthorized spinoffs from the text of the
novel itself—plagiarisms, "sequels," imitations, songbooks, the cobbled
texts of stage adaptations. Characters from the novels were portrayed
on a set of six of the so-called Mulready envelopes that were unsuccessfully introduced in 1841, immediately following the inauguration of the
penny post.

Dickens's next novel but one, *Nicholas Nickleby*, had a reception similar to, though less frantic than, that of *Pickwick*. Again there were crude
plagiarisms issued in penny weekly parts, "sets of extra illustrations, such
as Kenny Meadows' *Heads of Nicholas Nickleby sketched by Miss La Creevy*,"
and a sequel, *Nickleby Married*.[11] The contributions of Dickens's novels to
the fashions of the day were continued by the Dolly Varden dress, a style
popularized by W. P. Frith in his several portraits of the heroine of *Barnaby Rudge*.

Leech and Tenniel repeatedly used Dickens characters in their *Punch*
cartoons. In the latter's hands, says Jane Cohen,

> London officials became perfect Bumbles; Disraeli made a memorable Fa-
> gin; and various topical figures were cast as Sikes, Mrs. Nickleby, Smike,
> Mrs. Gamp, and even Mark Tapley. Gladstone especially served as a prime
> satirical target for Tenniel just as Peel and Russell had for Leech. For over
> three decades, Gladstone, an attentive, if not always admiring, reader of
> Dickens, had to submit to being caricatured as little Nell's weak grand-
> father, Micawber certain of "something turning up," a political Mrs. Gum-
> midge lamenting her misfortunes with Russia and Egypt, Betsey Prig,
> Sairey Gamp, and, most memorably, Scrooge-Sadstone observing the cha-
> otic spirit of Christmas Present. . . .[12]

Other novels from time to time captured the popular fancy in ways
that had nothing to do with their literary qualities. In 1860 there were

" *Well, Syusan, 'ow did yer like Aroorer Floyd last night!*"
" *Oh! so lovely, Jeames—I cried so! that wicked Conyers! . . . Oh, Jeames, you won't desert me for our young Missus, will you, dear!*"

The fame of many novels, including Scott's and Dickens's, was spread by the theatrical adaptations that were staged as soon as they were published—or, in Dickens's case, while they were still in the midst of their serial run. Mary Elizabeth Braddon's sensation novel, *Aurora Floyd*, completed its serialization in *Temple Bar* in January 1863; when this cartoon appeared in *Punch* on 2 May, at least two stage versions were playing in London.

Woman in White perfumes, cloaks, bonnets, waltzes, and quadrilles; and ten years later, aided no doubt by the political eminence of the author, who was then out of office between his first and second tenures as prime minister, Disraeli's *Lothair* inspired a song, a dance, and a perfume, and Baron Rothschild's race-winning filly was named after the novel's hero-

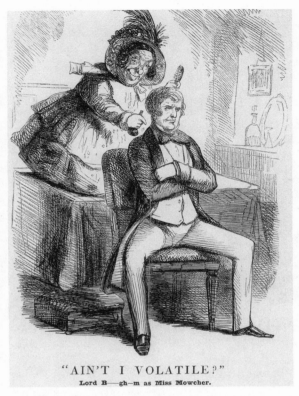

"AIN'T I VOLATILE?"
Lord B——gh—m as Miss Mowcher.

This political cartoon was published in *Punch* on 6 April 1850, only four months after Miss Mowcher appeared in the December 1850 number of *David Copperfield*—a good example of the speed with which a popular novel might provide graphic journalism with immediately topical references. The composition directly copies Phiz's illustration (page 614) and, what is more important, the accompanying selective quotation from the novel—"Bless you, man alive! I'm here and there, and where not, like the Conjuror's half-crown in the lady's handkercher. Aha! Umph! What a rattle I am!—Ain't I volatile?"—served as a timely hit at the politician Henry Brougham's notorious "volatility" (unpredictability). The particular case in point was his *volte face*, in the House of Lords a few days earlier, on the question of the proposed Great Exhibition; in an editorial comment in the same issue, *Punch* suggested that the building be topped by a monstrous effigy of Brougham in the form of a weathercock.

THE HUNT BALL — "ASK MAMMA POLKA"

At some point early in the serial publication of Surtees's *Ask Mamma* (1857–58), a prolific popular-song writer, William Henry Montgomery, composed a polka named for the novel. In its last number Surtees reciprocated by working the polka into the text—at the hunt ball it was played in the same set as "the enlivening 'La Traviata'" and the "Pelissier Galop"—and John Leech illustrated the scene.

ine, Corisande.[13] There was even, on the authority of Surtees's novel itself, an "Ask Mamma" polka.

Once in a while a novel might accidentally become topical for a reason unrelated to its contents or its popularity. When, in a French cause célèbre of the day, the Duchesse de Praslin was murdered in her bed by her husband in 1847, she had been reading Mrs. Gore's novel *Mrs. Armytage, or Female Domination* (1836). As a writer in the *New Monthly Magazine* said five years later, "The book was a favourite one with that ill-fated lady; and a volume of it being found on her bed, stained with her blood, and subsequently deposited in evidence at the trial, it acquired remarkable notoriety on the continent."[14] And not only there; never one to discount the monetary value of notoriety, Henry Colburn, the leading publisher of fashionable fiction in its heyday, reissued *Mrs. Armytage* in 1848, trusting to float it anew on the wave of the trial coverage. (Thackeray subsequently recalled l'affaire Praslin when Ethel Newcome, speaking of Sir Barnes's brutal treatment of his wife, said, "You remember that dreadful case in France of the Duc de ——, who murdered his duchess? That was a love-match, and I can remember the sort of screech with which Lady Kew used to speak about it; and of the journal which the poor duchess kept, and in which she noted down all her husband's ill-behaviour" [*The Newcomes*, 59:2.237]). (Lady Kew had died some years before the event, but no matter.)

3.

The developing affinity between fiction and journalism manifested itself in other ways besides periodicity of issue, the presence of editorial text and advertising within a single number, and the sharing of information about public events. By the 1840s it was recognized that the materials and even the techniques associated with the more sensational portion of the press, especially the Sunday papers with their high assay of crime, sex, and radical politics, were being borrowed by its counterpart in the popular fiction industry, the penny-a-portion novels of G. W. M. Reynolds and his fellow purveyors of printed excitement. Signs multiplied that the orbits of the novel and the newspaper were coming into (as some thought) dangerous conjunction, and that the respectable profession of novel writing was being infiltrated by persons whose outlook, if not actual occupation, was that of the inferior class of journalist.

Speedier communication and the enlargement of the reporting machinery made it possible for the daily press to follow an unfolding story from day to day, thus intensifying the suspense and drama that had been limited by slower and less thorough coverage. The larger format of newspapers, with their folio-sized pages and long columns of small, crowded type, provided room for a much larger budget of the day's happenings, described in greater detail. Conforming to a version of Parkinson's Law, the more space there was in newspapers, the more crime and catastrophe seemingly became available to fill it—thus lending credence to every piece of fiction that had these for its subject. As the author of a totally forgotten novel, *Gideon Giles the Roper*, affirmed in 1841:

> Let an author draw the character of a villain in the blackest colours he can use, such a one lives in the world. Let him paint murder in its most sanguine hues, writhing, brutal and horrible, the next month proves how much he fell short of reaching the actual colouring. Let him break hearts asunder, bleeding and aching with blighted love; draw the curtain and reveal all that is awful in suicide and death—then turn to the everyday world, and with a shudder he may view the selfsame picture. He outrages not nature, for nature is every day outraged; let those who disbelieve us sum up all the unnatural deeds which the last twelve moons have waxed and waned over, and which are recorded in almost every newspaper.[15]

A much better-remembered novelist, Thackeray, invoked the analogy between newspaper reporting and fiction writing to justify his touching on risky subjects. In the printed text of *The Newcomes* (31:1.341),
Thackeray defended the Duc d'Ivry's and Lady Kew's reminiscences of
the loose morality of Regency society—"Old scandals woke up, old
naughtinesses rose out of their graves, and danced, and smirked, and
gibbered again." But he had expunged, before printing, these additional
sentences:

> I am trying to tell this story, not in a sermonizing tone, wh. is a bore in
> society: where the fable is acted before us, and the observer must point his
> own moral. Admit that the novel is a newspaper; where the Editor utters
> his opinions only in a small part of the journal, the rest being filled up with
> advertisements, accidents offences fashionable news &c, and where Lady
> Brilliants last nights party: the running at Doncaster yesterday, Jack Split-
> skulls execution and behaviour at the Old Bailey: the price of peas at Cov-
> ent Garden: Captain Screwby's appearance at Bow Street for wrenching off
> knockers, and so forth are registered without comment. But now and then
> in the newspaper columns you must come on a dreadful story or two. Do
> your children not see it? [16]

"What a wonderful institution is 'The Times'!" exulted Surtees a few years
later, in *Plain or Ringlets?* (1860). "The second column of the supplement
contains hints for a hundred novels. The open, the mysterious, the anxious, the forgiving, the mandatory, the admonitory, the conciliatory"
(48:171). This was the agony column, "that mysterious corner of the
Times newspaper," as another novelist put it, "where husbands sue for
the return of wives one should think they were better without—mothers
promise forgiveness to sons, to whom a sound flogging would be the
wholesomer advertisement—and where notices of the loss of jewels and
money make one think how extremely idiotic the original possessors
must have been. . . ." [17]

It is tempting to think that it was after Trollope's fruitless visit to
Hurst and Blackett, recalled in Chapter 1, that he inserted into *The Three
Clerks*, issued by another publisher, a passage that enlarged into specifics
a fact of modern life—that novelists wishing to make a livelihood were
obliged to depend heavily on current topics, turning themselves willy-
nilly into crusading journalists. The editor of the new *Daily Delight*—this
was a time when cheap daily papers were beginning to proliferate, now
that the newspaper stamp tax was no longer a burden on the journalistic
economy—counsels Charley Tudor, a would-be contributor of fiction,
on what sells papers nowadays. "The editor says," Charley reports, "that
we must always have a slap at some of the iniquities of the times. He gave
me three or four to choose from [for his projected story]; there was the

adulteration of food, and the want of education for the poor, and street music, and the miscellaneous sale of poisons." Still another was "the absurdity of our criminal code" (19:218–19). Such muckraking topics had somehow to be worked into the story, however unrelated they might be to characters and plot.

> "We have polished off poison and petticoats pretty well," said the editor; "what do you say to something political? . . . This Divorce Bill, now—we could have half a dozen married couples all separating, getting rid of their ribs and buckling again, helter-skelter, every man to somebody else's wife; and the parish parson refusing to do the work; just to show the immorality of the thing. . . . Or the Danubian Principalities and the French Alliance— could you manage now to lay your scene in Constantinople? . . . Or perhaps India is the thing? The Cawnpore massacre would work up into any lengths you pleased. You could get a file of the *Times*, you know, for your facts." (46:547–48)

Two related developments between 1850 and 1870 gave impetus to this encroachment of journalism on the precincts of fiction: the harnessing of the novel to social causes and the appearance, as a distinctly named genre, of sensational fiction. Charles Reade especially, as we have seen, turned fiction into a vehicle for outright reformist propaganda, at times simply a lengthy supplement to leading articles in the press. Frankly recognizing how much he owed to the masses of newspaper clippings he pasted into his bulky scrapbooks,[†] he sent an unsolicited testimonial to the editor of the *Times* in 1871:

> For eighteen years the journal you conduct so ably has been my preceptor and the main source of my works; at all events of the most approved. A noble passage in the "Times" of September 7 or 8, 1853, touched my heart, inflamed my imagination, and was the germ of my first important work, "It Is Never Too Late to Mend." Some years later you put forth an able and eloquent leader on private asylums, and detailed the sufferings there in-

---

[†]These were components of Reade's imposing armory of documentation—facts on file—which he described in *A Terrible Temptation*. Mr. Rolfe, his alter ego in the novel (both were lawyers, novelists, and playwrights), held that every written scrap that came into his possession "ought either to be burned or pasted into a classified guard-book, where it could be found by consulting the index. . . . Underneath the table ["a gigantic writing-table, with the signs of hard labor on it, and of severe system"] was a formidable array of notebooks, standing upright, and labelled on their backs. There were about twenty large folios of classified facts, ideas, and pictures; for the very woodcuts were all indexed and classified on the plan of a tradesman's ledger. . . . Then there was a collection of solid quartos, and of smaller folio guard-books called Indexes. There was 'Index rerum et journalium,' 'Index rerum et librorum,' 'Index rerum et hominum,' and a lot more; indeed, so many that, by way of climax, there was a fat folio ledger entitled 'Index ad Indices'" (22:221–22).

flicted on persons known to you. This took root in me, and brought forth its fruit in the second volume of "Hard Cash." Later still your hearty and able but temperate leaders on trades unions and trade outrages incited me to an ample study of that great subject, so fit for fiction of the higher order, though not adapted to the narrow minds of bread-and-butter misses, nor of the criticasters who echo those young ladies' idea of fiction and its limits, and thus "Put Yourself in His Place" was written. Of "A Terrible Temptation" the leading idea came to me from the "Times," viz., from the report of a certain trial, with the comments of counsel, and the remarkable judgment delivered by Mr. Justice Byles.[18]

Authors of sensational novels were particularly grateful for the credibility that newspapers supplied to their accounts of murder, bigamy, forgery, white-collar crime of other descriptions, elaborate deceptions, the discovery of lost wills. In Wilkie Collins's *No Name*, Mrs. Vanstone rejected as "unaccountable" the inference drawn from a tidbit of gossip that "girls take perverse fancies for men who are totally unworthy of them." Her daughter's governess retorted, "Unaccountable, because it happens every day! . . . I know a great many excellent people who reason against plain experience in the same way—who read the newspapers in the morning, and deny in the evening that there is any romance for writers or painters to work upon in modern life" ("First scene," chap. 8 : 1.108–9).

Nowhere but in sensation fiction was there a plainer demonstration of art imitating life. In 1869 Albany Fonblanque, in a novel called *Cut Adrift*, expressed the truism (as it was becoming) with heavy irony:

> Bankers never do commit forgery out of sensation romances, and Sir John Dean Paul never did work at Portland.[†] Husbands never do poison their wives out of novels, and that affair of Dr. Smethurst was a myth. People do not go about and shoot each other in broad mid-day about women, and the Northumberland Street tragedy was a penny-a-liner's hoax. We who write these sort of books take human nature as we think we find it, taking our models out of those confounded newspaper reports, and supposing that what people tell my lords the Queen's Justices on their oaths, and on the strength of which men and women are hanged and transported may, after all, be true—and we have our reward.[19]

By this time, critics were coming to think that newspapers, freshly cheapened and deliberately written to suit the capacities and expectations of a mass market, were beating fiction at its own (sensational) game. If one wanted to read exciting stories, they could be found more readily,

[†]For the reason why the rich broker Sir John Dean Paul served time in one of Her Majesty's prisons, see pages 648–49 below.

more cheaply, and in greater quantities in the daily press from which novelists drew their topical material in the first place; that novelists by their intervention might somehow shape and add meaning to that press-fodder was close to irrelevant. One wonders, however, whether R. H. Hutton was wholly serious when he wrote in the *Spectator*:

> We suspect that as the mechanical appliances of communication improve, all kinds of light reading will be swallowed up by the most sensational of all, the hourly history of the world, its doings and its people. This tendency is already noted in America; and even in England, where people adhere longer to habits, the journal, and especially the journal of news, threatens to supersede the novel. People are, on the whole, more amused by seeing "what is going on" than by reading what imaginary people suffer, and that taste once acquired, lasts for life. It is as strong as a thirst for drams, and as a great many people think,—we do not agree with them,—is very little less deleterious to the mental palate. Owing to causes not worth discussing here, it has been very little fostered in England; but still the demand for newspapers which for any reason are readable increases till . . . the empire of the novel is already disputed, and but for the lingering distaste of women for newspapers, a distaste rapidly passing away, it would be seriously menaced. The reader in fact obtains, say in an evening paper, all that he obtains in an ordinary novel,—a distraction, and something else besides,—a distraction which is not based on a fiction. He finds as many stories, tragic or comic, as many characters, as many social sketches; and they are all real, all more or less true, and all described in the style which, be it bad or good from an artistic point of view, is the easiest and pleasantest to him to read.[20]

The increased readership of newspapers did not, as Hutton argued, presage the death of the novel. But by drawing off a portion of the audience for realistic reporting of the facts of contemporary life it may well have made room for the revival of the romance in the eighties under the auspices of such novelists as Robert Louis Stevenson and Rider Haggard.

Meanwhile, newspaper coverage of the kind of events depicted in realistic, and especially reformist, fiction proved repeatedly to be a convenient and convincing means of authenticating similar events when they occurred in novels. An early example of fortuitous corroboration had appeared in connection with Bulwer's *Paul Clifford* (1830), which contained several sharp thrusts against the existing penal system, including the arbitrariness of detention and the stony inhumanity of judges. Bulwer was able to cite an instance that had been publicized just before the novel went on sale. The *Morning Herald* had reported that a "poor woman" had been sentenced to seven days in prison on a charge of "*disrespectability.*" Her husband and their neighbors were able at once to disprove the accusation, but the justice said that since she would, in any case, be released in five days, "it will be scarcely worth while to release

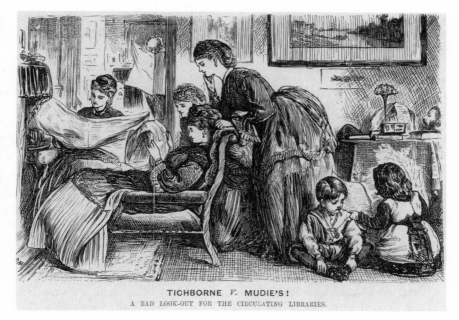

TICHBORNE *V.* MUDIE'S!
A BAD LOOK-OUT FOR THE CIRCULATING LIBRARIES.

This is an apt expression (*Punch*, 25 November 1871) of the current notion that journalism and real life were taking over the sensation novel's turf, thus reducing the trade at circulating libraries. The first of the two trials of Arthur Orton, the "Tichborne claimant," had begun on 11 May and would remain in the headlines until it was concluded on 5 March of the following year, setting a record for a single court hearing (102 days).

her now" (7:1.91). [†] A few years later, in *Ernest Maltravers* (1837), Bulwer appended a note to a passage in which Alice, a victim of child abuse on the part of a criminal father, revealed her shocking ignorance of basic religious principles, a deficiency prophetic of Jo's in *Bleak House*. "This ignorance—indeed, the whole sketch of Alice—," said Bulwer, "is from the life; nor is such ignorance, accompanied by what almost seems an instinctive or intuitive notion of right or wrong, very uncommon, as our police reports can testify. In the 'Examiner' for, I think, the year 1835,

[†]Bulwer seems to have been particularly fortunate in the way late-breaking news enhanced the topicality of his novels. On one occasion, Nature herself collaborated with him. In the week just prior to the publication of *The Last Days of Pompeii* (September 1834), the papers had been printing the first accounts received in London of "the most destructive eruptions of Vesuvius in modern centuries," which had occurred on 27–29 August. (James C. Simmons, "Bulwer and Vesuvius: The Topicality of *The Last Days of Pompeii*," *Nineteenth-Century Fiction* 24 (1969): 103–5.)

will be found the case of a young girl ill-treated by her father, whose answers to the interrogatories of the magistrate are very similar to those of Alice to the questions of Maltravers" (1.4:24).

In the same year (1837), news from a London jail furnished Dickens with an implicit, almost instantaneous reply to the disbelievers among his readers. In part 16 of *Pickwick Papers*, published 1 August, he described the death of a longtime captive debtor in the Fleet prison. On the twenty-fifth of that month, the newspapers reported an inquest on a female debtor who had been an inmate of King's Bench prison for over sixteen years. The jury's verdict was "Died of a nervous fever brought on through long confinement and excited feelings."[21] In the preface to the 1848 cheap edition of *Nicholas Nickleby*, Dickens reaffirmed and amplified the claim he had made in the preface to the original edition, that his depiction of conditions in the Yorkshire proprietary schools, based on his own investigation and corroborated by numerous eyewitnesses, fell short of the dreadful actuality. Had he seen fit at that time, he added, he could have quoted details of criminal cases stemming from the schoolmasters' practices that had been printed in "certain old newspapers."

That novelists sometimes availed themselves of newspaper material did not sit well with some critics. Kingsley was among the first to feel the sting of such criticism. In *Yeast*, his hero, Lancelot Smith, buried himself "up to the eyes in the Condition-of-the-Poor question—that is, in blue books, red books, sanitary reports, mine reports," then went into the countryside to see for himself the miserable conditions in which farm laborers existed. "What he saw, of course I must not say," continued Kingsley; "for if I did the reviewers would declare, as usual, one and all, that I copied out of the *Morning Chronicle*; and the fact that these pages, ninety-nine hundredths of them at least, were written two years before the *Morning Chronicle* began its invaluable investigations, would be contemptuously put aside as at once impossible and arrogant" (8:133–34).[†]

Dickens was peculiarly vulnerable to such criticism, which was part of the broader accusation that his was a mole's-eye view of society. Having made palpable use of newspaper material from time to time, he was thrust on the defensive when faced with the kind of complaint a reviewer of *Great Expectations* voiced in the *Rambler* in 1862: "It is the mere poverty of an imagination self-restrained to one narrow field of human nature, that makes him search curiously for such follies, and ransack newspapers for incidents to put into his books."[22] Five years earlier, in a

---

[†] This passage does not occur in the serialized version of *Yeast* (*Fraser's Magazine*, 1848); it was added, along with much else, when the novel was published in book form in 1851. For the *Morning Chronicle*'s "invaluable investigations," see page 94 below.

slashing attack in the *Edinburgh Review*, James Fitzjames Stephen had said, "Even the catastrophe in 'Little Dorrit' is evidently borrowed from the recent fall of houses in Tottenham Court Road, which happens to have appeared in the newspapers at a convenient moment."[23] For Dickens, smarting from the general hostility of the article, which was titled "The License of Modern Novelists," this was the last straw, and he replied in *Household Words* (1 August) under the caption "Curious Misprint [ironic euphemism for "Error"] in the *Edinburgh Review*": "The Novelist begs to ask him [the Reviewer] whether there is no License in his writing those words and stating that assumption as a truth, when any man accustomed to the critical examination of a book cannot fail, attentively turning over the pages of *Little Dorrit*, to observe that that catastrophe is carefully prepared for from the very first presentation of the old house in the story." Touché: as he wrote his serial story month by month, Dickens had indeed introduced several clear foreshadowings of the sudden eventual collapse of Mrs. Clennam's rickety old house. He undoubtedly remembered earlier instances of the same kind of urban spontaneous destruction, which were reported in the papers from time to time.

Still, Dicken's asperity as he denied the accusation that he cribbed from the papers did not prevent his citing newspaper or other documentary evidence when it served his interests to do so. In the defensive "Postscript in Lieu of Preface" he wrote for *Our Mutual Friend*, he contested, as was his wont, the "odd disposition in this country to dispute as improbable in fiction, what are the commonest experiences in fact," and asserted that "there are hundreds of Will Cases (as they are called), far more remarkable than that fancied in this book; and that the stores of the Prerogative Office teem with instances of testators who have made, changed, contradicted, hidden, forgotten, left cancelled, and left uncancelled, each many more wills than were ever made by the elder Mr. Harmon of Harmony Jail" (893). Responding specifically to charges that his attack on the administration of the Poor Law, in his description of Betty Higden's dread of dying as a pauper in a workhouse infirmary, had little basis in fact, Dickens referred his critics to "the records in our newspapers [and] the late exposure by *The Lancet*." When the twelfth number of the novel appeared (April 1865), the medical weekly, the *Lancet*, had announced the formation of its Sanitary Commission for Investigating the State of the Infirmaries of Workhouses, whose findings were being published week by week as the serialization of *Our Mutual Friend* drew to a close.

An astonishing coincidence of fiction and news report occurred in 1865–66. In the appendix to his sensation novel *Armadale* when it was published in volume form in the latter year, Wilkie Collins wrote:

"Remains of the fallen house, no. 184, Strand": graphic evidence, from the *Illustrated London News* for 10 September 1853, that the episode of the collapsing house in the final number of *Little Dorrit* (June 1857) was no figment of Dickens's imagination. Another example, in the same paper for 9 October 1858 ("Ruins of the Fallen House in Pilgrim-Street, City"), would have made the episode all the more credible to readers of the novel in volume form.

My readers will perceive that I have purposely left them, with reference to the Dream in this story, in the position which they would occupy in the case of a dream in real life: they are free to interpret it by the natural or the supernatural theory, as the bent of their own minds may incline them. Persons disposed to take the rational view may, under these circumstances, be interested in hearing of a coincidence relating to the present story, which actually happened, and which in the matter of "extravagant improbability" sets anything of the same kind that a novelist could imagine at flat defiance.

In November 1865, that is to say, when thirteen monthly parts of "Armadale" had been published, and, I may add, when more than a year and a half had elapsed since the end of the story, as it now appears, was first sketched in my notebook—a vessel lay in the Huskisson Dock at Liverpool which was looked after by one man, who slept on board, in the capacity of ship-keeper. On a certain day in the week this man was found dead in the deck-house. On the next day a second man, who had taken his place, was carried dying to the Northern Hospital. On the third day a third ship-keeper was appointed, and was found dead in the deck-house which had already proved fatal to the other two. *The name of that ship was "The Armadale."* And the proceedings at the Inquest proved that the three men had been all suffocated *by sleeping in poisoned air!* (574–75: italics in both cases are Collins's)

Collins referred to, but did not quote, an item in the *Times* for 30 November 1865:

POISONOUS GAS.—At the Liverpool Coroner's Court yesterday an inquiry was held touching the deaths of three men who were suffocated within a few days of each other while acting as shipkeepers on board the ship Armadale lying in the Huskisson Dock. Dr. Trench, medical officer of health, and Mrs. Ayrton gave evidence to the effect that death had been caused by the inhalation of carbonic acid gas, which, in consequence of the prevailing high winds, had been forced back into the deckhouse where the men slept, and where they had kindled fires. The jury returned a verdict "That death resulted from suffocation caused by defective ventilation."

The coincidence was this. In "Book the Last, Chapter III ('The Purple Flask')," the final installment of *Armadale* as printed in the *Cornhill Magazine* for June 1866, the evil Doctor Le Doux and his accomplice Miss Gwilt conspired to kill Allan Armadale by running a tube of poisonous gas, disguised as "fumigating apparatus," into his room. As it happened, Armadale and Ozias Midwinter had exchanged rooms, unknown to the would-be murderers, but both survived. If Collins was correct in saying that he had sketched the end of the novel in his notebook more than a year and a half before the Liverpool episode, art would seem to have anticipated life. What is equally striking is the coincidence of the name *Armadale*. That a ship bearing the name of the novel should have been the site of an episode resembling one the author had already planned was a near-incredible event, in the true spirit of sensation fiction.

4.

When the *Lancet* launched its investigation of workhouse infirmaries, it did so in response to the *Report of the Select Committee of the House of Commons on Poor-Law Medical Relief*, which had received newspaper publicity just as the serialization of *Our Mutual Friend* was getting under way. (It had, in effect, exonerated the present administration of the primitive health/welfare system, hence the *Lancet's* formation of its own unofficial ".commission.") This was one of the latest blue books to provide a background for, if not actually contribute to, the Victorian novel with a purpose.[24]

Blue books, so called from the color of their wrappers, were government publications that presented, along with other matter such as the reports of various arms of government, the full oral testimony and written evidence gathered by inquiries into matters of current concern by ad hoc committees of the House of Commons and the Lords and by royal commissions, whose respective modern American counterparts are congressional investigating committees and administratively appointed "blue ribbon" panels. Primarily intended for the use of members of Parliament, government officials, and any public men without office who might be interested in their contents, blue books were known to the general public through the newspapers, which often printed lengthy excerpts from them, as well as reports of the parliamentary debates they occasioned. No one ever claimed they made lively reading—many were laden with great, arid expanses of statistics—and none ever kept old men from the chimney corner, but one or two became best-sellers after they were first put on sale to the public in 1835.[25] The 1842 *Report on the Sanitary Condition of the Labouring Population*, prepared by Edwin Chadwick, the hero of Victorian reform in this nauseous area, stirred a popular fad called "the sanitary question." It was a subject, replete with details of the fearsome efficacy of open sewers and overflowing cess pits in spreading pestilence, that could not possibly be discussed, except in evasive terms, in fiction itself. The closest Kingsley dared come to it in *Yeast* was to propose that a truly modern epic might be called the *Chadwickiad*; his hero, Lancelot Smith, suggested that it might begin, "Smells and the Man I sing" (6:103).

Like newspapers, blue books were regarded as certifying the truth of otherwise incredible events and conditions. A writer in the *Quarterly Review* said of the *Report of the Commissioners for Inquiring into the Condition of Children Employed in Mines*, published in the same year as Chadwick's, that it "disclosed . . . modes of existence . . . as strange and as new as the wildest dreams of fiction."[26] But the facts could not be gainsaid, no matter what flaws there might have been in the procedures by which they were collected and presented or how differently they might be interpreted by various interested parties. Blue books were, on the whole, the most unimpeachable source on living and working conditions among the Victorian urban and rural poor, and novelists used them as such. Among the first was Frances Trollope, whose *Life and Adventures of Michael Armstrong, the Factory Boy* (monthly parts, 1839–40) borrowed harrowing descriptions of the exploitation of child labor from the so-called Sadler Report of 1832, formally known as the *Report of the Committee of the House of Commons on the Bill to Regulate the Labour of Children in the Mills and Factories of the United Kingdom*. Several years later, Disraeli had several recent blue books before him as he wrote *Sybil*.[27] The description of the mining town of "Marney," especially, owed much more to those volumes than to any on-site inspections Disraeli may have made, as he said he did in his preface. He copied into the novel, word for word, numerous passages from the *First Report from the Midland Mining Commissioners for South Staffordshire* by Thomas Tancred (1842) and took other material, though less verbatim, from Chadwick's report. The *Second Report (Trades and Manufactures) of the Children's Employment Commissioners* (1843) was formerly thought to have contributed a great deal to Disraeli's description of living conditions in the town of "Wodgate," but this claim has recently been modified.[28] There is no question, though, that that particular blue book, with its revelation of the barbarous conditions in which children of tender age slaved for long hours a day in the craft shops and factories, deeply affected both Elizabeth Barrett and Dickens. Miss Barrett wrote her "Cry of the Children," which she called her "bluebook in verse," and Dickens, the nascent reformer, was moved by it to write *The Chimes*. Later he read the *Second Report of the Metropolitan Sanitary Commission* (1848), which urged the establishment of a central authority to eradicate the most flagrant sources of epidemic disease. He also may well have seen the published results of several quasi-official or private investigations that backed up the blue books, setting forth in horrifying detail the contagious capabilities of the slums and graveyards described in *Bleak House*.[29] Still another pertinent blue book, the report of a royal commission appointed "to inquire into the Process, Practice, and System of Pleading in the Court of Chancery," became the subject of parliamentary debate just before the novel's first number appeared.

In 1865, George Eliot, doing research for *Felix Holt*, entered into her notebook numerous extracts from the *Reports from the Select Committee on*

Bribery at Elections (1835). But in those years the novelists who most often resorted to blue books, either citing them directly or assuming their readers' awareness of their contents, were Collins and Reade. Both men, as we shall see in another connection (pages 545–47), wrote in the shadow of three reports (1859–60) of a committee investigating the management of private madhouses. For *It Is Never Too Late to Mend* (1856) Reade drew liberally from the royal commissioners' report on Birmingham Borough Prison, the result of an inquiry instituted after a fifteen-year-old prisoner had hanged himself in 1853, as well as from *Times* articles commenting on the case.[30]

When Collins took up the questionable validity of a "Scotch" marriage in *Man and Wife* (1870), his inspiration, he told his readers, was a blue book issued two years earlier.[†] "There are certain readers," he said in a long note intruded into the middle of the narrative,

> who feel a disposition to doubt Facts, when they meet with them in a work of fiction. Persons of this way of thinking may be profitably referred to the book which first suggested to me the idea of writing the present Novel. The book is the Report of the Royal Commissioners on the Laws of Marriage. Published by the Queen's Printers. For her Majesty's Stationery Office. (London, 1868.) What Sir Patrick says professionally of Scotch Marriages in this chapter is taken from this high authority. What the lawyer (in the Prologue) says professionally of Irish Marriages is also derived from the same source. (20:1.327–28)

Collins went on to cite the exact passage in the report that bore upon his argument. Documentation of fiction in the manner of a learned historical work or a polemic tract could go no further.

It was not only as sources of factual information that blue books found their way into fiction. Dickens, predictably, had no high regard for their plodding style and all too frequent large servings of humbug. In *Bleak House* he parodied a typical examination of a witness, to satirize the ponderousness of governmental and legal procedures and, in the person of the funereally dressed lawyer Vholes, to mock the "respectability" of a profession that battened on the misery of Chancery's victims:

[†]The blue book was the end product of a legal controversy stemming from the notorious Yelverton trial in 1861. A "Scotch" marriage, the practice at issue, was one in which bride and groom married themselves by reading the Anglican service together, without the presence of a clergyman. The case recurred in the headlines for several years as it progressed through the courts (it eventually reached the House of Lords) and the state of the marriage laws in general was considered by the royal commission Collins mentions. The public was less interested in the legal angle than in the allegations that Major Yelverton, second son of Lord Avonmore, had committed bigamy. This mildly titillating offense was a leading theme in numerous sensation novels, most notably *Lady Audley's Secret*.

The respectability of Mr. Vholes has even been cited with crushing effect before Parliamentary committees, as in the following blue minutes of a distinguished attorney's evidence. "Question (number five hundred and seventeen thousand eight hundred and sixty-nine). If I understand you, these forms of practice indisputably occasion delay? Answer. Yes, some delay. Question. And great expense? Answer. Most assuredly they cannot be gone through for nothing. Question. And unspeakable vexation? Answer. I am not prepared to say that. They have never given *me* any vexation; quite the contrary. Question. But you think that their abolition would damage a class of practitioners? Answer. I have no doubt of it. Question. Can you instance any type of that class? Yes. I would unhesitatingly mention Mr. Vholes. He would be ruined. Question. Mr. Vholes is considered, in the profession, a respectable man? Answer"—which proved fatal to the inquiry for ten years—"Mr. Vholes is considered, in the profession, a *most* respectable man." (39:604)

The same heavy spirit of the blue books brooded over *Hard Times*, where they epitomized the fact-worshipping, doctrine-bound quality of Utilitarianism:

> Although Mr. Gradgrind did not take after Blue Beard, his room was quite a blue chamber in its abundance of blue books. Whatever they could prove (which is usually anything you like), they proved there, in an army constantly strengthening by the arrival of new recruits. In that charmed apartment, the most complicated social questions were cast up, got into exact totals, and finally settled—if those concerned could only have been brought to know it. . . . (1.15:131)

Even on such delicate private matters as marriage, when he discussed it with his sadly nubile daughter Louisa, a blue book was the supreme authority: "the statistics of marriage, so far as they have yet been obtained, in England and Wales" (1.15:134).

The chief descriptive usefulness of blue books, however, was in connection with fictional members of Parliament, for whom they were required reading—or at least nominally so. The "vast sideboard" in Sir Brian Newcome's house in Piccadilly "groan[ed] under the weight of Sir Brian's blue-books" (*The Newcomes*, 14:1.50). Application to them, despite their notorious Saharan dryness, was an unmistakable sign of the conscientious and/or ambitious legislator. On Pitt Crawley the younger's library table an orderly set of recent blue books stood alongside a file of printed bills submitted to the House, advocacy pamphlets, the current *Quarterly Review*, and the *Court Guide*—a model selection of professional reading matter for one in his position. "At home," Thackeray said later, "he gave himself up to the perusal of Blue Books, to the alarm and wonder of Lady Jane, who thought he was killing himself by late hours and intense application" (*Vanity Fair*, 45:441). Preparing to enter the House

of Commons, Arthur Pendennis told his friend Warrington that he had
been doing his homework by studying "some social questions . . . during
the vacation." "Don't grin, you old cynic," he said, "I *have* been getting
up the Blue Books, and intend to come out rather strong on the Sanitary
and Colonisation questions" (*Pendennis*, 69:2.326). In *Aurora Floyd*, the
dutiful M.P. for a Cornish constituency, Captain Talbot Bulstrode, was
repeatedly seen communing with his blue books, boning up for the next
session. Such devotion, even if in this case it was assumed by a self-
sacrificing wife, was an attribute of Clara Amedroz's ideal husband in
Trollope's *The Belton Estate*: "A Member of Parliament, with a small
house near Eaton Square, with a moderate income, and a liking for committees, who would write a pamphlet once every two years, and read
Dante critically during the recess, was, to her, the model for a husband.
For such a one she would read his blue books, copy his pamphlets, and
learn his translations by heart" (11:129).

Plantagenet Palliser, later Duke of Omnium and prime minister, is
Victorian fiction's most eminent devotee of blue books, to which he
undoubtedly contributed as a leading member of the Commons who
would have sat on various committees of inquiry and royal commissions,
such as the one on copyright on which Trollope served in 1876–77.
Palliser's pet cause was conversion of the coinage to the decimal system,
an especially suitable concern, given the constant stress on money that is
a hallmark of society in Trollope's fiction. Palliser's research would have
taken him into a series of blue books scattered across many years: the
royal commissions on decimalization in 1838 and 1843 were on record
as favoring the change, as was a select committee of the House of Commons in 1853, but the reports from the most recent inquiries, by royal
commissions in 1857[†] and 1868, opposed it. In both *The Eustace Dia-*

[†]This was the commission alluded to at the beginning of *The Three Clerks*, published
the next year. "And then that question of the decimal coinage! Is it not in these days of
paramount importance? Are we not disgraced by the twelve pennies in our shilling, by the
four farthings in our penny? One of the worthy assistant-secretaries [of the Board of Commissioners for Regulating Weights and Measures, within whose purview decimalization
presumably came], the worthier probably of the two, has already grown pale beneath the
weight of this question. But he has sworn within himself, with all the heroism of a Nelson,
that he will either do or die. He will destroy the shilling or the shilling shall destroy him"
(1:2). In the novel, this issue was eclipsed by the one involving a proposed Limehouse-
Rotherhithe bridge across the Thames, which promised to be a speculators' bonanza. But
this bubble burst when "A huge blue volume was . . . published, containing, among other
things, all Mr. Nogo's 2,250 questions and their answers; and so the Limehouse and
Rotherhithe bridge dropped into oblivion and was forgotten" (32:402). There was also a
committee looking into the momentous question of whether the British army should
supply its mess tables with potted peas imported from Germany rather than the native
product; it would inevitably generate another "huge blue volume" to take its place alongside the one on the bridge inquiry.

monds and *Phineas Redux* a bill to institute it was said to be on the verge of passage, but this was one of Trollope's historical inventions; it apparently stood little chance of enactment in those years. But Palliser's advocacy of it was a pleasantly quixotic touch in Trollope's characterization.

For every politician who actually studied the blue books there was at least one who detested them. The iniquitous James Harthouse in *Hard Times*, electioneering for the Coketown seat, made "a discreet use of his blue coaching" and "came off triumphantly, though with a considerable accession of boredom" (2.2:163), which must have been due as much to the blue books he skimmed through as to the people he was forced to glad-hand. Sir Leicester Dedlock's boredom was not only acute but soporific. Dickens shows him once in his library at Chesney Wold, where he "has fallen asleep for the good of the country, over the report of a Parliamentary committee" (*Bleak House*, 48:706). One article of the fun-loving young Lord Nidderdale's resolution to don a hair shirt after the Beargarden Club, his favorite haunt, has closed, is to "begin reading blue books tomorrow" (*The Way We Live Now*, 96:779). It may be doubted whether this sudden burst of virtue lasted longer than his determination at the same time to attend the House every day and limit himself to a cheap claret at 20*s*. a dozen. But blue books actually came to the therapeutic rescue of another nobleman, Lord Fawn in *The Eustace Diamonds*, who suffered a different kind of misfortune. After "a disappointment in love," says Trollope, "he . . . consoled himself with bluebooks, and mastered his passion by incessant attendance at the India Office" (3:62).

One of the earliest allusions to blue books and their conscientious or negligent recipients, however, remained the most telling. In *Ten Thousand a Year* (1839–41) Samuel Warren described an aftermath of election to the first reformed Parliament:

> 'Twas truly delightful to see the tables of these young gentlemen [newly elected M.P.s] groaning under daily accumulations of Parliamentary documents, containing all sorts of political and statistical information, collected and published with vast labor and expense, for the purpose of informing their powerful intellects upon the business of the country, so that they might come duly prepared to the important discussions in the House, on all questions of domestic and foreign policy.

Among them was the insufferable coxcomb Tittlebat Titmouse, formerly a London linen draper's assistant and now a country magnate.

> [H]e never relished the idea of perusing and studying these troublesome and repulsive documents—page after page filled with long rows of figures, tables of prices, of exchanges, etc., reports of the evidence, *verbatim et literatim*, taken in question and answer before every committee that sat; all sorts

of expensive and troublesome "returns," moved for by any one that chose; he rather contented himself with attending to what went on in the House; and at the close of the session, all the documents in question became the perquisite of his valet, who got a good round sum for them (uncut) as waste paper (28:783–84).

One other documentary source for mid-Victorian novelists was the part journalistic, part sociological reports of Henry Mayhew, whom Gertrude Himmelfarb has aptly called "a one-man Royal Commission."[31] Between October 1849 and December 1850, the *Morning Chronicle* published six articles a week by its "special correspondents," dealing with "labour and the poor" in London and the provinces: two from the mining and manufacturing districts, two from the agricultural countryside (it was these that Kingsley referred to in *Yeast*), and two from Mayhew—a total of eighty-two over the entire run of the series—on conditions in London, with ample attention to the sweated tailoring trade. In *Alton Locke* (10:91n), Kingsley implored "all Christian people to 'read, mark, learn, and inwardly digest'" Mayhew's findings, which in the articles printed on 14 and 18 December massively authenticated the picture the novel presented of London's airless, dimly lit sweatshops. Mayhew gathered these articles in the weekly numbers of *London Labour and the London Poor*, published between December 1850 and February 1852.

There is no absolute proof that Dickens read this now classic work, which was enlarged when reissued in four volumes in 1861–62, but there is good reason to suppose that he did.[32] There are, for instance, striking parallels between his description of Krook's occupation in *Bleak House*—that of a buyer and seller of rags, bottles, waste paper, and other reusable junk—and Mayhew's articles on the trade. In any case, Mayhew's starkly authentic account of life among the submerged population of the metropolis substantiated many observations that Dickens made independently during his compulsive explorations of the urban scene, and readers of Mayhew would have read novels like *Bleak House*, whose serial publication began only a month after that of *London Labour and the London Poor* concluded, with enlarged understanding. And when, a decade later, Dickens located certain scenes of *Our Mutual Friend* among the "golden dust heaps" of rubbish and worse just north of King's Cross station, acquaintance with Mayhew's many pages on the various departments of the scavenging trade would have told readers much more about Noddy Boffin's landfill empire than Dickens had space, or liberty, to tell. Here, as elsewhere, contemporary documents, insofar as readers knew them, did some of the novelist's work for him, adding resonant details to the sketch or small incidental hint that was all he needed to provide.

4
Events and Movements

1.

THE EVENTS and movements that provided part of the Victorian novelists' store of topical references fall into two categories, with no clear boundary between them. Some were what might be called strictly newspaper events, ephemeral affairs that occupied the headlines, and therefore the forefront of the popular mind, just long enough for novelists to exploit them for their strong immediate interest. Like most of the contents of a London daily paper on any given morning, they were occurrences that did not contribute in any appreciable way to "history in the making"; they were flotsam on the restless sea of human affairs, but their momentary impact was often greater than that of larger events. A selected few of these topics lingered in the communal memory long after the daily press had finished with them, there to join occurrences that were recognized at the time as having profound significance and that we realize today were landmarks in the history of Victorian England.

The earliest major event to be memorialized as a topicality in Victorian fiction was the bitterly fought campaign to free Roman Catholics from the civil disabilities under which they had labored ever since the late seventeenth century. "The Catholics, bad harvests, and the mysterious fluctuations of trade," wrote George Eliot as she described the climate of opinion at St. Ogg's in *The Mill on the Floss,* "were the three evils mankind had to fear," and the greatest of these was the coming backwash of "the Catholic question" (1.12:106). Only Mr. Deane's sanguine view of the nation's economic prospects mitigated, for a time, the popular conviction that "the country would become utterly the prey of Papists and Radicals" (1.7:67), because, as surely as night followed day, the passage of the Catholic Relief Bill in 1829 was to be followed by a still greater disaster, the passage of the First Reform Bill. A character in Bulwer's *Alice,* set in the same "unreformed years," similarly was convinced that "the ballot"—that is, the secret ballot, representing the total triumph of electoral reform and therefore of the widely dreaded democracy—was a logical consequence of Catholic emancipation (6.5:360). (In the event, it was staved off for another forty years.)

Far from settling "the Catholic question," the fait accompli of 1829 merely exacerbated the divisiveness stemming from the controversy. But "Mr. Peel's late extraordinary tergiversation in the fatal Catholic Relief Bill" was one of the numerous contemporary issues in which the widowed Amelia Sedley Osborne, in *Vanity Fair*, was wholly uninterested. "'She is dreadfully ignorant or indifferent,' said Mrs. Glowry, with a voice as if from the grave, and a sad shake of the head and turban—'I asked her if she thought that it was in 1836, according to Mr. Jowls, or in 1839, according to Mr. Wapshot, that the Pope was to fall: and she said—"Poor Pope! I hope not—What has he done?"'" (61:595). (The Reverend Giles Jowls was "the Illuminated Cobbler, who dubbed himself Reverend as Napoleon crowned himself Emperor" [33:322]; he and Mr. Wapshot represented the ultra-Protestant polemicists of the day.) In addition to the Jowlses' and Wapshots' prophetic exercises, the bill inspired a large body of fiction on both sides, none of which is remembered today.[1]

One imaginary product of the Catholic Relief debate was a poem written at that time by the youthful Arthur Pendennis, "On Saint Bartholomew's Day," "a tremendous denunciation of Popery," says Thackeray, "and a solemn warning to the people of England to rally against emancipating the Roman Catholics" (*Pendennis*, 3:1.26). Readers of the completed *Pendennis* two or three years after the first number, containing this reminiscence, appeared in November 1848, would have responded to it more emotionally than Thackeray anticipated: it was one of the numerous topical references in Victorian fiction to which later events lent a new charge of meaning. In the interim Pope Pius IX's announcement of the reinstatement of the Catholic hierarchy in Britain had dashed oil on the long-smoldering anti-Romish feeling in the nation, with the result that in August 1851 Parliament passed the Ecclesiastical Titles Act which forbade Catholic bishops to assume British titles. "Papal Aggression," as the issue was called, stirred a nationwide hysteria that was vented in extraordinarily scurrilous prose and cartoons (not least in *Punch*), in comparison with which Pen's poem would undoubtedly have seemed a model of restraint.

Catholic Emancipation was a domestic issue only, whereas Papal Aggression was international, involving as it did a sovereign state headquartered in Rome. The difference was reflected, though somewhat confusedly, in Mrs. Gaskell's *Cranford*, when Lady Glenmire admired Mrs. Forrester's lace collar. "'Yes,' said that lady, 'such lace cannot be got now for either love nor money; made by the nuns abroad they tell me. They say they can't make it now, even there. But perhaps they can now they've passed the Catholic Emancipation Bill'" (8:78).† In some mysterious way, Catholic Emancipation at home meant liberating Continental nuns from a (papal?) ban on lace-making.

To a larger portion of the Anglican communion than the ultra-Protestants who led the vilifying chorus against Papal Aggression, the Oxford Movement represented the fulfillment of the fears the people at St. Ogg's harbored: its logical end was Lambeth Palace's capitulation to the Vatican. Like the novels dealing with Catholic Emancipation, the considerable number inspired by Tractarianism have disappeared into oblivion.²

The leading novelists, having reflected in their respective ways these new developments in the Church of England, derided their lesser colleagues' exploitation of the topicality. In *Aurora Floyd*, Miss Braddon defined a High Church novel as one "in which the heroine rejected the clerical hero because he did not perform the service according to the Rubric" (14:135), but in Trollope's *The Three Clerks* a different scenario was proposed. In one of the stories that Charley Tudor wrote to order for the *Daily Delight*, "the end," as Charley told Harry Norman, "is rather melancholy. Sir Anthony reforms, leaves off drinking, and takes to going to church every day. He becomes a Puseyite, puts up a memorial window to the Baron, and reads the Tracts. At last he goes over to the Pope, walks about in nasty dirty clothes all full of vermin, and gives over his estate to Cardinal Wiseman" (19:219).

But the mainstream fiction of the day, although it did not use Tractarianism as a central theme, abounds with clergymen with such leanings who are described as "High Church" or "Puseyite"—Trollope's Mr. Oriel and Mr. Arabin, for example.† And from the Oxford Movement sprang, by a somewhat indirect route, the ritualism that was a recurrent topic in the fiction of the late forties and the fifties. Originally representing simply a revival of interest in the general architecture of

†The verb tense suggests that the passage of the bill was an event of the quite recent past, whereas, assuming that *Cranford* is set in the late 1830s or early 1840s (Mrs. Gaskell fudged the point), it had occurred at least a decade earlier. This is one of a number of means she employed to suggest how time stood still, or at best crept slowly, in the town. Topicalities that were outdated in the world at large were still fresh news there. On the other hand, it is conceivable that, under cover of the hazy chronology, Mrs. Gaskell slipped in a strictly up-to-date topicality, a palpable anachronism, for the sake of making Mrs. Forrester's confusion worse confounded. Might not readers in 1851 have suspected that she thought Catholic Emancipation and the controversial issue of the moment, Papal Aggression, were the same?

This picture of the furious Protestant crowd entering the London Guildhall for a mass meeting (*Illustrated London News*, 30 November 1850) conveys some idea of the intensity of feeling that met the Pope's reestablishment of the English hierarchy and influenced readers' responses to mentions of the issue in novels of the moment.

churches, in its full flower the movement concentrated on the decoration of the altar and the dress and ceremonial postures of the minister, and it was this aspect that particularly engaged novelists' attention. There is a retrospective, mildly anachronistic hint of developing ritualism in *Jane Eyre* (1848): Eliza Reed devotes three hours a day to "stitching, with gold thread, the border of a square crimson cloth, almost large enough for a carpet. In answer to my [Jane's] inquiries after the use of this article, she informed me it was a covering for the altar of a new church lately erected near Gateshead" (21:294). Dr. Kenn, the saintly rector of St. Ogg's, imperils his parishioners' respect for him by putting candles on the communion table and holding early prayers every morning.

†In unsympathetic mouths, "Puseyite" could become a powerful term of abuse, a possibility that must be kept in mind as one encounters it in novels: it was not merely descriptive but heavily judgmental. Surtees's characters, in particular, were given to applying it to people they despised, as when Lord Scamperdale, in *Mr. Sponge's Sporting Tour*, called Soapey Sponge "you perpendicular-looking Puseyite pig-jobber!" (20:110), the "perpendicular" perhaps alluding to the ritualist enthusiasm for medieval church architecture.

"Fashionable" clergymen were usually High Churchmen. In *Pendennis*, the hero's old tutor Mr. Smirke, brought up in Claphamite Evangelical circles, turns High Church with a vengeance:

> He cut off his coat collar, and let his hair grow over his back. He rigorously gave up the curl which he used to sport on his forehead, and the tie of his neckcloth, of which he was rather proud. He went without any tie at all. He went without dinner on Fridays. He read the Roman Hours, and intimated that he was ready to receive confessions in the vestry. The most harmless creature in the world, he was denounced as a black and most dangerous Jesuit and Papist, by Mr. Muffin of the Dissenting chapel, and Mr. Simeon Knight at the old church. Mr. Smirke had built his chapel of ease with the money left him by his mother at Clapham. Lord! lord! what would she have said to hear a table called an altar! to see candlesticks on it! to get letters signed on the Feast of Saint So-and-so, or the Vigil of Saint What-do-you-call-'em! . . . The post office never brought him any letters from the Pope; he thought Blanche, to be sure, at first, the most pious, gifted, right-thinking, fascinating person he had ever met; and her manner of singing the Chants delighted him. . . . (63:2.267)

Between them, Smirke and Blanche Amory exemplify the uses novelists like Thackeray made of the innovative religion of the 1830s and 1840s. However sincere Smirke's views may have been, his practices, both ecclesiastical and sartorial, smacked of opportunism; he followed the newest clerical fashion, just as Blanche did when she was constantly in attendance at his "pretty little church, of immense antiquity—a little Anglo-Norman *bijou*, built the day before yesterday, and decorated with all sorts of painted windows, carved saints' heads, gilt Scripture texts, and open pews" (63:2.266). Blanche began forthwith to work a most correct High-Church altar-cover, which may have been the occasion of the "conference of near two hours in the vestry" that Thackeray mentions.†

In *The Newcomes*, Charles Honeyman works the female trade for all it is worth. "The reverend gent," as Thackeray devastatingly dubs him (for the implication of "gent" see pages 244–48 below), is Victorian fiction's most accomplished parlor cleric, transferring to the mansions of Mayfair and Belgravia the ingratiating talents Dickens's Mr. Stiggins had devoted to his adoring lower-middle-class clientele in *Pickwick Papers*. One cannot help thinking that Honeyman's fictional prototype was the

---

†The amount of needlework and other services farmed out to pious women—or at least women to whom an affectation of piety was the vogue of the moment—was handy for novelists. It enabled them to bring a much discussed religious movement into the intimacy of the parlor or fireside, in the same way that the doctrines at issue were dramatized and literally "brought home" when a leading character was torn between, say, Tractarianism and Roman Catholicism, and a family crisis ensued, as it often did in real life.

FASHIONS FOR 1850; OR,

On the same day the preceding picture appeared in the *Illustrated London News*, *Punch* came out with this cartoon (above and opposite), one of the many anti-Popery, anti-Puseyite thrusts with which it fed the "Papal Aggression" hysteria. Especially notable is the manner in which it satirizes the fancy ecclesiastical dress associated with both Roman Catholicism and "Romish" Puseyism—what Dickens was later to call, in *Bleak House*, "Dandyism" in religion.

A PAGE FOR THE PUSEYITES.

Reverend Morphine Velvet in *Ten Thousand a Year*, whose Rosemary Chapel, near St. James's Square, attracted such blue-blooded communicants as the Earl of Dreddlington and his family. Warren described him and his sacred enterprise in terms almost indistinguishable from Thackeray's:

'Twas a fashionable chapel, a chapel of *Ease*; rightly so called, for it was a
very *easy* mode of worship, discipline, and doctrine that was there practiced
and inculcated. . . . Mr. Morphine Velvet's yoke was very "easy," his burden
very "light." He was a popular preacher; middle-aged; sleek, serene, solemn in his person and demeanour. He had a very gentleman-like appearance in the pulpit and reading-desk. There was a sort of soothing, winning,
elegance and tenderness in the tone and manner in which he *prayed* and
besought his dearly beloved brethren, as many as were there present, to accompany him, their bland and graceful pastor, to the throne of the heavenly grace. [And, as usual with Warren, much, much more.] (22:591)

As incumbent of Lady Whittlesea's chapel, Mayfair, Honeyman is the
central figure in the novel's cluster of satirical allusions to the religious
fashion of the day.[3] His sister, at the same time, is vehemently anti-
Catholic. So had the lowly Miss Higgs of Manchester been until she became the Princesse de Montcontour, when she found herself "not so
hostile to Rome as she had been at an earlier period of her religious
life; . . . she had migrated (in spirit) from Clapham to Knightsbridge, as
so many wealthy mercantile families have likewise done in the body"
(*The Newcomes*, 40:2.18)—the migration, that is, of leading Evangelicals,
"Saints" in the derisory parlance of the period, from their Clapham Zion
to the new venue of High Church Anglicanism. St. Paul's, Knightsbridge, consecrated in 1843, and its chapel of ease, St. Barnabas's, Pimlico, consecrated seven years later, were both in the hands of incumbent
priests whose innovations did not sit well with many of their parishioners, including Lord John Russell and his wife, or their representatives in
the vestry. At the former church, one of the wardens brought suit
against the rector to force him to remove the high altar and its ornaments. At St. Barnabas's, an enthusiastic young curate hired choir boys
to throw rotten eggs at a sandwich man employed by a churchwarden to
carry antiritualistic messages through the parish.

When Pendennis and Clive Newcome visited the Princesse de Montcontour at her hotel in Jermyn Street, they found her surrounded by "a
number of pretty little books in middle-age bindings, in antique type
many of them, adorned with pictures of the German School, representing demure ecclesiastics, with their heads on one side, children in long
starched nightgowns, virgins bearing lilies, and so forth. . . . A long strip
of embroidery, of the Gothic pattern, furthermore betrayed her present
inclinations . . ." (40:2.18).[†]

[†] At that point, Honeyman arrives, "sliding over the carpet" in a snakelike movement
that suggests the sinuous demeanor conventionally attributed to Jesuits. His ceremonious
entrance is announced by a gigantic footman bawling "Mr. 'Oneyman." One wonders if
readers of *The Newcomes* were reminded of another such entrance that had been depicted

Dickens paid his ironic respects to the newly resuscitated "Dandyism," "the newest fashion . . . in Religion" (*Bleak House*, 12:210) as represented by the ladies and gentlemen who gather at Chesney Wold in a dreary January—members of the select upper class that had distanced itself from the ecclesiastical heresies of the Oxford Movement but delightedly adopted its offspring, the theatrical trappings and ceremonies of ritualism. But this was only a passing reference, and elsewhere in the novel Dickens expressed his animus toward the newest fashion in the person of Mrs. Pardiggle, self-appointed missionary to the heathen of St. Albans and mother of five surly sons named for heroes and holy men particularly favored by the High Church—Egbert, Oswald, Francis, Felix, and Alfred. (Dickens never calls her a Puseyite, but everything he says about her invited his readers to apply to her that derogatory label.)

As late as 1885, George Meredith recalled the Tractarian furor as one of the distinguishing events of the forties, the setting of *Diana of the Crossways*. The heiress Constance Asper totters on the brink of Rome, and the "burly old shipowner" Quintin Manx, M.P., confides his worries to Lady Wathin:

> Constance, he said, had plunged into these new spangle, candle and high singing services; was all for symbols, harps, effigies, what not. Lady Wathin's countenance froze in hearing of it. She led Mr. Quintin to a wall-sofa, and said: "Surely the dear child must have had a disappointment, for her to have taken to those foolish displays of religion! It is generally a sign."
>
> "Well, ma'am—my lady—I let girls go their ways in such things. I don't interfere. But it's that fellow [Percy Dacier], or nobody, with her. She has fixed her girl's mind on him, and if she can't columbine as a bride she will as a nun. Young people must be at some harlequinade." (21:238–39)

Later, Meredith describes Constance's room as one that both Blanche Amory and the Princesse de Montcontour would have been at home in: "a saintly little room; and more impressive in purity, indeed it was, than a saint's, with the many crucifixes, gold and silver emblems, velvet *prie-Dieu* chairs, jewel-clasped sacred volumes; every invitation to meditate in

---

a year or two earlier in *Bleak House*, when the Rev. Mr. Chadband's arrival with his wife at the Snagsbys' was heralded, not by a gigantic footman, but by the wretched slavey from the orphan asylum: "Mr. and Mrs. Cheeseming, least which, Imeantersay, whatsername!" (19:316). Dickens added an inspired touch by having the Protestant, nonsacramental, and undoubtedly anti-Papist clergyman's advent announced by a tinkling of the bell at the inner door, as if in imitation of the moment when the Host is elevated. The same attractive line of interpretation would lead to the further hypothesis that the oiliness Chadband exudes represents not only an excessive application of Rowlands' Macassar Oil but an overdose of chrism.

A STAINED WINDOW FOR ROCHESTER CATHEDRAL.

We have been favoured with the inspection of a design for a painted window to be put up in Rochester Cathedral at the expense of the Dean and Chapter.

When we say, at the expense of the Dean and Chapter, we do not mean to insinuate that the Dean and Chapter are going to pay for the window.

The design is divided into compartments, each representing, in the mediæval fashion, a "Fytte," in "Ye Gestes of Maister Robert Whiston ye Confessour."

In *Compartment* 1, at the left hand corner of the window, the Master of the Cathedral School, Whiston, is seen standing beside a lectern or reading desk, whereon lie some scrolls of parchment inscribed with black letter, which he is supposed to be reading; although, in accordance with the principles of ancient art, he is delineated fronting the spectator. His arms are averted sideways, with the hands uplifted, and the palms open. He rests on the points of his toes, and his cap is raised from his head on those of his hair, which is standing on end. The contorted mouth and goggle eyes express horror and astonishment. Beneath is written,

Maister Roberte Whistone Discouerynge how ye Cathedrall Statutes were Ybroke.

In the next scene our hero appears pleading the cause of the Cathedral Scholars, in the Chapter-Room, before the Dean and his associates. With one hand (which is wide open) he extends the Statutes towards the capitular body; the other he stretches over the heads of a party of emaciated youths in academic costume, and angular postures, who are making dolorously wry faces, and have labels issuing from their mouths, inscribed with the legends, "Wee are Starving," "Gyv us over Stypends," and other appeals to pity and justice. "Ye Dene" is delineated in the centre of a number of fat fellows, who, seated at a table covered with great loaves of bread and large fishes, are thrusting their tongues out and poking one another in the ribs; whilst the Very Reverend Gentleman himself is responding to the appeal of Whiston by taking an energetic sight at him with both hands, the fingers of which are extended like spikes in a lateral direction from the decanal nose. This stage of the history is described, below, as

Maister Whyston hys Petycyon to ye Dene and Chapitre.

Division 3 represents the Rev. Mr. Whiston seated in his study, pen in hand, writhing, with dislocated limbs, in the agonies in composition. This effort of genius is described as meant to pourtray

Maistre Whyston wrytinge Cathedrall Crustes and theyr Fulfillmente.

"The fourth picture exhibits in one view the interior and exterior of the Cathedral School. In the school-room are a number of figures, who are recognised by their corpulence and shovel hats as identical with the occupants of the Chapter-House before depicted. A figure of superior obesity to the rest, whom, as their Coryphæus, there is no mistaking, is kicking the Confessor Whiston out of doors; the others are joining their hands in what seems devotion, but is intended for applause. The emaciated scholars are here introduced as trampled on and sprawling beneath their feet. The title under-written is

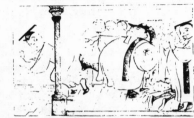

Maister Whistonne thrust forth of his Schoole by ye Deane and Chapiter.

Compartment Fifth displays the expelled Schoolmaster in his progress through the Courts of Law and Equity; the fat clerical figures already alluded to, aided by sundry monsters with tails and cloven feet, and wigs on their heads through which protrude horns, endeavouring to obstruct his progress with various legal instruments, labelled "Replycacyon," "Demmurrer," "Byll of Costes," and such like terms of Law. The denomination of this compartment is

Mayster Robt. Whyston seekyth Justyce.

This pseudo-medieval jeu d'esprit on the Whiston affair (above and opposite) appeared in *Punch* on 29 January 1853, only weeks after Whiston had been restored to his headmastership and six months before Trollope began to write *The Warden*. Its humorous treatment of the ecclesiastical tempest in a teapot harmonized with Trollope's allusions to it, interspersed with more frequent ones to the concurrent St. Cross scandal.

The succeeding division discovers our indomitable WHISTON having carried his case before the Bishop of the Diocese, who is pronouncing judgment to the effect of reinstating that ill-used clergyman in the Mastership of the Cathedral School. The mediæval style is here very appropriate, as strikingly expressive of the ill grace with which the prelate performs that act of tardy justice, namely, by thrusting the appellant down in an academic chair with his crozier, held between his wrists, whilst he exchanges mournful grimaces with the DEAN and CHAPTER. This representation is entitled,

Ɖe Bysschop restoryth Mastere Whistonn against ƥe Grayne.

The crowning scene is

Ɖe Dene and Chaptere eating Rumbil Pye.

The defeated dignitaries are seated in the Chapter-House as before; but in lieu of the loaves and fishes, their fare now consists of a large pasty, on which is written the word RESTITUCYON. In the right hand corner stands the REV. MR. WHISTON hugging a folio, indicated as his book on Cathedral Trusts; in the left there is a Cathedral scholar dancing for joy.

In "storied windows richly dight" there are generally too many stories illustrated that are not strictly accurate; but it will be allowed that the paintings in the new window of Rochester Cathedral will embody a true story.

luxury on an ascetic religiousness" (35:358). But her marriage to Dacier cures all that.

For readers who tired of the Tractarian and Papal Aggression controversies at mid-century, the ecclesiastical news in the press offered another diversion, one that was largely responsible for Trollope's first success as a novelist, *The Warden* (1855). A pair of long-running churchly scandals had lately been winding down.[4] Both were part of a politically inspired movement to inspect the closely guarded ledgers of the Church of England and find out if the rich income of the various churches and foundations was going where it was supposed to go. One case, mentioned by name at least nine times in the novel, stemmed from charges that the master of St. Cross Hospital at Winchester, the pluralist clerical son of a pluralist bishop, had enjoyed an inordinately large income from the foundation, well over £10,000 a year. The other was the Whiston affair, precipitated when the headmaster of the Rochester Cathedral grammar school, Robert Whiston, publicly attacked the dean and chapter for failing to abide by the foundation statute that required them to give scholarships out of cathedral funds to twenty pupils and also to support four ex-pupils who had gone on to university. For his pains, Whiston had lost his job, and he promptly sued. When Trollope began to write *The Warden* on 29 July 1853, Parliament had just completed its four-year investigation of the diversion of funds at St. Cross, and a few days later the Master of the Rolls delivered judgment on it. On the preceding 1 January, the nettlesome Whiston, having fought his dismissal through the whole chain of courts, had been reinstated in his post. Years later Trollope told his first biographer, T. H. S. Escott, that it was the day-to-day reports of these cases and the accompanying letters to the press that had inspired the novel's plot. Cleverly, by referring to the St. Cross and Whiston affairs by name at the outset, he implicitly denied that the Hiram's Hospital of the novel was simply a fictitious version of the real one: the two were wholly separate. At the same time, by mentioning Hiram's Hospital in the same pages that contained St. Cross, he placed it in the same world: if St. Cross was "real," as no newspaper reader could doubt, so was Hiram's Hospital.

2.

Contemporaneous with these religious developments was an equally influential movement in secular life, which novelists treated with a mixture of respect and derision. Here the aim was to improve the intellect of the masses rather than to arouse, amplify, enrich, and direct the spiritual life of the upper crust. The guiding force was not the Thirty-Nine Articles or the ninety theological-historical *Tracts for the Times* (the series title, like the subtitles of novels that echo it, testifies to the up-to-dateness of its interest) but the simple prudential doctrine that Self-Help and Knowledge combined could pave the shining road to Success and Power.

This moral principle was reflected in a variety of contexts. One of the stock figures in novels was the self-taught hero who made his way in adverse circumstances: Job Legh, the millworker-botanist in *Mary Barton*; Alton Locke, the book-reading tailor in Kingsley's novel; Leonard Fairfield in Bulwer-Lytton's *My Novel*; Dinah Maria Mulock's John Halifax—the modern version, in short, of the industrious apprentice in older literature and lore. The schoolmaster may have been abroad, as another cliché of the time (coined by Henry Brougham) had it, though more often than not the phrase was uttered ironically, by people whose belief in the efficacy or even the desirability of popular education was minimal; but the autodidact figure in fiction escaped his ministrations and was obliged somehow to acquire learning, and, more important in a commercial world, practical acumen, without benefit of formal schooling. His heroism bore a direct relation to the steepness of the obstacles he had overcome, an equivalence implied in another catch phrase associated with Brougham, "the pursuit of knowledge under difficulties." This was the title of a two-volume work, published anonymously in 1829–30 by the bustling Society for the Diffusion of Useful Knowledge but known from the title pages of its many later editions to have been written by George Lillie Craik. Dickens mocked it when he had the elder Weller in *Pickwick Papers* come upon his son in the desperate ink-smearing throes of composing his valentine: "But wot's that, you're a doin' of? Pursuit of knowledge under difficulties, Sammy?" (33:538) The phrase became deeply embedded in the Victorian vocabulary and was still current when Dickens borrowed it for the running title (added in the 1867–68 edition) of the second chapter of *Great Expectations*, in which Pip persists in asking questions about the convict hulks in the Medway.

The determined young man who pulled himself up by his own bootstraps (an item of masculine costume peculiar to the period) and the organizations that public-spirited groups formed to help him were the abiding symbol in fiction of the early Victorian confidence in the personally rewarding and socially beneficial powers of education, however obtained. On the opening page of *Pickwick Papers*, the Pickwick Club paid tribute to the author of the paper "Speculations on the Source of the Hampstead Ponds, with some Observations on the Theory of Tittlebats," averring that "inestimable benefits" were bound to accrue from that learned gentleman's "enlarging his sphere of observation, to the advancement of knowledge, and the diffusion of learning." The date was 12 May 1827, and the sentiment—and the terms in which it was expressed—could not have been more timely. The middle phrase implied the veneration of Francis Bacon that characterized the period, he having been the author of *The Advancement of Learning* and the supposed coiner of the Knowledge is Power platitude; the last referred to the Society for the Diffusion of Useful Knowledge, founded only the year before, with much fanfare, by Brougham and his radical-Benthamite associates. Later in the novel, when Mr. Pickwick visits the town of Muggleton, he sees, flanking the marketplace, "an auctioneer's and fire-agency office, a corn-factor's, a linen draper's, a saddler's, a distiller's, a grocer's, and a shoe-shop—the last-mentioned warehouse being also appropriated to the diffusion of hats, bonnets, wearing apparel, cotton umbrellas, and useful knowledge" (7:161). The many cheap instructive publications of the society were distributed through such unorthodox channels during the height of their popularity in the late 1820s and the early 1830s.[†] Many years later, in *Endymion*, Disraeli recalled the fad and the skepticism, if not outright antagonism, that the sponsoring organization inspired. Farmer Thornberry confides to his tenant, Mr. Ferrars, his worry over his son's unconventional, including politically liberal, sympathies. "[B]ut then he is young," he says. "But I am very much afraid he will leave me. I think it is this new thing the big-wigs have set up in London that has put him wrong, for he is always reading their papers." Ferrars: "And what is that?" Thornberry: "Well, they call themselves the Society for the Diffusion of Knowledge, and Lord Brougham is at the head of it." "Ah!" says Ferrars, "he is a dangerous man" (13:49).

In the period 1830–50, the growing "fashion of the age," as a character in *My Novel* remarked, was to "set up a mechanics' institute." In *Sybil* the "Temple of the Muses" in Mowbray was a mechanics' institute under a typically elegant title, as was the Hackney Parthenopaeon, where Frederick Bayham, the successful journalist in *The Newcomes*, had once picked up small fees "lecturing on the genius of some of our comic writers" when he was on his uppers as a briefless barrister and literary man who could not sell "the works of his brains" (12.1:139).

A prettified description of a mechanics' institute outing—honest laboring men and their families in a festive mood—was one of the several passages that lent Tennyson's *The Princess* (1847) greater topicality than most early- and mid-Victorian poems possessed; it has been traced to a particular occasion, a picnic on the grounds of a house near Maidstone on 6 July 1842.[5] At mid-century, these agencies for popular enlightenment were largely being taken over by the mercantile-manufacturing middle class in their respective communities, and in at least four novels in the next fifteen years opportune use was made of a typically upgraded institute. On his return to Clavering, Pendennis consoled himself for the absence of Dr. Portman, the village rector who had retired to Harrogate to favor his gout,

> by making acquaintance with Mr. Simcoe, the opposition preacher, and with the two partners of the cloth-factory at Chatteris, and with the Independent preacher there, all of whom he met at the Clavering Athenaeum,

[†]Encountering Mr. Pickwick in the Fleet debtors' prison, Jingle describes to him how he had pawned his last disposable possessions to keep body and soul together. "'Lived for three weeks upon a pair of boots, and a silk umbrella with an ivory handle!' exclaimed Mr. Pickwick, who had only heard of such things in shipwrecks, or read of them in Constable's *Miscellany*" (42:688–90). This commercial publication, like the books issued by the not-for-profit Society for the Diffusion of Useful Knowledge, catered to the current vogue for self-education.

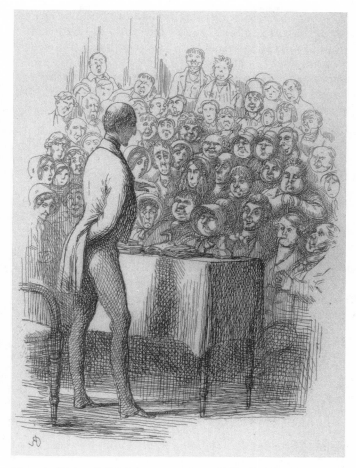

Here is Richard Doyle's conception of Sir Barnes Newcome discoursing on "the Affections" from the rostrum of the Newcome Athenaeum, "round about which the magnates of the institution and the notabilities of the town were rallied."

which the Liberal party had set up in accordance with the advanced spirit of the age, and perhaps in opposition to the aristocratic old reading-room, into which the *Edinburgh Review* had once scarcely got an admission, and where no tradesmen were allowed an entrance. (*Pendennis*, 65:2.284–85)

—the politicized double-track history of the mechanics' institute movement in a nutshell. In places like Clavering by mid-century, the former mechanics' institutes had been gentrified, and at the same time the institutes' elite precursors, the so-called Lit and Phil societies, had been downgraded, though retaining such fancy titles as "Athenaeum." Both trends attested to the predominance of the class that occupied the middle ground.

Gaining public exposure by lecturing, gratis, at an institute sometimes was part of a candidate's electioneering routine. Sir Barnes Newcome's appearance was announced thus in the *Newcome Independent*:

> Newcome Athenaeum. 1. For the benefit of the Newcome Orphan Children's Home, and 2. for the benefit of the Newcome Soup Association, without distinction of denomination. Sir Barnes Newcome Newcome, Bart., proposes to give two lectures, on Friday the 23rd, and Friday the 30th, instant. No. 1. The Poetry of Childhood: Doctor Watts, Mrs. Barbauld, Jane Taylor. No. 2. The Poetry of Womanhood, and the Affections: Mrs. Hemans, L.E.L. Threepence will be charged at the doors, which will go to the use of the above two admirable societies. (*The Newcomes*, 65:2.287–88)

The lectures were delivered as promised, and Thackeray gives a summary of their content, the eloquence "plapping on like water from a cistern" (66:2.300). The subsequent review of Sir Barnes's performance in the *Independent* did him no good in the public estimation, as we shall note in a later chapter.

A few years later, in *Framley Parsonage*, Trollope, perhaps not forgetting Sir Brian's addresses, arranged for Harold Smith, M.P., to deliver a lecture on the South Seas, with Bishop Proudie in the chair and the audience consisting mainly of Barchester tradesmen and their wives. Although satirically intended, Trollope's account of the lecture is no more exaggerated than Thackeray's, as contemporary reports of actual mechanics' institute performances assure us:

> "On the present occasion . . . our object is to learn something as to those grand and magnificent islands which lie far away, beyond the Indies, in the Southern Ocean; the lands of which produce rich spices and glorious fruits, and whose seas are embedded with pearls and corals, Papua and the Philippines, Borneo and the Moluccas. My friends, you are familiar with your maps, and you know the track which the equator makes for itself through those distant oceans. . . . But what . . . avails all that God can give to man, unless man will open his hand to receive the gift? And what is this opening of the hand but the process of civilization—yes, my friends, the process of civilization? These South Sea islanders have all that a kind Providence can bestow on them; but that all is as nothing without education. That education and that civilization it is for you to bestow upon them—yes, my friends, for you; for you, citizens of Barchester as you are."

But this harangue, whose florid eloquence grew as Harold Smith proceeded, had untoward consequences.

"It is to civilization that we must look," continued Mr. Harold Smith, descending from poetry to prose as a lecturer well knows how, and thereby showing the value of both—"for any material progress in these islands; and—"

"And to Christianity," shouted Mrs. Proudie, to the great amazement of the assembled people, and to the thorough wakening of the bishop, who, jumping up in his chair at the sound of the well-known voice, exclaimed, "Certainly, certainly. . . ."

"Christianity and Sabbath-day observance," exclaimed Mrs. Proudie, who, now that she had obtained the ear of the public, seemed well inclined to keep it. "Let us never forget that these islanders can never prosper unless they keep the Sabbath holy." (6:1.70–73)

Poor Mr. Smith completed his lecture, but in total disarray and without having had a chance to bring into play the "huge bundle of statistics, with which he had meant to convince the reason of his hearers, after he had taken full possession of their feelings." The next day, at a post mortem of the occasion, Smith confessed he had been so rattled that he did not hear what Mrs. Proudie said.

"She hoped you would not put the South Sea islanders up to Sabbath travelling," said Mr. Sowerby.

"And specially begged that you would establish Lord's-day schools," said Mrs. Smith; and then they all went to work and picked Mrs. Proudie to pieces from the top ribbon of her cap down to the sole of her slipper. (7:1.83)

Also testifying to the prominence of the mechanics' institutes in the Victorian consciousness—and to the low opinion some people had of them—was the interlude in Wilkie Collins's *A Rogue's Life* in which the narrator serves briefly as secretary of the Duskydale Literary and Scientific Institution between a spell in the bogus old-master painting racket and participation, albeit reluctant, in a more familiar kind of counterfeiting, the manufacture of unofficial coins. In Bulwer-Lytton's *What Will He Do With It?* the Gatesboro' Athenaeum and Literary Institute was the site of a performance by a learned dog attached to a strolling theatrical troupe.

Another offshoot of the popular education movement was the system of elementary schools which, beginning in 1833 with a miserly Treasury grant of £20,000, came to be partially subsidized from public funds and, for that reason, governed by rules and regulations handed down from Whitehall. The predecessors of these schools had been those sponsored by two bitterly contentious religious groups, the British and Foreign School Society (nonsectarian and Benthamite) and the National Society for the Education of the Poor in the Principles of the Established Church in England and Wales (Anglican). Ham Peggotty acquired his learning, such as it was, in the Yarmouth "national school." To alleviate the shortage of teachers willing to settle for wages many a skilled workman would have scorned, teacher-training institutions were established, the first at Battersea in 1840. The best-known graduates of such schools in fiction were Mr. M'Choakumchild in *Hard Times*, who Dickens said was one of "some one hundred and forty other schoolmasters [who] had been lately turned at the same time, in the same factory, on the same principles, like so many pianoforte legs" (1.2:52–53), and Bradley Headstone in *Our Mutual Friend*, the victim of the futile social ambition allegedly fostered by the spread of elementary schooling and the creation of a new breed of schoolmaster. The classroom scenes in both novels are the best evidence contemporary fiction provides of the wretched learn-by-rote theory of education in (faltering?) action. Within a few years, the government-trained and certified female teacher had become commonplace. Miss Peecher, presiding over her school in an outlying working-class neighborhood in *Our Mutual Friend*, had her counterpart in rural Wessex. Fancy Day, in *Under the Greenwood Tree*, had gone to a normal school, where "her name stood first among the Queen's scholars of her year," and "when she sat for her certificate as Government teacher, she had the highest of the first class" (4.2:154).

The first phase of the popular education movement, still fresh in many readers' memories, continued to serve as a useful period token. Reaching back to the 1840s in *The Return of the Native*, Hardy recalled the spread of such newfangled education, as it was regarded by Wessex countrymen. Olly the besom maker declares, "The class of folk that couldn't use to make a round O [i.e., write a legible hand] to save their bones from the pit can write their names now without a sputter of the pen, oftentimes without a single blot: what do I say?—why, almost without a desk to lean their stomachs and elbows upon" (1.3:17).

3.

As a quick fix for the manifold social problems that Victorian Britain had to cope with, free elementary education turned out to be a failure. But a backup solution presented itself toward the end of the 1840s: emigration, which had the attractive power to remove the problems en masse from British shores and dump them halfway round the world, where they could fend for themselves. For many years, of course, there had been a steady flow of English and Scottish emigrants to North America, and during the Great Famine hundreds of thousands of the Irish endured the long Atlantic voyage under slave-ship conditions. To

workingmen disaffected with Chartism, westward emigation offered an
escape route. Mrs. Gaskell contrived for her hero Jem Wilson, in *Mary
Barton*, what amounted, under the circumstances, to a truly luxurious
destiny in Canada. As "an intelligent man, well acquainted with mechanics," he was promised a job as instrument maker at the new agricultural college in Toronto—free passage, and house and land provided
when he arrived, in addition to a percentage on the instruments ·he
made (36:363). As Jem said, it was an offer he could not refuse.

By that time (1848) a new, endlessly absorbent destination had come
into the public view. Hitherto, Australia had been regarded only as a
conveniently remote place to which to ship convicted criminals—men,
women, and children, some guilty of major offenses, some (hapless victims of a grossly imperfect system of justice) of minor ones or none at
all. The flawed hero of Bulwer's *Paul Clifford* (1830) escaped from an
Australian convict camp and made his way to America and a fortune.
But in the middle of the century, as Coral Lansbury has shown, the continent, its population of social rejects notwithstanding, became the site
of a supposed Arcadian paradise such as even the most visionary re-
formers could no longer conceive as materializing in industrial England,
a vast land overflowing with milk, honey, and flocks of sheep to be nurtured and shorn for the profitable export market.[6]

The most energetic propagandists for Australian emigration were
Samuel Sidney, one of Dickens's associates in the early years of *Household
Words*, and Mrs. Caroline Chisholm, "the emigrant's friend," who had
greeted every ship arriving in New South Wales between 1840 and 1846
and tirelessly exerted herself to help the newly arrived men and their
families to settle in and to spare unaccompanied women the attentions
of waiting procuresses. On her return to England, she won the ears of
influential officials and founded the Female Colonization Loan Society,
underwritten by Coutts's Bank, which loaned migrants their passage
money at no interest and found work for them on their arrival. At this
moment the cause received welcome publicity in Bulwer-Lytton's *The
Caxtons*, which was serialized in *Blackwood's Magazine* from April 1848 to
October 1849. In it, several of the main characters go to Australia, prosper, and bring their wealth back to England, and in the course of the
narrative Bulwer-Lytton devoted two lengthy editorializing passages to
the pros and cons of emigration. Dickens met Mrs. Chisholm in 1850,
was converted, and gave her practical assistance by running no fewer
than six articles on Australian emigration in the first year of *Household
Words* and sending the Peggottys, the Micawbers, and Mr. Mell the flute-
playing schoolmaster in successful quest of modest antipodean fortunes.
That Mr. Micawber succeeded in the face of his unblemished record of

These news pictures of emigrants boarding ship and the ship's departure from the Waterloo Docks, Liverpool (*Illustrated London News*, 6 July 1850) (above), added immediacy and authenticity to Phiz's realization of a like scene in the October number of *David Copperfield* (opposite).

failure while in England was proof enough of the miraculous quality of life Down Under.

If this fictional turn of events strained credibility, credibility was soon strengthened by arriving news of a gold strike, first near Bathurst (12 February 1851) and some months later at several places in the newly constituted state of Victoria. The London press described the region as "one vast gold-field," and a year later the ship *Dido,* inbound with ten and a half tons of the precious metal aboard, passed vessels carrying early contingents of the emigrant flood which in the next eight years would deliver some 290,000 gold-seeking settlers to Australian ports. The novelists followed them and often brought them back. The hero of Kingsley's *Two Years Ago* (1857) returned with £1,500 in gold sovereigns in his purse, only to lose them, for almost the whole duration of the novel, when he was shipwrecked off the Cornish coast. The next year, Trollope's Alaric Tudor in *The Three Clerks,* newly released from prison after serving a term for embezzlement, went off to Australia as a matter of course; even when convicted criminals were not sent there under compulsion, it was becoming a customary place to which they would ex-ile themselves in a kind of expiation tempered by dreams of striking it (legitimately) rich.

The intensifying public interest in Australia was a windfall to sensation novelists. Alfred Austin wrote in *Temple Bar* (1870) that the modern reader

> knows nothing of the Hesperides, the inhospitable Caucasus, Ultima Thule, or the back of the North Wind; and he does not suppose that he knows anything about them. Moreover, he does not want to know anything about them. But he does know something about Australia, or he fancies he does; and he wants to know something more—or, at least, to hear it talked about—because he has a brother, son, cousin, or former servant there, and he is aware that hundreds of people have there made large fortunes. Accordingly, Australia is the very thing for the sensational novelist to conjure with. If such a distance does not quite lend enchantment to the view, it makes bigamy, missing letters, the rapid accumulation of money, and misreported deaths amazingly feasible. Australia has been a true goldfield to the Sensational School of novelists, and many a good "find" has it provided for them.[7]

Thus Charles Reade grafted one topicality onto another in *It Is Never Too Late to Mend*: when benevolence replaces sadism in the administration of the prison that was the central "problem" in the first part of the novel, the prisoner, transported to Australia, becomes a ticket-of-leave man in the goldfields. Once reformed, he becomes a recidivist—anything to prolong the narrative as it reached the public in 1856—and is finally re-reformed by a chance reading of a religious tract. The first 130 pages of Reade's and Boucicault's *Foul Play* (1868) were set in Australia and on the voyage home.

Wilkie Collins's early novel *Hide and Seek* (1854) was written well after news of the gold strike had arrived, but because his plot ended in 1851, he could not take advantage of it. He therefore did the next best thing by having his adventurer, Matthew Grice, returning to England with a cap on his head because his scalp had been removed by some Amazon Indians, report that he had "made a good time of it in California, where I've been last, digging gold" (2.1:275). George Talboys, Lady Audley's first husband in *Lady Audley's Secret* (1861–62), returned from Australia richer by £20,000, the price he received for a single nugget.

Australia was also convenient to the purposes of Surtees, whose Soapey Sponge, in *Mr. Facey Romford's Hounds* (1864–65), migrates there after his cigar and betting shop has failed. He digs a satisfactory amount of gold, and then, meeting Facey Romford in Melbourne, joins him in setting up a bank. Surtees left the sequel—what happened to the depositors and shareholders in a financial institution run by this precious pair—to the reader's imagination.

Emigration as a mass movement faded as a topicality in the 1870s, after which Australia was looked upon as a relatively settled colony, however distant, which was linked with the homeland by telegraph and where people went in the more or less ordinary course of business. Trollope traveled there twice, in 1871–72 and 1875, partly to gather material for travel books and partly to visit his son Fred, who had located at a remote sheep station. He took a more serious interest in the land than did his fellow novelists, who regarded it largely as a conveniently topical place to send characters whose continued presence in England was undesirable (either from their own point of view or that of society, or the necessity of the plot). He did follow their routine in sending John Caldigate to Australia after he sowed his wild oats at Newmarket—and in returning him after he had made an honest fortune in the goldfields (*John Caldigate* [1878–79]). It was not the prospect of instant riches, however, but that of a more democratic society, which sent the newly rich, formerly radical tailor, Daniel Thwaite, to Sydney with his bride (*Lady Anna* [1873–74]).

4.

The burst of interest in emigration at the halfway point of the century coincided with another topical event. In the third of his *Latter-Day Pamphlets* (1850), Carlyle had inveighed against the inbred bureaucracy that managed the nation's governmental business. Shortly afterward, a royal commission, headed by Sir Stafford Northcote and Sir Charles Trevelyan, was appointed to look into the matter. In its report, published in 1853, it recommended converting the Barnacle-encrusted offices, whose major accomplishment, in Dickens's view, had been to perfect ways of avoiding any constructive action, into a professional body open to all talents through genuinely competitive examinations. The controversy these radical proposals stirred was fed by the ensuing public indignation over the incompetence with which the agencies concerned had responded to the demands of the Crimean War.[8]

The Circumlocution Office in *Little Dorrit*, which began serialization in December 1855, was a satirical summation of the defects the Northcote-Trevelyan report found in the old system of patronage and sinecures. For this topicality Dickens paid a price, then and now. One of the main charges James Fitzjames Stephen leveled against him in the "License of Modern Novelists" article already mentioned (page 85 above) was what Stephen called his irresponsible animus against an institution which in its unreformed state, Stephen maintained, had served the nation well. More than a century later, a distinguished career official, C. P. Snow, supported Stephen's charge. The "cumulative mass of evidence ... about the condition of the English civil service in Dickens's period," he wrote, proves that "it was not much like what he imagined."[9] Still, far-reaching changes were needed, and the notoriety of Dickens's Circumlocution Office helped the Society for Administrative Reform, founded in 1855 before *Little Dorrit* began publication, to strengthen the Northcote-Trevelyan case for major reform. In 1870, the ultimate goal of abolishing all patronage and requiring competitive examinations for all aspirants to civil-service positions was achieved under Gladstone, leading to Hardy's simile ten years later in *A Laodicean*, "he felt himself as inconveniently crammed as a candidate for a government examination" (3.2 : 198).

Dickens brought an outsider's bias—an ignorant bias, in Stephen's opinion—to the controversy. Trollope's contrary bias was that of a seasoned insider, for he was a middle-level official of the Post Office, which was as patronage-ridden a bureaucracy as any. As soon as the report was issued, he wrote in his *Autobiography*, he resolved to "lean very heavily" on "that much loathed scheme of competitive examination."[10] He had no opportunity to do so in *The Warden*, his next novel, and in *Barchester Towers* he merely glanced at it when, deploring the Honorable George de Courcy's long-winded speech at the Ullathorne lawn party, he remarked, "either let all speech-making on festive occasions be utterly tabooed and made as it were impossible; or else let those who are to exercise the privilege be first subjected to a competing examination before the civil service examining commissioners" (39 : 448).

This unobtrusive hint of his opposition to competitive examinations was enlarged into a full-fledged attack in the early chapters of *The Three Clerks*, published the following year; and to leave no doubt as to where he stood, Trollope added to the novel a 6,200-word appendix, omitted from modern editions, on "The Civil Service." He wrote as a man whose career had begun and moderately flourished in the existing system but who could not even have entered the civil service if competitive examinations had been required in 1834, because he had been too wretchedly educated. "The prodigy of 1857," he wrote in *The Three Clerks*, "who is now destroying all the hopes of the man who was well enough in 1855 [that is, edging him out of his job or blocking his promotion on the basis of examination scores], will be a dunce to the tyro of 1860" (6 : 63). Not only did Trollope "lean very heavily" on the proposed reform: he loaded the dice against it. In the novel, he set up two contrasting government offices, the badly managed, examination-free Commissioners of Internal Navigation and the Weights and Measures Office, a model of reformed efficiency that was "exactly antipodistic of the Circumlocution Office" (1 : 1).

But the virtuous Weights and Measures, whose examination he describes in detail, was the breeding ground of iniquity. Alaric Tudor, the successful competitor, shoots to the top of the table of organization and becomes one of the "mighty trio" who constitute the examination board. In this supposedly reformed environment, however, he succumbs to temptation and, bribed with shares in the very company (Cornish tin mines) he is officially required to investigate, he enters a second career as speculator. In the end, nemesis overtakes him: he is arrested and convicted on an embezzlement charge and, after serving time, emigrates to Australia, as we have seen. Questionable though it may be, this is Trollope's case against competitive examinations: bright young men may pass them with honors, but that same brilliance can subsequently lead them astray, and no examination can measure a person's moral, as opposed to intelligence, quotient.

The Three Clerks was Trollope's reply to the Circumlocution Office theme in *Little Dorrit*, whose serial run was completed in June 1857, less than a year before Trollope's novel was published. What with the several passages of authorial commentary, and the eventually deleted appendix, Trollope may well have thought he had said his say on that topic. Although there were incidental references to the civil service in ensuing novels—in *Framley Parsonage*, for instance, he remarked sardonically that "in these days a young man cannot get into the Petty Bag Office without knowing at least three modern languages; and he must be well up in trigonometry too, in bible theology, or in one dead language,—at his option" (10:1.113)—it was not until *John Caldigate* (1878–79) that he again paid much attention to it, when he identified the Home Office as the new Circumlocution Office, with a bow to the originator of that derogatory name. Trollope probably meant the scene of Squire Caldigate's visit to that center of governmental business to be the counterpart of Daniel Doyce's getting the runaround at the original Circumlocution Office. But by then, having been passed over for promotion, he had been retired for a dozen years, and with the resultant detachment came a certain mellowing: his satire, while unmistakable, had none of Dickens's wonderful acrimony.

The eventual reform of the civil service could be counted as one of the by-products of the Crimean War. The war itself, which not only tried the resolution and institutions of the unprepared nation in 1854–56 but killed or mutilated many more soldiers than had been sacrificed in all the distant military engagements since Waterloo, had relatively little impact on fiction by the leading writers of the time. Depictions of actual scenes of war were left for novelists of now faded celebrity, such as George Alfred Lawrence in *Guy Livingston* (1857), George Whyte-Melville in *The Interpreter* (1858), Charles Kingsley's brother Henry in *Ravenshoe* (1861), and "Ouida," the future hostess of rakish Guardsmen, in the first of her many novels, *Held in Bondage* (*New Monthly Magazine*, 1861–63), in which the hero and his comrades take part in the charge of the Light Brigade.[†]

A few characters entered Victorian fiction with Crimean service behind them. Captain Talbot Bulstrode, in Braddon's *Aurora Floyd*, had been at Inkermann, where Captain Bellfield, in Trollope's *Can You Forgive Her?*, also claimed, unconvincingly, to have fought. It was only after twenty years had passed, however, that a genuine Crimean veteran played a leading role in a major novel, when, early in *Beauchamp's Career*, Meredith sketched his hero's military life before he turned to politics.

The war served as a continuous background for only one novel by a relatively important writer, Charles Kingsley, the action of whose *Two Years Ago* (1857) was concentrated in 1854–55. In the course of the narrative, ships are reported to be sailing to the Crimea; news comes of the battle of the Alma; the hero, the adventurous physician Tom Thurnall, actually goes out, followed by the heroine, Grace Harvey, as a nurse. Kingsley does not follow them there, but the historical value of the novel resides in the fact that it alone offers a fairly good idea of the way in which ordinary lives in England were affected by the far-off war. Otherwise, the lastingly important novels of the time provide only glimpses of the home front. War is said to be threatening in *Barchester Towers*, and, by a small trick of backdating, in *Doctor Thorne*.

In *The Warden*, Trollope joked, with a rather nasty edge, that Cobden and leading Quakers were appealing for funds to aid the Emperor of Russia, the nation's enemy: a proposal that, on the face of it, was tantamount to treason (10:68–69). The truth was that Cobden, John Bright, and the Quakers—whom nobody listened to—were lonely voices opposing the war; Cobden, as matter of fact, "fully shared the common antipathy to the Russian Emperor." Only weeks before *The Warden* was published (January 1855), he made a speech in the House of Commons (22 December), followed a month later by one at Leeds, urging that the war be ended.[11] In a somewhat different vein, Trollope mocked the reputed omniscience of Tom Towers, the sovereign editorialist of *The Jupiter*:

> Why should we look to Lord John Russell—why should we regard Palmerston and Gladstone, when Tom Towers without a struggle can put us right?

[†]Although Kingsley's *Westward Ho!* (1855) was set in Elizabethan times, its patriotic spirit was plainly applicable to the England of the current moment. As a writer on the Victorian historical novel has remarked, Kingsley served as "a recruiting agent . . . intent on impressing his readers with the view that the English fighting in the Crimea were worthy successors to the scourges of the Spanish Main." (Nicholas Rance, *The Historical Novel and Popular Politics in Nineteenth-Century England* [London, 1975], pp. 54–55.)

Look at our generals, what faults they make; at our admirals, how inactive they are. What money, honesty, and science can do, is done; and yet how badly are our troops brought together, fed, conveyed, clothed, armed, and managed. The most excellent of our good men do their best to man our ships, with the assistance of all possible external appliances, but in vain. All, all is wrong—alas! alas! Tom Towers, and he alone, knows all about it. (14:94)

William Howard Russell's famous dispatches from the war zone, revealing how the soldiers' and sailors' bravery had been undercut by the red tape and downright corruption in Whitehall, had just appeared in the *Times*.†

5.

The publicity that Russell gave to Florence Nightingale's heroic labors in the Crimea provided a timely boost to the slowly developing women's rights movement, a cause doubly handicapped in that it was in no way fashionable and enjoyed no support from the powerful religious and charitable organizations that brought about many other Victorian reforms.[12] Its origin in the 1790s was forgotten by all novelists except Thackeray, who mentioned, as one evidence of Miss Matilda Crawley's having been "a dreadful Radical for those days," that "she talked very lightly about divorce, and most energetically of the rights of women" (*Vanity Fair*, 10:93). The revival of Mary Wollstonecraft's cause in mid-century elicited as little sympathy from male novelists as did the spectacle of fashionable women lusting after dandiacal clerical showmen and enraptured by the theatrical spectacles they performed before the altar. At a party at the Jellybys' in *Bleak House*, John Jarndyce met a Miss Wisk, whose mission, he said, was "to show the world that woman's mission was man's mission"; Miss Wisk herself declared that "the idea of woman's mission lying chiefly in the narrow sphere of Home was an outrageous slander on the part of her Tyrant, Man" and that "the only practical

†There were scattered references in the next few years to the Sepoy Mutiny (summer 1857), when many British soldiers and male civilians were executed at Cawnpore, followed within weeks by the slaughter of their wives and children. In Bulwer-Lytton's *What Will He Do With It?* (1857–59), "the Colonel evinced no more compassionate feeling than any true Englishman, at the time I am writing, would demonstrate for a murderous Sepoy tied to the mouth of a cannon" (12.11:2.568–69)—this being the drastic form taken by the British army's subsequent revenge. In Surtees's *Ask Mamma* (1857–58), Jack Rogers says to Imperial John, "Two such mans as you, sare, could have taken Sebastopol. You could vop all de 'ell 'ound savage Sepoys by yourself" (51:259). And in *Lady Audley's Secret* (1861–62), Robert Audley says, "Do you know . . . that when some of our fellows were wounded in India, they came home, bringing bullets inside them" (7:33).

thing for the world was the emancipation of Woman from the Thraldom
of her Tyrant, Man" (30:479). According to this formulation, Mrs. Pardiggle was an emancipated woman: she pursued her mission far outside
the narrow sphere of Home, into the hovels of brickmakers. Mrs. Jellyby, on the other hand, was unemancipated in this sense, because she
operated from home. But the distinction became meaningless when the
project to turn the natives of Borrioboola-Gha into productive economic
units collapsed and Mrs. Jellyby was obliged at the end of the novel to
find a new mission, which proved to be "the rights of women to sit in
Parliament" (67:933). The full radicalism of this goal can be appreciated
only when it is remembered that a dozen years later the leading advocate
of women's rights, John Stuart Mill, limited the emancipated woman's
political role to possession of the franchise and, even then, restricted
eligibility to single women who met the same property qualification as
men. To Dickens, Mrs. Jellyby had simply traded one crazy cause for
another that was equally absurd.

Shortly after *Bleak House* completed its serial run, and at the very
moment when Florence Nightingale was attaining a kind of secular
sainthood, the pioneer feminist Barbara Leigh Smith (later Bodichon)
published a pamphlet (1854) summarizing, in layperson's language, the
state of the existing laws relating to women. She followed this up with a
petition to Parliament, signed by, among many others—twenty-six thousand of them—such well-known women authors as Elizabeth Barrett
Browning, Elizabeth Gaskell, Harriet Martineau, and Mary Howitt, urging the passage of legislation that would place women on an equal status
with men in certain respects. The blatantly discriminatory laws of divorce were, in that same year, the object of a swingeing attack stemming
from the hopeless position of Stephen Blackpool in *Hard Times*, married
as he was to an alcoholic woman from whom no divorce was possible
except through a cumbersome and expensive appeal to Parliament for a
special act.

The Matrimonial Causes Act of 1857[†] liberalized the procedure, but
it left untouched the double standard by which a husband could divorce
an adulterous wife but not the other way around, unless the husband's

---

[†]This, the first revision of the divorce laws since the Reformation, provided for the
dissolution of marriages to be granted by a new tribunal, organized and presided over by
the eminent judge Sir Cresswell Cresswell. This lawyer with the reduplicative name inspired a topical verb to figure in a hypothetical social gaffe in Surtees's *Plain or Ringlets?*
(1859–60): "How much better this is than calling Mr. Riffield Mr. Driffield, asking after a
man's children who has none, or hoping Mr. Bolter's good lady, who has just been Sir
Cresswell Cresswell'd, is quite well" (55:202). "Most marriages are fairly happy," remarked
Trollope in *Framley Parsonage* (1860–61), "in spite of Sir Cresswell Cresswell; and yet how
little care is taken on earth towards such a result!" (20:1.243)

MILL'S LOGIC; OR, FRANCHISE FOR FEMALES.

"PRAY CLEAR THE WAY, THERE, FOR THESE—A—PERSONS."

When *Punch* printed this cartoon on 30 March 1867, John Stuart Mill had already expressed in Parliament his advocacy of voting rights for women, and on 20 May he would formally offer an amendment to the Second Reform Bill on their behalf. Disraeli and Gladstone joined in opposing it, and it was defeated, 196 to 73.

dereliction was aggravated by other offenses. It conferred a greater benefit on the feminist movement simply by establishing "the woman question" in its various manifestations as an enduringly lively and debatable topic of the times. It was also a boon to novelists. In *The Belton Estate* (1865–66), a sympathetic link between Mrs. Winterfield and her nephew, a Conservative Member of Parliament, was their consensus that the new law was iniquitous and that it was his mission to "annul that godless Act of Parliament and restore the matrimonial bonds of England to their old rigidity" (8:92). The plot of *He Knew He Was Right* (1868–69) centered on a woman's right to keep her child in defiance of the unrelenting attempt of her mad husband, Louis Trevelyan, from whom she was separated, to obtain custody. As the law then stood, she enjoyed no such right. At one point in the novel, the American minister in Florence told

Charles Glascock, Trevelyan's friend, "Your John S. Mill is a great man. . . . He is a far-seeing man. . . . He is one of the few Europeans who can look forward, and see how the rivers of civilization are running on. He has understood that women must at last be put upon an equality with men." ("'Can he manage that men shall have half the babies?' said Mr. Glascock, thinking to escape by an attempt at playfulness") (55:521). This exchange occurred in part 18 of the novel, which appeared on 13 February 1869; it would have had extra point to readers coming to it a few months later, because Mill's *The Subjection of Women*, the prime Victorian women's rights manifesto, was published in May.

Meanwhile, in its issue for 14 March 1868, the *Saturday Review* had printed Mrs. Eliza Lynn Linton's sensational attack on "The Girl of the Period," which inflamed the feminist controversy in advance of Mill's book.[13] Linton was the most vehement antifeminist writer of her time, and as she followed up her initial assault on the liberated woman with several others she managed to offend every party of what men facetiously called "the sex." She came down particularly hard on face painting, hair dyeing, the free use of slang, the flaunting of the latest fashions no matter how tasteless or unladylike, and consorting on familiar terms with cigar-smoking members of the opposite sex. The giddy girl of the period, in fact, was no better than a queen of the demimonde infiltrating respectable society, trailing clouds of suspected immorality to cap her many breaches of decorum. In Linton's own words, "If we must have only one kind of thing, let us have it genuine, and the queens of St. John's Wood in their unblushing honesty rather than their imitators and make-believes in Bayswater and Belgravia. . . . [I]t cannot be too plainly told to the modern English girl that the net result of her present manner of life is to assimilate her as nearly as possible to a class of women whom we must not call by their proper—or improper—name." The article, reprinted as a pamphlet—a single printer is said to have sold forty thousand copies—caused an instant sensation, furnishing an amusing topic of dinner-table conversation and inspiring innumerable jokes in the comic papers, enough, if the metaphor is permissible, to curl any modern feminist's hair.

In the next few years several novelists exploited, or at least referred to, the titillating uproar. Trollope was among them.[14] In *He Knew He Was Right*, Wallachia Petrie says, "If you have a baby, they'll let you go and see it two or three times a day. I don't suppose you will be allowed to nurse it, because they never do in England. You have read what the Saturday Review says. In every other respect the Saturday Review has been the falsest of all false periodicals, but I guess it has been pretty true in what it has said about English women" (81:758). For good measure, in several later novels Trollope made not too heavily veiled allusions to

"EVIL COMMUNICATIONS," &c.

Trollope's satiric allusions to the women's rights movement, most immediately in *Is He Popenjoy?* (1877–78), comported well with *Punch's* antifeminist bias as expressed in such cartoons as this, published on 18 December 1875. The scene, says *Punch*, "is Mrs. Lyon Hunter's Drawing-Room, during a Lecture on 'Women's Rights.' *Modest Youth (in a whisper, to Young Lady looking for a Seat)*. 'Er—excuse me, but do you believe in the equality of the sexes, Miss Wilhelmina!' *Young Lady*. 'Most certainly I do, Mr. Jones.' *Modest Youth*. 'Haw! In that case of course I needn't give you up my chair!'"

the "girl of the period" controversy—it had spread from the intellectual magazines to *Punch*, the stage (in the form of farces), and even the ballroom (in the form of waltzes and galops so titled). Nora Rowley in *He Knew He Was Right* and Alice Vavasor in *Can You Forgive Her?* are generally sympathetic portraits of perfectly respectable yet spirited young women who would not escape Mrs. Linton's censure, and prominent among Miss Jemima Stanbury's numerous reactionary crotchets in *He Knew He Was Right* is ferocious criticism of the modern young woman.

Although Trollope was generally sympathetic to the feminist movement, in *Is He Popenjoy?* (1877–78) he made it a target of heavy satire. In the Marylebone Road there stood a "Rights of Women Institute. Established for the Relief of the Disabilities of Females," familiarly abbreviated as "Female Disabilities" and still further curtailed in the name of the nearest bus stop, "Disabilities." The leading spirit was a Ph.D. from Vermont with the Grouchomarxian name of Olivia Q. Fleabody, who twice a week worked up a band of "strongly-visaged spinsters and mutinous wives . . . to a full belief that a glorious era was at hand in which women would be chosen by constituencies, would wag their heads in courts of law, would buy and sell in Capel Court [the site of the Stock Exchange], and have balances at their banker's" (60:2.266).

Trollope squeezed the last topical drop out of feminism in *Mr. Scarborough's Family* (1882–83), when Mr. Prosper, a man with money to spare, engages in conversation with Miss Thoroughbung, who is interested in obtaining some. Fathers, brothers, uncles, and lawyers, she tells him, "intend to do right after the custom of their fathers and uncles. But woman's rights are coming up." "I hate woman's rights," says Prosper. "Nevertheless," she retorts, "they are coming up. A young woman doesn't get taken in as she used to do. . . . Since woman's rights have come up a young woman is better able to fight her own battle" (26:249).

The two best-known heroines in Victorian fiction who, according to their respective creators, typified the woman for whom the feminist movement existed—Dorothea Brooke in *Middlemarch* (1871–72) and Diana Warwick in *Diana of the Crossways* (1884)—came after the publication of *The Subjection of Women* in May 1869, and many readers doubtless responded to them with Mill's argument (if not Mrs. Linton's counterargument) in mind. The figure of Dorothea Brooke, yearning for emancipation from her rigidly prescribed feminine role in Loamshire society, was relatively timeless, and certainly did not allude to any feminist stirrings at the time of the First Reform Bill, the novel's setting, because there were none. Diana, by contrast, was imagined by a writer who took seriously, and sympathized with, the feminist movement as it had evolved since Mill. Meredith made her an exemplary feminist of the 1880s, forthright in speech and action, dispensing with chaperonage, and even traveling alone on trains, in subplebeian third class at that. Because the novel is set in the 1840s, however, she is also an anachronism: there were no exemplary feminists then, at least articulate ones. (Tennyson can hardly be said to have advanced the cause in *The Princess*.) But Diana's real-life original, Caroline Norton of the sensational case of Norton *versus* Melbourne in 1836 (see pages 148–51 below), had been active in the cause after her legal separation insofar as she publicly fought for the right of access to her children. She had died only seven years before *Diana of the Crossways* appeared.

In the meantime, Thomas Hardy had contributed a character of his own to the developing gallery of partially liberated young women. Neither a restless, pensive Dorothea nor a sexually attractive Diana removed

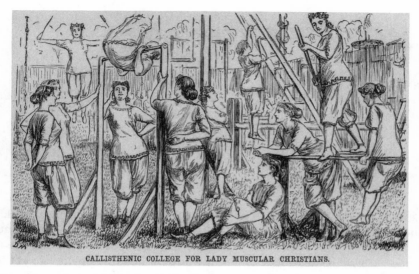

CALLISTHENIC COLLEGE FOR LADY MUSCULAR CHRISTIANS.

Paula Powers's athleticism in Hardy's *A Laodicean* was one of the typical "eccentricities" attributed to "emancipated" females, as demonstrated in this section of "Punch's Almanack" for January 1867. Like many of *Punch's* topical cartoons, this one had a second target, the "Muscular Christianity" (Christian Socialist) movement, formerly led by Charles Kingsley and Thomas Hughes.

in time from the present day, Paula Powers in *A Laodicean* (1880) was a precursor of the "new woman" of the 1890s without any of her ideological baggage. Her modernism was exemplified by what was strewn about her rooms in the habitable part of Stancy Castle: "popular papers and periodicals . . . not only English, but from Paris, Italy, and America . . . books from a London circulating library, paper-covered light literature in French and choice Italian, and the latest monthly reviews . . . and photographic portraits of the artistic, scientific, and literary celebrities of the day." She was no more a militant feminist than she was a bluestocking, but in one respect she was thoroughly unconventional. One wonders what Mrs. Lynn Linton, if she had happened to come upon Hardy's novel, would have made of a heroine who built on her castle grounds a gymnasium where she did acrobatics "in a pink flannel costume" (1.4:63–64; 2.7:183–84). It is perhaps not irrelevant that pretty fleshings-clad young women swinging on trapezes were among the favorite subjects of naughty postcards at the time.

5
Lapses of Time

1.

CONDITIONED BY THE COMMON BELIEF, sustained by subtitles and publisher's advertisements, that fiction's primary locale was present-day Britain, readers ordinarily opened a new novel expecting that it was indeed a "tale of the times." Unless the author furnished evidence to the contrary, as they turned the pages they automatically posited a contemporary setting. Aware of this expectation but refusing to be necessarily bound by it, novelists had three choices: (1) They could reinforce the effect of presentness by employing specific topical allusions, including details of physical setting, costume, and other indications of time; (2) they could use datable details so sparingly that the reader would be free to invent his own time-setting, assuming, if he wished, that it was near the present day, or, on the other hand, that it was some time in the past; (3) or while still purporting to write a "story of modern life" (in this context, any set in the nineteenth century), they could explicitly remove the action some distance from the present day, making the "pastness" clear by specifying the actual time of the plot and/or by introducing period color (historical events, details of the physical setting no longer seen, and so forth).

It was in the first and third alternatives that topicalities were brought into play, and the uses that novelists made of them reveal how flexible and how vital to the sought-for effect they were.

Topicalities are, by definition, temporal subjects, associated with a particular moment of time. Most quickly lose their effective strength, just as newspapers, initially immaculate from the press, soon become tattered and worn and their content outdated. But in every Victorian year, a small handful of fresh ones survived the ephemerality that was the fate of most and were absorbed into the storehouse of available allusions that novelists could rely upon as being readily intelligible to their readers even at a distance of years. The publicity some received from their early occurrences in fiction when they possessed the force of immediacy fed on itself, resulting in their acquiring a durable celebrity, as Daniel Boorstin would put it, through the simple fact that they were already celebrated. There was, in short, a selective tradition of topicalities.

When do topicalities lose their timeliness and shade into what eventually becomes period color, to be used by novelists seeking to evoke the scene and flavor of a time somewhat removed from the present? Unfortunately, in the psychology of neither communal consciousness nor literary response do we possess any such neat formulation as do nuclear physicists with their concept of an isotope's half-life. Some topicalities quickly diminish in strength, while others, which we might call "remembered" topicalities, retain a persistent resonance, a connotative aura that might even be intensified—and its emotional impact altered—as the perspective on it lengthens. Which fade, and which survive with unimpaired vitality, depends on the nature of each: on the depth to which it initially rooted itself in the popular mind, on its self-renewing magnetic power of attracting kindred associations to it, and on its regenerative quality as successive events, separated by some distance in time, seem to recapitulate the original event.[1]

The most important single aspect of Victorian fiction's strong orientation toward the contemporary scene is one that approaches the paradoxical: a surprising number of novels we call "Victorian" are nothing of the sort so far as their settings are concerned. Though published in the Queen's reign, they are set back as far as the opening years of the century. One of the greatest Victorian novels is, from this viewpoint, the very antithesis of the "typical" tale of the present. In *Wuthering Heights* (1847), the year in which Lockwood hears Nellie Dean's story is 1801; her narrative begins in 1778, and by chapter 25 it is within one year of the "present" in the novel's chronology—that is, 1801. Then Lockwood takes over, and the concluding events occur in 1802. That is the closest we get to 1847. Although there is plenty of circumstantial detail, none of it can be tied down to a specific era. Were no dates mentioned, the events could just as well have taken place in 1760, or for that matter in 1846, the year before *Wuthering Heights* was published. Lord David Cecil once wrote that the Brontës' Yorkshire was still "pretty well cut off from the influence of those forces that shaped the main trend of the time. Its life remained essentially the same as it had been in the days of Queen Elizabeth,"[2] and the same could be said of the novel. As many critics have observed, it is literally "timeless," dealing with a closed group of characters living on their self-destructive passions, with no sense of a world, a society, beyond Wuthering Heights and Thrushcross Grange.

There is no impingement of the life around them, which, if we accept the stated dates, is also the world of Jane Austen—and *Adam Bede*. One wonders why Emily Brontë chose the specific dates she did, for any span of about a quarter of a century would have served just as well in the absence of any topical connection with the world outside.

Her sister Charlotte's *Jane Eyre*, published the same year, is somewhat different, apart from the obvious fact that it is located inside society rather than enacted in severe isolation. It contains a few indications of time, though these are inconsistent: Millcote (Leeds) is "a large manufacturing town," but a cross-Channel steamboat is a novelty; St. John Rivers brings Jane a copy of the newly published *Marmion* (1808), but Eliza Reed's stitching an altar cloth for a church that observed saint's days and Brontë's characterization of her as "a rigid formalist" would indicate a date no earlier than the mid-1830s, when the Oxford Movement was beginning to have an impact on religious practices; the women's dress and wisps of Byronic suggestion such as the Corsair song on which Blanche Ingram "doated" suggest the period from 1820 to 1830, but there is also a clear allusion to the military presence in Sheffield in 1840, a topicality to which we will return in a few pages. Thus, although the most recent editors of the novel find it "clear that the action is set thirty or forty years before the time of publication" (611), it is no less likely that the novel's first readers would have found it to be a story of near-contemporary life, and if the few specific topicalities that attached it to the earlier period were overlooked, it might well have been read as a tale literally of "today"—1847. On the other hand, again overlooking the specific allusions, *Jane Eyre* could equally well have been read as a story of an eighteenth-century heroine, a contemporary, say, of Fielding's Sophia Western or Fanny Burney's Evelina Belmont, so little had the essentials of life changed in the interim. Even details that might appear to be early Victorian background topicalities (the needle factory and the iron foundry, and the village school where Jane briefly teaches when she is with the Rivers family) could equally well belong to the eighteenth century.

Wuthering Heights is not, by any stretch of the label, a "realistic" novel, and *Jane Eyre* is not much of one. But a truly realistic fiction purporting to be "modern" and unquestionably written and published for a Victorian audience might be set in a time several decades removed from the present. Yet it remained topical, even though the time allusions were mostly related to that earlier period, because it still reflected the ideas, interests, and manners of the time when it was written rather than those of its putative setting. Such fiction occupied the middle ground between the (journalistic) point of time that was the Victorian present and the spacious past, measured in centuries, of the historical romance. It was of the present yet not of the present—or, more likely, it was both. And in this removed time setting there was discernibly a more insistent thrust forward, toward the present day, a more marked community of interest, than there was a comparable reaching backward to a still earlier moment. This propellent effect of drawing the narrative closer to the present was subtly assisted by anachronisms involving events that occurred after the presumed time of the action. The gulf between past and present was not quite as absolute when such intervening events were mentioned.

It was Humphry House, I think, who first called attention to this common distancing effect, which he called "ante-dating." But he did not develop the point, and it was left for Kathleen Tillotson to illustrate the process in some detail, using examples from the single decade of the 1840s.[3]

When the scope is enlarged to include the several scores of Victorian novels, from the 1830s to the 1880s, that figure in the present study, the technique proves to be less incidental than almost characteristic. Strictly speaking, a distanced novel is one whose narrative ends an appreciable time before the present; its beginning is not set in the past merely to allow time for the events it describes to occur before reaching the present, and the span of time between its conclusion and the present is not filled in with the wrap-up events associated with epilogues. Under the looser definition of "any novel whose main action is set more than ten or a dozen years in the past," regardless of whether its narrative reaches the present, considerably more than half of the novels discussed in these pages can be called "distanced."

Although critics said much about contemporary novelists' devotion to the portrayal of life in their own times, almost nowhere in the great mass of reviews is there any mention of distancing. Reviewers took its presence for granted as a perfectly acceptable and widely employed literary device, not an innovation or a matter for discussion. Distancing a novel was not so much a breach of the understanding that it would occur in the present day as a quiet modification of it. The only time its existence was noted was by implication in connection with occasional anachronisms. Thus, in 1859, E. S. Dallas wrote in his *Times* review of *Adam Bede*, "the date of the incidents is thrown to the end of the last century, but the time is not strictly observed, and we are not very much surprised to be informed that Bartle Massey 'lighted a match furiously on the hob,' which is far from being the only anachronism in the tale."[4]

There was a tacit understanding that a dividing line separated the "modern" novel and the historical romance. The subtitle of Scott's *Wav-*

erley, "'Tis Sixty Years Since," supplied a convenient demarcation. As Leslie Stephen remarked in an essay on Defoe's novels in 1868, "That date [sixty years] just fixes the time after ["before" would be closer to what he meant] which the epoch must be handed over to the historical novelist; when few even of the greatest novelists have sufficient imaginative fire to burn up the antiquarian dust that has accumulated."[5] By a strict application of this rule of thumb, *Adam Bede,* published in 1859 but set in 1799, barely qualifies as a modern novel, and *Barnaby Rudge* (1841), whose central episode, the Gordon riots, is set in 1780, barely does not. But both *Barnaby Rudge* and *A Tale of Two Cities* (1859, set in 1780–93) were regarded quite apart from Dickens's other novels: they were the only ones whose settings were truly "historical."

No nominally "modern" novel announced the distancing element in its subtitle, as did genuine historical novels such as William Harrison Ainsworth's *Old Saint Paul's: A Tale of the Plague and the Fire*; *Saint James's, or the Court of Queen Anne*; *James the Second, or the Revolution of 1688*; *The Lord Mayor of London: or City Life in the Last Century*; *Cardinal Pole, or the Days of Philip and Mary*; *Boscobel, or the Royal Oak: A Tale of the Year 1651.* (A number of other Ainsworth novels were subtitled simply "A Romance" or "An Historical Romance.")

Dickens presents special problems in this connection. As Kathleen Tillotson observed, "It is not a matter of committing occasional anachronisms, in forgetfulness or fun, nor yet of a calculated *de te fabula*; the relation of Dickens's novels to the past and the present is complex and contradictory—'extensive and peculiar.' . . . [Dickens is] subject at once and in the same novels to the drag of the past and the pull of the present."[6] He had, said Humphry House,

> no exact historic sense, no desire to make his stories into accurate "period" records, and no particular fear of anachronisms. The stories often contain material which keeps the original colour of several different periods in his own experience; they also bring together widely spaced material that can be checked by outside evidence. But though he had little historic sense, he had a very acute sense of time; he liked to give his books a surface of tidiness and punctuality; he went out of his way to indicate precise dates and seasons of the year, and sometimes even used known historical facts to enforce the actuality of a moment. But in the next chapter he might use a second fact quite incompatible with the first.[7]

It is true that five of Dickens's first six novels *(Pickwick Papers, Oliver Twist, Nicholas Nickleby, The Old Curiosity Shop,* and *Martin Chuzzlewit*: the sixth was *Barnaby Rudge*) were set in the near present, within a decade of the time of publication. Of these, *Pickwick* (1836–37) was the least immediate in setting. The advertisement of the first number (*Athenaeum,* 26 March 1836) said that "The Pickwick Club . . . was founded in the year One Thousand Eight Hundred and Twenty-two" (exactly a decade before the British Association, of which it was a topical satire). But the action itself runs from May 1827 to October 1828. *Dombey and Son* (1846–48) was laid in the period, ten years earlier, when the Birmingham railway reached London (its terminal station, Euston, was opened in 1837). In *David Copperfield* (1849–50) the present serves as a point from which the autobiographical narrator recalls the past—private events (virtually no concurrent public ones are mentioned), beginning some forty years earlier, which gradually move toward the present but reach it only in the last hasty pages. The novel's early action occurs in the second and third decades of the century. The datable details, down to David's marriage to Agnes, agree with a period before 1830, and if mention of the King's Bench prison may be taken literally, the main plot ends before 1837, when the Queen took the throne. Ample time—a dozen years—is left for Micawber to make his fortune and thus realize the golden promise of the emigrants' Australia.

In *Bleak House* (1852–53), as in *David Copperfield*, all travel is by coach, a sufficient sign of Dickens's intention to locate the novel at some distance from the present. The omniscient narrator, whose Dickensian voice alternates with Esther Summerson's, seemingly is writing simultaneously with events, as his use of the present tense implies, but he also is gifted with a prescience which advances him, momentarily, from the time of the action he is describing to the present day. "[T]he far-famed Elephant," he says at one point, referring to the Elephant and Castle inn in Lambeth, an old staging point for coaches, ". . . has lost his castle formed of a thousand four-horse coaches, to a stronger iron monster than he, ready to chop him into mince-meat any day he dares" (27:438). At the same time, however, Dickens connected the pre-railway time of the action with the time of publication by a sprinkling of relatively up-to-date allusions that lend the novel its strong contemporaneous flavor. Never before had he taken up so many pressing subjects of the day in a single novel: the law's delays as exemplified by the glacial pace of suits in Chancery, the paralysis of government as ministries came and went through the revolving door of politics, the criminal abuse of orphaned children in workhouses and private for-profit asylums, the plague-generating powers of congested city churchyards, the smoke-polluted air—all topics immediate to the moment, although some of the issues, such as the urgency of Chancery reform, had prior histories and thus belonged to a chain of topicalities that linked the *Bleak House* present with the *Bleak House* past.[8] The most recent appearance of spontaneous combustion in the news had been in 1850, when the *Times* reported the conclusion of an investigation undertaken at Darmstadt three years earlier, of the death of one Countess Görlitz, who seemed to have suffered

Dickens's mention, in part 3 of *Bleak House* (May 1852), of five-year-old Alfred Pardiggle's belonging to the "Infant Bonds of Joy" would have reminded readers of this picture, captioned "London Temperance League: Great Juvenile Gathering of Bands of Hope, Etc., in Exeter Hall, on Monday," which had appeared in the *Illustrated London News* on the preceding 21 February. Presumably he is among those shown in attendance, however unwillingly. (For Exeter Hall and its connotations, see pages 423–26.)

the same vaporized fate as the drunken junk dealer Krook, but the scientific riddle had been debated back and forth for many years, even appearing elsewhere in fiction.[9] The Bands of Hope ("Infant Bonds of Joy" in the novel), the juvenile temperance league which the youngest Pardiggle child, aged five, was coerced into joining, dated from 1847. The detective branch of the Metropolitan Police, to which Inspector Bucket belonged, had been established in 1842. The "artist of a picture paper" who did quick sketches at the inquest on Nemo at the Sol's Arms public house represented an occupation created by the new illustrated journalism, whose specialty was on-the-scene drawings of news events. Humphry House mentions other "quite clear indications of time—all rather contradictory, though they seem to be so definite—" in support of his cogent argument that "Dickens seems to have gone out of his way to leave the imaginary time of the story vague."[10]

In the following years, Dickens sometimes distanced, sometimes wrote of the recognizable present day. A reader of *Hard Times* was entitled to assume that Coketown was one of the Black Country industrial cities in 1854. But the first words of the next novel, *Little Dorrit* (1855–57), were "Thirty years ago," and nearly all the topical clues are consistent with a setting in the late 1820s. The milieu of *Great Expectations* is less specific, though most of the evidence again points to the 1820s. That the scene is pre-1837 is indicated by the command "in the name of the King," and Wemmick's enumeration of the existing London bridges includes old London Bridge, which was demolished in 1831.

After distancing two novels in a row—three, if we count *A Tale of Two Cities*—Dickens returned to the immediate present in *Our Mutual Friend* (1864–65). He hedges in the opening sentence—"In these times of ours, though concerning the exact year there is no need to be precise"—but the novel's first readers could easily have supplied the precise year, namely the year stamped on the covers of their pocket diaries. The various topical themes are those of the present day; "newness" is the running Veneering motif, and new elementary schools dominate the suburban scene in Kent and Surrey. This is the bustling, building London of the mid-sixties. As for *The Mystery of Edwin Drood*, the few time indications in the unfinished text tend to ease the story toward rather than away from the year of its composition (1870).

Except in *David Copperfield* and *Great Expectations*, Dickens seldom adopted a reminiscential posture in his fiction. Thackeray, on the other hand, made remembrance of things past his very stock in trade as a "modern" novelist. Drawing on his memories of the time, and extrapolating further back to the years of his infancy, he set *Vanity Fair* (1847–48) unmistakably in the Regency and its lingering sunset. The frequent touches of period color that produced the justly admired verisimilitude of his social scene, beginning in 1813 and coursing through the years to 1830, were matched by an equal number of topicalities current at the moment Thackeray was writing: a reference to a "curtain lecture" that would have evoked memories of Douglas Jerrold's popular series of "Mrs. Caudle's Curtain Lectures" in *Punch* two years earlier; the celebrated Reform Club chef Alexis Soyer, who had recently been running a charitable soup kitchen in Ireland; an omnibus ride from Richmond "this present moment." Both *The History of Pendennis* (1848–50) and *The Newcomes* (1853–55) began roughly in the thirties and reached into the early or mid-forties; Pendennis, the hero of one novel and the narrator of the other, was a "gentleman of our age," Thackeray said in the preface to his fictional biography. Like *Vanity Fair*, both novels had a double set of references, to the more or less distanced past and to the present. The late *Adventures of Philip* (1861–62) maintained the same space between action and publication: the three years or so that are the site of Philip Firmin's adventures are the middle forties ("the times of

Louis Philippe the King," who abdicated in 1848)—a tight fit, because Philip was born in 1825 and during most of the action he is in his early twenties.

Elizabeth Gaskell's first novel, *Mary Barton* (1848), began "ten or a dozen years ago" (1838 to 1836) and straightforwardly progressed to about 1842. In *Cranford* (1851–52) she deliberately blurred the time setting for the sake of depicting that Cheshire town (Knutsford on the maps) as a backwater from which, as far as women's dress, manners, and ideas were concerned, the eighteenth-century tide had not wholly receded. "Modernity" at Cranford was represented by the railway that ran to "the great neighbouring commercial town of Drumble [Manchester] distant only twenty miles" (1:1), Captain Brown's unfortunate death under the wheels of a train while reading the latest number of *Pickwick Papers*, a reference to William IV's wife as "the Queen" (there was no mention of the Princess Victoria who succeeded her in 1837), and the publication of the two-volume collection of Tennyson's poems in 1842. But this general sense of the late 1830s and early 1840s was, as Gaskell created it, simply a fixed background against which she introduced the insistent wraiths of times further removed from the present.

Gaskell's *Ruth* (1853) was set "many years ago," ever a conveniently hazy time indication which in this instance meant the 1830s, because the topicalities included the new railways, electoral reform agitation, and a cholera epidemic. *North and South* (1853–54), resuming the rights-of-labor issue that was the leading theme of *Mary Barton*, contained a workers' riot and debates over living conditions, strikes, and unionization, all of which would place it no earlier than the forties; but it was almost devoid of explicit topicalities. The chronology of Gaskell's last novel, *Wives and Daughters* (1864–66), is provided by plain indications in the text. When the narrative opens "five and forty years ago," the heroine, Molly Gibson, is twelve, hence the date is 1819; ensuing mentions of her age or of the year bring the main action down to 1826, a date confirmed by the fact that in those years "Catholic emancipation had begun to be talked about by some politicians" (23:299).

Only one of George Eliot's novels, the late *Daniel Deronda* (1876), was set in contemporary England; all the rest were distanced, *Romola* most of all, to fifteenth-century Italy, in fact. Eliot began her regular distancing practice with the three stories that comprised *Scenes of Clerical Life* (1857). "The Sad Fortunes of the Rev. Amos Barton" was set "rather more than twenty years ago" (1:44), when "the New Poor-Law had not yet come into operation" (2:61) (thus before 1834)—and yet the complete *Pickwick Papers* had been published (1837). "Mr. Gilfil's Story," a costume piece, was laid entirely in 1788–90, except for a brief flashback to 1773. "Janet's Repentance" was set "more than a quarter of a century" ago (2:252), though after W. S. Gill's *Memoirs of Felix Neff* and Grace Kennedy's novel *Father Clement* (both 1832) had been published. *Adam Bede* (1859) began in 1799, as the first paragraph made clear, and ended in 1801, with a brief epilogue in 1807. *Silas Marner* (1861) was also set initially in Napoleonic times, then moved to a period sixteen years later as Eppie grew up. But the period Eliot knew best, the one she studied most closely and did most background research upon, was that of the First Reform Bill, the setting of three novels. *The Mill on the Floss*, set "many years ago," covered a span of ten years, from 1829, when Maggie was "gone nine" and all the talk at St. Ogg's was about Catholic Emancipation, to 1839, the year of her death at the age of nineteen. *Felix Holt, the Radical* was precisely dated, from September 1832 to April 1833. And *Middlemarch*, its plot carefully coordinated with references to public events, occupied the years 1829–32.

Distancing was a device alien to Trollope's art. As his novels came from the press in quick succession, his readers could rely on their being tales of the present moment. Their chronological scope was not only recent but limited. He seldom attempted the "chronicle" structure employed by Thackeray, the events strung out over a span of years. Antecedent developments such as the descent of estates were quickly and summarily dealt with in the first pages, making way for the main action, which ordinarily was concentrated within a year or two.

Meredith's practice varied. In *The Adventures of Harry Richmond* (1870–71), a Bildungsroman that covered a number of years, Harry's father is an admirer of Pitt and thus has sympathies reaching back to the beginning of the century, and at one point mention is made of a new railway station in Hampshire, which would place that phase of the action in the 1840s. *Evan Harrington* (1860) is set about the same time. Notwithstanding the up-to-dateness, especially of the feminist theme, in *Diana of the Crossways* (1884), that novel is firmly anchored in the mid-1840s. Other Meredith novels are located, inferentially or explicitly, in the present day. Allusions to the Italian Risorgimento, a topic in which England had intense interest in the late fifties and early sixties, clearly date both *The Ordeal of Richard Feverel* (1859) and *Emilia in England* (1864). *Beauchamp's Career* (1874–75) is loaded with implicit references to current strains of thought, especially in political matters, but the action is concentrated in the middle and late 1850s, beginning with Beauchamp's service in the Crimea.

2.

Distancing sometimes implied an affinity in some respect between the past setting and the present moment. That resemblance, whatever its

degree, was enhanced by the fact that among the large events and movements in nineteenth-century England were several that, in effect, repeated themselves at intervals. Their timeliness, for authorial purposes,
was renewed at each recurrence; the history of the century, viewed in
long enough perspective, seemed to possess an elemental rhythm.

Several novelists availed themselves of the short-term cyclic movements they could discern in their lifetimes, extended in some cases by
memories they acquired from the preceding generation. This repetition
of more or less similar events at a remove of two, three, or four decades
provided a dual topicality—the event in the past and its counterpart in
the present. Current topicalities thus acquired a retrospective, historical
dimension as well as a widened resonance. Conversely, an occurrence of
the earlier event in a novel set in that period invited readers to see it in
terms of the later one.

The impact of such retrospection depended on the strength of the
communal memory that preserved the past event's most prominent features and the popular emotions that accompanied it. Pat Rogers has described the way that the early eighteenth-century English imagination
was dominated by the "afterlife" of events that had taken place several
decades earlier: "Within the lifetime of men and women who were still
active, four great events had impinged deeply on the national consciousness . . . the Civil War, the Great Plague, the Fire of London and the
Glorious Revolution. These happenings had personal and imaginative
repercussions which were to last for generations. . . . [T]he recollection
of the disasters of a generation before still operated powerfully in
people's minds at the opening of the eighteenth century."[11]

The phenomenon was just as powerful in the Victorian era, when
landmark events, whether disastrous or fortunate, seemed to repeat
themselves. The earliest of these series of analogous events—bursts of
public excitement that stand out in the continuum of history—was the
one initiated by the French Revolution, which until at least the middle
of the century served the Victorians as the model of violent political
upheaval that combined millennial hope on some people's part with
fear of chaos and anarchy on that of others. Long after the English
generation who had lived through the revolutionary years as adults,
precariously safe but incurably apprehensive, had passed from the
scene—although the bookseller Sandy Mackaye, in *Alton Locke*, claimed
to remember those days—the days of the Jacobin rule were locked into
the communal memory. As Patrick Brantlinger has remarked,

> the first French Revolution was only a little over forty years old when Car-
> lyle wrote and was still as much a matter of lived experience for many as
> of the dead, hoary past. Histories of it—as opposed to memoirs and to po-

lemical essays like those by Burke and Paine—were new in the 1830s. . . .
Carlyle comes to the subject of the French Revolution . . . when it is particularly fluid and ambiguous—hovering dangerously between history and
lived experience, and between past politics and present controversy—and
he stresses the fluidity and ambiguity of it in every conceivable way, if only
in order to make "the haggard element of Fear" ever present to us.[12]

The timeliness of Carlyle's history (1837) resided in the fact that the
social turbulence and passionate ideological contention that France had
undergone in the 1790s had subsequently been enacted on a comparatively small yet potentially dangerous scale in England. First there had
been the radical activity in the immediate post-Waterloo years, resulting
in the mobilizing of the yeomanry, repression of civil liberties, spies and
arrests and trials. Then there had been the rioting, arson, and other
disturbances attending the agitation for the First Reform Bill that had
brought the nation to the verge of civil war in 1831–32. Now, only five
years later, militant Chartism was reviving the same fears, as thousands
upon thousands of workingmen, especially mill hands thrown out of employment and desperate to feed their families, followed the banners to
torchlit meetings where they cheered inflammatory speeches by their
leaders.

This was the climate of alarm, accreted from the past several decades,
that lay behind the allusions to Chartism in the fiction of the late 1830s
and the 1840s. In only three novels did the movement, as such, figure
very prominently: Disraeli's *Sybil*, in which Gerard, the leading working-
class character, is a Chartist leader and the attack on Mowbray Castle
resembles the one in which rioters sacked and burned Nottingham
Castle in 1831; *Mary Barton*, in which Chartist leaders of the Manchester
unions, including the heroine's father, attend the great national rally in
London in July 1839 and return confirmed in their determination to win
the political concessions demanded in the "Six Point Charter"; and *Alton
Locke*, the fictionalized tract in which the hero is a Chartist and most of
the argumentative matter is concerned with social justice as the Chartist
program conceived it.

The most suggestive appearances of Chartism in the novels of the
time, however, are not overt and extended but oblique, inferential, and
fleeting.[†] The torch-bearing and arson-bent mobs in *The Old Curiosity*

[†]Michael Slater has pointed out (Penguin edition, p. 937) that in the manuscript of
Nicholas Nickleby Dickens made a facetious allusion to Chartism. Mr. Gregsbury, M.P., is
being grilled by a deputation of his dissatisfied constituents, who claim that on the hustings
he had given "a voluntary pledge to vote for universal suffrage and triennial parliaments"
(the actual Chartist goals were universal manhood suffrage and annual parliaments).

At the time *The Old Curiosity Shop* was published (1840–41), many people sensed an unsettling, if usually subliminal, affinity between militant Chartism, depicted in this illustration by Phiz, and the French revolutionary spirit. The iconography is suggestive of such monuments of combative heroism as Dela-croix's *Liberty Leading the People* (1830) and Rude's bas relief on the Arc de Triomphe, *Departure of the Volunteers, 1792* ("La Marseillaise") (1833–36).

Shop (although mentioned only in passing in the text [45:424], their presence was amplified by Hablot K. Browne's accompanying illustration) and *Barnaby Rudge* would have aroused disturbing recollections of recent demonstrations, which were always fully covered by the press, and in the latter novel so would the mob scenes attending the 1780 "No Popery" riots in London. As the Chartist threat approached its climax, any mention of riots or attempts to suppress them would have evoked momentary responses appropriate to the situation, even if the allusion

Gregsbury tries to weasel his way out of his embarrassment by claiming that "An illiterate voter in the crowd enquired if I would vote for universal suffering and triangular parlia-ments. To which I replied (jestingly) 'by all means.'" But Dickens thought better of the joke (it was not a very good one) and it did not appear in print.

was a casual one and had no direct reference to Chartism. In *Jane Eyre*, Rosamund Oliver tells of her having danced until two in the morning at "S——": "The —th regiment are stationed there, since the riots; and the officers are the most agreeable men in the world: they put all our young knife-grinders and scissor-merchants to shame" (31:465). The town was actually Sheffield, and the date 1839–40: a detachment of 210 officers and men belonging to the First Royal Dragoons was billeted there as part of the widespread deployment of troops in the Northern District following the twelve-day Chartist riots at Birmingham the preceding summer.[13] (There was a Chartist disturbance in Sheffield itself on 12 January 1840, which the soldiers easily quelled.) By the time Charlotte Brontë's next novel, *Shirley*, was published (1849), the menace had finally been dissipated by the unexpectedly peaceful events of 10 April 1848, but no reader conditioned to associate mass violence with Chartism would have followed the melodramatic subplot of the Luddite machine-breaking riots, which Brontë derived from a borrowed file of the *Leeds Mercury* for 1812, without drawing the obvious parallel. She availed herself of a headline event from the present to intensify the effect of an episode laid thirty-six years earlier.

When the first readers of *Bleak House* heard Sir Leicester Dedlock mutter darkly about Wat Tyler being abroad in the land again—his refusal to entertain any complaint against the Court of Chancery on the ground that it "would be to encourage some person in the lower classes to rise up somewhere—like Wat Tyler" (2:61), they would have realized that Dickens intended a multiple reference, apart from the somewhat contrived historical word play on the name of Mrs. Rouncewell's ironmaster son, Watt. "[I]t is certain that he [Sir Leicester] only regarded him as one of a body of some odd thousand conspirators, swarthy and grim, who were in the habit of turning out by torchlight, two or three nights in the week, for unlawful purposes" (7:135). Actually young Rouncewell, a self-made engineer and a representative new man of the age, was named for James Watt, inventor of the steam engine and, as such, a revered father of the industrial revolution. That association alone would have disturbed Sir Leicester, a representative old Tory landowner. But the chiming of Watt/Wat led him in his baleful imagination to transform Watt Rouncewell from a go-ahead employer of industrial labor to a conspiring revolutionist, spiritually descended from the leader of the fourteenth-century peasants' revolt—in modern terms, a machine-breaking Luddite or, alternatively, a rick-burning farm-laborer follower of the mythical Captain Swing at the time of the First Reform Bill riots.

This would have been Sir Leicester's mental process at the distanced

time in which *Bleak House* was (more or less) set. But the eruption of
Chartism added more recent overtones to Sir Leicester's worry. The
name Wat Tyler had been back in the news in 1846, when one of the
leaders of the Chartist riots in the West Riding, Isaac Jefferson, used it
as a stealthy sobriquet. And so readers in 1852 would have extended Sir
Leicester's chain of association: Wat Tyler, medieval labor agitator, was
also Wat Tyler, bearer of a Chartist torch.[14] No wonder that when Watt
Rouncewell proposes to intervene in his son's love affair with Lady Dedlock's maid, "All Sir Leicester's old misgivings relative to Wat Tyler, and
the people in the iron districts who do nothing but turn out by torchlight, come in a shower upon his head: the fine grey hair of which, as
well as of his whiskers, actually stirs with indignation" (28:451).

The continuity of the Reform/Chartist theme across the first half of
the century thus was one historical circumstance that permitted novelists
to match an event in the present with a similar event in the past. Another
was the fact that periods of prosperity alternated every ten or a dozen
years with financial crises of various magnitudes. Two of these were especially severe, the one in 1825–26 which stemmed from the failure of
speculative ventures in Central and South America, and that in 1847,
when the bubble of hysterical enthusiasm for investing in railway building schemes came to its predestined bursting point, sending shock waves
through the entire financial establishment. Their contributions to the
topicality of Victorian fiction will be discussed in Chapter 17.

One of the most persistent topical subjects in Victorian fiction was
the Sabbatarian, or Sunday observance, issue, which dated as far back as
the seventeenth century but had come to renewed public attention in
1831, when the Evangelical crusade to keep the Sabbath uncontami-
nated by such secular activities as recreation, shopping, and traveling
was institutionalized by the founding of the Society for Promoting the
Due Observance of the Lord's Day.[15] Two years later, Sir Andrew Agnew, the Irish M.P. who represented the Sabbatarian cause in the national legislature, introduced the first of what proved to be a series of
annual bills to ban Sunday shop openings, travel except to divine service,
and any "pastimes" which might lead to some form of "public inde-
corum." Dickens wrote against the proposal in a pamphlet called *Sunday
Under Three Heads: As It Is; As Sabbath Bills Would Make It; As It Might Be
Made* (1836). Agnew lost his seat the next year and the issue became
dormant until the middle of the century, when the Sabbatarian party
scored a big victory by forcing the Great Exhibition of 1851, the most
popular place of instruction and enjoyment in the whole history of Britain, to be closed on Sundays.

Encouraged by this success, the new spokesman for the movement,

The unexpectedly peaceful climax to the Chartist crusade for drastic electoral reform—the orderly procession on 10 April 1848—was portrayed in the next issue of the *Illustrated London News* (15 April). Now that the ten-year-old threat of social revolution was dissipated, novelists could use Chartist allusions with a longer perspective, undominated by fright, as Dickens shortly was to do in *Bleak House*.

Lord Robert Grosvenor, introduced a fresh Sunday Trading Bill in June 1855. Although it was a comparatively mild version whose application was confined to London, working-class throngs, correctly identifying it as a measure directed against them, held a series of demonstrations in Hyde Park, beginning on Sunday, 24 June, when they went to see how the aristocrats customarily kept the Sabbath. The aristocrats paraded before them in their splendid carriages amidst hisses, yells, and cries of "Go to church." At the gathering the next Sunday, attended, one newspaper said, by 150,000 protesters, police reinforcements made a hundred arrests and a number of people were severely hurt. On the third Sabbath, the better classes, now more prudent, did not show themselves, so the mob invaded Belgravia, where they threw paving stones through the windows of mansions.

Palmerston saw to it that the hated bill was defeated. The following year, a bill designed to compensate for the continued closing of the Crystal Palace, now reerected at Sydenham, by opening the British Museum on Sunday also lost, by a margin of 328 to 48. But military band concerts that summer attracted large and orderly Sunday crowds to the London

Admirable Working of Lord Ashley's Measure.

"OH! I WISH I KNEW HOW MY DEAR GIRL IS?"

Wife. ART GOING OUT, TOM?"
Husband. "YES, LASS, I BE JUST GOING OVER TO RED LION TO HEAR WHAT'S A DOING. YOU SEE, SINCE THESE NEW FANGLED POST-OFFICE CHANGES, I CAN'T GET MY BIT OF A NEWSPAPER O' SUNDAYS NOW?"

"DEAR! DEAR! DEAR! I WONDER WHETHER WALKER'S BILL WAS PAID YESTERDAY."

Swindler (loq.) "HURRAH FOR THE PURITANS, I SAY. I'VE DONE EVERY BODY, AND NOW I'VE A CLEAR DAY'S START OF THE BRUTAL POLICE AND MY INFAMOUS CREDITORS. VIVAT CANT, NO MONEY RETURNED."

On the first day the Commons met in their new building, Lord Ashley introduced on behalf of the Lord's Day Observance Society a bill to prohibit the Sunday collection and delivery of mail. The vote was carried over the opposition of the Whig government, and, though the law was repealed at the end of the year, Ashley, long admired for his advocacy of philanthropic and humanitarian causes, became "one of the most unpopular men in England." *Punch*'s cartoon, published on 6 July 1850, suggests the reason.

parks, thus aiding the anti-Sabbatarian cause. It was against this background of ploys and counterploys that *Little Dorrit* appeared (December 1855–June 1857). For the past seven years Dickens had been campaigning against Sabbatarianism by publishing at least eleven articles on the subject under his editorship in *Household Words*. It was no accident, then, that the mordant satire in the third chapter of *Little Dorrit* was directed against the dismal *dimanche anglais* as illustrated by the grim Mrs. Clennam and her refusal to see her son, back in London after many years in the Orient, when he turned up at her door on Sunday. (Dickens also managed—clumsily—to involve the Sunday obsession in the denouement of the complicated plot.) Although the novel was set "thirty years ago," when Sabbatarianism was only working up steam, readers of *Little Dorrit* would have responded to the renewed topicality of the issue.

At the same time, Trollope inflated the Sabbatarian demands far beyond the actual provisions of proposed legislation. To readers of *Barchester Towers* in 1857, one of Mrs. Proudie's most telling characteristics as "a religious woman" was her comprehensive definition of Sabbath observance:

> Woe betide the recreant housemaid who is found to have been listening to the honey of a sweetheart in the Regent's park, instead of the soul-stirring evening discourse of Mr. Slope. Not only is she sent adrift, but she is so sent with a character which leaves her little hope of a decent place. Woe betide the six-foot hero who escorts Mrs. Proudie to her pew in red plush breeches, if he slips away to the neighbouring beer-shop, instead of falling into the back seat appropriated to his use. Mrs. Proudie has the eyes of Argus for such offenders. Occasional drunkenness in the week may be overlooked, for six feet on low wages are hardly to be procured if the morals are always kept at a high pitch; but not even for grandeur or economy will Mrs. Proudie forgive a desecration of the Sabbath. (3:166–67)

This was a subject on which the bishop's wife and the bishop's chaplain happily saw eye to eye. "Sunday observances" were the Reverend Obadiah Slope's obsession, not unassociated with his dreams of power:

> Sunday, however, is a word which never pollutes his mouth—it is always "the Sabbath." The "desecration of the Sabbath," as he delights to call it, is to him meat and drink:—he thrives upon that as policemen do on the general evil habits of the community. It is the loved subject of all his evening discourses, the source of all his eloquence, the secret of all his power over the female heart. To him the revelation of God appears only in that one law given for Jewish observance. . . . To him the New Testament is comparatively of little moment, for from it can he draw no fresh authority for that dominion which he loves to exercise over at least a seventh part of man's allotted time here below. (4:169–70)

THE CLUB.

Just a Sandwich and a Nice Glass of Hock and Seltzer Water.

[Dedicated to my Lord Robert Grosven

This double-page spread (above and opposite) in *Punch* for 7 June 1855 anticipated by six months chapter 3 of *Little Dorrit*, which began "It was a Sunday evening in London, gloomy, close, and stale." It is typical of many cartoons and editorial attacks directed against Lord Robert Grosvenor's Sabbatarian campaign in this year and the first half of the next.

THE ROADSIDE INN.
A Mouthful of Dust and a Pull at the Pump.
Dedicated to my Lord Robert Grosvenor.

Long after Slope had fallen from grace and retired to an obscure London parish, Mrs. Proudie remained a stalwart defender of what was to her the socially most urgent of the Ten Commandments. In *Framley Parsonage*, as we have seen, she disrupted Mr. Harold Smith's eloquent discourse on Polynesia by insisting that strict Sabbath observance should be the officially enforced way of life in that remote outpost of religious Britain.

By the end of the 1850s, the direction of the Sunday observance campaign had shifted from legislated compulsion to "moral suasion." But
the issue was still before the public in 1867–69, when *Phineas Finn* was
published. A Factory Acts Extension Bill included the bizarre provision
that women and children might not work in or about blast furnaces on
Sundays (cooler minds prevailed, and the clause was amended to read
"any factory"); recycled Sunday trading bills were repeatedly turned
down in committee; Lord Amberley introduced a bill that would have
exempted Sunday lectures from legislative prohibitions; and when that
failed, T. H. Huxley and some two hundred other intellectuals formed
the Sunday Lecture Society, which thrived and was untouched by the
law. All this activity supplied an immediately topical basis for Trollope's
selection of Sabbatarian mania as the chief symptom of Robert Kennedy's incipient madness in *Phineas Finn*.

As late as *Beauchamp's Career* (1874–75) Sunday observance was a
lively issue. In the latter year, a group of public men ranging from ecclesiastics (the Dean of Westminster) and philosophers (John Stuart Mill
and Herbert Spencer) to novelists (Wilkie Collins and Trollope) and artists (Holman Hunt and Rossetti) formed the Sunday Society, whose aim
was to liberate libraries, museums, and galleries on Sunday afternoons.
In Meredith's novel Sabbatarianism had, as in *Little Dorrit*, a dual time
reference, to both the time of publication and the time of the action in
the late 1850s, when the Lord Robert Grosvenor episode, with its Hyde
Park protest, would have been fresh in the characters' minds as Beauchamp, campaigning for the Bevisham seat in Parliament, debated the
issue with the stubborn Sabbatarian shoemaker Carpendike.

A single event, not a more or less cyclic movement, might also be
repeated, or at least recalled, in the mirror of fiction. In March 1855,
nineteen years after the sensational one-day "criminal conversation"
(adultery) trial of Norton *versus* Melbourne had found its way into *Pickwick Papers* in the satirical form of the Bardell *versus* Pickwick breach-of-
promise suit, Thackeray read the printed trial record in the library
of the Reform Club as he prepared to write of the wretched business of
Barnes Newcome and his tormented wife, Lady Clara. As we have seen,
the rights of married women under existing law were a timely subject in
those years; Thackeray's readers were not likely to have forgotten the
newspaper coverage of the trial, in the Westminster County Court in
August 1853, of a suit brought by a London coach-building firm against
Caroline Norton, who had failed to pay for repairs to her brougham.†

---

†The testimony centered on her claim that she would have paid for them if her husband, from whom she had been estranged, since the failure of his crim.con. suit against

Relief from the neglect or persecution of a husband in the form of divorce was then obtainable only through an act of Parliament—this was shortly before the passage of the Matrimonial Causes Act of 1857—and so the case of Newcome *versus* Newcome, having been appealed from the Court of Queen's Bench, became known as the "Newcome Divorce Bill" when it landed in the House of Lords, which formed the court of ultimate jurisdiction. Forty-eight years after Norton *versus* Melbourne and twenty-nine after Newcome *versus* Newcome, Meredith recalled the original trial in Warwick *versus* Dannisburgh, a central episode in *Diana of the Crossways* (1884).

Thackeray's and Meredith's adaptation of the same historical event differed significantly. In *The Newcomes*, Thackeray derided the courtroom histrionics of Serjeant Rowland, appearing for the plaintiff in the Queen's Bench phase, and noted the way the press lapped up the trial.

> Rowland wept freely during his noble harangue. At not a shilling under twenty thousand pounds would he estimate the cost of his client's injuries. The jury was very much affected; the evening papers gave Rowland's address *in extenso*, with some pretty sharp raps at the aristocracy in general. The *Day*, the principal morning journal of that period, came out with a leading article the next morning, in which every party concerned and every institution was knocked about. The disgrace of the peerage, the ruin of the monarchy (with a retrospective view of the well-known case of "Gyges and Candaules"), the monstrosity of the crime, and the absurdity of the tribunal and the punishment, were all set forth in the terrible leading article of the *Day*.

The next day, Mr. Oliver, Q.C., Lady Clara's defender, had his innings. "Many witnesses were mauled and slain. Out of that combat scarce anybody came out well, except the two principal champions, Rowland, Serjeant, and Oliver, Q.C. The whole country looked on and heard the wretched story, not only of Barnes's fault and Highgate's fault, but of the private peccadilloes of their suborned footmen and conspiring housemaids" (58:2.223–24).

Lord Melbourne in 1836, had continued to pay her the allowance stipulated in their separation agreement. His defense was that she was well off without it, considering the money she had been receiving from Melbourne (now dead) and her current income from her writing (to which George Norton laid claim). In the course of Mrs. Norton's testimony, many details of her financial situation were revealed, and the smouldering remembrances of her involvement with Lord Melbourne were revived. After the suit was thrown out of court, husband and wife continued their battle in the press. Caroline's three-columns-plus letter in the *Times* for 2 September and George's column-length reply on the twenty-fourth left her clearly in possession of the field, in the judgment of most readers: she was a lovely, victimized woman, and he was a cad.

Meredith, in his account of Diana Warwick's ordeal, picked up a detail of Norton *versus* Melbourne that Dickens had taken joyous advantage of but Thackeray overlooked or chose not to use: the brevity and absolute innocuousness of Melbourne's alleged "love letters." Dickens, whose coverage of the trial had occupied twenty-six closely printed columns in the next day's *Morning Chronicle* (the *Times* had room for only twenty and a half), transformed these blameless missives ("I will call about half past 4. Yours, Melbourne") into what Mr. Serjeant Buzfuz convinced the jury was prima facie evidence of Pickwick's guilt: "Dear Mrs. B.—Chops and Tomata sauce. Yours, Pickwick" (34:562). Lord Dannisburgh's notes, Diana exclaimed in fury, were "none very long, sometimes two short sentences—he wrote at any spare moment" (12:130), just as Melbourne, another busy cabinet minister, had done.

Meredith handled the scandalmongering in a way strikingly different from Thackeray's. The appearance in the gossip press of a mere paragraph of innuendo concerning Mr. and Mrs. W—— was enough to bring the big guns of her chivalric defenders into action. Meredith's emphasis was on the effective efforts Sir Lukin Dunstane made to suppress the story.

> [H]e began a crusade against the scandal-newspapers, going with an Irish military comrade straight to the editorial offices, and leaving his card and a warning that the chastisement for print of the name of the lady in their columns would be personal and condign. Captain Carew Mahony, albeit unacquainted with Mrs. Warwick, had espoused her cause. She was a woman— she was an Irishwoman—she was a beautiful woman [Caroline Sheridan Norton was all of these]. She had, therefore, three positive claims on him as a soldier and a man. Other Irish gentlemen, animated by the same swelling degrees, were awakening to the intimation that they might be wanted. Some words were dropped here and there by General Lord Larrian: he regretted his age and infirmities. (13:144)

Diana therefore was spared the trial-by-publicity that was Lady Clara's lot. And, indeed, unlike Thackeray, Meredith held the trial of Warwick *versus* Dannisburgh entirely offstage, forgoing even a summary—an interesting example of his genial perversity as a novelist-craftsman. He all but concealed the trial's outcome by placing it, with seeming casualness, last in a sentence reporting a series of other events:

> The Bull's Head, or British Jury of Twelve, with the wig on it, was faced during the latter half of a week of good news. First, Mr. Thomas Redworth was returned to Parliament by a stout majority for the Borough of Orrybridge: the Hon. Percy Dacier delivered a brilliant speech in the House of Commons, necessarily pleasing to his uncle: Lord Larrian obtained the command of the Rock: the house of The Crossways was let to a tenant ap-

proved by Mr. Braddock: Diana received the opening proof-sheets of her little volume, and an instalment of the modest honorarium: and, finally, the Plaintiff in the suit involving her name was adjudged to have not proved his charge. (14:159–60)

If a topical event could be said to have had a Janus-like quality when treated in fiction, the Norton-Melbourne sensation was one. Its comedic counterpart in *Pickwick Papers* was the essence of timeliness; in *The Newcomes* and *Diana of the Crossways*, the adultery trials were material salvaged from the past, but with strong pertinence to the present.

In the summer of 1839 the newspapers found much to write about in another vein, when Archibald William Montgomerie, thirteenth Earl of Eglinton, held a tournament at his Scottish seat, Eglinton Castle. It was an event to which the word *happening* in its modern pop-art meaning is entirely applicable. As one spinoff from the multifaceted and quixotic early Victorian effort to revive the medieval spirit in a nation of smoking factory chimneys, and to divert minds from the darkening clouds of Chartism and other worries, the Earl invited the cream of society to his castle, to participate in a glorious series of jousts and other festivities popular in the days of King Arthur. The cream of society brought with them a rich array of appropriate garb and weaponry, some of which had been bought or rented from London antique dealers and theatrical costumers. The Queen of Beauty, in private life Lady Georgiana Seymour, Duchess of Somerset and sister of Caroline Norton, was attended by the fairest maids and matrons of the aristocracy. Unfortunately, as had been the case many years earlier when Garrick mounted an extravagant "jubilee" tribute to Shakespeare at Stratford-on-Avon, much of the pageantry was washed out by storms that bemired not only the celebrants but the crowds of outsiders who had come to see what they could of Fashion disporting itself in antique costume. The press had a field day covering the glittering fiasco; the radical Sunday papers mingled their glee with severe observations on the unsuitability of such frivolity and lavish expenditure at a time of widespread unemployment, labor unrest, and privation.

The preposterous bout of lance-bearing and favor-wearing at Eglinton Castle quickly passed into what might be called topical legend.[16] Within a few years Tennyson introduced recognizable echoes of it in the course of the mechanics' institute picnic described in *The Princess*[17] and Surtees (*Mr. Sponge's Sporting Tour* [1849–51]) recalled the event in a description of a hunting horse which "decorated himself with a sky-blue *visite* trimmed with Honiton lace, which he wore like a charger on his way to the Crusades, or a steed bearing a knight to the Eglinton tournament" (12:62).

The rain-soaked Eglinton Tournament entered
history wrapped in popular derision. This cartoon, "The Eglinton Tomfooleryment," which appeared in *Cleave's Penny Gazette*, a working-class
paper, suggests the humorous undercurrent that
accompanied serious allusions to the event in fiction (Disraeli) and poetry (Tennyson).

Probably only an antiquarian like the late Sir Samuel Meyrick could
have distinguished the ritual "medieval" events at Eglinton from the
"Elizabethan" games at Ullathorne in *Barchester Towers*. A featured event
there was the quintan, which required an aspiring knight, presumably
sans peur et sans reproche, to tilt at a swinging sandbag without getting
hurt. Farmer Greenacre's son Harry, who attempted the feat, predictably got hurt. But this was only a fragmentary reprise of Eglinton,
which, however, every reader was bound to recognize and so more fully
appreciate the fiasco of Trollope's episode. The grand recapitulation
would await Disraeli's description in *Endymion*. There, forty years after
the event, the colorful extravagances of Eglinton were summoned up
again in three whole chapters (58–60) written in Disraeli's purplest
prose and with a full measure of the bright conversation—verbal joust-
ing—that was also a hallmark of the politician-novelist's style. Disraeli
omitted the rainy finale from this late revival of the Eglinton story, probably because he wanted to downplay the comic aspect that had always
been uppermost in readers' minds.

Another topical topos was inherently aqueous. Its origin was the story of Grace Darling, a lighthouse keeper's teenage daughter and a powerful rower, who in 1838 saved several persons from the wreck of a steamer off the Northumbrian coast. Grace became an instant heroine, one of the very first creations of the media; her deed was celebrated in songs and engravings, on the stage and in verse.[18] Even the elderly Wordsworth, caught up in the fever, composed a 97-line poem "carry-[ing] to the clouds and to the stars, / Yea, to celestial choirs, GRACE DAR-LING's name!" The ever opportunistic G. W. M. Reynolds published a bestselling melodramatic novel based on the event the next year. Grace's premature death four years later enhanced its sentimental luster. The heroic deed of a woman saving a man—or men—from drowning became the model for several later fictional incidents. In *Christie Johnson* (1853), Reade adopted the story to solve the problem, often found in novels of the time, of a love affair being frustrated by familial opposition: the young fishwife Christie plunged into the Firth of Forth and saved her artist-lover Charles Gatty from drowning, thus demonstrating that she was worthy of marriage to him despite their difference in social rank. Four years later, in Kingsley's *Two Years Ago*, the intrepid school-mistress, Grace Harvey (the name was transparent enough), saved the adventurous doctor Tom Thurnall from a shipwreck off the Cornish coast. The question of whether they would or would not marry after this dramatic introduction in the turbulent seas furnished a note of suspense throughout the remainder of the narrative.

In the very same year occurred another fictional rescue of the sort, when the intrepid and athletic American, Caroline Courtney, in Reade's story "The Bloomer" (in *The Course of True Love Never Did Run Smooth*), dove into a stream wearing bloomers (Turkish trousers) instead of heavy, water-absorbent skirts and plucked her fiancé from the jaws of watery death. In the next appearance of the topos, the conclusion of *The Mill on the Floss* (1860), Maggie Tulliver was the Grace Darling figure who, when the river Floss was flooded, strained at the oars in a desperate attempt to rescue the people at the mill and lost both her life and her brother's—the only tragic outcome in the Grace Darling series except for that in *Daniel Deronda* (1876), over which Grace's wraith seems to have presided. In that novel, the sexes of the protagonists were reversed when Grandcourt rescued Mirah Lapidoth from drowning in the Thames.[†] In a later episode, the climax of the Grandcourt-Gwendolen

---

[†]The reversal also appeared in Charlotte Yonge's *The Heir of Redclyffe* (1853), where, as in *Two Years Ago*, the scene was a shipwreck off a fishing village in the West Country. Here the Grace Darling part was played by the novel's hero, Sir Guy Morville.

Grace Darling, instantly famous for the "heroic nobility of
heart and conduct" with which she rescued several persons
from a sinking steamship in 1838, became the media-made
prototype of the intrepid life-saving heroine in Victorian fiction. The *Illustrated London News* (8 October 1842 and 22 January 1848) familiarized readers with (above) her appearance
while alive and (opposite) the tomb erected to her memory on
the Northumberland coast, near the scene of her deed.

plot was reached when Grandcourt fell overboard from their sailboat in
Genoese waters and Gwendolen, in marked contrast to Maggie Tulliver,
forsook the Grace Darling role that the circumstances clearly required
and let him drown.

In *Our Mutual Friend*, the event conformed more closely to the original: Lizzie Hexam, who saved her brutally beaten lover, Eugene Wrayburn, from almost certain death in the Thames weir, was no amateur

like Maggie Tulliver but a virtual professional, who almost as an infant had learned boatmanship and the art of fishing bodies out of swiftly flowing water from her father, who made a living at this unpleasant trade. Thanks to this early training, she ensured that Wrayburn would survive, though as a mere wreck of a man.

Another kind of shadow event, less personal than the Grace Darling story and hovering only in the background of several Victorian novels, was the long-running mystery of the fate of Sir John Franklin and his expedition that had set out to discover the Northwest passage to the Pacific. It had left England in the spring of 1845 to the accompaniment of much patriotic publicity, and when no word of it came back after many months, the admiralty dispatched three search expeditions in a single year (1847). It was at this very time that readers of *Dombey and*

Son, the real-life counterparts of Mr. Chick and his fellow newspaper readers in the novel, were worrying about what had happened to Walter Gay and the *Son and Heir*, on which he had shipped to Barbados. Dickens thus took advantage of an actual, widely felt anxiety to intensify the effect of his fictional suspense story, causing his readers to transfer the emotions stirred by the Franklin mystery to the question of what had happened to Walter Gay. The eventual return of the shipwrecked Walter represented a fulfilment of hopes which, in the case of Franklin, were destined not to be realized.

3.

The means by which novelists fixed the time of the action, distanced or not, ranged from the sharply specific to the mistily vague. Disraeli, like George Eliot later in *Middlemarch*, carefully coordinated his fictional plot with public events and, for additional veraciousness, frequently mentioned the precise year. In *Coningsby*, after a first book set firmly in 1833, the narrative reached from 1834 to 1841. In *Sybil*, Book 1 was set in 1837 and Books 4 and 5 in 1839, when the ascendancy of Chartism as a major social and political force was made alarmingly evident in the national convention held that summer, a meeting also attended by Elizabeth Gaskell's John Barton. Book 4, chapter 4, brought the narrative up to "the spring of last year."

Overt attention to chronology was one of the hallmarks of the sensation school, as Alfred Austin pointed out:

> If the novel is printed about 1860, care is taken to inform us, early in its pages, that "three days after this, the 14th of June, 1856," such an event occurred to the heroine; and then, to bring us still nearer, we are informed, a little further on, that it is late in the August of 1857. The reader may thus well hope to reach 1860 before the end of the third volume, by which means the mysterious occurrences detailed in all three [volumes] will be brought almost to his own door; and that is a great advantage.[19]

Austin may well have had Wilkie Collins in mind, because in several novels he went to unusual pains to specify the time setting. His early *Hide and Seek* (1854) began, "At a quarter to one o'clock, on a wet Sunday afternoon, in November, 1837. . . ." In *The Dead Secret* he went so far as to place the date of the initial action in the title of Book 1, chapter 1: "The Twenty-Third of August, 1829." Collins was similarly precise in *The Moonstone*—the specific dates in 1848–49 were noted in the various characters' narratives. In *Desperate Remedies*, Hardy's avowed attempt to write a sensation novel, he emulated Collins, his master, by turning his chapter and subchapter headings into a virtual calendar: "December and January, 1835–36"; "From 1843 to 1861"; "October the twelfth, 1863"; and so on, down to "Midsummer Night, 1867."[†] This practice was consonant with the spirit of the new school of "scientific" historiography, which laid much stress on temporal exactness. But it could also be traced to the older custom found in some historical romances, of conveying at least an initial semblance of veracity by pinpointing the date of the fictional action.

In place of explicit dates, novelists might use the looser reference to the regnant monarch in such phrases as "the King's Highway," "the Queen's subjects," "turning King's Evidence," and the legal formula "against the peace of our Sovereign Lord the King [or Queen]." The shift in appellation from His Majesty to Her Majesty occurred at a moment within a span of time that would subsequently figure in hundreds of novels. On 30 June 1837 the new queen gave her assent to the first forty acts of Parliament in her reign, and "La Reine le veult" and "Her Majesty" instantly replaced the familiar "Le Roy le veult" and "His Majesty" in official documents. In fiction written after that date the use of one or the other set of royal designations was, when accurately employed, a convenient and unambiguous indication of the time setting. But novelists sometimes inadvertently wrote "His Majesty" when the context clearly required "Her," and Dickens, writing and revising *Oliver Twist* at the very moment of the transition, sometimes fell into the trap of inconsistency. The plot of the novel, serialized in *Bentley's Miscellany* from February 1837 to April 1839, took place prior to Victoria's accession, and so the references to "the King" and "His Majesty" were quite correct. In an early passage of authorial commentary detached from the action ("Although the presiding Genii in such an office as this, exercise a summary and arbitrary power over the liberties, the good name, the character, almost the lives, of His Majesty's subjects" [11:123]), Dickens, again correctly, changed "His" to "Her" when revising the text for publication in volume form, but in a later passage, also of comment rather than dialogue or narration, he let "the king's subjects" stand.[20] In *The Old Curiosity Shop* (1840–41) he juxtaposed the two reigns in a single sentence: "David Quilp of Tower Hill, and Sampson Brass of Bevis Marks in the city of London, Gentleman, one of her Majesty's attorneys

[†]In the preface to the 1895 edition of another early novel, *The Return of the Native*, Hardy provided a time indication in the rare form of a statement outside the text: "The date at which the following events are assumed to have occurred may be set down as between 1840 and 1850, when the old watering-place herein called 'Budmouth' still retained sufficient afterglow from its Georgian gaiety and prestige to lend it an absorbing attractiveness to the romantic and imaginative soul of a lonely dweller inland."

Dating a novel's action by a specific calendar year contributed to its realistic effect, but the sense of immediacy could be also enhanced by allusion to an occurrence fresh in readers' memories, such as the celestial event by which Surtees dated his *Plain or Ringlets?* (1859–60). This picture of Londoners watching Donati's comet from Greenwich Park at 7:30 P.M. on 17 September 1858 was in the *Illustrated London News* for 25 September.

of the Courts of King's Bench and Common Pleas at Westminster" (13:152).

Other novelists at the time, as well as later, made the same kind of slip. Those writing close to the event could extenuate their lapses on the ground of long habit: the English mind and tongue had been attuned to the masculine style ever since the death of the last regnant queen in 1714, and to change this deeply ingrained custom was considerably harder than the annual revision required when one dates a letter in the first days of the new year.

Other chronological indications included readily recognizable allusions to the weather or a celestial event. When Surtees wrote *Hawbuck Grange* (1846–47), the weather in the past two years had been so dreadful that he adopted it as a malign presence in the book, the subject of repeated execration by the frustrated fox hunters and even of a four-page meteorological review by the author (15:191–94). Surtees began a later novel, *Plain or Ringlets?* (1859–60), with the sentence "It was the Comet year—a glorious summer hastened the seasons and forced the country into early maturity." (The astronomer Giovanni Battista Donati had discovered what proved to be the most spectacular comet of the century, its tail stretching across a quarter of the sky, on 2 June 1858.)

Such specific references occupied one compartment in the novelist's store of dating devices; in another, at a considerable distance, resided the sheer timbre of his prose, which might distance a narrative more effectively, though less precisely, than any number of small particulars. In *David Copperfield*, the several references to physical changes in London are of minor importance compared with the enveloping style, a masterpiece of reminiscential writing replete with evocations of David's poignant memories and associations. Thus, in the first nine chapters alone: "Look[ing] back . . . into the blank of my infancy. . . ." "Let me remember how it used to be. . . ." "All this appears to have gone round and round for years instead of days, it is so vividly and strongly stamped on my remembrance. . . ." "The rest of the half-year is a jumble in my recollection of the daily strife and struggle of our lives. . . ." "How well I recollect the kind of day it was! . . ." "All this . . . is yesterday's event. Events of later date have floated from me to the shore where all forgotten things will reappear, but this stands like a high rock in the ocean. . . ."

Great Expectations, Dickens's other novel cast as autobiography, was not written in the elegiac mood. Instead, the action was distanced by a smaller comparative device which was not uniquely Dickens's but which no other novelist except Thackeray employed to so moving an effect. The fourth sentence on the opening page at once removed the narrative from the present by a reference to a present-day novelty: "As I never saw my father or my mother, and never saw any likeness of either of them (for their days were long before the days of photographs). . . ." The unobtrusive distancing touches recur: "At a certain Assembly Ball at Richmond (there used to be Assembly Balls at most places then) . . ."; "[I] drove to the Hummums in Covent Garden. In those times a bed was always to be got there at any hour of the night . . ."; "but as the hours of the tide changed, I took towards London Bridge. It was Old London Bridge in those days . . ."; "At that time, the steam-traffic on the Thames was far below its present extent, and watermen's boats were far more numerous. Of barges, sailing colliers, and coasting traders, there were perhaps as many as now; but, of steam-ships, great and small, not a tithe or a twentieth part so many."[†] In such a manner, Dickens steadily held the past at arm's length from the present.

But he could also bring the present as close to the reader as the resources of language permitted. The celebrated present-tense survey of the fogbound London scene in the opening pages of *Bleak House* is largely responsible for the illusory assumption, sustained by all the chapters narrated in the present tense by the observer, that the novel is set in the present. Trollope used the historical present at the opening of *The Warden* and then mixed present and past tenses for a few paragraphs in chapter 2, thus sliding unobtrusively into the narrative mode in which the rest of the novel is cast.

Thackeray's constant use of "we" in addressing his readers was one of the major ways by which he maintained intimate rapport with them, making the witnessing of an action an experience shared by writer and reader who are living in the strictly contemporary world, and so reinforcing the "presentness" supplied by one set of topical allusions. Meredith also lavishly employed the device, as when in the prelude to *The Egoist* (to select one from thousands of instances) he wrote of "the malady of sameness, our modern malady. We have the malady, whatever may be the cure or the cause. We drove in a body to Science the other day for an antidote; which was as if tired pedestrians should mount the engine-box of headlong trains. . . ."

Few distanced novels were so completely separated from the time of publication as to allow their readers uninterrupted residence in the designated past era. If double-faced topicalities, set in the removed context but clearly having contemporary relevance, were not enough, authors might, writing in their own persons, insert topical allusions that were independent of the narrative and so could not be reckoned as anachronisms. Like Thackeray, in the course of pointing a moral or in a simple description George Eliot might add an updated authorial comment. In *The Mill on the Floss* she referred, in the setting of 1829, to "Mr. Broderip's amiable beaver, [which] as that charming naturalist tells us, busied himself as earnestly in constructing a dam, in a room up three pair of stairs in London, as if he had been laying his foundation in a

---

[†]This was one of the few points of London urban history on which Dickens was (surprisingly) ill informed. (He made the same error in *Little Dorrit* [see page 170 below].) Regular steamboat service on the Thames, mainly to suburbs downstream but also as far as Gravesend and Margate, was begun in 1815, when Dickens was three years old, and it steadily increased thereafter. By the 1830s Greenwich boats were running every quarter-hour in summer and every half-hour in winter. There was a similar increase in commercial, nonpassenger traffic.

stream or lake in Upper Canada" (2.1:122; W. J. Broderip: *Leaves from the Note Book of a Naturalist*, 1852). Later on, in approximately the same time context, she mentioned in a single sentence a cluster of topicalities appropriate to the time of writing (1860) rather than to the Catholic Emancipation era: ". . . good society . . . rides off its ennui on thorough-bred horses, lounges at the club, has to keep clear of crinoline vortices, gets its science done by Faraday, and its religion by the superior clergy who are to be met in the best houses . . ." (4.3:255).

An initial flurry of current topicalities before the narrative got under way could provide a baseline for what turned out to be a distanced plot. Trollope began *The Bertrams* (1859) with a compact series of allusions to politician-horsemen and race horses of recent memory:

> Were we to ask Lord Derby, or Lord Palmerston, or to consult the shade of Lord George Bentinck—or to go to those greater authorities on the subject, Mr. Scott, for instance, and the family of the Days—we should, I believe, be informed that the race-horse requires a very peculiar condition. It is not to be obtained quickly; and, when obtained, will fit the beast for no other than that one purpose of running races. Crucifix was never good at going in a cab; Ilone never took her noble owner down to the house of Parliament; nor has Toxophilite been useful in Leicestershire.[†]

The plot of the novel proved to be laid wholly in the 1840s, a dozen years or more before it was published. But the magnetic effect of these clustered references, like that of some anachronisms, would have been to draw it closer to the present, to reduce, however slightly, the gap between past and present. And, in fact, this was the usual tendency whenever a novelist, reaching back to the past for his plot, inserted up-to-date topicalities here and there.

No matter what the distance was between the time of publication and the time of the action, a Victorian novel—*Middlemarch* is an arguable exception—did not purport to recreate, as modern historians strive to do, the particular mental atmosphere, the basic attitudes and assumptions that prevailed in that earlier day. The application of period color did not reach that far, except that a character might express a prejudice well known to have existed then, such as the fears and superstitions about railways that George Eliot attributed to the farmers in *Middle-*

[†]Lord George Bentinck (d. 1848) was the firmest link between Parliament and racing: he kept a racing stud and was active in the management of race courses. John Scott was a prominent jockey and horse trainer of the time, and William Day, also a breeder, was famous for the number of winners he trained. In the year *The Beltons* was published, one of his horses won the Two Thousand Guineas stakes.

march. Otherwise, period flavor was achieved only through externalities such as physical appearances and landmark events. Distanced novels with strong ideological content were meant to be tracts for the (present) times, not experiments in historical reconstruction. When George Eliot wrote *Felix Holt* (1866), with its setting in the immediate aftermath of the First Reform Act, she intended it to be a commentary on the political situation and the state of opinion at the moment of writing in the mid-sixties, when the great political issue of the day was the Second Reform Bill. Pressed by John Blackwood, her publisher—"It strikes me," he wrote her, "that you could do a first-rate address to the Working Men on their new responsibilities"[21]—Eliot went so far as to expatiate on the novel's conservative message in just such an "Address to Working Men, by Felix Holt" in the January 1868 issue of *Blackwood's Magazine*, some months after the bill had become law. The novel's numerous passages of debate as the people at Treby Magna sought to digest the meaning of the newly achieved widening of the franchise and prepare for the impending election, the first to be held since the bill was passed, were less historical (1832) than argumentative (1866) in purpose. An early reviewer saw through the distancing:

> We are told that the date of the story is 1832, and the title is "Felix Holt, *the Radical*"—a good publishers' device, considering what political questions were mainly agitating the country when the book appeared. But the whole thing is a delusion. So far as connexion with the time goes, or with the prominent subject of the time, the date of the tale might as well have been 1732, and the title Felix Holt the Mahometan. We speak, of course, of a real connexion with the time—not of such outward matters as the fact that there is a general election, and that one man contests the county as a Tory, and another as a Radical. A careful and impartial representation of the state of feeling in this country after the passing of the Reform Bill; an estimate of what Radicalism then was—presenting, we should think, a curious contrast to what Radicalism now is,—these would have afforded material for much careful and interesting study. Nothing of the sort is attempted. There is much writing *about* politics, but nothing approaching to a real picture of the political life of the time. Mail-coaches, Dissenters' meeting-houses, many phases of life are represented; but that which especially ought to have been represented, namely, the political phase, has been omitted. As for the ideal Radical of 1832, he is an entirely modern figure—an utter anachronism—a sort of cross between Mr. Lowe and Lord Elcho.[22]

Beauchamp's Career was set in the 1850s, to which the particular topicalities are referable—the Crimean War, the agitation to open the British Museum on Sundays, the craze for carte-de-visite photographs. But the ideas are strictly those of the mid-seventies, centering on the current debate over the present condition and prospects of political liberalism.

Much of the authorial commentary and the dialogue between the characters sounds like paraphrases of articles in the *Fortnightly Review*, where, as a matter of fact, the novel was serialized. Thus a thick layer of political attitudes and biases characteristic of the time when Meredith was writing is superimposed on a setting twenty years earlier.[23]

One can be less certain about Disraeli's *Endymion*. In its conversations between quasi-fictional political leaders in the period 1830–50, the novel purported to be faithful to the ideas of that time, as had the trilogy Disraeli had written then. But he could scarcely have meant to write only a period piece, and his readers in 1880 could not have helped interpreting the book's ideological content in the light of its author's well-known views as an elder statesman who had resigned the premiership only months before *Endymion* was published.

4.

When novelists kept firm ties with the present even as they distanced their narratives, they produced a stereoscopic effect, that of two time-planes: "then" in the foreground, "now" in the background, or vice versa. Past and present could be seen simultaneously and compared, for whatever purpose the novelist had in mind. The technique occurs in its simplest form in James Payn's *Lost Sir Massingberd* (1864), where a dual system of references maintains the separation of past and present. "Nearly half a century has passed over my head since the time of which I write," says the narrator, and other indications are consistent with this. A character refers to the politician Castlereagh as still living (he died in 1822); another mentions "the new romance of 'Ivanhoe'" (1820); there is a quotation from Byron's *Mazeppa* (1819), "that poem which came down in the box of books . . . a week ago"; Lord Eldon is still Lord Chancellor (he occupied the woolsack until 1827); and so on. Against these period allusions, Payn counterpointed a set of references explicitly contrasting past and present: "The 'people' [then] were 'the Great Unwashed.' To build a Crystal Palace for such as they were held to be, would have seemed to be the height of folly"; a compassionate woman is "like some Miss Nightingale of a generation and a half ago"; "I do not think," says the narrator, "that the boys of my time, myself included, were quite so honourable and frank as Mr. Tom Brown [in Thomas Hughes's novels, *Tom Brown's Schooldays*, 1857, and *Tom Brown at Oxford*, 1861] describes those of the present day to be"; "In these days of Palmerston and Derby, of Tweedledum and Tweedledee, it is impossible for those who are not old enough to have witnessed it, to imagine the rancour of political parties half a century ago, or the despotism and flagrant injustice that were sanctioned under the convenient name of Order."†

The same result was obtained elsewhere in a more concentrated, local form, when in single paragraphs or longer passages "then" and "now" were juxtaposed. Victorian fiction acquired this contrasting technique—"Look upon this picture, and now upon this," as Hamlet commanded his mother—from other realms of literature. Analysts, pro and con, of the spirit of the age—Southey in his *Colloquies of Sir Thomas More*, Macaulay in his hatchet job on Southey's book in the *Edinburgh Reviews*—invoked some past epoch as a means of defining the characteristic quality of the present. In 1836 Augustus Welby Pugin published *Contrasts: or a Parallel Between the Architecture of the 15th and 19th Centuries*, in which a series of engravings placed the recreated beauty of the medieval scene side by side with the blatant ugliness of the present one: an old abbey contrasting with a new Poor Law workhouse, an old "Catholic town" with its heaven-pointing spires contrasting with its modern (Protestant) counterpart, all smokestacked factories and bleak, utilitarian warehouses with a grim prison in the foreground. Carlyle's *Past and Present* (1843) was structured on the discrepancy between English life under a benevolent ruler (the abbot of a Benedictine monastery in twelfth-century Suffolk) and the materialism, greed, and poverty of an industrialized nation living under the Chartist menace.

But the then-and-now technique that came closest to the fictional method was most notably exemplified by the organizing principle in the third chapter ("England in 1685") of the first volume of Macaulay's *History of England* (1849). Between the majestic second paragraph that announces the theme and the long coda that finally expands and summarizes it, Macaulay uses contemporary England to describe and evaluate his subject, England at the time of the Glorious Revolution. The rhetorical ground fabric is furnished by words that establish the present moment as the measure of all past things: "now," "at present," "our time," "modern," "our generation," "are still" (referring to a survival from 1685), and "not yet" (a kind of oblique "now," in connection with some familiar object or institution that was created or developed since that date).

---

†One allusion, intended to be a touch of period color, was actually a relatively recent topicality. One of the characters, speaking in the removed context of fifty years, quotes a nine-line passage of poetry beginning "Behold the harvest that we reap / From popular government and equality!" and remarks to his companion, "The author of those lines, my friend, is the greatest poet in Great Britain, and has never possessed an income of a hundred pounds a year" (9:94). This was Wordsworth; but the passage quoted is from *The Prelude*, first published in 1850.

From rural England as it was in a former day and as it is now, Macaulay passes, halfway through the chapter, to London: "Great as has been the change in the rural life of England since the Revolution, the change which has come to pass in the cities is still more amazing."

Whoever examines the maps of London which were published towards the close of the reign of Charles the Second will see that only the nucleus of the present capital then existed. The town did not, as now, fade by imperceptible degrees into the country. No long avenues of villas, embowered in lilacs and laburnums, extended from the great centre of wealth and civilisation almost to the boundaries of Middlesex and far into the heart of Kent and Surrey. In the east, no part of the immense line of warehouses and artificial lakes which now spreads from the Tower to Blackwall had even been projected. On the west, scarcely one of those stately piles of building which are inhabited by the noble and wealthy was in existence; and Chelsea, which is now peopled by more than forty thousand human beings, was a quiet country village with about a thousand inhabitants. On the north, cattle fed, and sportsmen wandered with dogs and guns, over the site of the borough of Marylebone, and over far the greater part of the space now covered by the boroughs of Finsbury and of the Tower Hamlets. Islington was almost a solitude; and poets loved to contrast its silence and repose with the din and turmoil of the monster London. On the south the capital is now connected with its suburb by several bridges, not inferior in magnificence and solidity to the noblest works of the Caesars. In 1685, a single line of irregular arches, overhung by piles of mean and crazy houses, and garnished, after a fashion worthy of the naked barbarians of Dahomy, with scores of mouldering heads, impeded the navigation of the river.[24]

Amidst all the respects in which modern England was incomparably superior to the England of Charles II, Macaulay had to confess there was one conspicuous instance of retrogression:

Johnson declared that a tavern chair was the throne of human felicity; and Shenstone gently complained that no private roof, however friendly, gave the wanderer so warm a welcome as that which was to be found at an inn.

Many conveniences, which were unknown at Hampton Court and Whitehall in the seventeenth century, are to be found in our modern hotels. Yet on the whole it is certain that the improvement of our houses of public entertainment has by no means kept pace with the improvement of our roads and of our conveyances. Nor is this strange; for it is evident that, all other circumstances being supposed equal, the inns will be best where the means of locomotion are worst. The quicker the rate of travelling, the less important is it that there should be numerous agreeable resting places for the traveller. A hundred and sixty years ago a person who came up to the capital from a remote county generally required twelve or fifteen meals, and lodging for five or six nights. . . . At present we fly from York or Exeter to

London by the light of a single winter's day. At present, therefore, a traveller seldom interrupts his journey merely for the sake of rest and refreshment. The consequence is that hundreds of excellent inns have fallen into
utter decay.[25]

Nostalgia in this unaccustomed Macaulayan key was the leitmotif of
the great then-and-now passages in Victorian fiction. It was as if the
novelists counterpointed the imperious, baying, brassy note of the stage-
coach guard's post horn with the shrill scream of the locomotive whistle.
Thackeray chose to embody his inveterate lament for times past in the
appropriate imagery of coaching and the railway that had spelled the
coaches' doom. I will quote only a parsimonious handful of examples
here, reserving others, no less eloquent, for the following chapter. The
earliest is from *Vanity Fair*:

> Where is the road now, and its merry incidents of life? Is there no Chelsea
> or Greenwich for the old honest pimple-nosed coachmen? I wonder where
> they are, those good fellows? Is old Weller alive or dead? and the waiters,
> yea and the inns at which they waited, and the cold rounds of beef inside,
> and the stunted ostler with his blue nose and clinking pail, where is he, and
> where is his generation? To those great geniuses now in petticoats, who
> shall write novels for the beloved reader's children, these men and things
> will be as much legend and history as Nineveh, or Coeur de Lion, or Jack
> Sheppard. For them stage-coaches will have become romances—a team of
> four bays as fabulous as Bucephalus or Black Bess. Ah, how their coats
> shone, as the stable-men pulled their clothes off, and away they went—ah,
> how their tails shook, as with smoking sides at the stage's end they demurely
> walked away into the inn-yard. Alas! we shall never hear the horn sing at
> midnight, or see the pike-gates fly open any more. (7:73)

One of Major Pendennis's several meditations on the flight of time
begins:

> The men, thinks he, are not such as they used to be in his time: the old
> grand manner and courtly grace of life are gone: "what is Castlewood
> House and the present Castlewood compared to the magnificence of the
> old mansion and owner? The late lord came to London streets with four
> post-chaises and sixteen horses: all the West Road hurried out to look at
> his cavalcade: the people in London streets even stopped as his procession
> passed them. The present lord travels with five bagmen [traveling sales-
> men] in a railway carriage, and sneaks away from the station, smoking a
> cigar in a brougham." (*Pendennis*, 67:2.308)

A similar elegiac passage is in *The Newcomes* (10:1.113). It was in that
novel, indeed, that Thackeray's nostalgic mood reached its climax, beginning with the very "Overture": "There was once a time when the sun
used to shine brighter than it appears to do in this latter half of the

nineteenth century . . ." (1 : 1.5–6). Past and present, and indeed future in the case of the schoolboys, were symbolically represented at Grey Friars (Charterhouse), where "then" and "now" were represented by widely separated generations. The boys' "life, bustle, and gaiety contrasted strangely with the quiet of those old men, creeping along in their black gowns under the ancient arches yonder, whose struggle of life was over, whose hope and noise and bustle had sunk into that grey calm" (7 : 1.71).

Thackeray's sense of halcyon days irrevocably gone was sharpest in London, the scene of his squandered youth, "the days when the 'Haunt' *was* a haunt," a favorite tavern frequented by artists and newspapermen, fairly reeking with pipe smoke and gemütlichkeit.

> Casinos were not invented, clubs were rather rare luxuries; there were sanded floors, triangular sawdust-boxes, pipes, and tavern parlours. Young Smith and Brown, from the Temple, did not go from chambers to dine at the "Polyanthus," or the "Megatherium," off potage à la Bisque, turbot au gratin, côtes-lettes à la What-d'you-call-'em, and a pint of St. Emilion; but ordered their beefsteak and pint of port from the "plump head-waiter at the 'Cock';" did not disdain the pit of the theatre; and for supper a homely refection at the tavern. . . . Those little meetings, in the memory of many of us, yet, are gone quite away into the past. Five-and-twenty years ago is a hundred years off—so much has our social life changed in those five lustres. (*The Newcomes*, 25 : 1.261)

London geography, which most of Thackeray's readers knew (and those who did not, still got the general idea), helped him visualize the past in terms of the present. In *Vanity Fair* he recalled Becky Sharp's early morning exit from London atop a coach, on the way to Queen's Crawley:

> how the carriage at length drove away [from the Swan with Three Necks inn]—now, threading the dark lanes of Aldersgate, anon clattering by the Blue Cupola of St. Paul's, jingling rapidly by the strangers' entry of Fleet-Market, which, with Exeter 'Change, has now departed to the world of shadows—how they passed the White Bear in Piccadilly, and saw the dew rising up from the market-gardens of Knightsbridge—how Turnham-green, Brentford, Bagshot, were passed—need not be told here. But the writer of these pages, who has pursued in former days, and in the same bright weather, the same remarkable journey, cannot but think of it with a sweet and tender regret. (7 : 73)

As late as 1880, Disraeli looked back, in *Endymion*, to the entertainments available in London at the very time of which Thackeray wrote. But he shared none of Thackeray's nostalgia, because, although the "bachelors about town" were in some ways more fortunate than the rest of the population, they enjoyed none of the variety of amusements that later years had brought:

The middle classes, half a century ago, had little distraction from their monotonous toil and melancholy anxieties, except, perhaps, what they found in religious and philanthropic societies. Their general life must have been very dull. Some traditionary merriment always lingered among the working classes of England. Both in town and country they had always their games and fairs and junketing parties, which have developed into excursion trains and colossal pic-nics. But of all classes of the community, in the days of our fathers, there was none so unfortunate in respect of public amusements as the bachelors about town. There were, one might almost say, only two theatres, and they so huge, that it was difficult to see or hear in either. Their monopolies, no longer redeemed by the stately genius of the Kembles, the pathos of Miss O'Neill, or the fiery passion of Kean, were already menaced, and were soon about to fall; but the crowd of diminutive but sparkling substitutes, which have since taken their place, had not yet appeared, and half-price at Drury Lane or Covent Garden was a dreary distraction after a morning of desk work. There were no Alhambras then, and no Cremornes, no palaces of crystal in terraced gardens, no casinos, no music-halls, no aquaria, no promenade concerts. Evans' existed, but not in the fulness of its modern development; and the most popular place of resort was the barbarous conviviality of the Cider Cellar. (20:86–87)

Perhaps benefiting from Thackeray's example, George Eliot too was a skillful manipulator of past and present. Her first exercises in the then-and-now vein appeared in *Scenes of Clerical Life* (1857). At the very opening of "The Sad Fortunes of the Rev. Amos Barton," after a paragraph describing the metamorphosis Shepperton church had undergone over a quarter of a century, she continued:

Immense improvement! says the well-regulated mind, which unintermittingly rejoices in the New Police, the Tithe Commutation Act, the penny post, and all guarantees of human advancement, and has no moments when conservative-reforming intellect takes a nap, while imagination does a little Toryism by the sly, revelling in regret, that dear, old, brown, crumbling, picturesque inefficiency is everywhere giving place to spick-and-span new-painted, new-varnished efficiency . . . (1:41)

In "Janet's Repentance," the last of the stories, there was an extended description of the process by which, again over a span of a quarter-century, Milby had been transformed from a sleepy, dull town to "a refined, moral, and enlightened" one (2:253).

Another large-scale descriptive passage occurred in *The Mill on the Floss*, when Eliot, having introduced the Tullivers and their relations, took her readers for the first time to St. Ogg's, "that venerable town with the red-fluted roofs and the broad warehouse gables," an ancient legend of a flood and a miracle-working saint, and communal memories of fighting in the streets during the civil wars.

Doubtless there are many houses standing now on which those honest citizens turned their backs in sorrow: quaint-gabled houses looking on the river, jammed between newer warehouses, and penetrated by surprising passages, which turn and turn at sharp angles till they lead you out on a muddy strand overflowed continually by the rushing tide. Everywhere the brick houses have a mellow look, and in Mrs. Glegg's day there was no incongruous new-fashioned smartness, no plate-glass in shop windows, no fresh stucco-facing or other fallacious attempt to make fine old red St. Ogg's wear the air of a town that sprang up yesterday. The shop windows were small and unpretending; for the farmers' wives and daughters who came to do their shopping on market-days were not to be withdrawn from their regular, well-known shops; and the tradesmen had no wares intended for customers who would go on their way and be seen no more. Ah! even Mrs. Glegg's day seems far back in the past now, separated from us by changes that widen the years. . . .

It was a time when ignorance was much more comfortable than at present, and was received with all the honours in very good society, without being obliged to dress itself in an elaborate costume of knowledge; a time when cheap periodicals were not, and when country surgeons never thought of asking their female patients if they were fond of reading, but simply took it for granted that they preferred gossip; a time when ladies in rich silk gowns wore large pockets, in which they carried a mutton-bone to secure them against cramp. (1.12:105–7)

Like Thackeray, Dickens used present-day London to realize the past more vividly. The chronology of *David Copperfield* rested on changes that occurred between the time of the events in the narrative and the time of writing. Those temporal landmarks were centered between Blackfriars and what was to become, about the time of David's brief marriage to Dora, Trafalgar Square—the region of the Strand and Charing Cross, where the real-life David, Dickens himself, once pasted labels on blacking pots, as the fictional David pasted them on wine bottles. Murdstone and Grinby's warehouse was in Blackfriars, before "modern improvements have altered the place." Mrs. Salmon's "perspiring Wax-work" was still being exhibited in Fleet Street; at Highgate, where Mrs. Steerforth lived, "the church with the slender spire, that stands on the top of the hill now, was not there then"; and while still at Murdstone and Grinby's, David sometimes lounged on "old London bridge" (demolished 1831).

In *Little Dorrit*, Arthur Clennam shadows Tattycoram and Rigaud/Blandois as they turn from the Strand into the Adelphi, "as if they were going to the Terrace which overhangs the river."

There is always, to this day [Dickens continued], a sudden pause in that place to the roar of the great thoroughfare. The many sounds become so deadened that the change is like putting cotton in the ears, or having the head thickly muffled. At that time the contrast was far greater; there being no small steam-boats on the river, no landing places but slippery wooden stairs and foot-causeways, no railroad on the opposite bank, no hanging bridge or fish-market near at hand, no traffic on the nearest bridge of stone, nothing moving on the stream but watermen's wherries and coal-lighters. . . . (2.9:585–86)[†]

Not only places and communities but individual people performed the same comparative function. Both Dickens and Thackeray depicted men and women who were living anachronisms, pathetically (in some cases) preserving vestiges of past appearances and manners in the degenerate present, a progressive time peculiarly inhospitable to human relics. Dickens created the absurd Turveydrop, the model of Deportment, the glass of Regency fashion and (padded) mold of form, who, like his role model Beau Brummell in exile at Calais, "kept up a ludicrous imitation of his past habits" (the words of the reminiscing Captain Rees Gronow);[26] Mrs. Skewton, the grotesquely aged Cleopatra whose claim to have been a Regency enchantress was as false as the contrivances of corsetry that held her together in public; Cousin Feenix, an M.P. in Pitt's time forty years earlier and now a well-preserved last representative of his old county family, living in retirement at Baden-Baden; Sir Leicester Dedlock and his company of outdated guests at Chesney Wold; Twemlow, the always available extra leaf in the Veneerings' dinner table, with his "neat little shoes and . . . neat little silk stockings of a bygone fashion" and, like Turveydrop, a strangulating "First-Gentleman-in-Europe collar and cravat" (*Our Mutual Friend*, 1.2:52); and the bony Lady Tippins, "relict of the late Sir Thomas Tippins, knighted in mistake for somebody else by His Majesty King George the Third, who, while performing the ceremony, was graciously pleased to observe, 'What, what, what? Who, who, who? Why, why, why?' . . ." (*Our Mutual Friend*, 1.10:164).

Thackeray, for his part, had Lady Kew, a coeval of Lady Tippins and Mrs. Skewton, who may have been suggested by his octogenarian friends the Berry sisters, Mary (1763–1852) and Agnes (1764–1852), who had

---

[†] In this densely allusive passage, Dickens was mistaken on one point: in the late 1820s, the setting of the novel, steamboats were common sights on the river, as we have seen. But his topographical references would have made complete sense to London readers in 1855–57. The "hanging bridge" was the Hungerford Suspension Bridge, opened in 1845; the "fish-market" was Hungerford Market, 1833; and the "nearest bridge of stone" was Waterloo, opened in 1817. The decision to build it of stone rather than wood had been the subject of controversy at the time. The "railroad on the opposite bank" was, at the moment, nonexistent but it was expected in the near future: it was the proposed extension of the South Eastern Railway westward from its terminus at London Bridge to Charing Cross, which became an actuality in 1864.

been close friends of Horace Walpole seventy years earlier and lived in his Little Strawberry Hill house, which he had bequeathed to them. In her *Autobiography* Harriet Martineau described them as she and Thackeray knew them: "While up to all modern interests, the old-fashioned rouge and pearl-powder, and false hair, and the use of the feminine oaths of a hundred years ago were odd and striking." (The feminine oaths were "O! Christ!" and "My God!")[27] Lady Kew took precedence of age, by a substantial margin, over Major Pendennis, who nevertheless was an "old buck," an "old man of the world," as Thackeray repeatedly characterized him. *His* breed, the breed of true gentlemen as he saw it, was gone: "there's no use for 'em; they're replaced by a parcel of damned cotton-spinners and utilitarians, and young sprigs of parsons with their hair combed down their backs" (*Pendennis*, 67:2.309). What a fall was there, from the days when coiffure, cosmetics, and costume proclaimed his proud status! Thackeray had taken up this theme earlier in the novel:

> If men sneer, as our habit is, at the artifices of an old beauty, at her paint, perfumes, ringlets; at those innumerable, and to us unknown, stratagems with which she is said to remedy the ravages of time and reconstruct the charms whereof years have bereft her; the ladies, it is to be presumed, are not on their side altogether ignorant that men are vain as well as they, and that the toilets of old bucks are to the full as elaborate as their own. How is it that old Blushington keeps that constant little rose-tint on his cheeks . . .? (36:1.365–66)

. . . and so into a long paragraph on the Old Buck phenomenon in modern life, ending with Major Pendennis's valet "set[ting] the old gentleman on his legs, with waistband and wig, starched cravat, and spotless boots and gloves," ready for the world's inspection.

But it was Thackeray's Lieutenant-General the Honourable Sir George Granby Tufto who provided the most explicit link between past and present. He was seen first in "On Some Military Snobs" (*Punch*, 2 May 1846; *BS*, 39–40), where he "dresses like an outrageously young man to the present moment, and laces and pads his bloated old carcass as if he were still handsome George Tufto of 1800." He reappeared in *Vanity Fair*, to figure as the officer with whom Becky Sharp flirts on the eve of Waterloo, and then thirty years later as a familiar, half-pathetic sight on the London streets.

> Those who know the present Lieutenant-General Sir George Tufto, K.C.B., and have seen him, as they may on most days in the season, padded and in stays strutting down Pall Mall with a ricketty swagger on his high-heeled lacquered boots, leering under the bonnets of passers-by, or riding a showy chestnut, and ogling Broughams in the Parks—those who know the present

Sir George Tufto would hardly recognise the daring Peninsula and Waterloo officer. He has thick curling brown hair and black eyebrows now, and
his whiskers are of the deepest purple. He was light-haired and bald in
1815, and stouter in the person and the limbs, which especially have shrunk
very much of late. When he was about seventy years of age (he is now
nearly eighty), his hair, which was very scarce and quite white, suddenly
grew thick, and brown, and curly, and his whiskers and eyebrows took their
present colour. (28:266–67)

By their very antiquity, unapologetic and often unconscious, characters
like Tufto and Turveydrop helped their creators not only to evoke the
past but to draw a sharper picture of the present scene in which they
were as much museum-quality curiosities as men and women in the living but aged flesh.

5.

As he concluded the action of his novel, the Victorian writer had three
choices available to him. If the plot of a distanced "novel of our times"
did not reach to the present, he could simply end it at a convenient point
and say nothing about what happened to the characters subsequently. If
he wished, however, he could fill in the intervening years in either of
two ways. He could inform his readers that this or that happened, the
surviving characters being assigned their respective deserts—ignominy
and ruin for the feckless or evil, appropriate rewards for the virtuous,
innocent, courageous, or repentant—without a specific time-frame being devised to contain this cluster of events. The reader would receive a
general sense of time having passed since the story ended without being
encouraged to question how many years actually elapsed. Or the novelist
could update his characters' fortunes in ways requiring specification,
such as careful calculation of the time necessary for the married hero
and heroine to produce a particular number of children—an important
consideration in that philoprogenitive age.

The latter was the riskier alternative, because once a novelist had
committed himself to a distanced past datable by topicalities, he might
have neglected to provide a sufficient time cushion between the end of
the action and the time of writing to contain all the subsequent occurrences about which he wanted to inform his readers. This was one of the
hazards of publishing in numbers, when the time of the action was specified early on and the chronology of the entire book had not been worked
out in advance; improvisation, in such circumstances, had its built-in
perils. No retrospective adjustment of chronology was possible unless

the author revised the text before publishing it in book form, and no novelist seems to have cared enough about temporal consistency to go to that much trouble.

The best-known instances of comprehensive epilogues, which became a typical feature of early Victorian fiction, are in Dickens's first half-dozen novels. As Humphry House observed, those "summaries of family history in the final chapters must never be taken too literally."[28] The action of *Pickwick Papers* ended in the autumn of 1828 and the last number was published in November 1837, leaving nine years to accommodate the diverse afterlives of all the main characters. The longest period required was for Sam Weller to remain single for two years, then to marry Mary, Mr. Nupkins's pert servant girl, and produce "two sturdy little boys." Pickwick acts as godfather to Snodgrass's, Winkle's, and Trundle's offspring, but Dickens does not say when, or how many occasions. Otherwise, he evades troublesome precision of dates (not including Bob Sawyer's and Benjamin Allen's having fourteen attacks of yellow fever), although the main impression his wording conveys as he bids farewell to various characters is of a fair amount of time passed: "ever afterwards" (Winkle), "to this day" (Snodgrass), "ever since" (Tupman), "never" (Mrs. Bardell), "still lives" (the elder Weller), "somewhat infirm now" (Pickwick himself).

The effect of such time-stretching terms as these was to recall the endings of the nursery stories that played so vital a role in feeding Dickens's imagination as a child: "ever afterwards" and "ever since" always implied an epilogue of uncertain, but considerable, duration. In the six novels he wrote between *Pickwick Papers* and *David Copperfield*, five, including *Barnaby Rudge*, fulfilled the expectations with which he credited his readers, similarly nurtured on stories with happy endings. The wrap-up chapters normally accounted for all the surviving characters in whose destinies readers might be interested, and covered a length of years commensurate with Dickens's statement in the last chapter of *Dombey and Son*, "Buried wine grows older, as the old Madeira did, in its time; and dust and cobwebs thicken on the bottles" (62:975).

And so, in *Oliver Twist*, Rose Fleming and Harry Maylie, having been married three months after the last scene, in time produce several "joyous little faces" to cluster around Rose's knee; Mrs. Maylie lives with her son and daughter-in-law for "the tranquil remainder of her days"; Monks goes to "a distant part of the New World" to squander his portion, undergoes "a long confinement for some fresh act of fraud and knavery," and sinks "at length" under a fatal disease; Charley Bates becomes, in turn, a farmer's drudge, a carrier's lad, and a merry Northamptonshire grazier; the Bumbles "gradually" become paupers, "finally" inhabiting the very same workhouse they had previously tyrannized over; Mr. Giles becomes bald, and Brittles grows "quite grey" (53:475–77)—always the strong suggestion of much time passing.

Apart from the simple appeal of the ritual fairy-tale ending, Dickens's early epilogues were subject to several more timely rules. One was that a duly married couple should produce as many healthy, red-cheeked children in as short a span of years as was biologically possible. A second was that deserving heroes should get rich as quickly as the unregulated operation of the economy enabled them to do. A third was that there should be sufficient years for other virtuous persons—including the Garlands' temperamental pony, who lived so long as to become the "very Old Parr of ponies" (*The Old Curiosity Shop*, "Chapter the last": 667)—to enjoy the rewards of their moral perseverance, and nonvirtuous ones to expiate their sins. Kit Nubbles and his wife, Barbara, were blessed with, in quick succession, Abel, Dick, Jacob, and Barbara junior, while Abel Garland and his bride had a family of indeterminate size (666, 671). Nicholas and Madeline Nickleby found themselves surrounded with "a group of lovely children" (*Nicholas Nickleby*, 65:932); and Mr. Toots and Susan Nipper had three, and Florence and Walter Gay, two (*Dombey and Son*, 62:973, 975)—Dickens might have added, in all cases, "at last count."

Before many years elapsed, Nicholas Nickleby became "a rich and prosperous merchant," carrying on the profitable business of his benefactors and partners, the Cheeryble brothers, who in the fullness of time retired to contemplate the golden record of their philanthropy, while Tim Linkinwater, who could "never" be persuaded to add his name to the firm's, "always" persisted in discharging his duties (*Nicholas Nickleby*, 65:930–31). It took some time for Sol Gills's seemingly doomed investments to redeem themselves, but they eventually did so. They were "coming out wonderfully well," Dickens reports, and "instead of being behind the time in those respects, as he supposed, he was, in truth, a little before it" (*Dombey and Son*, 62:971). The villainous Sir Mulberry Hawk "lived abroad for some years" for a reason to be noted later in these pages (536–37) before returning to England, only to be thrown into a debtors' prison and die there (*Nicholas Nickleby*, 65:932). The reprobates Sampson and Sally Brass disappear from sight for five years, during which he serves time in prison, and then are reunited, to spend the rest of their lives in squalid misery in a London rookery (*The Old Curiosity Shop*, "Chapter the last": 663–65).

If all the developments described in the last pages of these pre-

Copperfield novels were to be allotted the time they required, the action would in each case have had to be moved back several years, thus qualifying, to that extent, the impression that they are novels of the near present. In *David Copperfield*, the time squeeze is especially apparent. David, the narrator, has brought his story up to his present felicitous condition of popular author, Agnes's husband, and the father of "boys" as well as at least two daughters, Betsey and Dora. At the same time, he must report on not only the antipodean success of Mr. Micawber and Mr. Mell, which must have required some years, but the miscellaneous fates of (among others) Aunt Betsey, Mr. Dick, Peggotty, Mrs. Steerforth, and Rosa Dartle, all of whom have aged perceptibly (64:947–48). These retrospective fag ends of plot of course occurred simultaneously; still, they needed more time than David's autobiographical chronology provided.

Dickens's next distanced novel, *Bleak House*, was not as cramped. Since it was nominally set pre-1840, there was enough room for the specified seven years to elapse between Esther's marriage, the birth of her two children, and her writing the last chapter. On the other hand, the plot of *Hard Times*, which is easily read as being literally a novel of the present day (1854), would have to be moved back at least five years in order to provide for Bounderby's dropping dead in a Coketown street at that distance of time, and Dickens's vagueness about the time elapsed in the surviving characters' lives suggests a longer rather than a shorter period. In *Little Dorrit*, he compresses the epilogue into a few lines that provide only for Amy's caring for Fanny's neglected children, having an unspecified number of children herself, and being "a tender nurse and friend" to her unrepentant and unsalvageable brother, Tip. In *Great Expectations*, similarly distanced, there was ample time for a comprehensive epilogue, but there were not many characters left unaccounted for at the close of the action, and only eleven years of the total available were required for Pip to establish himself as a businessman with Clarriker and Company, foreign traders, and, on his return to England, to have a brief chance encounter with Estella, now married for the second time (the original ending), or, having met Estella in the ruined garden of Satis House, to see "no shadow of another parting from her," presumably because they will be married (the ending Bulwer-Lytton proposed and Dickens adopted).

In his last completed novel, *Our Mutual Friend*, which Dickens announced was set "in these very times of ours," the epilogue necessarily was dispensed with altogether. The "voice of Society" pronounces ex cathedra judgment on the late events, the Veneerings' company dis-

perse, and "Mortimer sees Twemlow home, shakes hands with him cor-
dially at parting, and fares to the Temple, gaily" (4.16:892). End of
novel.

At the outset of his career as a scrupulous literary craftsman, Trollope acknowledged the reading public's expectation of a satisfying epilogue, and in *The Warden* he obliged it:

> Our tale is now done, and it only remains to us to collect the scattered
> threads of our little story, and to tie them into a seemly knot. This will not
> be a work of labour, either to the author or to his readers; we have not to
> deal with many personages, or with stirring events, and were it not for the
> custom of the thing, we might leave it to the imagination of all concerned to
> conceive how affairs at Barchester arranged themselves. (21:142)

But the loose ends of the story—"It is now some years since Mr. Harding
left [Hiram's Hospital]" and other developments—were longer than the
available time between the up-to-date setting of the story, as suggested
by the topical references, and the date of publication (1855) allowed.
The epilogue to *The Warden* served, in effect, as the prologue to its sequel, *Barchester Towers* (1857), where "five years" (2:159) were said to
have elapsed since Harding left the hospital.

Was Trollope aware of this fuzzy chronology? He was, at any rate,
restive under "the custom of the thing." In the penultimate chapter of
Barchester Towers he wrote:

> We must now take leave of Mr. Slope, and of the bishop also, and of Mrs.
> Proudie. These leave-takings in novels are as disagreeable as they are in
> real life; not so sad, indeed, for they want the reality of sadness; but quite
> as perplexing, and generally less satisfactory. What novelist, what Fielding,
> what Scott, what George Sand, or Sue, or Dumas, can impart an interest to
> the last chapter of his fictitious history? Promises of two children and su-
> perhuman happiness are of no avail, nor assurance of extreme respect-
> ability carried to an age far exceeding that usually allotted to mortals. The
> sorrows of our heroes and heroines, they are your delight, oh public! their
> sorrows, or their sins, or their absurdities; not their virtues, good sense,
> and consequent rewards. When we begin to tint our final pages with *couleur
> de rose*, as in accordance with fixed rule we must do, we altogether extin-
> guish our own powers of pleasing. When we become dull we offend your
> intellect; and we must become dull or we should offend your taste. A late
> writer, wishing to sustain his interest to the last page, hung his hero at the
> end of the third volume. The consequence was, that no one would read his
> novel. And who can apportion out and dovetail his incidents, dialogues,
> characters, and descriptive morsels, so as to fit them all exactly into 930
> pages, without either compressing them unnaturally, or extending them
> artificially at the end of his labour? Do I not myself know that I am at this
> moment in want of a dozen pages, and that I am sick with cudgelling my

brains to find them? And then when everything is done, the kindest-hearted critic of them all invariably twits us with the incompetency and lameness of our conclusion. We have either become idle and neglected it, or tedious and over-laboured it. It is insipid or unnatural, overstrained or imbecile. It means nothing, or attempts too much. The last scene of all, as all last scenes we fear must be,

> "Is second childishness, and mere oblivion,
> Sans teeth, sans eyes, sans taste, sans everything."

I can only say that if some critic, who thoroughly knows his work, and has laboured on it till experience has made him perfect, will write the last fifty pages of a novel in the way they should be written, I, for one, will in future do my best to copy the example. (51:530–31)

Having got this off his chest, and incidentally made some progress toward taking up the slack of the remaining dozen pages, Trollope went on to write a conventional epilogue.

But having taken a stand against the device, Trollope proceeded to avoid it in subsequent novels. As he concluded the very next one, *Doctor Thorne* (1858), he forthrightly cut the Gordian knot by saying, "As the time of the story has been brought down so near to the present era, it is not practicable for the novelist to tell much of [Frank Gresham's] future career" (47:504). And that was that.[†]

As Trollope adopted the mode of the connected novel, first in the Barchester and then in the Palliser series, readers had less reason to expect the wrap-up conclusions found in free-standing novels; characters and themes carried over from one book to the next. The title of the concluding chapter in *Framley Parsonage* (1860–61), "How they were all Married, had two Children, and lived happy ever after," was obviously Trollope's tongue-in-cheek obeisance to the old practice, which by that time had fallen into desuetude; instead of a number of years, the chapter covered scarcely more than one, just enough time to briskly bring to the altar "four couple of sighing lovers" (47:2.286). The "children" were present only in the arch concluding sentence of the novel, "And the big room looking into the little garden to the south is still the nursery at Framley Court." Only infrequently, as in *He Knew He Was Right*, did

---

[†]Trollope's troubles were not over, however. Instead of an epilogue in *Doctor Thorne*, he inserted a flash-forward signal at the point where the narrative had clearly reached 1856: "Four years afterwards—long after the fate of Mary Thorne had fallen, like a thunderbolt, on the inhabitants of Greshamsbury; when Beatrice was preparing for her second baby . . ." (38:408). In his next novel, *The Bertrams* (1859), he avoided that particular hazard entirely, when he specified that Caroline and George, married at the end of the novel in the late 1840s, were childless.

Trollope fall back on the "Conclusion" chapter to bring the histories of his characters up to date.

The distancing technique always entailed the risk of anachronisms, but it was one that novelists generally did not much worry about. Dickens was especially inattentive to chronology at the very beginning of his career. In *Pickwick Papers*, whose action ended in October 1828, there are references to "the new patent cabs" (hansoms were patented in 1834), the Burke and Hare "resurrectionist" murders (discovered in November 1828), the "Captain Swing" rural riots of 1830–31, and the song "Black-eyed Susan" in Douglas Jerrold's melodrama of that name (first performed in 1829). These lapses escaped general notice, but one other, Jingle's declaration that he was present at the July Revolution in France in 1830, was called to Dickens's attention, and in the Cheap Edition of 1847 he wriggled out of the difficulty by dropping a footnote: "A remarkable instance of the prophetic force of Mr. Jingle's imagination" (2:79). Perhaps this early embarrassment had something to do with Dickens's later avoidance of datable public events as topical allusions.

Thackeray took a relaxed view of anachronisms. Explaining the delay in Warrington's response to Mr. Bows's letter telling him of Pen's serious illness, he first invoked a historical circumstance ("He [Warrington] had been from home when Bows's letter had reached his brother's house—the Eastern Counties did not then boast of a railway") and then added, in dry self-deprecation, "we beg the reader to understand that we only commit anachronisms when we choose, and when by a daring violation of those natural laws some great ethical truth is to be advanced . . ." (*Pendennis*, 52:2.142). (The anachronism was a fairly venial one: at the time Thackeray is referring to, the Eastern Counties Railway had already, in June 1839, begun service from a temporary station at Mile End.)

As the occasional illustrator of his own fiction, however, Thackeray had a special problem: the discrepancy between the costumes his men and women wore in *Vanity Fair*, set between 1813 and 1830, and fashions at the time the novel appeared (1847–48). All was well so long as he could describe the clothing in words, which he could choose carefully to avoid possible mistakes, but his artistic powers, confined as they were to idiosyncratic sketching and stopping far short of contemporary history painters' facility of period illustration, got in the way of the desired authenticity. He solved the problem by risking anachronism, as he declared, with overt disingenuousness, in a note in the first edition of *Vanity Fair* (later deleted):

> It was the author's intention, faithful to history, to depict all the characters of this tale in their proper costumes, as they wore them at the commence-

ment of the century. But when I remember the appearance of people in those days, and that an officer and lady were actually habited like this,

I have not the heart to disfigure my heroes and heroines by costumes so hideous; and have, on the contrary, engaged a model of rank dressed according to the present fashion. (6:65)

This did not dispose of the issue, and midway through *The Adventures of Philip*, which was serialized in the *Cornhill Magazine* in 1861–62, he dilated on it:

A fair correspondent—and I would parenthetically hint that all correspondents are *not* fair—points out the discrepancy existing between the text and the illustrations of our story [which he himself drew]; and justly remarks that the story dates more than twenty years back, while the costumes of the actors of our little comedy are of the fashion of to-day.

My dear madam, these anachronisms must be, or you would scarcely be able to keep any interest for our characters. What would be a woman without a crinoline petticoat, for example? an object ridiculous, hateful, I suppose hardly proper. What would you think of a hero who wore a large high black-satin stock cascading over a figured silk waistcoat; and a blue dress-coat, with brass buttons, mayhap? If a person so attired came up to ask you to dance, could you refrain from laughing? Time was when young men so decorated found favour in the eyes of damsels who had never beheld hooped petticoats, except in their grandmother's portraits. Persons who flourished in the first part of the century never thought to see the hoops of our ancestors' age rolled downwards to our contemporaries and children. Did we ever imagine that a period would arrive when our young men would part their hair down the middle, and wear a piece of tape for a neck-cloth? As soon should we have thought of their dyeing their bodies with woad, and arraying themselves like ancient Britons. So the ages have their dress and undress; and the gentlemen and ladies of Victoria's time are satisfied with their manner of raiment; as no doubt in Boadicea's court they looked charming tattooed and painted blue. (19:2.319)

Authenticity could go just so far.

The only Victorian novelist whose chronological errors were so numerous as to form a distinct entry in the modern critical ledger relating
to her fiction was Elizabeth Gaskell. She started well enough; *Mary Barton* was securely set in the past decade, the Chartist era, and the topical
signposts she chose were dependable. But her interest in plausible chronology as represented by incidental topicalities dwindled from that time
onward. In *Ruth* (1853), for instance, she mentions a railway train; yet
some years later in the action an accident is reported to the [London-]
Dover coach, which the railway had long since driven from the roads.
But most of Gaskell's slips occurred in *Wives and Daughters*, set in
1819–26. "Oh, but that he might keep a brougham!" exclaimed Mrs.
Gibson, referring to her physician husband (20:263); but broughams
were not seen on the roads until 1838. Gaskell nodded most deeply
when she had Lady Harriet Cumnor ask, "Didn't you hear that rich eccentric Mr. Crichton, who died some time ago, and—fired by the example of Lord Bridgewater, I suppose—left a sum of money in the
hands of trustees" for specified scientific purposes (32:405). The eighth
Earl of Bridgewater, as a matter of fact, had not yet died, leaving his
famous bequest to fund a prize for the best work on "The Goodness of
God as manifested in the Creation," so there was scarcely time for the
late Mr. Crichton to have been inspired by the example Bridgewater
had not yet set.[†] We shall have several further occasions to discover
Mrs. Gaskell momentarily nodding.[‡]

To conclude a lengthy but necessary survey of the manifold links the
Victorian "novel of our times" had with the past, and the opportunities
and pitfalls the distancing procedure held for novelists: Why did so
many writers distance as many novels as they did? The readiest answer,
which is limited, however, to autobiographical and family chronicle fiction, was the practical need for allowing enough time for the narrative
to develop. But although such chronicles included some of the most famous Victorian novels, they comprised only a small part of the total corpus of Victorian fiction. Another explanation, more widely applicable, is
suggested by J. I. M. Stewart in his notes to the Penguin edition of *Vanity
Fair*: "the novel contains a great deal of period detail designed to appeal
to the memory of the older among its first readers." This would have
been true of all distanced Victorian novels that fell short of being his-

---

[†]This was Sir Alexander Crichton, who published in 1825 a treatise *On the Climate of
the Antediluvian World, and Its Independence of Solar Influence; and on the Formation of Granite*,
seemingly a translation of Cuvier's monograph published in German three years earlier.

[‡]Her *Life of Charlotte Brontë* (1857), though in some respects it was, for its time, a
superior example of biographical writing, was notorious for the number of "facts" she
got wrong.

torical romances: the particularized (or even unparticularized, if at least implied) setting would have been remembered by older readers who, with their foreshortened view of time, would have recognized it as being "only yesterday"—not very far, after all, from the present.

The authors of fiction with some content of social criticism may well have been anxious to avoid the stigma of the social protest novel itself. W. R. Greg's severe review of *Mary Barton* in 1849 and the angry reaction in some quarters to Dickens's multipronged attack on imposing but clay-based institutions in *Bleak House* typified the kind of criticism most writers, reformist or not, sought to avoid; Reade was almost alone in relishing the stimulus it gave to his innate combativeness. As we have seen, most of the major "social abuses" freshly exposed in Dickens's novels, and sometimes others as well, were not unique to the moment of writing but had existed at the time in which the novel was set. The fact that history sometimes unpleasantly repeated itself—or that defects in the system in which the Victorians lived stubbornly resisted treatment over numerous decades—was a boon to novelists who had some social conscience but no stomach for combat. Distancing current scandals by referring them to an earlier epoch enabled them to make their points from the shelter furnished by the past setting. If pressed, they could disclaim any application to present controversy.

Novelists may also have felt unspoken, perhaps not even conscious, reluctance to associate themselves with the "realistic" school of everyday-life representation, which some influential critics continued to deplore even as its popularity grew. Such realism, inseparable from contemporaneity of subject, had a lingering aura of vulgarity, a legacy of the days when Dickens's early novels struck some reviewers as being embarrassing mixtures of genius and offensive coarseness. Were writers, or the spirit of literature at large, however it may have been defined, more at home in a somewhat distanced past, where the stigma of journalism did not apply? Was realism too new a mode to enlist their total commitment? Did they prefer the softened outlines of the past to the starker, sharper image of the present? Perhaps, in the long run, it was a case of eating their cake (acceding to the popular taste for up-to-dateness in subject matter) and having it too (enjoying the mild protection that distancing afforded).

With Dickens and Thackeray, the appeal of the past was deeply temperamental. Thackeray's mind had a peculiarly strong retrospective component, and so, in obedience, did those of some of his characters; and this was linked to his sense of mission, which took the form of comparing the morality of the present day with that of a past age. In *Vanity Fair* especially, his running interpretation of the action firmly rooted the book in the present despite its distanced setting, which was, however, indispensable to his method. He did not so much alternate between the past (the narrative) and the present (the authorial discourse) as merge the two. The puppet play was performed before a mirror, and readers could choose: did the puppets really represent the Crawleys and Sedleys and Dobbins, and the reflected images their counterparts in the fashionable life of mid-century England, or was it the other way round? In either case, Thackeray not only implied the two ages' similarity but explicitly stated it: "At the time whereof we are writing, though the Great George was on the throne and ladies wore *gigots* and large combs like tortoise-shell shovels in their hair, instead of the simple sleeves and lovely wreaths which are actually in fashion, the manners of the very polite world were not, I take it, essentially different from those of the present day: and their amusements pretty similar" (*Vanity Fair*, 51:491). Contemporary reviewers, commenting on the picture of society he presented in *Vanity Fair, Pendennis,* and *The Newcomes,* always assumed that it was essentially the society of the present day, despite the period trimmings, and they usually went on either to affirm or contest the implied resemblance. "His impressions," said the *Times* reviewer of *The Newcomes* in a typical comment, "appear to have been derived from that age which he himself calls 'the old fogeyfied times,' but of which the pretence and selfish worldliness were more than usually prominent. . . . But is society still what society was at that time? Is it as false in its relations and as hollow beneath the surface? For our own part we gladly believe in an improvement of which Mr. Thackeray appears to be still unconscious."[29]

Kathleen Tillotson was not quite accurate when she wrote that "the novelists' concern with past time deepened, if anything, in the sixties."[30] The examples of *The Mill on the Floss, Great Expectations, Silas Marner, Wives and Daughters,* and *Felix Holt,* all published in that decade, are markedly outweighed by the "modern," undistanced novels that appeared contemporaneously—*Our Mutual Friend,* Trollope's dozen or more stories of contemporary life, Meredith's *Emilia in England,* and the sensation fiction of Collins (*No Name, Armadale, The Moonstone*), Reade (*Hard Cash, Foul Play, Put Yourself in His Place*), Braddon (*Lady Audley's Secret, Aurora Floyd*). "Newspaper fiction," on the one hand, and a revival of historical romance, on the other, left the middle ground of distanced novels relatively unoccupied in the ensuing years. Thackeray had died in 1863, Dickens in 1870, and George Eliot was to die in 1880 after finishing *Daniel Deronda,* her only novel with a present-day setting. Among them, they had taught the reader to see in the earlier decades of the nineteenth century a selective but instructive pre-image of the Victorian present.

6
New Ways of Riding and Writing

1.

THE DISAPPEARANCE of the comfortable old coaching inn and the lumbering vehicles that stopped there before the railway juggernaut bulldozed them into dust became a veritable cliché as the customary sign of momentous and irreversible change in Victorian England. Thackeray was far from overstating the case when he said that in his generation the coming of the railway marked the end of the past and the beginning of the present. "Your railroad," he wrote in "De Juventute," one of his *Roundabout Papers* (*Cornhill Magazine*, October 1860), "starts the new era and we of a certain age belong to the new time and the old. . . . We elderly people have lived in that praerailroad world, which has passed into limbo and vanished from under us. I tell you it was firm under our feet once, and not long ago. They have raised those railroad embankments up, and shut off the old world that was behind them. Climb up that bank on which the irons are laid, and look to the other side—it is gone."

Thackeray was writing just thirty years after the first steam-driven, passenger-carrying railway was opened between Liverpool and Manchester. By the time he died (1863) the national network was virtually complete, although several thousand additional miles of feeder lines would continue to be built down to the end of the century. Extending the network, with its bridges, viaducts, deep cuttings, and tunnels ("grottos" as Theodora in Disraeli's *Lothair* romantically called them), required engineering works of unprecedented size, difficulty, and complexity. It has been said that building the London and Birmingham line in 1833–38 was "the largest public work ever to be undertaken in the whole history of man, with the possible exception of the Great Wall of China."[1] At the height of the construction boom, in the forties, an army of 250,000 navvies and other workmen was employed, with an annual wage bill of 16 million pounds. It was, Norman Gash has written, "as though an entire major industry had been temporarily added to the nation's resources."[2]

What was most amazing was the speed with which the railway transformed the face of England and the everyday life, not mobility alone, of the entire society.[3] It occurred in no longer a time than it took for a ten-year-old boy who had watched the departure of the first train from Liverpool to Manchester to grow up, marry, and begin a family: he would have had memories of an England that his children, born in the 1840s, never knew. The lines cut across the countryside, completely indifferent to the directions of roads, their chuffing, shrieking trains (the locomotive engines were wonders in themselves) leaving trails of smoke lingering in the air. The railways' accessibility, the cheapness of their fares, and above all their speed, revolutionized the nation's travel habits, erasing the provincial immobility that had tied most English people to the neighborhood where they had been born so long as travel by coach was expensive, uncomfortable, and slow.

But the disadvantages of coach travel when compared with what a reviewer of *Our Mutual Friend* in 1865 called "that great Macadamizing[†] spirit of change and progress, the railway line and station"[4] were suppressed when the two modes of transportation formed the basis of a then-and-now passage in fiction. The elegiac note is either overt or implicit in every such passage, though in some instances it is hard to tell whether the sentiment a novelist expressed was heartfelt or whether it had quickly become a conventional part of the comparison. In any case, no one captured the mood better or oftener than did Thackeray. In *Pendennis* he wrote:

> Coming back a few weeks since from a brief visit to the old University of Oxbridge, where my friend Mr. Pendennis passed some period of his life, I made the journey in the railroad by the side of a young fellow at present a student of Saint Boniface. He had got an *exeat* somehow, and was bent on a day's lark in London. . . . [W]hen we arrived at the terminus nothing would satisfy him but a Hansom cab, so that he might get into town the quicker, and plunge into the pleasures awaiting him there. Away the young lad went whirling, with joy lighting up his honest face; and as for the reader's

---

[†]The adjective recalled another transport novelty of a slightly earlier time. John Loudon Macadam, inventor of roadbeds made of broken stone surfaced with tar, which improved the speed of coaches and other horse-drawn vehicles as well as the smoothness of the ride, was something of a culture hero in the first half of the century. John Hamilton Reynolds, Keats's friend, celebrated him in a seven-strophe "Ode to Mr. M'Adam" that he contributed to Thomas Hood's *Odes and Addresses to Great People* (1825). He is several times referred to in Victorian fiction.

humble servant, having but a small carpet-bag, I got up on the outside of the omnibus. . . . *We* weren't in a hurry to get to town. . . .

There were no railroads made when Arthur Pendennis went to the famous University of Oxbridge; but he drove thither, in a well-appointed coach, filled inside and out with dons, gownsmen, young freshmen about to enter, and their guardians, who were conducting them to the University. . . . Pen sate on the roof, examining coach, passengers, and country, with great delight and curiosity. (17:1.162)

The old leisurely way of travel, surely, was better than the new, headlong way.

Railway works were prominent in the transformation of the old town of Newcome into a bustling industrial center. "Twenty years since," Thackeray wrote in *The Newcomes*,

Newcome Park was the only great house in that district; now scores of fine villas have sprung up in the suburb lying between the town and park. Newcome New Town, as everybody knows, has grown round the park gates, and the "New Town Hotel" (where the railway station is) is a splendid structure in the Tudor style, more ancient in appearance than the park itself; surrounded by little antique villas with spiked gables, stacks of crooked chimneys, and plate-glass windows looking upon trim lawns; with glistening hedges of evergreens, spotless gravel walks, and Elizabethan gig-houses. Under the great railway viaduct of the New Town goes the old tranquil winding London highroad, once busy with a score of gay coaches, and ground by innumerable wheels; but at a few miles from the New Town Station the road has become so mouldy that the grass actually grows on it. (63:2.200)

Shortly afterward, in *Doctor Thorne* (1858), perhaps taking a leaf from his admired master, Trollope wrote an extended description of the town of Courcy, which, unlike Newcome, had disastrously chosen not to accommodate the railway by putting up a "New Town" on its outlying line.

The town of Courcy . . . consisted of four streets, which were formed by two roads crossing each other, making at the point of junction a centre for the town. Here stood the Red Lion; had it been called the brown lion, the nomenclature would have been more strictly correct; and here, in the old days of coaching, some life had been wont to stir itself at those hours in the day and night when the Freetraders, Tallyhoes, and Royal Mails changed their horses. But now there was a railway station a mile and an half distant, and the moving life of the town of Courcy was confined to the Red Lion omnibus, which seemed to pass its entire time in going up and down between the town and the station, quite unembarrassed by any great weight of passengers. . . .

And how changed has been the bustle of that once noisy inn to the present death-like silence of its green court-yard! There, a lame ostler crawls about with his hands thrust into the capacious pockets of his jacket, feeding on memory. That weary pair of omnibus jades, and three sorry posters, are all that now grace those stables where horses used to be stalled in close contiguity by the dozen; where twenty grains apiece, abstracted from every feed of oats consumed during the day, would have afforded a daily quart to the lucky pilferer.

Come, my friend, and discourse with me. Let us know what are thy ideas of the inestimable benefits which science has conferred on us in these, our latter days. How dost thou, among others, appreciate railways and the power of steam, telegraphs, telegrams, and our new expresses? But indifferently, you say. "Time was I've zeed vifteen pair o' osses go out of this 'ere yard in vour-and-twenty hour; and now there be'ant vifteen, no, not ten, in vour-and-twenty days! There was the duik—not this 'un; he be'ant no gude; but this 'un's vather—why, when he'd come down the road, the cattle did be a'going, vour days an eend. Here'd be the tooter and the young gen'lemen, and the governess and the young leddies, and then the servants— they'd be al'ays the grandest folk of all—and then the duik and the doochess—Lord love 'ee, zur; the money did fly in them days! But now—" and the feeling of scorn and contempt which the lame ostler was enabled by his native talent to throw into that word, "now," was quite as eloquent against the power of steam as anything that has been spoken at dinners, or written in pamphlets by the keenest admirers of latter-day lights. (15:160–62)

The lame ostler went on in this vein for another paragraph. To him, the Red Lion omnibus, drearily shuttling between the inn and the railway station in the fields, was symbol enough of what had happened to rural England.

Eight years later, George Eliot devoted the whole introduction of *Felix Holt* to a sweeping panoramic comparison of the countryside around Treby Magna and the satellite village of Little Treby as it was at the time of the First Reform Bill with its present degenerate state:

Five-and-thirty years ago [Eliot began] the glory had not yet departed from the old coach-roads: the great roadside inns were still brilliant with well-polished tankards, the smiling glances of pretty barmaids, and the repartees of jocose ostlers; the mail still announced itself by the merry notes of the horn; the hedge-cutter or the rick-thatcher might still know the exact hour by the unfailing yet otherwise meteoric apparition of the pea-green Tally-ho or the yellow Independent; and elderly gentlemen in pony-chaises, quartering nervously to make way for the rolling swinging swiftness, had not ceased to remark that times were finely changed since they used to see the pack-horses and hear the tinkling of their bells on this very highway. . . . O youngsters! the elderly man has his enviable memories, and not the least of them is the memory of a long journey in mid-spring or autumn on the outside of a stage-coach. Posterity may be shot, like a bullet through a tube, by atmospheric pressure from Winchester to Newcastle: that is a fine result to have among our hopes; but the slow old-fashioned way of getting from one end of our country to the other is the better thing to have in the memory. The tube-journey can never lend much to picture and narrative; it is as barren as an exclamatory O! ("Introduction":5)[†]

The length of the ensuing comparison was sustained by the recurrent interwoven motifs of coach and rail travel: what a latter-day passenger saw from his train window, and what a coach passenger in 1832 had seen along the same route, with the coachman, a more philosophical colleague of Tony Weller, as commentator:

> His view of life had originally been genial, and such as became a man who was well warmed within and without, and held a position of easy, undisputed authority; but the recent initiation of Railways had embittered him: he now, as in a perpetual vision, saw the ruined country strewn with shattered limbs, and regarded Mr. Huskisson's death as a proof of God's anger against Stephenson. "Why, every inn on the road would be shut up!" and at that word the coachman looked before him with the blank gaze of one who had driven his coach to the outermost edge of the universe, and saw his leaders plunging into the abyss. ("Introduction":9)

[†] Eliot was referring most immediately to an experimental railway demonstrated in 1864 on the grounds of the Crystal Palace at Sydenham—a brickwork tunnel 600 yards long, through which a railway carriage was propelled by the alternate action of large fans at each end, the principle being the same as that of "the Pneumatic Despatch Company in the conveyance of letters and parcels" which depended on the creation of a vacuum in the closed tube. One admitted disadvantage, apart from the unappealing prospect of accomplishing a whole cross-country railroad journey inside a tunnel, was that when one of the fans was venting the air from inside, "an artificial hurricane" was created on the outside, "making the adjacent trees shake like reeds and almost blowing off his feet any incautious spectator who approaches too near it" (*Times*, 29 August 1864; there is a shorter account, with a picture, in the *Illustrated London News*, 10 September).

Eliot's older readers would have remembered a more famous attempt to use air pressure as a motive force. This was the "atmospheric caper," locally so called, by which the engineers of the Great Western Railway attempted to surmount the difficulties of the South Devon coastal terrain by substituting for steam working a vacuum-filled continuous tube between the rails, somewhat in the manner of cable cars with their grip on a moving cable. The first "atmospheric" train ran between Exeter and Teignmouth in September 1847, but because of high costs—nine times more than calculated—and insuperable mechanical problems, atmospheric working was abandoned after only a year. The eleven Italianate pumping engine houses along the route were promptly dubbed "Brunel's follies," after the great engineer whose celebrity stemmed from brilliant ideas that did work. (Frank Booker, *The Great Western Railway: A New History*, 2d ed. [Newton Abbot, 1985], pp. 63–68.) "Mr. Huskisson's death," in the next part of the passage, alludes to the long remembered episode at the opening of the Liverpool-Manchester line, when William Huskisson, M.P., a prominent politician, was killed by the first train, thus entering the national hagiography as the first martyr of the railway age.

The fact that the coach *versus* railway apposition was now a literary cliché did not discourage Hardy from writing his own version, in *Desperate Remedies* (1871):

> The Three Tranters Inn [in Carriford] . . . was an uncommonly characteristic and handsome specimen of the genuine roadside inn of bygone times; and standing on one of the great highways in this part of England, had in its time been the scene of as much of what is now looked upon as the romantic and genial experience of stage-coach travelling as any halting-place in the country. The railway had absorbed the whole stream of traffic which formerly flowed through the village and along by the ancient door of the inn, reducing the empty-handed landlord, who used only to farm a few fields at the back of the house, to the necessity of eking out his attenuated income by increasing the extent of his agricultural business if he would still maintain his social standing. (8:144–45)

Set pieces like these summed up the railway theme as, in its various forms, it had developed elsewhere in contemporary fiction. Although *Pickwick Papers* was set in the years immediately preceding the first run, Dickens wedged the topic of the moment into the heading of chapter 8: "Strongly illustrative of the Position, that the Course of True Love is not a Railway." It would have been remarkable if Dickens, writing in 1836, had not made some use of the timely fact that Tony Weller and his associates on the lofty boxes of the old intercity coaches were losing their jobs. Weller was not prescient enough to express his sentiments about the railway when he held center stage in the novel, but Dickens seized upon the occasion of his reappearance in *Master Humphrey's Clock* (1840) to rectify the omission. By then jokes about the railway, and particularly the sometimes delicious hazards of tunnels, had become as common as an older class of jokes Dickens had already worked into *Pickwick Papers*, those dealing with predatory widows, and now he combined them.

> "It wos on the rail," said Mr. Weller, with strong emphasis; 'I was a goin' down to Birmingham by the rail, and I wos locked up in a close carriage vith a living widder. Alone we wos; the widder and me was alone; and I believe it wos only because ve *wos* alone and there wos no clergyman in the conwayance, that that 'ere widder didn't marry me afore ve reached the half-way station. Ven I think how she began a screaming as ve wos a goin' under them tunnels in the dark,—how she kept on a faintin' and ketchin' hold o' me,—and how I tried to bust open the door as was tight-locked and perwented all escape—Ah! it was a awful thing, most awful! . . .
> "'I con-sider,' said Mr. Weller, 'that the rail is unconstitootional and an inwaser o' priwileges, and I should wery much like to know what that 'ere old Carter [? the political reformer John Cartwright (1740–1824)] as once stood up for our liberties and wun 'em too,—I should like to know wot he

vould say, if he was alive now, to Englishmen being locked up vith widders, or vith anybody again their wills. Wot a old Carter would have said, a old Coachman may say, and I as-sert that in that pint o' view alone, the rail is an inwaser. As to the comfort, vere's the comfort o' sittin' in a harm-cheer lookin' at brick walls or heaps o' mud, never comin' to a public-house, never seein' a glass o' ale, never goin' through a pike, never meetin' a change o' no kind (horses or othervise), but alvays comin' to a place, ven you come to one at all, the wery picter o' the last, vith the same p'leesemen standin' about, the same blessed old bell a ringin', the same unfort'nate people standin' behind the bars, a waitin' to be let in; and everythin' the same except the name, vich is wrote up in the same sized letters as the last name, and vith the same colours. As to the honour and dignity o' travellin', vere can that be vithout a coachman; and wot's the rail to sich coachmen and guards as is sometimes forced to go by it, but a outrage and a insult? As to the pace, wot sort o' pace do you think I, Tony Veller, could have kept a coach goin' at, for five hundred thousand pound a mile, paid in adwance afore the coach was on the road? And as to the ingein,—a nasty, wheezin', creakin', gaspin', puffin', bustin' monster, alvays out o' breath, vith a shiny green-and-gold back, like a unpleasant beetle in that 'ere gas magnifier[†]—as to the ingein as is alvays a pourin' out red-hot coals at night, and black smoke in the day, the sensiblest thing it does, in my opinion, is, ven there's somethin' in the vay, and it sets up that 'ere frightful scream vich seems to say, 'Now here's two hundred and forty passengers in the wery greatest extremity o' danger, and here's their two hundred and forty screams in vun!'"[5]

In the midst of the foolery there is a residue of serious comment, for Mr. Weller voiced a number of frequently heard complaints about this new mode of going from one place to another.

On the whole, the passage would have added no comic lustre to the pages of *Pickwick* if it had appeared there. It was not until *Martin Chuzzlewit* that Dickens approached his full powers on the subject. Like Tony Weller, Sairey Gamp took a highly personalized, and at the same time professional, view of the railway. In her magnificently addled diatribe delivered to an impromptu audience at the London Bridge steamboat wharf, which adjoined the terminus of the London and Greenwich Railway (opened seven years earlier, on 14 December 1836), she lumped steamboats and railway together as twin abominations:

"Them confugion steamers," said Mrs. Gamp, shaking her umbrella again, "has done more to throw us out of our reg'lar work and bring ewents on at times when nobody counted on 'em (especially them screeching railroad ones), than all the other frights that ever was took. I have heerd of one

---

[†] For this loudly touted scientific novelty of the moment, see page 498 below.

In the dawning age of steam transportation, the London Bridge wharf was one of the busiest places in London. Among the people shown in this picture from the *Illustrated London News* for 13 July 1844 may well have been Sairey Gamp, for this was the site of her denunciation of steamships and railways in part 15 of *Martin Chuzzlewit*, published in March.

young man, a guard upon a railway, only three years opened—well does Mrs. Harris know him, which indeed he is her own relation by her sister's marriage with a master sawyer—as is godfather at this present time to six-and-twenty blessed little strangers, equally unexpected, and all on 'um named after the Ingeins as was the cause. Ugh!" said Mrs. Gamp, resuming her apostrophe, "one might easy know you was a man's inwention, from your disregardlessness of the weakness of our naturs, so one might, you brute!" (40:701)

The most celebrated railway passages in Victorian fiction are the four in *Dombey and Son* (1846–48): the pair describing Staggs's Gardens, a small enclave in Camden Town, before and after it was razed to make way for the London and Birmingham Railway's approach to Euston Station, the set piece of Mr. Dombey's ride with Major Bagstock en route to

Leamington Spa, and the scene of Carker's annihilation under engine wheels on the London-Dover line, which had opened on 7 February 1844. In this powerful use of topicality for artistic purposes, Dickens induced his readers to bring into focus the various impressions and ideas that this portentous social phenomenon had so far generated in them. The several passages in *Dombey and Son* would have meant quite different things, and different combinations of things, to readers who had already journeyed on the railways and those who had not, to those who had watched the engineering operations that drastically altered the aspect of town and country, and to those who had invested in speculative railway shares. Readers who had seen Turner's *Rain, Steam, and Speed* at the Royal Academy exhibition in 1844 would have superimposed their memories of the painting's bold colors and indistinct forms on the imagery they found in Dicken's prose flights.[6]

Mr. Dombey and Bagstock were joined in their first-class carriages by the upper-crust characters in Disraeli's *Coningsby* and *Sybil*, whose combined narratives spanned the years 1837–42. Thackeray depicted the transition period between coach and rail in *Pendennis*. When Pen is eighteen and smitten by Miss Fotheringay, the actress—the internal chronology of the novel would place this phase at about 1830—his uncle rides the coach to the West Country town of Chatteris (Exeter), and when Pen shortly afterward goes off to Oxbridge, "There were no railways made" (17 : 1.162). But by the middle of the novel London has begun to stretch iron tentacles out in several directions, and Pen takes the train to Tunbridge Wells, as he could have done after 1843, when the line to Folkestone branched off the London-Southampton route at Reigate. The burst of prosperity that rewards the deserving at the end of the "typical" Victorian novel takes the form in this one of Pen selling some of his land "at a great figure" for the construction of the Clavering (Ottery St. Mary) and Chatteris branch of the Great Western Railway. This would date the conclusion of the novel in or after 1844, when the line from Paddington to Exeter was completed and rights-of-way were being purchased for GWR branch lines in the vicinity.

Although no other novelist wrote railway bravura pieces comparable to Dickens's, until well past mid-century a number used the sheer unaccustomedness of train travel as topical material—the exhilaration mingled with wonder and no little apprehension, the phantasmagoria of sights quickly passing before one's eyes, even the noise ("the hideous combinations of shriek and scream and throb and groan," as Mortimer Collins was later to describe it in *The Vivian Romance* [1870]).[7] Surtees's novels contain noticeably more railroad allusions than do Thackeray's, from which they differ in their lack of nostalgia for the good old days of coaching. Jorrocks's arrival by rail to take over as the Master of Fox Hunting at the new spa in *Handley Cross*, and the farcical encounter at the Golconda station of the Great Gammon and Spinach Railway in *Plain or Ringlets?*, are among the liveliest scenes Surtees ever wrote. In the latter novel he devoted an entire chapter (51) to listing the benefits country squires enjoyed from the coming of the railways which many of them initially fought against. Among these benefits was the ease with which fox hunters and their horses could now move from one venue to a distant one. But there was also a debit side to Surtees's ledger. He decried, for instance, the extravagances of some of the company directors, including their reckless expenditure on building fancy country stations in the popular Swiss Cottage style.

By the early fifties, railway travel had lost most of its novelty and become, instead, a routine accompaniment to life. Now the clergy of Barchester and their relatives went up to London by train as a matter of course, and the main characters in *The Woman in White* frequently passed through London stations in obedience to the twists and turns of the plot.

The presence of either the railway or coach travel was, to the reader, an instantaneously recognizable clue to the time setting of a novel's plot. Although the term "modern novel" antedated the railway age, the very definition of modernity in early Victorian fiction may be said to have hinged on the railway. It served as a key signature, a mechanism that automatically fixed the reader's sights, encouraging him to translate into contemporary terms all the other, time-neutral, details the author may have supplied. Once a train was mentioned, everything fell into place. It was the prime way by which an action could be fixed in the present, as surely as spikes held down the rails.

Conversely, mention of travel by coach was generally an indication that the action occurred on the far slope of Thackeray's great divide, because in most parts of the country coaches coexisted with railways for only a brief period. (Eventually these superannuated vehicles would be replaced by the country omnibuses, plying between villages and railway stations, as at Trollope's Courcy, which characters in fiction rode on the first or last laps of their journeys.) The characters in *Jane Eyre* travel exclusively by coach, which was one of a number of clues that the action took place considerably before the first train steamed into Gateshead, to great acclaim, on 18 June 1844.

In novels laid in certain parts of the country, however, the absence of railways and/or the presence of coaches did not necessarily require a setting before or in the 1840s, because the iron lines may not have reached that particular region until later. Railways threaded across the Midlands, for instance, before they reached the West of England, and although most of the east and north had service by 1850, the Great

Northern from London to York was not yet finished. This fact of railway history underlies Dickens's statement in *Bleak House* that is crucial to dating the novel: "Railroads shall soon traverse all this country [Lincolnshire], and with a rattle and a glare the engine shall shoot out like a meteor over the wide night-landscape, turning the moon paler; but, as yet, such things are non-existent in these parts, though not wholly unexpected. Preparations are afoot, measurements are made, ground is staked out. Bridges are begun . . ." (55:801). The first line in Lincolnshire, from Lincoln to Nottingham, was opened in 1846, and other local lines followed in 1848. As far as Dickens's allusion to ongoing railway construction in that part of the country is concerned, therefore, the novel could be said to be set no earlier than 1845–50. On the other hand, Esther says, apropos of her and Charley Neckett's journey to see Richard Carstone at Deal, "it was a night's journey in those coach times" (45:674). Since the rail line between London and the Kentish coast (Dover/Folkestone) was opened in 1844, this would argue for a prior date. But these two allusions conflict, in turn, with other dating evidence we have already seen. As Stephen Blackpool would say in another connection, in Dickens's next novel, "'Tis a' a muddle.'"

When the Pecksniffs, John Westlock, and later Tom Pinch come up to London from Salisbury *(Martin Chuzzlewit* [1843–44]), they have no choice of mode of public transport, because the railway did not arrive in that town, in the form of a branch from the main line at Basingstoke, until 1847, and the direct route, via Andover, was opened ten years later. Salisbury's last coach, the Quicksilver, perhaps the very one on which Dickens's characters rode, was in service until 1846. In the early 1850s, when Sir Guy Morville traveled to claim the Redclyffe estate in Cornwall as his inheritance (Charlotte Yonge's *The Heir of Redclyffe* [1853]), "Railroads had come a step nearer, even to his remote corner of the world, in the course of the last three years; but there was still thirty miles of coach beyond" (21:213). This is factually accurate: not until 1859, with the completion of the Plymouth-Truro section of the Great Western Railway, was a Cornishman able to travel across his county by a continuous rail line.

With each passing year, the usefulness of the railway as a strict indication of modernity diminished. In a novel published in 1870, it might only mean that the setting was any time in the past forty years. This was the case when Hardy began *The Hand of Ethelberta* (1875–76) by casually noting that Ethelberta "crossed the railway and soon got into a lonely heath." As it happened, the setting in this novel was contemporary, as several specific topicalities make clear. But the presence of the railway in itself proved nothing.

If railways steadily lost their prime value as symbols of up-to-dateness

after the middle of the century, this was compensated for by their growing usefulness as a distancing device, with the results we have already
noted. In chapter 56 of *Middlemarch*, George Eliot made much of the
approach of the London-Birmingham line, which in strict historical
terms had not yet reached Coventry, the "model" for her fictitious town.

> [O]ne form of business which was beginning to breed just then was the con-
> struction of railways. A projected line was to run through Lowick parish
> where the cattle had hitherto grazed in a peace unbroken by astonishment;
> and thus it happened that the infant struggles of the railway system entered
> into the affairs of Caleb Garth, and determined the course of this history
> with regard to two persons who were dear to him. . . .
>
> In the hundred to which Middlemarch belonged railways were as exciting
> a topic as the Reform Bill or the imminent horrors of Cholera, and those
> who held the most decided views on the subject were women and landhold-
> ers. Women both old and young regarded travelling by steam as presump-
> tuous and dangerous, and argued against it by saying that nothing should
> induce them to get into a railway carriage; while proprietors, differing from
> each other in their arguments as much as Mr. Solomon Featherstone dif-
> fered from Lord Medlicote, were yet unanimous in the opinion that in sell-
> ing land, whether to the Enemy of mankind or to a company obliged to
> purchase, these pernicious agencies must be made to pay a very high price
> to landowners for permission to injure mankind.
>
> But the slower wits, such as Mr. Solomon and Mrs. Waule, who both oc-
> cupied land of their own, took a long time to arrive at this conclusion, their
> minds halting at the vivid conception of what it would be to cut the Big
> Pasture in two, and turn it into three-cornered bits, which would be "no-
> how"; while accommodation-bridges and high payments were remote and
> incredible. (56:597–98)

While debate raged in the town—there are few better illustrations than
this of George Eliot's adroit conversion of the pros and cons of public
opinion into period color—in the fields surveyors were at work and the
farmers were greeting them with suspicion or downright hostility.

George Eliot was not the only novelist, however, to derive period
color from the railway's impact on her characters. In Mrs. Gaskell's *Wives
and Daughters* (1864–66) Molly Gibson and her father return to their
town of Hollingford after a visit to Squire Hamley. "I think I never wish
to be out of sight of it again," says Molly. "Nonsense!" replies her father.
"Why, you've all your travelling to do yet; and if these new-fangled railways spread, as they say they will, we shall all be spinning about the
world; 'sitting on tea-kettles,' as Phoebe Browning [an old maid] calls it.
Miss Browning wrote such a capital letter of advice to Miss Hornblower.
I heard of it at the Millers'. Miss Hornblower was going to travel by
railroad for the first time; and Sally was very anxious, and sent her di-

rections for her conduct; one piece of advice was not to sit on the boiler" (52:616). The joke was in the spirit of amused condescension with which people in the sixties recalled the fears of the thirties, the implication being, "We, including you, dear readers, who may be reading these very words on a speeding train, know better than our parents did. What timid souls they were!"[†]

The blunt antagonism of George Eliot's Lowick farmers and the trepidation of her Middlemarch women typified another important way in which the railway served the novelist—as a ready means of character delineation. In its earlier years, everyone in England had an opinion on the subject. If the railway's arrival drew a temporal line across the century, it also sharply differentiated men and women of conservative temperament from those of more liberal inclinations, who welcomed rather than feared or deplored the onward march of science and technology and its impact on institutions and habits—or, like Pendennis at Chatteris and Mr. Solomon and Mrs. Waule at Middlemarch, scented large profit in selling their land to the railway companies. The elder Mr. Weller and Sairey Gamp, like the farmers in *Middlemarch*, had strongly negative views, a mingling of ignorance, superstition, self-interest, and realism (the railways did deface the landscape, and their trains did have wrecks). Their respective opinions were in character; and so, at the opposite end of the social scale, were the mercenary and political ones expressed by the select company Disraeli assembled around a dinner table in *Sybil*:

> "You came by the railroad?" inquired Lord de Mowbray mournfully, of Lady Marney.
> "From Marham; about ten miles from us," replied her ladyship.

[†] Responding to the authentic "human touch," Gaskell's readers probably were disinclined to question its appropriateness to the time-setting, which was no later than 1826, when the perils of train-riding were not yet a subject of anxious correspondence, even between constitutionally timorous spinsters. As if on the principle that one anachronism deserved another, later in the novel Mrs. Gaskell had Lady Cumnor speaking of "the railway station on this new line between Birmingham and London" (57:661), which was still a dozen years in the future. And assuming that Cranford was the real-life Knutsford, Gaskell again anticipated events. The locomotive engine that killed Captain Brown at Cranford in the thirties would not arrive at Knutsford until the sixties. Evidently the railway was so universally appreciated an indication of modern time-setting that it seduced ordinarily careful authors (which Gaskell was not) into historical errors. In the explicit setting of 1825, Guy Halifax, in a Cotswold town, "refused his mother's companionship to London, even his father's across the country to the nearest point where one of those new and dangerous things called railways tempted travellers to their destruction" (*John Halifax, Gentleman*, 34:355). Such allusions were too laden with effective topicality to succumb to the niggling requirements of chronological accuracy. This could be said also of *Pendennis*, where the dates of the railway references do not quite fit the novel's internal time scheme.

"A great revolution!"

"Isn't it?"

"I fear it has a dangerous tendency to equality," said his lordship, shaking his head: "I suppose Lord Marney gives them all the opposition in his power."

"There is nobody so violent against railroads as George," said Lady Marney. "I cannot tell you what he does not do! He organised the whole of our division against the Marham line!"

"I rather counted on him," said Lord de Mowbray, "to assist me in resisting this joint branch here; but I was surprised to learn he had consented."

"Not until the compensation was settled," innocently remarked Lady Marney; "George never opposes them after that. He gave up all opposition to the Marham line when they agreed to his terms."

"And yet," said Lord de Mowbray, "I think if Lord Marney would take a different view of the case, and look to the moral consequences, he would hesitate. Equality, Lady Marney, equality is not our *métier*. If we nobles do not make a stand against the levelling spirit of the age, I am at a loss to know who will fight the battle. You may depend upon it that these railroads are very dangerous things."

"I have no doubt of it. I suppose you have heard of Lady Vanilla's trip from Birmingham? Have you not, indeed? She came up with Lady Laura, and two of the most gentlemanlike men sitting opposite her; never met, she says, two more intelligent men. She begged one of them at Wolverhampton to change seats with her, and he was most politely willing to comply with her wishes, only it was necessary that his companion should move at the same time, for they were chained together! Two gentlemen, sent to town for picking a pocket at Shrewsbury races."

"A countess and a felon! So much for public conveyances," said Lord Mowbray. (2.11:118−19)

But in *Tancred* three years later (1847), the Duke of Mellamont and his son sang a different tune as they complacently discussed the social impact of this new mode of public conveyance:

"There is no sort of doubt," said the duke, "that the state of England at this moment is the most flourishing that has ever existed, certainly in modern times. What with these railroads, even the condition of the poor, which I admit was lately far from satisfactory, is infinitely improved. Every man has work who needs it, and wages are even high."

"The railroads [adds his son] may have improved, in a certain sense, the condition of the working classes almost as much as that of members of Parliament. They have been a good thing for both of them. And if you think that more labour is all that is wanted by the people of England, we may be easy for a time." (2.1:51−52)

It was at this very moment, the mid-forties, that, according to the novel's time scheme, several of the characters in *Diana of the Crossways*

(1884) vented their opinions about the railway. A "melancholy ancient patriot" in Sussex declared, "It's the Devil come up and abroad ower all England!" "He saw with unerring distinctness," said Meredith, "the triumph of the Foul Potentate, nay his personal appearance 'in they theer puffin' engines'" (8:97). He refused to be cheered by Redworth, the up-and-coming railway builder and speculator in shares. "That the people opposing railways were not people of business, was his reflection, and it returned persistently: for practical men, even the most devoted among them, will think for themselves; their army, which is the rational, calls them to its banners, in opposition to the sentimental; and Redworth joined it in the abstract, summoning the horrible state of the roads to testify against an enemy wanting almost in common humanness" (8:94).

Lady Dunstane expressed, at some length, what was assumed to be the consensus among women—"a sex not much used to the exercise of brains," reflected Redworth, "and they hate railways!" (8:101)

> Ah, those railways! She was not long coming to the wailful exclamation upon them, both to express her personal sorrow at the disfigurement of our dear England, and lead to a little, modest, offering of a woman's counsel to the rash adventurer [Redworth]; for thus could she serviceably put aside her perplexity awhile. Those railways! When would there be peace in the land? Where one single nook of shelter and escape from them? And the English, blunt as their senses are to noise and hubbub, would be revelling in hisses, shrieks, puffings and screeches, so that travelling would become an intolerable affliction. "I speak rather as an invalid," she admitted; "I conjure up all sorts of horrors, the whistle in the night beneath one's windows, and the smoke of trains defacing the landscape; hideous accidents too. They will be wholesale and past help. Imagine a collision! I have borne many changes with equanimity, I pretend to a certain degree of philosophy, but this mania for cutting up the land does really cause me to pity those who are to follow us. They will not see the England we have seen. It will be patched and scored, disfigured . . . a sort of barbarous Maori visage— England in a New Zealand mask. You may call it the sentimental view. In this cause I am decidedly sentimental: I love my country. I do love quiet, rural England. Well, and I love beauty, I love simplicity. All that will be destroyed by the refuse of the towns flooding the land—barring accidents. . . . There seems nothing else to save us." (5:59–60)

Seen against this background of feminine timidity and outright disapproval, Diana's democratic insistence on riding third-class is all the more telling an indication of her fiercely independent character. When Percy Dacier sees her off at a country station after she has kept watch over Lord Dannisburgh's deathbed, she tells him,

> "unprotected no women is in England if she is a third-class traveller. That is my experience of the class; and I shall return among my natural protectors—

the most unselfishly chivalrous to women in the whole world. . . . It is not denied that you belong to the knightly class . . . and it is not necessary that you should wear armour and plumes to proclaim it: and your appearance would be ample protection for the drunken sailors travelling, you say, on this line; and I may be deplorably mistaken in imagining that I could tame them. But your knightliness is due elsewhere, and I commit myself to the fortune of war. It is a battle for women everywhere; under the most favourable conditions among my dear common English. I have not my maid with me, or else I should not dare."

Ensconced among her equals for the moment—two old women, a mother and her baby and little maid, and a laboring man—Diana watches with amusement Dacier's futile struggles to lower the window, for the sake of fresh air (with what that implies about the cleanliness of her fellow passengers). "His mouth sharpened its line while he tried arts and energies on the refractory windows. She told him to leave it. 'You can't breathe this atmosphere!' he cried, and called to a porter, who did the work, remarking that it was rather stiff" (20:207–9).

Stations provided up-to-the-minute locales that were endowed with diverse connotations fresh in the experience of most readers: the regimented hustle resulting from tight scheduling, so different from the relatively easygoing pace of coaches other than the mails; the presence of crowds of anonymous people, among them some who were unused to travel and found themselves in stressful situations with which they could barely cope; the dreadful food in the eating facilities, which reportedly outdid the worst that used to be obtainable in the most dismal of country inns. (Dickens wrote what may well be the definitive description of these flyblown railway oases in the third chapter of "Mugby Junction," his Christmas story for 1866.)

Trollope, a constant passenger who ran up as much mileage in the course of a year as the commercial travelers in *Orley Farm*, was vocal on this last point. "We are often told in our newspapers," he wrote in *He Knew He Was Right*,

> that England is disgraced by this and by that; by the unreadiness of our army, by the unfitness of our navy, by the irrationality of our laws, by the immobility of our prejudices, and what not; but the real disgrace of England is the railway sandwich,—that whited sepulchre, fair enough outside, but so meagre, poor, and spiritless within, such a thing of shreds and parings, such a dab of food, telling us that the poor bone whence it was scraped had been made utterly bare before it was sent into the kitchen for the soup pot. (37:351–52)

The new pressures of time, which required every traveler to carry a watch, generated a new impatience. More and more people wasted more

MANNERS · AND · CVSTOMS · OF · y^e ENGLYSHE · IN · 1849 · Nº 21.

A · RAYLWAY · STATYON. SHOWYNGE y^e TRAVELLERS. REFRESHYNGE · THEMSELVES.

Railway travel had its undoubted advantages, but these did not include opportunities for enjoying leisurely, appetizing, and well-served meals en route. Richard Doyle's station buffet scene appeared in *Punch* on 4 August 1849, at the height of the pleasure-travel season.

and more precious time waiting for trains. Trollope is an expert witness on the alternation of boredom and last-minute haste, in *The Bertrams*:

> I don't know of anything so tedious as waiting at a second-class station for a train. There is the ladies' waiting-room, into which gentlemen may not go, and the gentlemen's waiting-room, in which the parties generally smoke, and the refreshment room, with its dirty counter covered with dirtier cakes. And there is the platform, which you walk up and down until you are tired. You go to the ticket-window half a dozen times for your ticket, having been warned by the company's bills that you must be prepared to start at least ten minutes before the train is due. But the man inside knows better, and does not open the little hole to which you have to stoop your head till two minutes before the time named for your departure. Then there are five fat

farmers, three old women, and a butcher at the aperture, and not finding yourself equal to struggling among them for a place, you make up your mind to be left behind. At last, however, you do get your ticket just as the train comes up; but hearing that exciting sound, you nervously cram your change into your pocket without counting it, and afterwards feel quite convinced that you have lost a shilling in the transaction. (2.5:2.86)

At no previous time in history had sheer mobility brought together at one time so many people from so many different places bent on so many diverse errands. When Frith depicted the throng at Paddington station on a busy day in *The Railway Station* (1862) he not only captured a significant cross-section of social history; his collage of a number of separate incidents might have been taken from as many current novels.[†] Unfortunately, the two Paddington episodes in major fiction occurred just too late for Frith to have depicted them. In Trollope's *The Small House at Allington* (1862–64), Johnny Eames gives the scoundrel Crosbie a black eye on one of the station's platforms: "The bystanders, taken by surprise, had allowed the combatants to fall back upon Mr. Smith's book-stall [where copies of the *Cornhill Magazine*, in which the novel was being serialized, were displayed], and there Eames laid his foe prostrate among the newspapers, falling himself into the yellow shilling-novel depot by the over fury of his own energy" (34:2.41). In *Our Mutual Friend* (1864–65), Dickens chose a railway station for the important scene in which Frank Milvey reveals to the lurking Bradley Headstone that he has not managed to kill Eugene after all and, even worse, that Eugene is going to marry Lizzie.[‡]

Like newspapers, railways served novelists as topical means of turning plots in new directions, even, indeed, offering an up-to-date way of disposing of characters. Their victims were a morally mixed company: villains like Carker in *Dombey and Son* and Lopez in *The Prime Minister*, the suicidal victim of the Euston-Inverness express; inoffensive men like

---

[†] Thomas DeQuincey saw the new institution of the railway station in a different light. In his fantasia "The English Mail-Coach" (*Blackwood's Magazine*, October 1849) he described the excitement once caused in town after town when the mail coach went through, bearing news of great victories in the war against Napoleon. But the coming of the railway had changed all that: "Thus have perished multiform openings for sublime effects, for interesting personal communciations, for revelations of impressive faces that could not have offered themselves amongst the hurried and fluctuating groups of a railway station. The gatherings of gazers about a mail-coach had one centre, and acknowledged only one interest. But the crowds attending at a railway station have as little unity as running water, and own as many centres as there are separate carriages in the train."

[‡] The station is not named, but Paddington, as the nearest gateway to the western suburbs, would seem to be a logical choice. A recent annotator of the novel, however, has argued that the station was Waterloo. (Michael Cotsell, *The Companion to "Our Mutual Friend"* [London, 1986], p.269.)

Captain Brown, the Dickens lover in *Cranford,* and Mr. Vanstone, the troubled family man whose death in a wreck in West Somerset sets off the intricate plot of Collins's *No Name.* In *East Lynne,* Lady Vane's disfigurement, which conveniently accounts for her disguise when she returns as governess to her own children, is caused by a train wreck. She could equally well have been maimed and crippled in a coach accident, but by this time (1861) coaches were out and railways were in.

As Tony Weller observed at the very outset of the railway age, the enclosed carriages naturally conduced to a variety of romantic encounters, whether or not these were mutually agreeable to the parties involved. The less disturbing possibilities of the situation were a frequent subject of *Punch's* faint ribaldry. On a more serious note, the compartments, with no means of escape or succor while the corridor-less train was in motion and for a long time no means of communicating with the trainmen, could be the scene of immoral conduct, even of attempts on young women's virtue, as occasional news accounts of alleged "indecent assaults" testified. The danger was increased when the train went through a tunnel. In *The Newcomes,* Thackeray trod with typical lightness over this risky situation, making sure that Clive and Ethel were adequately chaperoned by her maid and two "young City gents, who smoked the whole way" from London to Brighton. Thackeray reported the tête-à-tête conversation of "hat" and "bonnet" from station to station—Croydon to Reigate and beyond. "I know what is going to happen today," says Ethel; "I am going to see papa and mamma, and be as happy as I can till Monday morning."

> "I know what I wish would happen now," said Clive,—they were going screaming through a tunnel.
> "What?" said the bonnet in the darkness; and the engine was roaring so loudly, that he was obliged to put his head quite close to say—
> "I wish the tunnel would fall in and close upon us, or that we might travel on for ever and ever."
> Here there was a great jar of the carriage, and the lady's maid, and I think Miss Ethel, gave a shriek. The lamp above was so dim that the carriage was almost totally dark. No wonder the lady's maid was frightened! but the daylight came streaming in, and all poor Clive's wishes of rolling and rolling on for ever were put to an end by the implacable sun in a minute.
> Ah, why was it the quick train? Suppose it had been the parliamentary train?†—even that too would have come to an end. . . . (41:2.34–36)

---

†So-called parliamentary trains were introduced as a result of a law, sponsored by Gladstone in 1844, that required each company to run one cheap train a day along its routes, charging a penny a mile fare and making all stops. The passenger accommodations, with narrow, hard benches, would really have taxed Clive's devotion.

Thackeray, as Whitwell Elwin remarked in a review of *The Newcomes*, was aware that the circumstances would "provoke the censure of rigorists."[8] But, again typically, Thackeray answered by anticipation "those austere judges who," in Elwin's words, "search for black hairs in the ermine of their neighbors": *Honi soit qui mal y pense*. "I ask any gentleman and father of a family, when he was immensely smitten with his present wife, Mrs. Brown, if he had met her travelling with her maid, in the mail, when there was a vacant place, what would he himself have done?" (41 : 2.36)—which neatly evaded the main issue (an ardent young man's facing temptation in a sudden blackout) by addressing a subordinate one, the propriety of a pair of prospective lovers chancing to sit together on a train. Only several pages later does Clive reveal, in a letter to his father, that he had made sure that temptation did come his way—by loitering in the London Bridge waiting room for three long hours until Ethel and her maid arrived.

Another situation that would have provoked the censure of rigorists, had its circumstances been fully known at the time, was the one from which several characters in *Our Mutual Friend* were lucky to escape with their lives. In the "Postscript in Lieu of a Preface" to the novel, dated 2 September 1865, Dickens told his readers:

> On Friday the Ninth of June in the present year, Mr. and Mrs. Boffin (in their manuscript dress of receiving Mr. and Mrs. Lammle at breakfast) were on the South Eastern Railway with me, in a terribly destructive accident. When I had done what I could to help others, I climbed back into my carriage—nearly turned over a viaduct, and caught aslant upon the turn—to extricate the worthy couple. They were much soiled, but otherwise unhurt. . . . I remember with devout thankfulness that I can never be much nearer parting company with my readers for ever, than I was then, until there shall be written against my life, the two words with which I have this day closed this book:—THE END.

What Dickens failed to mention was the presence, in the same precariously positioned carriage, of his mistress, Ellen Ternan, with whom he was returning from a holiday in France.

2.

When, in the preface to the 1902 edition of *Far from the Madding Crowd*, Hardy wrote of "a modern Wessex of railways, the penny post, mowing and reaping machines, union workhouses, lucifer matches, labourers who could read and write, and National school children," in giving precedence to railways and the penny post he was following an established consensus. The penny post was the second of the two great innovations that divided the present from the still remembered past. In her preface to *The Semi-Attached Couple* (1860), Emily Eden said, "This story was partly written nearly thirty years ago, before railroads were established, and travelling carriages-and-four superseded; before postage-stamps had extinguished the privilege of franking, and before the Reform Bill had limited the duration of the polling at borough elections to a single day."

With its adhesive prepaid stamps, its speeding mail trains, and, beginning in the early 1850s, its ubiquitous pillar boxes, the Victorian post was as much a true novelty, and as conspicuous a one, as the railroads without which it could not have existed. It became all the more important to English life as the incidence of literacy increased, thus enabling more and more men and women to take advantage of its cheap convenience, and as the volume of business correspondence climbed in this most mercantile of nations.[9]

Initially, in the late 1830s, Rowland Hill's proposal to democratize the communication system drew the same intensity of fire from conservative politicians that the railway received from adamant reactionaries in Parliament. In *Coningsby* Disraeli portrayed Rigby

> concocting, you could not term it composing, an article, a "very slashing article," which was to prove that the Penny postage must be the destruction of the Aristocracy. It was a grand subject treated in his highest style. His parallel portraits of Rowland Hill, the Conqueror of Almarez,[†] and Rowland Hill the devisor of the cheap postage, was enormously fine. It was full of passages in italics; little words in great capitals; and almost drew tears. The statistical details also were highly interesting and novel. Several of the old postmen, both twopenny and general, who had been in office with himself, and who were inspired with an equal zeal against that spirit of Reform of which they had alike been victims, supplied him with information which nothing but a breach of ministerial duty could have furnished. (8.6:504)

But there was equally vehement propaganda on the other side of the debate. Henry Cole, the promoter of many progressive causes, issued at irregular intervals a "Post Circular" in the form of a newspaper, full of practical arguments in favor of the penny post. One issue contained an imaginary scene at Windsor in which the Queen studies Hill's influential pamphlet, *Post Office Reform*, and confers with Lord Melbourne about the proposal. Forty thousand copies of this issue were stitched into the twelfth number of *Nicholas Nickleby* (March 1839).

In the end, Parliament approved, and the penny post was officially introduced on 10 January 1840. Rejoicing was widespread. Elizabeth

---

[†]This was General Rowland Hill, first Viscount Hill, who "gallantly stormed the works of Almaraz" during the Peninsular campaign (May 1812). It does not appear that the two were related.

Barrett wrote to Cornelius Mathews, the editor of *Graham's Magazine* (Philadelphia), in 1843: "Why will you not as a nation, embrace our great Penny Post Scheme & hold our envelopes in all acceptation? You do not know—cannot guess what a wonderful liberty our Rowland Hill has given to British spirits—& how we '*flash* a thought' instead of 'wafting' it from our extreme south to our extreme north, paying 'a penny for our thought' & for the electricity included.—I recommend you our Penny Postage as the most successful revolution since the 'glorious three days' of Paris." [10] (She did not foresee what lavish use she and Robert Browning would make of the London penny post in 1845–46.) On the other hand, a few diehards remained unreconciled to this new device of social leveling by which all persons were subjected to the same charge of a single penny for a universally available service. Thirty years after the first penny letter was sent, the crotchety Miss Stanbury, in Trollope's *He Knew He Was Right*, "regarded penny postage as one of the strongest evidences of the coming ruin" (7:67).

The fact that Dickens chose to describe Jaggers's professionally taciturn clerk Wemmick, in *Great Expectations*, as having a mouth like a post-office slot might symbolize the increasingly visible and important role the post office was playing in Victorian life. It is true that from the beginning of the English novel, most notably in the case of Samuel Richardson, the exchange of letters had been a favorite, though clumsy, way of advancing the action; so favorite, in fact, that a whole genre of "epistolary novels" was shelved in eighteenth-century circulating libraries. Literacy and money to pay the postage were largely privileges of the middle and upper classes, though in fiction the occasional servant was allowed to write for the sake of the laughable double entendres that might result, as they did from the pen of Smollett's Winifred Jenkins. But now letters became a much more familiar accompaniment to everyday living, because they cost less to send and, for the first time outside London, could be prepaid by the use of adhesive stamps.

The envelopes Elizabeth Barrett mentioned were something of a novelty, but not to the degree that Mrs. Gaskell, as usual over-confident of her facts, assumed when the ladies in *Wives and Daughters*, set in the 1820s, exchanged through the post "little quarter of sheet notes, without any envelopes—that invention was unknown in those days" (31:387). In the sense of "the cover of a letter," the word was used as early as the first years of the century. Before 1840, most letters were simply folded, closed with a wax seal, and addressed on the outer face of the sheet; if an envelope was used, it was counted as an extra piece of paper and charged accordingly. So unfamiliar were envelopes that Rowland Hill felt obliged to define the word in his 1837 pamphlet: "Those little bags called envelopes."

The "new fashioned envelopes" introduced in 1840 had the four corners of the folded paper meeting under the seal. At first they were closed the old-fashioned way, with sealing wax or an adhesive wafer. But because the new postage stamps were backed with gum, someone soon got the idea of putting gum on the envelope flap as well. Such adhesive-sealed envelopes could be had from commercial sources in the 1840s, but it was not until 1850 that stamped envelopes with gummed flaps were issued by the government.

The few people who used separate envelopes before 1840 were members of the bon ton, those who could afford the double charge (collectable upon delivery). But then the social distinction was turned upside down, the new envelopes with their gummed flaps becoming commonplace, while folded-over, wax-sealed letters were a fast-disappearing affectation. In Surtees's *Handley Cross*, Mr. Mountford, as he went through Mr. Barnington's mail, "casting an adhesiv'd one aside, as either a 'bill or a begging letter,' opened a fine glazed note with blue edges, sealed with a transfixed heart on green wax," which implied Gentility with a capital G. (12:91).

At the same time, as often happens, ostentation was linked with waste. Mrs. Gaskell said of a frugal old gentleman in *Cranford*, "Envelopes fretted his soul terribly when they first came in; the only way in which he could reconcile himself to such waste of his cherished article was by patiently turning inside out all that were sent to him, and so making them serve again" (5:40–41).

The cheap post and the sealable envelope play various roles in Victorian fiction. The penny-a-letter rate was a godsend to the begging-letter industry, which was already flourishing by 1840. (An extensive Mayhew-esque account of this busy cottage industry, published two years earlier, reported that one nobleman "of a very humane and benevolent disposition" had received nearly 350 begging letters—not prepaid—in the course of a single year, "all of which were dated from London, and detailed trumped-up cases of the deepest distress.")[11] Now the output of mendicant letters swelled, both in the sheer number of individually addressed appeals and in the number of writers employed, whether they took pen in hand in their private behalf or that of some other genuine or bogus charitable cause. It is sobering to reflect that without the penny post Mrs. Jellyby could scarcely have functioned. According to her admirer, Mr. Quale, she "received as many as from one hundred and fifty to two hundred letters respecting Africa in a single day" and "sent off five thousand circulars from one post-office at one time" (*Bleak House*, 4:89). To highly visible targets like Dickens, who enlarged his long paragraph on the nuisance of begging letters in *Bleak House* (8:149–50) to a veritable mini-essay on the subject in *Our Mutual Friend* (1.17:259–61), the very sight of Her Majesty's portrait on the morning's intake of stamped mail must have aroused fervently unpatriotic feelings. No doubt one of his mendicant correspondents was Captain Wragge in *No Name*, one of whose lucrative rackets was writing begging letters to easy touches. On the other hand, the penny post might figure in happier occasions, as when Bella Wilfer, newly become Mrs. John Rokesmith, notified her mother of the event by post from Greenwich. "John Rokesmith put the queen's countenance on the letter—when had Her Gracious Majesty looked so benign as on that blessed morning!—and then Bella popped it into the post-office . . ." (*Our Mutual Friend*, 4.4:733).

The postal revolution was responsible for a journalistic report, by Arthur Pendennis (in *The Adventures of Philip*), on "the decay of the sealing-wax trade in the three kingdoms (owing to the prevalence of gummed envelopes)" (16:1.277). And it is arguable that when, in the person of the footman C. Jeames de la Pluche in the *Yellowplush Correspondence* (*Fraser's Magazine*, 1837–38), Thackeray revived the Smollettian device of phonetic literacy with its inviting opportunities for broad orthographical humor, he intended a foretaste of the kind of epistolary expression that would flood the mails once the penny post was in operation. Anyone reading the correspondence after the fait accompli in 1840 would have done so with heightened relish of its timeliness.

Trollope, who spent most of his adult life as a postal official, might have observed 10 January as a professional feast day.[12] From his perspective, 1840 would have been the same kind of historical watershed that Thackeray identified the coming of the railway as having been. Readers who knew that Trollope was a post-office official would have found extra humor, a quiet kind of private joke, in the frequency with which he scattered allusions to the working of the mails throughout his novels. Thanks to it, Mary Thorne had to endure a full week of "terrible suspense" after writing Frank Gresham to break off their engagement. Determined that "all the Greshamsbury world should know of it . . . and having put her penny label on it, she handed it, with an open brow and an unembarrassed face, to the baker's wife, who was Her Majesty's postmistress at Greshamsbury" (*Doctor Thorne*, 42:450). In her innocence,

she doubtless thought that the baker's wife had nothing to do but to send it up to the house at Greshamsbury on the following morning. But this was by no means so. The epistle was posted on a Friday afternoon, and it behoved the baker's wife to send it into Silverbridge—Silverbridge being the posttown—so that all due formalities, as ordered by the Queen's government, might there be perfected. Now, unfortunately, the postboy had taken his departure before Mary reached the shop, and it was not, therefore, despatched till Saturday. Sunday was always a *dies non* with the Greshamsbury Mercury, and consequently, Frank's letter was not delivered at the house till

Monday morning; at which time Mary had for two long days been waiting with weary heart for the expected answer. (43:450–51)

But this was only the beginning of her undeserved anguish, because Frank, saying "Who ever got a letter that was worth waiting for?", had left for London that morning before the post-bag from Greshamsbury, via Silverbridge, arrived at Greshamsbury House.

Steeped as he was in the minutiae of post-office routine, Trollope was not averse to making much ado about little when he had to explain the slight miscarriage of a letter Mark Robarts, in *Framley Parsonage*, sent to his wife from Chaldicotes. Again the contretemps was complicated by the fact that it occurred over a weekend, when, for one reason or another, the postal service was not operating at top efficiency:

> I will follow the postman with that letter to Framley; not by its own circuitous route indeed, or by the same mode of conveyance; for that letter went into Barchester by the Courcy night mail-cart, which, on its road, passes through the villages of Uffley and Chaldicotes, reaching Barchester in time for the up mail-train to London. By that train, the letter was sent towards the metropolis as far as the junction of the Barset branch line, but there it was turned in its course, and came down again by the main line as far as Silverbridge; at which place, between six and seven in the morning, it was shouldered by the Framley footpost messenger, and in due course delivered at the Framley Parsonage exactly as Mrs. Robarts had finished reading prayers to the four servants. Or, I should say rather, that such would in its usual course have been that letter's destiny. As it was, however, it reached Silverbridge on Sunday, and lay there till the Monday, as the Framley people have declined their Sunday post. And then again, when the letter was delivered at the parsonage, on that wet Monday morning, Mrs. Robarts was not at home. As we are all aware, she was staying with her ladyship at Framley Court. (5:1.47–48)

This was, after all, an inexpensive way for Trollope to meet his self-imposed daily quota of wordage.

Trollope appears in his own person as a traveling postal inspector in the encounter, no doubt a frequent one in his experience, reported by the rural postmistress Mrs. Crump in *The Small House at Allington*: "Oh, letters! Drat them for letters. I wish there weren't no sich things. There was a man here yesterday with his imperence. I don't know where he come from,—down from Lon'on, I b'leeve: and this was wrong, and that was wrong, and everything was wrong; and then he said he'd have me discharged the sarvice. . . . Discharged the sarvice! Tuppence farden a day! So I told 'un to discharge hisself, and take all the old bundles and things away upon his shoulders. Letters indeed! What business have they with postmissusses, if they cannot pay'em better nor tuppence farden a day?" (60:2.355).

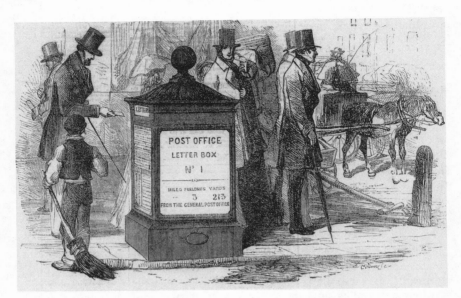

The pillar box for the convenient deposit of mail was a familiar token of the importance the post office had in Victorian life. Few, if any, readers of the *Illustrated London News*, 24 March 1855, would have known that the author of *The Warden*, published in January, was responsible for its recent introduction.

Trollope in his professional capacity reappeared in a more favorable light in *The American Senator*, when Mrs. Masters tried to retrieve an injudicious letter she had dropped into the post:

> ... she went to the Postmaster assuring him that there had been a mistake in the family, that a wrong letter had been put into a wrong envelope, and begging that the letter addressed to Mr. Twentyman might be given back to her. The Postmaster, half vacillating in his desire to oblige a neighbour, produced the letter and Mrs. Masters put out her hand to grasp it; but the servant of the public,—who had been thoroughly grounded in his duties by one of those trusty guardians of our correspondence who inspect and survey our provincial post offices,—remembered himself at the last moment and expressing the violence of his regret, replaced the letter in the box. (2.7:235)

In *He Knew He Was Right*, one of Miss Stanbury's bêtes noires was the pillar box.[†]

[†]This was not, as tradition has it, Trollope's invention. In an official report from the Channel Islands in November 1851 he wrote, "I believe that a plan has obtained in France of fitting up letter boxes in posts fixed at the road side." His superiors liked the idea, and

Miss Stanbury carried her letter all the way to the chief post-office in the city [Exeter], having no faith whatever in those little subsidiary receiving houses which are established in different parts of the city. As for the iron pillar boxes which had been erected of late years for the receipt of letters, one of which,—a most hateful thing to her,—stood almost close to her own hall door, she had not the faintest belief that any letter put into one of them would ever reach its destination. She could not understand why people should not walk with their letters to a respectable post-office instead of chucking them into an iron stump,—as she called it,—out in the middle of the street with nobody to look after it. Positive orders had been given that no letter from her house should ever be put into the iron post. (8:69)

In *John Caldigate* (1878–79), a true sensation novel with expertly managed suspense, Trollope obliquely referred to his travels on post-office business to Suez, the West Indies, and America. Unlike earlier novels in which the post-office allusions were incidental throwaways, the plot of *John Caldigate* hinged on the possible forgery of a postmark and stamp in the Sydney post office. Samuel Bagwax, the London clerk-technician who proves the forgery in a first-class piece of scientific detective work, is offered a six-month trip to Australia, all expenses paid in addition to his salary, to gather evidence that would clinch the case. But Caldigate is already in prison at home for bigamy—a charge resting solely on the fraudulent dating of a letter—and Bagwax sacrifices the attractive junket in order to present his findings at once to the authorities and thus get Caldigate freed. His immediate reward is to receive the hand of a fellow-clerk's daughter in marriage. In addition, he is sent to Australia anyway, to see that the post office there secures itself against further forgeries. (Trollope added a footnote to say he meant no offense to his antipodean colleagues.) Bagwax returns in triumph, bearing "a treasure in the shape of a newly-discovered manner of tying mail-bags" (64:611).

The inner workings of the post office also were integral to one of the concurrent plots in *Marion Fay* (1881–82). It was the old story of class differences standing in the way of true love, but Trollope gave it a new setting, the very office in St. Martin's-le-Grand in which he had worked with such clerks as he described, and under the top-level supervision of Lieutenant Colonel William Leader Maberly, the novel's Sir Boreas Bodkin. The hero, a "gentlemanly" clerk named George Roden, is in love with Lady Frances Trafford, sister of his liberal-minded friend Lord Hampstead. Her stepmother, the Marchioness of Kingsbury, is strongly

the first boxes were installed in Jersey and Guernsey a year later. "By the middle of the decade roadside letter boxes had spread all over the kingdom" and had become familiar street furniture in the towns. (R. H. Super, *Trollope in the Post Office*, pp. 26–27.)

opposed to the match, voicing the conventional view that such a marriage would demean a lady of gentle birth. Trollope reports Lady Frances's reasoning: "Rank was not so high as it used to be,—and in consequence those without rank not so low. The Queen's daughter had married a subject [the Marquis of Lorne]. Lords John and Lords Thomas were, every day, going into this and the other business. There were instances enough of ladies of title doing the very thing which she proposed to herself. Why should a Post Office clerk be lower than another?" (4:29) But the Victorian romancer's stock solution to a socio-amorous impasse arrives with the revelation, worthy of Gilbert and Sullivan, that the humble clerk is a genuine Italian duke by inheritance, despite his English upbringing. Now the burning issue is whether George Roden will abandon his democratic principles and aspire to a more dignified government office. Only in the novel's very last pages does Trollope wholly resolve the difficulty by allowing convention to triumph over scruple and finding George a place as Registrar of State Papers to the Foreign Office.

3.

In his late-in-life characterization of the Victorian age as one of "railroads, telegraphs, penny posts and penny newspapers" (*Endymion*, 12.45), Disraeli gave pride of second place to the telegraph rather than the penny post—a sign, perhaps, of the greater dependence which men of his station had come to have on that mode of instantaneous, not merely expeditious, communication. In fiction after 1850 or so, ordinary messages were sent by post, but urgent ones by telegraph—a choice not available to Richardson or Smollett and in any event scarcely suited to the verbosity of correspondence in eighteenth-century fiction. When Elizabeth Barrett playfully used the imagery of the electric telegraph in her letter to Cornelius Mathews in 1843, she was probably alluding to news reports that Samuel F. B. Morse had received from the United States Congress a grant of thirty thousand dollars to string an experimental line between Washington and Baltimore. In Britain, Sir William Fothergill Cooke and Charles Wheatstone had similarly connected the new Euston and Camden Town stations six years earlier (1837). The electric telegraph was then exclusively a railroading device, but beginning with the wire on the Great Western Railway between Paddington and Slough, the public gained access to the system, which quickly spread beyond the railway network to cover the whole country. For many years, the telegraph offices in the country were at railway stations; when Sir Barnes Newcome, M.P., was in residence at his country seat, the porter "daily brought telegraphic messages from his uncle and the bank in London" (*The Newcomes*, 60:2.247).

An implicit allusion to the new device—Arthur Hugh Clough called it, with belated Augustan elegance, the "magical missive electric" in *The Bothie of Tober-na-Vuolich* (1848)—was the most timely touch, timelier even than the railway, in *Dombey and Son*. During the party at the Blimbers', "Mr. Toots felt it incumbent on him to make a speech; and in spite of a whole code of telegraphic dissuasions from Mrs. Toots, appeared on his legs for the first time in his life" (60:947). "Telegraphic" had been used for many years to denote semaphoric or blinking-light messages in code, and here it clearly alludes to body language. But to Dickens's readers it had an extra, up-to-the-minute reference, which would have been reinforced by the novel's association with the railway. In 1847 the electric telegraph was treated as an educational toy in *The Princess*, along with other scientific novelties of the moment. When the local mechanics' institute held a picnic on the grounds of the squire's estate,

> A little clock-work steamer paddling plied round the lake
> And shook the lilies: perched about the knolls
> A dozen angry models jetted steam:
> A petty railway ran: a fire-balloon
> Rose gem-like up before the dusky groves
> And dropt a fairy parachute and past:
> And there through twenty posts of telegraph
> They flashed a saucy message to and fro
> Between the mimic stations; so that sport
> Went hand in hand with Science. . . .
>
> (Prologue, lines 71–80)

It is odd that although both *The Woman in White* and *The Moonstone* are set in the same short span of years, 1849–51 and 1848–50 respectively, and there is much long-distance communication in both, the characters in the former do not use the newly available telegraph while those in the latter take full advantage of it. Perhaps the high initial rates—eight or nine shillings for twenty words from London to Manchester, fourteen from London to Glasgow—were some deterrent to the characters in *The Woman in White*, although they were by no means poor and some of the messages they sent were urgent. In any case, by the 1860s the several telegraph companies had offices throughout London, connected by wires strung along the streets, and the nationwide network had grown to 21,751 miles. When Society, convened at the Veneerings' in *Our Mutual Friend* (1864–65), reviews and passes magisterial judgment on the late melodramatic events up the Thames, the Wandering Chairman opines that the proper reward for Lizzie Hexam's heroism in saving Eugene Wrayburn would be to get her "a berth in an Electric Telegraph Office, where young women answer very well" (4.17:890).

This bran-new occupation was one of the first that made it possible for women to enter the Victorian business world.

A deft little touch in *Barchester Towers* contributed to Trollope's stress on the gentle Mr. Harding's unworldliness. When he is given the responsibility of notifying the prime minister that old Bishop Grantly is dead, the bishop's son has to instruct him on the proper way to send a message. "'There,' said he, 'just take that to the telegraph office at the railway station, and give it in as it is; they'll probably make you copy it on to one of their own slips; that's all you have to do: then you'll have to pay them half-a-crown . . .'" (1:155). But as late as the sixties there were many places where "telegraphic messages" were rare, as at Plaistow Hall in Norfolk (Trollope's *The Belton Estate* [1865–66]). "[O]n the arrival of any that had as yet reached that house, something of that awe had been felt with which such missives were always accompanied in their earliest days. 'A telegruff message, mum, for Mr. William,' said the maid, looking at her mistress with eyes opened wide, as she handed the important bit of paper to her master" (20:251).

It will be noted that she did not say "telegram." That fresh coinage was edging its way into the everyday vocabulary against strong opposition. Lady Audley had cried out at one point in the novel bearing her name, "A telegraphic message!"—for, explained Miss Braddon, at the time of the action (1859) "the convenient word telegram had not yet been invented" (7:40). But in fact it had been, though barely. That same year had seen the publication of Bulwer-Lytton's *What Will He Do With It?*, in which Colonel Morley says, "I sent a telegram (oh, that I should live to see such a word introduced into the English language!)" (12.11:2.567). Debate over the propriety of the word had been a minor topic in the mid-fifties, classicists maintaining that it was not legitimately derived from the Greek. According to the *Oxford English Dictionary*, it was first substituted for "telegraphic dispatch" in 1855, in the correspondence of the secretary at war, Lord Panmure. The allegation that it was of American origin did not appreciably speed its acceptance. A correspondent wrote to the *Times* two years later, "May I suggest to such as are not contented with 'Telegraphic Dispatch' the rightly constructed word 'Telegrapheme'? I do not want it, but . . . I protest against such a barbarism as 'telegram.'"

But, as usual in the history of popular usage, convenience outweighed correctness, and "telegram" quickly entered the dictionaries and the ordinary vocabulary of novelists. Bulwer-Lytton's son, the poet "Owen Meredith," commemorated the brief tempest in the linguistic teapot, and connected it with another topicality, in a couplet in his popular *Lucile* (1860): "Ere a cable went under the hoary Atlantic, / Or the word *telegram* drove grammarians frantic." Given this vexed early history of the word, the use of it by a character in Reade's and Boucicault's *Foul Play* (1868)—"Oh, there was no time to write; and ladies do not use the telegram" (14:144)—had extra significance to contemporary readers. It not only reflected the fact that sending a message by wire involved, in some people's minds, the sacrifice of feminine modesty: the suspect word itself was a topicality.

In *Is He Popenjoy?* (1877–78) Trollope commented on the radical difference the common use of telegrams had made in the language of courtship, if not affairs in general:

> In olden times, fifteen or twenty years ago, when telegraph-wires were still young, and messages were confined to diplomatic secrets, horse-racing, and the rise and fall of stocks, lovers used to indulge in rapturous expressions which would run over pages; but the pith and strength of laconic diction has now been taught to us by the self-sacrificing patriotism of the Post Office. We have all felt the vigour of telegrammatic expression, and, even when we do not trust the wire, we employ the force of wiry language. "Wilt thou be mine?—M.N.," is now the ordinary form of an offer of marriage by post; and the answer seldom goes beyond "Ever thine—P.Q." (20:1.190–91)

But many years earlier (1850) *Punch* had seen it differently: telegraphic terseness merely served an inherent national trait. "The Englishman," it said, "is as laconic as an electric telegraph's message. The Frenchman is as lengthy and as pompous as an American President's message. . . . The English Policeman says briefly and sharply, 'Move on there.'" [13]

Toward the end of the era, Hardy substituted the telegraph for the railway as the prime symbol of modernity. In *A Laodicean* (1880–81) the ruinous Stancy Castle is linked with the outside world by a single telegraph wire, which the up-to-date heroine, Paula Powers, uses in the manner of a telephone.

> [F]rom the poles amid the trees it leaped across the moat, over the girdling wall, and thence by a tremendous stretch towards a tower which might have been the keep where, to judge by sound, it vanished through an arrow-slit into the interior. This fossil of feudalism, then, was the journey's-end of the wire, and not the village of Sleeping-Green.
>
> There was a certain unexpectedness in the fact that [the castle and all it represented] should be the goal of a machine which beyond everything may be said to symbolize cosmopolitan views and the intellectual and moral kinship of all mankind. In that light the little buzzing wire had a far finer significance to the student Somerset [the architect-hero] than the vast walls which neighboured it. But the modern fever and fret which consumes people before they grow old was also signified by the wire. . . . (1.2:50)

It was Thackeray and the railway all over again, though in a different, Hardyan key.

7
Consumer Goods

1.

IN THE NEW circumstances of nineteenth-century life, brand names of consumer products and the names of fashionable tradesmen became (literally) household words and thus entered the ready vocabulary of fiction depicting contemporary middle-class life with what came to be called "domestic realism." They first appeared in quantity in the fashionable novels of the Regency and early Victorian years as a form of name-dropping, assurance that the writer was fully au courant with the buying habits of the upper crust. Whether novelists were acquiescent or satirical as they described the snobbery that accompanied flamboyant disregard of the spirit or letter of the sumptuary laws ("conspicuous consumption" in a later age of economics), they constantly had ladies and gentlemen tossing off, for effect, the names of their favorite suppliers. Hazlitt singled out this hallmark of the silver fork novel for special comment:

> You dip into an Essay or a Novel, and may fancy yourself reading a collection of quack or fashionable advertisements:—Macassar Oil, Eau de Cologne, Hock and Seltzer Water, Otto of Roses, *Pomade Divine*, glance through the page in inextricable confusion, and make your head giddy. . . . A writer of this accomplished stamp, comes forward to tell you, not how his hero feels on any occasion, for he is above that, but how he was dressed, and makes him a mere lay-figure of fashion with a few pert, current phrases in his mouth. . . . Then he gives you the address of his heroine's milliner, lest any shocking surmise should arise in your mind of the possibility of her dealing with a person of less approved taste. . . .[1]

Catherine Gore was notorious for this practice. A notice of her *Pin-Money* (1831) in the *Westminster Review* said:

> A true lady of rank in a novel of fashionable life, not only has a constant demand for all the things we have mentioned [a list of some items], and

many more; but she must procure them from particular individuals, residing in particular districts of the town. A book like Pin Money is, in fact, a sort of London Directory: even we, careless of all but philosophy, and utterly ignorant of the arcana of fashion, should have no difficulty in addressing an aspirant to, at least Mrs. C. Gore's list of fashionable tradesmen; and it has sometimes occurred to us, that the persons who are really at the bottom of these singular productions, are no other than a certain set of dealers in articles of luxury, who know the value of getting notoriety, and of having their names in the mouths of the fashionable and titled. We are not sure the authoress of this work has made any bargain with her tradespeople; but we are very certain she might: the description of puffing (not mentioned by Sheridan), may be said to be invaluable. None of the persons commemorated would hesitate to give a popular authoress the run of the shop, for the sake of being down in her list; we are too much out of the world to know whether what we are suggesting may not be quite a common practice; and we may be recommending what is done every day, and what would really seem to be done in every page. . . .

"Good morning Mr. Storr! what put it into your head to send in my bill? I have not the least idea of paying it."
"Whenever you please Madam!"

Does not this, in the plainest manner, announce, that Messrs. Storr and Mortimer are accommodating creditors; and give any length of credit that may be agreeable to ladies of fashion . . . ?[2]

Thackeray briefly parodied Mrs. Gore's use of fiction as a spendthrift shopper's guide in "Lords and Liveries," one of the series of "Punch's Prize Novelists." In his late postscript ("Plan for a Prize Novel," *Punch*, 22 February 1851) he took another swipe at this amiable habit, addressing "the eminent novelist Snooks," who, he said, could make a killing simply by writing an advertisement novel:[†]

Look over the *Times* or the *Directory*, walk down Regent-street or Fleet-street any day—see what houses advertise most, and put yourself into communication with their proprietors. With your rings, your chains, your studs, and the tip of your chin, I don't know any greater swell than Bob Snooks. Walk into the shops, I say, ask for the principal, and introduce yourself, saying, "I am the great Snooks; I am the author of the *Mysteries of May Fair*;

[†]Bob Snooks, author of the smashing popular success *Mysteries of May Fair*, was obviously G. W. M. Reynolds, whose *Mysteries of London* (1847) and *Mysteries of the Court of London* (8 volumes, 1849–56) were published in penny numbers—624 all told. They thus belonged to the lowest level of commercial fiction, and readers would have appreciated Thackeray's satirical point in vulgarizing a device originally associated with high-society novels.

my weekly sale is 281,000; I am about to produce a new work called *The Palace of Pimlico, or the Curse of the Court*, describing and lashing fearlessly the vices of the aristocracy—this book will have a sale of at least 530,000; it will be on every table; in the boudoir of the pampered Duke, as in the chamber of the honest artisan. The myriads of foreigners who are coming to London [for the Crystal Palace exhibition, to open the first of May], and are anxious to know about our national manners, will purchase my book, and carry it to their distant homes. So, Mr. Taylor, or Mr. Haberdasher, or Mr. Jeweller—how much will you stand if I recommend you in my forthcoming novel?

Tradesmen who paid up might look forward to seeing their establishments casually, but it was to be hoped effectively, mentioned in the course of the story: "'We are poor, Eliza,' said Harry Hardhand, looking affectionately at his wife, 'but we have enough, love, have we not, for our humble wants? The rich and luxurious may go to Dillow's or Gobiggin's, but we can get our rooms comfortably furnished at Timmonson's for £20.'" Or: "Amramson, the tailor, waited upon Lord Paddington with an assortment of his unrivalled waistcoats, or clad in that simple but aristocratic style, of which Schneider *alone* has the secret." Or: "'Count Barbarossa is seventy years of age,' said the Earl. 'I remember him at the Congress of Vienna, and he has not a single grey hair.' Wiggins laughed. 'My good Lord Baldock,' said the wag, 'I saw Barbarossa's hair coming out of Ducroissant's shop, and under his valet's arm—ho! ho! ho!'" Thackeray invented those names, but some of the business names he used elsewhere were straight from the London signboards. Truefitt's, the hairdresser-parfumier establishment referred to several times in *Pendennis* and *The Newcomes* as the shop preferred by gentlemen of style and wealth, is still in Old Bond Street, where it opened its doors in 1805.

Thackeray's "modern" novels are replete with references to actual London purveyors of food, drink, clothing, and accessories, for the very good reason that he was describing the life-style of the fashionable and would-be fashionable in the tradition of the silver fork novel, and using its characteristic devices. As John Carey has said, "To annotate his stories you need a commercial directory of early Victorian London. Howell and James's (of Regent Street) and Gunter's were his favourite emporia, but scores of smaller vendors are cited, or invented, along with their addresses, specialities and usual advertisements. The carriages and flunkeys outside Howell and James's, like the women dripping with baubles inside, are a perpetual feature of his metropolitan scene."[3]

Of the fashionable tradesmen whose names were transparently disguised, the one that readers most immediately recognized was a jeweler and goldsmith who had earlier appeared, as Mr. Garnet, in Disraeli's *The Young Duke*, but who achieved wider fame in Thackeray's fiction as Mr.

Polonius, first in *The History of Samuel Titmarsh and the Great Hoggarty Diamond* (*Fraser's Magazine*, September-December 1841; better known as *The Great Hoggarty Diamond*, the title it will bear in these pages). It was to Polonius that Sam took his aunt's diamond, "the great jew'l of all Ireland," as an awestruck old lady in the shop called it, to be reset. And it was from him that Becky Sharp Crawley alleged she rented the jewels she wore at the royal levee—jewels that later figured in the showdown between Rawdon and Lord Steyne. As Thackeray makes clear, the diamonds actually came from Lord Steyne, who may well have bought them from Polonius, for Polonius specialized in providing wealthy men with costly, glittering little remembrances for their wives or mistresses. In real life Polonius was Thomas Hamlet, whose shop was first located in Leicester Square at the corner of Cranbourne Alley and later in the Oxford Street Bazaar, which he owned. The memorist Captain Gronow recorded some particulars of his contemporary fame:

His shop . . . exhibited a profuse display of gold and silver plate, whilst in the jewel room sparkled diamonds, amethysts, rubies, and other precious stones, in every variety of setting. He was constantly called on to advance money upon such objects, which were left in pawn, only to be taken out on the occasion of a great banquet, or when a court dress was to be worn. His gains were enormous, though it was necessary to give long credit; and his bills for twenty or thirty thousand pounds were eagerly discounted. In fact, he was looked upon as a second Croesus, or a Crassus, who could have bought the Roman empire; and his daughter's hand was sought in marriage by peers.[†] But all at once the mighty bubble collapsed. He had advanced money to the Duke of York, and had received as security property in Nova Scotia, consisting chiefly of mines, which, when he began to work them, turned out valueless, after entailing enormous expense. . . .

On the day after the coronation of George IV, Hamlet made his appearance at the house of Mr. Coutts, in Piccadilly, the corner of Stratton Street. It was during dinner; but owing no doubt to a previous arrangement, he was at once admitted, when he placed before the rich banker a magnificent diamond cross, which had been worn the previous day by the Duke of York. It at once attracted the admiration of Mrs. Coutts,[‡] who loudly exclaimed, "How happy I should be with such a splendid specimen of jewellery." "What is it worth?" immediately exclaimed Mr. Coutts. "I could not allow it to pass out of my possession for less than £15,000," said the wary tradesman. "Bring me a pen and ink," was the only answer made by the doting husband; and he at once drew a cheque for that amount upon the bank in the Strand, and with much delight the worthy old gentleman placed the jewel upon the fair bosom of the lady:—

[†] For a confirmation of this fact from an unexpected source, see page 618n below.

[‡] This was the former actress Harriot Mellon, the original of "Mrs. Million" in Disraeli's *Vivian Grey*. See pages 592–95 below.

"Upon her breast a sparkling cross she wore,
Which Jews might kiss, and infidels adore."[4][†]

Hamlet was an inveterate speculator, as well as a ready source of loans
to the most exalted debtors in the kingdom. At the height of his prosperity, his Cavendish Square mansion contained a rich collection of ob-
jets d'art.[5] But financial pressures such as Gronow mentioned forced
him to sell the Oxford Street Bazaar for a mere £15,000, and in 1841,
the very year *The Great Hoggarty Diamond* was published, he went bankrupt. The National Gallery acquired his priceless Titian, *Bacchus and Ari-
adne*, along with two lesser paintings, for the reduced price of £9,000.[6]
Hamlet was, in short, admirably qualified to be a walk-on character in a
Thackerayan novel, and with the utmost fitness he ended his days, like
Colonel Newcome, as a poor brother of the Charterhouse.

Since *Little Dorrit* was set in the late 1820s, when Hamlet was riding
high, Merdle might well have bought from his dazzling stock the jewels
that adorned his wife's famous bosom. "Mr. Merdle wanted something
to hang jewels upon, and he bought it [i.e., Mrs. Merdle, or at least the
bosom] for the purpose. Storr and Mortimer might have married on the
same speculation" (21:293)—Storr and Mortimer (as above, in the *Westminster Review* article on Mrs. Gore, and "Morr and Stortimer" in *The
Newcomes*) being another fashionable jeweler's shop.

While Hamlet's shop was obviously *the* place of first resort when one
was in the market for extravagantly priced baubles, for a broader assortment of goods Howell and James's in Regent Street, "silk mercers, etc., to
the Royal Family," had the same prestige and the same custom, though
as wealth became more widely distributed its clientele was similarly
broadened. It sold not only silks, wearing apparel, decorative accessories,
and a popular line of antique and modern silver and jewelry, but—a
specialty that fed its fame during the aesthetic movement in the 1870s
and 1880s—painted porcelain, art pottery, and metal work.[7] (Its association with the aesthetic fad won it additional, perhaps not entirely welcome publicity, in Gilbert and Sullivan's *Patience* [1881], when Grosvenor
identified himself as "a Howell and James young man," in other words,
a counter-jumper in the mold of Oscar Wilde.)

The firm was already established when, in a setting of about 1823,
Sam Titmarsh's aunt instructed her nephew to order for his prospec-
tive bride "three magnificent dresses . . . from the celebrated Madame
Mantalini of London [Thackeray's friendly bow to Dickens, who had in-

---

[†]The very lines (from *The Rape of the Lock*) that Lord Steyne murmured as he bowed
over the diamond-bedecked Becky at the royal levee.

troduced his readers to Mantalini's shop in the June 1838 number of *Nicholas Nickleby*], and some elegant trinkets and embroidered pocket-handkerchiefs from Howell and James's" (10:62). Howell and James at least conveyed the impression that their prices were not out of line; in his piece on "Clerical Snobs" (*Punch*, 16 May 1846; *BS*, 47), Thackeray contrasted a parson's laying out a little money for charitable causes with his nonclerical reader's succumbing to the temptation to buy "an ormolu-clock at Howell and James's, because it is such a bargain."

Like Hamlet's jewelry, not all of Howell and James's expensive goods flowed in morally impeccable channels. "If," said Thackeray in *Vanity Fair*, "Messrs. Howell and James were to publish a list of the purchasers of all the trinkets which they sell, how surprised would some families be: and if all these ornaments went to gentlemen's lawful wives and daughters, what a profusion of jewellery there would be exhibited in the genteelest homes of Vanity Fair!" (30:287) Thackeray's allusions to the firm acquired extra irony when knowledgeable readers considered the connection it had with the fate of Lady Blessington and her longtime housemate Count D'Orsay, whose Gore House, facing Kensington Gardens, was the scene of a brilliant fashionable and literary salon which Thackeray often attended. When Blessington moved into the mansion in 1836, she furnished it with elegant extravagance from Howell and James's ample stock. Because the firm had had long and sometimes painful experience in dealing with free-spending society, it took the precaution of securing her indebtedness by taking out an insurance policy on her life to the amount of £3,500. In 1849 (*Vanity Fair* had completed its serial run the preceding July), when rumors began to circulate that Blessington and D'Orsay were in deep financial trouble, Howell and James tried to collect what remained of the debt by issuing a writ of execution, the first of many to be served as other creditors closed in. The pair made good their escape to France. The firm then offered the policy to Blessington's agent for £800 plus interest. The agent agreed to pay the capital sum but not the interest; and just as they were negotiating, news came of Blessington's sudden death. Whereupon, Howell and James came away with the full £3,500.[8]

In the ensuing years, Howell and James continued to flourish and to win more mentions in contemporary fiction. Mrs. Carbuncle bought heavily there in anticipation of Lucinda Roanoke's marriage (*The Eustace Diamonds*), and it was there that Mary Wharton got her wedding veil (*The Prime Minister*). But the firm faced healthy competition. In Surtees's *Hillingdon Hall*, Jorrocks said of women with minds of their own, "I declares they drives me parfectly mad. Unless a man spends 'alf his time at 'Owell & James's, or Swan & Hedgar's, or some o' them man-milliner sort o' shop doors, waitin' for to see the gals get into their chays, he has no possible chance o' knowin' wot sort o' understandin's they have" (10:68). Since 1812 Swan and Edgar had been established at 10 Piccadilly, the former premises of the Western Mail Coach office in the Bull and Mouth tavern, which was the scene of a number of fictional arrivals and departures. When Jorrocks, in *Handley Cross*, found himself lagging far behind in a hunt, he "bump[ed] on, vowing all sorts of vows to Diana [goddess of the hunt], if she will only 'ave the kindness to assist him that once. He would give her a hat and feather! He would give her a swan's-down muff and tippet! Nay, he would stand a whole rig-out at Swan and Hedgar's; pettikits, bustle, and all!" (51:373). Later, people in Trollope's *Is He Popenjoy?* and *Lady Anna* patronized the firm.

2.

Robert Gunter of Berkeley Square was the Thomas Hamlet of the confectionery and catering trade.[9†] Although his and his family's name is indelibly associated with the silver fork novel and Thackeray's echoes of

---

†The business was founded in 1757 by an Italian pastry cook named Dominicus Negri, at the sign of the pineapple at 7 Berkeley Square, only a few doors from Horace Walpole's town house. James Gunter became a partner in the 1770s and subsequently took over the business, from which he proceeded to make a fortune. As "Captain Gunter the confectioner" he was one of several officers of the St. George's Volunteer Corps who tangled in 1798 with Lord Grosvenor, owner of Berkeley Square, over the rental of a plot of land they used for drills. The family—James died in 1819, his son Robert in 1852—became large landowners and developers on what came to be known as "the Gunter estate" on both sides of the Old Brompton Road, including the site of The Boltons, a fashionable square. (It is conceivable, incidentally, that the Brompton cottage to which the Sedleys in *Vanity Fair* were reduced after the father's calamitous bankruptcy was on Gunter land—which would have had its own considerable irony.) The Gunters were market gardeners and fruit growers as well, much of their produce being destined for the kitchen at their Berkeley Square shop. For their family home they bought Earl's Court Lodge from the estate of the anatomist John Hunter, who had kept a menagerie on the grounds. Lord Aberdeen's children, who lived nearby in the mansion known as Earl's Court House, called the Gunter lodge "Currant-Jelly Hall," for obvious reasons. Gunter's "exquisite ices," which came in many flavors and whose recipe remained a tightly guarded secret, continued to be a favorite Mayfair delicacy well into the twentieth century. In 1937 the tea shop was moved to Curzon Street, but it fell victim to the austerities of the Second World War and its aftermath and closed, finally, in the 1950s. As late as 1983, the Gunter Estate was still in the hands of the family, and their name is preserved in Gunter Grove, which connects the Fulham Road and the King's Road. (See *Survey of London*, vol. 39: *The Grosvenor Estate in Mayfair, Part 1* [London, 1977], pp. 42–43; vol. 41: *Southern Kensington: Brompton* [London, 1983]; and vol. 42: *South Kensington: Kensington Square to Earl's Court* [London, 1986], esp. chap. 13, "The Gunter Estate." There is an appreciative paragraph on the firm in Carol Kennedy, *Mayfair: A Social History* [London, 1986], pp. 88–89.)

it, one of the first glimpses we have of him is in surroundings some distance removed—the sporting world of *Jorrocks' Jaunts and Jollities* (1831–34). When the Surrey Hunt meets one morning at Croydon, one of the number cries, "Well, Gunter, old boy, have you iced your horse to-day?" (2:27).[†] Like Jorrocks, who was a wholesale grocer, Gunter represented "trade" and so bore a taint that was not wholly expunged even in the commercial heart of the nation. But "that splendid artist of sweet comestibles . . . the renowned ice and pastry-cook of Berkeley Square," as he was called, was a dedicated follower of the hounds, which meant that, whatever his social disadvantage, he had a spiritual kinship with the lofty clientele he served. He did, in fact, wear two hats: at the same time that he rode on terms of equality with Grantley Berkeley's stag hunt in the Vale of Harrow, he supplied cakes for the hunt balls held in the Home Counties.[10]

Gunter, his efficient and ultra-respectable-looking employees, and their elegant viands were indispensable to any pretentious social function, and thus to silver fork fiction as well. Young Disraeli, who as yet had little acquaintance with the rarified precincts of Regency fashion, imagined, quite rightly no doubt, that Gunter was a staple subject of smart chitchat there. Vivian Grey, on the social make, drawls:

> "If it were not for the General Election, we really must have a war for variety's sake. Peace gets quite a bore. Everybody you dine with has a good cook, and gives you a dozen different wines, all perfect. We cannot bear this any longer; all the lights and shadows are lost. The only good thing I heard this year was an ancient gentlewoman going up to Gunter and asking him for 'the receipt for that white stuff,' pointing to his Roman punch. I, who am a great man for receipts, gave it her immediately. 'One hod of mortar to one bottle of Noyau.'" (*Vivian Grey*, 2:10.48)

Mrs. Million, in the same novel, has Gunter supply her lavish parties with pineapples, Italian creams, trifles, and lobster salads. Her personal physician, Dr. Sly, declares, "There are few people for whom I entertain a higher esteem than Mr. Gunter" (2.15:74), and this seems to have been the consensus among those in the best position to evaluate his performance.

So necessary was Gunter to the ordering of affairs in society, not least

---

[†]This anecdote became part of the permanent lore of the hunting field. Surtees alluded to it again twenty years later, when he named the purported author of the witticism. In *Young Tom Hall* (1851–53) the hero was told that an excessively spirited mount was not as dangerous as he appeared to be, an assurance "which he interpreted as an intimation that the horse had had the fiery edge taken off him—iced, perhaps, as Lord Alvanley recommended Gunter to have done by his hot one . . ." (36:265).

weddings with their requisite monumental cakes, that when the heroine
of Charles White's *Almack's Revisited* (1828) considers eloping to Gretna
Green, a confidant objects: "But, my dear, if you are to be married by
that dirty blacksmith, you will have no bridesmaids, no fleurs d' orange,
no lace veils—and what will Gunter think of you for not ordering
cake?"[11] Although Disraeli, in *The Young Duke* (1.14:47), described the
London off-season as "the hour when trade grows dull and tradesmen
grow duller. . . . Oh, why that sigh, my gloomy Mr. Gunter!", the confectioner shared in the late harvest of the season's matchmaking, as one
of Mrs. Gore's characters described it in *Cecil*:

> It was a deuced hot day. . . . I sauntered into Gunter's, on my way to Cur-
> zon Street, for a white currant ice—the only safe species of nutriment in
> the dog-days. From the mere aspect of the counters in Berkeley Square one
> might have known that the season was over. Instead of vans at the door,
> clatterings of china and glass, cross porters swearing under their great
> trays, and thousands of white paper parcels, all addressed to the same
> happy house, destined that night to receive and refresh "five hundred per-
> sons of the highest ton," the tables were covered with white paper parcels,
> addressed severally to the five hundred persons of the highest ton, contain-
> ing the wedding-cake of the match of the morning—as sure a produce of
> the balls of the season as Sir Gabriel Winstanley's crops from his sowing in
> seed-time.[12]

It was in Thackeray's pages that Gunter reaped the most frequent
publicity.[†] In fact, if Thackeray had business dealings with that admirable pastry cook he would have been entitled to ask for a courtesy discount. When Mr. Brough, director of the West Diddlesex Insurance
Company, gave his annual grand ball at his house at Fulham, Gunter
provided the ices, supper, and footmen (*The Great Hoggarty Diamond*).
The erstwhile footman C. Jeames de la Pluche ordered his wedding cake
from Gunter as a matter of course when he came into money. The social
round in Vanity Fair, said Thackeray, included "the annual ball with a
supper from Gunter's (who, by the way, supplied most of the *first-rate*
dinners which J. [an archetypal social climber named Jenkins] gives, as
I know very well, having been invited to one of them to fill a vacant
place, when I saw at once that these repasts are very superior to the

---

[†]At the beginning of a letter to his mother, dated 16–20 February 1843, Thackeray
wrote of his being about to go "to an op, having on the brass buttons at this very minute,"
and later: "This is wrote after the hop mentioned in page 1, where there was a grand meet,
and supper by Gunter going on from 12 till 4—the finest thing, and the most wholesome
too: for it did me a world of good." There is no indication of where the op took place. (*The
Letters and Private Papers of William Makepeace Thackeray*, ed. Gordon N. Ray, 2:94–95.)

common run of entertainments for which the *humbler* sort of J.'s acquaintances get cards) . . ." (*Vanity Fair*, 11:350).

In *Pendennis*, ladies like Lady Clavering, seeking refreshment on a summer day, had their carriages parked on the shady side of Berkeley Square, and waiters from Hunter's (as it is called in that novel) went back and forth with trays of pink ices. And in *The Newcomes*, Gunter's elegant food and suave service provided almost a gustatory leitmotif, to various effects. "The true pleasure of life," Thackeray advised his readers, "is to live with your inferiors. . . . With a shilling's worth of tea and muffins you can get as much adulation and respect as many people cannot purchase with a thousand pounds' worth of plate and profusion, hired footmen, turning their houses topsy-turvy, and suppers from Gunter's" (9:1.96–97). "Who can be more respectable than a butler?" argues Lord Kew. "A man must be somebody's son. When I am a middle-aged man, I hope humbly I shall look like a butler myself. Suppose you were to put ten of Gunter's men into the House of Lords, do you mean to say that they would not look as well as any average ten peers in the House?" (19:1.196). The "clerical bachelor" Charles Honeyman, who demands the best that fashionable life has to offer—though he tells his guests, depreciatingly, that they must "put up with the Cenobite's fare"—entertains at a Gunter-catered lunch, with four bouquets on the table (Warrington's humbler entertainment boasted only two) and in addition "a great pineapple, which must have cost the rogue three or four guineas . . ." (23:1.239). The cake at Lady Clara Pulleyn's wedding breakfast is "decorated by Messrs. Gunter with the most delicious taste and the sweetest hymeneal allusions" (36:1.393–94). And when His Excellency the Bulgarian minister has a reception, "there was the same crowd in the reception room and on the stairs, the same grave men from Gunter's distributing the refreshments in the dining-room" (2:113).

Gunter's supremacy in the high-calorie trade lasted well into the mid-Victorian period. When preparations were made for Aurora's birthday ball in *Aurora Floyd* (1862–63),

> they drove to Mr. Gunter's in Berkeley Square, at which world-renowned establishment Mrs. Alexander commanded those preparations of turkeys preserved in jelly, hams cunningly embalmed in rich wines and broths, and other specimens of that sublime art of confectionary [*sic*] which hovers midway between sleight-of-hand and cookery, and in which the Berkeley Square professor is without a rival. When poor Thomas Babington Macaulay's New-Zealander shall come to ponder over the ruins of St. Paul's, perhaps he will visit the remains of this humbler temple in Berkeley Square, and wonder at the ice-pails and jelly-moulds, the refrigerators and stewpans, the hot plates long cold and unheeded, and all the mysterious paraphernalia of the dead art. (3:23)

BERKELEY SQUARE. 5 P.M.

Gunter's pastry and confectionery shop had been at the same location for over a
century when *Punch* ran this drawing (24 August 1867) of hungry street boys gazing at fashionable ladies in their barouche, "under the trees, . . . out of the sun, /
In the corner where GUNTER retails a plum bun," as the accompanying verses
put it. Social commentary in the form of a stark contrast between the luxury of
the rich and the wretchedness of the poor was one of *Punch's* specialties.

For Aurora's wedding, in the same novel, "Mr. Richard Gunter provided
the marriage feast, and sent a man down to Felden to superintend the
arrangements, who was more dashing and splendid to look upon than
any of the Kentish guests" (12:109).

But the elegiac note suggested by the image of the New Zealander
excavating Berkeley Square was not entirely fanciful. In retrospect, it
had a touch of more immediate prophecy, which was echoed in another
novel published only a year later (J. B. Harwood's *Lord Lynn's Wife*,
1864): "The supper was worthy of the ball. The force of Gunter—
people still swore by Gunter in 1858—could no further go." [13] If the
evidence of fiction is to be trusted, people now were swearing more by
Fortnum and Mason, the specialized grocers in Piccadilly, a much older
establishment than Gunter's; one of Queen Anne's footmen had opened
the shop in 1707. The fashionable world seems not to have patronized

Fortnum and Mason as much during the years of Gunter's ascendancy, but the plebeian John Jorrocks ordered "a dozen pots of marmeylad" from the firm in *Handley Cross* (28:217); one wonders if, as a wholesale grocer, he had sold them the ingredients. Lord Erith, Foker's uncle in *Pendennis*, got his wine there, and Pen bought a guinea's-worth of bonbons to send to Blanche Armory: "each sugarplum of which was wrapped in ready-made French verses, of the most tender kind" (39:2.6). At the same moment, in *Mr. Sponge's Sporting Tour*, when Mr. Puffington entertains the local meet, "There was a splendid breakfast, the table and sideboard looking as if Fortnum and Mason . . . had opened a branch establishment at Hanby House" (36:243). At a dinner party at Brighton in *Aurora Floyd*, the guests are seated around "a phalanx of glass and silver, and flowers and wax candles, and crystallized fruits, and other Fortnum-and-Mason ware!" (6:55).

While the two firms served the same select clientele, they were not direct competitors. The declining prominence of one firm and the increasing presence of the other in Victorian novels reflects a fundamental shift in social habits. Gunter made party food to order and served it; Fortnum and Mason packed and sold it. Gunter catered to a society whose entertainments mainly took place indoors, Fortnum and Mason to one that was finding its pleasure more and more in the open air. To Victorian readers, "Gunter" suggested gleaming silverware and snow-white tablecloths; Fortnum and Mason, well-packed hampers.

Hampers from Piccadilly were standard equipment at Ascot and the Derby. And when the fastidious Sir Hugh Clavering started to provision a yacht for a fishing trip off Norway, Trollope reports: "he had a good deal to do. . . . Fortnum and Mason, no doubt, would have done it all for him without any trouble on his part, but he was not a man to trust any Fortnum or any Mason as to the excellence of the article to be supplied, or as to the price" (*The Claverings*, 38:396). But the less demanding Frank Greylock in *The Eustace Diamonds* was unquestioningly loyal to the firm. He took with him to Scotland "two guns, two fishing rods, a man-servant, and a huge hamper from Fortnum and Mason's" (23:243).

Trollope's later reference to another, this time fictitious, firm marked the difference that separated him, and the altered system of social manners he described, from his master Thackeray's and Gunter's heyday. Lopez, in *The Prime Minister*, hires the firm of Stewam and Sugarscraps, of Wigmore Street, to cater the dinner party he arrogantly throws at his father-in-law's home in Manchester Square. This does not sit well with the old housekeeper, the butler, and the cook, who "resigned impetuously within half an hour after the advent of Mr. Sugarscraps' head man." "The butler expressed his intention of locking himself up in his own peculiar pantry, and the housekeeper took it upon herself to tell her young mistress that 'Master wouldn't like it.' Since she had known Mr. Wharton such a thing as cooked food being sent into the house from a shop had never been so much as heard." "I cannot say," Trollope commented, "that the dinner was good."

> It may be a doubt whether such tradesmen as Messrs. Stewam and Sugarscraps do ever produce good food;—or whether, with all the will in the world to do so, such a result is within their power. It is certain, I think, that the humblest mutton chop is better eating than any "Supreme of chicken after martial manner,"—as I have seen the dish named in a French bill of fare, translated by a French pastrycook for the benefit of his English customers,—when sent in from Messrs. Stewam and Sugarscraps even with their best exertions. Nor can it be said that the wine was good, though Mr. Sugarscraps, when he contracted for the whole entertainment, was eager in his assurance that he procured the very best that London could produce. (48:72–74)

Thackeray had said of Gunter what all the fashionable world knew, and his respectful references implied the social prestige enjoyed by a firm that responded with style and efficiency—at a matching price—to the luxurious needs of high society. By replacing that honored name, as well as Fortnum and Mason's, with an invented one, which is not among his successes in that treacherous vein, Trollope implied the great inferiority of the vulgarian Stewam and Sugarscraps to their eminent predecessors and competitors. An instructive chapter of social history is contained in the Victorian novelists' record of the prosperity and eventual decline of catering.[†]

3.

No fashionable novel ever contained advertisements for commodities or services other than the gratis ones its author inserted in the text. It is not

---

[†] While much is eaten in Victorian fiction, the fare is considerably more commonplace than in the novels of Regency society, whose authors delighted in reciting the cloying contents of gourmet menus, written mostly in caterers' ornamental French. Despite the changes in the English diet that resulted from new agricultural practices and the increasing importation of exotic foods, new or out-of-the-way dishes are seldom mentioned. (The modern reader can only envy the availability of oysters and inexpensive lobsters, which even Dickens's poor characters could buy as no more than a modest treat.) Although Dickens writes of the Veneerings' "excellent dinners," he does not tell us what was actually served at their board, which groaned with extravagantly tasteless and weighty ornaments. We are equally ignorant of what Merdle's highly placed guests ate at his dinners. Instead of the pineapples that were a costly delicacy in Thackeray's fiction, such food as we read

likely that purveyors to the rich like Thomas Hamlet and Robert Gunter advertised anywhere. Commercial promotion of any kind was, to say the least, not genteel.[†] Later in the century, under competitive pressure, fashionable retail establishments went in for discreet direct-mail advertising to their select clients. In 1873, Ruskin admired Howell and James's "lovely illuminated circular, printed in blue and red, . . . which respectfully announces . . . their half-yearly clearance sale."[14]

But the advertising leaves in the monthly numbers of Dickens's and Thackeray's novels were another matter. They were addressed for the most part to a much wider and socially inferior readership, whose limited incomes, if nothing else, prevented them from responding in any practical way to the snob appeal of the names that sparkled in the pages of silver fork novels. The advertisements in Thackeray's part issues, for example, promoted products associated less specifically with the superior social class to which the characters belonged than with the wider public. The demographic spread of Victorian advertising can be inferred from the variety of commodities touted in the *Newcomes Advertiser*: floral mantillas, trusses (fitted with "patent levers"), cod liver oil, cutlery, camomile pills, pocket sophonias (raincoats), respirators (anti-allergic masks), patent self-adjusting shirts, patent expanding-screw dining tables, patent barley and groats (invalid fare), invisible ventilating perukes (gentlemen's wigs). It is impossible to conceive of any of Clive's friends wearing a high-tech truss or an invisible ventilating peruke.[‡]

With the enlarging consumers' market and the invention of rudimentary mass production methods, entrepreneurs in a number of lines began to experiment with new forms of publicity as well as to intensify their exploitation of old-established ones. In the *New Monthly Magazine*

---

about in Trollope's is on the level of the "ice creams and sponge cakes [which] are things apart from the shillingless schoolboy" (*Rachel Ray*, 26:332–33).

[†]The contemporary theory and practice of advertising has not yet received the serious attention its importance in English social history warrants. The subject is discussed at length in only one Victorian novel, Trollope's *The Struggles of Brown, Jones, and Robinson*, serialized in the *Cornhill Magazine* in 1861–62. George Robinson, the junior member of this firm of haberdashers and linendrapers, is gung-ho for advertising in many forms, but the money he spends on it is no match for his partners' timidity and dishonesty, and the firm goes bankrupt.

[‡]Scholars bent on acquiring a firmer notion of the social distribution of the novel-reading Victorian public could do worse than consider the implications of those advertisements. Although advertisers then were not equipped with any of the tools of present-day market analysis, as shrewd businessmen they must have had a pretty accurate idea of who their prospective customers were, how large their disposable incomes were, and for what kinds of goods their station in life created a demand.

for May 1841, Thomas Hood, ever alert for fresh topicalities, wrote, in "A Tale of a Trumpet":

> 'Tis strange what very strong advising,
> By word of mouth, or advertising,
> By chalking on walls, or placarding on vans,
> With fifty other different plans,
> The very high pressure in fact of pressing,
> It needs to persuade one to purchase a blessing!
> Whether the Soothing American Syrup,
> A Safety Hat, or a Safety Stirrup,—
> Infallible Pills for the human frame,
> Or Rowland's O-don't-O (an ominous name!)
> A Doudney's suit which the shape so hits
> That it beats all others into *fits*;
> A Mechi's Razor for beards unshorn,
> Or a Ghost-of-a-Whisper-Catching Horn!

Brand names leapt from the pages of every paper that accepted advertising, their number multiplying with the repeal of the advertisement tax in 1853. "Leviathans of public announcement" (Dickens's description of the banners heralding Mrs. Jarley's touring waxwork) exploited every existing medium—the sides of buses, the boards of sandwich men, pavement inscriptions, the display vehicles that clogged the shopping streets, and every vacant wall space. For every proselytizing Drusilla Clack strewing her precious tracts over stony ground in *The Moonstone*, there was a shabby hireling who thrust circulars and price lists through the windows of cabs bearing shoppers in London for the day as they left the railway termini or were stalled in traffic. Magdalen and Mrs. Wragge received fliers for infant feeding bottles and hunting breeches in such a manner in Wilkie Collins's *No Name*.

In ways like these, brand-name locks, for instance, came insistently to the public notice. They were items for which there was an unprecedented demand in an era when more people had ever more real property to secure against theft. When locks were mentioned in conversation, people automatically thought of Chubb or Bramah. In *The Warden*, Archdeacon Grantly locked up, in a desk drawer, "his Rabelais, and other things secret, with all the skill of Bramah or of Chubb" (8:58), and Thackeray's returning revelers, in one of his "Club Snob" papers (*Punch*, 2 January 1847; *BS*, 172), let themselves into their silent houses at cockcrow with Chubb keys. ("I am not, by nature, of an incendiary mind," confided Thackeray to *Punch*'s women readers, "but if, my dear ladies, you are for assassinating Mr. Chubb and burning down the Club Houses

in St. James's, there is *one* snob, at least, who will not think the worse of
you.") Chubb's New Patent Detector Locks were advertised in the part
issues of *Nicholas Nickleby, Dombey and Son,* and *Bleak House,* but it appears that Joseph Bramah's were even better known.[15] The inventor
(1748–1814) laid the foundations of his prosperous career with an improved water closet that is said to have "remained the standard model
for over a century," and a beer engine which still survives at the bars of
a few present-day public houses that have been spared modernization.
But his name was, instead, indelibly associated with a precision lock, to
open which defied the skill of the best technicians. Only after sixty-one
years did an American expert meet the challenge Bramah had issued in
1790, and then only after sixteen days' full-time work with the aid of
specially designed tools. Few artifacts of the time appeared in such a
variety of contexts in fiction, from Lizzie Eustace locking the troublesome diamond necklace in her desk "with a patent Bramah key" (its subsequent disappearance was no fault of Bramah) to Mr. Weller in *Pickwick
Papers* complaining malapropically to Sammy of the siege he was undergoing from a buxom female: "I can't keep her avay from me. If I was
locked up in a fire-proof chest vith a patent Brahmin, she'd find means
to get at me, Sammy" (52:831).

Even more heavily advertised, and in a greater number of places,
were the several products bearing the name of a French émigré, one
Rowland (or Rouland), who was said to have come to London at the
outbreak of the Revolution and set up next door to the Thatched House
tavern in St. James's as a fashionable coiffeur, charging the large sum of
five shillings for a haircut. According to Captain Gronow, he returned
to France in 1814, but if he did so, he left his valuable name behind.[16]
Who took it over and applied it to a celebrated line of beauty needs for
men and women is not clear. The first product to bear the name Rowland was undoubtedly his own, the Macassar Oil which necessitated that
abiding symbol of Victorian quaintness, the "antimacassar" linen doily
that protected armchair upholstery from the greasy ravages of the oil
on a man's hair. Of the bluestocking paragon of learning, Don Juan's
mother, Donna Inez, Byron wrote in 1819, "In virtues nothing earthly
could surpass her, / Save thine 'incomparable oil, / Macassar!'" (*Don
Juan*, I.xvii) The quotation marks suggest that the slogan was already
familiar. It echoed down the corridors of Victorian time. In *Plain or
Ringlets?* (1859–60) Surtees remembered it: "Formerly the real professional book-making betting-men were few and far between, who operated largely on their own accounts; now there is a perfect myriad of
middle-men who advertise their infallible winning 'secrets' with as much

ingenuity and pertinacity as Rowland used to advertise his 'Incomparable Oil Macassar'" (19:63).[†]

The owners of this profitable line spent large sums to keep their name before the public, so successfully that more people recognized it than they did the names of current politicians, and so imitably that "Howland" and "Gowland" beauty preparations turned up on the market. After Macassar Oil, Rowlands' most famous product was Kalydor, which, as we saw in Chapter 4, was frequently advertised in the part issues of novels. In the ninth number of the *Nicholas Nickleby Advertiser* (December 1838), it was described as "An Auxiliary of Vital Importance to the Support of Female Loveliness [which] eradicates TAN, FRECKLES, PIMPLES, SPOTS, REDNESS, and all CUTANEOUS ERUPTIONS." (It was also recommended to gentlemen as an after-shave lotion.) In a later monthly part of the novel, the mad old gentleman pays extravagant court to Miss LaCreevy in these terms:

> "She is come at last—at last—and all is gas and gaiters! . . . All the wealth
> I have is hers if she will take me for her slave. Where are grace beauty
> and blandishments like those? In the Empress of Madagascar? No. In the
> Queen of Diamonds? No. In Mrs. Rowland, who every morning bathes
> in Kalydor for nothing?" (49:744)

Readers remembering the down-to-earth terminology in the Kalydor advertisement could hardly have resisted transposing the lunatic's Rowland reference to that decidedly unromantic key, even though "Kalydor" presumably was meant to recall Sir Calidore in *The Faerie Queene*. On occasion, it is true, the Rowland people used high-falutin language themselves, as when, in an *Illustrated London News* advertisement some years later (6 November 1845), they praised their celebrated trinity: "The exuberance of the feelings amid scenes of gaiety induces the fair and youthful to shine in advantage under the gaze of many friends, and therefore to devote increased attention to the duties of the toilet. Macassar Oil imparts a transcendant lustre and Kalydor a radiant bloom, while Odonto"—mentioned in the poem by Hood quoted above—"bestows a pearl-like whiteness on the teeth." The fact, however, was that ordinary

---

[†]The past tense was quite premature. The product was still being advertised in the monthly issues of *Our Mutual Friend* (1864–65). It was perhaps one of Rowlands' less credible products that the whiskerless Fascination Fledgeby, in that novel, daily anointed himself with: "the last infallible preparation for the production of luxuriant and glossy hair upon the human countenance (quacks being the only sages he believed in besides usurers) . . ." (3.1:492). Like Kalydor, it was a unisex remedy. "Rowland!" exclaimed the Countess of Saldar in Meredith's *Evan Harrington*: "I have great faith in Rowland. Without him, I believe, there would have been many bald women committing suicide!" (9:105)

readers thought of Kalydor in blunt terms of pimples and other cutaneous afflictions, which Thackeray alluded to by circumlocution as he described the callow Jim Crawley in *Vanity Fair*: "when the face not uncommonly blossoms out with appearances for which Rowland's Kalydor is said to act as a cure" (34:329).

A new Rowland vanity product in the late 1830s was the "Infallible Hair Dye." It was not mentioned by name in Warren's *Ten Thousand a Year*, and there were rival concoctions on the market; but readers of the early installments of the novel in *Blackwood's Magazine* in 1839 would have automatically supplied it, thanks to the lavish publicity given to the Rowland brand name. As Warren describes the fluid, it came in a small vial wrapped in a puffery leaf citing "numberless instances of its efficacy, detailed in brief but glowing terms—as—the 'Duke of ******— the Countess of ******—the Earl of, etc., etc., etc., etc.—the lovely Miss ——, the celebrated Sir Little Bull's-eye (who was so gratified that he allowed his name to be used)—all of whom, from having hair of the reddest possible description, were now possessed of raven-hued locks" (5:158). Redemption from red hair—a misfortune to be discussed in a later chapter—was essential to the upward mobility of the lowly shop assistant Tittlebat Titmouse. He applied the magic fluid to his "great crop of bushy, carroty hair" with discouraging sequential results: first his hair turned bright green, then, after further applications, purple— the eyebrows and whiskers, however, emerging snow white. In the end, liberal use of ordinary ink produced black whiskers, but nothing further could be done for the hair, which remained an arresting shade of purple until it grew out. Ignoring the doubts that this performance cast upon the dye's alleged infallibility, Rowlands continued to market it; it was recommended in the advertising pages of *Oliver Twist* when that novel was reissued in monthly parts (1846).

4.

Rivaling Rowland as trade names incised into the Victorian consciousness were those of two preeminent manufacturers and suppliers of boot (shoe) blacking, an important commodity at a time when boots were highly varnished and therefore frequently had to be relieved of their daily encrustation of urban mud and restored to a drawing-room gloss. It was a highly competitive branch of trade, with at least thirty different firms vying for the public's blacking custom. An American visitor recorded in the 1830s that the annual advertising expenditure for that item alone ran to a quarter of a million pounds ($1,250,000 American).

It was at a Warren's factory that the proud, sensitive twelve-year-old

Charles Dickens suffered the unforgettable indignity of having to label the bottles (for liquid polish) and pots (for paste) and wrap them in the puffery leaves mentioned by another Warren in *Ten Thousand a Year*, in full view of passersby. This, however, was not *the* Warren firm of "30, the Strand," but a rival firm set up nearby by the disgruntled brother of the successful proprietor. In the absence of any code of advertising ethics, the dissident Warren advertised his product as WARREN'S BLACK-ING, 30 Hungerford Stairs, STRAND. (When Dickens served his purgatorial term, however, the firm had moved to Chandos Street, Covent Garden.) It may have been this "Blacking Ware'us" that Joe Gargery and Wopsle went to see when they came to London (*Great Expectations*, 27:244), but the handsome building of a rival firm in High Holborn is a likelier possibility.

The name and address of the original and larger Warren's were painted in big letters on the walls of buildings along every road leading into London. The slogan WARREN'S IS THE BEST was chalked or painted on the very pavements and borne through the streets on large vans. In Surtees's *Hillingdon Hall* (1843–44) there was a timely exchange: "'You have heard of the great National Anti-Corn-Law League?' 'I have seen their advertising machine, . . . but I never thought more of it than I should of Tosspot's crockery cart, or Warren's matchless blacking van'" (5:27). The praises of the miraculous fluid were likewise inscribed throughout the nation and abroad as far as Egypt, though sometimes the publicity was contributed by the inevitable graffitists. In his *Journey from Cornhill to Cairo*, Thackeray reported that Pompey's Pillar at Alexandria bore "rude remarks" inscribed by "numberless ships' companies, travelling Cockneys, etc. . . . Some daring ruffian even painted the name of 'Warren's blacking' on it."

George Cruikshank designed for Warren's tireless campaign the first famous pieces of iconography in British advertising history, probably the earliest contribution that commercial advertising made to the popular imagistic vocabulary—a series of woodcuts showing an astonished cat viewing its reflection in the mirror of a freshly polished Hessian boot, a cock fighting his shadow, or a man using the boot as a shaving mirror. Thackeray said that the Hessians on Jos Sedley's "beautiful legs shone so, that they must have been the identical pair in which the gentleman in the old pictures used to shave himself" (*Vanity Fair*, 22:207) and Josiah Bounderby, in his fabricated reminiscences of his allegedly underprivileged youth, boasted, "For years upon years, the only pictures in my possession, or that I could have got into my possession by any means, unless I stole 'em, were the engravings of a man shaving himself in a boot, on the blacking bottles that I was overjoyed to use in cleaning boots with, and that I sold when they were empty for a farthing a-piece, and

Cruikshank's variations on the theme of
boots polished to a mirrorlike shine, of
which this is one, were among the earliest classics of brand-name advertising imagery. (The set of verses was by another
hand.)

glad to get it!" (*Hard Times*, 2.7:197) Georgiana Podsnap's "early views of life," said Dickens in *Our Mutual Friend* (1.11:76), were "principally derived from reflections of it in her father's boots."

An equally famous feature of Warren's advertising was (to grossly misuse the adjective) its literary penchant. Praises of the product usually took the form of snatches of doggerel or hyperbolic prose such as Byron referred to in *Don Juan*: in the don's Gothic bedchamber at Norman Abbey ". . . he took up an old newspaper; / The paper was right easy to peruse; / He read an article the king attacking, / And a long eulogy of 'patent blacking'" (XVI.xxvi). These eulogies sometimes were direct imitations of popular poems, often with a topical slant—the commercial equivalent of Hood's and Praed's light verse, though without those poets' metrical and stanzaic sophistications. To "write for Warren's blacking" was a customary way of describing the lowest form of Grub Street hack work. On 31 May 1831, Elizabeth Barrett published in the *Times* a set of eight stanzas entitled "Kings," in the current mode of sentimental, watery album verse. Several days later, she recorded in her diary that a friend said "that she wonders how I could *publish* such horrible verses, & that some of those on Warren's Blacking are as good." The reproach haunted her, even in her sleep; a full month later she dreamed that she was rewriting "the Warren-blacking lines."[17] In a similar vein, a number of years later, Eliza Lynn (Linton's) vicar-father, responding to her outrageous proposal that she be allowed to live an independent life as a London journalist, declared that it would be degrading for her, a lady, and the granddaughter of a bishop (of Carlisle), "to write poems for Warren's blacking, or scratch up Bow Street details for a dinner."[18]

Both firms bearing the Warren name bought custom-made copy from seedy verse-mongers, and there are fragments of evidence that as a youth, once he was emancipated from his shameful servitude in the factory window, Dickens turned out some himself. His uncle John Barrow, trying to find his nephew a place on a newspaper, cited this experience in writing to order as a sign of his journalistic talent, and many years later John Payne Collier, the Shakespeare scholar, declared that Dickens once told him that he had written some of Warren's puffs, including this specimen:

> I pitied the dove, for my bosom was tender,
> I pitied the sigh that she gave to the wind;
> But I ne'er shall forget the superlative splendour
> Of Warren's Jet Blacking, the pride of mankind.[19]

John Forster suggested that Dickens used one of the writers patronized by Warren as the model for Mr. Slum in *The Old Curiosity Shop*. Slum's greatest gift, like that of all freelance eulogists of nineteenth-century consumer products, is his adaptability. He offers his services to Mrs. Jarley, the waxwork lady, but she objects that his verses are overpriced and in any case questions their cost-effectiveness. He shows her "a little trifle here, thrown off in the heat of the moment, which I should say was exactly the thing you wanted to set this place on fire with. It's an acrostic—the name at the moment is Warren, but the idea's a convertible one, and a positive inspiration for Jarley" (28:282). He asks five shillings for this latest visitation of his muse, but she beats him down to three-and-six, and he retires to make the necessary alterations. It is regrettable that Dickens, with his putative experience in the form, did not share the finished product with us.

It has been suggested that Mr. Slum may have been specifically modeled after an actual "blacking laureate," one Alexander Kemp, a former civil servant who had been reduced to performing odd jobs in the literary way.[20] In June 1823, by coincidence only a few months before Dickens entered upon his hated employment, Kemp addressed a begging letter to Sir Walter Scott, noting that in his utter destitution he had been assisted only by the "benevolent sympathy" of Catherine Opie:

> My early years, and subsequent leisure opportunities, have been much devoted to literature; and my MS. Volume of Original Poetry has been submitted to the perusal and honored with the approbation of several eminent writers. From that Volume I presume to annex a few extracts; and add at the same time a specimen of puffing advertisement, of which I have written for Warren (30, Strand) above two hundred, all of different incident, but all embracing the same hacknied subject of eulogy, the "unparalleled Blacking"; for the remuneration of Two shillings and Sixpence each!

It would seem that Mrs. Jarley paid more than the going rate, unless Kemp's price was based on wholesale lots. Nothing more is heard of his mendicant campaign, which took one of the standard forms practiced for at least a century by this time—that of offering a likely Samaritan the choice of buying the wretched manuscript (as modern sidewalk beggars offer boxes of matches) or arranging to have it printed by subscription for the author's benefit. But there was an immediate sequel, the result of the manuscript's having gone the rounds of the "eminent writers" of the time. A journalist and novelist named William Frederick Deacon was inspired to put together a collection of parodies of such poets as Coleridge, Leigh Hunt, and Thomas Moore, the common theme of which was praise of Warren's blacking. It was published the next year (1824) under the title of *Warreniana*.[†]

[†] The prototype of this transparent hoax was James and Horace Smith's bestselling *Rejected Addresses* (1812), a series of parodies of currently famous poets which their sup-

Warren's most formidable rival was the firm of Day and Martin. Surtees described, in *Ask Mamma*, Billy Pringle's and Miss Willing's nighttime arrival in London: "At length, a sudden turn of the road revealed
to our friends, who were sitting with their faces to the horses, the first
distant curve of glow-worm-like lamps in the distance, and presently the
great white invitations to 'TRY WARREN'S,' or 'DAY AND MARTIN'S BLACK-
ING,' began to loom through the darkness of the dead walls of the outskirts of London" (5:27). Either because he wanted to be even-handed
or because, in a spirit of mild vengefulness, he wanted to give free publicity to the competition, Dickens alluded as often to Day and Martin as
he did to Warren. A hint of the latter motive occurs in the ambiguous
way in which he described Sam Weller's energetic application to his task
in the inn yard: he "brushed away with such hearty good will" that in a
few minutes he worked up "a polish which would have struck envy to
the soul of the amiable Mr. Warren (for they used Day and Martin at the
White Hart) . . ." (*Pickwick Papers*, 10:198–99). Was it the superior product, or Sam's elbow grease, that produced so high a gloss?

When the Saffron Hill gang embarked on its ill-fated burglarious
expedition to Chertsey, young Charley Bates complained to Fagin that
his top boots needed polishing: "See there, Faguey, not a drop of Day
and Martin since you know when; not a bubble of blacking, by Jove!"
(*Oliver Twist*, 25:233). Translated from the vernacular, this meant
simply that Charley was suffering from severe thirst. The street term for
cheap port was Day and Martin, and this subliminal association of wine
and boot blacking was behind Dickens's substitution of Murdstone and
Grinby, wine merchants, for Warren, blacking manufacturer, when he
revisited his childhood under the thinnest of disguises in *David Copperfield*. He repeated the Day and Martin/wine joke many years later in *Our
Mutual Friend*, when Mortimer gropes for the name of the place from
which the mysterious stranger came: "where they make the wine." "'Eugene suggests 'Day and Martin's.' 'No, not that place,' replies Mortimer,
'that's where they make the Port. My man comes from the country where
they make the Cape Wine'" (1.2:55). Eventually the Day and Martin
name, and indeed the explicit association, faded from the slang expression, so that one of the components became simply understood, not
voiced. In *The Mystery of Edwin Drood*, when Dickens described the hotel
behind Aldersgate Street where John Jasper checked in on arriving from
Cloisterham, he said of its advertising that "It bashfully, almost apolo-
getically, gives the traveller to understand that it does not expect him,

---

posed authors were said to have entered in a competition to find an address to be delivered
at the opening of the rebuilt Drury Lane Theatre.

on the good old constitutional hotel plan, to order a pint of sweet blacking for his drinking, and throw it away; but insinuates that he may have
his boots blacked instead of his stomach . . ." (22:265–66).

Perhaps, as the elder Mr. Weller implied when his son was struggling
to compose a valentine, Warren and his fellow advertisers gave poetry at
large a bad name: "Poetry's unnat'ral; no man ever talked poetry 'cept a
beadle on boxin' day, or Warren's blackin', or Rowland's oil or some o'
them low fellows" (*Pickwick Papers*, 33:540). If so, poetry labored under
a considerable disadvantage in early Victorian England. For in addition
to the several blacking companies, a ceaselessly self-publicizing tailoring
firm filled newspaper advertising columns as well as the advertising
supplements to serialized novels with its own brand of facetious, usually
versified, commercial messages. This was E. Moses and Sons, whose copy
writer—or fraternity of tame poets—Thackeray called "the delightful
bard of the Minories" in "A Plan for a Prize Novel."

The prominence of Moses' puffs in the various Dickens Advertisers—their correlation with the seasons and, in the case of *Bleak House*,
their tie-ins with the novel's text—has already been mentioned.[21] No Victorian advertiser made greater efforts to pick up news items that could
somehow be twisted into promotional prose or verse. In the first three
months of 1844 alone, for example, Moses' poems-cum-price lists in the
Illustrated London News bore such captions as "Ojibbeway Indians" (the
current entertainment rage—George Catlin's troupe of American "sav-
ages"), "The Queen's Speech" (at the opening of Parliament), "The State
Trials" (the trial of the Irish firebrand Daniel O'Connell on a charge of
"creating discontent and disaffection"), "The Mart of the East" (a parody
of "The Land of the West," a popular song of the day), and "The Giant's
Visit" (another show-business attraction, the seven-foot, one-and-one-
half-inch "Devonshire Giant"). One jeu d'esprit in the sartorial line, coming as it did on 27 April, only four months after Thomas Hood's poem
on shirt makers' sweatshops appeared in *Punch* (16 December 1843),
may strike one as being in doubtful taste under the circumstances:

THE SONG OF THE "SUIT"

> Attend to my ditty, attend, ev'ry one!
> For I owe my existence to MOSES and SON.
> I am view'd as the very "perfection of dress,"
> And wherever I go I am met with success.
> My fashion and elegance none will dispute,
> But all have pronounc'd me a "beautiful suit."
> The manner I fit round the waist and the shoulders,
> Is certain to captivate all the beholders.
> [There are sixteen more lines.]

The great motive behind E. Moses and Sons' year-in, year-out advertising campaign in middle-class media was their ambition to go upmarket, shedding the image of mere slop-sellers, makers of cheap clothing for men who could not afford tailors. They angled for a larger, more genteel clientele to whom, as "clothiers and outfitters," they sought to sell fashionable tailored coats, trousers, waistcoats, and accessories, as well as ladies' riding habits. The firm was nothing if not innovative: it opened an elegant furnished "bespoke" department with a separate waiting room for servants, experimented with a scheme for "self-measured," custom-tailored suits, and, most unorthodox of all, sold its wares at fixed prices that were plainly marked on each garment, with a money-back guarantee.[22]

Despite these ambitions, however, it appears that E. Moses and Sons boxed themselves in, first by persisting in the use of flamboyant advertising which, however clever it might sometimes have been, was still regarded as vulgar puffery by the very clientele they sought to attract, and secondly by continuing to stress their low prices: "ready-made suits that Beau Brummell would have been proud to wear at prices that a mechanic could afford to pay."

To judge from fictional references, it is likely that ill-paid clerks and shop assistants like Tittlebat Titmouse bought their weekend stepping-out suits off the rack at the familiar address in the Minories. Readers of Annie Edwards's novel *The World's Verdict* (1861) would have appreciated her description of a Brighton "tripper" in full fig: "People from the country might, possibly, have mistaken him for a swell-mobs-man: London men have hesitated as to whether he was a tailor arrayed in his own workmanship, or a banker's clerk newly fitted out by the Messrs. Moses. No one upon earth would ever have taken him for what he took himself—a London dandy of the very first water, and one of the finest gentlemen in the world."[23] The rival firms of Moses, Nicholl, and Doudney†—all heavy advertisers, as it happened—reclothed the Dandiacal Body at prices made possible, if not necessarily by sweated labor, certainly by large volume, low profit margin, and aggressive promotion.

As she sometimes did with familiar topicalities, George Eliot put this one to serious use. In the course of Daniel Deronda's search for his Jew-

---

†It was Doudney, who had a combined clothing and printing business in Lombard Street, rather than E. Moses and Sons, that William Edmonstoune Aytoun chose to memorialize in one of the "Bon Gaultier" ballads—"The Lay of the Doudney Brothers," a polished literary version of the typical Mosaic poem. The Doudney advertisements did not lend themselves to parody or pastiche because, according to Bernard Darwin (*The Dickens Advertiser*, pp. 39–40), only one of them, in a *Pickwick* number, was in verse.

ish identity (though he would not have put it thus at this stage of the novel), he contemplates one way in which it was possible to learn more about the Jewish character:

> Deronda's thinking went on in rapid images of what might be: he saw himself . . . in some quarter . . . under the breath of a young Jew talkative and familiar, willing to show his acquaintance with gentlemen's tastes, and not fastidious in any transactions with which they would favour him—and so on through the brief chapter of his experience in this kind. Excuse him: his mind was not apt to run spontaneously into insulting ideas, or to practise a form of wit which identifies Moses with the advertisement sheet. . . . (*Daniel Deronda*, 19:247)

A long time had passed since Moses and his ilk had first addressed themselves to cashing in on the Regency rage for gentlemen's fashion, and since the heyday of Stultz, the true gentleman's tailor, who was neither cheap nor promotion-minded, and whose extensive record in fiction we shall examine in the next chapter but one.

8

The Favorite Vice of the Nineteenth Century

1.

"GO TO THE SMOKING-ROOM," cried an exasperated Lady Janet Roy in Wilkie Collins's *The New Magdalen* (1872–73) as she pushed Horace Holmcroft toward the door. "Away with you, and cultivate the favorite vice of the nineteenth century. . . . Go and smoke! . . . Go and smoke!" (6:257). A few years earlier, in *The Belton Estate* (1865–66), Trollope had described Aylmer Park as "a country house in which people neither read, nor flirt, nor gamble, nor smoke, nor have resort to the excitement of any special amusement" (26:340)—in short, a place bereft of any of the pastimes that helped fill the vacancies of life in the Victorian leisured class. No other popular amusement, solitary or social, appears more often in Victorian fiction than smoking; and its chief instrument was the cigar, which was seen more frequently in those pages than any other artifact that was new to the century.

Later in the century the cigarette came into fashion. Preceding both was the pipe, which coexisted with them on a certain social plane. All three served novelists in a surprising variety of ways. The use of tobacco in any of these forms (snuff was another matter, more characteristic of the eighteenth century than the nineteenth) was, among other things, a sure indication of time-setting as well as personality and, often, social class. The difference in rank between two components of an election crowd in a country town could hardly be expressed in fewer words than George Eliot used when she said in *Felix Holt* that "some rough-looking pipe-smokers, or distinguished cigar-smokers, chose to walk up and down in isolation and silence" (2.30:246).

Down to the beginning of the nineteenth century, men who enjoyed the fragrance of smoldering tobacco had only one way of smoking, and that was the pipe, whose pleasures were sometimes celebrated in verse. In *A Pipe of Tobacco* (1736) Isaac Hawkins Browne parodied six well-

240

known authors of the day, including James Thomson, Swift, Pope, and Edward Young, in the form in which each might eulogize "the weed." In fiction, the archetypal pipe smoker was Tristram Shandy's Uncle Toby, whose habit harmonized with his eccentric, philosophical character. By the time the cigar arrived in England (about 1804), the pipe was increasingly associated, in literature at least, with rough-and-ready men, whose manners were diametrically opposed to those cultivated in fashionable society. Nothing in Thackeray's portrait of old Sir Pitt Crawley more positively identified him as a survivor of the hard-riding, hard-drinking, profane country gentry of Fielding's time—miserly to boot—than the fact that over his beer (a workingman's drink, not a gentleman's) he smoked not a cigar but a pipe. In Victorian times, pipe smoking remained a fixed attribute of countrymen, from sturdy farmers down to the lowliest day laborers. While Tennyson's and Carlyle's literary peers smoked fashionable cigars (Trollope, in particular, was a powerful smoker), Tennyson, who grew up in the remote Lincolnshire wolds, and Carlyle, a son of the Scottish soil whose earthy country manners long residence in London had failed to eradicate, smoked short-stemmed clay "cuttie" pipes, the manual laborer's companion, or long churchwardens.

As a rule, middle- and upper-class men in Victorian fiction scorned the pipe, except, possibly, as a reaction against the early vulgarization of the cigar (of which, more in a moment) and as a frugal alternative. In a deliberate inversion of social symbolism, undergraduates adopted it in part as a mark of class—their temporary membership in an elite little precinct of society. The pipe was favored, too, in mildly Bohemian artists' circles. "The smoking of a proper number of pipes," Pendennis said, sustained Clive Newcome and his fellow painters before their easels as they were finishing their artistic education in Rome. The habit carried over into adjacent territory. Pendennis remembered with nostalgia the companionable evenings he and other members of Clive's circle spent in the house the Colonel rented from Sherrick: "What cozy pipes did we not smoke in the dining-room, in the drawing-room, or where we would!" (*Pendennis*, 16:1.175)—a delicious liberty not available when ladies were present. Journalists, too, were partial to pipes: Pendennis's friend Warrington, for example, and in Trollope, Hugh Stanbury, a leader-writer for a down-market penny daily (*He Knew He Was Right* [1868–69]), though by this time, some newspapermen, like Nicholas Bourne, editor of the *Morning Breakfast Table* in *The Way We Live Now* (1874–75), were taking up cigarettes.

Otherwise, pipe smoking was associated with men on the periphery of intellectual circles—humble country schoolmasters, say, and reflective vicars, and, beyond them, with persons who fell into that capacious but amorphous class called by the Victorians "the inferior orders of society." Most of the smoke in *Great Expectations* comes from the pipes of Wemmick, secure in his moated cottage at Walworth, the returned convict Magwitch, and, most typically, Joe Gargery, the Kentish blacksmith. In *The Moonstone*, the Indian traveler Murthwaite, who is smoking a cheroot, asks Gabriel Betteredge, the faithful steward on Lady Verinder's Yorkshire estate, "Do you smoke, Mr. Betteredge?" "Yes, sir." "Do you care much for the ashes left in your pipe when you empty it?" "No, sir." "In the country those men [the mysterious Indians] came from, they care just as much about killing a man, as you care about emptying the ashes out of your pipe" ("First period," chap. 10:81). Murthwaite assumed, rightly, that a person in Betteredge's walk of life would smoke a pipe; to smoke a cigar would be the mark of a man who did not know his place.

Cigars were introduced into England more or less simultaneously by two fashion-setting groups, officers back from the Peninsular Wars (1804–13) and cheroot-smoking soldiers and nabobs home from India—Captain, later Major, finally Colonel Dobbin is several times seen with a cigar—and the novelty was taken up at once by stay-at-home dandies, who proceeded to violate the social rules long associated with pipe smoking. Contemporary satirical prints show them, negligently posed, smoking in the presence of ladies in the park and indoors. In one, a dandy puffing cigar smoke in the face of a lady sitting beside him says, "[T]he only reasonable objection I can see to smoking is, that one runs a risk of sing[e]ing one's mustachio's by it." [1] When Thackeray showed the aptly named Tom Raikes[†] trying to force his way into Becky Sharp Crawley's sitting room at Boulogne, he needed only to add the detail that he had "a cigar in his mouth" to underscore his boorishness (*Vanity Fair*, 64:620).

The German traveler Pückler-Muskau, a supposed model for Count Smorltork in *Pickwick Papers*, recorded that when he dined with the Duke of Sussex in 1824, "after the ladies left the table, cigars were brought in, and more than one smoked, which I never before saw in England." [2] The habit or affectation, as it may more properly be called in a Regency context, did not spread far into "respectable" circles at this time. Even at that famous haunt of the fast set, White's gambling house,

---

[†]The name was not only apt, it was real—one of the few names of actual persons to be found in the novel. Thomas ("Apollo") Raikes (1777–1848), a governor of the Bank of England, was a well-known clubman and dandy and a close friend of Beau Brummell. His diary, a valuable source for Regency society, was published in 1856–57.

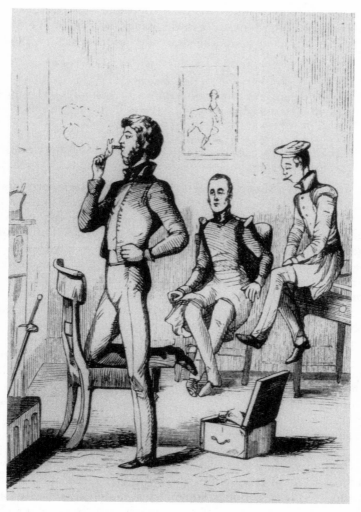

In the Waterloo era, cigar smoking was a distinctive habit of
military officers like George Osborne. Thackeray's illustration
for *Vanity Fair*, chapter 13, shows a practical use to which cigars
could be put: George Osborne is cavalierly destroying one of
Amelia Sedley's love letters, "to the horror of Captain Dobbin,"
says Thackeray, "who, it is my belief, would have given a bank-
note for the document."

smoking was forbidden until 1844. In the same year, a notice at the Surrey Zoological Gardens, a new version of the venerable Vauxhall Gardens that attracted a middle-class and upper-working-class clientele, read:

> TO GENTLEMEN,
> The Proprietor, anxiously solicitous to insure the comfort of all, respectfully suggests to Gentlemen (*especially subscribers*), whether his views would not be materially promoted, if they would refrain from
> SMOKING CIGARS.
> He is certain the respectability of the Gardens would be better insured, and the repeated complaints he is constantly receiving from Ladies be avoided.[3]

"Gentlemen" in the sober, accepted sense, though the word was standard in all such public addresses, did not frequent places like the Surrey Gardens. The true target of the management's polite request was the impudent breed of youth—and middle-aged men reluctant to concede that they were no longer in the first bloom of youth—called "gents," who did their best to ape their betters and succeeded only in drawing their ridicule. The fact is that the cigar-smoking habit, bypassing the respectable middle class, had been vulgarized into a practice peculiarly associated with them in the 1830s. Large, cheap,[†] and strong-smelling cigars, flourished with an extravagant air, were the hallmark of a gent, along with loud clothing (a little later, he would buy his suits from E. Moses and Sons) and a swaggering, impudent demeanor. These were characteristics also of the dandy's leisured middle-class imitator, the swell. The latter hung around raffish sporting establishments, "cigar divans" such as the one Mr. Harding in *The Warden* found refuge in when he took his innocence abroad to London, and downright dives. The gent, by occupation typically a lawyer's clerk, like those supreme exemplars of the type, Guppy and Bart Smallweed in *Bleak House*, or a bookkeeper or shop assistant, was much to Dickens's satirical taste.[4] He repeatedly depicted the gent in different guises and different aspects of his way of life outside business hours, though suppressing, in deference to his readers' sensibilities, one consequence of cigar smoking abetted by cheap liquor. An exchange in Surtees's *Jorrocks' Jaunts and Jollities*, published before *Sketches by Boz*, ran: "Take a cigar, sir?" "No; I feel werry much obliged, but they always make me womit" (2:34).

---

†Cheap cigars were made from the discarded stubs of others, scavenged in the streets by sub-poverty-level children, who made a halfpenny a pound for their findings, and adults who could command 6*d.* to 10*d.* for the same quantity if dry. Insofar as this early form of recycling was known to the world at large, it did nothing to enhance the reputation of cigar smoking.

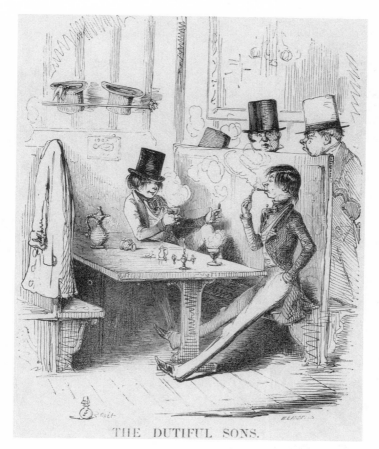

THE DUTIFUL SONS.

Dressing up like swells and ostentatiously smoking cigars was an adolescent ritual practiced, according to *Punch* (23 April 1842), even by scions of middle-class families. "Aint it prime Bill, being out o' nights?" asks one of the juvenile libertines. "I believe yer," replies the other, "—'specially when the Gov'nors don't know anything about it."

In *Sketches by Boz* Dickens portrayed a pair of clerks "Making a Night of It." After dinner in the eating house (restaurant) they patronize,

they went on, talking politics, puffing cigars, and sipping whiskey-and-water, until the "goes"—most appropriately so called—were both gone, which Mr. Robert Smithers perceiving, immediately ordered in two more goes of the best Scotch whiskey, and two more of the very mildest Havan-

GENTS.

(Suggested by the Frontispiece of *Punch's Pocket Book*; and the Poem of "Birds." in the *New Monthly Magazine*.

ENTS! Gents! ye are horrible things
With your slang-looking coats, and gaudy rings;
Where shall a gentleman wander or dwell,
Horrible Gents, but ye come there as well!
Ye swarm at the theatres' half-price to the slips,
And think that your style doth all others eclipse;
With glaring handkerchiefs tied round your neck,
And coarse common trowsers of violent check;
Ye fall the best prey to the cheap tailor's lures,
Whose pitiful doggrel your custom procures.
Horrible Gents, ye come thickly around
Wherever flash manners and habits are found;
Ye flourish in force when the shutters are up,
And think singing taverns good places to sup.

Pilgrim, say, who was it found
A ready pathway to the hill
Over Gravesend's town renown'd,
Christen'd from the windless' mill!
Tired and hungry friends had failed,
"Tea with shrimps" was their intent:
But thy presence there was hailed
By the dashing Sunday Gent!

* * * * *

Mariner! mariner! speed 'st thou on
From lively Folkestone to Boulogne,
(Or, if thou lov'st the word to coin
In foreign accent, to Bouloyne)
Or travel'st else, in homely sphere
To Woolwich from the Brunswick Pier;
Much thou 'lt tell when thou gett'st on shore,
Of that part of the boat which is called the "fore,"
From whence cheroots give forth a cloud

Which abaft the funnel is not allow'd;
And the tobacco's noisome scents
Comes from the mob of holiday Gents.
Out on the river, leagues away,
Saileth the dense and filthy fume,
The passengers cough—but what care they?—
They are free as the cloud, and out for the day,
They have money enough for a dozen to pay,
And leaves of the cabbage they can consume.

* * * * *

Up in the morning, ere the cads
Of duns begin to bore him,
The huntsman hies to "The Three Magpies," *
But the Gent is there before him.
He sings as he thinks he cuts a dash,
In a three-pound coat attired;
But the scarlet is free from stain or splash,
And the horse for the day is hired.
He rides o'er the dogs, and he tries a leap,
And drops in the ditch behind him;
Oh, the Gent's lament is loud and deep,
But the sportsmen never mind him.

Horrible Gents! they have coupled thy names
With cheap gaudy things in the bright window frames.
We have "Gent's newest Berlin," and "Gent's Opera Ties,"
With "Gent's Patent Alberts"—unnumber'd supplies.
The slop-selling clothesman has blouses quite rife,
For "Gents" who are leading "a business life;"
And similar objects are everywhere vended.
For Gents—not for Gentlemen—always intended.

Dismal attempters! upbraid ye I must,
Oh! where is the eye but is dulled with disgust
As it watches your trimmings—your cut-away coats,
The pins in your bosoms, and stocks at your throats.
Oh! I would not wish, as the old ballads sing,
To be fairy or butterfly—rich man, or king:
I only would pray that the Fates might consent
To save me from ever becoming A GENT!

The gent was a much ridiculed social phenomenon of the early Victorian years, as this caricature-in-verse (*Punch*, 25 November 1843) makes clear. The fourth stanza singles out his notorious addiction to cheap cigars.

nahs; and the goes kept coming in, and the mild Havannahs kept going out, until, what with the drinking, and lighting, and puffing, and the stale ashes on the table, and the tallow-grease on the cigars, Mr. Robert Smithers began to doubt the mildness of the Havannahs, and to feel very much as if he had been sitting in a hackney-coach with his back to the horses. ("Characters" chap. 11:268)

Medical students, in their off-duty hours, easily reverted to the habits of gents. In *Pickwick Papers*, when they were smoking and drinking by the kitchen fire in their lodgings,

> Mr. Bob Sawyer . . . had about him that sort of slovenly smartness and swaggering gait, which is peculiar to young gentlemen who smoke in the streets by day, shout and scream in the same by night, call waiters by their Christian names, and do various other acts and deeds of an equally facetious description. (30:493)

On his first hungover appearance in *The Old Curiosity Shop*, Dick Swiveller, who (though Dickens is not specific on the point) must have been as copious a cigar smoker as he was an imbiber of cheery liquids, was the very model of a spreeing gent, down to a "strong savour of tobacco smoke" (2:61). At old Trent's shop, he made philosophical conversation.

> He began by remarking that soda-water, though a good thing in the abstract, was apt to lie cold upon the stomach unless qualified with ginger, or a small infusion of brandy, which latter article he held to be preferable in all cases, saving for the one consideration of expense. Nobody venturing to dispute these positions, he proceeded to observe that the human hair was a great retainer of tobacco-smoke, and that the young gentlemen of Westminster and Eton, after eating vast quantities of apples to conceal any scent of cigars from their anxious friends, were usually detected in consequence of their heads possessing this remarkable property; whence he concluded that if the Royal Society would turn their attention to the circumstance, and endeavour to find in the resources of science a means of preventing such untoward revelations, they might indeed be looked upon as benefactors to mankind. (2:62)†

Another Dickensian gent, Bailey junior, riding behind the hackney coachman as he delivered a drink-befuddled Jonas Chuzzlewit to Todgers', "smoked his cigar with an air of particular satisfaction; the undertaking in which he was engaged having a free and sporting character about it, which was quite congenial to his taste" (*Martin Chuzzlewit*, 28:525).

Dickens was true to both the period (the late 1820s) and the character of John Chivery, his most sympathetically treated gent, when John, togged out in true gent's attire, took William Dorrit a handful of cigars

---

†Earlier, just as he arrived at the shop, he "observed that whilst standing by the post at the street-corner, he had observed a pig with a straw in his mouth issuing from out of the tobacco-shop, from which appearance he augured that another fine week for the ducks was approaching, and that rain would certainly ensue" (2:60). The Penguin editor rightly cites a weather proverb, "When pigs carry sticks, The clouds will play tricks; When they lie in the mud, No fears of a flood." But surely the image also suggests a fellow gent, in porcine form, with a thin cigar (straw) in his mouth.

as part of his campaign to win Little Dorrit's heart. To a gent, cigars were
the very emblem of the good life, but he failed to realize that such a gift,
at that date, impugned the old Marshalsea prisoner's obsessive conviction that he remained a gentleman and thus was neither a cigar-smoking
gent nor a cigar-smoking swell. Dorrit has John put the cigars on the
mantelpiece, and nothing further is said about them.

Daniel Quilp was not, by any stretch of the imagination, a gent, a
swell, or a dandy—he was far more objectionable than any of these—
but tobacco addiction served Dickens well as he developed the evil
dwarf's full grotesqueness. Quilp was one of the few characters in Victorian fiction, besides sailors, who chewed tobacco—a penchant inseparable in its grossness (not only because he ate watercress at the same
time) from eating "hard eggs, shell and all," devouring "gigantic prawns
with the heads and tails on," and downing boiling tea without a wink
(*The Old Curiosity Shop*, 5:86). Smuggling his cigars through customs, he
chain-smoked them in all-night sessions. When he took over the shop
during the old man's illness, he "deemed it prudent, as a precaution
against infection from fever, and a means of wholesome fumigation, not
only to smoke himself without cessation, but to insist upon it that his
legal friend did the like" (11:137). In this setting, he preferred his pipe
to cigars,

> throwing himself on his back upon the bed with his pipe in his mouth, and
> then kicking up his legs and smoking violently. . . . The legal gentleman
> [Sampson Brass] being by this time rather giddy and perplexed in his ideas
> (for this was one of the operations of the tobacco upon his nervous system),
> took the opportunity of slinking away into the open air where in course
> of time he recovered sufficiently to return with a countenance of tolerable
> composure. He was soon led on by the malicious dwarf to smoke himself
> into a relapse, and in that state stumbled upon a settee where he slept till
> morning. (11:140–41)

Cigar smoking at the beginning of the Queen's reign therefore suffered from its prejudicial association, on the one hand, with the dandy
(extravagantly profligate high life) and, on the other, with the gent
(cheaply profligate low life). There was also a more sharply moral bias
that stemmed from the fact that it entailed sensual pleasure, albeit one
with no subsequent price to pay. In an often quoted example of Victorian neo-Puritan austerity, Leslie Stephen wrote of his father, Sir James,
a pillar of the Evangelical Clapham sect, that he "was inexorably suspicious of pleasure. . . . He once smoked a cigar . . . and found it so delicious that he never smoked again."[5]

Smoking was also regarded—by Lord Melbourne, for one—as a
"dirty German habit" (though Pückler-Muskau's host, the elderly Duke
of Sussex, was "an inveterate smoker of German pipes"). The German

princeling who married Victoria, however, had other ideas. As Mark
Girouard has pointed out, he was an enthusiastic smoker himself, and
the smoking haven he installed at Osborne "was the only room with a
solitary 'A' instead of an entwined 'V & A' over the door."[6] He is generally credited with having rescued cigar smoking from the obloquy it had
accumulated since its introduction thirty years earlier. From him the
habit spread through court circles and so, within a few years, to the most
solid, respectable portion of the middle class—a process that took place
in the very years (1842–55) when Thackeray accustomed the reading
public to character after character who smoked with a regularity and
enjoyment that would have been worthy of the prince himself. In the
first of his "Fitz-Boodle's Confessions" (*Fraser's Magazine*, June 1842) he
devoted several pages to the reminiscences of a tobacco addict, a middle-
aged man-about-town who had been sent down from Christ Church and
discharged from the army for indiscretions associated with his habit. Beginning with an eloquent argument in behalf of making cigar smoking
respectable—evidence enough that this was a controversial issue at the
moment—the raconteur ended with a cautionary tale describing how he
had promised his betrothed, an adamant young lady who had £4,000 a
year to bring to her marriage, that he would refrain from smoking for a
year. At great cost to his morale, he clung to his rectitude for four
months and eleven days, the last of which saw him tricked by his rival
into appearing at her costume ball redolent with cigar smoke. He got the
boot, and the other man got the girl.

2.

Once cigars were freed from their demeaning associations and could be
seen in the mouths of the most prosperous and upstanding gentlemen
in the land (the acceptance was signalized by the sharply increased number of cigars figuring in *Punch* cartoons in the mid-1850s), they quickly
recommended themselves to novelists who, like Thackeray, specialized
in portraying men whose incomes were substantially above the national
median. Far from being merely time-specific accessories or stage props
and automatic indicators of class, cigars became protean accompani-
ments to social intercourse. On occasion they acquired their own sign
language, comparable to the language of flirtation attributed to ladies'
fans in *The Spectator* 102, or to the code of messages delivered by individual flowers in the Victorian sentimental schema. "[I]s there any
one besides Captain and Mrs. Torrington at Duplow?" Gwendolen asks
Grandcourt in *Daniel Deronda*, "or did you leave them *tête-à-tête*? I suppose he converses in cigars, and she answers with her chignon" (29:374).
    As they developed in the forties and fifties, the conventions affecting

By the time Surtees's *Mr. Sponge's Sporting Tour* was published (1849–51), cigar smoking was beginning to be regarded as a habit proper to gentlemen, who might indulge it in the snug privacy of the home. But in "respectable" circles its acceptability was still qualified by its strong association with fast-living sportsmen such as John Leech depicted in an illustration in the 1856 edition of the novel (above), and with bibulous occasions like seafood dinners down the Thames (*Punch*, 16 July 1853) (opposite).

the use of the cigar were to form an ineradicable part of the image of Victorian society that was to come down to us. What strikes us most forcibly, perhaps, was the ceremonial nature of cigar smoking. Unlike modern cigarette smoking, which is a largely automatic act, the lighting and smoking of cigars was deliberate and conscious event. Outside fiction, the most notable evidence of this is found in the diaries and letters of men of the time, such as Sir William Hardman, the so-called mid-Victorian Pepys. Whenever gentlemen gathered after dinner or some other entertainment, or when they strolled about the grounds of an estate or walked cross-country for exercise, or simply lounged, they often recorded afterward, "Of course we smoked," or, more specifically, "We smoked two cigars apiece." Often in fiction (and even in light verse, as in Thomas Hood's "Ode to Mr. Graham, the Aeronaut" [1825]), the consumption of a cigar or a series of cigars was used to measure elapsed time. In *Vanity Fair*, having put Becky in her carriage after her brilliant

THE GREENWICH DINNER.—A CONVIVIAL MOMENT.

debut at Lord Steyne's party, Rawdon Crawley accepts a cigar from his friend Wenham and they begin to walk down Gaunt Square. Rawdon is accosted by bailiffs, who arrest him for a debt of £66 6s.8d. he owes Mr. Nathan. Wenham cannot help his friend, whom the bailiffs bundle into a cab—"and Rawdon Crawley finished his cigar as the cab drove under Temple Bar" (51:501)

There was an especially noteworthy instance of this modern functional equivalent of the ancient hour glass at the very beginning of Reade's *A Terrible Temptation*, in which Sir Charles Bassett "smoked five cigars, and pondered the difference between the pure creature who now honored him with her virgin affections, and beauties of a different character who had played their parts in his luxurious life" (1:9–10). Immediately thereafter, when he and his solicitor discuss the matter, they do so through the heavy smoke generated by "the inevitable cigars," and their dialogue, as Reade reports it, is punctuated with "Puff, puff."[†]

[†]There was, however, some opinion that smoking could be injurious to one's health. The same Charles Bassett would end up being railroaded into an insane asylum, whose proprietor, an unusually enlightened alienist, weaned him, as Watts-Dunton weaned Swin-

The very process of lighting up was a ritual analogous to a piece of stage business called for in a playwright's script, as in Bulwer-Lytton's *The Caxtons*:

> he [Peacock] carefully twirled round a very uninviting specimen of some fabulous havanna, moistened it all over, as a boa constrictor may do the ox he prepares for deglutition, bit off one end, and lighting the other from a little machine for that purpose which he drew from his pocket, he was soon absorbed in a vigorous effort (which the damp inherent in the weed long resisted) to poison the surrounding atmosphere. Therewith the young gentleman, either from emulation or in self-defence, extracted from his own pouch a cigar-case of notable elegance,—being of velvet, embroidered apparently by some fair hand, for "From Juliet" was very legibly worked thereon,—selected a cigar of better appearance than that in favor with his comrade, and seemed quite as familiar with the tobacco as he had been with the brandy.
>
> "Fast, sir, fast lad that," quoth Mr. Peacock, in the short gasps which his resolute struggle with his uninviting victim alone permitted; "nothing but [puff, puff] your true [suck, suck] syl-syl-sylva—does for him. Out, by the Lord! 'the jaws of darkness have devoured it up;'" and again Mr. Peacock applied to his phosphoric machine. This time patience and perseverance succeeded, and the heart of the cigar responded by a dull red spark (leaving the sides wholly untouched) to the indefatigable ardor of its wooer.
>
> This feat accomplished, Mr. Peacock exclaimed triumphantly: "And now, what say you, my lads, to a game at cards? . . ." (4.4:1.131–32)

Victorian gentlemen, in short, took their cigar smoking seriously. They might have been more casual about it had the habit not been severely subject to domestic restrictions. Because the stale odor of smoke permeated the upholstered furniture and heavy drapery of Victorian drawing rooms, they had to repair to a distant room set aside for that purpose (Tennyson's successive homes had one), smoke up the chimney (as Tennyson and Carlyle did in the kitchen at the latter's Cheyne Row house), or go outdoors, thus eliminating whatever casualness the occasion might have otherwise had. The same property of tobacco smoke,

---

burne from the brandy bottle, from his customary daily consumption of twenty cigars. Along with judicious diet, exercise, and other wholesome therapy, "He came back from the asylum, much altered in body and mind. Stopping his cigars had improved his stomach" (25:246; 33:320). In the Australian bush, however, cigars served a purpose that was not deleterious but, under the circumstances, the next best thing to nutritious. A character in Reade's *It Is Never Too Late to Mend* offered his famished companion a cigar, saying, "We can't afford to smoke them; this is to chew. It is not food, George, but it keeps the stomach from eating itself" (20:2.192).

applied to hair and clothing, required men who could afford to do so to buy special wearing apparel, quilted and frogged smoking jackets (to be worn only among themselves, in quarters, such as the gun or billiard room, which were sacrosanct to them) and tasseled smoking caps, to keep their hair inviolate.

The offensiveness of the odor in women's nostrils was a powerful reason for enforced abstinence in their presence. Lady Blessington supposedly spoke for most women when, in her novel *Strathern*, she deplored "the filthy and unbearable habit of smoking, a habit which so unblushingly betrays a disregard to the comfort of women, by infecting them with the odour with which our clothes are impregnated. How ladies can submit to receive into their society men who, by this filthy and disgusting habit, render themselves totally unfit for it, has ever been to me a matter of utter surprise."[7] George Meredith, characteristically, put a reverse twist on this prejudice in *Emilia in England*, when Wilfrid Pole, a cigar smoker himself, is repelled by the tobacco odor in Emilia's hair, acquired when she was singing at a village beer party which ended in a brawl. Judith Wilt points out that "he rejects Emilia and the vitality of the Ipley set-to and the simplicity of Emilia's willingness to sing for the peasantry. Several times more Wilfrid finds the tobacco-smoke Emilia impossible to accept, refining on the difference in class and the differences between that image connected with a woman and with a man." His "comic enlightenment" comes when he lights another cigar: ". . . the first taste of the smoke sickened his lips. Then he stood for a moment as a man in a new world. This strange sensation of disgust with familiar, comforting habits, fixed him in perplexity, till a rushing of wild thoughts and hopes from brain to heart, heart to brain, gave him insight, and he perceived his state, and that for all he held to in our life he was dependent upon another: which is virtually the curse of love" (57:290). This exchange of roles is a fragment of a Bildungsroman; as Wilt says, "Wilfrid has made a gain, in any case; heart and brain have made a fledgling connection and something may be built on that."[8]

It was typical of the time that a cigar should have been the vehicle of Wilfrid's small epiphany, because it figured elsewhere in fiction in a related role. Initiation into the adult practice of smoking was a peculiarly Victorian kind of adolescent rite de passage (its survival throughout the twentieth century is one evidence of the persistence of certain Victorian rituals). One of the most memorable episodes of the sort in fiction, it is true, involved an old-fashioned pipe, but it might as well have been a cigar, and Victorian readers may have substituted the one for the other as they read of the ill-timed and disastrous indulgence of Bute Crawley's country-bred teenage son Jim in *Vanity Fair*. He visits his wealthy maiden

Thackeray's illustration to *Vanity Fair*, chapter 34, shows how the Bute Crawleys' expectation of Aunt Matilda's fortune went up in smoke.

aunt at Brighton for the laudable purpose of ensuring, by his ingratiating conduct, that at her death her fortune of £70,000 will fall to his father rather than into the alien hands of his Uncle Pitt. He behaves as he thinks a man of the world should, and ends up, on the fateful night, going tipsily to his room with the revised "notion that his aunt's money should be left to him in preference to his father and all the rest of the family."

Once up in the bed-room, one would have thought he could not make matters worse; and yet this unlucky boy did. The moon was shining very pleasantly out on the sea, and Jim, attracted to the window by the romantic appearance of the ocean and the heavens, thought he would farther enjoy them while smoking. Nobody could smell the tobacco, he thought, if he cunningly opened the window and kept his head and pipe in the fresh air. This he did: but being in an excited state, poor Jim had forgotten that his door was open all this time, so that the breeze blowing inwards and a fine thorough [*sic*] draft being established, the clouds of tobacco were carried downstairs, and arrived with quite undiminished fragrance to Miss Crawley and Miss Briggs.

That pipe of tobacco finished the business: and the Bute Crawleys never knew how many thousand pounds it cost them. (*Vanity Fair*, 34:335)

The other Thackerayan instances of early indulgence had no such disagreeable consequences, although they were useful as incidental touches of characterization. One was a fairly precocious event. In *Pendennis*, "The good-natured Begum's house was filled with a constant society of young gentlemen of thirteen, who ate and drank much too copiously of tarts and champagne, and rode races on the lawn, and frightened the fond mother, who smoked and made themselves sick, and the dining-room unbearable to Miss Blanche. She did not like the society of young gentlemen of thirteen" (53:2.266)—all the less so, she might have added, because they were the cronies of her son, already wild and undisciplined, an all too authentic chip off the block of his father, Sir Francis. Pendennis's own acquisition of the habit, as a young undergraduate of some means—and a doting mother—was more timely:

Pen brought a large box of cigars branded *Colorados, Afrancesados, Telescopios*, Fudson, Oxford Street, or by some such strange titles, and began to consume these not only about the stables and greenhouses, where they were very good for Helen's plants, but in his own study,—which practice his mother did not at first approve. But he was at work upon a prize-poem, he said, and could not compose without his cigar, and quoted the late lamented Lord Byron's lines in favour of the custom of smoking.[†] As he was smoking to such good purpose, his mother could not of course refuse permission: in fact, the good soul coming into the room one day in the midst of Pen's labours (he was consulting a novel which had recently appeared, for the cultivation of the light literature of his own country as well as of foreign nations became every student)—Helen, we say, coming into the room and finding Pen on the sofa at this work, rather than disturb him went for a

[†]These were in *The Island* (1823), II.xix, beginning "Sublime tobacco!" and ending with a rejection of elaborate pipes and hookahs, "Like other charmers, wooing the caress, / More dazzlingly when daring in full dress; / Yet thy [i.e., tobacco's] true lovers more admire by far / Thy naked beauties—Give me a cigar!"

light-box and his cigar-case to his bedroom, which was adjacent, and actually put the cigar into his mouth and lighted the match at which he kindled it. Pen laughed, and kissed his mother's hand as it hung fondly over the back of the sofa. "Dear old mother," he said, "if I were to tell you to burn the house down, I think you would do it." (18:1.173–74)

Given that the normal age for initiation into the adult pleasure of smoking was the middle or late teens, there was visible fatuity in Lady Ann Newcome's roguish exclamation when she inspected the cluttered den of Clive, already in his twenties (and, as an aspiring artist, favoring pipes over cigars): "You horrid young wicked creature, have you begun to smoke already?" (*The Newcomes*, 19:1.194).

Novelists used cigars most interestingly when they availed themselves of the lingering association "the weed" had with indolent self-indulgence or, at the extreme end of the moral scale, sheer villainy. Even the most incidental allusion to cigar smoking could contribute its mite to a developing portrait. Introducing Sir Felix Carbury in the third chapter of *The Way We Live Now*, Trollope gave him a cigar to warn readers of the iniquities they would be watching this young wastrel commit.

> Felix entered the room with a cigar in his mouth and threw himself upon the sofa.
> "My dear boy," said [his mother], "pray leave your tobacco below when you come in here."
> "What affectation it is, mother," he said, throwing, however, the half-smoked cigar into the fire-place. "Some women swear they like smoke, others say they hate it like the devil. It depends on whether they wish to flatter or snub a fellow."
> "You don't suppose that I wish to snub you?"
> "Upon my word I don't know. I wonder whether you can let me have twenty pounds?" (3:21)

In *The Prime Minister*, a cigar completes rather than initiates the portrait of Ferdinand Lopez as Trollope brings that scoundrel and his wife together in what proves to be the final confrontation of their wretched marriage. His scheme to make his fortune by distilling and marketing a Guatemalan spirituous drink called Bois having fallen through, he asks his wife what her plans now are:

> "It is not my duty to have any purpose, as what I do must depend on your commands," [she replies]. Then again there was a silence during which he lit a cigar, although he was sitting in the drawing room. This was a profanation of the room on which even he had never ventured before, but at the present moment she was unable to notice it by any words. "I must tell papa," she said after a while, "what our plans are." (60:2.186)

The issue of Lopez's first profanation of his wife's drawing room with cigar smoke, a belated desecration which she in her misery is unable to protest, is an ironically small one—he has been guilty of far greater transgressions, yet never before of this one—and it is trivial indeed in the shadow of his destroying himself the next day by jumping in front of an express train.

The cigar-smoking habit knew no moral bounds, and it would be perilous for the modern reader to categorize a smoker in a Victorian novel as honest or unscrupulous on that ground alone. In *The Adventures of Philip*, Thackeray ingeniously used an expressed abomination of cigars as an attribute of Philip Firmin's father, a physician who had been artificially elevated in society by running off with a peer's niece and thus was excessively class-conscious. Far from being a tobacco addict, "Dr. Firmin was an enemy to smoking, and ever accustomed to speak of the practice with eloquent indignation. 'It was a low practice—the habit of cabmen, pot-house frequenters, and Irish apple-women,' the Doctor would say, as Phil and his friend [Pendennis] looked at each other with a stealthy joy. Phil's father was ever scented and neat, the pattern of handsome propriety. Perhaps he had a clearer perception regarding manners than respecting morals . . ." (2:1.115–16). Readers need not have known of Thackeray's personal affection for cigars to appreciate his point; it was evident in the number of generally sympathetic characters in his novels, Phil and Pendennis among them, who shared it. To him, one who vocally abominated cigars was, like the musicless man whom Shakespeare's Lorenzo warned against, "fit for treasons, stratagems, and spoils . . . his affections dark as Erebus. Let no such man be trusted." And so, as events proved, the tobacco-hating physician was a despicable, not to say hypocritical, character.

Yet a generally sympathetic character in Thackeray might also be a tobacco-hater. Pendennis knew "full well that to smoke was treason in the presence of the Major" (*Pendennis*, 68:324), and Thackeray admits us to the Major's thoughts as he passed Chevalier Strong, "redolent of Havannah," on a street in St. James's: "Every fellow who smokes and wears mustachios is a low fellow" (62:255). There was a world of moral difference between the Major and George Firmin; but their sharing this deep prejudice simply was one confirmation, among countless others, of Thackeray's steady view of man's mixed, complicated, and inconsistent nature.

Addiction to cigars, along with laziness and the flashy but empty sophistication that his friend Mortimer Lightwood so admires, is among the main attributes of Eugene Wrayburn in *Our Mutual Friend*. Eugene eventually proves not to be a villain, but Dickens's skillful use of traits

The cigar as stage prop and clue to character: "Composedly smoking, he [Eugene Wrayburn] leaned an elbow on the chimneypiece, at the side of the fire, and looked at the schoolmaster" (*Our Mutual Friend*, book 2, chapter 6).

and habits associated with the type leaves the question hanging in the air during most of the novel. He enhances the theatrical quality of the scene in Eugene's and Lightwood's newly acquired rooms in the Temple, in which they are visited by the schoolmaster Bradley Headstone and his protégé Charlie Hexam, by recurrent references to Eugene's cigar, as if the blasé unemployed solicitor was blowing smoke in his humble visitors' faces, matching their truculence with his insolence. In addition, Eugene is several times glimpsed smoking in the street, something that was as yet "not done" in the best circles because it was too reminiscent of the gent and the swell who did. The fact that he no longer smokes cigars after Lizzie rescues his battered body from the river is an especially telling symbol of his moral regeneration. (Not that he could have smoked anyway unless Lizzie helped him, because both his arms were broken.)

A few years earlier, in *The Mill on the Floss*, the cigar served in another case of ambiguous character. Though lacking some of Wrayburn's distinctive traits, young Stephen Guest also was a potential rotter. After the walk in the garden with Maggie during which they realize their attraction for each other, "He spent the evening in the billiard-room, smoking one cigar after another, and losing 'lives' at pool" (6.6:357). Walking home afterward "in the cool starlight," he broods over his passion for

THE FAVORITE VICE OF THE NINETEENTH CENTURY 259

Maggie and his consequent disloyalty to Lucy, his betrothed, the "inner soliloquy" ending as he "threw away the end of his last cigar." There has been sharp critical disagreement over George Eliot's handling of Stephen and Maggie, many if not most readers feeling that she did not satisfactorily establish Stephen as worthy of drowning with Maggie— that her picture of Stephen went in the wrong direction, leaving him to be, in the words of one modern critic, "a vulgarian . . . a coxcomb and an insensitive egotist," and in those of another, "a worthless popinjay." (Swinburne, reading the novel when it first came out, was less restrained: "He should be horsewhipped!") In extenuation, it has been pointed out that Eliot's space restrictions did not allow her to do more than sketch in Stephen's character, no room being left to make him a credibly sympathetic figure.[9] It is noteworthy in any event that Eliot recognized the difficulty and sought, in one significant respect, to change the direction of her portrait: in the ensuing pages of the manuscript, she deleted no fewer than four allusions to Stephen's cigar smoking, as if she wished to downplay that side of his character. Although he had some traits of an incipient libertine, she did not intend him to be a villain.

But Grandcourt, in *Daniel Deronda*, was clearly a villain, as George Eliot made additionally clear by her several allusions to his cigar addiction. One telling touch as she gradually developed his portrait occurred in the archery scene: "he had begun a second large cigar in a vague, hazy obstinacy which, if Lush or any other mortal who might be insulted with impunity had interrupted by overtaking him with a request for his return, would have expressed itself by a slow removal of his cigar to say, in an under-tone, 'You'll be kind enough to go to the devil, will you?" (14:187). Later, in the painful scene in which Grandcourt demands from Lydia Glasher the diamonds he had given her, she tries to paper over the deep rift between them.

> She ventured to lay her hand on his shoulder, and he did not move away from her: she had so far succeeded in alarming him, that he was not sorry for these proofs of returned subjection.
> "Light a cigar," she said, soothingly, taking the case from his breast-pocket and opening it.
> Amidst such caressing signs of mutual fear they parted. The effect that clung and gnawed within Grandcourt was a sense of imperfect mastery. (30:399)

And when Grandcourt and Gwendolen quarrel over his insistence on Lush's presence in their home, and Grandcourt orders her to treat Lush civilly, he is met by "Silence. There may come a moment when even an excellent husband who has dropt smoking under more or less of a pledge during courtship, for the first time will introduce his cigar-smoke between himself and his wife, with the tacit understanding that she will put up with it. Mr. Lush was, so to speak, a very large cigar" (45:626). Deronda, by contrast, was not a smoker, but when he visited the Philosopher's Club of "poor men given to thought,"

> He looked around him with the quiet air of respect habitual to him among equals, ordered whisky and water, and offered the contents of his cigar-case, which, characteristically enough, he always carried and hardly ever used for his own behoof, having reasons for not smoking himself, but liking to indulge others. Perhaps it was his weakness to be afraid of seeming strait-laced, and turning himself into a sort of diagram instead of a growth which can exercise the guiding attraction of fellowship. (42:582)

More than once, as in the case of Grandcourt's Mr. Lush, cigars, like Yorick's skull, furnished a tangible metaphor around which a novelist, or a character in his behalf, could drape a psychological or philosophical observation. In Bulwer-Lytton's *My Novel*, "the stranger" (Lord L'Estrange) philosophizes as twilight falls over a deserted Hyde Park:

> He took out his cigar-case, struck a light, and in another moment, reclined at length on the bench,—seemed absorbed in regarding the smoke, that scarce colored, ere it vanished into the air.
> "It is the most barefaced lie in the world, my Nero," said he, addressing his dog, "this boasted liberty of man! Now, here am I, a free-born Englishman, a citizen of the world, caring—I often say to myself—caring not a jot for Kaisar [*sic*] or Mob; and yet I no more dare smoke this cigar in the Park at half-past six, when all the world is abroad,[†] than I dare pick my Lord Chancellor's pocket, or hit the Archbishop of Canterbury a thump on the nose. Yet no law in England forbids me my cigar, Nero! What is law at half-past eight was not crime at six and a half! Britannia says, 'Man, thou art free,' and she lies like a commonplace woman. O Nero, Nero! you enviable dog!—you serve but from liking. No thought of the world costs you one wag of the tail. Your big heart and true instinct suffice you for reason and law. You would want nothing to your felicity, if in these moments of ennui you would but smoke a cigar. Try it, Nero!—try it!" And, rising from his incumbent posture, he sought to force the end of the weed between the teeth of the dog. (5.4:2.72–73)

In *The Moonstone*, Franklin Blake seeks the company of the steward Betteredge, who recorded that

> he smelt my pipe, and was instantly reminded that he had been simple enough to give up smoking for Miss Rachel's sake. In the twinkling of an

---

[†] It is not clear whether there was an explicit restriction on smoking in the park during certain hours, or whether it was more informally forbidden, as at the Surrey Gardens.

eye, he burst in on me with his cigar-case, and came out strong on the one everlasting subject, in his neat, witty, unbelieving, French way. "Give me a light, Betteredge. Is it conceivable that a man can have smoked as long as I have without discovering that there is a complete system for the treatment of women at the bottom of his cigar-case? Follow me carefully, and I will prove it in two words. You choose a cigar, you try it, and it disappoints you. What do you do upon that? You throw it away and try another. Now observe the application! You choose a woman, you try her, and she breaks your heart. Fool! take a lesson from your cigar-case. Throw her away, and try another!"

I shook my head at that. Wonderfully clever, I dare say, but my own experience was dead against it. "In the time of the late Mrs. Betteredge," I said, "I felt pretty often inclined to try your philosophy, Mr. Franklin. But the law insists on your smoking your cigar, sir, when you have once chosen it." I pointed that observation with a wink. ("First period," chap. 22:194–95)

Blake's renunciation of tobacco (he was later a backslider, if Betteredge can be believed) had severe psychological and physical effects. Betteredge had earlier described the effect of cold-turkey withdrawal on a heavy smoker like Blake:

Though one of the most inveterate smokers I ever met with, he gave up his cigar, because she [Rachel] said, one day, she hated the stale smell of it in his clothes. He slept so badly, after this effort of self-denial, for want of the composing effect of the tobacco to which he was used, and came down morning after morning looking so haggard and worn, that Miss Rachel herself begged him to take to his cigars again. No! he would take to nothing again that would cause her a moment's annoyance; he would fight it out resolutely, and get back his sleep, sooner or later, by main force of patience in waiting for it. ("First period," chap. 8:61–62)

These withdrawal symptoms played a crucial part in the plot. Mr. Candy, the physician, offered to prescribe a tranquilizer to overcome Blake's sleeplessness, but Blake affronted him by saying that "taking medicine and groping in the dark mean one and the same thing" ("Second period, second narrative," chap. 10:430). In friendly retaliation, Candy slipped a dose of laudanum into his grog. It was under the influence of the drug that Blake sleepwalked that night and unconsciously removed the fateful moonstone from Rachel's cabinet.

To the extent that cigar smoking was regarded as a culpable indulgence, renunciation of the habit sometimes figured in male characters' vowing to turn over a new leaf. Protesting his love for Ethel Newcome, young Lord Farintosh cries to her, "I've given up everything—everything—and have broken off with my old habits and—and things you know—and intend to lead a regular life—and will never go to Tatter-sall's again; nor bet a shilling; nor touch another cigar if you like—that is, if you don't like; for I love you so, Ethel—I do, with all my heart I do!" (*The Newcomes*, 59:2.244).

On the other hand, cigar smoking could afford an acceptable substi-tute for a greater vice. In *The Claverings*, Trollope describes the Rever-end Henry Clavering as a model parson despite his too-comfortable cir-cumstances (he had £800 a year of his own, and his wife's fortune brought him double that). "Till within ten years of the hour of which I speak," says Trollope, "he had been a hunting parson,—not hunting loudly, but followed his sport as it is followed by moderate sportsmen. Then there had come a new bishop [it was Proudie!], and the new bishop had sent for him,—nay, finally had come to him, and had lectured him with blatant authority. . . . After that Mr. Clavering hunted no more, and never spoke a good word to any one of the bishop of his diocese. . . . Mr. Clavering hunted no more, and probably smoked a greater number of cigars in consequence . . . and he smoked cigars in his library." "I do not know," Trollope remarks, "whether the smoking of four or five ci-gars daily by the parson of a parish may now-a-day be considered as a vice in him, but if so, it was the only vice with which Mr. Clavering could be charged" (2:14–16). Trollope's readers would have appreciated his point more readily than we do. As a handbook on *The Habits of Good Society* put in 1855, "One must never smoke, without consent, in the presence of a clergyman, and one must never offer a cigar to any eccle-siastic over the rank of a curate."[10] This is capable of two interpretations: either proper clergymen did not smoke cigars—which would imply that though Clavering no longer followed the hounds, his new indulgence, like the former one, ill befitted his cloth—or churchmen, from vicars upward, were expected to supply their own.

The moral barometer had another, characteristically Thackerayan setting in a comparable event in *The Newcomes*, when Clive, prey to his "unsatisfied longing" for Ethel, "passed hours in his painting-room, though he tore up what he did there. He forsook his usual haunts, or appeared amongst his old comrades moody and silent. From cigar-smoking, which I own to be a reprehensible practice [Thackeray's irony is obvious], he plunged into still deeper and darker dissipation; for I am sorry to say he took to pipes and the strongest tobacco, for which there is *no* excuse" (51:2.139).

A word should be added about American cigar smokers in England. Evidently the elaborate etiquette governing the use of cigars once they had become respectable—there were even right and wrong ways of actually smoking them—had no counterpart in the United States, if

Trollope, admittedly not an unbiased observer, is to be believed. A major element in the British stereotype of American politicians and go-getting businessmen during the Ulysses S. Grant era (president, 1869–77) was their ferocious, uncouth smoking manners. Part of Trollope's initial characterization of Senator Elias Gotobed (*The American Senator* [1876–77]) was devoted to this regrettable lack of the polish expected in English society. "Mr. Gotobed, lighting an enormous cigar of which he put half down his throat for more commodious and quick consumption, walked on to the middle of the drive. . . . Then [after a page of dialogue], having nearly eaten up one cigar, he lit another preparatory to eating it, and sauntered back to the house." In a later scene, "It was quite clear that as quickly as the Senator got through one end of his cigar by the usual process of burning, so quickly did he eat the other end. . . . 'I'm sorry to say that I haven't a spittoon,' said Mounser Green, 'but the whole fireplace is at your service'" (1.8:54–55; 2.1:195).[†] A year or two earlier (*The Way We Live Now* [1874–75]), Hamilton K. Fisker, the American speculator-swindler, was seen "smoking a very large cigar, which he kept constantly turning in his mouth, and half of which was inside his teeth" (9:67). English gentlemen, we are to believe, neither chomped nor swallowed their modest medium-sized cigars.

3.

Objectionable though tobacco smoke was to many women, some were prepared to put up with the habit. Indeed, cigars occasionally assisted the course of true love, as when Jane Eyre followed the scent of Edward Rochester's cigar into the moonlit orchard—where it mingled with the fragrance of sweetbriar, jasmine, pink, and rose—and found herself finally in her lover's arms. Elsewhere, a woman's toleration of her lover's or husband's cigar smoking was a readily available expression of her sacrificial love. The fervently anti-nicotinian Lady Blessington spoke from the grave, in her posthumously published novel *Country Quarters* (1850), when she had her heroine grit her teeth and tolerate her fiancé's smoking: "Although the disgusting odour was odious to her, and she turned

---

[†]The discrepancy between American and English cigar customs was not so vast that England could afford to dispense with the spittoons that were so notorious a fixture in American homes and public buildings. "In England the spittoon was usually a circular pan of metal or porcelain, either open or enclosed in a wooden case with a hinged lid, which was covered with leather or some patterned material, so it could masquerade as a footstool. The genteel name *salivarium* was invented, and thus disguised the appliance could and did appear in the dining-room and the study." (John Gloag, *Victorian Comfort: A Social History of Design from 1830–1900* [1961; reprint, Newton Abbot, 1973], pp. 79–80.)

with loathing from the noisome vapour that filled the carriage, infecting her clothes and even her hair, she made it a case of conscience to make no complaint."[11] Some women, handy with the needle, went so far as to embroider personalized cigar cases for favored gentlemen, as we saw above, in the quotation from *The Caxtons*.

The most overt sign of a woman's capitulation, as it was the most loving, was the very act of lighting her man's cigar or pipe. To contemporary readers, there may have been no more affecting passage in *The Cricket on the Hearth*, Dickens's Christmas book for 1845, than the one in which Dot Peerybingle performs this office for her husband, the carrier (modern: truck driver):

> She was, out and out, the very best filler of a pipe, I should say, in the four quarters of the globe. To see her put that chubby little finger in the bowl, and then blow down the pipe to clear the tube; and when she had done so, affect to think that there was really something in the tube, and blow a dozen times, and hold it to her eye like a telescope, with a most provoking twist in her capital little face, as she looked down it; was quite a brilliant thing. As to the tobacco, she was perfect mistress of the subject; and lighting of the pipe, with a wisp of paper, when the Carrier had it in his mouth—going so very near his nose, and yet not scorching it—was Art: high Art, Sir. ("Chirp the First," Penguin edition of *The Christmas Books*, 2:48–49)

Dutch art might be nearer the mark, so full of domestic contentment is the scene, which is the acme, if that is the word, of Dickensian sentimentality. When Thackeray transposed it into scenes in his own novels, altering the setting and substituting a cigar for the cherished, blackened old pipe, he elevated socially, and in effect modernized, a familiar domestic vignette. Helen Pendennis, as we saw, happily fussed about as she indulged her promising undergraduate son, even to putting his cigar in his mouth before lighting it. In the days before she became Clive Newcome's termagant mother-in-law, Mrs. Mackenzie added to Colonel Newcome's enjoyment of a musical evening by lighting his cigar "with her own fair fingers," and later, when her Rosie has married Clive, she—Rosie—takes over the "little kind office" of administering the Colonel's cigar to him "in the daintiest, prettiest way" (*The Newcomes*, 23:1.239; 65:2.282).

But these were only little domestic gestures, and the greatest distance between Dickens and Thackeray in this respect had already been measured off in *Vanity Fair*, two years after Dot Peerybingle lighted John's pipe for him. At Queen's Crawley the little governess, Becky Sharp, is walking with the dashing Captain Rawdon Crawley, son of old Sir Pitt, who observes the proceedings from his window as he takes his pipe and beer:

"O those stars, those stars!" Miss Rebecca would say, turning her twinkling green eyes up towards them. "I feel myself almost a spirit when I gaze upon them."

"O—ah—Gad—yes, so do I exactly, Miss Sharp," the other enthusiast replied. "You don't mind my cigar, do you, Miss Sharp?" Miss Sharp loved the smell of a cigar out of doors beyond everything in the world—and she just tasted one too, in the prettiest way possible, and gave a little puff, and a little scream, and a little giggle, and restored the delicacy to the Captain; who twirled his moustache, and straightway puffed it into a blaze that glowed quite red in the dark plantation, and swore—"Jove—aw—Gad— aw—it's the finest segaw I ever smoked in the world aw," for his intellect and conversation were alike brilliant and becoming to a heavy young dragoon. (11:107)

Becky would take it from there. The next step would be to light Rawdon's cigars, and the step after that would be to light still another man's cigars—George Osborne's, husband of her dear friend Amelia. "How delicious they smell in the open air," she breathed to him as they drank in the moonlit beauty of the sea at Brighton: "How calm the sea is, and how clear everything. I declare I can almost see the coast of France!" (25:234).[†] History is silent as to whether she performed the same service for Lord Steyne, but the odds are strongly in favor of her having done so. But later, after her marriage has suffered numerous vicissitudes, she, Rawdon, and their "little brat," as she calls him with something less than maternal affection, are going down to Queen's Crawley for Christmas. Rawdon senior proposes to take the boy to ride with him on the outside.

"Where you go yourself because you want to smoke those filthy cigars," replied Mrs. Rawdon.

"I remember when you liked 'em though," answered the husband.

Becky laughed; she was almost always good-humoured. "That was when I was on my promotion, Goosey," she said. "Take Rawdon outside with you, and give him a cigar too if you like." (44:433)

The impact on *Vanity Fair's* first readers of Becky's initial feat of female derring-do, her actually taking one puff of Rawdon's cigar, can best be appreciated in the light of a letter Dickens wrote to Forster from

---

[†]There was a reprise of this romantic moment in *Pendennis*, when Pen, smoking out his bedroom window at Lady Clavering's Tunbridge Wells villa, dreams of Blanche. ". . . [H]e hummed a tune which Blanche had put to some verses of his own. 'Ah! what a fine night! How jolly a cigar is at night! How pretty that little Saxon church looks in the moonlight!'" (63:2.269). Allowing for his greater age, Mr. Rochester may have felt a similar euphoria, induced by the synergy of moonlight and nicotine, when he met Jane Eyre in the moonlit orchard.

Lausanne on 11 October 1846, six months before that number of the novel appeared (March 1847). In it, Dickens gave an uproarious description, unfortunately too long to quote here, of a cigar-smoking orgy at his hotel, led by an English pair—a titled mother and her daughter—and joined in by an American lady and two Frenchmen. The daughter alone smoked six or eight cigars, a single one of which, Dickens said, "would quell an elephant in six whiffs." "Conceive this," Dickens urged Forster, "in a great hotel, with not only their own servants, but half a dozen waiters coming constantly in and out! I showed no atom of surprise, but I never *was* so surprised, so ridiculously taken aback, in my life; for in all my experience of 'ladies' of one kind or another, I never saw a woman—not a basket woman or a gipsy—smoke, before!"[12] The scandalous equivalent in our day would seem almost to be a participant's account of group sex performed in that proverbial locale, Macy's window. Becky's transgression was comparatively minor and momentary, but its shock value can hardly be overestimated.

Dickens was no innocent; his experience of the world was as wide as the phrase "'ladies' of one kind or another," including the quotation marks, seems to suggest. In this respect, however, Thackeray was more the man of the world. Three years later, in the February 1850 number of *Pendennis*, he mentioned "ladies"—daughters of Harry Foker's maternal uncle, "the respectable Earl of Rosherville"—one of whom "was a horsewoman and smoked cigars" (39:2.2). Among Harry's guests at dinner up the river at Richmond was the actress Miss Rougemont, a cigar between "her truly vermilion lips," and in a later scene (in the April number) Foker, "expressing his opinion against sporting females" to Blanche Amory at a ball at Clavering House, pointed out "Lady Bullfinch, who happened to pass by, as a horse-godmother, whom he had seen at cover with a cigar in her face" (45:2.70). Notwithstanding Dickens's contrary testimony, ladies, in quotation marks, did smoke cigars, and openly at that, as Thackeray well knew. And in Surtees's *Mr. Sponge's Sporting Tour*, serialized (January 1849–April 1851) in part concurrently with *Pendennis*, readers met Lady Scattercash, formerly the equestrienne Miss Spangles of the Theatre Royal, Sadler's Wells: "she used to do scenes in the circle (two horses and flags)—and she could drive, and she could smoke, and she could sing, and she could swear, and drink not a little."[†] When she brought several of her former colleagues down

---

[†]Thus the serialized text, in the *New Monthly Magazine* for September 1850. When Surtees revised it for book publication, he toned down many such descriptions. This one was altered to ". . . and she could drive, and smoke, and sing, and was possessed of many other accomplishments" (46:324–25), an emendation that simultaneously made Miss Spangles more genteel and more open to suspicion. Was it only the now suppressed swearing and drinking that constituted her "many other accomplishments"?

Fast Young Lady (to Old Gent). "HAVE YOU SUCH A THING AS A LUCIFER ABOUT YOU, FOR I'VE LEFT MY CIGAR LIGHTS AT HOME!"

In 1857, when this drawing appeared (*Punch*, 29 August), "fast young ladies," if they smoked at all, were coming to prefer cigarettes, which were now manufactured domestically.

from London, "the tableau that presented itself to Mr. Sponge" as he returned with Sir Harry's drunken hunting party was "Lady Scattercash, with a cigar in her mouth, and several elegantly-dressed females around her" (in the book, Surtees equipped them all with cigars), who "conversed with them from the open drawing-room windows on the first floor, while sundry good-looking servants ogled them from above," a scene scarcely to be witnessed in any respectable country setting. Here, as elsewhere, a cigar flourished by a female set the tone of the whole description.

At the midpoint of the century, the conventional wisdom was that a cigar-smoking woman could only be an actress or a sporting horse-woman, to whom the habit came naturally through her association with the sort of men who typically smoked cigars. Because certain notorious demimondaines, especially "Anonyma" (Catherine Walters: see pages 537–39 below), were famous for their equestrian skill—"horsebreaker" became in Victorian slang a euphemism for high-class prostitute—that chain of associations permitted novelists like Thackeray and Surtees to convey by implication what they could not say outright.

The habit spread slowly, but eventually it reached the edge of conventional circles.[†] In Lady Blessington's *Marmaduke Herbert* (1847), a venturesome hoyden learned "to smoke cigars, which I have got to like at last, though I hated them at first,"[13] and in Charlotte Yonge's *The Heir of Redclyffe* (1853), reference is made to "a story of a lady who had a cigar-case hanging at her chatelaine, and always took one to refresh her after a ball" (5:47). By the time Miss Braddon wrote *Lady Audley's Secret* (1861–62), it was common knowledge that some generally respectable women indulged in the habit. Finding himself smoking an inferior specimen that his ordinarily reliable tobacconist in Chancery Lane had sold him, Robert Audley advised his aunt, "If ever you smoke, my dear aunt (and I am told that many women take a quiet weed under the rose), be very careful how you choose your cigars" (15:79).

4.

But the sheer size of cigars, if nothing else, preserved the idea that smoking them was "unladylike." By a fortunate accident, it was at this very time that a more suitable alternative became available. Cigarettes were not wholly unknown before then. Admittedly, Thackeray verged on the anachronistic in *The Newcomes* when he had Lord Kew roll a cigarette, the context being the 1840s; but Kew had traveled abroad and no doubt learned to like them there. In the same description of the mixed-company cigar smoking at Lausanne that he sent Forster, Dickens said that "Lady A's" daughter, who must have been a pioneer liberated woman indeed, offered him cigarettes—"good large ones, made of pretty strong tobacco; I always smoke them here, and used to smoke

---

[†]Mark Girouard quotes Constance de Rothschild, aged fifteen, in her diary for 1858: "We talked about ladies smoking in general and about Julia's in particular. We all agreed that we did not like to see a lady smoke regularly day after day but that at times a chance cigar is very pleasant." Girouard hastens to add, however, "Rothschild young ladies were not typical." (*The English Country House*, rev. ed. [New Haven, 1979], p. 36n.)

them at Genoa, and I know them well." (Later, when cigarettes became generally available in England, Dickens smoked them "insatiably" when he was working in the *Household Words* and *All the Year Round* offices; at home and in the company of his male friends, he preferred cigars).[14] University students in the forties imported cigarettes as a faddish alternative to cigars and pipes. In a now forgotten novel, Chichester's *Two Generations* (1851), an undergraduate's sister, "Miss Simper," having examined his Turkish pipes and cigar cases, "actually put a paper cigarette in her mouth and declared it must be 'so funny' to smoke."[15]

Cigars might be unladylike, but no longer were they un-English. Cigarettes, on the other hand, were decidedly "foreign," and the English attitude toward them was heavily colored by the xenophobia that was continually waxing and waning in the Victorian years. This prejudice deepened as more and more men and women from the Continent, the Latin countries particularly, immigrated to London and took over such highly visible neighborhoods as Leicester Square. Spaniards were less in evidence than Frenchmen and Italians, but in *Bleak House* Dickens said that in Somers Town, where Harold Skimpole had his tatty lodgings, there were "a number of poor Spanish refugees walking about in cloaks, smoking little paper cigars" (43:649). (These were probably Carlist exiles.)

The Crystal Palace of 1851 attracted flocks of Latin sightseers with their eternal cigarettes which, contrary to staid English custom, they freely smoked in the streets. Hundreds of thousands of Londoners saw and smelled them for the first time that summer, an experience that would lend familiarity later on to Thackeray's affectionate portrait of the Vicomte de Florac, in *The Newcomes*, who lodged in Leicester Square and "would roll and smoke countless paper cigars, talking unrestrainedly when we [Arthur Pendennis and Warrington] were not busy, silent when we were engaged" (36:1.397).

This association of cigarette smoking with an amiable, honest character was unusual at the time; Florac's attractive personality outweighed his foreignness. In English fiction, as far back as the Gothic romance, a well-established type of villain was the slippery, calculating, conspiring Frenchman or Italian, adept at unspeakable evil. The type still flourished in the Victorian novel, with cigarettes added. In *The Moonstone*, Count Fosco's chainsmoking of the cigarettes rolled to order by his devoted wife is unmistakable evidence of his villainy, even if it is supplanted in the second half of the novel by more eccentric appurtenances—his pet mice, canaries, and vicious cockatoo. Similarly, the first appearance in *Little Dorrit* of Rigaud, chain smoking in the Marseilles prison, identifies him as a potential troublemaker. It is true that his companion, John Baptist Cavalletto, falls under the reader's suspicion for the same reason—which adds to the uncertainty that is part of Dickens's strategy, as would later be the case with Wrayburn and his cigars. But whereas Rigaud, now alias Blandois, continues to smoke while he pursues his machinations in London, and the subservient Cavalletto continues to the end to give him lights, honest Cavalletto himself is no longer seen smoking, an act that would not comport well with either his affectionate standing as "Mr. Baptist" in the Bleeding Heart Yard community or his eventual employment as a skilled pattern-maker in Clennam's machine shop.

Cigarettes began to be domesticated in England when naval officers and soldiers brought them back from the Crimea (1854–56), where they had found them being smoked by the Turks and Russians. That circumstance made it possible for George Meredith to depict a cigarette-smoking *hero*, for Captain Nevil Beauchamp had served in the Crimea, and when he and his friend Palmet take a lunch break from their electioneering, they "smoked a cigarette or two afterward [and] conjured away the smell of tobacco from their persons as well as they could" (*Beauchamp's Career*, 19:1.200).

The smell of tobacco was still objectionable, at least to the electors of Bevisham, and the cigarette-smoking man remained suspect, even though the demand for the product in the wake of the war had increased to the point that the first English cigarette factory was established at Walworth in 1856. The stereotype of the cigar-smoking idler was now remade into the stereotype of the cigarette-smoking idler. Maurice Maule, the middle-aged, occupationless spendthrift in Trollope's *Phineas Redux* (1873–74), killed time between a late breakfast and two o'clock by smoking two cigarettes—a modest enough number—over a new French novel. But after a distressing interview with his son, the soothing routine failed him: he "immediately lit another cigarette, took up his French novel, and went to work as though he was determined to be happy and comfortable again without losing a moment. But he found this to be beyond his power. He had been really disturbed, and could not easily compose himself. The cigarette was almost at once chucked into the fire, and the little volume was laid on one side" (21:186). In *Is He Popenjoy?*, published several years later, the thoroughly unsatisfactory Marquis of Brotherton, who prefers to live in Italy rather than England and has married under questionable circumstances a self-styled Italian marchesa, goes about "all the afternoon in a dressing-gown, smoking bits of paper" (22:1.215).

Lord Silverbridge in the last of the Palliser novels, *The Duke's Children*

(1879–80), also smokes cigarettes—"half-a-dozen . . . one after another" during a single sitting on a bench in St. James's Park (30:237). This was suitable to his youthful character, as the unfledged heir to the family estates and a novice politician. But later in the novel, Trollope portrayed him switching to cigars, as a token of his growing maturity. The sign to readers was unmistakable, for Meredith likewise had Beauchamp take up cigars later in his novel. Cigarettes, in that respect, had not yet come of age. Indeed, in *A Laodicean* (1880–81) Hardy returned to first principles when he tipped off the reader that the brash, young, self-styled citizen of the world, William Dare, was up to no good by making him a cigarette smoker. After watching him perform this operation several times, no reader would have been surprised when the full extent of his villainy—abetted by the fact that he was the illegitimate son of another scoundrel—was disclosed.

The evolving attitudes toward smoking in the middle Victorian years enable us to evaluate the characters more precisely on the basis of their opinions on the matter. We have noticed in other connections the way Trollope used strongly expressed views on topical questions to characterize such persons as Miss Jemima Stanbury, the sixty-year-old possessor of a considerable fortune, in *He Knew He Was Right* (1868–70). In most matters, Miss Stanbury's opinions are notably conservative, not to say reactionary; she is at least a generation behind the "best" current ideas in her thinking on political and religious questions. When her nephew Hugh, a pipe smoker who has deserted the law for penny journalism, visits her in Exeter, he risks her disfavor. "It's past eleven o'clock," he says, "and I must go and have a smoke."

> "Have a what?" said Miss Stanbury, with a startled air.
> "A smoke. You needn't be frightened, I don't mean in the house."
> "No;—I hope you don't mean that."
> "But I may take a turn round the Close with a pipe;—mayn't I?"
> "I suppose all young men do smoke now," said Miss Stanbury, sorrowfully.
> "Every one of them; and they tell me that the young women mean to take to it before long."
> "If I saw a young woman smoking, I should blush for my sex; and though she were the nearest and dearest that I had, I would never speak to her;—never. Dorothy, I don't think Mr. Gibson [a decidedly wishy-washy young clergyman] smokes."
> "I'm sure I don't know, aunt."
> "I hope he doesn't. I do hope that he does not. I cannot understand what pleasure it is that men take in making chimneys of themselves, and going about smelling so that no one can bear to come near them." (31:299–300)

Miss Stanbury is always outspoken, but her opinions, however conservative, usually are not eccentric. Here, however, she is less representative of current thought on one aspect of the matter than on the other. By this time, it had become the accepted thing that "all young men do smoke now"; she spoke for an older generation. But in her refusal to contemplate women smoking, she was in the mainstream. Whether or not, as Stanley Weintraub has observed, "smoking had become, for some women, a feminist statement,"[16] the fact was that with the cigarette coming into general circulation, more women did smoke. This, as Bulwer-Lytton archly put it in *What Will He Do With It?* (1857–59), complicated the relation of the sexes:

> Flora, too, was an heiress; an only child,—spoiled, wilful, not at all accomplished (my belief is that accomplishments are thought great bores by the *jeunesse dorée*), no accomplishment except horsemanship, with a slight knack at billiards, and the capacity to take three whiffs from a Spanish cigarette. That last was adorable,—four offers had been advanced to her hand on that merit alone.—(N.B. Young ladies do themselves no good with the *jeunesse dorée*, which, in our time, is a lover that rather smokes than "sighs like [a] furnace," by advertising their horror of cigars.) (7.1:2.32–33)

Flora represented that alarming phenomenon of the late 1850s, the "fast girl" (see the song quoted by Emily Eden in 1859, page 467 below), who at the end of the next decade was to be metamorphosed into her giddier cousin, Mrs. Lynn Linton's despised Girl of the Period. Although such "liberated" women are sometimes seen in books by both major and decidedly submajor novelists, they seldom smoke cigarettes in the presence of the reader. But lively and semiliberated women inhabit once-popular novels that are now utterly forgotten:

> Cecilia used to be ladylike and good-natured, but now she is always making herself sick with cigarettes; while Julia almost swears at her, and tells her that she makes herself look as ugly as the deuce. (Houstoun, *Recommended to Mercy* [1862])

> In an easy chair sat a very showy young lady, about twenty-five years old, smoking a cigarette. (Mortimer Collins, *Who Is the Heir?* [1865])

> She was leaning back, and had lighted her cigarette, which she was smoking with half-closed eyes and a look of intense satisfaction; her delicate little hand, covered with gems, gleamed soft through the trailing smoke. (Wood, *Rosewarn* [1866])

> She was very fast, and had once been seen under the marble colonnade at the Fountains puffing daintily at a coquettish little cigarette. But it is only fair to add that the daring exploit resulted in deadly pallor and unpleasant

Visitors to the Royal Academy exhibition in 1870 would have found a wider applicability in Frith's painting *At Homburg, 1869* than the localized title suggested. The falling woman, after all, might just as well have been English as, say, a Frenchwoman to whom the habit came naturally, and the subject of "Her First Cigarette" (the painting's informal alternate title) was almost as disturbing to Victorian moralists as a seduction scene.

faintness, and that the experiment was not repeated. (Braddon, *The Lady's Mile* [1866])

Maria [sent] some smoke out at her nostrils, a feat that was immediately followed by a paroxysm of distressing cough. (Brooks, *The Gordian Knot* [1868])[17]

These were books written for the day's market, and it was only to be expected that they would introduce a topicality that was deliciously, but not dangerously, risqué. No young woman who smoked cigarettes could be regarded as a paragon of maidenly virtue, but paragons were not what the circulating library clientele of the 1860s most wanted to read about. They wanted to read about "Ouida's" women, who were not ladies but entertained roistering Guardsmen and smoked any number of cigarettes. It will be noted, however, that in the last two quotations (as perhaps in the other novels cited, if one were to read them) there is a safety net of moralism: women smoked only at the peril of their feminine appeal.

What finally legitimized women's smoking, or at least gave it irrefutable social cachet, was its spread into the Royal family. The Queen herself had gone on record as opposing such a betrayal of the womanly virtues, but one of her daughters, Princess Beatrice, chainsmoked cigarettes as her fiancé, Prince Henry ("Liko") of Battenberg, chainsmoked cigars. "If the pair had a passion for anything at the start," observes the Queen's latest biographer, "it was tobacco." Like her father the Prince Consort before her, who had rehabilitated the cigar, the princess set an example for others to follow, if with occasionally troubled consciences. And eventually the Queen herself came round: on picnics late in life, she is reputed to have smoked cigarettes "to keep the flies away."[18]

9

The Way They Looked

1.

IN THE DAYS of *Sartor Resartus* ("the tailor re-tailored") and Beau Brummell, one man dominated the highest reaches of tailordom. George Stultz was almost providentially named, because Stultz is a mere vowel-slippage away from *stolz*, the German word for "proud," "splendid"—the sort of off-name that Thackeray so often licensed himself to invent. References to him in fiction greatly outnumber the few hard facts we possess. His shop, we know, was at 10 Clifford Street, Bond Street, from 1809 onward. After his retirement or death, the business, subsequently styled Stultz, Binnie, and Company, remained at the same address until 1915. He was not the only fashionable tailor in London—such names as Delcroix and Nugée also occur in Regency records—and he was not even Brummell's (that honor fell to a Mr. Weston of Old Bond Street), but he was by far the most publicized, and his was the only name in his occupation to find its way into so many varied literary contexts over so long a period of time. Stultz was reputed to have become rich catering to the whims and vanities of masculine haute couture, and one book of contemporary gossip, *The English Spy* (1825) by "B. Blackmantle" (Charles Molloy Westmacott), predicted that he would retire with a fortune of £100,000. One of the rare glimpses we have of the actual person is found in the memoirs of the American sculptor G. A. Storey, who recalled seeing him sitting for a bust to be presented to some almshouses he was building in Kentish Town for the relief of less prosperous members of his trade.[1]

The most exalted of Stultz's clients was none other than the Prince Regent. In a letter to her mother in 1831, the novelist Maria Edgeworth wrote of his unlamented death (as George IV) and the preparations necessary to get the royal corpulence in shape so that David Wilkie could paint the official picture of his last days:

it took 3 hours to get him into those clothes!—to lace up all the bulgings
and excrescencies!—The horrid ideot of a Dandy of 60—and what do you
think his last coat cost? A blue silk coat it was charged by *Stultz*—six hundred pounds. The Duke of Wellington was in a tow'ring passion about it
and swore it should not be pe'd [paid?] but when he came to examine into it
Stultz charged no more than he had a right to. For there he was at Windsor
he and two of his men for 3 weeks or more residing o' purpose to try this
coat on every succeeding day and cut it and coax it and fine draw it upon
the old dying dandy and an alteration and fresh seaming at every sitting for
the picture. Why when he was well even he always looked like a great sau-
sage stuffed into the covering but what it must have been at the last—Think
o'n't. The Duke agreed that Stultz had not overcharged—You know the
most fashionable London tailor and his 2 men—Their time worth as much
as a minister o' states and two secretaries'.[2]

Among Stultz's other clients were Wordsworth's sister-in-law, for whom
he made a riding habit in 1829, and John Ruskin, who made his first
appearance on the lecture platform (Edinburgh, 1853) in a Stultz coat,
notwithstanding his frugal wife Effie's opinion of Stultz's prices. In a
letter to her parents from Venice the preceding year, she reported, "I
bought him trowsers and vest of Turkish 'gane', white crossed with
black; it looks so glossy, clean & nice with a blue tie that I shall buy him
another set as they are very cheap & nice in comparison with Stulz's." As
late as 1871–74 the name retained its snob appeal. The artist W. P. Frith
later recalled knowing someone who sympathized with the claim of the
putative "Sir Roger Tichborne" to the title and estate that would be his
if he could prove his identity. "By the way, Sir Roger," said one Captain
N—— whom Frith quoted, "what tailor did you patronize when you
were in London? Were your clothes made in London?" "Sometimes—
generally indeed," he replied. "Do you remember the name of your tailor?" "Yes, Stultz, always."[3]

This was far from proof that the claimant was actually the former
man-about-town he purported to be, because to any reader of fiction
Stultz would have been the first fashionable tailor to come to mind in a
pinch. The name began to acquire its legendary quality when it figured
in run-of-the-mine silver fork fiction in the twenties, and it was doubtless
present also in military novels in which officers ordered their resplendent uniforms and mufti from the best shops in Mayfair. The best-
known novel to contain an early reference to Stultz was Bulwer's *Pelham*
(1828), in which the delicate distinctions of sartorial snobbery were satirized by the disdain that Russelton (= Beau Brummell) expressed for
Stultz's product: "Pray, Mr. Pelham," asks Russelton, "did you try Staub
when you were at Paris?" "Yes," Pelham replies, "and thought him one
degree better than Stultz, whom, indeed, I have long condemned as fit

This pair of dandies might have walked out of any silver fork novel of the time (1838). The odds are better than even that they have been outfitted by George Stultz.

only for minors at Oxford, and majors in the infantry." "True," says Russelton judiciously. ". . . Stultz aims at making *gentlemen*, not *coats*; there is a degree of aristocratic pretension in his stitches, which is vulgar to an appalling degree. You can tell a Stultz coat anywhere, which is quite enough to damn it: the moment a man's known by an invariable cut, and that not original, it ought to be all over with him. Give me the man who makes the tailor, not the tailor who makes the man" (32 : 1.169). Nevertheless, according to Bulwer, the tailor *did* make the man. Describing

Lord Mute, the typical *élégant,* in *England and the English* (1833), he wrote, "He is six feet of inanity enveloped in cloth! You cannot believe God made him—Stultz must have been his Frankenstein."[4]

To other connoisseurs, Stultz's work should have not been dismissed so summarily; the best practice was to make up an eclectic ensemble. In another silver fork novel, T. H. Lister's *Arlington* (1832), the insufferable Arthur Davison, "an overgilt piece of mere ballroom furniture, fitted out under the auspices of Stultz and Delcroix," announces that "Nugée makes my coats, and Stultz my waist-coats, and there is another man who builds my trousers. No tailor can furnish one really well who professes more than one of these departments."[5] Tittlebat Titmouse in *Ten Thousand a Year* was not so finicky. He vowed that his very first mission, once he acquired the aristocratic title that was about to fall into his lap, was to be "rigged out in Stulze's tiptop" (1.12)—a lord of the realm could wear nothing less.

Carlyle borrowed generously from *Pelham* (which he knew from reviews, especially William Maginn's in *Fraser's Magazine,* though there is no evidence that he actually read the book) in the famous passages on the dandy in *Sartor Resartus.* But oddly, in view of what became a veritable obsession with Dandyism and Tailordom as a symbol of the flamboyant phenomena that concealed and distracted attention from the noumenal reality, he did not mention Stultz in *Sartor,* famous though the name was by that time. In 1838, however, when he resumed the clothes-and-dandy metaphor in his essay on Scott in the *Westminster Review,* Carlyle invoked the name when he hoped that two centuries hence "the Stulz swallow-tail . . . will seem as incredible as any garment that ever made ridiculous the respectable back of man."

Disraeli, having alluded in passing to Stultz in *The Young Duke* (1831), made a more substantial reference to him in *Coningsby* (1844), when he described his hero's inexplicable sense of inferiority in the presence of Mr. Melton:

> The genius of the untutored inexperienced youth quailed before that
> of the long practised, skillful, man of the world. What was the magic of
> this man? What was the secret of this ease, that nothing could disturb and
> yet was not deficient in deference and good taste? And then his dress, it
> seemed fashioned by some unearthly artist; yet it was impossible to detect
> the unobtrusive causes of the general effect that was irresistible. Conings-
> by's coat was made by Stultz; almost every fellow in the sixth form had his
> coats made by Stultz; yet Coningsby fancied that his own garment looked as
> it had been furnished by some rustic slopseller. (3.5:183)

Stultz was indispensable to Thackeray's Regency scene. The Hon. Algernon Percy Deuceace, C. J. Yellowplush's employer, owned a "curious

colleckshn of Stulz and Staub coats." The temporarily affluent Sam Titmarsh bought two "Von Stiltz" suits in anticipation of his wedding, and
when the Independent West Diddlesex Fire and Life Insurance Company failed, and Titmarsh with it, Stiltz was the first to sue for his bill.
(Titmarsh's other creditors included Madame Mantalini of *Nicholas
Nickleby* fame, Howell and James, and Polonius the jeweler.) One Colonel
Fitzstultz is mentioned in Thackeray's "A Visit to Some Country Snobs"
(*Punch*, 7 November 1846; *BS*, 139). Major Pendennis's chest was "man-
fully wadded with cotton by Mr. Stultz" (*Pendennis*, 8:1.86), and on his
return to London after many years in India, Colonel Newcome was
looked upon as being somewhat out-of-date, because "he has no mufti
coat except one sent him out by Messrs. Stultz to India in the year 1821"
(*The Newcomes*, 8:1.79). This long-wearing coat, in fact, was one of the
most important single items of clothing in Victorian fiction, epitomizing
as it did the good Colonel's character and his unsettled position in the
unfamiliar society to which he has returned after long absence. Thackeray stressed its functional significance by describing it more particularly
than almost any other garment in his characters' wardrobes:

> a blue swallow-tail, with yellow buttons, now wearing a tinge of their native
> copper, a very high velvet collar, on a level with the tips of the Captain's
> ears, with a high waist, indicated by two lapelles, and a pair of buttons high
> up in the wearer's back, a white waistcoat and scarlet under-waistcoat, and
> a pair of the never-failing duck trousers. . . . We have called him Captain
> purposely, while speaking of his coat, for he held that rank when the gar-
> ment came out to him; and having been in the habit of considering it a
> splendid coat for twelve years past, he has not the least idea of changing his
> opinion. (8:1.79–80)

When he first wears it in the presence of Binnie, his friend and shipmate
on the recent homeward voyage, Binnie chaffs him:

> "It is you, you gad-about, is it? How has the *beau monde* of London
> treated the Indian Adonis? Have you made a sensation, Newcome? Gad,
> Tom, I remember you a buck of bucks when that coat first came out to Cal-
> cutta—just a Barrackpore Brummel—in Lord Minto's reign was it, or when
> Lord Hastings was Satrap over us?"
> "A man must have one good coat," says the Colonel; "I don't profess to be
> a dandy; but get a coat from a good tailor, and then have done with it." He
> still thought his garment was as handsome as need be.
> "Done with it—ye're never done with it!" cried the civilian.
> "An old coat is an old friend, old Binnie. I don't want to be rid of one or
> the other." (8:1.90)

But reflecting on the course of true young love (as he thinks) between
Clive and Ethel, the Colonel realizes that he must keep up with the
times—their times: "I must wear gloves, by Jove I must, and my coat *is*

CARTOON FOR THE MERCHANT TAILORS.

MOSES AND SON ATTIRING YOUNG ENGLAND.

THE novel of Coningsby clearly discloses
The pride of the world are the children of MOSES.
Mosaic, the bankers—the soldiers, the sailors,
The statesmen—and so, by-the-by, are the tailors.
Mosaic, the gold—that is worthless and hollow ;
Mosaic, the people—the bailiffs that follow.
The new generation—the party that claim
To take to themselves of Young England the name' ;
In spite of their waistcoats much whiter than snow,
It seems after all are the tribe of Old Clo !
Then where in the world can Young England repair
To purchase the garments it wishes to wear—
Unless to that mart whose success but discloses
The folly of man, and the cunning of MOSES ?

Disraeli's *Coningsby* (1844)—part silver fork, part political
novel—offered *Punch* a chance to satirize a whole row of sitting ducks, as it did on 22 June of that year (above): Disraeli,
the Young England movement with which he was prominently associated, dandyism, and Moses's cheap clothing. The
strong element of anti-Semitism that linked Disraeli with
Moses cannot be overlooked. It is present, by more than
implication, in Thackeray's illustration (opposite) for "Codlingsby," his parody of *Coningsby* (*Punch*, 24 April 1847),
where the figure of "Rafael Mendoza" (Moses) might easily
be taken to be a caricature of the dandyish Disraeli himself.

"D'you vant to look at a nishe coat?" a voice said, which made him start; and then some one behind him began handling a masterpiece of STULTZ's with a familiarity which would have made the Baron tremble.

old-fashioned, as Binnie says; what a fine match might be made between that child and Clive!" And so he asks his servant, "I say, Kean, is that blue coat of mine very old?"

"Uncommon white about the seams, Colonel," says the man.

"Is it older than other people's coats?"—Kean is obliged gravely to confess that the Colonel's coat is very queer.

"Get me another coat, then—see that I don't do anything or wear anything unusual. I have been so long out of Europe that I don't know the customs here, and am not above learning."

Kean retires, vowing that his master is an old trump. . . . (15:1.169)

Thackeray anticipates an implicit irony at the end of the novel, when the last coat the Colonel wears is not a fashionable new product of Stultz's workshop but the humiliating uniform of a Poor Brother of Grey Friars (Charterhouse).

Kingsley singled out Stultz as one of the "few master tailors, who have built workshops fit for human beings and have resolutely stood out against the iniquitous and destructive alterations in the system of employment" that resulted in the sweatshops he deplored in *Alton Locke* (2:22). Despite whatever inroads E. Moses and Sons and their competitors made in the respectable but not ultrafashionable clothing market, at mid-century the name Stultz remained one to be conjured with. Lord Scamperdale in Surtees's *Mr. Sponge's Sporting Tour* (1849–51) "had an uncommonly smart Stultz frock-coat, with a velvet collar, facings, and cuffs, and a silk lining" (34:226).

Stultz had had a long run, first as a topical and then as a half-legendary figure. Surrounding his symbolic image in the Victorian mind was an active cluster of social, philosophical, and political associations having to do with the tailoring trade. Carlyle's elaborate structural metaphor in *Sartor Resartus* of clothing, particularly dandiacal clothing, as the symbol of the rag-husks that fatally obscure and inhibit the vital activity of man's soul, was part of the permanent furniture of every well-read Victorian's mind. Even apart from its transcendental message, the clothing figure emblematized the essential nature of the slowly evolving social democracy. Breeches were the mark of the old regime: the French revolutionaries were the sans culottes, the men who wore pantaloons—the immediate ancestors of trousers, which were almost universally worn in England after about 1820 except by gentlemen of the old school.[†] And at the center of this sartorial revolution was the man who made it all possible, the tailor.

The tailoring trade and its close partner, shirtmaking, recurred in the headlines of the 1840s because of revelations of the sweated conditions that prevailed in some workshops. Following Hood's "The Song of the Shirt" in *Punch* (1843), the plight of both male and female pieceworkers in the tailoring and haberdashery trades was, as we have seen, brought to the renewed attention of the public by the series of *Morning Chronicle* articles by Henry Mayhew in 1849–50. The hero of *Alton Locke* (1850) was a tailor who turned radical (Chartist) as a result of his experience in a trade that cried out for some kind of intervention. Even if *Punch*, the *Times*, and the *Morning Chronicle* had never published a word on this festering subject, and if *Alton Locke* had never been written, the tailoring trade would have labored under a stigma from which most oth-

---

[†] "Pantaloons" came to be an actual synonym for trousers, seemingly without the mildly comic suggestion the word has today.

ers were free. "Of all the tradesmen in London," wrote Trollope in *Can You Forgive Her?*, "the tailors are, no doubt, the most combative,—as might be expected from the necessity which lies upon them of living down the general bad character in this respect which the world has wrongly given them" (52:553). People in other lines of work—confectioners, wholesale grocers, jewelers—might reasonably aspire to gentility, surmounting the stigma of "trade." But not tailors, perhaps because they came into more intimate physical contact with their clients and, like personal servants, acquired anatomical secrets (as well as choice gossip) they could not divulge. If, as was often said, no man was a hero to his valet, still less was he to his tailor.

This was the leading theme of Meredith's *Evan Harrington*, the definitive account of a socially ambitious Victorian youth's attempt to overcome the disability of being "in trade." The story, a study of a variety of social neurosis that might well be called occupation anxiety, may have been largely fictional, but the emotional fever was all too genuine, because Meredith came from a family of Portsmouth naval tailors, and that shame was as heavy a burden to him in his impressionable years as the memory of the blacking warehouse remained to Dickens throughout his life. "Tailordom" is the word that echoes throughout that early novel of Meredith, and the book is haunted by the ghost of the late Melchisedek ("old Mel" or "the Great Mel") Harrington, a robust, life-loving "character."

In Trollope's *Lady Anna*, too, the word *tailor* echoes through the book as if it had its own peculiar timbre of scorn bordering on outrage. The lone social issue in the novel is the acceptability of a tailor as the husband of a supposed heiress, and in many places Trollope, both authorially and in the speeches of his characters, substitutes the loaded word for the name of his hero, Daniel Thwaite, the son of a Keswick tailor, who himself works in a shop in Wigmore Street, London. If any of Trollope's novels can be said to have a verbal leitmotif, it is the constant iteration of the single statement "I don't think a tailor can be a gentleman." In a letter to a friend while *Lady Anna* was running in the *Fortnightly Review*, he said that the trade he selected for Thwaite best suited his purpose:

> The story was originated in my mind by an idea I had as to the doubt which would, (or might) exist in a girls mind as to whether she ought to be true to her troth, or true to her leneage [*sic*], when, from early circumstances the one had been given in a manner detrimental to the other—and I determined that in such case she ought to be true all through. To make the discrepancy as great as possible I made the girl an Earls daughter, and the betrothed a tailor. All the horrors had to be invented to bring about a condition in which an Earls daughter could become engaged to a tailor without glaring fault on her side.[6]

But social class was not the only issue. The tailoring trade had a long history of political radicalism. Alton Locke was in a line of descent that included John Thelwall, the tailor (and attorney's clerk) who, with the polemic clergyman Horne Tooke, was sent to the Tower in 1794 for his "seditious utterance" but was subsequently acquitted by a courageous jury, and Francis Place, "the radical tailor of Charing Cross," who had begun as an English Jacobin in the 1790s, helped lead the agitation for the First Reform Bill, and ended up as a militant Chartist in the 1830s. Such well-remembered figures doubtless lay behind the remark of one character about another in Payn's *Lost Sir Massingberd*, "One can't hang him, you know, like a radical tailor" (34:318).[†] The Great Mel Harrington, their contemporary, did not share those radical heroes' advanced ideology (at least Meredith does not specify that he did), but the simple fact that he had political ambitions of any kind was radical enough. Mrs. Barrington in the novel recalled that

> ". . . he tried to stand for Fallowfield once. I believe he had the support of Squire Uploft—George's uncle—and others. They must have done it for fun! Of course he did not get so far as the hustings; but I believe he had flags, and principles, and all sorts of things worked ready. He certainly canvassed."
>
> "A tailor—canvassed—for Parliament?" remarked an old Dowager, the mother of Squire Copping. "My! what are we coming to next?" (*Evan Harrington*, 22:274)

In *Lady Anna*, the Thwaites, father and son, conformed to a familiar pattern. The father, said Trollope, "had been a Radical all his life, guided thereto probably by some early training, and made steadfast in his creed by feeling which induced him to hate the pretensions of an assumed superiority." With radicalism came book-reading that concentrated on subversive writings: the two were indelibly associated in the Victorian image of the dangerous tradesman. "Daniel Thwaite was a thoughtful man who had read many books. More's Utopia and Harrington's Oceana, with many a tale written in the same spirit, had taught him to believe that a perfect form of government, or rather of policy, under which all men might be happy and satisfied, was practicable on earth . . ." (4:34–35).

[†]This is doubtless a reminiscence of an episode in French revolutionary days, when the quintessential radical Thomas Paine, a former staymaker, was hung in effigy all over England after the publication of *The Rights of Man*, part 2, in February 1792. The memory of these ritual executions was preserved in numerous caricatures. There is no record that Paine was also a tailor, but the speaker in the novel may have confused him with Francis Place, the actual "radical tailor," who, however, escaped both vicarious and actual hanging.

A little earlier, in *Ralph the Heir* (1870–71), Trollope had introduced as a leading character the prosperous Conduit Street breeches-maker Thomas Neefit, whose products were to the lower half of a fashionable foxhunter's attire what Stultz coats were to the upper. But Neefit's bourgeois ambition was to move up in the world and see his daughter marry in furtherance of that end; it did not drift in the imprudent direction of politics. Elsewhere in Trollope, tailors or their sons did cast their eyes toward Parliament. In *Doctor Thorne* the Barchester election was contested by Sir Roger Scatcherd, a railway-building magnate, and Gustavus Moffat, a tailor's son who had already been a member of Parliament and was a wealthy man to boot.

The advent of working-class M.P.s in the seventies (Thomas Burt, a coal miner, sat for Morpeth from 1874 to 1918) was signalized in Trollope's *Marion Fay* (1881–82), where two radical noblemen, the Marquis of Kingsbury and his son Lord Hampstead, having "doubts about a Parliament of which one section was hereditary," respond by getting a tailor elected from the vestigial pocket borough of Edgware. Unfortunately, this experiment in grass-roots representation does not work out, the tailor forfeiting his chances by turning up drunk on the hustings. Young Lord Hampstead, however, remains attracted to the trade. "I ought to have been a tailor," he ruminates. "Tailors I think are generally the most ill-conditioned, sceptical, and patriotic of men" (1:3–5; 10:70).

2.

Tailors, none more than Stultz, were also the means by which men sought to associate themselves visually with a particular class. Through descriptions of clothing, novelists constantly sent to their readers messages that are not always clear today. As even the best-informed historians of costume, especially women's, confess, there were nuances in the choice of apparel at a given date that only contemporary readers were equipped to detect. Many descriptions, especially of Regency dress, function simply as assurances that the wearers were conforming to the current fashion. On the surface, the diversity of designs, colors, and accessories affected by the male characters in fashionable novels says little more about them than that they were à la mode; it furnishes no information about personality beyond that.

Significant distinctions, however, were at least implied, then and later. Strictly speaking, it was only the dandy who set masculine fashion in his time, which entered its twilight no later than the early 1840s. Almost by definition, it was he alone who was obsessed by the subject of clothes, forever talking of the precise cut of coats and the delicate art of

PRIVATE OPINIONS.

Two *Punch* drawings illustrate the sartorial affinity of the swell and his callow imitator, the gent. (top) "London idlers" (swells) in the issue for 2 July 1842. (bottom) A brisk exchange of compliments between a pair of gents and a shopkeeper (14 January 1843): "GENTS. 'Did you ever see such a rhinoceros?'—RHINOCEROS—'Vell, I never seed sich monkeys!'"

cravat-tying. He was the walking embodiment of the axiom that clothes maketh the man. A swell, on the other hand, while emulating the dandy's dashing demeanor and taste for extravagance, was, in respect to clothes-consciousness, a derivative product: he simply took over the dandiacal wardrobe, stripped it of its essential fastidiousness and restraint, and vulgarized it with loud colors and fancy, eccentric cuts that a true patron of Stultz would never be seen wearing. The third and lowliest member of the triumvirate, the gent, wore the cheapest, ready-made versions of swell attire, its calico shirts with their false fronts complemented by flashy costume jewelry, dirty ears, hair greasy with the products of Rowlands (or one of the firm's down-market competitors), and, as we have seen, foul-smelling cigars.[7]

All three breeds of costumed coxcombs were in evidence in the 1840s. The full-rigged dandy was fading from view; his social inferior, the swell, was more in evidence as he patronized gambling clubs, illegal prize fights, and race courses; the gent did his best, on a severely limited budget, to emulate the swell. The raffishness with which sartorial splendor was associated led to its becoming more and more confined by mid-century to the country sporting set.

This is the background that Thackeray's readers brought to his novels set in the Regency and the following two decades. Sometimes he could provide, by a single phrase or a telling detail, such as Colonel Newcome's blue Stultz coat, the clue from which a reader might construct a complete image of a man, in this case a typical officer, past middle age, who had been abroad for many years. But Thackeray often went into more detail, and where his description departed in one respect or another from the norm, a reader would have been able to differentiate that wearer with a knowledgeability that is sometimes beyond our reach.

Jos Sedley's wardrobe—elegant, splendid, and a bit more obtrusive than was considered in the best of taste—was as sure an index of his character as any of his speeches or actions. "Jos," said Thackeray, "was as vain of his person as a woman, and took as long a time at his toilette as any fading beauty" (*Vanity Fair*, 57:555). When he and Dobbin return from India, his first order of business, even before proceeding to London to see his mother and sister, is to outfit himself anew:

> There are some splendid tailors' shops in the High Street of Southampton, in the fine plate-glass windows of which hang gorgeous waistcoats of all sorts, of silk and velvet, and gold and crimson, and pictures of the last new fashions in which those wonderful gentlemen with quizzing glasses, and holding on to little boys with the exceeding large eyes and curly hair, ogle ladies in riding habits prancing by the Statue of Achilles at Apsley House. Jos, although provided with some of the most splendid vests that Calcutta could furnish, thought he could not go to town until he was supplied with

Dickens's prototypical gents, when they were in pocket, had as much of an appetite for the good things of life as did their betters. (above) Dick Swiveller, in *The Old Curiosity Shop*, momentarily renounces that appetite, vowing to "abstain from all intoxicating and exciting liquors." (opposite) William Guppy, Bart Smallweed, and Tony Jobling, in *Bleak House*, treat themselves to dinner at a restaurant "of the class known among its frequenters by the denomination Slap-Bang."

> one or two of these garments, and selected a crimson satin, embroidered with gold butterflies, and a black and red velvet tartan with white stripes and a rolling collar, with which, and a rich blue satin stock and gold pin, consisting of a five-barred gate with a horseman in pink enamel jumping over it, he thought he might make his entry into London with some dignity. For Jos's former shyness and blundering blushing timidity had given way to a more candid and courageous self-assertion of his worth. "I don't care about owning it," Waterloo Sedley would say to his friends, "I am a dressy man. . . ." (59:570)

This, Thackeray implies, was an understatement.

Three characters in *Pendennis* dressed in styles that represented varieties of dandiacal dress. Major Pendennis, now out of uniform, wore a kind of mufti that still identified him as a retired officer:

At a quarter-past ten the Major invariably made his appearance in the best blacked boots in all London, with a checked morning cravat that was never rumpled until dinner time, a buff waistcoat which bore the crown of his sovereign on the buttons, and linen so spotless that Mr. Brummel himself asked the name of his laundress. . . . Pendennis's coat, his white gloves, his whiskers, his very cane, were perfect of their kind as specimens of the costume of a military man *en retrait*. (1 : 1.1)

Pendennis's old schoolfellow Harry Foker, in contrast, had no military record to affect his choice of dress, and therefore, says Thackeray, when he turned up at Chatteris after a year's absence he

appeared before Pen in one of those costumes to which the public consent, which I take to be quite as influential in this respect as Johnson's Dictionary, has awarded the title of "Swell." He had a bulldog between his legs, and in his scarlet shawl neckcloth was a pin representing another bulldog in gold: he wore a fur waistcoat laced over with gold chains; a green cut-away with basket buttons, on each of which was engraved some stirring incident of the road or the chase; all of which ornaments set off this young fellow's figure to such advantage, that you would hesitate to say which character in life he most resembled, and whether he was a boxer *en goguette*, or a coachman in his gala suit. (*Pendennis*, 3:1.31)

Much more a man of the world than the youthful Foker, Monsieur Alcide Mirobolant, the chef at Clavering, walked out

> in his usual favourite costume, namely, his light-green frock or paletot, his crimson velvet waistcoat with blue glass buttons, his *pantalon Écossais* of a very large and decided check pattern, his orange satin neckcloth, and his jean-boots, with tips of shiny leather,—these, with a gold embroidered cap, and a richly-gilt cane, or other varieties of ornament of a similar tendency, formed his usual holiday costume . . . in which he considered that he exhibited the appearance of a gentleman of good Parisian *ton*. (23:1.231)

—the laudable ambition of any follower of fashion of English soil.

After these dazzling versions of dandiacal costume, readers may have found something likable in Thackeray's more restrained description of what Pen wore, even though he too was "dandified": "His white duck trousers and white hat, his neckcloth of many colours, his light waistcoat, gold chains, and shirt-studs, gave him the air of a prince of the blood at least" (49:2.109). There were, Thackeray seems to be saying, dandies and dandies; and Pen was of the better—salvageable—breed.

In some circumstances other novelists of Thackeray's generation continued the silver fork tradition of elaborately describing male attire. In his capacious send-up of (among other things) the fashionable novel, *Ten Thousand a Year*, Samuel Warren devoted many long paragraphs to the successive dandyish ensembles Tittlebat Titmouse donned, with Stultz's assistance, in his gaudy progress from lowly draper's assistant to spurious aristocrat. Surtees described the dress of his sporting characters, aptly named "the fancy," with faithful minuteness; some of his inventories, in *Mr. Sponge's Sporting Tour* for example, ran to more than a full page each, beginning with the hat, ending with the boots, and lingering over every button in between. In his sharp-eyed delineations of riders to the hounds, Surtees followed his forerunner, "Nimrod" (G. L. Apperley), in differentiating the classes involved. "The *style* of your Meltonian fox-hunter," wrote Nimrod, "has long distinguished him above his brethren of what he calls the *provincial* chace. When turned out of the hands of his valet, he presents the very *beau-idéal* of his *caste*. The exact Stultz-like fit of his coat, his superlatively well-cleaned leather breeches and boots, and the general apparent high breeding of the man, can seldom be matched elsewhere."[8]

But as Surtees made plain to readers who could appreciate the differences, there were also ignorant, clumsy interlopers and hangers-on, no true sportsmen, who joined the attendant festivities from self-interested motives. He looked with an equally informed and critical eye at what they wore, betraying their ignorance of the true mode, and at non-sporting partygoers who happened to have links with the hunting set. When he said that Mr. Stotfold in *Mr. Facey Romford's Hounds* (1864–65) dressed "in the brightest, gaudiest colours: pea-green coat, with canary-coloured vest, sensation ties, Garibaldi shirts" (42:271)—the latter two being particularly topical items of dress, the first reflecting the current rage for "sensation" in fiction and the theatre, the other the Italian patriot's ongoing struggle to liberate his nation from Austria—no further "placing" was needed. Given this comprehensive word-coverage, John Leech's illustrations for *Handley Cross, Mr. Facey Romford's Hounds*, and *Mr. Sponge's Sporting Tour* seem almost superfluous.

Dickens's male characters wore clothing that ran the whole gamut of styles from the 1820s to the 1860s, and from old-fashioned lawyers and sober-suited businessmen to thieves and gents. Nothing could be more indulgently indicative of John Chivery's moonstruck character as he hopelessly pursued Amy Dorrit than the dandyish outfit he wore in the 1820s.

> He was neatly attired in a plum-coloured coat, with as large a collar of black velvet as his figure could carry; a silken waistcoat, bedecked with golden sprigs; a chaste neckerchief much in vogue at that day, representing a preserve of lilac pheasants on a buff ground; pantaloons so highly decorated with side-stripes that each leg was a three-stringed lute; and a hat of state very high and hard . . . a pair of white kid gloves, and a cane like a little finger-post, surmounted by an ivory hand marshalling him the way that he should go. . . . (*Little Dorrit*, 1.18:258)

John was merely the son of the gatekeeper at the Marshalsea prison, and as such had no claim to be a dandy, though he was a prototypical gent. In Mr. Dombey, the incongruity of dress and station worked in another way. Dombey was wealthy enough to qualify for the latest fashions, but he was also middle-aged and coldly calculating, in no way romantic, in his successful courtship of the haughty Edith Skewton. The splendid costume he chose for their wedding was, under these circumstances, heavily ironic in its unsuitability: "Gorgeous are Mr. Dombey's new blue coat, fawn-coloured pantaloons, and lilac waistcoat; and a whisper goes about the house, that Mr. Dombey's hair is curled" (*Dombey and Son*, 31:520).

No other Dickens character, it is safe to say, affected dandiacal dress because his social position entitled him to do so, least of all Montague Tigg as he is first seen in *Martin Chuzzlewit*:

> The gentleman was of that order of appearance which is currently termed shabby-genteel, though in respect of his dress he can hardly be said to have been in any extremities, as his fingers were a long way out of his gloves,

and the soles of his feet were at an inconvenient distance from the upper
leather of his boots. His nether garments were of a bluish grey—violent
in its colours once, but sobered now by age and dinginess—and were so
stretched and strained in a tough conflict between his braces and his straps,
that they appeared every moment in danger of flying asunder at the knees.
His coat, in colour blue and of a military cut, was buttoned and frogged
up to his chin. His cravat was, in hue and pattern, like one of those mantles
which hairdressers are accustomed to wrap about their clients, during the
progress of the professional mysteries. His hat had arrived at such a pass
that it would have been hard to determine whether it was originally white
or black. . . . He was very dirty and very jaunty; very bold and very mean;
very swaggering and very slinking; very much like a man who might have
been something better, and unspeakably like a man who deserved to be
something worse. (4:97)

The very nature of his dress proclaimed the man. And so did the
spectacular metamorphosis that occurred when, having lighted on a
highly promising form of swindling, he reversed his name and bought—
undoubtedly on credit—a new wardrobe:

He had a world of jet-black shining hair upon his head, upon his cheeks,
upon his chin, upon his upper lip. His clothes, symmetrically made, were
of the newest fashion and the costliest kind. Flowers of gold and blue, and
green and blushing red, were on his waistcoat; precious chains and jewels
sparkled on his breast; his fingers, clogged with brilliant rings, were as un-
wieldy as summer flies but newly rescued from a honey-pot. The daylight
mantled in his gleaming hat and boots as in a polished glass. And yet,
though changed his name, and changed his outward surface, it was Tigg.
Though turned and twisted upside down, and inside out, as great men have
been sometimes known to be; though no longer Montague Tigg, but Tigg
Montague; still it was Tigg: the same Satanic, gallant, military Tigg. The
brass was burnished, lacquered, newly-stamped; yet it was the true Tigg
metal notwithstanding. (27:496–97)†

The most fraudulent adoption of dandiacal dress, of course, was Turveydrop's, the spurious Regency buck who had long outlived the fashion
but still clung to it, a grotesque effigy complete with a padded-breasted
waistcoat, big neckcloth, wig, white gloves, cane, quizzing glass, wristbands, a hat of "great size and weight" and a form so tightly laced that
there were creases in his eyeballs (*Bleak House*, 14:242–44).

---

†Robert Colby has ingeniously argued that the attire of the crooks in *Oliver Twist* represents an inversion of the dandiacal. "Bill's overdressed accomplice Toby Crackit, with his
'smartly cut snuff-coloured coat, with large brass buttons; an orange handkerchief,' and
his red-dyed hair 'tortured into long corkscrew curls,' is a grotesque version of a Regency
fop." (*Fiction with a Purpose* [Bloomington, Ind., 1967], p. 115.)

Dickens made a specialty of old men who retained the fashions of the age preceding the Regency, the last years of the eighteenth century, although in some instances, such as that of Mr. Brownlow, the "old gentleman" in *Oliver Twist*, Dickens may be implying that the clothing was not so much outmoded as simply conservative, the style that older men preferred. Brownlow's irascible friend Mr. Grimwig, who was forever threatening to eat his head, "was dressed in a blue coat, striped waistcoat, nankeen breeches and gaiters, and a broad-brimmed hat, with the sides turned up with green. A very small-plaited shirt-frill stuck out from his waistcoat, and a very long steel watch-chain, with nothing but a key at the end, dangled loosely below it" (14:147).

These were, roughly speaking, Mr. Pickwick's contemporaries, as were Dr. Blimber in *Dombey and Son*, with his old-fashioned black suit and breeches, the Cheeryble brothers and their foil, the miserly Gride, in *Nicholas Nickleby*, Dr. Strong in *David Copperfield*, and the ancient clerk Chuffey in *Martin Chuzzlewit* (a dreary contrast to the resplendent, retailored Tigg Montague). In one case, that of Tulkinghorn in *Bleak House*, Dickens used a selection of clothing as an insistent motif, introduced early on and periodically repeated whenever Tulkinghorn made an important reentrance: "He is of what is called the old school—a phrase generally meaning any school that seems never to have been young—and wears knee-breeches tied with ribbons, and gaiters or stockings. One peculiarity of his black clothes, and of his black stockings, be they silk or worsted, is, that they never shine. Mute, close, irresponsive to any glancing light, his dress is like himself" (2:58–59). The knee breeches tied with ribbons, the gaiters or stockings (Dickens will later add a "wisp" of limp white handkerchief and designate the general effect of the dull black coat and waistcoat as "rusty") are part of Dickensian old men's standard attire. Readers could fill out their images of Tulkinghorn by borrowing additional details from other characters of the same age: gold spectacles and powdered head (Brownlow), hair gathered behind with a black ribbon (Gride). Ralph Nickleby was younger, but he affected an old-fashioned sprinkling of powder on his hair, thus borrowing from persons like Brownlow the suggestion (deceptive, in Ralph's case) of benevolence.

Black suits such as Tulkinghorn wore were, for the most part, the giveaway uniforms of men who were not to be trusted, among them Pecksniff and the lawyers Conversation Kenge and the vulturelike Vholes in *Bleak House*. That Dickens, introducing Pancks in *Little Dorrit*, clothed him in "black and rusty iron-gray," was clearly intended as a stroke of ambiguity: would the dirty rent collector for his slumlord boss, Casby, conform to the established pattern, or turn out to be on the side of the angels?

Individual items of dress carried their own implications. Dickens was much concerned with neckwear: neckerchiefs colored (red with Sam Weller, brightly checked with Dick Swiveller), white (with Cheeryble); frilled shirts (Ralph Nickleby, Wickfield, Tulkinghorn); stiff, starched cravats (Carker and Dombey—in the latter case, an unmistakable expression of his stiff-necked character). The possession of a silk handkerchief was an ambiguous indication of status. Handkerchiefs were, as Dickens pointed out in *Oliver Twist*, "decided articles of luxury" that were "for all times and ages, removed from the noses of paupers by the express order of the [workhouse] board, in council assembled" (3:59). Millions of people who were not paupers could not afford to buy them in pristine condition at the steep price of four or five shillings. But they were, for that reason, valuable items in the thieves' market, as Oliver soon discovered; one that was stolen from a gentleman's pocket could bring the light-fingered purloiner ninepence, and even with the severe markup applied by a fence like Fagin, when it resurfaced on the secondhand market, a silk handkerchief was no longer the luxury item it had once been.

Dickens paid most attention to what his under-class characters wore—the poor, the petty criminal, even the shabby genteel. Their clothing, like that of the families and friends straggling through the gate of the Marshalsea to bring food to the insolvent prisoners, was both miscellaneous and fortuitously assembled: "Such threadbare coats and trousers, such fusty gowns and shawls, such squashed hats and bonnets, such boots and shoes, such umbrellas and walking-sticks, never were seen in Rag Fair. All of them wore the cast-off clothes of other men and women, were made up of patches and pieces of other people's individuality, and had no sartorial existence of their own proper" (*Little Dorrit*, 1.9:131).

The condition of the clothing worn by men and women and the air with which they wore it were as potent clues to their characters as the nature of the individual items. Bill Sykes wore a dirty belcher neckerchief (named for a famous pugilist) and "very soiled" drab breeches; Quilp's white neckerchief was limp, crumpled, and dirty; Chuffey's black suit was "decayed"; Dick Swiveller's handkerchief was large and dirty, and he had to wear his hat the wrong side foremost to hide a hole. Dr. Strong's clothes were "not particularly well brushed, and his hair not particularly well combed; his knee-smalls unbraced; his long black gaiters unbuttoned . . ." (*David Copperfield*, 16:282).

In the strongest possible contrast, Dickens's description of old Nandy, the workhouse inmate in *Little Dorrit*, is a masterpiece of nonspecification, intensifying his conception of a human being living perilously on the very margin of existence, bewildered, meager, featureless. His clothing belongs to no time: it is the very antithesis, the negation, of "fashion":

> If he were ever a big old man, he has shrunk into a little old man; if he were always a little old man, he has dwindled into a less old man. His coat is a colour, and cut, that never was the mode anywhere, at any period. Clearly, it was not made for him, or for any individual mortal. Some whole-sale contractor measured Fate for five thousand coats of such quality, and Fate has lent this old coat to this old man, as one of a long unfinished line of many old men. It has always large dull metal buttons, similar to no other buttons. This old man wears a hat, a thumbed and napless and yet an obdu-rate hat, which has never adapted itself to the shape of his poor head. His coarse shirt and his coarse neck-cloth have no more individuality than his coat and hat; they have the same character of not being his—of not being anybody's. Yet this old man wears these clothes with a certain unaccustomed air of being dressed and elaborated for the public ways; as though he passed the greater part of his time in a nightcap and gown. (1.31:413)

The closer Dickens's men came to the present time-setting, the less colorful their outfits were. Mr. Brownlow's and Ralph Nickleby's coats had been bottle green; Micawber had worn a brown surtout, and both Captain Cuttle and Wickfield had blue suits, though the cuts probably differed, as befitted an old salt and a Kentish lawyer. One of the Cheer-ybles had a broad-skirted suit of the same color. Even though the tone was dull, Sam Weller's, Cheeryble's, and Flintwinch's "drab" (yellowish brown) breeches and gaiters relieved the stark white and black items of their costumes. But Ralph Nickleby's grey mixture pantaloons and the pepper-and-salt ones worn by Morfit, Dombey's office clerk, were symp-tomatic of the great change that came over "respectable" masculine dress in the early Victorian years. As the painter Frith was later to lament, distinctive details of material, ornament, and color gave way to mo-notony in all except the portion of contemporary society described by Surtees. Beau Brummell's eccentric dictum that black and white were the only colors suitable for evening wear, no matter how bright a man of fashion's daytime apparel might be, had become orthodoxy even in the daylight hours, when brown and gray coats and perhaps pepper-and-salt or checked trousers made out of heavier material than heretofore, were a favored kind of middle-class garb. The other kind was, appro-priately enough, called "ditto," the entire suit being made of the same material and color. "Ditto" also may have referred to the fact that the cuts of garments too were standardized, so that by the sixties male dress had become, in effect, a mufti uniform, noteworthy for its very incon-spicuousness and impersonality, as well as its shapeless, baggy trousers.

Thus the schoolmaster Bradley Headstone, a representative, though

particularly ill-paid, white-collar worker of the 1860s, embodied the extreme reaction against multicolored dandyism, "in his decent black coat
and waistcoat, and decent white shirt, and decent formal black tie, and
decent pantaloons of pepper and salt, with his decent silver watch in
his pocket and its decent hair-guard round his neck"—"a thoroughly
decent young man of six-and-twenty," as Dickens summed him up, who
"was never seen in any other dress . . ." (*Our Mutual Friend*, 2.1:266).
This was the conventional garb of the professional man, a status to which
he had no claim but toward which he fervently aspired. But Dickens
neatly undercut the pretension with the iterated "decent," which was the
standard term of condescending approval used by journalists when they
described a workingman who had somehow figured in a news event as
"decently dressed" and thus an exceptional member of his class. The
word had ineradicable class connotations, as did "respectable," which
replaced it later in the novel, in a short reprise (2.6:342).

In this latter-day society of conformist fashion, little was left for a
novelist to describe. Readers of Trollope would have known what his
men wore without his telling them, because their real-life counterparts,
wearing sack coats or lounge suits in the later novels, crowded every
respectable street and inhabited every respectable home. And in any
case, the illustrations that now accompanied many Victorian novels, including the four of Trollope's for which Millais drew, would have afforded whatever visualization was needed.

One other item of masculine fashion was facial hair. In the century's
earliest decades, mustaches (or, in tribute to their foreign associations,
mustachios) were affected mainly by military types and fops; they were
occasionally a sign of fraudulence, as with Mr. Mantalini and Tigg Montague. Jos Sedley grew one to identify himself as a soldier when he
escorted his sister Amelia to Brussels on the eve of Waterloo, hastily
removed it in order to join the exodus of noncombatants when the heat
of battle came too close for comfort, and resumed it when, back in India,
he assumed the role of self-described "Waterloo veteran." Rawdon
Crawley, as an army officer, was fully entitled to wear mustachios and
was one of those who habitually twiddled them. Colonel Newcome wore
them on the same basis, and his son Clive on another. "In his youth,"
says Thackeray, Clive "was of the ornamental class of mankind—a cus-
tomer to tailors, a wearer of handsome rings, shirt-studs, mustachios,
long hair, and the like" (*The Newcomes*, 24:1.251). On his return from
Italy, he had Truefitt the barber remove "a great portion of the flowing
locks and yellow beard which he had brought with him from Rome," but
"with his mustachios he would not be induced to part; painters and cavalry officers having a right to those decorations" (40:2.16).

Whiskers were more common, and so widely distributed in the male population that they were virtually classless. Many muddy-booted countrymen wore them. Hobson Newcome, "a good old country gentleman," "allowed his red whiskers to grow wherever Nature had planted them, on his cheeks and under his chin" (*The Newcomes*, 6:1.63), a fitting accompaniment to his thick, hobnailed shoes, broad-brimmed hat, and the samples of beans or corn he carried in the pocket of his cutaway coat. Red whiskers ran in the family: Hobson's twin brother, Sir Brian, M.P., bore them in the best London drawing rooms. The townsman Fred Bayham, in the same novel, had "great red whiskers" that "curl[ed] freely round his capacious jowl" (12:1.138). Arthur Pendennis sported them as a young man, as did his Oxford friend Pysent. So did, among others, Alfred Lammle, the frustrated fortune hunter in *Our Mutual Friend*, the ex-soldier Bagnet in *Bleak House*, and Morfin, the clerk in *Dombey and Son*, whose whiskers were prematurely white.

The full beard appeared in fiction just after the middle of the century; like the domestication of cigarettes, it was thought of as a by-product of the Crimean War, although Trollope attributes to another exotic source, the Holy Land, the glossy, patriarchal beard that Bertie Stanhope wore as he precipitated the debacle at Mrs. Proudie's reception. "Such clothes and such a beard!" thought the scandalized elderly clergymen whom he brashly tried to engage in conversation (*Barchester Towers*, 11:221).† Wilkie Collins noted the beginnings of the hirsute

†The frequently seen statement that beards arrived in England when the army returned from the Crimea must be modified in light of the fact that when Britain declared war on Russia at the end of March 1854, they had already appeared on civilians' cheeks and chins. As early as the preceding 5 November, *Punch* ran a cartoon on "The Beard and Moustache Movement," and during the next year it published at least ten cartoons and satirical paragraphs on the new vogue. A light-hearted piece in the *Illustrated London News* for 4 February 1854 derided the conservatism that had inhibited Englishmen from adopting a fashion that had appeared on the Continent a dozen years earlier: "it was an abomination in English eyes, and was never seen, unless occasionally in aged eccentrics ripe for Bedlam, or on the chins of ancient Hebrews who cried 'Old Clo' through the streets of the metropolis." Now stokers, masons, and even policemen in some towns gloried in their hirsuteness. Countering the claim that the fashion was "unscriptural" because the Bible contained no word on whether men should or should not shave, the writer remarked, "Adam must have worn his beard. Abraham is always represented as having had a large and flowing one; and Moses and Aaron are never portrayed, by painter or sculptor, without the manly, and in them, the venerable appendage. . . ." He also pointed out that in Charles Mackay's *Memoirs of Extraordinary Popular Delusions* it was said that "shaving the face was a Monkish innovation; and that Protestantism ought, in reality, to protest against the razor"—all of which was doubtless in the minds of the Barchester clergy as they gazed upon Bertie Stanhope.

THE BEARD AND MOUSTACHE MOVEMENT.

Punch saluted the new hirsute fashion before it spread to all social classes in the aftermath of the Crimean War. If these drawings are authentic documentation, two of the earliest occupational groups to cultivate beards were (above) railway guards and porters (5 November 1853)—the apprehensive old lady, mistaking the porter for a brigand, tells him to take all her luggage, "but spare, oh spare our lives!"—and (opposite) policemen ("Punch's Almanack" printed in the first issue of 1854).

revolution in *The Dead Secret*, serialized in *Household Words* in 1857, the year after the war ended:

> In the year eighteen hundred and forty-four [he wrote], the fact of a man's not shaving was regarded by the enlightened majority of the English nation as a proof of unsoundness of intellect. At the present time, Mr. Treverton's beard would only have interfered with his reputation for respectability. Thirteen years ago, it was accepted as so much additional evidence in support of the old theory that his intellects were deranged. He was at that very time, as his stockbroker could have testified, one of the sharpest men of business in London; he could argue on the wrong side of any question with an acuteness of sophistry and sarcasm that Doctor Johnson himself might have envied; he kept his household accounts right to a farthing, . . . but what did these advantages avail him, in the estimation of his neighbours . . . when he wore a hairy certificate of lunacy on the lower part of his face? We have advanced a little in the matter of partial toleration of beards since that

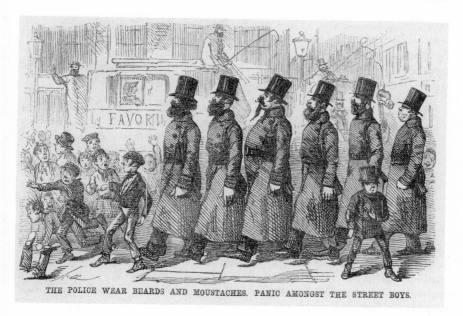

THE POLICE WEAR BEARDS AND MOUSTACHES. PANIC AMONGST THE STREET BOYS.

time; but we have still a great deal of ground to get over. In the present
year of progress, eighteen hundred and fifty-seven, would the most trustworthy banker's clerk in the whole metropolis have the slightest chance of
keeping his situation if he left off shaving his chin?

(In the 1861 edition [3.1 : 118], the text was appropriately revised, "thirteen years" being replaced by "seventeen years" and "eighteen hundred
and fifty-seven" by "eighteen hundred and sixty-one.")

But Collins did not allow for the irresistible contagion that fashion
brings with it. Within a short time he and his friend Dickens were
wearing beards, and even bankers' clerks, trustworthy or not. Carroty
Kebbel, the peripatetic, roistering attorney in Surtees's *Ask Mamma*
(1857–58), was "Crimean-bearded," as were a number of men in minor
novels that made special efforts to be timely. "[N]ow even the shopkeepers wear them," remarked a character in a novel called *The Marstons*
(1868).[9] Before the great change, a bearded man in fiction raised questions; afterward, the only safe inference to be drawn from his beard was
that he was a creature of a new habit.

3.

Ordinarily, as we have noted, a modern reader can interpret with reasonable confidence the messages that descriptions of men's clothing con-

veyed to a novel's contemporary audience. The case is quite different
with women's dress, which involved a whole system of nuances that have
evaporated with the passage of more than a century and can be reconstructed only through the expertise of professional historians of costume; and even they, in the end, confess bafflement:

> Some colours [write C. Willett and Phillis Cunnington] were more ladylike
> than others; some were unsuitable for certain regions of the dress; some
> were unfit for the widow or the maiden; or for particular seasons of the
> year, and there were some that were never correct for the Perfect Lady.
> One had to distinguish between a "warm" and a "cold" colour, the two
> never to be placed in juxtaposition on a dress but separated by a "neutral."
> A gloomy satisfaction was derived from the proper use of black for mourn-
> ing, and the precise depth of crape to be worn was subject to rule. . . . In
> short, colours had a significance which is now lost.[10]

Thackeray ordinarily mentioned that his women wore bonnets, pel-
isses, and robes of certain colors (he had a definite bias toward pink),
and let it go at that. Dickens could be more specific on occasion, although
none of his descriptions of female dress could be mistaken, as Trollope's
might, for literal translations of hand-colored fashion plates into words.
His eye was always on the exceptional costume, the one that told more
about its wearer's peculiar physicality and manifestations of feminine
vanity than about her affiliation with a certain social class. Thus he introduced the thirty-five-year-old Sally Brass, she of the "gaunt and bony
figure," "dirty-sallow" complexion, and unforgettably "deep and rich
voice":

> Her usual dress was a green gown, in colour not unlike the curtain of the
> office window, made tight to the figure, and terminating at the throat,
> where it was fastened behind by a peculiarly large and massive button.
> Feeling, no doubt, that simplicity and plainness are the soul of elegance,
> Miss Brass wore no collar or kerchief except upon her head, which was in-
> variably ornamented with a brown gauze scarf, like the wing of the fabled
> vampire, and which, twisted into any form that happened to suggest it-
> self, formed an easy and graceful head-dress. (*The Old Curiosity Shop*, 33:
> 320–21)

Fanny Squeers, too, was a special case. When, "in a desperate flutter as
the time approached" for Nicholas Nickleby to take tea with her and her
friend Tilda Price,

> she was dressed out to the best advantage: with her hair—it had more than
> a tinge of red, and she wore it in a crop—curled in five distinct rows up to
> the top of her very head, and arranged dexterously over the doubtful eye;
> to say nothing of the blue sash which floated down her back, or the worked

apron, or the long gloves, or the green gauze scarf worn over one shoulder and under the other, or any of the numerous devices which were to be as so many arrows to the heart of Nicholas. (*Nicholas Nickleby*, 9:170)

Refashioning herself at the Saracen's Head inn on arriving in London after riding in the same coach as Tilda and her new husband, John Browdie, Fanny built on the foundation already laid and produced a masterpiece of fine excess:

> To have seen Miss Squeers now, divested of the brown beaver, the green veil, and the blue curl-papers [which she had worn during the overnight journey], and arrayed in all the virgin splendour of a white frock and spencer, with a white muslin bonnet, and an imitative damask rose in full bloom on the inside thereof: her luxuriant crop of hair arranged in curls so tight that it was impossible they could come out by any accident, and her bonnet-cap trimmed with little damask roses, which might be supposed to be so many promising scions of the big one—to have seen all this, and to have seen the broad damask belt, matching both the family rose and the little ones, which encircled her slender waist, and by a happy ingenuity took off from the shortness of the spencer behind,—to have beheld all this, and to have taken further into account the coral bracelets (rather short of beads, and with a very visible black string) which clasped her wrists, and the coral necklace which rested on her neck, supporting outside her frock a lonely cornelian heart, typical of her own disengaged affections—to have contemplated all these mute but expressive appeals to the purest feelings of our nature, might have thawed the frost of age, and added new and inextinguishable fuel to the fire of youth. (39:589–90)

Little Miss Tox, in *Dombey and Son*, was much better connected socially. She was also, as the Victorians would say, of a certain age, and as Dickens did say, "a lady of what is called a limited independence," and therefore his account of "her habit of making the most of everything" had more than a hint of pathos:

> Miss Tox's dress, though perfectly genteel and good, had a certain character of angularity and scantiness. She was accustomed to wear odd weedy little flowers in her bonnets and caps. Strange grasses were sometimes perceived in her hair; and it was observed by the curious, of all her collars, frills, tuckers, wristbands, and other gossamer articles—indeed of everything she wore which had two ends to it intended to unite—that the two ends were never on good terms, and wouldn't quite meet without a struggle. She had furry articles for winter wear, as tippets, boas, and muffs, which stood up on end in rampant manner, and were not at all sleek. She was much given to the carrying about of small bags with snaps to them, that went off like little pistols when they were shut up; and when full-dressed, she wore round her neck the barrenest of lockets, representing a fishy old eye, with no approach to speculation in it. (1:56)

As was to be expected, women novelists were more attentive to the nice points of female fashion. They found costume and coiffure a convenient way of establishing time-settings and quietly intimating the character of their women insofar as it was manifested by their conformity with, or detachment from, the styles of their day. Charlotte Brontë said of Maria Temple, the superintendent of the Lowood School in *Jane Eyre*, "on each of her temples her hair, of a very dark brown, was clustered in round curls, according to the fashion of those times, when neither smooth bands nor long ringlets were in vogue; her dress, also in the mode of the day, was of purple cloth, relieved by a sort of Spanish trimming of black velvet; a gold watch (watches were not so common then as now) shone at her girdle" (5:52–53). A little later, a pupil's hairstyle, supposedly inappropriate in such a setting, offends Mr. Brocklehurst, the school visitor: "Julia Severn, ma'am!" he exclaims to Miss Temple. "And why has she, or any other, curled her hair? Why, in defiance of every precept and principle of this house, does she conform to the world so openly—here in an evangelical, charitable establishment—as to wear her hair one mass of curls?" "Julia's hair curls naturally," Miss Temple quietly replies (7:71).

Elizabeth Gaskell also used fashions in her sedulous effort to establish Cranford as a backwater of time, where women's fashions arrived late, if they arrived at all:

> Their dress is very independent of fashion; as they observe, "What does it signify how we dress here at Cranford, where everybody knows us?" And if they go from home, their reason is equally cogent: "What does it signify how we dress here, where nobody knows us?" The materials of their clothes are, in general, good and plain, and most of them are nearly as scrupulous as Miss Tyler, of cleanly memory [Robert Southey's aunt, in his *Life and Correspondence*, 1849]; but I will answer for it, the last gigot, the last tight and scanty petticoat in wear in England, was seen in Cranford—and seen without a smile. (*Cranford*, 1:2)

Describing Mrs. Tulliver in the opening pages of *The Mill on the Floss* (1860), George Eliot said she was "a blond comely woman in a fan-shaped cap (I am afraid to think how long it is since fan-shaped caps were worn—they must be so near coming in again. At that time [1829], when Mrs. Tulliver was nearly forty, they were new at St. Ogg's, and considered sweet things)" (1.2:9). Later, when her sister, Mrs. Pullet, takes off her cap, she displays "the brown silk scalp with a jutting promontory of curls which was common to the more mature and judicious women of those times" (1.9:81). A "trait of Miss Brooke's asceticism" as Eliot described her in the early pages of *Middlemarch* was that "she wore her brown hair flatly braided and coiled behind so as to expose the out-

Thackeray's illustration for his parody "prize novel," "Crinoline"
(*Punch*, 4 September 1847), was among the earliest of the scores
of caricatures the vogue inspired.

line of her head in a daring manner at a time when public feeling required the meagreness of nature to be dissimulated by tall barricades of
frizzed curls and bows, never surpassed by any great race except the
Feejeean" (3:49).

The single fashion in women's costume extensively memorialized in
Victorian fiction was the crinoline, of which Thackeray spoke in his ex-
postulation in *The Adventures of Philip* already quoted (page 179).[11]
During the crinoline's run of two decades in the middle of the century,
it was the object of incessant ridicule. As early as *Punch*'s issue for 10 October 1846 (*BS*, 123), in "A Visit to Some Country Snobs," Thackeray
noted the presence of these novel contrivances at an evening entertain-

ment: "Very broad backs [of the musical ladies] they were too, strictly according to the present mode, for crinoline or its substitutes is not an expensive luxury, and young people in the country can afford to be in the fashion at very trifling charges. Miss Emily Ponto at the piano, and her sister Maria at that somewhat exploded instrument, the harp, were in light blue dresses that looked all flounce, and spread out like Mr. Green's balloon when inflated." One of Thackeray's "Punch's Prize Novelists" parodies (*Punch*, 4 September 1847) was titled "Crinoline, by Je——mes Pl——sh, Esq."

The word *crinoline* originally referred to petticoats of flannel or cotton stiffened with horsehair (French: *crin*) that women wore, instead of more expensive petticoats of down or feathers, to achieve the desired dome-like amplitude of the dress skirt, which at the height of the fashion might be twelve feet in circumference and required twenty yards of material. Unfortunately, several of the cheaper garments were needed where a single costlier one would serve. This was a considerable burden for a woman, supposedly the "weaker vessel," to bear, but British engineering and metallurgical know-how came to her rescue with a cross-barred "cage" or "steel" crinoline, which replaced the weighty petticoats. This was made possible in 1856 by Sir Henry Bessemer's opportune perfecting of a method of making sprung steel, which evidently was the ideal structural material for the purpose. The *Times* soberly reported the following year that forty thousand tons of high-grade Swedish iron had been imported to meet the demand. Queen Victoria denounced the crinoline as an "indelicate, expensive, dangerous, and hideous article."† George Meredith, writing in the *Ipswich Journal*, denounced its effects, how seriously we cannot tell: ". . . morally worse than a *coup d'état*. It has sacrificed more lives [through combustion?]; it has utterly destroyed more tempers; it has put an immense division between the sexes. It has obscured us, smothered us, stabbed us." Florence Nightingale, the clergy, and the medical profession vehemently concurred.[12]

Assisted by *Punch's* relentless campaign of gibes and cartoons, the crinoline became a stock joke, which novelists, always eager for a universally understood touch of timeliness, delighted in exploiting. In *Hide and Seek* (1854), Wilkie Collins described "an emaciated fine lady, who de-

† Indelicate it was, and dangerous too. The steel cage improvement was a boon to casual voyeurs, because as it tipped, it exposed its wearer's ankles, and even more; "Women getting into omnibuses," wrote the observant Sir William Hardman, "servant-girls cleaning door-steps, and virgins at windy seaside watering places, all show their —— on occasion." (*A Mid-Victorian Pepys*, p. 262.) A crinoline also made it possible for a lady to ignite. Lady Dorothy Nevill caught fire in her Hampshire home while showing a friend an engraving of Richard Cobden that hung over the fireplace. With admirable presence of mind, she saved herself by rolling up in the hearth rug. (Duncan Crow, *The Victorian Woman*, p. 125.)

EASIER SAID THAN DONE.

Master of the House. "OH, FRED, MY BOY—WHEN DINNER IS READY, YOU TAKE MRS. FURBELOW DOWN STAIRS!"

When the amplitude of crinolines was increased by the invention of the steel cage in 1856, so was the scope of the cartoonists' hyperbole. Here John Leech depicts one of the numerous practical problems the new structure created (*Punch*, 19 July 1856).

ceitfully suggested the presence of vanished charms by wearing a balloon under her gown—which benevolent rumor pronounced to be only a crinoline petticoat" (2.5 : 337). Blithely disregarding the anachronism (*Little Dorrit* [1855–57] was set thirty years earlier), Dickens included among the guests at the Merdles' grand dinner party "a countess who was secluded somewhere in the core of an immense dress, to which she was in the proportion of the heart to the overgrown cabbage. If so low a simile may be admitted, the dress went down the staircase like a richly brocaded Jack in the Green,[†] and nobody knew what sort of small per-

---

[†]Explained by the Penguin editor as "A traditional May-day figure who went in the spring procession hidden inside a framework of newly-cut leafy branches."

son carried it" (1.21:295). The heroine of the short fiction that Charley
Tudor wrote for the new halfpenny paper in *The Three Clerks* (1858) was
named Crinoline.

Surtees's last novels, especially *Plain or Ringlets?* (1859–60), were full
of complaints against the crinoline on the dual grounds of gross imprac-
ticality and incongruity. In a quadrille, he wrote,

> Great was the wheeling, and circling, and spreading, and guiding of crino-
> line, and divers the apologies of the fair obstructionists for stopping each
> other's ways. But with a little patience and mutual concession, each fair lady
> at length got through her portion of the figure. Better have been stopped
> altogether than not have carried her full complement of crinoline. Wonder-
> ful fashion! We suppose we shall have the other extreme next, and dresses
> as scant as they are now inflatedly full. (10:24–25)

Dress, Surtees said in another place in *Plain or Ringlets?*,

> has made a marvellous spring since the introduction of railways. Ladies,
> whose mothers used to get all their things into a moderate sized box and
> a carpet-bag, travel with great piano-forte-case-like packages, so numer-
> ous that they are obliged to be numbered for fear they forget how many
> they have. And the more they take the more they want to take, till each
> lady looks as if she ought to have a luggage-van to herself. Then, to see
> them attempt the entry of a moderate sized carriage; the utter dispropor-
> tion of the door to the "object," as it may well be called, that seeks admis-
> sion! The absurdity of fashion might be tolerated if it inconvenienced only
> the wearer; but when one lady extends herself to the size of two, she nec-
> essarily takes up the room of two, and must exclude some one else from
> a seat. . . . The only advantage we see in the absurdity is, that it forms a
> sort of graduated scale of gentility; the more extravagant a woman is in
> her hoops, the less inclined we are to think her a lady. It is only the vulgar
> who go into extremes, and make themselves look like curtains to bathing-
> machines. (32:121)

In addition, said Surtees at various places, there was the nuisance of "oft-
recurring collisions" when the space available for maneuvering was insufficient for the number of ambulant hoops. Narrow doorways could
be negotiated only with difficulty, certainly at some expense to dignity,
and at the dinner table a lady's crinoline overflowed onto the lap of the
gentleman sitting next to her, thus preventing him from spreading his
napkin. Caught in a wind, ladies descending from the carriages were
"driven past their port like peacocks with their tails up on a windy day."
These "rotatory haystacks" inspired a spate of Surteesian metaphors:
"moving balloons," "bell-glasses," "inflated" ladies sitting "looming on
their chairs, like hens upon broods of chickens."

Mrs. Gaskell joined the satirical fun with a piece called "A Cage at
Cranford," published in *All the Year Round* in 1863, ten years after the

NEW OMNIBUS REGULATION.

Crinolines were as inconvenient to women traveling as they were in the drawing room. "Werry sorry 'm," says the conductor to his fair prospective passenger, "but yer'l 'av to leave yer Krinerline outside" (*Punch*, 2 October 1858). Presumably the garments ladies shed before boarding a bus were carried free.

book appeared. One of her Parisian friends was Madame Mohl, the eccentric widow of an Orientalist, who kept a salon in the rue du Bac, where Mrs. Gaskell wrote parts of *Wives and Daughters*. One of Madame Mohl's phobias was the crinoline, which she regarded as "the downfall of society. With its coming she observed a shift from intelligence, esprit and politics to dress."[13] Gaskell did not take the crinoline all that seriously, and in her *All the Year Round* contribution she revived the *Cranford* character of Miss Pole, who received from a friend in France a "cage" which was, in fact, the by then familiar wired structure designed to support the vast yardage of dress material, but which, in her Cranford innocence, she took to be a birdcage.

Crinolines were still modish in 1864–65, when Mrs. Greenow, the young widow in *Can You Forgive Her?*, who had no reason not to be fashionable, included one in her mourning finery. But now, at last, the decline began. In 1866 a well-known corsetiere advertised "a thousand crinolines at half-price. . . . Beautiful shapes but a little dusty." (The historian of nineteenth-century shopping who reports this sensibly wonders where she stored a cool thousand of those monstrous structures.)[14] *Punch* ran pictures of maidservants discarding their crinolines in imitation of their mistresses, and householders using their daughters' outmoded wardrobe to protect their garden shrubs from frost.

By the time of *The Eustace Diamonds* (1871–73), the crinoline had become totally passé, having been replaced by the bustle, which Trollope described as "a dorsal excrescence appended with the object surely of showing in triumph how much absurd ugliness women can force men to endure" (35:358). The bustle had been in fashion in the 1830s and 1840s—Surtees mentioned it in *Hillingdon Hall*—but the crinoline had then, in a quite literal sense, eclipsed it. In its resurrected form, it achieved heroic dimensions in the 1880s, when it could reputedly accommodate a good-sized tea tray on its shelf-like surface.

Only once did another fashion momentarily divert humorists and novelists from their—at that time nascent—crinoline obsession. This was provided from America in the late summer of 1851, when Mrs. Amelia Bloomer, having failed to persuade her countrywomen to wear trousers—so much more practical and healthful than any skirts, not to say crinolines—arrived in London with several fellow enthusiasts. When they began handing out circulars addressed to the "Mothers, Wives and Daughters of England" at the Crystal Palace and in St. James's Park, they were threatened with a ducking or worse. They soon gave up their crusade, leaving behind only a fresh topic for antireformers and moralists to hash over and the *Punch* crowd, assisted by Leech's busy pencil, to hone their wit upon in a season when the Crystal Palace was exhausting its immediate topicality and they needed a new sure-fire comic theme. Among the numerous timely references Surtees included in the reissue in monthly parts of *Mr. Sponge's Sporting Tour* (1852–53)—the original serialization had concluded in April 1851, before the arrival of Mrs. Bloomer's liberating cadre—was the added characterization of the poetry-writing Miss Grimes, "a young lady of a certain age—say liberal thirty" and desperate to find a cause that would stave off the prison-house shades of middle age, as "an ardent Bloomer" (38:264). In the extended version of *Handley Cross* (1853–54), two other Bloomerites turned up, in the persons of the hostess of the Turtle Doves Hotel and the lovely Constantia, who "may afternoonly [*sic*] be seen reclining elegantly on a rose-coloured sofa, in the full-blown costume of a Bloomer" (62:438). At her wedding both she and her bridesmaids wore Turkish trousers.

About this time, Charles Reade wrote a short story, "The Bloomer," which was first published in his volume *The Course of True Love Never Did*

Run Smooth (1857). In it, Caroline Courtenay is a convinced Bloomerite, who gives a drawing-room lecture demonstration during which she invokes historical precedent for the garment by comparing it with the "very spacious trousers" of Persian women, concluding that "pantaloons are not necessarily masculine nor long skirts feminine." Her insistence on wearing what her fiancé averred "three-fourths of her sex think indelicate" has blighted their romance and in fact postponed their marriage until, by a fortunate turn of events, Reginald finds himself in imminent danger of drowning (4:129, 121). The betrousered Caroline plunges into the water and, unhampered by heavy skirts, saves him. It is all very light-hearted and topical, but one remembers that neither Grace Harvey that same year (in Kingsley's *Two Years Ago*) nor Lizzie Hexam afterward wore pantaloons, yet they too saved their men.

Succeeding the bloomer as a fashion issue which in fictional situations, at least, might prevent the course of true love from running smooth was a new fashion in women's coiffures. As the quotations from *Jane Eyre, The Mill on the Floss*, and *Middlemarch* earlier in this chapter have shown, curls (or ringlets) alternated or coexisted with braids and smooth bands as standard hairstyles during the early decades of the century, and as contemporary engravings affirm, this alternative fashion lasted down to the fifties. The plot of *Plain or Ringlets?* hinged on the choice the heroine, Rosa McDermott, had to make between two suitors, Jack Bunting, who liked her to dress her hair in the plain fashion, and Jasper Goldspink, who preferred her in ringlets. But a development in the middle and late sixties would render the issue moot and at the same time compensate for the fading of the crinoline as a stock subject of masculine humor. This was the chignon, a large lump or coil worn on the back of the head or lower, on the nape of the neck, which had last been in vogue in the century's opening years. All three of the styles from which a fashionable lady could choose—"massed coils; massed plaits; or the chignon 'à marteaux' consisting of a row of vertical sausage-shaped curls pinned down to prevent their floating loose"—required more hair than nature ordinarily supplied, and so the difference had to be eked out by "false hair" (false, that is, insofar as it was not indigenous to the wearer), an imported commodity whose price rose sharply as a consequence.[15] The total product, including the net to hold it, cost from thirty to sixty shillings over the counter.

"Charming old Lady Tippins," in *Our Mutual Friend* (1864–65), was up to the fashionable minute: "a dyed Long Walk[†] up to the top of her

---

[†] A reference to the three-mile avenue, then lined with stately elms, in Windsor Great Park. The walk terminated at the summit of Snow Hill with its famous prospect of the Thames Valley.

BLOOMERISM—AN AMERICAN CUSTOM.

In *Punch*'s eyes, the Bloomer fad in 1851 had two counts against it: it arrived, uninvited, from America, always the breeding ground of odd—that is to say, un-English—practices, and its proponents could be envisioned as stalwart females whose penchant for cigars identified them as "fast women" and therefore, by another associational leap, feminists. The cartoon (top) (5 July) is by John Tenniel, the other (bottom) (27 September) by Leech.

While the "Bloomers" Leech drew for *Punch* were ill-favored Amazons, in conformity with that paper's prejudices, the one he portrayed in an illustration for Surtees's *Handley Cross* was simply a pretty girl—neither an American nor a proto-feminist—who happened to be wearing trousers beneath her abbreviated crinoline as, under something of a handicap, she attempted a curtsy before the gouty Sir Thomas Trout.

head" served as "a convenient public approach to the bunch of false hair behind" (1.2:53). A few years later, in *He Knew He Was Right* (1868–69), Trollope enlarged the new style from an incidental topicality into a major theme that contributed to both characterization and plot. The opinionated Miss Jemima Stanbury is as obsessed with chignons as David Copperfield's Aunt Betsey was with donkeys, or for that matter Mr. Dick with King Charles's own, but chignonless, head.

> In the days of crinolines she had protested that she had never worn
> one,—a protest, however, which was hardly true; and now, in these later
> days, her hatred was especially developed in reference to the head-dresses
> of young women. "Chignon" was a word which she had never been heard
> to pronounce. She would talk of "those bandboxes which the sluts wear
> behind their noddles;" for Miss Stanbury allowed herself the use of much
> strong language. (7:64)

She used similarly strong language on the same topic at least eight times in the course of the novel: the obsession seems to have been as much Trollope's as her own. As she grows more and more tiresome on the subject, the chignon, like the controversial bloomer in Reade's story, be-

JEMIMER HANN'S LAST SWEET THING IN HEAD-DRESSES!

By 1861, when this cartoon appeared in *Punch* (2 November), the humorous potential of the crinoline was finally being exhausted, but the newest women's fashion, the chignon, supplied a fresh butt for masculine ridicule. Women may well have found the "Balaclava helmet" worn by the dustman, an article of clothing brought back from the Crimea, equally absurd.

comes a bargaining chip in Arabella French's amatory negotiations with Mr. Gibson, the parson. Arabella's hair

> was very thin in front, and what there was of supplemental mass behind,— the bandbox by which Miss Stanbury was so much aggrieved,—was worn with an indifference to the lines of beauty, which Mr. Gibson himself found to be very depressing. A man with a fair burden on his back is not a grievous sight; but when we see a small human being attached to a bale of goods which he can hardly manage to move, we feel that the poor fellow has been cruelly over-weighted. Mr. Gibson certainly had that sensation about Arabella's chignon. And as he regarded it in a nearer and a dearer light,—as a chignon that might possibly become his own, as a burden which in one sense he might himself be called upon to bear, as a domestic utensil of [*sic*]

GREAT SHOW OF CHIGNONS.

Although one or two details suggest a show of the Horticultural Society, this satire of chignons in *Punch* (21 July 1866) drew upon a more immediate topicality. The annual exercises of volunteers organized as the National Rifle Association took place that month at Wimbledon, and one of the major events was a ceremonial inspection of the ranks.

> which he himself might be called upon to inspect, and, perhaps, to aid the shifting on and the shifting off, he did begin to think that that side of the Scylla gulf ought to be avoided if possible. (47:440)

He broaches the matter in an ensuing scene, subsequent to which Arabella, in the privacy of an interview with her mirror, reluctantly capitulates. Trollope notes and satirizes the resulting absence of Arabella's bulky ornament in deference to Mr. Gibson's views. But then Mr. Gibson jilts her and marries her sister instead. Miss Stanbury immediately lights upon the reason why women have such bad luck as to fall in love with parsons who don't know their own minds and have no scruples against jilting one sister in favor of another: "It all comes from their wearing chignons." But at least Arabella has the tact to leave her chignon at home when she visits Miss Stanbury in her sickroom.

One would think that by this time Trollope had exhausted the comic possibilities of the chignon, but he still could not quite let it go. In his next novel but one, *Ralph the Heir*, Clarissa Underwood wore her hair "according to the fashion of the day, with a chignon on her head; but"—and here we may detect a hint that the joke was indeed growing thin—"beneath that there were curls which escaped, and over her forehead it was clipped short, and was wavy, and impertinent,—as is also the fashion of the day" (2:1.21), and an indication of Clarissa's "impertinent" (= saucy) temperament.

In *The Eustace Diamonds* the very absence of the chignon was used to characterize both Lady Eustace and Lady Linlithgow, to different effects. Trollope stressed Lady Eustace's physical attractiveness: "very lovely," he called her at the outset of his long description, in which he constantly undercut his praise with more than a mere hint of deception: "Her hair, which was nearly black—but in truth with more of softness and of lustre than ever belong to hair that is really black—she wore bound tight round her perfect forehead, with one long love-lock hanging over her shoulder.[†] The form of her head was so good that she could dare to carry it without a chignon, or any adventitious adjuncts from a hairdresser's show. Very bitter [i.e., condescendingly sarcastic] was she in consequence when speaking of the headgear of other women" (2:55). Lady Linlithgow, who had her own faults, nevertheless was honest, as her refusal to submit to deceitful fashion suggested: "Her appearance on the whole was not prepossessing, but it gave one an idea of honest, real strength. What one saw was not buckram, whalebone, paint, and false hair. It was all human—hardly feminine, certainly not angelic, with perhaps a hint in the other direction—but a human body, and not a thing of pads and patches" (6:89). Later in the novel, Lady Linlithgow, like Miss Stanbury before her, communicates her opinion of chignons to a younger woman, but Lucy Morris proves, happily, to be no Arabella French:

> "Perhaps you consider yourself pretty [she says to Lucy]. It's all altered now since I was young. Girls make monsters of themselves, and I'm told the men like it;—going about with unclean, frowzy structures on their head, enough to make a dog sick. They used to be clean and sweet and nice—what one

---

[†] These details illustrate how freely novelists followed one another in putting together their pen-portraits of women. The styling of Lady Eustace's "nearly black" hair emulated that of black-haired Aurora Floyd's and red-haired Lydia Gwilt's "plaited coronets." Gwilt, too, wore "one vagrant love-lock, perfectly curled, that dropped over her left shoulder" (see below, pages 319 and 323). A methodical analysis of the way women looked in Victorian fiction would reveal the extent to which such descriptions, like the women described, depended on the clichés of current fashion. They might have been derived as much from colored engravings as from life.

would like to kiss. How a man can kiss a face with a dirty horse's tail all whizzling about it, is what I can't at all understand. I don't think they do like it, but they have to do it."

"I haven't even a pony's tail," said Lucy. (34:348)

4.

It is not surprising that reflections of the coming and going of hairstyles should have contributed to the contemporaneous "feel" of Victorian fiction; this would have been true of any period in which changing fashions of dress were a significant part of social life. It was less to be expected that evolving attitudes toward the very color of a woman's or a man's hair—and, more important, the words used to describe it—should not only add to a novel's timeliness but provide the writer with a further means of quick characterization. But so it was in Victorian England.

A variety of words was used to describe acceptable tints for the hair of women of all ages short of terminal gray or white: black (usually called either "jet" or "raven"), dark brown (including "nut-" and "chestnut-" brown), light brown, "flaxen," "tawny," and "golden." As the crowning glory of an extended line of women in folklore, literature, and art, golden hair had a complex set of meanings to the Victorians. Elisabeth Gitter has recently noted that when Rossetti says of Lilith, "her enchanted hair was the first gold,"

> he is alluding not to any legend about Lilith herself but to a long literary tradition of gold-haired ladies. . . . While women's hair, particularly when it is golden, has always been a Western preoccupation, for the Victorians it became an obsession. . . . Golden hair, through which wealth and female sexuality are inevitably linked, was the obvious and ideal vehicle for expressing their notorious—and ambivalent—fascination both with money and with female sexual power.[16]

But all the hair that glittered in Victorian fiction was not gold. Some of it was red, and red hair too had special meaning to contemporary readers. The unidentified author of an essay titled "Red Hair" in the May 1851 issue of *Bentley's Miscellany* (the date, as we shall see, is significant, coinciding as it did with the growing controversial fame of the Pre-Raphaelite painters) recognized that the term had its own ambivalence:

> In the general category of "red" the greater part of people one meets confound every description of hair which is neither black, nor brown, nor white, nor whity-brown. It may be the fiery Milesian [Irish] shock—it may be the paly amber—it may be the burnished gold—it may be the "Brown in the shadow, and gold in the sun;"—*c'est égal*—it is all "red"—they have no other word.

And yet, under this general term are confounded the two extremes of
beauty and ugliness—the two shades which have been respectively made
the attributes of the angel and of the demon—we find that while, on the
one hand, red hair (or rather a certain shade of it) has been both popularly
and poetically associated with all ugliness, all vice, and all malignity, a more
pleasing variety of the same hue has been associated with all loveliness, all
meekness, and all innocence.

What the writer does not make clear is the crucial fact that the word *red*
was in fact not applied to hair that was an attribute of a beautiful woman
(the customary word here was *golden*) or of a handsome man; it referred
only to "a certain shade" that bore a strong connotation of physical and,
in many instances, moral ugliness.

The origins of the prejudice are obscure. The *Bentley's* writer, drawing on his or her acquaintance with what was not yet known as cultural
anthropology, noted that "Among all nations the ancient Egyptians
stand preeminent for the violence of their aversion to red hair," Diodo-
rus recording that they annually burned alive "an unfortunate individual whose only crime was the colour of his hair." The writer imagined
the sad case of an ancient Egyptian whose hair wasn't all that red but
who, the supply of the truly fiery kind having dried up, was executed
anyway: "fancy him, more eagerly than Titmouse [in *Ten Thousand a
Year*: see page 231 above], grasping at every receipt warranted to produce a deep and permanent black."

Probably the anti-red hair bias drew some of its strength from the
convention according to which devils in medieval drama were red-
haired, if not red all over and, by extension of association, also Jewish
villains such as Barabbas in Marlowe's *The Jew of Malta* and Dickens's
Fagin. (By further extension, "Jew boys" were often redheaded, as in
Thackeray: when Rawdon Crawley was inducted into Moss's sponging
house in Cursitor Street, "A little pink-eyed Jew-boy, with a head as
ruddy as the rising morn, let the party into the house" [*Vanity Fair*,
53:510].) The *Bentley's* writer cited the demon of Cruelty in Southey's
The Maid of Orleans ("His coarse hair was red . . .") and associated red
hair also with executioners, such as Richard the Lionhearted's headsman
in Scott's *The Talisman* ("a huge red beard, mingling with shaggy locks of
the same colour"). In Spanish painting, the traitor-disciple Judas was
depicted with red hair, a fancy reflected in Rosalind's remark in *As You
Like It* (III.iv) that Orlando's "very hair is of the dissembling colour" and
Celia's tactful reply, "Something browner than Judas'."

While golden-haired heroines abounded in literature and art,
women with unequivocally red hair were rare. In *The Ordeal of Richard
Feverel*, Richard says of Mrs. Mount, whom Meredith describes as "a glo-

rious dashing woman . . . with shining black hair, red lips, and eyes not afraid of men," "Now that's my idea of Bellona. . . . Not the fury they paint, but a spirited, dauntless, eager-looking creature like that." "Bellona?" replies Adrian. "I don't think her hair was black. Red, wasn't it? I shouldn't compare her to Bellona; though, no doubt, she's as ready to spill blood" (37:384).

Down to the middle of the nineteenth century, a woman possessing a head of red hair, bluntly so called, was severely disadvantaged in the marriage market. This was the unmistakable message conveyed whenever a novelist allotted red hair, instead of golden, to a girl or woman: no female could be red-haired and at the same time be considered attractive. Witness Fanny Squeers ("her hair . . . had more than a tinge of red") and Sally Brass, who "carried upon her upper lip certain reddish demonstrations . . . which might have been mistaken for a beard" (*The Old Curiosity Shop*, 33:320–21); one assumes that the hair on her head was of the same unacceptable hue. Sally Leadbitter in *Mary Barton* was "vulgar-minded to the last degree; never easy unless her talk was of love and lovers; in her eyes it was an honour to have had a long list of wooers. So constituted, it was a pity that Sally herself was but a plain, red-haired, freckled girl; never likely, one would have thought, to become a heroine on her own account. But what she lacked in beauty she tried to make up for by a kind of witty boldness . . ." (8:84).

It is in Thackeray's pages that we learn most about the plight of red-haired women in the marriage market, and therefore, given the centrality of that market in the society of the time, their disadvantage in life itself. In their first appearance en masse, to be sure, they seem at first glance to contradict the general rule. In the brooch whose adventures spin the plot of *The Great Hoggarty Diamond*, the portrait of the red-faced Mick Hoggarty was, as the old lady pointed out to Sam in Mr. Polonius the jeweler's shop, surrounded by locks of matching hair: "These thirteen sthreamers of red hair represent his thirteen celebrated sisters,— Biddy, Minny, Thedy, Widdy (short for Williamina), Freddy, Izzy, Tizzy, Mysie, Grizzy, Polly, Dolly, Nell, and Bell—all married, all ugly, and all carr'ty hair" (2:17). That they were all ugly, according to the current prejudice, went without saying; that they were also all married need cause no surprise, because they were Irish, which meant that normal conventions did not apply. An Irishman, or thirteen Irishmen, had to take their wives as they found them.

In England, however, where golden-haired brides were available, red-haired ones could be had at a severe discount. In "Club Snobs" (*Punch*, 23 January 1847; *BS*, 185) Thackeray's young man-about-town, Waggle, spoke of the daughter of a wealthy owner of a ham-and-beef shop whom only a suitor who was more susceptible than intelligent could think of marrying: "She's five-and-forty. She's red hair. She's a nose like a pump-handle." Writing to Mrs. Bute Crawley concerning the possibility of her hiring, as governess, an alumna of her Hammersmith finishing school (but actually to learn whatever she could to Becky's discredit), Miss Barbara Pinkerton had to admit that one of the candidates, Miss Letitia Hawky, "is not personally well-favoured. She is twenty-nine; her face is much pitted with the small-pox. She has a halt in her gait, red hair, and a trifling obliquity of vision" (*Vanity Fair*, 11:97). Becky Sharp's hair, on the other hand, was an acceptable, if not very glamorous, sandy or yellow, but when she returned to Queen's Crawley following the elder Sir Pitt's death, her former pupils, having sized her up, indulged in a little cattiness even as their late, unlamented father lay unburied in the house:

> "She's hardly changed since eight years," said Miss Rosalind to Miss Violet, as they were preparing for dinner.
> "Those red-haired women look wonderfully well," replied the other.
> "Hers is much darker than it was; I think she must dye it," Miss Rosalind added. (41:404)

In *Pendennis*, Blanche Amory, whose hair was "fair," sounded the true depth of her despair over having received no bids during the open season in London: "[I]t was the end of the season and nobody had proposed to her: she had made no sensation at all, she who was so much cleverer than any girl of the year, and of the young ladies forming her special circle. Dora who had but five thousand pounds, Flora who had nothing, and Leonora who had red hair, were going to be married, and nobody had come for Blanche Amory!" (44:2.62)

The chasm that separated desirability as a wife and possession of red hair (except in such instances as the undeservedly lucky Leonora) was illustrated by an exchange between Captain Talbot Bulstrode and his fellow officer Francis Maldon, who has been proclaiming to him the perfection of Aurora Floyd, with whom he is madly in love and whom they are about to meet at a party. "'I don't want to stand in your way, my boy,' said Captain Bulstrode. 'Go in and win, and my blessing be upon your virtuous endeavours. I can imagine the young Scotchwoman[†]—red

---

[†]Although one would expect the prejudice to have been associated with the Irish, as it certainly was with Thackeray's baker's dozen of Hoggartys ("the nine graces, and four over"), red hair was, in fact, oftener thought of as a Scottish attribute. The *Bentley's* writer observed that "among some of the Highland clans, red hair is regarded with so much aversion as to be considered a positive deformity. . . . It is probable that this bitter aversion may have originated in some quarrel between the different clans, as we find that there are

hair (of course you'll call it auburn), large feet, and freckles!' "'Aurora Floyd—red hair and freckles!'" The young officer laughed aloud at the stupendous joke. 'You'll see her in a quarter of an hour, Bulstrode,' he said" (*Aurora Floyd*, 3:26). When Bulstrode did see her, to his surprise (and relief) she turned out to have a "coronet of plaits dead black against the purple air," an attribute to which Miss Braddon repeatedly called her readers' attention in the course of the novel.

The topicality of Bulstrode's mischievous description was centered in the parenthetical "of course you'll call it auburn." The use of this adjective was due to the inescapable fact that in life, many women had hair that was simply too reddish to be called golden. What, then, should it be called? "Carrotty" would do for Irishwomen—Thackeray first described Mick Hoggarty's miniature portrait in the brooch as "a great fat red round of beef surrounded by thirteen carrots" (1:3)—but certainly not for respectable Englishwomen, or indeed, women of any respectable nation. Red, then? In one of Thackeray's "Club Snob" papers (*Punch*, 9 January 1847; *BS*, 177) Captain Spitfire, R.N., reported to his dinner companion, Minns, the Draconian punishment administered to the Princess Scragamoffsky, who had failed to turn up at Lady Palmerston's party:

> "The Princess Scragamoffsky's back is flayed alive, Minns—I tell you it's raw, Sir! On Tuesday last, at twelve o'clock, three drummers of the Preobajinski Regiment arrived at Ashburnham House, and at half-past twelve, in the yellow drawing-room at the Russian Embassy, before the Ambassadress and four ladies' maids, the Greek Papa, and the Secretary of Embassy, Madame de Scragamoffsky received thirteen dozen. She was knouted, Sir, knouted in the midst of England—in Berkeley Square, for having said the Grand Duchess Olga's hair was red." ("Minns: 'Good Ged!'")

The undiplomatic princess could have gone unscathed to the party if she had merely substituted the by then widely used euphemism "auburn." In 1839, for example, Kate Aubrey, a daughter of the exemplary county family who were dispossessed of house and home by the red-haired Tittlebat Titmouse's machinations in *Ten Thousand a Year*, had "auburn tresses" (11.307). Because her hair was officially auburn, not red, she made a good marriage at the end of the novel.

Thackeray's women, as often as not, were auburn-haired, either by nature or artifice: the poetess Clementina Clutterbuck in "Party-Giving Snobs" ("florid auburn hair"), Lady Bareacres in *Vanity Fair* ("a beautiful

---

clans in which red hair preponderates." Sandy M'Collop, one of the art students at Gandish's school (*The Newcomes*), was a "huge red-haired" Scotsman.

golden auburn," formerly "dark"), Martha Coacher, the first wife of
Laura Bell's father in *Pendennis* ("auburn ringlets"), Lady Agnes Foker
in the same novel ("meek auburn fronts"). It is likely that Thackeray was
deliberately exploiting what was rapidly becoming a popular joke. In a
scene in *Pendennis* (1848–49), Fanny Bolton and her mother had just
had a brief encounter with Pen, who recalled with pleasure their recent
excursion to Vauxhall with Captain Costigan. Mrs. Bolton, who had once
been a bit-part actress at Sadler's Wells, recalled that "there was a young
gentleman from the City, that used to come in a tilbry, in a white 'at, the
very image of him, ony his whiskers was black, and Mr. P's is red." "Law,
Ma!" Fanny exclaimed, "they are a most beautiful hawburn" (48:2.101).

Mrs. Proudie's daughters, said Trollope in *Barchester Towers* (1857),
were "tall and robust like their mother, whose high cheekbones, and—
we may say auburn hair, they all inherit" (3:166). He alluded to the same
semantic distinction without a difference in *The Struggles of Brown, Jones,
and Robinson* four years later (1861): "At that time," he said of his heroine, Maryanne Brown, "she was about twenty-four years of age, and was
certainly a fine young woman. She was particularly like her mother, a
little too much inclined to corpulence, and there may be those who
would not allow that her hair was auburn. Mr. Robinson, however, who
was then devotedly attached to her, was of that opinion, and was ready
to maintain his views against any man who would dare to say that it was
red" (2: *Cornhill Magazine*, 5:186–87).

Whatever distinctions between the two were or were not implied, all
references to auburn or red hair from the early 1850s onward were rendered immediately topical by the acrimonious debate over PreRaphaelite painting. Thackeray had anticipated it, in a way, in his burlesque of a
Disraelian description of a Jewish beauty in "Codlingsby" (*Punch*, 22 May
1847): "Her hair had that deep glowing tinge in it which had been the
delight of all painters, and which, therefore, the vulgar sneer at. It was
of burning auburn. Meandering over her fairest shoulders in twenty
thousand minute ringlets, it hung to her waist and below it." "Burning
auburn" became as much a hallmark of the PreRaphaelite style as the
women's elongated necks. Rossetti depicted a seductive company of
women with reddish-brown, or titian, hair—Lady Lilith, Helen of Troy,
Fazio's mistress, Lucrezia Borgia, Mary Magdalene. But the copper coin,
as it were, had another side. As part of their subversive defiance of outworn and empty convention, Rossetti and his followers gave virtuous,
even saintly, women the same red—not golden—hair: Rossetti, the Virgin and the angels, in his *Girlhood of Mary Virgin* and *Ecce Ancilla Domini*;
Arthur Hughes, the wistful, purple-skirted figure in *April Love*; Millais,
The Bridesmaid with her cascading tresses. In *The Awakening Conscience*,

Holman Hunt had it both ways: the prostitute's red hair linked her immoral past with her possible repentance.

This new prominence of flaming red hair had several consequences in fiction. One was that it invested the very term "red hair" with new meaning.[†] Charged as it was with derogatory connotations, it gave art critics an extra stick with which to beat the iconoclasts, serving a polemic purpose of which the innocuously conventional "golden" and "auburn" were incapable. In fictional descriptions, therefore, the association of red hair with PreRaphaelitism and the controversy it stirred gave red hair additional meaning. Another effect was that in attributing red hair to virtuous women the PreRaphaelites disturbed the accepted moral categories. And a third was that the publicity attending the furor generated a new fashion: hair that was undeniably, indeed defiantly, red, not merely auburn, became the mode of the moment, thus inviting novelists to make fresh topical use of a familiar physical attribute that now enjoyed a heightened status.

As Mrs. H. R. Haweis put it in *The Art of Beauty* (1878)—by then, Rossetti had painted two more flaming-haired beauties, in *The Bower Meadow* and *Veronica Veronese* (both 1872)—"Morris, Burne-Jones, and others, have made certain types of face and figure, once literally hated, actually the fashion. Red hair—once, to say a woman had red hair was social assassination [as in the case of the unfortunate Princess Scragamoffsky]—is all the rage."[17] Mrs. Lynn Linton, for one, was furious. Along with "talking slang as glibly as a man, and by preference leading the conversation to doubtful subjects," the "Girl of the Period" she excoriated in her famous *Saturday Review* diatribe proclaimed her "loud and rampant modernisation" by flaunting a head of "*false* red hair" (my italics), thus compounding the sin: where nature refused to assist the degenerate new vogue, artifice—unmitigated, unwomanly deceit—rushed in to supply the lack.

Adopting a more temperate tone, Justin McCarthy implied the same devious practice in an article on "The Pre-Raphaelites in England" that he contributed to an American periodical, *The Galaxy* (June 1876). One could see in the drawing rooms of the moment women who looked as if

---

[†]There is an echo of this in *The Newcomes*. Although Clive was not a PreRaphaelite, Ethel momentarily associated him with the group when, as they neared Croydon on their exhilarating train ride to Brighton, she remarked, "You painters always pretend to admire girls with auburn hair, because Titian and Raphael painted it. Has the Fornarina red hair?" (41:2.34). Ethel is not only perceptive in art matters: her forthright use of the lexical distinction is another indication of her lively mind. (She was thinking, incidentally, of Sir Augustus Wall Callcott's popular *Raffaelle and la Belle Fornarina*, exhibited at the Royal Academy in 1837.)

they had just stepped out of the frames of PreRaphaelite paintings, "bright red hair" and all. "How," McCarthy wondered, "did all these pre-Raphaelite girls manage to come to life so suddenly? Were they all born with that red hair, those high cheekbones, those straight lank shapes, which shape have none, and which you are compelled to see, outlined as they are so sharply in the close and clinging drapery?" The rage, he added, had extended even to Christmas cards, by which "we cheer each other by interchanging illustrations of the stiff and lean young woman in various ungainly attitudes, and seeming to be all angles, joints, and fuzzy red hair."

At the end of the first PreRaphaelite decade, George Eliot gave the outdoor preacher Dinah Morris (*Adam Bede*, [1859]) "smooth locks of pale reddish hair" (2:21), not, of course, to imply kinship with any other red-haired heroines of recent art or fiction, but to add a distinctive, and by this time not necessarily degrading, physical touch to her portrait. The next year, in *Evan Harrington*, Meredith played with the piquant new ambiguity of red hair when he presented Mrs. Evremonde, "a lovely person with Giorgione hair, which the Countess [Evan Harrington's sister] intensely admires, and asks the diplomatist [her husband] whether he can see a soupçon of red in it." Later in the novel the Countess described her—fastidiously avoiding the "auburn" joke—as "A fine-ish woman with a great deal of hair worn as if her maid had given it one comb straight down and then rolled it up in a hurry round one finger. Malice would say carrots. It is called gold" (18:233; 19:243).

Lesser novelists in those years signalized the relaxation of the taboo against calling red hair by its name, and at the same time its persistence, in several ways, depending on the context:

> "Oh, that long, long lovely sunbright hair!" taking the comb out, and letting it fall its full length down. "I never saw hair at all to be compared to it! with that peculiar golden sparkle on it, and yet no one could possibly call it red!" (Mrs. Stirling, *Sedgley Court* [1865])

> Her dark brown hair (fortunately at that time it was not considered necessary for beauty to have a red head), taken off behind the ears in two tight bands, showed the exquisite shape of her head. . . . (Edmund Yates, *Running the Gauntlet* [1865])

> There was a red glory—not a golden one, but a dark red glory—in the hair that crowned that head. (Annie Hall Cudlip, *On Guard* [1865])

> Now that lime-and-lemon-juice blanche our women's hair, and that auricomus and other fluids bring it back to yellow or red, one gets sceptical on the subject of gold-tinted locks; but Archie's were of a hue that all the *artistes* in London could never so much as imitate: nut-brown in shade, red-gold in

sunshine, supple, plenteous, exquisitely soft. (Annie Edwards, *Archie Lovell* [1866])

Neither wholly red nor wholly brown, were those well-plaited locks. Brown was, of the two, their predominant hue, with just a dash of red to keep them warm a-glow. (Rhoda Broughton, *Not Wisely But Too Well* [1867])[18]

Although red hair, adding flame to the customary gold, was now legitimized as an occasional attribute of the maidenly, marriageable heroine, PreRaphaelite practice had also strengthened its old association with seduction, a relation parodied, while the future painter of Lilith was still a child, in Dickens's figure of the redheaded would-be femme fatale, Fanny Squeers. T. J. Edelstein has plausibly argued that "the immoral connotations of reddish hair," its suggestion of brazenness and evil, even of female fiendishness, made it valuable to the writers of sensation novels.[19] In Collins's *Armadale* (1864–66), Lydia Gwilt wore her hair in the same style that the blameless Aurora Floyd preferred, but the color made all the difference. "The luster of her terrible red hair showed itself unshrinkingly in a plaited coronet above her forehead, and escaped in one vagrant love-lock, perfectly curled, that dropped over her left shoulder" (3.7:2.62). Gwilt was a poisoner, forger, and bigamist; even her name chimed "guilt" and "gilt." At the age of thirty-five, having already been tried on a murder charge and served time for theft, she was still beautiful—and dangerous.

Risking overkill, Collins made the association of flaming hair with female villainy clear to even the most inattentive reader: "This woman's hair, superbly luxuriant in its growth, was of the one unpardonably remarkable shade of color which the prejudice of the Northern nations never entirely forgives—it was *red!*" (The excited italics this time are Collins's.) Collins may have been (fortunately) alone among his fellow novelists in seizing on still another supposed synonym for the controversial hue: "Her magnificent hair flashed crimson in the candle-light. . . ." Elsewhere in the novel he called it "hideous." Under the circumstances, Lydia Gwilt was indulging in dry understatement when she explained to her London landlady why she was wearing a veil as she left for the railway station: "One meets such rude men occasionally in the railway. . . . And though I dress quietly, my hair is so very remarkable" (2.10:1.470; 3.7:2.72; 2.10:1.460; 3.12:2.210). So remarkable, in fact, that readers of *Armadale* might well have concluded that her proper habitat would be a freak show. But one can understand why Mrs. Lynn Linton was so exercised over the Girl of the Period's deliberate adoption of false red hair: this abandoned creature was bent on turning herself into, if not a femme fatale, a reduplicated Lydia Gwilt.

In *A Terrible Temptation*, Reade used the red hair-temptress association to generate an ambiguity within the plot. Lady Bassett, with "a
skin like satin, and red hair," is suspected through most of the novel of
having had an adulterous relationship which resulted in a difficult, un-
English "son." At the end, it is proved that she was unfairly accused, "a
chaste woman passionately in love with her husband" and totally without
fault (34:334; "Note":475). But the fact that she had red hair would
have kept before the reader in 1871, through most of the novel, the
nagging question, Did she have the morals of a certain notorious type of
red-haired woman?

Meanwhile, redheaded men had been appearing in fiction in equally
unsympathetic roles: Fagin, the burglar Tony Crackit (also in *Oliver
Twist*), Sampson Brass ("hair of a deep red"), Jonas Chuzzlewit, Uriah
Heep, Blandois/Rigaud ("a quantity of dry hair, of no definable colour,
in its shaggy state, but shot with red"), Rugg (also in *Little Dorrit*; Dickens
forgot that earlier he had written of Rugg's "ragged yellow head like a
worn-out hearth-broom"), the taxidermist Venus in *Our Mutual Friend*
("a tangle of reddish-dusty hair"). Once in a while, Dickens attributed
red hair to youths who may have been incipient gents, such as young
Bailey in *Martin Chuzzlewit*, but whose moral tendencies, unlike those of
Samuel Warren's flaming-haired Cockney-on-the-make, Tittlebat Titmouse, were at least unobjectionable.

On the highest level of society there was the dissolute Marquis of
Steyne, whose fringe of red hair around his "shining bald head" proclaimed him a traitor to his class: noblesse oblige required a true, morally
impeccable aristocrat *not* to have red hair (*Vanity Fair*, 37:366).[†] The

---

[†] Later, residing on the Continent after his roughing-up by Rawdon Crawley, Steyne's
"red whiskers were dyed of a purple hue, which made his pale face look still paler"
(64:627). Evidence of dye jobs was a customary mark of both kinds of Regency bucks—
those well up in years, who sought to obscure the ravages of time by coloring gray hair
and whiskers a youthful black, and aspiring dandies whom an uncooperative nature had
endowed with unfashionable red. When the cast of subordinate characters more or less
reassembles toward the end of *Vanity Fair*, "Lady Bareacres' hair which was then dark was
now a beautiful golden auburn, whereas Lord Bareacres' whiskers, formerly red, were at
present of a rich black with purple and green reflections in the light" (62:597), the same
effects, one remembers, that Tittlebat Titmouse obtained in his early efforts to transform
himself into a dandy. Once more, what had begun as a fashionable habit soon spread to a
demotic level, as in the case of gents and their abominable cigars. Towler, the former
groom of the chambers in Lord Levant's family, was a "tall red-'aired man—but dyes his
'air," said Morgan, Major Pendennis's manservant (*Pendennis*, 36:1.368). And when Blan-
dois/Rigaud turned up in London, "He had a quantity of hair and moustache—jet black,
except at the shaggy ends, where it had a tinge of red—and a high hook nose" (*Little Dorrit*,
1.29:393). Dickens later explicitly describes his hair as "dyed."

crowning glory, such as it was, was more typically the attribute of, say, political agitators like the unnamed one at Treby Magna in *Felix Holt*, "a grimy man in a flannel shirt, hatless and with turbid red hair," who lectured a group of "men in very shabby coats and miscellaneous head-coverings . . . insisting on political points with much more ease than had seemed to belong to the gentlemen speakers on the hustings . . ." (2.30:245–46).

Undecimus Scott, the unprincipled rogue in *The Three Clerks*, had red hair in his genes: his whole family, who seem not to have been noted for their probity, were distinguished, Trollope says, by their "red hair, bright as burnished gold." Undy himself was "hirsute with copious red locks, not only over his head, but under his chin and round his mouth"—a characterization that occurred, significantly, in the midst of Trollope's detailed rehearsal of his sullied record. Red hair comported well with his having been unseated from Parliament, for good reasons, by "the independent electors of the Tillietudlem burghs" and serving as vice-president of one of those Victorian businesses whose reliability was inversely proportional to the length of its title, "the Caledonian, English, Irish, and General European and American Fire and Life Assurance Society" (8:84–90 passim). Undy's red hair lighted the reader's way as he followed the tortuosities of his subsequent career.

Candor in such matters was, Thackeray averred, the obligation of the veracious novelist. "The describer and biographer of my friend Mr. Philip Firmin," he wrote in the person of Arthur Pendennis in *The Adventures of Philip*, "has tried to extenuate nothing; and, I hope, has set down naught in malice. If Philip's boots had holes in them, I have written that he had holes in his boots. If he had a red beard, there it is red in this story. I might have oiled it with a tinge of brown, and painted it a rich auburn" (23:2.373). As a matter of fact, he had already done so; on an earlier page, describing the portrait of Philip's mother, he wrote, "Philip Firmin had the same violet odd bright eyes, and the same coloured hair of auburn tinge; in the picture it fell in long wild masses over the lady's back as she leaned with bare arms on a harp" (2:1.112). As with Undy Scott's family, the trait was markedly genetic. Philip's red hair was inherited from both his mother and his paternal grandfather, Brand Firmin, "one of the handsomest men in Europe," Major Pendennis reminisced. "Firebrand Firmin they used to call him—a red-headed fellow—a tremendous duellist; shot an Irishman—became serious in after life, and that sort of thing—quarrelled with his son, who was doosid wild in early days. Gentlemanly man, certainly, Firmin [i.e., Philip's father]. Black hair: his father had red" (1:1.101).

Even though they may have been of impeccable character, redheaded clergymen were at a particular disadvantage. Charles Honeyman's temporary vicar at Lady Whittlesea's fashionable chapel, the Reverend Simeon Rawkins, simply didn't pan out, according to Sherrick, who used the wine vaults under the building for storage: "the lowest of the Low Church, sir—a red-haired dumpy man, who gasped at his *h*'s and spoke with a Lancashire twang—he'd no more do for Mayfair than Grimaldi for Macbeth" (*The Newcomes*, 25 : 1.267). In one case, however, the disability proved to have a silver, if not positively golden, lining for the cleric involved. When pressed by her family to marry her cousin, Harry Foker (in *Pendennis*), Lady Ann Milton in desperation runs off to be married to "Mr. Hobson, her father's own chaplain and her brother's tutor; a red-haired widower with two children" (71:2.345), bringing with her, in all probability, a dowry sufficient to cancel out the social disparity and the widower's disability.

At least two reviewers of *Barchester Towers* singled out Obadiah Slope's red hair for special mention. Trollope had spared no detail in harmonizing it with the rest of Slope's person, as well as inviting recollections of another unctuous, red-haired fraud, Uriah Heep. The egregious Obadiah's hair, Trollope specified, was "lank, and of a dull pale reddish hue. . . . His face is nearly of the same colour as his hair, though perhaps a little redder: it is not unlike beef,—beef, however, one would say, of a bad quality." His nose, to top off the repulsively ruddy ensemble, "had a somewhat spongy, porous appearance, as though it had been cleverly formed out of a red coloured cork" (4:170). Trollope underscored Mrs. Proudie's initial affinity with Slope by endowing both her and her daughters with what Trollope delicately called auburn hair. When a match was set to this tindery combination—one red-haired man, three red-haired women—trouble was bound to erupt in the precincts of Barchester Cathedral, as it soon did. In his next novel, *Doctor Thorne*, Trollope allotted red hair to the boorish and alcoholic heir to the railway building fortune, Louis Philippe Scatcherd: "His hair was dark red, and he wore red moustaches, and a great deal of red beard beneath his chin, cut in a manner to make him look like an American" (24:260).

The burden of bias in the middle of the century, therefore, was strongly against redheaded males as well as females. It was reflected in one item of Dickens's notorious assault on PreRaphaelite painting (*Household Words*, 15 June 1850). In Millais's picture of *Christ in the House of His Parents* ("*The Carpenter Shop*"), then being examined by throngs of curious, and in many cases indignant, viewers at the Royal Academy exhibition, one of the foreground figures—Christ himself—was, to Dickens, "a hideous, wry-necked, blubbering, red-haired boy." In a painting allegedly filled with sacrilege—what had happened to the Holy Family of traditional religious art?—this last, Faginesque detail, reminiscent more immediately of Thackeray's Jew boy at the sponging house, was the most sacrilegious of all.

Nevertheless, redheaded men were on the way to partial redemption. On the very eve of the PreRaphaelite revolution, Thackeray had used hair color in the same way that Reade was later to do in *A Terrible Temptation*, to introduce a substantial element of ambiguity. Describing the sixteen-year-old Pendennis, he said that "His hair was of a healthy brown colour, which looks like gold in the sunshine, . . . his whiskers were decidedly of a reddish hue; in fact, without being a beauty, he had . . . a frank, good-natured kind face" (*Pendennis*, 3:1.22). Which way was Pen to go, then—the way of his "healthy brown" hair or that of his "reddish" whiskers, with all that "reddish" suggested in 1848? (Admittedly, reddishness of whisker was not as culpable as reddishness of thatch: witness, as above, the Oxford undergraduate Pysent, Hobson Newcome, and Fred Bayham.) Thackeray meant Pen's reddish whiskers (auburn in the eyes of so enamored a beholder as Fanny Bolton) as a preliminary signal to the reader that Pen's was a mixed nature, as the rest of his history would amply demonstrate.

Early in *Villette* (1853), Charlotte Brontë availed herself of the same ambiguity that "auburn" then conveyed in the case of men as well as women. Paulina Hume said to Graham Bretton:

"I think you queer."
"My face, ma'am?"
"Your face and all about you. You have long red hair."
"Auburn hair, if you please. Mamma calls it auburn, or golden, and so do all her friends. But even with my 'long red hair'" (and he waved his mane with a sort of triumph,—tawny he himself knew it was, and he was proud of the leonine hue), "I cannot possibly be queerer than is your ladyship."

While Millais's portrayal of the youthful Christ as a redhead initially shocked the conventionally minded, in the long run, once they were reconciled to so drastic an iconographic innovation, it helped to rehabilitate the breed.[†] Red-haired males appeared in other well-known paintings of the day, as Claudio in Holman Hunt's *Claudio and Isabella*, and as Arthur Hughes's Brave Geraint. In time, the new tolerance filtered down as far as Christmas cards, in whose scenes, as Justin McCarthy reported in his *Galaxy* article, red-haired PreRaphaelite women were

[†]The developing ambivalence toward red-haired men in the 1850s must have complicated the effect produced on eyewitnesses by Algernon Swinburne's mop of "orange red" or "flaming red" hair, so bright that it was practically fluorescent. Even if his behavior at Oxford in 1856–59, and subsequently in London social and literary circles, had been unexceptionable, his hair alone would have ensured that he would not be overlooked.

joined by men with the same high cheekbones, gaunt faces—and red hair. The old prejudice which had made it extremely unlikely that gentlemen with red hair would be found pictured in fashion magazines and silk-bound drawing-room table books was not renounced, but in fiction it was relaxed to the extent that red hair sometimes was included in the portrait of a hero whose character and conduct did not always match the moral norm but who proved himself a gentleman before a novel's end. Red hair need not always be associated with loutishness or worse, as with Lord Steyne; it might conceal a kind of rough honesty, an integrity that would disprove the signal it customarily sent.

Red-haired men, therefore, were given another chance; they might be allowed not only to live comfortably with their conspicuous physical characteristic but to transcend it. Thus Meredith, in *Emilia in England* (1864), could, without prejudice, endow Tracy Runningbrook with "hair . . . red as blown flame" (4:24). Trollope joined the revisionists when, three years later in *Phineas Finn* (1867–69), he used Lord Chiltern's red hair to set the whole tone of his portrait, not at all to Chiltern's discredit. And he could drop the jocularity he had once felt obliged to use in describing Mrs. Proudie and her daughters when he turned to portraying Chiltern's sister, Lady Laura Kennedy. Early in the novel, Phineas is in love with Mary Flood Jones, the young woman he is later to marry—"a little girl about twenty years of age, with the softest hair in the world, of a colour varying between brown and auburn,—for sometimes you would swear it was the one and sometimes the other" (2:61). It is only natural, under the circumstances, that he should accordingly derogate Lady Laura Standish, "about six feet high," he tells Mary, and "as unlike you as possible in everything. She has thick lumpy red hair [in manuscript, Trollope added and then deleted ". . . which in all probability has been died" (*sic*)], while yours is all silk and softness" (2.63).

But later Trollope corrected Phineas's enthusiastic distortion of Lady Laura's appearance:

> Phineas had declared at Killaloe that Lady Laura was six feet high, that she had red hair, that her figure was straggling, and that her hands and feet were large. She was in fact about five feet seven in height, and she carried her weight well. There was something of nobility in her gait, and she seemed thus to be taller than her inches. Her hair was in truth red,—of a deep thorough redness. Her brother's hair was the same; and so had been that of her father, before it had become sandy with age. Her sister's had been of a soft auburn hue, and hers had been said to be the prettiest head of hair in Europe at the time of her marriage. But in these days we have got to like red hair, and Lady Laura's was not supposed to stand in the way of her being considered a beauty. (4:74)

It was in his late novel *Ayala's Angel* (1881), however, that Trollope made the most prominent use of the (male) ruby-in-the-rough theme. Ayala Dormer meets Colonel Jonathan Stubbs,

> the youngest Colonel in the British army, who had done some wonderful thing,—taken a new province in India, or marched across Africa, or defended the Turks,—or perhaps conquered them. She knew that he was very brave,—but why was he so very ugly? His hair was ruby red, and very short; and he had a thick red beard: not silky, but bristly, with each bristle almost a dagger,—and his mouth was enormous. His eyes were very bright, and there was a smile about him, partly of fun, partly of good humour. But his mouth! And then that bristling beard!

Ayala's good friend Nina Baldoni sees him differently, saying he is "perfectly lovely. The fire comes out of his eyes, and he rubs his old red hairs about till they sparkle. Then he shines all over like a carbuncle [a red gem]" (16:146, 149). The motif of sheer ugliness, exacerbated by the bristling red beard, appears every time Stubbs is onstage. But Ayala's conviction that "he was the ugliest man she had ever seen" gradually melts; she is bewitched despite her bias, and in the end they are romantically united. He is the angel's Prince Charming, even though Trollope, tongue in cheek, insists that the true hero of the tale is the poor besotted Tom Tringle, who, in retrospect, never had a chance.

Still, the impediment remained, and whether love would conquer redheadedness was a tossup. Red-haired women continued to be conscious of their lingering disadvantage and took whatever means they could to reduce it. In *The Hand of Ethelberta* Hardy described his heroine as "squirrel-haired," an original enough adjective. He went on to portray the decoration of the London house in which she lived as a young widow: "The decorations tended towards the artistic gymnastics prevalent in some quarters at the present day. ["Written in 1875"—Hardy's footnote.] Upon a general flat tint of duck's-egg green appeared quaint patterns of conventional foliage, and birds, done in bright auburn, several shades nearer to redbreast-red than was Ethelberta's hair, which was thus thrust further towards brown by such juxtaposition—a possible reason for the choice of tint" (17:133). Trollope to the contrary notwithstanding, heroines still could not afford to flaunt their red hair when means of softening the effect were available.

5.

That novelists went to so much trouble to describe what their characters looked like was, according to Reade, the result of the fact that women comprised most of the fiction-reading audience. In a letter addressed to him in his self-portrait character of Rolfe, by the central figure in *A Terrible Temptation*, he wrote,

> [I] doubt whether philosophers are not mistaken in saying that women generally have more imagination than men. I suspect they have infinitely less; and I believe their great love of novels, which has been set down to imagination, arises mainly from their want of it. You writers of novels supply that defect for them, by a pictorial style, by an infinity of minute details, and petty aids to realizing, all which an imaginative reader can do for himself on reading a bare narrative of sterling facts and incidents. (25:248)

Whether or not novelists subscribed to this theory, they exerted themselves to compensate for whatever deficiencies of imagination their readers might have. George Eliot and Trollope, especially, offered them detailed Identikit inventories of a woman's features, her eyes, nose, teeth, complexion, the shape of her face, above all her hair—and even a gingerly, one-word classification of her figure. In this method of working, novelists were following a convention introduced into English fiction at the beginning of the century as a result of the vogue of physiognomy, which purported to associate character traits with physical features.[20] A montage of these discrete components, constructed by the reader herself, sufficed for ordinary purposes. This was the implication of Walter Bagehot's remark about Dickens in 1858: "Mr. Dickens is not only unable to make lovers talk, but to describe heroines in mere narrative. As has been said, most men can make a tumble of blue eyes and fair hair and pearly teeth, that does very well for a young lady, at least for a good while; but Mr. Dickens will not, probably cannot, attain even to this humble measure of descriptive art."[21]

Once in a long while, a novelist might rely on the reader's acquaintance with older art to provide an instantaneous portrait, as Mrs. Gaskell did when she wrote that at Jem Wilson's trial Mary Barton's "look, and indeed her whole face, was more like the well known engraving from Guido's picture of "Beatrice Cenci'" (*Mary Barton*, 32:312–13) than any other picture with which it might be compared. Much later, in *Desperate Remedies* (1871), Hardy invoked Greuze's "Head of a Girl" in an attempt to suggest Cytherea's expression at a certain moment. But nowhere in an existing eighty-page anthology of extracts describing women's appearances in Victorian fiction can one find any reference to contemporary models, which would render such descriptions topical and at the same time obviate the need for sketches synthesized by the reader from the detached details the novelist spread out before him. Yet novelists had an abundance of labor-saving opportunities close at hand, in the various forms of graphic art that would have enabled them to say simply, "Lady A. bore a striking resemblance to the actress Harriot Mellon, the late

Duchess of St. Albans," or "Mr. B., except for the angularity of his features, might have been mistaken for Mr. Palmerston." The real-life components of such topical look-alikes were familiar to readers in widely distributed separate engravings (publicly seen in the shop windows of print-sellers and booksellers, who often displayed portraits of popular authors), *Punch* caricatures, portraits in the illustrated press beginning in the 1840s (the *Illustrated London News* ran hundreds of them), Parian ware busts, Staffordshire figurines, and, after mid-century, camera studies sold in photographers' shops.[22] In *Mr. Sponge's Sporting Tour* (41.289), Jogglebury Crowdey, the country squire who had a mania for cutting down blackthorn shrubs to make "curious-handled walking-sticks [which he] would cut into the heads of beasts or birds, or fishes, or men," including such celebrities as Wellington, O'Connell, Brougham, and Lord John Russell, depended on such sources. At one point in the serialized novel, deleted from the subsequent book, he "contemplated immortalising the Pope and all his band of make-believe bishops [i.e., the newly created and fiercely controversial English hierarchy], but he waited for the 'Illustrious London News,' as he called it, to furnish him with the necessary designs to go by."

No matter how obtained—vicariously through reproductive art or from personal acquaintance—images of famous men were part of many readers' mental equipment, and, as Thackeray testified in *Pendennis*, the images led some to emulate them, as Major Pendennis did the Duke of Wellington:[†]

> We have all of us, no doubt, met with more than one military officer, who has so imitated the manner of a certain Great Captain of the Age; and has, perhaps, changed his own natural character and disposition, because Fate had endowed him with an aquiline nose. In like manner have we not seen many another man pride himself on having a tall forehead and a supposed likeness to Mr. Canning? many another go through life swelling with self-gratification on account of an imagined resemblance . . . to the great and revered George IV? many third parties, who wore low necks to their dresses because they fancied the Lord Byron and themselves were similar in appearance? (36:1.371–72)

[†]Trollope no doubt relied on his reader's familiarity with the many portraits and busts of the Duke of Wellington when he said of Sir Lionel Bertram, a soldier of fortune who "held a quasi-military position in Persia," that "considering his age, he was very well preserved. He was still straight; did not fumble much in his walk, and had that decent look of military decorum which, since the days of Caesar and the duke, has been always held to accompany a hook-nose" (*The Bertrams* [1859], 2.9:2.143). From the clue of the hook nose, a reader could, if he wished, model his impression of Sir Lionel after Wellington, as he could earlier have done with Major Pendennis, whose "nose was of the Wellington pattern" (*Pendennis*, 1:1.1).

Seldom, however, despite the availability of models, did a novelist paint a face or demeanor by analogy, and instances in which one did were notable for their rarity rather than for their effectiveness. When, in *Paul Clifford* (1828), Bulwer said of Long Ned's face, "There was a mixture of frippery and sternness in its expression: something between Madame Vestris and T. P. Cooke [two well-known theatrical personalities], or between 'lovely Sally' and a 'Captain bold of Halifax' [two popular ballads]" (6:1.67–68), he assumed his readers' acquaintance with theatrical iconography.[†] In the expanded version of *Handley Cross* (1854) Surtees said of a character that "he was an immensely tall, telescopic kind of man, so tall, that he might pass for the author of Longfellow's poems" (30:228). This implied that readers were acquainted with engraved portraits of England's favorite American poet, as they in fact were. Charlotte Brontë once painted a face in part by what might be called denied analogy. In *Shirley* she described the curate Mr. Malone as "a tall, strongly-built personage, with real Irish legs and arms, and a face as genuinely national; not the Milesian face—not Daniel O'Connell's style, but the high-featured, North-American-Indian sort of visage, which belongs to a certain class of the Irish gentry, and has a petrified and proud look, better suited to the owner of an estate of slaves, than to the landlord of a free peasantry" (1.1:11).

There seldom was even any cross-genre borrowing such as might occur if a novelist referred readers to a woman's portrait in one of Browning's or Tennyson's poems. It was evidence, then, of the immediately contemporary fame of PreRaphaelite art when Miss Braddon described a fictional woman, Lady Audley, as she would have been painted by one of the brotherhood. To visualize Lady Audley, one had only to remember a portrait painted by a certain kind of avant-garde artist, lately seen in an exhibition or a dealer's showroom:

My lady's [unfinished] portrait stood on an easel, covered with a green baize in the center of the octagonal chamber. It had been a fancy of the artist to

---

[†]Madame Vestris was one of the many theatrical figures whose likenesses were known to a wide public. "Song-sheets carrying her picture, often in costume, were sold everywhere and would be seen and bought by many people who never got to a theatre to see the lady in person," a biographer has said. (Clifford John Williams, *Madame Vestris: A Theatrical Biography* [London, 1973], pp. 71–73.) But such portraits were not much more authentic than the cruder ones sometimes seen in playbills. Moreover, these pictures were usually full-figure, not close-up busts, and more attention was paid to the costume than to the subject's features. (It was of no help that in the case of breeches parts—Vestris as Don Juan in the "comic extravaganza" hit *Giovanni in London*, or in the title role of *Oberon*—her legs were the focus of attention.) Like the female portraits in gift albums, theatrical portraits were stylized. The best a novelist could do would be to refer his reader to whatever characteristic features the various portraits of a given actor or actress had in common.

paint her standing in this very room, and to make his background a faithful reproduction of the pictured walls. I am afraid the young man belonged to the pre-Raphaelite brotherhood, for he had spent a most unconscionable time upon the accessories of this picture—upon my lady's crispy ringlets and the heavy folds of her crimson velvet dress. . . .

Yes, the painter must have been a pre-Raphaelite. No one but a pre-Raphaelite would have painted, hair by hair, those feathery masses of ring-lets, with every glimmer of gold, and every shadow of pale brown. No one but a pre-Raphaelite would have so exaggerated every attribute of that deli-cate face as to give a lurid brightness to the blonde complexion, and a strange, sinister light to the deep blue eyes. No one but a pre-Raphaelite could have given to that pretty pouting mouth the hard and almost wicked look it had in the portrait.

It was so like, and yet so unlike. It was as if you had burned strange-colored fires before my lady's face, and by their influence brought out new lines and new expressions never seen in it before. The perfection of fea-ture, the brilliancy of coloring, were there; but I suppose the painter had copied quaint mediaeval monstrosities until his brain had grown bewil-dered, for my lady, in his portrait of her, had something of the aspect of a beautiful fiend.

Her crimson dress, exaggerated like all the rest in this strange picture, hung about her in folds that looked like flames, her fair head peeping out of the lurid mass of color as if out of a raging furnace. Indeed the crimson dress, the sunshine on the face, the red gold gleaming in the yellow hair, the ripe scarlet of the pouting lips, the glowing colors of each accessory of the minutely painted background, all combined to render the first effect of the painting by no means an agreeable one. (8:46–47)

Especially noticeable is Braddon's deftness in exploiting the prejudice against PreRaphaelite art as an indirect means of intensified character-ization. It was the sort of art, she implies—and she was right—that was peculiarly adaptable to portraying femmes fatales. If the PreRaphaelites had not existed, what other contemporary painter could she have seized upon for her particular purposes?

Later the picture was finished and "hung in the post of honor oppo-site the window, amidst Claudes, Poussins, and Wouvermans, whose less brilliant hues were killed by the vivid coloring of the modern artist. The bright face looked out of that tangled glitter of golden hair, in which the Pre-Raphaelites delight, with a mocking smile . . ." (25:141). Still later, after Robert Audley has put pressure on her, Lady Audley sits down to think, and in so doing, provides a model for another PreRaphaelite painting:

If Mr. Holman Hunt could have peeped into the pretty boudoir, I think the picture would have been photographed upon his brain to be reproduced by-and-by upon a bishop's half-length for the glorification of the pre-

Raphaelite brotherhood. My lady in that half-recumbent attitude, with her elbow resting on one knee, and her perfect chin supported by her hand, the rich folds of drapery falling away in long undulating lines from the exquisite outline of her figure, and the luminous, rose-colored firelight enveloping her in a soft haze, only broken by the golden glitter of her yellow hair—beautiful in herself, but made bewilderingly beautiful by the gorgeous surroundings which adorn the shrine of her loveliness. (31:194)

In her next novel, *Aurora Floyd*, Braddon briefly revisited the Pre-Raphaelites in order to depict Captain Bulstrode as differing from his comrades in the 11th Hussars in several laudable respects, including this one:

The young men who breakfasted with him in his rooms trembled as they read the titles of the big books on the shelves, and stared helplessly at the grim saints and angular angels in the pre-Raphaelite prints upon the walls. . . . Talbot Bulstrode's ideal woman was some gentle and feminine creature crowned with an aureole of pale auburn hair; some timid soul with downcast eyes, fringed with golden-tinted lashes; some shrinking being, as pale and prim as the mediaeval saints in his pre-Raphaelite engravings, spotless as her own white robes, excelling in all womanly graces and accomplishments, but only exhibiting them in the narrow circle of a home. (4:33–34)

That ideal woman turns out to be Aurora Floyd's cousin Lucy, the banker Archibald Floyd's "fair-haired niece . . . with the sunshine upon her amber tresses ["amber," not auburn or red], and the crisp folds of her peach-coloured dress, looking for all the world like one of the painted heroines so dear to the pre-Raphaelite brotherhood" (19:182).

To characterize the novel's villain, the jockey and horse-trainer James Conyers, Braddon reached back to the iconography of Byronic subjects. He posed, she said, as a Byronic hero, looking "as sentimental as if he had been ruminating upon the last three pages of the 'Bride of Abydos.' He had that romantic style of beauty peculiar to dark-blue eyes and long black lashes. . . . He looked like an exiled prince doing menial service in bitterness of spirit and a turned-down collar. He looked like Lara returned to his own domains to train the horses of a usurper" (17:159–60). But such forthright analogizing, as I have said, was rare.

Surtees once proposed that the newly fledged photographer, or daguerreotypist, could perform the same function as the illustrator. "If we had a Daguerreotype machine," he remarked in *Hawbuck Grange* (1846–47), "we would sketch him [Dolores Brown] as he sits under the stunted, crooked, decaying ash-tree, and impale him on our page; but that not being practicable, and our friend 'Phiz' not being at hand, we will just do what we can with the pen" (11:134). (In the event, however,

"Phiz," Hablot K. Browne, did illustrate the one-volume edition.) The coming of photography must have had some impact on novelists' descriptive technique, just as it had on the PreRaphaelite painters', perhaps, as is usually the effect of a new form of representational art, by sharpening their powers of observation and making its exercise more self-conscious.

From 1839 onward, photography was constantly in the news and more and more present in everyday life, beginning with the daily demonstrations of picture-taking that were among the attractions of the Adelaide Gallery, London's first applied science and technology museum. In its first years, this miraculous art of recording images was confined to portraits, outdoor scenes in which no motion would disturb the slow action of the chemicals on the plate, and inert objects like the coin collection, photographs of which (not the collection itself!) the valetudinarian Mr. Fairlie donated to the Carlisle Mechanics' Institute in *The Woman in White*. As a scientific wonder, the invention of Daguerre and his English counterpart, Fox Talbot, ranked with the telegraph. Surtees wrote in *Plain or Ringlets?* that those were "days of wonderful science and discovery, when sighs are wafted on wires 'From Indus to the Pole,' and the sun condescends to take portraits as low as a shilling a minute" (17:56).

By mid-century, the commercial possibilities of cheap, almost instantaneous portraiture had attracted scores of entrepreneurs who set up studios in the vicinity of Regent Street, and soon thereafter Julia Margaret Cameron began taking her now celebrated gallery of photographs of her eminent friends. "Likenesses of every living creature from the Pope down to the latest beauty of the ballet can be had in these happy days for a mere song," observed a writer in the *Saturday Review* in 1867.[23] Pioneer outdoor cameramen took their cumbersome equipment on location, even to the Crimea. In the social sphere, photography had an impact on manners, in that leafing through richly bound albums of daguerreotypes, as Mrs. Lammle and Twemlow did in *Our Mutual Friend*, replaced the old drawing-room pastime of paging through books of engravings. In appropriate circumstances, this decorous ritual could be a pretext for courting couples to sit close together on a sofa, as Mrs. Greenow and her imperious suitor Captain Bellfield did in the same year, in *Can You Forgive Her?* (1864–65). But such ardor as leafing through a book of photographs stirred was dampened in this instance by the presence in it of a carte de visite of her late husband. The current rage for distributing calling cards bearing a miniature photograph of oneself, a singular indulgence of vanity, had by this time become a nuisance, which Trollope denounced in *Phineas Finn*: "That bringing out

Photographer. "Now, sir! Ave yer Cart de visit done?" In the early 1860s, the fad
of exchanging calling cards bearing miniature portraits swept the nation, from
Trollope's middle class to (if we are to believe *Punch*, 29 June 1861) sanitation
workers. But it may be that this picture was drawn merely for the sake of the pun.

and giving of photographs, with the demand for counter photographs,
is the most absurd practice of the day" (57:544). But the exchange of
photographs had its serious private uses in a nation that sailed the seven
seas and colonized many of their shores. "Captain Beauchamp," reported Meredith, "encouraged the art of photography, as those that
make long voyages do, in reciprocating what they petition their friends
for. Mrs. Rosamund Culling had a whole collection of photographs of
him, equal to a visual history of his growth in chapters, from boyhood
to midshipmanship and to manhood" (*Beauchamp's Career*, 26:1.282).

In fiction as in life, the photographer came on the scene with his
magical apparatus. "From today, painting is dead!" exclaimed the popular French portraitist Paul Delaroche, who once dined at the Tuileries
with Ethel Newcome and Lady Kew (*The Newcomes*, 42:2.109). In Kingsley's *Two Years Ago*, the successful painter Claude Mellot, recognizing, as
he thought, the wave of the future, took up the art. "I yield to the new
dynasty," he said. "The artist's occupation is gone henceforth, and the
painter's studio, like 'all charms, must fly, at the mere touch of cold philosophy.'" When he set up his "tall three-legged box and a little black

tent" on the pier of a West Country fishing village, "'I say!' quoth one of the fishing elders, after long suspicious silence; 'I say, lads, this won't do. We can't have no outlandish foreigners taking observations here!'" (The Crimean War had brought on a spy scare.) "And then dropped out one wild suspicion after another. 'Maybe he's surveying for a railroad!'" (15:239, 255)

Normally, photography was welcomed as a pleasant adjunct to domestic life, particularly because of the way it enabled a family to amass inexpensively, across the years, its own visual archive. In nearly all respects, the camera and wet plates represented the life-enriching face of technology. But photography took a nasty turn in Hardy's *A Laodicean* (1880–81), when William Dare, one of the novel's two villains, uses a product of his machine to discredit the young architect Somerset in the eyes of the woman he loves, Paula Powers: "It was a portrait of Somerset; but by a device known in photography the operator, though contriving to produce what seemed to be a perfect likeness, had given it the distorted features and wild attitude of a man advanced in intoxication. No woman, unless specially cognizant of such possibilities, could have looked upon it and doubted that the photograph was a genuine illustration of a customary phase in the young man's private life" (5.4:311). A local photographer, to whom Paula's friend showed the picture, "told her that such misrepresentations were quite possible, and that they embodied a form of humour which was getting more and more into vogue among certain facetious persons of society. . . . 'I consider them libellous myself. Still, I have one or two samples by me, which I keep merely as curiosities.—There's one,' he said, throwing out a portrait from a drawer. 'That represents the German Emperor in a violent passion: this one shows the Prime Minister out of his mind; this the Pope of Rome the worse for liquor'" (5.13:367). But this, along with the associated under-the-counter art of pornophotography, constituted an aberration otherwise unseen in fiction.

The words *daguerreotype* and *photograph* were coined just in time to be pressed into service, along with another opportune invention, *Pre-Raphaelite*, as the critical discussion of realism grew livelier. The photograph was a convenient, comprehensible, and topically flavored symbol of realistic representation, and as such it became a permanent part of the critical vocabulary, reviewers using the words as nouns, adjectives, and verbs to signify fidelity to the eye's report. (Charlotte Brontë is reputed to have been the first to use *daguerreotype* as a verb, in *Shirley*.) Elizabeth Rigby, writing in the *Quarterly Review* in December 1848, described *Vanity Fair* as "a literal photograph of the manners and habits of the nineteenth century," and the phrase "sketched with all the fidelity of a daguerreotype portrait" was already on the verge of becoming a cliché when Surtees used it in 1845, in *Hillingdon Hall* (12:105). For the next thirty years, reviewers of Trollope's and George Eliot's novels in particular—Dickens's and Thackeray's somewhat less so—could scarcely have done their job without those words in their inkwells. (Eventually they were supplanted by *realism* and *realist*, first used in French art criticism in the 1830s, which came into general acceptance in England at the end of the fifties.) Whether they were used approvingly or disparagingly depended on how the critic stood on the all-important issue of realism.

At the same moment that Kingsley's Claude Mellot was exulting over the impending demise of his art and the rise of a modern replacement, Trollope, in a more ruminative mood, was considering the possibility that photography was capable of more physical and moral portraiture than any artist in words could hope to accomplish; in which case, would his own occupation be gone? As he began the second volume of *Barchester Towers*, he proposed to paint a word-picture of the Reverend Francis Arabin, late of Oxford:

> It is to be regretted that no mental method of daguerreotype or photography has yet been discovered by which the characters of men can be reduced to writing and put into grammatical language with an unerring precision of truthful description. How often does the novelist feel, ay, and the historian also and the biographer, that he has conceived within his mind and accurately depicted on the tablet of his brain the full character and personage of a man, and that nevertheless, when he flies to pen and ink to perpetuate the portrait, his words forsake, elude, disappoint, and play the deuce with him, till at the end of a dozen pages the man described has no more resemblance to the man conceived than the sign-board at the corner of the street has to the Duke of Cambridge?
>
> And yet such mechanical descriptive skill would hardly give more satisfaction to the reader than the skill of the photographer does to the anxious mother desirous to possess an absolute duplicate of her beloved child. The likeness is indeed true; but it is a dull, dead, unfeeling, inauspicious likeness. The face is indeed there, and those looking at it will know at once whose image it is; but the owner of the face will not be proud of the resemblance.
>
> There is no royal road to learning; no short cut to the acquirement of any valuable art. Let photographers and daguerreotypers do what they will, and improve as they may with further skill on that which skill has already done, they will never achieve a portrait of the human face divine. Let biographers, novelists, and the rest of us groan as we may under the burdens which we so often feel too heavy for our shoulders; we must either bear them up like men, or own ourselves too weak for the work we have undertaken. There is no way of writing well and also of writing easily. (20:280)

10

The Sense of Place

1.

RAILWAY STATIONS, telegraph wires, pillar boxes, and, in towns of some size, omnibuses were among the most visible signs of change on the broad Victorian scene, just as Rowlands' Kalydor, Gunter's ices, Stultz's coats, crinolines, and chignons were, in their various ways, emblems of modernity that men and women wore or consumed. But there also were new aspects of locale, public and domestic, that novelists enlisted in behalf of contemporary realism.

In 1807 a company called The New Patriotic Imperial and National Light and Heat Company, a title that would have filled an engraved business letterhead with as many flourishes as the United Metropolitan Improved Hot Muffin and Crumpet Baking Company in *Nicholas Nickleby*, successfully demonstrated how brightly streets could be lighted by a newly developed form of coal gas. The London site chosen for the display was the south side of Pall Mall, a neighborhood where many fashionable people, including some of the royal entourage, lived—a shrewd move because it not only generated maximum publicity but attracted investors and influential backers. Between 1817 and 1826, at least ten companies were formed to illuminate streets, shops, business offices, and some public buildings, although gas would not be introduced into any private homes for some years.

In his *Sketches by Boz* piece on "Gin-Shops," Dickens called attention to the "epidemic," originating six or eight years earlier—that is, about 1830—whose primary symptoms, he said, "were an inordinate love of plate-glass, and a passion for gas lights and gilding." The first trades affected were the linen-drapers and haberdashers, but the disease "attained a fearful height" as it spread to chemists' and hosiers' establishments ("Scenes," chap. 22 : 182–83). Gas lighting provided shopkeepers with a welcome threefold effect. There was the interior lighting itself, which not only showed up the colors of the goods but, in combination

339

The association of gas lighting with gin palaces was strengthened by
such graphic evidence as this, one of George Cruikshank's illustrations for *Sketches by Boz*.

with plate-glass mirrors, multiplied, if only by illusion, the amount of
goods in stock; there was added illumination from the street lamps; and
there was still more from exterior gas jets with reflectors directed toward
the show windows, which averted the nuisance of soot spoiling the goods
inside. But, Dickens went on to say, it was at certain forward-looking
wine vaults and public houses that the craze for gas and glass was most
conspicuous, turning those venerable places of refreshment into a new

species, called gin palaces. Their frosted windows not only screened the interior from the pavement but allowed the brilliant interior lighting, again multiplied by mirrors, to flood into the street, supplementing the flaring exterior jets that were an identifiable sign of the trade. The lamp outside one gin palace, about 1838–40, was said to be ten feet high and to contain seventy jets: a well-nigh irresistible beacon on a dull, rainy London night.

These lights, which in the absence of adequate street illumination outshone everything else in the poorer sections of any town, were standard fixtures in Victorian novelists' descriptions of lower-class neighborhoods at night. They symbolically juxtaposed alcoholic sociability, which according to most moralists lighted the road to debauchery and neglect—even abuse—of wife and children, with the realities of the dark, cold, wretched world outside. No other concise image carried so deep a tincture of implicit social criticism.

To a certain degree, therefore, gas lighting was associated in the public mind with the great drink-sodden underclass which people of standing preferred not to be reminded of. Combined with a conservatism that distrusted innovations in general, this was the main reason why, in some quarters, there was a strong prejudice against what Dickens called in *Bleak House* "the upstart gas."[1] Disraeli was remembering accurately when, in *Endymion*, one of Zenobia's (Lady Jersey's) favorite members of Parliament, arriving at her reception, announced, "I have some good news for you. We have prevented this morning the lighting of Grosvenor Square by gas by a large majority." "I felt confident that disgrace would never occur," replied Zenobia. "And by a large majority!" (1.5:23). This was in 1830, or shortly thereafter; the last oil lamps vanished from Grosvenor Square only in 1846.

On this high level of society, whether or not one had gas laid on in one's house served novelists as an instantly recognizable discriminant of rank and character. When Florence Dombey, after a stay with the Skettleses at Fulham, returned to the house her father was having completely redecorated and furnished for his new bride (who couldn't care less), "The garish light was in the long-darkened drawing-room" (*Dombey and Son*, 28:483). For "garish," Dickens's readers would have read "gas," because the pejorative adjective was habitually applied to gas at that time, except by the few who had had it installed. The adoption of gas lighting as an ostentatious token of wealth perfectly fitted Dombey's character.

The detail of "most of the lamps [being] lighted two hours before their time—as the gas seems to know, for it has a haggard and unwilling look" in the majestic overture to *Bleak House* announced a theme that would recur throughout the novel. The very fact that Sir Leicester Dedlock's town house was still lighted by candles, not even by oil lamps, when gas flared elsewhere in the fogbound city—at the gate of the awful graveyard, in the Sol's Arms public house, Snagsby's law stationery shop, and Trooper George's shooting gallery—would have identified him in the minds of the novel's first readers as, if not a moss-backed conservative, certainly not one on the cutting edge of modernity. Of him it could be said, as was said of the Duke of Donkeyton in Surtees's *Hillingdon Hall*, "His Grace didn't use gas—the only piece of sense he was known to be guilty of" (11:84). The old-fashioned lawyer Tulkinghorn lived in a Lincoln's Inn Fields mansion that was equally innocent of oil lamps, let alone gas jets. By contrast, the typical "new men" in Coketown, like Dombey in London, boasted this paragon of Victorian modern conveniences. At his house a mile or two outside town, Gradgrind presided over "A lawn and garden and an infant avenue, all ruled straight like a botanical account-book. Gas and ventilation, draining and water-service, all of the primest quality" (*Hard Times*, 1.3:54–55). Similarly, a "bright gaslight" was fixed over the steps in Bounderby's house in town.

Both gas and circulating hot water were lacking at the bishop's palace when Mrs. Proudie arrived at Barchester. That she was so upset by this discovery immediately notified Trollope's readers of her ambitiously modern set of values: no self-respecting person's abode, least of all that of the wife of a high-ranking ecclesiastic, should be without either of these amenities. She made sure that one omission was rectified, so that what turned out to be her disastrous housewarming was bathed in the merciless light of several gigantic twelve-burner gas chandeliers, the bishop's palace thereby acquiring the look of a gin palace. (As for the plumbing, we hear no more about it; conceivably this other pet project got sidetracked as the complications of the plot demanded Mrs. Proudie's full attention. Her husband is later seen washing his hands in his dressing room, but Trollope does not say whether the water was piped in or lugged upstairs in cans. Curiously, Sir Leicester Dedlock, who refused to have gas laid on in his London house, enjoyed the luxury of circulating hot water at Chesney Wold.)

Soon after the middle of the century, some venerable country homes were fitted for gas. Joseph Paxton, fresh from his Crystal Palace triumph, equipped the Duke of Devonshire's Chatsworth in 1852. In emulation, rich commoners installed gas in their new country houses, as did the banker Archibald Floyd in his "great mansion" in Kent (*Aurora Floyd* [1862–63]). But there were other considerations than its ambiguous role as status symbol (was it more fashionable to have gas or to refuse it?) that affected its reception in this sphere of society. One was its expense and

The prominently displayed gas chandelier in Marcus Stone's picture of the Veneerings' dinner party in *Our Mutual Friend* attests to the fact that this bright but garish source of illumination was de rigueur in households of the pretentious nouveaux riches.

another was its unpleasantly pungent odor, as Sir Walter Scott had discovered to his regret when he installed it at Abbotsford as early as 1823. George Eliot alluded to another effect, the consumption of oxygen, in one of her characteristic timely analogies in *The Mill on the Floss*: "Such glances and tones bring the breath of poetry with them into a room that is half-stifling with glaring gas and hard flirtation" (6.10:386). A partial remedy was provided about 1840, with the invention of the atmospheric burner.

In addition, the supply of gas was erratic; it emitted too much heat if the ventilation was inadequate, the pipes clogged, and the burners silted up. Nor could gas illuminate a large room with the pleasant softness of improved candles. As in gin palaces, it brought out the brilliance of mirrors and drinking glasses, and in these social elevations, of jewels as well (the newly rich Veneerings lighted their dining room with gas as a matter of course), but at the same time it lent a Tussaud-like waxen look to flesh and called unwelcome attention to women's wrinkles. All these were facts of everyday life that the mere mention of gas lighting would have evoked in readers' minds.

Still, its convenience appealed even to normally unadventurous and penny-pinching middle-class householders. Carlyle's hard-won (relative) affluence enabled him to have two jets installed at his house in Cheyne Row in 1852, despite the high cost of feeding them; at 15s. per thousand cubic feet it was close to a domestic extravagance.[2] But the distribution was spotty, and in some houses gas, oil lamps, and even candles coexisted. In the same year that Carlyle installed gas, Wilkie Collins described, in *Basil*, a newly built London suburb where "the gas lamps were lighted far and near"—one assumes he meant indoors—but in one of them "a servant brought candles into the room, and drew down the Venetian blinds" (1.7:58). In *Our Mutual Friend* a dozen years later, the Wilfers' house in Holloway lacked gas, yet Boffin's Bower, John Harmon's former house amid the Battlebridge dumps, rejoiced in it. This is doubtless an indication of Noddy Boffin's newfound wealth and his wife's good-natured inclination toward "Fashion." As late as 1874–75 (*The Way We Live Now*) there was gas in one London upper-middle-class house but not in another. Only when new techniques made it possible to burn gas at much greater heat and thus more economically, and the rates came down, did it come to be taken for granted in the kind of home where so much of the action in Victorian novels occurred.

The presence or absence of gas, then, was a social fact to be noted in fiction, in settings ranging from London streets and gin palaces to towns[†] and country houses, with their self-contained gas-making outfits

[†]There is a gas works at Yarmouth when David Copperfield first visits the Peggottys. It was at such a place that Phil Squod, Trooper George's aide-de-camp at the shooting gallery, acquired one of his coatings of scar tissue and grime: ". . . what with being scorched in a accident at a gas-works; and what with being blowed out of winder, case-filling at the firework business; I am ugly enough to be made a show on!" (*Bleak House*, 26:422)

that required a resident technician, as at Abbotsford and Chatsworth. It provided novelists with a constant store of timely, diversified, and sometimes curiously conflicting glimpses of the contemporary scene. The inherently gloomy precincts of the Fleet prison are brightened by gas as early as 1836–37 (*Pickwick Papers*), but the Colonial Office is lighted by candles as late as 1867–69 (*Phineas Finn*). Martin Chuzzlewit the younger, lodging over a tavern as he tries to find a job, lights his candle at the gas jet at the bar before going upstairs to open a letter the landlord has given him ("It was not sealed, but pasted close," and was prepaid, Dickens specifies as an extra up-to-date touch). At night, a newspaper office in the Strand had "windows . . . in a blaze of gas" (*Pendennis*). In Manchester about 1840 (*Mary Barton*), the Weavers' Arms, where the millworkers' union meets, is illuminated by "flaring gaslight," but candles are still used in the home of their employers, the Carsons.

Few of the articles of furniture that were bathed in the light of the gas jets were absolute novelties in the nineteenth century. Chairs, sofas, tables, sideboards, beds differed only in style from those the Victorians' grandparents had lived with, though sometimes those differences were arresting. Pianos were the only pieces of domestic furniture whose increasingly widespread distribution spoke of a new age.[3] In Jane Austen's novels, where nearly all of the ladies played, they were a distinct novelty, having begun to replace the harpsichord of Sophia Western's day only in the last quarter of the eighteenth century. Though they were status symbols—the cachet having as much to do with cultural pretensions and the implication that the household included talented ladies of leisure as with actual wealth—they were not ruinously expensive. A "piccolo pianoforte," designed for small rooms, cost thirty guineas, and larger models, such as "a pillared and leafy-legged monster that leans forward as though about to spring upon and bite the hand that opens it," could be had for seventy.[4] Becky Sharp, who was very well informed in such matters, said that the piano John Sedley bought for Amelia when she left Miss Pinkerton's school cost only thirty-five pounds. (Was it a Broadwood or a Stodart? Thackeray wasn't sure: he mentioned both names.) Thackeray's having Dobbin buy the same piano for twenty-five pounds at the auction of the Sedley chattels, and anonymously return it to Amelia to play in the Brompton lodgings to which the family was reduced, was an inspired touch. Not only did it express Dobbin's self-effacing generosity and his unspoken love for Amelia: it was a token of continuity, ensuring the fallen Sedley family a valued possession which proclaimed that, though in deeply reduced circumstances, they were still gentlefolk.

Among farmers, possession of a piano ranked as a status symbol with

This is Richard Doyle's realization of Charles Honeyman's *déjeuner musical* in *The Newcomes*: Mrs. Sherrick, a "famous artiste" who performed at La Scala and other opera houses before her marriage, is at the piano, her daughter possesses "a noble contralto voice," and together they "sing . . . magnificently."

buying smart gigs for their wives, a form of putting on airs that was always unkindly commented on by envious neighbors. Near Pendennis's West Country town of Clavering, the ambitious representative of an old family of yeomen and farmers "pulled down the old farmhouse; built a flaring new white-washed mansion, with capacious stables; had a piano in the drawing-room; kept a pack of harriers; and assumed the title of Squire Hobnell" (*Pendennis*, 50:2.116). Such emblematic breaches of the social contract that kept people in their places complicated entertaining arrangements, for example. Describing Miss Thorne's fête champêtre in *Barchester Towers*, Trollope commented: "To seat the bishop on an arm chair on the lawn and place Farmer Greenacre at the end of a long table in the paddock was easy enough; but where will you put Mrs. Lookaloft, whose husband though a tenant on the estate hunts in a red coat, whose daughters go to a fashionable seminary in Barchester, who calls her farm house Rosebank, and who has a piano forte in her drawing-room?" (35:410). (After much agonizing on Miss Thorne's part, "Mrs. Lookaloft was asked into the Ullathorne drawing-room merely because she called her house Rosebank, and had talked over her husband into buying pianos and silk dresses instead of putting his money by to stock farms for his sons" [39:443]. Strong-minded women must be rewarded.)

Eventually the stigma of ostentation wore off and keeping a piano in farmhouse or village cottage became a proud rural tradition, as in Hardy's Wessex. In *Under the Greenwood Tree*, Maybold, pressing the schoolmistress Fancy Day to marry him, knew precisely what terms to offer: "Your musical powers shall be still further developed; you shall have whatever pianoforte you like; you shall have anything, Fancy, anything to make you happy . . ." (6:171). Gabriel Oak's amatory approach to Bathsheba, in *Far from the Madding Crowd*, followed, though a bit more cautiously, the same presumably time-tested pattern: "You shall have a piano in a year or two—farmers' wives are getting to have pianos now . . ." (4:27). When Bathsheba inherits her uncle's farm, as she shortly does, she gets a piano, and a new one at that.

The make and style of a piano made some difference. The great name remained Broadwood, but in *Aurora Floyd*, Miss Braddon described a conservative taste that preferred another brand: "Mrs. Lofthouse was rather a brilliant pianist, and was never happier than when interpreting Thalberg and Benedict upon her friends' Collard-and-Collard [the name under which the famous pianist-composer Clementi's old firm then marketed its instruments]. There were old-fashioned people round Doncaster who believed in Collard and Collard, and were thankful for the melody to be got out of a good honest grand, in a solid rosewood case, unadorned with carved glorification, or ormolu fretwork" (23:231). At the time of the novel, "good honest grands" had fallen from favor; they accounted for only five to ten percent of the annual English production, the world outside Doncaster now having an overwhelming preference for uprights.

Clocks were to the working class what pianos were to the relatively well–off. At one time these household timekeepers were taxed as luxury items, but in the early Victorian years the English market was flooded with cheap clocks from Holland and then Connecticut (the latter also bearing the generic name of "Dutch"), until, as G. R. Porter observed in *The Progress of the Nation* (1847), they were "often pointed out as the

certain indication of prosperity and personal respectability on the part
of the working man."[5] In Coventry, it was said, "If an artisan could afford no bacon, he was badly off. If he could afford bacon, but no meat,
then he was doing middling well. If he could afford butcher's meat, and
had a clock in the house, then he was very well off indeed."[6] The prototypical dwelling of an honest workingman was the one described in
Vivian Grey: "the neat row of plates, and the well-scoured utensils, and
the fine old Dutch clock, and the ancient and amusing ballad, purchased
at some neighbouring fair, or of some itinerant bibliopole, and pinned
against the wall" bespoke "the very model of the abode of an English
husbandman" (2.11:52). In *Sybil*, the cottage of the factory hand Gerard
boasted "an oaken table, some cottage chairs made of beech-wood, and
a Dutch clock" (2.16:155), and at the same time, in a London working-
class quarter, the Toodle family's mantelpiece was graced with a clock
and a castle "with red and green windows in it, susceptible of illumination by a candle-end within" (*Dombey and Son*, 6:125). Conversely, to the
unsympathetic or censorious, the absence of a clock in a lower-class
dwelling was inferential evidence of moral decline, because when a man
or woman needed money for drink, the household timepiece was the
first item to be presented at the pawn shop.[†]

2.

Comprehensive views of domestic mise-en-scènes are not often found in
the writings of the greater Victorian novelists, who preferred such small
indicative touches as have just been described. Dickens, with all his zest
for deploying descriptive detail, seldom gave his readers the kind of assembled and particularized middle-class interiors that popular painters
of domestic genre subjects routinely produced. When he did, it was in

[†]There was another angle to the clock-drink relation, a joke repeated in several novels.
Esther Summerson and Ada, after their night in the Jellybys' chaotic household, "met the
cook round the corner coming out of a public house, wiping her mouth. She mentioned,
as she passed us, that she had been to see what o'clock it was" (*Bleak House*, 5:96). And in
Our Mutual Friend, Bella Wilfer comes upon an elderly charwoman, employed at her father's office, "wiping her mouth, and account[ing] for its humidity on natural principles well
known to the physical sciences, by explaining that she had looked in at the door to see
what o'clock it was" (3.16:667). The point was that during the years when clocks were
taxed beyond most people's reach, public houses installed them as required by law (thus
some clocks, as well as some railway trains, were called "parliamentaries"). A domestic
servant, returning from an unauthorized absence, might always explain to his or her mistress that a quick trip to the corner had been made for the sake of a time check, a specious
excuse in view of the fact that by the Victorian era any household that could afford a
servant could also afford a clock below stairs as well as in the family's quarters.

the interest of the familiar axiom that surroundings, like clothing, bespeak the person. He fully described John Jarndyce's Bleak House with its cluttered interior, a predecessor of the high Victorian overstuffed parlor rather than an example of it; he presented it as comfortable, a repository of many objects with sentimental, "homely" associations—a distance away from the cold grandeur of the Dedlocks' town and country houses, on the one hand, and the disheveled anarchy of the Jellybys' quarters, on the other. The Meagleses' "cottage" at Twickenham, in *Little Dorrit*, likewise testified to the warm, familiar atmosphere that prevailed there, the accumulations of bric-à-brac and souvenirs reminding the reader of their love of travel despite their refusal to learn a word of a foreign tongue. The innocent tastelessness of the furnishings of Harmony Jail, shortly to be dignified as Boffin's Bower, provided an early clue to the newly rich Boffins' amiability and lack of culture.

Congestion, combined with wild eclecticism, was the very quintessence of the middle- and upper-class Victorian domestic scene. Parlors and drawing rooms were so crowded with large pieces of furniture and miscellaneous objects that the inhabitants scarcely had space to walk, let alone escape in case of fire. Thackeray waxed ironically eloquent on the "fine house in Tyburnia, . . . as gorgeous as money could make it" into which Clive and Rosey Newcome moved at the height of their prosperity:

> An Oxford Street upholsterer had been let loose in the yet virgin chambers; and that inventive genius had decorated them with all the wonders his fancy could devise. Roses and Cupids quivered on the ceilings, up to which golden arabesques crawled from the walls; your face (handsome or otherwise) was reflected by countless looking-glasses, so multiplied and arranged as, as it were, to carry you into the next street. You trod on velvet, pausing with respect in the centre of the carpet, where Rosey's cipher was worked in the sweet flowers which bear her name. What delightful crooked legs the chairs had! What corner-cupboards there were filled with Dresden gimcracks, which it was part of this little woman's business in life to purchase! What étagères, and bonbonières, and chiffonières! What awfully bad pastels there were on the walls! What frightful Boucher and Lancret shepherds and shepherdesses leered over the portières! What velvet-bound volumes, mother-of-pearl albums, inkstands representing beasts of the field, prie-dieu chairs, and wonderful nicknacks I can recollect! (*The Newcomes*, 63: 2.268–69)

In 1861–62 Miss Braddon extravagantly catalogued the "little Aladdin's palace" that was Lady Audley's boudoir, crammed with ormolu, porcelain, Gobelins, and every other kind of fashionable objet d'art that money could buy. Like their predecessors of the silver fork school, the so-called minor Victorian novelists knew that their readers hungered for detailed, highly colored, and supposedly authoritative pen-pictures of elegant interiors they never expected to see in person. But these novelists ranged beyond the upper crust to portray, with equal particularity, the homes of comfortably fixed middle-class families.

What strikes one most forcibly in descriptions of domestic interiors is the general lack of specifically contemporary touches. The congestion and eclecticism were themselves "period": no Victorian interior bore any resemblance to the comfortable, relatively open ones seen in seventeenth-century Dutch paintings, or to the undescribed but easily imaginable parlors in a Jane Austen novel. These predated the great expansion of middle-class consumerism and the sharpening realization on the part of suppliers that money was to be made from the new enthusiasm for keeping up to the minute, when fashion after fashion swept the household furnishings market, as it did the market for women's clothing. But the greater novelists, at least, seldom note the presence of new styles. The products of such manufacturers as the Patent Decorative Carving Company, a firm dedicated to making carved furniture by machinery whose failure in the 1840s robbed Alfred Tennyson of his scanty patrimony, do not appear in fiction, nor do many of the miscellaneous items that individually and in the aggregate were assumed to beautify the domestic scene. A rich and gaudy inventory, however, could be compiled from the novels of Surtees, always observant of the period physical detail: floss silk pheasants, Kidderminster rugs, gaudy bell pulls, electroplated candlesticks, inlaid Indian work tables, wax flowers, needlework pictures of such sentimental landscapes as Melrose by moonlight (products of the accomplished young daughters of the house), mahogany cellaret sideboards with patent locks, papier-mâché or imitation Dresden porcelain vases—some of these and their innumerable companion items were among the new household accessories, some exclusively and exuberantly decorative, others allegedly functional, that were admired at the Crystal Palace.

There is an oblique allusion to a new type of furniture—new in material if not in design—in the name of the Veneerings in *Our Mutual Friend* as well as that of the furniture dealer Vineer in *The Newcomes*.[7] Veneering was a brand-new method of making cheap furniture (a thin layer of choice wood, which gave its name to the whole piece, on the surface, and inferior wood underneath), and its applicability to the family in Dickens's novel would have been obvious to all readers. In *Orley Farm*, Trollope had timely fun with the figure of a commercial traveler (member of a fraternity called less grandly, in Dickens's early days, bagmen) whose line was patent iron "Louey catorse" furniture—an attempt

John Everett Millais drew this illustration for Trollope's *Orley Farm*, showing Mr. Kantwise, sales representative for the Patent Steel Furniture Company, demonstrating the solid virtues of his product to his fellow "commercials." "There's nothing like iron, sir, nothing; you may take my word for that. . . . I don't think any lady of your acquaintance, sir, would allow you to stand on her rosewood or mahogany loo table."

to introduce into the parlor an admittedly long-wearing material whose domestic uses hitherto had been confined to garden seats and benches, umbrella stands, door stops, and boot scrapers. Packed disassembled in three boxes and priced at £15 10s., with the reusable boxes thrown in, the suite allegedly had "never [been] seen equalled in wood for three times the money." It consisted of an easy rocking chair, eight other chairs, a music stand with matching stool, a pair of stand-up screens, and three tables, one with a blue top with a bird of paradise in the middle and a two-inch border in the same yellow color as the pillar and the three legs; a second was a chess table with blue and light pink squares; and the third was "a 'sofa,' of proper shape, but rather small in size" (6:53–54; 23:204). To say that the various components of this "metallic set of painted trumpery" matched was, in a sense, true, but it gave the wrong impression of their actual hideousness as an ensemble.

The most noteworthy domestic innovation (except for gas) in Victorian times had only a much delayed impact on personal habits, and it appeared as infrequently in fiction as it did in actual life until near the end of the century. Readers of *The Moonstone* in 1868 must have raised their eyebrows, at the very least, when they read of the indefatigable tract-distributor Drusilla Clack's saturation coverage of Lady Verinder's London house. She arrived eventually in Lady Verinder's bedroom, where she put one tract near the matches and another under a box of chocolate drops. "But one book was now left at the bottom of my bag," she recounted, "and but one apartment was still unexplored—the bath-room, which opened out of the bed-room. I peeped in; and the holy inner voice that never deceives, whispered to me, 'You have met her, Drusilla, everywhere else; meet her at the bath, and the work is done.' I observed a dressing-gown thrown across a chair. It had a pocket in it, and in that pocket I put my last book" ("Second period, first narrative," chap. 4:252). ("Bath room" meant exactly what it said; water closets were totally absent from the universe of Victorian fiction, though their existence in actual life could be inferred from nonliterary sources in which working-class recipients of religious tracts indicated the practical use to which such material was customarily applied.)

Bathing did not occupy much time in ordinary Victorians' lives, except among those who had acquired the habit while living in warm climates where daily immersions were almost a necessity. Not the least of the Duke of Wellington's well-publicized idiosyncrasies was his daily bath, and although a few fastidious—or emulative—men adopted the habit, the common opinion was that of the old barrister Grump in *Pendennis*, who declared that the practice of daily bathing was "an absurd, new-fangled, dandified folly. . . . He had done without water very well, and so had our fathers before him" (29:1.294). So long as most people confined their ablutions to a "daily wash" and, in the middle classes, a weekly bath, no elaborate provisions had to be made, the usual bedroom apparatus (basins, jugs, soap dishes, sponge trays, and wash-hand stands) sufficing for the former and a portable hip-bath or its equivalent for the latter.

Rooms set apart for this purpose were extremely rare as the Victorian years approached. In *Pelham* (1828), Bulwer described Reginald Glanville's palatial quarters: "Beyond this library (if such it might be called), and only divided from it by half-drawn curtains of the same colour and material as the cushion, was a bath room. The decorations of this room were of a delicate rose colour; the bath, which was of the most elaborate workmanship, represented, in the whitest marble, a shell, supported by two Tritons" (2.9:183). But practical considerations would suggest that this sybaritic neoclassic installation was for display rather than use: its location off a reception room, for one thing, and for another, the evident difficulty of cleansing oneself in a marble conch.

In 1838 John Claudius Loudon's *The Suburban Gardener and Villa Companion* included a judicious passage on the advantage of locating a house's bath room on the ground floor, adding that "Where there are dressing-rooms to the bed-rooms, a bath may be placed in each of these, or in such of them as may be thought necessary."[8] But this was an option found oftener in architectural pattern books than in the houses that were actually built. Only health freaks, as their commonsensical friends would have called them had the term been known, were impervious to medical opinion that attributed the "alarming increase in rheumatic fever, lung complaints, and other ailments" to excessive bathing.[9] John Jarndyce, in *Bleak House*, slept in a plain room "all the year round, with his window open, his bedstead without any furniture standing in the middle of the floor for more air," and had a "cold bath gaping for him in a smaller room adjoining" (6:116). This probably was a tub, a modest replica of the "enormous dishpan affair," constructed of mahogany lined with sheet lead and weighing a ton, that Lord John Russell was known to use in his London house. But patent shower baths were also to be had. At first, the gravity flow of water came from a tank filled from heavy cans toted upstairs by servants; later—the date is uncertain and the advertisements of these domestic novelties are not always helpful—the water was piped in from the very latest amenity, a hot- and cold-water system. One such adjunct to gracious living was among the day's novelties discussed by Mrs. Tibbs's lodgers in *Sketches by Boz*:

> "Capital things those shower baths!" ejaculated Wisbottle.
> "Excellent!" said Tomkins.
> "Delightful!" chimed in O'Bleary. (He had once seen one, outside a tinman's.)

THE NEW PATENT SHOWER BATH.

R. AND J. SLACK, 336, STRAND,

(Opposite Somerset House)

Beg to call attention to their new Shower Bath as an article far superior to any bath ever introduced, its action being so simple that a child can fill it. The great inconvenience in the old shower bath was the difficulty in raising the water, the pump requiring great labour, and consequent liability to get out of order ; all these objections are obviated in this bath. May be seen in operation at 336, Strand, where may be inspected the most extensive assortment of baths, toilet sets, nickel and electro-plated ware, and every article in furnishing ironmongery at prices much lower than any other house where quality is considered. Sponging Baths, from 7*s.* 6*d.* ; Hip ditto, 19*s.* and 21*s.* ; Portable Shower Baths and Curtains, 7*s.* 6*d.*

Their Catalogue, containing Two Hundred Drawings and Prices, may be had gratis, or sent, post-free, to any part.

This advertisement in the June 1849 number of *Pendennis* fortuitously prepared readers for the passage in the novel's August number in which Pen and Warrington rig up a newfangled shower bath in their lodgings. Neither the advertiser nor Thackeray, however, pointed out that the invention delivered only an invigorating stream of *cold* water. The figure in the *Punch* cartoon (opposite) (8 December 1849) cheerfully makes the most of this deficiency.

"Disgusting machines!" rejoined Evenson, who extended his dislike to almost every created object, masculine, feminine, or neuter.

"Disgusting, Mr. Evenson!" said Gobler, in a tone of strong indignation.—"Disgusting! Look at their utility—consider how many lives they have saved by promoting perspiration!"

"Promoting perspiration, indeed," growled John Evenson. . . . "I was ass enough to be persuaded some time ago to have one in my bedroom. 'Gad, I was in it once, and it effectually cured *me*, for the mere sight of it threw me into a profuse perspiration for six months afterwards." ("Tales," chap. 1:305)

In 1838 Thomas Hood published in his *Comic Annual* "Stanzas Composed in a Shower-Bath," which began:

> Trembling, as Father Adam stood
> To pull the stalk, before the Fall,
> So I stand here, before the Flood,
> On my own head the shock to call:
> How like our predecessor's luck!
> 'Tis but to pluck—but needs some pluck!

"Quite a new Sensation for the Luxurious, these cold Mornings.
Use Hot Water, and look at your Shower-Bath !"

At the same moment, the late thirties, Pendennis and Warrington installed a pair in their digs on the top floor of Lamb Court, Temple,
beneath which old Grump "used to be awakened by the roaring of the
shower-baths . . . part of the contents of which occasionally trickled
through the roof into Mr. Grump's room" (*Pendennis*, 29:1.294).† Some

---

†Thackeray later had a shower in his house in Onslow Square. In 1851, renovating his
new London residence, Tavistock House, Dickens installed for his daily ablutions "a cold
shower of the best quality, always charged to an unlimited extent" from rooftop water
tanks. As a newly published letter discloses, the presence of a toilet in the same room

larger houses at the time had piped-in water set in the recess of a bed-room or dressing room, as did the royal suite at Osborne. At least once in fiction, however, an existing bathroom was partly reconverted. When more room was needed in the Bradshaws' house in the West Country town of Eccleston (Gaskell's *Ruth* [1853]), "the 'ingenious' upholsterer of the town . . . [came] in to give his opinion, that 'nothing could be easier than to convert a bathroom into a bedroom, by the assistance of a little drapery to conceal the shower-bath,' the string of which was to be care-fully concealed, for fear that the unconscious occupier of the bath-bed might innocently take it for a bell-rope" (22:251).

As possessors of a reconvertible bath room, the Bradshaws were decidedly avant-garde. Although Thomas Cubitt, the famous London builder, claimed he had installed water closets in all his houses since about 1824, his response to a tenant in Lowndes Square who wanted a *bath* room was that while it was "unusual for him," he would install one for an additional £3 per year in the rent.[10] Even the model home that Philip Webb built for William Morris and his bride six years later (1859) had no bath room. In successive novels, Surtees specified bathing facili-ties as the hallmark of what he portrayed as truly luxurious establish-ments. At Hanby House, Mr. Soapey Sponge—a fitting name for a character in this context—found that "the bed-rooms possessed every imaginable luxury. . . . In Sponge's room, for instance, there were hip-baths, and foot-baths, a shower-bath, and hot and cold baths *adjoining*" (*Mr. Sponge's Sporting Tour*, 37:253; emphasis mine). A few years later (*Ask Mamma* [1857–58]), young Billy Pringle, reputedly "the richest Commoner in England," wrote to his mother from Tantivy Castle in Wales that it was "a splendid place . . . more like Windsor than anything I ever saw. . . . I've got a beautiful bedroom with warm and cold baths and a conservatory attached" (18:71).

The clear inference to be drawn was that such provision was by no means to be expected even in luxuriously appointed houses. Even in the newly built homes of the nation's wealthiest families, rooms explicitly designed for bathing were far from universal. The enormous Thoresby House in Nottinghamshire, built in the mid-sixties, had none, and even in the seventies, some new country houses had them and some did not. Carlton Towers in Yorkshire lacked them, yet at Wykehurst, Sussex, a bath room was attached to each bedroom suite.[11] Perhaps the difference

---

complicated matters, but a solution was found in the form of a curtain to conceal "the box in the corner." (Fred Kaplan, *Dickens: a Biography* [New York, 1988], p. 271.) Later (1869), Tennyson luxuriated in the plumbing arrangements in his new home, Aldworth—"a per-ennial stream which falls through the house and where I take three baths a day." (Charles Tennyson, *Alfred Tennyson* [New York, 1949], p. 382.)

was attributable to the sources of the respective owners' wealth: Carlton Towers was built for a Catholic nobleman (old money) and Wykehurst for a City banker (new money). All of which adds timely pertinence to Aurora Floyd's "weary sigh" in 1862–63 as she contemplated the luxury with which her husband, a bluff, honest, and wealthy Yorkshireman, had literally (in part) showered her at his place near Doncaster: "How pretty the rooms look! . . . how simple and countrified! It was for *me* that the new furniture was chosen,—for me that the bath-room and conservatory were built" (*Aurora Floyd*, 28:278).

Given this history of the bath room down to the time of *The Moonstone*, one obvious point about Drusilla Clack's planting her tracts is the gall it took for her to do so in what had become the most private part of the house, not a reception room open to anyone who happened to be visiting, but one that could be entered only from a certain bedroom that was sacred to anyone who occupied it. In short, she had no business being there. Another point is that the simple presence of such a room in her London house marked Lady Verinder as one in advance of the general fashion. And that, in turn, would have implied to the Victorian reader, for whatever it was worth, that she had a greater concern for personal cleanliness than was common at the time.[†]

The interiors of shops were largely taken for granted in fiction. The social historian who wants to know more about the physical aspects of the Victorian retail trade—the enlarged size of the display windows, now that plate glass had become untaxed and thus less costly; their interior arrangements and appointments; the way goods were displayed, and the difference that gas lighting made—must look elsewhere than in the novels of the time. The Bishopsgate haberdashery and linen-drapery in Trollope's *The Struggles of Brown, Jones, and Robinson* is one of the few exceptions to the rule. Dickens described some shop interiors, but seldom of premises that respectable females would venture to enter. In *Sketches by Boz*, for example, he took his readers by proxy into ornate gin palaces, pawnbrokers', and marine store shops. The establishments whose looks he took pains to describe in his novels typically were specialized ones, and whatever else they were, these Dickensian interiors were picturesque to a fault. Many had the dusty aura of age, and almost all were outside the mainstream of Victorian commerce: the Old Curiosity Shop, a dusty, crowded mishmash of battered antiques and second-

---

[†]Or, for that matter, for many years to come. Mark Girouard reports that in 1906 Raymond Asquith, writing from Chatsworth, complained that in that enormous pile there was only one bathroom, "which is kept for the King." Girouard adds that "Bathrooms did not really establish themselves adequately [in country houses] until the 1920s—and then only in some houses." (*A Country House Companion* [New Haven, 1987], pp. 57, 168.)

hand goods; Poll Sweedlepipe's combination barber and bird-dealer's
shop; Sol Gills's nautical instrument shop at the sign of the wooden midshipman, where money passed from hand to hand only when a passerby
came in for change; and the dark, grotesque premises of Mr. Venus,
"Preserver of Animals and Birds and Articulator of human bones."

3.

Novelists seldom noted the proliferation of new public and commercial
buildings that resulted from the revival of the construction industry following the Napoleonic Wars and the subsequent surge of prosperity that
transformed several provincial centers into reduced-scale Londons. The
economic and political power that these cities now possessed was sym-
bolized by the railway termini, town halls, financial exchanges, auditori-
ums, hospitals, office buildings, and sprawling multistoried factories and
warehouses that crowded the cityscape. But fiction set in the new industrial cities, such as Mrs. Gaskell's two Manchester novels, *Mary Barton*
and *North and South*, did not so much as glance at those imposing and
already soot-blackened monuments of commercial prosperity and municipal pride. Thackeray explicitly avoided "a description of that great
and flourishing town of Newcome, and of the manufactures which
caused its prosperity . . . the magnificent brokers and manufacturers
who had their places of business in the town, and their splendid villas
outside its smoky precincts" (*The Newcomes*, 2:188–89). The only typically Victorian buildings to be mentioned—and even then novelists did
not pause to describe them—were railway stations.

The prominence of these buildings was due not only to the scale and
grandeur with which their architects had endowed them but to their
contrasting surroundings. Although the chief business streets in London
and the provincial capitals witnessed much demolition and new construction, a great deal remained that was old. Despite all the clichés that
hovered in the Victorian air about the unprecedented, to some actually
dizzying, pace of change, the total physical scene, with the single but
conspicuous exception of the railway, was marked more by continuity
than by novelty. Churches in both town and country, the setting of innumerable episodes in fiction, belonged much more to the preserved
past than to the innovative present. Until mid-century, with few exceptions, nothing had happened to their venerable interiors to distinguish
them from the edifices in which the Reverend Laurence Sterne had
preached and Jane Austen had prayed. Nowhere in fiction does one see
the fruits of the Church Building Act of 1818, which allocated a million

pounds to build 214 "Commissioners' churches" in underserved London
suburbs and the new towns of the industrial Midlands and North, or any
but a handful of the two thousand or other privately financed churches
built between 1800 and 1850, most of which were confidently asserted
to be neo-Gothic and many of which were constructed, not of traditional stone, but of the more efficiently utilized, and cheaper, brick and
cast iron.[12†]

In Hardy's early fiction, by contrast, church buildings, like railways,
have a sharp topical significance. The aspiring novelist was then earning a living as an employee of a London architectural firm specializing in church restoration, an activity that had begun in the 1840s as
"Cambridge ecclesiology," an offshoot of tractarianism, and in later
years had come to be much deplored because, among other depredations, it involved removing from the stone surfaces, both exterior and
interior, all the supposedly disfiguring encrustations of age; hence William Morris's description of the opposing preservation movement, which
he spearheaded, as "Anti-Scrape." In *A Pair of Blue Eyes* (1872–73), the
progress of the plot was marked by the stages in the rebuilding of a
Wessex church to modern (misguided) specifications intended to restore
it to its original appearance. The novel, Hardy wryly noted in his preface
to a new edition in 1895, was "written at a time when the craze for indis-
criminate church restoration had just reached the remotest nooks of
England."

Eight years later, the controversial movement furnished the major
plot theme for another of Hardy's novels, *A Laodicean* (1880–81). The
railway construction heiress Paula Powers hired the young architect
Somerset to restore old Stancy Castle. An erroneous news story to the
effect that she was to "demolish much, if not all, that was interesting in
that ancient pile, and insert in its midst a monstrous travesty of some
Greek temple" evoked a letter in one of the morning newspapers. "In

†The churches in Dickens's novels are invariably old, an important illustration of his
penchant for selecting whatever was quaint or antique in the Victorian visual experience.
Even when he set scenes in actual churches that were identifiably new, he suppressed
evidence of their recent origin and lent them the usual aura of age. If readers of *Dombey
and Son* wished to identify the icy church, "in the region between Portland Place and
Bryanstone Square," that was the site of the successive baptism, funeral, and wedding
scenes, they would have thought of either All Souls', Langham Place, or St. Marylebone
parish church, neither of which was old, the former having been built in 1822–24, the
latter in 1817. Of course, it is not necessary to assume that he had either in mind. One
London church he definitely identified was St. George's, Southwark, the scene of Little
Dorrit's overnight "party." It was built between 1733 and 1736.

the name of all lovers of mediaeval art, conjured the simple-minded writer, let something be done to save a building which, injured and battered in the Civil Wars, was now to be made a complete ruin by the freaks of an irresponsible owner." Paula's architect was on the side of the angels. "Somerset," Hardy wrote approvingly, "had not attempted to adapt an old building to the wants of the new civilization. He had placed his new erection beside it as a slightly attached structure, harmonizing with the old; heightening and beautifying, rather than subduing it. His work formed a palace, with a ruinous castle annexed as a curiosity" (1.14:127; 2.2:154). Under such circumstances, Hardy intimated, that was the way to go.[†]

One senses a certain irony in the use of this particular topicality—a controversial large-scale effort to restore to the English scene a sense of the past—to enforce a novel's sense of the present. There was similar irony in the physical appearance of new suburbs that were spreading out, usually ribbon-wise along the major roads, from the old town centers. They were an incongruous mixture of the new and the old. The mortar between the bricks of the jerry-built "villas" and "semi-detacheds" may not have dried, and the wood of their frames may have been unseasoned, but the styles in which they were built intentionally smacked of tradition. The idioms that dominated the architectural pattern books from which most of the new housing was designed were Greek revival, "Old Scotch (mini-baronial)," Gothic, Swiss chalet, bogus—and eclectic—Queen Anne; there was, in fact, no such thing as a contemporary domestic style, any more than there was an identifiably modern style in public buildings.

In the countryside, as soon as one moved beyond sight of the railway lines with their cuttings, tunnels, and viaducts, little bespoke change except the immemorial procession of the seasons. There were, it is true, several thousands of miles of comparatively new canals, but in appearance these were little more than artificially straightened streams, and they easily blended into the landscape. In some parts of the country the landscape had been modified in comparatively recent times by a belated and final surge of enclosure, the open arable land being divided into fields by hedges or post-rail fences; and what natural woodland had re-

---

[†]Much earlier (1860), Wilkie Collins had opportunely used church restoration as a topical link in the chain of events. In *The Woman in White*, the fast-spreading fire in the tumbledown Hampshire church which kills Percival Glyde originated in straw-bedded packing cases that contained old carvings awaiting funds necessary to send them to London for restoration.

mained at the beginning of the century had been reduced by the insatiable demands of wartime shipbuilders. But this partial, local transformation of the physical scene had happened so slowly that none but the oldest inhabitants were aware of it, and in any case there was no William Cobbett or Richard Jefferies among the novelists to call attention to it.

Although in thriving little towns on the railway lines there was some new construction in the different styles that Trollope noted from time to time, in most sleepy villages old landmarks remained unchanged: a tavern (its custom much diminished since coaches no longer stopped there), a wheelwright's shop, a blacksmith's, a saddler's, perhaps an ancient church in bad repair, possibly a mill and a tiny shop. The cottages in which weavers and spinners had worked in prefactory times survived, but only as dwellings, not sites of home industry. "In comparison with cities," said Hardy in *Far from the Madding Crowd*, the town of Weatherbury, near Casterbridge, was immutable.

> The citizen's *Then* is the rustic's *Now*. In London, twenty or thirty years ago are old times; in Paris, ten years, or five; in Weatherbury three or four score years were included in the mere present, and nothing less than a century set a mark on its face or tone. Five decades hardly modified the cut of a gaiter, the embroidery of a smock-frock, by the breadth of a hair. Two generations failed to alter the turn of a single phrase. In these Wessex nooks the busy outsider's ancient times are only old; his old times are still new; his present is futurity. (22:127)

The thriving market town of Casterbridge itself, Hardy was at pains to emphasize, was an "antiquated borough . . . at that time [the mid-1840s], recent as it was, untouched by the faintest sprinkle of modernism. It was compact as a box of dominoes. It had no suburbs—in the ordinary sense. Country and town met at a mathematical line" (*The Mayor of Casterbridge*, 2:21). Casterbridge is the most perfectly realized country town in Victorian fiction, and one of its most striking features is the absolute lack of novelty. It was then, Hardy intimates, just as it had been a century earlier, finished and finite, unlike town suburbs elsewhere, which represented the instability of modern times.

It was inside the great country houses, above all, that time stood still, or seemed to do so in fiction. These seats of landowning wealth, the locale of many of Disraeli's and Bulwer-Lytton's novels between 1840 and 1860, and of Trollope's from then to the 1880s, contained nothing, except in service areas like the kitchen, that distinguished them from their condition a century earlier. In a presumably typical mansion described in Bulwer's *Alice*, "the only modern article in the room" was a grand piano.

Many fine Tudor mansions, redolent of the past, and Stuart ones built retrogressively in the Tudor style, survived in Trollope's Barsetshire, some of which he described in considerable detail with an appreciative architectural eye that was both history-oriented and comparative. Greshamsbury House was "built in the richest, perhaps we should rather say in the purest, style of Tudor architecture; so much so that, though Greshamsbury is less complete than Longleat, less magnificent than Hatfield, it may in some sense be said to be the finest specimen of Tudor architecture of which the country can boast" (*Doctor Thorne*, 1:8). The "purest" hybrid was Humblethwaite Hall (*Sir Harry Hotspur*), on which Trollope lavished his most extended description. Its oldest part dated from Henry VIII's time, although "the great body of the house," like Chaldicotes in *Framley Parsonage*, was *temp*. Charles II, with Queen Anne and early nineteenth-century additions. In between were Ullathorne Court (*Barchester Towers*), Carbury Manor House (*The Way We Live Now*), and Christopher Dale's Great House at Allington (*The Small House at Allington*). Courcy Castle (*Doctor Thorne* and elsewhere) was later: "a huge brick pile, built in the days of William III."

The nineteenth century saw the pulling down or radical alteration of many great country houses, less for the sake of comfort than because of their owners' dislike of architectural styles that were then out of fashion. Early in the century, Bulwer's own mother had demolished much of Knebworth, which dated from the sixteenth century, and built a baronial pseudo-Gothic mansion in its place. But Victorian fiction contains few hints of these local operations, which sacrificed the authentic look of one past epoch for the usually spurious look of another. Only two come to mind. When Lord Scamperdale, in *Mr. Sponge's Sporting Tour*, succeeded to his grandfather's earldom and Woodmansterne, his estate; he "sent to London for a first-rate architect . . . who forthwith pulled down the old brick-and-stone Elizabethan mansion, and built the present splendid Italian structure, of the finest polished stone" (24:141). And when John Mellish installed Aurora Floyd at Mellish Park, the interior luxury, bath rooms and all, was enclosed in a remodeled shell that was "half Gothic, half Elizabethan," with a "semi-Gothic, semi-barbaric portico of the great door" (*Aurora Floyd*, 15:142; 12:111).

Trollope noted, with open disapproval, the advent in Barsetshire of huge new houses, pretentious, ruinously expensive, and totally lacking the patina of centuries. The Duke of Omnium's seat, Gatherum Castle, was "a new building of white stone, lately erected at an enormous cost by one of the first architects of the day. It was an immense pile, and seemed to cover ground enough for a moderate-sized town" (*Doctor*

Thorne, 19:205). These monstrous buildings often emblematized the passage of great wealth from the landowning class to the new plutocracy. The exterior of Boxall Hall in the same novel, evidence of the riches Sir Roger Scatcherd acquired from his railway construction business, was a fitting crown to the career of a man who had started life as a stonemason; it was as grand as the showy rooms within, which were set apart for the titled company that never came.

Surtees's novels in the forties provide other evidence of the impact of the times on country life. *Hillingdon Hall* (1843–44, completed 1845) offers a colorful view of English agriculture at the time of Corn Law repeal. Surtees, a landowner in County Durham, was an enthusiast for the scientific farming techniques advocated by the Royal Agricultural Society (founded in 1838), which were expected to take up the slack in agricultural income once grain was exposed to the operation of a free market, but he evenhandedly satirized both sides of the issue through a variety of voices.

"[S]cience is the ticket," exclaimed Jorrocks, the London grocer now transplanted into the soil, in the same novel, "neat genuine unadulterated science. Everything now should be done by science. The world's on the wing, and why shouldn't farmers take flight?" He dreams extravagantly of a "monster reaper," a proto-combine that delivers grain into, and through, the mill; "the same monster engine wot does all this upstairs, ploughs the land by machinery down in the area, so that reapin' and sowin' go 'and in 'and, like the Siamese twins, or a lady and gen'lman advancin' in a quadrille, or the poker" (16:143–44). No such multipurpose machine existed, the nearest thing to it being a mechanical marvel that, for the moment, brought the breath of modernity to Casterbridge—

> the new-fashioned agricultural implement called a horse-drill, till then unknown, in its modern shape, in this part of the country, where the venerable seed-lip was still used for sowing as in the days of the Heptarchy. Its arrival created about as much sensation in the corn-market as a flying machine would create at Charing Cross. The farmers crowded round it, women drew near it, children crept under and into it. The machine was painted in bright hues of green, yellow, and red, and it resembled as a whole a compound of hornet, grasshopper, and shrimp, magnified enormously. Or it might have been likened to an upright musical instrument with the front gone. That was how it struck Lucetta. "Why, it is a sort of agricultural piano," she said. (*The Mayor of Casterbridge*, 24:128)

Another key to extracting riches from the land was using the right fertilizer, a subject on which there was a sharp conflict of opinion. Beginning in 1840, great quantities of guano were imported from the sea-coast of Peru. To true believers, this bird-produced substance was infi-nitely superior to the native manure on which English agriculture had hitherto relied. Two such enthusiasts were Archdeacon Grantly and Mr. Thorne, who talked animatedly in *Barchester Towers* (23:313–14) about guano, which Thorne ordered from Bristol, and the archdeacon from a local dealer whom he suspected of giving short weight. (Guano, turnip-drillers, and new reaping machines were not proper subjects of conversation on a Sunday, but they were more attractive than ecclesias-tical ones.)[†] Elsewhere, however, opinion was strongly in favor of ma-nure. In *Hillingdon Hall*, Jorrocks's huntsman, the drunken James Pigg, repeatedly roars out the militant slogan, "Sink your guarno! Muck's your man!" (29:284)

After the middle of the century, Trollope occasionally reported on changes other inventions wrought in country life. "A telegraph message makes such a fuss in the country," complained Sowerby in *Framley Par-sonage*, "frightening people's wives, and setting all the horses about the place galloping" (32:2.110). The introduction of central heating in the Duchess of Bungay's country seat is the subject of a running joke in *Can You Forgive Her?*. But Trollope's consuming country interest was fox hunting, of which Surtees had already given an ample account in his sporting novels. Victorian fiction at large preserved the immemorial ritual as if in amber, resistant to the environing world of relentless prog-ress. In the character of Jorrocks, Surtees had signalized the one impor-tant development in the sport during the post-Waterloo years, the en-largement of the field by interlopers who swelled the traditional small complement of country squires whose private recreation it had been since Fielding's time. Trollope noted the Victorian acceleration of this process in *Doctor Thorne*:

> The Honourable John was not known in Barsetshire as one of the most for-ward of its riders. He was a man much addicted to hunting, as far as the get-up of the thing was concerned; he was great in boots and breeches; wondrously conversant with bits and bridles; he had quite a collection of saddles; and patronised every newest invention for carrying spare shoes, sandwiches, and flasks of sherry. . . . But when the work was cut out, when the pace began to be sharp, when it behoved a man either to ride or visibly to decline to ride, then . . . in those heart-stirring moments, the Honourable John was too often found deficient. (5:65)

[†]Miss Thorne and Eleanor Grantly Bold, who were present at this conversation, would have sympathized with Lady Attenbury in *The Ordeal of Richard Feverel* when she was "sub-

In *Can You Forgive Her?* six years later, Trollope remarked that "that taking of brushes of which we used to hear" (it is a ceremony often observed in Surtees) "is a little out of fashion" (17:212). But it was not until the end of the seventies that Trollope had to concede that the gentlemen's sport to which he was so passionately addicted was, to borrow a phrase from the nonhunting Mr. Mantalini, going to the demmed bowwows. In *The Duke's Children* he finally substituted for the timeless details of pink-coated men and women in pursuit of the fox or animatedly discussing chases past and to come, despondent evidence of "the perils at large to which hunting in these modern days is subjected; . . . the perils from outsiders, the perils from new-fangled prejudices, the perils from more modern sports, the perils from over-cultivation, the perils from extended population, the perils from increasing railroads, the perils from literary ignorances, the perils from intruding cads, the perils from indifferent magnates,—the Duke of Omnium for instance;—and that peril of perils, the peril of decrease of funds and increase of expenditure!" (62:495–96).

By this time, the made-over face of the Victorian outdoors—country house and villa gardens with their tennis courts and croquet lawns, village commons with their cricket pitches, rivers with their rowing courses—was being peopled by new enthusiasts for open-air recreation and sport. Fox hunting and shooting, still the chosen pursuits of the elite despite the infiltration of the unqualified and unskilled, were joined by a number of more democratic pastimes involving more or less vigorous physical activity and competition. To Trollope, however, they all shared with hunting a pretentious, expensive materialism and a snob appeal that were alien to the whole spirit of English sport.

> I hold that nothing is so likely to be permanently prejudicial to the interest of hunting in the British Isles [he wrote in *Marion Fay* (1881–82)] as a certain flavour of tip-top fashion which has gradually enveloped it. There is a pretence of grandeur about that and, alas, about other sports also, which is, to my thinking, destructive of all sport itself. Men will not shoot unless game is made to appear before them in clouds. They will not fish unless the rivers be exquisite. To row is nothing unless you can be known as a national hero. Cricket requires appendages which are troublesome and costly, and by which the minds of economical fathers are astounded. To play a game of hockey in accordance with the times you must have a specially trained pony and a gaudy dress. Racquets have given place to tennis because tennis is

---

jected to the gallantries of Sir Miles [Papworth], who talked land and steam-engines to her till she was sick" (4:27).

costly. In all these cases the fashion of the game is much more cherished
than the game itself. But in nothing is this feeling so predominant as in
hunting. (13:91–92)

All of which was but the prelude to a long lament for the decadence in
particular of his own beloved sport.[†]

4.

The means by which people moved from place to place in town and
country were among the Victorian novelists' most readily recognizable
social indicators as well as tokens of character. Upper- and prosperous
middle-class Victorians were known by the carriages they kept. And, just
as in our day certain makes of automobiles are prized in various select
"markets" as symbols of social and financial standing, private vehicles
of various types—broughams, phaetons, barouches, landaus, gigs—had
their individual class associations. A substantial list of acceptable kinds
of carriages in the 1830s and 1840s could be compiled from Thackeray's
novels alone. He does not usually explain their social nuances, but these
may be inferred from the kind of people who favor one type or another.
In one's private rolling stock, the twin impulses of ostentation and emulation could be manifested in more than one way. The brougham, introduced in 1838 and named for the former lord chancellor, who ordered
the prototype and was said to have been largely responsible for its design, was unquestionably the carriage of choice among the very rich
and/or pretentious. In *Endymion*, the envious St. Barbe says to the hero,
"You have got a brougham! Well, I suppose so, being a member of parliament, though I know a good many members of parliament who have
not got broughams" (77:349). There was obviously a pecking order, with

---

[†]Except for novels of school and university life, headed by Thomas Hughes' *Tom
Brown's School Days* and *Tom Brown at Oxford*, Victorian fiction seldom recognizes the growing presence of athletics on the contemporary scene. Dickens alludes in *Little Dorrit* to a
man who had won a bet in 1851 by walking 1,000 miles in as many consecutive hours.
Country cricket matches are described at some length in *Pickwick Papers*, Meredith's *Evan
Harrington* (more briefly in *Diana of the Crossways*), and Reade's *A Terrible Temptation*, and in
several late novels—*The Duke's Children*, *Dr. Wortle's School*, *Ayala's Angel*, and *Mr. Scarborough's Family*—Trollope's youthful characters play lawn tennis. In *The Duke's Children*, indeed, a romantic contest of love takes place on the court. In Hardy's *A Laodicean*, "some
young people . . . were so madly devoted to lawn-tennis that they set about it like day-
labourers at the moment of their arrival" (1.15:133). A croquet game is played near the
opening of Wilkie Collins's *Man and Wife*, one of whose themes is the pernicious effects of
fame on a superb but morally flawed athlete, a product of the rage for *mens sana in corpore
sano* that stemmed from the "muscular Christianity" movement in the late sixties.

barouches second to broughams in stylishness. In *Our Mutual Friend*, the arriviste Veneerings begin at the top; nothing short of a brougham could proclaim their riches. The Boffins, however, start at the bottom, inheriting from the miserly Harmon, monarch of the dust mounds, a four-wheeled carriage in the last stages of decrepitude. When they are firmly ensconced in their wealth, they buy a "superb," "bang-up" chariot, in which Bella Wilfer rides around in style. Meanwhile, the Podsnaps use a "custard-coloured phaeton," which was not the most fashionable type of vehicle they might have bought; but at least its color was an offshade of a voguish one: the Boffins' chariot was painted light yellow.

This was one aspect of social rivalry that had numerous ramifications. At what point in one's improving circumstances did having one's own carriage cease to be a censurable affectation and become an accepted perquisite of rank? A case in point occurred in *Orley Farm*, where it played a delicate part in the front the accused forger, Lady Mason, presented to the world. "She had never kept any kind of carriage," said Trollope, "though her means, combined with her son's income, would certainly have justified her in a pony-chaise. Since Lucius had become master of the house he had presented her with such a vehicle, and also with the pony and harness complete; but as yet she had never used it, being afraid, as she said to him with a smile, of appearing ambitious before the stern citizens of Hamworth," a town twenty-five miles from London. As her friend Mrs. Arkwright argued, "your having the pony chaise just at this time will make everybody see that you are quite comfortable yourself," and therefore that the charge of forging a will to obtain wealth could not hold water (4:36; 15:130).

In London, the vast majority of people could not afford to keep a carriage. Throughout most of the Victorian period, most everyday locomotion was on foot, as the peregrinations of many fictional characters, as well as pictures of the rush-hour pedestrian traffic across London Bridge, attest. Although mass transportation by omnibus and underground railway was introduced in 1829 and 1863, respectively, the hired cab remained the mode of urban travel for most men and women in novels. It took urgent business and disregard of comfort to make them settle for the notorious old-style hackney, often a cast-off carriage of the rich that had dirty straw on the floor and was driven by legendarily rapacious, foul-mouthed members of a despised race who bore the biblical name of Jehu—a far cry from the aristocrats of the road, the long-distance coach drivers who helplessly found their occupation slipping away from them in the 1830s. Fortunately, at the beginning of the period (1834) Joseph Aloysius Hansom, an architect who had lost his money building Birmingham's town hall, came to Londoners' rescue by invent-

In "The Last Cab-Driver, and the First Omnibus Cad" (*Sketches by Boz*), Dickens prophesied
that with the coming of omnibuses London cab-
bies would find their occupation gone; hence
Cruikshank's illustration of the (supposedly) last
survivor with skeletonlike jacket and death's-
head face. But in actuality the cab and the bus
came to coexist and compete for space in the
London streets, as they do today.

ing a new type of "safety" cab, dashingly designed, with a little trap
through which passengers could communicate with the driver, and
doors that kept out the weather more effectively than in any preceding
model. Hansoms, as they came to be called, were an immediate hit, and
the number of them on the streets steadily grew, but it was many years
before the rickety, filthy hackneys disappeared. "Hackney" remained
the generic term for all vehicles for hire, and so it is not always possible

to determine whether a fictional character on a London errand rides in an old or new model. The fares were the same, but if a novelist specifies that the journey was made in a hansom, he seems to imply that the hirer was more genteel, or luckier, than one who settled for a hack.

The very fact that a character hired a coach at all added a touch of meaningful description as well as placing him or her more accurately on the social scale. In some circumstances, taking a cab, as Mrs. Nickleby did when she went from her lodgings in the Strand to see Nicholas off to Yorkshire from the Saracen's Head inn, Snow Hill, might be viewed as an indefensible extravagance. "*I* never pay a hackney coach, ma'am," said her brother-in-law Ralph, "I never hire one. I haven't been in a hackney coach of my own hiring for thirty years, and I hope I shan't be for thirty more, if I live as long" (*Nicholas Nickleby*, 5 : 108). (In the course of the novel he does in fact hire cabs, an indication of the heightened urgency of the journeys he is obliged to make.) Readers would have agreed with Ralph that Mrs. Nickleby, in her reduced circumstances, had no business squandering money on cab fare; that she did so without questioning whether or not she could afford it was an additional revelation of her all-encompassing lack of realism.

Characters in novels seldom hired self-drive vehicles to use in London, as many did in the country. Pecksniff was an exception when he took his two daughters and Mrs. Todgers to visit Ruth Pinch, governess in a wealthy brass and copper founder's family at suburban Camberwell. He might have hired a hackney for the occasion, but the fare for such a distance would have been high. He might also have taken his party by short-run coach, but the round trip would have cost him eight fares. He therefore settled on the cheapest conveyance possible, a one-horse fly.

Of the various forms of London transport, however, it was the omnibus that most often provided novelists with an immediately understandable social discriminant, the urban equivalent of the distinction that had long been made in the country between well-to-do "coaching" people, who rode in their own vehicles, and "posting" people, who had to endure the ignominy of using public transportation in the form of mail or stage coaches. The same distinction applied to transport in London, and by a process familiar in many other realms of life, prejudices characteristic of the top layer of society filtered down to the middle class. Members of the aristocracy and gentry would no more consider riding on a bus than they would, if they could avoid it, riding in a public long-distance coach or its successor, a railway carriage. (Carrying the bias to its logical extreme, in the early years of railroading, some families, as fastidious as they were rich, avoided contact with other passengers by riding in their own coaches secured to flat wagons.) This social prejudice

In Phiz's illustration for *Martin Chuzzlewit*, Tom Pinch drives
Pecksniff's new pupil, Martin, in a "gig with a tumour" (i.e., a
hood that was extra equipment). Since the vehicle could barely
accommodate the two men and Martin's trunk, readers might
well have wondered how, later in the novel, the parsimonious
Pecksniff contrived to compress himself, Mrs. Todgers, and his
two daughters into a similar conveyance.

carried over into the omnibus era, beginning in 1829 when an entrepreneur named George Shillibeer, who had successfully put a new form of passenger-bearing vehicle on the streets of Paris a few years earlier, introduced his invention to London. For at least two decades, to ride in one was regarded, in the higher levels of society, as utterly demeaning. It would have brought blue bloods into enforced physical contact with their nearest inferiors, the middle class of people who had not previously been able to afford to hire cabs but who now enjoyed public transportation at the rate of a sixpence for a short trip and a shilling for a longer one.

Circumstances excluded two other groups of potential riders. The bus fares were too steep for workingmen and their families, who continued to go about as they had always done, on foot. Even if they could have afforded it, the men's rough and dirty clothing, to which clung evidence of their occupations—flecks of plaster or mortar, dirt and mud from excavations, encrusted sawdust—and their generally uncouth appearance, manner, and odor made them thoroughly undesirable fellow passengers. Few of their wives and children were, to use the Victorians' favorite, if never explicitly defined, criterion of acceptability, "decently dressed." Moreover, there was a deepening prejudice, part of the Victorian code of propriety, against women coming into too close contact with strangers, and this difficulty was compounded by the structure of the early buses. Their roofs were accessible only by ladder, and so women could only ride in such crowded interior space as was available. But Mrs. Nickleby rode the bus at least once, and so did plucky little Miss LaCreevy when she went to visit her and Kate at Bow. On one such occasion, Dickens depicted a small incident than which none could be truer to everyday London life as his readers knew it. Miss LaCreevy, having said goodbye to Kate and Mrs. Nickleby at the bus stop, boarded the vehicle and

> pulled out of her reticule ten-pennyworth of half-pence which rolled into all possible corners of the passage, and occupied some considerable time in the picking-up. This ceremony had, of course, to be succeeded by a second kissing of Kate and Mrs. Nickleby, and a gathering together of the little basket and the brown-paper parcel, during which proceedings, "the omnibus," as Miss LaCreevy protested, "swore so dreadfully, that it was quite awful to hear it." At length and at last, it made a feint of going away, and then Miss LaCreevy darted out and darted in, apologising with great volubility to all the passengers, and declaring that she wouldn't purposely have kept them waiting on any account whatever. (*Nicholas Nickleby*, 38:573)[†]

[†] This comic confrontation was the precursor, indeed the virtual archetype, of literally hundreds of *Punch* cartoons, set either at the rear end of a bus where the conductor ex-

It may be that it was that very same profane conductor ("cad" in the slang of the day), with a glazed hat and a wart on his nose, who later caught Mrs. Nickleby's particular attention as the possible bearer of a message to Mrs. Browdie at "the Saracen with Two Necks" (typically, she merged the names of two separate inns).

In its "Monthly Supplement" for 28 February–31 March 1837, the mass-circulation *Penny Magazine* described for the benefit of its country readers the class of passengers who then rode the buses. They conveyed, it said,

> the merchant to his business, the clerk to his bank or counting-house, the subordinate official functionaries to the Post Office, Somerset House, the Excise, or the Mint, the Custom House, or Whitehall. An immense number of individuals, whose incomes vary from 150*l.* to 400*l.* or 600*l.*, and whose business does not require their presence till nine or ten in the mornings [service began at 8 A.M.], and who can leave it at five or six in the evenings; persons with limited independent means of living, such as legacies or life-rents, or small amounts of property; literary individuals; merchants and traders, small and great; all, in fact, who can, now endeavour to live some little distance from London.

All accounts of early and mid-Victorian London transport, factual and fictional, agree that the typical bus riders were men in the £150–£600 income range cited by the *Penny Magazine*—City clerks and their grandly named public-sector counterparts, "subordinate government functionaries," who packed the vehicles during the mid-morning and afternoon rush hours. The fondest fantasy of many young civil servants, such as those in the Weights and Measures Office in Trollope's *The Three Clerks*, was to rise high enough to afford a loving little wife and a newly built suburban cottage along a bus line. Endymion Ferrars, in Disraeli's novel, daydreamed of marrying Imogene, the daughter of a rich man who kept a four-horse coach.

> Six hundred a year, he thought, was not a very large income; but it was an income, and one which a year ago he never contemplated possessing until getting grey in the public service. Why not realise perfect happiness at once? He could conceive no bliss greater than living with Imogene in one of those little villas, even if semi-detached, which now [1880] are numbered by tens of thousands, and which were then beginning to shoot out their suburban antennae in every direction of our huge metropolis. He saw her in his

---

ercised his impudent wit on boarding or alighting passengers, or at the front, where the driver, equally loose of tongue, presided on his box. No other single aspect of London life generated as much *Punch* humor, year in and year out.

mind's eye in a garden of perpetual sunshine, breathing of mignonette and bright with roses, and waiting for him as he came down from town and his daily labours, in the cheap and convenient omnibus. (*Endymion*, 48:210)

Having a bus at the door, however, could be seen as something other than a utilitarian enhancement of an idyllic, albeit suburban, castle in the air. In *Ten Thousand a Year*, the Oxford Street draper Mr. Tag-rag lived in a Pooteresque villa in Clapham, where the dullness was so oppressive that the "only amusement" at times was "the numberless dusty stage-coaches [in this case, short stages, or extended-run buses] driving every five minutes close past their gate (which was about ten yards from the house)." Visiting his employer, Tittlebat Titmouse, who at this stage of his still humble career was given to committing one egregious gaffe after another, remarked "how cheerful the stages going past must make the house" (6:178). Mr. Tag-rag had no choice but to agree with him, whatever private feelings he might have entertained.

Thackeray advantageously used the social nuances attached to bus riding in the 1840s. Though Major Pendennis had returned from India a number of years earlier, he was still unaccustomed to this new mode of transport and needed directions from his manservant. "And after having ascertained from Morgan that he could reach the Temple without much difficulty, and that a City omnibus would put him down at the gate . . . the Major one day entered one of those public vehicles, and bade the conductor to put him down at the gate of the Upper Temple" (*Pendennis*, 28:1.289). The lordly air with which he presumably addressed the cad underscores the incongruity of a gentleman riding in a cheap public conveyance; and remembering this, the reader sees extra significance in Thackeray's later explanation of how Miss Bunion, the author of "Passion-Flowers" and other works of sentimental poesy, got to Mr. Bungay's dinner in Paternoster Row.

> Wagg instantly noted the straw which she brought in at the rumpled skirt of her dress, and would have stooped to pick it up, but Miss Bunion disarmed all criticism by observing this ornament herself, and, putting down her own large foot upon it, so as to separate it from her robe, she stooped and picked up the straw, saying to Mrs. Bungay, that she was very sorry to be a little late, but that the omnibus was very slow, and what a comfort it was to get a ride all the way from Brompton for sixpence. Nobody laughed at the poetess's speech, it was uttered so simply.
>
> Indeed, the worthy woman had not the least notion of being ashamed of an action incidental upon her poverty.
>
> "Is that 'Passion-Flowers?'" Pen said to Wenham, by whom he was standing. "Why, her picture in the volume represents her as a very well-looking young woman."

"You know passion-flowers, like all others, will run to seed," Wenham said; "Miss Bunion's portrait was probably painted some years ago."

"Well, I like her for not being ashamed of her poverty."

"So do I," said Mr. Wenham, who would have starved rather than have come to dinner in an omnibus; "but I don't think that she need flourish the straw about, do you, Mr. Pendennis?" (*Pendennis*, 34:1.348–49)

Major Pendennis understandably never became a regular bus rider. If, as a gentleman of the old school, he could not or did not wish to keep his own carriage, he had wealthy friends who did, and they generously shared their equipages with him. Seeing Sir Hugh Trumpington's "dark blue brougham, with that tremendous stepping horse," parked outside Bays's club, he remarks to Pen that Sir Hugh "was never known to walk in his life; never appears in the streets on foot—never" and would take the brougham merely to go next door. But, the Major says, his friend would put the vehicle and driver at his disposal any day between four and seven: "Just as much mine as if I jobbed it from Tilbury's [a fashionable livery stable], begad, for thirty pound a month" (*Pendennis*, 36:1.372–73). Later, however, he drove the convalescent Pen and his mother to Richmond for the medically prescribed "change of air," using the "antiquated travelling chariot" in which she and Laura had come up from Chatteris upon learning of Pen's serious illness. Laura and Warrington followed in the bus. We hear no more of the chariot, however, because while Pen, his mother, and Laura are still at Richmond, the Major and Warrington ride the bus back and forth.

When taxation on buses was reduced (they had initially been lumped with hackney cabs on the tax schedule), and their capacity was increased by installing knifeboard benches on the roof, fares declined; in 1847 a mere penny could take one from Charing Cross to Camden Town. Patronage naturally increased, and when London was flooded with Crystal Palace visitors in 1851, buses really came into their own as a gloriously democratic means of transportation, though still excluding the rougher class of day laborers, who would be taken care of only when railways instituted cheap workmen's trains in the early sixties. "The fat man in the twopenny omnibus" became for politicians the archetypal voter. Walter Bagehot quoted a saying, "Public opinion is the opinion of the bald-headed man in the back of the omnibus," and in 1855, attacking what *Punch* called the "incredible imbecility, incompetence, and mismanagement" in the conduct of the Crimean War, Mr. Punch himself reminded Palmerston, the beleaguered prime minister, in a letter of advice, "I don't go below the omnibuses . . . I speak for the omnibuses—*and the omnibuses have votes.*" [13]

Once the London bus was established as a symbol of middle-class

An "improved" model omnibus, with knifeboard (longitudinal) seating on the roof, appeared on the London streets in 1847. By then, men of higher social station than City clerks and minor-grade civil servants were beginning to ride the bus to and from work.

supremacy, novelists in the fifties used it for a variety of purposes, chiefly to illustrate, in a literary tradition reaching all the way back to Chaucer, the variety of people to be found in a fortuitous assembly of travelers. By this time, buses were an acceptable mode of transport for respectable women, although in *Basil* (1852) Wilkie Collins stressed how self-consciously some bore themselves in these unaccustomed surroundings:

> I had often before ridden in omnibuses to amuse myself by observing the passengers [said his twenty-four-year-old narrator]. An omnibus has always appeared to me to be a perambulatory exhibition-room of the eccentricities of human nature. I know not any other sphere in which persons of all classes and all temperaments are so oddly collected together, and so immediately contrasted and confronted with each other. . . . Two middle-aged ladies, dressed with amazing splendor in silks and satins, wearing straw-colored kid gloves, and carrying highly scented pocket-handkerchiefs, sat apart at the end of the vehicle, trying to look as if they occupied it under protest, and preserving the most stately gravity and silence. They evidently felt that their magnificent outward adornments were exhibited in a very unworthy locality, and among a very uncongenial company. (1.7:43–44)

William Maw Egley's *Omnibus Life in London* was exhibited at the British
Institution in 1859. When the *Illustrated London News* printed this engraving of the painting in its issue for 11 June, it remarked, "There is scarcely
a London omnibus that does not carry its hundred passengers a day—
six hundred a week!—more than thirty thousand souls per annum!
Could it set before us the passions, emotions, hopes, fears, and sorrows
of a tithe of that vast multitude, what a picture of life would be set before
us!" In other words, it was grist for three thousand novels.

Inspector Bucket's wife and Lady Dedlock's dismissed maidservant,
Hortense, in *Bleak House*, who went down to a Greenwich tea garden
by bus, were more typical of bus-riding womanhood. The vehicles' interiors were, if not luxurious or spacious, at least not as Spartan in decor
and comfort (the seats were now cushioned) as the first Shillibeers that
plied the streets. In the mid-sixties the substitution of stairs for ladders

theoretically gave women access to the roof, although the crinoline fashion discouraged them from attempting that athletic feat (as well as reduced the companies' profit margin by occupying two spaces for the price of one).

A typical full load of passengers presented a cross-section of middle-class life, as William Maw Egley demonstrated in his popular painting *Omnibus Life in London*, exhibited in 1859. Two years earlier, a novel by a writer named Kortright had exploited the same rich vein of genre painting:

> One hears and sees such droll things in the omnibus. There's always the fat man that takes up the room of three; always the woman with the big bundle hugged up to her like a baby, and the bigger basket that she sets on her neighbour's toes. There's always the mother with a baby that you are assured is a good as *goold*, but that will squall all the way. Then there's the dandy clerk coming home from his office or bank, who wears mosaic gold rings and paste, and runs his fingers through his macassared hair to show the said mosaic and paste. Then there's the young lady opposite to him, with seven flounces that will get rumpled and the bonnet that won't keep on. There's the impatient gentleman that swears at the conductor because he stops to take up anybody but himself. There's the child that's thrust in like a foundling and stands up right in the middle (till the fat woman that's nursing the bundle makes room for him on the other knee), and stares round bewildered, and wonders if he is really a boy, or a parcel, or a hamper, that he's shipped off that way by an undutiful aunt.[14]

Broadly based though it now was, this social mix was not so complete as to leave no room for occasional incongruities. Trollope availed himself of one such—a gentleman in full clerical dress as a passenger in a succession of London buses—when he described how Mr. Harding in *The Warden* passed the time during his "long day in London" awaiting his late-evening consultation with Sir Abraham Haphazard. (The whole passage is an oblique commentary on the notorious absence of places to sit down, without charge, in London. For a country clergyman, park benches and grass were clearly unsuitable, even if the season was, and everywhere else, as in public houses, some purchase was required.) Upon his arrival the previous day, he had ridden from Westminster to his hotel near St. Paul's "in a clattering omnibus, wedged in between a wet old lady and a journeyman glazier, returning from his work with his tools in his lap" (16:109). After dinner, he had made another round trip in a futile attempt to beard Sir Abraham in the House of Commons. On the day itself, determinedly eluding Dr. Grantly, who had come to London in pursuit, he rode a bus to Westminster Abbey, which he had never before entered, and hid out there for six endless hours, encountering "the very same damp old woman who had nearly obliterated him in the omnibus, or some other just like her." That evening, after an awkward meal at a filthy supper house in the Strand, "he thought of getting into an omnibus, and going out to Fulham for the sake of coming back in another." But he was too tired to adopt this desperate remedy, and settled instead for an unplanned nap in a cigar divan, after which he walked to Sir Abraham's chambers in Lincoln's Inn. Trollope clearly relished the extended comedy of the gentle elderly clergyman taking bus after bus. It was unlikely that many metropolitan parsons, Anglican ones at any rate, rode omnibuses, and even less likely that a precentor of a cathedral would have sacrificed his dignity in such a manner. That Mr. Harding did so was, like his not knowing how to send a telegram, a measure of his simple nature, innocent of the little sophistications of modern life.

Other men, fully sophisticated Londoners, had not reconciled themselves to the democracy of bus travel. In *The Moonstone*, Franklin Blake and the lawyer Mr. Bruff tailed a strange man they saw at the Bank. "The man in the grey suit," Blake related, "got into an omnibus, going westward. We got in after him. There were latent reserves of youth still left in Mr. Bruff. I assert it positively—when he took his seat in the omnibus, he blushed!" ("Second period, fifth narrative," chap. 1, p. 483). On the other hand, Sir William de Vescie, in Emily Eden's *The Semi-Detached House*, was not too proud to be seen there; asking Lady Sarah Mortimer to make him a purse, he explained that "he lost a shilling yesterday when he took some silver out of his waistcoat pocket to pay the omnibus fare" (17:151). And when Lord Nidderdale, in *The Way We Live Now*, contemplated a thoroughgoing reformation when the Beargarden Club closed, one of his resolutions was to go about London, not in a cab, but economically, on the top of a bus. (Trollope offers no evidence that in the event he was actually seen there.)

Deeply rooted prejudices are a long time dying, and in 1881 *The Builder*, a trade paper, commented: "There was a time when it was considered to be hardly respectable to be seen on an omnibus, and even yet there is a certain *mauvaise honte* visible in a man whose richer or more luxurious friend meets him as he emerges from the interior of a public omnibus."[15] The temporarily virtuous Lord Nidderdale notwithstanding, peers ordinarily did not patronize public buses, as Trollope's portrait of Lord Hampstead, the democratically minded hero of *Marion Fay*, makes clear. A bus line ran past the lodge gate of Hampstead's father's estate in the north London suburb of Hendon, and the young lord rode the vehicles, "saying that an omnibus with company was better than a private carriage with none." At one point in his pursuit of Marion Fay, the daughter of a Quaker who was chief clerk to a City firm, "He thought of finding out the Quaker chapel in the City and there sitting out the whole proceeding,—unless desired to leave the place,—with the Quixotic idea of returning to Holloway with her in an omnibus," which would have been a highly unconventional way for a peer of the realm to escort his beloved to her simple abode in a prosaic lower-middle class neighborhood (2:10; 17:120). The very next day he actually made it to Holloway, evidently going by underground railway via Baker Street and King's Cross to Islington, from which point he went to his destination by bus. This was a prudent move, because a coach with a coronet on its side would have attracted undesirable attention in what Trollope describes as an extremely nosy neighborhood.

Trollope's final use of London buses as a clue to character occurred in *Mr. Scarborough's Family* (1882–83). Mr. Grey, the impeccably honest old lawyer in the sordid case of the Scarborough will, "at this time was living down at Fulham in a small old-fashioned house which overlooked the river, and was called the Manor House. He would have said that it was his custom to go home every day by an omnibus, but he did in truth almost always remain at his office so late as to make it necessary that he should return by a cab." By this date no stigma evidently was attached to a professional man's riding a bus, but women of good family were still under some constraints. Grey's unmarried daughter, with whom he was accustomed to talk over his cases when he got home at night, was, in this respect, a self-liberated woman. One of her "vagaries," as Trollope called it, was that she "would . . . go up and down in the omnibus, and would do so alone without the slightest regard to the opinion of any of her neighbours" (16:145–50 passim).

In the country, meanwhile, omnibuses had supplanted the last of the decrepit stagecoaches that had been reduced to shuttling between village inns and the nearest railway station. "'Neat carriages by the day, month, or year,'" wrote Surtees in *Hillingdon Hall*, "are unknown in the country, and post-chaises are fast disappearing. Omnibuses are all the go. An omnibus for a picnic is all very well, but for a morning visit rather incongruous. Besides, they don't leave a certain line or road; all drawing towards the railway stations, as true as the needle to the pole" (33:334). These, too, were vehicles, so to speak, of class consciousness, and women who avoided riding London buses carried their prejudices with them when they left town. Sometimes a great lady had no choice but to ride in a country bus—something not to be thought of when she was in London. Surtees, in another novel (*Mr. Facey Romford's Hounds*), let his readers imagine the hauteur with which, in the absence of any more suitable mode of transportation, the Countess of Caperington endured the experience of the Dirlingford station bus. "One disadvantage of the new universal use of public conveyances," he remarked, "undoubtedly is, that consequence does not get properly attended to. When that the maid dresses so much finer than the mistress, it is difficult at first sight to distinguish between them—to say which is which. The Countess, however, was not one of that sort, and always dressed as became her exalted station, and the 'bus had scarcely stopped at the 'Lord Hill' hotel and posting-house door ere it was bruited throughout that a great lady had come" (59:382).

The first glimpse Trollope gave his readers of the imperious and wealthy young widow Mrs. Greenow, in *Can You Forgive Her?*, was of her alighting from a train at Yarmouth station. The first words she spoke were "Omnibus;—no, indeed. Jeannette, get me a fly" (7:100). Later in the same novel Alice Vavasor reaches Matching station en route to a visit with Lady Glencora and her husband. "Outside, on the broad drive before the little station, she saw an omnibus that was going to the small town of Matching, intended for people who had not grown upwards as had been her lot" (22:245). But she was spared that abasement when Lady Glencora drove up, handling the reins of "a little low open carriage with two beautiful small horses." That so high a personage as the wife of the heir to the Palliser estate chose to drive a spanking team to meet her guest at the train rather than be driven in a stately carriage was one of Trollope's shrewdest strokes as he went about developing Lady Glencora's selectively unconventional character.

When Meredith had Diana Warwick insist on riding in a third-class railway carriage as a token of her fiercely independent nature, he carried things a bit too far. However much they sympathized with her, readers would have boggled at the idea of so intelligent and well-brought-up a lady fixing on so primitive an accommodation for the sake of making a point. They would, on the other hand, have appreciated the cleverness with which Wilkie Collins used the social distinctions associated with travel in *Armadale*. In a Norfolk village, the rector is accosted by a veiled woman wearing a red Paisley shawl who asks to be directed to Mrs. Armadale's house. Later he passes her as she is about to enter the village inn. He goes around to the stable and asks if the lady is going away. "Yes," the landlord tells him, "she had come from the railway in the omnibus, but she was going back again more creditably in a carriage of her own hiring, supplied by the inn" (1.1:1.111). The reader was to wonder, as part of the thickening mystery, what had happened in the interim, during the lady's visit to Mrs. Armadale, that caused her to upgrade her mode of travel from a cheap omnibus to an expensive hired carriage. Many chapters would pass before the elated woman was identified as Miss Gwilt, the beautiful but evil spider in the center of the web.

Novelists often used a character's choice of mode of travel for such purposes. Two related instances occur in a single chapter (47) of *Barchester Towers*. In the first, Obadiah Slope buys a *first-class* ticket to London, a sign of his euphoria after a week of suspense over who was to be the new dean: at this moment, the odds seem to favor him, and his investment in luxury travel is therefore a celebration—unjustified, as things turn out—of his golden prospects. A few pages later, Mr. Harding arrives at the Grantlys' home at Plumstead driving, not his accustomed one-horse green fly, but a splendid hired post chaise drawn by two horses. He, too, seems to be in a celebratory mood, and the message he brings is that it is he, not Slope, who has been named to the deanship. The salient fact, however, is that he has refused the office that the purchaser of a first-class ticket to London thought was his. Trollope has playfully led his readers down the garden path, even as the gentle Harding's unwonted extravagance has led his daughter and son-in-law.

11
The Great Metropolis

ɝ

1.

THE COMING OF THE RAILWAY reinforced London's centrality, in geographical fact as well as in people's minds. There was appreciable symbolism in the fact that all "up" trains, like the coaches before them, were headed for the metropolis and all "down" trains started there. London remained what it had been since the Middle Ages, the seat of the court and the legislature; it was the English cultural capital; and it was soon to become the commercial center not only of the nation but of the expanding empire and, in some respects, the whole world. Despite the growth of industrial cities like Manchester, Birmingham, Sheffield, and Leeds, modern London, with a population in 1871 six times as large as that of the next biggest city, Liverpool, was ever more of a presence in the national consciousness. While the provincial press flourished, mail trains sped London papers, with their detailed coverage of metropolitan news, to breakfast tables throughout Britain. To the millions of people who lived in countryside and town, London constituted the "outer world" that dominated their imagination; or, to put it another way, "all England," as a modern writer has said, "was a suburb of London."[1]

The sprawling metropolis was also the chief mise en scène of Victorian realistic fiction. In 1859 David Masson distinguished the London-rooted novel as a separate category in his taxonomy of current fiction:

The Novels of Dickens and Thackeray are, most of them, novels of London; it is in the multifarious circumstance of London life, and its peculiar humors, that they move most frequently and have their most characteristic being;—a fact not unimportant in the appreciation of both. As the greatest aggregate of human beings on the face of the earth, as a population of several millions crushed together in one dense mass on a space of a few square miles—this mass consisting, for the most part, of Englishmen, but containing also as many Scotchmen as there are in Edinburgh, as many Irishmen

382

as there are in Dublin, and a perfect Polyglott [*sic*] of other nations in addition—London is as good an epitome of the world as anywhere exists, presenting all those phenomena of interest, whether serious or humorous, which result from great numbers, heterogeneousness of composition, and close social packing. . . . If any city could generate and sustain a species of Novel entirely out of its own resources, it might surely be London; nor would ten thousand novels exhaust it. After all the mining efforts of previous novelists in so rich a field, Dickens and Thackeray have certainly sunk new shafts in it, and have come upon valuable veins not previously disturbed. So much is this the case that, without injustice to Fielding and others, Dickens and Thackeray might well be considered as the founders of a peculiar sub-variety of the Novel of English Life and Manners, to be called "The British Metropolitan Novel."[2]

It was this combination of newly probed veins of urban life and London's intrinsic importance as the focus of cultural and commercial activities that made it an inexhaustible source of topicality.

To Londoners, the novelists' use of urban materials had significances that were sometimes quite different from those they conveyed to other readers. Londoners were acquainted well enough with most of the locales mentioned (though not, as we shall see, with some that Dickens described), and they were familiar with local character types and customs or "manners"; what was new to them was, as Masson suggested, certain social classes and aspects of city life hitherto untouched by novelists. Dickens and Thackeray especially, although not exclusively—when Masson wrote, Wilkie Collins and Kingsley had also produced London novels—saw fresh and often depressing meanings in the London scene. Not since Hogarth, working in a different medium, had exposed the seamy and downright brutal side of London life had artists of any kind developed a clear "image of the city," which in practice meant London alone, in their critical interpretation of modern society.

Readers outside London, while not unaffected by the social or philosophical implications that London-based novelists found in their local material, saw the city from a different perspective, although one that was less complex than that which modern critics attribute to the novelists themselves, Dickens in particular. The pioneer student of English urban history, H. J. Dyos, stressed how little we actually know about that perspective:

London invited more sharply divided opinions, more deep-seated ambivalence than any other city or town in Victorian England. It is an interesting speculation whether London did not perform some necessary Freudian function for provincial minds. How hungrily were George W. M. Reynolds's

entrancing *Mysteries of London* (1846–50)—or Mayhew, Greenwood, Hollingshead, Sala, Sims, or Stead, for that matter[†]—devoured in provincial
places, and how securely lodged in provincial prejudices were their metropolitan melodramas and side-shows and stereotypes? One cannot tell.
But . . . London occupied a unique and identifiable place in the national
psyche which someone has got to probe very thoroughly before we can
understand properly its relations with the provinces, either then or now.[3]

This much, at least, is clear: The ordinary company of people who read
fiction, whether in the rural homes of the lesser squirearchy or in the
middle-class villas on the outskirts of the bustling industrial towns,
thought of the city in predominantly moral terms, a reductive version of
the old literary tradition that drew a stark Manichean contrast between
the "evil" city and the "innocent" countryside. Ultimately, this tradition
reached back to Roman times, and most recently it had been revived in
Romantic poetry, inspiring, healing, transcendental Nature now finding
its antithesis in Wordsworth's "dissolute city."[4] The phrase "modern
Babylon" must have rolled from the tongues of the Reverend Mr. Stiggins and the Reverend Mr. Melchisedech Howler, who made livings
there, as orotundly as it did in fact from that of Mr. Micawber, and it
would have hovered in many readers' minds as they read Dickens's
novels.

Thackeray said that "Helen Pendennis was a country bred woman,
and the book of life, as she interpreted it, told her a different story to
that page which is read in cities" (*Pendennis*, 7 : 1.70). The relevant pages
in her "book of life" were likely synthesized from vestiges of the old
Miltonic-Bunyanesque distrust of, or outright aversion to, the Earthly
City as Mammon's abode, the seat of Vanity, the polar opposite of the
City of God—in short, a dystopia even before the word, in that sense,
entered the language.

Miss Browning, the old maid in Gaskell's *Wives and Daughters*, "had
got many of her notions of the metropolis from the British Essayists,
where town is so often represented as the centre of dissipation, corrupt-
ing country wives and squires' daughters, and unfitting them for all their
duties by the constant whirl of its not always innocent pleasures. London
was a sort of moral pitch, which few could touch and not be defiled. . . .
'As far as I can judge of London,' said Miss Browning, sententiously
continuing her tirade against the place, 'it's no better than a pickpocket
and a robber dressed up in the spoils of honest folk'" (41 : 500–501).

[†]Journalists who wrote much, from various points of view, on contemporary London
life.

Her apprehensions were shared by Tom Pinch in *Martin Chuzzlewit*, who came up to London after a number of years' absence in the country only to discover, somewhat to his disappointment, that they were groundless.

> He was particularly anxious, among other notorious localities, to have those streets pointed out to him which were appropriated to the slaughter of countrymen; and was quite disappointed to find, after half-an-hour's walking, that he hadn't had his pocket picked. . . . (36:641)
>
> Tom's evil genius did not lead him into the dens of any of those preparers of cannibalistic pastry, who are represented in many standard country legends as doing a lively retail business in the Metropolis; nor did it mark him out as the prey of ring-droppers, pea and thimble-riggers, duffers, touters, or any of those bloodless sharpers, who are, perhaps, a little better known to the Police. He fell into conversation with no gentleman who took him into a public-house, where there happened to be another gentleman who swore he had more money than any other gentleman, and very soon proved he had more money than one gentleman by taking his away from him: neither did he fall into any other of the numerous man-traps which are set up, without notice, in the public grounds of this city. But he lost his way. (37:651)

About the same time, Mary Barton's father went to London as a delegate to the Chartist convention of 1839. He had none of Tom Pinch's fears (although he and his friends were hassled by the police for obstructing the carriages going to a drawing-room at the palace), but his report when he returned to Manchester was bleak: "One-sixth may be made up o' grand palaces, and three-sixth's o' middling kind, and th' rest o' holes o' iniquity and filth, such as Manchester knows nought on, I'm glad to say" (*Mary Barton*, 9:93).

But if Victorian readers cherished the idyllic picture of rural surroundings and society drawn by poets like Thomson and Goldsmith (still widely read), it was not necessarily at the expense of another compelling myth, that of Dick Whittington. If London was, from one viewpoint, a human warren compact of squalor, vice, misery, and crime, to say nothing of sinful luxury, it was also the fountain of opportunity for youth imbued with the self-help creed, where fulfillment in the form of wealth awaited the dedicated, the industrious, and the shrewd, not to say the ruthless. This was the heady expectation of the speaker in Tennyson's "Locksley Hall,"

> Eager-hearted as a boy when first he leaves his father's field,
>
> And at night along the dusky highway near and nearer drawn,
> And sees in heaven the light of London flaring like a dreary dawn;

And his spirit leaps within him to be gone before him then,
Underneath the light he looks at, in among the throngs of men.
                                                                    (lines 112–16)

There were other considerations, besides the literary, moral, and social ones, that colored readers' responses to the modern London presented in novels. One such bias was primarily aesthetic: the idea of London as a "great foul city . . . rattling, growling, smoking, stinking,—a
ghastly heap of fermenting brickwork, pouring out poison at every
pore—a cricket ground without the turf, a huge billiard table without
the cloth, and with pockets as deep as the bottomless pit"—the judgment
in 1865 of a somewhat overwrought Ruskin, who would not have denied
that the factory cities also qualified on every count.[5] Male readers of
fiction in the provinces could rationalize urban ugliness as being the
price an industrial nation had to pay for its prosperity, but they had other
prejudices to replace Ruskin's, those arising from civic pride and the
envy and resentment it generated, as of a brawny young David chafing
against the overlordship of a Goliath. No matter how imposing the
wealth that accumulated in the Midlands and the North, and no matter
how much political power the new cities had managed to acquire, the
City, the little square mile in the heart of the metropolis, was still the
economic fulcrum of the nation, and from legislative Westminster and
administrative Whitehall came the laws and fiats that governed its life.
    Resident Londoners that they were, Dickens, Thackeray, Trollope,
Collins, and Reade naturally would have their fellow residents in mind
as they wrote. There is no evidence that any novelist consciously made
any allowance for that portion of his audience which resided beyond
commuting distance of London. Nor do we know how large that portion
was. Between one-sixth and one-fifth of the total English population
lived in London, but it by no means followed that an identical proportion of the audience for fiction resided there. For whatever the guess is
worth, a reviewer of *Nicholas Nickleby* in 1838 remarked: "we suspect that
the circulation of Boz takes certain channels, beyond which he is not
greatly relished or read. It would be curious, were it attainable, to know
respectively the demand for his publications in the metropolis, in large
provincial towns, and in the country. In the latter we suspect it would be
small, of course supposing the district removed beyond the town impulses."[6] But those impulses affected an increasing number of people.
Decade by decade, hundreds of thousands flocked from the relatively
isolated countryside into the provincial towns, if not into London itself,
where books, magazines, and newspapers were more readily available.
    John Sutherland has said that half of the pressrun of the weekly *All*

the Year Round "stayed in the metropolis."[7] Perhaps this even split applied to books as well. Until some kind of distributive breakdown is made of surviving publishers' sales accounts, we cannot know how many copies of a given edition went to London readers and how many to those in the provinces. To complicate matters, a significant portion of London's book output went neither to buyers in the metropolis nor elsewhere in Britain but to India and the colonies. There is the further complication that a substantial part of an edition of a popular novel went to Mudie's circulating library, to whose large London walk-in trade was added the out-of-town clientele served by the branches that were established in almost every large town and by the "country boxes" sent down from London by rail. And there were competing libraries as well.

Whatever the true size of the audience for fiction outside London may have been, its members responded to London topicalities in various ways, depending on their knowledge of the city. How familiar were they with the metropolis's sights, streets, and neighborhoods?

One class of country and provincial-town readers offers no great problem. These were the families of landowners—the aristocracy and superior gentry—who spent as much as half the year in London, either in their town houses or in rented accommodations. The vanguard went up for the opening of Parliament in February, followed by large numbers when hunting tapered off in March. The Royal Academy summer exhibition, which opened at the end of April or the beginning of May, initiated the height of the "season," during which marriageable daughters were marketed and other social negotiations conducted in a steady round of balls and "at homes." The reverse migration to the country began in August, when Parliament rose and the partridge-shooting season opened. During those spring and summer months in town, county families acquired a familiarity with the landmarks, fashionable neighborhoods, and shopping streets that was equal to that of any year-round resident.

Until the spread of the railway network, comparatively few men and women outside the privileged circle of provincial society went to London except on urgent business. Travel by coach was uncomfortable, slow, and expensive; even the richest families, who could afford their own carriages, were relieved when the long, jolting trip was over.[†] Meanwhile,

---

[†]This was the general state of affairs, but it must be remembered that on the verge of the Victorian period macadamized all-weather highways and the introduction of faster, more comfortable coach service portended a new era in long-distance transport. Like the new canal system, this promising development was aborted by the advent of speedier, ever more comfortable railway trains.

however, nontraveling readers could acquire a vicarious if spotty knowledge of contemporary London through books borrowed from local libraries or bought at bookshops such as the two in Salisbury that Tom Pinch patronized, and through periodicals and part-issues of new novels sold by town and village agents. Over the years, they built up enough secondhand familiarity with the London scene to envision the localities mentioned in current fiction and to understand references to customary events such as the ceremonial opening of Parliament, Greenwich Fair down the river, and the Lord Mayor's Day procession.

The illustrations of exterior scenes in the monthly numbers of Dickens's novels would have assisted visual realization. So would whatever urban topographical prints the country reader happened to have on his walls or in portfolios in his library or drawing room.[8] The beauties of eighteenth-century London, many of them architectural landmarks still extant, were portrayed in Augustus Pugin's and Thomas Rowlandson's prints. More up-to-date scenes were represented in two albums of engravings made from Thomas Hosmer Shepherd's topographical paintings: James Elmes's *Metropolitan Improvements* (1827) and *London and Its Environs in the Nineteenth Century* (1829). There was also John Britton and Pugin's *Public Buildings of London* (1828); and another set of engravings appeared in Thomas Boys's *Original Views of London as It Is* (1842). Their high price and the fact that they were issued in small editions limited the audience such pictures would reach, but a mass readership was served by the weekly *Penny Magazine*, which, beginning in 1832, featured many engravings of London scenes.

A decade later two large new sources of pictorial information began publication. Between them, *Punch: or the London Charivari* (1841) and the *Illustrated London News* (1842) printed hundreds of pictures of contemporary London each year, thus disseminating up-to-date visual impressions through a large section of the middle-class public, although *Punch*'s were limited to drawings whose tinge of caricature could distract readers' attention from whatever visual authenticity they possessed. These supplemented the casual, fragmentary glimpses to be gained through such souvenirs of the city as small juvenile "guidebooks" and Peggotty's "work-box with a sliding lid, with a view of St. Paul's Cathedral (with a pink dome) painted on the top" (*David Copperfield*, 2:65). When the *Illustrated London News* gave away with its issue for 7 January 1843 a panoramic view of London from the top of the Duke of York's Column, the *Times* commented: "There could not be a more appropriate and acceptable present in so portable a form for country friends; and we can imagine the interest with which the 'young ones' to whom London is but a dream would gaze at this fine picture of its glories." The *Morning Ad-*

Country readers' ideas of what the great metropolis looked like were formed in part by pictures like this of Fleet Street in the *Illustrated London News* (8 January 1848). The same scene, looking toward St. Paul's Cathedral, was later depicted in a frequently reproduced engraving by Gustave Doré (1872).

vertiser remarked on the same occasion, "this the most eligible picture of London which has ever been produced . . . is in short the sole means by which foreign and country readers can form to themselves [i.e., in a single picture] any idea of the grandeur of the British metropolis."[9]

At that very moment, the means were being provided by which country readers could see for themselves the metropolis shown in this and other views-from-the-sky. London was becoming more accessible physically than anyone would have thought possible a decade or two earlier. Main railway lines struck into the city from every direction. A year after the first panoramic engraving was published, the "parliamentary trains" act (1844) made travel to London available to anyone having the penny-a-mile fare the law stipulated. On Whit Monday of the same year, the first holiday excursions by rail were staged: a train consisting of fifty carriages and pulled by six engines hauled a huge crowd of Londoners on a day trip to Brighton, and other trains took thirty-five thousand more to Greenwich.[†] These excursions, it is true, were away from London rather than to it, but their instant popularity led to many being arranged inbound from the provinces. By 1850 the *Times* could observe, "There are thousands of our readers, we are sure, who, in the last three years of their lives, have travelled more and seen more than in all their previous life taken together. Thirty years ago not one countryman in one hundred had seen the metropolis. There is now scarcely one in the same number who has not spent the day there."[10] This was, of course, no more than a rhetorical flourish, but it came close to being substantiated in 1851, when cheap excursions, as many as twenty a day steaming into a single London terminal, made London at large a reality as wonderful to millions of men, women, and children from the country as the gleaming Crystal Palace they had particularly come to see.

2.

In an often-quoted phrase, Walter Bagehot once said of Dickens that he "describes London like a special correspondent for posterity." From the very outset of his career, with the street scenes in *Sketches by Boz*, Dickens became the Victorian reader's chosen guide to London. An obscure "country cousin" relating her first visit to the metropolis wrote, "I saw wealth, and beauty, and power, so closely connected with crime, suffering and poverty, that I thought the enjoyment of the former must be

---

[†]This is the received figure, but one wonders if the company's rolling stock had so large a "passenger capacity" at that date, even assuming that the excursioners were packed as tightly into the unroofed third-class "waggons" as contemporary pictures indicate.

marred by the presence of the latter. Perhaps I looked on everything with an intensity which might be attributed to my having seen it all in fancy's glass, by the aid of that masterly delineator, Charles Dickens."[11] John Forster, reviewing *Nicholas Nickleby*, couched his appreciation in more elaborately literary terms:

> Who that has read his descriptions of the various localities of London . . . can ever expect to forget them more? A fresh glow of warmth and light plays over the cheerful and familiar places, a deeper mist of misery and blackness settles on the darker scenes. With him, we pass along misty streets in some cold and foggy morning, while but a few meager shadows flit to and fro or now and then a heavy outline of coach or cab or cart looms through the dull vapour, yet were it only for the noises he strikes from time to time upon our ears, distantly and indistinctly as though the fog had muffled them, we could not doubt that it was LONDON. . . . At all times, and under every aspect, he gives us to feel and see the great city as it absolutely is. Its interior life is made as familiar to us as its exterior forms. We come to know better the very places we have known best. We observe more smoking and hear more singing in Golden square; the Saracen's Head on Snow hill relaxes into a grim cordiality; the Alphonses of Cadogan place reveal themselves plain Bills to our practised eye; and the sight of even a real butterfly, fluttering among the iron heads of dusty area railings in some retired and noiseless City square, startles us no more.[12]

The shock of recognition was common to both visitor and Londoner, but it took different forms: in the one case, the realization of the actuality behind the graphic or literary images that had fed fireside visions; in the other, sudden awareness of the strangeness that had hitherto been hidden in the everyday-familiar.

Even lifelong inhabitants learned from Dickens's pages much about London that they had not known before. Not only did they see accustomed sights from a totally new, inimitable viewpoint: they saw other locales, in the heart of the city, that they had never had the occasion or the temerity to visit. In the course of his routine life, a middle-class reader might have become well acquainted with, say, the legal quarter between the Temple and Lincoln's Inn Fields, the "labyrinth near Park Lane" where the Barnacles lived, and Golden Square, where Ralph Nickleby had his office. But there would have been few occasions when a respectable Londoner of either sex penetrated into such neighborhoods as the misery-, disease-, and crime-ridden Saffron Hill and Jacob's Island (*Oliver Twist*), the fictitiously named but all too real Tom-All-Alone's (*Bleak House*), Bleeding Heart Yard (*Little Dorrit*), the enclave of railway workers that replaced Staggs's Gardens in Camden Town (*Dombey and Son*), or the Millbank riparian wasteland, strewn with rusting junk,

The construction of the London-Birmingham Railway's approach to Euston sta-
tion on the site of the obliterated "Staggs's Gardens," described by Dickens in
Dombey and Son, was the subject of this on-the-spot sketch by George Scharf.
Reproduced by courtesy of the Trustees of the British Museum.

where David Copperfield and Mr. Peggotty overtook the outcast Martha
in their continuing search for Em'ly, or the dockland localities, grim by
day and sinister by night, in *Bleak House* and *Our Mutual Friend*.

Although London topographical scenes provided a fair number of
Victorian artists with a sideline, they seldom if ever painted Dickens's
most characteristic low-life locales, which were beyond the pale of art as
well as the tolerance of people who bought pictures for household decoration. Social realism came late to Victorian art, and even then, it seldom
ventured into neighborhoods where even policemen, Dickens's friends,
feared to tread unless in pairs. Shepherd's and Boys's topographical
paintings, like the engravings in the *Penny Magazine* and most of the
news-related pictures in the *Illustrated London News*, concentrated on
quasi-architectural renderings of public edifices and well-known streets.
Moreover, except for the recently rediscovered George Scharf, these visual chroniclers made no attempt to portray life surging through the
streets as it did in Dickens's fiction. It is true that they showed groups of
well-dressed pedestrians and a judicious sprinkling of road traffic, but
these were obviously not studied from life but inserted after the architectural subjects had been completed, to enhance the effect of verisimilitude. And although panoramic views of the city were photographed as
early as 1843, when they constituted the basis of the *Illustrated London
News*'s famous engraved giveaway, street scenes, with their disturbing
movement, were not satisfactorily recorded by the camera until near the
end of Dickens's life.

The unique flavor of Dickens's descriptions of streets and neighborhoods, unattainable by any artist's pencil or any black-shrouded camera,

stemmed from the way in which his preternaturally acute sense of place was vivified by another extraordinary gift, that which led him to attribute life to inanimate objects, including whole locales. The realistic merged with the fantastic. Streets and buildings acquired distinctive personalities of their own from the people who passed through or lived in them. In part following his example, the minor fiction of Dickens's day was replete with descriptions of London, especially at various specific times of day and seasons of the year, but no one but he—and occasionally Thackeray, for example, in his descriptions in *Pendennis* of "Shepherd's Inn" and of the Temple on a quiet Sunday evening—was capable of conveying so authentically the atmosphere of contemporary London. Certainly no other novelist dwelt so insistently on what every Londoner was all too conscious of but seldom wrote about, its smells (which Dickens forthrightly called by that word), from sources ranging from ill-ventilated kitchens to stables too close to living quarters. "To the sense of smell," he wrote, the Tite Barnacles' house in Mews Street, Grosvenor Square, "was like a sort of bottle filled with a strong distillation of mews; and when the footman opened the door, he seemed to take the stopper out" (*Little Dorrit*, 1.10:151). Nor, as far as that is concerned, did any other novelist take as much note as Dickens rightly did of people's personal dirtiness.

During the tireless, absorptive walks that took him into every street and byway in metropolitan London, Dickens cultivated an awareness of the relation between people and their habitat that would do credit to a modern urban environmentalist. In his novels he first anticipated, then followed, Disraeli's succinct recommendation in *Tancred* (1847): "One should generally mention localities, because very often they indicate character" (2.12:132). It was not uncommon for novelists to begin as Reade and Boucicault did in *Foul Play*, whose first sentence read: "There are places which appear at first sight inaccessible to romance: and such a place was Mr. Wardlaw's dining room in Russell Square." Mr. Wardlaw had not yet been introduced, but the simple fact that he lived in Russell Square was enough to categorize him; he clearly belonged to a well-defined, in this case superior, social class.

The class system was overlaid on the London map to produce social geography, which served the novelists well as they sought to define character and social position (the two were inseparable) by indirection rather than plain statement. Nowhere, before Trollope at least, was the Victorian penchant for differentiating social standing on the basis of postal addresses better exemplified than in Dickens's choice of Cadogan Place, Sloane Street, as the Wititterlys' chosen place of residence—an exquisitely ambiguous neighborhood:

Cadogan Place is the one slight bond that joins two great extremes; it is the
connecting link between the aristocratic pavements of Belgrave Square and
the barbarism of Chelsea.† It is in Sloane Street, but not of it. The people in
Cadogan Place look down upon Sloane Street, and think Brompton low.
They affect fashion too, and wonder where the New Road is. Not that they
claim to be on precisely the same footing as the high folks of Belgrave
Square and Grosvenor Place, but that they stand with reference to them
rather in the light of those illegitimate children of the great who are content to boast of their connexions, although their connexions disavow them.
Wearing as much as they can of the airs and semblances of lofty rank, the
people of Cadogan Place have the realities of middle station. It is the conductor which communicates to the inhabitants of regions beyond its limit,
the shock and pride of birth and rank, which it has not within itself, but
derives from a fountain-head beyond; or, like the ligament which unites the
Siamese twins, it contains something of the life and essence of two distinct
bodies, and yet belongs to neither. (*Nicholas Nickleby*, 21:339)

Cadogan Place, in short, was a prototypical tertium quid—or limbo—in
London's social geography.

Out of the steadily growing number of old neighborhoods and formerly detached villages that were being swallowed up in the great con-
urbation, the novelists selected comparatively few for the sake of their
social connotations, but they used those few repeatedly, so that experienced country readers could soon pick up the signal intended. Evicted
from their Bloomsbury Eden by old John Sedley's bankruptcy, his
family was reduced to lodging in "a humble cottage" (or "a terrace
house"—one of Thackeray's trifling inconsistencies) owned by his former clerk: St. Adelaide's Villas, Anna-Maria Road, West, "one of those
streets . . . where the houses look like baby-houses, where the people,
looking out of the first-floor windows, must infallibly, as you think, sit
with their feet in their parlours" (*Vanity Fair*, 17:163). Thackeray's precise location of the Sedleys in Brompton, several times repeated so that
no reader could miss the prejudicial point, "in a street *leading from* the
Fulham Road" (my emphasis) carried its own message to knowledgeable
Londoners. Fulham, two miles west of Hyde Park Corner, was then a
community of villas occupied by families who, though they could afford
to live in then-fashionable Bloomsbury, preferred the *rus in urbe* air of

---

†"Barbarism" here does not mean what it would later mean to Matthew Arnold, whose
"barbarians," whatever their severe deficiencies, had solid socioeconomic credentials. Dickens's London readers would have known that at this time Chelsea was an area whose small
houses, so compact that they did not require servants, were occupied by artisan-class families. Their convenient size is in part responsible for the extravagant prices the surviving
ones command today.

the suburb. It continued to attract people of this highly respectable class
throughout the life of the Victorian novel. Mr. Brough, the insurance
executive in *The Great Hoggarty Diamond*, lived there, in a house called
The Rookery; among his neighbors were the Sir Barnet Skettleses in
Dombey and Son. In later years, one of the Floyd brothers, partners in a
great City bank (*Aurora Floyd*), had a villa at Fulham, as did Sir Thomas
Underwood, M.P., in Trollope's *Ralph the Heir* and the lawyer John Grey
in his *Mr. Scarborough's Family*. Readers of *Vanity Fair*, not only when it
was first published but for many years thereafter, would have understood Thackeray's subtle point: by living *off* the Fulham Road, the
Sedleys lived near the road leading to Bloomsbury's Arcadian counterpart. The traffic *to* Fulham, where affluent families like their forner
selves enjoyed their villas, passed them by, at the bottom of the street.

Their actual address—Brompton, absorbed in today's South Kensington—only intensified their humiliation. From the superior vantage
point of the Wititterlys' Cadogan Place, it was unquestionably "low."
When the Sedleys moved there, the neighborhood was given over to
modest dwellings and market gardens (the Gunters had their gardens
and greenhouses there), and by his insistent repetition of the name
Thackeray underscored the fact that they clung to the perilous nether
edge of petit-bourgeois respectability. In the forties, after the Sedleys'
time, there was a development boom during which many of the truck
gardens were built over, and the region became known as the abode of
workaday artists and theatrical people. (An appendix to the volume devoted to the area in the monumental *Survey of London* [1983] lists "Actors, Musicians, and Writers Resident in Brompton between 1790 and
1870.") In *Pendennis* the poet Miss Bunion lived there, as did Harry
Foker's fast girl friends, Miss Pinckney, a lady of the *corps de danse*, and
Miss Rougemont, an actress who posed as Venus, presumably in the
tableaux vivants that were the early Victorian precursor of the strip-
tease. In the fifties, exploiting Brompton's reputation for "pleasant and
salubrious . . . health-bestowing air," speculative builders, the Gunters
among them, metamorphosed it into a "district of tall Italianate mansions" while still retaining, though on a higher economic level, its association with the arts.[13] The combination of its ineffaceably shabby-
genteel past with its haut-bohemian present led to *Punch*'s derisive
coinage of "passionate Brompton" when it came to satirize the aesthetic
craze in the seventies. By finding the precise location, artists could have
the best of both worlds. In Trollope's *Ayala's Angel* (1881), the painter
Isadore Hamel chose to live in "A small house, very prettily furnished,
somewhat near the Fulham Road" (surely not the very house where the
Sedleys had once lived?) "or perhaps verging a little towards South Ken-

sington" because he preferred "the conventional mode of life" (17:156).
Fine discriminations were the essence of London's social topography.

Dickens used a less suburban neighborhood in north London to undercut the factitious aestheticism of a dabbler in the arts. Harold Skimpole, otherwise Leigh Hunt (who was living in "unsalubrious quarters" in Brompton when *Bleak House* began its serial run), occupied a set of rooms in the Polygon, Somers Town, near Euston station. London readers in 1853 would have got the message. It was a neighborhood filled with cheap houses already falling into decay and occupied by somewhat seedy literary and artistic types who lived on a shoestring of debt. Mere mention of the location not only drew attention to the discrepancy between Skimpole's pose as a professional lover of the beauties of life and the squalor of his surroundings but exposed the pretension itself, as effectively as did Esther Summerson's ingenuous descriptions and Skimpole's disingenuous chatter put together.

For forty years Dickens, the inveterate London observer, watched the ups and downs of particular neighborhoods. When Mr. Brownlow rescued Oliver Twist from Magistrate Fang's clutches, he took him to his house on a "quiet, shady street" near Pentonville, which was then a fashionable suburb, due north of Bloomsbury and east of Somers Town. But when Pentonville reappeared in *David Copperfield*, it had plainly come down in the world, because the penurious Micawbers had lodgings there; and subsequently Dickens arranged for both Guppy (in *Bleak House*) and Pancks (in *Little Dorrit*) to lodge there also, the correct implication being that by that time it was a vicinity specializing in such cheap accommodations.

A reader knowing the relative social standings of various London localities would have been able instantly to contrast Micawber's escalating ambition with his declining circumstances. He and his family left Pentonville to sojourn at Canterbury, where he had hoped to find his fortune in the Medway coal trade, and when that bubble duly burst, they returned to London, where they found humble accommodations in working-class Camden Town. This was certainly not a move in the right direction, socially speaking, though Micawber euphemized the result by simply saying that he found the neighborhood "inconvenient." The contrary upward curve of his fantasy accordingly steepened.

> He mentioned a terrace at the western end of Oxford Street, fronting Hyde Park, on which he had always had his eye, but which he did not expect to attain immediately, as it would require a large establishment. There would probably be an interval, he explained, in which he should content himself with the upper part of a house, over some respectable place of business— say in Piccadilly,—which would be a cheerful situation for Mrs. Micawber; and where, by throwing out a bow-window, or carrying up the roof another

story, or making some little alteration of that sort, they might live, comfortably and reputably, for a few years. (*David Copperfield*, 28:483)

The dream house facing Hyde Park would have been in new, fashionable Tyburnia, on the edge of old, still fashionable Mayfair. Having risen so far in the world, the suddenly (and unaccountably) rich Micawbers would doubtless have ended up in the most desirable neighborhood of all, the ultrafashionable Belgravia, which Thomas Cubitt had begun building in the 1820s and would complete just as *David Copperfield* was published.

Notwithstanding the great amount of time Trollope's characters spend in the country, he can fairly be called a London-centered novelist.[14] This was the opinion of R. H. Hutton, who contrasted Trollope with Jane Austen in this respect in his obituary article in the *Spectator* (16 December 1882):

> In Mr. Trollope's novels—the Irish ones, of course, excepted—nothing can be done without London. Even "The Warden" depends wholly for its plot on the articles of Tom Towers in the "Jupiter," and poor Mr. Harding's visit to London is the turning-point of the story; while ten out of every dozen of Mr. Trollope's stories turn chiefly upon London life. Even his evangelical Bishops go up to London, while his statesmen, politicians, Civil servants, money-lenders, commercial travellers, barristers, boarding-house keepers, and policemen, all, of course, live there. Nothing is more remarkable, in reading the two series of novels together [i.e., Trollope's and Austen's], than the self-centredness of the country in Miss Austen, and the constant reference to London in Mr. Trollope. . . .
>
> In a word, the society which in Miss Austen's tales seems to be wholly local, though it may have a few fine connections with the local capital, is in Mr. Trollope's a great web of which London is the centre, and some kind of London life for the most part the motive-power. The change from Miss Austen to Mr. Trollope is the change from social home-rule to social centralization.[15]

In novel after novel set largely or partly in London, Trollope had occasion to consider the niceties of London addresses; one sometimes feels that beneath his gruff and overbearing exterior lurked the soul of an estate agent. Unlike the cynics in Oscar Wilde's famous definition, his worldly-wise characters know not only prices but values in the prestige-neighborhood market, though those values, being intangible, have nothing to do with the monetary worth of a property and the added expense its location entails. In *Lady Anna*, the complicated legal situation involving the contested will of the wicked Earl Lovel and a problem of legitimacy brought Lady Anna's counsel, Sir William Patterson, to weigh the relative advantages of two different outcomes when the case was litigated—either the distant heir to the title would receive virtually the whole of the late earl's fortune, or he would have only the leavings, a meager income from some land. "Earl Lovel with a thousand a year, and that probably already embarrassed," said Trollope, "would be a poor, wretched creature, a mock lord, an earl without the very essence of an earldom. But Earl Lovel with fifteen or twenty thousand a year would be as good as most other earls. It would be but the difference between two powdered footmen and four, between four hunters and eight, between Belgrave Square and Eaton Place" (5:46–47).

Even within neighborhoods whose high place in the pecking order was fixed for the time being, subtle distinctions had to be made; one address was more fashionable than another only one or two streets away. In *The Small House at Allington* there is a lengthy canvassing of fashionable trends in London neighborhoods as of 1862–64—a new development in Bayswater (which acquired its cachet by osmosis from Tyburnia on the east), St. John's Wood, Belgravia, and the Pimlico streets that bordered on it. Trollope says of Adolphus Crosbie and Lady Alexandrina, "If, indeed, they could have achieved Eaton Square, or a street leading out of Eaton Square,—if they could have crept on to the hem of the skirt of Belgravia—the bride would have been delighted . . . . Her geographical knowledge of Pimlico had not been perfect, and she had nearly fallen into a fatal error. But a friend had kindly intervened. 'For heaven's sake, my dear, don't let him take you anywhere beyond Eccleston Square!'" (40:2.111).

Toward the end of *The Three Clerks*, Trollope had a bit of fun with such distinctions:

> The Tudors . . . lived in one of the quiet streets of Westbournia, not exactly looking into Hyde Park, but very near to it; Mrs. Val [Scott], on the other hand, lived in Ebury Street, Pimlico; her house was much inferior to that of the Tudors; it was small, ill built, and afflicted with all the evils which bad drainage and bad ventilation can produce; but then it was reckoned to be within the precincts of Belgravia, and was only five minutes' walk from Buckingham Palace. Mrs. Val, therefore, had fair ground for twitting her dear friend with living so far away from the limits of fashion. "You really must come down somewhat nearer to the world; indeed you must, my dear," said the Hon. Mrs. Val.
>
> "We are thinking of moving; but then we are talking of going to St. John's Wood, or Islington," said Gertrude [Tudor], wickedly.
>
> "Islington!" said the Honourable Mrs. Val, nearly fainting.
>
> "Is not Islington and St. Giles' the same place?" asked the innocent Clem, with some malice, however, to counterbalance her innocence. (35:429)†

---

† Islington had formerly been a favorite suburb because it could easily be reached from merchants' and stockbrokers' offices in the City, but by this time it was in decline as its

In *The Eustace Diamonds*, Frank Greystock, debating whether he should marry Lizzie Eustace for money or the little governess, Lucy Morris, for love, casts his dilemma in real-estate terms:

> He could look out and see two altogether different kinds of life before him, both of which had their allurements. There was the Belgrave-cum-Pimlico life, the scene of which might extend itself to South Kensington, enveloping the parks and coming round over Park Lane, and through Grosvenor Square and Berkeley Square to Piccadilly. . . . And then there was that other outlook, the scene of which was laid somewhere north of Oxford-street, and the glory of which consisted in Lucy's smile, and Lucy's hand, and Lucy's kiss, as he returned home weary from his work. (13.156)

The point of Trollope's distinction is that Frank's dream of setting up a cozy home north of Oxford Street was by no means as sacrificial as the contrast with the Belgravia-Pimlico axis suggested. So long as Mayfair remained the heart of fashion, and even when it was losing ground to Belgravia, Oxford Street was the dividing line between the realm of the truly rich and fashionable and the northerly quarter which housed families who, while no less respectable and hardly less affluent, lacked the very best credentials. For Frank to renounce the cachet of Belgravia for the supposed modesty of north-of-Oxford Street would have meant some loss of status, but not a severe one. He was also being unrealistic, because to settle there would have required Lizzie Eustace's money just the same; he could not have afforded it on his income alone.

It was across this barrier—under the circumstances, it was almost a frontier—that the two branches of the Newcome family despised each other. Sir Brian Newcome, Bart., and Lady Ann in Park Lane hardly condescended to notice Hobson Newcome and his Evangelical wife, Maria, residing in Bryanston Square, several streets north of the upper end of Park Lane, Mayfair's western boundary. "Bryanstone Square," as Thackeray put it, "could not forget the superiority of Park Lane's rank; and the catalogue of grandees at dear Ann's parties filled dear Maria's heart with envy" (5:1.46). Dear Maria, for her part, welcomed her nephew Barnes to her party—also attended by Colonel Newcome in his (t)rusty Stultz swallowtail coat—with these less than cordial words:

---

affluent residents moved farther out, leaving their houses to be converted into multifamily dwellings such as the lodging house Mrs. Lirriper, in Dickens's Christmas story for 1863, conducted after her husband's death. St. Giles's, for many years a notorious inner-city slum and criminal haunt, had been demolished in 1844–47 when New Oxford Street was cut through. The exchange is a subtle mixture of sociogeographical awareness and playfully assumed ignorance. Clem knew that St. Giles's no longer existed, but its evil reputation long survived its demise.

"What, Barnes; is it possible that you do me the honour to come all the way from Mayfair to Marylebone? I thought you young men never crossed Oxford Street" (*The Newcomes*, 8:1.82).

The house at the corner near Portland Place where Silas Wegg had his pitch was located with the usual Dickensian aptness, for its subsequent role as the luxurious mansion bought and furnished with the proceeds of Noddy Boffin's dust heaps: it was north of Oxford Street, but close enough to Mayfair to borrow some of its exclusive air. The Podsnaps, too, were correctly located near Portland Square. Dickens, however, does not specify where the parvenu Veneerings lived with their monstrous set of dinnerware. He merely says that it was in a "bran-new house in a bran-new quarter of London."

3.

When the Peggottys and Micawbers set sail for Australia from the Tilbury docks, another migration, a movement covering no more than two or three miles but much more important in the fortunes of characters in Victorian fiction, was taking place in London. There were two actual separate streams of horizontal social mobility with, as it were, a socially upward inclination. Both involved classes of people who had social ambitions, or at least were financially able to follow the flow if they wished.

Historically, men whose occupations lay in the City, from bankers to small tradesmen, had always lived close to their work, either in the same houses, the back and upper rooms of which were their family living quarters, or in separate dwellings. But as early as the eighteenth century well-heeled City merchants and Westminster gentlemen had built weekend or summer retreats to the west, particularly in or near Thames-side villages like Twickenham. In 1782 William Cowper satirized the trend:

> Suburban villas, highway-side retreats,
> That dread th' encroachment of our growing streets,
> Tight boxes neatly sash'd, and in a blaze
> With all a July sun's collected rays,
> Delight the citizen, who gasping there,
> Breathes clouds of dust, and calls it country air.[16]

As rents and the value of property in the City rose, townsmen began to move their permanent residences to these supposedly more salubrious vicinities, to which, from the 1830s onward, the growing network of omnibus and railway lines gave cheap and easy access. Commuting from home to work became a widespread London habit, although a few men scorned both forms of public transportation; James Carker, Dombey's manager, rode horseback between his office and his villa in the leafy suburb of Norwood.

It was not only City inhabitants who migrated, however, nor only the upper class of merchants and financiers; prosperous West End tradesmen did likewise. The breeches-maker Neefit, in *Ralph the Heir* (1870–71), was one of the last holdouts, but eventually he too became a contented commuter.

> Our readers [said Trollope] may be told in confidence that up to a very late date Mr. Neefit lived in the rooms over his shop. This is certainly not the thing for a prosperous tradesman to do. Indeed, if a tradesman be known not to have a private residence, he will hardly become prosperous. But Neefit had been a cautious man, and till two years before the commencement of our story, he had actually lived in Conduit Street,—working hard, however, to keep his residence a deep secret from his customers at large. Now he was the proud possessor of a villa residence at Hendon, two miles out in the country beyond the Swiss Cottage; and all his customers knew that he was never to be found before 9.30 A.M., or after 5.15 P.M. (1.5:51)†

The departure of these shopkeeper-citizens from the City and regions farther east left a vacuum that was filled at once by a humbler class of people who occupied their former homes. Nobody with any pretension of fashionableness lived there any longer. When Kate Nickleby, ending her second day of employment at Madame Mantalini's shop near Cavendish Square to return to the Thames Street dwelling Ralph

---

† "What tradesman now resides over his shop in the City?" rhetorically demanded Mrs. J. H. Riddell in her novel *The Race for Wealth* (1866) (Brightfield, 1:406). One of the few who did was the stubbornly independent shopkeeper whose preference for an after-hours life of self-expression and avocations, happily pursued, provided the framework metaphor in Browning's "Shop" (1876):

> . . . Nor Mayfair residence
> Fit to receive and entertain,—
> Nor Hampstead's villa's kind defence
> From noise and crowd, from dust and drain,—
> Nor country-box was soul's domain!
> . . . .
> 'Twas lodging best to live most nigh
> (Cramp, coffinlike as crib might be)
> Receipt of Custom; ear and eye
> Wanted no outworld: "Hear and see
> The Bustle in the shop!" quoth he.

Nickleby, its owner, lent her mother and herself, the forelady, Miss Knag, asked:

> "Which way are you walking, my love?"
>
> "Towards the city," replied Kate.
>
> "The city!" cried Miss Knag, regarding herself with great favour in the glass as she tied her bonnet. "Goodness gracious me! now do you really live in the city?"
>
> "Is it so very unusual for anybody to live there?" asked Kate, half smiling.
>
> "I couldn't have believed it possible that any young woman could have lived there under any circumstances whatever, for three days together," replied Miss Knag.
>
> "Reduced—I should say poor people," answered Kate, correcting herself hastily, for she was afraid of appearing proud, "must live where they can."
>
> (*Nicholas Nickleby*, 18:288)

Westward the course of the social empire, to adapt Bishop Berkeley's phrase, took its way. Much of the Bedford estate (Bloomsbury) had begun to be occupied in the late eighteenth century by rich City merchants, bankers, and lawyers, replacing the nobility that had clustered around Bedford House, on the north side of Bloomsbury Square.[17] Russell Square, the jewel of the estate and its most fashionable quarter in the later Napoleonic years, was built in 1800–1814. But already the established haunts of the true *haut monde* farther west beckoned, and members of the *haute bourgeoisie* gradually infiltrated Mayfair and adjacent neighborhoods for the sake of associating with the aristocracy and benefiting from the even more prestigious address.

It was against this background of change that Thackeray placed the Osbornes and Sedleys in Russell Square when *Vanity Fair* opened. Fellow residents of Bloomsbury as they once had been, they were united in their detestation of the West End. The view of Mayfair from Brompton, where the Sedleys now lived in a cramped cottage off the Fulham Road, was not identical with that from Russell Square, but both were imbued with a nagging sense of the gulf that separated commoner from aristocrat. At the peak of his fortunes, Sedley, Osborne's former clerk and now a bankrupt stockbroker, presumably could once have afforded to move to Mayfair, but it was too late now. Sedley denounces George Osborne to Dobbin as "the stiff-necked prig, with his dandified airs and West-End swagger" and forbids him to court Amelia, and for his part old Osborne, when his son insists on remaining true to Amelia, storms, "If I had kept the company *some folks* have had through *my means*, perhaps my son wouldn't have any reason to brag, sir, of his superiority and *West End* airs" (20:192; 21:203). Osborne, meanwhile, could still have afforded the move that was beyond Sedley's reach, but he chose to torture himself with a deep-seated combination of insecurity and envy: the classic outsider's complex. Entertaining visions of George making an advantageous match with the rich mulatto Rhoda Swartz, he somewhat dampens that lady's enthusiasm by warning her that "you can't find . . . that splendour and rank to which you are accustomed at the West End, my dear Miss, at our humble mansion in Russell Square" (21:196). When his daughter Maria marries Frederick Bullock, scion of a banking family, and they take a house near Berkeley Square, she pleads with him to "quit that odious vulgar place," which she now avoids. "So Russell Square is not good enough for Mrs. Maria, hay?" he growls to her sister Jane as they drive away from one of her glittering dinners "to meet City folks and littery men" while she "keeps the Earls and the Ladies, and the Honourables to herself. I am a plain British merchant I am: and could buy the beggarly hounds over and over. . . . And they won't come to Russell Square, won't they?—ha! ha!" (42:413–14).

Around the time that Osborne was making his last-ditch stand in Russell Square, the wealthy gentry were being displaced by a lower, commercial class that nevertheless was prosperous enough to afford its rents. "Old Puffington," in Surtees's *Mr. Sponge's Sporting Tour*, a prosperous starchmaker who first lived with his wife in a "sweet little villa" near his factory in Stepney—now a totally unacceptable place of residence—found his balance sheets becoming ever more favorable. His wife accordingly "insisted . . . upon migrating to the 'west,' as she called it, and at one bold stroke they established themselves in Heathcote-street, Mecklenburgh-square. Novelists had not then written this part down as 'Mesopotamia,'[†] and it was quite as genteel as Harley or Wimpole-street are now [i.e., at the time the novel was written, 1849–51]" (32:206–7).

Vanity Fair's first readers in 1847–48 would have responded to the Russell Square passages in the light of what Bloomsbury had become in those intervening years. It had grown and declined almost simultaneously. Developing its remaining unoccupied land was Cubitt's first major project before Belgravia, but he had to contend with both an ill-timed slump in the housing market and the shift in fashion toward the West

[†]The word seems to have been used loosely as a topographical designation. In Disraeli's *Vivian Grey*, mention is made of "an invitation to an assembly, or something of the kind, at a place, somewhere, as Theodore Hook or Mr. Croker would say, 'between Mesopotamia and Russell Square'" (2.9:48), which may have been a clever distinction without a difference, because Mecklenburgh Square and Russell Square are only a few hundred feet apart. At that date (1826–27), it could scarcely have referred to Belgravia, which Cubitt was only beginning to build, although it later did so. According to Eric Partridge's *Dictionary of Slang*, Belgravia was also called Asia Minor, the New Jerusalem, and Cubittopolis. One wonders if the last name was associated, as a kind of pun, with the biblical "cubitt"—a measure of length and therefore appropriate in a surveying and building context.

End, taking with it the very tenants for whom he had undertaken to build his fine houses. In 1842 he wrote, "The fact is the place is become unfashionable. Everybody is running away to the west, and though my Houses may be classed with the best that have ever been built anywhere; and the situation is really good and airy, yet I cannot get rid of the Houses."[18] As the leading trade paper, *The Builder*, pointed out two years later, "the houses are now being rapidly deserted—are converted or are converting into shops, lodging-houses, and chambers, and in a few years, when age begins to stamp its mark upon them, the last traces of aristocratic, commercial, or professional opulence will vanish from among them."[19]

By then, the "Mesopotamia" Surtees spoke of was at best a betwixt-and-between neighborhood, comparable to Cadogan Place farther west. Surtees further records that when Jorrocks, the wholesale grocer in St. Botolph's Lane, City, got rich enough, he took up residence in Great Coram Street, Russell Square. "This," said Surtees in *Handley Cross* (1853–54), "is rather a curious locality,—city people considering it west, while those in the west consider it east. . . . Neat unassuming houses form the sides, and the west end is graced with a building that acts the double part of a reading-room and swimming-bath; 'literature and lavement' is over the door. In this region the dazzling glare of civic pomp and courtly state are equally unknown. . . . It is a nice quiet street, highly popular with Punch and other public characters. A smart confectioner's in the neighbourhood leads one to suppose that it is a favourite locality for citizens" (7:58).

The "Gaunt Square" of *Vanity Fair* had witnessed such a decline, enabling Thackeray's readers to relate, ever more closely, the past to the present.[†] The three remaining sides of the square—Gaunt House occupied the fourth—

> are composed of mansions that have passed away into Dowagerism. . . . Little light seems to be behind those lean, comfortless casements now: and

---

[†]Joan Stevens, tracking down Gaunt House and the square it dominated through Thackeray's many hints, concluded that it was "a creative amalgam of . . . elements in the history of Cavendish, Berkeley, and Manchester Squares" rather than a single identifiable locality ("A Roundabout Ride," *Victorian Studies* 13 [1969]:70). These squares are all in the West End, but what happened to Gaunt Square followed a pattern equally typical of Bloomsbury. For whatever it is worth, one might note that if the traditional identification of Lord Steyne with the Marquis of Hertford (see pages 595–600 below) is accepted, the claim of Manchester Square as an "original" of Gaunt Square is strengthened, because Manchester House was one of Hertford's two London mansions. Later renamed Hertford House, it is now the home of the Wallace Collection.

hospitality to have passed away from those doors as much as the laced lacqueys and link-boys of old times who used to put out their torches in the black iron extinguishers that still flank the lamps over the steps. Brass plates have penetrated into the Square—Doctors, the Diddlesex Bank Western Branch—the English and European Reunion, &c.—it has a dreary look— nor is my Lord Steyne's palace less dreary. (47:451)

Little wonder, then, that after Bloomsbury's brief prime, fashionable novels, which Thackeray had very much in mind when writing *Vanity Fair*, had abounded with snide references to it as a region no longer tolerable to men and women who thought themselves as belonging to, or wished to associate with, the crème de la crème of London society. Russell and Bedford Squares were nowhere; Grosvenor or Berkeley Square, Mayfair, was where the action was.

One distinct class, however—one to which Thackeray tangentially belonged and in which he had a special interest, the nabobs who had made their fortunes in India and now lived in clannish retirement at home—migrated on a somewhat different route. Once "the Indian magnates" flourished in Bedford Square, Bloomsbury; then they moved successively to Portland Place, Baker Street, and Harley Street (thus bypassing Mayfair in favor of Marylebone), ending up, at the time *The Newcomes* was written, in Tyburnia, which, Thackeray points out (8:1.89), was convenient to Kensal Green cemetery.

The precarious gentility of London neighborhoods, their vulnerability to forces beyond personal control, was as much a part of Thackeray's elegiac theme as his melancholy reflections on the passing of the ways of life they had once witnessed. The superficially jaunty tone of his comment on the phenomenon of artists finally taking over formerly fashionable neighborhoods does not conceal his sense of loss:

> There are degrees in decadence: after the Fashion chooses to emigrate, and retreats from Soho or Bloomsbury, let us say, to Cavendish Square, physicians come and occupy the vacant houses, which still have a respectable look, the windows being cleaned, and the knockers and plates kept bright, and the doctor's carriage rolling round the square, almost as fine as the countess's, which has whisked away her ladyship to other regions. A boarding-house, mayhap, succeeds the physician, who has followed after his sick folks into the new country; and then Dick Tinto comes with his dingy brass-plate, and breaks in his north window, and sets up his sitters' throne. (*The Newcomes*, 17:1.176)

But the whirligig of time brought its revenge. Though Mayfair had stolen the glory that once was briefly Bloomsbury, its social supremacy was not absolute. Indeed, Bloomsbury, even so late, had its holdouts. In

Trollope's *Castle Richmond* (1860), Mr. Prendergast, a solicitor, "was one of those old-fashioned people who think that a spacious substantial house in Bloomsbury Square, at a rent of a hundred and twenty pounds a year, is better worth having than a narrow, lath and plaster, ill-built tenement at nearly double the price out westward of the Parks. A quite new man is necessarily afraid of such a locality as Bloomsbury Square, for he has no chance of getting any one into his house if he do not live westward. . . . But Mr. Prendergast was well enough known to his old friends to be allowed to live where he pleased" (3.5:3.108−9).

By the time Disraeli described it in *Tancred* (1847), Mayfair was no longer the exclusive haunt of fashion that it had been in the Regency. It was now possible for dedicated socialites to leap over Mayfair en route to the peak of early Victorian prestige. The paradigmatic route was that of the ambitious Guy Flounceys in *Tancred*, who began in Park Crescent, Marylebone, a good but not top-drawer Regency address, then moved to Portman Square, farther south but still north of Oxford Street, and finally, soaring above Mayfair and Hyde Park Corner, landed in a "'splendid mansion' in Belgrave Square" (2.7:98). They now were perched at the top of the heap—looking superciliously down on Mrs. Wititterly in Cadogan Place as she, in turn, looked down on low Brompton.[†]

4.

Although there is much truth in the common belief that Victorian London lives for us most of all in Dickens's pages, his contemporaries would have put firm limitations on the idea. His is an accurate and vivid picture of London so far as it goes, but there are large blanks in this wide canvas, including sections of the metropolis that people knew best. To every one of his London readers his was a very selective reflection of the actuality. Regardless of the date of the action, the London of Dickens's novels is substantially the one he grew up in, from the moment his parents brought him from Chatham to settle permanently in the city (1822) to the years in which as a peripatetic reporter he produced his first kaleidoscopic view of London in *Sketches by Boz*.

[†]Even Caddy and Prince Turveydrop participated in the migration. At the very end of *Bleak House* (67:933), as an indication of their honestly earned prosperity, Dickens sets them up in a house "full two miles further westward than Newman Street," which would place them in the fashionable neighborhood of Tyburnia or Bayswater—as improbable a sociogeographical transmigration as Micawber's taking up residence in the same vicinity would have been. To further ice the belated wedding cake, Caddy "keeps her own little carriage."

As it happened, both this book and *Pickwick Papers*, set in the years just before the beginning of the Victorian period, depicted a London that was on the verge of sweeping changes. In the next quarter-century, when the money and labor that had been pent up during the Napoleonic Wars and the subsequent economic depression were released, some London locations changed beyond recognition. The Houses of Parliament burned in 1834, and the neo-Gothic pile that replaced them took fifteen years to finish. A large area at the western end of the Strand, with which the boy Dickens had become miserably familiar during his term in the blacking factory, was swept away to make room for Trafalgar Square, the Nelson Column, and the National Gallery.

In his fiction, however, Dickens seldom recognizes the presence of new construction, the major exception being his two-part, before-and-after description in *Dombey and Son* of the razing of Staggs's Gardens and the rise, in its place, of a bustling but wholly unpicturesque working-class neighborhood serving the newly arrived railway. Otherwise, though he witnessed the progressive alteration of the face of London, Dickens did not report it except in his occasional journalism. "Dickens's London" was the London filled with quaint vestiges of the past, not the new landmarks that were gradually being built around them or on their very sites. The landmarks and scenes that made the deepest impression on him, contributing most to his prodigious fund of local color, were those that had survived through several centuries, or at best had been new many years before—the London familiar to those tireless perambulators, Dr. Johnson and Charles Lamb. Those scenes were the prime material of the picturesque views portrayed in the antiquarian engravings that became increasingly popular in those years, as "modern improvements" threatened to engulf the metropolis: ancient churches, crooked byways in the City, old wharves in the river, almshouses, charity schools, inns of court, tumbledown tenements. It is noteworthy that in the panoramic view from Todgers's commercial boardinghouse near the Monument (*Martin Chuzzlewit*), not a "modern" detail can be seen, no hint of new building. The newness enters only in the form of resistance to it: the inhabitants of the "queer old taverns" "were much opposed to steam and all new-fangled ways, and held ballooning to be sinful, and deplored the degeneracy of the times" (9:187).

Thackeray, who knew the more comfortable parts of London as well as Dickens knew those into which the respectable or timorous never penetrated, used many small details from the metropolitan scene, especially, as we saw in Chapter 5, to reinforce his elegiac theme and to measure the passage of time. In *Vanity Fair*, the vicinity of Hyde Park Corner marked two widely separated turns of the action.[20] When in 1815 Cap-

tain George Osborne rode with his manservant to his wedding in a chapel near the Fulham Road, the carriage took "the road down Piccadilly;
where Apsley House and St. George's Hospital wore red jackets still
[their brickwork was not yet covered with stone]; where there were oil-
lamps; where Achilles was not yet born; nor the Pimlico arch raised; nor
the hideous equestrian monster which pervades it and the neighbourhood" (22:206). When Dobbin returns to London after ten or twelve
years in India (Thackeray gives both figures, and the incidental references becloud rather than clarify the point), he finds that "The arch and
the Achilles statue were up since he had last seen Piccadilly: a hundred
changes had occurred which his eye and mind vaguely noted" (58:560).
Westmacott's fifteen-foot nude bronze statue of Achilles, honoring the
Duke of Wellington, had been erected at Hyde Park Corner in 1822;
Decimus Burton's triumphal "Pimlico" arch, in 1828.

Reference to the latter, and the "hideous equestrian monster," stirred
an instant response in *Vanity Fair*'s first readers, when the controversy
over the new and notorious statue of Wellington himself still raged.
Financed by a subscription drive launched in 1838, Matthew Wyatt, the
well-known sculptor, had produced a colossal forty-ton, thirty-foot-high
statue of the Duke on horseback to be placed atop Burton's arch. The
statue was ridiculed even when it was still in the casting stage, and when,
on 29 September 1847, it was delivered to the site on a wagon pulled by
twenty-nine stout horses for what was promised to be a three-week trial
period, this instant eyesore touched off a burst of public derision and
indignation. *Punch* devoted as many as three or four jokes, lampoons,
and cartoons to the monstrosity in every issue. But the furor, which was
not without its political overtones, was in vain. The statue remained on
the arch until 1883, when it was discreetly rusticated to "a deserted heath
at Aldershot." The event added fortuitous topicality to the central position in the novel of the Battle of Waterloo and the crucial turns it gave
to the lives of several of the principal characters. From this viewpoint,
the symbolic center of *Vanity Fair* is Hyde Park Corner, on which faced
Wellington's Apsley House, several times mentioned in the novel. The
design on the wrapper of the monthly numbers carried out the same
theme, with the notorious arch and statue on the right.

Only rarely did a novelist pause to comment on the transformation
the city as a whole was undergoing, as Disraeli did at the same moment
in *Tancred*. He denounced the architecture of the new public buildings,
which should represent the nation at its grandest to the increasing number of visitors from abroad and be "monuments to which all should be
able to look up with pride, and which should exercise an elevating influence upon the spirit of the humblest." But, he said,

Though London is vast, it is very monotonous. All those new districts that have sprung up within the last half-century, the creatures of our commercial and colonial wealth, it is impossible to conceive anything more tame, more insipid, more uniform. Pancras is like Mary-le-bone, Mary-le-bone is like Paddington; all the streets resemble each other, you must read the names of the squares before you venture to knock at a door. This amount of building capital ought to have produced a great city. What an opportunity for Architecture suddenly summoned to furnish habitations for a population equal to that of the city of Bruxelles, and a population, too, of great wealth. Mary-le-bone alone ought to have produced a revolution in our domestic architecture. It did nothing. It was built by Act of Parliament. Parliament prescribed even a façade. It is Parliament to whom we are indebted for your Gloucester Places, and Baker Streets, and Harley Streets, and Wimpole Streets, and all those flat, dull, spiritless streets, resembling each other like a large family of plain children, with Portland Place and Portman Square for their respectable parents. . . . In our own days we have witnessed the rapid creation of a new metropolitan quarter, built solely for the aristocracy by an aristocrat [Viscount Belgrave, since 1845 the Marquis of Westminster]. The Belgrave district is as monotonous as Mary-le-bone; and is so contrived as to be at the same time insipid and tawdry. (2.10:116–17)

But Disraeli had more favorable words for the Strand ("perhaps the finest street in Europe, blending the architecture of many periods") and the City. "The Inns of Court, and the quarters in the vicinity of the port, Thames Street, Tower Hill, Billingsgate, Wapping, Rotherhithe, are the best parts of London; they are full of character; the buildings bear a nearer relation to what the people are doing than in more polished quarters." The last comment points toward Corbusier in one direction—and back to Dickens in another. His choice of locales was, after all, a discriminate one.

As Disraeli's comments indicate, some judges deplored the current tastes in urban domestic architecture. A decade later, in *What Will He Do With It?* (1857–59), Bulwer-Lytton satirized the wild eclecticism then in vogue:

Eleven o'clock, A.M., Samuel Adolphus Poole, Esq., is in his parlor,—the house [named Alhambra Villa], one of those new dwellings which yearly spring up north of the Regent's Park: dwellings that, attesting the eccentricity of the national character, task the fancy of the architect and the gravity of the beholder,—each tenement so tortured into contrast with the other, that, on one little rood of ground, all ages seemed blended, and all races encamped. No. 1 is an Egyptian tomb!—Pharaohs may repose there! No. 2 is a Swiss *châlet*,—William Tell may be shooting in its garden! Lo! the severity of Doric columns,—Sparta is before you! Behold that Gothic

THE PROPOSED STATUE OF THE IRON DUKE.

These pictures of the Wellington statue suggest the composite image that Thackeray's allusion to it may have evoked in the first readers of *Vanity Fair*. (above) The statue as *Punch* humorously envisioned it (13 June 1846)—the profile wittily merges Wellington and Mr. Punch, who shared a hawk nose. (opposite) The statue after it was completed in Wyatt's foundry, the dwarfing of the men and women below it providing unimpeachable evidence that it was indeed "colossal" (*Illustrated London News*, 3 October 1846).

porch,—you are rapt to the Norman days! Ha! those Elizabethan mul-
lions,—Sidney and Raleigh, rise again! Ho! the trellises of China,—come
forth, Confucius, and Commissioner Yeh! (7.5 : 2.57)

While individual contractors were putting up those monstrosities north
of Regent's Park and Cubitt was devoting his construction forces to lin-

ing the streets of Belgravia and Pimlico with hundreds of imposing terrace houses, a host of speculative jerry-builders were converting outlying
areas into housing tracts. This was one up-to-date urban phenomenon
that Dickens singled out in *Our Mutual Friend* (1864–65):

> The schools—for they were twofold, as the sexes—were down in that dis-
> trict of the flat country tending to the Thames, where Kent and Surrey
> meet, and where the railways still bestride the market-gardens that will soon
> die under them. The schools were newly built, and there were so many like
> them all over the country, that one might have thought the whole were but
> one restless edifice with the locomotive gift of Aladdin's palace. They were
> in a neighbourhood which looked like a toy neighbourhood taken in blocks
> out of a box by a child of particularly incoherent mind, and set up anyhow;
> here, one side of a new street; there, a large solitary public-house facing
> nowhere; here, another unfinished street already in ruins; there, a church;
> here, an immense new warehouse; there, a dilapidated old country villa;
> then, a medley of black ditch, sparkling cucumber-frame, rank field, richly
> cultivated kitchen-garden, brick viaduct, arch-spanned canal, and disorder
> of frowziness and fog. As if the child had given the table a kick, and gone to
> sleep. (2.1:267–68)

Here Dickens borrowed a theme from Wilkie Collins, who had discovered a decade earlier the topicality of settings in the raw housing
developments where green fields were disappearing under the multitudinous Laburnum Groves, Acacia Gardens, Hawthorn Roads, and
Mayfield Avenues lined with semidetached houses cheaply built from
pattern books, drab and dreary and, almost from the day they were finished, shabby without the mild saving grace of actual gentility. It was
perfect material for the writer of realist fiction; one might give the bleak
descriptions it inspired the name of "suburban naturalism." This was the
beginning, following a brief prologue, of Collins's *Hide and Seek* (1854):

> At the period when the episode just related occurred in the life of Mr. Za-
> chary Thorpe the younger—that is to say, in the year 1837—Baregrove
> Square was the furthest square from the city, and the nearest to the coun-
> try, of any then existing in the north-western suburb of London. But, by the
> time fourteen years more had elapsed—that is to say, in the year 1851—
> Baregrove Square had lost its distinctive character altogether; other squares
> had filched from time those last remnants of healthy rustic flavor from
> which its good name had been derived; other streets, crescents, rows, and
> villa residences had forced themselves pitilessly between the old suburb and
> the country, and had suspended forever the once neighborly relations be-
> tween the pavement of Baregrove Square and the pathways of the pleasant
> fields.
>   Alexander's armies were great makers of conquests; and Napoleon's ar-
> mies were great makers of conquests; but the modern Guerilla regiments

of the hod, the trowel, and the brick kiln are the greatest conquerors of all; for they hold the longest the soil that they have once possessed. How mighty the devastation which follows in the wake of these tremendous aggressors, as they march through the kingdom of nature, triumphantly bricklaying beauty wherever they go!

Collins went on in this vein for more than seven pages, a length unmatched by any other such discourses on the increasingly visible urban sprawl. In *Armadale* (1864–66), he initially established the modern credibility of a building that had the potential of being the scene of a latter-day Gothic horror episode by placing it in a commonplace housing tract.

Fairweather Vale proved to be a new neighborhood, situated below the high ground of Hampstead, on the southern side. The day was overcast, and the place looked very dreary. We approached it by a new road running between trees, which might once have been the park avenue of a country house. At the end we came upon a wilderness of open ground, with half-finished villas dotted about, and a hideous litter of boards, wheelbarrows, and building materials of all sorts scattered in every direction. At one corner of this scene of desolation stood a great overgrown dismal house, plastered with drab-colored stucco, and surrounded by a naked, unfinished garden, without a shrub or a flower in it, frightful to behold. On the open iron gate that led into this inclosure was a new brass plate, with "Sanitarium" inscribed on it in great black letters. (4.3:2.425)

One especially deplored feature of the housing boom was the inescapable ugliness of the building process itself. Miss Braddon described the rise of "Crescent Villas" in West Brompton:

The houses were large, but they lay half imbedded among the chaos of brick and rising mortar around them. New terraces, new streets, new squares led away into hopeless masses of stone and plaster on every side. The roads were sticky with damp clay, which clogged the wheels of the cab and buried the fetlocks of the horse. The desolations—that awful aspect of incompleteness and discomfort which pervades a new and unfinished neighborhood—had set its dismal seal upon the surrounding streets which had arisen about and intrenched Crescent Villas. . . . (*Lady Audley's Secret*, 26:149)

To compound the misery, the initial incompleteness may have lasted for years. Underfinanced speculative builders often had to suspend operations until they could scrape together more capital; hence the prominence of hideous weathering carcases in developments that had run into trouble.

Trollope was totally uninterested in the spread of dreary suburbia, where his characters seldom had either the occasion or the desire to visit, let alone live. His milieu was the city itself, but for some reason the keen architectural eye he exercised in the country, resulting in detailed sketches of buildings from manor houses to vicarages, did not operate in town. Instead of describing London cityscapes, he applied his topographical knowledge to making routes for his characters to follow. Much earlier, Dickens had traced, street by street, the route the Artful Dodger followed in conducting Oliver Twist to Fagin's hangout, and subsequently the town portions of the housebreaking expedition to Chertsey and Bill Sikes's hasty exit from London. Now Trollope did the same thing with characters of a markedly higher social class, and in a newer London. His first effort of the kind was the most memorable, the affectionate account of Mr. Harding's "long day in London." In later novels, Trollope's male figures had a habit of taking long walks through central London as they mulled over their personal problems. Trollope and his readers followed Will Benton in *The Belton Estate*, "a very unhappy gentleman," in a nocturnal walk from St. James's Square across Jermyn Street and Piccadilly, up Bond Street and thus to Portman Square and Baker Street and as far beyond the beaten path as the other side of the New Road (Euston Road) before winding up in his Bond Street lodgings (14:179–82). The ruminating Phineas Finn, in his turn, once walked a different route, from Great Marlborough Street through Poland Street, Soho Square, and Long Acre to Old Square, Lincoln's Inn. Like his creator, Finn was sensitive to the differences of London locales. "His morning walk was of a piece with his morning studies, and he took pleasure in the gloom of both. But now the taste of his palate had been already changed by the glare of the lamps in and about palatial Westminster, and he found that St. Giles's was disagreeable. The ways about Pall Mall and across the Park to Parliament Street, or to the Treasury, were much pleasanter, and the new offices in Downing Street [were] already half-built . . . " (*Phineas Finn*, 7:103–4).

Reliable London cartographer though he was, Trollope did not convey to his readers any awareness of the way London was being torn up and further transformed in the 1860s, when novel after novel, some with London settings, flowed from his breakfast-time pen. Sir John Summerson has said that in those years "London was more excavated, more cut about, more rebuilt and more extended than at any time in its previous history,"[21] what with massive excavations for arterial sewers and the first underground railway, the building of huge new railway terminals (Broad Street, Cannon Street, Holborn Viaduct, St. Pancras, Charing Cross, Victoria) and the lines leading into them, and the cutting through of broad thoroughfares like Queen Victoria Street and Holborn Viaduct. "[F]amiliar thoroughfares have been closed," said the *Daily*

One of the large-scale and highly visible events in mid-Victorian London that went unmentioned in contemporary novels was the excavations for the underground railway, new railway stations, and arterial sewers, and the protracted disruption of traffic these caused in the midst of the metropolis. The *Illustrated London News* for 15 February 1862 showed the construction of the first segment of the underground beneath the Fleet Ditch sewer.

News, "familiar streets have disappeared in clouds of dust, familiar lines of traffic have been diverted into tortuous byways, and one of the chief thoroughfares of the metropolis has been a fine high road through a waste and howling wilderness, with a long vista of hoarding stretching on either side, and behind it ruin and desolation."[22] Although Trollope's characters are constantly on the move, somehow their cab or carriage drivers manage to avoid all the delays and roundabout routes such projects entailed. No Trollopian scene began late because of these manifold inconveniences, the most impressive physical evidence the Victorians had yet had of the headlong pace of their vaunted progress.

Trollope did, however, frequently refer to other matters of current local interest. In *Orley Farm* (1861–62) there is talk of a subsequently abandoned plan to build a new art gallery at Charing Cross. George

THE RIOT IN HYDE PARK.

The railings around Hyde Park, erected long before to keep "the mob" from casually entering this preserve of the fashionable, who took the air there in their carriages or on horseback, had become by the sixties an emblem of the growing division between the working class and the rich and powerful. Here they are being demolished by rioters reacting to the closure of the park by police "to prevent the meeting announced by the Reform League," of which Trollope's Ontario Moggs was a member (*Illustrated London News*, 4 August 1866).

Vavasor, standing for Parliament in "the new Chelsea districts" (*Can You Forgive Her?* [1864–65]), promised the artisan-class voters that he would have the River Thames embanked in their area, thus incomparably improving its amenities and property values.[†] The controversial railings at Hyde Park, then in the public eye because they were the site of the Second Reform Bill disturbances that occasioned Matthew Arnold's *Culture*

[†]The scheme to embank the river from Westminster to Chelsea had been bruited about since the 1840s, but no work was done until 1849–53, when Thomas Cubitt, tiring of delays from various sources, built a half-mile of the proposed two-mile stretch at his own expense. The rest of the project was still pie in the sky when Vavasor campaigned, and the embankment was only brought to completion a decade later, in 1874.

and Anarchy (1869), were denounced by the radical Ontario Moggs in *Ralph the Heir* (1870–71): "Down with them!" was his predictable cry. In the distanced context of the 1830s, Trollope speaks of Lady Anna receiving parcels "from Swan and Edgar's,—Marshall and Snellgrove were not then, or at least had not loomed to the grandeur of an entire block of houses" (*Lady Anna*, 13:131). The latter firm, though not made a partnership until 1848, had been in business in Vere Street since 1837; Trollope is referring to the subsequent expansion by which the firm took over adjoining properties so that by the 1870s it had frontage on both Vere Street and Oxford Street.

One perennial subject of London conversation in the mid-Victorian years formed a running joke in Trollope's fiction: the long-drawn-out project to build new law courts in the vicinity of the Temple. In *The Warden* (1855), the *Jupiter* newspaper had announced the impending doom of Temple Bar (it was actually to remain in situ, constituting a formidable traffic bottleneck between the Strand and Fleet Street, until 1878) and reported rumors of "some huge building" to be erected nearby (14:96). In *Phineas Finn* (1867–68), an exhibition of architectural drawings for the proposed edifice occasioned mention of "the suggested but uncommenced erection of new Law Courts in the neighborhood of Lincoln's Inn" (7:104). In *The Vicar of Bullhampton* (1869–70), the barrister Quickenham cherished the ambition to sit on the bench "in the new Law Courts" (42:266). Finally, in *The Prime Minister* (1875–76), Arthur Fletcher went to "the Jolly Blackbird,—a very quaint, old-fashioned law dining-house in the neighbourhood of Portugal Street, which had managed not to get itself pulled down a dozen years ago on behalf of the Law Courts which are to bless some coming generation" (36:1.339). By this time, work on Street's Decorated Gothic confection in the Strand had actually begun (1874), but it progressed so slowly that Trollope, who shared Dickens's mordant opinion of the law's delays, barely lived to see it opened in state by the Queen. He died a few months later, in December 1882.

One other topic of conversation and press comment in Trollope's time was more localized and seasonal, but to the important people it affected it was far more inconvenient, not to say offensive, than the great construction upheaval of the 1860s. This was the summer stench of the Thames, recipient of the sewage produced by three million people and many industries—Dickens called it "a deadly sewer" in *Little Dorrit* (1.3:68)—which in hot weather was so oppressive that sheets soaked in chloride of lime had to be hung across the river-facing windows of the Houses of Parliament. In the summer of 1858, a dramatic scene in the

TEMPORARY BUILDING IN NEW-SQUARE, LINCOLN'S-INN, FOR EXHIBITING THE DESIGNS FOR THE NEW LAW-COURTS.

OUR Illustrations show the exterior and interior of the temporary building within the raised inclosure of New-square, Lincoln's Inn, where the designs of the several architects competing for the building of the proposed new Courts of Law are now exhibited to public view.

The competitors are eleven in number, it will be remembered—namely, Mr. Abraham, Mr. E. M. Barry, Mr. Raphael Brandon, Mr. Burges, Mr. Deane, Mr. Garling, Mr. Lockwood, Mr. Seddon, Mr. G. G. Scott, Mr. Street, and Mr. Waterhouse. The drawings of

each competitor are hung in a separate chamber, formed right and left of a central pathway, and lighted from the top. The exhibition is altogether well arranged, and daily attracts a multitude of visitors. We shall publish some illustrations of the architects' designs.

THE DESIGNS FOR THE NEW LAW COURTS.

These pictures of the exterior and interior of a temporary structure built to display competing architects' drawings for the proposed new law courts (*Illustrated London News*, 16 February 1867) provided background for Trollope's mention of that much-delayed project in chapter 7 of *Phineas Finn* (*St. Paul's* magazine, November).

House of Commons finally overcame the members' inertia. As the *Times* reported on 3 July, "the Chancellor of the Exchequer [Disraeli] . . . with a mass of papers in one hand and with his pocket handkerchief clutched in the other, and applied closely to his nose, with body half bent, hastened in dismay from the pestilential odour, followed closely by Sir James Graham, who seemed to be attacked by a sudden fit of expectoration; Mr. Gladstone also paid particular attention to his nose." Some onlookers, however, made light of Parliament's distress, viewing it as merely an opportune excuse to rise early. Dating the action of *Plain or Ringlets?* (1859–60), Surtees specified that it occurred in "the Comet year," when Donati discovered the brightest of his six comets, and "harvest-bitten M.P.'s magnified the aroma of the bouquet de mille sewers of the Thames, in order to get away to their turnips, their tares, and under shade of their umbrageous trees" (1:1).

Within a month after the distressing episode in the Commons, a bill Disraeli introduced to clean up the "Stygian pool reeking with ineffable and intolerable horrors"—his language as he addressed the Commons, not that of the bill itself—was enacted into law. It authorized the Metropolitan Board of Works to raise rates to pay for building a comprehensive drainage system, and work got under way more or less promptly, creating some of the traffic chaos already mentioned. But relief was slow in coming. Before Sir Joseph Bazalgette's massive undertaking was completed in the mid-seventies, Parliament still suffered during hot, dry weather. When the "protracted" session of Parliament ended in *Phineas Finn* (1867–69), Ratler, the parliamentary whip, said to Phineas, "I shall never get over it . . . never. I don't suppose such a session for work was ever known before. Think what it is to have to keep men together in August, with the thermometer at 81° and the river stinking like,—like the very mischief" (48:455). Nor did any alleviation occur the next year: "In the early days of July, when the weather was very hot . . . people were beginning to complain of the Thames, and members were becoming thirsty after grouse . . . " (63:600).

Another peril of London life, less offensive to the nose but more melodramatic in execution, was garrotting, a particularly vicious form of mugging. The *Annual Register* for 1862 said for the benefit of readers at a distance that it consisted "in one ruffian seizing an unsuspecting traveller by the neck and crushing in his throat, while another simultaneously rifles his pockets; the scoundrels then decamp, leaving their victim on the ground writhing in agony, with tongue protruding and eyes starting from their sockets, unable to give an alarm or to attempt pursuit."[23] This is what happened to Robert Kennedy while walking along Park Street, Mayfair (*Phineas Finn*); fortunately, Phineas had been following him and frightened the assailant away before Kennedy was seri-

DIPHTHERIA.   SCROFULA.   CHOLERA.

FATHER THAMES INTRODUCING HIS OFFSPRING TO THE FAIR CITY OF LONDON.

Week after week in the hot summer of 1858, *Punch* printed grim cartoons complaining of the stench arising from London's main sewer, the River Thames. The one above appeared on 3 July, the same day that Disraeli fled the House of Commons clutching his handkerchief to his nose. (Father Thames's offspring are named Diphtheria, Scrofula, and Cholera.) The sub-caption, not reproduced here—"A Design for a Fresco in the New Houses of Parliament"—refers to a less momentous topicality, the attempt by the Prince Consort and Sir Charles Eastlake to persuade the highly respected artist Daniel Maclise to paint historical frescoes in the Royal Gallery of Parliament. The cartoon on the opposite page was published on 10 July.

ously injured. Less than a decade later (*The Prime Minister*), Everett Wharton was garrotted and robbed by a man and two women in St. James's Park, a notoriously dangerous locale at night, and Ferdinand Lopez received the same treatment when attempting to rescue him.

On the brighter side, London gained a secure place for unaccompanied women to take the air, free of the unwanted attentions of predatory men. "It is generally understood," said Trollope early in *Ayala's Angel* (1881), "that there are raging lions about the metropolis, who would certainly eat up young ladies whole if young ladies were to walk about

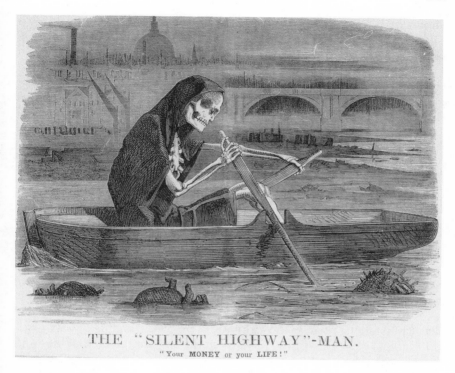

THE "SILENT HIGHWAY"-MAN.
" Your MONEY or your LIFE ! "

the streets or even about the parks by themselves" (4 : 31)—the beginning of a long paragraph whose import was that it had now become
permissible for a respectable young lady to walk alone in Kensington
Gardens. Whether this was a result of liberalized custom or improved
policing does not appear. But the event was sufficiently notable as of
1881 to lead Trollope to refer to it several times later in the novel, when
Ayala's daily walks take her to the park, which becomes a trysting place,
first for Gertrude Tringle and Frank Houston, and later for Gertrude
and Captain Ben Batsby.

The most memorable London event in the middle of the century, the
Great Exhibition of 1851, figured less prominently in Victorian fiction
than one would expect. Of the considerable amount of frothy literature-
for-the-moment the Crystal Palace spun off in that festive summer of
1851, only a novel by Henry Mayhew and John Binny, with Cruikshank
illustrations, *The Adventures of Mr. and Mrs. Sandboys Who Came up to London to "Enjoy Themselves" and to See the Great Exhibition*, is occasionally remembered. As Butt and Tillotson point out, the exhibition is noticeably

absent from *Bleak House*, that treasury of topicalities current around that time. Only later, in *The Woman in White*, did the Crystal Palace excitement figure in an important novel's plot. Mr. and Mrs. Rubelle come to London from Lyons and take a house near Leicester Square "to be fitted up as a boarding house for foreigners, who were expected to visit England in large numbers" (2.2:328). There is more here than meets the casual modern eye. London readers when the novel appeared in 1859–60 would have remembered the widespread fear that when the exhibition opened, London would be a mecca for conspiratorial foreigners bent on all kinds of trouble, from industrial espionage and grand larceny to terrorism and rape. This attack of xenophobia was not justified in the event—no crime wave ever materialized—but in the novel it was, insofar as Count Fosco was revealed to be a member of an Italian secret society.

Otherwise the Crystal Palace turned up in novels by major authors only in the form of throwaway references. One of the few topical events in *Armadale*, whose main narrative extends from May to December 1851, is a brief mention of a visit two of the characters propose to make to the palace. (They never get there.) In *Barchester Towers*, Archdeacon Grantly gives his daughter, on her marriage to Mr. Arabin, "a new pony chair that had gained a prize in the Exhibition" (53:542), and in *The Newcomes* J. J. Ridley's painting of Mrs. Clive is "in the Crystal Palace Exhibition in Fable-land" (80:2.422)—that is, in the imaginary world into which the novel dissolves in its last pages; the real Crystal Palace did not admit the fine arts to its spacious precincts.[†]

As several contemporary sources suggest—cartoons in *Punch*, Tennyson's reference in *Maud* (1855) to a mid-Victorian dandy as "That jewell'd mass of millinery, that oil'd and curl'd Assyrian bull," and Rossetti's poem "The Burden of Nineveh" (*Oxford and Cambridge Magazine*, 1856)—a leading topic of those years was the installation at the British Museum of the monumental sculptures and bas reliefs the archaeologist Austen Henry Layard had brought back from his well-publicized excavations at

---

[†] In the installment of *Mr. Sponge's Sporting Tour* published in the *New Monthly Magazine* for March 1851, when the building was barely completed, Surtees had Watchorn exclaim, "I'm dashed if one mightn't as well be crashin' over the Christial Palace as ridin' over a country fence froze in this way!" In the same issue of the magazine began a serial by Dudley Costello titled *All the World and His Wife; or, What Brought Everybody to London in 1851*. Its first words were, "On the morning of the third of February last," and its subject was the adventures of some French visitors to London to see the exhibition, which opened three months later, on 1 May. Writing up to the very moment, Costello achieved what was probably the tightest fit of all between events and an ongoing narrative. The novel wound up in the August issue of the *New Monthly*, when the show was still in full swing.

Babylon and Nineveh. Trollope used the event to contrast Alaric Tudor's mind with Harry Norman's in *The Three Clerks* (1858): "Alaric's mind was of a different cast; he panted rather for the great than the beautiful; and was inclined to ridicule the growing taste of the day for torsos, Palissy ware, and Assyrian monsters" (7:76). Later, in *The Hand of Ethelberta* (1875–76), Hardy set a scene in the basement room of the museum in which the Nineveh bas reliefs were displayed. By that time, replicas of some of Layard's treasures had been placed in the reerected Crystal Palace at Sydenham, and in *Daniel Deronda* (1876) Hans Meyrick, perhaps remembering Tennyson's line, expressed his hope that Mirah's brother would not turn out to be "a fellow all smiles and jewellery—a Crystal Palace Assyrian with a hat on" (47:640).

5.

Few of the standard London tourist attractions figured to any significant extent in Victorian fiction. St. Paul's Cathedral (the predecessor of Wren's masterpiece, to be sure) and the Tower of London provided the background for historical romances like Ainsworth's, but that is another matter. One familiar building that had no such associations with the remote past but served instead as a topical symbol was Exeter Hall, an instant landmark opened in the spring of 1831 in the Strand, on the site of old Exeter Change.[24] Financed by a company of rich Evangelicals, including prominent members of the Clapham sect, it was for fifty years the evangelical Zion, the first purpose-built convention center in Britain, if not the world. Its opulent Great Hall, with a mighty organ and seats for four thousand and additional benches for a choir of five hundred, was the venue of mass rallies and the annual meetings of religious, missionary, and philanthropic organizations, including the Society for Promoting the Due Observance of the Lord's Day, the powerful Sabbatarian lobby, which had its headquarters there. During the "May meeting" season extending from April through June, the adjoining conference rooms were the scene of as many as twenty meetings a day of smaller societies rendering up the accounts of their stewardship. In the London calendar, the May meeting was to the religious (Low Church and Dissenting) population what the Royal Academy's exhibition, held in those same weeks at the nearby National Gallery, was to the fashionable set.

In fiction, conforming to the store of topographical associations that readers brought to a novel, Exeter Hall was more than a building with a certain street address. Like Tattersall's horse auction room off Hyde Park Corner, the favorite gathering place of sportsmen, and Gunter's Berkeley Square confectionery shop, it was a symbol, a focus for a par-

The annual May meeting of various Nonconformist church bodies and their associated evangelistic and philanthropic organizations was covered by the daily press as a straight news story, without the pronounced satirical edge that usually accompanied mention of Exeter Hall in novels. This picture appeared in the *Illustrated London News* on 18 May 1844.

ticular state of mind or way of life, as, for that matter, was St. John's Wood, the abode of well provided-for demimondaines. When novelists mentioned Exeter Hall, as they often did in passing, they automatically activated the vein of prejudice the name evoked. The painter of miniature portraits, Miss LaCreevy, who lived close by, told Nicholas Nickleby—using the word "flat" to denote the shape of a nose, and, in current slang, a stupid person—that "Snubs and Romans are plentiful enough, and there are flats of all sorts and sizes when there's a meeting at Exeter Hall" (*Nicholas Nickleby*, 5 : 104).

Exeter Hall was the site of Godfrey Ablewhite's spellbinding addresses in behalf of his numerous philanthropic and morals-enforcing causes, and the various female charitable committees he chaired, such as the British-Ladies'-Servants'-Sunday-Sweetheart-Supervision Society, met there. Such facts, announced early in *The Moonstone*, subliminally prepared readers for the denouement, in which the organization man with the sex appeal of a matinee idol was exposed as the true purloiner of the precious diamond, a forger and embezzler who, in Sergeant Cuff's words, was also "a man of pleasure, with a villa in the suburbs which was not taken in his own name, and with a lady in the villa, who was not taken in his own name, either" ("Second period, sixth narrative," chap. 3:503). To the properly biased, it was only to be expected that so smooth a double-dealer and hypocrite was harbored in the sanctimony of Exeter Hall.

Readers carried over whatever prejudices *The Moonstone* aroused to *The Mystery of Edwin Drood*, published two years later. There, Exeter Hall appeared as "the Haven of Philanthropy," the site of the meetings of the "Convened Chief Composite Committee of Central and District Philanthropists," over which Luke Honeythunder presided. While leaving his readers, for the most part, to draw their own conclusions as to Honeythunder's possible moral affinity to Godfrey Ablewhite, Dickens concentrated on what Exeter Hall itself stood for, as exemplified by Honeythunder "the Philanthropist":

> Though it was not literally true, as was facetiously charged against him by public unbelievers, that he called aloud to his fellow-creatures: "Curse your souls and bodies, come here and be blessed!" still his philanthropy was of that gunpowderous sort that the difference between it and animosity was hard to determine. You were to abolish military force, but you were first to bring all commanding officers who had done their duty, to trial by court martial for that offence, and shoot them.[†] You were to abolish war, but were to make converts by making war upon them, and charging them with loving war as the apple of their eye. You were to have no capital punishment, but were first to sweep off the face of the earth all legislators, jurists, and judges, who were of the contrary opinion. You were to have universal concord, and were to get it by eliminating all the people who wouldn't, or conscientiously couldn't, be concordant. You were to love your brother as your-

---

[†]Of the several current public controversies whose wrong side—from his point of view—Dickens lays at the doorstep of Exeter Hall, more for the sake of rhetoric than with historical justification, this was the most inflammatory. The "Governor Eyre case," involving allegations that the governor of Jamaica, Edward John Eyre, had used excessive brutality in putting down a Negro rebellion there in 1865, had divided the literary-intellectual community more deeply perhaps than any other issue reflected in Victorian fiction. It hovers as well in the background of *The Moonstone*. See K. J. Fielding, "Edwin Drood and Governor Eyre," *Listener* 48 (1952): 1083–84, and Sue Lonoff, *Wilkie Collins and His Victorian Readers* (New York, 1982), pp. 178–79.

self, but after an indefinite interval of maligning him (very much as if you
hated him), and calling him all manner of names. Above all things, you
were to do nothing in private, or on your own account. You were to go to
the offices of the Haven of Philanthropy, and put your name down as a
Member and a Professing Philanthropist. Then, you were to pay up your
subscription, get your card of membership and your riband and medal, and
were evermore to live on a platform, and evermore to say what Mr. Honeythunder said. . . . (6:85–86)

A much older landmark acquired a proverbial association that found
its way into London lore and thence into Victorian novels. The Monument on Fish Street Hill, whose gallery provided a view of London superior to that which could be had from Todgers's boardinghouse not far
away, had been a tourist attraction ever since it was completed in 1677
as a memorial of the Great Fire of 1666. In 1874 Lewis Carroll, explaining to a correspondent his long delay in sending a promised photograph, quoted the familiar words from *Twelfth Night*, "like patience on
a monument, smiling at grief." He went on to make a mock-erudite
Carrollian joke:

> This quotation, by the way, is altogether a misprint. Let me explain it to
> you. The passage originally stood "*They* sit, Like patients on *the* Monument,
> smiling at *Greenwich*." In the next edition "Greenwich" was printed short
> "Green*h*" and so got gradually altered into "Grief." The allusion of course is
> to the celebrated Dr. Jenner, who used to send all his patients to sit on the
> top of the Monument (near London Bridge) to inhale fresh air, promising
> them that, when they were well enough, they should go to "Greenwich
> Fair." So of course they always looked out towards Greenwich, and sat smil-
> ing to think of the treat in store for them. A play was written on the subject
> of their inhaling the fresh air, and was for some time attributed to him
> (Shakespeare), but it is certainly not in his style. It was called *The Wandering
> Air*, and was lately revived at the Queen's Theatre. The custom of sitting
> on the Monument was given up when Dr. Jenner went mad, and insisted
> that the air was worst up there, and that the *lower* you went the *more airy* it
> became.[25†]

---

†*The Wandering Air*, like the textual emendation, was Carroll's jocose invention. As the
editor of his letters points out, the actual play at the Queen's Theatre was Charles Reade's
The Wandering Heir, starring Ellen Terry and based on the sensational Tichborne Claimant
case which had occupied the headlines for several years. At the time Carroll wrote, the
claimant, Arthur Orton, was being tried for perjury, in a court action that lasted for 188
days. Trollope alluded to the case in *John Caldigate* (1878–79). George Eliot and George
Henry Lewes had attended the earlier, 102-day trial (1872), and Eliot drew from the story
the episode in *Middlemarch* in which Joshua Rigg, Peter Featherstone's illegitimate son,
suddenly turns up to claim Featherstone's estate. I have not so far been able to explain the
Jenner reference, except as part of the extravagant jape. Dr. Edward Jenner, the cele-

In Dickens's *Barnaby Rudge*, published as part of the serial *Master Humphrey's Clock* between 13 February and 27 November 1841, Joe Willet, who dislikes his son, sends him off to London with one shilling sixpence in his pocket, the shilling to be reserved for emergencies. "The other sixpence," he says, "is to spend in the diversions of London; and the diversion I recommend is going to the top of the Monument, and sit there. There's no temptation there, sir—no drink—no young women—no bad characters of any sort—nothing but imagination" (chap. 13).

To readers in 1841, this passage had a highly topical implication. In Dickens's "The Egotistical Couple," originally published in *Sketches of Young Couples* (1840) and collected in later editions of *Sketches by Boz*, a gentleman recalled "walking down Fish Street Hill, a few weeks since" and saying to his wife "—slightly casting up his eyes to the top of the Monument—'There's a boy up there, my dear, reading a Bible. It's very strange. I don't like it.—In five seconds afterwards, Sir,' says the egotistical gentleman, bringing his hands together with one violent clap—'the lad was over!'" (590) Some months before Dickens's sketch was published, he wrote to Forster (18 September 1839), "What a strange thing it is that all sorts of fine things happen in London when I'm away! I almost blame myself for the death of that poor girl who leaped off the Monument—she would never have done it if I had been in town."[26] A week earlier (11 September), the daughter of a baker in St. Martin's Lane had jumped from the Monument, the third or fourth such suicide in the column's history.[27] In the first number of *Nicholas Nickleby*, published in April 1838, Dickens had already used its macabre celebrity to add topical meaning to Nicholas Nickleby's father's considering the idea, when hard pressed for money to support his family, of "a little commercial speculation of insuring his life next quarter-day, and then falling from the top of the Monument by accident" (1:60).

The allusions in "The Egotistical Couple" and *Barnaby Rudge* were prompted most immediately by the next suicide, that of a boy named Hawkes, said to have been of unsound mind, who had been discharged by his master, a surgeon (18 October 1839). One more event of the sort

brated inventor of inoculation, did have a side interest in mental illness, but according to his recent biographer, his therapy leaned toward the administration of tartar emetic, not fresh air, to insane patients (it "moderated their violence"). (Paul Saunders, *Edward Jenner: The Cheltenham Years 1795–1823* [Hanover, N.H., 1982], p. 47.) He did not go mad himself. The more immediate reference is to Sir William Jenner, K.C.B. (1815–98), physician-in-ordinary to Queen Victoria, who had attended the Prince Consort in his last illness and, more recently, the Prince of Wales in his near-fatal bout with typhoid fever (1871). But his professional record reveals no interest in insanity.

TOP OF THE MONUMENT.

The latest suicide from the top of the Monument had occurred two weeks before this picture ran in the *Illustrated London News* on 3 September 1842. Either the cage ordered by the City authorities "in order to prevent other persons from precipitating themselves from the top of this pillar" had not yet been installed or the engraving was taken from stock rather than freshly made.

was yet to come. On 19 August 1842, a seventeen-year-old servant girl from Hoxton paid her sixpence and was accompanied to the top by one of the men who had been appointed to supervise visitors after the two proximate incidents in 1839. She pretended for fifteen minutes to admire the view, and then, when the guard's attention was relaxed, went over the railing. Five days later, the City Lands Committee ordered the installation of "some strong iron bars fixed sufficiently close over the head of the visitor to leave no chance of squeezing through."[28]

In these circumstances, it is tempting to believe that readers of *Barnaby Rudge* in 1841–42 would have suspected an extra, sinister suggestion in Joe Willet's seemingly innocuous speech. In effect, he was saying to his unloved son, Go jump off the Monument. Such an interpretation is fully in the spirit of early Victorian comedy, which unapologetically embraced what is today called black humor. The despondent speaker in R.H. Barham's "Misadventures at Margate" (*Ingoldsby Legends*, second series, 1842) exclaimed, "And now I'm here, from this here pier it is my fix'd intent / To jump, as Mister Levi did from off the Monu-ment!"[†]

The association of the Monument with suicide had become ineradicable. Although it is not explicit in Tom Pinch's encounter with the "Man in the Monument," the sinister figure who collects the admission fee at the base (*Martin Chuzzlewit* [1843–44]), it lingered in the air. A man who takes grim pleasure in receiving two tanners from an unwary couple who "don't know what a many steps there is" (37:652) and shutting the door behind them as they make their way up the tight, dark spiraling stairs, may be seen, not too fancifully, as the ticket-seller at the gates of hell.

Even though it was out of service in this respect, the Monument's former role as a suicidal venue was not forgotten. When Charley Tudor, faced with a sea of troubles, contemplates suicide in *The Three Clerks*, he considers his options: " . . . he would again think of Waterloo Bridge, and the Monument, and of what might be done for threepence or fourpence in a pistol gallery" (30:372). Twice within a month in 1861, in different contexts, the association was revived, in one case with the additional suggestion of lunacy. Reviewing *Adam Bede* in its July number, the *London Quarterly Review* asked: "Why do the horrors of war and shipwreck continually tempt boys into the army and navy? Why does one

[†]Curiously (because of metrical necessity? the more recent suicides had monosyllabic names, Moyes and Hawkes), Barham reached back to 1810 for his allusion. In that year, Lyon Levi, a Jewish diamond merchant, had taken the plunge. But Barham's choice illustrates how securely such events, and the actual names of people associated with them, were preserved in the communal memory.

semi-madman's shooting at the Queen,[†] or jumping off the Monument,
incline others to the same insanity?"[29] Perhaps inspired by this allusion,
a writer in the *Saturday Review* for 3 August, dilating on the same topic
of copycat crimes, remarked, "When people begin to throw themselves
from the Monument, a fashion of this sort of suicide springs up."

The Monument, in this role, repeatedly turned up in Trollope's novels. Of Roger Carbury he said, "No man in England could be less likely
to throw himself off the Monument or to blow out his brains" (*The Way
We Live Now*, 8:65), and in the late *Mr. Scarborough's Family* (1882–83),
as the no-good gambling son of the family climbs the stairs to Mr. Grey's
room, "he did feel thoroughly ashamed of himself . . . 'It would be better
that I should go back,' he said, 'and throw myself from the Monument'"
(49:469–70). But Trollope, who presumably had no such urges himself,
realized that London provided alternative means of suicide. In *Marion
Fay* (1881–82), the clerk Daniel Tribbledale, at a low point in his pursuit
of Clara Demijohn, considers them:

> "They've caged up the Monument, and you're so looked after on the Duke
> of York's [Column] that there isn't a chance. But there's nothing to prevent
> you from taking a header at the Whispering Gallery of Saint Paul's. You'd
> be more talked of that way, and the vergers would be sure to show the
> stains made on the stones below. 'It was here young Tribbledale fell,—a
> clerk at Pogson and Littlebird's, who dashed out his brains for love on the
> very day as Clara Demijohn got herself married.'" (30:216)

(Here Trollope touched on another, much older fragment of London
lore, the vergers of St. Paul's and Westminster Abbey as cheapjack show-
man-guides.)

With the near completion of the Albert Memorial in 1872, London
acquired a monument that was destined to become as famous as the one
to the Great Fire. It was instantly more controversial: was it an admirably
conceived and executed tribute to the Queen's much lamented consort,
or was it the pompous eyesore that opinion, until very recently, has
branded it? A few years later, shortly after the colossal statue of Prince
Albert it was built to shelter was unveiled (1876), Trollope took adroit
advantage of the memorial's topicality in *Is He Popenjoy?* (1877–78). The
dashing Captain Jack de Baron,[‡] the dean of Brotherton Cathedral, his

---

[†] The latest attempt to assassinate the Queen had occurred in 1850. Two had preceded
it (1840 and 1841) and three more were to follow, two in 1872 and a final one in 1882.

[‡] There is an in-joke in Trollope's invention of the name. It was at this very moment—
1877—that the speculative empire of the company promoter Albert ("Baron") Grant, né
Albert Gottheimer, collapsed and he faced eighty-nine separate legal actions. Earlier, to
the extent that he was a partial model for Augustus Melmotte in *The Way We Live Now*,

daughter Mary, and her husband, Lord George Germain (who, says Trollope, "was simple, conscientious, absolutely truthful, full of prejudices, and weak-minded" [1:1.7]), are on the steps of the monument. "'I think it's the prettiest thing in London,' said the Dean, 'one of the prettiest things in the world.' 'Don't you find it very cold?' said Lord George." Trollope's readers were at liberty to apply their own aesthetic standards to interpreting what each opinion revealed about the person who expressed it. Subsequently a small crisis occurs between Lady George and her husband when Captain Jack plays the fool. His "describing the persons represented on the base of the monument, . . . after some fashion of his own that . . . infinitely amused not only Lady George but her father also. 'You ought to be appointed Guide to the Memorial,' said the Dean." But Lord George is not amused.

> [H]e was not satisfied that his wife should play like a child, and certainly not with such a playfellow. . . . She ought not to want playfellows. If she would really have learned the names of all those artists on the base of the Memorial, as she might so easily have done, there would have been something in it. A lady ought to know, at any rate, the names of such men. But she had allowed this Jack to make a joke of it all, and had rather liked the joke.

"There is a levity which is often pretty and becoming in a girl," he tells her as they walk down Constitution Hill, "in which a married woman in some ranks of life may, perhaps, innocently indulge, but which is not appropriate to higher positions."

"This is all because I laughed when Captain De Baron mispronounced the men's names," Lady George replies. "I don't know anything peculiar in my position. One would suppose that I was going to be made a sort of female bishop . . ." (19:1.182–87).

There was something decidedly unsuitable in Kensington Gardens' imposing new memorial to royal connubial harmony becoming the occasion of a marital spat.

One London site that repeatedly figured in Victorian fiction lay across the river in Lambeth. The history of Vauxhall Gardens had had a literary component since the middle of the eighteenth century. Ever since 1729, when it was opened on the site of an earlier entertainment

---

readers would have associated him with another London topicality. In the summer of 1874, just as the novel began to appear in monthly parts, he had bought the open space originally known as Leicester Fields, which in recent times had degenerated into a convenient dumping site, and public-spiritedly transformed it into a park, replacing its notoriously vandalized statue of George III with one of Shakespeare that remains the focal point of today's Leicester Square. Trollope's association of "de Baron" with London statuary had thus been prepared for three years earlier.

place that Pepys knew, its wooded groves and winding paths, statuary, refreshment stands and supper boxes, thousands of colored lanterns, mechanical cascades and every other attraction that an eighteenth-century admission-charging park could boast, drew, on a summer evening, throngs of Londoners of every class, from Royalty (the fun-loving Prince of Wales and his entourage) down to household servants. Henry Fielding praised "the particular Beauties of these Gardens" in *Amelia*, Goldsmith described its pleasures in *The Citizen of the World* (Letter 70), and in Smollett's *Humphry Clinker* Matthew Bramble and his party visited it. Lydia Melford later communicated her wide-eyed wonderment to her correspondent Laetitia Willis, though she had also to report that the evening was cut short by a rainstorm and the ensuing confusion in which Humphry Clinker, their footman, lost his periwig and got a broken head into the bargain. Wordsworth, recalling in *The Prelude* his residence in London in 1793, wrote of its "green groves, and wilderness of lamps, . . . gorgeous ladies, fairy cataracts, and pageant fireworks" (MS. 1804–6:7.124–26).

It was this glamorous Vauxhall that Thackeray portrayed in the early pages of *Vanity Fair*, when Jos and Amelia Sedley, Becky Sharp, Captain Dobbin, and George Osborne spend an evening there. Thackeray used the occasion as a preliminary means of sorting out his characters, especially Jos, who gets drunk on rack punch and reveals himself to be a thoroughgoing, however amiable, slob. The description of Vauxhall is colored with the romantic feeling with which Thackeray so often invested the pleasures of Regency youth seen from the perspective of middle age.[†] But the fact was that in 1813, when the *Vanity Fair* excursion took place, the gardens, then some eighty years old, were beginning to fray at the edges. Although the numerous accounts of visitors, particularly foreign ones, are generally enthusiastic, as early as 1778 the hero-

---

[†] Perhaps because he wished to leave unbroken the prevailing tone of "pastness," Thackeray excised from the manuscript of the Vauxhall scene a reference to the garden as it was at the time of writing: Simpson's ghost—Simpson having been the longtime manager and master of ceremonies, whose thirty-sixth year in that capacity was marked by a gala benefit in 1833—"may wander about now in the Ghost of a royal property where the spirit of Madame Sacqui is still dancing on the apparition of a tight rope, and the old departed ham-cutters are carving slices scarcely more visionary than those wh. in life they supplied" (Tillotson Riverside ed., p. 677). This was replaced by a past-tense inventory of the "delights of the garden" in its prime, ending with "the twinkling boxes, in which the happy feasters made believe to eat slices of almost invisible ham;—of all these things, and of the gentle Simpson, that kind smiling idiot, who, I daresay, presided even then over the place—Captain William Dobbin did not take the slightest notice" (6:56–57). The transparency of the ham slices in Vauxhall sandwiches was the oldest joke in the metropolitan repertory.

On their eventually disastrous excursion to Vauxhall Gardens, Jos Sedley wins Becky Sharp to the point of her hand being placed on his heart, but this promising development is cut short when "the bell rang for the fireworks, and, a great scuffling and running taking place, these interesting lovers were obliged to follow in the stream of the people" (*Vanity Fair*, part 2, February 1847). This picture of the scene, a nightly occurrence at Vauxhall during the summer for over a century, appeared in the *Illustrated London News* for 13 June of the preceding year.

ine of Fanny Burney's *Evelina* was unpleasantly accosted by a man in one of the dark wooded paths, and four years later a German tourist, admittedly a clergyman who may have been more easily scandalized than most observers, was disturbed by evidence of immorality among the pleasure seekers.

Vanity Fair's first readers in 1847 would have superimposed on Thackeray's evocation of Vauxhall's gracious atmosphere early in the century their knowledge of what it had since become. From the late 1820s onward, at the beginning of every season the London papers lamented its decline, almost as if they were witnessing in the Lambeth Eden a latter-day recapitulation of the primal fall. In the thirties its proprietors (the Tyers family, who had owned it from its earliest days, sold out in 1821) sought to revive its flagging fortunes by making it a launching site for balloons, the latest entertainment rage, and—fatal miscalculation—opening it in the daylight hours, thus exposing its legendary festive nighttime face to the merciless glare of the sun. Dickens reported the disillusionment he suffered on visiting the place soon after the new policy was adopted ("Vauxhall Gardens by Day," published in the *Morning Chronicle* for 26 October 1836 and reprinted in *Sketches by Boz*).

What with the growing dilapidation, the introduction of flashy attractions like panoramic spectacles and reenactments of famous battles, and the falling away of the respectable clientele, by the forties going to Vauxhall had acquired the flavor of a libertine adventure rather than a family treat. As a gay blade in *Tancred* (1847) remarked when he resisted going to a house party in the country, " . . . you will have dancing enough at Montacute; it is expected on these occasions: Sir Roger de Coverley, tenants' daughters, and all that sort of thing. Deuced funny, but I must say, if I am to have a lark, I like Vauxhall" (1.3:21).

In *Pendennis*, Thackeray explicitly adopted the now tacky Vauxhall as the symbol of the lost pleasures of youth: "Sometimes, perhaps, the festivity of that period revives in our memory; but how dingy the pleasure-garden has grown, how tattered the garlands look, how scant and old the company, and what a number of the lights have gone out since our day! Grey hairs have come on like daylight streaming in—daylight and a headache with it. Pleasure has gone to bed with the rouge on her cheeks" (30:1.304). Whereas the Vauxhall of *Vanity Fair* represented the innocent-cheeked past, the Vauxhall of *Pendennis* belonged irremediably to the berouged present. Readers of the former novel were free, if they liked, to modify Thackeray's idyllic picture by what they knew of the garden of their own day; readers of *Pendennis* had no choice. The Vauxhall in that book was the Vauxhall they themselves knew.

On their visit to Vauxhall Gardens in 1813, Jos Sedley and his party would not have seen a balloon ascension; that attraction was introduced at a later date, in time for Pendennis and his fun-seeking friends to have seen it (the April 1850 number of *Pendennis*). The *Illustrated London News* printed a picture of the veteran aeronaut Charles Green's departure on the preceding 25 August.

Hence, when the young surgeon Huxter (he of the dirty hands and vulgarian manners and values), Captain Costigan, Mrs. Bolton and her daughter Fanny, and Sir Francis Clavering's valet go there, Thackeray's readers could assume that they—or the men at least—were on the prowl for tawdry entertainment. The fact that Pendennis runs into them there precisely indicates his moral condition at the moment; he is indulging in proclivities that the prevailing moral climate of fiction prevented Thackeray from specifying except through this indirect means—no further than a fleeting mention of the "poor outcasts" who haunt the place. Though Pen is wiser in the ways of the world than he had been during his callow infatuation with Captain Costigan's actress daughter, his eventual salvation is by no means assured, and his new infatuation with the working-class charmer Fanny Bolton, viewed against the sleazy background of present-day Vauxhall, seems to place his residual virtue at further risk. The company he finds himself in—men and women drawn as if by magnetic attraction to the increasingly notorious haunt of London lowlife—increases the doubt.

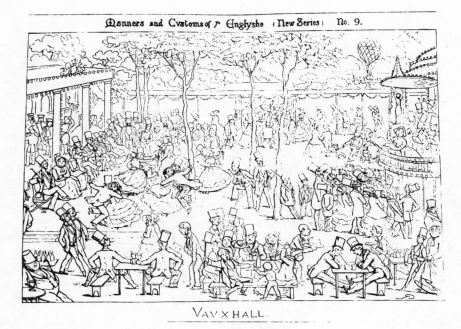

Manners and Customs of ye Englyshe (New Series) No. 9.

VAVXHALL.

Four months after the Vauxhall scene in *Pendennis*, Richard Doyle's drawing in *Punch* (27 July 1850) admirably caught the spirit of the place in its increasingly disreputable decline, epitomized by the whirling abandon of the polka and the number of stovepipe-hatted swells and gents drinking and seeking female companionship. Apart from the dancers, however, the only women represented here are firmly attached to their husbands. None are "loose" in either the physical or the moral sense of the word, a fact that does not tally with eyewitness accounts. But *Punch* was, after all, a family paper.

To round off the picture, Thackeray depicts Sir Francis Clavering himself, no model of culture or virtue, as being an habitué of Vauxhall. His valet tells Major Pendennis's man, "A few nights ago I sor him at Vauxhall, where I was a-polkin with Lady Hemly Babewood's gals—a wery pleasant room that is, and an uncommon good lot in it, hall except the 'ousekeeper, and she's methodisticle—I was a-polkin—you're too old a cove to polk, Mr. Morgan—and 'ere's your 'ealth—and I 'appened to 'ave on some of Clavering's *'abberdashery*, and he sor it too: and he didn't dare so much as speak a word" (60:2.233).

Vauxhall's death throes were prolonged until 1859, when, to the regret of no one but riffraff and elderly, hard-core sentimentalists, its decrepit structures were torn down and speculative builders took over the land.

"And here," wrote Wilkie Collins in *No Name* three years later, " . . . on the site where thousands of lights once sparkled; where sweet sounds of music made night tuneful till morning dawned; where the beauty and fashion of London feasted and danced through the summer seasons of a century—spreads, at this day, an awful wilderness of mud and rubbish; the deserted dead body of Vauxhall Gardens mouldering in the open air" ("Third scene," chap. 1 : 1.372–73). The event provided an opportune metaphor to the critic William C. Roscoe, writing of "Sir E. B. Lytton, Novelist, Philosopher, and Poet" in the April 1859 issue of the *National Review*:

> The thoughts of a great poet are like the stars in heaven. At the first glance they seem but shining adornments of the sky; but the more you penetrate their secrets, the vaster grow their proportions, and the deeper the significance of their being. The lucubrations of Bulwer may be compared to the illuminations of Vauxhall. They seem bright as the stars at a little distance; but go nearer and nearer, and they prove to be a modicum of rag and oil in a coloured glass. They shine but to ornament the place in which they are hung, and light up only blind alleys and circumscribed commonplace pathways.[30]

It is not at all certain that Bulwer-Lytton would have appreciated this criticism of his literary art, least of all the likening of it to the famous, now extinguished, array of Vauxhall lamps. But Vauxhall's usefulness to writers persisted to the very end.†

6.

A durable source of topicality throughout the Victorian era was the development of London mass transportation. In Pepys's time and thereafter, the Thames provided the quickest route between the City and Westminster in one direction and downstream points in the other. Boswell and Johnson routinely availed themselves of the service of boatmen rowing what would now be called water taxis. The coming of steam boats early in the nineteenth century displaced these wave-borne hackney coaches both for short trips and for longer excursions up and down

---

† It is odd that Cremorne Gardens, between the Thames and the King's Road in Chelsea, which contributed to Vauxhall's decline by siphoning off its major attractions and roistering clientele, are not mentioned in mainstream Victorian fiction. (They are better remembered from Hardy's lines in "Reminiscences of a Dancing Man": "Who now remembers gay Cremorne, / And all her jaunty jills, / And those wild whirling figures born / Of Jullien's grand quadrilles?", and from Phoebus (?) Levin's painting *The Dancing Platform at Cremorne Gardens* [1864].) The principal summer venue of mid-Victorian fast-track entertainment, Cremorne ran into licensing trouble in the early 1870s and closed finally in 1877.

the Thames; they docked mainly where Sairey Gamp saw and denounced them, at London Bridge. In *Sketches by Boz* Dickens seized on
these services as a timely locale in which to set no fewer than three of his
earliest comic sketches, including one called "The Steam Excursion." In
this he reported the opening gambit of a conversation between two
strangers aboard a Gravesend packet: "'Wonderful thing steam, sir.'
'Ah! (a deep-drawn sigh) it is indeed, sir.' 'Great power, sir.' 'Immense—immense!' 'Great deal done by steam, sir.' 'Ah! (another sigh at
the immensity of the subject, and a knowing shake of the head) you may
say that, sir.' 'Still in its infancy, they say, sir.' Novel remarks of this kind,"
said Dickens, "are generally the commencement of a conversation which
is prolonged until the conclusion of the trip . . ." ("Scenes," chap. 10:103).
Novelty had already become a banal subject in casual discourse.

On land, as we saw in Chapter 10, the only forms of public transportation prior to 1829 were hired hackney coaches and scheduled short-
stage coaches, some six hundred of them in 1825, which carried passenger traffic from such suburban districts, as they then were, as Paddington, Clapham, and Camberwell, to the City and Westminster. David
Copperfield rode them from Covent Garden to Highgate and Putney.
But the fares were high (1*s.* 6*d.* or 2*s.* from Paddington), the service was
limited (by law, these coaches could not pick up or set down passengers
within the paved area of the city, which was, as it had long been, the
monopoly of the hackney cabs), and the pace was slow: "away went the
coach up the hill," wrote Dickens in *Sketches by Boz*, "with that beautiful
equanimity of pace for which 'short' stages are generally remarkable"
("Tales," chap. 10:436).

The introduction of omnibuses in 1829 was a topic of conversation
less grave than the current overriding one of Catholic Emancipation.
The new word served Dickens for a typical Pickwickian joke. The elder
Mr. Weller has inherited the estate of his late wife, proprietress of the
Marquis of Granby public house, Dorking. He now proposes to sell the
business and, he tells his son,

> "out o' the money, two hundred pound, agreeable to a rekvest o' your
> mother-in-law's [i.e., stepmother's] to me a little afore she died, vill be in-
> wested in your name in—wot do you call them things again?"
> "Wot things?" inquired Sam.
> "Them things as is always a goin' up and down, in the City."
> "Omnibuses?" suggested Sam.
> "Nonsense," replied Mr. Weller, "Them things as is alvays a fluctooatin',
> and gettin' theirselves inwolved somehow or another with the national debt,
> and the checquers bills, and all that."
> "Oh! the funds!" said Sam. (*Pickwick Papers*, 52:833)

London buses—at least, those shown here—operated on the pay-as-you-leave system. Here two buses discharge their passengers at the Bank, clogging the roadway to the annoyance of the cabby at the left.

The word was one of those Latinate coinages that would shortly begin to inspire a numerous class of *Punch* jokes, the kind that assumed, no doubt correctly, that a fair number of that periodical's devoted readers had a smattering of the classical tongues. Writing in the immediate wake of *Pickwick*, in *Handley Cross* (1838–39), Surtees attributed the same—in this case fragile—erudition to his sporting characters, and capped the Weller joke with one of his own. In one of his "sporting lectors" before an appreciative audience, Jorrocks, not otherwise known for his learning, asserted:

> "Gentlemen wot take their ideas of 'unting from Mr. Hackermann's pictor-shop in Regent's Street must have rum notions of the sport . . . Danger is everywhere! An accomplished frind o' mine says, 'Impendet *omnibus* periculum'—Danger 'angs over an omnibus: and 'Mors *omnibus* est communis,'—You may break your neck in an *omnibus*: but are we, on that account, to shun the vehicle of which the same great scholar says, 'Wirtus parvo pre-

tio licet ab *omnibus*,'—Wirtue may ride cheap in an *omnibus*? Surely not!"
(32:259)

The new omnibuses figured repeatedly in *Sketches by Boz*, along with
the old hackneys (the sketch entitled "Hackney-Coach Stands") and the
short-stage coaches ("Early Coaches"). Dickens wrote of cab drivers
"wondering how people can prefer 'them wild beast cariwans of homni-
buses, to a riglar cab with a fast trotter,'" and a little later of the "theatre
omnibuses" that mingled with private carriages and hackney cabs in
the 1 A.M. traffic, when the customarily lengthy performances ended
("Scenes," chap. 1:50; chap. 2:56). He noted also the advent of a new
kind of London character, the "omnibus cad" who hung on the rear step
and snatched prospective riders away from the competition.

At mid-century, by which time buses were thick in the main thoroughfares, Surtees invented a topical hobby for the hero of *Mr. Sponge's
Sporting Tour*, an engaging parasitical rogue whose interest in horses,
unlike that of Surtees's riders to the hounds, was limited to their value
as objects to be haggled over—and as the motive power in front of London buses. At the beginning of chapter 2, Soapey Sponge, in the course
of his daily walk through the West End,

> had gone along Oxford Street at a somewhat improved pace to his usual
> wont—had paused for a shorter period in the "'bus" perplexed "Circus,"
> and pulled up seldomer than usual between the Circus and the limits of
> his stroll. Behold him now at the Edgeware Road end, eyeing the 'busses
> with a wanting-a-ride like air, instead of the contemptuous sneer he gen-
> erally adopts towards those uncouth productions. Red, green, blue, drab,
> cinnamon-colour, passed and crossed, and jostled, and stopped, and
> blocked, and the cads telegraphed, and winked, and nodded, and smiled,
> and slanged, but Mr. Sponge regarded them not. He had a sort of "'bus"
> panorama in his head, knew the run of them all, whence they started,
> where they stopped, where they watered, where they changed, and, won-
> derful to relate, had never been entrapped into a sixpenny fare when he
> meant to take a threepenny one. In cab and "'bus" geography there is not a
> more learned man in London. (2:5–6)

Soapey Sponge was the robust ancestor of the comparatively colorless
modern train spotter. His vade mecum, the London equivalent of *Bradshaw's Railway Guide*, was *Mogg's Ten Thousand Cab Fares*, more formally
known as *Mogg's Omnibus Guide and Hackney Coach and Cab Fares*, a shilling booklet, complete with routes, schedules, and fares, with which
(among other uses) a passenger could confront an extortionate cabby.
While in the country as the novel progressed, he often improved the
time by reading Mogg, just as Gabriel Betteredge, in *The Moonstone*, com-

pulsively consulted his oracle, Robinson Crusoe. "In idea he transferred himself to London, now fancying himself standing at the end of Burlington Arcade, hailing a Fulham or Turnham Green 'bus; now wrangling with a conductor for charging him sixpence when there was a pennant flapping at his nose with the words 'ALL THE WAY 3d.' upon it . . . " (21:113–14). Another devotee of Mogg's must have been Wilkie Collins, who, it is said, did much of his topographical research perched on the top of London buses.

In the same novel, Surtees spoke of "walking down Bond-street . . . of a glorious summer's day, when you could not cross Conduit-street under a lapse of a quarter of an hour, and carriages seemed to have come to an interminable lock at the Piccadilly end of the street" (32:207). Jorrocks described the same scene more enthusiastically in *Handley Cross*: "Vot a sight! All the world compressed into Bond Street! carriages blocked, cabs locked, 'ossmen driven on to the footway, and the foot-people driven into the shops" (59:418). As pictures like Doré's of Ludgate Circus at the rush hour testify, traffic gridlocks were common occurrences in central London. A surplus of omnibuses, drays, carts, cabs, and private carriages brought traffic in the old narrow streets to a standstill. Advertising vans, pasted over with bold, eye-catching announcements and sometimes bearing enlarged replicas of the product being touted (hats or patent medicines, for instance), were particular nuisances, because the tradesmen who hired them naturally wanted them to move at the slowest possible pace, and sometimes as many as nine such vehicles might collect at a single spot. Thackeray humorously moved this indigenous feature of the Victorian urban scene back a century, when, in "George de Barnwell, By Sir E.L.B.L., Bart" ("Punch's Prize Novelists," *Punch*, 3 April 1847), he parodied Bulwer-Lytton's high-flown and sometimes anachronistic attempts to create period color:

> 'Twas noonday in Chepe [Cheapside]. High Tide in the mighty River City!— its banks well-nigh overflowing with the myriad-waved Stream of Man! The toppling wains, bearing the produce of a thousand marts; the gilded equipage of the Millionary; the humbler, but yet larger, vehicle from the green metropolitan suburbs (the Hanging Gardens of our Babylon), in which every traveller might, for a modest remuneration, take a republican seat; the mercenary carouche, with its private freight; the brisk curricle of the letter-carrier, robed in royal scarlet; these and a thousand others were labouring and pressing onward, and locked and bound and hustling together in the narrow channel of Chepe.

But again, as with the congestion caused by the building boom of the sixties, no crucial appointment in a Victorian novel was missed, or a last-minute rescue aborted, because of a gridlock.

REGENTE· STRETE· ·AT FOVR OF Ɣᵉ CLOCKᵉ· P. M.

Richard Doyle's impression of central London's busiest shopping street, congested with carriages, buses, and mobile advertisements on foot and on wheels, appeared in *Punch* on 25 August 1849. It could well have illustrated Thackeray's parody, two years earlier, of Bulwer-Lytton describing rush hour in Cheapside.

Beginning in 1863, with the opening of the line between Paddington and Farringdon Street, the underground railway began to supplement the omnibus system. Trollope periodically recorded its progress, as line after line was opened in the next two decades.[31] In *The Claverings* (1866–67), Theodore Burton, the head of an engineering and land surveying firm in the Adelphi, is "very fully engaged,—having to meet a synod of contractors, surveyors, and engineers, to discuss which of the remaining thoroughfares of London should not be knocked down by the coming railways" (31:330), a very timely touch, because it was at that moment that most of the Metropolitan Inner Circle route was being dug, although its eastern loop, around Tower Hill and Aldgate, was not finished until later. "He was very keen at the present moment about Met-

A trial run on the first segment of the underground railway was pictured in the *Illustrated London News* on 13 September 1862. Four months later (10 January 1863) the line was opened to the public, and from that time onward, the new and steadily expanding underground figured prominently in novelists' tracing of their characters' movements from one part of the city to another.

ropolitan railways," Trollope continued, "and was ridiculing the folly of those who feared that the railway projectors were going too fast" (43:450)—a possible allusion to newspaper correspondence that was appearing at the time. "He'd like to make a line from Hyde Park Corner to the Tower of London," said his wife (32:332), a journey that cannot be made even today without a change of trains.

By the time of *Ralph the Heir* (1870–71), the Northern line of the underground had been extended to "within two miles" of the suburb of Hendon. In *The Eustace Diamonds* (1871–73), Frank Greystock, contemplating a reduction in his present scale of living, thinks he will "take a small house somewhere, probably near Swiss Cottage, [and] come up and down to his chambers by the underground railway" (18:201), a short trip to Baker Street now that the Swiss Cottage station had been opened (1868). A few years later, Hetta Carbury in *The Way We Live Now*

(1874–75), unaccustomed to using public transportation, "trusted herself all alone to the mysteries of the Metropolitan underground railway, and emerged with accuracy at King's Cross" (91:734–35). Ferdinand Lopez's last trip on earth (*The Prime Minister*, 1875–76) took him by underground to Euston station and thence to the fatal Tenway (Willesden) Junction.

A reader of *Ayala's Angel* (1881) who was familiar with the existing state of the system would have been tempted to interpret the character of Uncle Dosett, the Admiralty clerk, in light of the way he chose to return to his "genteel house" in Notting Hill. He took the underground to Temple station and then walked along the Embankment, through St. James's Park, Green Park, Hyde Park, and Kensington Gardens; but he might just as well have traveled the Inner Circle line all the way to Notting Hill Gate, via South Kensington, a route that had become fully operational a decade earlier. (The impecunious sculptor Isadore Hamel, in the same novel, wrote of his "descend[ing] into the underground cavern at the Gloucester Road Station" on that line [34:320].) That Uncle Dosett preferred to walk that distance could be attributed either to his desire for healthful exercise or his wish to maintain his modestly comfortable way of life by saving on fares. In *Mr. Scarborough's Family* (1882–83), finally, Mr. Barry, John Grey's law partner, dreams of the "pleasant genteel residence" at Putney to which he might take Dolly Grey as his wife—even though she has just firmly turned him down. He might, he thinks, take the railway from Putney and ride it to the Temple station (which must have been busy with Trollope characters), from which it was only a five-minute walk to his chambers. Here again, Trollope was on top of developments: the District line's Putney Bridge station, offering direct service to the Temple, had opened only the year before (1 March 1880).

12
Names in the Cultural News

1.

THE VICTORIAN READER'S fund of topically allusive names was boundless. Yet what strikes us most forcibly is the small number of choices novelists made when they drew upon this fund. A selective process was continually at work. Gunter had no monopoly as a fashionable confectioner and caterer; there were rival firms, but in fiction the ices and pastries at wedding receptions and "at homes" came from Gunter's and nowhere else. Stultz was only one of number of tailors patronized by the fashionable, but few of his competitors are ever heard of outside the pages of silver fork novels.

Nowhere is this winnowing of each year's harvest of names for fictional purposes more evident than in the novelists' choice of allusions to the nation's ongoing cultural life, specifically (to begin with) its literary affairs. In the course of the century, hundreds of thousands of book titles, from paperback comicalities to pass the time on a train trip to multivolumed histories and biographies addressed to a small, highly cultivated audience, entered the public consciousness at one time or another, if only with the casualness of a placard on a bus or in a display at a newsagent's or bookshop window, or an advertisement in a weekly paper. Of this huge output, only a tiny handful of names and titles was ever alluded to in fiction. The winnowing was done by a force that, whatever else it may have been, was amazingly prescient.

The most notable instance of this inspired selectivity was an early one, in a novel predating the Victorian era. In 1826, the London bookshops stocked, fresh from the press, such characteristic publications of the day as a Welsh translation of Pope's *Messiah;* Polwhele's *Tradition and Recollections, Dramatic, Domestic, Clerical, and Literary*; an epic poem on the Swedish hero Gustavus Vasa; a didactic work titled *The Best Intentions, or Reflections and Thoughts for Youth, Maturity, and Age;* a religious novel called *Going Too Far; a Tale for All Ages;* and *The Progress of Licentiousness:*

A Satirical Poem. On the same shelves appeared a new novel, T. H. Lister's *Granby*, featuring the usual complement of dandies who ate Gunter ices, ordered their suits from Stultz, and paraded as "walking essence bottles" (one such character was named Count Kalydor). And what did these gentlemen talk about in a literary way? None of the above ephemera, as they soon proved to be, but the writings of "the Opium Eater," serialized several years earlier in the *London Magazine* (September–October 1821), Coleridge's "Christabel," Byron's "epitaph on his Newfoundland dog," and the novels of Maria Edgeworth, Ann Radcliffe—and Jane Austen.

Literary chitchat, light, witty, and involving if possible a piquant mystery of authorship, was a staple of the fashionable novel, as it was of the society it portrayed. In *Vivian Grey*, published no more than a year after *Granby* (1826–27), Disraeli had his characters indulge in bits of literary gossip:

"... if ever you write a novel, Miss Manvers, mind you have a rookery in it. Since Tremaine and Washington Irving, nothing will go down without."
"By-the-bye, who is the author of *Tremaine?*"
"It is either Mr. Ryder, or Mr. Spencer Percival, or Mr. Dyson, or Miss Dyson, or Mr. Bowles, or the Duke of Buckingham, or Mr. Ward, or a young officer in the Guards, or an old Clergyman in the North of England, or a middle-aged Barrister on the Midland Circuit."[†]

Miss Manvers asks Vivian to get Washington Irving's autograph for her. He playfully forges one on the spot, and asks whose else she wants—"One of Sir Walter's, or Mr. Southey's, or Milman's, or Mr. Disraeli's? or shall I sprawl [scrawl?] a Byron?" She says, Make me a Scott. Backtracking a little, Vivian replies:

"Poor Washington! I knew him well. He always slept at dinner. One day, as he was dining at Mr. Hallam's, they took him, when asleep, to Lady Jersey's: and to see the Sieur Geoffrey, they say, when he opened his eyes in the illumined saloons, was really quite admirable! quite an Arabian tale!"
"How delightful! I should have so liked to have seen him! He seems quite forgotten now in England. How come we to talk of him?"
"Forgotten! Oh! he spoilt his elegant talents in writing German and Italian twaddle with all the rawness of a Yankee. He ought never to have left America, at least in literature; there was an uncontested and glorious field for him. He should have been managing director of the Hudson Bay Company, and lived all his life among the beavers." (2.19:47)

[†]Correct answer: Robert Plumer Ward (1825).

Not that all characters in silver fork fiction talked this way. *Vivian Grey* is something of a special case, being the early, anonymously published effort of an upwardly mobile young commoner to break into that society by depicting it in a novel replete with real names, including those of currently talked-about writers. Only a novelist as brash as Disraeli would have had the impudence to include his own name among the literati mentioned, as he did. But the testimony of other fashionable novels, not *Granby* alone, assures us that Disraeli was otherwise taking a page from life.

Twenty years later, when his reputation as a novelist was established, he revived the device of literary chitchat, this time with scathing wit. In *Tancred* (1847) he reported a conversation hinging on the stir created three years earlier by a best-selling book called *Vestiges of the Natural History of Creation*, which popularized recent evolutionary thought, to the scandal of many pious readers. One dotty lady readily explained the gist of the unnamed author's argument (he was actually the Edinburgh publisher Robert Chambers):

> "But what is most interesting, is the way in which man has been developed. You know, all is development. The principle is perpetually going on. First, there was nothing, then there was something; then, I forget the next, I think there were shells, then fishes; then we came, let me see, did we come next? Never mind that; we came at last. And the next change there will be something very superior to us, something with wings. Ah! that's it: we were fishes, and I believe we shall be crows. But you must read it. . . . We are a link in the chain, as inferior animals were that preceded us: we in turn shall be inferior; all that will remain of us will be some relics in a new red sandstone.[†] This is development. We had fins; we may have wings." (2.9:113)

But such *jeux d'esprit* were in the mode of silver fork fiction rather than in that of the Victorian novel proper. Allusions to nineteenth-

---

[†] The speaker was alluding, in her confused way, to Hugh Miller's *The Old Red Sandstone* (1841), another contribution, this time from the creationist side, to the controversy over the geological evidences of evolution. The fame of the book was such that it inspired a joke in *Martin Chuzzlewit*, in Lafayette Kettle's invitation to young Martin to address the Young Men's Watertoast Association: "The Society would not be particular in limiting you to the Tower of London. Permit me to suggest that any remarks upon the Elements of Geology, or (if more convenient) upon the Writings of your talented and witty countryman, the honourable Mr. Miller would be well received" (22:429). The Penguin editor of the novel, sharing Lafayette Kettle's misapprehension, erroneously identifies Mr. Miller as "Joe Miller of the Jest Book (1739)."—The reference to the Watertoast Association was particularly timely: as Dickens recalled in his preface to the Cheap Edition in 1852, "the proceedings of a certain Brandywine Association . . . were printed in the Times newspaper

century books and authors served a number of purposes, but serious consideration of current issues discussed in particular books was not one of them. Instead, offhand mentions of new books helped reinforce the prevailing sense of presentness; and in distanced novels they furnished strokes of period color. Because all the books mentioned in a removed context continued to be read or were well remembered at the time the novel was published, an additional link was forged between present and past. The occurrence of a popular author or title initially as a timely topic in the present and subsequently as one that memorialized an earlier year often testified to the strong continuity of literary preferences that marked nineteenth-century English cultural life.

This was true of both the books that made a great splash in their time but eventually sank without a trace except for the survival of their authors' names in the more capacious literary histories, and those that were proclaimed classics in their own time and continue to be venerated today in the fixed pantheon of the nation's literary heritage. (A shrine, not a reading room: many pay dutiful obeisance to the inscribed names; few actually read the books.)

In *Paul Clifford* (1830), for example, Bulwer quoted the then greatly admired sentimental poet Letitia Elizabeth Landon's "The History of the Lyre," which had been published only a few years before. Landon's fame faded after her mysterious death on the Gold Coast shortly after her marriage in 1838 and the demise of the fashionable gift-book annuals to which she had contributed much of her now unreadable output, but her older contemporary, Felicia Hemans, was longer remembered. To fix the scene of *Wives and Daughters* (1864–66) in the middle and late 1820s, Mrs. Gaskell pictured Molly reading "this last poem of Mrs. Hemans," which may have been in any of the several volumes she published in that decade. "To be 'nearly as good as Mrs. Hemans,'" commented Gaskell, "was saying as much to the young ladies of that day, as saying that poetry is nearly as good as Tennyson's would be in this" (6:96–97). A musical setting of Hemans's "The Landing of the Pilgrim Fathers" is sung in Kingsley's *Two Years Ago*, which has a contemporary locale: "that glorious melody," Kingsley said, "which has now become the national anthem to the nobler half of the New World" (15:257).

The names of three better-remembered best-selling authors of the century's first decades, Scott, Byron, and Moore, entered fiction as topics of current conversation and subsequently became convenient time-

---

in June and July 1843." It must have required some resolution on Dickens's part not to name the fictitious temperance organization after the real one. Readers unaware of the latter's existence would have credited him with a "peculiarly Dickensian" invention.

markers. Susan Ferrier's *The Inheritance* (1824) had a comic theme involving an old Scotsman who is a closet devotee of Scott's novels and is
"embarrassed to have it [known] throughout the town that he was a
novelle reader!" Bulwer referred to Scott, still living, in *Paul Clifford*
(1830), and St. John Rivers brought Jane Eyre a copy of the newly published *Marmion*, "one of those genuine productions," said Charlotte
Brontë, "so often vouchsafed to the fortunate public of those days—the
golden age of modern literature. Alas! the readers of our era [1847] are
less favoured" (*Jane Eyre*, 32:473).† Scott's popularity in the 1820s, so
vividly recalled, gave two other novelists an easy means of locating the
action in those years. Young Pendennis's horse was named Rebecca after
the heroine of *Ivanhoe*, and Mrs. Gaskell's Molly Gibson read *The Bride
of Lammermoor*.

Byron appeared as a person, either under his own name or transparently disguised, in a number of novels, including the obsessively infatu-
ated Lady Caroline Lamb's *Glenarvon* and Catherine Gore's *Cecil*. The
popularity of his poetry was several times reflected in fiction. In *Sketches
by Boz*, a "hospital walker" (medical student) spouted *Don Juan*; and a
decade later, in Surtees's *Hillingdon Hall* (1843–44) the leisured wife of
Jorrocks's bailiff was seen reading the poem. Cynthia Gibson, in *Wives
and Daughters*, could "repeat 'the Prisoner of Chillon' from beginning to
end'" (24:307). (Earlier in the novel, when Lord Cumnor quoted the
phrase "To make a Roman holiday" from *Childe Harold*, his wife remarked that "Byron was a very immoral poet" [12.173]—the tense being
barely accurate, because Byron died in April 1824 and Mrs. Gaskell's
narrative had progressed just beyond that date.) In *Aurora Floyd*, which
contains noticeably more literary references than most Victorian novels
of any date—did Miss Braddon toss them in to assert the respectability
of sensation fiction at a time when it was coming under critical attack?—Byron appeared as a remembered public figure rather than
as a poet. Contradicting the facile assumption that Aurora would be
"wretched" as the wife of "a gentleman who had neither a straight nose

---

†Thackeray, writing only a year or two later in *Pendennis*, was ironic where Brontë was
nostalgic. Of Fanny Bolton's reading tastes he said, "Many novels had Fanny read, in secret
and at home, in three volumes and in numbers. Periodical literature had not reached the
height which it has attained subsequently, and the girls of Fanny's generation were not
enabled to purchase sixteen pages of excitement for a penny, rich with histories of crime,
murder, oppressed virtue, and the heartless seductions of the aristocracy; but she had had
the benefit of the circulating library which, in conjunction with her school and a small
brandy-ball and millinery business, Miss Minifer kept,—and Arthur appeared to her at
once as the type and realisation of all the heroes of all those darling greasy volumes which
the young girl had devoured" (47:2.96).

nor dark hair," Lucy Floyd thought, "Some women never outlive that school-girl infatuation for straight noses and dark hair? Some girls would have rejected Napoleon the Great because he wasn't 'tall,' or would have turned up their noses at the author of 'Childe Harold' if they had happened to see him in a stand-up collar. If Lord Byron had never turned down his collars, would his poetry have been as popular as it was? If Mr. Alfred Tennyson were to cut his hair, would that operation modify our opinion of 'The Queen of the May'?" (19:185).

Dickens attested to the popularity of the third of the triumvirate, Thomas Moore, when in *Sketches by Boz* ("Tales," chap. 1:283) he quoted the conversation around the dinner table in a "genteel" boardinghouse during which the merits of Moore's "The Fire Worshippers" and "Paradise and the Peri" were canvassed. "Lalla Rookh" was one of the adolescent Pendennis's favorite poems, although his mother preferred Bishop Heber's poems and sermons, Mrs. Hemans's poems, and John Keble's *The Christian Year*. And if Pendennis's horse was named Rebecca, Molly Gibson's, in *Wives and Daughters*, was named Nora Creina, after the heroine of one of Moore's ballads. (To follow the equine-literary bloodline one step further, Surtees named an elderly horse in *Young Tom Hall's Heart-Aches and Horses* after Major Pendennis.)

The Christian Year (1827), the most popular versified expression of religious sentiment before *In Memoriam*, served as a chronological landmark almost as often as Catholic Emancipation. George Eliot, who habitually used books, like various events, to enhance the historical authenticity of her narratives, included it among the publications—others being three Scott novels, Pinnock's *Catechisms* (1820–30), Southey's *Life of William Cowper* (1835), and Buckland's Bridgewater treatise on geology (1837)—that marked the temporal progress of *The Mill on the Floss*.

Earlier, in *Adam Bede*—the time context is 1799–1800—Captain Donnithorne recommended to his godmother, Mrs. Irwine, a book that "came down in a parcel from London the other day. I know you are fond of queer, wizard-like stories. It's a volume of poems, 'Lyrical Ballads:' most of them seem to be twaddling stuff; but the first is in a different style—'The Ancient Mariner' is the title. I can hardly make head or tail of it as a story, but it's a strange, striking thing" (5:57).[†] In *Felix Holt*,

---

[†]Only a bibliographical pedant would be moved to point out the unlikelihood of any such occurrence. The first edition of *Lyrical Ballads* (1798), printed at Bristol, was taken over by a London firm, and few of the five hundred copies could have drifted back into the country except as makeweight thrown into a parcel by a bookseller's whim. There would seem to be a greater possibility that Donnithorne received the 1800 edition, which was published by the eminent London firm of Longman. The difficulty here, however, is that "The Ancient Mariner" was no longer the lead-off poem, having been displaced by

the action begins on 1 September 1832, and soon thereafter Miss De-
barry and Miss Selina are said to be "feeling rather dull than otherwise,
having finished Mr. Bulwer's 'Eugene Aram,' and being thrown back on
the last great prose work of Mr. Southey, while their mamma slumbered
a little on the sofa" (7:87). *Eugene Aram* had been published the preceding December, and thus was a likely book to have found its way to Treby
Manor. This story of a murderous schoolmaster was the sensation of the
day, and the first edition sold out within months. Presumably "the last
great prose work of Mr. Southey" was his *Sir Thomas More: or Colloquies
on the Progress and Prospects of Society* (1829–31), which doubtless held
less interest for the young ladies, or their mamma, on the sofa than it
had for Macaulay, who wrote a famous slashing article on it in the *Edinburgh Review*.

George Eliot devoted her great fund of literary knowledge chiefly to
distancing references like these; she seldom mentioned books that had
recently come to the attention of her readers. Kingsley, on the other
hand, used literary topicalities to strengthen the contemporaneity of his
novels. In *Yeast* he several times quoted his mentor Carlyle's *Chartism*
(1839) and *Past and Present* (1843), along with a reference to Harriet
Martineau's *Feats on the Fiords* (1844), which the gamekeeper Tregarva
had been reading. *Two Years Ago* had a quotation from Emerson, one of
whose works Mrs. Gaskell had earlier pictured, with some improbability,
in the hands of a daughter of the mill-owner Carson in *Mary Barton*. (She
promptly fell asleep.) In the same book, Kingsley mentioned the novels
of Charlotte Yonge, whose popular *The Heir of Redclyffe* had been published three years earlier, "those novels of Currer Bell's, and her sister,"
and "that Marquesas romance of Herman Melville's" (*Typee* [1846]) ("In-
troductory":13; 8:124; 19:327).

In 1842, with the appearance of a two-volume collection of his
poems, Tennyson established himself as a poet worth reading. A decade
later, in *The Newcomes*, Thackeray breached chronology (the setting of
the passage is no later than the last years of the thirties) to insert a mention of his former fellow Cantabrigian in the course of a literary conversation in which Warrington, Honeyman, and Pendennis scandalize the
Colonel with their up-to-date literary opinions:

"The Idiot Boy." The subsequent fame of both Wordsworth and Coleridge deluded at least
one other novelist into believing that they were a common topic of conversation so early,
even in a part of the country as remote as Dinah Mulock's Cotswolds. In *John Halifax,
Gentleman*, a character mentioned, in the setting of 1800, "Mr. William Wordsworth, and
some anonymous friend," authors of a "collection of Lyrical Ballads," and later in the novel
John Halifax says of his self-acquired literary culture, "Think of a man of business liking
Coleridge" (12:115; 24:236). It does indeed boggle the mind.

He heard. . . . that a young gentleman of Cambridge, who had lately published two volumes of verses, might take rank with the greatest poets of all. . . . Mr. Keats and this young Mr. Tennyson of Cambridge, the chief of modern poetic literature! What were these new dicta, which Mr. Warrington delivered with a puff of tobacco smoke; to which Mr. Honeyman blandly assented, and Clive listened with pleasure? Such opinions were not of the Colonel's time. He tried in vain to construe "Oenone," and to make sense of [Keats's] "Lamia." "Ulysses" he could understand; but what were these prodigious laudations bestowed on it? (21:1.213–14)

From 1842 onward, writers could depend on their readers' knowing many of Tennyson's poems. Mrs. Gaskell ended a chapter of *Mary Barton* with a snatch of "Mariana in the Moated Grange," and in *Cranford* she quoted from "The Gardener's Daughter" and alluded to a review of the collection that had appeared in *Blackwood's Magazine*. (None had, as a matter of fact.) In the same passage Miss Matty fell asleep while Mr. Holbrook read "Locksley Hall" aloud. This poem was a special favorite with characters in fiction. When Warrington fumed to Pendennis about the way the operation of the marriage market forced young people into unions that were advantageous but contrary to their natural preferences (Clive Newcome and Rosey Mackenzie were the case in point), he quoted the poem, without implied quotation marks, as if the words were a familiar part of everyday discourse: "Rather than have such a creature I would take a savage woman, who should nurse my dusky brood" (*The Newcomes*, 43:2.56). A more favorable judgment of the poem than Miss Matty's implicit one was to be found in *The Heir of Redclyffe*, when one of the characters declared, "There is nonsense, there is affectation in that . . . ; there is scarcely poetry, but there is power, for there is truth" (3.27).

In *Two Years Ago* a rural railway station is named "Shalott"; *The Princess* figures in a love passage between the curate Frank Headley and Valentia St. Just; another character could "repeat Tennyson from end to end"; and regret was expressed that "Tennyson's Palace of Art is a true word [*sic*]—too true, too true," because art, alas, has no place in a society in which "the most necessary human art, next to the art of agriculture," is "the art of war" (19:315; 23:381).

Aurora Floyd was shot through with Tennysonian allusions. When it appeared (1862–63), the laureate's latest work was the first four books of *Idylls of the King*, published in 1859. Lucy Floyd, the heroine's cousin, was a "pale Elaine of modern day; and she never told Talbot Bulstrode that she had gone mad and loved him, and was fain to die. . . . But the Lily Maid of Astolat lived in a lordly castle, and had doubtless ample pocket-money to buy gorgeous silks for her embroidery, and had little on earth to wish for, and nothing to do; whereby she fell sick for love of Sir Lancelot, and pined and died" (7:65). But "Guinevere [Aurora] was lady of his [Bulstrode's] heart, and poor Elaine was sadly in the way. Mr. Tennyson's wondrous book had not been given to the world in the year fifty-seven, or no doubt poor Talbot would have compared himself to the knight whose 'honour rooted in dishonour stood'" (8:80–81). Local talk at Beckenham when Aurora was about to marry Mellish reportedly took a literary turn: "She was a very lucky woman, they remarked, in being able, after jilting one rich man, to pick up another; but of course a young person whose father could give her fifty thousand pounds on her wedding-day might be permitted to play fast and loose with the male sex, while worthier Marianas moped in their moated granges till grey hairs showed themselves in glistening *bandeaux*, and cruel crow's feet gathered about the corners of bright eyes" (12:107). Bulstrode, reading of Aurora's marriage and emulating the distraught lover in "Locksley Hall," "took his gun and went out upon the 'barren, barren moorland,'[†] as he had done in the first violence of his grief, and wandered down to the dreary sea-shore, where he raved about his 'Amy, shallow-hearted,' and tried the pitch of his voice against the ides of February should come round," and—anticlimactically—Parliament would meet and he could promote the sole piece of legislation in which he was interested, a bill for the relief of the Cornish miners (12:110). Later in the novel, a whole paragraph of philosophizing in the manner of George Eliot began, "There is a great deal of vicarious penance done in this world. Lady's-maids are apt to suffer for the follies of their mistresses, and Lady Clara Vere de Vere's French Abigail is extremely likely to have to atone for young Laurence's death" (22:214).

Tennyson continued to be to the Victorian woman reader what Byron had been to her mother or grandmother. In *The Eustace Diamonds* (1871–73), Lizzie Eustace reads *The Holy Grail*, hot from the press—

> a volume of poetry. . . . the story of certain knights of old, who had gone forth in quest of a sign from heaven, which sign, if verily seen by them, might be taken to signify that they themselves were esteemed holy, and fit for heavenly joy. One would have thought [Trollope continues] that no theme could have been less palatable to such a one as Lizzie Eustace; but the melody of the lines had pleased her ear, and she was always able to arouse for herself a false enthusiasm on things which were utterly outside herself in life. She thought she too could have travelled in search of that

---

[†] Braddon was evidently quoting from memory, because the couplet actually reads "O my cousin, shallow hearted! O my Amy, mine no more! / O the dreary, dreary moorland! O the barren, barren shore!"

holy sign, and have borne all things, and abandoned all things and have
persevered—and of a certainty have been rewarded. But as for giving
up a string of diamonds—in common honesty—that was beyond her.
(19:208–209)

Notwithstanding the phenomenal popularity of *Pickwick Papers* and,
to varying degrees, of his next several novels, Dickens's books were slow
to figure as topicalities in other people's fiction. Mrs. Gaskell led the way
in *Mary Barton*, when she unflatteringly described a union organizer
from London as "a disgraced medical student of the Bob Sawyer class,
or an unsuccessful actor, or a flashy shopman" (16:178). In *Cranford*,
Captain Brown's nose had been deep in the latest number of *Pickwick
Papers* an instant before he snatched a child from the path of an oncom-
ing train, slipped, and was himself run over. According to Charlotte
Yonge in *The Heir of Redclyffe*, if a young lady was able to read without a
tear Paul Dombey's death scene, "the part of Dombey that hurts women's
feelings most," she was proved to be "stony hearted" and a disgrace to
her sex (3:23). At the same moment, in the expanded text of *Handley
Cross* (1853–54), Surtees declared (11:85) that "the great and renowned
Mr. Jorrocks" was "a name familiar to our ears as Mr. Dickens's household words," a play on the title of Dickens's weekly paper and the
Shakespearean phrase from which it was derived (". . . our names, / Familiar in his mouth as household words" [*Henry V*]). Soon afterward,
Thackeray used an early Dickens novel as a time-marker in *The Newcomes*. When Lord Kew was convalescing from the wound he received in
a duel on an island in the Rhine,

> Good Lady Walham was for improving the shining hour by reading amus-
> ing extracts from her favourite volumes, gentle anecdotes of Chinese and
> Hottentot converts, and incidents from missionary travel. George Barnes,
> a wily young diplomatist, insinuated *Galignani* [an English-language news-
> paper published in Paris, precursor of today's *International Herald Tribune*],
> and hinted that Kew might like a novel; and a profane work called "Oliver
> Twist" having appeared at about this time, which George read out to his
> family with admirable emphasis, it is a fact that Lady Walham became so
> interested in the parish boy's progress, that she took his history into the
> bedroom (where it was discovered, under Blatherwick's "Voice from Meso-
> potamia," by her Ladyship's maid), and that Kew laughed so immensely
> at Mr. Bumble, the Beadle, as to endanger the reopening of his wound.
> (38:1.412)

It was under Trollope's auspices, however, that Dickens appeared
most memorably in fiction outside his own pages. This was in *The
Warden*, which contained a purported excerpt from the latest work of
Mr. Popular Sentiment, "a gentleman," as the *Spectator*'s reviewer said,

"who reforms society by means of novels published in numbers, and who brings out the first part of 'The Almshouse,' glaringly coloured up to the taste of the million."[1] "The Almshouse" would prove to be *Little Dorrit*, whose part-publication would begin in December 1855 (*The Warden* had been published in the first days of the year). In choosing ecclesiastical malfeasance as the target of "Mr. Popular Sentiment"'s next reformist novel, Trollope did not reckon on the possibility that Dickens would, in fact, take up a subject on which, as we have seen, they had quite different opinions—the Circumlocution Office.

The parodic allusion to Dickens would have reminded readers that in the 1840s Thackeray had published his series of parodies, "Punch's Prize Novelists," in which he skewered several popular novelists of the day, including Bulwer-Lytton, Disraeli, G. P. R. James, and Mrs. Gore. At the same moment, a pair of phenomena tending the other way had appeared in the workaday world of novel writing. One was a spirit of camaraderie that manifested itself in a form of back-scratching, a welcome relief from the private and public knifing that had infected the literary-journalistic cliques of the twenties and early thirties. The other was the development of a sense of professional solidarity, as it became evident that the increasing monetary rewards of authorship were being inequitably divided between writer and publisher.

Authors, including novelists, became acutely aware of the exploitation to which they were subjected by people who took advantage of the deficiencies of the existing copyright law and of the outdated system under which publishers bought literary properties outright rather than sharing their profits with authors through royalties. In *Nicholas Nickleby*, Dickens editorialized on the current campaign of a number of well-known authors to obtain a copyright law more favorable to their interests. His butt of the moment (August 1838), Mr. Gregsbury, M.P., summarized, in fatuous terms that came uncomfortably close to the truth, the opposition's argument that accepting payment for the fruit of divinely bestowed inspiration was beneath the dignity of a genius:

> "For instance, if any preposterous bill were brought forward for giving poor grubbing devils of authors a right to their own property, I should like to say, that I for one would never consent to opposing an insurmountable bar to the diffusion of literature among *the people*,—you understand?—that the creations of the pocket, being man's, might belong to one man, or one family; but that the creations of the brain, being God's, ought as a matter of course to belong to the people at large—and if I was pleasantly disposed, I should like to make a joke about posterity, and say that those who write for posterity, should be content to be rewarded by the approbation *of* posterity. . . . " (16:267)

Later in the novel, Dickens used Nicholas as his vehement mouthpiece to vent a related complaint to "a literary gentleman . . . who had dramatised in his time two hundred and forty-seven novels as fast as they had come out—some of them faster than they had come out":

> "you take the uncompleted books of living authors, fresh from their hands, wet from the press, cut, hack, and carve them to the powers and capacities of your actors, and the capability of your theatres, finish unfinished works, hastily and crudely vamp up ideas not yet worked out by their original projector . . . all this without his permission, and against his will; and then, to crown the whole proceeding, publish in some mean pamphlet, an unmeaning farrago of garbled extracts from his work, to which you put your name as author. . . . Now, show me the distinction between such pilfering as this, and picking a man's pocket in the street: unless, indeed, it be, that the legislature has a regard for pocket handkerchiefs, and leaves men's brains, except when they are knocked out by violence, to take care of themselves." (48:726–28)

Despite the opposition of Mr. Gregbury and others, in 1842 Parliament passed the Copyright Amendment Act, which in some respects clarified and strengthened the rights of authors vis-à-vis their own creations but in other respects left them as dubious as before. As a result, Dickens, Bulwer-Lytton, and other prominent writers organized an "Association for the Protection of Literature" which kept the issue alive throughout the 1840s.

In 1849, Thackeray signified his enlistment in the cause by depicting Pendennis and Warrington as professional authors resentful of the economic restraints and lack of recognition under which they and their fellow writers labored. It is a theme that, as two recent scholars have independently demonstrated,[2] runs through the whole of *Pendennis*. In the eleventh number (September 1849), for instance, Warrington, assuming for the moment the role of devil's advocate, argued the publisher's case. He cited the episode reported by Boswell in which the necessitous Samuel Johnson dined on a plate of food his host, the publisher Edward Cave, was obliged to send behind a screen because "Johnson, dressed so shabbily, . . . did not choose to appear" with the other guests:

> "Do you want [he asks Pendennis] a body of capitalists that shall be forced to purchase the works of all authors who may present themselves manuscript in hand? . . . You couldn't force the publisher to recognise the man of genius in the young man who presented himself before him, ragged, gaunt, and hungry. Rags are not a proof of genius; whereas capital is absolute, as times go, and is perforce the bargain-master. It has a right to deal with the literary inventor as with any other. . . I may have my own ideas of the value of my Pegasus, and think him the most wonderful of animals; but the

dealer has a right to his opinion, too, and may want a lady's horse, or a cob for a heavy timid rider, or a sound hack for the road, and my beast won't suit him." (32:1.335)

That this was a timely topic was confirmed only a few months later (3 January 1850), when the *Morning Chronicle* printed a strong editorial endorsing the received opinion that in a laissez-faire society, authors were obliged to compete as did the producers of any other marketable commodity, and too bad for them if they failed. John Forster replied to this blast two days later in the *Examiner*, and Thackeray in a letter to the *Morning Chronicle* (12 January). The exchange, brief though it was, undoubtedly increased the topicality of the remaining numbers of *Pendennis*, in which the hero and his friend pursue their literary careers; and it has been suggested that it was in response to this current interest that Dickens chose to make David Copperfield a professional author in the later portion of his novel, which concluded in November.[3]

Meanwhile, perhaps as evidence of the growing feeling in the profession that we're all in this together, "us" against "them," novelists were freely expressing their appreciation of their rivals' work. In 1840 Thackeray wrote to his mother, "There is a story called Ten thousand a year in Blackwood that all the world attributes to me, but it is not mine—only better: it is capital fun: of a good scornful kind."[4] In "On Literary Snobs" (*Punch*, 20 June 1846; *BS*, 65) he put his opinion in print. "I don't know anything more delicious," he wrote, "than the pictures of genteel life in *Ten Thousand a Year*, except perhaps the *Young Duke* and *Coningsby*. There's a modest grace about *them*, and an air of easy high fashion, which only belongs to blood, my dear Sir—to true blood." And again in "Snobs and Marriage" (12 December 1846; *BS*, 157): "In that noble romance called *Ten Thousand a Year*, I remember a profoundly pathetic description. . . . The elegant words I forget. But the noble, noble sentiment I shall always cherish and remember."

Among Thackeray's friends was Surtees, with whom he corresponded, exchanged books, and dined when the sporting squire from the North was in London, and who distributed compliments of his own in his novels. "[I] have often wished," he wrote in *Hawbuck Grange*, "for the pencil of Thackeray to sketch the delightful complacency with which he [Mr. Trumper] sits listening to all the handsome things that are said of him." "[H]alf the world should be put under 'Titmarsh,' to learn how to see things," he wrote a few pages further on, thinking it necessary here to drop an explanatory footnote: "The clever author of a *Journey from Cornhill to Grand Cairo*, etc., who saw more in a month than most travellers see in a year" (7:99; 8:104). Two years later, in *Mr. Sponge's Sporting Tour* (1849–51), Surtees paid tribute to *Vanity Fair*, which had concluded its part issue in July 1848: "Mr. Thackeray, who bound up all the home truths in circulation, and many that exist only in the inner chambers of the heart, calling the whole 'Vanity Fair' . . . "; later on, on another subject: "'But what good,' as our excellent friend Thackeray eloquently asks, 'ever came out of, or went into, a betting book? If I could be CALIPH OMAR for a week,' says he, 'I would pitch every one of those despicable manuscripts into the flames . . . '" (16:83; 58:434).

In *The Adventures of Philip* (1861–62), Thackeray sacrificed chronology for the sake of dropping a compliment to Trollope. Pendennis, here acting as Philip Firmin's "biographer," says that Philip wears on his watch chain a little gold locket. "As for the pretty hieroglyphical A.T. at the back, these letters might indicate Alfred Tennyson, or Anthony Trollope, who might have given a lock of *their* golden hair to Philip, for I know he is an admirer of their works" (14:1.251). At that moment in the novel (in the 1840s), neither Philip, Pen, nor anyone else was in a position to admire Trollope's work, for he was then an obscure post-office inspector in Ireland, who had published, or was about to publish, only the first of his novels, *The Macdermots of Ballycloran* (1847). But when Thackeray wrote *The Adventures of Philip*, *The Warden* and *Barchester Towers* had appeared, and he and Trollope had become friends, and he had lately given the younger man's career an opportune boost by serializing *Framley Parsonage* in his *Cornhill Magazine*. The timing of the reference to Trollope may have been off by ten or fifteen years, but it was a graceful gesture all the same.

Mary Elizabeth Braddon also nodded amiably in the direction of her fellow novelists. "With what wonderful wisdom," she exclaimed in *Aurora Floyd*, "has George Eliot told us that people are not any better because they have long eyelashes!" (16:152), and in *Lady Audley's Secret*, the amateur detective Robert Audley mutters as he goes about his sleuthing, "I haven't read Alexander Dumas and Wilkie Collins for nothing. . . . I'm up to their tricks, sneaking in at doors behind a fellow's back, and flattening their white faces against window panes, and making themselves all eyes in the twilight" (38:263).

Apart from the Dickens parody, Trollope seldom alluded to his fellow writers in his own fiction, though he did write a study of his master Thackeray and dealt with other literary subjects in his occasional journalism. But, fittingly enough in view of his well-known interest in his books' commercial value, he referred oftener than other novelists did to the great Victorian institution whose label was inside many, if not most, copies of their books: Mudie's Select Circulating Library. In *The Bertrams* (1859) Trollope indicated the success of George Bertram's controversial "bookling," *The Romance of Scripture*, by stating that Mudie had stocked no fewer than two thousand copies, a figure that readers could readily compare with the publicly announced number of copies the library then had of the third and fourth volumes of Macaulay's *History of England* (2,400) and Tennyson's *Enoch Arden* (2,500); the next year Mudie would take two thousand copies of *The Mill on the Floss.*

Subscribing to Mudie's was a handy social indicator, a cachet available to anyone who could afford the modest annual subscription. From a certain perspective, to be sure, money thus spent was wasted, because it was a kind of domestic expense that added little to the image a family presented to the world. There was no more telling clue to Ferdinand Lopez's calculating eye to the main chance than the fact that "He would have [his wife] save out of her washerwoman and linendraper, and yet have a smart gown and go in a brougham. He begrudged her postage stamps, and stopped the subscription at Mudie's, though he insisted on a front seat in the Dovercourt church, paying half a guinea more for it than he would for a place at the side" (*The Prime Minister*, 47 : 2.59). In *Ayala's Angel* Trollope contrasts the modest circumstances in which Lucy, Ayala's sister, finds herself after her father's death with the affluence Ayala enjoys. Her aunt Dosett "did not subscribe to Mudie's. The old piano had not been tuned for the last ten years," whereas at their father's house "That Mudie's unnumbered volumes should come into the house as they were wanted had almost been as much a provision of nature as water, gas, and hot rolls for breakfast. A piano of the best kind, and always in order, had been a first necessary of life, and, like other necessaries, of course, forthcoming" (1 : 10; 2 : 11).

Victorian novels contain few allusions to another prime means by which the expanding reading public was served—the periodicals that lay alongside them on middle-class library tables, including the magazines in which those very novels often appeared. Once in a while, a popular periodical is mentioned in passing. In Wilkie Collins's *No Name* (1862–63), Magdalen is given an illustrated paper, supposedly the *Illustrated London News*, although there were several shorter-lived ones at the moment, to amuse her as she recovers from a serious illness, and in Emily Eden's *The Semi-Detached House* (1859), Mrs. Hopkinson says of a gossip column she has read in the *Weekly Lyre* (the pun is almost too obvious), "it is not much worse than paragraphs I have read in the most decent papers—I have seen things like that in the *Illustrated*" (2 : 14), by which she probably meant the *Illustrated London News*, although *Cassell's Illustrated Family Paper*, the *Illustrated Times*, and the *Illustrated News of the World* were also current at the time. In *Two Years Ago*, Kingsley referred to the "cynical pedants in the *Saturday Review*" (7 : 100), and Trollope spoke in *The Vicar of Bullhampton* of the "Saturday Reviewers" (37 : 237).

The latter, however, was a special case, because Trollope specifically had in mind Mrs. Linton's notorious article on "The Girl of the Period," which made the periodical famous far beyond its usual audience and lent timeliness to the treatment of "the woman question" in the novel.

In accordance with the premise that a man or woman is known by what he or she reads, mentions of current periodicals were among the details by which novelists could indicate social class or fill in the description of a character. Thus Mary Barton's father, a militant Chartist, was seen smoking his pipe over an old copy, borrowed from a nearby public house, of the *Northern Star*, the movement's principal organ and the very symbol, at the moment, of inflammatory radicalism. That Aurora Floyd was not a completely conventional romantic heroine was brought home to readers by her poring over the sportsmen's weekly scripture, *Bell's Life in London*, much to the horror of a more staid lady, "who had a vague idea of the iniquitous proceedings recited in that terrible journal" (*Aurora Floyd*, 5:45). *Bell's* was the preferred, and often the only, paper seen in the hands of male and female devotees of the fast life. Interest in its contents was as sure a clue to character as similar absorption in the latest issue of the *Morning Post* was in a different social sphere, where the latest news of the fashionable world took precedence over all other events. Typically, Sir Francis Clavering, the dissolute gambler in *Pendennis*, sequestered himself behind double doors in his imposing library, "smoked cigars, and read *Bell's Life in London*" (37:1.381). George Vavasor in *Can You Forgive Her?* doubtless subscribed to the same weekly potpourri of sporting news, scandal, and coarse humor, but Trollope chose instead to have him "perusing" *Bell's* close relations, the equally widely circulated Sunday sheets, a sufficient indication of his low character. And when Henry Grantly and Johnny Eames shared a compartment in a train to Guestwick in *The Last Chronicle of Barset*, Trollope contrasted them by their respective purchases at the Paddington news stall: Grantly bought the *Times* and the conservative *Saturday Review*, Eames the *Daily News* and the liberal *Spectator*, although, Trollope added, both had copies of that "enterprising periodical" the *Pall Mall Gazette* (the real one, not the Thackerayan one from which it got its title); perhaps it was his sly way of saying that it had something for every taste. In any event, the allusion was a particularly timely one. The *Pall Mall* was a relatively new newspaper, its first issue having appeared on 7 February 1864, and the novel's serialization began in December of the following year.

While such mentions of periodical reading were usually statements capable of only one interpretation, the situation regarding books was not quite so simple. Normally, a topical literary allusion consisted of no more than a remark that he or she read or quoted this or that book, with, possibly, his or her opinion couched in an offhand, throwaway line. Little could be inferred from such fleeting expressions of literary taste beyond the unexciting fact that those characters were like many people of their time. As far as the novelists were concerned, a mere handful of books, some of which have already been mentioned, constituted the golden treasury of popular literary taste. The contents of "the little library," dating from a generation earlier, that Allan Armadale found at Thorpe Ambrose were the most standard assortment imaginable: "The Waverley Novels, Tales by Miss Edgeworth, and by Miss Edgeworth's many followers, the Poems of Mrs. Hemans, with a few odd volumes of the illustrated gift-books of the period" (*Armadale*, 2.3:1.306). It would be hard to deduce much about the former owners of these books except that they were obedient to current custom. Similarly, when Aurora Floyd's governess read aloud for her delectation "'Marmion' and 'Childe Harold,' 'Evangeline,' and 'The Queen of the May'" when she was recovering from an illness, the reader of the novel learned only that the governess's tastes were those of the great majority of poetry lovers in the 1860s. Braddon added, however, that Aurora did not like poetry in general; she would have preferred to "listen to a lively dispute between a brood of ducks round the pond in the farm-yard, or a trifling discussion in the pigsty, to the sublimest lines ever penned by poet, living or dead" (*Aurora Floyd*, 10:97).

Convention, then, rather than a desire to suggest idiosyncrasy, governed novelists' attribution of literary interests to their characters when they were in a reading mood. But once in a while these allusions are worth pausing over. A short passage in *The Eustace Diamonds* (34:347–49) points two ways at once. When Lucy Morris begins her tenure as Lady Linlithgow's companion, she can find nothing better to read while her employer busies herself with her accounts than "Tupper's great poem," as Trollope will call it several times in the course of the novel, taking care that no reader should miss the irony. Martin Tupper's *Proverbial Philosophy* (1838–42), which by that time had sold over two hundred thousand copies, was an egregiously moralized guide to material success, and that it failed to grip Lucy's interest certainly counted in her favor, as Trollope expected his supposedly discriminating readers to understand. Lady Linlithgow, for her part, was decidedly old-fashioned in her taste, as was revealed by her recommendation that Lucy read the novels of Maria Edgeworth or Jane Austen, both dating from the beginning of the century. That she no longer subscribed to Mudie's because "when I asked for 'Adam Bede,' they always sent me the 'Bandit Chief'" was a little joke appreciated by whichever of Trollope's readers may have been annoyed by what they considered Mudie's less than efficient response to their wishes.[†]

Some messages from novelist to reader were unmistakable. In an aside, George Eliot wondered, and then explained, why Mr. Stelling, Tom Tulliver's schoolmaster in *The Mill on the Floss*, "deferred the execution of many spirited projects—why he did not begin the editing of his Greek play, or any other work of scholarship, in his leisure hours." The answer was that "after turning the key of his private study with much resolution [he] sat down to one of Theodore Hook's novels" (2.4:151), these being prime examples of the scandalmongering fiction popular at the time of the novel's action, though whatever actual salacity they may have contained could only be detected, with difficulty, between the lines.

One of the few extended attempts to depict character through literary conversation occurred in *Felix Holt*, when the hero visits Esther Lyon in the home of her father, a Dissenting minister. He accidentally spills her work basket, and a small volume falls between the table and the fender.

> This last had opened, and had its leaves crushed in falling; and, with the instinct of a bookish man, he saw nothing more pressing to be done than to flatten the corners of the leaves.
>
> "Byron's Poems!" he said, in a tone of disgust, while Esther was recovering all the other articles. "'The Dream'—he'd better have been asleep and snoring. What! do you stuff your memory with Byron, Miss Lyon?"
>
> . . . She reddened, drew up her long neck, and said, as she retreated to her chair again,
>
> "I have a great admiration for Byron."
>
> . . . "He is a worldly and vain writer, I fear," said Mr. Lyon. He knew scarcely anything of the poet, whose books embodied the faith and ritual of many young ladies and gentlemen.
>
> "A misanthropic debauchee," said Felix, lifting a chair with one hand, and holding the book open in the other, "whose notion of a hero was that he should disorder his stomach and despise mankind. His corsairs and

---

[†]Few of Trollope's readers or Mudie's subscribers would have noticed a possible joke within the joke. Unless there was a more recent novel with the same title, the unwelcome book was *The Bandit Chief; or, Lords of Urvino*, published anonymously in 1818 by the Minerva Press, which specialized in melodramatic and violently sentimental novels. Lady Linlithgow's old-fashioned taste doubtless did not extend as far as such gaudy reading matter, and in any case it is most unlikely that Mudie's would have had a copy of a fifty-three-year-old book on their shelves.

renegades, his Alps and Manfreds, are the most paltry puppets that were ever pulled by the strings of lust and pride."

"Hand the book to me," said Mr. Lyon.

"Let me beg of you to put it aside till after tea, father," said Esther. "However objectionable Mr. Holt may find its pages, they would certainly be made worse by being greased with bread and butter." (5:61–62)

Over tea, the conversation turns to the subject of "fine ladies" such as the lawyer Jermyn's daughter. "A real fine-lady does not wear clothes that flare in people's eyes," says Esther, "or use importunate scents, or make a noise as she moves: she is something refined, and graceful, and charming, and never obtrusive." "O yes," Felix retorts. "And she reads Byron also, and admires Childe Harold—gentlemen of unspeakable woes, who employ a hairdresser, and look seriously at themselves in the glass" (5:64). The passage is a masterstroke of compact, implicit characterization. Felix Holt's bookishness is tainted by his priggishness, his narrow sympathies; and George Eliot drove home her point with Mr. Lyon's surprisingly mild reaction to his discovery that Esther had a copy of the poems. The poet's notoriety was such that even though the minister was little acquainted with his works, he might well have scolded Esther for her indulgence in what, to stricter Nonconformists, was a species of forbidden literature.

Novels themselves, of course, were out of bounds to a considerable segment of the total reading public. And even to those who had no scruples in that respect, a "given" of the time, that fiction was an inferior kind of literature and novel-reading a lazy way of passing time that could better be devoted to self-improvement or some other form of constructive activity, was built into the very structure of morally oriented criticism. It had inherent irony whenever it appeared in the novels. In 1817, Coleridge had expressed a widely held view, which was to persist for many years, when he described readers of circulating-library novels as a "comprehensive class characterized by the power of reconciling the two contrary yet co-existing propensities of human nature, namely indulgence of sloth, and hatred of vacancy." To call their favorite "kill-time" by the name of reading, said Coleridge, was to dignify it beyond its deserts. "Call it rather a sort of beggarly day-dreaming, during which the mind of the dreamer furnishes for itself nothing but laziness, and a little mawkish sensibility." Such activity was on the same plane as "gaming, swinging, or swaying on a chair or gate; spitting over a bridge; smoking, snuff-taking; tête-à-tête quarrels after dinner between husband and wife; conning word by word all the advertisements of a daily newspaper in a public house on a rainy day, &c. &c. &c."[5]

In this initial vignette for an installment of his "Mr. Brown's
Letters to a Young Man" in *Punch*, 12 May 1849, Thackeray
drew his conception of an idle young man killing time reading the latest number of a novel—which happens to be *Pendennis*, part 7 of which had appeared at the beginning of
the month. The youth might be Pendennis himself, whom
Thackeray had described in the preceding number (April)
as lounging at home during the long vacation and devouring "works of English 'light literature.'"

Idling away a vacant hour with a light novel became the standard
sign of directionless, unambitious, unproductive youth. Wiggle, a "club
snob" (*Punch*, 23 January 1847; *BS*, 182), "passes his mornings in
a fine dressing-gown, burning pastilles, and reading *Don Juan* and
French novels. . . . He has twopenny-halfpenny French prints of women

with languishing eyes, dressed in dominoes,—guitars, gondolas, and so forth—and tells you stories about them." Pendennis passed up the French prints, but otherwise he conformed to type. In the long vacation, he brought home from Oxbridge "boxes of the light literature of the neighbouring country of France; into the leaves of which when Helen dipped, she read such things as caused her to open her eyes with wonder," and when he was rusticated, he lounged about Fairoaks "yawning over his novel in his dressing-gown" (*Pendennis*, 18:1.174; 21:1.203). George Eliot captures the essence of Fred Vincy's character in the simple act of his carelessly "taking up a novel" and throwing himself into an armchair (*Middlemarch*, 3:38–39). In Trollope's *The Belton Estate*, Clara Amedroz and Will Belton call on Colonel Askerton and his wife at their country place:

> "How is Colonel Askerton?" asked Clara.
> "He's in-doors [replied his wife]. Will you come and see him? He's reading a French novel, as usual. It's the only thing he ever does in summer. Do you ever read French novels, Mr. Belton?"
> "I read very little at all, and when I do I read English."
> "Ah, you're a man who has a pursuit in life, no doubt."
> "I should rather think so,—that is, if you mean, by a pursuit, earning my bread. A man has not much time for French novels with a thousand acres of land on his hands; even if he knew how to read French, which I don't."
> (3:38–39)

Time taken off from serious pursuits was more culpably wasted if devoted to French novels than the same time spent in reading English ones. James Payn was in sure touch with his readers' prejudices when, in the rousing finale of *Lost Sir Massingberd*, the narrator and others break into the parlor in which, many years before, "the lost baronet had passed his last hours within the house, and thither he had intended to return" and find "A scurrilous French novel [which] had engaged the last hours of the wretched old man, ere he went forth—to his doom" (32:307, 309). A more tolerant modern reader would be inclined to feel a disproportion between the offense and the punishment: the Gothic "doom" was the lingering death Sir Massingberd suffered when he climbed into a hollow tree on his estate and found himself inextricably trapped. The habit was even more reprehensible when clergymen indulged in it. At the same time (1855) that Archdeacon Grantly was furtively perusing his Rabelais, and Bishop Blougram, in Browning's poem, his Balzac, the Reverend Charles Honeyman, said Thackeray in *The Newcomes*, "was well enough read in profane literature, especially of the lighter sort; and, I dare say, could have passed a satisfactory examination in Balzac,

Dumas, and Paul de Kock himself, of all whose works our good host
[Colonel Newcome] was entirely ignorant" (21:1.213).

2.

In fiction as in life, the middle-class Victorian home resounded with
songs sung at the pianoforte or, in the earlier years, the harp. Music was
an indispensable accompaniment to social life in the "superior classes."
From time to time, novelists used particular songs as time-indicators,
general period color, or, less often, sidelights on character. The favorite
ones, by Thomas Moore, were as inescapable in parlors as Musak is today in public places. At Highgate, the scarred, embittered Rosa Dartle,
at the harp, sang to Steerforth and David Copperfield an "Irish song,"
which David said was "the most unearthly I have ever heard in my life,
or can imagine. . . . It was as if it had never been written, or set to music,
but sprung out of passion within her; which found imperfect utterance
in the low sounds of her voice, and crouched again when all was
still"—after which, when Steerforth laughingly put his arms around her,
she threw him off "with the fury of a wild cat" and burst from the room
(*David Copperfield*, 29:496). In India, Glorvina O'Dowd in *Vanity Fair*
assisted her parents' campaign to get her engaged to Major Dobbin:
"She sang Irish Melodies at him unceasingly. She asked him so frequently and pathetically, will ye come to the bower? that it is a wonder
how any man of feeling could have resisted the invitation. She was never
tired of inquiring, if Sorrow had his young days faded. . . " (43:420).[†]
In *John Halifax, Gentleman*, Phineas Fletcher spoke of "light songs written
by an Irishman, Mr. Thomas Moore, about girls and wine, and being
'far from the lips we love,' but always ready enough 'to make love to the
lips we are near'" (34:348–49). In a decidedly unromantic context,
"Eveleen's Bower" figured in the repertory of popular ballads Silas Wegg
displayed at his sidewalk pitch, and the tart-tongued Lavvy Wilfer, in
Our Mutual Friend, flung a questionably appropriate fragment of "The
Fire Worshippers" in the face of her suitor, George Sampson: "If you
mean to say . . . that you never brought up a young gazelle, you may save
yourself the trouble, because nobody in this carriage supposes that you
ever did" (4.16:877).

Mrs. Gibson remarks in *Wives and Daughters*, "'There's no place like
home,' as the poet says. 'Mid pleasures and palaces although I may

---

[†]Geoffrey and Kathleen Tillotson identify the first song as one attributed to Moore;
the second is from *Irish Melodies*. The singer was patriotically named after the heroine of
Lady Morgan's popular novel, *The Wild Irish Girl* (1806).

roam,' it begins, and it's both very pretty and very true" (45:540). This was an authentic touch for the setting of about 1830: Henry Bishop's song in *Clari, or The Maid of Milan* had been an instant hit when the opera was first performed in 1823. Equally credible was Molly Gibson's playing of a "beautiful piece of Kalkbrenner's" (24:312)—Friedrich Wilhelm Kalkbrenner's piano pieces were widely known, and Molly's distaste for the composition's "eighteen dreary pages" might have been mitigated had she known that their composer would shortly become the dedicatee of Chopin's E Minor Concerto. In *The Mill on the Floss*, Stephen Guest brings Maggie some sheet music from Balfe's latest opera, *The Maid of Artois* (1836). Isabelle Carlyle, in *East Lynne*, sings one of the ballads from that composer's most famous opera, *The Bohemian Girl* (1843).

When Emily Eden's *The Semi-Detached House* was published in 1859, the tune of the moment was the anthemlike "Partant pour la Syrie," whose words and music were attributed to Napoleon III's mother. It had been played and sung incessantly during the state visit, four years earlier, of the Emperor and the Empress Eugénie; either its popularity had not diminished or Eden was a little behind the times. In the same novel, she used an alarming new development in popular music and the related emergence of a new, liberated kind of "girl" to fix the setting in the immediate present. "Now," said Emily Eden, "if there is one thing more than another conducive to low spirits, it is that depressing invention—a comic song! The mere advertisements—'I'm a merry laughing girl,' or 'I too, am seventeen, mamma!' if read early in the morning, particularly before breakfast, produce a degree of nausea that affects the health for the whole day." As well it might, considering the quality of the sample offered: "Yes, Sir! I can waltz! I can flirt! / I'm out of the schoolroom at last! / Pa' says I'm a romp, Ma' says I'm a pert, / I say, I am fast! I am fast!" (14:122–23)

Conceivably, many people would have preferred, to this, even the vapidity of the sound track to David Copperfield's courtship of and marriage to the mindless child-bride Dora Spenlow: the "Affection's Dirge" that her friend Julia Mills copied from new sheet music and, worst of all, Dora's incessantly trilling, to the strumming of her guitar, "enchanted ballads in the French language, generally to the effect that, whatever was the matter, we ought always to dance, Ta ra la, Ta ra la!" (*David Copperfield*, 26:453–54)

During the boating picnic in the Norfolk Broads in *Armadale*, young Pedgift ("Gustus Junior") obliges with a series of songs familiar to the novel's first readers.

> He began . . . not with songs of the light and modern kind, such as might have been expected from an amateur of his age and character, but with de-

clamatory and patriotic bursts of poetry, set to the bold and blatant music
which the people of England loved dearly at the earlier part of the present
century, and which, whenever they can get it, they love dearly still. "The
Death of Marmion," "The Battle of the Baltic," "The Bay of Biscay," "Nelson," under various vocal aspects, as exhibited by the late Braham [the famous tenor, composer of the patriotic song "The Death of Nelson," had
died in 1856]—these were the songs in which the roaring concertina and
strident tenor of Gustus Junior exulted together.

He winds up, however, with the sentimental "The Mistletoe Bough" and
"Poor Mary Anne." Allan Armadale then contributes "Eveleen's Bower,"
explaining "My poor mother used to be fond of teaching me Moore's
Melodies when I was a boy . . . " "Aha!" the deaf Mrs. Pentecost rejoins,
"I know Tom Moore by heart" (2.8 : 1.425–27).

Music, choral this time and in a mildly disreputable, urban setting,
contributed topical notes to *The Old Curiosity Shop*. Some of the songs in
Dick Swiveller's extensive repertory were old—a full century old, in the
case of those from *The Beggar's Opera*—and some, notably Moore's, relatively new. The "harmonic meetings" of the "Glorious Apollers" (named
for Samuel Webb's glee "Glorious Apollo") represented a new form of
convivial gathering; Dickens first described them in *Sketches by Boz*. The
initial scene of *The Newcomes*, at the roistering "Cave of Harmony," sets
the tone for the many ensuing contrasts between present and past, as
the Colonel, newly returned from India, delights in his and others' ren-
dition of innocent old favorites—"The Derby Ram," "The Old English
Gentleman," "Wapping Old Stairs"—until he is outraged and the evening spoiled by the drunken Captain Costigan's howling out a "ribald"
song that Thackeray refrains from quoting.

George Eliot's musical "Saturday afternoons" at her and Lewes's
house near Regent's Park brought together the two Victorian novelists
whose serious musical interests exceeded the norm for the time: the
hostess herself, and Wilkie Collins.

His understanding of the subject [writes Kenneth Robinson] was not particularly profound and we have Dickens' word, for what it is worth, that he
was virtually tone-deaf, but at least it is to his credit that his favourite composer was Mozart. . . . Laura Fairlie and Walter Hartwright [in *The Woman in
White*] play Mozart piano-duets; Uncle Joseph's music box [in *The Dead Secret*] plays—rather too often, one must confess—"Batti, batti," the air from
Don Giovanni; the blind Lucilla in *Poor Miss Finch* plays a Mozart sonata on
the piano. He liked Italian opera, particularly Rossini, Donizetti, Bellini and
Verdi, and shared the fashionable enthusiasm for Meyerbeer. For Wagner,
whose music-dramas were soon to make their impact on the London opera-
goer, he conceived a violent dislike. Neither did he apparently appreciate
Beethoven. . . .[6]

It was fitting, then, that the two scenes in Victorian fiction in which music
plays a pivotal role in the plot occur in Collins's novels. Both are opera
performances in the same year, 1851. In the one, a London production
of Donizetti's *Lucrezia Borgia*, Count Fosco recognizes his nemesis, Professor Pesca, in the audience, and knows he is in mortal danger (*The
Woman in White*). In the other, a performance of Bellini's *Norma* at the
San Carlo opera house in Naples, Lydia Gwilt, now Mrs. Midwinter,
spies in the chorus of Druids her former husband, Manuel, "the one
man on earth whom I have most reason to dread ever seeing again!"
(*Armadale*, 4.2:2.370).

Collins's liking for Italian opera was reflected in the musical allusions
of his fellow novelists, although they sometimes referred to the German
and French repertories as well. The one opera that may be said to dominate a Victorian novel, forming a true leitmotif in its repeated occurrence, is Bellini's *I Puritani* (1835), the airs from which haunt Diana
Warwick in *Diana of the Crossways*. Recounting his disillusioning visit to
Vauxhall in daylight (*Sketches by Boz*), Dickens reports hearing "A small
party of dismal men in cocked hats . . . 'executing' the overture to
[Rossini's] *Tancredi*" (1813), and in another sketch, arias from Auber's
Masaniello (*La Muette de Portici*) are sung, with indifferent success, at a
charity entertainment ("Scenes," chap. 14:127; chap. 19:165). Stephen
Guest and Philip Wakem, in *The Mill on the Floss*, sing a duet arranged
from the same opera—it was new in 1828—and Philip plays and sings
the tenor aria, "Ah! perchè non posso odiarti" from an even newer one,
Bellini's *La Sonnambula* (1831) (6.7:363, 365). Later, Collins, in *The Law
and the Lady* (1874–75), praised another air from Bellini's masterpiece,
"Come per me sereno" (9:95). Mr. Tupman attends Mrs. Leo Hunter's
public breakfast ("fête champêtre") "in full Brigand's costume," alluding
to Meyerbeer's *Fra Diavolo*, which was first performed in 1830 (*Pickwick
Papers*, 15:279). The opera turns up also in *The Newcomes*. Watching
Rosey Mackenzie playing the coquette in the company of predatory
women at Colonel Newcome's party on the eve of his losing his fortune,
Arthur Pendennis, juxtaposing a reminiscence of a nursery rhyme (actually a "fine lady," not an old woman) with characters in a modern opera, ruefully comments, "An unconscious little maid, with rich and rare
gems sparkling on all her fingers, and bright gold rings as many as belonged to the late Old Woman of Banbury Cross—still she smiled and
prattled before these banditti—I thought of Zerlina and the Brigands,
in 'Fra Diavolo'" (70:2.330).

Fra Diavolo was one of the several operas of those same memorable
years in London's musical life that Thackeray recalled when he described the youth of his heroes and heroines, and his own self as

Music for the masses: the band at Vauxhall as described by Dickens and illustrated by Cruikshank (*Sketches by Boz*). Dickens wrote unenthusiastically of a daytime concert in which "a particularly small gentleman . . . led on a particularly large lady . . . and forthwith commenced a plaintive duet." Ten years later, in *Vanity Fair*, Thackeray revived the romantic glamor of Vauxhall music by returning it to the evening and infusing it with affectionate memory: "the fiddlers, in cocked-hats, who played ravishing melodies under the gilded cockle-shell in the midst of the gardens; [and] the singers, both of comic and sentimental ballads, who charmed the ears there."

well—and he might have included Princess Victoria's, because in those seasons she attended the very operas and ballets Thackeray mentions. In the night party at Oxbridge which sees Pendennis initiated into the dangerous delights of gambling, he joins his friends in belting out the chorus from Meyerbeer's *Robert le Diable*, "an opera then in great vogue" (it was first performed in Paris in 1831), and on another occasion, toping with his tutor, the Reverend Mr. Smirke, he sings the drinking song from Weber's *Der Freischütz* (1821) (*Pendennis*, 16:1.153; 19:1.187). Writing *Jorrocks' Jaunts and Jollities* in 1831–34, Surtees mentioned "the fading notes of the 'Huntsman's Chorus' in *Der Frieschutz*" [*sic*], and in the prologue to *Armadale*, set explicitly in 1832, Wilkie Collins described the opera's waltz as *the* popular tune of the day. (Weber's opera remained in the standard repertory for many years. In *Mr. Facey Romford's Hounds* [1864–65], a gong summoning guests to dinner at a country house, "A most scientific roll of thunder," reminded Lucy Sponge of "the cavern scene in *Der Freischütz*" [32:194].)

Rossini's *Il Barbiere di Siviglia* (1816) was another well remembered, and often revived, opera in the salad days of Thackeray's characters. At the end of *Vanity Fair*, Becky Sharp Crawley, now a time-worn adventuress, recalls it when the widowed Amelia Osborne blushingly confesses to her that she has written Dobbin, inviting him to join her in Ostend. "Becky screamed with laughter,—'*Un biglietto*,' she sang out with Rosina, '*eccolo qua!*'—the whole house rang with her shrill singing" (67:659).[†] Blanche Amory sang "two or three songs of Rossini" to Laura Bell (*Pendennis*, 24:1.244). Rosey Mackenzie's tastes in opera were, predictably, conventional and vague: "Does she love music? Oh yes. Bellini and Donizetti? Oh, yes" (*The Newcomes*, 24:1.256).

Thackeray himself, he admitted in *Vanity Fair*, had no taste for "the milk-and-water *lagrime, sospiri*, and *felicità* of the eternal Donizettian music with which we are favoured nowadays" (4:40). Donizetti had succeeded Bellini and Rossini as the master of the bel canto style. In *The Heir of Redclyffe* (1853), Charlotte Yonge mentioned Donizetti's *La Figlia del Reggimento*, which had premiered thirteen years earlier, and when Collins wished to add a touch to his characterization of a liberal clergyman in the Kingsleyan mode (*The New Magdalen* [1872–73]), he not only had him whistle—a notable infraction of clerical dignity—but whistle "La donna è mobile," from *Rigoletto*. Another Verdi work, *La Traviata*

[†] In some highly unlikely performance of the opera, in whatever circle of hell their sins may have required they inhabit, Becky might well have sung Rosina to the Figaro of Count Fosco in *The Woman in White*, who had a habit of singing "Largo al factotum" in his rich Italian baritone.

(1853), was the most popular opera of its time in England. Surtees alluded to it in the book-form text of *Ask Mamma* (1857–58), as did Thackeray, with some distaste, in *The Adventures of Philip* (1861–62): "Well, I am not mortally angry with poor Traviata tramping the pavement, with the gas-lamp flaring on her poor painted smile, else my indignant virtue and squeamish modesty would never walk Piccadilly or get the air" (9:1.189).

If the years around 1830 glowed in the memory of people like Thackeray, it was not only because of the operas themselves: their enduring fame was due in no small part to the galaxy of singers who performed in them. As a rule, the silver fork novelists paid scant attention to the operatic scene of their day, but one exception was Disraeli, who glanced obliquely at it in *The Young Duke* (1831), when, in the course of a bout of amateur musical theatricalism, the actress-stage manager-producer Miss Dacre, responding to bravos from the socialite audience, "led on her companion as Sontag would Malibran" (2.11:112). These were the two reigning sopranos of their day, Henriette Sontag and Maria Malibran, who had made their London debuts three years apart (1825, 1828) in the same role, Rosina in *Il Barbiere di Siviglia*. One wonders which star Disraeli had in mind when he created "the Bird of Paradise," the glamorous prima donna in the novel who seemingly was the young duke's mistress, comfortably ensconced at Brighton. Perhaps the odds are slightly in favor of Sontag, to whom, it was said, the Duke of Devonshire proposed marriage. (She left the operatic stage in 1830 in order to acquire the "respectability" necessary for her to become the wife of a Sardinian diplomat.)

In a substantial paragraph toward the end of *Vanity Fair* (62:603), Thackeray described a performance of *Fidelio* at the Royal Grand Ducal Pumpernickelisch Hof (Weimar) starring Wilhelmine Schröder-Devrient, whose London debut in the title role he had attended in 1832. But the only operatic star to be repeatedly referred to in subsequent Victorian fiction was the soprano Giulia Grisi. Pendennis proposed going to hear her in *Norma* (Warrington: "Are you going to meet anybody there?" Pen: "No—only to hear the music, of which he was very fond") but in the event he went to Warrington's digs in Lamb Court, the beginning of their close friendship (*Pendennis*, 29:1.302). Grisi, who had sung the first Adalgisa to Pasta's Norma in 1831, made her London debut in the title role three years later.

Another Thackerayan admirer of Grisi was the Princesse de Montcontour in *The Newcomes*. "When first I was took to the Opera," she reminisced, "I did not like it—and fell asleep. But now, oh, it's 'eavenly to hear Grisi sing!" (47:2.100). Using Grisi for period color, Mrs. Gaskell

Giulia Grisi might fairly be called the presiding prima donna of
Victorian fiction. She is pictured here in the title role of Bellini's
Norma, one of the operas with which she was most closely iden-
tified during her long career.

saw to it that Lady Cumnor, in *Wives and Daughters*, would include
"Grisi's concert" in her social plans. The setting in the novel, however,
was 1825, when Grisi was in fact only fourteen, and nine years before
she appeared on the London stage—another of Gaskell's carefree anachronisms. The soprano's long career was especially convenient for novel-

ists. Besides contributing to the distancing effect, as in Thackeray and Gaskell, she remained immediately topical because in the years 1834–61 she missed only one London season. In April 1846 she joined two other great singers, Mario (he used only his given name), and the buffo bass Luigi Lablache (who, Thackeray said in *The Newcomes*, might have envied Frederick Bayham his voice), in what a critic called "one of the most exquisite performances of the melodious and effective opera *I Puritani* that has ever been heard."[7] It was this memorable revival, in the appropriate time context of *Diana of the Crossways*, that inspired Meredith to have airs from the opera echo in his heroine's mind. No more than a month later (16 May), in his *Punch* sketch "On Clerical Snobs" (*BS*, 47), Thackeray included "a box at the Opera, because Lablache and Grisi are divine in the *Puritani*" in his list of contemplated private indulgences, along with buying an ormolu clock on sale at Howell and James's. In 1849 Grisi began a series of farewell appearances that continued for over a dozen years. Allusions to her were therefore still timely in the late fifties, when she sang at a Queen's concert in 1858 (*The Semi-Detached House*), and Captain Bulstrode, Aurora Floyd, and others had a box at the "pretty little theatre" at a seaside resort "to hear Grisi and Mario" (*Aurora Floyd*, 5:46).

The durable Grisi was to the fond operatic memories of Thackeray's generation what Marie Taglioni was to their memories of the ballet at the same moment. On the third and last night of Pendennis's stay in London during the Easter vacation, "why, Taglioni was going to dance at the Opera,—Taglioni! and there was to be 'Don Giovanni,' which he admired of all things in the world: so Mr. Pen went to 'Don Giovanni' and Taglioni" (*Pendennis*, 19:1.188). Taglioni's name was brought up later at Sir Francis Clavering's dinner table. "Seen Taglioni in the Sylphide, Miss Amory?" said Harry Foker. "She's clipping in the Sylphide, ain't she?" and, says Thackeray, "he began very kindly to hum the pretty air which pervades that prettiest of all ballets, now faded into the past with that most beautiful and gracious of all dancers. Will the young folks ever see anything so charming, anything so classic, anything like Taglioni? 'Miss Amory is a sylph herself,' said Mr. Pen" (38:1.386).

In Meredith's *Emilia in England* and George Eliot's *Daniel Deronda*, there are glimpses, fleeting in one case, recurrent in the other, of professional musical life in Victorian England (Emilia's proper career begins only at the end of the novel when she goes off to study in Milan), but these are woven into the narrative rather than serving as isolated allusions. The major operatic composers and Grisi apart, the fiction of the period contains fewer incidental references to composers and performers than one would expect, as if their names had little place in the common store of information to which novelists appealed. No novelist mentions Clara Novello, the first-rank oratorio specialist of the time; and Mendelssohn, whose sojourns in England were well publicized and whose music was extremely popular, was alluded to only in passing, as when Julia Sherrick's mother proposed to Charles Honeyman, in *The Newcomes*, that her daughter contribute an unspecified Mendelssohn hymn to the Sunday service ("Julia sings it splendid!") (44:2.68). Lady Audley, who in her former occupation of governess had taught her charges to play Beethoven sonatas, played her husband to sleep with these and songs by Mendelssohn.

As far as novelists were concerned, oratorios and symphony concerts simply did not figure in the Victorians' musical experience. The only conductor referred to is the flamboyant Jullien, recalled in Hardy's poem (page 437n above), who conducted huge orchestras, three or four hundred strong, at the Surrey Gardens and somewhat smaller forces at public balls held at the theatres during the off season in the late forties and early fifties. The Drury Lane promenade concerts that Disraeli mentions in *Endymion* as being among the novelties of his time were Jullien's invention. In *Hawbuck Grange*, the music of the hounds at a bright, early-morning hunt was heard "reverberating like Mons. Jullien's band of a hundred and twenty performers at a 'Bal Masqué'" (8:109), and in the updated version of *Handley Cross*, the baying hounds' "melody" echoing from the walls of an old castle was true music to Jorrocks's ears: "A Jullien concert's nothin' to it. No, not all the bands i' the country put together" (36:282).

The immediately contemporary theatre served no oftener as a source of topicalities. Characters in Victorian novels go to the play as seldom as they attend concerts or, except in Thackeray's fiction—and even here the reference is to only a few years around 1830—the opera. (Most Victorians' knowledge of the operas of the day was derived largely at second hand, from vocal and piano arrangements of popular melodies.) Kit Nubbles proudly took his little family party to the hippodrome performance—a spectacle, not a drama—at Astley's Royal Amphitheatre, which acquired fortuitous topicality by burning down only four months after the final number of *The Old Curiosity Shop* was published, and Colonel Newcome took his nephews and nieces there—but the difference between the two family visits is significant. Dickens treats the one in *The Old Curiosity Shop* with unqualified, affectionate enthusiasm: a wonderful time was had by all. But while Uncle Thomas Newcome, Sir Brian's daughters and sons, and Clive and Ethel at the back of the box had a wonderful time too—each proportionate to his or her generation—Thackeray, in the interests of characterization, introduces a sour note,

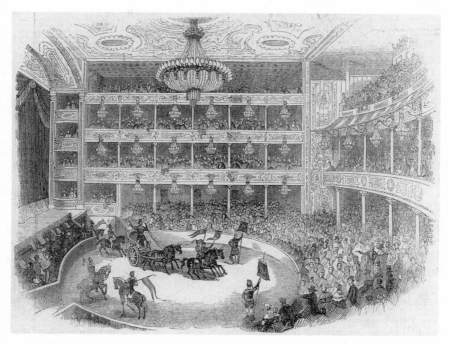

Astley's new building was depicted in the *Illustrated London News* for 1 April 1843. Although it was larger and more splendid than its destroyed predecessor, the layout preserved the same social distinctions. The Nubbles party presumably would have been in the top gallery at the right, and the Newcomes in a stage box on the left.

contrasting with the orange that Colonel Newcome enjoyed between the acts: "I wonder what sum of money Mr. Barnes Newcome would have taken to sit for five hours with his young brothers and sisters in a public box at the theatre and eat an orange in the face of the audience?" (*The Newcomes*, 16:1.170).

Pendennis hovered on the fringes of the theatre in the provinces

(opposite) Astley's Royal Amphitheatre attracted a socially mixed audience to the equestrian performances that were its longtime specialty. In his illustration for *The Old Curiosity Shop* (top) Phiz pictured the Hogarthian crowd that surrounded Kit Nubbles and his party as they were enthralled by what was essentially a variety bill with strong emphasis on horses. For *The Newcomes*, by contrast, Richard Doyle portrayed (bottom) the select little group who occupied a box at a reenactment of an enduringly topical event, the Battle of Waterloo.

during his feverish pursuit of The Fotheringay, and Dickens took his readers inside the provincial playhouse when Nicholas Nickleby toured with Mr. Crummles's select company. Although neither Collins nor Hardy attempted to create, as Dickens did with such great success, the intimate theatrical atmosphere, each introduced the same somewhat unusual kind of solo performer. In *No Name*, the heroine, Magdalen Vanstone, a born—and gentle-born—actress deprived of home and fortune by the death of her father and her proved illegitimacy, takes to the road in a one-woman multi-role entertainment inspired by the "At Home" entertainments in which the singing comedian Charles Mathews rose to stardom earlier in the century. A decade later, the young widow Ethelberta (*The Hand of Ethelberta* [1875–76]) makes a reputation for herself as a professional "story-teller" (monologist) on the platform of London's "Mayfair Hall."

But allusions to contemporary real-life plays and players were rare. In *The Newcomes* (1853–55) Thackeray mentioned Sir Harry Courtly, a character in Boucicault's melodrama of fifteen years earlier, *London Assurance* (25:1.263). In *Two Years Ago* (1857) Kingsley glancingly referred to Rachel and Adelaide Ristori at the moment when the celebrated French tragedienne was being eclipsed by the new star (10:168). Miss Braddon, in *Aurora Floyd*, noted the presence in Doncaster during race week of huge posters, printed in bright blue ink, announcing "Mr. and Mrs. Charles Matthews, or Mr. and Mrs. Charles Kean, for five nights only" (22:212).

Most theatrical topicalities were retrospective, and like operatic allusions they are found most often in Thackeray's fiction. In *The Great Hoggarty Diamond*, set in 1822–24, one of Titmarsh's fellow clerks "was always talking about Vestris and Miss Tree." These were the same actresses advertised in the Doncaster posters forty years later. The patent theatre favorite, Lucy Vestris, would marry Charles Mathews's namesake son, and Ellen Tree, the popular Olivia in the Covent Garden production of *Twelfth Night* in 1823, would marry Charles, the second son of Edmund Kean. Both couples were prominent on the stage and in management at the time of *Aurora Floyd*. Sam Titmarsh was given to singing "one of Charles Kemble's famous songs in 'Maid Marian'; a play that was all the rage then, taken from a famous storybook by one Peacock, a clerk in the India House; and a precious good place he has too," added Thackeray, in one of his asides (2:10). (Thomas Love Peacock was a friend of Thackeray. His *Maid Marian*, published in 1822, was adapted the same year for the stage by J. R. Planché, with music by Henry Bishop.) After Becky Sharp Crawley's triumphant appearance as Iphigenia in the charade at Gaunt House, a French duke declared that

"Madame Crawley was worthy to have been a pupil of Vestris, or to have figured at Versailles" (*Vanity Fair*, 51:498). Master Cuff, "the great chief and dandy of the Swishtail Seminary," a precocious man of the world whom little Dobbin faced down, "had been to the Opera, and knew the merits of the principal actors, preferring Mr. Kean to Mr. Kemble" (*Vanity Fair*, 5:46). Fanny Bolton, in *Pendennis*, could not forget Macready's production of Bulwer's *The Lady of Lyons* in 1838: "Oh, Ma! how I did love Mr. Macready when I saw him do it; and Pauline, for being faithful to poor Claude, and always thinking of him; and he coming back to her an officer, through all his dangers! And," Fanny continued, applying the stage story to her present lovesickness, "if everybody admires Pauline—and I'm sure everybody does, for being so true to a poor man—why should a gentleman be ashamed of loving a poor girl? Not that Mr. Arthur loves me—Oh, no, no! I ain't worthy of him; only a princess is worthy of such a gentleman as him" (51:2.128).

In *Aurora Floyd*, Miss Braddon wrote a then-and-now passage in the uncommon form of a comparison between the English stage as it once was and its present condition. Aurora was the daughter of an actress "on the dirty boards of a second-rate theatre in Lancashire" who married a wealthy banker—a clear reprise of the story of Harriot Mellon and Thomas Coutts (see pages 217–18 above and 592–95 below). Archibald Floyd "nourished a traditional, passive, but sincere admiration for the British Drama. Yes, the *British* Drama; for he had lived in a day when the drama was British, and when 'George Barnwell' and 'Jane Shore' were amongst the favourite works of art of a play-going public. . . . It was not the fashion in those days to make 'sensation' dramas of Shakespeare's plays. There was no 'Hamlet' with the celebrated water scene, and the Danish prince taking a 'header' to save poor weak-witted Ophelia. . . .[†] Archibald Floyd knew that she [his wife] was as bad an actress as ever played the leading characters in tragedy, comedy, and farce for five-and-twenty shillings a week." Like Pendennis's Fotheringay, she did not live her roles; when *Romeo and Juliet* was being played, she could be seen "laughing and talking in the white-washed little green room before she ran on to the stage to wail for her murdered kinsman and her banished lover. They tell us that Mr. Macready began to be Richelieu at three o'clock in the afternoon, and that it was dangerous to

---

[†]Unless there actually was a "sensational" *Hamlet*, the reference is to Dion Boucicault's thriller *The Colleen Bawn*, first performed in London in September 1860, which was famous for the scene in which the heroine was pitched into the waters of a lake (represented by waves of blue gauze operated by a score of boys) to be rescued by the hero after a death-defying dive.

approach or to speak to him between that hour and the close of the performance." In any case, said Braddon, "It was a repetition of the old story. It was Arthur Pendennis at the little Chatteris theatre bewitched and bewildered by Miss Fotheringay all over again" (1:10–12).

The past glories of the British theatre were most often recalled by allusions to Sarah Siddons. In *Vanity Fair* (40:397), Thackeray described Lady Southdown's departure from the family fight consequent upon old Sir Pitt's death "as magnificent as Mrs. Siddons in Lady Macbeth," the role she had assumed for her farewell performance in 1812, just ten years earlier. In *John Halifax, Gentleman*, Dinah Mulock, fixing the action in the year 1800, had her playing Lady Macbeth in a Cotswold town. There was also an oblique but immediately recognizable reference to her in Bella Wilfer's description of her mother, who habitually bound her face in a handkerchief, as "the Tragic Muse with a Toothache," Siddons having been Sir Joshua Reynolds's model for his painting of *The Tragic Muse*.

3.

Fictional characters occasionally attend exhibitions of paintings, the most memorable episode of the sort occurring in *The Newcomes*, when Ethel, all too conscious of her vulnerable presence in the marriage market, purloins a green "sold" ticket from the frame of a painting at the Gallery of Painters in Water-colours and pins it on her frock, explaining to her father, "I am No. 46 in the Exhibition"—and, inferentially, up for sale (28:1.299). The youthful civil servants in *The Three Clerks* go to picture shows, as do Lord and Lady George in *Is He Popenjoy?*, who drop into a dealer's in Bond Street to see a new picture exhibited by gaslight before going on to shop at Swan and Edgar's.

Two Victorian novelists had a more than casual interest in art for personal reasons, Wilkie Collins as the son and biographer of a successful artist, Thackeray a failed one. Collins's fiction occasionally referred to the contemporary art world, most notably in his lengthy description of the bogus Old Masters racket in *A Rogue's Life*. There the eponymous hero, after brief careers as a portrait painter and a caricaturist, turned to the fabrication of paintings that were touted as being from the brushes of the great names in Renaissance art.

Thackeray brought to his novels the firsthand knowledge of the London and Paris art scene of the late thirties and the forties that he had acquired as a critic for *Fraser's Magazine* and other periodicals. In the eighth number of *Vanity Fair* (August 1847), his description of the countryside of Waterloo on the eve of the battle ("All looked as brilliant and harmless as a Hyde Park review") led to the timely observation, "As our painters are bent on military subjects just now, I throw this out as a good subject for the pencil, to illustrate the principle of an honest English war" (28:262).†

The Newcomes is replete with references to contemporary art, and it provided its readers with the best description of mid-Victorian artists' society to be found in any novel. The high-spirited students at Gandish's school lived as close to a *vie de bohème* as the London of the day permitted. In the novel there is at least one allusion that only a reader well acquainted with the art scene would have recognized. Visiting his son's studio one day, Colonel Newcome "found Clive and his friend Ridley engaged in depicting a Life-Guardsman, or a muscular negro, or a Malay from a neighbouring crossing, who would appear as Othello . . ." (22:1.220). The reference was to a story that must have long been current—the artist tells it in his late autobiography—of Frith's actually using a Malay crossing-sweeper as the model for his painting of Othello with Desdemona, exhibited at the Royal Academy in 1840.

Allusions to portraiture almost had to involve Sir Thomas Lawrence—whether as a sign of a family's rank, a standard of comparison, a means of indirect description, or, in Becky Sharp Crawley's case, strategic evidence of loyalty to the monarch, George IV. She went to Colnaghi's, the famous printsellers, and "ordered the finest portrait of him that art had produced, and credit could supply"—an engraving of Lawrence's 1822 portrait, "in which the best of monarchs is represented in a frock-coat with a fur collar, and breeches and silk stockings, simpering on a sofa from under his curly brown wig" (*Vanity Fair*, 48:463). But actual portraits by Lawrence were outnumbered in Victorian fiction by a veritable shadow-oeuvre that novelists invented for him: the portrait of the Marquis of Carabas in *Vivian Grey* ("one of Sir Thomas' happiest efforts" [2.2:28]); "the Lawrence portraits, tawdry and beautiful, and, thirty years ago, deemed as precious as works of real genius" that hung side by side with "the magnificent Vandykes" and "the noble Reynolds pictures" at Bareacres Castle, before which Lawrence depicted the present Lord Bareacres waving his saber (*Vanity Fair*, 49:471); that of the Earl of Ringwood in *The Adventures of Philip*, whose countenance, even under Lawrence's tactful brush, remained "very ill-favoured" (5:1.139);

†Thackeray was remembering here a piece he had contributed a few weeks earlier to *Punch* (10 July) in which, writing as "Professor Growley Byles," an artist who failed to get his work into the annual exhibitions, he complained of the excessive violence displayed in the cartoons (large sketches) then being displayed in connection with the ongoing competition for the honor of painting the frescoes in the new Houses of Parliament. "If the government grants premiums for massacres," he said, "of course I can have no objection."

that of Lady Florence Lascelles in Bulwer's *Ernest Maltravers*, whom the Duke of —— assures, in a suave compliment, that her "picture in the exhibition scarcely does you justice, Lady Florence; yet Lawrence is usually happy" (6.3:326); and the youthful portrait of Sir Hugh Mallinger in *Daniel Deronda*, in which, says George Eliot, the artist "had done justice to the agreeable alacrity of expression and sanguine temperament still to be seen in the original, but had done something more than justice in slightly lengthening the nose, which was in reality shorter than might have been expected in a Mallinger" (16:204–5).[†]

Other allusions to Lawrence served comparative ends. In *Felix Holt*, George Eliot, always perceptive in art matters and here witty as well, described Harold Transome as looking "like a handsome portrait by Sir Thomas Lawrence, in which that remarkable artist had happily omitted the usual excess of honeyed blandness mixed with alert intelligence, which is hardly compatible with the state of man outside of paradise" (46:373). Introducing the Earl of Dreddlington, who was to play a prominent role in *Ten Thousand a Year*, Warren sought to capture the essence of his physical bearing in hardly more than a dozen words: "Had he been standing to Sir Thomas Lawrence, he could not have disposed himself more effectively" (22:599). This is baldly stated, and in striving for the same effect in his particularized description of Tite Barnacle, Dickens was more adroit. Having inventoried his "folds and folds of white cravat," his "oppressive" wristbands and collar, his "large watch-chain and bunch of seals, a coat buttoned up to inconvenience, a waistcoat buttoned up to inconvenience, an unwrinkled pair of trousers, a stiff pair of boots," he summed it up in a masterly sentence: "He seemed to have been sitting for his portrait to Sir Thomas Lawrence all the days of his life" (*Little Dorrit*, 2.10:152). Dickens could have used precisely the same words to describe the ineffable Mr. Turveydrop; instead, he made the same point by indirection, saying that his pose when seated was "in imitation of the print of his illustrious model on the sofa" (*Bleak House*, 14:174)—an allusion to Lawrence's portrait of George IV which so attracted Becky Sharp. (It will be noticed that most allusions to Lawrence's portraiture dwelt not on the faces but the stiff poses as a revelation of character.)

Another Regency portrait painter, not of Sir Thomas's stature, was

---

[†]The picture of Lady Ann Newcome "leaning over a harp, attired in white muslin" (*The Newcomes*, 14:1.150) was by the other portraitist by that name, as Thackeray's spelling—Laurence—and the novel's time scheme make clear. Lady Ann's portrait was doubtless among the many that Samuel Laurence exhibited at the Royal Academy at some date after 1836 (he continued to exhibit until 1882).

his pupil George Harlow, who painted the Newcome brothers' mother, "with her two sons simpering at her knees" (*The Newcomes*, 14:1.150), the formidable old Lady Kew, and (in *The Adventures of Philip*, 1:107) Mrs. Firmin, "that year he was at Rome, and when in eighteen days he completed a copy of the 'Transfiguration' to the admiration of all the Academy," a feat so celebrated in its time that it eventually found its way into the *Dictionary of National Biography*.

Harlow could not have been a personal friend of Thackeray, because he died in 1819. But in some other Thackerayan references one may suspect a gentle attempt to advance certain artists' fame, as when Ethel Newcome and Lady Kew, visiting the annual show of the Watercolour Society, see a new picture by Cattermole and discover that "all Mr. Hunt's pictures are sold," including one of "a friendless young girl cowering in a doorway, evidently without home or shelter" (*The Newcomes*, 28:1.298). (In view of the setting, in the 1840s, this would have been the popular artist William Henry Hunt [1790–1864], not William Holman Hunt, who had not yet arrived and whose forte, in any case, was not sentimental genre.)

Scattered throughout Victorian fiction were more or less casual mentions of other artists. When Disraeli's fashionable men and women in *Vivian Grey* tired of literary chitchat, they turned to affected talk of the art of the moment. Largely forgotten now (he died in a Chelsea madhouse in 1835), the Nova Scotia-born Gilbert Stuart Newton enjoyed a vogue in the 1820s. As they idly glance through a sheaf of his languishing lithographed beauties, Vivian asks Miss Manvers, "You would not call these exactly Prosopopoeias of Innocence? Newton, I suppose, like Lady Wortley Montague, is of opinion, that the face is not the most beautiful part of a woman; at least, if I am to judge from these elaborate ankles. Now, the countenance of this Donna, forsooth, has a drowsy placidity worthy of the easy chair she is lolling in, and yet her ankle would not disgrace the contorted frame of the most pious faquir." Miss Manvers replies, "Well! I am an admirer of Newton's paintings." And Vivian, unabashed, smartly changes sides and modifies his opinion: "Oh! so am I. He is certainly a cleverish fellow, but rather too much among the blues. . . " (2.9:46).

The name of Landseer was, in some quarters, synonymous with supreme authority. When the obsequious Andrew Smee, Esq., R.A., was shown a selection of Clive Newcome's sketches, he exclaimed, "What a genius the lad has, what a force and individuality there is in all his drawings! Look at his horses! capital, by Jove, capital! and Alfred on his pony, and Miss Ethel in her Spanish hat, with her hair flowing in the wind! I must take this sketch, I positively must now, and show it to Landseer"

(*The Newcomes*, 17:1.178). He brought back word that "the great painter had been delighted with the young man's performance."

"Sir Edwin Landseer might have been proud of such spirit and dash," says the doting John Mellish of his wife Aurora Floyd's pencil sketch of her dog Bow-wow (13:120–21). In *Doctor Thorne*, Sir Roger Scatcherd, addressing a rough crowd from the hustings, points first to a scurrilous caricature of himself and then to one of his opponent, Gustavus Moffat, the London tailor's son: "But now, having polished off this bit of a picture, let me ask you who Mr. Moffat is? There are pictures enough about him, too; though Heaven knows where they all come from. I think Sir Edwin Landseer must have done this one of the goose; it is so deadly natural" (17:186). The crude picture seems to have been a visual pun on a tailor's goose, a smoothing iron.

William Etty, the foremost early Victorian painter of nudes, had a more controversial reputation. The "formal lady" in Dickens's *Sketches of Young Couples*, later added to *Sketches by Boz* (562), echoed the widespread opinion that "it really is high time Mr. Etty was prosecuted and made a public example of." His picture of *Phaedria and Cymocles on the Idle Lake*, for example, was denounced as sheer pornography when it was shown at the Royal Academy in 1835. If, as is likely, Carker in *Dombey and Son* was a collector of contemporary rather than older art, we can recognize a submerged allusion to Etty, for whose paintings the word *voluptuous* was particularly reserved at the time. In Carker's opulent house "the prints and pictures do not commemorate great thoughts or deeds, or render nature in the poetry of landscape, hall, or hut, but are of one voluptuous cast—mere shows of form and colour—and no more" (33:554). A man so stained by this taste deserved the retribution he ultimately suffered under the wheels of a locomotive.

By the middle of the century, when it was well known that the Queen and her husband bought paintings by Etty's protégé, William Frost, that featured bevies of topless beauties suggested by passages in Spenser or Milton, the issue of nudity in art, while scarcely moot, was no longer inflammatory. The housekeeper at Lord Heartycheer's castle in Surtees's *Young Tom Hall's Heart-Aches and Horses* was unembarrassed as she explained to visitors the "voluptuous Etty" that hung in the castle's picture gallery:

"This is the great Mr. Apollo, a gent much given to the ladies. He co'abited with Wenus in the Island of Rhodes, where it rained gold, and the earth was clothed, as you see, with lilies and roses. Among other young ladies he made love to was Miss Daphne, who, 'owever, liked a youngerer gent better nor him. Mr. Apollo, therefore, who was an artful man, persuaded the youth to dress up as a gal, and keep company with the nymphs. They, you see, want him to bathe with them in the river near London, which the youth refusing to do, his sex was discovered, and he was stabbed to the heart with many daggers." (40:318–19)

Thackeray defined the characters of Clive Newcome and his friend J. J. Ridley, the idle and industrious apprentices respectively, in terms directly derived from the current climate of artistic taste. Granting the obvious differences between fifteenth- and sixteenth-century Florence and mid-nineteenth-century London, Clive was a latter-day avatar of Browning's "Pictor Ignotus" (1845), a convention-bound artist adhering to outmoded ideals of art, while the dedicated Ridley was a mid-Victorian Fra Lippo Lippi. (Browning's poem was published in his *Men and Women* collection on 17 November 1855, only months after *The Newcomes* had wound up its serial run.) The parallel, of course, is incomplete. Browning's nameless painter was the victim of the sclerotic condition of postmedieval religious art, while Clive's incubus was the notion, increasingly rejected even as Benjamin Robert Haydon continued to champion it, that grand-scale history painting was the pinnacle of artistic ambition; and Ridley was no prophet of a new realism, as, in Browning's view, Fra Lippo Lippi had been in his time. But Clive's limitation as a painter would have been apparent to any reader of *The Newcomes* who followed trends in the fine arts in early Victorian England. He sends his pictures to the British Institution—second-best to the Royal Academy, perhaps a sign, therefore, that he shrank from competing for a place on the Academy's august walls, even as the timid Pictor Ignotus had sought refuge in painting "These endless cloisters and eternal aisles / With the same series, Virgin, Babe, and Saint." And the pictures—machines, really, they are so "enormous"—are of such pretentious and threadbare subjects as "Combat of Chivalry" and "Sir Brian the Templar Carrying off Rebecca." Later he paints the equally heavy and stale subject of Belisarius. Meanwhile, Ridley is doubly blessed, being not only truly devoted to art and a diligent worker but profitably attuned to the taste of the moment, which runs strongly to fairy pictures. His "Oberon and Titania" at the Academy is described by the *Pall Mall Gazette* as "one of the most charming and delightful works of the present exhibition," showing "not only the greatest promise," but "the most delicate and beautiful performance" (22:1.230).

Thackeray used his strong feelings on the subject of artists' being entitled to a full measure of social respect to emphasize the stodgy intolerance of other characters. Hobson Newcome, speaking of Clive, complains to his nephew Barnes, "But since he has taken this madcap freak of turning painter, there is no understanding the chap. Did you ever see such a set of fellows as the Colonel had got together at his party the other night? Dirty chaps in velvet coats and beards? They looked like a set of mountebanks. And this young Clive is going to turn painter! . . . I don't care what a fellow is if he is a good fellow. But a painter! hang it—a painter's no trade at all—I don't fancy seeing one of our family sticking up pictures for sale" (*The Newcomes*, 20:1.201). Major Pendennis likewise protests: "Nothing could show a more deplorable ignorance of the world than poor Newcome supposing his son could make such a match as that with his cousin. Is it true that he is going to make his son an artist? I don't know what the dooce the world is coming to. An artist! By Gad, in my time a fellow would as soon have thought of making his son a hair-dresser, or a pastry-cook, by Gad" (*The Newcomes*, 24:1.249).

Describing the London art scene of the 1840s from the perspective of 1853–55, Thackeray looked across a divide that was almost as marked in its particular realm of contemporary life as the other he described, the one that separated coaches from railway trains. Bridging it was the increasingly controversial figure of J. M. W. Turner, who had died in 1851. Novelists had usually mentioned him with respect, and they continued to do so on some occasions, as when Bulwer-Lytton associated him with three more popular painters, Wilkie, Landseer, and Maclise, in *What Will He Do with It?* (1857–59).[†] He fell from general favor, however, when his late landscapes exceeded permissible limits of nonrepresentationalism. "Worthy reader," asked Charles Lever in his novel *Davenport Dunn* (1859), "have you stood by while some enthusiastic admirer of Turner's later works has, in all the fervour of his zeal, encomiumized one of those strange, incomprehensible creations, where cloud and sun, atmosphere, shadow, and smoke, seem madly commingled with tall masts piercing the lurid vapour, and storm-clouds drifting across ruined towers?"[8] This was now the popular view of Turner's art, and it added timely point to readers of *Lady Audley's Secret* two years later, when they were told that as a governess she had taught her pupils to "paint from nature after Creswick" (a thoroughly conventional—and popular—watercolorist), but now, as a lady moving in the best circles, spent a leisure hour "copying a water-colored sketch of an impossibly Turner-esque atmosphere" (1:4; 15:79). It does not appear that her model was an actual Turner picture, but to desert safe Creswickian conventionality

[†] In the serialized version of *Yeast* (*Fraser's Magazine*, December 1848), the artist Claude Mellot said, "You English must learn to understand your own history before you paint it. Rather follow in the steps of your Landseers, and Stanfields, and Creswicks, and add your contribution to the present noble school of naturalist painters. This is the niche in the temple which God has set you English to fill up just now." One wonders what led Kingsley to insert Turner's name before Landseer's when he revised the text for publication in book form in 1851.

for unnatural Turneresque luridness represented an unmistakable decline in taste, and who could say it was not meant to be a quiet reflection of her unnatural (unfeminine) character as a would-be murderess?

Public attention was partly diverted from the supposed madness of Turner's last paintings by the controversy that brought the Victorian art world into the limelight as no other event had done. In 1848 the Pre-Raphaelite Brotherhood, setting out to revolutionize modern art, denounced the very academic shibboleths that Clive and his friends at Gandish's and in Rome embraced in their uncritical ways. Initially greeted with laughter rather than alarm, the PreRaphaelites' notoriety—many found their canvases ludicrous, and some entertained grave suspicions about the personal lives of these impudent subverters of artistic orthodoxy—furnished novelists with a new and highly topical means of suggesting character. In *The Warden*, Tom Towers, editor of the omnipotent *Jupiter* newspaper, lived in a four-room suite in the Temple, "furnished, if not with the splendour, with probably more than the comfort of Stafford House [the palatial St. James's home of the Duke of Sutherland]. Every addition that science and art have lately made to the luxuries of modern life was to be found there." The chamber in which he usually sat

> contained but two works of art—the one, an admirable bust of Sir Robert Peel, by Power[s], declared the individual politics of our friend; and the other, a singularly long figure of a female devotee, by Millais, told equally plainly the school of art to which he was addicted. This picture was not hung, as pictures usually are, against the wall; there was no inch of wall vacant for such a purpose: it had a stand or desk erected for its own accommodation; and there on her pedestal, framed and glazed, stood the devotional lady looking intently at a lily as no lady ever looked before.
>
> Our modern artists, whom we style Prae-Raffaellites, have delighted to go back, not only to the finish and peculiar manner, but also to the subjects of the early painters. It is impossible to give them too much praise for the elaborate perseverance with which they have equalled the minute perfections of the masters from whom they take their inspiration: nothing probably can exceed the painting of some of these latter-day pictures. It is, however, singular into what faults they fall as regards their subjects: they are not quite content to take the old stock-groups—a Sebastian with his arrows, a Lucia with her eyes in a dish, a Lorenzo with a gridiron, or the virgin with two children. But they are anything but happy in their change. As a rule, no figure should be drawn in a position which it is impossible to suppose any figure should maintain. The patient endurance of St. Sebastian, the wild ecstacy of St. John in the Wilderness, the maternal love of the virgin, are feelings naturally portrayed by a fixed posture; but the lady with the stiff back and bent neck, who looks at her flower, and is still looking from

hour to hour, gives us an idea of pain without grace, and abstraction without a cause. (14:97)[†]

The point? "It was easy, from his rooms, to see that Tom Towers was a
Sybarite, though by no means an idle one." To readers who equated a
taste for PreRaphaelitism with Sybaritism and Sybaritism with illicit sen-
suousness—a long leap, to be sure—the journalist's addiction to characteristic PreRaphaelite art was a decided count against him.

The next year (1856), Charles Reade took momentary advantage of
the growing tendency to use "PreRaphaelitism" as an all-purpose smear
term when, in *It is Never Too Late to Mend*, he applied it to a worsted-work
sampler in a farmhouse (2:1.44). The sampler's "two moral common-
places" and a "forbidden fruit-tree" no more qualified it as a typical
product of the school than the homely material of which it was made.

Kingsley professed to see through the PreRaphaelite pretense: it was
opposed to common reason. In *Two Years Ago* (1857) his physician hero,
Tom Thurnall, "arriv[ed], on pre-Raphaelite grounds, at a by no means
pre-Raphaelite conclusion. 'A picture, you say, is worth nothing unless
you copy nature. But you can't copy her. She is ten times more gorgeous
than any man can dare represent her. Ergo, every picture is a failure;
and the nearest hedge-bush is worth all your galleries together" (14:215).
Earlier in the novel, Kingsley had staged a scene at the Royal Academy
"in front of one of those pre-Raphaelite pictures, which Claude [Mellot,
the artist] does not appreciate as he should." Mellot enlightens his friend
Stangrave at considerable length, one of his arguments being that the
PreRaphaelite painters "forget that human beings are men with two
eyes, and not daguerreotype lenses with one eye, and so are contriving
and striving to introduce into their pictures the very defect of the daguerreotype which the stereoscope is required to correct. . . . [T]he only
possible method of fulfilling the Pre-Raphaelite ideal would be, to set a
petrified Cyclops to paint his petrified brother" (9:134–36).

The ambivalent position on PreRaphaelitism was expressed more or
less satirically by the very minor novelist George Herbert, in *Gerald
Fitzgerald* (1858):

[†]Trollope seems to be describing an imaginary painting here: no picture that Millais
exhibited before 1855, the date of *The Warden*, wholly conforms to the specifications given.
Perhaps it is a composite of paintings by two, or even three, PreRaphaelites. The "singu-
larly long figure" with "the stiff back and bent neck" is recognizable as Millais's Mariana
(1851), but she is not a devotee and she is not looking fixedly at a lily. The lily gazer is the
Virgin Mary in Rossetti's *Ecce Ancilla Domini* (1850). Two varieties of lilies are prominent
in Charles Allston Collins's *Convent Thoughts* (1851), and the nun (devotee) is gazing at one
of them, a water lily.

Freely translated, it might be understood as—painting after a certain style that was before a certain other style; but the great critics, with Mr. Buskin [*sic*] at their head, gave to it a grand and mysterious meaning that took it beyond the range of common intelligence and made it awfully comprehensive! One characteristic of this heretical art was its nicety of detail. Nothing escaped the brushes of its disciples. That woman was unfortunate who, with a mole on her back or a pimple on her nose, should happen to sit to one of the new school. As sure as fate the mole would go in, or the pimple would be picked out with a skill that might merit the good word of a man learned in cutaneous disorders! Yet some of these painters were poets withal, and conceived lovely things.[9]

But Thackeray's daughter Anne, in one of her novels (*The Village on the Cliff* [1867]), allowed a character no such tolerance: "[B]ut what is this violet female biting an orange, and standing with her toes turned in and her elbows turned out? P.R.B.'s. I have no patience with the nonsense."[10]

The reference to "Mr. Buskin" in *Gerald Fitzgerald* was one of a number (correctly spelled) found in fiction, especially in connection with Ruskin's championship of Turner and the first PreRaphaelites. Describing a supposedly typical intellectual conversation of the day, Frank Smedley wrote in *Harry Coverdale's Courtship* (1855):

Alice, thus deserted, fell into the hands of a tall, gaunt, blue woman, rejoicing in a red nose and a long fluent tongue, who began to talk high art to her, and confused her about transcendentalism and Carlyle—the Oxford Graduate (*viz.*, Turner's single and singular disciple, wonderful Mr. Ruskin), and pre-Raphaelism—the meaning of Tennyson, when he condescends to be obscure (for he can write real poetry which he who runs may read and feel)—and of the dark Brownings, and Macaulay and the romance of history, and many other hackneyed pseudo-literary topics of the day.[11]

"Do you really so admire Ruskin?" asked a character in *Money* (1860), by a novelist styling himself or herself "Kennaquhom" ("I don't know who"). "Yes," came the reply; "I dote upon him because he has such an opinion of himself—he is always morally certain that he is right, and everybody else wrong."[12]

Several individual paintings were mentioned in fiction, the novelist in each case relying on his reader's acquaintance with either the original or a widely circulated engraving, perhaps in one of the illustrated papers. "Everyone knows the picture," wrote Walter Thornbury, Turner's first and appallingly incompetent biographer, in his novel *The Vicar's Courtship* (1869), "—the little ferry tug is carelessly dragging the old phantom of the war ship to her last anchorage; the spars of the *Téméraire* stand out pale against the sky, while below the last crimson radiance of

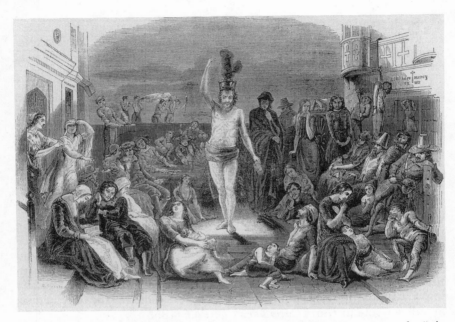

Paul Falconer Poole's *Solomon Eagle Exhorting the People to Repentance* was the "picture of the year" at the Royal Academy in 1843, and the *Illustrated London News* featured an engraving of it as part of its coverage of the show (10 June 1843). Elizabeth Gaskell implicitly urged the readers of *Mary Barton* to visualize the dying mill hand as the central figure in the painting.

autumn sunset, the thin blue mist steals up the river and shrouds the distant forest of masts."[13]

In Reade's *Love Me Little, Love Me Long* (1859), Lucy Fountain came down the stairs and entered the room brandishing a new gown her aunt hoped to wear to a ball—"holding this female weapon of destruction as high above her head as Judith waves the sword of Holofernes in Etty's immortal picture," which was first exhibited at the Royal Academy in 1827 (1:11). In *East Lynne* (1861), there was mention (48:500) of "Martin's pictures of the Last Judgment" being shown at "Lynneborourgh": a chronologically exact reference, because John Martin's huge apocalyptic canvases had recently been toured throughout the provinces. Landseer's popular painting of *Bolton Abbey in the Olden Times* (1834) was spoken of in Trollope's *Lady Anna,* set in the 1830s.

Elizabeth Gaskell slipped an allusion to a currently talked-of painting into *Mary Barton* (1848) without mentioning it by name. She wrote of a dying mill hand whom John Barton watched over in the wet and evil-smelling cellar of a Manchester tenement: "Every now and then he started up in his naked madness, looking like the prophet of woe in the fearful plague-picture . . . " (6:57). This was Paul Falconer Poole's melodramatic rendering of *Solomon Eagle Exhorting the People to Repentance, During the Plague of the Year 1665,* which had caused a sensation at the Academy exhibition in 1843. Gaskell and some of her readers may have seen it either there or when it was shown in Manchester two years later; in any case, an engraving of it had already appeared in the *Illustrated London News.*

The best instance of a novelist's relying on readers' prior knowledge of a painting is to be found in *John Halifax, Gentleman,* in which the narrator, Phineas Fletcher, describes the hero discussing with his wife the possibility of their moving to a small landed estate in accordance with his growing wealth and position in Norton Bury (Tewkesbury):

> He spoke gently, laying his hand on his wife's shoulder, and looking down on her with that peculiar look which he always had when telling her things that he knew were sore to hear. I never saw that look on any living face save John's; but I have seen it once in a picture—of two Huguenot lovers. The woman is trying to fasten round the man's neck the white badge that will save him from the massacre (of St. Bartholomew)—he, clasping her the while, gently puts it aside—not stern, but smiling. That quiet, tender smile, firmer than any frown, will, you feel sure, soon control the woman's anguish, so that she will sob out—any faithful woman would—"Go, die! Dearer to me than even thyself are thy honour and thy duty!" When I saw this noble picture, it touched to the core this old heart of mine—for the painter, in that rare expression, might have caught John's. (29:299–300)

The picture is not identified, but every reader who recognized Millais's *The Order of Release,* exhibited at the Academy four years earlier (1852), would have noticed that Dinah Mulock was relying on that acquaintance to heighten the visual quality of her prose description.

Another famous PreRaphaelite painting almost, but not quite, found its way into fiction. When Dickens was writing *Little Dorrit* in 1856, he concluded the twelfth number with William Dorrit, now a rich man, harping at the family's Roman breakfast table "on his wish to know Mr. Merdle, with the contingent view of benefiting by the advice of that wonderful man in the disposal of his fortune." Amy Dorrit, Dickens wrote, "began to . . . entertain a curiosity on her own part to see the shining light of the world" (2.7:568). But on second thought he deleted the two last words and substituted "his time." The intent of the original wording, as Harvey Sucksmith has noted, was satirical: "Contemporary Englishmen and women, as depicted in the novel, are venerating and worshipping Mr. Merdle as if he were divine, as if he were Christ," the reference being to Holman Hunt's *The Light of the World*, the picture of the year at the Academy show of 1854. "[T]he strong graphic identification of Holman Hunt's Christ with . . . Mr. Merdle would arouse so powerful an incongruity and introduce so painful an element of blasphemy into the comparison as to quite swamp its ironic meaning." [14]

When novelists went beyond the narrative content of familiar paintings and sought to invoke artistic instances of the use of particular colors, they doubtless assumed more acquaintance with the originals than many, if not most, of their readers had, especially those who lived in the country. Several times in his early novels, Hardy, a frequenter of London art exhibitions, used this kind of analogy: "a reddish brown, as if the blue component of the grey had faded, like the indigo from the same kind of colour in Turner's pictures" and "In an instant Bathsheba's face coloured with the angry crimson of a Danby sunset" (both in *Far from the Madding Crowd*, 5:31 and 20:117); "Gaslights glared from butcher's stalls, illuminating the lumps of flesh to splotches of orange and vermilion, like the wild colouring in Turner's later pictures" (*A Pair of Blue Eyes*, 13:148). But the full force of these allusions, as is true also of Braddon's description (pages 332–33 above) of Lady Audley's portrait and her definition of Talbot Bulstrode's special brand of idealism in PreRaphaelite visual terms, depended on readers' having seen the original pictures in all their bright coloring. If they knew a few of them only from chromolithographic reproductions, they would have a crude sense—no more—of what the originals were like. But most readers would have seen only black-and-white engravings, either in illustrated papers or separately sold copies, and to them, Hardy's references would have been meaningless.

13
Popular Entertainments

1.

IN ALL OF THE TIMELY ALLUSIONS that bespeckle the comic-journalistic verse that Thomas Hood ground out between 1825 and 1844, the one aspect of modern everyday life most often referred to was not books, music, the theatre, or the fine arts, but a great variety of nondramatic entertainments, most of which took the form of pay-as-you-enter exhibitions.[1] This was no private eccentricity; Hood knew his audience well, and knew that such shows, so diverse, numerous, attention-grabbing, and (in some cases) freshly contrived, animated his readers' consciousness of the current scene. And those same readers belonged also to the novelists' audience. It is true that many exhibitions intended to catch the pennies and shillings of "the masses"—performing animals, for instance, or acts by fire-eaters or men who played tunes by tapping their chins[†]—were despised by cultivated men and women as vulgar and meretricious. Yet some of the most exalted members of Victorian society patronized them. The Queen herself went to Drury Lane Theatre no fewer than six times in 1838–39 to see the performances of Isaac Van Amburgh, the young American lion trainer, and later she summoned George Catlin's troupe of Red Indians and the American midget General Tom Thumb, P. T. Barnum's profitable protégé, to Windsor. The Duke of Wellington was a familiar sight at every new attraction of the sort—panoramas, Madame Tussaud's, the ever-changing

---

[†]This was the peculiar specialty of an entertainer named Michael Boai, the "Chin Chopper," who performed at several London sites around 1830 with his wife accompanying him on the guitar. Dickens alluded to the art twice in *Sketches by Boz.* In "The Tuggses at Ramsgate" Miss Tippin, a juvenile member of a theatrical family, played "variations on the guitar . . . accompanied on the chin by her brother Master Tippin," and in "The Steam Excursion" the "funny gentleman," Mr. Hardy, "could sing comic songs, imitate hackney-coachmen and fowls, play airs on his chin, and execute concertos on the Jew's-harp" ("Tales," chap. 4:351; chap. 7:385).

bill of exhibitions and performances at the foremost venue of such entertainment, the Egyptian Hall in Piccadilly—and Lord Stowell, the renowned authority on maritime law, had a lifelong addiction to all shows that charged no more than a shilling (few did).

Some well-known kinds of Victorian street shows had a long history. Punch puppetry, which Thackeray memorably adopted as a mock framework for *Vanity Fair*, was familiar to everyone, and casual allusions to particular episodes in the traditional script found their way into a number of novels. Waxworks, such as David Copperfield took Peggotty to see when she visited London, had been on the urban scene since the early eighteenth century. In *Ask Mamma*, Surtees, describing his hero as "neither a tradesman nor a gentleman," explained that his family, "like the happy united family we meet upon wheels; the dove nestling with the gorged cat, and so on—all pulled well together when there was a common victim to plunder" (1:10). Readers would have recognized the "happy family," a mobile collection of birds and animals living peaceably together in a single cage, even though they were antipathetic in nature. These, too, had been seen on the London streets in the previous century. Henry Mayhew was told that there were five separate extended families of the kind being exhibited in the 1850s, and one of them, based in the Waterloo Road, appeared in Frith's painting of holiday crowds on the beach at Ramsgate.

Eighteenth-century pleasure seekers had also gaped at learned pigs and industrious fleas, the latest generations of which Dickens mentioned in *Sketches by Boz*, and automatons—robotlike machines that imitated human actions such as playing a musical instrument, writing, drawing, or engaging living persons in games of chess. Improved models of these mechanical men, capable of new feats, were introduced in the early Victorian years. One of the most publicized in 1846 was Professor Faber's Euphonia, a machine that imitated the spoken voice in approximations of five languages. Thackeray, to whose ears "Hurray for Queen Victoria" came out as "Hourrah for Figdoria," had fun with it in *Punch*. The next year, Charlotte Brontë described Mr. Rochester's frightening reaction to Jane Eyre's mention of the mysterious stranger who had called at the house: "'Mason!'—the West Indies!' he said, in the tone one might fancy a speaking automation to enounce its single words . . ." (*Jane Eyre*, 19:255). In *Our Mutual Friend*, Dickens revived the old-line musical automaton by converting the piano player at the Podsnaps' dancing party into one, and in *Dombey and Son* he alluded to a more common form of mechanical music in the person of Mr. Feeder, B.A., the downtrodden assistant at Dr. Blimber's select academy, who ground away at a figurative hand organ fitted with barrels (ancestors of modern cassettes) that gave forth, not little tunes, but dreary excerpts from the Greek and Roman classics.

The most respectable ornament of the London entertainment scene in the first half of the nineteenth century was the panorama, a huge circular canvas depicting a battle, a city, or some other locale or event currently in the news, such as David Copperfield saw when his new chum Steerforth showed him the sights of London. Initially praised, and for a time seriously regarded, as a new art form and soon adapted for spectacular effects in the theatre, the panorama in its final (360 degree) form was first seen in 1792, two years before it was transferred to a purpose-made building just off Leicester Square that was to be known for over sixty years as "the panorama," even though there were rival canvases elsewhere. The name, coined at the inventor's request, promptly entered the general vocabulary as an up-to-date synonym for the old "prospect," but not as quickly as Dinah Mulock assumed when, in a passage in *John Halifax, Gentleman* set in 1800, she had a character exclaim of the view from Nunnely Hill, "There's a panorama!" (10:100). Another neologism was *diorama*, a word originally coined to denote a semitransparent painting, the size of a theatrical scene, that could be transformed by manipulating the light sources before and behind it. In the course of time, the application of both terms widened, *panorama* coming to mean also a lengthy rolling canvas depicting a trip down the Nile or the Mississippi or on the new Overland route to India, and *diorama* any series of pictures within a large single frame, one dissolving into the next. In the theatre, both words were used loosely to apply to any kind of painted background that moved or was transformed by lighting tricks. Thus Surtees could write, in *Hawbuck Grange*, "The field had now a perfect panoramic view of the chase, without more trouble than they would be put to at the diorama, or any London show" (8:109).

These large-scale painted and lighted pictures with their spectacular illusive effects in turn planted new figurative images in novelists' minds. In *Adam Bede*, George Eliot adopted these effects to describe images in Adam's private consciousness: "While his muscles were working lustily, his mind seemed as passive as a spectator at a diorama: scenes of the sad past, and probably sad future, floating before him, and giving place one to the other in swift succession" (4:42). Toward the end of the novel, she revived the image; "These were Arthur's chief thoughts, so far as a man's thoughts through hours of travelling can be compressed into a few sentences, which are only like the list of names [in the program supplied to spectators] telling you what are the scenes in a long, long panorama full of colour, of detail, and of life" (44:367). Later on, in *Middlemarch*, Eliot picked up the *Adam Bede* image again: "The memory has as many moods as the temper, and shifts its scenery like a diorama" (53:566).

Eliot's effective use of such imagery was matched by Hardy in *The Return of the Native*, when he described Diggory Venn and Wildeve gambling: "The aspect of the two opponents was not singular. Apart from motions, a complete diorama of the fluctuations of the game went on in their eyes. A diminutive candle-flame was mirrored in each pupil, and it would have been possible to distinguish therein between the moods of hope and the moods of abandonment, even as regards the reddleman, though his facial muscles betrayed nothing at all" (3.8:183).

In the same novel Hardy wrote, "As Eustacia crossed the firebeams she appeared for an instant as distinct as a figure in a phantasmagoria—a creature of light surrounded by an area of darkness" (5.7:272). The phantasmagoria, in which lighting tricks in a darkened room produced eerie effects of ghosts materializing and then vanishing, had a brief vogue in one or more London theatres early in the century and then subsided into a form of domestic entertainment. Dickens had used the figure in *The Old Curiosity Shop* (Quilp "looked fixedly at him, retreated a little distance without averting his gaze, approached again, again withdrew, and so on for half-a-dozen times, like a head in a phantasmagoria" [48:455]), as did Mrs. Henry Wood in *East Lynne* ("The old scenes passed through her mind, as the changing pictures in a phantasmagoria" [58:601]). Two other visual entertainments familiar in Victorian homes were the phantasmagoria-derived dissolving views ("But now she had known Felix, her conception of what a happy love must be had become like a dissolving view, in which the once-clear images were gradually melting into new forms and colours"—*Felix Holt* [22:197]) and the kaleidoscope, a best-selling toy derived from a scientific device invented by Sir David Brewster in 1832 and mentioned in *Ten Thousand a Year*: "These were the few little bits of different colored glass in a mental kaleidoscope, which, turned capriciously round, produced those innumerable fantastic combinations out of the simple and ordinary events of the day, which we call *dreams*" (4:106).

Hardy's description of a bull that ran loose through the Casterbridge streets, "His horns were thick and tipped with brass; his two nostrils like the Thames Tunnel as seen in the perspective toys of yore" (*The Mayor of Casterbridge* [29:157]), referred to a peepshow representing the most famous London engineering feat of the time, the tunnel connecting Wapping and Rotherhithe. Commenced in 1825, it was finally opened to pedestrians in 1843 as an innovative tourist attraction. (Its souvenir stands, where such toys could be purchased, entitled it to be regarded as the world's first underwater shopping mall.) The tunnel itself furnished a simile to Jorrocks in *Handley Cross*. After being lost in the woods during a hunt, he finally arrives at Pigg's house, exclaiming, "Werry clever of the chap . . . runnin' to ground here—seems a capital house—wot a passage! like the Thames tunnel" (26:190).

Two by-products of the panorama idea catered to the public craving for geographical information entertainingly presented. One was James Wyld's Great Globe, a monstrous hollow sphere erected in Leicester Square to attract the crowds that flocked into London for the Crystal Palace exhibition in 1851. Wyld was a prominent map seller, and the structure was mainly intended as an advertising stunt. The globe's interior surface bore a colored relief map of the world, enabling spectators to view the earth inside out, as it were. A decade later, having outlived its novelty, it was a deteriorating eyesore, dominating a squalid neighborhood known as London's French quarter, when Thackeray wrote in *The Adventures of Philip* of his armchair travels at panoramas: "Algiers I have only seen from the sea; but New Orleans and Leicester Square I have visited; and have seen [in a rolling panorama-travelogue] a quaint old France still lingering on the banks of the Mississippi"—adding that he had also seen "a dingy modern France round that great Globe of Mr. Wyld's, which they say is coming to an end" (21:2.346)—as it soon did (1861). In *Mr. Facey Romford's Hounds*, Surtees used Wyld's unique structure as a timely means of describing another topicality, the crinoline. Mrs. Gowleykins, he wrote, wore "a hoop that made her look like 'the Great Globe itself'" (39:248).

Another derivative from the panorama was the popular entertainment conceived by, and starring, a prominent figure on the mid-century literary-theatrical scene, *Albert Smith's Ascent of Mont Blanc*, first produced at the Egyptian Hall in 1852. The recent completion of the railway to Chamonix, giving ready access to the mountain, had made Alpinism a topic of the day, which Smith promptly exploited by creating a show in which he recited comic monologues and sang topical songs against a background of Swiss scenery. In the expanded version (1853–54) of Surtees's *Handley Cross*, Jorrocks, now a master of foxhounds, likened a successful country hunt to an Albert Smith performance:

> "Dash my vig, if I could but get a clever feller like Leech to draw me a panorama o' the chase, with all my beauties goin' like beans—'eads up and sterns down, and a lot o' trumps ridin' as they should do—near enough to 'ear their sweet music, but not too near to prevent their swingin' and spreadin' like a rocket to make their own cast, I'd—I'd—I'd—bowl Halbert

Smith and his wite mountain and his black box right down Sin Jimses street into the Thames, and set hup i' the 'Giptian 'All myself." (32:260)

Later in the novel, faced with a steep hill in his pursuit of the fox, Jorrocks exclaimed, "Might as well try to follow Halbert Smith hup Mont Blanc as Arterxerxes [his mount] hup this incorrigible mountain . . . " (44:336).

Around 1830–35 there was a spate of mechanical exhibitions in London of whose presence Dickens took note, as he did other varieties of shows. Sam Weller was of the opinion that "The have-his-carcase [habeas corpus], next to the perpetual motion, is vun of the blessedest things as wos ever made. I've read that 'ere in the newspapers, wery of'en" (*Pickwick Papers*, 43:701). ("Blessedest" may reflect that fact that each new version of that perennial gleam in the nineteenth-century inventor's eye, the perpetual-motion machine, was regarded as a landmark on the way to that ultimate Utopia, a world run by inexhaustible and not only inexpensive but literally cost-free energy. In other contexts, though probably not here, it was a polite euphemism for "damnedest.") On another occasion, Sam again revealed his acquaintance with the newest sensations among London attractions: "Yes," he tells the ferociously cross-examining Serjeant Buzfuz during the trial of Bardell *versus* Pickwick, "I have a pair of eyes, and that's just it. If they wos a pair o' patent double million magnifyin' gas microscopes of hextra power, p'raps I might be able to see through a flight o' stairs and a deal door; but bein' only eyes, you see, my wision's limited" (34:573). At the moment *Pickwick Papers* appeared, rival proprietors of oxyhydrogen microscopes were locked in a battle of advertising in the course of which they raised the alleged magnifying power of their respective instruments from an initial 20,000–30,000 to an even higher figure than the one Sam cites, 2,500,000. During her research in newspapers of the early 1830s for *Middlemarch*, George Eliot undoubtedly came across mentions of the gas microscope (it was introduced early in 1833) and she made it figure, presciently, in Lydgate's mind in 1829 as he dreamed of the great work he might achieve in cellular research: "Here would be another light, as of oxyhydrogen, showing the very grain of things, and revising all former explanations . . ." (15:177–78).

In the 1830s and 1840s the chief site for the exhibition of inventions was the new Adelaide Gallery just off Trafalgar Square. In *Tancred* (1847) Disraeli said of the socially ambitious Mrs. Guy Flouncey, "Her self-possession . . . was the finest work of art [i.e., artifice] of the day, and ought to be exhibited at the Adelaide Gallery" (2.7:107). One of the most famous inventions shown at the gallery was the American entrepreneur Jacob Perkins's steam gun.[†] First demonstrated there in 1832, it was still emitting a fearful racket every hour on the hour when Dickens remarked in *Martin Chuzzlewit*, apropos of Jonas's assertion that no conscientious man's life should exceed the biblical threescore-and-ten, "Is any one surprised at Mr. Jonas making such a reference to such a book for such a purpose? Does any one doubt the old saw, that the Devil (being a layman) quotes Scripture for his own ends? If he will take the trouble to look about him, he may find a greater number of confirmations of the fact in the occurrences of any single day, than the steam-gun can discharge balls in a minute" (11:233), the advertised rate then being 1,050.

At this time, another application of steam—to nurturing life, not destroying it—was the patent egg hatchery, an early model of which was shown in London in 1824. In *The Caxtons* (1849) Bulwer-Lytton invented a paper called *The Capitalist*, which was devoted to various get-rich-quick schemes, including a machine that would enable the poor "to hatch chickens in ovens like the ancient Egyptians" (10.6:2.37). In that year a certain Cantelo was shrilly advertising and demonstrating his new and improved egg incubator under the slogan "Poultry for the Million!!" but readers might also have recalled the publicity for an earlier machine, the Eccaleobion (1839), "which," said its proprietor, "in the ungenial climate of England, realizes the greatest wonder of Egypt," though he did not say how its daily rate of production, a hundred chicks per machine, compared with the ancients'.

The name of George Wombwell (1778–1850) was synonymous with animal shows. From a nucleus of two boa constrictors he exhibited in London in 1804 he built up the largest menagerie in Britain, which he toured decade after decade through the provinces. According to the 1845 key to *Coningsby*, he was the gouty Mr. Cassilis in that novel. He was well remembered in Cranford for a visit when one of his lions ate a little child's arm, and in *Felix Holt* George Eliot wittily observed that to Mr. Pink, the saddler, the arrival of an official sent to monitor Treby Magna's first election "was like the existence of the young giraffe which Wombwell lately brought into those parts—it was to be contemplated, and not criticized" (28:228).[‡]

[†]An earlier reference to the American inventor occurred in T. H. Lister's *Granby* (1826). Two years earlier, Perkins had set up his "safety steam engine manufactory" at the junction of Albany Street and the New Road. It was there that he demonstrated his machine gun to the Duke of Wellington and other high-ranking military men (6 December 1825).

[‡]Here George Eliot momentarily nodded. Wombwell did not have a giraffe at that time. There had been one, a gift of the Pasha of Egypt in 1827, in the Royal Menagerie at

In the first thirty years of the century, the old Tower of London menagerie having lost most of its small company of neglected, despondent beasts, including the lions that had long ago provided the generic term for tourists' "sights," the mecca for animal-gazers was Exeter Change in the Strand. This smelly indoor zoo was the home of Londoners' favorite quadruped, the elephant Chunee. During the elder Sedley's merciless ribbing of his pompous son Jos, newly returned from India, he facetiously demanded that his elephant be ordered from Exeter Change. One of Chunee's engaging tricks was recalled in *Pickwick Papers*, when the roaring of the crowd during the Eatanswill election was, said Dickens, "like that of a whole menagerie when the elephant has rung the bell for the cold meat" (13:239).

Chunee unfortunately had to be killed in 1826—an event that plunged all London into mourning—and Exeter Change was torn down two years later. Simultaneously, the newly formed Zoological Society opened its spacious grounds in Regent's Park, an establishment whose topicality would grow as the collection of animals, and later birds and reptiles, increased. Having initially been open to members only, it became a popular public attraction, enjoying, year by year, ample coverage in the press. Dickens used the presiding lion of the day as a lead-in to his piece on literary lions in *Sketches by Boz* ("The Mudfog and Other Sketches," 676). Novelists found the animals and the people who gazed at them especially useful when they needed metaphors to describe some form of human body language. Zach Thorpe said of Mat Marksman in Collins's *Hide and Seek* that he "bolts his dinner like the lion in the Zoological Gardens" (2.10:440), and in *Armadale*, Lydia Gwilt wrote to her evil friend, Mother Oldershaw, "Did you ever see the boa-constrictor fed at the Zoological Gardens? They put a live rabbit into his cage, and there is a moment when the two creatures look at each other. I declare Mr. Bashwood reminded me of the rabbit!" (2.11:1.490). Emily Eden said of Mr. Willis in *The Semi-Detached House*, "The Hopkinsons all looked at him with the greatest commiseration, and with some curiosity, just as people stare when a fresh beast arrives at the Zoological Gardens" (22:195).

The Zoo acquired an aquarium in 1853, thus giving authoritative sanction to what a recent historian of naturalist studies in Britain has called "that enormously popular invention, the marine aquarium." Readers of the popularized books and articles the craze evoked in the early fifties "rushed off in . . . masses in frantic search of sea-anemones

Sandpit Gate, Windsor, but it died before these animals were transferred to the Regent's Park Zoo in 1830. The zoo did not acquire specimens of its own—four noble beasts that stirred great enthusiasm—until 1836.

and ferns. . . . Then, at length, the enthusiasms faded. Nine out of ten aquaria were thrown out or abandoned; . . . 'to all appearances, in the words of the Rev. J. G. Wood, the aquarium fever had run its course, never again to recur, like hundreds of similar epidemics.'"[2] It was this rage that Collins recalled in *No Name* (1862–63). In his house in Vauxhall Walk, Lambeth, Magdalen Vanstone's wicked cousin Noel kept on a table in his study

> a glass tank filled with water, and ornamented in the middle by a miniature pyramid of rock-work interlaced with weeds. Snails clung to the sides of the tank; tadpoles and tiny fish swam swiftly in the green water, slippery efts and slimy frogs twined their noiseless way in and out of the weedy rock-work; and on top of the pyramid there sat solitary, cold as the stone, brown as the stone, motionless as the stone, a little bright-eyed toad. (3.2:1.393)

"The art of keeping fish and reptiles as domestic pets," said Collins, "had not at that time [1846–48] been popularized in England," and so the aquarium was not attributed to Vanstone—he was himself a collector of inanimate foreign curiosities—but to his housekeeper's late husband, "Professor Lecomte, the eminent Swiss naturalist," who had bequeathed it to her as her sole legacy. Evading anachronism in this easy manner, Collins availed himself of his readers' remembrance of the recent craze to make a timely metaphor, an objective correlative really, for the slippery, slimy nature of the intrigue in which his assortment of villainous characters was engaged.

Concurrent with the marine biology vogue was one for fern collecting, which sent droves of amateur naturalists and commercial exploiters of the fashion into the shaded countryside in quest of specimens. This fleeting enthusiasm, too, left its imprint in fiction. In *Evan Harrington*, Mr. Goren, the London tailor in whose shop Evan worked, was "an enthusiastic fern-collector. Not that Mr. Harrington shared the passion, but the sight of these brown roots spread out, ticketed, on the stained paper, after supper, when the shutters were up and the house defended from the hostile outer world; the old man poring over them, and naming this and that spot where, during his solitary Saturday afternoon and Sunday excursions, he had lighted on the rare samples exhibited: this contrast of the quiet evening with the sordid day humanized Mr. Goren to him" (39:487).

2.

Unlike spending an afternoon looking at the big and little creatures in Regent's Park, staring at human freaks could not be rationalized as contributing to one's education, although showmen often advertised their grotesque attractions in an edifying vein. Until late in the century there was little of today's abhorrence of exhibiting nature's cruel mistakes for profit, and they could be written about without any embarrassment that might spring from pity; they were simply curiosities who happened to be alive.

Dickens and Surtees were especially given to making references to exhibited freaks. Miss Biffin, in particular, haunted Dickens's imagination—the woman born in 1784 without arms or legs who nevertheless taught herself to draw pencil and watercolor sketches with a pencil or brush held between her teeth. Featured in the several early nineteenth-century printed collections of stories about men and women remarkable for their peculiar physiques or accomplishments, Miss Biffin toured widely to demonstrate her incredible talent, and so she would have been known to most readers of *Nicholas Nickleby*, even though at the time Dickens wrote the novel she had been retired for a number of years.[†]

Miss Biffin had a place in Mrs. Nickleby's surreal confusion, which is nowhere better displayed than in her remark about her mad wooer on the other side of the fence: "There can be no doubt that he *is* a gentleman, and has the manners of a gentleman, and the appearance of a gentleman, although he does wear smalls and grey worsted stockings. That may be eccentricity, or he may be proud of his legs. I don't see why he shouldn't be. The Prince Regent was proud of his legs, and so was Daniel Lambert [of whom, more in a moment], who was also a fat man; *he* was proud of his legs. So was Miss Biffin: she was—no," Mrs. Nickleby reconsidered, "I think she had only toes, but the principle is the same" (*Nicholas Nickleby*, 37:567). In *Martin Chuzzlewit*, the theatrical Mr. Pip speaks of a mythical "Viscount" coming behind the scenes in search of an actress friend, "rather slued," and free-associating in the manner of Mrs. Nickleby:

> "Shakespeare's an infernal humbug, Pip! What's the good of Shakespeare, Pip? I never read him. What the devil is it all about, Pip? There's a lot of feet in Shakespeare's verse, but there ain't any legs worth mentioning in Shakespeare's plays, are there, Pip? Juliet, Desdemona, Lady Macbeth, and all the rest of 'em, whatever their names are, might as well have no legs at all, for anything the audience know about it, Pip. Why, in that respect they're all Miss Biffins to the audience, Pip." (28:523)

In *The Old Curiosity Shop*, meanwhile, Dickens had described the arrival at the Jolly Sandboys inn of two rain-soaked showmen, one of whom

---

[†]She had been married in 1824. Two years after *Nicholas Nickleby* was published, she returned to public notice when it was learned that she was living in "reduced circumstances" in Liverpool, her only income being a royal annuity of £12.

was "the proprietor of a giant, and a little lady without legs or arms" (19:203). Though Miss Biffin is not named, every reader would have known whom Dickens meant. He referred to her once more, in *Little Dorrit*, when Mr. Merdle, who walked around with each hand clasping the opposite wrist as if he were handcuffed, "came creeping in with not much more appearance of arms in his sleeves than if he had been the twin brother of Miss Biffin . . ." (2.18:691).

When Jorrocks spoke of her in *Handley Cross* he felt obliged to explain who she was: "Rot ye, do ye think I'm like Miss Biffin, the unfortunate lady without harms or legs, that I can't 'elp myself?" (39:309) Obviously, on this occasion at least, Surtees did not have Dickens's confidence in his readers' ability to interpret his allusions. Neither he nor any other novelist, it seems, felt obliged to identify Miss Biffin's closest rival among famous nineteenth-century English freaks, who played the heavy to her fragile, pathetic ingenue part. This was Daniel Lambert, the fattest man ever exhibited in England (1806–9), 714 pounds at the top of his form. Mrs. Nickleby notwithstanding, he could not have been proud of his legs for the simple reason that he never saw them; whatever pride he felt must have derived from the reports of disinterested observers. He immediately became the abiding exemplar of terminal obesity. Mr. Wardle's Fat Boy (*Pickwick Papers*, 7:157) was called "the infant Lambert" (during the real Lambert's first London season, an outsize infant named Master Wybrant had been exhibited as "Mr. Lambert in Miniature"). When the drunken Jos Sedley sang a song during the disastrous evening at Vauxhall, the bystanders cried "Brayvo, Fat un! Angcore, Daniel Lambert!" (*Vanity Fair*, 6:58). In Thackeray's *Lovel the Widower* (1860), his persona, "the bachelor of Beak Street," exclaimed of a waistcoat he had worn long ago at a Dublin ball, "Lord!—Lord! it would no more meet round my waist now than round Daniel Lambert!" (1:64)

But Lambert as a standard of comparison came into his own most often in Surtees's novels. It was either poverty of imagination or an obscure fixation that led Surtees, throughout his writing career, to invoke the celebrated fat man, beginning with *Jorrocks' Jaunts and Jollities*: "His male *vis-à-vis* [dancing aboard an excursion steamer] was a waistcoatless young Daniel Lambert, in white ducks, and a blue dress-coat, with a carnation in his mouth" (7:113). Lambert's substantial ghost reappeared at least nine times in Surtees's succeeding novels, and on five of those occasions in identical metaphors:

> In an instant, two tall, highly-powdered footmen, in rich scarlet and white lace-bedaubed liveries, threw wide the folding-doors as though they expected Daniel Lambert, or the great Durham ox [another celebrated showpiece], exhibiting a groom of the chamber and a lusty porter, laying down the newspapers. . . . (*Handley Cross*, 26:189)

Although Daniel Lambert died in 1809, the image of his commanding figure was preserved in numerous show-business pictures and political cartoons. There was no need for an artist like Leech to refresh readers' memories on the numerous occasions on which his name was invoked in Surtees's novels.

Spigot, with his attendants in livery, here put a stop to the confab by hurrying past, drawing the bolts, and throwing back the spacious folding doors, as if royalty or Daniel Lambert himself were "coming out." (*Mr. Sponge's Sporting Tour*, 22 : 123)

". . . a couple of gigantic footmen threw back the portals, as if Daniel Lambert or the Durham ox were about to emerge instead of his slim antiquated lordship." (*Young Tom Hall's Heart-Aches and Horses*, 38 : 291)

". . . the powdered footmen threw back the folding-doors as if they expected Daniel Lambert or the Durham Ox to enter." (*Ask Mamma*, 19 : 73)

. . . the great doors . . . were thrown open as if Daniel Lambert himself were coming. (*Plain or Ringlets?*, 43:153)

A contemporary of Lambert, whose weight, however, was concentrated in one part of the anatomy, was Saartje Baartmann, a South African woman known professionally as "the Hottentot Venus," whose "posterial luxuriance," as Carlyle called it in *Sartor Resartus*, was exhibited to great acclaim, and only mild disapproval, in London in 1810. When George Osborne's father presses him to marry the rich mulatto, Miss Swartz, who was Becky Sharp's schoolmate, George bursts out, "Marry that mulatto woman? I don't like the colour, sir. Ask the black that sweeps opposite Fleet Market, sir. *I'm* not going to marry a Hottentot Venus" (*Vanity Fair*, 21:204). Elderly readers of *Vanity Fair* in 1847–48 would have enjoyed a mental image unavailable to younger readers unless they happened to have run across one of the several contemporary political caricatures in which Baartmann was featured. They would also have appreciated, as younger readers could not, the allusion in *Young Tom Hall's Heart-Aches and Horses* to Lord Heartycheer's prizing in his gallery a copy of Hiram Powers's statue of the Greek Slave, "that," in his words, "was so much run after by all the young gentlemen at the Great Exhibition. . . . The figure's beautiful—very beautiful, certainly—full and voluptuous, without Hottentot Venusish exaggeration about it" (40:319–20). This was an instance, certainly, of a topical allusion serving to clarify a mental image. Lingering memory of her remarkable attribute added a slightly ribald overtone to one of Surtees's several jokes about crinolines in *Plain or Ringlets?*: "We often think it fortunate for the Hottentot Venus that she lived when she did, for she would never have made anything by showing herself now-a-days" (7:14). Perhaps the oldest readers of fiction in the 1870s, contemplating the latest fad in "dorsal excrescences," as Trollope called them—bustles—would have regarded it as Saartje rediviva.

At the other end of the scale (literally) was Claude Seurat, the fearfully emaciated Frenchman, victim of some wasting disease, who was exhibited as "the living skeleton" in 1825. He aroused more pity than did most of his fellow freaks, but this is not apparent in Dickens's allusions to him. "Here's your servant, sir," said Sam Weller to Mr. Pickwick. "Proud o' the title, as the Living Skellinton said, ven they show'd him" (*Pickwick Papers*, 15:288). (Sam was referring with some exaggeration to Seurat's purported reply to humanitarians who denounced his exhibitors that, far from feeling exploited, he would earn enough money to "return and live at my ease in my native country.") This was meant as pure humor, however tasteless it strikes us today. But when Mr. Dombey remarked, in reference to little Paul's aching bones, "He is not a living

The Editor's Visits to Claude Ambroise Seurat,

EXHIBITED IN PALL MALL UNDER THE APPELLATION OF THE

ANATOMIE VIVANTE; or, **LIVING SKELETON!**

Thou com'st in such a questionable shape,
That I will speak to thee.   *Shakspeare.*

No. 33.

Incongruous or even shocking as it may seem, this is the
mental image Dickens's readers would have had when Mr.
Dombey made his ill-judged remark about little Paul and the
living skeleton. The picture is from William Hone's *Every-
Day Book* (1825–27).

skeleton, I suppose," (*Dombey and Son*, 8:156)† readers' memory of
Seurat, long since mercifully dead, would have induced them to respond
to Dombey's unwitting callousness as Dickens wanted them to do.

Next in the procession of sensational freak shows that contributed
topicalities to fiction were the Siamese Twins, Chang and Eng, first exhibited in London in 1829. As genuine anomalies, they attracted serious
scientific attention, and, like panoramas, dioramas, phantasmagorias,
and kaleidoscopes, they enriched the language, furnishing a term that
could be applied, jokingly or in earnest, to any kind of close connection.
In *Nicholas Nickleby*, Dickens used them in an unusually sophisticated
way when he likened Cadogan Place's relationship to aristocratic Belgravia and "the barbarism of Chelsea" to "the ligament which unites the
Siamese twins, [and which] contains something of the life and essence of
two distinct bodies, and yet belongs to neither" (21:339). In *Martin
Chuzzlewit*, the twins served another purpose, graphic rather than geographical, as they completed Dickens's description of a stove in Mrs.
Pawkins's New York boardinghouse, "garnished on either side with a
great brass spittoon, and shaped in itself like three little iron barrels set
up on end in a fender, and joined together on the principle of the Siamese Twins" (16:329). In *Handley Cross*, Surtees described the peculiar
walk of Jorrocks and Captain Doleful: "thereupon they joined hands
and advanced into the balcony, like the Siamese twins, amid the uproarious applause of the meeting" (11:85).

After the death of the sea captain who brought them to London, the
twins fell under the management of P. T. Barnum, who turned them
into one of his most lucrative attractions. Less is heard in the novels of
another celebrated Barnum property, General Tom Thumb. Jorrocks,
however, presumably believing that any freak, however diminutive, was
a cannibal, used him as the ogre with whom to frighten a page boy
into swearing a solemn oath: "mind you speak the truth, otherwise
I'll—I'll—make a present on you to General Tom Thumb" (*Hillingdon
Hall*, 30:302).

Another of Barnum's ventures, a decidedly less successful one, left a
small mark in fiction. Hervio Nano, the Gnome Fly, otherwise known as
Hervey Leech, was a misshapen but agile American performer whom
the great impresario brought to London in 1846 as "the Wild Man of
the Prairies" or the "What Is It?". Clothed in a hairy ape's costume and
touted as the long missing and now finally discovered link between man

†The term had become generic in show-business parlance following Seurat's pitiable
notoriety. Sairey Gamp described a specimen of the type as being exhibited at Greenwich
Fair, in company with a "sweet infant . . . kep in spirits in a bottle," "the pink-eyed lady,"
and the "Prooshan dwarf" (*Martin Chuzzlewit*, 52:893).

and the orang-utan, he uttered blood-curdling cries, devoured raw meat, and rattled the bars of his cage at the Egyptian Hall. The press discovered the deception within a week and the exhibition hastily closed, but Charles Reade remembered the Gnome Fly ten years later in *It Is Never Too Late to Mend,* when he described the central locale of this thesis novel on prison reform, a "massive castellated building, glaring red brick with white stone corners," with the gatekeeper's lodge at the entrance, "a small house constructed in the same style as the grand pile." "The castle," Reade wrote, "is massive and grand: this, its satellite, is massive and tiny, like the frog doing his little bit of bull,—like Signor Hervio Nano, a tremendous thick dwarf now no more" (10:1.128). (He had died, some said of embarrassment, soon after the fraud was exposed.)

Reade seems to have had the same taste for freaks of a later vintage that Dickens and Surtees had for earlier ones. Julia Pastrana, the bearded "Baboon Lady," another alleged type of missing link said to have been reared by her Indian mother among bears and monkeys somewhere in Central America, was exhibited in London in 1857. In *A Terrible Temptation* (1871), Reade, in the persona of the lawyer-novelist Rolfe, expounds to Lady Bassett his theory, relevant to the plot, of "reversion in race":

> Perhaps there is Moorish blood in your family, and here [in the person of her putative son] it has revived: you look incredulous, but there are plenty of examples, ay, and stronger than this; every child that is born resembles some progenitor: how then do you account for Julia Pastrana, a young lady who dined with me last week, and sang me 'Ah, perdona,' rather feebly, in the evening.[†] Bust and figure like any other lady, hands exquisite, arms neatly turned, but with long silky hair from the elbow to the wrist. Face, ugh! forehead made of black leather, eyes all pupil, nose an excrescence, chin pure monkey, face all covered with hair; briefly, a type extinct ten thousand years before Adam, yet it could revive at this time of day." (37:361–62)

In all probability Reade took this description from a handbill or newspaper advertisement he had pasted into one of his enormous scrapbooks. Understandably, he suppressed the grisly sequel to Julia Pastrana's story, which the newspaper advertising columns reported in 1861. She had died in Moscow and was then brought, in an embalmed state, to be reexhibited in Piccadilly, "attired in the costume and placed

---

[†]The stronger voice of a collaborative tenor could have compensated for the weakness of hers, because "Ah, perdona al primo affetto" is a duet, not an aria, as Reade implies. *La Clemenza di Tito,* where it occurs, was one of Mozart's most popular operas in early Victorian England.

in the attitude of a danseuse," and so, said her posthumous manager, there was "nothing in the Exhibition to offend the taste or disturb the sensibility of even the most fastidious lady."

Whatever faint performing talents curiosities like Julia Pastrana (and even the Living Skeleton) possessed were decidedly secondary to their bizarre physical traits. The two celebrated male performers outside the theatre who were remembered in Victorian fiction had splendid physiques, but what they did was more important than how they looked. Giovanni Belzoni, mendaciously billed as "the Patagonian Samson," was a weight lifter who toured England during the Napoleonic Wars and then entered a second, more widely publicized career as an explorer and collector of antiquities in Egypt. It was in the latter role that Dickens several times referred to him. He supplied a comparison in *Sketches by Boz*. "The stranger who finds himself in 'The [Seven] Dials' for the first time, and stands Belzoni-like, at the entrance of seven obscure passages, uncertain which to take . . ." (Scenes," chap. 5:69) alluded to an episode Belzoni described in his *Narrative of the Operations and Recent Discoveries within the Pyramids, Temples, Tombs, and Excavations in Egypt and Nubia*, published in connection with the exhibition of his booty in 1821. Belzoni died two years later, but as late as 1855, in *Little Dorrit*, Dickens depended on his readers to recognize the name when he described "the illuminated windows of a Congregationless Church [in the City] that seemed to be waiting for some adventurous Belzoni to dig it out and discover its history" (1.3:70). Belzoni's Egypt was one of the subjects about which Miss Twinkleton, proprietress of the young ladies' boarding school at Cloisterham in *The Mystery of Edwin Drood*, was lengthily boring. "Tiresome old burying-grounds!" complained Rosa Bud, one of her pupils, "Isises, and Ibises, and Cheopses, and Pharaohses; who cares about them? And then there was Belzoni or somebody, dragged out by the legs, half choked with bats and dust. All the girls say serve him right, and hope it hurts him, and wish he had been quite choked" (3:59). The intrepid Egyptologist's adventures still were not forgotten, but it is evident that some young ladies thought it high time they were.

Toward the end of his early career as a circus performer, Belzoni invented an act in which he used his magnificent musculature to strike poses that imitated famous antique statues, of the Gladiator, Hercules, and Achilles among others. Within a few years, the other great athlete-showman of the time, Andrew Ducrow, put Belzoni's act on horseback and enlarged it into a daring equestrian display in which, posing as Mercury or Zephyr, he rode five galloping horses at once and drove a total of nine. For many years this was the star turn at Astley's Royal Amphitheatre, which Kit Nubbins and his guests in *The Old Curiosity Shop*

Even at a time when a man could change his occupation with relative
ease, Giovanni Belzoni's seemingly effortless metamorphosis from professional strong man to renowned Egyptologist was bound to attract
attention and preserve his name long after his death in 1823.

watched in amazement. (When Colonel Newcome took his nieces and
nephews there, the bill was headed by a depiction of the battle of Waterloo, featuring, of course, the great cavalry charge.) Setting the time of
one scene in *Sketches by Boz*, Dickens noted that Astley's "was not a 'Royal
Amphitheatre' in those days, nor had Ducrow arisen to shed the light of
classic taste and portable gas over the sawdust of the circus" ("Scenes,"
chap. 11 : 104).

Ducrow's expert melding of daring horsemanship with show business

naturally was not overlooked by Surtees. In *Handley Cross* he described
Captain Doleful's mare: "A rare-actioned beast it was too! Up and down,
up and down, it went, so light and so easy, and making so little progress withal, that Ducrow himself might have envied the possession of
it" (9:76). In *Plain or Ringlets?* he recalled an anecdote about "poor
Ducrow," who had died seventeen years earlier (1842). He "was overheard exclaiming one night, when it was his turn to go upon the stage
to represent Autumn in the allegorical piece called the 'Seasons,' "Ow the
'ell can I play Hautumn without the happles?'" (52:193).[†] Meredith
probably had Ducrow in mind when, adding a dash of period color to
Evan Harrington, he had a wagoner chuckle, "Warn't he like that Myzep-
per chap, I see at the circus, bound athert gray mare!" (10:121). Ducrow
was equally famous for his wild ride, inspired by Byron's *Mazeppa*, which
was first performed at Astley's in 1831. Numerous Victorian horses, including John Mellish's in *Aurora Floyd*, were named for the hero.

With the notable exception of Sleary's Horse Riding in *Hard Times*,
traveling circuses seldom figured in Victorian fiction. In Collins's *Hide
and Seek*, published in the same year (1854), there was a brief scene in a
circus that starred the "Mysterious Foundling," a deaf and dumb girl
who was named "Madonna" and served as the mute heroine, a rather
challenging role for a novelist to make credible. In the early scenes of
What Will He Do With It? Bulwer-Lytton described, though with none of
the vivid authenticity Dickens achieved in the Crummles and Jarley episodes in *The Old Curiosity Shop*, a fair in a Surrey village, where a grandfather and granddaughter exhibit a learned dog.

By Victorian times, the waxwork side of the entertainment business
was dominated by Madame Tussaud, who settled in London in 1834
after many years on the road. Her second-rate rivals on the country
circuit, typified by Mrs. Jarley, had been relatively uninterested in keeping up with the times in their selection of famous people to be exhibited
in wax. It is true that Mrs. Jarley had once shown the great comedian
Joseph Grimaldi, who died in 1837, three years before *The Old Curiosity
Shop* was published, but she had since converted him into Lindley Mur-

[†]This seems to be one of the anecdotes told of the profane and uncultured Ducrow
that floated in the oral tradition but was not printed except in Surtees's novel; at least, it is
not included in the large roundup of Ducrow apocrypha in A. H. Saxon's exhaustive biography of the star equestrian. The most famous Ducrowism undoubtedly is one that
illustrated his gift for malapropism: "Cut out the dialect [dialogue] and come to the 'osses,"
spoken on some occasion when a literary work was being trimmed down to the capabilities
of Astley's tanbark riding space. In the corrupt form in which it comes down to us, as in
George Moore's *A Mummer's Wife*—"cut the cackle and get to the 'osses"—its malapropian
origin is lost. (*The Life and Art of Andrew Ducrow* [Hamden, Conn., 1978], p. 179.)

ray, the grammarian (died 1825), as she also converted a celebrated murderess into Hannah More, the author of improving tales for the young (died 1833), in deference to the putative interests of Miss Monflathers's pupils. Some of the girls screamed when they detected vestiges of Lord Byron in the made-over figure of Mary Queen of Scots. The costumed and ferocious-looking brigand figure that was used to advertise the show in the town streets probably was meant to exploit the fashion for robber-outlaws that was reflected in James Robinson Planché's adaptation of a French brigand story, *The Brigand Chief*, first performed at Drury Lane Theatre in November 1829, and shortly thereafter in Auber's opera *Fra Diavolo*, among other manifestations.

Unlike Mrs. Jarley, and in harmony with the novelists, Madame Tussaud sought—and found—riches in exploiting the public's ever-growing interest in current events. One of the centerpieces in her display was a richly costumed and mounted tableau of the Queen's coronation, and among the figures there and elsewhere on the platforms were realistic effigies of politicians (Peel, O'Connell, Brougham, Lord John Russell, Cobbett) and men and women of the stage (Charles Kean, Macready, Ellen Tree, Jenny Lind). Although some of these were permanently installed, signifying their lasting fame, many others came and went as public interest in them fluctuated. There was no more reliable index of popular topicality in Victorian London than the current mix of personalities at Tussaud's.

One public attraction, balloon ascents, was free to all, unless one wished to watch the event close up at one of London's several launching sites—Vauxhall, Surrey Gardens, or occasionally some other pleasure garden with the requisite space. Strictly speaking, manned balloons were no novelty, the first ascent from London having taken place as long ago as 1784. But it was not until the post-Waterloo years that they were taken more or less seriously, as a futuristic form of transport. Notwithstanding a few abortive attempts to demonstrate the practicality of air travel, however, ballooning amounted to no more than an adjunct to show business in the Victorian era. The big, brightly colored, spinning-top-shaped bags with one or two venturesome aeronauts in the swaying wicker basket underneath were as much new signs of man's conquest of natural forces as were steam locomotives, but they had no such place in the store of topicalities as railways did. The only description of a balloon ascension in remembered fiction was Emily Eden's in *The Semi-Attached Couple*, in which, as was often the custom, it was the highlight of a local celebration, in this case the grand opening of a town bridge.

Most of the references to balloons in novels were incidental, used as recognizable symbols of modernity or convenient metaphors of daredevilry or airborne speed. The "ancient inhabitants" in the neighborhood

When *Sketches by Boz* was reissued in parts in 1837–39, the publishers were well advised to have a wrapper featuring a balloon ascension. It was their way of intimating to potential buyers that one of the book's chief delights was its topicality.

of Todgers' boardinghouse "held ballooning to be sinful, and deplored the degeneracy of the times," and Sairey Gamp, discoursing learnedly to Poll Sweedlepipe on the symptomatology of "fevers of the mind," declared, "You may make yourself as light as any gash balloon, [b]ut talk, when you're wrong in your head and when you're in your sleep, of certain things; and you'll be heavy in your mind" (*Martin Chuzzlewit*, 9:187; 29:533). The names of famous aeronauts were sometimes invoked, as personalities repeatedly in the news. Dickens mentioned one of them, Charles Green, in *Sketches by Boz*, and in *Jorrocks' Jaunts and Jollities* Surtees spoke of Mrs. Graham, a member of the husband-and-wife team who often lifted off from the Sadler's Wells tea garden. Thackeray brought ballooning into his excursus in *Pendennis* on the professional author as economic man: "When you want to make money by Pegasus (as he must, perhaps, who has no other saleable property), farewell poetry and aërial flights; Pegasus only rises now like Mr. Green's balloon, at periods advertised beforehand, and when the spectators' money has been paid" (36:1.361.). But balloon metaphors were most frequently useful during the crinoline craze, when time after time, as the examples from Thackeray, Collins, and Surtees have already shown, they provided a ready hyperbolic analogue to that voluminous—and from the male viewpoint ridiculous—article of a woman's costume.

3.

One of Madame Tussaud's stellar attractions as she put down her roots in London was her models of the Edinburgh "resurrection men" Burke and Hare, the revelation of whose wholesale traffic in fresh cadavers for the anatomical lecture room had shocked the nation in the last days of 1828. In response to popular demand, she made a practice of displaying effigies of celebrated malefactors alongside royalty and politicians. Setting aside two rooms formerly devoted to Napoleonic relics, whose topicality was beginning to fade, she developed what by 1843 came to be called the Chamber of Horrors, a gruesome and always well-patronized three-dimensional supplement to the newspapers' crime coverage. Here relevant weapons and other artifacts added realism to the waxen figures of a notorious murderer and his (occasionally her) victim, sometimes dressed in the very clothes they had worn. In *Pendennis*, Arthur walked past the window of Bays's Club in St. James's Street with his friend Popjoy, an aspiring novelist.

> "Look!" said Popjoy to Pen, as they passed, "did you ever pass Bays's at four o'clock, without seeing that collection of old fogies? It's a regular museum. They ought to be cast in wax, and set up at Madame Tussaud's"—

"—In a chamber of old horrors by themselves," Pen said, laughing.
"—In the chamber of horrors! Gad, dooced good!" Pop cried.
"They *are* old rogues, most of 'em, and no mistake . . ."
They were only momentarily discomfited when one of the old rogues in the window proved to be Pen's uncle. (36:1.370)

The Victorians inherited from their fathers an insatiable relish for reading about murders in newspapers and the so-called gallows literature of ad hoc pamphlets and broadsides hawked in the streets, visiting the scene of the crime, and seeing it reenacted on the stage and frozen in waxworks. Homicide was an impromptu entertainment industry, the avid spectator never knowing when, where, or under whose auspices the next sensational episode would unfold. Fascination with murder—always domestic, never political, as on the Continent—knew no bounds of class or gender. Tennyson, Browning, Edward FitzGerald, Walter Pater, and Thomas and Jane Carlyle, among others, eagerly scanned the newspaper coverage of especially engrossing murders. George Eliot read the newspaper crime columns and discussed selected cases in letters to her friends.

In Emily Eden's *The Semi-Detached House* (1859) the genteel, elderly Mrs. Hopkinson made no apology for her taste:

"it seems there is such a grand murder in the paper—you must find it and read it to me, girls; a whole family poisoned by the father—just think of John poisoning us at breakfast, or, indeed, of his meddling with my tea-pot; and Lord Chester and Doctor Ayscough said such clever things about poisons; I thought I would remember them for fear of accidents; but I am not quite certain whether I have not forgotten part. However, I know it is not wholesome to take strychnine in any great quantity, so mind that, girls; arsenic, which is very apt to get into puddings and gruel, should be avoided, and you should take something after it, if you do swallow any—but I forget what. It was really very interesting, and I like a good murder that can't be found out; that is, of course, it is very shocking, but I like to hear about it." (17:147–48)

The lady had recently had ample opportunity to learn about poisons; in three successive years (1856–58) there had been as many sensational cases involving murder by poison, and the newspapers and magazines were full of articles about the alleged efficacy of arsenic for clearing the complexion, the pretext under which more than one female murderer, then and later, obtained the largely uncontrolled toxic substance.

Sir Walter Scott's keen interest in crime, which led him to collect criminal narratives and printed records of trials for his library at Abbotsford, set a distinguished example for Victorian novelists. Dickens as a child devoured the weekly issues of a rousing periodical called *The Terrific Register*, "making myself unspeakably miserable, and frightening

THIRST FOR——INFORMATION.

" Please, Ma'am, have you done with Yesterday's Paper? There 's a
dreadful Murder in it, I should like to read about."

Beginning with a trio of sensational domestic murders in 1856–58, middle-class women were thought to have become as avid followers of homicide in the news reports as their husbands had long been. According to this drawing in *Punch* for 4 July 1874, maidservants unapologetically came to share this taste with their mistresses.

the very wits out of my head, for the charge of a penny weekly; which considering that there was an illustration to every number, in which there was always a pool of blood, and at least one body, was cheap."[3] In *Household Words* he printed several of his own articles on contemporary

FATAL FACILITY; OR, POISONS FOR THE ASKING.

Even before the murders in the mid-fifties revealed the ease with which poison could be bought over the counter for "household purposes," including homicide, *Punch* (8 September 1849) commented on the absence of regulation. "*Child*. 'Please, Mister, will you be so good as to fill this bottle again with Lodnum, and let Mother have another pound and a half of Arsenic for the rats(!).' *Duly Qualified Chemist*: 'Certainly, Ma'am. Is there any other article?'" "Lodnum" (laudanum), an uncontrolled substance, was often used as aspirin is today, and in appropriately large dosage it could, like arsenic, be administered with lethal intent.

murderers. Like Scott, he visited murder scenes—in Norfolk, the Jermy-Rush tragedy; in America, at the Harvard Medical School, the Webster-Parkman affair; near his Kentish home, the spot in Cobham Park where the deranged young artist Richard Dadd fatally stabbed his father. Thackeray indulged in the not always appreciated whimsy of giving the footman the name of a currently celebrated murderer when he was about to be announced at an evening party. Newspaper clippings and other printed documents relating to murders abounded in Charles Reade's scrapbooks of source material.

Although hundreds of homicides were reported in the press each year, only a dozen or so achieved classic status by virtue of their having peculiar, crowd-pleasing features that set them apart from the ruck. The selective fame of these few great murderers, whom novelists alluded to again and again, was assisted by Madame Tussaud's memorializing them in permanent exhibits in the dimly lighted Chamber of Horrors.

When a mid-Victorian novelist mentioned a famous murder committed several decades earlier, only elderly or middle-aged men and women may have remembered reading newspaper accounts or seeing one of the melodramas loosely based on it, but its outlines and salient particulars remained the common possession of new generations. In Payn's *Lost Sir Massingberd* (1864), set early in the century, the narrator and his friend, searching for the missing evil baronet in London, come upon a procession bearing a corpse that is accompanied by a howling mob. The lost Sir Massingberd? No: a murderer named Williams, who "had committed suicide two days before, to escape, it was thought, not so much the scaffold, as the execrations of his fellow-creatures" (26:243). Although the crime had occurred over a half-century earlier (1811), Payn's readers would have recognized it at once—the gruesome Ratcliffe Highway murders, immortalized, on the highest level of literary interest, by Thomas DeQuincey in "On Murder, Considered as One of the Fine Arts" (*Blackwood's Magazine*, February 1827), and on a lower level by more than the usual outpouring of cheap pamphlets.

The historian G. M. Trevelyan once remarked that the event that most caught the public fancy in the dozen years between the trial of Queen Caroline in 1820 and the passage of the First Reform Bill was the murder in 1823, in an obscure Hertfordshire lane, of a gambler and promoter of crooked fights, William Weare, by an equally shady sportsman named John Thurtell. Sir Walter Scott made a pilgrimage to the scene—it might almost be called a sentimental journey—five years after the event. The name Thurtell, or recognizable variants of it, repeatedly turned up in novels in the next few years. Tyrrell was the villain in Lister's *Granby* (1826), and two years later, in Bulwer's *Pelham*, a gambler,

Sir John Tyrrell (whose name Bulwer had actually taken from his friend William Godwin's novel *Caleb Williams*—the echo of "Thurtell" was a windfall), was murdered in a lonely lane for the £2,000 he had on his person. The real-life Thurtell provided the partial model for the novel's gambler-sportsman murderer, Tom Thornton. As Albert Borowitz has recently pointed out in his definitive account of the case, Bulwer's description of Pelham's discovery of Tyrrell's body mirrored the press reports of the discovery of Weare's five years earlier.[4] There are also sinister reminders of Thurtell and Weare in *Martin Chuzzlewit*: Jonas's receiving instruction from Dr. Jobling on the technique of throat-slitting, his carriage ride in a storm, and his waylaying and murdering his accomplice Tigg Montague in a dark wood.

Only a most attentive reader, however, and one steeped in the trial record, would have noticed Dickens's hidden allusion to the case long afterward in *Our Mutual Friend*, when, at a fair in a Thames-side village, "A Fat Lady, perhaps in part sustained upon postponed pork, her professional associate being a Learned Pig, displayed her life-size picture in a low dress as she appeared when presented at Court, several yards round" (a crinoline, no doubt) (4.5:757–58). The "postponed pork" referred to an exchange between a lawyer and a witness, the maidservant at the house to which the murderers repaired after stowing their victim's body under a hedge. It was supper time, but Thurtell, nauseated by memories of Weare's copiously flowing blood, had no appetite. "Was the supper postponed?" asked the lawyer. "I don't know," the girl replied. "It was pork."

Following Thurtell there were Burke and Hare, caterers to Dr. Knox's anatomical demonstration room. In addition to the combined frisson and revulsion that the Edinburgh resurrection men stirred in the entire British population as their systematic murders for profit were revealed in the courtroom and thence in the press, one of the partners gave the English language a new word. When Sam Weller told Mr. Pickwick about the "Celebrated Sassage factory" "where the mysterious disappearance of a 'spectable tradesman took place four year ago," Pickwick was brought up short: "You don't mean to say he was burked, Sam?" (*Pickwick Papers*, 31:509). The verb, which Pickwick used several years before it was invented, referred to the nefarious pair's preference for suffocating their victims. The "Celebrated Sassage factory" alluded to another gruesome item in murder lore, the legend of Sweeney Todd, the barber in Fleet Street whose chair was equipped to dump an unlucky occupant into the cellar, where he was converted into oven-fresh pies for the restaurant trade. It was to Sweeney Todd that Dickens referred in *Martin Chuzzlewit*, when, as we saw earlier (page 385), he described Tom

Pinch's arrival in London: "Tom's evil genius did not lead him into the dens of any of those preparers of cannibalistic pastry, who are represented in many standard country legends as doing a lively retail business in the Metropolis. . . ."

It was about this time that Becky Sharp Crawley, as Thackeray later reported in *Vanity Fair*, employed a firm of solicitors named Burke, Thurtell, and Hayes. The junior partner was named for Christopher Hayes, an innkeeper who was murdered by his wife Catherine in 1725. This famous murder story was revived in a popular Surrey Theatre melodrama in 1833, *Jonathan Bradford; or, The Murder at the Roadside Inn*, and it was retold in fictional form in *Catherine* (*Fraser's Magazine*, 1839–40), Thackeray's response to the current glamorizing of criminals in the Newgate novels of Bulwer-Lytton and Ainsworth.

After Burke and Hare came James Greenacre, who murdered his washerwoman-mistress and deposited parts of her body at several London sites (1836). In "Sketches of Young Couples" (*Sketches by Boz*, 590), a character bragged that he rode "in the same omnibus with Mr. Greenacre, when he carried his victim's head about town in a blue bag" (as attested to by Greenacre himself), and later in the same series Mr. Blubb delivered a lecture before the Mudfog Association "upon the cranium before him, clearly showing that Mr. Greenacre possessed the organ of destructiveness to a most unusual extent" ("The Mudfog and Other Sketches," 666)—one of the many references to the pseudoscience of phrenology found in the fiction of the time. (The supposed skull turns out to be a coconut.) Thackeray's use of the same crime was more clever. In *Catherine* the fictive narrator, Ikey Solomons, Jr., referred to the bucolic atmosphere of the Edgware Road on the edge of London, as it was at the time of the story. "Here, then, in the midst of green fields and sweet air—before ever omnibuses were, and when Pineapple Turnpike and Terrace were alike unknown—here stood Tyburn: and on the road towards it, perhaps to enjoy the prospect, stood, in the year 1725, the habitation of Mr. John Hayes" (8:613). Behind the approaching murder of Hayes lurked another, more recent atrocity: Greenacre's. Thackeray's readers would have picked up the multiple clues. The Pineapple Turnpike on the Edgware Road was one of the places where Greenacre had disposed of his victim's remains; "before omnibuses were" slyly alluded to the unusual parcel he carried on successive buses; and "green fields" had obvious overtones of "Greenacre." Thus Thackeray brought into momentary conjunction a century-old London murder and one that had barely disappeared from the newspapers as he wrote.

At that same time, unknown to the public, a new candidate for celebrity in the criminal line had been busy.[5] Early in the year 1828, at whose close the Burke and Hare operation came to light, Thomas Griffiths

Wainewright, painter, art critic, and member of literary circles to which
Lamb, Hazlitt, and DeQuincey belonged, did away with his uncle, from
whom he expected to inherit a large sum—larger, in fact, than the estate
proved to contain. Two years later, an insurance fraud he cooked up
claimed the lives (by poisoning) of his wife's sister and his mother-in-law.
The Eagle Insurance Company, its suspicions aroused, declined to pay,
whereupon the brazen Wainewright, who had meanwhile fled to France
to escape his creditors, sued it. When the case was finally tried in 1835,
the poisoning episodes were disclosed, but the evidence was insufficient
to make a case and so Wainewright was not charged; the jury found for
the insurance company in the civil action. But the case did not end there.
In 1837, only days before the new Queen's accession, Wainewright was
convicted of having forged a power of attorney by which to defraud the
Bank of England and was sentenced to a life term in Van Diemen's Land.
Six years later, Dickens interwove elements of the story with those derived from Thurtell in *Martin Chuzzlewit*, in which Jonas tries to poison
his father to hasten receipt of his estate.

Almost simultaneously (1844), Bulwer-Lytton used Wainewright as
the model for Gabriel Varney, the villain in *Lucretia*. Although Varney's
career differed widely from Wainewright's, the novelist, in the true spirit
of Victorian documentary realism, went to the length of obtaining from
the Eagle Company the papers it had recovered from his French refuge
when he was arrested. Later, in *Ask Mamma* (1857–58), Surtees worked
the poisoner into a passage commenting on the current rage for speculative joint banks and the inflation that affected people's notions of how
much they could comfortably live on—or pretend to possess:

> Since our friend Warren wrote his admirable novel, *Ten Thousand a Year*,
> that sum has become the fashionable income for exaggerators. Nobody that
> has anything a year has less, though we all know how difficult a sum it is to
> realize, and how impossible it is to extract a five-pound note, or even a sov-
> ereign, from the pockets of people who talk of it as a mere bagatelle. . . .
> When Wainwright, the first of the assurance office defrauders by poison,
> was in prison, he said to a person who called upon him, "You see with what
> respect they treat me. They don't set me to make my bed, or sweep the
> yard, like those fellows," pointing to his brother prisoners; "no, they treat
> me like a gentleman. They think I'm in for ten thousand pounds." Ten
> thousand pounds! What would ten thousand pounds be nowadays, when
> men speculate to the extent of a quarter or maybe half a million of money?
> Why, Wainwright would have had to clean out the whole prison on the
> present scale of money delinquency. (79:376)

Two years later, in *All the Year Round*, Dickens revived memories of the
affair when he modeled Julius Slinkton on Wainewright in the short
story "Hunted Down."

At the very middle of the century there was a rash of sensational murders. In 1848 a Norfolk tenant farmer named James Blomfield Rush, threatened with eviction by Isaac Jermy, an Oxford-educated lawyer whose ownership of the land he disputed, killed Jermy and his son and seriously wounded the latter's wife and a maidservant. This deed was recalled by the scoundrel George Vavasor in Trollope's *Can You Forgive Her?* when he entertained the possibility of murdering John Grey. He had, said Trollope, often expressed in company his high opinion of Rush, declaring that "the courage of Rush had never been surpassed. 'Think of him,' he would say with admiration, 'walking into a man's house, with pistols sufficient to shoot every one there, and doing it as though he were killing rats! What was Nelson at Trafalgar to that? Nelson had nothing to fear!'" (51:541–42) Rush's trial abounded with interesting forensic points, not the least intriguing of which was the crucial issue of timing in Rush's alibi and the alleged quarter-hour difference between the clock at his farm and the one at Jermy's Stanfield Hall. The testimony of a bumbling rural constable and the judge's impatience over it added comic spice to the proceedings which Wilkie Collins drew from his memory when he wrote *Poor Miss Finch* (1871–72). In the murder trial that provided the early background to the story, there were recognizable reminiscences of Rush's, the most prominent of which was the question of timing (chapter 8 was titled "The Perjury of the Clock").

Hard on the heels of the Rush affair came the Manning sensation (1849), involving the murder in London of a customs employee and petty usurer by Frederick Manning and his Swiss-born wife, Maria. Part of the extraordinary stir the case caused was due to the novel means by which the fugitive Maria was apprehended in Edinburgh (it was the first time the police used the telegraph for such a purpose), Manning's attempt to pin the blame on his wife, her hysterics in prison and in the courtroom, and finally their execution. Maria's choice of a black satin gown for her going-away outfit was said to have cast black satin gowns beyond the pale of fashion for many years. Dickens, who wrote two furious letters to the *Times* protesting the primitive brutality of their public execution, modeled the French maid Hortense, murderer of the lawyer Tulkinghorn in *Bleak House*, after Maria, who had been a maid in the household of the Countess of Sutherland.

In 1856 the Reverend Francis Eden, in Reade's *It Is Never Too Late to Mend*, preached a sermon obviously inspired by the Manning case. In *The Woman in White* (1859–60), in a particularly neat chronological fit—the Mannings were hanged on 13 November 1849 and the diary entry is dated 15 June 1850, so they would still have been very much in people's minds at the time of the story—Marian Halcombe tried to arrive at some moral estimate of the corpulent Count Fosco: "I have asked whether Henry the Eighth was an amiable character? Whether Pope Alexander the Sixth was a good man? Whether Mr. Murderer and Mrs. Murderess Manning were not both unusually stout people . . ." ("Narrative of Marian Halcombe": 167). At the same moment that Collins was writing, Surtees recalled the affair in a lighter vein, in *Plain or Ringlets?*. Jasper Goldspink's father said to his errant son, "I dread the very name [of the Rag and Famish Club, known outside fiction as the Army and Navy]—it must be shocking, a frightful place—a place where they would very likely cut you up into quarters and drop you quietly over Blackfriars Bridge in the dead of the night"—there had been such a disposal of a dismembered body at the Waterloo Bridge two years earlier—"or shoot you through the head and bury you in the back kitchen, as somebody did Mr. Manning or Mr. Manning did somebody, I forget which way it was" (49:179).

When Robert Audley, the self-appointed detective, begins to put the heat on his cousin Lady Lucy, he warns her that outward respectability is no guarantee of innocence: "If I were to go to-morrow into that commonplace, plebeian, eight-roomed house in which Maria Manning and her husband murdered their guest, I should have no awful prescience of that bygone horror. Foul deeds have been done under the most hospitable roofs . . ." (*Lady Audley's Secret*, 18:94).

After the Mannings came (1856) Dr. William Palmer, who was accused of killing a minimum of six persons—popular indignation, prompted by inflammatory pre-trial pamphlets, raised the figure to sixteen—at Rugeley, Staffordshire. Dickens's immediate response, drawing on the copious newspaper coverage and his childhood memories of Thurtell (he was eleven years old at the time of the Weare murder), was to write for *Household Words* (14 June 1856) a lengthy comparison of the two murderers' personalities and conduct. He spoke of Palmer only as "the Poisoner," but everyone knew whom he meant. The next year, he and Wilkie Collins went on holiday to the north of England and, among other adventures, joined the crowds at Doncaster in race week. In "The Lazy Tour of Two Idle Apprentices" (*Household Words*, 31 October 1857), Dickens revealed that he still had those two turf-addicted murderers in mind:

An awful family likeness among the Keepers [bettors], to Mr. Palmer and Mr. Thurtell. With some knowledge of expression and some acquaintance with heads . . . I never have seen anywhere, so many repetitions of one class of countenance and one character of head (both evil) as in this street at this time. Cunning, covetousness, secresy [*sic*], cold calculation, hard callousness and dire insensibility, are the uniform Keeper characteristics. Mr. Palmer passes me five times in five minutes, and, as I go down the street, the back of Mr. Thurtell's skull is always going on before me.

As later references attest, it continued to haunt him throughout the week.

Mary Elizabeth Braddon had the case very much in mind when she wrote *Aurora Floyd* six years later. "If Mr. William Palmer had known that detection was to dog the footsteps of crime, and the gallows to follow at the heels of detection," she said, "he would most likely have hesitated long before he mixed the strychnine-pills for the friend whom, with cordial voice, he was entreating to be of good cheer" (20:203). Places associated with Palmer had the same magnetic attraction as those that had once enticed Scott and Dickens. "People are apt," said Braddon, "to take pride out of strange things. An elderly gentleman at Doncaster, showing me his comfortably-furnished apartments, informed me, with evident satisfaction, that Mr. William Palmer had lodged in those very rooms" (25:244). Another allusion in *Aurora Floyd* was to a "scientific" custom that then prevailed in criminal cases: "The phrenologists who examined the head of William Palmer, declared that he was so utterly deficient in moral perception, so entirely devoid of conscientious feeling, that he could not help being what he was. Heaven keep us from too much credence in that horrible fatalism!" (25:250).

In his murderous broodings, George Vavasor in *Can You Forgive Her?* linked Rush with Palmer. Of Palmer

> he declared that he was a man of genius as well as courage. He had "looked the whole thing in the face," Vavasor would say, "and told himself that all scruples and squeamishness are bosh,—child's tales. And so they are. Who lives as though they fear either heaven or hell? And if we do live without such fear or respect, what is the use of telling lies to ourselves? To throw it all to the dogs, as Palmer did, is more manly." "And be hanged," some hearer of George's doctrine replied. "Yes, and be hanged,—if such is your destiny. But you hear of the one who is hanged, but hear nothing of the twenty who are not." (51:542)

In a later novel (*Phineas Redux* [1873–74]), Trollope recalled a tantalizing feature of the Palmer trial, the question of whether he had actually killed John Parsons Cook, the fellow racing man he was specifically charged with having killed, no matter how many others whose involuntary demise he had certainly brought about. (Before he was executed, Palmer put on record the ambiguous declaration, "I am innocent of poisoning Cook by strychnine.") On the eve of Phineas Finn's own trial for the murder of Bonteen, the criminal lawyer Chaffanbrass, who was supposedly modeled after a real-life courtroom star, Serjeant

William Ballantine, and whom Trollope described at length in *The Three Clerks*, said: "What we should all wish to get at is the truth of the evidence about the murder. The man is to be hung not because he committed the murder,—as to which no positive knowledge is attainable; but because he had been proved to have committed the murder,—as to which proof, though it be enough for hanging, there must always be attached some shadow of doubt. We were delighted to hang Palmer,—but we don't know that he killed Cook. A learned man who knew more about it than we can know seemed to think that he didn't" (*Phineas Redux*, 60: 483–84).

The year after the Palmer sensation (1857), Madeleine Smith, daughter of a Glasgow architect, was tried for killing her lover with hot chocolate spiked with arsenic. Not the least controversial aspect of this case was the ambiguity inherent in the jury's resort to the verdict, peculiar to Scottish jurisprudence, of "Not proven." Among the novelists who followed the proceedings with rapt attention were George Eliot and Henry James. But Madeleine Smith left less trace in the fiction of the day than did Palmer, her immediate predecessor, or Dr. Thomas Smethurst, who followed her into the dock the next year.

The most scandalous feature of Smethurst's trial for poisoning his wife was the all too evident incompetence of the chief scientific witness for the prosecution. The doctor was convicted but the evidence against him was so flimsy and the trial had been conducted with such palpable bias that there was a great outcry in the medical and legal professions and the press. The Home Secretary, with the reluctant acquiescence of the judge, was forced to turn the case over to Sir Benjamin Brodie, a highly respected surgeon—but not a forensic scientist, let alone a lawyer—who proceeded to adjudicate, not the controversial medical evidence alone but the jury's verdict itself, "a most unprecedented course," as the newspapers quickly pointed out. The upshot was that Smethurst was granted a pardon, but since the proverbial pound of flesh had somehow to be extracted, he was rearrested, and tried and convicted on a charge of bigamy.

All this was in the minds of Wilkie Collins's readers when, in *Armadale*, they read of Lydia Gwilt's having been convicted of poisoning her husband before the novel began. After the verdict was rendered, said Bashwood the detective, "Doctors who had *not* attended the sick man, and who had *not* been present at the examination of the body, declared by dozens that he had died a natural death. Barristers without business, who had *not* heard the evidence, attacked the jury who had heard it, and judged the judge, who had sat on the bench before some of them were born" (3.15:2.330–33). (It is obvious that Collins, bucking the tide of public opinion, thought Smethurst had been fairly convicted.) The up-shot, as in the real-life case, was that the Home Secretary submitted "the conflict of medical evidence . . . to one great doctor; and when the one great doctor took the merciful view, after expressly stating, in the first instance, that he knew nothing practically of the merits of the case, the Home Secretary was perfectly satisfied." Lydia Gwilt was pardoned, but to satisfy the popular feeling that she should be punished a little, she was tried and convicted on a charge of robbery.

Collins gathered a number of elements remembered from this and other domestic poisoning cases in the central episode of *The Law and the Lady*, the retrospective narration of a "famous trial" at Edinburgh in the form of a printed transcript which the heroine uses during her cam-paign to prove that her husband had not poisoned his first wife. Collins's propagandist purpose was to attack the "Not proven" verdict which doomed the defendant to the legal limbo in which, like Madeleine Smith, he was neither convicted nor judged innocent. (At the end of the novel, a fortuitously recovered and reconstructed document proves his inno-cence.) Emily Eden's Mrs. Hopkinson would have found the array of evidence in *The Law and the Lady* gratifyingly familiar—the victim's acute symptoms as the arsenic took effect, the evidence of the medical wit-nesses, the testimony of the chemist who sold the poison, and the usual defense claim that it was bought for cosmetic or pesticidal purposes.

There was, finally, the Road mystery of 1860, in which the teenage daughter of a government official was accused of killing her four-year-old stepbrother. Collins appropriated several features of it for *The Moon-stone*: the stained nightgown that was one of the pieces of evidence most closely linking the girl with the crime, the household laundry book, and the friction between Superintendent Seegrave and Sergeant Cuff, which recalled the equally uneasy relations between the inept country police-man, Superintendent Foley, and the man from Scotland Yard, Inspector Whicher. In the novel, Sergeant Cuff, having failed to solve the mystery, resigns from the force, just as, in actuality, Inspector Whicher, whose conviction that Constance was indeed the murderer was overruled by local sentiment, left Scotland Yard.

Not all fictional murders suggested by ones in real life were topical in the sense that most readers would have recognized their sources and thus filled in the outlines of the fictional events with such details as they remembered reading about the actual ones. Some murders, the subjects of headlines for a season, faded from public memory and so did not qualify as classics. This was true of the one from which Mrs. Gas-kell—unconsciously, she claimed—derived the killing of the Manchester mill-owner Carson's son by an unknown assailant, who in the end is revealed to have been Mary Barton's father, a strong union man. Probably only Gaskell's Manchester readers and others with very retentive memories would have noticed that the episode resembled the murder in January 1831 of the son of a Manchester cotton manufacturer, Thomas Ashton. The perpetrators of the crime proved to have been hired by the Spinners' Union, one of whose members Ashton had discharged for union activity. An earlier novelist, Elizabeth Stone, had already used the outlines of the story in her *William Landshawe, the Cotton Lord* (1842).

In *Mary Barton* occurs another allusion to a murder, one that in 1831 had aroused almost as much popular indignation as had Burke and Hare two years earlier. Just after the heroine's lover, Jem Wilson, had been arrested on suspicion of murdering Carson, Mary was walking home, distraught, when

> her impetuous course was arrested by a light touch on her arm, and turning hastily, she saw a little Italian boy, with his humble show-box,—a white mouse, or some such thing. The setting sun cast its red glow on his face, otherwise the olive complexion would have been very pale; and the glittering tear-drops hung on the long curled eyelashes. With his soft voice, and pleading looks, he uttered, in his pretty broken English, the word—"Hungry! so hungry!"
> And as if to aid by gesture the effect of the solitary word, he pointed to his mouth, with its white quivering lips.
> Mary answered him impatiently, "Oh, lad, hunger is nothing—nothing!"
> And she rapidly passed on. But her heart upbraided her the next minute with her unrelenting speech, and she hastily entered her door and seized the scanty remnant of food which the cupboard contained, and she retraced her steps to the place where the little hopeless stranger had sunk down by his mute companion in loneliness and starvation, and was raining down tears as he spoke in some foreign tongue, with low cries for the far distant "Mamma mia!" (20:221–22)

Mention at this time of hungry little Italian boys with show-boxes of white mice was bound to arouse memories of the real-life victim of another pair of body snatchers, John Bishop and Thomas Head, alias Williams, who were charged with his murder in London and were subsequently hanged. Dickens, in his journalistic piece on "A Visit to Newgate" (*Sketches by Boz*), reported seeing there "casts of the heads and faces of the two notorious murderers, Bishop and Williams; the former, in particular, exhibiting a style of head and set of features, which might have afforded sufficient moral grounds for his instant execution at any time, even had there been no other evidence against him" ("Scenes," chap. 25:202–3).

The moral grounds for Bishop's instant execution, apart from his unattractive face, were the fact that in December 1831 he and Williams were convicted of having murdered a fourteen-year-old Italian boy, Carlo Ferrari, who had been showing in West End streets a squirrel cage containing two white mice, and delivering his body to the dissecting room of King's College. The pair were veteran resurrectionists; in his confession Bishop said that in the past twelve years he had handled between five hundred and one thousand corpses, "all," he virtuously added, "obtained after death"—with the solitary exception of the one with which he was charged.[6] Coming so soon after the Burke and Hare sensation, with the victim in this case being an innocent child beggar rather than the wornout and elderly adults whose passing the earlier pair had hastened, Bishop's and Williams's chances of escaping the gallows were nil.

In the wake of the murder it was reported that "no fewer than four thousand of these boys . . . pursued their avocation by means of a hand-organ, a white mouse, or something else to afford an excuse for begging," while their masters, enriched by their earnings, returned to Italy and enjoyed lives of leisure on the small estates they bought.[7] However that may have been, one detail of the episode especially gave Thackeray cause to reflect. He moralized in *Catherine*: "Surely our novel-writers make a great mistake in divesting their rascals of all gentle human qualities: they have such—and the only sad point to think of is, in all private concerns of life, abstract feelings, and dealing with friends, and so on, how dreadfully like a rascal is to an honest man. The man who murdered the Italian boy, set him first to play with his children whom he loved, and who doubtless deplored his loss" (5:580).

A number of such emotional considerations must have been present in *Mary Barton*. To Gaskell's readers in 1848, mention of an Italian boy and his white mouse, particularly with a murder in the background, would have triggered a rush of sympathy, for Mary as much as for the boy. Thanks to the publicity it received, the pathetic incident seventeen years earlier and the figure of the victim were firmly fixed in the popular mind, so that wisps of the murder clung to the very notion of Italian boy-beggars. Perhaps in time the connection with murder was forgotten, but it had succeeded in establishing the figure as a familiar archetype of the victimized child. Flora Finching, learning from Arthur Clennam that Amy Dorrit is in Italy with her family, says in her free-associational way, "In Italy is she really?, with the grapes growing everywhere and lava necklaces and bracelets too that land of poetry with burning mountains picturesque beyond belief though if the organ-boys come away from the neighbourhood not to be scorched nobody can wonder being so young and bringing their white mice with them most humane . . . " (*Little Dorrit*, 2.9:590). At one point in Marian Halcombe's description of Count

Fosco's peculiar obsession with white mice in *The Woman in White*, she wrote that he had "all the small dexterities of an organ-boy in managing his white mice" ("Narrative of Marian Halcombe": 169).[8]

4.

Accompanying famous murders into novels was a related occupation, brand-new in name if not in function.[9] The Bow Street Runners, created by the novelist Henry Fielding when he was a magistrate at the Bow Street police court, constituted a primitive kind of detective force, but by the beginning of the nineteenth century they had become increasingly inefficient (although it was one of their number, George Ruthven, who tracked down and arrested Thurtell). Following the passage of Peel's Metropolitan Police Act in 1829, which set up a disciplined body of uniformed men to take over the policing functions of both the runners and the much-ridiculed parish constables, the Bow Street contingent was phased out during the next decade. Dickens, marking the occasion, said farewell to them in the person of the comedy team of Blathers and Duff, who signally failed to solve the mystery of the Chertsey break-in in *Oliver Twist*.

The detective branch of the Metropolitan Police was formed in 1842, but the first sleuth Dickens introduced into his fiction after that was not an official one. He was the mysterious Nadgett in *Martin Chuzzlewit*, the counterpart of the investigator for the Eagle Insurance Company who worked on the Wainewright case. "He was always keeping appointments in the City," said Dickens, "and the other man never seemed to come" (27:517): not Godot, surely? The first fictional detective on a provincial force was the Manchester plainclothesman who gathered evidence against Jem Wilson in *Mary Barton*.

Dickens's subsequent love affair with Scotland Yard, reflected in his journalism as well as his novels, embraced both the detective and the uniformed branches. Inspector Bucket, in *Bleak House*, was followed at some distance by a less prominent colleague, the unnamed "Mr. Inspector" in *Our Mutual Friend*, a sympathetically portrayed plainclothesman who is "trepanned into an industrious hunt on a false scent" (4.16:875). By this time, sensation novel plots had employed so many members of official force, private investigators, and amateurs that the detective had become a stock character. As Fitzjames Stephen wrote in a peppery article on "Detectives in Fiction and Real Life" (*Saturday Review*, 11 June 1864),

> Of all forms of sensation novel-writing, none is so common as what may be called the romance of the detective. Indeed, one very popular author seems to think that the only striking incident that ever varies the monotony of

every-day life is the discovery [i.e., the solution] of a mysterious murder by a consummate detective. Whether the contrast between the stern prose of the officer and the awfulness of the offence, or whether a Pre-Raffaellite delight in the representation of familiar objects, is the true source of the popularity of this kind of plot, it would be rash to decide.

Stephen was quite possibly referring to the detective in *Lost Sir Massingberd*, which had concluded its run in *Chambers's Journal* a few weeks earlier (16 April). There, James Payn enlisted the current vogue of the new type-character in the interest of distancing. In a chapter titled "A Detective of Half a Century Ago," he introduced Townshend, "the famous Bow Street officer," who "was faithful as a watch-dog to the government which employed him":

> When Townshend fairly settled himself down upon the track of an offender, the poor wretch felt like the hare whose fleeting footsteps the stoat relentlessly pursues; he might escape for the day, or even the morrow, but sooner or later his untiring foe was certain to be up with him. In those early days, when the telegraph could not overtake the murderer speeding for his life, and set Justice upon her guard five hundred miles away, to intercept him, and when the sun was not the slave of the Law, to photograph the features of the doomed criminal, so that he can be recognized as easily as Cain, thief-catching was a much more protracted business than it is now; nevertheless, it was at least as certain. (26:253–54)

Writing in *Armadale*, which began serialization only a few months later, Collins presented young James Bashwood, another exemplar of the new type-figure, in a considerably less glamorous light. He was repellent to strict morality, and a depressing sign of the times:

> No eye for reading character, but such an eye as belongs to one person, perhaps, in ten thousand, could have penetrated the smoothly deceptive surface of this man, and have seen him for what he really was—the vile creature whom the viler need of Society has fashioned for its own use. There he sat—the Confidential Spy of modern times, whose business is steadily enlarging, whose Private Inquiry Offices are steadily on the increase. There he sat—the necessary Detective attendant on the progress of our national civilization; a man who was, in this instance at least, the legitimate and intelligible product of the vocation that employed him; a man professionally ready on the merest suspicion (if the merest suspicion paid him) to get under our beds, and to look through gimlet-holes in our doors; a man who would have been useless to his employers if he could have felt a touch of human sympathy in his father's presence; and who would have deservedly forfeited his situation if, under any circumstances whatever, he had been personally accessible to a sense of pity or a sense of shame. (3.15:2.305–6)

Most readers, eager to follow detectives in their pursuits, would not have subscribed to this severe judgment. They relished Sergeant Cuff in *The Moonstone*; the amateur Robert Audley in *Lady Audley's Secret*, whose "generous nature," as Miss Braddon put it, "revolted at the office into which he had found himself drawn—the office of spy, the collector of damning facts that led on to horrible deductions" involving his own cousin (23:128); the detective whom Mrs. Dodd, in Reade's *Hard Cash*, employs to track down her addled husband; Major Mackenzie of Scotland Yard, who gives Lady Eustace a hard time, and his colleagues Bunfit and Gager; the ex-policeman Samuel Bozzle in *He Knew He Was Right*, whom Louis Trevelyan hires both to spy on his estranged wife and to arrange for the abduction of their son; Prodgers, in *Mr. Scarborough's Family*, whom the moneylender Tyrwhitt employs to find Captain Scarborough; the unnamed (walk-on) police inspector in *North and South*; and the detective who appears briefly at the end of *Desperate Remedies*.

The most overlooked field representative of justice in Victorian fiction, apart from Payn's Townshend, was Joseph Grimstone, who appeared at the end of *Aurora Floyd* (1862–63), thus antedating Sergeant Cuff by several years. He did some fine-tooth investigating in quite the modern manner, with particular attention to tracing a rusty waistcoat button that was a crucial piece of evidence. It is true that the mystery was solved fortuitously, before he had a chance to do it on his own; perhaps, if the serialization of the novel in *Temple Bar* could have been stretched out an extra month or so, Miss Braddon would have let him triumph.

Taken all together, the novelists' exploitation of current crime represents one of the clearest cases of symbiosis in Victorian literary history. Both they and the newspapers, always ready to light upon a crime that had out-of-the-way features and to devote as many daily columns to it as the diligence of its reporters and the cooperation of the police and the courts allowed, thrived on the public's consuming appetite. What novelists read along this line in their morning papers might well mean added prosperity if they could but work it into their current books. Sometimes fate played directly into their hands. In 1876 the papers were full of the mysterious death of a young barrister named Charles Bravo, who had succumbed to a dose of poison at his villa in the London suburb of Balham. There were three suspects: his wife, who had formerly been the mistress of an elderly hydropathic physician; the physician himself; and the wife's paid companion. One inquest came to nothing, and a second was called for. At that moment (May), the veteran novelist William Harrison Ainsworth wrote to William Tinsley, his publisher, concerning his just completed novel: "There is a poisoning case in *Chetwynde Calverley* which bears a curious resemblance to the great sensational case now before the public, so that the book will appear very apropos. . . . If you can get an early notice of *Chetwynde Calverley* into some papers, drawing attention to the remarkable resemblance between the poisoning case in that story and 'The Balham Mystery,' you might quote it in your advertisements with effect. . . . A notice just now in *The Daily Telegraph* would sell an edition." [10]

Whether or not the Bravo case helped the sale of Ainsworth's novel—I have seen no evidence that Tinsley adopted his suggestion—is unknown. So, officially at least, was the murderer. After the second inquest, which lasted a record twenty-three days (it lacked only an indictment to qualify as a full-fledged trial), the coroner's jury decided that "evidence to fix the guilt upon any person or persons" was lacking, and so the case was filed away in the thick dossier of unsolved Victorian murders.

14

The Shady Side

1.

ONE GENERALIZATION made about Victorian fiction which has withstood intense scrutiny by modern scholars is that the prevailing code of morality and propriety inhibited novelists from depicting large areas of private and social experience. The cast of mind that has been (too facilely) summed up as "Victorian prudery" discouraged, effectively for the most part, explicit description of aspects of life that readers wished not to be reminded of. "It is all among workhouses and pickpockets and coffinmakers," complained Lord Melbourne after glancing into *Oliver Twist*. "I do not *like* those things: I wish to avoid them. I do not like them in reality and therefore do not like to see them represented."[1] The best that novelists could do was cautiously to imply what they could not say outright. In this effort they were sometimes assisted by topical parallels, drawing from contemporary newspapers and gossip the hints by which knowledgeable readers could fill in the gaps in a novel's text.

Thackeray lamented, in his famous preface to *Pendennis*, that since Henry Fielding no English novelist was at liberty to portray "a MAN" (i.e., one vulnerable to normal sexual and other temptations). It was the same Thackeray who occasionally conveyed with a wink what could not be made explicit. The superannuated courtesan Emily Montanville, in *Lovel the Widower*, who had once enjoyed "an elegant little cottage in the Regent's Park" and "a brougham with a horse all over brass harness," "*may*," he said, stressing the conditional, "under another name, keep a trinket-shop in the Burlington Arcade, for what you know, but this secret no torture shall induce me to divulge" (1:60). Some readers would have felt no need to apply thumbscrews or any other torture to the innuendo-confiding novelist: they knew that rooms over millinery and "trinket" shops in London's fashionable enclosed shopping mall were used for daytime prostitution. Between three and five o'clock in the afternoon, the "prima donnas" of their profession could be seen patrolling the arcade, alert for signals from strolling gentlemen, on receipt of which they would enter a shop and rendezvous upstairs. The Burlington's notoriety as a place of assignation was sufficiently widespread as to deter gentlemen of discretion from being seen there during those hours.

Although there is no evidence that the milliners' shop assistants had any direct part in the traffic through these premises, the ill-paying millinery/dressmaking trade at large (dressmakers were also called milliners at this time) had a reputation of which Dickens availed himself when he portrayed the first threat to Kate Nickleby's chastity. The very fact that Ralph Nickleby found his niece a job at Madame Mantalini's dressmaking establishment would have been, to contemporary readers, a clear sign of his villainy. It was well known that girls so unprotected were exposed to the wiles of men, both inside the shop—the proprietress's sleek husband in this case, who seemed capable of offering an intramural threat, his voluble uxoriousness notwithstanding—and outside, on the pavement. Conventional wisdom held that, just as men in their unredeemed state were potential seducers, so young women in dressmakers' shops, yearning to bedeck themselves in the finery they made for the more fortunate members of their sex, were their natural prey. "Consider," wrote a contributor to *Fraser's Magazine* in March 1846, "how the image of Mammon and worldliness was constantly before them. . . . It is inconceivable how many of those unfortunate beings who live on the wages of prostitution, might refer the first step taken towards the downward path to the house of the milliner or dressmaker."

To this widely assumed cause-and-effect relationship between the needlework trade and immorality, social investigations in the years following the publication of *Nicholas Nickleby* added a new and equally horrifying element: the sweated conditions under which young needlewomen worked, both in fashionable establishments like Mantalini's and in the slum garrets where, at starvation rates, they did piecework brought to them by slop-sellers and other tyrannous employers.[2] Conditions in the trade were documented in the appendix to the *Second Report of the Children's Employment Commission*, which inspired both Hood's "The Song of the Shirt" and the formation in the same year (1843) of the Association for the Relief and Protection of Young Persons Employed in the Dressmaking and Millinery Departments in London, to which "an impressive list of influential ladies of rank" subscribed.

Primed with information supplied by periodical articles commenting on the 1843 blue book, readers in 1847–50 would have recognized the urgent topicality involved in direct or oblique allusions to the perils of the dressmaking trade in several new novels. They would have realized, though Charlotte Brontë did not overtly make the point, that Jane Eyre put her virginity at risk when, after leaving Mr. Rochester's employment,

The Needlewoman at Home and Abroad.

AT HOME.   ABROAD.

Punch, which had ignited the social issue of exploited needlewomen by printing Thomas Hood's "The Song of the Shirt" in 1843, returned to the attack with this searing cartoon in its issue for 12 January 1850, only weeks after Henry Mayhew's exposé of conditions in the trade was published in the *Morning Chronicle*.

she sought work first as a dressmaker and then as a plain sewer. In the rakish world of *Vanity Fair*, milliners were the standard prey of idle youth: Dobbin assured his messmates that George Osborne was "not going to run off with a Duchess or ruin a milliner" but marry Amelia as he had promised, and Rawdon Crawley entertained himself by "courtships of milliners, opera-dancers, and the like easy triumphs" (13:116; 30:284). At the same moment, readers of *Mary Barton* would have been able to appreciate more keenly the danger to which the heroine, a Manchester seamstress, was exposed when she fell under the eye of the seduction-bent son of Carson, the mill owner.

A year later, when *Pendennis* and *David Copperfield* were appearing in monthly parts, Henry Mayhew's articles in the *Morning Chronicle*, especially the one on 23 November 1849, which reported the testimony at a meeting he convened of "needlewomen forced to take to the streets," called fresh attention to the scandal.[3] Thus two references in Thackeray's and Dickens's current novels had particular timeliness. In *Pendennis*, Harry Foker, possessed of more money than rectitude, carried his London habits with him when he visited the sedate town of Clavering and "flattened his little nose against Madame Fribsby's window to see if haply there was a pretty workwoman in her premises" (15:1.143)—an innocent enough gesture in itself, but given a more disturbing implication when readers took account of what could happen to pretty workwomen, even in the country. And in *David Copperfield*, Little Em'ly's vulnerability to Steerforth, a considerably more polished seducer than the residually decent, and for all we know inexperienced, Foker, was automatically enhanced by the very fact that she was an apprentice dressmaker; never mind that she was articled to the merry, benevolent Mr. Omer.

But Dickens made more of Kate Nickleby's vulnerability than he did of Little Em'ly's. In locating her, with her uncle Ralph's assistance, at Madame Mantalini's, he was, in effect, laying the groundwork for the later development in which the danger of seduction became alarmingly clear, as Kate became the prey of Sir Mulberry Hawk and his witless young dupe, Lord Frederick Verisopht.

In the Hawk-Verisopht plot Dickens again relied on his readers' topical knowledge.[4] A year before the first number of *Nicholas Nickleby* appeared in 1838, the newspapers reported a court case involving an aristocratic adventurer, Henry William, twenty-second Baron de Ros, who sued for libel a man who had publicly accused him of cheating at cards. De Ros's ill fame—as early as 1824 the diarist Thomas Creevey had called him "one of the cleverest and most hardened villains" in London[5]—had already earned him a covert place in fiction, as Harry Finish in Bulwer's *Paul Clifford* (1830). In the mid-thirties clubland gossip had it that he had seduced a woman and then made her available to a friend in part payment of a gambling debt. Fanny Kemble used this story for the plot of her play *An English Tragedy*, which Macready admired when she submitted it to him in December 1838 but declined to produce because he himself feared a libel action. It was this episode that Browning eventually used in his narrative poem *The Inn Album*.[6]

The aspect of De Ros's dissolute character that was most in the public eye at the time Dickens created Sir Mulberry Hawk was related to the charge of cheating at cards.[†] But it was the other two of De Ros's special-

---

[†] As with Wainewright when he sued the insurance company a few years earlier, and Oscar Wilde when he sued the Marquis of Queensberry for libel many years later, De Ros's subscription to the theory that the best defense is a preemptive strike backfired. The jury at the court of Queen's Bench needed only fifteen minutes to find against him, and he had to flee to the Continent, where he died a year later.

ties, seducing women and fleecing gullible youths, that Dickens stressed in his portrait from life. His readers would have found the identification irresistible. "Sir Mulberry Hawk," he wrote, "was remarkable for his tact in ruining, by himself and his creatures, young gentlemen of fortune—a genteel and elegant profession, of which he had undoubtedly gained the head" (19:309). De Ros's notoriety would have rendered all the more culpable in readers' minds the fact that Mrs. Nickleby was completely taken in by Hawk. At one point, she "indited a long letter to Kate, in which she expressed her entire approval of the admirable choice she had [supposedly] made, and extolled Sir Mulberry to the skies; asserting, for the more complete satisfaction of her daughter's feelings, that he was precisely the individual whom she (Mrs. Nickleby) would have chosen for her son-in-law, if she had had the picking and choosing from all mankind" (28:435). Dickens could hardly have found a more effective means of underscoring her total lack of even rudimentary perception.

De Ros also probably lies behind the story that Mrs. Bute Crawley, in *Vanity Fair*, tells her sister-in-law Miss Matilda to discredit Rawdon, who, she fears, may inherit her fortune. Included in her recital of Rawdon's "manifold sins" (Thackeray takes care to brand the story an "invention of scandal") was this: "the unhappy Lord Dovedale, whose mamma had taken a house at Oxford, so that he might be educated there, and who had never touched a card in his life till he came to London, was perverted by Rawdon at the Cocoa Tree, made helplessly tipsy by this abominable seducer and perverter of youth, and fleeced of four thousand pounds" (19:181).

Living in the same ambience of "fast" society, but at a later date, were two beautiful women who successively furnished models for a single character in Reade's *A Terrible Temptation* (1871). One was Catherine Walters, better known to the Victorian demimonde as "Skittles."[7] The height of her public notoriety came in 1862, when a man-about-town and *Times* staffer named Matthew James Higgins ("Jacob Omnium") contributed to his paper a profile of this charmer, an expert horsewoman who rode with the exclusive Quorn hunt and was, at that moment, stopping traffic as she starred in the daily parade of the fashionable in Hyde Park's Rotten Row. Higgins called her only "Anonyma," but people in the know recognized her as the beauty recently celebrated in a pastiche of Alexander Pope by the future poet laureate, Alfred Austin:

> Gone the broad glare, save where with borrowed bays
> Some female Phaeton sets the Drive a-blaze:
> Or, more defiant, spurning frown and foe,
> With slackened rein swift Skittles rules the Row.
> Though scowling matrons champing steeds restrain,
> She flaunts Propriety with flapping mane.

"Skittles" (Catherine Walters) was the prototype of the mid-Victorian "fast woman," a celebrated demimondaine whose liaisons and unconventional behavior added lurid specificity to Mrs. Lynn Linton's notion of the "girl of the period" and gave moralists a stick with which to beat the developing feminist movement. In the view of respectable society, a "liberated" woman was, by virtual definition, a sexual delinquent.

The next year, Skittles was living in Paris, the recipient of a £500 annuity from the family of the young Marquis of Hartington, eldest son of the seventh Duke of Devonshire. Hartington had set her up in accommodations convenient to Devonshire House, an arrangement that was entirely acceptable to the fast-track sector of mid-Victorian nobility, but his expressed desire to actually marry her carried things too far, hence the subsidized exile. It was then that Wilfrid Scawen Blunt met her and conceived the first grand passion of his life, eventually memorializing the short-lived liaison in two sonnet sequences. They remained friends, her letters filling him in on society and court gossip, until her death in 1920.

Acquaintance, however achieved, with Skittles's lively personality— she had intellectual as well as amatory interests—and with her scandalous life in high society, would have enhanced readers' appreciation of the character of Rhoda Somerset, "the vixen of Hyde Park and Mayfair," in *A Terrible Temptation*. Once the action was well under way, however, Somerset disappeared from Reade's pages, to reappear, surprisingly, near the end as a female preacher, a kind of upscale Dinah Morris—"a lady richly dressed, tall and handsome, but with features rather too commanding," holding a Bible in her "white, and finely formed" hand (41:422). But Skittles was unregenerate at the time (like Blunt, she later converted to Roman Catholicism), and the new Rhoda Somerset was in fact modeled on another well-known courtesan, Laura Bell.[8] Sharing with Skittles the title of "the Queen of London Whoredom," as the memorist Sir William Hardman called her, this lady, too, adorned the daily Hyde Park processional, stopping, as was the custom, to chat with the swells gathered near the Achilles statue, but only from her carriage; there is no evidence that she had any of Skittles's equestrian talent. In 1852 she married the elegantly, almost parodically, named Captain Augustus Frederick Thistlethwayte, who set her up in luxury in Grosvenor Square. (A decade later, Skittles drew even with her in the onomastic sweepstakes by eloping to New York with a married man named Aubrey DeVere Beauclerk.) Several times in the ensuing years her extravagant spending reached such a peak that her husband advertised that he would not be responsible for her debts.

In the early 1860s, however, Laura Bell acquired both a social conscience and religious fervor, and from then on she exercised her considerable newfound oratorical gifts on the revivalist platform. Some said she rivaled the great drawing card at the Metropolitan Tabernacle, the Reverend Charles Spurgeon. The incongruity of a born-again lady of pleasure treating her auditors, as one of them wrote, to the sight of "the sparkling of an array of large diamond rings, which adorned her fingers, as she raised them in eloquent exhortation to her audience to follow the path that alone leads to salvation" and signing herself "A sinner saved by grace through faith in the Lamb of God" was not, therefore, one of Reade's less likely inventions. There actually was such a person, and Reade quite possibly knew, though he could scarcely reveal it, that his bejeweled revivalist often entertained the high-principled Gladstone at tea; at her death in 1894 she left behind a large box of his letters.

The topicality represented by Rhoda Somerset was not limited to her resemblance to Laura Bell. It also reminded readers of the current "pulpit controversy," which hinged on women's right to preach, if not to be actually ordained, and centered at the time on Catherine Booth, an excommunicated Wesleyan who drew capacity audiences at such large assembly places as the dome in Brighton (1868). Reade's decision to model the later Rhoda on a reformed demimondaine rather than the well-known evangelistic founder (1865) of the Christian Revival Association, the precursor of the Salvation Army, doubtless reflected his sardonic view of the controversy, as Dinah Morris had presumably reflected George Eliot's quite different one a dozen years earlier.

Not much can be made of the initially startling fact that Thackeray gave Laura Bell's name to the wholly virtuous heroine of *Pendennis*. Perhaps somewhere in the annals of mid-century lowlife there is a record of her already having been the subject of ribald songs as the night hours passed, cigar smoke thickened, and liquor flowed at the haunts Thackeray knew and was to portray as the Cave of Harmony in the opening pages of *The Newcomes*. But it was not his habit to subvert a chosen fictitious name in a serious context by tipping a wink to the roisterers among his readers. The coincidence of name was nothing more than an unlucky accident, though it is conceivable that Thackeray drew it from his subconscious and adopted it without ever realizing its origin. After 1850 he must have been acutely embarrassed to find his heroine's name debased by the scandal attached to its real-life bearer.

Reade gives no hint that Rhoda Somerset's beauty faded as she pursued her evangelistic career. But many other ladies, in life as in fiction, were not so fortunate, and it was the more desperate among them who would have had recourse to the shadowy Mrs. Oldershaw in Wilkie Collins's *Armadale*. A confidante of the criminal Miss Gwilt, she dated her letters from the "Ladies' Toilet Repository, Diana Street, Pimlico," and boasted of having had "twenty years' experience among our charming sex in making up battered old faces and worn-out old figures to look like new" (2.1:1.264, 266). Late in the novel the detective Bashwood describes her as "the most eminent woman in England, as restorer-general of the dilapidated heads and faces of the female sex" (3.15: 2.340). "Mother" Oldershaw, or "Mother Jezebel," as Collins calls her,

Madame Rachel takes a Hint from the Cheap Tailors and Picture-Cleaners.

Like people in other lines of work, *Punch* is saying (12 July 1862), Madame Rachel should hire sandwich men, or in this case sandwich women, accoutered to personify the message on the boards. The lady second in line presumably represents "before" and the one in the foreground, a spectacularly successful "after."

exploiting the sinister suggestion of witchcraft the epithet had acquired as early as the legendary Mother Shipton, "the Yorkshire Nostradamus," and Mother Sawyer in the Elizabethan drama *The Witch of Edmonton*, was transparently Madame Rachel, known outside business hours as Mrs. Sarah Rachel Leverson.[9] This energetic lady was formerly the proprietress of a fish-and-chip shop in Clare Market, and by night a procuress working the corridors of Drury Lane Theatre. By 1859–60, she was already famous as, in Surtees's phrase in *Plain or Ringlets?*, a "great lady-renovator." At her shop in New Bond Street she sold a comprehensive line of beauty products, some sixty items in all, ranging from face creams, kohl (eye shadow), and dentifrices to hair rinses, soaps, and perfumes, none priced at less than a guinea. Among the services she offered to ladies past the bloom of youth were hair-dyeing, wrinkle-removing, and a mysterious process called "enamelling."

In an anti-feminist passage in *Lady Audley's Secret* (1861–62)—"Better the influence of the tea cups and saucers gracefully wielded in a woman's hand than all the inappropriate power snatched at the point of the pen from the unwilling sterner sex"—Mary Elizabeth Braddon enhanced her rhetoric with a timely reference: "Imagine all the women of England elevated to the high level of masculine intellectuality, superior to crinoline; above pearl powder and Mrs. Rachael Levison [*sic*]; above taking the pains to be pretty; above tea-tables and that cruelly scandalous and rather satirical gossip which even strong men delight in; and what a drear, utilitarian, ugly life the sterner sex must lead" (25:147).

Madame Rachel enriched the mid-Victorian vocabulary with a catch-phrase that originated in the title of a promotional brochure she distributed in 1863, *Beauty Forever*—a quick review of female pulchritude through the ages, from Eve and Madame du Barry to Florence Nightingale and Queen Victoria.[†] (Patriotism, in this instance, was truly the refuge of a scoundrel.) When, in Trollope's *Ralph the Heir*, the prosperous breeches-maker Neefit recommended his virginal daughter Polly to the favorable attention of Ralph Newton, the heir in question, he exclaimed, "There ain't no mistake there, Mr. Newton; no paint; no Madame Rachel; no made beautiful for ever!"(6:1.75)

Skeptics might have suspected, as later proved to be the case, that the two-guineas-a-bottle Magnetic Rock Dew Water of Sahara was not the miraculous rejuvenator it purported to be; it was actually a mixture of carbonate of lead, starch, fuller's earth, hydrochloric acid, and distilled water costing the manufacturer no more than sixpence; and an equally expensive bath preparation consisted of nothing more exotic than bran and pump water. Whether Collins and the first readers of *Armadale* in 1864–66 had deeper suspicions—that the New Bond Street shop was not merely a swindle but a front for blackmailing and procuring— cannot be known, but Collins certainly managed to imply a good deal. When Allan Armadale and Pedgift Junior went round to Mrs. Oldershaw's Pimlico address, they found that "the face of this house was essentially furtive in its expression. The front windows were all shut, and the

---

[†] It would do Madame Rachel less than justice to suppose she was unaware that "Beauty Forever" echoed the title of Covèntry Patmore's poem *Faithful For Ever*, published in 1860 and subsequently incorporated into *The Angel in the House*, the supreme Victorian celebration of domestic bliss.

front blinds were all drawn down. . . . It affected to be a shop on the ground-floor; but it exhibited absolutely nothing in the space that intervened between the window and an inner row of red curtains, which hid the interior entirely from view." Their cabman commented, "There's the only shop window I ever saw with nothing at all inside it." Adjoining the shop door was the private door, "with a bell marked Professional; and another brass plate, indicating a medical occupant on this side of the house, for the name on it was, 'Doctor Downward.' If ever brick and mortar spoke yet, the brick and mortar here said plainly, 'We have got our secrets inside, and we mean to keep them.' " Downward, said Collins when he appeared, was "one of those carefully constructed physicians in whom the public—especially the female public—implicitly trust. He had the necessary bald head, the necessary double eyeglass, the necessary black clothes, and the necessary blandness of manner, all complete. His voice was soothing, his ways were deliberate, his smile was confidential. What particular branch of his profession Doctor Downward followed was not indicated on his door-plate; but he had utterly mistaken his vocation if he was not a ladies' medical man" (3.3 : 1.573–77). At one point in her diary, Lydia Gwilt noted "the risks the doctor runs in his particular form of practice" (3.14 : 2.275). Collins, for his part, was unwilling to accept the risk that naming the doctor's illicit specialty would have entailed, but his more worldly readers would have supplied the word.

Madame Rachel may not, in fact, have been involved in an abortionist racket, and in one other respect, as her gaudy career unfolded, Collins proved to have embellished the facts in a false direction. Anticipating Reade and his born-again Rhoda Somerset, he had Mother Oldershaw wind up as a Sunday evening lecturer (suggested donation: half a crown) on "the Pomps and Vanities of the World, by A Sinner Who Has Served Them," "a narrative of Mrs. Oldershaw's experience among dilapidated women, profusely illustrated in the pious and penitential style" ("Epilogue," chap. 1 : 2.568). In 1867, the year after *Armadale* finished its serial run, Madame Rachel was tried at the Old Bailey for obtaining money under false pretenses, her victim having been a haggard elderly widow of an army officer whom she undertook to make young again at an escalating cost that finally totaled seven thousand pounds, so that in her restored beauty she could captivate the seventh Viscount Ranelagh, who, Madame Rachel alleged, was in love with her. In order to sustain the fiction as long as the money held out, Rachel contrived an exchange of amorous letters between her victim and Ranelagh, who, though a habitué of the establishment, was not a party to the deception. During the trial, many scabrous particulars about the New Bond Street operation were offered in evidence, including the fact that when one of her other customers complained that all her valuable jewelry had disappeared from her dressing room while she was taking a "beauty bath," Madame replied, "How would you like your husband to know the real reason for your coming here, and about the gentleman who has visited you here?"

The first trial resulted in a hung jury, but a fresh prosecution was brought, this time with success. The elegant con artist was sentenced to a term of penal servitude, from which she emerged unrepentant and still ambitious. She reestablished her business not far from the old location, only to find herself in trouble again when a woman who had prepaid a course of beauty treatments with a pair of necklaces tried to get them back. Madame Rachel no longer had them, the new victim sued, and the beautician was again convicted.

Belated readers of *Armadale* therefore could read more into the character of Mrs. Oldershaw than was supplied by the known facts at a time when, riding high, her original was impudently advertising herself as "Purveyor to the Queen." Madame Rachel's trials attracted wide press coverage, so wide in fact that some homesick antipodean humorist named a New Zealand spring Madame Rachel's Bath. By the time Trollope came to write *The Eustace Diamonds* (1871–73), he and his readers had the advantage of knowing all that had transpired in the last half-dozen years, and he therefore could use it as background for his introduction of the handsome and formidable Mrs. Carbuncle:

> But perhaps the wonder of her face was its complexion. People said— before they knew her—that, as a matter of course, she had been made *beautiful for ever*. But, though that too brilliant colour was almost always there, covering the cheeks but never touching the forehead or the neck, it would at certain moments shift, change, and even depart. When she was angry, it would vanish for a moment and then return intensified. There was no chemistry on Mrs. Carbuncle's cheek; and yet it was a tint so brilliant and so transparent, as almost to justify a conviction that it could not be genuine. (36:366–67; emphasis added)

If Mrs. Carbuncle had not actually been one of Madame Rachel's clients, she was a walking advertisement for the kind of wonders Madame Rachel supposedly could, at an extortionate price, perform. Either way, Trollope left a pointed doubt as to her real character hanging in the air.

The cases of Laura Bell and Madame Rachel illustrate in different ways the retrospective turn that topicalities could take. Knowing who the real Laura Bell was, informed readers of *Pendennis* in the 1850s would have had trouble eliminating the extraneous elements from Thackeray's portrait of his fictional heroine; no doubt many of them would have been confused by the opposite tendencies life and art took in this instance. "Mother Oldershaw," on the other hand, was already a full-fledged topicality when *Armadale* appeared, and to later readers

Madame Rachel's highly publicized subsequent adventures simply confirmed and amplified the portrait Collins had already painted.

2.

While Mrs. Oldershaw edified her Sunday evening audiences with intimate reminiscences of the wealthy but time-ravaged women she had magically rejuvenated, Dr. Downward, assuming a new name (Le Doux) and a new specialty, became proprietor of a newly established private "sanitarium" in suburban Hampstead: "This is not a mad-house; this is not a licensed establishment; no doctors' certificates are necessary!" he exclaims. This was the topical issue that led to Alfred Austin's observation in 1870 that "lunatic asylums are a mine of wealth" to the sensation school of novelists to which Collins and Reade belonged. A lunatic asylum by another name was still a madhouse, and the regulation of these establishments was a recurrent item on the social-reform agenda of the 1850s and 1860s. While government, through the Commissioners in Lunacy, exercised loose control over licensed facilities, the proprietors of private institutions were free to admit patients without requiring a medical certificate or inquiring into the motives of those who sought to commit an inconvenient relative.[10]

In *Armadale*, however, Collins used the Hampstead sanitarium as the scene of the novel's melodramatic climax for its topical value without direct reference to the legal issue. Possession of a license would not necessarily have forestalled the bungled murder attempt, in which Dr. Le Doux taught Miss Gwilt how to mix a lethal batch of chemicals for the alleged purpose of fumigation—actually to kill the entirely sane Allan Armadale, whom they had decoyed into spending a night in a patient's room. Nor was the issue specifically raised in Collins's earlier employment of a private asylum in *The Woman in White*, although its first readers in 1859–60 would undoubtedly have found more food for thought than was evident on the surface. In the summer of 1858 three well-publicized cases of alleged improper confinement came to public attention. One was that of a Mrs. Turner, a patient in an asylum near York, who was subsequently found to be of sound mind. A second concerned a Mr. Ruck, confined in another institution, who was also judged to be sane. The third, which proved to be most closely connected with fiction, was that of a young man named Fletcher, a hard-drinking wastrel who claimed £35,000 from his late father's firm. The surviving partners had him pronounced insane and committed to a madhouse, but he escaped and, scenting a sensational topic for a novel, Charles Reade interviewed him. The firsthand information he received from Fletcher served as the basis of a series of letters he sent to the press between

August and December on "Our Dark Places"—the unregulated mad-houses.

By sheer concidence, there occurred in the same summer the newest episode in the protracted affliction visited upon another famous novelist by his more-than-half-mad wife. (Her few sympathizers, to be fair about it, contended that she was saner than he.) Ever since their legal separation in 1836, Rosina Bulwer-Lytton had conducted a guerrilla campaign against her husband, writing novels in which he was the instantly recognizable villain, blackmailing him for a bigger allowance, and, most recently, addressing letters to him at his club and elsewhere, sometimes as many as twenty a day, with obscenities written on the envelopes. On 8 June she fought her way to the platform from which he was addressing his constituents at Hertford and once more publicly denounced him. Armed with the opinions of six different doctors, none of whom had examined her but all nevertheless concurring with his assurance that she was out of her mind, Bulwer-Lytton had her removed to a private asylum, where she was kept for three weeks. In part for political reasons—he was then Colonial Secretary and therefore vulnerable to partisan attack—some London and provincial papers took up his wife's cause, which neatly fitted into the current furor. Skillful maneuvering by his colleagues in the government kept the case out of the courts, and his son, obtaining Rosina's release, spirited her abroad.

The upshot of all this was the appointment of a Select Committee of Commons on the Operation of the Acts and Regulations for the Care and Treatment of Lunatics and Their Property. The results of its investigations were published in April and August 1859 and July 1860, just before and during the serialization of *The Woman in White* in *All the Year Round* (26 November 1859–25 August 1860).

In July 1859, after a hearing in law, Reade's Exhibit A, Arthur Fletcher, was proved to be of sound mind, whatever his moral deficiencies might have been. Having pamphleteered for the reform of the entrepreneurial madhouse system, Reade now began to amass a great stock of printed material, letters, oral interviews, and other kinds of evidence that he hoarded until he used them as the basis for *Hard Cash* (1863), in which he typically overreached himself, writing in a shrill register and allowing his readers no opportunity to put two and two together for themselves.[11] Although he insisted, as usual, that his narrative was supported by facts, a *Times* reviewer declared that "the incautious reader is apt to imagine mad doctors to be scientific scoundrels, lunatic asylums to be a refined sort of Tophet, and the commissioners in lunacy and visiting justices to be a flock of sheep."[12] Reade's treatment of the same theme in a subsequent novel, *A Terrible Temptation*, was open to a

LAW AND LUNACY;
Or, A Glorious Oyster Season for the Lawyers.

Properly speaking, there seems to have been no formal "lunatics inquiry" (by an appointed investigative body) when this cartoon was published in *Punch* on 25 January 1862. But a "Lunacy Regulation Bill," supported by an "Official Return of Lunatics and Idiots" in custody, was before the House of Commons, and the publicity they received would have sharpened public interest in *The Woman in White* and, a year later, *Hard Cash*.

like objection, and seemingly it was less timely; but because the action was spread well over two decades, Reade might justifiably have argued, with *Hard Cash* as evidence, that it had been a burning issue at that time. And he was not, in any case, disposed to sacrifice a proved attention-getter. Not surprisingly, the revived topic stimulated a newspaper correspondence which Reade included, as part of the documentary record, in the volume that followed serialization.

Legitimate claimants to the title of "doctor" abounded in Victorian fiction as walk-on characters whenever a figure in the plot fell ill—Trollope's eminent society physician Sir Omicron Pie, for example—but only once in a while were their professional acquirements and wisdom made much of. The one to whom a novelist paid the most handsome tribute was Thackeray's personal physician, Dr. John Elliotson, who is mentioned by name, as an expert mesmerist, in *Vanity Fair*. Thackeray dedicated *Pendennis* to him as a token of gratitude for his "constant watchfulness and skill" and "great goodness and kindness" during the novelist's recent serious illness, and he appears several times in the novel as Dr. Goodenough, Pen's physician. In *The Newcomes* he attends Sir Brian's family. Only in *Middlemarch* does the medical profession come into real prominence, when George Eliot pits Lydgate, the apostle of scientific medicine, against his stodgy, old-fashioned, or downright incompetent fellow practitioners. Lydgate is so far in the vanguard of his profession that even good physicians (for their time) seem quacks in comparison.[13]

It was the practitioners of false medicine whose names, not personalities, occurred most often in Victorian fiction. The charlatan-physician, who concocted and dispensed remedies of dubious therapeutic powers, often, early on, with the equally questionable assistance of astrology, was of course not new to the English scene. Earlier manufacturers of specific or all-purpose medicines had earned fame if not necessarily fortune: Dr. Robert James's (1705–76) powder and pill were relied on by several generations of British families, and Godfrey's opium-loaded pacifier, euphemistically called a "cordial," served nineteenth-century mothers of high and low estate, the latter being thus freed to go out to work in factories while their malnourished and drugged babies slept an unnatural sleep from which, all too often, there was no awakening.

Although Godfrey's preparation is the one most often mentioned in historical accounts of Victorian working-class life, Daffy's Elixir, another powerful soporific, is met frequently in fiction, to a variety of effects. Amelia Sedley Osborne's mother "surreptitiously" administered the potion to little George, her grandson, thereby precipitating a bitter scene between them, one of the few occasions when the normally passive Amelia showed any spirit.

> Amelia flung the bottle crashing into the fire-place. "I will *not* have baby poisoned, mamma," cried Emmy, rocking the infant about violently with both her arms around him, and turning with flashing eyes at her mother.
> "Poisoned, Amelia!" said the old lady; "this language to me?"
> "He shall not have any medicine but that which Mr. Pestler sends for him. He told me that Daffy's Elixir was poison."
> "Very good: you think I'm a murderess then," replied Mrs. Sedley. "This is the language you use to your mother. I have met with misfortunes: I have sunk low in life: I have kept my carriage, and now walk on foot: but I

did not know I was a murderess before, and thank you for the *news*" (*Vanity Fair*, 38:375–76).

Writing in *The Newcomes* of the kinds of life to which the children of various social classes were committed, Thackeray cited as an example a "pauper child in London [who] at seven years old knows how to go to market, to fetch the beer, to pawn father's coat," and perform other domestic tasks, and "is dosed with Daffy's Elixir, and somehow survives the drug" (53:2.162). Advising Eleanor Bold on little Johnny's teething problems, Miss Thorne in *Barchester Towers* first recommends a coral rubbed well with carrot juice, but since Eleanor doesn't have a coral, she asks, "with almost angry vehemence," "Have you got Daffy's Elixir?" "Eleanor," says Trollope, "explained that she had not. It had not been ordered by Mr. Rerechild, the Barchester doctor whom she employed; and then the young mother mentioned some shockingly modern succedaneum, which Mr. Rerechild's new lights had taught him to recommend. Miss Thorne looked awfully severe. 'Take care, my dear,' she said, 'that the man knows what he's about; take care he doesn't destroy your little boy'" (23:312). Miss Thorne obviously had more faith in Daffy's Elixir than she did in Eleanor's pediatrician: after all, the mixture had been time-tested for almost two centuries (the brainchild of a Leicestershire clergyman, Thomas Daffy [died 1690], it was being administered at bedsides as early as 1673). In a lighter vein, during a New Year's party in *Mr. Sponge's Sporting Tour*, Captain Seedeybuck, pouring out an adult-size jolt of whiskey for young George Cheek, pupil at the "classical and commercial academy" of Flagellation Hall, jovially recommended it in these terms: "Now, young man, this is the real Daffy's Elixir that you read of in the papers. It's the finest compound that ever was known. It will make your hair curl, your whiskers grow, and you a man before your mother . . ." (63:404).

The venerable quack-medicine trade had been one of the chief early supports of the primitive advertising industry, as early as the seventeenth century: like the alliance of Chaucer's physician and apothecary, the one between quackery and puffery was not "new to begin." With increasing literacy and cheap access to printed means of communication in the nineteenth century, quackery, in the right hands, might prove a road to easy riches. Advertisements for various nostrums appeared everywhere, from circulars, wall posters, pavement stencilings, and the sides of buses to the columns of newspapers and the part issues of Dickens's and Thackeray's novels.[†]

[†]Browning paid tribute to the sloganeering of quack-remedy advertising when, in *Pippa Passes* (1841), one of the foreign students jauntily alluded to "Hebe's plaister—One

The more widely the advances of scientific knowledge in other fields
were proclaimed, the more the continuing relative inability of the medical profession to cure illness became apparent, and in any event, medical
help of any kind was beyond the reach of millions of the poor and isolated. And so the pill-maker's incessant advertising, aided as always by
word-of-mouth testimony, exploited a popular reliance on self-help doc-
toring that was not only deep-seated but spreading. Even people who
could easily afford the services of the most fashionable and expensive
physicians patronized the vendors of Podgers' Pills, Rodgers' Pills, and
Pokey's Elixir. These were among the remedies Lady Southdown in
Vanity Fair, a practitioner of "quack theology and medicine" (33:323),
recommended to her friends; if they failed to produce bodily improvement, she provided a backup in the form of religious tracts for the improvement of her friends' souls. "Becky first accepted the tracts, and
began to examine them with great interest, engaging the Dowager in a
conversation concerning them and the welfare of her soul, by which
means she hoped that her body might escape medication. But after the
religious topics were exhausted, Lady Macbeth would not quit Becky's
chamber until her cup of night-drink was emptied too . . . " (33:323).

The Lady Macbeth angle was too precious to waste, and so to appreciative audiences in her Mayfair drawing room Becky merged Lady
Southdown with Mrs. Siddons in the sleepwalking scene (Doctor: "This
disease is beyond my practice. . . . More needs she the divine than the
physician"): "Becky acted the whole scene for them. She put on a night-
cap and gown. She preached a great sermon in the true serious manner:
she lectured on the virtue of the medicine which she pretended to
administer, with a gravity of imitation so perfect, that you would
have thought it was the Countess' own Roman nose through which she
snuffled. . . . And for the first time in her life the Dowager Countess of
Southdown was made amusing" (41:406).

The very concept of quackery was enlarged, thanks particularly to
Carlyle's use of it in his vituperative diagnosis of contemporary social ills
in *Past and Present*. To him, the tragic "condition of England" in modern
times was its domination by quacks of one stripe or another; it was
no accident that two of the chapters of *Past and Present* were titled
"Morrison's Pill" and "Morrison Again." The nation's soul, he cried,
could be saved only by "a total change of regimen, change of constitution
and existence from the very centre of it; a new body to be got, with
resuscitated soul": "This is sad news to a disconsolate discerning Public,

---

strip Cools your lip. Phoebus' emulsion—One bottle Clears your Throttle. Mercury's bo-
lus—One box Cures—" (Browning pulled up short of a mild Victorian naughtiness).

hoping to have got off by some Morrison's Pill, some Saint-John's corrosive mixture and perhaps a little blistery friction on the back!"

Each of the two sovereign remedies Carlyle mentioned had a colorful
history behind it. James Morison (the correct spelling; Carlyle always got
it wrong, as, following him, did some novelists) was a retired Baltic and
West Indian merchant who in 1825 put on the market a product that
would perform cures where doctors had failed, as Morison testified
they had done in his case after thirty-five tedious years of suffering.[14]
Morison's Vegetable Universal Pill came in two varieties, one containing
aloes, cream of tartar, and gum, the other fortified with gamboge and
colocynth. These mixtures were of universal application indeed: they
were claimed to be effective against, among other fleshly ailments, fevers, scarlatina, smallpox, consumption, and senility. Their purgative
effect was well known and apparently more desired than feared. John
Jorrocks, addressing a political meeting as a drafted candidate for Parliament in the Corn Law interest, recalled a time when the very mention
of Napoleon Bonaparte's name "worked one wuss nor a whole box o'
Morrison's pills" (*Hillingdon Hall*, 46:458).

The pill's initial success encouraged its inventor to set up his headquarters under the name of the British College of Health in London's
New Road.[†] From then on until his death in 1840, Morison—if not all
his vicarious patients—moved from strength to strength. He even went
so far as to hire Exeter Hall, with its odor of Evangelical sanctity, for
"Hygiene meetings" in which he preached independence of conscience,
the virtues of his pill, and the wickedness of ignorant doctors who bled
their patients to death. In 1834 the record of his purchases of revenue
stamps (1 1/2*d*. per box) indicated that he sold more than 1.1 million
boxes annually. His successors were reputed to clear £80,000 a year.

The Carlylean use of Morison's pill as an emblem of ceaselessly promoted but ineffectual social panaceas persisted in fiction. In Reade's *It Is
Never Too Late to Mend*, the idealistic prison reformer, Mr. Eden, recalled
as he recovered from an illness a dialogue he had had with a fever-
created apparition on "the good points of every system, and others of
his own": "'Yes,' said he in answer to his imaginary companion, 'there
shall be both separation and silence for those whose moral case it
suits,—for all, perhaps, at first,—but not for all always. Away with your

---

[†]Guarded by a sculptured lion that no doubt was a cousin of the better-known ones in
Trafalgar Square, it was still a landmark in 1868, when Matthew Arnold referred to it in
his essay "Anarchy and Authority" (later included in *Culture and Anarchy*) in the July issue
of the *Cornhill Magazine*. Earlier, in "The Function of Criticism at the Present Time" (*National Magazine*, 1864), he had dismissed it, justly enough, as "the grand name without the
grand thing."

The circumstances of this squib (*Punch*, 3 April 1852) are, for
the moment, obscure. The accompanying text asserted that
the "People of England" were being urged in a series of advertisements to erect a monument to Morison, who had died in
1840. But why the tribute was delayed for a dozen years is
unexplained.

Morrison's pill-system, your childish monotony of moral treatment in
cases varying and sometimes opposed'" (18:1.298).

Carlyle's allusion to "Saint-John's corrosive mixture" would have been
as intelligible to his readers as was "Morrison's pill," even though no
reference work identifies Saint John under that name. Every reader
knew that Carlyle meant John St. John *Long*, a man whose name had
been much in the news a dozen years before, and whose memory was

still vivid.[15] Long was a tall, gaunt Irishman with a stutter, who after failing to become a painter (he was one of John Martin's few pupils), turned with spectacular success to medical charlatanism. His drastic form of treatment won him a large, hopeful clientele. His all-embracing therapeutic theory was simplicity itself: a disease is centered in a particular organ, therefore it can be cured by applying to that organ, through the skin, a special "corrosive mixture." Properly administered, it was recommended primarily for consumption, but also for stubborn cases of rheumatism, gout, abscesses of the lungs and liver, and insanity. In the case of consumption, the proper administration was to have the patient breathe hot air through red morocco leather tubes while the physician rubbed his or her chest or back with the caustic liniment. In the case of an already amputated limb—the leg that the Marquis of Anglesey lost at Waterloo—Long rubbed the liniment on the place where it had been severed, to no great effect, unless we accept the contemporary rumor that a toe grew out of the stump, somewhat in the manner of Mrs. Nickleby's conception of Miss Biffin.

Scientific diagnosis was still in its infancy in Long's time, and however erroneous most of his interpretations of his patients' symptoms may have been, he cannot also be faulted for having overlooked an affliction that was as yet unrecognized and unnamed. What brought most of his patients, money in hand, to his consulting room was sheer masochism. In 1830, not surprisingly, one of his patients died, and he was haled into court on a charge of manslaughter. Appearing in his behalf were several titled men and women who had not only survived but, they testified, been cured of whatever ailed them. Despite the strong support of his carriage trade, Long was convicted, but he was let off with a £250 fine. Soon thereafter, he was charged in another case but acquitted. The newspapers were full of the subject, and *Fraser's Magazine* ran articles on Long by Carlyle's physician brother. The combative Thomas Wakley, editor of the *Lancet*, waged against Long a campaign as corrosive as his salve.

Long came to a melancholy, if ironically fitting, end. He contracted (or perhaps already had) tuberculosis, and notwithstanding his patients' faith in his cure, he refrained from risking his own skin with the corrosive mixture. As a consequence, he died in 1834, leaving an estate composed mainly of his precious recipe (50 percent acetic acid, 25 percent spirits of turpentine suspended in egg yolk, and the remainder miscellaneous), which reputedly was sold for £10,000.

Repeated allusions by writers other than Carlyle demonstrate how durable was the public memory of Long. Thackeray referred to him in "The Snobs of England" (*Punch*, 14 November 1846; *BS*, 144). Lady

Blanche Fitzague, he wrote, "has tried everything [in a medical way] on her own person. She went into Court, and testified publicly her faith in St. John Long; she swore by Doctor Buchan, she took quantities of Gambouge's Universal Medicine, and whole boxfulls of Parr's Life Pills."[†] As late as the 1870s Long's name appeared in *Middlemarch* and *Far from the Madding Crowd.* George Eliot swept together much information on him during her research into the headline events of 1831–32, and her brief allusion to him helped fill out her pattern of contrasting the medically avant-garde Lydgate with his contemporaries:

> The medical aversion to Lydgate was hardly disguised now. Neither Dr. Sprague nor Dr. Minchin said that he disliked Lydgate's knowledge, or his disposition to improve treatment: what they disliked was his arrogance, which nobody felt to be altogether deniable. They implied that he was insolent, pretentious, and given to that reckless innovation for the sake of noise and show which was the essence of the charlatan.
>
> The word charlatan once thrown on the air could not be let drop. In those days the world was agitated about the wondrous doings of Mr. St. John Long, "noblemen and gentlemen" attesting his extraction of a fluid like mercury from the temples of a patient.

"There's St. John Long," chimed in Mr. Toller, who had not been paying attention, "that's the kind of fellow we call a charlatan, advertising cures in ways nobody knows anything about; a fellow who wants to make a noise by pretending to go deeper than other people. The other day he was pretending to tap a man's brain and get quicksilver out of it." ("Good gracious!" exclaimed Mrs. Taft, "what dreadful trifling with people's constitutions!") (45:493–94)

[†]"Gambouge," of course, was Morison. The other two allusions are straight from life. William Buchan's *Domestic Medicine* was a popular home medical guide first published as long before as 1769; it was to Mrs. Tickit, the Meagles's housekeeper in *Little Dorrit*, what Robinson Crusoe was to that other faithful servant, Gabriel Betteredge in *The Moonstone*, a veritable icon in book form. But while Betteredge used his book as a kind of secular Sortes Biblicae, Mrs. Tickit stored her spectacles between the pages of Buchan, "the lucubrations of which learned practitioner, Mr. Meagles implicitly believed she had never yet consulted to the extent of one word in her life" (1.16:242). Parr's Life Pills were touted as possessing an aperient action which acted against both constipation and diarrhoea, thus enhancing a woman's beauty and lending new vigor to her body. Herbert Ingram, a Nottingham printer, bookseller, and newsagent, reputedly bought the formula from a descendant of the celebrated Thomas Parr, who was said to have lived to the age of one hundred fifty two, thanks to regular dosage with this pharmaceutical wonder-worker. To widen the market for his product, Ingram moved to London and there (1842) founded the *Illustrated London News*, where Parr's advertisements often appeared. There seems, however, to have been no other connection between the pill and the paper, which Ingram had been planning for some time, originally as a crime sheet rather than a general-news weekly.

Hardy, too, relied on his reader's recognition of an allusion that, by the time he wrote *Far from the Madding Crowd*, was more than forty years old. Farmer Boldwood's "deep attachment" to Bathsheba after having been for many years "the perfect exemplar of thriving bachelorship . . . was an anticlimax somewhat resembling that of St. John Long's death by consumption in the midst of his proofs that it was not a fatal disease" (22:131).

It was said that when Long was convicted he paid the fine by peeling £250 in notes from a large roll in his pocket. The fact that over-the-counter medicines paved the way to some men's wealth made quackery something of a scandal, ready for novelists' polemic or satiric use. That their advertisements appeared in, among other places, radical papers with a working-class audience added fuel to Kingsley's Carlylean outburst (in the person of Alton Locke) to O'Flynn, the editor of the *Weekly Warwhoop*:

> "You a patriot? You are a humbug. Look at those advertisements, and deny it if you can. Crying out for education, and helping to debauch the public mind with Voltaire's 'Candide' and Eugène Sue—swearing by Jesus, and puffing Atheism and blasphemy—yelling at a quack government, quack law, quack priesthoods, and then dirtying your fingers with half-crowns for advertising Holloway's ointment and Parr's life pills—shrieking about slavery of labor to capital, and inserting Moses and Son's doggerel-ranting about searching investigations and the march of knowledge. . . ." (*Alton Locke*, 23:203)

Thomas Holloway's ointment, first marketed about 1838, and somewhat later his pills were probably the most heavily advertised of all Victorian remedies. According to George Robinson, the advertising enthusiast in Trollope's *The Struggles of Brown, Jones, and Robinson*, in 1860 the proprietor had the biggest promotion budget in the nation—£30,000 a year, compared with the £10,000 spent by each of two firms, E. Moses and Sons and the makers of Rowlands' Kalydor. Fifteen years later, it was between £40,000 and £50,000.[†] Holloway, a notable collector of contemporary art, died a millionaire in 1883; his chief memorial is the Royal Holloway College for women, a component of the University of London that is now merged with Bedford College.

[†] In the November 1848 number of the *Pendennis Advertiser*, Holloway's pills were represented as providentially offering, in a season when cholera was ravaging the London slums and everyone lived in fear of contagion, a specific preventive for the disease. One had only to take five or six at night, repeat the dose in the morning for fifteen days, and take dietary precautions. Nothing was said about abstaining from the London drinking water, which was the true vector of cholera.

Bubbles of the Year.—Patent Life Pills.

In "Punch's Almanack" for 1845, appearing in the year's first issue, Mr. Punch took aim at the most famous proprietors of patent medicines, whose names were increasingly famous, thanks to widespread advertising. The death's-head and ironic inscription on the cannon wheel ("Licensed by Government") refer to the lack of regulation of these potentially harmful curealls.

It was typical of the times that when the resourceful and resilient Captain Wragge, in Collins's *No Name*, after engaging in several dubious enterprises, finally came upon the pot at the end of the rainbow, it proved to be filled not with gold but with packets of pills of at least equivalent value.

> "Here I am [he says], with my clothes positively paid for; with a balance at my banker's; with my servant in livery, and my gig at the door; solvent, flourishing, popular—and all on a Pill. . . . There is not a single form of appeal in the whole range of human advertisement which I am not making to the unfortunate public at this moment. Hire the last new novel, there I am, inside the boards of the book. Send for the last new Song—the instant you open the leaves, I drop out of it. Take a cab—I fly in at the window in red. Buy a box of tooth powder at the chemist's—I wrap it up for you in blue. Show yourself at the theatre—I flutter down on you in yellow. The mere titles of my advertisements are quite irresistible. Let me quote a few from last week's issue. Proverbial Title: 'A Pill in time saves nine.' Familiar Title: 'Excuse me, how is your Stomach?' Patriotic Title: 'What are the three characteristics of a true-born Englishman? His Hearth, his Home, and His Pill.' Title in the form of a nursery dialogue: 'Mamma, I am not well.' 'What

is the matter, my pet?' 'I want a little Pill.' Title in the form of a Historical Anecdote: 'New Discovery in the Mine of English History. When the
Princes were smothered in the Tower, their faithful attendant collected all
their little possessions left behind them. Among the touching trifles dear to
the poor boys, he found a tiny Box. It contained the Pill of the Period. Is it
necessary to say how inferior that Pill was to its Successor, which prince and
peasant alike may now obtain?'—Et cetera, et cetera. The place in which my
Pill is made is an advertisement in itself. I have got one of the largest shops
in London. Behind one counter (visible to the public through the lucid medium of plate-glass) are four-and-twenty young men, in white aprons, making the Pill. Behind another counter are four-and-twenty young men, in
white cravats, making the boxes. At the bottom of the shop are three elderly accountants, posting the vast financial transactions accruing from the
Pill in three enormous ledgers. Over the door are my name, portrait, and
autograph, expanded to colossal proportions, and surrounded in flowing
letters, by the motto of the establishment, 'Down with the Doctors!' Even
Mrs. Wragge [a gigantic imbecile] contributes her quota to this prodigious
enterprise. She is the celebrated woman whom I have cured of indescrib-
able agonies from every complaint under the sun. Her portrait is engraved
on all the wrappers, with the following inscription beneath it: 'Before she
took the Pill you might have blown this patient away with a feather. Look at
her now!!!'" ("Last scene," chap. 2:2.446–48)

Collins doubtless meant Captain Wragge to be a composite figure, recalling Morison, Holloway, and who knows what other contemporary large-
scale manufacturers of patent medicines who saturated the public consciousness with their advertising and thereby struck it rich.

One other successful entrepreneur of the sort in fiction, though he
is never seen, was the late father of Martha Dunstable, the humorous, loud-voiced, "kind, generous, and open-hearted" heiress in *Doctor
Thorne* and *Framley Parsonage*. An apothecary by trade, he had become
the proprietor of a money-spinning preparation called the Oil (or Balm)
of Lebanon; Trollope does not pause to describe its properties or the
maladies to which it was applied. The elder Dunstable would have been
an interesting addition to Trollope's gallery of plutocrats, had the novelist chosen to portray him. But Trollope's interest lay in his daughter
and the position in which she found herself as, in her own deprecatory
words, "a quack doctor," "a woman who sold the oil of Lebanon." She
had inherited over £200,000, "a great deal of money, certainly," said
Lady Arabella Gresham (*Doctor Thorne*, 6:71–72), but not nearly as
much as the "half a dozen millions of money" with which some people
credited her. (To Dr. Thorne she was simply "the richest woman in England.") Though she came to visit Courcy Castle with an entourage and
equipment reminiscent of the banker's (merry) widow Harriot Mellon

Coutts (pages 593–94 below)—her own carriage, horses, coachman, footman, and maid, as well as "half a score of trunks full of wearing apparel; some of them nearly as rich as that wonderful box which was stolen a short time since from the top of a cab" (16:168)[†]—she was still not as rich as Sir Roger Scatcherd, whose fortune came into Mary Thorne's possession after his son's death. But it was a sufficiency, permitting her, as it did, to continue living in her father's London house, known to the populace as "Ointment Hall" (cf. Gunter's Currant Jelly Hall), an enormous mansion that "had been built by an eccentric millionaire at an enormous cost, and the eccentric millionaire, after living in it for twelve months, had declared that it did not possess a single comfort, and that it was deficient in most of those details, which . . . are necessary to the very existence of man" (*Framley Parsonage*, 29:2.61).[‡]

The trouble was, the origin of Martha Dunstable's fortune stigmatized her. The Scatcherd money had been obtained from a perfectly legitimate form of Victorian enterprise, although it was still questionable in the minds of people who clung to the belief that the only really defensible fortunes were based on the land. Rough and rich adventurers like Scatcherd, self-made and contributing at home and abroad, through their contracts for building foreign railways, to the nation's economic might, belonged to a new class of heroes. But wealth derived from patent medicines was another matter. Freely though the ailments they purported to cure were enumerated in advertising, at a time when any kind of commercial publicity that was less than decorous offended discrimi-

[†]Trollope was referring to a recent heist (December 1857) that the press had treated in a deservedly seriocomic fashion. The elderly Countess of Ellesmere, on her way to visit at Windsor Castle, sent ahead of her to Paddington station a cab on whose roof was loosely secured a trunk containing £15,000-worth of "her ladyship's grandeur" in clothing and jewels. Happening to notice this inviting cargo as it trundled through Grosvenor Square, a self-described house painter hopped aboard and, unobserved by the driver or the maids inside, delivered it into the willing arms of his mate, a "labourer," and his wife. Embarrassed by the riches they discovered when they opened the trunk in the back parlor of a Shoreditch oil shop, they got rid of them at deep discounts, selling Lady Ellesmere's wardrobe for three pounds and some jewels to "a Jew" for £300. They threw away other jewelry, including a pair of diamond earrings that landed in a field near Whitechapel. Detected and arrested, these incompetent practitioners were convicted of theft and received sentences of various lengths. (*Annual Register 1857*, Chronicle pp. 243–46.)

[‡]In a notable case of art anticipating life, this fictional invention of 1870 became an actual much talked about topicality in ensuing years. The shady financier "Baron" Albert Grant (pages 430–31n, above) erected, on a parcel of sites in Kensington, a French-style palace that cost the huge sum of £300,000 and, according to contemporary witnesses, was in proportionally bad taste. But it stood empty for six years, and when its owner ran into serious money difficulties, it was demolished (1882) without ever having been occupied.

nating taste, illness was a subject that respectable, Trollopian people were not inclined to talk about with any particularity in their drawing rooms. From that point of view, therefore, the Dunstable fortune was suspect. On the other hand, it was indubitably a fortune, safely invested in a thriving business, and in the estimate of the comparatively impecunious county families, the DeCourcys and Greshams, its sheer size easily neutralized the stigma attached to its source. Wealth on that majestic scale is a powerful solvent of prejudice.

Trollope presents Martha Dunstable as a woman whose strong character enables her to transcend the aura of quackery and puffery that she inherited along with the money. She had in fact, said Trollope, "a thorough love of ridiculing the world's humbugs." That she was already thirty years old (in *Doctor Thorne*; in *Framley Parsonage*, published only two years later, she was "well past forty") would ordinarily have reduced her eligibility for marriage, but her possession of such riches stopped the clock, if it did not actually set its hands back. There was pleasant irony in the fact that eventually the Oil of Lebanon money landed, by marriage, in the lap of a competent, though not brilliant, legitimate physician, Dr. Thorne himself. His stuffy rival, Dr. Fillgrave, recognized that irony but transformed it into acid sarcasm. "He has been little better than a quack all his life," he said, "and now he is going to marry a quack's daughter" (*Framley Parsonage*, 47:2.292).

Somewhere between the legitimate medical profession and the lucrative charlatanism of Morison and Holloway (and, beginning at midcentury, Thomas Beecham, whose pills, as everyone knew, were "worth a guinea a box!") lay homeopathy. Homeopathic physicians, disciples of Charles Gottfried Samuel Hahnemann (1755–1843), based their treatment on the so-called law of similars, which held that a disease could be cured by a dose of whatever drug produced the same symptoms in a healthy person, so that malaria, for example, could be cured by quinine, which also induced high fever. Hahnemann also maintained that, contrary to common belief, less was more; the efficacy of a drug was inversely proportional to the amount administered, hence gradual and careful reduction of the dosage, down to a microscopic amount, hastened the cure. (In *Oliver Twist* [42:380], Dickens used the term as a synonym for stinginess when Noah Claypole administered "homeopathic doses" of cold beef and porter to the exhausted and famished Charlotte.) Orthodox physicians opposed homeopathy as a more than ordinarily pretentious branch of quackery that wrapped itself in the mantle of science, and in the 1850s it narrowly escaped being declared illegal. None of its practitioners could be admitted to the British Medical Association. It was in this atmosphere of distrust and controversy that

THE HOMŒOPATHIC MINISTER.

"YOU SEE, MR. JOHN BULL, LARGE DOSES OF REFORM ARE BAD FOR YOUR CONSTITUTION. BUT HERE
IS A GLOBULE, OR INFINITESIMAL BILL, WHICH," ETC., ETC.

"Homeopathic" was a byword for caution and stinginess, obviously unsuited to
the figure of a well-fed John Bull, and it also had a strong connotation of quackery, here applied to Disraeli, who had just achieved his first cabinet post as chancellor of the exchequer in Derby's short-lived ministry (*Punch*, 7 February 1852).

Thackeray, in *Pendennis*, classified it with mesmerism and hydropathy. Shortly afterward (*My Novel* [1852–53]), Bulwer-Lytton created the character of Dr. Morgan, "an able and warm-hearted man" but a homeopath. There was no reason why the novelist should have assigned the doctor to a heretical sect rather than to the respectable community of British physicians, except that doing so provided a means of easing into the book a lengthy debate on homeopathy.

This was the only substantial passage on the subject in Victorian fiction, but devotion to homeopathy served once in a while as a characterizing device. "One year," wrote Disraeli in *Tancred*, "Lady Hampshire never quitted Leamington [spa]; another, she contrived to combine the infinitesimal doses of Hahnemann with the colossal distractions of the metropolis" (1.5:31). Thackeray's Lady Blanche Fitzague, that fervent devotee of St. John Long's fiery balm and Parr's pills, extended her medical catholicity so far as to wear a picture of Hahnemann in her bracelet, and a woman in Emily Eden's *The Semi-Attached Couple* declared herself "a great homoeopathist."†

3.

However acute their philosophical differences may have been, homeopaths and their allopathic opponents shared one problem: the unpre-

---

†Another topical enthusiasm, taken seriously by some but easily lending itself to charlatanism, was phrenology, the supposed science of reading character from the contours of the cranium, based, as Dickens put it in "Our Next-Door Neighbour" (*Sketches by Boz*, "Our Parish," chap. 7:40) on the assumption that "the agitation of a man's brain by different passions, produces corresponding developments in the form of his skull." He played fancifully with this and the related pseudoscience of physiognomy (the art of reading character in the face) in his paragraphs on door knockers in this essay. (See also the quotation from "The Lazy Tour of Two Idle Apprentices" [pages 523–24 above].) The main British advocate of phrenology was George Combe—"the sagacious Mr. Combe," as Bulwer called him in *Paul Clifford*—who had been spreading the news through a society, a journal, lectures, and books in the 1820s. The Brontë sisters were much affected by both phrenology and physiognomy, to which they frequently referred in their novels. A few years before these appeared, Surtees wrote a substantial passage on the subject in *Hillingdon Hall* (1843–44), and a decade later, Colonel Newcome's friend Binnie drew a phrenological profile of Clive's fitness for a profession: "I place his qualities thus:—Love of approbation, sixteen. Benevolence, fourteen, Combativeness, fourteen. Adhesiveness, two. Amativeness is not yet of course fully developed, but I expect will be prodigiously strong. The imaginative and reflective organs are very large; those of calculation weak. He may make a poet or a painter, or you may make a sojer of him, though worse men than him's good enough for that—but a bad merchant, a lazy lawyer, and a miserable mathematician. He has wit and conscientiousness, so ye mustn't think of making a clergyman out of him" (*The Newcomes*, 8:1.91). That Dickens and Thackeray, in addition to the sporting squire Surtees and

dictable quality of the drugs they prescribed. Apothecary chemists like
Pendennis's late father (whose own record was clean, so far as we are
told), enjoyed the same lack of governmental regulation that allowed the
makers of pills, powders, and ointments to pile up riches while they en-
dangered the health, indeed the very lives, of countless men, women,
and children. Prescriptions written by physicians like Dr. Thorne might
well be contaminated with often dangerous additives without their
knowledge.

This was one part of a problem which encompassed large portions of
the nation's food and drink trade.[16] As early as 1820, Friedrich Christian
Accum, the librarian of the Royal Institution, wrote a book exposing the
widespread practice of adulteration, with special reference to druggists'
and wholesale grocers' selling extraneous materials to breweries. The
book, naming names, went into four editions in two years, but Accum
was charged with purloining leaves from rare books he had in his
care—one cannot help suspecting a frame-up—and, jumping bail, he
fled to his native Germany. Because at that time novelists had no interest
in any such questions of the public weal, the event went unnoticed in
fiction, and when the brief uproar had subsided, the merchants of im-
purities, who had in fact broken no laws, resumed their profitable ways.

In 1848, however, one John Mitchell published a *Treatise on the Falsi-
fications of Food, and the Chemical Means Employed to Detect Them*, evidence
of either a continuing or a revived interest in the subject. Whether or
not George Meredith remembered the book, adulteration was one of the
topicalities that figured in *Diana of the Crossways*, which was set in those
very years. On a blazing summer afternoon in London, the perspiring
Thomas Redworth, walking to a City bank, overheard "a couple of jour-
neymen close ahead of him":

> One asked the other if he had ever tried any of that cold stuff they were
> now selling out of barrows, with cream. His companion answered that he
> had not got much opinion of the stuff of the sort; and what was it like?
>   "Well, it's cheap, it ain't bad; it's cooling. But it ain't refreshing."
>   "Just what I reckoned all that newfangle rubbish."
>   Without a consultation, the conservatives in beverage filed with a smart
> turn about, worthy of veterans at parade on the drill-ground, into a public-
> house; and a dialogue, chiefly remarkable for absence of point, furnished
> matter to the politician's head of the hearer. Provided that their beer was
> unadulterated! Beer they would have; and why not, in weather like this?

the sheltered young women in the Haworth parsonage, had a common interest in phrenology is evidence of how widely it was disseminated—and credited—in early Victorian
years.

But how to make the publican honest! And he was not the only trickster preying on the multitudinous poor copper crowd, rightly to be protected by the silver and the golden. Revelations of the arts practised to plump them with raw-earth and minerals in the guise of nourishment, had recently knocked at the door of the general conscience and obtained a civil reply from the footman. Repulsive as the thought was to one still holding to Whiggish Liberalism, though flying various Radical kites, he was caught by the decisive ultra-torrent, and whirled to admit the necessity for the interference of the State, to stop the poisoning of the poor. (41:457–58)

Meredith here—in 1884—was treating the adulteration issue as it had developed over the past thirty-plus years. It was a component in the cluster of public-health issues that were at the center of the debate over the proper function and limits of government. From breweries and public houses the practice of introducing inappropriate substances had spread, by mid-century, to dairies, bakeries, and retail grocery shops. Between 1851 and 1854, Thomas Wakley, the West Middlesex coroner who was remembered as St. John Long's nemesis twenty years earlier, published in the *Lancet*, side by side with examples of blatant untruth-in-advertising, the findings of the paper's "Analytical and Sanitary Commission" headed by two analytical chemists who were also M.D.s. One was Arthur Hill Hassall, who assembled all the documents in a 659-page volume expansively entitled *Food and Its Adulterations . . . Being Records of the Results of Some Thousands of Original Microscopical and Chemical Analyses of the Solids and Fluids Consumed by All Classes of the Public; and Containing the Names and Addresses of the Various Merchants, Manufacturers, and Tradesmen of Whom the Analysed Articles Were Purchased*. This exposé was discussed at length in the *Quarterly Review* (March 1855), and additional publicity was generated by the findings of a select committee of Commons the same year. Popularized books with such titles as *Tricks of the Trade in the Adulteration of Food and Physic* (1856) reraked the muck.

The scandal, extending as it did into every kitchen, dining room, sickroom, and public house in the realm, aroused more concern than any of the kind since the publication of Chadwick's blue book on sanitation. In *Alton Locke*, Sandy Mackaye complained of "Bread full o' alum and bones, and sic filth" (6:56), and Tennyson wrote in *Maud*, ". . . chalk and alum and plaster are sold to the poor for bread, / And the spirit of murder works in the very means of life. . . ." The brewers of Burton's ales, which had been specifically exempted from the *Lancet*'s censure, bought advertising pages in the monthly numbers of *Bleak House*—no fewer than eight in the one for November 1852—to display further testimonials to the purity of their pale and bitter. Reade transferred the topicality to a scene in the Australian goldfields when, in *It*

THE USE OF ADULTERATION.

Little Girl. "IF YOU PLEASE, SIR, MOTHER SAYS, WILL YOU LET HER HAVE A QUARTER OF A POUND OF YOUR BEST TEA TO KILL THE RATS WITH, AND A OUNCE OF CHOCOLATE AS WOULD GET RID OF THE BLACK BEADLES?"

Now that the widespread adulteration of food and drink had become a burning public issue, *Punch* (4 August 1855) brought back the little girl who had bought arsenic "for the rats" (see illustration, page 517), this time to buy tea—a universal household beverage—for the same deadly purpose.

Is Never Too Late to Mend (1856), he had a pair of hard-bitten prospectors buy from a peddler a packet of books that he assured them were "spicey." To their disappointment, "There was not even a stray hint or an indelicate expression for the poor fellows' two shillings. The fraud was complete. It was not like the ground coffee, pepper, and mustard in a London shop—in which there is as often as not a pinch of real coffee, mustard, and pepper, to a pound of chiccory [*sic*] and bullock's blood, of red-lead, dirt, flour, and turmeric. Here the do was pure" (47:1.531).

In *Barchester Towers* (1857) Miss Thorne complained that she offered her guests "good honest household cake, made of currants and flour and eggs and sweetmeat; but they would feed themselves on trashy wafers from the shop of the Barchester pastry-cook, on chalk and gum and adulterated sugar" (36:417)—there was junk food even then. "Nothing," said the philosophical artist, Vance, in Bulwer-Lytton's *What Will He Do With It?* (1857–59), "is pure and unadulterated in London use; not cream, nor cayenne pepper—least of all fame—mixed up with the most deleterious ingredients" (6.1:1.547).

In cheap story papers, the ingredients of up-to-date melodrama might include the administration of poisons whose purchase was uncontrolled by law, as testimony at the Palmer, Smith, and Smethurst trials, among others, was dramatically revealing, year by year. In a passage in *The Three Clerks* already quoted (pages 79–80), Charley Tudor, author of the story "Crinoline and Macassar," read to Harry Norman another tale he had been working on. He reached the point where the hero is "lying with an open bottle [of poison] in his hand."[†]

> "Having committed suicide?" asked Norman.
> "No, not at all. The editor says that we must always have a slap at some of the iniquities of the times. He gave me three or four to choose from; there was the adulteration of food, and the want of education for the poor, and street music, and the miscellaneous sale of poisons."
> "And so you chose poisons and killed the knight?"
> "Exactly; at least I didn't kill him, for he comes all right again after a bit. He had gone out to get something to do him good after a hard night, a Seidlitz powder, or something of that sort, and an apothecary's apprentice had given him prussic acid in mistake."
> "And how is it possible he should have come to life after taking prussic acid?"
> "Why, there I have a double rap at the trade. The prussic acid is so bad of its kind, that it only puts him into a kind of torpor for a week. Then we

---

[†]The image suggests Henry Wallis's well-known painting of the death of Chatterton, exhibited at a particularly timely moment, 1856.

THE GREAT LOZENGE-MAKER.

A Hint to Paterfamilias.

This drawing, in *Punch* for 20 November 1858, was in direct response to a letter to the *Times* (11 November) in which Arthur Hill Hassall reaffirmed information he had published in his book-length exposé of adulteration: that plaster of paris was often introduced into "several kinds of sugar confectionery." It would appear that Miss Thorne in *Barchester Towers*, published the previous year, had good reason to suspect the purity of the party fare supplied by the Barchester pastrycook.

have the trial of the apothecary's boy; that is an excellent episode, and gives me a grand hit at the absurdity of our criminal code."

"Why, Charley, it seems to me that you are hitting at everything."

"Oh! ah! right and left, that's the game for us authors." (19:218–19)

The agitation Wakley had begun ten years earlier resulted finally in the passage of the Act for Preventing the Adulteration of Articles of Food and Drink (1860), followed by supplementary legislation in later sessions. But the law continued to have many loopholes, and the subject remained uncomfortably topical for a number of years. Simultaneously, in 1864–66, both Dickens and Trollope referred to it. In *Our Mutual Friend*, Dickens created the butler he dubbed "the Analytical Chemist," whose glum demeanor as he poured wine at the Veneerings' resplendent dinner table and asked "Chablis, sir?" seemed to say "You wouldn't if you knew what it's made of" (1.2:52). Dickens's readers would have relished the irony of this unspoken commentary on the wine's purity taking place at the dinner table of Veneering, of all people—partner in the drug house of Chicksey, Veneering, and Stobbles, a trade known for its adulterative practices.

In *Can You Forgive Her?* Trollope, describing the generally sleazy atmosphere of curbside politics in metropolitan London, had Grimes, the publican at the Handsome Man in the Brompton Road, complain to George Vavasor about the unprofitability of his trade. As the proprietor of a tied house, he had to order his beer from Meux's. "But if I sells their stuff as I gets it," he said, "there ain't a halfpenny coming to me out of a gallon. Look at that, now."

"But then you don't sell it as you get it. You stretch it" [replied Vavasor].

"That's in course. I'm not going to tell you a lie, Mr. Vavasor. You know what as well as I do, and a sight better, I expect. There's a dozen different ways of handling beer, Mr. Vavasor. But what's the use of that, when they can take four or five pounds a day over the counter for their rot-gut stuff at the 'Cadogan Arms,' and I can't do no better nor yet perhaps so well, for a real honest glass of beer. Stretch it! It's my belief the more you poison their liquor, the more the people likes it!" (12:157)

Four years later (1869–70), Wilkie Collins incorporated the still current topicality in the advice Sir Patrick Lundie, in *Man and Wife*, offered to Arnold Brinkworth, who was in love with Sir Patrick's niece. This otherwise desirable lady was tainted by the fact that she had earlier entered into a questionably legal marriage, a leading reform theme in the novel.

"You go to the tea-shop and get your moist sugar [says Sir Patrick]. You take it on the understanding that it is moist sugar. But it isn't anything of the sort. It's a compound of adulterations made up to look like sugar. You shut your eyes to that awkward fact, and swallow your adulterated mess in various articles of food; and you and your sugar get on together in that way as well as you can. Do you follow me so far? . . . Very good. You go to the marriage shop, and get a wife. You take her on the understanding—let us say—that she has lovely yellow hair, that she has an exquisite complexion, that her figure is the perfection of plumpness, and that she is just tall enough to carry the plumpness off. You bring her home, and you discover that it's the old story of the sugar over again. Your wife is an adulterated article. Her lovely yellow hair is—dye. Her exquisite skin is—pearl powder. Her plumpness is—padding. And three inches of her height are—in the boot-maker's heels. Shut your eyes, and swallow your adulterated wife as you swallow your adulterated sugar—and, I tell you again, you are one of the few men who can try the marriage experiment with a fair chance of success." ("First scene," chap. 6: 1.117–18)

When Dickens remarked, in *The Mystery of Edwin Drood* (1870), that among other ways local news was speedily disseminated in Cloisterham was "the milkman deliver[ing] it as part of the adulteration of his milk" (9: 107), he was not using a mere leftover joke. The topicality was well preserved.

15
Real People, More or Less

𝒜

1.

IN RECENT CHAPTERS we have noticed how often Victorian novelists made incidental reference, by name, to well-known contemporary figures and well-remembered earlier ones in the luxury trades, the performing and fine arts, the exhibition business, and crime. These were part of a larger pattern which was to some extent a legacy of Sir Walter Scott. In his best-selling romances, Scott had shown how useful men and women in the public domain of history could be to creating a believable setting in the past. The presence, either as leading characters or in cameo roles, of Charles II and Titus Oates in *Peveril of the Peak*, Queen Elizabeth, the Earl of Leicester, and Amy Robsart in *Kenilworth*, the Earl of Northumberland in *The Monastery*, Mary Queen of Scots in *The Abbot*, and the Earl of Montrose in both *Old Mortality* and *A Legend of Montrose* lent veracity to the imaginary characters with whom they mingled in Scott's pages. Taking a leaf from Scott's book in his own historical novels, Thackeray brought Addison and Steele, Mrs. Bracegirdle, Dr. Arbuthnot, and other celebrities of the Queen Anne period into *Henry Esmond*, and an even larger gallery of generals, noblemen, and literary men, Dr. Johnson conspicuous among them, into *The Virginians*. Other novelists, writing fictionalized history, adopted the same practice. Among the Dissenters assembled on Finchley Common in Ainsworth's *James the Second*, for example, were such religious figures as John Bunyan, George Fox, and Richard Baxter. The cast of characters in Kingsley's *Westward Ho!*, a tale of Elizabethan England, included Sir Philip Sidney, Sir Richard Grenville, Sir Francis Drake, and Edmund Spenser.

Meanwhile, Macaulay was providing novelists with stiff competition as he sought to bring history alive to Victorian readers. In his *History of England* (first two volumes, 1849) he depicted historical figures of the Restoration with a vividness and seeming intimacy that, it was often said, novelists would be hard pressed to match. For that reason, many patrons of Mudie's circulating library found his narrative as engrossing as any of the novels that crowded its shelves.

There was, then, excellent precedent for introducing the names, if not the actual personalities, of living persons into fiction with contemporary settings. If Scott, Thackeray, and Macaulay demonstrably added realism to their evocations of the past by such means, how much more effective would be the introduction of men and women whom novel readers read about in the newspapers and magazines and might well pass in the London streets!

One universally recognized celebrity of the early Victorian years who repeatedly turned up in fiction, either by name or by unmistakable reference, was the Duke of Wellington. As the *Quarterly Review* said at the time of his death, he was "the best known man in London; every one knew him by sight: like a city built on a hill, or his own colossal statue on the arch, he could not be hid. He was the observed of all observers, and the object of universal royal-like homage, which he neither courted nor shunned." [1] For thirty-five years he rode or walked about London, not a commanding figure—he was only five feet eight—but identified always by his fresh color, silver hair, hook nose, and the characteristic one- or two-fingered salute (the authorities, writers of both fact and fiction, differ: it was, in any case, economical) by which he returned the greetings of passersby.

No other famous name was dropped more often. Archer, the politician in *Pendennis*, explains that he had not been at the House of Commons one evening because his presence was required (dinnerless) elsewhere:

> "I hate your grandees who give you nothing to eat [he tells Pen and Warrington]. If it had been Apsley House, it would have been quite different. The Duke knows what I like, and says to the Groom of the Chambers, 'Martin, you will have some cold beef, not too much done, and a pint bottle of pale ale, and some brown sherry, ready in my study as usual; Archer is coming here this evening.' The Duke doesn't eat supper himself, but he likes to see a man enjoy a hearty meal, and he knows that I dine early."
> (30:1.312–13)

In *Endymion*, Disraeli's late-in-life retrospect of the Reform Bill era, Mr. Rodney recalled that "he had been so fortunate as perhaps even to save the Duke's life during the Reform Bill riots [when a London mob broke the windows of Apsley House]. 'His Grace has never forgotten it, and only the day before yesterday I met him in St. James' Street walking with Mr. Arbuthnot, and he touched his hat to me'" (19:77). In Bulwer-Lytton's *The Caxtons*, Uncle Roland, a Waterloo veteran, encountered, fittingly enough, in Waterloo Place, "a slight but muscular figure buttoned up across the breast like his own canter[ing] by on a handsome bay horse; every eye was on that figure. Uncle Roland stopped short, and lifted his hand to his hat; the rider touched his own with his forefinger, and cantered on; Uncle Roland turned round and gazed" (5.4 : 1.173)— as did every Londoner who happened to see the Duke on his mount, one of the metropolis' cherished familiar sights. In *The Adventures of Philip*, the Duke having died ten years earlier (1852), Thackeray dated the time of the action with a fanciful hypothesis: "It is after lunch, and before Rotten Row ride time (this story, you know, relates to a period ever so remote, and long before folks thought of riding in the Park in the forenoon) . . . perhaps, Philip has just come from Hyde Park, and says, 'As I passed by Apsley House, I saw the Duke come out, with his own blue frock and white trousers and clear face . . .'" (9 : 1.189,192).

It was not really necessary to name so instantly recognizable a public figure. In *Ten Thousand a Year*, Samuel Warren introduced a character identified only as the Duke of————, who acknowledged the bystanders' removal of their hats "by touching his hat in a mechanical sort of way with his forefinger . . . an elderly, middle-sized man, with a somewhat spare figure, dressed in plain black clothes, with iron-gray hair, and a countenance which, once seen, was not to be forgotten. That was a great man; once, the like of whom many previous centuries had not seen; whose name shot terror into the hearts of all the enemies of old England all over the world . . ." (7 : 184). The encomium also was superfluous. The gentleman's identity had been established at the outset, as it was, also, in what was perhaps Wellington's most memorable appearance in major Victorian fiction. Pendennis and his old soldier uncle, walking along St. James's Street on a bright summer morning,

> got bows from a Duke, at a crossing, a Bishop (on a cob), and a Cabinet Minister with an umbrella. The Duke gave the elder Pendennis a finger of a pipe-clayed glove to shake, which the Major embraced with great veneration; and all Pen's blood tingled as he found himself in actual communication, as it were, with this famous man (for Pen had possession of the Major's left arm, whilst that gentleman's other wing was engaged with his grace's right), and he wished all Grey Friars School, all Oxbridge University, all Paternoster Row and the Temple, and Laura and his mother at Fairoaks, could be standing on each side of the street, to see the meeting between him and his uncle, and the most famous Duke in Christendom.
>
> "How do, Pendennis?—fine day," were his Grace's remarkable words, and with a nod of his august head he passed on—in a blue frockcoat and spot-

Two of the postures in which the late Duke of Wellington was
best known to Londoners. (above) "A very characteristic portrait of the Duke, as he appeared in our metropolitan rides
half a score of years since" (1842). (opposite) The Duke paying
his annual visit to the spring exhibition of the Royal Academy
(*Illustrated London News*, 25 September and 9 October 1852).

less white duck trousers, in a white stock, with a shining buckle behind.
(*Pendennis*, 36:1.371)[†]

Allusions to the Prince Regent and his subsequent self, George IV,
were often used for retrospective dating. In novels with immediately

[†] In *The Newcomes*, Wellington makes a cameo *non*appearance, which Thackeray arranged partly for the sake of a weak *Punch*-type joke. When Colonel Newcome has a party,
one of the guests is Frederick Bayham, who notices among the company Sir Thomas de
Boots, K. G. "'Stars and garters, by jingo!' cries Mr. Frederick Bayham; 'I say, Pendennis,

contemporary settings, mention was sometimes made of current activities such as might be found in the daily Court Circular or reported in
the press. Describing the status-prizing old Duke of Omnium in *Doctor
Thorne*, Trollope remarked, "He was very willing that the Queen should
be queen so long as he was allowed to be Duke of Omnium. Nor had he
begrudged Prince Albert any of his honours till he was called Prince

have you any idea, is the Duke coming? I wouldn't have come in these Bluchers, if I had
known it. Confound it, no—Hoby himself, my own bootmaker, wouldn't have allowed
poor F. B. to appear in Bluchers, if he had known that I was going to meet the Duke'"
(13:1.143).

Consort" (15:165)—a reference to an event of the preceding year, Victoria's appointing her husband Prince Consort by patent. Much later, Hardy used, as one means of dating the action of *The Mayor of Casterbridge*, the Prince's brief stay in Dorchester on the way to dedicating the foundation stone of Portland Breakwater in 1849. (In the novel, the festive visit was moved back two or three years.)

Similarly, the itinerant salesman Bob Jakin's assurance to Mrs. Glegg in *The Mill on the Floss*, that a piece of goods he was tempting her to buy was "a muslin as the Princess Victoree might ha' wore" (5.2:280), was one more small touch by which George Eliot established the novel's historical setting (the passage can be dated 1836, the year before the princess came to the throne). In Emily Eden's particularly up-to-date *The Semi-Detached House* (1859), several socially qualified persons attend functions at court; she mentioned Prince Albert, the Duchess of Cambridge, and Princess Mary by name, and alluded to the "Prussian politics" attending the prospective marriage of Princess Alice to Prince Louis of Hesse-Darmstadt. In *Marion Fay*, Trollope involved the Prince of Wales in a rumored situation that may have meant more to his gossipwise readers than it does to us: "It had been reported that the Prince had declared that he had hoped to be asked to be godfather [to an offspring of Lord Llwddythlw, a Welsh peer] long ago" (19:137).

Public interest in the leading politicians of the day waxed and waned according to the temperature of the current parliamentary debates and the personal colorfulness of the men involved. It was only to be expected that Dickens, a former shorthand reporter in the House of Commons, would include in *Sketches by Boz* several readily recognizable penportraits of prominent members of the first reformed Parliament. The most picturesque of the men thus profiled was the eccentric reactionary Tory, Colonel Waldo de Laet Sibthorp, who occupied one of the Lincoln seats during the years (1832–41) when the other was held by the much talked-about young novelist, Edward Lytton Bulwer. Readers of *Nicholas Nickleby* would have recognized Sibthorp as the true-life model for Mr. Gregsbury, M.P., whose platform promises were recalled by an outraged constituent, Mr. Pugstyles: "Question number three—and last. . . . Whether, sir, you did not state upon the hustings, that it was your firm and determined intention to oppose everything proposed; to divide the house upon every question, to move for returns on every subject, to place a motion on the books every day, and, in short, in your own memorable words, to play the devil with everything and everybody?" (16:262–63). These were, indeed, the "very words" that Sibthorp used, time and again, to describe his intentions, as the pages of *Hansard's Parliamentary Debates* bear adequate witness; he gloried in his long career of ferocious obstructionism.

Sibthorp, however, was more famous for his flamboyance than for his political influence, which, except in this negative way, was nil. Among the early Victorian politicians with true clout, apart from Wellington, only two repeatedly appeared under their own names or by unmistakable allusion. One was the Irish member, Daniel O'Connell. In *Ten Thousand a Year* he was O'Gibbet, the venal politician who corrupted a parliamentary investigation into electoral corruption (see pages 723–24 below). He appeared as "the Liberator" in *Sybil*, and in *Martin Chuzzlewit* the American membership of the Young Men's Watertoast Association came out in strong sympathy with "a certain Public Man in Ireland" (21:425)—an early instance of the favorite Yankee pastime of twisting the British lion's tail. But the association hastily backed off when news arrived of the Public Man's having declared himself in favor of Negro emancipation. Nine years after O'Connell's death in 1847, Dinah Mulock used his early career ("making a commotion in Ireland") as a chronological landmark in *John Halifax, Gentleman*.

But among all early Victorian politicians it was Henry Brougham who appeared in fiction most often, over the longest stretch of time, under the most guises, and for the largest variety of purposes. Unlike Wellington, who was no longer the controversial figure he had once been as a leader of the right-wing Tories in the Reform Bill era, allusions to Brougham were bound to arouse strong reactions, personal or partisan, in readers of fiction. A man of formidable intellect and insatiable ambition, tirelessly energetic, mercurial, combative, and a spell-binding orator, albeit in a style better suited to Burke's day than his own, Brougham was in the public eye for over fifty years, as a political leader (first as a Whig, then as a Tory, and finally, in the diarist Charles Greville's phrase, "a political Ishmaelite"), lawyer (he defended Queen Caroline at her sensational trial in 1820), legal and social reformer, prolific writer. Tumult was a way of life for him, and with so controversial and checkered a career and so changeable a personality, what Brougham meant to the writers who alluded to him—and readers who responded to the allusions—depended largely on what office he held, what he was doing, and what he stood for at the moment the allusion was made. He was Mr. Foaming Fudge in Disraeli's *Vivian Grey* (1826–27), where it was said of him that "Foaming Fudge can do more than any man in Great Britain; that he had one day to plead in the King's Bench, spout at a tavern, speak in the House, and fight a duel; and that he found time for everything but the last" (2.12:56).

A few years later, in Thomas Love Peacock's *Crotchet Castle* (1831), Brougham, the most vocal proponent of adult education in the form of mechanics' institutes, was obviously the man behind the "Steam Intellect Society" (the Society for the Diffusion of Useful Knowledge) whom the

Reverend Doctor Folliott denounced as his "learned friend who is for doing all the world's business as well as his own, and is equally well qualified to handle every branch of human knowledge. I have a great abomination of this learned friend; as author, lawyer, and politician, he is *triformis*, like Hecate; and in every one of his three forms he is *bifrons*, like Janus; the true Mr. Facing-both-ways of Vanity Fair."[2] By this time, Brougham had been elevated to the woolsack and to the peerage as Baron Brougham and Vaux. As one of the strongest proponents of the popular cause of electoral reform, he was at the height of his celebrity; Macaulay said of him in November 1831, "He is, next to the King, the most popular man in England. There is no other man whose entrance into any town in the kingdom would be so certain to be [met] with huzzaing and taking off of horses."[3] Referring to him by name, in a passage briefly evaluating other politicians such as George Canning, Sir Francis Burdett, and the rising Sir Robert Peel, Disraeli editorialized in *The Young Duke*,

> I think the lawyer has spoiled the statesman. He is said to have great powers of sarcasm. From what I have observed there [from the House of Commons gallery—he was not yet a member], I should think very little ones would be quite sufficient. . . . The fault of Mr. Brougham, is, that he holds no intellect at present in great dread, and, consequently, allows himself on all occasions to run wild. Few men hazard more unphilosophical observations; but he is safe, because there is no one to notice them. On all great occasions, Mr. Brougham has come up to the mark; an infallible test of a man of genius. (5.6:309)

In 1834 Brougham's public image darkened when he engaged in an undignified squabble with the *Times* and undertook a three-week tour of the North, speechifying in an eccentric vein and undergoing what Disraeli was to call his "vagrant and grotesque apocalypse." Soon afterward he gave up the great seal. It was this fallen hero whom Phiz caricatured as Mr. Pott, the firebrand editor of the *Eatanswill Gazette*, full of sound and fury but signifying very little, in plate 14 of *Pickwick Papers*. (This was an identification Dickens did not make in the text of the novel, but the first purchasers of the monthly part who were familiar with the literally hundreds of caricatures of Brougham that had been circulated between 1812 and 1836 would have detected it at once. Buyers of later copies of the part would not have done so, however, because in the second state of the plate Phiz expunged the likeness.)[4]

But Brougham remained a power at the bar, and it was in this role that he next appeared, in *Ten Thousand a Year*. Samuel Warren, himself a lawyer, had much opportunity to study him, and he figured as Mr. Quicksilver, who appears at the York Assizes to back up the deplorable London firm of Quirk, Gammon, and Snap in their successful effort to deliver the Aubrey fortune, on an obscure legal technicality, into the slimy hands of Tittlebat Titmouse: "a man of great but wild energy. . . . The first and the last thing he thought of in a cause was—himself" (13:341). Warren dwelt on his political hypocrisy, especially his denunciation of rotten and pocket boroughs while occupying the seat for one himself. Later in the novel (27:718) mention is made of his having become "Lord Chancellor Blossom [Brougham (pronounced "broom")→ bloom→Blossom] and Box [Vaux]." It appears that in the manuscript Warren handled Brougham more roughly than in the published text; in an exchange of letters on the possibility of libel, Warren told Alexander Blackwood, his publisher, that he was "on the whole glad that you struck out the stinging portion of the passages alluding to him."[5]

Some of Brougham's ideas, if not his personality, figured in Dickens's portrayal of Sir Joseph Bowley, "The Poor Man's Friend," in *The Chimes* (1844). In a recent parliamentary debate on a bill designed to put a cap on the number of hours factory hands could work in a day, Brougham had revealed how limited his understanding of the true plight of the laboring poor was. In his character of Bowley, Dickens turned Brougham into an advocate of paternalism which, in fact, was a thin disguise for social laissez-faire.

In the ensuing decade and a half, Brougham disappeared from fiction, though not from public notice—he was frequently caricatured and alluded to in *Punch* squibs. When Trollope published *The Bertrams* in 1859 (the setting is the 1840s, so the focus of the conversation is clearly anachronistic), Brougham, at the age of eighty-one, was having his last hurrah, not as a politician but in another of his longtime roles, that of a social reformer. The Society for the Diffusion of Useful Knowledge having long since vanished, he now was back in the news as the founder of the National Society for the Promotion of Social Science. In a Peacock-like exchange of opinions over the wine and walnuts, Trollope demonstrated that "Lord Boanerges"'s power to divide opinion was unimpaired. This is a fragment of the exchange between "Mr. Stistick," Boanerges's admirer, "the Baron," a high-court judge, and their host:

THE BARON. Well, Mr. Stistick, if Sir Henry will allow us, we'll drink Lord Boanerges.

STISTICK. With all my heart. He is a man of whom it may be said—

THE BARON. That no man knew better on which side his bread was buttered.

STISTICK. He is buttering the bread of millions upon millions.

[THE HOST]. Or doing better still, enabling them to butter their own. Lord Boanerges is probably the only public man of this day who will be greater in a hundred years than he is now.

THE AMAZON (B—G—M) ATTACKING CHANCERY ABUSE.

(BEING HIS L—D—P'S FIRST APPEARANCE THIS SEASON.)

One of the many cartoons (this one was in *Punch*, 28 June 1851) by which the name and figure of Lord Brougham were kept constantly before the public, many years after he had ceased to be a mover and shaker in politics. Here he anticipates Dickens's *Bleak House* in his determination to reform the Court of Chancery.

THE BARON. Let us at any rate hope that he will at that time be less truculent.

(2.11:2.186–88)

The timeliness of this dialogue is indicated by the fact that between April and December of the following year, *Fraser's Magazine* serialized Peacock's late satire *Gryll Grange*, in which Brougham again was "Lord Facing-both-ways" and his new organization was devoted to "the Science of Panto-pragmatics."

Quite probably the cleverest use that any novelist made of the names of current public figures was Trollope's, in *The Warden*. Here he named the three teenage Grantly boys after contemporary bishops, Charles James Blomfield (London), Henry Phillpotts (Exeter), and Samuel ("Soapy Sam") Wilberforce (Oxford). Writing much later, Henry James deplored Trollope's "inspiration to convert Archdeacon Grantly's three sons . . . into little effigies of three distinguished English bishops of that period, whose well-known peculiarities are reproduced in the description of these unnatural urchins. The whole passage, as we meet it, is a sudden disillusionment; we are transported from the mellow atmosphere of an assimilated Barchester to the air of ponderous allegory."[6] James evidently overlooked the reductio ad absurdum, as readers of *Punch* in the 1850s did not (even though the association may have been subliminal). Among Victorian caricaturists' staple devices was the portrayal of grown, and preferably grave, public men as mischievous boys. The year before *The Warden* appeared, the 29 July 1854 issue of *Punch* had a cartoon entitled "The Holiday Letter," in which "masters" Aberdeen and Russell were seen as two loutish schoolboys whose "Royal Mistress" was writing a letter home—"the most extreme idleness has characterized the whole year" (the same complaint Dickens was then making about the inertia of Parliament and the Aberdeen ministry). Sir James Graham was repeatedly depicted as "Peel's Dirty Little Boy" who was "always in trouble," and six months after *The Warden* appeared, another *Punch* cartoon (2 June 1855) was devoted to "Jamie Gr-h-m, the Unpleasant Boy, Who Made a Dirt-Pie and Ate It." Thus Trollope's satire acquired an extra dimension: the verbal thrust against three eminent churchmen had an imagistic context provided by the leading comic periodical of the day. It was a case of witty topicality by both direction and indirection.[†]

[†]Events immediately following the publication of *The Warden* in the first days of 1855 fortuitously increased the topical pertinence of the allusion. In February, Lord Palmerston (Whig, Evangelical) succeeded Lord Aberdeen (Tory, High Church) in the prime ministership, with its bishop-making power. The prospect was that, in his appointments to the

A few years earlier, Thackeray had employed another technique of religious reference. Whereas Trollope used comic indirection in the case of the Grantly boys, endowing fictitious characters with allusive "real" names, Thackeray chose not to name names at all but to rely on his readers' grasping a hidden implication. In *Pendennis* (61:2.245–52), Arthur and his friend Warrington chat in a philosophical mood about two supposedly hypothetical brothers who have chosen to follow divergent religious paths. They were, in fact, as Robert Lee Wolff pointed out some years ago,

> sensitive descriptions of John Henry Newman and his younger brother, Francis. It was the elder Newman who had been the leader in the Church of England, "with the respect of any army of churchmen," and who had given up everything to join the Roman Catholic Church ("the enemy"). . . . Francis Newman, on the other hand, had joined the Plymouth Brethren, one of the strictest Calvinist sects among Dissenters, and eventually (after trying vainly to "reconcile an irreconcilable book"—the Bible, of course) became a Freethinker. His religious pilgrimage was by no means over, but in 1850, only a few months before this passage in *Pendennis* was written [it appeared in the September number of the novel], he had published his own book, *Phases of Faith*, in which he told his own story.[7]

The number of nonpolitical figures alluded to in fiction sharply increased after the middle of the century. Novelists seldom referred to any of their personal traits, as they did with Wellington and Brougham. These people were simply, and literally, names in the news, useful as topical tags to add point to a general remark. Ruskin's name, for example, was invoked in at least three different connections. As "Buskin" he was, as we have seen, the elucidator of the "grand and mysterious meaning" of PreRaphaelitism in George Herbert's *Gerald Fitzgerald*. Rightly spelled, Ruskin was the lawgiver of art whom, along with the entire Royal Academy, "first-rate country artists [were] quite ready to set . . . at defiance" (Surtees's *Mr. Facey Romford's Hounds*, 56:363). The name served Kingsley for a literary/artistic analogy when, in *Two Years Ago*, he wrote of Vavasour's poems:

> They are more and more full of merely sensuous beauty, mere word-painting, mere word-hunting. . . . The art, it may be, of his latest poems is greatest: but it has been expended on the most unworthy themes. The later

company of the Lords Spiritual, Palmerston would favor the Evangelical party, and the whole issue of the "Palmerston bishops" inflamed the political scene. The controversy, authoritatively described by Owen Chadwick (*The Victorian Church* [New York, 1966–70], 1:468–76), in turn provided the ecclesiastical background for *Barchester Towers*, where, says Chadwick, the "single absolute impossibility . . . occurs when Lord Palmerston appoints a Tractarian clergyman to the deanery of Barchester."

are mannered caricatures of the earlier, without their soul; and the same change seems to have passed over him which (with Mr. Ruskin's pardon) transformed the Turner of 1820 into the Turner of 1850. (10:144–45)

Other figures were associated with headlined deeds. Florence Nightingale's name appeared now and again in novels when she was at the height of her fame.[†] News of her heroic labors in the Crimean hospitals had no sooner reached England than Thackeray, commenting in the April 1855 number of *The Newcomes* on the "sweet, kindly sisterhood of Misfortune and Compassion"—women like Ethel Newcome and Pendennis's wife—declared, "the world is full of Miss Nightingales; and we, sick and wounded in our private Scutaris, have countless nursetenders" (2.29:2.240). Recalling his illness on a voyage, Arthur Chester, in *The Semi-Detached House* (1859), remarked, "Florence Nightingale herself could not have made a better nurse" than the captain of the *Alert* (1:7). In *Orley Farm* (1861–62), Madeline Staveley's mother, pressuring her to be married, equated Nightingale with sacrificial spinsterhood, arguing that she did not want her to "take to the Florence Nightingale line of life"; she should not "give up to sick women what was meant for mankind" (58:517–18). In *Aurora Floyd*, published the next year, Miss Braddon, referring to the lovelorn Lucy Floyd, demanded, "Did the LADY WITH THE LAMP cherish any foolish passion in those days and nights of ceaseless toil, in those long watches of patient devotion far away in the East?" "Remember . . . Florence Nightingale in the bare hospital chambers, in the close and noxious atmosphere, amongst the dead and the dying" (7:65; 25:261).

Still other familiar names emblematized new social phenomena. No one knew or cared much about the personality of Thomas Cook, who organized the first railway excursion in 1841 and founded the travel agency that bore his name, but that name was synonymous with the new institution of tourism. "[T]o go to Scotland in August, and stay there, perhaps, till the end of September," said Trollope in *The Eustace Diamonds*, "is about the most certain step you can take towards autumnal fashion. Switzerland and the Tyrol, and even Italy, are all redolent of Mr. Cook, and in those beautiful lands you become subject at least to suspicion" (32:329). Tourists—"a distinct species" of the old established

---

[†] Her name appeared in fiction even before she had any fame at all. In Surtees's *Tom Hall's Heart-Aches and Horses*, serialized in the *New Monthly Magazine* in 1851–53, and thus predating Crimea, an itinerant sign painter has settled down as a portraitist in the town of Fleecyborough: "The ladies then came trooping to have their portraits painted . . . . Good, strong, bold, hard-featured, tea-boardy, stiff-ringleted things they were, with just that provoking degree of resemblance that enables a spectator to say, 'Ah, I suppose that's meant for Miss Nightingale,' or, 'That's not unlike Mrs. Crossfinch'" (29:207). The name Nightingale here seems to be Surtees's invention, in ornithological harmony with "Crossfinch."

and respected genus of travelers, as Hardy observed in *Far from the Madding Crowd*—were a symptom of the new affluence of the bourgeoisie, and as the foremost caterer to their desire to see the world without inconvenience or risk Cook was always mentioned rather sniffishly. Trollope again, in *The Prime Minister*: "The travelling world had divided itself into Cookites and Hookites;—those who escaped trouble under the auspices of Mr. Cook, and those who boldly combated the extortions of foreign innkeepers and the anti-Anglican tendencies of foreign railway officials 'on their own hooks'" (67:2.250).

At home, and catering to some of the same clientele on another level of life, was the unordained Baptist preacher Charles Spurgeon, who had come to London in 1854 and soon attracted such crowds that the four-thousand-seat Exeter Hall could not hold them all. Exchanging persiflage with Martha Dunstable in *Framley Parsonage*, Mark Robarts assures her that her ambition to "get up into a pulpit, and preach a sermon" (as Reade's Rhoda Somerset had not yet done) would soon pall. "That would depend upon whether I could get people to listen to me," she replies. "It does not pall upon Mr. Spurgeon, I suppose" (3:1.32). The size of the preacher's audiences became, for the moment, a standard comparison. In *The Three Clerks* (1858), Mr. Jobbles, the enthusiastic proponent of civil service examinations being thrown open to all comers ("the whole adult male population of Great Britain"), "longed to behold, crowding around him, an attendance as copious as Mr. Spurgeon's" (27:333). At the same moment, in Surtees's *Ask Mamma*: "as a ball can always begin as soon as there are plenty of gentlemen, there are not those tedious delays and gatherings of nothing but crinoline that would only please Mr. Spurgeon" (91:446).

2.

But it was none of these public figures who were mentioned most often, under their own names, in Victorian novels. That distinction was held jointly by three businessmen, itself a significant commentary on the Victorian social scene. Only one of them, however, is "real" in the sense that in fiction he is a living presence, with distinctive personal traits. The other two, Stultz the master tailor and Gunter the master confectioner, are represented in fiction only by their names; one had a busy shop in Clifford Street and the other in Berkeley Square, but that is virtually all we know about them. They are quasi-legendary figures, bearers of famous names rather than flesh-and-blood human beings, each representing an aspect of what would much later be called conspicuous expenditure.

The man whom contemporary accounts enable us to see in the flesh, sanguine, busy, and voluble, is George Robins, the prince of auctioneers. Like Stultz and Gunter, he was a legacy of the silver fork era. The tailor and the confectioner served their fashionable clients when they were spendthrift consumers; Robins more often than not served them when their life-style had gone sour, at least temporarily. Catherine Gore, in *Preferment* (1840), represented him as presiding over the obsequies of the dandy. Of the great men illustrating the dandy epoch of Adolphus Egerton's youth, she wrote, "Some were in exile—some in the grave. . . . George Robins had disposed of the paraphernalia of a dozen or so, whose place remembered them no longer . . . whose names were forgotten amid their daily haunts and ancient neighbourhood, except in the defaulter-lists of the clubs."[8] Like Thackeray's Mr. Polonius (Thomas Hamlet the jeweler, who also acted as a high-level pawnbroker, receiving glittering objects of value as collateral for loans), Robins was at hand when material wealth in the form of landed and other properties urgently needed to be transmuted into cash. One of the cruelest ironies in the last days of Regency society occurred when Hamlet, overwhelmed in 1834 with debt, had to sell his Old Master paintings, armor, and a dozen elaborate silver salvers reputedly by Cellini; who but George Robins auctioned them off for a total of a thousand guineas? By contrast, Robins left an estate of no less than £140,000, even though out of his reputed annual income of £12,000 to £15,000 he had given much to charity.

A measure of Robins's fame is found in his presence among the celebrities profiled in James Grant's *Portraits of Public Characters* (1841). In the second of the two volumes, he was one of a company that included Carlyle, William Macready, George Cruikshank, Count D'Orsay, Thomas Moore, and the playwright Sheridan Knowles. Grant described Robins as being tall and athletic, bald except at the back of his head, with small, shrewd, sly eyes and a complexion "rough and ruddy as if he were the bailiff on one of those estates which he describes with such graphic effect. He has all the appearance of one who, notwithstanding the extent and importance of his business, enjoys the pleasures of life."[9]

Robins's headquarters, accommodating a crowd of a hundred and fifty prospective bidders, was his Auction Mart in Bartholomew Lane, just opposite the Bank of England. In action, he eschewed both theatrical gestures and the loud voice of an actor trying to fill the cavernous Drury Lane Theatre.† His only histrionic gesture was to throw himself

---

†Although Grant describes Robins only in his professional role of auctioneer, he was also active in theatrical circles, having a financial interest in Drury Lane, where he was associated with Byron, Kemble, Colman, and other literary-dramatic personalities. In the

into a comfortable armchair he kept on the rostrum, as if fatigued by his effort to get top prices for his client. When the bidding lagged, said Grant,

> he will heave two or three sighs, which are wonderfully good, considering they are manufactured for the occasion, and declare, with the utmost conceivable gravity of countenance, that in the whole course of his professional experience he never met with anything so discouraging, and that it must surely be owing to some want of perspicuity of expression, or deficiency of professional ability on his part, that the audience do not see their own interests, which are as clear to his view as the noon-day sun.[10]

Grant made a special point of Robins's manner suggesting an attorney manqué. Among other things, he was "partial to the use of legal phraseology," talking with great gusto, in conversation, of "his fees, his retainers, his briefs, his clients, his pleadings, and so forth." It was not the lawyerly element in his language that was most famous, however, but its sheer ornateness. As his obituary in the *Illustrated London News* (20 February 1847) put it:

> The wonderful skill and tact with which every advantage connected with the property he had to describe was seized upon and turned to profit, in his glowing descriptions and his ready wit and *repartee* in [*sic*] the rostrum are well known. His announcements were unlike those of any of his contemporaries; they were highly-coloured, graphic, and often clever, and that they were his own productions there is ample reason to believe. Overwrought as they were, he has been heard to say in no instance was ever a purchase repudiated on the ground of mis-description; whilst in many cases bargains to a heavy amount have been made by persons who had never seen or heard of the estate when they entered the auction room, but were overcome by his persuasive eloquence.

The deception issue aside, Robins was a sort of plutocrats' Barnum, and in sheer floridity and hyperbole of language he outdid the American showman. His advertising style may have lacked the wit and terseness that characterized the publicity of E. Moses and Sons and the leading manufacturers of boot blacking, but it could never be overlooked. He

---

same passage of Byron's "Detached Thoughts" in which he recorded the celebrated anecdote of the watchman finding Richard Brinsley Sheridan dead drunk in a gutter and asking his name ("Wilberforce!"), the poet mentioned that he had met Sheridan at George Robins's, among other places. It was at one of the auctioneer's "splendid dinner[s] full of great names and High spirits" that Byron saw Sheridan in tears over "some observation or other upon the subject of the sturdiness of the Whigs in resisting Office and keeping to their principles." (*Byron's Letters and Journals*, ed. Leslie A. Marchand [London, 1973–82], 4:297; 9:16, 32.)

was an untaught master of a certain kind of prose, a frustrated (but well-heeled) poet warbling his native woodnotes wild.[†]

Unfortunately, there is no tape recording to tell us what George Robins sounded like in full oratorical flight. But we do have the copious evidence of his newspaper advertisements, and it assures us that his peculiar fame was not undeserved. This is how he announced the auction of a desirable London property (in need of minor repairs) in the *Times* for 15 April 1842:

> MR. GEORGE ROBINS is empowered to SEEK by public COMPETITION, at the Auction Mart on Thursday, April 28, at 12, the distinguished FREEHOLD MANSION, for a lengthened period the favoured habitation of the Right Hon. the Earl of Lichfield, on the west and preferable side of St. James's square, being No. 13, and extending through to Duke-street. This abode is so well known and so highly appreciated that it is believed it does not require a long detail with a view to enlist the public attention. It is really altogether, from its size and importance, a princely habitation, and decidedly one that does not succumb to anything in London. It has a magnificent and imposing stone front, embellished with elegant Ionic stone columns; indeed, the architectural decorations throughout are of the most approved order. Within the accommodation for a family of distinction will be found perfect and in the most comprehensive interpretation. The following is a brisk summary:—the noble entrance hall and quadrangular stone staircase, demonstrating the correctness of the architectural design, has uniformly been greatly eulogised, and the dimensions are very ample, and the best taste is evinced throughout. On the ground and principal floor the grand suites of five elegant and spacious rooms have always been eulogised for their capability to accommodate a soiree to an unlimited extent. [T]hey are in communication with each other; the bed room department is numerous and excellent, and the domestic arrangements fully adequate to the legitimate establishment of the first family in England. The mansion is favoured beyond most of its rivals by possessing a large garden at the rear, communicating with the court yard, a 12 stall stable, and standing for five carriages, which is approached by a separate entrance and folding door from Duke-street. It will be found that the noble entrance under review stands in need of a small outlay for ornamental reparation, thus presenting an opportunity to display a little tact in contradistinction to bygone taste; beyond this nothing is required, since it is a solid finely built structure perfect, in all its de-

---

[†]Dickens paid tribute in *Sketches by Boz* to the combined verbal and typographical splendor of Robins's placards when Mrs. Tibbs put her furniture up for sale: ". . . the transcendent abilities of the literary gentlemen connected with his establishment are now devoted to the task of drawing up the preliminary advertisement. It is to contain, among a variety of brilliant matter, seventy-eight words in large capitals, and six original quotations in inverted commas" ("Tales," chap. 1:311).

partments, with three stone staircases, and the envied possessor will be the
more inclined to encounter a moderate expense in embellishing, when he
remembers it is one of the splendid mansions in London, and as the tenure
is freehold, it is not subject to any outgoings.

Robins's commercial effusions naturally had a special savor to professional users of the language, such as poets and novelists. Thomas Hood
celebrated him as a fellow craftsman in his comic masterpiece "Miss
Kilmansegg and Her Precious Leg" (*New Monthly Magazine*, September 1840):

> . . . to paint that scene of glamour,
> It would need the Great Enchanter's charm,
> Who waves over Palace, and Cot, and Farm,
> An arm like the Goldbeater's Golden Arm
>   That wields a Golden Hammer.
>
> He—only *he* could fitly state
> *The Massive Service of Golden Plate*,
>   With the proper phrase and expansion—
> The rare selection of *Foreign Wines*—
> The *Alps of Ice* and *Mountains of Pines*,
> The punch in *Oceans* and sugary shrines,
>
> The *Temple of Taste* from *Gunter's Designs*—
> In short, all that *Wealth* with a *Feast* combines,
>   In a *Splendid Family Mansion*.
>
>   (lines 1195–1208)

When novelists sought to describe locales, they often thought of Robins,
even in contexts far removed from London mansions and country
houses. In *Paul Clifford* Bulwer said of the highwaymen's cave, "In a
thinly-peopled country, surrounded by commons and woods, and yet (as
Mr. Robins would say, if he had to dispose of it by auction) 'within
an easy ride' of populous and well frequented roads, it possessed all
the advantages of secrecy for itself, and convenience for depredation"
(26:2.92). Even ordinary words like *advantages* and *convenience* came to
be associated with Robins's professional vocabulary, and still more did
his genteel borrowings from the French. "Even the carpet exhibited on
its pale grey ground," wrote Mrs. Gore in *Cecil*, "the same design, and
the Worcester plain china was what George Robins would call *en suite*." [11]

It was fitting, therefore, that his *faux-élégant* prose should have provided the literary model which Sam Titmarsh, the brash young insurance clerk, aspired, in vain, to emulate. Carrying his natty "Von Stiltz's
dress-coat" in a bag, he arrived at his employer's Fulham villa: "If I had
the pen of a George Robins, I might describe the Rookery properly:

suffice it, however, to say, it is a very handsome country place; with handsome lawns sloping down to the river, handsome shrubberies and conservatories, fine stables, outhouses, kitchen-gardens, and everything belonging to a first-rate *rus in urbe*, as the great auctioneer called it when he hammered it down some years after" (*The Great Hoggarty Diamond*, 1:48).

This was in *Fraser's Magazine* for October 1841. The next year (July 1842), in the same periodical, Thackeray devoted part of his satirical piece, "Professions by George Fitz-Boodle. Being Appeals to the Unemployed Younger Sons of the Nobility," to recommending the auctioneering "pulpit" as "just the peculiar place where a man of social refinement, of elegant wit, of polite perceptions can bring his wit, his eloquence, his taste, and his experience of life, most delightfully into play." Robins's name did not occur until the very end: "Look round, examine THE ANNALS OF AUCTIONS, as Mr. Robins remarks, and (with every respect for him and his brethren) say, is there in the profession SUCH A MAN?" But knowledgeable readers must have detected him hovering in the background throughout the piece, an identification made all the more positive by Thackeray's repeated references to his famous eighteen-day sale, concluded only weeks before, of Horace Walpole's medieval-pastiche showplace, Strawberry Hill, and its contents—"the late sale . . . which made some noise in the world (I mean the late Lord Gimcrack's at Dilberry Hill.)"[†]

> Poor Horace Waddlepoodle! to think that thy gentle accumulation of *bricabrac* should have passed away in such a manner! by means of a man who brings down a butterfly with a blunderbuss, and talks of a pin's head through a speaking-trumpet! Why, the auctioneer's very voice was enough to crack the Sèvres porcelain and blow the lace into annihilation. Let it be remembered that I speak of the gentleman in his public character merely, meaning to insinuate nothing more than I would by stating that Lord Brougham speaks with a northern accent, or that the voice of Mr. Sheil [a voluble Irish politician] is sometimes unpleasantly shrill.

In the May 1847 number of *Vanity Fair*, Thackeray wrote of "those public assemblies, a crowd of which are advertised every day in the last page of the 'Times' newspaper, and over which the late Mr. George Robins"—he had died in February—"used to preside with so much dignity" (17:159). Much later in the novel, Thackeray referred to him once

---

[†]At the outset, at least, the noise was largely Robins's own creation. The preliminary publicity he orchestrated in cooperative newspapers and magazines was, in his own complacent words, "without parallel—there is nothing upon record to approach it." (See Wilmarth S. Lewis, *Rescuing Horace Walpole* [New Haven, 1978], pp. 94–95.)

Thackeray's portrait (top) of "Mr. Hammerdown," the auctioneer who sold John Sedley's possessions, appeared in the May 1847 number of *Vanity Fair*. It was undoubtedly meant to represent George Robins, whom Thackeray mentioned in the text and whose picture (bottom) had accompanied his obituary in the *Illustrated London News* for 20 February.

again, as the "late celebrated auctioneer" who had once sold "the wonderful furniture" at the Marquis of Steyne's "humble place of residence"
in Hampshire upon that corrupt worthy's demise (47:452)

Meanwhile, Surtees had begun the string of allusions to Robins's art
of advertising that, like those to Daniel Lambert, came to be a hallmark
of his novels:

> . . . the description is as accurate as if George Robins had drawn it himself.
> (*Jorrocks' Jaunts and Jollities*, 7:125)

> "'I 'opes I haven't come to 'Andley Cross to inform none on you what an
> 'oss is, nor to explain that its component parts are four legs, a back-bone,
> an 'ead, a neck, a tail, and other etceteras, too numerous to insert in an
> 'and-bill, as old Georgey Robins used to say." (*Handley Cross*, 18:130)

> . . . in addition to all the tenants being described as most opulent and re-
> spectable, Mark Heavytail, the largest, who farmed what was called the 'pet
> farm,' was stated by the rural Robins who 'did' the printed particulars, to be
> a man of such *respectability* and independence of character, as to be above
> asking or accepting a reduction of rent. (*Hillingdon Hall*, 6:39)

> Puff now turned his attention to the country, or rather to the advertise-
> ments of estates for sale, and immortal George Robins soon fitted him with
> one of his earthly paradises. . . . Hanby House was a very nice attractive sort
> of place, and seen in the rich foliage of its summer dress, with all its roses
> and flowering shrubs in full blow, the description was not so wide of the
> mark as Robins's descriptions usually were. (*Mr. Sponge's Sporting Tour*,
> 32:211)

> The Golconda Station of the Great Gammon and Spinach Railway, as the
> reader—at all events the shareholders are well aware—was built, as George
> Robins used to say, "regardless of expense," the architect having apparently
> taken his idea of the edifice from some scene in the Arabian Nights enter-
> tainment. (*Plain or Ringlets?*, 61:224)

Robins eventually faded from the fictional memory. He once more
appeared by name, however, in Reade's story of the "The Bloomer" in
The Course of True Love Never Did Run Smooth (1856), as the man who sells
Courtenay Court. He had, said Reade, painted "the wood and water of
the estate . . . in language as flowing as the one and as exuberant as the
foliage of the other" (2:101).

3.

When novelists brought the Duke of Wellington briefly onstage or had
their characters refer to him in familiar terms, they were using a contemporary celebrity as Scott had used historical figures. When they alluded

to Brougham, though avoiding his name, they were conforming to the roman à clef tradition of the fashionable novel. It was the latter device, of introducing living originals under invented names, that dominated Victorian practice when novelists sought to authenticate their narratives by giving a character an implied resemblance to an actual person. The effectiveness of this use of models depended on two variables. One was the amount of knowledge that readers had of the original, whether through a printed source or hearsay. The other was the degree of resemblance to be inferred between model and character, whether it amounted simply to borrowing the living original as a type (a railway magnate, a demimondaine, a politician) irrespective of individual traits, or using well-known personal qualities as a means of shorthand characterization, knowledge to be expanded to fill out the bare sketch in the text. To put it in the most practical terms possible, novelists used real-life models as a labor-saving device. A recognized affinity of this sort was worth a thousand words of descriptive text.

So-called originals ranged from "public" ones, people whom even minimally informed readers could discern behind the names novelists gave them, to "private" ones, who were totally unknown to their readers. The latter can be dealt with summarily, because they were topical only in the limited sense that they figured in a novelist's personal experience: they may never have been names in the news, but they fed his imagination.

Gordon Ray devoted an entire book (*The Buried Life*, 1952) to showing how Thackeray "drew many of his principal characters from life, quite often choosing as models persons to whom he was bound by close emotional ties." The wife of his friend Whitwell Elwin recorded after he visited them at Norwich in 1857 that he "tells a story [about one of those persons], and then adds that it suggested such and such a trait of one of his characters. He said, 'People tell me such and such a character is not natural; but I *know* it is natural, that it is to the life.'"[12] Thus Amelia Sedley was derived from Thackeray's wife, Miss Crawley from his maternal grandmother, Jos Sedley from a cousin, Laura Bell and Lady Castlewood from Mrs. Brookfield, Helen Pendennis from his mother, Major Pendennis from his uncle by marriage, and Colonel Newcome from his stepfather.

In some instances, not Thackeray's alone, the supposed real-life private models meant a great deal to the novelist, whether in affection or aversion. No matter what a reader's response to a model-based character of this kind may have been, however, it would have been unaffected by any knowledge of what the model was like. This fully applies, as well, to self-portraits. No reader except the few who happened to be personally acquainted with Charles Reade would have been aware of the resemblance between him and the figure of Rolfe in *A Terrible Temptation*. And so the large class of private originals may, without regret, be set aside.

There remain the real-life people, given fictitious names, who were known to at least some portion of the novelist's audience and who were therefore of some topical interest, evoking, as they did, a response affected by information outside the novel's text. The gamut covered by the "public" original was extensive. At one extreme there were figures who were known to the widest portion, if not the totality, of the reading audience. At the other, which abutted on the realm of the wholly private original, were persons known to only a small handful of readers, who for that reason shared privileged knowledge with the novelist as a sort of in-joke.

The most extensive matching of fictional characters with real-life models occurred in the fashionable novels, and especially in Disraeli's political trilogy of the 1840s, which contained substantial silver fork elements.[13] One of the earliest nineteenth-century romans à clef was Lady Caroline Lamb's *Glenarvon* (1816), which sold three editions in a single week on the strength of its notoriety as a thinly veiled narrative of the author's mad pursuit of Byron, about which all society was talking. (The poet would reappear in Catherine Gore's *Cecil* [1841].) Ten years later, in *Vivian Grey*, the ambitious but still obscure Disraeli mingled mention of actual persons under their real names—Southey, Scott, Byron, Washington Irving—with others whose fictional names were easily interpreted: the Duke of Waterloo for Wellington, Lord Past-Century for the reactionary Lord Eldon, Stanislaus Hoax for the unprincipled practical joker, satirist, and editor Theodore Hook. But because not all characters were so recognizably named, a key was needed to identify the entire cast, and this was furnished, perhaps by Disraeli himself, in a short-lived (eight issues) scandal sheet, *The Star Chamber*. There one could learn that the Marquis of Carabas was Lord Lyndhurst, the lord chancellor, and Charlatan Gas was the Tory politician Canning.

On the eve of publication, *Vivian Grey* ("a sort of Don Juan in prose," as the publicity called it) was helped along by a barrage of titillating publicity masterminded by its publisher, Henry Colburn, the leading impresario of fashionable fiction.[14] In addition to paid advertising, he customarily ran extended puffs posing as reviews in the *New Monthly Magazine*, which he owned, and the *Literary Gazette*, in which he had an interest. "A very singular novel of the satirical kind," ran a preliminary puff. "We understand nearly all the individuals at present figuring in fashionable society, are made to flourish, with different degrees of honour, in the pages of this new work."[15] This was part of Colburn's usual package. He would publish a book anonymously, hinting that "the author moved in the highest circles of society," and, once public curiosity was whetted to the point of inspiring parlor guessing games, would issue a "key" purporting to name all the disguised originals.

Bulwer introduced a refinement on the hidden-original device in his Newgate novel *Paul Clifford* by imposing a pattern on the cast of real-life figures in the manner of Gay's *Beggar's Opera* a century earlier, where the band of pickpockets and highwaymen satirized the in-fighting politicians of Sir Robert Walpole's ministry. (More recently, caricaturists like Gillray had grouped their characters in similar arrangements derived from well-known nursery tales or literary works.) The band of highwaymen in *Paul Clifford* included Gentleman George (George IV, the former Prince Regent), Fighting Attie (Wellington), Bachelor Bill (the Duke of Devonshire), and Mobbing Francis (Sir Francis Burdett, the populist radical).

Each of the three parts of Disraeli's trilogy continued the practice he had adopted in *Vivian Grey*. The largest assemblage of fictional characters equivalent to known originals was in the first of the series, *Coningsby* (1844), the published key to the first reissue of which contained no fewer than sixty-two identifications. Here the device was carried to a self-defeating extreme. The only intrinsic value of such keys, the purely commercial one of capitalizing on gossipy curiosity, was realized to its utmost, but the individual points of the identifications, such as they were, were overwhelmed by their sheer number. Disraeli's talents did not lie in the direction of either satire or psychological perception, so a reader had little to gain, apart from the satisfaction of an idle, fleeting inquisitiveness, by trying to read hidden meaning in those scores of vignettes.

All fashionable novels that came with an actual or implied key were, naturally, replete with titled and/or wealthy figures. One was "Mrs. Million" in *Vivian Grey*, whom we have already met as the buxom lady whose indulgent elderly husband bought her a £15,000 diamond cross when Hamlet the jeweler called on them at dinnertime. This was the former comedienne Harriot Mellon, who married the banker Thomas Coutts, reputedly one of the richest men in England, in January 1815.[16]

Coutts died in 1822 at the age of eighty-seven, leaving his wife a fortune of £600,000, a partnership in his bank, and other substantial legacies. After eighteen months of mourning, she signaled her return to the glittering precincts of fashion by holding a party at her Highgate mansion, the seven hundred names on the guest list including "the Duke of York, three European princes, three other dukes, six marquises, and 12 earls, with their ladies." The two thousand coachmen and footmen

The face of Harriot Mellon was well known to readers in
Regency years through the several theatrical portraits that
had been painted of her and, even more, the acid caricatures inspired by her meteoric rise into high society and
her lavish entertainments. This portrait appeared in the
European Magazine for May 1815. She and Thomas Coutts
had been secretly married in January, four days after his
invalid first wife's funeral.

who brought them to Highgate were entertained, on a reduced scale, at
nearby houses of refreshment. In the course of her new revelrous life,
Mrs. Coutts met Lord Burford, heir to the Duke of St. Albans, with
whom she visited Sir Walter Scott at Abbotsford, an event described in
detail in Lockhart's life of Scott.[17] The retinue she brought with her on
that occasion found its way into *Vivian Grey*, where Mrs. Million arrived
at Lord Carabas's country place, Chateau Désir, with an entourage of

ten attendants distributed among three carriages—of which there were two less, it was noticed, than on her previous visit there. "So modest," people said (2.11:51). Trollope probably remembered the pages in Lockhart when, as we have seen, he arranged for the patent medicine heiress Martha Dunstable to arrive at Courcy Castle with a retinue fit for a princess.

The Duke of St. Albans died in 1825, and his son married Mrs. Coutts, who gave him £30,000 as a memento of the occasion. As a duchess, she continued to entertain on an opulent scale, sometimes giving three or four sumptuous dinners a week, until her death in 1837. But all this social climbing, party giving, and wild but not crippling expenditures (she retained most of her fortune, which she left to Angela Burdett Coutts, her first husband's granddaughter, who became Dickens's close friend) was a bit much, even for those extravagant, hedonistic times. Some of the most resplendently titled ladies of the realm refused to have anything to do with her, and she was relentlessly vilified in Theodore Hook's *John Bull* newspaper and in a swarm of scurrilous prints.

Pendennis's first flame, the actress Miss Fotheringay, was luckier. Married to the senile, infirm, and rich Sir Charles Mirabel, G.C.B., former envoy to the Court of Pumpernickel, she enjoyed the reputation, said Major Pendennis, of being "a most respectable woman, received everywhere—everywhere, mind. The Duchess of Connaught receives her, Lady Rockminster receives her—it doesn't become young fellows," he admonished Pen, "to speak so lightly of people in that station. There's not a more respectable woman in England than Lady Mirabel" (*Pendennis*, 44:2.55). That Thackeray had Harriot Mellon in mind is unquestionable; or, more precisely, he drew upon the topos over which she presided by virtue of the fact that, alone among her peers, she had been a double-dipper, first marrying an aged banker rich beyond dreams of avarice and then acquiring a second husband who bore a title first conferred by Charles II on a son of his by Nell Gwyn. By the time Thackeray wrote *Pendennis*, novelists had inherited a long tradition of real-life actresses marrying fortunes or titles—preferably both—and retiring from the stage, but Harriot was the only one to marry twice to achieve separate goals. It had begun almost a century ago (1751), when Lavinia Fenton, the first Polly Peachum, married the third Duke of Bolton. Since then, Elizabeth Farren had married the twelfth Earl of Derby (1797); Louisa Brunton, the first Earl of Craven (1807); Mary Catherine Bolton had become Lady Thurlow (1813); Eliza O'Neill had married William Becher, M.P., large Irish landholder and later baronet (1810); Maria Foote, the fourth Earl of Harrington (1831); and, most recently, Louisa Brunton had become Countess of Essex in 1838.[18] The stories behind these unions had more to do with the long-standing desirability, among fast-living noblemen, of actresses as mistresses and even, in extreme cases, wives, than in the men's interest in what occurred on stage; but at least two of the husbands in fiction were definitely stage-struck. Sir Charles Mirabel, said Major Pendennis, had been "occupied with theatricals since his early days. He acted at Carlton House when he was Page to the Prince—he has been mixed up with that sort of thing" (*Pendennis*, 44:2.55), and Aurora Floyd's banker father was, as we have seen (page 479), a constant theatregoer.

The figure of Mrs. Million, who had her counterpart in other silver fork novels, represented one side of Regency life, in which magnificent display degenerated into magnificent vulgarity. Another side, that of the rich roué and borough-monger, was represented by the Marquis of Grandgout in *Vivian Grey* and, more famously, by Lord Monmouth in *Coningsby* and Lord Steyne in *Vanity Fair*. Everyone in touch with the world in which Disraeli's (and later Thackeray's) characters moved recognized the man behind the fiction, who, of all the aristocrats in Victorian novels, did least honor to his blue blood: Francis Charles Seymour-Conway, third Marquis of Hertford. Conceivably he has received more credit—if that is the right word—than he deserves. Even at the peak of Victorian respectability, when the dignity incumbent on rank was taken more seriously than during libertine Regency days, there were more than a few titled rakes and wastrels. But unless there were identifying marks to the contrary, it was generally accepted that one real-life original served for all the fictional portraits of the type, if only because Lord Hertford—erstwhile vice chamberlain to the Prince Regent himself, an office for which nobody was better qualified—sinned so compulsively, extravagantly, and ostentatiously. (Some authorities find in Lord Steyne a soupçon of Hertford's father, the second marquis [died 1822], the Prince Regent's lord chamberlain and boon companion, whose dissoluteness seems to have compared very favorably with his son's.)

Hertford died at one of his London mansions, Dorchester House, on 1 March 1842. By that time, novelists who were privy to fashionable gossip and read the scandalmongering press of the day would have possessed much of the information that the man-about-town Charles Greville included in the private obituary he confided to his diary:

A pompous funeral left Dorchester House three days ago, followed by innumerable carriages of private individuals, pretending to show a respect which not one of them felt for the deceased; on the contrary, no man ever lived more despised or died less regretted. His life and his death were equally disgusting and revolting to every good and moral feeling. As Lord Yarmouth he was known as a sharp, cunning, luxurious, avaricious man of the world, with some talent, the favorite of George 4th (the worst of Kings) when Lady Hertford, his mother, was that Prince's mistress. . . . He was a Bon Vivant. . . . But after he became Lord Hertford and the Possessor of an enormous property he was puffed up with vulgar pride, very unlike the real scion of a noble race; he loved nothing but dull pomp and ceremony, and could only endure people who paid him court and homage. After a great deal of coarse and vulgar gallantry, generally purchased at a high rate, he formed a connexion with Lady Strachan, which thenceforward determined all the habits of his life. She was a very infamous and shameless woman, and his love after some years was changed to hatred. . . .

All of this, so far, was the kind of gossip common to silver fork novels, though seldom so bluntly expressed. But Greville continued:

There has been, as far as I know, no example of undisguised debauchery exhibited to the world like that of Lord Hertford, and his age and infirmities rendered it at once the more remarkable and the more shocking. Between sixty and seventy years old, broken with various infirmities, and almost unintelligible from a paralysis of the tongue, he has been in the habit of travelling about with a company of prostitutes, who formed his principal society, and by whom he was surrounded up to the moment of his death, generally picking them up from the dregs of that class, and changing them according to his fancy and caprice. Here he was to be seen driving about the town, and lifted by two Footmen from his carriage into the Brothel, and he never seems to have thought it necessary to throw the slightest veil over the habits he pursued . . . [E]very day at a certain hour his women, who were quartered elsewhere, arrived, passed the greater part of the day, and one or other of them all the night in his room . . .† [W]hat a life, terminating in what a death! without a serious thought or a kindly feeling, lavishing sums incalculable on the worthless objects of his pleasures or caprices, never doing a generous or a charitable action, caring and cared for by no human being, the very objects of his bounty only regarding him for what they could get out of him; faculties, far beyond mediocrity, wasted and degraded, immersed in pride without dignity, in avarice and sensuality; all his relations estranged from him, and surrounded to the last by a venal harem, who pandered to the disgusting exigencies *lassatae sed nondum satiatae libidinis.*[19]

No reader of the *Times*, without access to private lines of communication, would have known any of this, though the items the paper did print within the next year pointed in the right direction. After a brief obituary that was strictly factual (3 March 1842), it reprinted a brief no-

---

†T. B. Macaulay, in a letter to Macvey Napier, 3 January 1843: "Lord Hertford's house was as scandalous a nuisance as ever the Key in Chandos Street or the White House in Soho Square [two notorious brothels] were." (*The Letters of Thomas Babington Macaulay*, ed. Thomas Pinney [Cambridge, 1974], 4:89.)

tice from *The Scotsman* that described Hertford as "a clever but dissolute man. He was one of the chief companions of George IV in early life, and revelled in all the voluptuous orgies of the period. Of late years he resided abroad, the greater part of each year in Italy. Since the Reform Bills [*sic*] he conceived a great dislike to his own country . . . [He was] the largest proprietor of rotten boroughs," with a total of eight at his disposal.[†]

A few days later the *Times* reported that he had left two million pounds "of money" and that among the provisions in his "extraordinary will" was a bequest to Lady Strachan, of £800 per annum for life as well as £100,000 "in money" as an outright gift, and another legacy to Lady Strachan's maid of £12,000 per annum, plus "a number of legacies to foreign ladies of his acquaintance to an immense amount." When the will, originally made in 1823, was probated in May, it was shown to contain thirty-five confused, altered, inconsistent, unwitnessed, or otherwise problematic codicils appended to it over the last decade of his life. The joke of the moment was that Hertford had amused himself with the game of codicil-writing as a way of passing dull hours at French or German inns in the course of his travels. Lord Lyndhurst, who had been among the luminaries in the funeral procession, said that the will with its numerous afterthoughts seemed to have "been prepared with the express object of benefiting the legal profession." Hence the throwaway remark in one of Thackeray's "Fitz-Boodle's Confessions" papers (*Fraser's Magazine*, June 1842): referring to his boyhood passion for a certain L—ra R-ggl-es, FitzBoodle declared, "I would not write her whole name to be made one of the Marquess of Hertford's executors," who were paid handsomely to sort out the mess.

At least one beneficiary was unsatisfied with what she got. Matilda, Countess of Berchtholdt, was one of Admiral Sir Richard Strahan's three daughters, whose mother, as Greville said, had been Hertford's mistress. She had received three legacies of £20,000 each, but a year after Hertford's death she went to court and held out her gruel bowl for more. Her suit, however, was of minor significance compared with the one the executors, desperately attempting to trace large sums of money that Hertford was known to have possessed, had earlier brought against a Frenchman named Nicolas Suisse, a longtime general factotum of the deceased marquis, who, they alleged, had stolen "a large quantity of inscriptions and coupons for the payment of French Rentes, to the amount of upward of 100,000 *l*." At the trial at the old Bailey on 24 August

---

[†]He had extensive land holdings in Ireland as well as in England. One of his Irish bailiffs had a daughter, Laura Bell, who made a name for herself in the manner noted in the preceding chapter. A flourishing libido seems to have come with the territory.

1842, Suisse put on public record the abominable inside history of the Hertford ménage in his employer's latter years. Influenced by the advice of Lord Abinger, presiding over the bench of three judges, that "they would find great difficulty in saying the prisoner was guilty," the jury acquitted him in short order. But the damage was done—the night soil, to use a trope every early Victorian city-dweller would have understood, had splashed from the cart, and the middle-class readers of the press, hungry for relief from the ominous dispatches flowing from Midland factory towns that were seething with strikes and bloody riots, welcomed this authoritative substantiation of old clubroom gossip, now laid before the public at large.

This was the sort of material that contemporary novelists had at their disposal. Little of it found its way into the first Hertford-like character sketched after his death, Lord Monmouth in *Coningsby*. Disraeli's picture was discreet indeed compared with the one in John Mill's *chronique scandaleuse, D'Horsay; or Follies of the Day*, published the same year. In one episode, a modern scholar reports:

> the marquis, knowing that he is on the point of death from an unnamed disease, has a valet arrange a tryst with two prostitutes at a hotel in Richmond as a last fling. So feeble has he become that he can only recline in a moribund state while the ladies of the evening cavort naked before him. "Poor old man! What, pity *him*!" comments the author, "the debauched sensualist, the heartless *roué*, the gamester—he who never evinced a latent spark of virtue among his glaring vice, revelling in crime even in his impotent age and dotage."[20]

Compared with this, Thackeray's depiction of Hertford as Lord Steyne seems almost an encomium. But then, Mills's book was suppressed, and *Coningsby* and *Vanity Fair* were not. What Disraeli's biographer, Lord Blake, says of Monmouth fits Thackeray's creation as well in most respects:

> He may be larger than life, but he lives intensely and vividly, the very quintessence of the old aristocratic order that was passing away, the arrogant grandee with his palaces, his mistresses, his minions, unscrupulous in his determination to secure a dukedom despite the loss of his rotten boroughs, hard and relentless in his fearful family feuds; but a man of polish, charm and breeding who could fascinate when he chose and who would do anything to avoid a scene.[21]

(Lord Steyne, too, might have been averse to scenes, but Rawdon Crawley allowed him no choice when he surprised him tête-à-tête, if not more, with Becky in the Crawleys' Curzon Street house.)

In the light of what Greville and Mills said of Hertford, it is obvious

This figure of Lord Steyne, present in the first edition of *Vanity Fair*, was missing from the second, perhaps because the woodblock was damaged, but more probably because Thackeray or his publishers thought it too closely resembled Lawrence's portrait of the Marquis of Hertford. This same figure appeared, half hidden by another, in a later illustration, "The Triumph of Clytemnestra."

that Thackeray liberally exercised his bowdlerizing pen in respect to Steyne's sexual habits. But what he was forbidden to say outright, he depended on his readers' knowledge of Steyne's "original" to supply. The identification enabled them to resolve the issue that Thackeray carefully left unclear: of course Becky and the lecherous lord were lovers.

Hertford, or someone resembling him, returned to fiction at least twice after *Vanity Fair* and *Pendennis*, where the image was notably sanitized. In *John Halifax, Gentleman* he was the evil aristocrat Lord Luxmore, a spendthrift owner of rotten boroughs and huge debts—usual attributes of the type—but Dinah Mulock alluded only indirectly to what was, in Victorian terms, the most reprehensible of moral shortcomings, his grand-scale sexual delinquencies.

The systematic peopling of novels with casts of publicly identifiable originals died out with the decline of fashionable fiction and the completion of Disraeli's trilogy. It was revived only by Trollope, in his Palliser series (in respect only to political figures), and by Disraeli, in the two novels he wrote late in life. In *Lothair* (1870) the titular character bears some resemblance to the third Marquis of Bute, whose conversion to Roman Catholicism two years earlier had caused some stir. "The Bishop" "is" (in the usual loose sense) Wilberforce; Mr. Phoebus is the artist Frederic Leighton; and Cardinal Grandison is Cardinal Manning, against whom Disraeli had a grudge stemming from a misunderstanding over the funding of an Irish Catholic university. There was a larger assembly of originals ten years later, in *Endymion*. Palmerston appeared as Lord Roehampton; Louis Napoleon (as he was at the time of the action; Napoleon III when the book was published) as the young King Florestan; Disraeli's friend Lady Jersey as Zenobia; the Rothschilds as the Neuchatels; and Manning again, who was back in Disraeli's good graces because he had quarreled with Gladstone in the interim, as the more sympathetically portrayed Nigel Penruddock, Archbishop of Tyre. It was assumed that the compulsively envious and ungrateful novelist St. Barbe was Disraeli's belated revenge for Thackeray's burlesque of *Coningsby* in "Punch's Prize Novelists" and his reviews of both that novel and *Sybil* in the *Morning Chronicle*, but this identification has recently been questioned on the reasonable ground that Disraeli had made "friendly gestures" to Thackeray after the parody and the reviews had appeared, and in any case thirty-three years was a long time to nurse a grievance.[22] Lord Hertford also was present in *Endymion*, as Lord Montfort, but after the passage of four decades and with the mellowing of Disraeli's memory, he was but a pale shadow of his former vigorous self.

In Dickens's early novels few characters were drawn from well-known public characters, and such renamed originals as did appear were apt to be more readily identified by Londoners than by provincial readers. Until the greater availability of the London press after the middle of the century enabled readers outside the metropolis to share its news on a roughly equal basis, "London figures" were not necessarily "national figures" as well.

One of the first Dickens characters alleged to be modeled after a living original was Fagin in *Oliver Twist*. Tradition identified him with Ikey Solomons, "the prince of fences," who after an apprenticeship in the pocket-picking trade became a receiver of stolen goods, an occupation in which Fagin excelled. Solomons turned up periodically in the news, notably in connection with appearances in the law courts and his consequent voyages on convict ships to Van Diemen's Land and return. At the peak of his fame, in 1827–30, at least three pamphlets sold in the streets recounted his diversified career; a typical comprehensive title was *Only Correct Edition! The Life and Exploits of Ikey Solomons, Swindler, Forger, Fencer, and Brothel-Keeper. With Accounts of Flash and Dress Houses, Flash Girls and Coves of the Watch, Now on Town; With Instructions How to Guard Against Hypocritical Villains, and the Lures of Abandoned Females. Also, Particulars of Mrs. Ikey Solomons, and the Gang Who Infested London for Nineteen Years.*

Ikey Solomons, now permanently under governmental detention at Hobart Town, Tasmania, where he was to die in 1850, was still fresh enough in the public memory in 1839–40 for Thackeray to use his name facetiously as the putative author of *Catherine*. It was only natural that readers of *Oliver Twist*, published just previously (1837–39), should have associated Fagin with Solomons, and that the identification would become hardened into a received assumption, as it did. But Solomons's modern biographer, after comparing Dickens's description of Fagin with the known facts of the eminent fence's appearance and character, has concluded that Dickens "*could* have remembered him; but there is no evidence that he did." The identification existed only in readers' imaginations, which of course was sufficient, despite its gratuitousness, to add interest in the character.[23]

Of another reputed original in *Oliver Twist*, however, there remains no doubt, because the name of the harsh Magistrate Fang, of the Hatton Garden police court, was clearly meant to echo that of Magistrate Laing of the same court. Laing's bullying of the wretched persons brought before him and the stiff sentences he handed out so offended the public sense of humanity and rudimentary justice that the press was already agitating for his removal when the novel began its serialization. Indeed, when Oliver was haled into his court, Fang/Laing "was at that moment perusing a leading article in a newspaper of the morning, adverting to some recent decision of his, and commending him, for the three hundred and fiftieth time, to the special and particular notice of the Secretary of State for the Home Department," Lord John Russell (11:120). Six months after the appearance of the chapter in which Laing figured, Russell dismissed him. Dickens, the budding reformer, had the satisfac-

SIR PETER LAUREUS.

Sir Peter Laurie, the original of Alderman Cute in Dickens's *The Chimes*, had earlier been mildly caricatured by Thackeray in his short-lived paper, *The National Standard* (top). He was pictured, simply as "a name in the news" (bottom), in the *Illustrated London News* for 21 January 1843, and was pilloried at the end of the year in *The Chimes*.

tion of knowing that his shaft had hit the mark, even if other bowmen's arrows were already fixed there.[24]

Another occupant of a London bench of justice provided the instantly recognized model for Alderman Cute in *The Chimes*: the Middlesex magistrate Sir Peter Laurie, a former Lord Mayor who had won himself the satiric attention of *Punch* as "the City Solon" partly by virtue of his widely ridiculed determination to "put down suicide."[25] Whether or not he actually uttered those words, his severity in dealing with men and women whose determination to do away with themselves was less than successful had become a London joke. (It is true that staging suicides with failure aforethought was, as Philip Collins has said, "a spectacular form of begging.") At the moment Dickens was writing *The Chimes*, Laurie had dealt in his accustomed summary fashion with a miserable woman who had failed to kill herself with poison, and at the same time was announcing statistics to prove that his tough dealing had considerably reduced the number of attempted suicides—though the erection of a railing at the top of the Monument certainly contributed to the decline at that particular site. Dickens was not entirely fair to Laurie, who had his humane side and was well-meaning even if misguided (and misquoted), but readers of *The Chimes* saw Cute solely in the indignant terms propagated by *Punch* and editorials in the press.

4.

After the middle of the century, fictional originals were increasingly found in two classes of nationally known men: the new generation of politicians, who were no longer necessarily distinguished by the statesmanlike posture and devotion to principle that Disraeli had attributed to many of them, and relative newcomers to fiction, the emblems of the burgeoning age of capitalistic enterprise, the financial moguls in the City who dealt in enormous sums at scarcely less enormous risks.

Embarking on his career in the fifties, Trollope wrote, as he always would, for readers who he could assume saw the *Times* or the new *Daily Telegraph* regularly. In *The Warden*, his first novel to be set in contemporary England, he mentioned leading politicians of the day by name—Lord John Russell, Palmerston, Gladstone, Lord Derby. The number of "originals" who can be detected in his political novels has been a subject on which scholars have not always agreed.[26] Trollope repeatedly denied having deliberately introduced into his casts well-known politicians under other names, but his disavowals are not persuasive. Followers of the news from Westminster, especially from 1867–69 onward, when *Phineas Finn*, the first of the parliamentary novels, appeared, would have detected many resemblances between the fictional politicians and the actual ones. Turnbull, in *Phineas Finn*, was a readily identifiable portrait of John Bright, and in this and later novels Daubeny was Disraeli, who was always Trollope's bête noire; Gresham was Gladstone; and Mr. Mildmay was Lord John (by that time, Earl) Russell.

With the exception of Bright as Turnbull, however, Trollope avoided endowing his created characters with the personal traits of their real-life counterparts, so that, as a recent critic has observed, "they tend to appear remote, slightly larger than life, even slightly mysterious, compared to the ordinary mortals—including the underlings of politics—with whom we are allowed to rub shoulders."[27] Contemporary readers identified them largely from the spaces they occupied, and the moves they made, on the political chessboard. But just as often Trollope exercised a novelist's license to rearrange the chronology of current issues and events for artistic purposes. To avoid the pretense of writing a mere veracious historical chronicle, he dissociated his characters from the specific opinions and causes to which their models were attached, thus additionally blurring the sharp one-to-one identifications to be found in comparable pairings in Disraeli's novels.

Preeminent among the financier-politicians who sat in Parliament chiefly to defend and advance their commercial interests was the most notorious mid-century magnate, the "Railway King," as Carlyle, following Sydney Smith, called him.[28] George Hudson, projector of railway companies, buccaneer stock speculator, financial manipulator, and the motive force behind the great "railway mania" of 1844–47 (Chapter 17 below), was what Trollope, referring to Sir Roger Scatcherd in *Doctor Thorne*, called a "newspaper hero, . . . one of those 'whom the king delighteth to honour'" (9:99). The hysterical nationwide adulation he received had originated at York, where his swift rise as a civic leader and benefactor made him a living municipal patron saint, and where a proposal to erect a statue in his honor elicited a public subscription of £25,000 and became the object of Carlyle's vituperative ridicule in the July 1850 number ("Hudson's Statue") of his *Latter-Day Pamphlets*.† Hud-

---

†Hudson treated York handsomely by making it an important railway center, but this boon was not unmixed. Wilkie Collins grumped, in *No Name*: "That entire incapability of devising administrative measures for the management of large crowds, which is one of the characteristics of Englishmen in authority, is nowhere more strikingly exemplified than at York. Three different lines of railway assemble three passenger mobs, from morning to night, under one roof; and leave them to raise a traveler's riot, with all the assistance which the bewildered servants of the company can render to increase the confusion" ("Second scene," chap. 1:1.268). As grateful stockholders in one of Hudson's companies—they had bought shares in the York and North Midland Railway Company in 1843—Emily and

MR. G. HUDSON, M.P.—"THE RAILWAY KING."

KING HUDSON'S LEVEE.

Two views of George Hudson at the peak of his celebrity as a financial wizard: (top) The news picture in the *Illustrated London News* for 6 September 1845; (bottom) *Punch*'s dissent from the general adulation, in its issue for 29 November of the same year.

son's paper empire came apart in 1849, when the public learned that he had fiddled his accounts on a truly superhuman scale. Among other malpractices, he had been paying railway company dividends out of principal, which, it might have been observed, was no way to run a railroad. He was also a pioneer in the art of privileged trading. Since fully two-thirds of the members of the House of Commons speculated in railway shares, they undoubtedly sought the constant advice of their front-bench colleague, whom the borough of Sunderland had the repeated honor of electing to Westminster. By virtue of his being an M.P., he was protected from his creditors, and no criminal prosecution could be brought against him because no existing statutes were applicable to the particular forms of fraud he practiced.

In 1855 the ruined Hudson, no longer enjoying parliamentary immunity, "retired to the continent," to use the favorite Victorian expression for putting the width of the English Channel between oneself and one's troubles, and though he lived on until 1871, he faded from public view, though not from public memory. He would have been recognized as bearing a strong resemblance in some respects to Sir Roger Scatcherd in *Doctor Thorne* (1858), the chief difference being that the one manipulated the finances of railways, existing or envisaged, and the other actually built them. Scatcherd, too, sat in Parliament, where he was esteemed, said Trollope, "as the greatest living authority on railway matters" before he lost his seat on a charge of corruption; both were self-made men, and both were heavy drinkers. But Trollope did not intend to reproduce Hudson's whole personality or duplicate his career in Scatcherd's. Instead, Hudson served him, as he did later novelists, as a type-figure, the embodiment of qualities that could shoot a man to the pinnacle of public esteem and then, as swiftly, bring catastrophic retribution. In Scatcherd's case, however, his fortune remained intact, passing by way of his son to Mary Thorne, the illegitimate daughter of his brother; and the newspaper obituary that Trollope invented for him was of the studiously *nil nisi bonum* variety.

At least the shadow of Hudson also appeared briefly in another novel Trollope published the same year as *Doctor Thorne*. In *The Three Clerks* we read of Mr. M'Buffer (the name refers to a piece of railway equipment) who had represented the corrupt borough of Tillietudlem for a number of years, meanwhile serving also as "a managing director of a bankrupt

---

Anne Brontë subscribed a guinea apiece toward the statue, which was never erected. They resisted Charlotte's urging that they sell their shares when Hudson's fortunes began to totter; it seems not to be known if their modest investment was entirely lost in the ensuing crash. (Winifred Gérin, *Emily Brontë* [Oxford, 1971], p. 142.)

George Hudson had been so venerated that his reputed birthplace in York was looked upon as a secular shrine almost coequal with Shakespeare's in Stratford, which had recently been auctioned off by George Robins's son and bought for the nation. But this picture in the *Illustrated London News* for 14 April 1849 was printed in conjunction with a front-page editorial, titled "Railway Morality," after his extravagant wheeling-dealing had brought catastrophe. "With all this wealth and fame, very likely he says, with hundreds of others, 'I wish I had minded my shop, and not speculated in railway shares.'"

swindle, from which he had contrived to pillage some thirty or forty thousand pounds." When the swindle was exposed, M'Buffer, unlike the more brazen Hudson, could not show his face either at Tillietudlem or the House of Commons, and therefore applied for the Chiltern Hundreds, the euphemistic equivalent of resigning one's seat. "After all," Undy Scott, who craved M'Buffer's place in the Commons, told Alaric Tudor, "he did not do so very badly. Why, M'Buffer has been at it now for thirteen years. He began with nothing; he had neither blood nor money; and God knows he had no social merits to recommend him. He is as vulgar as a hog, as awkward as an elephant, and as ugly as an ape. . . . [F]or the five years he has been in Parliament, his wife has gone about in her carriage, and every man in the city has been willing to shake hands with him" (24:282–86).

Just as M'Buffer had a wife who went about in her own carriage, so Sir Roger Scatcherd had a Lady Scatcherd, whom Trollope described as an amiable vulgarian, "no fit associate for the wives of English baronets . . . no doubt by education and manners much better fitted to sit in their servants' halls; but not on that account was she a bad wife or a bad woman" (*Doctor Thorne*, 10:108). Some knowledgeable readers of *Doctor Thorne* would have amplified and altered Trollope's portrayal of her in the light of the circulating gossip about Mrs. George Hudson, who came from the same humble roots as her fictional counterpart. Mrs. Hudson's gaffes were legendary: told that a bust in the Marquis of Westminster's town house was of Marcus Aurelius, she inquired whether "he was the late Markiss," her host's father, who had died a year or two earlier. She was said to have returned a pair of globes, celestial and terrestrial, to James Wyld, the mapmaker and proprietor of Wyld's Great Globe in Leicester Square, on the grounds that they didn't match. But she was a famous hostess, so long as her husband still had his Midas touch. When he bought their mansion in Albert Gate from Thomas Cubitt, the builder, for £15,000, she spent an additional £14,000 furnishing and decorating it to serve as the new headquarters of the cream of London society, headed by the Duke of Wellington himself.

Thackeray appears to have had Mrs. Hudson in mind when he created two characters, in *Pendennis* and *The Newcomes*, respectively. Lady Clavering ("the Begum") in *Pendennis* is a thoroughly bourgeois type who has come into sudden wealth. Thackeray describes in detail the appointments in her "gorgeous" dining room and drawing room in Grosvenor Place, the former "fitted up, Lady Clavering couldn't for goodness gracious tell why, in the middle-aged style, 'unless,' said her good-natured Ladyship, laughing, 'because me and Clavering are middle-aged people.'" Throughout his satirical description, Thackeray plays, Dickens-fashion, with the words *taste* and *chaste* ("that being the proper phrase") and ends, ". . . everybody who saw Lady Clavering's reception rooms was forced to confess that they were most elegant: and that the prettiest rooms in London—Lady Harley´ Quin's, Lady Hanway Wardour's, Mrs. Hodge-Podson's own, the great Railroad Croesus' wife, were not fitted up with a more consummate 'chastity'" (37:1.381).†

---

† Here Thackeray uses a novelist's familiar device to counter the reader's suspicion that he has a certain model in mind: if "Mrs. Hodge-Podson, the great Railroad Croesus's wife,"

The Princesse de Montcontour in *The Newcomes*, "née Higg of Manchester," is married to a French nobleman who becomes director of the Great Anglo-Gallic, subsequently inflated to Anglo-Continental, Railway. She is "a good natured body who drops her *h*'s"—Thackeray might have added that she fractured her French with a broad Lancashire accent; Mrs. Hudson fractured hers with the Yorkshire variety—and, like Lady Clavering, she does not quite know what to make of the luxurious surroundings into which fortune has thrust her. When she and her husband occupy the first floor of his father's Paris *hôtel*, she has "a bedchamber which, to her terror, she is obliged to open of reception evenings, when gentlemen and ladies play cards there. It is fitted up in the style of Louis XVI," which in its own way, with "Cupids and nymphs, by Boucher, sporting over the door-panels," is as overwhelming as the decoration in any other railway Croesus's house. "'Ah, mum,'" says old Betsy, the Princesse's maid, "'what would Mr. Humper at Manchester, Mr. Jowls of Newcome' (the minister whom, in early days, Miss Higg used to sit under) 'say if they was browt into this room!'" (46:2:82–83).

It is odd that Dickens, who loved to ridicule the pretensions of the newly rich, did not visibly incorporate Mrs. Hudson into his portrait of Mrs. Merdle in *Little Dorrit*. But Hudson was not much in the forefront of Dickens's mind when he wrote that novel. Instead, the financial background was provided by events that occurred as Dickens was in the very process of planning and writing the novel. From the outset he had planned a plot that would involve several characters in financial disaster, a most timely subject, since the bitter finale of the railway mania had done nothing to dampen the high-flying speculative fever in banking circles. In June 1855, as he was beginning to write *Little Dorritt*, the supposedly granite-solid house of Strahan, Paul, and Bates closed its doors, and within a week the partners were arrested and charged with fraudulent conversion. After a short trial in late October, they were sentenced to fourteen years' penal servitude.

The first number of the novel appeared in December. Then occurred, at least from Dickens's point of view, a lucky accident. In the middle of the following February the Tipperary Joint-Stock Bank failed, and three days later the partner John Sadleir, Hudson's successor as the new Midas, committed suicide by poison on Hampstead Heath. Like

---

obviously refers to Mrs. Hudson, then Lady Clavering can't be Mrs. Hudson too. But the red herring is as plain as the implied identification, and in any case no law of fiction requires that only one character per novel be traceable to a given original. This was the same dodge Trollope used when he mentioned Hiram's Hospital and the St. Cross charity on the same level of reality.

Hudson, he had possessed a kind of publicity-generated charisma that led thousands of investors to commit their savings to him, and many more to watch in admiration as he rose to the post of junior Lord of the Treasury. Dickens now had, straight from the newspapers, a character providentially qualified to precipitate the catastrophe he had planned— the swindling financier Merdle, whom he promptly introduced in the number he was then writing for May publication. "I shaped Mr. Merdle himself out of that precious rascality," he wrote Forster. "Mr. Merdle's complaint, . . . fraud and forgery, came into my mind as the last drop in the silver cream-jug on Hampstead Heath." Readers from that point onward could superimpose on the fictional character of Merdle the image of Sadleir they received from the daily press. Merdle "was in everything good, from banking to building. He was in Parliament, of course. [Sadleir had successively represented the Irish constituencies of Carlow and Sligo.] He was in the City, necessarily. He was Chairman of this, Trustee of that, President of the other . . ." (*Little Dorrit*, 1.21:293). Dickens stressed his celebrity, which rested solely on the popular will to believe, and therefore to idolize, not on any tangible benefits he had conferred on society:

> The famous name of Merdle became, every day, more famous in the land. Nobody knew that the Merdle of such high renown had ever done any good to any one, alive or dead, or to any earthly thing; nobody knew that he had any capacity or utterance of any sort in him, which had ever thrown, for any creature, the feeblest farthing-candle ray of light on any path of duty or diversion, pain or pleasure, toil or rest, fact or fancy, among the multiplicity of paths in the labyrinth trodden by the sons of Adam; nobody had the smallest reason for supposing the clay of which this object of worship was made, to be other than the commonest clay, with as clogged a wick smoldering inside of it as ever kept an image of humanity from tumbling to pieces. All people knew (or thought they knew) that he had made himself immensely rich; and, for that reason alone, prostrated themselves before him, more degradedly and less excusably than the darkest savage creeps out of his hole in the ground to propitiate, in some log or reptile, the Deity of his benighted soul. (2.12:611)

So far as can be determined, Merdle did not resemble Sadleir personally; as Trollope had done with Hudson, Dickens used him principally as a representative of a class that typified the free-wheeling Mammonism of the City in the mid-fifties. The Sadleir figure reappeared shortly afterwards in Charles Lever's *Davenport Dunn*, which began publication in monthly parts in July 1857.

Melmotte, in Trollope's *The Way We Live Now*, though as skillfully developed as Merdle, was also a type-figure, reminiscent of both Sadleir and Hudson, whose several forms of fraud he combined in a single conglomerate enterprise. In one respect he was likely to have reminded readers of Hudson rather than Sadleir, because one of his promotions was the South Central Pacific and Mexico Railway of London and San Francisco, which nobody in his right mind expected to be built.

Hudson appeared in fiction once more as Mr. Vigo in *Endymion*, Disraeli doubtless thinking that no picture of life among the movers and shakers in the late 1840s would be complete without a Hudson figure. He stopped short, however, of portraying the calamitous bursting of the bubble. By this time, Hudson's machinations had begun to fade from the public memory, eclipsed by more recent chicanery centering in City banking and business houses, and a new breed of respectable railway magnates had come into view. As a result the figure was treated more sympathetically in fiction. In Hardy's *A Laodicean*, whose run in the European edition of *Harper's Monthly Magazine* began in the same year in which *Endymion* was published (1880), the figure of the late Mr. Powers, who came upon the ruined Stancy Castle in the course of his surveying and diverted the new line so as not to disturb it, was *not* modeled on George Hudson. He was, said Hardy, "a great Nonconformist, a staunch Baptist up to the day of his death," and, among other beneficences, "built the people [of the neighborhood] a chapel on a bit of freehold be bought for them" (4:60). Readers would have recognized the real-life figure of Sir Samuel Morton Peto (1809–89), who, like Powers, was said to have "made half the railways in Europe." He too was a strong Baptist, and his best-known charitable deeds were providing the funds for building the denomination's chapel in Bloomsbury and converting to the same use the building on the edge of Regent's Park that had formerly housed the famous Diorama. Like Trollope's Scatcherd, Peto had begun to learn the construction business as a manual laborer, but with a significant difference: Scatcherd was a stone mason without any connections, whereas the young Peto was apprenticed to his uncle, a London builder, whose business he inherited in 1830. Peto also was an M.P., sitting for a succession of constituencies in 1847–68, and he had the opportunity, denied to Scatcherd, of serving his country in the Crimea; the railway line he built between Balaclava and the entrenchments won him a baronetcy in 1855. But eleven years later he was ruined when his firm was caught in the debacle of Overend, Gurney, and Company, the last of the great mid-Victorian bank failures. There was no such event in Powers's career.

Into the amalgam that produced the latter-day image of the railway mogul went a trace of still another real-life figure, Thomas Brassey (1805–70), who built many miles of the Great Western Railway and other lines in the 1840s, as well as doing much foreign business. It is noticeable that the writer of his life in the *Dictionary of National Biography* went out of his way to extol Brassey's honesty: he "made a large fortune without suspicion of unfair dealing," in addition to being a paragon of courtesy and diplomacy, and enjoying a "perfect domestic life."

The Hudsonian stigma, though fading, took a long time to be totally eradicated, notwithstanding both Disraeli's and Gladstone's personal tributes to Peto's character after his business failed. After all, in 1857 there had been the case of Leopold Redpath, a clerk in the share transfer office of the Great Northern Railway Company and "a man of unblemished reputation of great charity" who was discovered to have issued a quarter of a million pounds of forged stock. He was convicted of embezzlement and sentenced to transportation for life. When Meredith gave the name Tom Redworth to the railway promoter and company director in *Diana of the Crossways* (1884), he must have expected his readers to respond appropriately: here, they would think, was the well-established topos once again—the pride of great riches derived from involvement in railway shares pointing inexorably toward a great fall. But Meredith, always the subverter of preconceptions, tricked his readers. Far from being an unscrupulous manipulator, making free with other people's money and eventually being caught with them in the ruins, Redworth, a man of unblemished integrity, enjoys the deserved rewards of integrity and intelligence and becomes the true hero of the novel. He is, for one thing, the only man who discerns and understands "the fire of positive brain-stuff" in the emancipation-hungry Diana, and in the end he marries her. Hardy cracked the mold; Meredith broke it.

5.

Midway between the wholly private original, known to the novelist but to none of his readers, and the public one, known to the widest possible audience, lay what may be called the semipublic one, a man or woman known to a limited part of that audience, who alone possessed the information that would enable them to appreciate and respond to the similarity between a fictional character and his or her real-life counterpart.

The Cheeryble brothers in *Nicholas Nickleby* are a good example. "These potbellied Sir Charles Grandisons of the ledger and day-book," as a reviewer called them, were inspired by a pair of Manchester merchants and factory owners, William and Daniel Grant, with whom Dickens dined in 1838. Their fame as philanthropists was strictly local until, many years after the novel was published, Samuel Smiles described them in his best-selling book of success stories, *Self-Help* (1859). Like the Ashton murder Mrs. Gaskell indirectly alluded to in *Mary Barton*, the Grants were topical only in Manchester, and so the Cheerybles, who needed all the credibility they could get, for many years went unauthenticated everywhere else that *Nicholas Nickleby* was read.[29]

Miss Mowcher, in *David Copperfield*, was recognizable only by those who were familiar with a certain portion of the London scene. In the eighth number of the novel (December 1849), Dickens introduced her as a dwarf who made a living as a manicurist and chiropodist and additionally, he implied, as a procuress. Her original was a neighbor of Dickens near Regent's Park, Mrs. Jane Seymour Hill, whom a gossip sheet, *The Town*, had once described as "the most eminent amongst female operators" in the corn-cutting line: "This interesting *little* lady is one of the *greatest* London characters; she may be seen in all parts of the town, riding in a chaise in company with her brother, who is also a dwarf."[30] Out of a sense of personal injury as well as fearing the possible impairment of her employment, Mrs. Hill immediately wrote Dickens a letter of protest: ". . . widowed in all but my good name you shew up my personal deformities with insinuations that by the purest of my sex may be construed to the worst of purposes. . . . May your Widow and Children never meet with such Blighting wit as you have poured on my miserably nervous head." Dickens replied with an attempt at some soothing remarks: "I assure you that the original of a great portion of that character is well known to me and to several friends of mine and is wholly removed from you and a very different person. Indeed I never represent an individual but always a combination of individuals in one."† He promised to make amends in a future number, but this would have to await an opportunity in the natural course of the narrative. This was eventually forthcoming, and Dickens, whatever his first intention had been, redeemed Miss Mowcher.

Contemporary readers who patrolled the London pavements as habitually as Dickens did, and had something of his eye for the picturesque in human appearance and behavior, would have seen in several other of his memorable characters more than was otherwise apparent. They would have associated the preposterous Mr. Turveydrop in *Bleak House*, an elderly parasite in the dress of a Regency buck and the very exemplar of elegant "deportment," with a real-life model. John Henry Skelton was

---

†Dickens was disingenuous here, not for the first time or the last. In the preface to the original edition of *Nicholas Nickleby*, he had assured his readers that the Cheeryble brothers "are drawn from life . . . the BROTHERS CHEERYBLE live." Yet later he denied, in the face of considerable evidence, that he had modeled Inspector Bucket in *Bleak House* on a Scotland Yard officer he knew and admired, Inspector Charles Frederick Field.

Phiz's picture of the dwarf Miss Mowcher dressing Steerforth's
hair may or may not have been faithful to the original, but Dickens's description of her clearly was meant to refer to Mrs. Davis,
the "interesting little lady" who was a familiar London figure.

a bankrupt woollen draper who, "possessed of the fixed idea that he was
destined to become the instructor of mankind in the true art of etiquette," published in 1837 a guidebook to that laudable end, *My Book;
or, The Anatomy of Conduct*. Skelton, decked out in the old Regency fashion, was a familiar sight on London streets as late as 1855, and two of
Dickens's contemporaries, the publisher and bookseller John Camden
Hotten and the theatrical man-about-town John Hollingshead, left descriptions of him that tally so closely with Dickens's portrait of Turveydrop as to make the identification certain.[31]

In contrast, the essence of Miss Havisham's fascination as a character in *Great Expectations* was her total invisibility to the world outside her perpetually darkened room. More "originals" have been proposed for her than for any other character in Dickens.[32] Whatever their individual credibility, there is little question that in creating her Dickens drew upon, and fused, a number of disparate recollections, ranging from the account of an Oxford Street recluse in the *Annual Register* for 1778 to his memory of a playlet performed once only in 1831, in which two characters, "Rouge et Noire" and "the White Woman," were suggested by demented women who were actually living at the time. The latter, a jilted bride who dressed entirely in white and was "constantly on parade" in Berners Street, was described by Dickens in an essay in *Household Words* (1 January 1853). But the fragments of London lore and life that Miss Havisham's situation would most immediately have recalled to readers of *Great Expectations*—though even so, their memories would have had to be fairly long—were two. One was the legend of "Dirty Dick," the well-to-do son of a Leadenhall Street ironmonger whose engagement feast was abruptly canceled by news of his intended's death and who sealed, undisturbed, the dining room in which the banquet had been set out. (Unlike Miss Havisham, he did not immure himself but became an unwashed "wanderer" until his death fifty years later.) The other suggestion appeared in the January 1850 issue of the "Household Narrative" (news magazine) supplement to *Household Words*, where a paragraph mentioned the death of a Havisham-like eccentric, one Martha Joachim of York Buildings, Strand.

To a large extent, then, Miss Havisham is a composite figure. Jo, the miserable, homeless crossing-sweeper in *Bleak House*, is both composite and generic. His numerous counterparts, not only small boys and girls but grown beggar women and otherwise unemployable men, could be seen wherever the mud and manure lay deepest in the principal London streets, earning pennies from pedestrians by clearing paths across the soggy mess that were instantly eradicated by the next surge of traffic. In addition to his day-to-day observation of this ragged band and visits to schools that attempted to lend them a modicum of civilization, Dickens learned about these outcasts from such sources as a review, in *Household Words*, of a book on *Reformatory Schools* (1851) which had passages specifically on street arabs, and a review in the *Westminster Review* (1852) of the same book together with a blue book, the *Report of the Select Committee of the House of Commons on Criminal and Destitute Juveniles*. For one aspect of Jo's portrait however, the benighted answers he gave when examined at the "inkwitch" on Nemo, Dickens seems to have had a particular boy in mind, one George Ruby, whose answers to questions addressed to

him, as a witness in a Guildhall hearing (January 1850) involving a savage assault on a policeman, were imbued with as much ignorance
as Jo's.[33]

A fair number of fictional characters were suggested by figures in the
restricted circle of literary and publishing London. It is difficult to say
how many readers unacquainted with that circle would have detected
the originals and understood the various kinds of comment on the literary personalities and politics of the day that the associations implied.
Some relatively innocuous gossip found its way into the pages of the
literary weeklies and, as a few successful authors became as newsworthy
as politicians, into the general press. But much of the significance of
the pairings must have been lost upon the novelists' readers at large.
They represented nothing more than pawns in a semi-private game
novelists played, either to satirize or denigrate unliked fellow authors
or exigent editors or publishers or in other ways to settle scores in the
intimate little world that centered in the Paternoster Row publishing
houses, the *Times* office in Printing House Square, the *Punch* office in
Fleet Street, and such meeting places of the literati as the Athenaeum
and the Garrick Club.

In Thackeray's fiction, indeed, the literary-journalistic world supplanted the beau monde and political world of Regency days as a prime
source of "originals." His portrait of Theodore Hook as Mr. Wagg in
Vanity Fair and *Pendennis* provides a handy test case by which to estimate
how much Thackeray's Victorian readers at large might have known of
a detectable original. The many-sided Hook—a quotable but acid wit,
fabulous improvisatore at dinner parties, editor of the scandalmongering weekly *John Bull*, author of numerous fashionable novels and other
books—had been one of the flashiest presences on the Regency literary
scene.[34] His death in 1841 had evoked several memoirs in periodicals,
including one shortly afterward in *Fraser's Magazine* and a lengthy article
by John Gibson Lockhart in the *Quarterly Review* for May 1843, which
was separately published in volume form in Murray's reprint series,
Reading for the Rail. There was also a memoir of Hook prefixed to Colburn's edition of his *Fathers and Sons* (1842), and Hook had figured
prominently in the *Memoirs of Charles Mathews*, the comedian, by his
widow (1839). All these could have been read, and remembered, by the
first purchasers of *Vanity Fair* (1847–48). Readers of *Pendennis*, in addition, could have read the biography of Hook written by Richard H. D.
Barham, published just as that novel began to appear in monthly parts
(November 1848). Thackeray's portrait of Wagg was comparatively brief
and simplified, as well as expurgated in deference to early Victorian
standards of propriety. But so, to varying degrees, were the memoirs

that presented the "real" Wagg; Hook's nasty jokes and his professional vending of scandal and innuendo gave way to a more respectable version of the man.

Few readers of *Pendennis* outside London literary circles would have fully appreciated Thackeray's satire, in the rivalry of the publishers Bacon and Bungay, of the extravagant puffery and sharp business practices for which the real-life firm of Colburn and Bentley had been notorious. This was, in any case, a dated topicality, because the firm had been acrimoniously dissolved as long ago as 1832, although the former partners, still bitterly unreconciled, maintained separate businesses at the time *Pendennis* was published. But, regardless of its specific application, the public would have relished Thackeray's picture of the fictional pair simply as an exposé of the realities of contemporary publishing.

Semiprofessional readers—persons with some kind of connection with the literary world—would have been best positioned to appreciate the thrust of Dickens's several characterizations inspired by contemporary writers. Preeminent among these was Harold Skimpole in *Bleak House*.[35] For many years, Skimpole's original, the poet and essayist Leigh Hunt, had been known to the book-reading public as the political martyr who had spent two years in jail for libeling the Prince Regent as a "fat Adonis of fifty," among other compliments, and as the intimate of Byron and Shelley, whose overly candid book recounting his association with them had stirred a tempest in literary circles in 1828. Hunt's personality, a mixture of charm, childish innocence of practical matters, and inveterate mendicancy, was known to the public at one remove through reviews of his successive volumes and a sketch in Richard Henry Horne's *New Spirit of the Age* (1844). By the time Dickens came to write *Bleak House*, Hunt's name still figured in publishers' advertisements and reviewing columns; his *Autobiography* had appeared in 1850. But like other writers who outlived the high-water mark of their fame, the man Leigh Hunt now dwelt in such obscurity that readers outside London's literary circles were surprised to hear he was still alive.

When Dickens developed the character of Skimpole, therefore, he could have been reasonably sure that comparatively few readers would recognize Leigh Hunt. Not that it mattered: he had already caricatured the pompous author and editor Samuel Carter Hall as Pecksniff without untoward consequences, and in 1864–65 he was to gather a number of his friend John Forster's less admirable qualities—his rudeness, chauvinism, complacency—in the portrait of Podsnap.[36] In none of these instances, however, does it appear that ordinary readers recognized the living originals, although reviewers, accredited members of the literary profession, may well have done so but kept their peace.

Caroline Chisholm, the "original" of Mrs. Jellyby in *Bleak House*, is a rather special case. Thanks to the publicity Dickens and others gave to her activities in behalf of female emigration to Australia, she was at least a semipublic figure. But the specific qualities he transferred to his portrait of Mrs. Jellyby were strictly private knowledge. "I dream of Mrs. Chisholm, and her housekeeping," he wrote to Angela Burdett Coutts in March 1850. "The dirty faces of her children are my continual companions."[37]

In contrast to such pairing of public and fictitious figures as Laing/Fang, Laurie/Cute, and Hook/Wagg, where novelists rightly assumed that the sharing of known personal traits would make identification unmistakable, the application of private knowledge diminished the artistic usefulness of public originals. Hunt's reliance on others' largess and Chisholm's domestic dishevelment were traits central to the portrayal of the respective characters, but none of their impact on the reader could be traced to his acquaintance with the models. The figures stood by themselves, and owed nothing to any comparison a reader could make: the resemblance was present only in the novelist's mind.

Identification of the real and the imagined characters often went no further than the activity or opinion they had in common. It was the simplest of equivalences: not who a man or woman was (as an individual, a living compound of personal characteristics), but what they were and what they did (their station, their occupations, their views on matters of current interest). The poisoner Wainewright served as an original only to the extent that Dickens used his story in "Hunted Down"; he provided a plot, not a personality. Count Smorltork in *Pickwick Papers*, a foreign visitor making a quick tour of England before hastily writing and publishing a supposedly authentic account of the nation and its people, was suggested by both Prince Pückler-Muskau[†] and Professor Friedrich von Raumer, who had written and published such books just before Dickens

---

[†]On one occasion, when it doubly intersected with the "real" world, the world of Victorian fiction proved to be small indeed. It is a matter of record that Dickens's Count Smorltork courted the daughter of Thackeray's Mr. Polonius. That is, Pückler-Muskau, visiting England in 1827 for the specific purpose of finding an heiress who could pay off his enormous debts, discovered the only daughter of Hamlet, the wealthy jeweler. She was worth £200,000—the richest prospect he came across—and her father, who was well acquainted with titled personages in his way of business and would have prized a princeling as a son-in-law, was all for the match. His daughter, however, had already turned down two lords and remained adamant in her determination to marry only for love. "The father," wrote Pückler, "took leave of me with tears in his eyes, as I did from his £200,000." (*Pückler's Progress: The Adventures of Prince Pückler-Muskau in England, Wales and Ireland Told in Letters to His Former Wife, 1827.–29*, trans. Flora Brennan [London, 1987], pp. 154–55.)

wrote his novel; but none of those gentlemen's personal qualities, whatever they may have been, entered Dickens's fleeting vignette.[38] John Paul
Jefferson Jones, the intrusive "correspondent of the New York *Dema-
gogue*" in *Vanity Fair*, was suggested by Nathaniel Parker Willis, the dandiacal American journalist who wrote a long series of letters to the
New York *Mirror* purporting to give its readers the lowdown on the frequenters of fashionable London salons in the 1830s. But like Count
Smorltork, he was a type-figure: Thackeray describes him only in
his professional capacity of gossip-for-profit, not as an individualized
person.

The "third gentleman" in the schoolroom scene in *Hard Times* was
inspired by Henry Cole, at that time an active force in the Marlborough
House movement, which was "dedicated (among other things) to curing
mid-Victorian design of its tendency toward excessive representational-
ism."[39] This commitment to a particular idea was all that the unnamed
gentleman and Cole had in common; a reader of the novel was simply
invited to fill in what the gentleman stood for by recalling what he knew
of Cole's own pronouncements. (Actually, as has recently been pointed
out, Dickens misunderstood his position—he was "merely protesting
against the horrible vulgarities of mid-Victorian decoration and was
an advocate of color and fancy.")[40] Dickens, in short, meant nothing
personal.

In *The Three Clerks*, Trollope introduced Sir Gregory Hardlines and
Sir Warwick Westend, high officials in Whitehall, who, he admitted
in his *Autobiography*, were modeled on Sir Charles Trevelyan and Sir
Stafford Northcote, authors of the report urging that the method of
selecting civil servants be radically reformed. But there was no suggestion that the fictitious pair personally resembled the real-life ones, although Trollope, in view of his opposition to the reform they advocated,
may have intended some sort of private comment whose nature is lost
to us.

On the whole, although Victorian novelists freely employed living
originals for the purposes of characterization, they seldom did so in
great detail. *Diana of the Crossways* was the only Victorian novel of
consequence to be largely based on the life of a well-known original
(Caroline Norton).[41][†] Otherwise, the largest roles that real-life models

[†]Among the episodes in the novel that most closely identified Diana Warwick with
Caroline Norton was the one in which she leaked the secret of Peel's plan to repeal the
Corn Laws, the most controversial political issue of the day, to "Mr. Tonans," editor of the
(unnamed) *Times*—Trollope's *Jupiter* newspaper. It was widely believed at the time that
Caroline Norton, along with Sidney Herbert, had been similarly instrumental in giving the

played in fictional narrative, as opposed to brief allusions, were—to draw
from the disreputable category alone—those of Lord Steyne/Lord Hertford in *Vanity Fair*, Madame Rachel/Mother Oldershaw in *Armadale*,
Skittles-cum-Laura Bell/Rhoda Somerset in *A Terrible Temptation*, and
Lord DeRos/Sir Mulberry Hawk in *Nicholas Nickleby*. They were, at most,
instruments of plot or protagonists in isolated episodes. Otherwise, the
reflection was not that of a full-length mirror but of a mere fragment of
a looking glass. But even in this limited compass, there was always the
possibility that the perceived resemblance between the original and the
invention might be so marked as to distract the reader's attention. Reviewing Disraeli's *Tancred*, Richard Monckton Milnes wrote, ". . . the immediate interest which these personalities confer on his works is dearly
purchased; for, the moment a character is known to represent Lord —
—— or Mr. ——, it loses all power as a work of art. The 'historical
picture' becomes the 'portrait of a gentleman'; the fidelity of the likeness
is the only object of attention, not the moral fitness, the entireness, the
beauty, or the grandeur of the character."[42] This would have been especially true of novels like Disraeli's, allegedly so replete with real-life
men and women under other names that systematic keys were needed
to elucidate the references. Perhaps it was this risk, as well as the disappearance of the silver fork novel itself, that led Victorian novelists to be
relatively unconcerned about "the fidelity of the likeness" to known originals. At any rate, Milnes's comment was virtually unique in the entire
corpus of Victorian literary criticism.[†] Like the distancing technique, the

---

Times its sensational scoop on 4 December 1845, when it reported that the cabinet had
unanimously agreed on the measure. But modern research has virtually exonerated her,
assigning the leak to Lord Aberdeen instead.

[†]Twenty years earlier, however, Robert Plumer Ward addressed himself to another
consideration in the preface to his novel of eighteenth-century life, *DeVere, or The Man of
Independence* (1827):

> [T]he production of ministers and public men on the scene, however ideal, or
> removed from the passing time, or however distant from real likeness to individual
> character at any time, can hardly fail to produce effects which may be made most
> painful to the Author's feelings. . . . He therefore desires most seriously, distinctly,
> and without a reserve, to declare in the outset, once and for ever, that no particular
> person is meant to be pourtrayed by any of the Dramatis Personae of this work. . . .
>
> But it may be said that certain known traits and anecdotes have been introduced,
> in connexion with particular characters; and that these characters, therefore, must
> surely be intended to represent the persons (whether alive or dead), to whom the
> anecdotes actually apply. . . .
>
> Yet surely a real anecdote of one person may be engrafted on the history of an-

use of models was an aspect of the fictional art that went unnoticed by reviewers as well as the more magisterial authors of summary articles on contemporary novelists. They simply did not care.

---

other, without identifying the two; and to suppose the contrary, is as illogical as it may be uncharitable.

(Quoted in *Nineteenth-Century British Novelists on the Novel,* ed. George L. Barnett [New York, 1971], p. 54.) The necessity for this disclaimer, so familiar to modern readers from its routine appearance on the verso of the title page of novels—"Any resemblance to persons living or dead . . ."—seems not to have been the "topic of fearful consequence" to Victorian novelists that it was to Ward; at least, I have not met it elsewhere.

16
Money and Occupations

1.

FROM TIME TO TIME we have noticed the part that social rank played in Victorian novelists' efforts to make their product timely. Once a late-twentieth-century reader fully grasps the nature of the biases that determined social attitudes and decisions, especially those of the upper and rising middle classes, the novels make the sense they made to their first readers; characters are placed, motivations become clear. Sometimes the problem of class is overt and central, as in *Evan Harrington*, whose dominant theme is "tailordom" and how it governs the ambitions, anxieties, and choices of the characters. But more often it is an unarticulated but omnipresent consideration, the implicit premise on which the action rests. It determines the characters' estimate of self, and indeed defines for them the world in which they move and the strategy they must adopt to cope with it. And at the root of it all is money.

At the beginning of the century, Jane Austen's men and women constantly talked about the size of the yearly income, estates, and marriage settlements that characterized the class to which they belonged and that differentiated one family from another.[1] The economics of land-based wealth and its impact on life in the squirearchal drawing rooms was the novels' major social theme. Allowing for altered circumstances more than half a century later, including the more worrisome sense of insecurity these entailed, this was even more true of Trollope's novels, where innumerable men and women are quietly obsessed with money as the one great indicator and instrument of class. A number of Trollope's love plots, for example, are based on the troubled situation of the young, attractive woman of good family who is a dependent without money of her own.

Dickens's characters are no less obsessed. "Money," Humphry House said, "is a main theme of nearly every book that Dickens wrote: getting, keeping, spending, owing, bequeathing provide the intricacies of his plots; character after character is constructed round an attitude to money. Social status without it is subordinate."[2] Whole books have been written on this theme, but what is to be noted here is the difference between Dickens's and Trollope's "worlds." In this respect they overlap a little—waiving the small chronological discrepancy, the Dedlock galaxy might well have been acquainted, in town and on the country-house circuit, with the best families of Barsetshire—but on the whole the Dickensian preoccupation is grubbier, more down-to-earth, than the Trollopian.

Money, in any case, supported the whole imposing structure of upper-class society, and within that structure it defined gradations. A man with a title, from duke down to baronet (or an untitled member of an old county family), who had ample wealth ranked higher on the social ladder than a man with the same title but less income. On the next lower level, money was a governing consideration as middle-class people of some substance decided and then acted on those decisions: money owed, money paid, money lost, money as a bargaining chip in marriage negotiations, money as a god, money as a devil. Little Paul Dombey exhibited truly preternatural insight into the values of early Victorian England when he confronted his father with the simple, confounding question, "What is money?". The elder Dombey, had he been less taken aback, might have replied, "For our purposes, it is everything."

An author's citing precise sums of money as an indication of status was a particular convenience to the contemporary reader. It was a reliable measure unthreatened, as it would be in our day, by steeply rising costs of living and inflation, subjects that are never mentioned in Victorian fiction. If there was a single store of topical knowledge universally shared by author and reader, it was a practical awareness of what money would buy. They could calculate to a nicety just what standard of living a given annual income would allow, based on their knowledge of wages and prices, the manner of life customary in a given bracket of society, and so forth. Converting Victorian sums of money into their modern equivalents, a very uncertain process at best because of the complications involved in the concept of the price index, is no substitute for the knowledge of comparative values that ordinary Victorian readers possessed. Only they could tell us precisely what kind of house Trollope had in mind when he wrote of an Islington lodging house simply that it was "such a house as men live in with two or three hundred a year" (*The Way We Live Now*, 26:206). Only such persons could recognize that when Nicholas Nickleby began his prosperous career in the Cheeryble brothers' business at an annual salary of £120 with a house thrown in, he was being paid an amount markedly higher than the prevailing scale for a clerk with no previous experience. Sam Titmarsh, occupying a similar position at the Independent West Diddlesex Fire and Life Insurance Company, made £80, which his aunt considered "a liberal salary," and after the collapse of that company he found a civil service post in the Tape and Sealing-Wax Office that paid exactly the same.

Nor could anyone but a Victorian reader aware of the going rates for shelter, commodities, and services appreciate that when Lady Dedlock tipped Jo a sovereign for leading her to Nemo's grave she gave him two hundred and forty times what he could have expected for sweeping a crossing in front of a pedestrian (Melmotte paid a penny in *The Way We Live Now*, and there is no evidence that he was a miser). That Mr. Garland in *The Old Curiosity Shop* gave Kit Nubbles all of sixpence for holding his wayward pony was a clear sign of his generosity. When Mrs. Bangham, the Marshalsea charwoman-messenger in *Little Dorrit*, returned from an errand short ninepence, after deducting the legitimate expenditure she had made from the amount with which she had been entrusted, readers would have understood why she was found "comatose on pavements": ninepence bought three neat tots of gin. Only a Londoner acquainted with Mogg's fare tables governing the price of cab journeys would have noticed that when Paul Montagu in *The Way We Live Now* paid the cabby half a crown after riding from Suffolk Street, Pall Mall, to Islington, he was giving him, in effect, a hundred percent tip.

A half-crown piece was a standard measure of parlor largess, as every schoolboy knew. In *The Egoist*, Young Crossjay told Clara Middleton that Sir Willoughby Patterne gave him "generally half-crown pieces," although he added that on exceptional occasions he had received tips as large as a sovereign. That being the case, any lingering doubt of Scrooge's change of heart must have been dispelled by the fact that, on a much lower social level, he gave no less than half a crown to the boy who went to buy the prize turkey, "twice the size of Tiny Tim," that he sent to the Cratchits. A boy hired for such an errand would have felt amply rewarded by, say, sixpence. In *Bleak House*, several transactions involve half-crowns, each time adding a significant touch to characterization. None of Mr. Snagsby's mannerisms or habits are more revealing than his giving Jo a half-crown on no fewer than four separate occasions, a token of his embarrassed benevolence as well, perhaps, as a sop to his troubled social conscience. When Skimpole goes by coach to Lincolnshire with Esther and John Jarndyce and the coachman comes round for his tip, "he pleasantly asked him," says Esther, "what he considered a very good fee indeed, now—a liberal one—and, on his replying, half-a-crown for a single passenger, said it was little enough too, all things considered" (18:297–98). The coachman seems to have recognized Skimpole as an easy touch and therefore quoted a high if not exorbitant sum, which he in fact received—though from John Jarndyce, not Skimpole. In the nature of things, hostlers would have expected less than coachmen, those monarchs of the box; but Inspector Bucket gave a half-crown to one at an inn near St. Albans where he and Esther stopped during their snowy pursuit of Lady Dedlock. (He was not out of pocket, because he could charge all his expenses to Sir Leicester.) In *Can You Forgive Her?* the same sum is handed over under very different circumstances. One of Burgo Fitzgerald's few altruistic deeds, inserted by Trollope to keep alive a modicum of sympathy for a man who is in general a wastrel and fortune hunter, is to give "out of his very narrow funds . . . half a crown to comfort the poor creature who had spoken to him in the street" (29:328–29).

Incomes and valuations in five figures had their own significance. When Samuel Warren titled his novel *Ten Thousand a Year*, he set a kind of magical figure, to be used by both the public and novelists, as Surtees pointed out in a passage in *Ask Mamma* quoted above (page 521). "Nobody that has 'anything' has less, thanks to the liberal talent of Mr. Warren," he said in *Hawbuck Grange* (10:124). Although the high-figure financial speculation of mid-Victorian times may have somewhat diminished the awesomeness of a mere ten thousand pounds, to upper-class people it remained a benchmark of value. The enormity of two crimes involving jewels was easily apparent when readers considered their valuations as constituting the yearly income of a wealthy member of mid-Victorian society. The stated value of the moonstone (diamond) in Collins's novel was £20,000, although the jeweler-moneylender Luker later estimated it to be worth £30,000, and Lady Eustace's necklace was usually quoted at £10,000, though rumor at least once doubled that amount.

In Thackeray and Trollope, annual incomes constitute the major criterion of social class (in Thackeray's case, it is also the prices of objects bought from this income or from the purchaser's overburdened credit line). In Trollope, particularly, characters who have unearned income come with a price tag attached: a figure of so many pounds per annum is an indispensable element in characterization, instantly placing the character in a social structure that is based on economic worth. A *Who's Who in Trollope* could be arranged in descending order of income, beginning with the Duke of Omnium, the richest man in the nation, with room reserved at the bottom of the ladder for those who, like some of Thackeray's characters, manage to live carefree and well on nothing a year.

The source of a family's wealth made a great deal of difference when it was a matter of status (in the country especially) or a consideration in marriage negotiations. In *Doctor Thorne*, the ancient Gresham family of Greshamsbury has entered on hard times, and to restore its former glory—and solvency—advantageous marriages are an absolute necessity. Enter Martha Dunstable, the Oil of Lebanon heiress, good for more than two hundred thousand pounds, who at once becomes the target of hopeful machinations despite the unrespectable source of her enviable fortune. Enter also Sir Roger Scatcherd the railway contractor, whose fortune is not beyond cavil either, conjuring up as it does disagreeable images of rough Irish navvies swarming from camp to camp as a line is built. Between them, they manage inadvertently to throw the settled Barsetshire county society into a turmoil in which the received and prized conception of a hierarchical society securely based on land income (including coalfields and London real estate) is confronted with an emerging new society based on commercial and industrial income, including all the fruits of venture capital. In the end, the two modern-type fortunes go to unanticipated beneficiaries, Miss Dunstable's to Dr. Thorne, whom she marries in the following novel, *Framley Parsonage*, and Sir Roger's to Mary Thorne and thus to her true love, Frank Gresham, when they marry—thus justifying in his mother's eyes the suit she had hitherto bitterly opposed on the ground that there was no money in it.

The prime economic discriminant of class was the inexorable prejudice in the upper reaches of society against "trade." It institutionalized what had developed into a veritable superstition, the aversion to physically handling cash. (The avoidance now was facilitated by the new system of credit, which in some kinds of transactions had created an alternative method of transferring money, from ledger to ledger rather than from hand to hand.) To the first readers of *Past and Present*, Carlyle's phrase "cash payment nexus" meant much more than the catchphrase it soon became; it epitomized the idea that the only remaining bond between human beings in these sorry times was coarsely economic, the transfer of coins and currency from one pocket to someone else's. The prejudice was so strong in Victorian times that it impelled discharged debtors leaving the Marshalsea to wrap in bits of paper the "tribute" pittances they slipped old Dorrit, and later in the book observance of form required Mrs. General to receive her honorarium from him, now a rich man, not in cash but by way of her banker.

What disqualified tradesmen from the ultimate dignity of gentility, a fact underlying the countless condescending allusions to trade throughout the whole realm of Victorian fiction, was therefore the simple circumstances that their business, whatever it was, routinely involved the exchange of cash for goods or, in the case of some artisans, services. And it was this same association of the passing of cash with despised "trade" that lay at the core of Dr. Thorne's own disadvantage at Greshamsbury, one of Trollope's most subtle studies of the interaction of money and status.

Physicians of solid standing in a community were paid in a prescribed ceremony. Their fee for a visit, usually a guinea (a denomination that was socially superior to the pound by the margin of a shilling), was discreetly handed them in a piece of paper as they left their patient's bedside, a custom that adds trenchant irony to Dickens's report of the rule of etiquette in the humble quarters of the Marshalsea. This ritual was itself a sign of status within the profession, sharply differentiating the physician from the apothecary, who served in his place in rural districts and the less elegant parts of towns. Because an apothecary had no educational qualifications, he could not charge for the medical advice he dispensed but made his living by selling drugs, herbal remedies, and other commodities that were understood to be related to bodily health or illness. He was therefore a tradesman, on the same humble level as an ironmonger or linen-draper, a fact of Victorian life that was responsible for the ambiguity of Pendennis's inherited social position at the opening of Thackeray's novel. Pen's father had been a successful apothecary at Bath, that mecca of the valetudinarian and convalescent, who, thanks to "frugality and prudence" and fortunate investments in property and copper-mine stocks, was able to retire in middle age and turn landowner. In that new station in life, the courtesy title of "Doctor," which was often bestowed on respected apothecaries, had no savor for him. "It was now his shame, as it formerly was his pride," said Thackeray, "to be called Doctor, and those who wished to please him always gave him the title of Squire" (*Pendennis*, 2:1.10).

Dr. Thorne seemingly had a legitimate claim to his honorific, though Trollope does not tell us precisely how he qualified to be a medical doctor. But his position in Barsetshire society was rendered ambiguous by the fact that, like many physicians, especially in the country, he doubled as an apothecary. Highly regarded medical men such as the painfully respectable Dr. Fillgrave never did so, sending their patients off to apothecaries with written directions instead. By doubling as an apothecary—a tradesman—Dr. Thorne compromised himself. Moreover, unlike Dr. Fillgrave with his customary guinea fee, Dr. Thorne charged a plebeian 7s.6d., with zoned increments for calls more than five miles distant. He also did not hesitate to make change, a vulgar evocation of the marketplace that additionally went against the ingrained prejudices of conservative Greshamsbury. Says Trollope, summing up: "The guinea fee, the principle of *giving* advice and of selling no medicine, the great resolve to keep a distinct barrier between the physician and the apothecary, and, above all, the hatred of the contamination of a bill [a tradesmanlike statement of services rendered and payment due], were strong in the medical mind of Barsetshire. Dr. Thorne had the provincial medical world against him" (*Doctor Thorne*, 3:28).

Although these distinctions and customs were of long standing, they were also immediately topical, at a moment when Dr. Thorne's profession was on the verge of drastic change that would sweep away some of the outworn conventions that affected his career. In the very year the novel was published, Parliament passed the landmark Medical Act of 1858, thus ending eighteen years of frustration during which proponents of professional reform had introduced no fewer than seventeen bills, all of which foundered on the rocks of professional (or antiprofessional) and political expedience. Among other reforms, the 1858 act devised the distinctive title of "registered medical practitioner" for anyone who had passed the examination given by any of the twenty-one existing licensing bodies, set up a General Medical Council to maintain the register and exert disciplinary powers over errant practitioners, and finally excluded apothecaries from the profession. Dr. Thorne, in this sense, was a representative man of the hour. His profession was about to take a long step away from the obloquy of "trade."

In society at large, wholesalers labored under a somewhat less burdensome weight of social prejudice than did the retailers to whom they sold their goods. The firm of Dombey and Son, it appears, straddled both branches of trade; Dickens suggested its diversification in the description he gave it on the novel's title page: " . . . Wholesale, retail and for exportation." (We never see the retail branch in operation, and have only the vaguest notion of the rest of the business.) A socially ambiguous firm cast its shadow across the whole of Trollope's *Miss Mackenzie*:

Thomas Mackenzie . . . had engaged himself in commercial pursuits—as his wife was accustomed to say when she spoke of her husband's labours; or went into trade, and kept a shop, as was more generally asserted by those of the Mackenzie circle who were wont to speak their minds freely. The actual and unvarnished truth in the matter shall now bé made known. He, with his partner, made and sold oilcloth, and was possessed of premises in the New Road, over which the names of "Rubb and Mackenzie" were posted in large letters. As you, my reader, may enter therein, and purchase a yard and a half of oilcloth, if you were so minded, I think that the free-spoken friends of the family were not far wrong. Mrs. Thomas Mackenzie, however, declared that she was calumniated, and her husband cruelly injured;

and she based her assertions on the fact that "Rubb and Mackenzie" had
wholesale dealings, and that they sold their article to the trade, who re-sold
it. (1 : 1−2)

At Dr. Swishtail's academy in *Vanity Fair*, William Dobbin, called "Figs"
because his father was a grocer, was taunted by "all the circle of young
knaves, usher and all, who rightly considered that the selling of goods
by retail is a shameful and infamous practice, meriting the contempt and
scorn of all real gentlemen. 'Your father's only a merchant, Osborne,'
Dobbin said in private to the little boy who had brought down the storm
upon him," which was scant consolation, because George Osborne could
justifiably retort, "My father's a gentleman, and keeps his carriage"
(5 : 45). (He was, in fact, a wholesale merchant in the tallow and Russian
trades.)

Subsequently Dobbin's father became rich, an alderman, and colonel
of the City Light Horse, and, in recognition of these accomplishments,
was knighted. Perhaps (though Thackeray does not say so) his business
had prospered so that, like John Jorrocks, he had entered the wholesale
line and thus qualified as a merchant. The son, having meanwhile made
good in the army, would doubtless have regretted flinging that epithet
at George Osborne when they were children. In the hierarchy of status,
stockbrokers (who dealt with abstractions in the form of stock certificates
and columns of figures in ledgers) were superior to merchants (who
dealt in tangible commodities)—it was the difference between keeping
one's hands fastidiously clean and dirtying one's hands, symbolically at
least, by touching articles of commerce. Such was the implication behind
old Osborne's hatred of old Sedley, even after the latter had lost his
money. Osborne was a merchant, Sedley a stockbroker. One was, and
remained, rich, the other was now poor. But theoretically the rich man
was, by virtue of their respective occupations, the poor man's inferior,
and always would be.

Some occupations had particular Victorian attributes. Tailors, as we
saw in Chapter 9, were notorious for their radical politics. And for some
reason (the fact that they were wholesalers is insufficient; other kinds of
merchants dealing in quantity did not enjoy the same prospects), brewers were uniquely qualified to rise in the social scale. Of all middle-class
commercial aspirants to the rank of gentleman, they had the best chance
of making it. This fact of contemporary life was not lost on Mrs. Micawber. "I will not conceal from you, my dear Mr. Copperfield," she said,
"that I have long felt the Brewing business to be particularly adapted to
Mr. Micawber. Look at Barclay and Perkins! Look at Truman, Hanbury,
and Buxton! It is on that extensive footing that Mr. Micawber, I know
from my own knowledge of him, is calculated to shine; and the profits,

I am told, are e-NOR-mous! But if Mr. Micawber cannot get into those firms—which decline to answer his letters, when he offers his services even in an inferior capacity, what is the use of dwelling upon that idea?" (*David Copperfield*, 28:479)

Several years earlier, Lady Joan Fitz-Warene remarked to Sir Vavasour Firebrace, in *Sybil*, "A baronetcy has become the distinction of the middle class; a physician, our physician for example, is a baronet; and I dare say some of our tradesmen; brewers, or people of that class" (2.11:122). Lady Joan did not venture to explain the curious phenomenon, and fifteen years later, in *Great Expectations*, Herbert Pocket was at a loss to do so. Miss Havisham's father, he told Pip, "was a country gentleman down in your part of the world, and was a brewer. I don't know why it should be a crack thing to be a brewer; but it is indisputable that while you cannot possibly be genteel and bake, you may be as genteel as never was and brew. You see it every day" (22:203).

You saw it, for example, in the person of Harry Foker, Pendennis's friend, whose family's product, Foker's Entire, brought him between fourteen and twenty thousand pounds a year (the reputed figure varied from speaker to speaker, but his own was fourteen). In his depressed moments, Foker was convinced that although his brewery association provided the material trappings of gentility, it did nothing to improve his chances of winning Blanche Amory, heiress to a far greater fortune: "What am I, compared to her? She's all soul, she is, and can write poetry or compose music, as easy as I could drink a glass of beer. Beer?—damme, that's all I'm fit for, is beer. I am a poor, ignorant little beggar, good for nothing but Foker's Entire" (*Pendennis*, 39:2.12). But the supposed disgrace had not harmed Isabella, the only daughter of ———— Grains, Esq., a partner in Foker & Company, when Lord Hercules O'Ryan, a former childhood suitor (at the age of nine) of Ethel Newcome, claimed her hand; though, to be sure, her marriage portion may well have neutralized the stigma. And the sagacious Major Pendennis considered wealth derived from a brewery to be just as desirable as wealth derived from any other trade. "I should say," he told his nephew, "that young Foker won't have less than fourteen thousand a year from the brewery, besides Logwood and the Norfolk property. I have no pride about *me*, Pen. I like a man of birth certainly, but dammy, I like a brewery which brings in a man fourteen thousand a year; hay, Pen? Ha, ha! that's the sort of man for me" (*Pendennis*, 40:2.16). Rawdon Crawley's aunt shared the major's tolerance. "What a pity that young man has taken such an irretrievable step in the world!" she exclaimed on hearing of his marriage to Becky; "with his rank and distinction he might have married a brewer's daughter with a quarter of a million—like Miss

Grains; or have looked to ally himself with the best families in England" (*Vanity Fair*, 33:316).

In *Evan Harrington*, Meredith posed an explicit contrast between the persistent ignominy of the tailoring trade and the superior status of brewing. Brewers might not be top-drawer socialites, but at least they could lord it over lowly tailors. Mrs. Melville, as sensitive to the word as Sir Leicester Dedlock was to "ironmaster," says, "My brother-in-law—my sister, I think, you know—married a—a brewer! He is rich; but well! such was her taste!" But the gentleman in question later says to Evan, stoutly upholding the dignity of his trade, "I'm a brewer, Van. Do you think I'm ashamed of it? Not while I brew good beer, my boy!—not while I brew good beer! They don't think worse of me in the House for it [he was, indeed, a Member]. It isn't ungentlemanly to brew good beer, Van" (4:37, 5:55).

To Trollope, in *Can You Forgive Her?*, a brewer might rank as high as some professional men, including novelists like himself. He put the case in a rather backhanded manner: "Why Grindley [a "would-be fast attorney"] should have been inferior to Mr. Maxwell the banker, or to Stone, or to Prettyman who were brewers, or even to Mr. Pollock the heavyweight literary gentleman, I can hardly say. An attorney by his trade is at any rate as good as a brewer, and there are many attorneys who hold their heads high anywhere" (16:196). But Miss Marrable, in *The Vicar of Bullhampton*, had stricter, more old-fashioned notions. She was convinced that "brewers, bankers, and merchants, were not gentlemen, and the world . . . was going astray, because people were forgetting their landmarks" (9:56). Nevil Beauchamp, too, voiced his social fastidiousness in the matter, uttering, Meredith says, "contempt of the brewer's business, and of the social rule to accept rich brewers for gentlemen" (*Beauchamp's Career*, 20:178).

2.

A comparable system of distinctions prevailed lower down in the social hierarchy. There was, for example, the difference between a tradesman, an independent businessman who was paid for his goods or services by his customers, and a mere wage earner who was paid for his labor by his employer. The fall from one category to a lower was not the least of the blows suffered when the lawyer Wakem took over the bankrupt Tulliver's mill and proposed, out of charity, to hire him as an employee. Said Mrs. Tulliver, "a little tear making its way," "O dear, sir, it's hard to think of, as my husband should take wage. But it 'ud look more like what used to be, to stay at the mill than to go anywhere else" (*The Mill on the*

Floss, 3.7:220). Still, this cold comfort did nothing to alleviate the shock of adversity. If anything, the lot of the bankrupt mill-owner Thornton in Gaskell's *North and South* was even more bitter: he had to give up his business "in which he had been so long engaged with so much honour and success; and look out for a subordinate situation" (25:426), presumably in the business of one of his competitors.

In *Sketches by Boz*, Dickens defined a shabby-genteel man as one who "may have no occupation, or he may be a corn agent, or a coal agent, or a wine merchant, or a collector of debts, or a broker's assistant, or a broken-down attorney. He may be a clerk of the lowest description, or a contributor to the press of the same grade" ("Characters," chap. 10: 265). Among all these unrewarding occupations, one in particular was taken to be a token of character, an association several novelists used for the shorthand message it conveyed. Popularly reputed to be an especially lucrative business, the coal trade attracted more than its share of misfits and incompetents. Selling at wholesale was where the money lay, but one hopefully could begin in the retail end of the business and work up. Selling coal in small quantities therefore appealed to men who were unequipped for or averse to earning money by the strength of their bodies, the skill of their hands, or the sharpness of their brains.

Dickens clearly fixed the Chuzzlewits' social position at the very outset of the novel's first chapter: "It is a notable circumstance that in these later times, many Chuzzlewits, being unsuccessful in other pursuits, have, without the smallest rational hope of enriching themselves, or any conceivable reason, set up as coal-merchants; and have, month after month, continued gloomily to watch a small stock of coals, without, in any one instance, negotiating with a purchaser" (*Martin Chuzzlewit*, 1:52). It was inevitable that at one stage in Micawber's downward progress his wife should have seized on the Medway coal trade as one in which a man of his talent could make his fortune if the brewery trade saw fit not to avail itself of his services. That was why they went to Canterbury, only to discover that in addition to talent, capital was required. It may have been only a little capital, but it was more than Micawber had available. And so he turned to an occupation in which it was not necessary—selling corn on commission, but of course with no greater success.

Thackeray availed himself of the same bit of Victorian occupational lore in *Vanity Fair*, when old Sedley, after losing his fortune, became, to quote the cards he distributed, "Sole Agent for the Black Diamond and Anti-Cinder Coal Association, Blunker's Wharf, Thames Street, and Anna-Maria Cottages, Fulham Road West" (37:372). According to the circulars Amelia devotedly wrote out for him, he "could supply his friends and the public with the best coals at ——s per chaldron"

(38:380). That Thackeray took pains to reintroduce the subject later on underscores the significance it had for his audience. Miss Dobbin wrote to her brother the Major in India, "The wretched place they [the Sedleys] live at, since they were bankrupts, you know—Mr. S., to judge from a *brass-plate*[†] on the door of his hut (it is little better) is a coal-merchant" (43:426). One can imagine the little shudder with which she wrote those last words. The senior Osborne was more blunt: he called Sedley "the old pauper, the old coal-man, the old bankrupt, and by many other such names of brutal contumely" (56:548).

Other men, like Mr. Brawler, the Brighton lodging-house keeper in *The Newcomes*, had to sell coal as a sideline to eke out a living. And to still others, like Micawber, it was simply one entry on a lengthening résumé of futile employment. If a down-at-heel entrepreneur tried to peddle one line and failed, he switched to another, often wine selling. Sedley's tattered business files, which he carried around with him, included "documents relative to the Wine Project (which failed from a most unaccountable accident, after commencing with the most splendid prospects)[‡] [and] the Coal Project (which only a want of capital prevented from becoming the most successful scheme ever put before the public . . .") (*Vanity Fair*, 59:568). Natchett, the seedy private eye in *Martin Chuzzlewit*, carried in "his musty old pocket-book" "contradictory cards, in which he called himself a coal-merchant, in others a wine-merchant, in others a commission-agent, in others a collector, in others an accountant: as if he really didn't know the secret himself" (27:517). He may have carried these cards for professional purposes, to support assumed identities. If so, several of the hand-to-mouth occupations named—the lower reaches of the coal and wine trades (uncapitalized commission agents) and door-to-door collectors (Lillyvick in *Nicholas Nickleby* collected water rents, Pancks in *Little Dorrit* house rents)—harmonized perfectly with his shabby appearance.

Several characters in Surtees's novels had similarly varied work records, which together constituted a comprehensive list of Victorian occupations that were chancey or simply dead-end. In *Handley Cross*, the auctioneer at a horse sale "was a burly, big-faced, impudent fellow, with a round of whisker, a consequential sort of hat, and a corporation so large as to look as if he had thriven in all the occupations he had turned

[†]According to Henry Mayhew (*London Labour and the London Poor* [1861–62; reprint, New York, 1968], 2:83), commission agents like Sedley, distinct from common street-sellers of coal, were called "brass-plate merchants."

[‡]Namely, one profitable sale, when Dobbin secretly bought a generous quantity of his stock at an inflated price.

his hand to—Hatter, Wine Merchant, Coal Merchant, Accountant, Land Agent, Temperance Hotel Keeper, Stationer, Broker, and General Negotiator" (49:351). The corporation must have owed most of its generous dimensions to attendance at public houses rather than to prosperity. In *Plain or Ringlets?* Surtees introduced "Mr. Tim Boldero, the auctioneering, coal-dealing, electioneering, ale-store-keeping clerk of the [racing] course" (20:67). Still another Surtees character, Captain Doleful, the master of ceremonies at the new Handley Cross spa, was luckier, or sharper, than most of his fellow workers in that generally unrewarding channel of Victorian commerce. After a hitch in the militia, "he had afterwards turned coal-merchant (at Stroud, we believe), an unprosperous speculation, so he sold the good-will of a bad business to a young gentleman anxious for a settlement, and sunk his money in an annuity" (*Handley Cross*, 2:16–17).

It is surprising that the population of the debtors' prisons in fiction did not have as high a count of failed coal merchants as this dismal record suggests; among the former inhabitants of Marshalsea, Dickens mentions only a single "agreeable coal-merchant who was remanded for six months" (*Little Dorrit*, 1.8:123). It is even more surprising that in the imposing list of brief jobs the rootless Tip Dorrit had—in a warehouse, a market garden, the hops trade, lawyer's offices (on five separate occasions), an auctioneer's, a brewery, a stockbroker's, a coach office, a waggon office, a general dealer's, a distillery, a wool house, a dry goods house, the Billingsgate trade, the foreign fruit trade, the docks—coal selling was not included. It might have been the very one in which, against heavy odds, he had a chance of prospering.

Some men, in fact, did. In one of the *Mudfog Papers*, eventually added to *Sketches by Boz*, the chief figure, Mr. Tulrumble, was a successful coal merchant who became mayor of the infelicitously named town of Mudfog. Supposedly he was a wholesaler, with his own wharf or coal yard, not a mere salesman on commission, which made a great difference. When Thackeray, writing as George Fitz-Boodle in *Fraser's Magazine* (July 1842), embarked on his description of the "Second Profession" open to younger sons of the nobility ("gastronomic agents," or arrangers of gourmet feasts)—the first, as we have seen, being the auctioneering trade—he said, "Take the twenty-four first men who come into the club, and ask who they are, and how they made their money? There's Woolsey-Sackville, his father was lord-chancellor, and sat on the woolsack, whence he took his title; his grandfather dealt in coal-sacks, and not in wool-sacks,—small coal-sacks, dribbling out little supplies of black diamonds to the poor." (One assumes, though Thackeray is not clear on the point, that the grandfather, beginning in a humble way, had so far multiplied the number of "small coal-sacks" he distributed as to become a wealthy wholesaler. Otherwise, how would his son have received the education that qualified him to become lord chancellor?) But several years later, in one of his papers on "Club Snobs" (*Punch*, 6 February 1847: *BS*, 191), Thackeray, reviving the Sackville name if only for the sake of the pun on sack-full, insisted that no matter how far a family had risen from its beginnings among the coal-sacks, the damned carbonaceous spot would not out. His persona, a connoisseur of snobbery in all its manifestations, asks his friend Wagley, at a ball, who the "charming young woman whisking beautifully in a beautiful dance" may be.

> "Which?" says Wagley.
> "That one with the coal-black eyes," I replied.
> "Hush!" says he, and the gentleman with whom he was talking moved off, with rather a discomfited air.
> When he was gone Wagley burst out laughing. "*Coal-black* eyes!" said he; "you've just hit it. That's Mrs. Sackville Maine, and that was her husband who just went away. He's a coal merchant, Snob, my boy, and I have no doubt Mr. Perkins's [the host] Wallsends are supplied from his wharf. He is in a flaming furnace when he hears coals mentioned."

In the next "Club Snobs" piece (*Punch*, 13 February 1847; *BS*, 195–96), the writer and others succeed in getting the man of business elected to their club, the Sarcophagus.

> It was not done without a deal of opposition—the secret having been whispered that the candidate was a coal merchant. You may be sure some of the proud people and most of the parvenus of the Club were ready to black-ball him. We combated this opposition successfully, however. We pointed out to the parvenus that the Lambtons and the Stuarts sold coals. . . .[†] [W]e carried our man, with only a trifling sprinkling of black beans in the boxes: Byles's, of course, who black-balls everybody; Bung's, who looks down upon a coal-merchant, having lately retired from the wine trade.

Trollope went to considerable trouble to redeem Martha Dunstable from the disgrace of her Oil of Lebanon fortune. But he left it to his readers to decide how they should regard the Hon. Mrs. George de Courcy in *The Small House at Allington*, who had £30,000: "Very young she was not,—having reached some years of her life in advance of thirty. . . . The lady herself was not beautiful, or clever, or of imposing manners—nor was she of high birth. But neither was she ugly, nor un-

---

[†]John Sutherland points out, in his annotated edition of *The Book of Snobs*, that the Earl of Durham (Lambton) and the Marquis of Londonderry (Stewart) "had estates in the coal-mining north-east."

bearably stupid. Her manners were, at any rate, innocent; and as to her birth,—seeing that, from the first, she was not supposed to have had any,—no disappointment was felt. Her father had been a coal-merchant" (17:1.187). The toneless last sentence said it all—whatever a Victorian reader might have interpreted it as meaning.

Perhaps, by the time Trollope wrote his series of articles on "London Tradesmen" for the *Pall Mall Gazette* in the summer of 1880, the much-maligned occupation had risen in status so that it was no longer inferior to the wine trade at least. He said nothing about the stigma of which Dickens and Thackeray had made so much, focusing instead on the plethora of advertising circulars that rival companies sent around, thus adding to the cost of the product: "We have heard of the annual tens of thousands expended on Holloway's pills and ointment, on Rowland's Kalydor, and Revalenta Arabica.† And we have not been much moved by these disclosures, not wanting these articles ourselves, and feeling in regard to such nostrums that it did not much matter in what way the money obtained was applied. But we must all use coals"[3]—a common-sense statement of a fact that was of small solace to the Chuzzlewits, Micawbers, and Sedleys of the world, and no more to the Sackville Maines, who could not buy social acceptance for all their grimy fortunes.

A number of Dickens's characters followed occupations which, though they existed earlier, became more visible in Victorian times: detectives, bill discounters, ironmasters. Two other occupations were absolutely novel. Dickens cast Toodle as a locomotive-engine stoker (later promoted to driver) partly because, as a novelist with a journalist's eye, he was alert to the newest presences on the social scene, and partly because it fitted in with the several extended passages on the railway. The other new occupation, that of teacher in the developing system of governmentally supported elementary schools, was of considerably greater usefulness to him.[4] Bradley Headstone in *Our Mutual Friend* was, like his protégé Charley Hexam and M'Choakumchild, the Coketown schoolmaster in *Hard Times*, a product of the teacher-training schools, also governmentally funded, the prototype of which had been established at Battersea in 1839. In the years just preceding the publication of *Our Mutual Friend* in 1864–65, the increasingly numerous band of teachers trained and paid at public expense, so different from the several other breeds familiar in fiction, had been much in the public eye for several reasons. In 1861 the Newcastle Commission, after three years of study,

---

†This widely advertised "health food" purported to alleviate a wide variety of afflictions, including nervousness, constipation, dyspepsia, asthma, debility, flatulence, spasms, and coughs.

had recommended that formal examinations be instituted in governmentally aided elementary schools to determine the cost-effectiveness of the education these teachers provided. In response, the Committee of Council on Education promulgated the so-called Revised Code of 1863, which made grants to each school contingent on the results of examinations conducted by a visiting government inspector, typified by the "third grown person" in M'Choakumchild's schoolroom. Among the major effects of the "payment by results" system was a large increase in the membership of the two professional organizations, as angry teachers, who got all the blame if their pupils failed and none of the money if they passed, rose to arms. The newspapers publicized their grievances, and Parliament debated their claims along with the merits and iniquities of the Revised Code. Robert Lowe, who as deviser of the code and its most voluble and prominent apologist was one of the most-hated men of the day, was driven from office in April 1864, just before the first monthly part of *Our Mutual Friend* appeared.

Schools and schoolmasters, then, were very much in the news. What engaged Dickens most, as a portrayer of character, was the socially ambiguous position of the new teacher, typically a member of the working or artisan class who, by virtue of his employment, was knocking at the door of the professional class in quest of the prestige that joining the ranks of lawyers, physicians, and clergymen might promise. Headstone served Dickens well in one of his most skillful exploitations of a topical subject. He was an individualized representation of a new form of employment. More important, he presented a challenging problem in psychology, as a person professional in theory and aspiration but stigmatized by the accident of his humble birth. At the same time, in the scene of his chief confrontation with Eugene Wrayburn, Dickens used Headstone's plight to fill out the portrait of Wrayburn that he had begun to draw in the second chapter. In his supercilious, contemptuous way, time after time he flung at Headstone the opprobrious epithet "Schoolmaster," reflecting the current scorn of the base-born schoolteacher (the prim Miss Peecher is Headstone's female counterpart) in the dreary setting of teacher-training schools, governmentally ordained syllabi, and bureaucratic management—an up-to-date form of social prejudice. In a larger sense, Wrayburn's derogation of Headstone's pathetic ambition, mixed as it was with an ineradicable sense of unbelonging, is Dickens's latest mockery of the endemic aspiration toward respectability.

17
Speculation and Bankruptcy

1.

OF THE BROAD TOPICAL THEMES in Victorian fiction, the two most pervasive were elections (Chapters 18 and 19 below) and bankruptcy. The latter was the Victorian version of Fortuna's wheel, the vulnerable power figures being no longer princes and conquerors but bustling, astute, and above all sanguine English merchants, bankers, speculators, investors—the new plutocracy who amassed wealth and then calamitously lost it: the worst fate, short of losing one's soul (and even here, the choice was difficult) that could befall a man playing by the non-rules of laissez-faire.[1]

"Trying to compile a full account of bankruptcy in Victorian fiction," a recent historian of the capitalist in literature has remarked,

> would mean listing every other novel of the age,[†] so the task would be pointless. Bankruptcy, it can be simply said, is an omnipresent calamity in the whole creative writing of the age, as central to the poem "Maud" (1855), for instance, as to "Dombey and Son," and is portrayed as horrendous to think about, devastating to endure. This exaggeration itself tells us that it was a reversal feared rather then experienced; for if the event had been as common as all that it would have lost much of its terror. We are dealing here with the haunting of the age of the self-made man. Parallels might be suggested with the image of imprisonment in eighteenth-century fiction and poetry, and of sexual inadequacy in the literature of our own time, cases too, both of them, in which an anxiety characteristic of the culture of the times is being voiced.[2]

[†]This is obvious hyperbole, but the reality is impressive enough. Approximately one in every five of the one hundred fifty novels that form the basis of this study has passages relating to bankruptcy, the same incidence in which election scenes occur. More than a few novels have both.

More than a century before Victoria came to the throne, with the bursting of the South Sea Bubble (1710–20), closely echoed by its French equivalent, the Mississippi Bubble (1717–20), economic ruin had replaced fire and plague as the kind of disaster, personal rather than communal, that dominated the English imagination in its most fearful mood. But down to the beginning of the nineteenth century this specter had affected the lives of relatively few people, those best able to invest in grandiose but (too often) ultimately ruinous projects and speculations. It was only when the traditional land-based economy had to give room to the expanding British commerce, sustained by industry and foreign trade and attracting throngs of new entrepreneurs and investors, that the risks as well as the rewards of sharing in the national prosperity came to have a widespread impact on ordinary lives.

In 1836, following a denunciation of commercial "puffery"—pushing the image rather than the product—that might have been written today, John Stuart Mill commented: "The same intensity of competition drives the trading public more and more to play high for success, to throw for all or nothing; and this, together with the difficulty of sure calculations in a field of commerce so widely extended, renders bankruptcy no longer disgraceful, because no longer a presumption either of dishonesty or imprudence: the discredit which it still incurs belongs to it, alas! mainly as an indication of poverty."[3] As the years passed, the "trading public" grew steadily larger, sharing risks which themselves steadily increased. Among its temporarily successful members were more and more self-made men, whose fall, when it occurred, was all the more calamitous because their rise to wealth seemed to have justified the prudential morality whose Holy Writ was Smiles's *Self-Help*. It had been mightily assisted by the almost total absence of regulation. The only note of caution applied in this heady free-market climate was caveat emptor, and even this was too often unheard, not to say unheeded.

From the beginning of the century, English prosperity, based initially on the uncertain grounds of a war economy, had been interrupted from time to time by financial crises that well served the purposes of Victorian novelists who wished to distance their action and yet remain topical. In fact, financial calamities, the most violent manifestations of a systaltic economy, were among the most visible of the recurrent events described in Chapter 5.

The first of these nineteenth-century sequences of speculative schemes and failures, occurring in the mid-twenties, was so well remembered more than a quarter of a century later as to provide a plausible background or major episode in a number of novels that were set in those years. What distinguished it from those in the Victorian age proper was the exotic or bizarre nature of the visionary cornucopias. The crisis of 1825–26 stemmed mainly from trouble in what would to-day be called the developing countries of Colombia, Mexico, Brazil, Peru, Chile, and Guatemala. These former Spanish colonies, once their sovereignty was recognized by the Canning government, floated, among them, twenty national loans. These were soon joined by the stock flota-tion of many private companies seeking capital to exploit the reputed fabulous richness of the region's gold and silver mines.[†] This aspect of the late Regency get-rich-quick mania remained topical as late as 1859, when Charles Reade suspended the narrative of *Love Me Little, Love Me Long* for eleven pages while he treated his readers to a ponderous dis-course on the economic history involved in the South American metals speculation.

The illusory sense of security generated by the Bank of England's resuming cash payment for notes in 1821 fed the speculative fever. In 1824–25 alone, 624 schemes were proposed for companies with a re-markable variety of stated purposes, including, among others almost equally fanciful, a project for draining the Red Sea to recover the trea-sure the Hebrews had jettisoned during their precipitate exodus from Egypt. The shock wave originating in the failure of these imaginative shortcuts to Golconda spread throughout the economy, and investors in even the most traditional and conventional kinds of financial insti-tutions and commercial enterprise suddenly found themselves in, to put it mildly, reduced circumstances. The publishing business was par-ticularly hard hit. Sir Walter Scott's publishers, Archibald Constable and Company, failed, and along with them the printing firm of James Bal-lantyne and Company, in which he was a partner. Scott, who had over-spent his income in buying Abbotsford and turning it into a baronial estate, had to choose between bankruptcy, which would have meant that although his creditors went unpaid he could start over with a clean ledger, and insolvency. His sense of gentlemanly obligation dictated the latter course, which meant that he committed himself to paying off his debts by whatever means he could. His effort to do so, which took the form of grinding out more and more novels, eventually succeeded, but it also killed him. The memory of his personal financial disaster and

---

[†] Those wishing to invest in metal shares closer to home could risk their money in West Country copper mines. In the backwater of Shepherd's Inn in *Pendennis*, the former offices of legal firms had been taken over by the headquarters of two firms, the Polwheedle and Tredyddlum Copper Mines and the twin-titled Registry of Patent Inventions and Union of Genius and Capital Company. The copper mines, still awaiting pumps, were as nugatory as the inventions were impractical. At an earlier date, however, Pendennis's father had

his honorable determination, fully disclosed in Lockhart's biography in 1837–38, undoubtedly colored many later Victorian readers' responses as they encountered echoes of the calamitous events of 1825–26 in the fiction of their own day.

A much younger and as yet obscure aspirant to fame as a novelist was also caught: Benjamin Disraeli, who in January 1825 bought South American mining shares with such small capital as he possessed. To boost the market value of the company's stock, he wrote—these were his first published works—three of the many pamphlets pretending to be disinterested market analyses that were circulated on behalf of such schemes. His *Enquiry into the Plans, Progress, and Policy of the American Mining Companies* went through several printings. But less than six months after he bought his shares at what turned out to be the peak price, he and his two partners had lost £7,000.

The fictional record illustrates the variety of ways in which one could lose money in this pre-Victorian rage for riches and the variety of people who did so, from Squire Bayham in *The Newcomes*, "who had the estate before the Conqueror, and who came to such a dreadful crash in the year 1825" (11:1.125) to the lady in *Cranford* who had money in "Peruvian bonds." (Mrs. Gaskell does not explicitly say that she suffered the common fate of such investors, but readers would have drawn their own conclusion.) Mrs. Pipchin's late husband in *Dombey and Son* broke his heart, as Miss Tox put it, pumping water out of Peruvian mines and thus reduced his widow to the occupation of keeping "an infantine Boarding-House of a very select description" (8:159).

Aunt Betsey Trotwood, referring to herself in third person, told David Copperfield that, not trusting her former man of business, Mr. Wickfield, to invest her money prudently,

"she took it into her head to lay it out for herself. So she took her pigs . . . to a foreign market; and a very bad market it turned out to be. First, she lost in the mining way, and then she lost in the diving way—fishing up treasure [from the Red Sea?] or some such Tom Tiddler nonsense . . . and then she lost in the mining way again, and, last of all, to set the thing entirely to rights, she lost in the banking way. I don't know what the Bank shares were worth for a little while . . . cent per cent was the lowest of it, I believe; but the Bank was at the other end of the world, and tumbled into space, for what I know; anyhow, it fell to pieces, and never will and never can pay sixpence; and Betsey's sixpences were all there, and there's an end of them." *(David Copperfield,* 35:573–74)

---

made considerable money in copper stocks, as, in real life, William Morris's father had done in Cornish tin shares.

Aunt Betsey's story was plausible enough in the novel's distanced time-context. But it turned out to be a fib, designed to conceal her suspicion that Wickfield had made off with the money and at the same time to prevent David from having any expectations. Actually, it had found its way from Wickfield to Uriah Heep's sticky hands, and eventually, thanks to Micawber's brilliant maneuvering, back to her.

Aunt Betsey would not have had to send her money halfway around the world to commit it to a failing bank: during the 1825–26 crisis, no fewer than eighty English country banks closed their doors. One that came perilously close to doing so was the bank in *John Halifax, Gentleman*. Just as Guy Halifax's twenty-first birthday was being celebrated by a happy crowd on his father's estate, news came of the failure of a London bank with strong ties to this Cotswold town. Many of the celebrants would be affected if the dire domino effect came into play ("Ten Bank failures in the *Gazette* to-day"). The townspeople threatened a run on the local bank, a private one conducted by an honest gentleman, Mr. Jessop, who was strapped for cash and dared not open his doors. John Halifax came to the rescue, dramatically riding to another town, stuffing £5,000 in cash into canvas bags, and returning with it to save the day, and the bank. As an unerringly prudent man of affairs, his own withers were unwrung. While the disastrous news from the City continued to flow in, he congratulated himself on his sagacity: "those Mexican speculations I refused to embark in" (30:307–8).

Others were not so shrewd or fortunate. The failure of the Town and County Bank reduced Miss Matty Jenkyns, in a central episode in *Cranford*, to an income of five shillings a week, and instead of being able to afford five sovereigns for a new silk gown she had to sell tea from her cottage. Surtees, predictably, took a lighter view of the event that caused so much heartache elsewhere in fiction. In *Plain or Ringlets?* (1859–60) he recalled, "During the great bubble year of 1825–6, a bank in the City was ruined in consequence of a butcher's pony falling down before the door just at the time of the high change, and the public mistaking the crowd gathered round the pony for a run upon the establishment" (97:403).

All the business projects, as grandly named as they were undercapitalized, that formed satirical fodder for early- and mid-Victorian novelists were wrapped in an inferential public and private aura of memories. Humphry House once suggested that the United Metropolitan Crumpet and Muffin Banking and Punctual Delivery Company in *Nicholas Nickleby*, a proposed attempt to corner the market for this appetizing and widely distributed food product, recalled "the speculative rage . . . when steam-ovens, steam-laundries, and milk-and-egg companies competed with canals and railroads for the public's money."[4] The full audacity of this particular set of would-be monopolists can be fully appreciated only when it is realized that its proposed capitalization of five million pounds was, for the time, a huge figure, exactly equal to that of Nathan Rothschild's Alliance Fire and Life Assurance Company, founded in 1824.

In *Little Dorrit*, set in those years, there are two business failures, one immediately appropriate to the period, the other having occurred earlier. The Merdle crash is an additional example—others were cited in Chapter 5—of a novelist's using a particular kind of event on two time planes: to readers in 1855–57 it echoed the day's headlines, and it also fitted in with the distanced setting of the middle and late twenties, when insolvencies like Merdle's were commonplace, though not on the same grandiose scale. The casualty that had brought William Dorrit to the Marshalsea, like that which reduced Sedley to a cramped cottage in Brompton, was connected with the Napoleonic Wars. He had been a merchant, "a partner in a house in some large way," according to Ferdinand Barnacle, "—in spirits, or buttons, or wine, or blacking, or oatmeal, or woollen, or port, or hooks and eyes, or iron, or treacle, or shoes, or something or other that was wanted for troops, or seamen, or somebody—and the house burst," the Barnacle clan being prominent among its creditors (2.12:620). It is conceivable that Dickens intended a modern parallel in Dorrit's case, as in Merdle's: this was, after all, a time when the supply demands of the Crimean War were enriching numerous balance sheets.

From their very first appearance on the English market, railway shares were favored speculative instruments. Stock in a number of proposed lines was floated on the very eve of the panic of 1825–26, and that in the Liverpool-Manchester line was one of the few issues to survive the great shakeout. Once it was successfully opened in 1830, private bills for other companies flooded Parliament, representing what would later be called, in the shadow of a far greater craze, the "little" railway mania. In 1836 alone, the thirty-five bills that were passed cost the company promoters an estimated fifteen million pounds for incorporation rights alone; M.P.s' pockets had to be lined before a single shovelful of earth was dug. (John Sadleir made his start up life's slippery ladder by acting as a parliamentary agent—lobbyist and money-dispenser—in behalf of Irish railway bills.) In October 1837, Dickens mentioned, in his "Full Report of the First Meeting of the Mudfog Association," a piece later added to *Sketches by Boz*, that "Mr. Jobba produced a forcing-machine on a novel plan, for bringing joint-stock railway shares prematurely to a premium" (643)—presumably on the model of the patent egg incubator that was several times exhibited in London to attract investors.

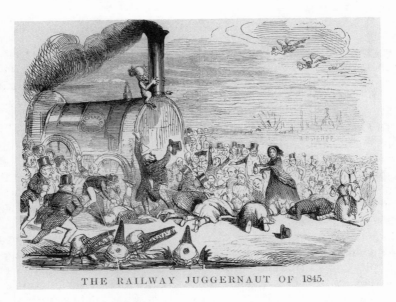

THE RAILWAY JUGGERNAUT OF 1845.

LEPORELLO RECOUNTING THE RAILWAY LOVES
OF DON JOHN.

Punch's numerous graphic satires of the railway mania employed a variety of allusive frameworks, from Hindu religion (top) (26 July 1845) to Mozart opera (bottom). The latter (9 December 1848) referred to a production of *Don Giovanni* at the Italian Opera House, Covent Garden, earlier in the year. George Hudson, of course, is Leporello, Britannia is Elvira, and Don John (unseen) is John Bull.

But the highest pitch of frenzy generated by popular faith in the ability of inventions like steam locomotion to coin money was reached in 1845–47, George Hudson's palmiest years. "Nobody," observed Tancred in Disraeli's novel (1847), "now thinks about heaven. They never dream of angels. All their existence is concentrated in steamboats and railways" (2.12:135). "Railway Shares! Railway Shares!" exclaimed the *Illustrated London News* on 11 October 1845,

> Hunted by Stags and Bulls and Bears—
> Hunted by women—hunted by men—
> Speaking and writing—voice and pen—
> Claiming and coaxings—pray'rs and snares—
> All the world mad about RAILWAY SHARES!

This was the year the word *stag*, subsequently defined in the *Oxford English Dictionary* as "A person who applies for an allocation of shares in a joint-stock concern solely with a view to selling immediately at a profit," entered the slang vocabulary. In a single six-month period in 1845, the word and the image associated with it occurred more than twenty times in *Punch*, where, at the same moment, Thackeray's "Diary of C. Jeames de la Pluche, Esq." was recounting the dizzying rise to riches of a footman named James Plush, who made a paper fortune of thirty thousand pounds in railway shares from an initial investment of twenty pounds lent him by a fellow servant.

In the November 1846 number of *Dombey and Son*, Dickens took his readers to "Staggs's Gardens," the working-class neighborhood, almost a shanty town, that was to be (actually, had been) demolished to make way for the London and Birmingham Railway's approach to Euston station. No one in the vicinity was likely to have invested in railway shares, but under the circumstances the name was an inspired choice: Staggs's Gardens was the Fool's Paradise of the 1840s.[5] Many thousands of investors, large and small, put their money into Hudson's companies or others that were ripe for his takeover; at the peak of the hysteria, half the private investment of the nation was channeled into railway shares.

The railway mania echoed through Victorian fiction for many years; as late as 1880, Disraeli retrospectively described the beginnings of the popular madness, but not its denouement, in *Endymion*. Captain Wragge, the engaging self-styled swindler in Wilkie Collins's *No Name* (1862–63), was caught in the ruins, but other rascals emerged unscathed, as did the loathsome valetudinarian Noel Vanstone in the same novel, whose railway investments "survived the panic of eighteen hundred and forty-six, and are rapidly rising in value. He is said to be a bold speculator" ("Between the Scenes," chap. 5:1.350). In *Hard Cash* (1863), Charles Reade

"A strange spectacle was witnessed in the metropolis on Sunday last," said the *Illustrated London News* on 6 December 1845. The holy day of rest was transformed into one of frenzied activity, as hundreds of railway directors and projectors tried to beat the midnight deadline for submission of plans for new lines to the Board of Trade.

traced the career of a buccaneer speculator bent on recovering the losses he had suffered when his railway shares turned into mere paper. And in *Our Mutual Friend*, which was set in the mid-sixties, the "Shares" that Dickens ironically celebrated ("As is well known to the wise in their generation, traffic in Shares is the one thing to have to do with in this world. Have no antecedents, no established character, no cultivation, no ideas, no manners; have Shares . . ." [2.10:159–60]) may well have been, in view of Veneering's "new race of intimate friends" whom he acquired when he entered Parliament, railway stocks. Among these magnates, "Fathers of the Scrip-Church," was a contractor who was reputed to employ, directly and indirectly, no fewer than half a million laborers (3.17:690).

Although a law passed in 1844 requiring all joint-stock companies to be listed by an official registrar went a small way toward restraining enterprises like Tigg Montague's Anglo-Bengalee Disinterested Loan and Life Insurance Company (the insurance industry was especially hospitable to dubious joint-stock setups), investors were almost wholly unprotected against stock market losses. Until the Limited Liability Act of 1856 came to their rescue, stockholders were liable, not to the amount of their individual holdings but to the total amount of their wealth. If a company went bankrupt, everything a shareholder owned—house, land, chattels—could be seized if this were necessary to satisfy the creditors' claims. This meant that the greater the number of investors, the more widely the misery was shared when a company failed.

What distinguished the speculative frenzy of the middle and late forties from all that had gone before, apart from its sheer intensity, was the number of people involved and their social distribution. The *Annual Register* for 1846, commenting on a report made to the House of Commons that named all persons subscribing in the last session for sums under two thousand pounds, characterized that public as "a combination of peers and printers, vicars and vice-admirals, spinsters and half-pays, M.P.s and special pleaders, professors and cotton spinners, gentlemen's cooks and Q.C.s, attorneys' clerks and college-scouts, waiters at Lloyd's, relieving officers and excisemen, barristers and butchers, Catholic priests and coachmen, editors and engineers, dairymen and dyers, braziers, bankers, beer-sellers and butlers, domestic servants, footmen, and mail guards; with a multitude of other callings unrecorded in the Book of Trades."[6] When, a decade later, *Little Dorrit* reached its climax with the catastrophe of the great Merdle, now revealed to have been a common forger and robber, Dickens did not need to particularize. "Numbers of men in every profession and trade," he wrote, "would be blighted by his insolvency; old people who had been in easy circum-

stances all their lives would have no place of repentance for their trust
in him but the workhouse; legions of women and children would have
their whole future desolated by the hand of this mighty scoundrel. . . .
[A] solitary watcher on the gallery above the Dome of St. Paul's would
have perceived the night air to be laden with a heavy muttering of the
name of Merdle, coupled with every form of execration" (2.25:776).
Remembering how many thousands of innocent but overly optimistic
men and women lost their money in railway offerings, readers required
no further indication of the scope of Merdle's depredations. It was, in a
way, a measure of how far social democracy had progressed in England.

Thackeray, writing *The Newcomes* only a year before Dickens wrote
Little Dorrit, made the same point in a somewhat different context. As in
Little Dorrit, a number of named characters were among the sufferers.
Shareholders in the Bundelcund Banking Company of Calcutta included Colonel Newcome, Clive, James Binnie, the Vicomte de Florac,
Miss Cann, Miss Honeyman, J. J. Ridley and his father, Mrs. Mackenzie
on behalf of herself and her daughters, not to mention the banking
houses of Hobson Brothers and Newcome in London and Higg in the
towns of Newcome and Manchester. Beyond these were the nameless
but exceedingly numerous investors, as vulnerable when their money
evaporated half a world away as when it was entrusted to a London
house for the use of railway speculators. The Bundelcund fraud, wrote
Thackeray,

> was one of the many similar cheats which have been successfully practiced
> upon the simple folks, civilian and military, who toil and struggle—who
> fight with sun and enemy—who pass years of long exile and gallant endur-
> ance in the service of our empire in India. Agency-houses after agency-
> houses have been established, and have flourished in splendour and
> magnificence, and have paid fabulous dividends—and have enormously
> enriched two or three wary speculators—and then have burst into bank-
> ruptcy, involving widows, orphans, and countless simple people who trusted
> their all to the keeping of these unworthy treasurers (2:332).

One of the novelists whom Thackeray had once parodied, the ever-
busy Mrs. Catherine Gore, had an experience that provides a striking
example of prescient topicality. In 1843 she published a novel entitled
The Banker's Wife, the story of a scion of an old Lombard Street banking
family, who "inherited a large landed estate which the weakened bank
cannot maintain. He misappropriates funds in a desperate effort to save
his fortunes. After deserting his party in the Commons, he is killed in a
duel, and the bank's failure is disclosed." Mrs. Gore dedicated the book
to her own trustee and banker, Sir John Dean Paul. Four years later, Sir

John urged her to lend the money he managed in her behalf to his prestigious firm, Strahan, Paul, and Bates, for them to lend to their clients.
She declined to do so, preferring that her hard-earned savings should
be salted away in gilt-edged Exchequer bills or consols (government se-
curities). Sir John died in 1852, and his place in the firm was taken by
his namesake son, the second baronet. When the firm crashed three
years later, Mrs. Gore discovered that her money, instead of being safely
invested, had been diverted to the firm's uses and she was out the very
large sum, for an individual, of nineteen thousand pounds. In an effort
to recoup a small part of her loss, she reprinted *The Banker's Wife*, can-
celing the dedication and remarking in a new preface that she had been
"far from foreseeing that her own fortune would become partially involved in a catastrophe similar to the one described in its pages." The
second baronet, guilty son of a guilty father, got a stiff jail sentence.[7]

The year after Strahan, Paul, and Bates wound up its affairs in the
criminal courts, the Tipperary Joint-Stock Bank failed, leading John
Sadleir to drink his fatal potion on Hampstead Heath; and managers of
several other important banks, finding themselves in deep trouble, either somehow escaped prosecution or fled the country. In *The Three
Clerks*, the mutually beneficial but shady partnership of unscrupulous
financiers, civil servants, and politicians was exposed at length, beginning with mine shares and proceeding to a proposed bridge between
Limehouse and Rotherhithe and a jail sentence for one of the principals.
Though long-overdue legislation, notably the Limited Liability Act of
1856, was beginning to cramp the style of such adventurers, still other
failures and exposures followed, several of which Trollope would later
combine in the story of Augustus Melmotte.

Dickens's and Trollope's treatment of the speculative frenzy of those
years, unlike that of Thackeray and Reade, who sometimes could not
resist the urge to sermonize, was not overly didactic; nor did it have to
be. The moral was as plain as it was amply authenticated by the press
coverage of the public events spawned by the mad rush to uncertain
wealth. Their novels in fact interpreted to a lay readership what might
not have been clear in the newspapers, as might be inferred from Emily
Eden's *The Semi-Detached House*: "The *Times* of the following morning
announced two more failures of large banking-houses, and there were
dark hints in the City article about a great capitalist, which were perfectly
unintelligible to those who had not been brought up to talk Stock Exchange fluently . . ." (22:194). And if the moral did have to be spelled
out, Eden was the writer to do it: "Is money worth all the misery, the
struggles it brings? Those Pauls, and Strahans, and Redpaths, have more
to answer for than the pecuniary ruin they have wrought. They have

ruined all confidence, all trust; they have made dishonesty the rule, and not the exception" (13:110–11).

This was wisdom Catherine Gore acquired the hard way; and so, belatedly in the sequence of Victorian novels, did another woman author, Meredith's Diana Warwick. Although her story was set in the 1840s, Meredith involved her in an older "speculative mania," for South American mining shares, rather than in the historically appropriate one, the railway investment craze. (Otherwise the presence of a good, as well as successful, railway speculator, Tom Redworth, who marries Diana in the end, would have sent the plot off in a direction Meredith obviously did not intend.) Separated from her husband and in acute need of money, Diana hears of the "rush for allotments" set off by the directors' claim that the mining shares would pay a conservative minimum of forty or fifty percent, although they had every expectation that it would reach a cool hundred. "Thus five thousand pounds invested would speedily bring five thousand pounds per annum. Diana had often dreamed of the City of London as the seat of magic; and taking the City's contempt for authorcraft and the intangible as, from its point of view, justly founded, she had mixed her dream strangely with an ancient notion of the City's probity. Her broker's shaking head did not damp her ardour for shares to the full amount of her ability to purchase." The upshot was that the mine "collapsed almost within hearing of the trumpets of prospectus, after two punctual payments of the half-yearly interest," and Diana "had to sit down in the buzz of her self-reproaches and amazement at the behavior of that reputable City, shrug, and recommence the labour of her pen" (*Diana of the Crossways*, 27:312–13).

2.

It was, of course, the failure of epic dimensions that claimed the most attention in the press, especially because there usually was a mastermind head of a bank or merchant firm who could personify the calamity, the kind of tycoon whose Hogarthian rise and fall was traced in W. P. Frith's series of paintings (1871) now known as *The Race for Wealth*. But such men were few compared with the ordinary run of bankrupts who failed on a more modest scale—a few hundred pounds, perhaps, like old Trent in *The Old Curiosity Shop*—but failed nonetheless. Even in the century's first years, to judge from the *Times*'s lists of declared bankrupts and the cases disposed of in the court, these were numerous enough to constitute an unending chronicle of shattered hopes. But as the years went by, the lists grew inexorably longer, requiring, in the fifties and sixties, as many as five or six double-columned pages in the *Times*'s quarterly index. Except in the recurrent years of general crisis, these modest bankruptcies were, as a rule, not directly connected with events in the City. Many of the men who thrust themselves upon the mercy of the Bankruptcy Court would have failed even when times were good and City crime more or less quiescent.

It may well be that, as the authority quoted at the beginning of this chapter says, bankruptcy was a disaster more feared than experienced; a far larger portion of the total population remained solvent throughout their lives than did not. But few of the lucky ones were without relatives or friends who at one time or another went into Bankruptcy Court, as did Colonel Newcome, or declared themselves insolvent and thus, in the earlier Victorian years, were exposed to the possibility of ignominious detainment in a debtors' prison. One did not have to lose one's own money to know the feelings induced by the event.

Apart from the obvious discomfort of finding oneself penniless— and, as likely as not, with a family to feed and house—there was the class stigma this entailed. Until 1861 the legal definition of bankruptcy was that it applied only to the "trading" classes (never precisely defined). The alternative, chosen by ten times as many persons in financial trouble as chose bankruptcy, was to have one's debts processed through the Insolvent Debtors' Court, through liquidation of assets and understandings with creditors. (In fiction, no distinction was made between the two: insolvency was synonymous with bankruptcy.) It was understandable that respectable people who were hopelessly in debt would try to escape appearing in the bankruptcy lists if it was at all possible. Losing money was bad enough, but to be associated with "trade" was worse, a contingency to be avoided if one's social status, or the illusion thereof, was to be preserved.

In 1861 the distinction between bankruptcy and insolvency was abolished and all persons owing debts they could not pay were subjected to a uniform procedure, a leveling effect that did not sit well with "private gentlemen," who regarded their financial difficulties as being of an entirely different order from those of businessmen, and therefore entitled to preferential handling. There was immediate topicality, therefore, in Trollope's highlighting of the failure of the Bishopsgate Street haberdasher-draper's firm whose vicissitudes are the subject of *The Struggles of Brown, Jones, and Robinson* (1861–62). Trollope devoted a whole page to the special sadness of bankruptcy on the level of the humble tradesman:

> [In] an ordinary way, I know nothing more sad than the fate of men who have embarked all in a trade venture and have failed. It may be, and probably is, the fact, that in almost all such cases the failure is the fault of the bankrupts; but the fault is so generally hidden from their own eyes, that

they cannot see the justice of their punishment; and is often so occult in its causes that that justice cannot be discerned by any without deep scrutiny. They who have struggled and lost all feel only that they have worked hard, and worked in vain; that they have thrown away their money and their energy; and that there is an end, now and for ever, to those sweet hopes of independence with which they embarked their small boats upon the wide ocean of commerce. The fate of such men is very sad. Of course we hear of bankrupts who come forth again with renewed glories, and who shine all the brighter in consequence of their temporary obscurity. These are the men who can manage to have themselves repainted and regilded; but their number is not great. One hears of such because they are in their way memorable, and one does not hear of the poor wretches who sink down out of the world—back behind counters, and to menial work in warehouses. Of ordinary bankrupts one hears nothing. They are generally men who, having saved a little with long patience, embark it all and lose it with rapid impotence. They come forward once in their lives with their little ventures, and then retire never more to be seen or noticed. Of all the shops that are opened year after year in London, not above a half remain in existence for a period of twelve months; and not a half ever afford a livelihood to those who open them. (22: *Cornhill Magazine*, 5:296)

This street-level perspective on bankruptcy was rare in Victorian fiction. When failures occurred on the petit-bourgeois plane, they were usually mentioned in a sentence or two, not developed or philosophized about as Trollope did here. The wealth that was lost in Victorian fiction was typically not of the kind earned directly from the sale of goods at wholesale or retail or of services, but the unearned kind that underlay the upper-class economy—the proceeds of land rental or of invested funds. Within these limits, however, the theme had numerous variations, significances, and social applications. As the occupational and class distribution of railway investors proved, it could be adapted to a wide range of characters like Merdle and "every servile worshipper of riches who had helped to set him on his pedestal" down to poor Mr. Jellyby, fortune's fool, in *Bleak House*.

And so readers, whether they were principals in enterprises or simply trustful shareholders, had all too good reason to accept the veracity of every case of financial disaster they encountered in novels. It was among the direst of topicalities, and they reacted to its insistent repetition in fiction in accordance with their private, perhaps only subconscious worries: no better instance could be found of a topical theme that evoked the classic Aristotelian combination of pity and fear. By contrast, the reverse action—the sudden, unmotivated acquisition of great wealth, as in old Dorrit's case—belonged to the realm of fairy stories rather than the daily headlines, of surrogate wish fulfillment rather than sober reality.

The sudden loss of wealth was a device, as credible as it was convenient, to explain, with no elaboration, the present situation of a character or to effect a planned turn of plot. The statement on the first page of Tennyson's poem *Maud* (1855) epitomized the convention adopted by many novelists before and after. The mental distraction of the speaker was caused by the perhaps suicidal death of his father in a "pit": "Did he fling himself down? who knows? for a vast speculation had failed." But the fateful event in a novel need not have been a speculation, vast or small, to bring ruin; it might have involved mere imprudence, or even sheer misfortune—the result was the same. Mrs. Nickleby and her children were impoverished because a short time before the story opened, says Dickens, "a mania prevailed, a bubble burst, four stockbrokers took villa residences at Florence, four hundred nobodies were ruined, and among them Mr. Nickleby" (*Nicholas Nickleby*, 1:63). Sol Gills in *Dombey and Son*, proprietor of the marine instrument shop at the sign of the wooden midshipman, became insolvent, a counterpart in miniature of Mr. Dombey's resounding crash. John Sedley's stockbroking firm failed, and he and his family were reduced to a penurious existence in a Brompton cottage. In *Jane Eyre*, St. John Rivers's family, scions of old county-gentry stock, were forced to live in reduced circumstances because the father had "lost a great deal of money, by a man he had trusted turning bankrupt" (29:438). The proud Lancelot Smith's fortune, in *Yeast*, was lost in the failure of his uncle's bank. The threat of bankruptcy hung over the cloth manufacturer Robert Moore in Charlotte Brontë's *Shirley*, to be dissipated only at the last moment in the novel when the repeal of the Orders in Council in 1812 restored the American market for his goods. Colonel Newcome was ruined in the failure of the Bundelcund Bank—perhaps the very bank in which Aunt Betsey claimed she had been caught.

The very fact that Emily Eden wound up the romantic plot of so light-hearted a novel as *The Semi-Detached House* (1859) with a bankruptcy suggests how topical such occurrences were. In that comedy of manners, nobody of any account got hurt—a drastic departure from the usual inexorable chain of events. In the very next year, at the climactic end of *Evan Harrington*, the brewing partners Andrew and "old Tom" Cogglesby staged the elaborate pretense of a bankruptcy, a "farce" as they called it. Like Noddy Boffin's later impersonation of a miser in *Our Mutual Friend*, it was a joke arranged in a good cause.

But financial failures were seldom treated so comically in the ensuing

The failure of the supposedly rock-solid credit bank of Overend, Gurney & Co. on 11 May 1866, a day that would long be remembered as "Black Friday," ruined thousands of shareholders, including those of other financial houses that came down with it. The *Illustrated London News* pictured some of them in its next issue (19 May).

years. In *The Mill on the Floss*, George Eliot used Tulliver's bankruptcy as the early pivotal catastrophe, a prime means of characterizing not only the Tullivers themselves but their various relations as they gathered to survey, with pharisaical crocodile tears as well as sincere commiseration, the ruins of the Tullivers' inoffensive prosperity. In *The Adventures of Philip*, Philip's unpleasant, class-conscious father, a society physician who had eloped with the niece of a peer, overspeculated and lost, fleeing first to the Continent and then to New York. In *Hard Cash*, in an obvious reprise of Dickens's description of the Merdle catastrophe, Reade de-

COMMITTED FOR TRIAL.

RUINED SHAREHOLDER. "YES, THEY ARE COMMITTED FOR TRIAL; BUT WE, MY CHILD, TO *HARD LABOUR FOR LIFE!*"

Two and a half years after Overend, Gurney's failure, six of its directors were accused of a variety of frauds, including selling stock to
the public when they knew the house was bankrupt. A panel presided over by the Lord Mayor of London sent the case on to the
criminal courts for prosecution, a development that evoked John
Tenniel's trenchant comment in *Punch* for 6 October 1869. (At the
conclusion of the ensuing trial at the Old Bailey, in December, the
defendants were acquitted.)

scribed the ripple effect on the people caught in the closing of the bank owned by the hero's father, who had rashly speculated with its funds. In *Our Mutual Friend*, published the next year, the newly rich Mr. Veneering joined the ranks of the insolvent. At the beginning of Hardy's *Desperate Remedies*, Cytherea Graye's father lost everything she might have inherited in what was, in fiction as in life, a rather uncommon gamble: "bottomry security," in which an investor financed a ship's voyage on the security of the ship itself. The vessel sank, and Cytherea was left penniless. Five years later (1876), the second chapter of *Daniel Deronda* opened with a letter to Gwendolyn Harleth announcing that "Grapnell & Co. have failed for a million and we are totally ruined" (2:43). No plot could have been got under way with greater dispatch, or less need for the author to explain.

These instances by no means exhaust the roll of bankruptcies in the fiction of well-remembered Victorian writers. Several more remain to be mentioned, and there are innumerable others in forgotten novels of the time. But the list helps to explain the noticeably matter-of-fact manner in which Hardy handles the failure of Henchard's corn-and-seed business in *The Mayor of Casterbridge*. Steadily developing his tragic hero, Hardy availed himself of this conventional turn of fortune to stress Henchard's integrity: his fall was nothing if not honorable. When he offered his creditors his last remaining assets—his watch and purse (a "yellow canvas money-bag, such as was carried by all farmers and dealers")—they refused to accept them. "I am bound to admit," said a senior commissioner (adjudicator of bankruptcy), "that I have never met a debtor who behaved more fairly" (31:168). It is not a climactic episode, being used simply as a device to make Henchard revert from his proud position as a leading citizen of his town to his original station as a farm laborer. There are no theatrics, no overt bid for sympathy or blame. Nor was there, at this late stage of a theme that had run through the fiction of the past fifty years, any need for these. Remembering Dombey, John Sedley, Colonel Newcome, Merdle, Tulliver, and the other well-described victims of their own or others' avarice or overweening self-confidence, readers of *The Mayor of Casterbridge* could supply for themselves what Hardy left unsaid, each shaping and seasoning the story of Henchard's fall according to his own moral tastes.

Whatever the pros and cons of his own case, Henchard was in good company. Too often in Victorian fiction, as in life, disaster in this form struck the undeserving, whose only fault was naiveté in a cutthroat world. In a moral society, Colonel Newcome would have escaped ruin in the Bundelcund Bank. But his fortitude enabled him to survive the test, as did Arthur Clennam, whose first response to the fall of the house of

Merdle was to try to protect his friend, the inventor Daniel Doyce, another innocent victim among the many whom he had urged to join the fatal speculation. Such men were true heroes, according to Victorian moral principles. If their ambition to make fortunes without working for them was reprehensible, they were adequately punished and, most important, they emerged from the ordeal purged and strengthened. This was the experience of Mr. Dombey, whom Dickens ultimately, however improbably, transformed into a sympathetic, feeble, white-haired character once he was crushed by adversity. Not as much could be said of Mr. Tulliver, whose dignity after he lost his lawsuit with Wakem, and his property with it, was stiff-necked rather than truly tragic.

> Mr. Tulliver, you perceive [wrote George Eliot], though nothing more than a superior miller and maltster, was as proud and obstinate as if he had been a very lofty personage, in whom such dispositions might be a source of that conspicuous, far-echoing tragedy, which sweeps the stage in regal robes and makes the dullest chronicler sublime. The pride and obstinacy of millers, and other insignificant people, whom you pass unnoticingly on the road every day, have their tragedy too; but it is of that unwept, hidden sort, that goes on from generation to generation, and leaves no record. . . . (*The Mill on the Floss*, 3.1:173–74)

Tulliver was not made of the same mettle as Samuel Pickwick, whom Mr. Lowten the lawyer admired as that gentleman was en route to the Fleet prison on another charge: "What a bankrupt he'd make, sir. How he would bother the commissioners! He'd set 'em at defiance if they talked of committing him, sir" (*Pickwick Papers*, 40:660).

Able, as they were, to associate the elaborately named enterprises in fiction with their fraudulent counterparts in the financial news of the 1830s and 1840s, readers could have anticipated plot developments. They could have foreseen, for example, that Sam Titmarsh's employer, the Independent West Diddlesex Fire and Life Insurance Company, would fail, with the result that he would be not only thrown into debtors' prison but struck from the will of his aunt, who had £3,000 invested in the firm (*The Great Hoggarty Diamond* [1841]). Although Thackeray, plausibly enough, moved the crash back to 1823–24, he was writing from the day's headlines. Responding to an exposé campaign in the press, a select committee of the House of Commons had just been appointed to look into the affairs of the West Middlesex General Annuity Company, which a recent historian has called "the most gigantic and impudent insurance fraud ever perpetrated."[8] Readers of *Martin Chuzzlewit*, published only three years later, would have been equally confident that disaster lay not far down the road when Tigg Montague launched the

Anglo-Bengalee Disinterested Loan and Life Insurance Company. The title of Merdle's pretentious empire was never given in *Little Dorrit*, but in the atmosphere of 1855–57 Dickens really telegraphed the future development of the story. Merdle had risen so high as to become, like Hudson, an object of public adulation, the very personification of invulnerable riches; that he was bound to fall, like Sadleir, before the novel's end was a foregone conclusion.

In *The Newcomes* Thackeray went further than Dickens in forgoing whatever surprise value a financial disaster might contain. "I disdain, for the most part, the tricks and surprises of the novelist's art," he wrote late in the novel. "Knowing, from the very beginning of our story, what was the issue of this Bundelcund Banking concern, I have scarce had patience to keep my counsel about it; and whenever I have had occasion to mention the company, have scarcely been able to refrain from breaking out in fierce diatribes against that complicated, enormous, outrageous swindle" (70:2.231–32)—which he then proceeded to do. Thakeray had signaled imminent trouble by mentioning more than once the excessive confidence of London stockbrokers and shareholders in the great bank. In addition, he had gone out of his way to mention the partners who sold their shares in India when the shares still commanded a high price, and returned home as rich nabobs, unscathed by the catastrophe they had foreseen.

A few novelists besides Emily Eden and Meredith found a comic side to the speculation-bankruptcy theme that extended beyond the ornate, but not untypical, names with which shady enterprises were christened. Shortly after Sir Matthew Pupker, M.P., pushed a private bill to float his crumpet and muffin monopoly in *Nicholas Nickleby*, other promoters, in *Ten Thousand a Year*, formed an Artificial Rain Company whose product was insecurely based on the supposed scientific know-how of Dr. Diabolus Gander, a thinly disguised version of Dionysius Lardner, an eccentric proponent of questionable scientific notions who was a familiar butt of satire at the time. (The company had a short life.) Titmarsh's loss in the West Diddlesex crash was more amusing than serious; Sam, after all, was young and resilient. Bulwer-Lytton's enumeration of Uncle Jack's amiable speculations in *The Caxtons* likewise was more caricature than censure. It described a whole stewpot of schemes designed for simultaneous private profit and public weal: the Grand National Benevolent Clothing Company, which was to steam-produce "inexpressibles" (trousers) at 7*s*. 6*d*. per pair and superfine coats at £1 18*s*.; the New, Grand, National, Benevolent Insurance Company, for the Industrial Classes, which promised a 24½ percent return on invested savings; the Grand

National Anti-Monopoly Coal Company, which proposed to break the monopoly enjoyed by the London Coal Wharves; a new daily newspaper modeled on the *Times*, but "devoted entirely to Art, Literature, and Science"; and the Grand Anti-Publisher Confederate Authors' Society ("every author is to be his own publisher"), a project that readers would have recognized as a burlesque of the agitation Dickens, Forster, and Thackeray were stirring at that very moment (1848–49) in behalf of "the dignity of literature," which included an author's right not to be cheated by a publisher.

There was humor, too, though it had a bitter taste, in the notion that under some circumstances bankruptcy carried with it not stigma but social cachet; even if a man lost his money, he had once possessed it, and that was a count in his favor. "Mrs. Pell," said her (widowed) husband in *Pickwick Papers*, "was very much attracted to me—very much—highly connected, too; her mother's brother, gentlemen, failed for eight hundred pounds as a Law Stationer" (55:870). Towlinson, the Dombey footman, counted on enjoying extra prestige in the London servants' world by sheer virtue of the size of his master's unpayable debt: "As soon as there is no doubt about it, Mr. Towlinson's main anxiety is that the failure should be a good round one—not less than a hundred thousand pound" (*Dombey and Son*, 59:924). The debt collector Rugg in *Little Dorrit* preferred, for the sake of his own reputation, that Arthur Clennam choose to be confined in a superior debtors' prison such as the King's Bench—one to which large-scale defaulters gravitated. In *Far from the Madding Crowd*, the ancient maltster said to Joseph Poorgrass, ". . . I knowed the man and woman both well. Levi Everdene—that was the man's name, sure. 'Man,' saith I in my hurry, but he were of a higher circle than that—'a was a gentleman-tailor really, worth scores of pounds. And he became a very celebrated bankrupt two or three times." Joseph: "Oh, I thought he was quite a common man!" The maltster: "O, no, no! That man failed for heaps of money; hundreds in gold and silver" (8:55).

Still, during its long run in Victorian fiction bankruptcy, whether or not it was the consequence of unwise or unlucky speculation, was not to be taken lightly. In novels, as in life, to go bankrupt or even be touched by bankruptcy—Mr. Pell, Towlinson, and John Stuart Mill notwithstanding—was to be disgraced. Old Osborne forbade George to marry the daughter of a hapless but despised bankrupt. Amelia Sedley, a latter-day Ophelia, had to return George's presents, and when Dobbin tried to arrange things on George's behalf, Osborne père stormed: ". . . you don't mean that he's such a d—— fool as to be still hankering after that swindling old bankrupt's daughter? You've not come here for to make me suppose that he wants to marry *her*? Marry *her*, that *is* a good one. My son and heir marry a beggar's girl out of a gutter" (*Vanity Fair*, 24:220).

The very terminology was offensive. After Wakem took over Tulliver's property, George Eliot noted that young Tom felt the humiliation even more keenly than did his father: "To 'have the bailiff in the house,' and 'to be sold up,' were phrases which he had been used to, even as a little boy; they were part of the disgrace and misery of 'failing,' of losing all one's money, and being ruined—sinking into the condition of poor working people. . . . His father must not only be said to have 'lost his property,' but to have 'failed'—the word that carried the worst obloquy to Tom's mind" (*The Mill on the Floss*, 3.2:178; 3.7:216).

To Thackeray, as to Elizabeth Barrett, whose family was forced to vacate Hope End and rent a house in Sidmouth when her father's creditors put up his £50,000 estate at auction in 1832, loss of fortune and the inevitable disgrace had a more personal meaning than it did to the other novelists who had used it simply because it was a widely appreciated topicality. Like Tennyson, Thackeray knew what it was like to suffer adversity when his patrimony suddenly vanished; in his case, with the collapse in the early 1830s of several great India-agency houses, typified in *Vanity Fair* by "the great Calcutta house of Fogle, Fake, and Cracksman," which "failed for a million, and plunged half the Indian public into misery and ruin" (60:578–79). The aspect of financial disaster that most affected him, as it affected the author of *The Cherry Orchard* half a century later, was the spectacle of a family's house and possessions being cruelly dispersed, the first step in the process usually being the arrival of a pair of uncouth bailiffs, unwelcome intruders from the outside world, whose sordid mission was to take possession and make an inventory of the chattels. Dickens introduced, in connection with the Mantalini bankruptcy in *Nicholas Nickleby*, a pair of walk-on characters named Scaley and Tox, avatars of the Jewish secondhand dealers, hats on heads, who would soon become stock figures that added an extra dose of unfeeling vulgarity to such scenes. In *Dombey and Son*, Dickens described the paying off of the servants and the sale of the expensive pieces Dombey had bought to furnish the mansion to which he brought his haughty bride. The same Towlinson who had basked in the glorious magnitude of Dombey's debt now let it be known that "he does not think it over-respectable to remain in a house where Sales and such-like are carrying forwards" (59:927). It was a fastidiousness comparable to that expressed by Merdle's butler, who gave notice the moment news of his ruined master's suicide arrived. Forced sales and suicides, alike, gave people a bad name—not the victims alone, but their servants, whose pocketbooks,

"When the sale of Colonel Newcome's effects took place . . ."—so began chapter 72 of *The Newcomes*, but Thackeray dismissed the event in two sentences, and it was left for Richard Doyle to picture it.

though small, were untouched, even if they now had to look for new situations.

Two of Victorian fiction's most memorable selling-up sequences fortuitously gained extra timeliness and emotional depth from events in the real world. The serialization of *Dombey and Son* and *Vanity Fair* ended in

April and July 1848, respectively. In August and September, the newspapers ran long stories about the sale of Stowe House, seat of the prodigiously bankrupt Duke of Buckingham and Chandos. A long leading article in the *Times* on 14 August, marking the end of "the tumultuous invasion of sight-seers" and the start of the actual sale the next day, began:

> During the past week the British public has been admitted to a spectacle of a painfully interesting and gravely historical import. One of the most splendid abodes of our almost regal aristocracy has thrown open its portals to an endless succession of visitors, who from morning to night have flowed in an uninterrupted stream from room to room, and floor to floor—not to enjoy the hospitality of the lord, or to congratulate him on his countless treasures of art, but to see an ancient family ruined, their palace marked for destruction, and its contents scattered to the four winds of Heaven. We are only saying what is notorious, and what therefore it is neither a novelty nor a cruelty to repeat, that the Most Noble and Puissant Prince, his Grace the Duke of Buckingham and Chandos, is at this moment an absolutely ruined and destitute man.

Readers of this journalistic threnody would have been struck by the way the novelists had anticipated it in their reports of the fall of two rich commoners, Dombey the merchant and Sedley the stockbroker. Thackeray had devoted several pages in the May 1847 number of *Vanity Fair* to the selling up of "Lord Dives'" (Sedley's) house as a regrettably splendid example of "those public assemblies, a crowd of which are advertised every day in the last page of the 'Times' newspaper, and over which the late Mr. George Robins[†] used to preside with so much dignity" (17:159). Dickens's comparable account of the Dombey event had appeared in the final (double) number of his novel in April 1848.

The next year (30 April 1849), Dickens wrote to his and Thackeray's friend, the cartoonist and illustrator John Leech, "I passed Gore House to day, and saw the bills up for a Sale (in the East Wing) with a very doleful eye."[9] Thackeray saw the same bills with an eye that was more than doleful; in the light of his close friendship with the occupants of Gore House, Count D'Orsay and the Countess of Blessington, famous hostess and sometime author, his eye brimmed over. Perhaps, at this moment, he was too overcome to recall a bitter irony. Twenty-seven

---

[†]The name of Robins was ineffaceably associated with these occasions. But for the clear inapplicability of the word to his loquacious self, he might have been called a mute, attending if not presiding over the obsequies of a departed fortune. He was to the sad end of a landed family's tenure of a "valuable and extensive country property" what Capability Brown had been during its expansive, improving heyday.

Bankruptcy and its sad sequel, the selling-up of a household, had a more poignant meaning to Thackeray than to any of his fellow novelists. His drawing of "the man in possession" was made for an episode in his Christmas book, *Our Street* (1848), in which such a fate is visited on an ex-captain of Dragoons, "director of the Cornaro Life Insurance Company, of the Tregulpho tin-mines, and of four or five railroad companies," who has fled to Boulogne to escape his creditors, leaving his wife and young children behind.

years earlier (1822), Lady Blessington had included in her *The Magic Lantern, or Sketches of Scenes in the Metropolis* a description of the selling up of a private house, which even then was an occasion of melancholy note. She thus proved to have anticipated the fate of her own house, which had to be sold as a result of what the *Dictionary of National Biography* calls D'Orsay's "pecuniary embarrassments." (He had already fled to the Continent.) When the house and its contents were laid open for inspection prior to the sale, wrote her biographer, "Every room was thronged. The well-known library salon, in which the conversaziones took place, was crowded . . . People as they passed through the room, poked the furniture, pulled about the precious objects of art and ornaments. . . . And some made jests."[10]

Thackeray was there. He wrote to his friend Mrs. Brookfield, "I have just come away from a dismal sight—Gore House full of Snobs looking at the furniture—foul Jews, odious bombazeen women. . . . Brutes keeping their hats on in the kind old drawing-rooms—I longed to knock some of 'em off: and say Sir be civil in a lady's room. . . . Ah it was a strange sad picture of Wanaty Fair."[11] Life had illustrated art in a peculiarly apposite fashion, and Thackeray's readers were the beneficiaries of life's intervention.

Ten years later, in 1860–61 alone, three well-known novels included the arrival-of-the-bailiffs scene, a coincidence that one is tempted to relate to the exhibition in the earlier year of Robert Braithwaite Martineau's painting *The Last Day in the Old Home.* The bailiffs, to be sure, do not appear in the picture, but the aftermath of their visit is shown in all its pathetic detail. In *The Mill on the Floss* their intrusive presence is essential to George Eliot's development of Mrs. Tulliver's character as she faces, in Tom's presence, the sacrifice of what Eliot calls, in the chapter heading, her "Teraphim, or Household Gods" with all their poignant domestic associations:

> "O my boy, my boy!" she said, clasping him round the neck. "To think as I should live to see this day! . . . To think o' these [table] cloths as I spun myself, . . . and Job Haxey wove 'em, and brought the piece home on his back, as I remember standing at the door and seeing him come, before I ever thought o' marrying your father! And the pattern as I chose myself—and bleached so beautiful, and I marked 'em so as nobody ever saw such marking—they must cut the cloth to get it out, for it's a particular stitch. And they're all to be sold—and go into strange people's houses, and perhaps to be cut with the knives, and wore out before I'm dead." (3.2 : 179)

In *Framley Parsonage* a pair of rural bailiffs arrived to inventory the parsonage itself as a consequence of Mark Robarts's incautiously endorsing bills of acceptance for Nathaniel Sowerby. The reader was prepared for the worst, but Trollope spared Robarts the customary grief by having the debt paid off before the chattels were put up for sale. (A similar resolution would occur ten years later in *Middlemarch*, when an execution was issued on Lydgate's house and a precautionary inventory of his furniture was made. His indebtedness, too, was erased by a so-called loan from Bulstrode.)

It was in Mrs. Henry Wood's *East Lynne*, however, that the most brutal use was made of the bailiff convention. When Lord Mount Severn died penniless, "a shoal of what the late earl would have called harpies . . . arrived to surround East Lynne. There were creditors for small sums and for great, for five or ten pounds, up to five or ten thousand. Some were civil; some impatient; some loud and rough and angry; some came in to put executions on the effects, and some—*to arrest the body!*" (11:104; Mrs. Wood's italics.) A pair of hook-nosed Israelites stood guard over the body for some time, until the new earl's lawyer, though he failed to dislodge them from their occupation of the house, succeeded in getting his client's grandfather decently interred.[†]

The last of the large-scale selling-up scenes in Victorian fiction occupied chapter 60 of *Middlemarch*. Dickens's and Thackeray's had been stylish London events, worthy of being presided over by an auctioneer of Robins's nationwide prestige. George Eliot described an equivalent event in a provincial town, which brought out the best in the local auctioneer, Mr. Borthrop Trumbull. Here, exceptionally, the occasion of the sale was not someone's financial necessity or someone else's death but the purchase by Mr. Larcher, a successful carrier (proprietor of an over-the-road hauling firm), of an already well-furnished mansion from "an illustrious Spa physician" and his consequently having to sell his present property.

> At Middlemarch in those times a large sale was regarded as a kind of festival. There was a table spread with the best cold eatables, as at a superior funeral; and facilities were offered for that generous drinking of cheerful glasses which might lead to generous and cheerful bidding for undesirable articles . . . In short, the auction was as good as a fair, and drew all classes with leisure at command: to some, who risked making bids in order simply to raise prices, it was almost equal to betting at the races. (60:649–50)

The humorous focus of this genre picture, which would have furnished an admirable subject for David Wilkie's or William Mulready's brushes, was on the variety of works of art offered, from an engraving of Wellington and his staff at Waterloo to a representation of the supper at Emmaus "by the celebrated *Guydo*, the greatest painter in the world, the chief of the Old Masters," as Mr. Trumbull described it. It was knocked down to Ladislaw for ten guineas.

Except for George Eliot's affectionate variation on the theme, where

---

[†]There was literary precedent for this grisly episode. In Maria Edgeworth's *Castle Rackrent* (1800) a body was seized for debt as the funeral cortege made its way through the Irish town, and more recently, in *Vanity Fair* (but in the same time context as *Castle Rackrent*), Thackeray had mentioned the corpse of Becky Sharp's father, lately dead of delirium tremens, being "quarrelled over" by two bailiffs (2:20).

nobody grieved and everybody had a good time, whether or not they came away with bargains, these almost formulaic scenes struck a powerful domestic chord. It was not only that they represented a fall from high, or at least highly respectable, estate, or the incurring of disgrace in the eyes of the all too readily censorious. They also entailed a grim violation of the sanctity that contemporary domestic mores prized over all others—a desecration, not a consecration, of the house. In the particular case of families in society's uppermost range, the house with its costly furnishings may have been an ostentatious status symbol, as it certainly was in *Dombey and Son*, and therefore to be deplored by the thoughtful and tasteful. But it still was, with all its luxurious appointments, a home, a scene of family life, however fraught it might have been with disappointments, conflicts, selfishness, and other bitter associations. At the public view it was seen devoid of its inhabitants, who were suffering shame, if not facing actual privation, as a consequence of deeds which may or may not have been the result of wanton imprudence or excessive ambition—or of capricious Fate. Only the furnishings remained in the silent shell, mute testimony to the life which had departed, and muddy boots tracked up the rich carpeting, salvagers pawed the fabrics and mentally calculated the value of the splendid silverware. However an individual reader might react to such scenes, whether with a satisfied sense of justice done or sympathy for the dispossessed—there but for the grace of God, and so on—his response to the fictional event would have been intensified when he imbued it with what he had read of scenes like those at Stowe and Gore House.

Such viewings also represented a violation of the privacy so jealously guarded by most upper- and middle-class Victorian families. Even when no financial crisis was involved, to the hypersensitive the mere advertising of a house for rental or sale, however routine, was an offense against taste and propriety. Rosalind Lydgate found the public announcement that their house was for sale "degrading." The town of Middlemarch perhaps had not heard of George Robins's auctioneering magniloquence—Mr. Borthrop Trumbull suited very well—but it doubtless lay behind Lady Dunstane's aversion, in the 1840s, to real-estate puffery (*Diana of the Crossways*). Because she disliked the house in Surrey that her husband had inherited,

> it was advertized to be let, and the auctioneer proclaimed it in his dialect. Her taste was delicate; she had the sensitiveness of an invalid: twice she read the stalking advertizement of the attractions of Copsley, and hearing Diana call it "the plush of speech," she shuddered; she decided that a place where her husband's family had lived ought not to stand forth meretriciously spangled and daubed, like a show-booth at a fair, for a bait; though

the grandiloquent man of advertizing letters assured Sir Lukin that a public agape for the big and gaudy mouthful is in no milder way to be caught; as it is apparently the case. She withdrew the trumpeting placard. (4:44)

"Take notice: This building remains on view, / Its suites of reception every one, / Its private apartment and bedroom too"—thus Browning, in his poem "House" (1876), sardonically adopting the phraseology of newspaper advertising. But his answer, as a man fiercely protective of his privacy, was forthright: ". . . please you, no foot over threshold of mine!" It was a sentiment most Victorians shared, and it was among the feelings most painfully aroused when an "earthquake" (read: selling up as a result of bankruptcy) came:

> The whole of the frontage shaven sheer,
> The inside gaped: exposed to day,
> Right and wrong and common and queer,
> Bare, as the palm of your hand, it lay. . . .
>
> Friends, the goodman of the house at least
> Kept house to himself till an earthquake came:
> 'Tis the fall of its frontage permits you feast
> On the inside arrangement you praise or blame.
>
> Outside should suffice for evidence:
> And whoso desires to penetrate
> Deeper, must dive by the spirit-sense. . . .

But the shabby, irreverent bailiffs, totally lacking in "spirit-sense," penetrated the domestic arcana just the same, and that is what Victorian families most dreaded.

18
The Free and Independent: I

1.

WHILE BANKRUPTCIES were the Victorian version of the turns of Fortuna's wheel, elections were the (not always) bloodless domestic equivalent of battles. "I like electioneering better than hunting—second only to war," said Disraeli's hero and alter ego, in *A Year at Hartlebury, or The Election* (1834) (2.7:140).† Admittedly, elections lacked some of the appeal to novelists that bankruptcies possessed. The latter came closer to home than did elections, which after all were institutionalized events whose outcome immediately affected only the candidates; the eventual impact, in the form of new laws or governmental policies, was diffused and delayed, whereas a financial crash could plunge a man and his family from wealth to penury in the course of a single day. One could read about elections with detachment, but unless one was so fortunate as to be permanently exempt from financial vicissitudes, stories of lost fortunes struck to the very heart of one's own precious sense of security.

On the other hand, the contemporary electoral process had much to recommend it to topicality-minded novelists.[1] Elections furnished authors with up-to-date illustrations of an old theme, one that had energized literature from Greek tragedy all the way down to the present: the conflict of man against man, group against group, with the outcome hanging in doubt. They also provided occasions for the staging of what is nowadays called political theatre—the manipulation, as by a candidate's agent, of individuals or groups for a private end. Like bankruptcies, they made available to a novelist a convenient plot device, to be resorted to if the status and fortunes of individual men had to be altered to advance the story—a kind of *deus ex hustings*. They provided occasions

---

†The novel was published under the pseudonyms of "Cherry" and "Fair Star," and only in 1979 was it discovered that the authors were Disraeli and his sister. Disraeli seems to have written the election chapters.

for tests of character when probity or courage was in question. And, even if elections served no more serious purpose, they gave scope to a novelist's penchant for lively narrative and rural or town genre painting. The humors of Hogarth's four-picture *Election Entertainment* (1754) were transferred to Victorian soil and lent plausibility by each real-life contest that novel readers witnessed or read about in the press.

Elections figured in at least as many novels as bankruptcies did, the length of the allusion reaching from a few paragraphs to the forty-five double-columned pages they occupied in three issues of *Blackwood's Magazine* (January–March 1841) when Warren's *Ten Thousand a Year* was serialized there. The Eatanswill election, half satire, half sheer farce, was among the episodes that contributed most to the unprecedented success of *Pickwick Papers*. The one at Treby Magna was the central theme of *Felix Holt*, and that at Bevisham, a generation later, of the first half of *Beauchamp's Career*. And the persistently, almost ritually corrupt elections in the years before and after the passage of the Second Reform Bill in 1867 were reflected in no fewer than ten of Trollope's forty-seven novels, most notably *Ralph the Heir*.

An early prototype of the fictional Victorian election, a description complete with speeches from the hustings, had appeared in the third and ninth chapters of Smollett's *The Life and Adventures of Sir Launcelot Greaves* (1760–62), and forty years later an Irish election figured briefly in Maria Edgeworth's *Castle Rackrent* (1800). Until the enactment of the First Reform Bill in 1832, however, elections were of comparatively little immediate interest to novelists and their middle-class readers. The qualities that, dramatically speaking, constitute the essence of free elections, combat and suspense, were largely lacking under the old system. It was estimated that at the end of the eighteenth century no fewer than half the seats in Parliament were controlled by the landed class. Genuine contests accordingly were rare.

In most boroughs before 1832, voters were numbered in mere three figures, or even fewer. The notorious rotten boroughs, such as Old Sarum, had no electorate at all except for the lonely handful of inhabitants necessary to sustain the fiction that they were an actual constituency. In Peacock's satirical *Melincourt* (1817), there were only two types of borough: Onevote, a "solitary farm, of which the land was so poor and untractable, that it would not have been worth the while of any human being to cultivate it, had not the Duke of Rottenburgh found it very well worth his to pay his tenant for living there, to keep the honourable borough in existence,"[2] and the city of Nonvote, a manufacturing town of fifty thousand population, which went totally unrepresented in Parliament.

In addition to the close ("pocket" or nomination) boroughs and downright rotten ones, there were safe seats, such as those produced when a pair of influential families on opposite sides of the fence amicably agreed to split a pair of county or borough seats, one going to a Tory candidate and the other to a Whig, or reached some other kind of accommodation. In such places, contests were largely pro forma. In Bulwer-Lytton's *My Novel*, the one for the borough of Lansmere

> had been, to use the language of Lord Lansmere, "conducted in the spirit of gentlemen,"—that is to say, the only opponents to the Lansmere interest had been found in one or the other of two rival families in the same county; and as the Earl was a hospitable, courteous man, much respected and liked by the neighboring gentry, so the hostile candidate had always interlarded his speeches with profuse compliments to his Lordship's high character, and civil expressions as to his Lordship's candidate. (1.10:1.54)

In *A Year at Hartlebury*, Disraeli depicted a similar pre-Reform coziness:

> For many years the borough of Fanchester had been represented by two wealthy and respectable individuals, who seldom appeared among their constituents. They came to be chaired at each election, and every now and then when they were travelling that road, they spent the morning in calling on their friends. Every year each sent a buck, and every year one of them, who considered himself an orator and was fond of spouting after dinner, banquetted with the Corporation: the other who was more silent and diffident, sent an additional present of rich fruits from his hot-houses. The flattering speeches and the rich fruits balanced the affair, both were equally popular. One was a Tory, the other a Whig, but side by side they bowed in amity to their constituents, and nothing would have disturbed their friendship but the overturning Reform Bill. (1.20:79)

A few boroughs, some thirty-eight in 1830, enjoyed so-called scot and lot representation, all adult males being entitled to vote if they paid certain local taxes. Among the largest were the London boroughs of Westminster and Southwark, the periodic scenes of genuine, and on occasion riotous, contests of the kind that inspired Hogarth. Individual occasions formed the subjects of numerous satirical prints by his successors, Rowlandson, Gillray, and George Cruikshank. Accompanying them, in the heat of an electoral combat, were equally numerous squibs, songs, and other forms of polemic. In the aggregate these comprised the half-graphic, half-verbal tradition of election sub-literature that the novelists inherited and whose place was filled by fictional descriptions when, in the 1830s, the printed and engraved missiles faded from the political air and the partisan journalism of earlier days found a new home in the weekly issues of *Punch*.

Meanwhile, elections found their way into many silver fork novels, providing, as it turned out, a link between that genre and the political fiction typified by Disraeli's trilogy. Although they were a stock ingredient, indigenous to fashionable novels on the ground that some of the characters would naturally be politicians by virtue of their social rank, they were largely fluff, their only serious function being to convey the prevailing aristocratic disdain for the principal instrument of democratic governance. Henry Pelham's summation of the process by which he won his seat in Bulwer's novel (1828) could almost be said to have represented the glass through which novelists of the time customarily saw elections: ". . . after the due quantum of dining, drinking, spouting, lying, equivocating, bribing, rioting, head-breaking, promise-breaking, and—thank the god Mercury, who presides over elections—*chairing* of successful candidateship, I found myself fairly chosen member for the borough of Buyemall!" (*Pelham*, 1.36 : 1.194).

Buyemall, as it happened, had only recently been thrown open to competition. As Pelham explained:

> The borough . . . had long been in undisputed possession of the Lords of Glenmorris, till a rich banker, of the name of Lufton, had bought a large estate in the immediate neighborhood of Glenmorris Castle. This event, which was the precursor of a mighty revolution in the borough of Buyemall, took place in the first year of my uncle's accession to his property. A few months afterwards, a vacancy in the borough occurring, my uncle procured the nomination of one of his own political party. To the great astonishment of Lord Glenmorris, and the great gratification of the burghers of Buyemall, Mr. Lufton offered himself in opposition to the Glenmorris candidate. In this age of enlightenment, innovation has no respect for the most sacred institutions of antiquity. The burghers, for the only time since their creation as a body, were cast first into doubt, and secondly into rebellion. The Lufton faction, *horresco referens*, were triumphant, and the rival candidate was returned. From that hour the borough of Buyemall was open to all the world. (35 : 1.183)

In John Galt's *The Member*, published in January 1832, as the struggle to enact the Reform Bill was nearing its climax, Archibald Jobbry, having once bought the Frailtown seat outright, was challenged by an unexpected rival the second time round. The election for a pocket borough that the principled John Halifax forced in Mulock's novel was almost revolutionary in its import: "A contested election! truly, such a thing had not been known within the memory of the oldest inhabitant" (*John Halifax, Gentleman*, 24 : 242).

The events at Buyemall and Frailtown reflected the fact that even prior to the electoral reforms of 1832 dissatisfaction with the old system

In its first issue, for 17 July 1841, *Punch* prophetically established elections as a topicality to which it would return time after time in the course of the Victorian era. At top, left to right: "Canvassing" ("What a love of a child") and "The Deputation" ("If you think me worthy"). Bottom row: "The Successful Candidate" ("Constituents—rascals"), "The Hustings" ("Dont mention it I beg"), and "The Public Dinner" ("The proudest moment of my life").

had reached the point where more elections were contested than ever before. No longer, observed Endymion Ferrars in Disraeli's retrospective novel, was it "possible to step into parliament as if you were stepping into a club" (*Endymion*, 69:312). But the drama inherent in the multiplied number of open contests was only one reason for the heightened interest that novelists and their readers took in elections after 1832. There were also the turbulent events—nationwide demonstrations, riots, military interventions, the sacking and burning of castles and whole sections of towns (notably Bristol)—that had preceded the passage of the First Reform Bill in May 1832. Never before had a proposed act of Parliament brought the nation as close to revolution as it had in the past eighteen months. "Thus," wrote George Eliot, "Treby Magna, which had lived quietly through the great earthquakes of the French Revolution and the Napoleonic Wars, which had remained unmoved by the 'Rights of Man,' and saw little in Mr. Cobbett's 'Weekly Register' except that he held eccentric views about potatoes, began at last to know the higher plains of a dim political consciousness; and the development had been greatly helped by the recent agitation about the Reform Bill" (*Felix Holt*, 3:44). It would be helped further by the volatile politics of the ensuing decade, 1832–41; no sooner was one election over with, it seemed, than another was required.

As a rule, only in London's scot and lot boroughs, composed of the largest and socially the most diversified electorate existing at the time, had elections previously stirred passionate feelings. With few exceptions, the customary transactions in the country, involving as often as not the rental and sale of seats, had aroused only ephemeral popular interest, if that. To the old shepherd in *Felix Holt*, "that mysterious system of things called 'Government,' . . . whatever it might be, was no business of his, any more than the most out-lying nebula or the coal-sacks [a galaxy] of the southern hemisphere" ("Introduction":6); once the ceremony and chicanery were out of the way, a borough could relapse into its normal apolitical condition. But the effects of the Reform Act reached into every corner of the nation; electoral apathy gradually became a thing of the past. With 217,000 new voters on the polling lists, an increase of some 80 percent, more and more members of the middle class, and therefore of the reading public, had a personal interest in the electoral process. Their stake in the outcome of elections grew as the power and influence of government was increasingly felt in everyday life through such matters of common concern as banking, industrial working hours and conditions, the health hazards in cities, and elementary education. Under a centralized government, national elections were more important to more people than ever before, and more of them lived and voted in the

Most of the pictures in the *Illustrated London News* were intended as sober graphic reportage, as in its depiction (above) of Guildford High Street at election time (29 September 1849). But in its earlier years, seeking to compete with *Punch*, it occasionally ran humorous drawings of topicalities. The Dickensian flavor of the pair (opposite) that appeared in its issue for 26 July 1852 was not accidental: they were drawn by Phiz, who had illustrated the Eatanswill election (see illustration, page 747) sixteen years earlier.

country. In the work of the major novelists the typical constituency being contested was a country borough (Eliot's Duffield, to which the hitherto unfranchised Treby Magna was attached by the act of 1832, or Middlemarch) or a small manufacturing or mining town (Percycross in Trollope's *Ralph the Heir*, Tankerville in his *Phineas Redux*). The only two fictional London elections are in Trollope's *The Way We Live Now* and *Can You Forgive Her?*.

Following the sweeping redistricting of 1832, many more boroughs than those represented by Pelham's Buyemall and Galt's Frailtown escaped from the local magnate's pocket (and some seats, such as the two Sir Pitt Crawley in *Vanity Fair* had owned by descent from his father, were done away with altogether). In the first reformed election in December of that year, genuine contests outnumbered those whose outcome was sealed in advance by two to one, a ratio that was maintained in 1837 and 1847.

The Reform Act reduced the number of pocket boroughs and other

THE SUCCESSFUL CANDIDATE.—DRAWN BY PHIZ.

THE REJECTED CANDIDATE.—DRAWN BY PHIZ.

varieties of safe seats but by no means eliminated them. Old-line borough-mongers like the Marquis of Hertford and the Duke of Newcastle emerged from 1832 almost unscathed. The early fictional accounts of Victorian elections recognize this survival of old practices, but usually by way of showing how unpredictable the electoral process had become. In Bulwer's Lansmere instance, cited above, the former placid accommodation, like that at Fanchester, was rudely disturbed:

> thanks to successive elections, one of these two families had come to an end, and its actual representative was now residing within the Rules of the Bench [i.e., as an insolvent debtor: perhaps he had overspent to protect the seat?]; the head of the other family was the sitting member, and, by an amicable agreement with the Lansmere interest, he remained as neutral as it is in the power of any sitting member to be amidst the passions of an intractable committee. Accordingly, it had been hoped that Egerton would come in without opposition, when . . . a handbill, signed "Haverill Dashmore, Captain, R.N., Baker Street, Portman Square," announced, in very spirited language, the intention of that gentleman "to emancipate the borough from the unconstitutional domination of an oligarchical faction, not with a view to his own political aggrandizement,—indeed, at great personal inconvenience,—but actuated solely by abhorrence to tyranny, and patriotic passion for the purity of election." (*My Novel*, 1.10:1.54)

The unexpected appearance of a challenger to a candidate who, according to local practice, was not expected to be opposed, provided a convenient and credible plot device in more than one novel. In *Hillingdon Hall*, the Duke of Donkeyton's easy assumption that his imbecile son Jeems, the Marquis of Bray, would be sent to Parliament without a contest was destroyed by the sudden advent of William Bowker, whom the cover story accompanying him claimed to be a rich London merchant but who actually was the proprietor of a small snuff shop.

> "God bless us! who ever heard such a thing!" exclaimed the Duke, dropping the paper lifelessly from his hand. "Who ever heard of such a thing!" repeated he, with a sigh; "bearded in one's own county by the Lord knows who! These are the blessings of the Reform Bill. To think that I should have lived to see such a thing! Told Grey and Russell, and all of them, that they were going too far. Never thought to get such a return for giving up my boroughs" (41:407).[†]

[†]Surtees wrote from personal experience to some extent. In 1837 he presented himself as a Tory candidate for Gateshead, seeking to displace the sitting member, a Liberal whom his own party was trying to unseat because of "the irregularity of his private life." A second Tory stood with Surtees, who eventually withdrew from the race to avoid splitting the party's vote. The man with the irregular private life was returned. (Leonard Cooper, *R. S. Surtees* [London, 1952], pp. 69–79.)

That latter-day super-magnate of landowners, the "great Lama" the Duke of Omnium, most men believed, "could send his dog up to the House of Commons as member for West Barsetshire if it so pleased him" (*Framley Parsonage*, 37:2.165). As late as 1867–69, Phineas Finn, who had previously lost, through his acceptance of a government post, the Loughshane seat to which he had been elected, thanks to the influence of the Earl of Tulla, was returned from Loughton. "It was manifestly a great satisfaction to Lord Brentford that he should still have a borough in his pocket, and the more so because there were so very few noblemen left who had such property belonging to them" (*Phineas Finn*, 32:325). But times were changing, and the cruder forms of electoral persuasion, such as evicting tenants who voted the wrong way, were being replaced by subtler forms of tacit understanding. Old Lord Tulla told Phineas: "There isn't a house in the town, you know, let for longer than seven years, and most of them merely from year to year. And, do you know, I haven't a farmer on the property with a lease,—not one; and they don't want leases. They know they're safe. But I do like the people round me to be of the same way of thinking as myself about politics" (33:338). Plantagenet Palliser, the new Duke of Omnium, renounced the influence immemorially vested in men of his rank. As Lady Glencora wrote Ferdinand Lopez, "We used to run a favourite, and our favourite would sometimes win,—would sometimes even have a walk over; but those good times are gone" (*The Prime Minister*, 29:1.269). The seat for Silverbridge was up for grabs—a notable manifestation of the Duke's quiet acceptance of the changed political climate and, incidentally, a radically revised notion of what constituted noblesse oblige. Going a step further than Lord Tulla, he disclaimed any intention of affecting any voter's decision, even as a landlord:

> "I trust [he wrote in a letter] that no elector will vote for this or that gentleman with an idea that the return of any special candidate will please me. The [secret] ballot will of course prevent me or any other man from knowing how an elector may vote;—but I beg to assure the electors generally that should they think fit to return a member pledged to oppose the Government of which I form a part, it would not in any way change my cordial feelings towards the town. I may perhaps be allowed to add that, in my opinion, no elector can do his duty except by voting for the candidate whom he thinks best qualified to serve the country." (*The Prime Minister*, 34:1.312–13)

This was in 1876. Three years later, in the next and concluding Palliser novel, *The Duke's Children*, Trollope reported that "The borough did not altogether enjoy being enfranchised." "Silverbridge had been proud to be honoured by the services of the heir of the house of Omnium, even while that heir had been a Liberal,—had regarded it as so much a matter of course that the borough should be at his disposal that no question as to politics had ever arisen while he retained the seat" (14:105, 104). In its new unfettered condition, the borough "began to feel Conservative predilections," and when young Lord Silverbridge decided to renounce the family's Liberalism and run as a Conservative, there was a natural disposition to vote for him. But the borough's old loyalties, in this case at least, remained strong: The rich local brewer Mr. Du Boung (born Bung) was a strong Liberal and could have run Silverbridge a good race had he, Du Boung, chosen to oppose him; but, recognizing, with Mr. Sprugeon, that the borough "was anxious to sink politics altogether for the moment" (14:111) so as to give the young man a good start in politics, he withdrew and Silverbridge was duly elected.

2.

If the election passages in fiction shared any constant theme, it was the contest between the "old" power—the landed magnates and their extended families—and the "new"—the prosperous townsmen, manufacturers, and financiers represented among the candidates: the industrialist Millbank in *Coningsby*, the (unseen) colliery owner Peter Garstin in *Felix Holt*, the millionaire railway builder Scatcherd in *Doctor Thorne*, the pharmaceutical tycoon Veneering in *Our Mutual Friend*. Whatever their other motives, these men valued the privilege of adding the magic letters M.P. after their names as the surest way of being transformed into gentlemen. Trollope reduced this widespread ambition to absurdity, in the terms of his day, when he wrote of the golden vision of the bootmaker Ontario Moggs in *Ralph the Heir*: "To be a member of Parliament, to speak in that august assembly instead of wasting his eloquence on the beery souls of those who frequented the Cheshire Cheese, to be somebody in the land at his early age,—something so infinitely superior to a maker of boots! A member of Parliament was by law an esquire, and therefore a gentleman" (21:1.250).

It was the nineteenth-century social revolution in microcosm, and nowhere was it more succinctly presented than in *Bleak House*. Sir Leicester Dedlock, unopposed as usual for his own seat, deploys his family forces from Chesney Wold to make doubly sure that his candidates will be elected to the two other "little" seats which "he treats as retail orders of less importance; merely sending down the men, and signifying to the tradespeople, 'You will have the goodness to make these materials into two members of parliament, and to send them home when done.'" But Tulkinghorn brings news: "They [the opposition] have brought in both their people. You are beaten out of all reason. Three to one"—and, worst of all, beaten through the electioneering activity of a prosperous ironmaster, the energetic Watt (Tyler!) Rouncewell, and his son. The lord of Chesney Wold has good reason to snort, stare, and give incoherent voice to the anguished spirit, if not the precise words, of the Duke of Wellington once his campaign against the Reform Bill was lost: "... then upon my honour, upon my life, upon my reputation and principles, the floodgates of society are burst open, and the waters have—a—obliterated the landmarks of the framework of the cohesion by which things are held together!" (40:624–28). Thus Sir Leicester, in the March 1853 number of *Bleak House*. Less than a year later, readers of the fifth part of *The Newcomes* heard from Sir Brian in the same apocalyptic vein:

> "The spirit of radicalism abroad in this country," said Sir Brian Newcome, crushing his eggshell desperately, "is dreadful, really dreadful. We are on the edge of a positive volcano." Down went the egg-spoon into its crater. "The worse sentiments are everywhere publicly advocated; the licentiousness of the press has reached a pinnacle which menaces us with ruin; there is no law which these shameless newspapers respect; no rank which is safe from their attacks; no ancient landmark which the lava flood of democracy does not threaten to overwhelm and destroy." (14:1.159)

To the extent to which Sir Brian's rhetoric, like Sir Leicester's, echoed the flights of some newspaper editorialists, readers would have found appreciable irony in his directing his clichés against the very place where he found them.

At first, it was not easy for the triumphant Liberals to find candidates who would contest seats in behalf of the newly enfranchised business interest. Although the Darlford (Bradford) seat in *Coningsby* was presumed to be safe for the Tory politician Rigby,

> the Liberal deputation from Darlford—two aldermen, three town counsellors, and the Secretary of the Reform Association, were walking about London like mad things, eating luncheons and looking for a candidate. They called at the Reform Club twenty times in the morning, badgered whips and red-tapers, were introduced to candidates, badgered candidates; examined would-be members as if they were at a cattle show, listened to political pedigrees, dictated political pledges, referred to Hansard to see how men had voted, inquired whether men had spoken, finally discussed terms. But they never could hit the right man. If the principles were right, there was no money; and if the money were ready, money would not take pledges. (5.3:331)

But eventually the desired "very rich man" with the correct principles turned up, in the person of Millbank, who had the public-relations advantage (at least from the Liberal standpoint) of being the "personal, inveterate, indomitable foe" of the crusty old borough-monger, Lord Monmouth. Under the old dispensation, the political power centers in the country were at the country houses of the aristocracy and higher squirearchy, and in the towns at the homes or business places of men who were pillars of their community by virtue of their wealth, social standing, or dignity of office, such as the "genteel" Reverend Combermere St. Quintin and the "bluff, hearty, radical wine-merchant" Briggs whom Bulwer's Pelham canvasses in the borough of Buyemall. When a considerable weight of power was transferred to the newly enfranchised boroughs, the "High Street oligarchs," as Disraeli called them in *A Year at Hartlebury*, acquired new importance. They may not have actually had the power to swing the vote, but the presumption that they could do so was reason enough for candidates to single them out for special attention in the course of their electioneering. Once pledged to a candidate, they would, it was assumed, influence electors who were beholden to them to vote the same way. At Fanchester in Disraeli's novel, the Tory leader was the mayor, a jolly brewer named Chumfield, and the senior alderman was Baggs, a retired businessman.

Nowhere else in Victorian fiction can one find so variegated and realistic an assortment of bourgeois characters as in the novelists' sketches of these electors, especially the newly enfranchised ones, who were feeling their oats. In *Felix Holt*, George Eliot painted a whole gallery of them, beginning with Chubb, the publican at the Sugar Loaf, who "was already a forty-shilling householder, and was conscious of a vote for the county. He was not one of those mean-spirited men who found the franchise embarrassing, and would rather have been without it: he regarded his vote as part of his investment, and meant to make the best of it" (11:112–13). This was the self-interested attitude generally expressed at the weekly ordinary at the Marquis inn, Treby Magna, where a whole company of substantial citizens aired their respective views on the political situation as of late 1832: a brewer, a rich butcher, a retired London hosier, a gentleman farmer, a miller, a wool factor—a veritable forum of provincial wise men. George Eliot's fullest portrait of the representative voter, however, is that of the self-important Middlemarch grocer Mawmsey, whom Mr. Brooke canvasses at considerable length, the result being that "Mr. Mawmsey went up and boasted to his wife that he had been rather too many for Brooke of Tipton, and that he didn't mind so much now about going to the poll" (*Middlemarch*, 51:544).

Gradually, as the years passed, the center of gravity of the electorate fell, socially speaking. At least, that is the impression the novelists convey; and one cannot help noticing a certain condescension on their part, as if they wished to imply that such voters as their candidates visited and tried to beguile were not men whom they would be comfortable with in their own homes. Trollope makes clear how the power was distributed in mid-century Barchester:

The aristocracy of Barchester consisted chiefly of clerical dignitaries, bishops, deans, prebendaries, and such like: on them and theirs it was not probable that anything said by Sir Roger would have much effect. Those men
would either abstain from voting, or vote for the railway hero, with the view
of keeping out the De Courcy candidate. Then came the shopkeepers, who
might also be regarded as a stiff-necked generation, impervious to electioneering eloquence. They would, generally, support Mr. Moffat. But there
was an inferior class of voters, ten-pound freeholders, and such like, who,
at this period, were somewhat given to have an opinion of their own, and
over them it was supposed that Sir Roger did obtain some power by his gift
of talking. (*Doctor Thorne*, 17:184)

Three years later (1861), Thackeray, writing as Arthur Pendennis, described Philip Firmin's old Grey Friars schoolmate, Hornblow, working
the old town of Whipham Market:

Baker Jones would not promise no how: that meant Jones would vote for
the Castle, Mr. Hornblow's legal aide-de-camp, Mr. Batley, was forced to
allow. Butcher Brown was having his tea,—his shrill-voiced wife told us,
looking out from her glazed back parlour: Brown would vote for the Castle.
Saddler Briggs would see about it. Grocer Adams fairly said he would vote
against us—against *us?*—against Hornblow. . . . (*The Adventures of Philip*,
42:2.632)

The Second Reform Act of 1867 added 938,000 men, including all
householders and lodgers paying ten pounds a year or more in rent, to
the electoral rolls. The commercial interest, whether that of large-scale
manufacturers or small tradesmen in a market town, now dominated the
electorate. In the Silverbridge of *The Prime Minister*, Sprugeon the ironmonger and Sprout the maker of cork soles called the tune. In the Percycross of *Ralph the Heir*, the centers of power were Spicer the mustard-
maker, Spiveycombe the papermaker, and four boot manufacturers.
The labor they employed were "excellent men, who went in a line to the
poll, and voted just as the master paper-makers and master mustard-
makers desired," though the men in the bootmaking trade were unpredictable, since "All the world over, boots do affect Radical sentiments"
(20:1.238, 239). Griffenbottom, the veteran representative of the borough in Parliament, told his agent Trigger that he would predict "how
nineteen out of twenty men here would vote, if you'd tell me what they
did, and who they were" (25:1.303). The present difficulty at Percycross
stemmed not from the understanding between men and masters, imple-
mented by free beer and half-crowns, which resulted in 324 men duti-
fully voting for one candidate and 272 for the other, but from the presence in the electorate of a whole new segment of voters whose political
leanings and susceptibility to persuasion were as yet untested. The old-

time voters, Trollope said, could be depended upon to follow the established voting pattern, "But among that godless, riotous, ungoverned and
ungovernable set of new householders, there was no knowing how to
act. They would take the money and then vote wrong. They would take
the money and then split." (29:2.2).

When Trollope wrote this in 1870–71, it was possible to know
whether a man gave value for the money received, because the old system of casting one's vote verbally before a registrar was still in effect. But
in 1874, when the secret ballot was first used in national elections, the
uncertainty became absolute. In novels appearing within a year of each
other in 1874–75, Trollope and Meredith made the same point. "Men
who heretofore had known, or thought that they knew, how elections
would go, who counted up promises, told off professed enemies, and
weighed the doubtful ones, now confessed themselves to be in the dark,"
remarked Trollope in *The Way We Live Now* (63:505–6). Seymour Austin, the Tory agent, confessed to Colonel Halkett in *Beauchamp's Career*
that "the number for him who appealed to feelings and quickened the
romantic sentiments of the common people now huddled within our
electoral penfold, was not calculable." "No one," he said, "could tell the
effect of an extended franchise. The untried venture of [the present
contest] depressed him" (18:1.177–78).

The fiction of the period, especially Trollope's, faithfully recorded
these momentous changes in the nation's political base and the recurrent
uncertainties, the upsetting of assumptions derived from long experience, that they entailed. In their narratives of elections in fictitious boroughs, the novelists dramatized phenomena that otherwise were chroni-
cled more diffusely, and on the whole less entertainingly, in the political
columns of the press.[†]

3.

The fixed sequence of events in an electoral contest gave novelists a
ready-made framework on which to hang a segment of their narrative.

[†] Because the malpractices and downright venality of elections in Victorian fiction will
occupy an increasing proportion of the space in the rest of this chapter and the entire next
one, a word should be said here about their truth to life. Historians sometimes accuse
novelists of misrepresenting the actuality, but in this case the misrepresentation takes the
unusual form of understatement rather than exaggeration. "The traditional Eatanswill
picture of early Victorian elections," says Norman Gash, "is in fact not so much an exaggerated as a pale and euphemistic version of the contemporary scene. No doubt it was
jocularly characteristic of some smaller rural boroughs but in comparison with what actu-

First there was the candidate's decision to run, followed by his appointment of a committee and an agent (campaign manager), the publication of his "address" (announcement of his candidacy) on posters and in the local press, and the beginning of arduous canvassing of the electors on the poll books. On nomination day the candidates delivered speeches to the crowd of voters and nonvoters, usually from the balcony of a tavern that served as the campaign headquarters or of another conveniently situated building. At the end of the speechifying a show of hands was called for. Sometimes a winner was declared on the spot, but more often, at least in fictional accounts where the suspense had to be maintained, the loser demanded a formal poll on the following day. The man at the top of the poll—two, in the case of boroughs with multiple representation—then went to Parliament. But sometimes there was an epilogue in the form of a petition to Parliament alleging corruption, and the issue was submitted to a committee appointed by the speaker of the House of Commons. (In 1852 these were replaced by ad hoc royal commissions, which gave way in turn, in 1868, to the regular courts of law.) If bribery or other criminal offenses were proved, the candidate would lose his seat and perhaps pay a heavy fine, and in particularly flagrant cases the borough might be disfranchised.

Prospective candidates might issue their addresses whenever an election was anticipated, but the first formal notification to the electors, following the dissolution of Parliament or an incumbent's vacating his seat before the end of the session, was a writ sent down from Westminster. Then the placards proliferated in a riot of eye-catching color, both in the paper stock itself and in the scarehead type of the captions. They were pasted on local walls with the lavishness equaled only, in the larger towns at any rate, by advertisements of boot blacking and quack medicines. In contested elections, the battle between rival candidates was joined with these opening salvos, which had been a customary feature of elections for more than a century; parodies of their content and style had often been printed as opposition propaganda in the course of especially heated campaigns. Addresses belonged to either of two classes: those composed of florid rhetoric that concealed—or failed to conceal—a total lack of ideas, or at least of any that a reasonable person

---

ally happened in many constituencies Dickens's account is under-drawn, conventional, and staid." (*Politics in the Age of Peel*, p. 147.) Gash provides impressive documentation of all the electoral abuses (down to 1850) described in fiction. Or, put another way, the present pages draw from fiction a series of toned-down "illustrations" of the corrupt and violent practices that are spread at large in the historical record.

Most news pictures of Victorian elections sought to communicate the excitement on the streets and before the hustings, but this one, in the *Illustrated London News* for 28 February 1846, is remarkable for its almost apathetic quality. Appearances, however, are deceiving. The election at Newark, where the county seat for South Nottinghamshire was being contested, was of almost unique interest, because it pitted the borough-mongering Duke of Newcastle against his own son, the incumbent. See the illustration on page 777.

could take exception to, and those that clearly set forth a candidate's position on current issues. Agents favored the kind of address that was adroitly noncommittal, "espoused no principle, and yet professed what all parties would allow was the best." Such was Pelham's vacuous address to the electors of Buyemall:

> In presenting myself to your notice, I advance a claim not altogether new and unfounded. My family have for centuries been residing amongst you, and exercising that interest which reciprocal confidence and good offices may fairly create. Should it be my good fortune to be chosen your representative, you may rely upon my utmost endeavors to deserve that honor. One word upon the principles I espouse: they are those which have found their advocates among the wisest and the best; they are those which, hostile alike to the encroachments of the crown and the licentiousness of the people, would support the real interests of both. Upon these grounds, gen-

tlemen, I have the honor to solicit your votes; and it is with the sincerest respect for your ancient and honorable body, that I subscribe myself your very obedient servant,

HENRY PELHAM"

(*Pelham*, 1.35:1.184)

Sir Barnes Newcome's address to his late father's constituents was a shade more specific but still a masterpiece of fence-sitting to which only a convinced Chartist, or some other inveterate malcontent, could object when it appeared in the local papers the day after Sir Brian's funeral:

That he was a staunch friend of our admirable constitution need not be said. That he was a firm but conscientious upholder of our Protestant religion, all who knew Barnes Newcome must be aware. That he would do his utmost to advance the interests of this great agricultural, this great manufacturing county and borough, we may be assured he avowed; as that he would be (if returned to represent Newcome in Parliament) the advocate of every rational reform, the unhesitating opponent of every reckless innovation. (*The Newcomes*, 48:2.112)

"[T]he less we put in it the better," the Duke of Donkeyton advised Mr. Smoothington, his lawyer, as they began to concoct an address for the Marquis of Bray, and Surtees describes the caution with which they weighed each phrase (*Hillingdon Hall*, 41:402–7). The product was flawless from the Duke's point of view, except that it omitted any mention of the Corn Laws at a time when every candidate was expected to take a stand on the repeal question no matter how evasive he might be on every other issue. Letters of inquiry from the Anti-Corn Law League went unanswered, and the omission impelled the league to bring down the London snuff dealer to contest the seat.

In contrast to the studied evasiveness of the Buyemall and Donkeyton documents and the sweeping, safe generalities of the Newcome one, Surtees's own address when he stood for Gateshead in 1837 was a model of forthrightness, as an excerpt dealing with the current debate over ecclesiastical reform demonstrates:

As a friend to the Church, I would support such a Measure of Reform as will provide for the improved Discipline of the Establishment, the Abolition of Sinecures, the apportioning of Emoluments to Duty, and the Prohibition of Pluralities, at the same time, I am desirous of relieving the Dissenters from Payments to which they entertain conscientious Objections, provided such Measure of Relief does not tend to compromise the Principle of a National Religion. I will not support any Measure either for this country or Ireland that appropriates any Portion of the Revenues of the Church to other than Religious Purposes, or that in any way weakens the Protestant Institutions of the Land.[3]

Faced with the choice between the address that said nothing and the one that said much, Samuel Warren decided to have both Tittlebat Titmouse (Reform) and Geoffrey Lovel Delamere (Tory) lay their respective positions on the line when they fought for the Yatton seat.[†] Forty years later, Nevil Beauchamp's address was, on Meredith's authority, forthright and explicit: "ultra-Radical: museums to be opened on Sundays; ominous references to the [Irish] Land question, etc.; no smooth passing mention of Reform, such as the Liberal, become stately, adopts in speaking of that property of his, but swinging blows on the heads of many a denounced iniquity" (*Beauchamp's Career*, 11:1.104).

As the electioneering progressed, the pasted-up addresses (which were also printed in the local newspapers that supported the respective candidates) were supplemented from day to day with freshly printed posters and handbills in which the candidates stoked the fires by trading insults and propagating rumors and warnings, and condensed their views into reductive slogans: JORROCKS THE FARMER'S FRIEND![‡] and TITMOUSE AND PURITY OF ELECTIONS! TITMOUSE AND NEGRO EMANCIPATION! TITMOUSE AND CHEAP ALE! TITMOUSE AND QUARTERLY PARLIAMENTS, VOTE BY BALLOT, AND UNIVERSAL SUFFRAGE! (*Ten Thousand a Year*, 27:707)—these last constituting a package that went beyond the imaginings of the most far-out Radicals. The half-crazy ex-poacher and pot-

[†]Warren recorded the purpose of the extended election narrative in *Ten Thousand a Year* in a letter to Alexander Blackwood, publisher of *Blackwood's Magazine*, on 7 January 1841: "It was only last night that I began my new chapter. I shall now paint an election to my own perfect satisfaction. I don't mean the mere external humors of one, which have been done a million times; but as one has never hitherto been painted. I mean *real*, the philosophy and the fact of elections, the true agencies at work, as by manoeuvring, management, bribery, etc., etc. Gammon on one side and Mr. Crafty, a skillful electioneering agent, on the other. How these two admirable heads really fight the whole battle under cover of the humbug of the usual display of bands, placards, canvassing, etc. It will be hard, true, exciting; for I am going to make the election uncertain to the last moment. Then comes the election [i.e., petition] committee and I will show them up in *fine style*." Fearing prosecution, Blackwood hesitated to publish the narrative as it stood, but Warren cited the opinion of friends at the bar, including the eminent lawyer Sir Frederick Pollock, that "Not a tittle of it should be lost to the public and to posterity," and after some further discussion Blackwood capitulated and the election narrative was published, with what changes we do not know. (Margaret Oliphant, *Annals of a Publishing House* [New York, 1897], 2:217–25.) Later, Warren, a practicing lawyer, published a *Manual of the Parliamentary Election Law of the United Kingdom* (1852) and a *Manual of the Law and Practice of Election Committees* (1853). He was M.P. for Midhurst, 1856–59.

[‡]This was the famous sobriquet conferred on the Duke of Buckingham and Chandos, a leader of the protectionist cause, by his fellow agriculturalists. It was altered and parodically applied to fictional characters such as Sir Joseph Bowley (= Lord Brougham) in *The Chimes*, "The Poor Man's Friend."

house frequenter Tommy Trounsem in *Felix Holt*, who was hired to paste up bills in the Transome interest, had a larger role in the novel than as the victim of a trick by which he unknowingly—because he was illiterate—put up those of the rival candidate: he was the crucial agent in the denouement of the Transome inheritance plot.

At Barchester, the voters were forcibly reminded of Scatcherd's notorious failing:

> There was . . . a great daub painted up on sundry walls, on which a navvy, with a pimply, bloated face, was to be seen standing on a railway bank, leaning on a spade, holding a bottle in one hand, while he invited a comrade to drink. "Come, Jack, shall us have a drop of some'at short?" were the words coming out of the navvy's mouth; and under this was painted in huge letters, "THE LAST NEW BARONET."
>
> But Mr. Moffat hardly escaped on easier terms. The trade by which his father had made his money was as well known as that of the railway contractor; and every possible symbol of tailordom was displayed in graphic portraiture on the walls and hoardings of the city. He was drawn with his goose, with his scissors, with his needle, with his tapes; he might be seen measuring, cutting, stitching, pressing, carrying home his bundle, and presenting his little bill; and under each of these representations was repeated his own motto, "England's honour." (*Doctor Thorne*, 17:180)

In *Can You Forgive Her?* Mr. Smithers, a London printer in a small way of business, complains to Scruby, George Vavasor's agent, that he has not been paid for the thirty thousand posters he had printed for another candidate in the recent Marylebone election. (Candidates of a given party were usually held responsible for their predecessors' unpaid expenses.) Even granting the wide expanses of London walls that beckoned bill stickers, so great a quantity would seem to represent overkill, if not large-scale waste. But the experienced agent believed in the efficacy of these as well as the six-foot-high pasteboard placards, bearing the slogan VOTE FOR VAVASOR AND THE RIVER BANK, that towered over the men he hired to carry them—twenty-four men, in fact, walking in close single file.

The battle of posters and handbills was no less rough at Bevisham when Beauchamp contested the seat. His much gossiped-about relation with Renée, the young French widow, made him vulnerable to the Tory attack. The electors were handed a verse broadside: "O did you ever, hot in love, a little British middy see, / Like Orpheus asking what the deuce to do without Eurydice?" "The middy" (Meredith wrote) "is jilted by his FRENCH MARQUEES, whom he 'did adore,' and in his wrath he recommends himself to the wealthy widow Bevisham, concerning whose choice of her suitors there is a doubt: but the middy is encouraged to

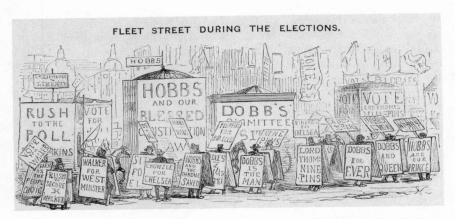

FLEET STREET DURING THE ELECTIONS.

Election time in London intensified the traffic congestion, because the sandwich men and vans hired by shopkeepers and brand-name manufacturers (see illustration, page 442) had to compete with the additional contingents hired by cancandidates. "Fleet Street," said *Punch* (17 July 1847), "will represent a series of placards which those who run may read, if running in Fleet Street were not always made impossible by the blockage to which it is subjected."

persevere: "'Up, up, my pretty middy; take a draught of foaming Sillery; / Go in and win the widdy with your Radical artillery'" (17:1.171).

Posters could accommodate no more than a paragraph or so, and handbills not much more, but their messages were elaborated by the speeches candidates delivered from the hustings. As professional users of language, novelists naturally had as keen an ear for bombast as for George Robins's promotional panegyrics, and some had a relish for writing pastiche, so that their election scenes not only contain suitably crafted initial addresses but abound with speeches—harangues would often be a more accurate word—delivered to audiences that were anything but docile or inattentive, even though a single speech, by Aubrey Bohun or Rigby, for example, might last two hours. In *Pickwick Papers*, Dickens set the tone of much subsequent fictional reporting of election speeches:

> The speeches of the two candidates, though differing in every other respect, afforded a beautiful tribute to the merit and high worth of the electors of Eatanswill. Both expressed their opinion that a more independent, a more enlightened, a more public-spirited, a more noble-minded, a more disinterested set of men than those who had promised to vote for him, never existed on earth; each darkly hinted his suspicions that the electors in the opposite interest had certain swinish and besotted infirmities which rendered them unfit for the exercise of the important duties they were called

upon to discharge. Fizkin expressed his readiness to do anything he was wanted; Slumkey, his determination to do nothing that was asked of him. Both said that the trade, the manufactures, the commerce, the prosperity of Eatanswill, would ever be dearer to their hearts than any earthly object; and each had it in his power to state, with the utmost confidence, that he was the man who would eventually be returned. (13:254–55)

Dickens retained the strong antipathy to electioneering verbiage that he had acquired during his brief stint reporting elections in Essex and Suffolk for the *Morning Chronicle* in 1835–36.[†] His parody of Veneering's speech at Pocket-Breaches, thirty years later, shows that his disrespect for politicians and their mouthed platitudes and downright absurdities had not diminished in that time.

Some novelists treated the views expressed in their election sequences more seriously. The lengthy speeches (though not by candidates) in *Felix Holt*, first by the unidentified "grimy man in a flannel shirt, hatless and with turbid red hair, who was insisting on political points with much more ease than had seemed to belong to the gentleman speakers on the hustings" (30:245), and then by the well-washed Felix Holt in rebuttal, embodied important issues, no matter how unsystematically and colloquially expressed.

Trollope increased his readers' respect for the crude-mannered Sir Roger Scatcherd by depicting his capability on the hustings. The railway builder's "eloquence," Trollope wrote, "was of a rough kind; but not perhaps the less operative on those for whom it was intended" (*Doctor Thorne*, 12:184). Uneducated and alcoholic though he was, he was no fool; on the contrary, he proved himself an adroit rhetorician as he exploited his hearers' prejudice against both tailors and London interlopers as personified by his opponent, Moffat. His device was the familiar and effective one of making a tactical concession in order to set up his adversary for a knockout punch:

"Why, he isn't even a tailor. I wish he were. There's always some good in a fellow who knows how to earn his own bread. But he isn't a tailor; he can't even put a stitch in towards mending England's honour. His father was a tailor; not a Barchester tailor, mind you, so as to give him any claim on your affections; but a London tailor. Now the question is, do you want to send the son of a London tailor up to parliament to represent you?" (17:187)

[†] He also had an excellent chance to watch corruption in action in towns long notorious for venality. At Sudbury, for example, from which he dated a dispatch on 14 January 1835, it was said that "the total sums spent on bribery averaged over £30 per voter." At Ipswich, also visited by Dickens on this assignment, the result was declared void on grounds of bribery.

One short step backward, then a long step forward: Sir Roger knew no more of Quintilian than Mrs. George Hudson knew of Marcus Aurelius, but his instinctive mastery of the classical method would have enabled him to hold his own with Oxbridge graduates on the hustings.

One constantly senses in the fictional descriptions of elections an undercurrent of derision, even if it applies to the occasion—the central event in the still suspect ceremonial of democratic politics—more than to the ideas advanced. If George Eliot could be in dead earnest in *Felix Holt*, she could also write the funniest election scene in all Victorian fiction, Mr. Brooke's disastrous attempt at speechmaking to the assembled weavers and tanners of Middlemarch. His self-diagnosis, that "his ideas stood rather in the way when he was speaking," was an inadequate view of the case. For George Eliot to have had her speakers in *Felix Holt* interrupted by heckling would have subverted her ideological intention, but since Mr. Brooke's speech was without content, there was no harm in her bringing into the Middlemarch fiasco a genuinely inspired form of heckling, one involving a ventriloquist and a painted effigy, though these worked separately, not as in a puppet show:

> At one and the same moment there had risen above the shoulders of the crowd, nearly opposite Mr. Brooke, and within ten yards of him, the effigy of himself; buff-coloured waistcoat, eye-glass, and neutral physiognomy, painted on rag; and there had arisen apparently in the air, like the note the cuckoo, a parrot-like, Punch-voiced echo of his words. Everybody looked up at the open windows in the houses at the opposite angles of the converging streets; but they were either blank, or filled by laughing listeners. The most innocent echo has an impish mockery in it when it follows a gravely persistent speaker, and this echo was not at all innocent; if it did not follow with the precision of a natural echo, it had a wicked choice of the words it overtook. (*Middlemarch*, 51:547–48)

"The invisible Punch" persisted in its echoing of Brooke's fatuous remarks, with ironic interpolations of its own, until Brooke had to retreat, the final indignity being "a hail of eggs, chiefly aimed at the image," some of which splashed the original as well.

Another well-aimed egg, landing on Gustavus Moffat's "well-plaited shirt" and reducing him "to speechless despair," concluded the election scene in *Doctor Thorne*. He too was a victim of incessant heckling, but in the course of the scene Trollope had made a striking distinction between the candidate who could take it and the one who could not. Sir Roger Scatcherd met the constant irreverent interruptions from the crowd with the same aplomb with which he parried with his stick a dead cat flung from their midst; the repeated references to his love of brandy never fazed him. And so, having converted his would-be tormentors into true

This picture of John Jorrocks addressing the crowd from the hustings prior to the Sellborough election in *Hillingdon Hall* is surprisingly decorous when compared with Surtees's text. It conveys none of the boisterousness of Jorrocks's extemporaneous remarks or the interjections of his cheerleader, the irrepressible Pigg (foreground).

believers from the portico of his headquarters inn, the Dragon of Wantley, he handed them over to his rival at the White Horse, with the result represented by the egg.

Sir Roger had doubtless steeled himself for his ordeal by recourse to his favorite stimulant. We do not know whether Moffat had taken anything, but it is clear that Mr. Brooke's incapacity to dominate, let alone persuade, an audience was intensified by the imprudent glass or two of sherry he had taken before he rose to what was to have been his great moment. John Jorrocks, like Scatcherd a master of rough eloquence, drew considerable sustenance from the same source as Sir Roger. His relaxed, unrehearsed speech to the voters of Sellborough, with his drunken, tobacco juice-drooling aide-de-camp Pigg bellowing clerklike responses, brought *Hillingdon Hall* to a tumultuous final curtain.

One of the most farcical aspects of the Eatanswill election, as the countless readers of *Pickwick Papers* remembered it, was the pitched battle between the town's rival newspapers, the *Gazette* and the *Independent*.

Fine newspapers they were. Such leading articles, and such spirited attacks!—"Our worthless contemporary, the Gazette"—"That disgraceful and
dastardly journal, the Independent"—"That false and scurrilous print, the
Independent"—"That vile and slanderous calumniator, the Gazette"; these,
and other spirit-stirring denunciations were strewn plentifully over the columns of each, in every number, and excited feelings of the most intense
delight and indignation in the bosoms of the townspeople. (13:238)

Nowhere else in Victorian fiction did journalists' political differences
take so comic a turn. But the newspapers of a town undergoing an election were often brought into the picture, thus adding to the reader's
general sense of verisimilitude. At Treby Magna in 1832, the *North Loamshire Herald* and the *Duffield Watchman* were the "large-minded guides of
public opinion" that judiciously, but with intemperate language, interpreted Harold Transome's embracing the liberal cause. At Newcome, a
Mr. Potts—no relation to the editor of the *Eatanswill Gazette*—edited the
Independent, which came out strongly against Sir Barnes Newcome, the
sitting member and choice of the opposition *Sentinel*, and in favor of
the untested, impractical Colonel Newcome. A smashing editorial contained a thread of innuendo that was intelligible to any reader who had
heard the local rumors of Barnes's cruel treatment of his wife and read,
in an adjacent column, a critical article, written by Warrington, on
Barnes's late lecture at the Newcome Athenaeum:

The performance of our talented representative last night was so pathetic
as to bring tears into the eyes of several of our fair friends. We have heard,
but never believed until now, that Sir Barnes Newcome possessed such a
genius for *making women cry*. Last week we had the talented Miss Noakes
from Slowcome, reading Milton to us; how far superior was the eloquence
of Sir Barnes Newcome Newcome, Bart., even to that of the celebrated actress! Bets were freely offered in the room last night that Sir Barnes would
beat any woman,—bets which were not taken, as we scarcely need say, so well
do our citizens appreciate the character of our excellent, our admirable
representative. (*The Newcomes*, 67:2.305)

The most prominent role a newspaper played in the narrative of a
Victorian election was that of the *Middlemarch Pioneer*, which Mr. Brooke
secretly bought to further his political ambitions. "What business has an
old county man to come currying favour with a low set of dark-blue
freemen?" demanded Mr. Hawley, the lawyer. "As to his paper, I only
hope he may do the writing himself. It would be worth our paying for."
Hawley was to be disappointed. Brooke brought in—a dangerous choice
for staid Middlemarch—Will Ladislaw, "a very brilliant young fellow,"
according to Mr. Hackbutt, the rich tanner. "who can write the highest
style of leading article, quite equal to anything in the London papers";

but once he took on the editorship, Middlemarch saw in him "a quill-driving alien, a foreign emissary, and what not" (*Middlemarch*, 37:393; 38:414)—the "what not" including a striking resemblance to a Byronic hero. Ladislaw might compose eloquent arguments for Reform and publish them in the *Pioneer*, but the *Trumpet*, the rival, anti-Reform paper, kept the attention of the town by its attack on Brooke (unnamed) as "the most retrogressive man in the county" and, later, by an assault on Ladislaw himself, as a dangerous Radical. "What can you expect with these peddling Middlemarch papers?" asked the wise rector, Mr. Cadwallader (38:417, 415).

Despite all the attention Trollope devotes to contemporary politics, his allusions to the press do not, as a rule, reflect the power it had by then acquired. The only local paper he refers to is the *Baslehurst Gazette* in *Rachel Ray*, which printed letters "which advocated the right of any constituency to send a Jew to Parliament if it pleased, but which proved at the same time that any constituency must be wrong to send any Jew to Parliament, and that the constituency of Baslehurst would in the present instance be specially wrong to send Mr. Hart [a Jewish clothing merchant with shops in Houndsditch and Regent Street] to Parliament" (24:313–14). In subsequent novels, national newspapers, real or fictitious, figured in various contexts, though none had the prominence that the *Times* enjoyed, as the *Jupiter*, in the Barchester novels. After Phineas Finn declines Quintus Slide's proposal that he vacate the Loughton seat at the next election in his, Slide's, favor, that odious journalist publishes in his rag, the *People's Banner*, "a startling article, a tremendous article, showing the pressing necessity of immediate reform, and proving the necessity by an illustration of the borough-mongering rottenness of the whole system" (*Phineas Finn*, 33:346)—an argument weakened, for Trollope's readers, by their knowledge that the coveted seat was for a pocket borough, and Slide was ready enough to sacrifice his high principle if he could obtain it.

Ontario Moggs was the only Trollope candidate, running for a provincial borough, to have his speeches reported in the national press. But his was a special case—he had been dropped as a Liberal candidate because of his outspoken radicalism, and thus was an outsider—and he was variously useful to the London papers:

> The record of his election doings would have been confined to the columns of the *Percycross Herald* had he carried on his candidature after the usual fashion; but, as it was now, his doings were blazoned in the London newspapers. The *Daily News* reported him, and gave him an article all to himself; and even the *Times* condescended to make an example of him, and to bring him up as evidence that revolutionary doctrines were distasteful to the electors of the country generally. (*Ralph the Heir*, 26:1. 312–13)

Trollope says nothing about the press's coverage of the subsequent official inquiry into the perennial Percycross corruption, but he does note
how the national papers handled the later investigation into the electoral
sins of the equally corrupt Tankerville (in *Phineas Redux*):

> Two or three London papers had printed leading articles, giving in detail
> the salient points of the old sinner's [Browborough's] criminality, and ex-
> pressing a conviction that now, at least, would the real criminal be pun-
> ished . . . Some papers boldly defended him, ridiculed the Commissioners,
> and declared that the trial was altogether an absurdity. The People's Ban-
> ner, setting at defiance with an admirable audacity all the facts as given in
> the Commissioners' report, declared that there was not one tittle of evi-
> dence against Mr. Browborough. . . . (44:359)

The election in *The Way We Live Now* pitted the company promoter Augustus Melmotte against a London journalist, Ferdinand Alf, editor of
the *Evening Pulpit*. But the power of the press, which manifested itself
by way of printing damaging rumors about Melmotte, the Merdle of the
new day, fell short of sending Alf to Parliament: Melmotte beat him by
"something not much less than a thousand votes" (64:520).†

The provincial press assumed an important role once more in Victorian fiction when Beauchamp, a novice in politics, reads a leading article in the *Bevisham Gazette*, extolling him in language usually found only
in the great national papers. The author turns out to be Timothy Turbot, veteran of many campaigns—Corn Law repeal, Reform, "and all
manifestly popular movements requiring the heaven-endowed man of
speech, an interpreter of multitudes, and a prompter." His place was on
the platform, since he had a golden tongue and mesmeric presence. He
should have been more than the editor of a country newspaper, but "the
report was that he worshipped the nymph Whisky" (*Beauchamp's Career*,
14:1.136, 139). However that might have been, Turbot was a master of
practical politics, and his advice furnished Beauchamp with a much-
needed insight into the way seats were actually won.

4.

Masterminding the election was the candidate's agent, a real-life figure
who turned up so often in fictional narratives that he can be fairly said

---

†Two novelists seized upon the occasion furnished by elections to illustrate, facetiously,
the discrepancy between what actually was said at a news event and what the papers
printed. In *Ten Thousand a Year*, Warren printed the text of one of Titmouse's incoherent
speeches as taken down by a shorthand reporter and the same speech as it was printed in
the *Yorkshire Stingo* (stingo = strong beer). In *Hillingdon Hall*, Surtees compared the cov-

to be a stock character—a genuinely new one, as much of a novelty as an engine driver or a photographer. The profession he represented was a spinoff from the type of London lawyers who handled landowners' business and family affairs. Among these affairs were the pocket boroughs their clients owned and wished to profit by, and one of the agent's tasks was to find a person like Archibald Jobbry, in *The Member*, who was in the market to rent or buy a sure seat. This function widened in time, so that some attorneys set themselves up as brokers, or political dating bureaus, matching boroughs and would-be candidates when both were in the market. Then, by another natural evolution, agents, who came euphemistically to be called "parliamentary attorneys," hired themselves out to manage campaigns in individual boroughs, even going so far as to advertise their services in metropolitan newspapers.

Beginning in the mid-1830s, such men were among the most prominent witnesses before the special committees that investigated charges of bribery in especially venal constituencies, and the testimony elicited from them indelibly associated them, as a class, with unsavory electoral goings-on. The connotative names borne by some of their fictional counterparts are sufficient evidence of the kind of reputation they had: Crafty and Barnabas Bloodsuck (*Ten Thousand a Year*), Nearthewinde and Closerstil (*Doctor Thorne*), Scruby (*Can You Forgive Her?*—an especially apt name, with its multiple suggestions of twistiness, applying pressure, haggling, and, in the slang of the time, tipsiness), Molescroft (*Phineas Redux*: a combination of stealth and craftiness), Sharpit and Longfite (*Rachel Ray*). There were, in addition, Perker in *Pickwick Papers*, Scrimshaw in *The Semi-Attached Couple*, Chace in *A Year at Hartlebury*, Pilson in *Ruth*, Trigger in *Ralph the Heir*, and Johnson, Jermyn, Makepiece (later spelled Makepeace), and Putty in *Felix Holt*.

Crafty in *Ten Thousand a Year* personified this shady branch of the legal profession, success in which required resourcefulness, guile, and lack of scruple, the condoning if not the overt encouragement of a variety of questionable practices. He was seen at his best when engaged in deep machinations against Oily Gammon, Titmouse's lawyer, a partner in the Saffron Hill firm of Quirk, Gammon, and Snap. The highest accolade a candidate—especially one with an inactive conscience—could bestow on an agent was the one that Undecimus Scott, in *The Three Clerks*, conferred on his own, one M'Cleury: "a thorough rascal, but no man does better work" (29:351).

Trollope argued that the strengthening of the laws against bribery in

---

erage of Jorrocks's hustings performance in the *Dozey Independent* with that in the *Church and State Gazette*.

1854 left a candidate with no choice but to hire a lawyer who knew how to skirt them: "All these stringent bribery laws only enhance the value of such very safe men as Mr. Nearthewinde. To him, stringent laws against bribery are the strongest assurance of valuable employment. Were these laws of a nature to be evaded with ease, any indifferent attorney might manage a candidate's affairs and enable him to take his seat with security" (*Doctor Thorne*, 22:236).

George Eliot, ever the moralist, took a more serious view of the professional agent:

> To have the pleasure and the praise of electioneering ingenuity, and also to get paid for it, without too much anxiety whether the ingenuity will achieve its ultimate end, perhaps gives to some select persons a sort of satisfaction in their superiority to their more agitated fellow-men that is worthy to be classed with those generous enjoyments of having the truth chiefly to yourself, and of seeing others in danger of drowning while you are high and dry, which seem to have been regarded as unmixed privileges by Lucretius and Lord Bacon. (*Felix Holt*, 30:243)

Eliot was referring to Johnson, the London agent, and Jermyn, the local one who was also lawyer to the Transome family. These conspiring attorneys, unlike such figures as Crafty and Perker, were not mere stock figures in a comic plot; they were deeply involved in the Durfey-Transome inheritance intrigue.

No novelist depicted a professional agent who was genuinely committed to whatever principles were espoused by the candidate he worked for. An election was an election, and once his job of work was over, the agent was free to sign up with whatever fresh candidate or party required his services. One character in fiction, however, served as a self-appointed, unpaid agent for a cause to which he was devoted, that of ousting Barnes Newcome from his seat and replacing him with his uncle the Colonel. Though a total novice in the trade, Frederick Bayham quickly learned its tricks. "I am afraid, in his conduct of the Colonel's election," wrote Thackeray in the person of Arthur Pendennis,

> Mr. Bayham resorted to acts of which his principal certainly would disapprove, and engaged auxiliaries whose alliance was scarcely creditable. Whose was the hand which flung the potato which struck Sir Barnes Newcome, Bart., on the nose as he was haranguing the people from the "Roebuck"? How came it that whenever Sir Barnes and his friends essayed to speak, such an awful yelling and groaning took place in the crowd below, that the words of those feeble orators were inaudible? Who smashed all the front windows of the "Roebuck"? Colonel Newcome had not words to express his indignation at proceedings so unfair. (*The Newcomes*, 69:2.321)

In contrast to the low-keyed scene from *Hillingdon Hall*, Richard Doyle's exuberant portrayal of the contest between "Old Tom" Newcome and his nephew, Sir Barnes, enhances the effect of Thackeray's text (chapter 69, "The Election"), which is achieved by an orderly narrative and series of vignettes rather than by the riotous mob scene Doyle supplied.

These were routine devices, to be sure. But no old pro could have topped Bayham's most inspired stunt—driving through the streets a brougham in which was comfortably ensconced an ancient family retainer, Mrs. Mason. Now senile, she wore a shawl and brooch the Colonel had sent her from India, tangible evidence of his affectionate attention during the long years when he was abroad and Barnes totally neglected her. "Look at him, boys!" cried Bayham as the carriage, now drawn by enthusiastic members of the crowd, pulled up at the King's Arms, from which the Colonel emerged to greet the old lady. "Look at him; the dear old boy! Isn't he an old trump? Which will you have for your Member, Barnes Newcome or Old Tom?"† (69:2.325).

Since the polling had already shown a strong trend toward the Colonel, this touching stage-managed reunion was not needed to ensure his victory. That the borough voted Barnes out and his old uncle in was due to the strong local feeling that had developed against Barnes. This animosity outweighed the fact that Bayham was an interloper from London, and the Colonel somewhat so, because, though his roots were here, he had been absent for many years. Agents and candidates from outside the electoral district had a built-in disadvantage, a result of the xenophobia which led people in settled rural or town communities to regard Londoners with suspicion and outright resentment. As far as the voters were concerned, an election was their private turf. Traditionally, at least one of the candidates, if not actually a resident, was attached to the borough by virtue of being sponsored by the leading magnate. Therefore, men without any such ties who came down from the metropolis to manipulate the borough's electoral strength, whether as candidates or candidates' agents, were unwelcome. Johnson, in *Felix Holt*, was from Bedford Row,

---

†Bayham's fine Macchiavellian hand is discernible in another trick on the same occasion, when two ragamuffins were presented to the crowd as "Barnes's children." "What can a factory girl expect from such a fine high-bred, white-handed, aristocratic gentleman as Sir Barnes Newcome, Baronet," a factory-hand orator demanded, "but to be cajoled, and seduced, and deserted, and left to starve! When she has served my lord's pleasure, her natural fate is to be turned into the street; let her go and rot there, and her child beg in the gutter" (69:2.323–24). Barnes instantly denounced the attribution, and the speaker admitted that the children were "a precious pair of lazy little scamps" belonging to someone else, but the damage was done. The stunt inevitably recalled to voters' minds a more or less forgotten scandal in Barnes's youth, when he was known both in the town of Newcome and in the London clubs to have seduced a poor factory girl, who followed him to London "with a child on each side of her" and could be removed from his father's Park Lane doorstep only by his promise to maintain them. She reappeared in a pew at St. George's, Hanover Square, when Barnes was being married to Lady Clara Pulleyn in the presence of an invited fashionable crowd, and was removed by two policemen, who "laughed at one another, and nodded their heads knowingly as the poor wretch with her whimpering boys was led away" (30:1.323; 36:1.394).

London; his local colleague had to assure Harold Transome that he was a "a first-rate man . . . who understands these matters thoroughly—a solicitor of course—he has carried no end of men into Parliament" (2:38). Crafty and Nearthewinde, among others, came down from London.

And so with candidates. When Prigmore, an emissary from the Whig stronghold in London, came down to Hartlebury he was met with cries of "Send him back to town!" (*A Year at Hartlebury*, 2.2:112) In *Rachel Ray*, a man whose forefathers had sat in dozens of parliaments found himself opposed by one who had two counts, perhaps three, against him: he was a Londoner, a Jew, and a rich tradesman (a clothier). In Bulwer-Lytton's *My Novel*, Captain Dashmore was called "the Man from Baker Street," with clearly disparaging intent. The fat Carbottle, standing for Polpenno in *The Duke's Children*, may have had no inconvenient fixed opinions, but what really damned him were Frank's pointed questions: "Who was Mr. Carbottle? Why had he come to Polpenno? Who had sent for him? Why Mr. Carbottle rather than anybody else? Did not the people of Polpenno think that it might be as well to send Mr. Carbottle back to the place from whence he had come?" (55:439) Even the inoffensive Sir Thomas Underwood, seeking to be returned from Percy-cross, had the onus of being an alien. "He's got a handle to his name," said Pile the bootmaker, "and money, I suppose, and comes down here without knowing a chick or a child. Why isn't a poor man, as can't hardly live, to have his three half crowns or fifteen shillings, as things may go, for voting for a stranger such as him?" (*Ralph the Heir*, 26:1.315)

The best agents were both shrewd strategists and expert publicists. Because, until the secret ballot was introduced in parliamentary elections in 1874, they could keep their eyes on voting trends as they were periodically announced, they could manage their pledged voters like troops of soldiery, keeping them in reserve or sending them into the booths as the tallies required.

> It was strongly urged upon Mr. Crafty to bring up a strong body of voters at the commencement, in order to head the polling at the end of the first hour. "Not the least occasion for it," said Crafty, quietly—"I don't care a straw for it; in a small borough no end can be gained, where the voters are so few in number that every man's vote is secured long beforehand, to a dead certainty. There's no *prestige* to be gained or supported. No. Bring up *first* all the distant and most uncertain voters—the timid, the feeble, the wavering; secure them early, while you have time and opportunity. Again, for the first few hours poll languidly; it *may* render the enemy over easy. You may perhaps make a sham *rush* of about twenty or thirty between twelve and one o'clock, to give them the idea that you are doing your very best.

Then fall off, poll a man now and then only, and see what *they* will do, how *they* are playing off their men. If you can hang back till late in the day, then direct, very secretly and cautiously, the bribery oath and the questions to be put to each of their men as they come up; and, while you are thus picking their men off, pour in your own before they are aware of your game, and the hour for closing the poll *may* perhaps arrive while some dozen or so of their men are unpolled." (*Ten Thousand a Year*, 28:746–47)

The shrewdness necessary to regulate the flow of a candidate's voters was ideally accompanied by a schoolboy-level talent for crude devices that ingratiated one portion of the electorate or discouraged the other, or both. A good agent, in short, arranged and oversaw the tricks-and-treats aspect of a country election. During the spirited contest at Eatanswill, Mr. Perker, Skumkey's agent, monopolized the public houses in the town, leaving only the disreputable beer shops to serve free refreshments to possible voters for Fizkin; Fizkin's people, on the other hand, locked thirty-three voters in the White Hart's coach house until they were needed.[†] Perker openly admired this tactic. "The effect of that is, you see," he told Mr. Pickwick, "to prevent our getting at them; and even if we could, it would be of no use, for they keep them very drunk on purpose. Smart fellow Fizkin's agent—very smart fellow indeed" (*Pickwick Papers*, 13:240–41). But this was not a fail-safe device. In *Coningsby*, Rigby's agent got four of Millbank's voters "very drunk" in order to spirit them from the site of the poll, but they "recovered their senses, made their escape, and voted as they originally intended" (5.4:344–45). This was a serious blow to the Millbank forces, who had already polled their dead men (a less common tactic, but by no means unheard of) and found themselves seven behind—the margin, as it proved, of Rigby's victory.

For a shilling a head, Sam Weller assisted in resuscitating, under a pump, a contingent of independent voters who had been wined and dined, too well, by one of the candidates' committees. But, he went on to report to Pickwick, this was nothing: "The night afore the last day o' the last election here, the opposite party bribed the bar-maid at the Town Arms, to hocus [put laudanum in] the brandy and water of four-

---

[†]This practice was called "cooping." When a candidate's agents had already bribed a number of voters but were not convinced of their probity—i.e., not assured that they would vote the right way when the time came—they were rounded up a few days before the poll, sequestered, and lavishly treated to food, drink, and tobacco as compensation for their involuntary detention until they could be delivered to the booth and their votes recorded under strict supervision. At Nottingham in 1841, for instance, a number of voters were cooped in, among other places, Lord Melbourne's garden, ten or twelve miles from the borough. (Gash, *Politics in the Age of Peel*, pp. 138–39.)

teen unpolled electors as was a stoppin' in the house. . . . Blessed if she didn't send 'em all to sleep till twelve hours arter the election was over. They took one man up to the booth, in a truck, fast asleep, by way of experiment, but it was no go—they wouldn't poll him; so they brought him back, and put him to bed again." Sam reported, furthermore, that when his father the coachman was hired to bring a load of voters (free-men of a borough who had retained their franchise when they moved away) from London, he was offered twenty pounds to dispose of them on the way, the road being so bad that any accident would be instantly plausible. "We're all wery fond o' you," the agent told the elder Weller, "so in case you *should* have an accident when you're a bringing these here woters down, and *should* tip 'em over into the canal vithout hurtin' of 'em, this is for yourself." Weller accepted the twenty pounds, virtuously intending not to spill the coachload. "You wouldn't believe, sir," said Sam, "that on the wery day as he came down with them woters, his coach *was* upset on that 'ere wery spot, and every man on 'em was turned into the canal." (All were saved except one old gentleman, whose hat was found, but "I ain't quite certain whether his head was in it or not") (*Pickwick Papers*, 13:246–48).[†]

Among the agent's duties was that of stage-managing, almost choreo-graphing, the indispensable ritual of canvassing, during which, in some novels, the opinions elicited from prospective voters were meant to rep-resent a portion of the vox populi. Canvassing was no novelty; it had been part of the electioneering process long before 1832. In a footnote in the 1835 edition of *Pelham*, Bulwer, referring to the hero's visits to the clergyman and the wine merchant, remarked:

> It is fortunate that Mr. Pelham's election was not for a rotten borough; so that the satire of this chapter is not yet obsolete nor unsalutary. Parliamen-tary Reform has not terminated the tricks of canvassing,—and Mr. Pel-ham's descriptions are as applicable now as when first written. All personal canvassing is but for the convenience of cunning,—the opportunity for manner to disguise principle. Public meetings, in which expositions of opin-ion must be clear, and will be cross-examined, are the only legitimate mode of canvass. (1.36:1.194)

Nevertheless, it remained an axiom of practical politics—still adhered to in the late twentieth century, when candidates wearing the rosettes of their respective parties and accompanied by an entourage of reporters

---

[†]A variant of this device is documented. At York, an agent arranged for coaches bring-ing voters from London to be stopped at Tadcaster, where those committed to vote for the opposition were paid off on the condition that they return to the city forthwith. (H. K. Cooke, *The Free and Independent Voter*, pp. 73–74.)

and TV crews tour the shopping streets and doorsteps of the nation—
that a candidate's soliciting a man's vote in a one-on-one encounter was
the most effective, if not necessarily the sincerest, form of flattery. This
was the part of electioneering that candidates faced with private loathing. The motions had to be gone through even when, as in the cases of
Endymion Ferrars, Phineas Finn at Loughton, and Veneering standing
for the borough of Pocket-Breaches, there was no opposition.

"'Canvasses are nasty things,' observed the Duke [of Donkeyton, who
had stood for his own pocket borough before ceding the privilege to his
son]. 'Remember a drunken fish-fag taking me in her arms, and hugging
and kissing me before the crowd,' added he, with a shudder . . . 'Nasty
business canvassing altogether, . . . should have abolished it with the Reform Bill'" (*Hillingdon Hall*, 41:404). One can reasonably assume that
even Samuel Slumkey had trouble repressing a slight shudder as, acting
on the advice of his agent, he worked the crowd at Eatanswill:

> "He has come out," said little Mr. Perker, greatly excited; the more so as
> their position did not enable them to see what was going forward.
> Another cheer, much louder.
> "He has shaken hands with the men," cried the little agent.
> Another cheer, far more vehement.
> "He has patted the babies on the head," said Mr. Perker, trembling with
> anxiety.
> A roar of applause that rent the air.
> "He has kissed one of 'em!" exclaimed the delighted little man.
> A second roar.
> "He has kissed another," gasped the excited manager.
> A third roar.
> "He's kissing 'em all!" screamed the enthusiastic little gentleman. (*Pick-
> wick Papers*, 13:250)

The decline of pocket boroughs and the consequent increase in the
number of contested elections and undecided voters made canvassing
ever more indispensable. In 1858 Sir Roger Scatcherd, in a temporary
remission of his alcoholism, had to endure "the dreadfully hard work of
canvassing and addressing the electors from eight in the morning till
near sunset" (*Doctor Thorne*, 17:184). The extension of the franchise in
1867 "made the work a deal harder than ever," as Trollope remarked in
Ralph the Heir. He spoke from bitter experience, for he had undergone
the same kind of slow torture as a Liberal candidate in the Beverley by-
election of 1868. In his autobiography he recalled:

> When the time came I went down to canvass, and spent, I think, the most
> wretched fortnight of my manhood. In the first place, I was subject to a
> bitter tyranny from grinding vulgar tyrants. They were doing what they

could, or said that they were doing so, to secure me a seat in Parliament, and I was to be in their hands for at any rate the period of my candidature. . . . From morning to evening every day I was taken round the lanes and by-ways of that uninteresting town, canvassing every voter, exposed to the rain, up to my knees in slush, and utterly unable to assume that air of triumphant joy with which a jolly, successful candidate should be invested.[4]

Trollope repeatedly tried to exorcise his traumatic memories in subsequent novels, above all *Ralph the Heir*. It was at Percycross (Beverley), for example, that his alter ego, Sir Thomas Underwood, learned the wisdom of his Tory fellow candidate, Griffenbottom, in respect to efficient canvassing:

Griffenbottom was very good at canvassing the poorer classes. He said not a word to them about politics, but asked them all whether they didn't dislike that fellow Gladstone, who was one thing one day and another thing another day. "By G——, nobody knows what he is," swore Mr. Griffenbottom over and over again. The women mostly said that they didn't know, but they liked the blue [the Conservative color]. "Blues allays was gallanter nor the [Liberal] yellow," said one of them. They who expressed an opinion at all hoped that their husbands would vote for him, "as 'd do most for 'em." "The big loaf;—that's what we want,"[†] said one mother of many children, taking Sir Thomas by the hand. There were some who took advantage of the occasion to pour out their tales of daily griefs into the ears of their visitors. To these Griffenbottom was rather short and hard. "What we want, my dear, is your husband's vote and interest. We'll hear all the rest another time." (25:1.305–6)

The seemingly foreordained electoral weather—the rain pouring down, the byways becoming muddier and muddier—topped up a candidate's flagon of misery. As Trollope put it in *The Duke's Children*, canvassing

is a nuisance to which no man should subject himself in any weather. But when it rains there is superadded a squalor and an ill humour to all the party which makes it almost impossible for them not to quarrel before the day is over. To talk politics to Mrs. Bubbs under any circumstances is bad, but to do so with the conviction that the moisture is penetrating from your greatcoat through your shirt to your bones, and that while so employed

---

[†]The "big loaf" was a slogan and graphic symbol familiar to voters from the Anti-Corn Law League agitation in the 1840s. The league's candidate at Sellborough, in *Hillingdon Hall*, was called "Big-Loaf Bowker," and he campaigned under signs to the same effect. Even after the Corn Laws were repealed (1846), the idea of cheap bread was so effective an electioneering point that it was retained as an emblem of prosperity. "Peace abroad and a big loaf at home" was Scatcherd's slogan in 1858. So the woman's political opinions were not as outdated as might appear at first glance.

In behalf of his own candidacy, Trollope worked the "cottages, hovels, and lodgings of poor men and women" at Beverley in 1868. If he remembered this placid rural-genre scene of Mr. Bowker, the Anti-Corn Law candidate, canvassing for votes in *Hillingdon Hall*, he would have found it intolerably idealized. For the reality, see the facing page.

> you are breathing the steam from those seven other wet men at the door, is abominable. To have to go through this is enough to take away all the pride which a man might otherwise take from becoming a member of Parliament. . . . To go through it and to feel that you are probably paying at the rate of a hundred pounds a day for the privilege is most disheartening. (55:444)

The only novelist to write zestfully of canvassing was the young Disraeli, who, by the time he and his sister wrote *A Year at Hartlebury* in 1833–34, had already campaigned twice, unsuccessfully, for the High Wycombe seat, and was to do so again shortly after the novel was published. Aubrey Bohun and his friend George Gainsborough, said Disraeli, "scampered agitating, over downs and commons, highways and byeways; hedges did not stop them; the astonished farmers were prepossessed in favour of a candidate who always rode on before his committee, and without any ceremony leaped the five-bar gates of their

One can easily conceive Trollope's wry appreciation when, two weeks after his defeat at Beverley, his eyes lighted upon this cartoon in *Punch* for 28 November 1868; it might have served as an illustration for any of the canvassing scenes in his subsequent novels, and the dialogue might almost have been from his pen:

The Missus (affably). "My 'usban's out just now, Sir. Can I give him any message?"

Liberal Candidate. "Ah—I have called with the hope that—ah—he'd promise me his vote at the approach—"

The Missus. "Oh, yes, Sir. You're Cap'm Blythe, the 'Yellow,' I s'pose, Sir! Yes, I'm sure he'll be most 'appy, Sir!"

The Captain (delighted). "Ya—as—I shall be much obliged to him—and—ah—he may depend upon my—"

The Missus. "Yes, I'm sure he'd promise you if he was at home, Sir; 'cause when the two 'blue' gents called and as'ed the other day, Sir, he promised 'em d'rec'ly, Sir!"

farm-yards" (2.1:102). But three years later, Disraeli was elected from Maidstone, and in the following decades he had ample—too ample— electioneering experience. At the end of his career he recalled the price he had repeatedly paid for his seat in Parliament when, in *Endymion*, he described his hero's tribulations:

> Although Endymion had no rival, and apparently no prospect of a contest, his labours as a candidate were not slight. The constituency was numerous, and every member of it expected to be called upon. To each Mr. Ferrars had to expound his political views, and to receive from each a cordial assur-

ance or a churlish criticism. All this he did and endured, accompanied by
about fifty of the principal inhabitants, members of his committee, who
insisted on never leaving his side, and prompting him at every new door
which he entered with contradictory reports of the political opinions of the
indwellers, or confidential intimations how they were to be managed and
addressed.

The principal and most laborious incidents of the day were festivals
which they styled luncheons, when the candidate and the ambulatory committee were quartered on some principal citizen with an elaborate banquet
of several courses, and in which Mr. Ferrars' health was always pledged in
sparkling bumpers. After the luncheon came two or three more hours of
what was called canvassing; then, in a state of horrible repletion, the fortunate candidate, who had no contest, had to dine with another principal citizen, with real turtle soup, and gigantic turbots, *entrées* in the shape of vol-
canic curries, and rigid venison, sent as a compliment by a neighbouring
peer. This last ceremony was necessarily hurried, as Endymion had every
night to address in some ward a body of the electors. (71:321–22)

Imperfectly concealed beneath such complaints as this was the chief
reason for a candidate's hatred of canvassing—that it was a demeaning
ordeal to which no true gentleman should be subjected. Beauchamp,
said Meredith,

> canvassed the borough from early morning till near midnight, and nothing
> would persuade him that his chance was poor. . . . Only conceive Nevil
> Beauchamp knocking at doors late at night, the sturdy beggar of a vote!
> or waylaying workmen, as he confessed without shame that he had done,
> on their way trooping to their midday meal; penetrating malodoriferous
> rooms of dismal ten-pound cottagers, to exhort bedraggled mothers and
> babes, and besotted husbands; and exposed to rebuffs from impertinent
> tradesmen; and lampooned and travestied, shouting speeches to roaring
> men, pushed from shoulder to shoulder of the mob! (*Beauchamp's Career*,
> 17:1.174)

Like Trollope, Meredith wrote of canvassing from personal experience.[5] In 1868 his friend Captain Maxse stood for Southampton as a
Radical, and Meredith went down to electioneer for him. Canvassing, he
wrote another friend, was "a dismal business, but I take to it as to whatever comes."

> It is not possible [he wrote in *Beauchamp's Career*] to gather up in one vol-
> ume of sound the rattle of the knocks at Englishmen's castle-gates during
> election days; so, with the thunder of it unheard, the majesty of the act of
> canvassing can be but barely appreciable, and he, therefore, who would
> celebrate it must follow the candidate obsequiously from door to door,
> where, like a cross between a postman delivering a bill and a beggar craving
> an alms, patiently he attempts the extraction of the vote, as little boys pick
> periwinkles with a pin. (18:1.180)

This was the prelude to one of the numerous fits of editorializing in the novel. Here, with his typical convolutions of argument, Meredith weighed the pros and cons of canvassing, concluding that it was a regrettable but necessary part of the British electoral process. He then proceeded to write what became the longest continuous narrative of a day's canvassing that any Victorian novelist put to paper, following Beauchamp, as he had proposed, through the streets of Bevisham, accompanied by Beauchamp's friend Lord Palmet, whose mind is much more preoccupied with beautiful women than the gritty realities of politics, and conversing with a variety of people holding a variety of views.

Rain, mud, housewives (blowzy and ignorant), voters (opinionated, truculent, mercenary), and sheer weariness of the flesh aside, the canvassing ritual appealed to novelists because of the possibility for dramatic encounters by the way. To judge from the number of such scenes they wrote, they seemed to believe that their readers expected an extended election narrative to include, as a matter of course, an accidental face-to-face meeting of the rival candidates and the light it shed on each man's character. During a particularly torrential day at Polpenno in *The Duke's Children*, a canvassing party consisting of Frank Tregear, the candidate, his friend Lord Silverbridge, a local tailor who served as "electioneering guide, philosopher, and friend," and other advisers, confer "under seven or eight wet umbrellas at the corner of a dirty little lane leading into the High Street" and decide to slog on,

> when suddenly, on the other side of the way, Mr. Carbottle's cortege made its appearance. The philosophers at once informed them that on such occasions it was customary that the rival candidates should be introduced. "It will take ten minutes," said the philosophers; "but then it will take them ten minutes too." Upon this Tregear, as being the younger of the two, crossed over the road, and the introduction was made. There was something comfortable in it to the Tregear party, as no imagination could conceive anything more wretched than the appearance of Mr. Carbottle. He was a very stout man of sixty, and seemed to be almost carried along by his companions. He had pulled his coat-collar up and his hat down till very little of his face was visible, and in attempting to look at Tregear and Silverbridge he had to lift up his chin till the rain ran off his hat on to his nose. He had an umbrella in one hand and a stick in the other, and was wet through to his very skin. What were his own feelings cannot be told, but his philosophers, guides, and friends would allow him no rest. "Very hard work, Mr. Tregear," he said, shaking his head.
>
> "Very hard indeed, Mr. Carbottle." Then the two parties went on, each their own way, without another word. (55:445–46)

The meeting of the two opponents in *Ten Thousand a Year* was thoroughly in harmony with a sustained theme of the novel, Tittlebat Titmouse's superhuman lack of common civility (not that it required to be demonstrated anew at this advanced juncture). At Yatton,

> as the hostile companies neared each other, that of Delamere observed some one hastily whisper to Titmouse, who instantly stuck his chased gold eye-glass into his eye, and stared very vulgarly at Mr. Delamere—who, on passing him, with the courtesy he conceived due to an opponent, took off his hat, and bowed with politeness and grace, his example being followed by all of his party. Titmouse, however, took not the least notice of the compliment; but without removing his glass from his eye, throwing an odious sneer into his face, stared steadily at Mr. Delamere, and so passed on. Mr. Barnabas Bloodsuck ably seconded him. Mudflint, with a bitter smirk, touched his hat slightly. Centipede affected to look another way. (27:721)

When Colonel Newcome and Barnes met, it was the Montagues and Capulets all over again, even though they were uncle and nephew. Their respective entourages executed the hostile gestures, without, however, any bloodshed:

> the two parties would often meet nose to nose in the same street, and their retainers exchange looks of defiance. With Mr. Potts of the *Independent*, a big man, on his left; with Mr. Frederick, a still bigger man, on his right; his own trusty bamboo cane in his hand, before which poor Barnes had shrunk abashed ere now, Colonel Newcome had commonly the best of these street encounters, and frowned his nephew Barnes, and Barnes's staff, off the pavement. (*The Newcomes*, 69:2.320)

Two other chance meetings—or in the first case nonmeeting—contributed to the stark opposition of good and evil that Mrs. Henry Wood and Trollope, respectively, sought to embody in the characters involved. In *East Lynne*, Sir Francis Levison, the deep-dyed villain of the piece,

> his agent, and the friend from town, who, as it turned out, instead of being some great gun of the government, was a private chum of the baronet's, named Drake, sneaked about the town like dogs, for they were thoroughly alive to the odour in which they were held; their only attendants being a few young gentlemen and ladies in rags, who commonly brought up the rear. The other party presented a stately crowd: county gentry, magistrates, Lord Mount Severn. Sometimes Mr. Carlyle [the "good" candidate] would be with them, arm in arm with the latter. If the contesting groups came within view of each other, and were likely to meet, the brave Sir Francis would disappear down an entry; behind a hedge; anywhere: he could not meet Mr. Carlyle and that condemning jury around him. (45:473)

In *The Prime Minister*, avoidance gave way to dramatic confrontation. Arthur Fletcher, standing for the borough of Silverbridge, is opposed by Lopez, the husband of Emily Wharton, with whom Fletcher has been—and continues to be—in love.

On the third day of his canvass Arthur Fletcher with his gang of agents and
followers behind him met Lopez with his gang in the street. It was probable
that they would so meet, and Fletcher had resolved what he would do when
such a meeting took place. He walked up to Lopez, and with a kindly smile
offered his hand. The two men, though they had never been intimate, had
known each other, and Fletcher was determined to show that he would not
quarrel with a man because that man had been his favoured rival. In comparison with that other matter this affair of the candidature was of course
trivial. But Lopez who had . . . made some threat about a horsewhip, had
come to a resolution of a very different nature. He put his arms a-kimbo,
resting his hands on his hips, and altogether declined the proffered civility.
"You had better walk on," he said, and then stood, scowling, on the spot till
the other should pass by. Fletcher looked at him for a moment, then bowed
and passed on. At least a dozen men saw what had taken place . . . and before they had gone to bed that night all the dozen knew the reason why. . . .
No doubt the incident added a pleasurable emotion to the excitement
caused by the election at Silverbridge generally. A personal quarrel is attractive everywhere. The expectation of such an occurrence will bring together the whole House of Commons. (34:315)

And, Trollope might have added, such an expectation, though not
necessarily fulfilled, spiced every election narrative in fiction, not least
his own.

19

The Free and Independent: II

1.

WHEN LADY TIPPINS, in *Our Mutual Friend*, went canvassing in behalf of her dear friend Mr. Veneering, she ended her set speech to women (who had no vote) with, "And above all, my dear, be sure you promise me your vote and interest and all sorts of plumpers for Pocket-Breaches; for we couldn't think of spending sixpence on it, my love, and can only consent to be brought in by the spontaneous thingummies of the incorruptible whatdoyou callums" (2.3:301). It is not clear whether this implies the seat's true worth or reflects the growing public sentiment in the 1860s that something really should be done about election expenses. Seats in Parliament never had come cheap. In pre-Reform days, candidates spent enormous sums for the lucrative privilege of representing a borough; seats were bought, sold, and rented like any marketable commodity. "[T]he sales of seats in Parliament," said Archibald Jobbry in *The Member*, as he began to haggle for one of his own, "are as plain as the sun at noon-day, and would make the bones of our ancestors rattle in their coffins to hear of it" (3:10). In the 1807 Yorkshire contest, which became famous as "the Austerlitz of electioneering," Lords Lascelles and Milton between them spent £200,000 and the antislavery crusader William Wilberforce somewhere near £30,000, of which between £8,000 and £9,000 was his own money and the rest contributed by the "independent freeholders" of the county. A Northumberland seat went for £80,000 in 1826, and four years later the going price in Gloucester was £20,000 and in Leicester, £30,000. After Huskisson's death on the first railway in 1830, the two men contesting his Liverpool seat spent £30,000 each. It is little wonder that in the borough of Shoreham the astute electors formed themselves into a joint stock company to receive and distribute among themselves the profits accruing from contests there.

In Galt's novel a knowledgeable politician advised Jobbry:

"at the very utmost . . . a few thousand pounds at a general election should do the business; or, if you would sooner take your seat, I should think that from twelve hundred to fifteen hundred pounds per session would be reasonable terms. . . . ye have just to give an inkling that if a convenient borough was to be had, ye would not mind about going into Parliament. Speeches of that sort are very efficacious; and it's not to be told how it will circulate that you would give a handsome price for an easy seat in the House of Commons. Keep your thumb on the price, and just let out that you have no relish for the clanjamfrey of a popular election, but would rather deal with an old sneck-drawer† in the trade than plague yourself with canvassing: depend upon it ye'll soon hear of some needful lord that will find you out, and a way of treating with you."(2:7)

"The most expensive hobby in the world," declared Mrs. Cadwallader in *Middlemarch* (38:419) at the same time, recalling that a candidate in the town's most recent election had spent £10,000—and lost.

The widespread publicity given to the huge sums that figured in the traffic in parliamentary seats was among the major stimuli behind the Reform agitation in 1830–32. Although the bill as enacted far from abolished the trade, it created many more seats, and by the simple operation of the law of supply and demand the average price was markedly reduced. Even so, it was steep enough to discourage many aspiring candidates. In *Coningsby* (1844) part of the Liberals' difficulty in finding a man to stand for Darlford was the reluctance of those who presented themselves to commit suitably large sums. One said he would pay only legal expenses; another "would go as far as £1,000, provided the seat was secured. Mr. Juggins, a distiller, £2,000 man; but would not agree to annual subscriptions" (i.e., to local charities) (5.3:332).

At Treby Magna, in the first election after the Reform Bill passed, when the average price of a seat was estimated to be £6,000, Harold Transome's expenses were between £8,000 and £9,000, the outlay proving at the end of the poll to have been merely "the price of ascertaining that he was not to sit in the next Parliament . . ." (*Felix Holt*, 34:278). In the 1837 election the cost to the candidates at Bedford totaled £28,000, a sum, said the Duke of Bedford, that "makes my hair stand on end." The going price of a seat continued to vary from place to place and year to year, as it had done in the bad old days, albeit seldom on the same princely scale. In 1858 the cost to the candidate of being elected from the obscure borough of Tillietudlem, where "The men . . . knew the

---

†Defined in the *O.E.D.* as "a crafty, flattering, or sly fellow"; in this context, a parliamentary agent or seat-broker.

value of their votes, and would only give them according to their consciences," was a modest £2,000, which included the expenses inflicted
on a successful candidate if the election was formally challenged (*The
Three Clerks*, 24:283). In London, on other hand, the costs could run
considerably higher, depending on the district. George Vavasor's agent,
Scruby, was well informed on the state of the London market:

> "You can't do it cheap for any of these metropolitan seats; you can't, indeed,
> Mr. Vavasor. That is, a new man can't. When you've been in four or five
> times, like old Duncombe, why then, of course, you may snap your fingers
> at such men as Grimes. But the Chelsea districts ain't dear. I don't call them
> by any means dear. Now Marylebone is dear,—and so is Southwark. It's
> dear, and nasty; that's what the borough is. Only that I never tell tales, I
> could tell you a tale, Mr. Vavasor, that'd make your hair [like the Duke of
> Bedford's] stand on end; I could indeed." (*Can You Forgive Her?*, 13:164)

In the end, Vavasor won the Chelsea seat by a wide margin. "You've
done it very cheap," Scruby told him, "considering that the seat is metropolitan. I do say that you have done it cheap. Another thousand, or
twelve hundred [on top of the "few modest hundreds" he had already
received on account], will cover everything—say thirteen, perhaps, at
the outside" (44:478).

At that very time (1864–65) the prevailing cost of a "safe" seat (which
meant, in practice, one within the gift of an electorate that, given the
proper incentives, could be relied upon to vote the right way) was specified in *Our Mutual Friend*: "Britannia mentions to a legal gentleman of
her acquaintance that if Veneering will 'put down' five thousand pounds,
he may write a couple of initial letters after his name at the extremely
cheap rate of two thousand five hundred per letter" (2.3:295). This cor-
responds exactly to the price mentioned a decade later, in *Beauchamp's
Career*, when it was said that the only chance to win the borough of Bevisham was to have "five thousand pounds in a sack with a hole in it"
(20:1.209). At the same time, however, Ferdinand Lopez reckoned that
the Silverbridge seat could be his for no more than £1,000 (*The Prime
Minister*). His withdrawal from the contest before the election prevented
his testing the estimate's accuracy.

It was typical of Scruby's slipperiness that he made George Vavasor
think he had got more of a bargain than was actually the case. The worth
of a seat was determined in part by the prospective duration of the current session, and when Vavasor entered the Commons the session was
already half over. A would-be candidate had, therefore, to read the political portents to decide whether he would be in the House long enough
before dissolution to get an acceptable return on his investment. When
Jobbry bargained for his seat, the chief consideration was just that. The

broker, Mr. Probe, originally demanded three or four thousand pounds for the two remaining sessions, but Jobbry pointed out that "a whole Parliament can be got, as ye said yourself, for about five thousand pounds, divide that by seven sessions, and ye'll then come nearer what the mark should be" (*The Member*, 3–5:11–18). The price finally agreed upon was five hundred in guineas and an additional hundred pounds.

Like canvassing, the expenditure of substantial sums was required by custom even when a candidate was unopposed, as was Phineas Finn at Loughton.

> He made one speech from a small raised booth that was called a platform, and that was all that he was called upon to do. Mr. Grating made a speech in proposing him, and Mr. Shortribs another in seconding him; and these were all the speeches that were required. The thing seemed to be so very easy that he was afterwards almost offended when he was told that the bill for so insignificant a piece of work came to £247 13s. 9d. He had seen no occasion for spending even the odd forty-seven pounds. (*Phineas Finn*, 33:337–38)

But that was the way the political mechanism worked.

A candidate's agent supervised the distribution of the expense money and sometimes advised him on the forms the expenditures should assume. The fact that he served as a conduit channeling money from the campaign fund to destinations that may or may not have been lawful—the operation we call laundering—was responsible in no small part for the unsavory reputation his profession had acquired. The least reproachable purpose to which electioneering money might be devoted (the spending might occur between elections, as a provident exercise in casting bread upon the waters) was community relations. Candidates saw fit to project the image of a local benefactor. In *Coningsby*, Sir Baptist Placid, one of the prospective bidders for the honor of representing Darlford, said he was willing to subscribe a guinea a year to the infirmary and every religious society, but he had a principled objection to subscribing an annual hundred pounds to the races (5.3:332). He fell short, by that amount, of qualifying as the Liberal candidate. Local claims upon a candidate's purse could be costly enough, but they were as nothing compared to those he faced if he ran for a whole county. "County representations," the lawyer Smoothington told Bowker in *Hillingdon Hall*, "are very troublesome . . . ; people never done asking—schools, churches, hospitals, infirmaries, races, plays, farces, devilments of all sorts—no gratitude either" (42:421).

In Percycross, "Old Mr. Griffenbottom, the Tory, had been very generous with his purse, and was beloved, doubtless, by many in the borough. It is so well for a borough to have some one who is always ready with a fifty-pound note in this or that need! It is so comfortable in a borough to know that it can always have its subscription lists well headed!" (*Ralph the Heir*, 20:1.236) It was a lesson his running mate, Sir Thomas Underwood, had to learn the hard way. When canvassed, Mr. Pabsby, the Wesleyan minister, played infuriatingly coy (in "a voice made up of pretence, politeness, and saliva"). After the election, he put the bite on Underwood for a subscription—a "first" one, with others to follow, to his chapel building fund, claiming that "Sir Thomas's return had been due altogether to Mr. Pabsby's flock, who had, so said Mr. Pabsby, been guided in the matter altogether by his advice." He received a check for twenty pounds. By Christmas time, "it seemed to Sir Thomas that there was not a place of divine worship in the whole of Percycross that was not falling to the ground in ruins. He had not observed it when he was there, but now it appeared that funds were wanted for almost every such edifice in the borough. And the schools were in a most destitute condition" (39.2.118–119).

Often a candidate's largess was bestowed on individuals. In *The Member*, Archibald Jobbry, M.P., sat on a committee looking into the case of Galbon, his former adversary at Frailtown, who had just been returned for the borough of Wordham. "[T]he petitioners alleged against him such things as might have made the hair on the Speaker's wig stand on end 'like quills upon the fretful porcupine,' had they not been so well accustomed to accusations of the same kind." The particular trick exposed here was one that had been used with success at Frailtown. It involved a mock quack doctor who dispensed, along with pills and salves, printed notes saying that he "would be consulted by the freemen and their families gratis, every day till the election was over" (25:83–86). What they received during those consultations, contingent on the freemen's promise to vote for Galbon, were "inoculations" in the form of gold sovereigns.

The Marquis of Bray likewise, pouring out money to counteract Jorrocks's popularity, bought, for the hugely inflated sum of £20, a parrot from an old lady whose voter-husband was "difficult to come over" (*Hillingdon Hall*, 46:444). Frank Gresham advanced Moffat's cause at Barchester by ordering bonnets for all the ladies from the milliner wife of Bagley the cathedral chorister. If Moffat declined to pay for them out of his campaign funds, said Frank, he would foot the bill himself (*Doctor Thorne*, 16:173).

Local tradesmen made a good thing out of the electioneering. There were posters and handbills to be printed, flags and banners to be sewn and distributed, ribbons and rosettes made up to adorn the candidates, their committees, and their followings. At Eatanswill, ladies who attended a tea party financed by the candidate Samuel Slumkey left with favors in the form of green parasols. "Fact, my dear sir, fact," Slumkey's agent, Mr. Perker, assured Pickwick. "Five-and-forty green parasols, at seven and sixpence a-piece. All women like finery,—extraordinary the effect of those parasols. Secured all their husbands, and half their brothers—beat stockings, and flannel, and all that sort of thing hollow. My idea, my dear sir, entirely. Hail, rain, or sunshine, you can't walk half a dozen yards up the street, without encountering half a dozen green parasols" (*Pickwick Papers*, 13:241).†

But the tradesmen who profited most from campaign expenditures were the publicans and innkeepers, in whose houses the candidates' committees had by long custom had their headquarters until the Corrupt Practices Act of 1883 finally made the practice illegal. Beer in unlimited quantities, paid for by a candidate, was assumed to be the most efficacious way of ensuring the good will of the populace. At Eatanswill, "Exciseable articles were remarkably cheap at all the public-houses; and spring vans paraded the streets for the accommodation of voters who were seized with any temporary dizziness in the head—an epidemic which prevailed among the electors, during the contest, to a most alarming extent, and under the influence of which they might frequently be seen lying on the pavements in a state of utter insensibility" (*Pickwick Papers*, 13:255). This was the aspect of democratic elections that continued to stir Dickens's most vehement disgust. Eighteen years later, adding one more damning touch to his portrait of Merdle, that of borough-monger, he wrote of "three little rotten holes in this Island, containing three little ignorant, drunken, guzzling, dirty, out-of-the-way constituencies, that had reeled into Mr. Merdle's pocket" (*Little Dorrit*, 2.12:620).

Just where the voters (and often their unfranchised sympathizers as well) got their beer implied a distinct social difference. Perker, Slumkey's manager at Eatanswill, made a point readily comprehensible to Dickens's readers when he reported that he had rounded up all the public houses, leaving only the beer shops to his opponent. Both of these classes of drinking establishments could be "open houses" where, during an election campaign, voters wearing the right colors were served an unlimited number of drinks at a candidate's expense. But the public houses, whose

†Elsewhere, if not at Eatanswill, the ladies graciously reciprocated. At Yatton, for example, Delamere's headquarters in *Ten Thousand a Year* were decorated with "an ample and very rich blue silk banner, on which was worked, in white silk, the figure of a Bible, Crown, and Sceptre, and the words, 'Delamere for Yatton.'" It was "the workmanship of some fifteen of as sweet, beautiful girls as could have been picked out of the whole county of York" (27:724).

management was regulated by the local magistrates, were respectable, and the beer houses were disreputable. The latter were of topical interest when *Pickwick Papers* appeared, because they had been created by the Beer Act of 1830, which repealed the tax on beer and permitted any ratepayer to buy from the local exciseman a two-guinea license that permitted him to sell beer free from magisterial control. The reverend wit Sydney Smith reported, soon after the law took effect, "Everybody is drunk. Those who are not singing are sprawling. The sovereign people are in a beastly state." [1]

The new law was inextricably linked with the Reform agitation of 1830–32, a fact that explains, for one thing, the slogan TITMOUSE AND CHEAP ALE! The cheapened beer was served more liberally in electioneering contests than it had been when taxed and its outlets limited, thus fortuitously providing, as the workingman's tipple of choice, an additional democratic element to the politics of the time; and this led to the grateful recipients' assuming some kind of causal connection between electoral reform and free beer. At Chubb's Sugar Loaf inn, in *Felix Holt*, a collier nicknamed Mike Brindle said that he had heard that "'lection men" were "up and down everywhere, and now's the time, they say, when a man can get beer for nothing." "'Ay, that's sin' the Reform,' said a big, red-whiskered man, called Dredge. 'That's brought the 'lections and the drink into these parts; for afore that, it was all kep up the Lord knows wheer'" (11:117).

The beer houses continued to thrive, most of all at election time. In the Barchester election (*Doctor Thorne*), "all the beer-houses were open, and half the population was drunk. . . . Mr. Nearthewinde assured [Moffat] triumphantly that 'half at least of the wallowing swine were his own especial friends; and that somewhat more than half of the publicans of the town were eagerly engaged in fighting his, Mr. Moffat's, battle'" (17:178–79).

These bar bills no doubt were a major item in the expenditures that lay behind the dramatic scene at Chesney Wold when Sir Leicester Dedlock, complacent owner of three pocket boroughs, tells his assembled cousins that "the Party has not triumphed without being put to an enormous expense." (This is just before Tulkinghorn brings the incredible news that, far from triumphing, two party stalwarts have been beaten three to one.) "Hundreds of thousands of pounds!" Sir Leicester exclaims. "Impelled by innocence," Dickens continues, Volumnia asks, "What for?"

> "Volumnia," remonstrates Sir Leicester, with his utmost severity. "Volumnia!"
> "No, no, I didn't mean what for," cries Volumnia, with her favourite little scream. "How stupid I am! I mean what a pity!"

"I am glad," returns Sir Leicester, "that you do mean what a pity."
Volumnia hastens to express her opinion that the shocking people ought
to be tried as traitors, and made to support the Party.
"I am glad, Volumnia," repeats Sir Leicester, unmindful of these mollify-
ing sentiments, "that you do mean what a pity. It is disgraceful to the electors. But as you, though inadvertently, and without intending so unreason-
able a question, asked me 'what for?' let me reply to you. For necessary
expenses. And I trust to your good sense, Volumnia, not to pursue the subject, here or elsewhere."
Sir Leicester feels it incumbent on him to observe a crushing aspect towards Volumnia, because it is whispered abroad that these necessary expenses will, in some two hundred election petitions, be unpleasantly connected with the word bribery. . . . (*Bleak House*, 40:624–25)

As they should have been. Because, as Emily Eden was to put it a few
years later, with a succinctness matching Dickens's, "expense" was simply
"a gentlemanlike term for bribery" (*The Semi-Attached Couple*, 36:177).

All the kinds of expenditure mentioned so far were, in a strict interpretation of the term, corrupt; but in Victorian politics there were infi-
nite gradations of corruption. To a rigorous moralist, the line often
drawn between "treating" and bribery was a distinction without a difference. Both, after all, were intended to influence the outcome of an election. But there was a world of difference between the distribution of
parasols to Eatanswill ladies or Jorrocks's contribution to the local hunt
and the kind of persuasion described by one of the fifteen (pre-Reform)
voters in *John Halifax, Gentleman:*

"Sir, I be a poor man. I lives in one o' my lord's houses. I hanna paid no
rent for a year. Mr. Brown zays to me, he zays—'Jacob, vote for Vermilye,
and I'll forgive 'ee the rent, and here be two pound ten to start again wi'.'
So, as I zays to Matthew Hales (he be Mr. Halifax's tenant, your honour,
and my lord's steward ha' paid 'un nigh four pound for his vote), I sure us
be poor men, and his lordship a lord and all that—it's no harm, I reckon."
(24:243)

Such grosser forms of bribery as the forgiveness of rent due gradually
disappeared, assisted by the lasting notoriety of the Duke of Newcastle's
eviction of some forty tenants and their families for voting the wrong
way in 1829: inducement and retaliation were two sides of the same
coin.[†] But other forms of indirect bribery persisted, though allowance
must be made for Samuel Warren's exaggeration for satirical effect in
Ten Thousand a Year:

[†]One of the little quirks of history is the fact that at the next election (1832), the Duke's
hand-picked candidate for the same seat (Newark, which remained a pocket borough under the new law) was William Ewart Gladstone. His success at the poll marked the beginning of his long political career.

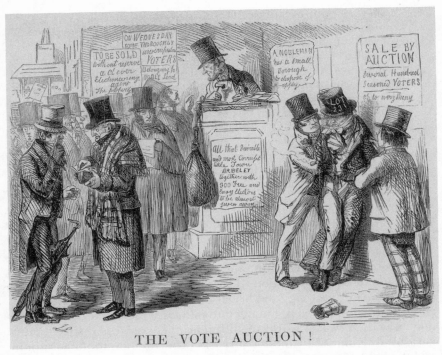

THE VOTE AUCTION!

In March 1853, readers of *Bleak House* had in their hands the latest number (13) in which Sir Leicester Dedlock complains of the "enormous expense" elections entailed. In the same month, *Punch* printed this cartoon and the one opposite in successive issues (12 and 19 March). At the very least, they helped drive Dickens's point home.

A small tinker and brazier at Warkleigh had received, with a wink, ten pounds from a member of Mr. Titmouse's committee, in payment of an old outstanding account—Heaven save the mark!—delivered in by him three years before for mending . . . pots, kettles, and saucepans. . . . The wife of a tailor at Grilston received the same sum for a fat tom-cat, which was a natural curiosity, since it could wink each eye separately and successively. A third worthy and independent voter was reminded that he had lent the applicant for his vote ten pounds several years before, and which that gentleman now took shame to himself, as he paid the amount, for having so long allowed to remain unpaid. Mr. Barnabas Bloodsuck, with superior astuteness, gave three pounds apiece to three little boys, sons of a voter, whose workshop overlooked Messrs. Bloodsuck's back offices, on condition that they would desist from their trick of standing and putting their thumbs to their noses and extending their fingers toward him, as he sat in his office,

THE PARTY WHO, ETC.   FREE AND INDEPENDENT, ETC.

THE ORDINARY LEGAL EXPENSES OF AN ELECTION.

and which had really become an insupportable nuisance. Here was, therefore, a *valuable consideration* for the payment, and bribery was out of the
question. (27:716)

It was coins above all—shining copies of the King's likeness, as the agent
Johnson in *Felix Holt* put it, in the days before a queen's likeness was
substituted—that energized the electoral process.

The first statute against electoral bribery, making it an offense at common law, had been enacted toward the end of the seventeenth century, but the penalties it prescribed were too severe to enforce, and the machinery for doing so was, in any case, too cumbersome. It remained a dead letter throughout the eighteenth century, when an indeterminate but unquestionably large portion of the expenditure for a seat took the form of monetary bribes. The First Reform Bill contained no provisions against corruption; ironically, bribery in all its current forms was more prevalent in the immediate wake of "reform" than ever before, for the simple reason that the large increase in the number of contested seats meant that there were just that many more opportunities for the illicit exchange of money for votes.† Seven years after the bill was passed, Palmerston declared in Parliament, "I verily believe that the extent to which bribery and corruption was carried at the last election [1839], has exceeded anything that has ever been stated within these walls." The parliament elected in 1841 was forthrightly called "the Bribery Parliament." It is understandable, therefore, that Warren devoted so much space to uninhibited chicanery in his novel, whose serialization spanned those very years (1839–41). No subject could have been more timely. The saga of the "Quaint Club," a body of 109 new voters who hold the balance of power under the new redistricting, sell themselves to Oily Gammon for £10 a head and, after complex negotiations, resell themselves to Crafty for £30 with a pledge (unhonored in the event) *not* to vote, may have been overstated, but in its essence it came uncomfortably close to the headlines of the day. At Stafford, near the close of the poll in 1835, votes went for £14, and in the same year Conservative electors claimed an identical sum at Bristol. And at Liverpool in 1834, the top Yatton figure was much exceeded: 1,300 freemen collected from ten to sixty pounds each. Judged on this scale, the seat for Swillington, in *Hillingdon Hall*, was a veritable steal. Bowker, the Anti-Corn League candidate, was informed that it could be had for "nothing but a dinner, and a guinea a head to the voters; five hundred pounds would do it" (42:421).

† In the first "reformed" election, held six months after the bill's passage, venality was more evident than virtue. At Stafford, admittedly a special case since its corruption had long been notorious, the newly enfranchised ten-pound householders demanded their fees as vociferously as did the old-established electorate. "Even before the election started 5s. and 10s. tickets had been distributed to about 800 electors. There was evidence that one side alone had paid out about £150 in 5s. tickets a week before polling day. But this was chicken feed compared with what was to come. When the election actually started, the price of votes began at £2 10s. for a single and £5 for a plumper [a double vote for a single candidate], and gradually rose to £4, £7, and even £10 for a vote. One agent alone paid out over £1,000 in bribes to between 400 and 500 voters. Of the 1,000 odd voters . . . it was calculated that 850 were bribed." (Gash, *Politics in the Age of Peel*, p. 158.)

Trollope says the most about the market in votes in the 1870s. The Polpenno electors in *The Duke's Children* could be had for ten shillings a head. Their rationalization for being receptive to douceurs, as explained in another novel (*The Prime Minister*), was simple: "Hints were made by honest citizens of the pleasure they would have in supporting this or that gentleman,—for the honest citizens assured one gentleman after the other of the satisfaction they had in seeing so all-sufficient a candidate in the borough,—if the smallest pecuniary help were given them, even a day's pay, so that their poor children might not be injured by their going to the poll" (34:1.315).[†] The Percycross workingmen in *Ralph the Heir* expected three half-crowns under ordinary circumstances, but in the heat of the election an agent named Glump paid no fewer than a hundred voters ten shillings each between one and two in the afternoon. When Phineas Finn contested the colliery town of Tankerville, he was running ahead until his opponent appealed to an as yet untapped pocket of grimy voters with an offer of £2 10s. per man. Phineas lost by seven votes.

Meanwhile, Bevisham was reputed to be "the dearest of boroughs." The voters, Beauchamp, was told, walked the streets "with their figures attached to them like titles. Mr. Tomkins, the twenty-pound man; an elector of uncommon purity . . . has never been known to listen to a member under £20, and is respected enormously . . ." (*Beauchamp's Career*, 11:1.105). But run-of-the-mine Bevisham votes cost considerably less.[‡] One "Morality Joseph," a rag and dust man, was known to campaign officials as a "five-pound-note man" who was also a "four o'clock man," that is, one who "waited for the final bids to him upon the closing hour of the election day" (19:1.200). (Disraeli's sardonic term for this type of procrastinator-for-profit was "thoughtful voter.")

Some voters, like the bootmaker Pile who drifts in and out of *Ralph the Heir*, looked upon the antibribery laws as a sign of decadence, the death of the good old days when men were brothers bonded by customary corruption: "And what's the meaning of it all? It's just this,—that folks wants what they wants without paying for it. I hate Purity, I do. I hate the very smell of it. It stinks. When I see the chaps as come here and talk of Purity, I know they mean that nothing ain't to be as it used

---

[†]This was an argument Sir Thomas Underwood, in *Ralph the Heir*, refused to buy. "Half an hour," he said, "would take a working man to the poll and back" (20:1.244).

[‡]The practice of fixing the size of the bribe according to the recipient's social rank was no figment of Meredith's imagination. In Cornwall in 1841, the modestly circumstanced voters of Penryn were paid at the fixed rate of four pounds, but the wealthier inhabitants of Falmouth demanded, and got, "larger sums more in keeping with their standards of living." (Gash, *Politics in the Age of Peel*, p. 124.)

to be. Nobody is to trust no one. There ain't to be nothing warm, nor friendly, nor comfortable any more." Pile, says Trollope, maintained that "It was the old-fashioned privilege of a poor man to receive some small consideration for his vote in Percycross, and [he] could not endure to think that the poor man should be robbed of his little comforts." Contemplating the encroaching immaculacy of elections as reflected by the increasingly strict enforcement of the statutes, Pile grew positively maudlin. "I did think it [bribery] would last my time," he said, coming close to tears as he lamented the days that were no more (26:1.314–15; 29:2.4).

2.

Even though the total cost of a bought election after the First Reform Act was but a fraction of what it had been in the late eighteenth and early nineteenth centuries, more fuss was made over the disbursement of a few hundred pounds to venal voters than had ever been made over larger-scale bribery earlier. The act generated a new atmosphere in which all forms of coercion were publicly deplored and some steps were even taken to eradicate it—an admittedly formidable task, given its deep roots in the English electoral process. In 1835 a select committee of the House of Commons, the first of its kind, was appointed to investigate the low state of electoral morality, and its report, as well as those of succeeding committees and royal commissions for the next thirty years, documented the disturbing extent of corruption.

The device by which, it was fondly hoped, electoral corruption could be publicized and effectively punished was already in place: the petition sent to Parliament by the aggrieved—that is, the losing—party, asking that an ad hoc committee of the Commons be appointed to investigate the complaint. Accustomed to corruption as they were, readers of fiction could well expect such a sequel to the main election narrative, and novelists often provided it. As early as 1828, Pelham had scarcely taken his seat when his opponent "preferred a petition against me, for what he called undue means. Heaven knows what he meant; I am sure the House did not, for they turned me out" and declared the other man the winner (*Pelham*, 47:1.248–49).

Petitioning was a notoriously costly process, and the possibility of its being resorted to after a given election required adding a substantial amount to a candidate's estimate of what a seat would cost him. In *The Three Clerks*, Undecimus Scott alleged that "What with the election and petition together," Tillietudlem, for which he had sat until his unsatisfactory performance in the Westminster patronage-and-perks game led the Government to prevent his being returned, "never cost me less than £2,000" (29:358–59). In *Rachel Ray*, the possibility that Hart might win the election forced the Cornbury party to project what it would cost to unseat him: £1,200 for the election itself, plus £5,000 for the petition.[†] The agent Trigger in *Ralph the Heir* reckoned that Sir Thomas Underwood would have to pay £1,500 to defend his victory at Percycross.

In *Ten Thousand a Year*, the exceedingly malodorous wheeling and dealing connected with the election itself was crowned by the fresh corruption connected with the petition. Delamere, the loser at Yatton, protested that Titmouse's minions had stolen the election, and he had a formidable array of evidence to prove it. But a politician named Swindall O'Gibbet took Titmouse aside and undertook, for a consideration of £3,000, to get him off. Which he proceeded to do, by suborning some members of the committee. As O'Gibbet pointed out to Titmouse, the money was well spent; if the decision had gone the other way, he could have been fined £10,000.

The O'Gibbet business was an instantly recognizable cut at the Irish politician Daniel O'Connell, against whom several charges of corruption had been brought. In the so-called Raphael affair (1836), he was accused of selling the Irish seat of Carlow, but an investigating committee absolved him of any wrongdoing. In a speech in 1838 he "asserted that the decisions of parliamentary election committees were always partisan and challenged the House of Commons to deny that the issue of every case depended always on the constitution of the committee and never on the merits of the petition." The partisanship of Tory committees was notorious, but for this aspersion he cast on his colleagues' integrity O'Connell received a vote of censure, 293 to 85.[2]

In their earlier treatments of elections, say, down to the early fifties, there is little evidence that novelists were outraged by the malpractices they described, with ample documentation from the press. Corruption was so ingrained in "the system" that it was exempt from moral censure. The writers of silver fork novels, including Disraeli and Bulwer-Lytton, were as unmoved by the possible immorality, not to say illegality, of bribing as were their fictional characters. Seemingly, no reform impulse actuated Dickens's depiction of the comedy of Eatanswill, and in Warren's protracted narrative of the Yatton election the satire was likewise under-

[†] In this case, there was the additional difficulty, not uncommon in actual practice, that the petitioner before the bar of justice had to have clean hands if his accusations were to have any weight. Hart, having lost to Butler Cornbury by a single vote, declared he would petition. "But as it was known that every possible electioneering device had been put in practice on his behalf during the last two hours of the poll, the world at large in Baslehurst believed that young Cornbury's position was secure" (25:322).

cut by the farce that degenerated into sheer absurdity. (The subsequent petition episode, with its obvious personal attack on O'Connell, was another matter.) Whether or not the widespread corruption constituted a fatal flaw in the system, it was a fact of political life, and nowhere in fiction at that time was there a sense that something of a permanent nature could, and should, be done about it. The early social protest novels—*Sybil, Mary Barton, Yeast, Alton Locke*—did not include electoral reform on their agendas.

The note of passionate indignation enters fiction only with *Bleak House*, by which time it appears that mid-Victorian morality had become a powerful enough force in public life to pose a considerable threat to the old ways of doing electoral business. In the midst of all the objects of Dickens's execration, bought elections have a minor place, a small thread in the Dedlock theme. But there is no mistaking where Dickens stood when he alluded to the stasis in public affairs caused by Aberdeen's inability to form a new government.

> Doodle has found that he must throw himself upon the country—chiefly in the form of sovereigns and beer. In this metamorphosed state he is available in a good many places simultaneously, and can throw himself upon a considerable portion of the country at one time. Britannia being much occupied in pocketing Doodle in the form of sovereigns, and swallowing Doodle in the form of beer, and in swearing herself black in the face that she does neither—plainly to the advancement of her glory and morality—the London season comes to a sudden end, through all the Doodleites and Coodleites dispersing to assist Britannia in those religious exercises. (40:619–20)

That the beer and sovereigns, in the novel, helped bring in candidates representing the new order of men—liberals backed by such industrial wielders of influence as the elder Rouncewell—was neither here nor there. Dickens knew that the same order of spending might just as well bring about a Tory victory, reinforcing the power of the Sir Leicester Dedlocks. But in the nineteen months that saw the novel appearing in parts (March 1852–September 1853) there was a renewed effort to purify elections. Elizabeth Gaskell made opportune use of it in *Ruth* (1853), when she used Donne's hypocrisy as a know-nothing, see-nothing candidate to further darken her portrait of the heroine's seducer. "Better speak as little about such things as possible," he advised his local backer, Mr. Bradshaw; "other people can be found to arrange all the dirty work. Neither you nor I would like to soil our fingers by it, I am sure. Four thousand pounds are in Mr. Pilson's [the agent's] hands, and I shall never inquire what becomes of them; they may probably, very probably, be absorbed in the law expenses, you know. I shall let it be clearly understood from the hustings that I most decidedly disapprove of bribery, and leave the rest to Hickson's management"—Hickson being a briefless barrister and friend of Pilson (22:260).

Just before Parliament was dissolved for the election of 1852, it passed a bill providing for a royal commission to be appointed to inquire into any constituency where "the House Election Committee suspected that corrupt practices prevailed." Commissions were appointed in six especially flagrant cases, and their reports made it clear that something more had to be done. The "something" proved to be the Corrupt Practices Act of 1854, which for the first time not only spelled out exactly what electoral bribery consisted of but described almost every conceivable form that it might take—a remarkable tribute to the lively imaginations of its framers, who perhaps were novelists manqués. It also prescribed realistic—i.e., collectable—penalties and additional machinery to deal with complaints.[†]

Four years later (1858), Trollope took aim at the Corrupt Practices Act in a half-serious, half-satiric mood. The first part of *Doctor Thorne* is specifically set in 1854, in the months just after the bill was passed. The question of corruption therefore is particularly urgent in several characters' minds during the Barchester contest. The colorless but reasonably honest Moffat had earlier won his seat at a cost he could not forget:

In one way or another money had been dragged from him for purposes which had been to his mind unintelligible; and when, about the middle of his first session, he had, with much grumbling, settled all demands, he had question with himself whether his whistle was worth its cost.

He was therefore a great stickler for purity of election; although, had he considered the matter, he should have known that with him money was his only passport into that elysium in which he had now lived for two years. He probably did not consider it; for when, in those canvassing days immediately preceding the [present] election, he had seen that all the beer-houses were open, and half the population was drunk, he had asked Mr. Nearthewinde whether this violation of the treaty [which had specified "no treat-

---

[†] It is possible that Dickens's choice of St. Albans as the site of the wretched brickmakers' hovels in *Bleak House* was prompted by the current notoriety of the borough, which had long been in the forefront of illegal electoral activity. It was one of the six boroughs to be visited by a royal commission after the 1852 election, as a consequence of which it was disfranchised. Among the reasons for this drastic action was the fact that its political life was in the hands of agents who kept for themselves the money their respective candidates had given them to distribute to loyal voters. Even Lord Verulam, the chief influence at St. Albans, told Parliament that it was impossible to oppose the disfranchisement and that he "was sorry for the counsel who tried to do so." (Charles Seymour, *Electoral Reform in England and Wales*, p. 222.)

HORROR OF THAT RESPECTABLE SAINT, ST. ALBANS,

At Hearing the Confession of a St. Albans' Elector.

In this cartoon (22 November 1851) *Punch* combined two topical issues, as it often did. The "confessor" is the stock figure of a fat, gluttonish monk who is seen in numerous *Punch* allusions to "Papal Aggression," and the reference to the St. Albans elector echoes the current scandal over flagrant irregularities in the election held there at the end of the previous year.

ing; no hiring of two hundred voters to act as messengers at twenty shillings a day in looking up some four hundred other voters; no bands were to be paid for; no carriages furnished; no ribbons supplied"] was taking place only on the part of his opponent. . . . (17:178)

Now, with the strengthened law on the books, even the slightest appearance of suborning must be avoided, on which basis Gresham's purchase of bonnets from the chorister's wife would seem to have bordered on the felonious.

A candidate [Trollope wrote on a later page] must pay for no treating, no refreshments, no band of music; he must give neither ribbons to the girls nor ale to the men. If a huzza be uttered in his favour, it is at his peril; it may be necessary for him to prove before a committee that it was the spontaneous result of British feeling in his favour, and not the purchased result of British beer. He cannot safely ask any one to share his hotel dinner. Bribery hides itself now in the most impalpable shapes, and may be effected by the offer of a glass of sherry. (22:235–36)

But on election day, "it certainly did appear . . . as though some great change had been made in that resolution of the candidates to be very pure. . . . [I]f the horses and postboys were not to be paid by the candidates, the voters themselves were certainly very liberal in their mode of bringing themselves to the poll. . . . Beer was to be had at the public-houses, almost without question, by all who chose to ask for it; and rum and brandy were dispensed to select circles within the bars with equal profusion" (17:179). One of the publicans profiting from the general open house was the conscientious Mr. Reddypalm, who was determined to preserve his neutrality by not voting at all. But in the course of resisting the blandishments of Romer, a solicitor in the Scatcherd interest, Reddypalm revealed that he had never been fully paid for the hogsheads of ale bought and consumed for political ends in the election two years before, and Romer quickly offered to pay the bill. The votes of Reddypalm and his son were assured, and Scatcherd won the election by precisely that margin.

Sir Roger was promptly unseated by petition, and Trollope took the opportunity to editorialize for a page or two on the timely issue his plot raised: "The sin of bribery is damnable. It is the one sin for which, in the House of Commons, there can be no forgiveness." But money was still needed to win elections, and "All these stringent bribery laws only enhance the value of such very safe men as Mr. Nearthewinde," who protected their clients, resolute in their blindness to misdeeds committed in their behalf, by knowing their way around such legal minefields (22:235, 236).

THE OLD REAL REFORMER.

"THERE WAS NO STOPPING THE SLAVE-TRADE UNTIL I MADE IT *FELONY*, AND SO IT WILL BE WITH ELECTION BRIBERY."—*Lord Brougham at Bradford.*

Trollope's *Doctor Thorne* (1858) exposed at length the continuing presence of bribery in elections; even though the Corrupt Practices Act of 1854 was the most serious attempt yet made to stem the flow of money from candidate to voter, the penalties prescribed were too lenient, and they were easily evaded. In this cartoon (*Punch*, 22 October 1859) notice is taken of Lord Brougham's recommendation that they be stiffened and stringently enforced.

In 1857 the number of petitions dropped off sharply (nineteen,[†] as against forty-nine in 1852), and though it rose to thirty in 1859, and a select committee appointed the next year to check on the working of the Corrupt Practices Act found defects persisting, the corruption issue lay dormant for the next several years.

The election of 1866, which saw the most contests (204) since 1841, was also the most expensive—£752,000 in the official returns alone, and nobody knew how much more was not reported—and it resulted in the largest number of petitions ever, sixty-one. A new royal commission report declared that "the deluge of corruption has been more universal and has reached a higher level of society than ever before." Its conclusion, that the law regarding election expenses was a dead letter despite the consternation it had at first caused, revived the agitation for reform measures that would stick.

It was in this atmosphere that George Eliot's portrayal of Harold Transome in *Felix Holt* (1866) had particular relevance. A candidate standing for Treby Magna in 1832 may or may not have had Transome's scruples about a clean election, but Eliot—and, as we shall see, Trollope—clearly thought that a candidate in the 1860s should. The scene in which Jermyn delivers a lengthy and specious defense of bribery to Harold Transome, with Felix Holt present, was one of those passages in the novel that readers would have recognized as a message for the immediate moment. The ethical dilemma of a candidate who, like Thackeray, was a man of principle yet was aware that corruption was practiced in his behalf might have been that of any number of candidates in 1866:

> The real dignity and honesty there was in him made him shrink from this necessity of satisfying a man with a troublesome tongue [Felix Holt, who alone had broached the matter]; it was as if he were to show indignation at the discovery of one barrel with a false bottom, when he had invested his money in a manufactory where a larger or smaller number of such barrels had always been made. A practical man must seek a good end by the only possible means; that is to say, if he is to get into Parliament he must not be too particular. It was not disgraceful to be neither a Quixote nor a theorist, aiming to correct the moral rules of the world; but whatever actually was, or might prove to be disgraceful, Harold held in detestation. (17:162)

[†] It might have been twenty if Thackeray, running for one of the two Oxford seats in a by-election, had won. The seat had been vacated when his friend Charles Neate was proved to have committed bribery. Thackeray's expenditure of £887 was insufficient to acquire it for himself (he lost, 1,070 to 1,005), and he subsequently admitted that even if he had won, "I should have been turned out, my agents, in spite of express promises to me, having done acts which would have ousted me." And so, by a margin of sixty-five votes, Thackeray missed becoming the first English man of letters to be charged with vote-buying. (*Letters and Private Papers of Thackeray*, ed. Ray, 4:64–66.)

The easiest way out, as Gaskell's Donne had said, was for a candidate not to know what his agent, who was hired for that tacit purpose, was doing with the campaign funds. "You are aware, my dear sir," Transome said to Felix, "that a candidate is very much at the mercy of his agents as to the means by which he is returned, especially when many years' absence has made him a stranger to the men actually conducting business" (16:159).

The "disgraceful disclosures" of the royal commission revived the corruption issue, and a bill applying to it accompanied the Second Reform Bill that was making its tortuous way through Parliament, but for tactical reasons it was withdrawn before the larger bill's enactment in 1867. The omission was made good the next year by Disraeli's Election Petitions and Corrupt Practices Act, one of whose chief provisions was that election petitions should be heard by a court appointed for the purpose.

It was under the supposed protection of the (once more!) strengthened laws against corruption that Trollope sought, as we saw in the preceding chapter, to fulfill his ambition to sit in the Commons by running for the Yorkshire seat of Beverley in 1868.[3] His agent, he recalled in his *Autobiography*, was a seasoned politician who had sat in Parliament himself.

> He understood Yorkshire,—or at least the East Riding of Yorkshire, in which Beverley is situated,—certainly better than any one alive. . . . "So," said he, "you are going to stand for Beverley!" I replied gravely that I was thinking of doing so. "You don't expect to get in!" he said. Again I was grave. I would not, I said, be sanguine, but nevertheless I was disposed to hope the best. "Oh no!" continued he, with good-humoured raillery, "you won't get in. I don't suppose you really expect it. But there is a fine career open to you. You will spend £1000, and lose the election. Then you will petition, and spend another £1000. You will throw out the elected members. There will be a commission, and the borough will be disfranchised. For a beginner such as you are, that will be a great success."[4]

Under such a definition, Trollope was indeed successful. He did come out at the bottom of the poll, the two successful candidates were unseated on petition, and the borough was disfranchised. "In this way Beverley's privilege as a borough and my Parliamentary ambition were brought to an end at the same time," he drily concluded.

Having trudged through the Beverley mud and thoroughly demeaned himself to no avail, Trollope henceforth could write of elections in a dark mood fed by firsthand experience, a mood of which we have already had glimpses in various connections. His fictive self, Sir Thomas Underwood in *Ralph the Heir*, stands for the borough of Percycross, whose past predilection for shady electoral dealings has been such that it has narrowly escaped disfranchisement. It was, said Trollope, as "rotten as a six-month-old egg" (44:2.193), a description that tightly fitted Beverley itself. That borough had long been notorious for its venality. As long ago as 1807, it was proved that of the 1,010 votes cast, only 78 were unsubsidized. In all but one of the six elections preceding 1868, corruption prevailed (the exception was 1854, but as the *Times* said, the momentary purity was "quite an accident").[5] The omens in the novel's Percycross, however, are faintly favorable to municipal reformation, because, says Trigger the agent, who naturally is against it, "Here are these judges, and you know that new brooms sweep clean." Sir Thomas's running mate as a Conservative (Trollope ran as a Liberal) is the longtime, thoroughly corruptible incumbent Griffenbottom, who is against petitions as a matter of principle ("un-English, ungentlemanlike, and unpatriotic—'A stand-up fight, and if you're licked—take it.' That was his idea of what an election should be") (39:2.130; 25:1.305).

More honestly than Harold Transome and Gustavus Moffat, Sir Thomas commits himself to a strict policy of nonbribery. In their first interview he tells Trigger, "It's as well that we should understand each other at once. . . . I should throw up the contest in the middle of it,—even if I were winning,—if I suspected that money was being spent improperly. . . . I desire to have it absolutely understood by all those who act with me in this matter." But Trigger warns him that raising the issue is bad politics: "Gentlemen when they're consulted don't like to be told of those sort of things" (20:1.240–41). Sir Thomas nevertheless proclaims his insistence on "purity" at every opportunity. He quickly learns the facts of electoral life, however, as illustrated by experiences such as have been mentioned earlier in this chapter.

Meanwhile, a more strongly motivated idealist, Ontario Moggs the bootmaker, a strong trades-union man and Reform Leaguer, has come down from London imbued with a pair of enthusiasms, "Purity [of Elections] and Rights of Labour." He creates a stir in Percycross, but the town's tradesmen, Liberal and Conservative alike, though they "did not understand much in the world of politics . . . did understand that such a doctrine as that, if carried out, would take them to a very Gehenna of revolutionary desolation" (26:1.312), and the Liberals among them abruptly withdraw their support. He perseveres, however, only to find himself plunging on election day from the head of the poll at 9:30 A.M. to the very bottom at 4 P.M. Sir Thomas is elected, along with Griffenbottom, but the ordeal, subsequently protracted through petition and trial, entirely disillusions him. In following him through the whole sorry business, from the initial address to his unseating because of his indelible

association with Griffenbottom, Trollope dramatized for his readers his
conviction that the electoral laws, even as newly energized through Disraeli's bill, were totally inadequate. "There was a night train up to London at 10 P.M., by which on that evening Sir Thomas Underwood travelled, shaking off from his feet as he entered the carriage the dust of
that most iniquitous borough" (44:2.195).

In *Phineas Redux*, published three years later (1873–74), Trollope's
disillusionment hardened into cynicism. Browborough, who had beaten
Phineas at Tankerville, was unseated as the result of a petition and Phineas seated in his stead. A royal commission came to Tankerville, "swept
very clean, being new brooms," and recommended that a criminal prosecution be brought against Browborough. In chapter 44 Trollope described the proceedings at the Durham assizes. Despite the legal skill of
Sir Gregory Grogram and against all the evidence, Browborough was
acquitted. Trollope read hypocrisy first in the law itself, and then in the
ineffectual way in which it was enforced:

> The House had been very hot against bribery,—and certain members of
> the existing Government, when the late Bill had been passed, had ex-
> pressed themselves with almost burning indignation against the crime. But,
> through it all, there had been a slight undercurrent of ridicule attaching
> itself to the question of which only they who were behind the scenes were
> conscious. The House was bound to let the outside world know that all cor-
> rupt practices at elections were held to be abominable by the House; but
> Members of the House, as individuals, knew very well what had taken place
> at their own elections, and were aware of the cheques which they had
> drawn. Public-houses had been kept open as a matter of course, and no-
> where perhaps had more beer been drunk than at Clovelly, the borough
> for which Sir Gregory Grogram sat. (44:358)

However serious the intention of its makers may have been, when the
law was applied it evoked only frivolity, as in Dickens's Court of Chancery, when the unsinkable case of Jarndyce *versus* Jarndyce surfaced
once more.

> The general flavour of the trial at Durham was one of good-humoured rail-
> lery. . . . Nobody scolded anybody. There was no roaring of barristers, no
> clenching of fists and kicking up of dust, no threats, no allusions to wit-
> nesses' oaths. A considerable amount of gentle fun was poked at the wit-
> nesses by the defending counsel, but not in a manner to give any pain.
> Gentlemen who acknowledged to have received seventeen shillings and six-
> pence for their votes at the last election were asked how they had invested
> their money. Allusions were made to their wives, and a large amount of
> good-humoured sparring was allowed, in which the witnesses thought that
> they had the best of it. The men of Tankerville long remembered this trial,
> and hoped anxiously that there might soon be another. (44:361–62)

But the true depth of Trollope's own cynicism was expressed, paradoxically enough, in connection with the only contest that was really clean, almost in spite of itself. It was the last election he would describe, that at Polpenno (*The Duke's Children*, [1879]). In accordance with the newly developed respect for the bribery laws, Frank Tregear's tailor friend had "kept his eyes so sharply open to the pecuniary doings of the Carbottleites, that Mr. Carbottle's guides and friends had hardly dared to spend a shilling" (61:446). Having not done what the Polpenno voters expected him to do, fat Carbottle, the Liberal, was beaten.

> Therefore, the Conservatives were very elate with their triumph. There was a great Conservative reaction. But the electioneering guide, philosopher, and friend, in the humble retirement of his own home, . . . knew very well how the seat had been secured. Ten shillings a head would have sent three hundred true Liberals to the ballot-boxes! The mode of distributing the money had been arranged; but the Conservative tailor had been too acute, and not half-a-sovereign could be passed. The tailor got twenty-five pounds for his work, and that was smuggled in among the bills for printing. (61:447)

3.

The election scenes in Victorian novels were written when the modern party system was only slowly evolving, and by and large the contests described centered on persons, who were tied only loosely to the parties they represented, rather than on the issues with which the parties were associated in parliamentary debate. At the time of the First Reform Bill there were no sharp distinctions between the Tories and the Whigs. "[A] Tory," said Jobbry in Galt's *The Member*, "is but a Whig in office, and a Whig but a Tory in opposition, which makes it not difficult for a conscientious man to support the government" (2:7), a dictum echoed in the later, more famous remark that Disraeli put in Taper's mouth in *Coningsby* and Surtees promptly quoted in *Hillingdon Hall*: "A sound Conservative government. I understand: Tory men and Whig measures" (2.6:124). The parties were simply two portions of the same ruling class, composed of family and interest groups vying among themselves for the control and the resulting private benefits of government.

Elaborately organized parties in the modern sense, with agreed programs, were to emerge only in the course of the Victorian years. As far as voters were concerned, it was labels, not principles, that mattered. As the political consciousness of Treby Magna developed in 1832, wrote George Eliot in the retrospect of more than thirty years, "Tory, Whig, and Radical did not perhaps become clearer in their definition of each other; but the names seemed to acquire so strong a stamp of honour or infamy, that definitions would only have weakened the impression" (*Felix Holt*, 3:44).

However strong and effective party discipline may or may not have been in Westminster, partisanship in local elections was not enforced by appeals to a voter's loyalty. The sense of liberation that accompanied the Reform Bill dissolved the former presumption that if one was so lucky as to have a vote, the vote should be cast as the local magnate desired.

> In Treby [continued George Eliot], as elsewhere, people were told they must "rally" at the coming election; but there was now a large number of waverers—men of flexible, practical minds, who were not such bigots as to cling to any views when a good tangible reason could be urged against them; while some regarded it as the most neighbourly thing to hold a little with both sides, and were not sure that they should rally or vote at all. It seemed an invidious thing to vote for one gentleman rather than another. (3:45)

Even after the parties had achieved stronger identities, individual personalities and deviant opinions made their presence felt. Trollope repeatedly noted this phenomenon. In *Rachel Ray*, the brewer Tappitt "was no doubt a Liberal as was also Mr. Hart; but in small towns politics become split, and a man is not always bound to vote for a Liberal candidate because he is a Liberal himself" (17:213). At Percycross, "Moggs was separated from Westmacott [the other Liberal candidate] quite as absolutely as was Westmacott from the two Conservative candidates." The split cut another way as well: " . . . there was almost as much ill-feeling between the old-fashioned Griffenbottomites and the Underwooders as there was between Westmacott's Liberals and Moggs's Radicals" (*Ralph the Heir*, 29:2.1,3).

While Trollope was writing these novels, the attention of political observers was concentrated on what was happening, or had already happened, to the Whig party. By the sixties, it had lost the identity it had acquired when the First Reform Bill triumphed under its auspices, and ceasing to be a "creed," it had become instead a "caste" in which, in a nation steadily deserting tradition for pragmatism, there was no mileage for ambitious young politicians. The decline of the Whigs and their replacement by the Liberals, a party which officially assumed the name that had hitherto been borne informally by the Whigs, was the leading theme of some passages in *Beauchamp's Career*, serialized in the *Fortnightly Review* in 1874–75. These constituted in the aggregate, among other things, an exercise in the fresh definition of parties, in which Meredith had the editor Timothy Turbot, Colonel Halkett, the "exuberant Tory" Blackburn Tuckham, and the irascible and vociferously opinionated Dr. Shrapnel talk brilliantly (in the mode of the interlocutors in the novels of Peacock, Meredith's father-in-law) in an effort to distinguish between the Conservatives (Tories), Liberals, and Radicals of 1874–75.

Beauchamp's Career was the most "political" novel since Disraeli's trilogy. No novelist in the interim had devoted so much attention as Disraeli did to contemporary political issues, especially as these were raised during the progress of an election. When party labels were used (and many novelists avoided doing so, in order not to muddy the waters with partisan biases), the positions on current questions that they respectively represented were ignored. Only a small handful of such issues were ever mentioned, and of these, suitably enough, the one that most often appeared dealt with the electoral machinery. Once the franchise had been extended in 1832, the left wing of the Whig party and, toward the end of the decade, the far more radical Chartists agitated for widening it still further, but this campaign subsided in the late forties and was not revived until the mid-sixties. Meanwhile, the great panacea for the ills of the electoral system that the First Reform Act had failed to cure was thought to be the secret ballot, which would end, once and for all, the threat of intimidation and the occasion for bribery, the efficacy of which could not be verified once a man's vote was cast in privacy.

For seven years after 1832, George Grote, M.P. for the City of London, annually introduced a bill to institute "the ballot" (the word *secret* seldom accompanied it), and in *Coningsby* "going for the ballot" was talked of as a shrewd Liberal tactic; but the proposal was always solidly defeated. The fact that it was one of the Chartists' six demands did not recommend it to the middle class. Even patrician legislators generally well disposed toward radicalism (read: liberalism) gagged at the idea. The Duke of Bungay, dining at the Pallisers' Matching Priory, told Alice Vavasor, "I've voted for every liberal measure that has come seriously before Parliament since I had a seat in either House," but, he added, "I hate it [the ballot] with so keen a private hatred, that I doubt whether I could vote for it. . . . Palliser," he called down the table to his host, "I'm told you can never be entitled to call yourself a Radical till you've voted for the ballot." But Plantagenet Palliser refused the bait: "I don't want to be called a Radical,—or to be called anything at all" (*Can You Forgive Her?*, 23 : 257–58).

That the ballot was recognized from the outset as the principal unfinished business of Reform was clear in *Felix Holt*. (A provision relating to it had been stripped from the bill before enactment.) In the intoxicating atmosphere in the autumn of 1832, "the speakers at Reform banquets were exuberant in congratulation and promise: Liberal clergymen of the Establishment toasted Liberal Catholic clergymen without any allusion to scarlet, and Catholic clergymen replied with a like tender reserve. Some dwelt on the abolition of all abuses, and on millennial blessedness generally; others, whose imaginations were less suffused with exhalations of the dawn, insisted chiefly on the ballot-box." It was the subject of debate between Harold Transome, who had "too much respect for the freedom of the voter to oppose anything which offers a chance of making that freedom more complete," and the Reverend Mr. Lyon, who argued that "it would be futile as a preservative from bribery and illegitimate influence; and . . . that it would be in the worst kind pernicious, as shutting the door against those influences whereby the soul of a man and the character of a citizen are duly educated for their great functions" (16:158).

This was one of the passages in *Felix Holt* that bore most directly on the political situation in 1866. The time was ripe for new reform measures, and agitation for the secret ballot was revived as the proposal to enlarge the franchise wound its way through Parliament. *Phineas Finn* (1867–69) reported the debate on the ballot, dramatized by the delivery to the House of Commons, in fifteen cabs, of a huge petition in favor of the bill. Here Trollope reached back twenty years for his topicality, enlarging it by a factor of five as he implicitly reminded his readers of the historic three-cab cortège that in April 1848 bore the monster Chartist petition from Kennington, the site of an unexpectedly peaceful demonstration, to Westminster. The petition's lukewarm reception there proved, in retrospect, to have marked the demise of Chartism as a political force.

Neither in the fictional version nor in fact did the ballot bill pass at that time. As had happened in 1832, that provision was removed from the larger Reform Bill, but it was passed as a separate act in 1872. Two years later the secret ballot was first used in a national election, and no sooner had the first papers been marked and counted than Trollope incorporated in *The Way We Live Now* (1874–75) a scene at the Covent Garden polling place, which Melmotte visits as he tries to brazen out the scandalous rumors that had gathered around his name.

Even before it was officially settled, however, the ballot issue was passé as far as the most forward-looking radicals were concerned. To Ontario Moggs it gave way to two other questions, neither of them really new but now possessing fresh value as ammunition for an idealistic young politician.

> The ballot was almost nothing to him. Strikes and bribery were his great
> subjects; the beauty of the one and the ugliness of the other. The right of
> the labourer to combine with his brother labourers to make his own terms

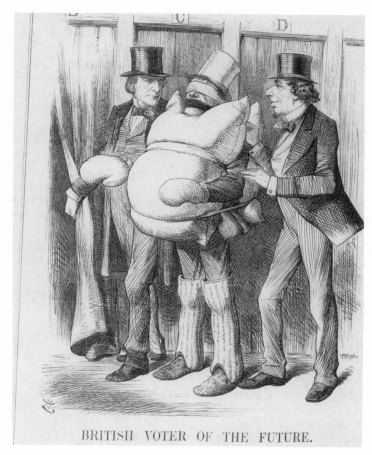

BRITISH VOTER OF THE FUTURE.

Punch (5 August 1871) anticipated the passage, the following year, of the law that abolished public vote-casting in favor of the secret ballot. The solicitous politicians, representing "Collective Wisdom" (Parliament), say, "Now, what more CAN we do to protect him?"

for his labour, was the great lesson he taught. The suicidal iniquity of the labourer in selling that political power which he should use to protect his labour was the source of his burning indignation. That labour was the salt of the earth, he told the men of Percycross very often;—and he told them as often that manliness and courage were necessary to make that salt productive. (*Ralph the Heir*, 26:1.310)

In the first part of Victoria's reign, Norman Gash has remarked, "National issues were growing in importance but they still had to compete with local issues and local methods of control; and the precise importance accorded to them in the provinces was not necessarily that attached to them in parliament or the national press." "It is unlikely under any circumstance," he says at another place, "that the ordinary farmer of the thirties and forties took a great interest in or had much knowledge of home and foreign policy."[6] The evidence of fiction supports this view and extends it to all classes of voters; no matter what national issues were placed before them, local ones were of much greater moment. (The most conspicuous exception to the rule was the proposed abolition of the Corn Laws in the forties, a literally bread (and butter) issue that affected the very pocketbooks of the producers in the agricultural regions and the consumers in the towns. It figured in *Hillingdon Hall* and, retrospectively, in *Endymion*.) And even when the subjects of fierce debates in Parliament found their way into the country, people often got them wrong. The Sproxton colliers' interpretation of Reform, according to George Eliot, was that if it was good for anything, it "must at last resolve itself into spare money—meaning 'sport' and drink, and keeping away from work for several days in the week" (*Felix Holt*, 11:120). The drunken farmer Dagley in *Middlemarch*, his truculence ignited by his landlord Brooke's mild punishment of his son for killing a leveret, extrapolates all his grievances into things the newly crowned king will "put a stop to" through the magical instrument of "Rinform":

> "An' I meean as the King 'ull put a stop to't, for them say it as knows it, as there's to be a Rinform, and them landlords as never done the right thing by their tenants 'ull be treated i' that way as they'll hev to scuttle off. An' there's them i' Middlemarch knows what the Rinform is—an' as knows who'll hev to scuttle. Says they, 'I know who *your* landlord is.' An' says I, 'I hope you're the better for knowin' him, I arn't.' Says they, 'He's a close fisted un.' 'Ay, ay,' says I. 'He's a man for the Rinform,' says they. That's what they says. An' I made out what the Rinform were—an' it were to send you an' your likes a-scuttlin'; an' wi' pretty strong-smellin' things too. An' you may do as you like now, for I'm none afeared on you. An' you'd better let my boy aloan, an' look to yoursen, afore the Rinform has got upo' your back." (39:432)

Mr. Brooke, who prided himself on his conscientious study of the day's issues, knew, as well as "them i' Middlemarch," what Reform was all about—or so he thought. When Will Ladislaw told him that with the approaching election the town "will have got more ideas into its head," he affirmed his support of Lord Grey and Reform, but added, "Only I want to keep myself independent about Reform, you know: I don't want to go too far. I want to take up Wilberforce's and Romilly's line, you

"A BRAVE LADY."

"Strong-minded Young Person (escorts the little Vicar and her Aunt to Vote).
'I'm *astonished* at your being Nervous *this* Year, Aunt! Why, we have only to put
our Papers in a Box!'" The light humor of this scene in *Punch* (23 November
1872) obscures the momentousness of the two changes in British electoral practice that it represents. In local elections, beginning that year, the secret ballot
was first used and women were allowed to vote in accordance with a law enacted
in 1869 that admitted them to the municipal franchise.

know, and work at Negro Emancipation, Criminal Law—that kind of
thing" (46:499–500). Whether this is an instance of his ingrained habit
of gliding from one subject to another without pausing over any, or of a
simple assumption that "Reform," which in the parlance of the time referred explicitly to the electoral system, also embraced Negro emancipation and law reform, is immaterial: either way, Brooke's incurable fuzzi-
ness of mind was exposed. Ladislaw, whose suppressed impatience can
easily be imagined, tries to set his employer straight in a single sentence:
"It [the country] wants to have a House of Commons which is not
weighted with nominees of the landed class, but with representatives of
the other interests." It was as simple as that, but neither the loose-
mouthed farmer nor the muddle-headed landowner—nor, one suspects,
many of the voters in 1832—thought that was what Reform really meant.

As in many elections, the one at Eatanswill made up in parochial
ferocity what it lacked in ideological substance.

Every man in Eatanswill, conscious of the weight that attached to his example, felt himself bound to unite, heart and soul, with one of the two great parties that divided the town—the Blues and the Buffs.† Now the Blues lost no opportunity of opposing the Buffs, and the Buffs lost no opportunity of opposing the Blues; and the consequence was, that whenever the Buffs and Blues met together at public meeting, Town-Hall, fair, or market, disputes and high words arose between them. With these dissensions it is almost superfluous to say that everything in Eatanswill was made a party question. If the Buffs proposed to new sky-light the market-place, the Blues got up at public meetings, and denounced the proceeding; if the Blues proposed the erection of an additional pump in the High Street, the Buffs rose as one man and stood aghast at the enormity. There were Blue shops and Buff shops, Blue inns and Buff inns;—there was a Blue aisle and a Buff aisle, in the very church itself. (*Pickwick Papers*, 13:237–38)

There is no hint that the minds of Messrs. Fizkin and Slumkey and their respective supporters were troubled by the momentous issues of the day.

The local pocketbook issue figured fairly often in elections, reaching beyond the ephemeral effect a hotly fought and adequately financed contest had on the borough's economy. This was the bottom line in the single-issue campaign in *Can You Forgive Her?*: "Vote for Vavasor and the River Bank." It was not the prospective amenities of a Chelsea embankment but the promise of jobs that would win over the voters. "No young Member can do anything without a subject," the experienced Scruby advised George Vavasor. "And it should be local;—that is to say, if you have anything of a constituency. Such a subject as that, if it's well worked, may save you thousands of pounds—thousands of pounds at future elections. . . . Only look at the money that would be spent in the districts if that were done! It would come to millions, sir!" (44:473). Trollope noted an inducement of a related kind in *Ralph the Heir*: Mr. Spicer and his obedient workmen would vote for the candidate who could get them government contracts for mustard.

4.

From the viewpoint of the market-conscious publisher of fiction, it was a happy accident that women, voteless though they were, figured, often

---

†"Blues" and "buffs" may be taken to mean the Tories and the Whigs, respectively, as they did also in *Ten Thousand a Year* three or four years later, but these identifications were not entirely fixed. At Hartlebury earlier in the decade, Mr. Chace, the agent, said "Blue and yellow are the engaged colours, Blue the Whig," and in later novels the partisan colors vary widely, seemingly being chosen locally for the occasion, as at Barchester, where they were scarlet and yellow (*Doctor Thorne*, 17:179). In *Ralph the Heir* (1870–71) blue is definitely the Tory (by that time, Conservative) color.

prominently, in the electioneering process. Elections were a topicality about which women could read with appreciation, some even recalling their own informal participation in local contests. If they lacked the franchise, they were uniquely situated—possessors, as they were, of the traditional "womanly wiles," whatever form these may have taken—to advance their men's careers or help swing an election for a favorite candidate or party. It might be, as Bulwer-Lytton snidely put it in *My Novel*, that in involving themselves in a province of public affairs that was dominated by men, ladies were simply indulging in "that intense interest which those gentle creatures usually do take in all matters of strife and contest" (1.10:1.58). It was true that a fairly large portion of Victorian society endorsed the rebuke the Dissenting preacher Mr. Prong, in *Rachel Ray*, delivered to his fiancée, the widow Dorothea Prime: "Voting for Members of Parliament is a thing which ladies naturally are not called upon to understand" (24:315). Pendennis had made the same point to Laura Bell some years earlier: "Women don't understand about politics, my dear" (*Pendennis*, 66:2.301).

But in fashionable society there was a long tradition of women taking part in heated contests. The coup of the beautiful Georgiana Spencer, Duchess of Devonshire, in the Westminster election of 1784 was legendary. The voting had been going on for six weeks, as was permissible then, and by the time the polling list was exhausted, the Duchess's favorite, Charles James Fox, was one hundred votes behind his opponent. Fox's only hope was to draw support from freemen living in the suburbs. According to a contemporary, "The Duchess instantly ordered out her equipage, and with her sister, the Countess of Duncannon, drove, polling list in hand, to the houses of the voters. Entreaties, ridicule, civilities, influence of all kinds were lavished on these rough legislators; and the novelty of being solicited by two women of rank and remarkable fashion, took the popular taste universally."[7] The final tally showed that Fox had won by the same margin by which he had earlier trailed.

The Duchess's exploit was immediately celebrated in a flurry of lampoons and caricatures, and it put ideas into the heads of later politicians. As Joseph Grego, the Victorian historian of parliamentary elections, elegantly put it, "a certain grace was lent to the generally discordant elements of electioneering by the zealous participation of Beauty in the canvassing department, where the seductive wiles of female charms and persuasions were relied upon."[8]

Electioneering therefore came naturally to ladies in fashionable novels, whose interest in politics—or, more accurately, certain politicians—took them upstairs to "the ventilator" in the old House of Commons, where they could hear, if not see, the debate. At Disraeli's Hartlebury, ladies, like their medieval ancestresses at jousts, made favors to bestow on their chosen combatants in the electoral lists, and, clad in green riding habits and accompanied by their grooms, put winsome pressure on shopmen-voters designated by Aubrey Bohun, who assured them that "A pretty woman . . . especially on horseback, is worth more than a whole committee" (*A Year at Hartlebury*, 2.4:125).

This wisdom, put more crudely by Gossip Faddle in the same novel——"If the men have the votes, the women have the influence" (2.7:135)—was handed down, undiluted, through the Victorian years. At the behest of his agent, Gustavus Moffat in *Doctor Thorne* spent three whole days in Barchester "looking up the electors' wives and daughters" (15:166). In *The Duke's Children*, to illustrate his heartfelt conviction that "Parliamentary canvassing is not a pleasant occupation," Trollope cited a hypothetical conversation between a rain-drenched candidate and a workingman's wife:

> "I think I am right in supposing that your husband's principles are Conservative, Mrs. Bubbs." "I don't know nothing about it, you'd better call again and see Bubbs hissel." "Certainly I will do so. I shouldn't at all like to leave the borough without seeing Mr. Bubbs. I hope we shall have your influence, Mrs. Bubbs." "I don't know nothing about it. My folk at home allays vote buff; and I think Bubbs ought to go buff too. Only mind this; Bubbs don't never come home to his dinner. You must come arter six, and I hope he's to have some'at for his trouble. He won't have my word to vote unless he have some'at." (55:443)

Such was the price a candidate paid for seeking a seat in Parliament at a time when the franchise had been extended to the likes of Mr. Bubbs. Regardless of their social position, women were valuable to candidates not for any appreciation of the issues involved, which they might discuss in a rational way with their open-minded husbands—as Mrs. Proudie perhaps expressed her views on current questions in the couple's connubial bed—but simply for the pressure they might exert, down to the requisite "some'at" to buy a square meal for the family. It was only late in the period, and in the special context of George Meredith's feminism, that "what a woman thinks in politics" was to be seriously considered. Beauchamp, said Meredith, "deemed it of great moment. Politically, he deemed that women have souls, a certain fire of life for exercise on earth. He appealed to reason in them; he would not hear of convictions. He quoted the Bevisham doctor: 'Convictions are generally first impressions that are sealed with later prejudices,' and insisted there was wisdom in it" (*Beauchamp's Career*, 17:1.174).

But the proven way to a woman's vicarious vote, genuinely practical politicians were convinced, was through her vanity. No candidate, it is true, could have brought himself to kiss Mrs. Bubbs—the soft cheeks of the Eatanswill babies were much to be preferred—but in general, before the informal inclusion of workingmen's wives complicated the electoral situation, it was agreed that woman-kissing was a productive adjunct to canvassing, assuming that the woman's husband (or brother or father) was as receptive to her subsequent entreaty as she was to this degree of flattering public attention.[†] It was one talent that could serve a candidate who was otherwise largely unqualified for office. Captain Dashmore, in *My Novel*, turned out to be

> a most capital electioneerer for a popular but not enlightened constituency. It is true that he talked the saddest nonsense ever heard from an open window; but then his jokes were so broad, his manner so hearty, his voice so big, that in those dark days, before the schoolmaster was abroad, he would have beaten your philosophical Radical and moralizing Democrat hollow. Moreover, he kissed all the women, old and young, with the zest of a sailor who has known what it is to be three years at sea without sight of a beardless lip . . . .

But the captain's proficiency in the art, if that is what it was, had the effect of making him more vulnerable on his own ground. When, in the absence of his rival, his prospects of election looked more favorable by the hour, a proxy for the missing man was found in the person of the Squire of Hazeldean, "the only mortal who could cope with the sea-captain,—a man with a voice as burly and a face as bold; a man who, if permitted for the nonce by Mrs. Hazeldean, would kiss all the women no less heartily than the Captain kissed them; and who was, moreover, a taller, and a handsomer, and a younger man,—all three great recommendations in the kissing department of a contested election" (1.10: 1.55–57).

Some candidates, to be sure, abstained from this form of canvassing. One was Gustavus Moffat, who, perhaps hypersensitive to the newly strengthened law against bribery, refrained from kissing not only the chorister's wife, from whom his opponent Frank Gresham had ordered the bonnets, but her two "very pretty" daughters as well. Instead, said the Honorable George DeCourcy, "he begged to give them his positive assurance as a gentleman, that if he was returned to parliament he would vote for an extension of the franchise, and the admission of the

[†] In some circumstances the action was reciprocal. When Thomas Attwood, the Chartist, worked Birmingham in 1837, he wrote that "he had received about 10,000 kisses, chiefly from old women although some had come from the most beautiful women in the world. 'My lips,' he added 'are quite sore with the kisses of yesterday.'" (Gash, *Politics in the Age of Peel*, p. 117.)

Jews into parliament." "Well, he is a muff!" exclaimed Gresham, dismissively (*Doctor Thorne*, 15:167).

When Victorian ladies went out canvassing on their own, they often did so in the way exemplified by Mrs. Nevill and Helen Molesworth at Hartlebury, by putting economic pressure, implicit or overt, on tradesmen. Emily Eden's ladies at Boroughford studied poll lists "all day to see if there are any of our tradespeople or old friends in the village whom we could persuade to vote for [Ernest]." They conspired to order a bonnet from Mrs. Vere, whose husband "pretends to have opinions about church reform," and a set of iron hurdles, to encircle the pleasure ground, from the ironmonger. Mr. Birkett, the physician, might lose the prospect of vaccinating a baby in the family if he continued to refuse to pledge his vote. As the contest heated up, Lady Eskdale and her daughters

> drove into the town constantly, and seemed suddenly to have discovered that they were without any of the necessaries or luxuries of life, for the extent of their dealings with well-thinking tradespeople was prodigious, and it might have been supposed that they were covertly sullying the purity of election; but, as they justly alleged, shopping was what every woman was born for, and could not, under any circumstances, be considered illegal. . . .
> (*The Semi-Attached Couple*, 36:179–80; 37:183)

On other occasions, ladies went out frankly soliciting votes, in direct emulation of their exemplary forebear, the Duchess of Devonshire. When the election at Hartlebury neared its end with the vote tied, Helen Molesworth made a dramatic visit to the single holdout, old Mr. Gainsborough, and persuaded him to vote for her suitor, Aubrey Bohun. Bohun won by that margin. Many years later, Patty Cornbury, wife of the Conservative candidate for Baslehurst, paid a similar visit to the brewer Tappitt, a known Liberal; but she made the mistake of involving in her plea Tappitt's mortal enemy, Luke Rowan, who wanted to buy Tappitt out—and was in love with Rachel Ray, Patty's friend. In this case, local politics and a love affair could not be satisfactorily reconciled, and Tappitt was obdurate. Whereas Helen Molesworth heroically delivered the goods, Butler Cornbury was obliged to admit that his wife had "made a mess of it" (*Rachel Ray*, 18:232).

The most memorable intervention of the kind in Trollope's novels, however, was Lady Glencora Palliser's attempt to assist Lopez's candidacy in defiance of her husband's order that the hitherto close seat of Silverbridge be thrown open. Her defense—"I suppose I may have my political sympathies as well as another. Really you are becoming so autocratic that I shall have to go in for women's rights" (*The Prime Minister*, 32:1.301)—was considerably in advance of its time as far as the novel-

A HINT FOR POLITICAL MENDICANTS.

The spectacle of women canvassing for votes in behalf of relatives
or friends elicited humorous comment in the mid-1860s, perhaps
because it was associated with the burgeoning "female emancipation" movement. Mrs. Veneering recruited Lady Tippins in her
husband's cause in the first number of *Our Mutual Friend* (May
1864), and a year later (15 July 1865) *Punch* printed this cartoon,
in which even the sisters' lapdogs beg votes for "Pa."

reading public at large was concerned, but it may well have been spoken
privately on other, real-life occasions in which spirited Victorian ladies
asserted their right to political activism. Perhaps Lady Glencora, Duchess of Omnium, was thinking of that other duchess a century earlier.
But in Trollope's treatment of the episode she bore a greater resemblance to Eve as she disobeyed her prime minister husband in the garden of Gatherum Castle.

In *Our Mutual Friend*, women canvass furiously in behalf of Veneering's candidacy for the Pocket-Breaches seat. "A woman's tact is invaluable," says Twemlow. "To have the dear sex with us, is to have everything
with us" (2.3:297). Accordingly, Mrs. Veneering entreats Lady Tippins
to lend her valuable hand, and lends *her* the Veneering carriage and

horses, with which she "clatters about town all day, calling upon every-body she knows, and showing her entertaining powers and green fan to great advantage, by rattling on with, My dear soul, what do you think? What do you suppose me to be? You'll never guess. I'm pretending to be an electioneering agent. And for what place of all places? Pocket-Breaches. And why? Because the dearest friend I have in the world has bought it . . . " (2.3:300–301). The effort, however, is wholly wasted, because the canvassing is conducted in the wrong place (London) and in any event Veneering has, as Lady Tippins says, already bought the seat.

The number of Victorian women who campaigned for candidates, whether frivolously or in dead earnest, was infinitesimal compared with those who watched from the sidelines or simply were uninterested in such contests. Perhaps the most astute summary of the average woman's view came from a decidedly un-average lady who had watched from the distance of her invalid's sofa the curious spectacle of English democracy in action—Signora Nerini in *Barchester Towers*, whose observations had led her to define a constituency as "the people that carry you about in chairs and pelt you with eggs and apples when they make you a member of Parliament" (45:500).

5.

"[T]he humors of a country election," wrote Samuel Warren in *Ten Thousand a Year*, " . . . have employed already thousands of able and graphic pens and pencils. Surely, what else are *they* than the sticks and straws which float along the eddying and roughened surface? The whole mass of water is moving along; and our object should be rather to discover its depth, its force, and direction. Principles are in conflict; the fate of the nation is, in a measure, involved in a popular election" (27:708)—which in the English style was more entertainment than a serious exercise in communal decision making. Warren's "thousands" was a palpable exag-geration, but his point was well taken. It was the "humors" of elections that engaged novelists, not their deeper political significance.

One of the earliest and, despite much competition later on, still the best concentrated description of an election scene was Dickens's single-paragraph report of the Slumkey rally in the Town Arms stable yard:

> There was regular army of blue flags, some with one handle, and some with two, exhibiting appropriate devices, in golden characters four feet high, and stout in proportion. There was a grand band of trumpets, bassoons and drums, marshalled four abreast, and earning their money, if ever men did, especially the drum beaters, who were very muscular. There were bod-ies of constables with blue staves, twenty committee-men with blue scarfs, and a mob of voters with blue cockades. There were electors on horseback,

Phiz's portrayal of the Eatanswill election in *Pickwick Papers*, part 5 (August 1836), was drawn, as was always to be the case during their long collaboration, under Dickens's close supervision. It doubtless captures the robust anarchy of the elections that Dickens had observed the preceding year when he covered the Sudbury and Ipswich elections for the *Morning Chronicle*. Both of these East Anglian boroughs were deservedly famous for their flagrant and persistent corruption.

and electors a-foot. There was an open carriage and four, for the honourable Samuel Slumkey; and there were four carriages and pair, for his friends and supporters; and the flags were rustling, and the band was playing, and the constables were swearing, and the twenty committee-men were squabbling, and the mob were shouting, and the horses were backing, and the post-boys perspiring. . . . (*Pickwick Papers*, 13:248)

Here were some of the most familiar ingredients of the later set pieces. Bands hired by each of the candidates paraded up and down, playing popular tunes that included marches and the indispensable "See the Conquering Hero Comes." Not only did a band draw attention to the candidate who was paying it: on cue, it could drown out his opponent's speech, as Slumkey's band, "performing with a power to which their strength in the morning was a trifle," obliterated Fizkin's. Everybody wore the colors of his or her candidate: cockades, ribbons, rosettes, and whatever other kinds of insignia—flags, banners, streamers—lent themselves to color coding. Officious constables with their staves, sometimes as devoid of dignity as a later age's Keystone Kops, sought, often to no avail, to maintain or restore order, and exerted themselves in arresting the ringleaders of disturbances to the number, in little Eatanswill, of two hundred and fifty. Their pàrticular bêtes noires were the town urchins, who reveled in the relaxation of discipline which, the police presence notwithstanding, inescapably accompanied an election; the impudent nuisances were given to shouting rude remarks, and the special constables at Hartlebury "broke the heads of all the boys in the town under ten years of age" for these and other offenses (*A Year at Hartlebury*, 2.5:130).

A borough undergoing an election campaign registered a high decibel level. Not only were there the rival bands and unorganized blowing of horns, beating of drums, and tooting of penny whistles: the street echoed with the sound of church bells pealing (it is sometimes not clear whether they were rung on behalf of a particular candidate, a vigorous defender of the Established Church, or administered impartially), and at Eatanswill the town crier wielded an "enormous bell" in the interests of commanding silence. The crowd cheered incessantly, their standard cry being "———For Ever," which, to a reasonable mind, took account of neither of life's ineluctable realities, mutability and mortality. At Hartlebury, "Even the children in arms were taught by their enraptured mothers to lisp, 'Bohun for ever', . . . [and] not an urchin passed the dwelling of a Whig leader without saluting the trembling owner with the odious watchword" (2.1:102). When dissatisfaction with the show of hands required a formal vote the next day, the clamor, steadily intensified by free beer flowing like water, lasted the whole night, while indoors the agents and their candidates held brainstorming sessions to plan their last-minute strategies.

Even the walls cried out, covered over as every one in the town was with sloganeering and often libelous allegations in gaudily colored posters. We have already noticed the battle of graphics that accompanied the Barchester contest between Moffat and Scatcherd. Earlier, at Yatton in *Ten Thousand a Year*, the Quaint Club, advertising its readiness to be bought by the highest bidder, carried a banner stretched between two poles, showing "an enormous man's face with an intense squint, and two hands, with the thumbs of each resting on the nose, and the fingers spread out toward the beholder" (27:724). Like Scatcherd, Hart, the Jewish clothing dealer in *Rachel Ray*, adroitly fended off a prank that might have embarrassed a candidate with less aplomb. Far from being the stereotyped Jew that the people of Baslehurst expected when he turned up to canvass, he "only laughed aloud when some true defender of the Protestant faith attempted to scare him away out of the streets by carrying a gammon of bacon up on high" (24:308).

Speeches proved a candidate's mettle, if nothing more, because he was at the mercy of his auditors, who were capable of sustaining indefinitely a barrage of hoots, groans, hisses, and what Thackeray called "odious hiccups" (studiously contrived burps?). These were inarticulate but effective; even more effective, if practiced by accomplished polemicists or wits among the audience, was the heckling that any candidate entered in a genuine contest had to endure. Mr. Brooke retired in confusion before the mockery of the ingenious ventriloquist and effigy; Scatcherd gave as good as he got, and won.

There were safer places than the hustings at election time. Accompanying the derisive chorus was a standard assortment of missiles, ranging from innocuous nutshells and bags of flour through dead cats, rotten eggs, and cabbage stalks, to brickbats and stones. Delamare, in *Ten Thousand a Year*, received a stone on his upper lip, the copious bleeding from which aroused sympathy for him if not for his cause; Barnes Newcome's nose caught a potato; and Sir Thomas Underwood actually had his arm broken at Percycross.[†] Once missiles began to be hurled at speakers, there was a good chance that a gathering that had begun in a festive spirit would get out of hand, as it several times did in fiction. The potential was always there, given the quantities of beer and spirits that were consumed, and it was increased when nonvoters were invited to join the fun. Diana Mulock's allusion to "the un-voting, and consequently unbribable portion of the community" in *John Halifax, Gentleman* (24:240) reveals a surprising lack of acquaintance with the way things actually

---

[†]Other missiles, attested to by reliable historical sources, were understandably omitted from narratives meant for family reading. At a county election at Wolverhampton in 1835, one voter had, in his own words, "an immense quantity of horse soil thrown all over me which got into my shirt and was very obnoxious," and a shopkeeper was assaulted by ruffians who disapproved of the way he had voted the day before. "They spit upon me," he said "and some made water in their hands and threw it at me." (Gash, *Politics in the Age of Peel*, pp. 149–50.)

were managed at an election. Nonvoters may not have been bribable, but they were employable. Muscular men, whose readiness to be hired to throw their weight around compensated for their absence from the polling list, had various uses. Chubb the publican in *Felix Holt*, said George Eliot, was "enlightened enough to know that there was a way of using voteless miners and navvies at Nominations and Elections" (11:114). This is spelled out to them in all its populist glory by the agent Johnson:

> "You've got no votes, and that's a shame. But you *will* have some day, if such men as Transome are returned; and then you'll be on a level with the first gentlemen in the land, and if he wants to sit in Parliament, he must take off his hat and ask your leave. But though you haven't got a vote you can give a cheer for the right man, and Transome's not a man like Garstin; if you lost a day's wages by giving a cheer for Transome, he'll make you amends. That's the way a man who has no vote can yet serve himself and his country: he can lift up his hand and shout 'Transome forever'—'hurray for Transome.' Let the working men . . . join together and give their hands and voices for the right man, and they'll make the great people shake in their shoes a little; and when you shout for Transome, remember you shout for more wages, and more of your rights, and you shout to get rid of rats and *sprats* and such small animals, who are the tools the rich make use of to squeeze the blood out of the poor man."

But Johnson cunningly warns his auditors:

> "No pommelling—no striking first. There you have the law and the constable against you. A little rolling in the dust and knocking hats off, a little pelting with soft things that'll stick and not bruise—all that doesn't spoil the fun. If a man is to speak when you don't like to hear him, it is but fair you should give him something he doesn't like in return. And the same if he's got a vote and doesn't use it for the good of the country; I see no harm in splitting his coat in a quiet way. A man must be taught what's right if he doesn't know it. But no kicks, no knocking down, no pommelling. . . . Why, sirs, for every Tory sneak that's got a vote, there's fifty-five fellows who must stand by and be expected to hold their tongues. But I say, let 'em hiss the sneaks, let 'em groan at the sneaks, and the sneaks will be ashamed of themselves." (11:122–23)

Advised with such sweet reasonableness, the miners and navvies are well prepared for their role on election day, when they provide a gauntlet of jeers, and even physical intimidation, to prevent opposition voters from getting to the polling booth, and, conversely, a platoon of bodyguards to protect the electors who are about to vote the right way.

Paradoxically, in the Darlford election in *Coningsby*, toughs were hired to keep the peace, not disturb it. The nominal enemies Bully Bluck and Magog Wrath "were in fact a very peaceful police, who kept the town in awe, and prevented others from being mischievous who were more inclined to do harm. Their hired gangs were the safety valves for all the scamps of the borough, who received a few shillings per head for their nominal service, and as much drink as they liked after the contest, were bribed and organised into peace and sobriety on the days in which their excesses were most to be apprehended" (5.4:342).

Once the pushing and shoving had begun, the next step, lacking a strong presence of constables, could be sheer riot. The election in Peacock's *Melincourt* broke up in a battle of (mock) epic proportions, which ended in the burning of the only tenant house in Rottenborough. There was fighting in the streets of Eatanswill, accompanied by Slumkey's band and the crier's bell, during Horatio Fizkin's attempted speech, though no serious casualties resulted. But the most extensive description of democracy in violent action occurred, once more, in *Felix Holt*, the only Victorian novel known to me in which the Riot Act had to be repeatedly read in an effort to quell an electoral disturbance. George Eliot's description of the turmoil at Treby Magna, which led to the death of a constable and the hero's going to jail on a charge of manslaughter, can too easily be dismissed as a routine piece of topical melodrama. Eliot had firsthand knowledge of what was likely to happen when a crowd, inflamed by drink if not ideology, got out of hand. She was at school at Nuneaton in December 1832, when the first post-Reform election there saw an "Extraordinary Interference of the Military at the Polling Booths," as the *Times* headline on 1 January described it. According to the account in the *Birmingham Journal*, which the *Times* quoted, the magistrates of the town, acting, it seems, on behalf of favored candidates, gratuitously called in the Scots Greys at a time when "the polling was orderly and quietly proceeding, and unoffending men, women, and children were cut down and trampled under the hoofs of the horses."

Eliot's memories of that turbulent occasion, including its aftermath, the trial of militiamen for the death of an elderly freeholder-elector (quite possibly the inspiration for Tommy Trounsem's death in *Felix Holt*), must have been vividly refreshed when, thirty-three years later, she went through the files of the *Times* in preparation for writing the novel. She would also have been reminded of a later electoral eruption in 1835 at Wolverhampton, which included repetition of the events she had observed as a schoolgirl at Nuneaton and was now to incorporate into *Felix Holt*: the barrage of hard missiles and dead rooks, the crowds "yelling, jostling, spitting, hooting, and making 'gross and indecent observations' as voters started to make their way up to the polling booth," the belated swearing-in of deputy constables, the summoning of a party of dragoons, the reading of the riot act, and the soldiers firing on the mob.[9]

DEGENERATE DAYS!!

"*Publican.* 'Call this a general election? Why it's all over in about a fortnight, and—' *Free and Independent Voter.* 'And not a fi—pun—note among 'em.'" To the mutual disgust of Tenniel's publican and bribable voter (*Punch*, 14 February 1874), the finally successful application of "pure election" laws delivered a mortal blow to a half-institutionalized custom that had served novelists well for a half-century.

Such scenes clearly touched readers' subliminal fears of unruly crowds, a phenomenon we glanced at in Chapter 4. They largely disappeared after fictional elections set in the 1830s—not that violence faded from the electoral proceedings (it cropped up now and again), but later novelists were less interested in this particular aspect of elections. Still, as late as 1864, in *Can You Forgive Her?*, "the entire Vavasorian army with its placards . . . was once absolutely driven ignominiously into the river mud" (44:478)—an unintended additional argument, incidentally, for Vavasor's campaign to embank the Thames.

A decade later, Meredith took a dyspeptic view of the moveable feast of election day, whose humors, he said, "are those of a badly-managed Christmas pantomime without a columbine—old tricks, no graces" (*Beauchamp's Career*, 27:1.292). The tricks, by that time, were indeed old, and the adoption of the secret ballot had "at one stroke robbed the British election of half of its character as a popular public festival and made of its culminating ceremony merely a series of private rendezvous with the citizens' consciences."[10] The tighter laws governing bribery, capped by the Corrupt Practices Act of 1883, spoiled what fun remained and further diminished the appeal that political contests held for novelists. Elections no longer had the atmosphere of rural holiday, with the whole community of men, women, and children in festive mood, notwithstanding the heat of personal and partisan animosities. But in their time, with all their movement, color, and noise, they had served many novelists well as sources of local color and comedy and as occasions for rudimentary drama and indirect social commentary.

Sometimes, too, they assisted characterization, as when, in the penultimate pages of *The Newcomes*, the rift between Clive and his father was healed during the electioneering, but not so thoroughly that Clive would have anything to do with the Colonel's quixotic campaign, and Thackeray's description of the latter's hopelessly eclectic opinions adds one final touch to the portrait he has so carefully drawn. The Colonel comes out for household suffrage and other, less radical, liberal causes, but they are so mixed with stock Tory ideas that in the end nobody knows where he really stands. One of the numerous milestones in John Halifax's progress toward the moral and social status of a gentleman is the incident in which he refuses to accept a pocket borough from the local magnate in the face of Victorian wisdom, which, as we have noted, held that becoming an M.P. was an easy way to become a gentleman as well. Subsequently, blocking the automatic election of another hand-picked man, he nominates his own candidate, who wins: a clear case of probity triumphing over venality. The short election episode in Meredith's *The Adventures of Harry Richmond* is an illustration, albeit a minor one, of the novel's theme, the formative influence of a man of ambiguous, mercurial, and complicated character—a "serio-comic genius," as his son describes him—on the character of the son. A few years later, Meredith brought an election to center stage when he used Beauchamp's candidacy under the tutelage of the eccentric Dr. Shrapnel as the means by which Beauchamp somewhat belatedly comes to terms with real life.

It was under the auspices of an election, too, that George Eliot further sharpened the contrast between the bumbling, leaky-brained Brooke and the sharply intelligent Will Ladislaw. Perhaps no other strain of the *Middlemarch* plot is so effective in revealing that Brooke was, as the grocer Mawmsey said, "not too 'clever in his intellects' " (51:543): his heart was in the right place, but his mind had no fixed address. Ladislaw's effort to put starch into the prospective candidate's mind, to impose a modicum of coherence on his political views, is a hopeless enterprise, and while George Eliot fully exploited the comic potentiality of the situation, she also used Brooke as a foil against whom to develop, stroke by stroke, Ladislaw's character.

No fictional election left the affected characters precisely as they were before the contest was run. Each was a turning point, however incidental, in a candidate's life. And with their topical appeal elections served as well as any other device a novelist possessed to change the direction of the plot. In *Ruth*, electioneering was the pretext by which Mrs. Gaskell arranged for Ruth's seducer to come back into her life. A number of elections, indeed, like that in *Beauchamp's Career*, were central to a novel's whole plot. By all odds the most pivotal is that in *Felix Holt*. George Eliot wrote,

> if the mixed political conditions of Treby Magna had not been acted on by the passing of the Reform Bill, Mr. Harold Transome would not have presented himself as a candidate for North Loamshire, Treby would not have been a polling-place, Mr. Matthew Jermyn would not have been on affable terms with a Dissenting preacher and his flock, and the venerable town would not have been placarded with handbills, more or less complimentary and retrospective—conditions in this case essential to the "where," and the "what," without which, as the learned know, there can be no event whatever.
>
> For example, it was through these conditions that a young man named Felix Holt made a considerable difference in the life of Harold Transome, though nature and fortune seemed to have done what they could to keep the lots of the two men quite aloof from each other. (3:46)

And, George Eliot might have added, some of the persons most closely involved in the electioneering were woven into the inheritance plot as well.

By their very nature, elections provided plots with the always desirable element of suspense. In pre–secret ballot days, the time in which the great majority of election scenes were set, running totals were periodically made available through the respective candidates' poll watchers. In a tight contest, the aggregate number of votes cast up to a given time, compared with the total number of electors on the books, sometimes resulted in a frantic search for new expedients, including scouring the town and countryside for laggards open to monetary persuasion. In several novels—*Ten Thousand a Year, Doctor Thorne, The Semi-Attached Couple*, and *Can You Forgive Her?*—novelists extracted the maximum benefit from the built-in suspense by displaying in prominent tabular form, not merely embodying in the text, the vote count as it changed during the day. (Close votes occurred oftener in fiction than in practice, one small respect in which considerations of craft led novelists to depart from the reality of elections.)

At least twice, elections were instrumental in bringing about the denouement, in the melodramatic manner of a sensation novel. In *East Lynne*, the election is a clear contest, though its issue is never in doubt, between virtue (Archibald Carlyle) and villainy (Sir Francis Levison). Levison, whose desperately needed sinecure as a government lackey is contingent on his getting into Parliament, announces for West Lynne (the borough; East Lynne is the name of Carlyle's estate); he does so with extreme reluctance, because he is locally remembered, and vilified, as the seducer of Lady Isabel Vane, Carlyle's wife. The climax of the novel comes when Levison is arrested—and handcuffed—on the very hustings, for another crime: as Captain Thorn, he had committed a murder that had been pinned on an innocent man.

East Lynne (1861) heralded the sensation craze of the 1860s, and it was not accidental that Thackeray decided to put a similarly rousing end to *The Adventures of Philip*, serialized in the *Cornhill Magazine* from January 1861 to August 1862. The election contest at Ringwood is between Philip Firmin's old friend, Hornblow, and the local magnate's candidate, a mulatto named Grenville Woolcomb. Pendennis, J. J. Ridley, and Philip, watching the electioneering with mounting distaste and alarm, contrive a purposeful prank in which a cart, drawn by two donkeys and driven by a black itinerant fishmonger, all decorated with Woolcomb's colors, carries about "a placard, on which a most undeniable likeness of Mr. Woolcomb was designed: who was made to say, 'VOTE FOR ME! AM I NOT A MAN AND A BRUDDER?'" (42:2.636)[†] The recklessly driven cart collides with Lord Ringwood's old post chaise, in which Woolcomb is riding; the impact splits the carriage's side, to reveal a secret compartment in which is found a lost will that miraculously makes Philip the heir to the

---

[†]The line had entered the popular vocabulary in the eighteenth century, when it often occurred in antislavery propaganda. Caddy Jellyby, enslaved as an unpaid amanuensis to her mother who is bent on redeeming the blacks of Borrio-boola Gha, complains to Esther Summerson, "I have no peace of my life. Talk of Africa! I couldn't be worse off if I was a what's-his-name—man and a brother!" (*Bleak House*, 14:236)

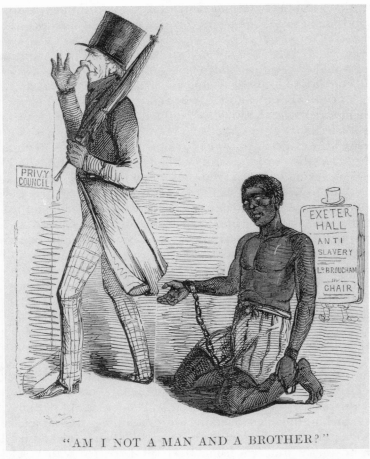

"AM I NOT A MAN AND A BROTHER?"

The slogan "Am I Not a Man and a Brother?" had energized the antislavery crusade for a century. Although slavery was forbidden in British territory by a law of 1834, its persistence elsewhere, including the United States, caused the catchphrase to echo through the May meetings of philanthropic organizations in Exeter Hall. *Punch* (1 June 1844) was miffed that Brougham, who had a long and honorable record in the abolitionist cause, failed to turn up at this one, pleading urgent public business in the Privy Council.

great estate. (But the villainous mulatto, who is the subject of a number of racist remarks which Thackeray does not disavow, wins the election.)

Victorian fiction being what it was, there were times when elections were made to serve the love interest in a novel. Disraeli and his sister set a pattern of sorts in *A Year at Hartlebury*, when Helen Molesworth arranges for the vote that will break the tie and send her beloved Aubrey Bohun to Westminster. In Meredith's novel, Harry Richmond's reason for wanting to enter Parliament is that he may thus be brought nearer to the Princess Ottilia, and it is the same motive, adjusted for differing circumstances, that leads Tittlebat Titmouse to contest Yatton; merely running for Parliament would "redeem and elevate him in the estimation of his fastidious and lofty mistress," Lady Cecilia Aubrey, with whom he is fatuously in love. On the lower level of society from which Titmouse liberated himself, Ontario Moggs the bootmaker acted on the expectation that "Surely if he were to go to Polly Neefit as a member of Parliament Polly would reject him no longer!" (*Ralph the Heir*, 21 : 1.250) There was romantic interest around the edges of the elections at Barchester (*Doctor Thorne*) and Baslehurst (*Rachel Ray*), but the only other Trollope novel in which an election was important to the love theme was *The Prime Minister*, in which Emily watched her husband, Lopez, challenged by Arthur Fletcher, the man whose honest love she had downgraded into mere "friendship." Characteristically, Trollope evaded the dramatic denouement that a more romantic novelist would have seized upon. Instead of bringing the combatants down to the wire, he had Lopez withdraw from the contest—a lame and impotent conclusion.

And so Victorian fiction would be much the poorer had it not had at its disposal so colorful and dramatic an institution as the contemporary form of participatory democracy. Apart from their treatment of such associated routines as canvassing and bribery, what opinions did the novelists hold about the assumptions and practices of the new polity of which elections were the recurrent outward signs? Seldom, if ever, does one find a novelist celebrating English elections as evidence of national progress; more often, the implication is that they are an imperfect part of the new political machinery, but, as Meredith said of canvassing, one that must be tolerated as a necessary evil. No novelist was without his or her implicit reservations about what the Great Reform Bill had wrought. No doubt the prevalence of underhanded practices in real elections substantiated whatever deep doubts the novelists may have entertained about the philosophical justification for or the practical workability of democratic politics. One can read between the lines of most novels the sense, prevalent among conservatives at any rate, that the political center, as they defined and located it, no longer held now that the admission of multitudes of new voters to the polling lists had destroyed the stability, however illusory, that had been supplied by the old electoral system, however restrictive and corrupt.

Perhaps the most untrammeled attack in fiction on the assumption that the 1832 act represented the genuine victory of the people over the entrenched interests was Samuel Warren's, who concluded a typically wordy diatribe with sentences that perfectly matched the ex cathedra tone of the political pronouncements in *Blackwood's Magazine*, where the novel was serialized: "The influence of property is inevitable as that of gravitation; and losing sight of this, people may split their heads in vain, and chatter until the arrival of the Greek kalends, about extending further and further the elective franchise, shortening Parliaments, and voting by ballot. Whether it *ought* to be so, signifies little, when we know that it is, and *will* be so . . ." (*Ten Thousand a Year*, 27:709–10). The results of what Warren called "the great BILL FOR GIVING EVERYBODY EVERYTHING" fueled Carlyle's reactionary vehemence and inspired the rhetorical flights of Sir Leicester Dedlock and Sir Barnes Newcome. But it must be remembered that the sentiments of that pair of baronets—one crusty, the other on the make—were meant to be satire. If no Victorian novelist was wholeheartedly committed to democracy on the leveling American pattern, Dickens and Thackeray at least distanced themselves from the Sir Leicesters and Sir Barneses of their world.

20
Language

1.

THE AGE put its indelible stamp on the language of Victorian fiction. Some of its effects are easily recognizable, others less so. Modern books on the language of Dickens, Thackeray, and Trollope, for instance, examine with justifiable assurance their uses of vocabulary and grammar as indicators of social class, and held-over archaisms as evidence of a speaker's conservatism. Often, however, the implication of a certain choice of words is too subtle to be reconstructed with any certainty. The definitions in the largest authority, the *Oxford English Dictionary*—itself a majestic product, in part, of late Victorian industry—generally provide the kernel of objective meaning only, with the outer wrappings of connotation added only when they seem to have represented a widely adopted usage. But even when these period connotations are noted, lexicography cannot take into account the extra aura of suggestion they acquired in a particular literary context. These special, local meanings and implications—nuances whose intention in dialogue, accompanied perhaps by an inflection of voice that is totally unrecoverable from the printed page—often expressed social distinctions on a wavelength to which Victorian readers were attuned and we are not. Whether the speech was cast in the rhetorical mode of Dickens's theatricalized characters, the concise, flexible correctness of Trollope's upper-class ones, or the blunt simplicity of George Eliot's country men and women, the meaning shared by character (and author) and contemporary reader is part of the novel's subtext.

In *Dombey and Son*, Mrs. Chick says, "Would anyone believe that when he [Mr. Dombey] received news of the marriage and emigration of that unnatural child . . . he should then turn round upon me and say he had supposed, from my manner, that she had come to my house?" (59:930). Actually, Florence, "that unnatural child," has gone out to China with her husband, Walter Gay, who has the responsible position

759

of supercargo (seagoing business manager), a quite different thing from "emigration," which was something done by the lower classes and, in addition, was unpleasantly suggestive of another, involuntary, form of home-leaving, penal transportation. To Mrs. Chick, Florence had lost caste by "emigrating": the current social connotation of the word made all the difference. As she no doubt uttered it, the word amounted to a verbal grimace.

Thackeray borrowed something of the prejudice that *emigration* bore in the middle of the century when, as we have seen (page 405), he remarked in *The Newcomes*, "There are degrees in decadence: after the Fashion chooses to emigrate, and retreats from Soho or Bloomsbury, let us say, to Cavendish Square, physicians come and occupy the houses . . . [etc.]" (17:1.176). Emigration, at that date, had so strong an association of poor families sailing off to Australia or America (as in Ford Madox Brown's painting *The Last of England* [1860]), that to use it in connection with Fashion was decidedly infra dig.

Dickens underscored his characters' biases by the more obvious device of having them choke over words. Sir Leicester Dedlock's patrician vocal apparatus is hardly capable of articulating "Ironmaster," a word that as he uttered it epitomized the landowning class's conviction that modern society had been catastrophically transformed by the industrial revolution. And in *Little Dorrit*, civil servants and their superiors gagged at the very name of the national constituency that, in theory, they were paid to serve: "'The Department is accessible to the—Public.' Mr. Barnacle was always checked a little by that word of impertinent signification, 'if the—Public approaches it according to the official forms; if the—Public does not approach it according to the official forms, the—Public has itself to blame'" (1.10:153–54).

Dickens's ear was especially sensitive to the ironic potentiality of phrases indigenous to the marketplace, such as the formulaic language of house agents' and auctioneers' newspaper advertisements, placards, and catalogues. The pompous series of announcements woven into the prose of *Dombey and Son*, "The Capital Modern Household Furniture, &c., is on view," "The Capital Modern Household Furniture, &c., is on sale," and "The Capital Modern Household Furniture, &c., is in course of removal," marked, like a tolling bell, the four-day piece-by-piece sale of the Dombey household furnishings and its aftermath, when "One of the pen-and-ink gentlemen goes over the house as a last attention; sticking up bills in the windows respecting the lease of this desirable family mansion, and shutting the shutters." Later, Polly Toodle, the last survivor of the household staff, locks the house, which stands "frowning like a dark mute on the street; baulking any nearer inquiries with the staring announcement that the lease of this desirable Family Mansion was to be disposed of" (59:929, 942).

Dickens used one house agent's cliché phrase to more devastating effect in his description of Tom-all-Alone's, the disease-ridden slum where the houses are literally falling down: "This desirable property is in Chancery, of course . . ." (*Bleak House*, 16:273). The irony was intensified when Dickens counterpointed the theme of the wretchedness that permeated the life of the London poor against a contrasting motif, the words "Fashionable Intelligence" applied to the onlooking, rumor-mongering high-society chorus that follows the stately progress of Sir Leicester and Lady Dedlock from Chesney Wold to London and Paris and back again. "Fashionable Intelligence" was the caption under which London newspapers printed the daily doings of the "Brilliant and distinguished circle," another cliché of which Dickens made mordant use in *Bleak House*. The ironic intent of such phrases was so obvious as to leave no doubt where Dickens stood.[†]

This was true of another prejudice-laden word, found in a very different context, whose special nineteenth-century meaning is now obsolete. *Serious* in the sense of "truly religious" was a favorite way by which evangelicals (Low Church and Dissenters) stressed their separateness from the larger community of believers. But like Exeter Hall, the physical symbol of all that "seriousness" stood for, it inevitably became charged with anathema when used by leading novelists who despised what they considered to be an especially intolerable form of contemporary humbug, the self-righteous sanctimoniousness, indeed the pharisa-

---

[†] Readers of *Bleak House* would have heard other echoes, tired cadences this time, of familiar, nonliterary language. When Rosa, the pretty maid at Chesney Wold, takes Guppy and Jobling on the standard tour of the mansion, the rhythms of her memorized talk (today it would be taped for renters of headsets) are true to the potted patter delivered to tourists at such houses as were then open to the public on visiting days. "The picture on the right is the present Sir Leicester Dedlock. The picture on the left is his father, the late Sir Leicester. . . . The terrace below is much admired. It is called, from an old story in the family, The Ghost's Walk" (7:138–39). The rote quality spills over into Mrs. Rouncewell's ensuing private narration of the legend to Rosa and young Watt. And in *Pendennis*, Mrs. Blenkinsop conducts Sir Francis Clavering through the dilapidated mansion he has inherited: ". . . that on the right is Theodosia, wife of Harbottle, second baronet, by Lely, represented in the character of Venus, the Goddess of Beauty,—her son Gregory, the third baronet, by her side, as Cupid, God of Love, with a bow and arrows . . ." (22:1.213). (Thackeray undoubtedly meant his readers to envision Lely's famous painting of Nell Gwyn as Venus and her son, the Duke of St. Albans, as Cupid. He had prepared himself for this passage by burlesquing, very clumsily, it must be admitted, the spiel of the housekeeper at Castle Carabas ["On Some Country Snobs," *Punch*, 31 October 1846; *BS*, 135–36].)

ism, that marked the Bible-reading evangelical, and in particular the Dissenting Christian. (The clear analogue in our own day is the way in which evangelical and fundamentalist sects have appropriated the label "Christian" for their particular use.) Serious people, so called, turn up again and again in Victorian fiction. The Reverend Obadiah Slope is identified by Trollope, almost tautologically, as a "serious young evangelical clergyman," and Miss Drusilla Clack, the tireless tract distributor in *The Moonstone*, uses the word as a badge of honor in referring to her proselytizing sisterhood.

Middle-class and even upper-class men and women holding serious views are found most often in the subgenre of religious novels, where they are presented respectfully, but several appear in Thackeray's fiction, where they are not. The elderly Countess of Southdown was "that strong-minded woman so favourably known in the serious world" (*Vanity Fair*, 33:320). The whole Southdown family, in fact, was famously serious, and when Lady Ann married Pitt Crawley the younger, she brought the infection with her. It is noteworthy that when Thackeray first describes Pitt, it is primarily in terms of his seriousness, which, given Thackeray's fixed attitude toward such sectarians, serves to intimate his limitations. When Pitt's character was later developed, as he inherited his father's estate, became an M. P., and entered London society, readers were not likely to forget the baseline, so to speak, from which it began. For her part, Becky, long since estranged from her husband and forced, once more, to live by her wits, found it tactically necessary to embrace the seriousness she had formerly ridiculed in her celebrated impersonation of Lady Southdown preaching in her nightgown. She ingratiated herself with Mrs. Newbright, an occasional correspondent of the Dowager Countess of Southdown, by expressing "her proper views upon serious subjects, concerning which, in former days, at Queen's Crawley, Mrs. Becky had had a good deal of instruction.—Well, she not only took tracts, but she read them." But when Mrs. Newbright learned from the Dowager Countess the true state of affairs vis-à-vis Becky, "all the serious world of Tours, where this misfortune took place, immediately parted company with the reprobate" (64:622).

In *Pendennis*, the widow Pendennis's lawyer, Mr. Tatham, was serious in both of the then current senses, an earnest, sober member of his profession and a Dissenter as well. But the word is most conspicuous in *The Newcomes*. It first occurs in the course of a general description of Clapham, the seat of the rich evangelical party, where the Newcome family's "palace"—perhaps a glancing ironic allusion to the name applied to the official residences of Anglican bishops—was "a serious paradise. . . . The lodge-keeper was serious, and a clerk at the neighbouring

Richard Doyle's addition to Thackeray's description of the "serious paradise" presided over by Sophia Newcome, née Hobson: her husband passes out tracts in her behalf, even though, says Thackeray, "I think he grew weary of the prayer meetings, he yawned over the sufferings of the negroes, and wished the converted Jews at Jericho."

chapel. . . . The head-gardener was a Scotch Calvinist, after the strictest order . . ." (2:1.17–18). The butler was serious too. In another connection Colonel Newcome's friend Binnie, a freethinking "disciple of David Hume," was denounced by the serious "as a man of dangerous principles, though," adds Thackeray, "there were, among the serious, men much more dangerous than James Binnie" (8:1.90, 52:2.148). Later, old Lady Kew tells Barnes Newcome, "You should have married some woman in the serious way" (as his aunt was). The seriousness of the old town of Newcome proved a formidable obstacle to his political ambitions. "In spite of his respectful behaviour to the gentlemen in black coats [the town's leading citizens], his soup tickets and his flannel tickets, his own pathetic lectures and his sedulous attendance at other folk's sermons, poor Barnes could not keep up his credit with the serious interest at Newcome, and the meeting-houses and their respective pastors and frequenters turned their backs upon him" (69:2.322).

In view of Thackeray's jaundiced opinion of seriousness, a certain ambiguity hovers over his reports of how two of his prominent male characters improved spiritually or morally. Major Pendennis, he records on the last page of that novel, "became very serious in his last days," and Clive Newcome wrote his father from Brighton that young Lord Kew's wound, sustained in a duel with a Frenchman, and his subsequent illness "have altered him a good deal. He has become much *more serious* [Thackeray's italics] than he used to be; not ludicrously so at all, but he says he thinks his past life has been useless and even criminal, and he wishes to change it. He has sold his horses, and sown his wild oats. He has turned quite a sober quiet gentleman" (*The Newcomes*, 42:2.37). To devout society at large, this would seem to have been a comforting development, but Thackeray was not devout, and in both instances of worldly men seeing the light one suspects a lack of conviction on Thackeray's part. How conventional—and hollow—a sinful man's overtly seeking the consolations of evangelical religion might be was clearly indicated in Major Pendennis's later reminiscence (in *The Adventures of Philip*) of the way "Firebrand" Firmin, "a tremendous duellist," "shot an Irishman [and] became serious in after life, and that sort of thing" (1:1.101).[†]

In mainstream fiction it was only in Thackeray's novels that people of substance fell prey to the sanctified enticements of seriousness,

---

[†]A leading student of Thackeray's language notes that *serious* in its religious application disappeared from his later novels, and cites Thomas Hughes's preface to the sixth edition of *Tom Brown's Schooldays*: "Boyishness in the highest sense is not incompatible with seriousness, or earnestness, if you like the word better." In a footnote Hughes added, "To [Thomas Arnold] and his admirers we owe the substitution of the word *earnest* for its predecessor *serious*" (K. C. Phillipps, *The Language of Thackeray* [London, 1979], pp. 54–55). But *pace* Hughes, who should have known, the two words were far from synonymous as they occurred in Victorian fiction; they could not have been, so long as *serious* retained its current association with a religious community, and so long as novelists like Dickens, Thackeray, and Trollope used it sardonically and satirically. *Earnest* had little religious reference except as it was an ideal promoted by Arnold at Rugby and subsequently by the Muscular Christianity movement. It denoted a secular virtue, closely akin to "manliness," and as such was ordinarily treated as praiseworthy. It entered a satirical phase only with the reaction against Victorian orthodoxy, as when two writers exploited its homophone quality (earnest/Ernest), Oscar Wilde in his play (1895) and Samuel Butler in *The Way of All Flesh* (1903), whose hero is Ernest Pontifex.

though there was one exception, "poor Willis," a leading character in Emily Eden's *The Semi-Detached House*, who

> fairly grumbled poor gentle Mrs. Willis out of the world, and then grumbled at her for dying. But still her death was a gain to him. He took up the high bereaved line, was at all hours and in all societies the disconsolate mourner, wore a permanent crape round his hat, a rusty black coat in the city, and a shining one when he dined out. He professed himself "serious," and proved it by snubbing his friends when they were prosperous, and steadily declining to take the slightest interest in their adversities. (2:8–9)

Because hers was a light-hearted novel, Eden saw to it that this gentleman eventually snapped out of his antisocial gloom and rejoined cheerful society.

Thoroughgoing, offensively flaunted seriousness was chiefly attributed to the trading and servant classes, an association with vulgarity that rendered its occasional cropping up in Thackeray's haut monde all the more incongruous. Socially, Lady Southdown, Lord Kew, and Major Pendennis had little in common with, say, one of Tittlebat Titmouse's fellow counter-jumpers in the Oxford Street draper's shop, "a serious youth, in a white neckerchief, black clothes, and with a sanctified countenance—the only professing pious person in the establishment—[who] took an occasion to ask him, in a mysterious whisper, 'whether he had not got *converted*'" (*Ten Thousand a Year*, 4:126).

Novelists' derision of seriousness took various forms. In *Nicholas Nickleby*, Dickens reported a dialogue between Tom, a clerk in an employment agency, and a fat lady looking for work:

> "Mrs. Wrymug," said Tom [reading from a ledger]. "Pleasant Place, Finsbury. Wages, twelve guineas. No tea, no sugar. Serious family—"
> "Ah! you needn't mind reading that," interrupted the client.
> "'Three serious footmen,'" said Tom, impressively.
> "'Three,' did you say?" asked the client, in an altered tone.
> "'Three serious footmen,'" replied Tom. "'Cook, housemaid, and nursemaid; each female servant required to join the Little Bethel Congregation three times every Sunday—with a serious footman. If the cook is more serious than the footman, she will be expected to improve the footman; if the footman is more serious than the cook, he will be expected to improve the cook.'" (16.255)

When Mark Tapley parts from Tom Pinch in Wiltshire to seek his fortune in London, he targets a particular class of employer who might offer the best scope for his talents: "I must look for a private service, I suppose, sir. I might be brought out strong, perhaps, in a serious family, Mr. Pinch" (*Martin Chuzzlewit*, 7:168). In *Dombey and Son*, Towlinson, the footman, momentarily sobered by Paul's death, aspires to lead "an altered and blameless existence as a serious greengrocer in Oxford Market" (18:313). At the end of the novel, after the Dombey household is dissolved, he again intends to "settle in Oxford Market in the general greengrocery and herb and leech line" (59:924), but because no bereavement is now involved, he says nothing about turning serious.

Wilkie Collins, like Dickens and Thackeray, exploited the comic potential of the word and the image it evoked to unsympathetic readers. In *The Dead Secret* he described a Sabbath outing from the servants' hall: ". . . Mr. Munder turned solemnly into the passage that led to the foot of the west staircase, walking with that peculiar, slow strut in which all serious-minded English people indulge when they go out to take a little exercise on Sunday. The housekeeper, adapting her pace with feminine pliancy to the pace of the steward, walked the national Sabbatarian Polonaise by his side, as if she was out with him for a mouthful of fresh air between the services" (4.3:269–70). But, as Trollope pointed out in *The Belton Estate*, not all classes of servant were serious:

> Mrs. Winterfield was always unhappy about her gardener. Serious footmen are very plentiful, and even coachmen can be found who, at a certain rate of extra payment, will be punctual at prayer time, and will promise to read good little books; but gardeners, as a class, are a profane people, who think themselves entitled to claim liberty of conscience, and who will not submit to the domestic despotism of a serious Sunday. They live in cottages by themselves, and choose to have an opinion of their own on church matters. (7:88)

Many such words in the vocabulary of Victorian fiction prove on examination to be tight little parcels embodying one or another of the day's social attitudes. Only rarely, however, does one meet in a novel a word of multiple significances, a cluster of related meanings such as rewarded the explicatory searches that the New Critics of the 1950s conducted in the texts of seventeenth- and eighteenth-century poetry. An outstanding example occurs in *Dombey and Son*, in which the unhappy Rob Toodle is sent, courtesy of Mr. Dombey, to the Charitable Grinders School, an institution founded, that is, by the trade guild of cutlery grinders.[1] It is not overingenious to assume that Dickens meant the noun *grinder* to suggest the gesture described in *Pickwick Papers*, when Jackson, Dodson and Fogg's clerk, "applying his left thumb to the tip of his nose, worked a visionary coffee mill with his right hand: thereby performing a very graceful piece of pantomime (then much in vogue, but now, unhappily, almost obsolete), which was familiarly denominated 'taking a grinder'" (31:507). This salute, also known as "taking a sight," "Queen Anne's

A visual pun, extending the play on one of the meanings of *grinder* in the text of *Dombey and Son*. In Phiz's illustration, the wooden midshipman is simultaneously "taking a sight" and "taking a grinder"—two slang terms for thumbing the nose. Florence Dombey, on the left, is "receiving," says Dickens, "the whole shock of his wooden ogling!" The streetwise Susan Nipper, behind her, seems to apprehend the impropriety of the gesture, minus the sextant.

fan," and "cocking a snook" (the nose thumbing was compulsory, the rotatory motion of the unengaged hand optional), was a mute but unmistakable expression of disbelief or defiance. We have already noticed (pages 718 and 749) its occurrence in the course of the rambunctious electoral campaign at Yatton.[†]

All the other contemporary meanings of *grind* and *grinder* are relevant to *Dombey and Son*. In the sense of "tooth," *grinder* clearly suggests Carker, the conspicuously toothy villain of the novel—given his character, the teeth are indubitably false—and indeed Rob's teeth are explicitly referred to as "grinders." There is also the obvious link with Mr. Feeder, B. A., the tutor at Dr. Blimber's school, who operates in the classroom a figurative barrel organ, turning on the Virgil stop and "slowly grinding the tune to four young gentlemen," and whose name, in university slang, meant "coach" or "grinder." Carlyle's coinage, "gerund grinder," fitted him exactly. In the schoolroom sense, *grinder* draws upon the meaning of the verb *to grind*—"to crush, oppress, to harass with exactions"—and refers, in its more specialized application, to both crammer and crammed. Another use of the word in the Blimber context, "Briggs is still grinding in the mill of knowledge," suggests a docile beast harnessed to a revolving millstone. *Grinder* in the name of Rob's school thus is a complete shorthand indication of the kind of force-fed education it purveys, although the charitable guild may not have insisted on a classical curriculum.

But *grinders* also had a specialized immediate significance to the first readers of *Dombey and Son*, because the Sheffield grinding (cutlery) industry had lately been in the news, as it would be periodically down to the time of Charles Reade's novel about its labor troubles, *Put Yourself in His Place* (1869–70).[†] Within three months in 1843–44 there had been half a dozen cases of arson and use of explosives in Sheffield, attributed to striking workingmen. Friedrich Engels, writing with pronounced

[†] *Pace* Dickens, the gesture was not on its way out. It was especially associated with impudent street urchins or persons like Chuckster in *The Old Curiosity Shop*, who sometimes honored Kit Nubbles "with that peculiar form of recognition which is called 'taking a sight'" (38:365). But as its frequent occurrence in cartoons in *Punch*, a family magazine, in the 1840s demonstrates, it was admissible to domestic firesides in graphic form even though its actual execution was deemed vulgar. Thus, Mr. Punch cocked a snook at a pair of undergraduates in Thackeray's vignette for his piece on "University Snobs" (*Punch*, 7 June 1846). Although the gesture appeared less frequently after mid-century, it was still within the pale of propriety if the occasion warranted. In an 1854 *Punch* cartoon, the British lion thumbed its nose at the Russian bear; in 1861 Palmerston thus expressed his detestation of one Father Daly, a pudgy Irish priest who participated in a scam involving a government subsidy to the Galway Steam Packet Company; and in 1864 John Tenniel portrayed Napoleon III so addressing an infuriated John Bull.

bias, saw in these occurrences "the hatred of the workers for their employers," while Beatrice and Sidney Webb, closer to our own day, saw them as extensions of the local unions' custom of "rattening," that is, of forcibly compelling workmen to pay their union dues and abide by union regulations. "Recalcitrant workmen were terrorized by explosions of cans of gunpowder in the troughs of their grinding wheels, or thrown down their chimneys. . . . The various Grinders' Unions . . . enjoyed an unhappy notoriety for outrages of this nature."[2] When we recognize that this notoriety was ineffaceably attached to the word *grinder* in the minds of those who read *Dombey and Son* along with their newspapers, and when we recall in addition that in the novel the epithet "charitable" is prefixed to the term, we realize that Dickens was extracting dependable irony from an equally dependable topical association.

2.

Of the various kinds of linguistic phenomena we find in Victorian fiction, slang, by virtual definition the ephemeral language of the moment, was the most topical, both as it figured in a novel's text (especially in dialogue) and as a subject of critical comment. As a form of "substandard" speech, it was closely linked with prevailing social attitudes. Self-consciously respectable people avoided it because it was the language of the streets or of "fast" society, and those whose superior education had sensitized them to the decorous glories of literary, or at least cultivated, English denounced it for its supposedly corruptive effect on the mother tongue. Slang was a verbal symptom of the forces that were undermining the old social structure and vulgarizing its culture.

The gadabout characters in Pierce Egan's popular depictions of Regency sporting, gambling, and night-house life, especially *Life in London; or The Day and Night Scenes of Jerry Hawthorn Esq. and Corinthian Tom* (1821), spouted a lively and colorful froth of slang. But such books appealed to a comparatively limited audience, which cared little for the conventions of cultivated English and was not affronted by high-spirited deviations from it. In the early stages of his career, Dickens was reproached for his liberal indulgence in colloquial language. "Boz," said a severe contributor to the *Quarterly Review* in 1839, "is regius professor

---

[†]Dickens may or may not have known of a little book published some two decades earlier (1823) called *Tom and Charles, or the Grinders: The History of Two Boys Educated at the Charity School at Sheffield*. Nor had he necessarily seen a painting exhibited at the Royal Academy in 1841 by Robert Turner, an artist living near Sheffield, *An Applicant for Admission into the Boy's Charity School, Sheffield*. In other years this artist showed pictures entitled *The Grinders* and *Sheffield Grinders' Christmas Dinner, with Mummers*.

of slang, that expression of the mother-wit, the low humour of the lower classes, their Sanscrit, their hitherto unknown tongue, which, in the present phasis of society and politics, seems likely to become the idiom of England. Where drabs, house-breakers, and tavern-spouting patriots play the first fiddle, they can only speak the language which expresses their ideas and habits."[3] "The Cockney pronunciation, the cant words, the slang expressions interwoven in his pages," said another critic in 1838, "will lose their zest as soon as they are superseded by other; but as long as they are current, they produce an effect, even upon those who can analyze their nature and detect their worthlessness."[4]

So much for the easygoing talk of *Sketches by Boz* and *Pickwick Papers*. When, in *Oliver Twist*, Dickens had Fagin and his associates speak "flash" language, the criminal-argot variety of slang, reviewers taxed him with carrying realism unacceptably far. To describe underworld characters through their dress, expressed attitudes, and physical setting was well enough, assuming—the question was hotly debated then—that a novelist had any right to portray so seamy an aspect of modern life, but to put almost unintelligible and certainly "low" expressions in their mouths was simply offensive. To some critics, the association with crime was indelible. "[S]lang," declared a reviewer of Dickens's writings to date in the *North British Review* in 1845, "arose in towns, amid thieves and gamblers, who had need of an obscure phraseology; it was adopted by those who wished to be thought initiated into secrets not known to every one; it came to be used as a cheap substitute for wit; but wherever it goes, it bears the stamp of its nativity, and an impress of crime, concealment, and baseness. The man of pure and honourable feeling cannot use it; and its spread will be an index of the departure of these qualities from society."[5]

As Dickens's popularity proved to be no mere flash in the pan but a permanent fact of Victorian literary life, however, his early mastery of slang came no longer to be held against him. "[N]o one else," asserted Richard H. Horne in *The New Spirit of the Age* (1844), "ever had the same power of using an abundance of 'slang' of all kinds, without offence, and carrying it off, as well as rendering it amusing by the comedy, or tragic force of the scene, and by its unaffected appropriateness to the utterers."[6] Six years later, an anonymous writer in *Fraser's Magazine* credited Dickens with having made slang almost respectable, even in the talk of cultivated people: "We began by using *Wellerisms* and *Gampisms* in fun, till they have got blended insensibly with our stock conversational phrases; and now in our most serious moments we talk *slang* unwittingly, to the great disgust of the old school, who complain that, instead of seeking the 'well of English undefiled' by Twickenham, we draw at haphazard from the muddy stream that washed Mile End."[7]

The eventual acceptance of Dickens's slang doubtless smoothed Thackeray's path, though admittedly his brand had social credentials that Dickens's notoriously lacked. Down to the middle of the century, the only realm of respectable society where slang was marginally acceptable was that of university undergraduates, whose acquisition of a racy vocabulary was, like initiation into the use of tobacco, a customary rite de passage as well as a sign of belonging to an elite group. Thackeray's admirer David Masson wrote in his joint review of *Pendennis* and *David Copperfield*:

> In the ease, and, at the same time, thorough polish and propriety with which Mr. Thackeray can use slang words, we seem especially to detect the University man. Snob, swell, buck, gent, fellow, fogy—these, and many more such expressive appellatives, not yet sanctioned by the Dictionary, Mr. Thackeray employs more frequently, we believe, than any other living writer, and yet always with unexceptionable taste. In so doing he is conscious, no doubt, of the same kind of security that permits Oxford and Cambridge men, and even, as we can testify, Oxford and Cambridge clergymen, to season their conversation with similar words—namely, the evident air of educated manliness with which they can be introduced, and which, however rough the guise, no one can mistake.[8]

Some critics nevertheless hesitated to include adept use of slang among Thackeray's credits. Whereas Margaret Oliphant, writing in the January 1855 issue of *Blackwood's Magazine*, praised his portrayal in *Pendennis* of "the English of the present day, careless and easy, just touched with the slang for which our author has a special gift," nine months later Whitwell Elwin, a Cambridge graduate and ordained clergyman, allotted his friend Thackeray a distinctly limited measure of praise on that score. The author of *The Newcomes*, he said, "even manages to give additional raciness by the not unfrequent use of colloquial vulgarisms, which if they were introduced with less skill would debase his style. It is with reluctance we confess that he has turned language to good account which in all other hands has hitherto revolted every person of cultivated mind, for we fear the evil effects of his example, and are sorry the black patches should heighten the beauty."[9]

The only women before mid-century who freely used slang were actresses and other female members of the fast set. In *Pendennis*, Harry Foker puts on "dreary entertainment" at Richmond for a few intimates of both sexes, including the actress Miss Rougement and her friend Miss Pinckney, a danseuse. He thinks, "I wonder how the deuce I could ever have liked these people? Why, I can see the crows'-feet under Rougemont's eyes, and the paint on her cheeks is laid on as thick as Clown's in a pantomime! The way in which that Pinckney talks slang is quite disgusting. I hate chaff in a woman" (40:2.13).

But now slang could be heard issuing from lips that were not, like Miss Rougemont's, truly vermilion, but a natural, maidenly hue. Slang was coming to be tolerated, but Trollope for one was aware that this new liberality was by no means universal and that it brought the novelist pitfalls as well as advantages. In 1859 he remarked in *The Bertrams*, "If I were to use the word 'flabbergasted' as expressing Miss Baker's immediate state of mind, I should draw on myself the just anger of the critics, in that I had condescended to the use of slang; but what other word will so well express what is meant?" (2.9:2.135) The occasional use of slang became a hallmark of his livelier heroines. When Martha Dunstable assures Mary Thorne that she will be at her wedding by saying, "I shall certainly come and see you turned off" (executed by the common hangman), Trollope conceded, "Miss Dunstable . . . was a little too fond of slang; but then, a lady with her fortune, and of her age [a mature thirty], may be fond of almost whatever she pleases" (*Doctor Thorne*, 47:501). But freedom to use slang was not the exclusive prerogative of wealthy ladies, their "fast" sisters, and undergraduates. When Lily Dale in *The Small House at Allington*, a modest maiden of no wealth at all, calls Crosbie a "swell" and is reproached by her sister Bell, she replies, "I fancy I do like slang. I think it's awfully jolly to talk about things being jolly. Only that I was afraid of your nerves I should have called him stunning. It's so slow, you know, to use nothing but words out of a dictionary" (2:1.16).

In the fifties and sixties the developing social acceptability of slang was a delightfully effervescent, not inconveniently weighty, topic of conversation. In Gaskell's *North and South* (1854–55) there was an exchange between Mrs. Hale and her daughter Margaret, who had just said of a young millworker, "She is very slack of work":

> ". . . But, Margaret, don't get to use these horrid Milton [Manchester] words. 'Slack of work': it is a provincialism. What will your aunt Shaw say, if she hears you use it on her return?"
> "Oh, mamma! don't try and make a bugbear of aunt Shaw," said Margaret, laughing. "Edith picked up all sorts of military slang from Captain Lennox, and aunt Shaw never took any notice of it."
> "But yours is factory slang."
> "And if I live in a factory town, I must speak factory language when I want it. Why, mamma, I could astonish you with a great many words you never heard in your life. I don't believe you know what a knobstick is."
> "Not I, child. I only know it has a very vulgar sound; and I don't want to hear you using it." (2.4:237)

A decade later, in Meredith's *Emilia in England* (1864), Lady Charlotte Chillingworth rebukes Wilfrid Pole for his attentions to Emilia: "I

Early Victorian bus drivers were notorious for their reckless passage through the narrow and congested London streets. This cartoon appeared in *Punch* for 13 October 1849, accompanied by a set of verses titled "The War-Song of the Wild 'Bus Man."

am sure you're a manly fellow, who would never have played tricks with a girl you were bound to protect; but you might have—pardon the slang—*spooned*,—who knows? You might have been in love with her downright" (36:2.91).

Originating in the superior levels of society described by Trollope, Gaskell, and Meredith, the purity-of-speech issue filtered downward. But whereas their independent-minded ladies maintained that they were entitled to utter a slang word or two, those of lower station perversely rejected that mild license in behalf of the gentility toward which they aspired. The world was turned upside down: now it was in the upper reaches of society that slang was faddishly regarded as "in," and in the lower classes, allegedly its natural habitat, that it was "out." When George Sampson, in *Our Mutual Friend*, ventured to exclaim, "Go it, Miss Lavinia Wilfer!" in that lady's presence, he was promptly reproved: "What you may mean, George Sampson, by your omnibus-driving expressions, I cannot pretend to imagine" (4.16:877). (Lavinia was referring to the expression that London bus conductors addressed to their drivers—or the drivers, a notoriously competitive and reckless lot, to their horses—as they raced to beat a rival bus to the next waiting passengers.)

The modern young person's freedom of speech—something of which poor Georgiana Podsnap would have been incapable, even in the extreme unlikelihood that her mother countenanced it—was duly deplored by Mrs. Lynn Linton in her celebrated assault on "The Girl of the Period" (1868). "Her conversation," she wrote, "is full of slang—so repulsive in a feminine mouth. We actually know of a young lady of fifteen who talks about being 'squisshy'; and of a gentleman having 'D.Ts.'" In Bulwer-Lytton's late novel *Kenelm Chillingly; His Adventures and Opinions* (1873), the hero philosophically surveyed the deteriorating situation: "I don't think nearly so many ladies six years ago painted their eyelids and dyed their hair; a few of them there might be, imitators of the slang invented by schoolboys and circulated through the medium of small novelists; they might use such expressions as 'stunning,' 'cheek,' 'awfully jolly,' etc. But now I find a great many who have advanced to a slang beyond that of verbal expressions—a slang of mind, a slang of sentiment, a slang in which very little seems left of the woman, and nothing at all of the lady."[10]

In light of these developments, it is clear that the Vincys' exchange on the subject of slang in *Middlemarch* was one of those passages in the novel that were more appropriate to the time it was published than to the time in which it was set. This is a conversation of 1871–72, not 1830–31. Rosamund has remarked to her mother that she would marry no Middlemarch man:

> "So it seems, my love, for you have as good as refused the pick of them; and if there's better to be had, I'm sure there's no girl better deserves it."
> "Excuse me, mamma—I wish you would not say, 'the pick of them.'"
> "Why, what else are they?"
> "I mean, mamma, it is rather a vulgar expression."
> "Very likely, my dear; I never was a good speaker. What should I say?"
> "The best of them."
> "Why, that seems just as plain and common. If I had had time to think, I should have said, 'the most superior young men.' But with your education you must know."
> "What must Rosy know, mother?" said Mr. Fred, who had slid in unobserved. . . .
> "Whether it's right to say 'superior young men,'" said Mrs. Vincy ringing the bell.
> "Oh, there are so many superior teas and sugars now. Superior is getting to be shopkeepers' slang."
> "Are you beginning to dislike slang, then?" said Rosamond, with mild gravity.
> "Only the wrong sort. All choice of words is slang. It marks a class."
> "There is correct English: that is not slang."
> "I beg your pardon: correct English is the slang of prigs who write history and essays. And the strongest slang of all is the slang of poets."
> "You will say anything, Fred, to gain your point."
> "Well, tell me whether it is slang or poetry to call an ox a *leg-plaiter*."

"Of course you can call it poetry if you like."

"Aha, Miss Rosy, you don't know Homer from slang. I shall invent a new game; I shall write bits of slang and poetry on slips, and give them to you to separate."

"Dear me, how amusing it is to hear people talk!" said Mrs. Vincy, with cheerful admiration. (10:126)

George Eliot obviously did not have the "girl of the period" in mind when she drew the fair Rosamund, nor did Trollope intend Lady Glencora Palliser to have any true kinship with Mrs. Linton's abomination. But by allowing Lady Glencora a moderate freedom of utterance, he implied some resemblance, and one reviewer of *Phineas Redux* (1873–74) took him to task for his injudiciousness. "Nothing," he wrote, "can be, on the whole, happier than the picture of Lady Glencora in this book, wherein she becomes Duchess of Omnium, though her manners, when in the retirement of her private interviews with her husband the Duke, are surely a little too fast and bounceable. For instance, when she says to the Duke, 'I'll tell you what. If he [Phineas Finn] is passed over, I'll make such a row that some of you shall hear it,' we think there is more of slang than of piquancy in her language; and Lady Glencora, though brusque and piquant, should never be slangy." [11]

3.

Catchphrases, which multiplied and circulated more widely as the printed media (and, later, such other disseminators of popular speech as the music hall) proliferated, were often indistinguishable from slang. Quotable remarks that at one point figured prominently in the day's news acquired in the course of time a proverbial quality, displacing the classical tags that had lent elegance to English writing in centuries when it was addressed to a more limited and cultivated audience. When Carlyle wrote *Past and Present* (1843), with its dense fabric of early Victorian topicalities, he made particularly effective use of what had already become a catch phrase, though its ultimate origin was the Gospel of Saint Matthew, 20:15. Fourteen years earlier, the bigoted, fanatical, reactionary fourth Duke of Newcastle had acquired extraordinary notoriety when he evicted forty of his tenants for failing to vote the way he desired in a by-election at Newark. In itself, this was not a matter of great moment in contemporary terms, because an English version of the droit du seigneur, though seldom exercised, was the supposed right of a landlord, including such infamous borough-mongers as the Duke, to dispossess tenants for electoral insubordination. To be sure, the deed was excessively high-handed, because the houses in question were not really

Newcastle's—he merely leased them from the Crown. But even this arrogance might have been overlooked had not his way of expressing it stuck in the public craw. When his unhoused tenants petitioned the Crown to revoke the leases and sell the properties to them, he replied, "Is it presumed, then, that I am not to do what I will with my own?" Even this single display of hauteur in a letter read at an indignation meeting at Newark and quoted in the *Times*'s detailed coverage of the event in its issue for 7 October 1829, might eventually have faded from the public memory had he not been so stubborn as to repeat it in the House of Lords five months later (1 March 1830), adhering to the very letter of the gospel verse: "Is it not lawful for me to do what I please with mine own?" asked the lord of the vineyard when his workers took exception to his paying them each a (biblical) penny, regardless of the number of hours they had worked.

Regardless of its scriptural origin, in the feverish climate of the moment the ill-chosen quotation was bound to stir up bitter resentment. It probably was on the tongues of the rioters who in October 1831 sacked and burned the Duke's seat as Lord-Lieutenant of Nottinghamshire. Disraeli, writing anonymously, exploited its notoriety in fiction as early as 1834, in *A Year at Hartlebury*, when a rustic character, self-important because he erroneously assumes that the recent Reform Act has added him to the electoral rolls, replies to a man soliciting his vote, "Am I woter, or am I not?—If a woter I be, I suppose I may do what I like with my wote" (2.2:107).

From Disraeli's pages the phrase leaped to Carlyle's. In *Past and Present* it achieved the prominence of a recurrent motif. On the Duke of Newcastle's first appearance as a typical "Master Unworker" he was unnamed, as he was to be throughout, but every reader would have recognized him in Carlyle's description of him as "coercing, bribing, cajoling; doing what he likes with his own." Later on, as part of his running strategy of contrasting the altruistic idealism of the past with the self-seeking ethos of the present, Carlyle put the "doing what he likes with his own" phrase into the mouth of the benevolent ninth-century East Anglian king (and landlord) Edmund. But here the context was radically altered; Carlyle had the saintly king use the phrase to justify a man's sacred right to sacrifice his life in a noble cause. The reader's appreciation of Carlyle's mordant irony depended on his responding, not to the words of Jesus' parable itself, but to the topicality that had associated them with a landlord who was totally lacking in social concern. Carlyle, in effect, enlarged the Newcastle figure into an emblem of a whole social class or phenomenon. In this case the effect was deepened by the topical use of a familiar quotation that had fallen from the wrong mouth and was grossly misapplied.

NEWCASTLE'S FREEDOM OF ELECTION.

THE PROPOSER, SECONDER, AND 900 FREE AND INDEPENDENT ELECTORS OF NEWARK.

In a by-election in 1846, the fourth Duke of Newcastle, a fervent protectionist, went to great lengths to remove his hated Peelite son, Lord Lincoln, from the seat for South Nottinghamshire (see illustration, page 684). *Punch*'s cartoon (21 February) shows that the Duke's peremptory eviction of his Newark tenants and his subsequent self-justification by quoting Saint Matthew were far from forgotten seventeen years later. No wonder the notorious question was repeated time after time in Victorian novels.

In some novels where the notorious question occurred thereafter, it is not always possible to determine whether the character who uttered it had its original or its topical association in mind. It was in the mental store of everyone who knew the Bible, as most literate persons, and even some illiterates, did. But at the very least, the angry publicity given it in the Reform Bill era and its recurrence in Carlyle's book were responsible for keeping it afloat, ready to be used in contexts that may or may not have resembled the one that first made it topical.

The words, whether or not they were consciously mediated through the Duke of Newcastle, served fictional characters in a variety of situations involving disputed possession and the rights of the possessor. In Mrs. Gaskell's *Ruth* (1853), Miss Benson describes Donne's first encounter with Leonard, his illegitimate child by the heroine. In the presence of others, he gives the boy his own watch and chain. She says: "I could see Mr. Bradshaw [a local businessman] was annoyed, and he and the other gentleman spoke to Mr. Donne, and I heard them say, 'too barefaced'; and I shall never forget Mr. Donne's proud, stubborn look back at them, nor his way of saying, 'I allow no one to interfere with what I choose to do with my own.' And he looked so haughty and displeased, I durst say nothing at the time" (24:290). This might be taken merely as evidence that the biblical phrase was on the common tongue, with no necessary reference to Newcastle. On the other hand, it might well be a touch of quiet Gaskellian irony. Not only might "my own" refer both to the watch *and* to the fact that the speaker was the boy's unacknowledged father; the words implicitly associated Donne, a seducer, with another unsympathetic character, the recently deceased Duke of Newcastle, and in a new electoral context, because Donne was at that time canvassing for votes.

The context of another, later use of the phrase allows no doubt that Trollope meant his readers to remember Newcastle. In *The Vicar of Bullhampton* (1869–70), forty whole years after the inflammatory episode, he twice attributed it to an imperious landlord and proprietor of pocket boroughs; "he held it [the seat] absolutely in his breeches pocket, to do with it as he liked," and "It was proper that the dissenters at Bullhampton should have a chapel [which he built for them on what turned out to be glebe land attached to the vicar's living], and he had a right to do what he liked with his own" (1:3; 43:277). In such references, the association with highhanded behavior on the part of dictatorial landowners remained firm.

For some reason, Trollope seems to have been enamored of the phrase at the time. In *He Knew He Was Right* (1868–69), a defender of Miss Stanbury's formidable decisiveness in respect to people over whom she holds some power protests, "She has got a right to do what she likes with her own, Uncle Barty" (35:326). In *Ralph the Heir* (1870–71) the words were placed in the mouth of a master bootmaker faced with a strike by "men who were attempting to dictate to him what he should do with his own" (16:1.195); and in *The Eustace Diamonds* (1871–73) Lady Eustace's repeated plea as she defends her right to the diamonds is "They are my own. Surely I might do what I liked with my own?" (51:500). Two or three years later, in *The Way We Live Now* (1874–75),

Ruby Ruggles's grandfather, a disagreeable character, protests to Joe Mixet, the baker, "I don't see why I ain't to do as I likes with my own," meaning Ruby (94:758).

In most applications the tag had a negative intent, to cast the character using it in an unfavorable light. But not in *John Halifax, Gentleman* (1856), where its two occurrences, one explicit and the other clearly implied, are the most interesting of all. First, in the anachronistic setting of 1800, twenty-nine years before the Duke's monumental gaffe, hungry workers threaten to burn the house of Halifax's master, a Quaker who has a large store of corn. "What do you do it for?" demands John. "All because he would not sell you, or give you, his wheat. Even so—it was *his* wheat, not yours. May not a man do what he likes with his own?" (8:79) Readers must have heard the peremptory voice of the Duke of Newcastle, but his line was spoken, this time, by a typical Victorian hero, a young man of humble origins but sterling character who educates himself and by loyalty to his employers makes his prosperous way in the world. Carlyle had left no doubt in his readers' minds what the sentiment should mean to anyone devoted to social justice, but what were Dinah Mulock's to think when John Halifax used it as a defense of his master? The ambiguity or irony, whichever it was, grew deeper in retrospect when, in a later phase of the novel, Mulock developed a situation obviously inspired by the Newcastle incident. When the evil Lord Luxmore bribes several tenants to vote for his candidate, Halifax persuades them to return the money and vote for the opposition man instead; whereupon Luxmore ejects them from their cottages. Halifax then provides a remedy not granted the unlucky voters in the actual case at Newark: as one of the numerous enlightened deeds he performs as a once homeless orphan who has made himself into a true (and wealthy) gentleman, he installs them in cottages *he* owns. While the scriptural tag does not appear in this connection, the repetition (with happy concluding variation) of the Newcastle story would have been plain to every reader who remembered it.[†]

Carlyle was responsible for popularizing another phrase long current in the Victorian literary lexicon. During the sensational Thurtell murder trial in 1823, the London newspapers had reported testimony to the

---

[†]In the preceding year (1855), James Russell Lowell used the famous question in describing to Charles Eliot Norton his telling Thackeray that marrying Clive and Ethel in *The Newcomes* was "an artistic blunder. He acknowledged that it was so. 'But then, you see, what could a fellow do? So many people wanted 'em married. To be sure, I had to kill off poor little Rosey rather suddenly, but shall not a man do what he will with his own?'" (*Letters of James Russell Lowell*, ed. Charles Eliot Norton [New York, 1893], 2:239.)

effect that the victim, Weare, "always maintained an appearance of respectability and kept a gig." Five years later, in the January 1828 issue of the *Quarterly Review*, a footnote appended to an article on New South Wales converted the simple affirmation into a fictitious exchange between counsel and witness: "Q. What do you mean by 'respectable'?" "A. He always kept a gig." In its new form of a definition rather than a loose association, the idea of respectability consisting of nothing more than means to keep a gig tickled Carlyle's sardonic sense of humor when he read it, and in the years to come he repeatedly invoked it, sometimes in the form of his coinage, *gigmanity*, as Carlylean shorthand for petit-bourgeois social pretension. (Modern readers, to whom horse-drawn vehicles are nothing more than curious historical artifacts, are likely to miss the full implications of "gig." Keeping a carriage had long been, and remained, an accepted sign of affluent gentility, requiring, in addition to the initial expense; horses to be fed and stabled and a coachman to drive them. When George Osborne in *Vanity Fair* boasted to Dobbin, "My father's a gentleman, and keeps his carriage," he was simply repeating a familiar measure of social worth. A gig, on the other hand, was at the time the lowliest and cheapest conveyance obtainable, and association with it robbed "respectability" of whatever dignity it otherwise possessed.)

The phrase quickly became proverbial. In *Pickwick Papers* Dickens invented a variation: "'He must be respectable—he keeps a man-servant,' said Miss Tomkins . . ." (16:306). Mrs. Gaskell wrote of Miss Betty Barker, who after coming into a modest competence "set up her cow; a mark of respectability in Cranford, almost as decided as setting up a gig is among some people" (*Cranford*, 7:61). Trollope used the phrase in an exotic context in *The Bertrams*, when he repeated the story told an Englishman by a "dragoman" (interpreter), of an Egyptian "great man" who killed his cook in a rage: "De sahib, him vera respecble man. Him kill cook, Solyman, this morning. Oh, de sahib particklar respecble!" "After all," Trollope commented, "it may be questioned whether this be not a truer criterion of respectability than that other one of keeping a gig" (2.16:2.244).

Novelists could depend on readers' recognizing the saying even when one of its terms was suppressed. Thus, in *Mr. Sponge's Sporting Tour*, Surtees could write of one Enoch Wriggle, who, having passed from one unrewarding occupation to another, found a mildly profitable métier in selling racing tips, "So the 'offending soul' prospered; and from scarcely having shoes to his feet, he very soon set up a gig" (58:434).

But the most skillful use of the Carlylean phrase was George Eliot's in *The Mill on the Floss*, where she juxtaposed, though at some distance, two contrasting measures of prosperous respectability in St. Ogg's. In the unpretentious social and familial milieu of the Dodsons and Tullivers, "one has conventional worldly notions and habits without instruction and without polish—surely the most prosaic form of human life: proud respectability in a gig of unfashionable build: worldliness without side-dishes" (4.1:238). But the Deanes aimed higher. When the family gathered to survey the ruin of Tulliver's modest fortune, "Mrs. Dean appeared punctually in that handsome new gig with the head to it, and the livery-servant driving it, which had thrown so clear a light on several traits in her character to some of her female friends in St. Ogg's" (3.3:182). There were different levels of respectability, and now different grades of gigs.

4.

George Meredith's and (to a lesser degree) George Eliot's novels apart, the prose style of Victorian fiction was not notably metaphorical; the figures of speech the novelists used were, on the whole, commonplace, although they play their usual significant role in any close textual exegesis. The figures in Meredith's coruscating aphoristic prose in, for example, *The Ordeal of Richard Feverel*, were almost never based on topicalities, and few of George Eliot's quieter ones were—the several she drew from visual shows such as panoramas were quite exceptional. And although modern critics have discerned large symbolic patterns in a few Victorian novels, these again lacked any timely reference. Dickens managed two or three, the most impressive being his use in *Our Mutual Friend* of a conspicuous site in the London of his day, the many-acred rubbish heaps north of the City, as a looming emblem of literally filthy lucre, the moral dirtiness of ill-acquired wealth. Although Dickens did not point out the fact, attentive Londoners reading the novel might have reflected that the liquid residue of the dumps that made old Harmon rich drained eventually into the already heavily polluted Thames, where river rats like Gaffer Hexam scavenged drowned corpses for whatever money and valuables they bore. In such a manner, Dickens physically as well as symbolically united two locales where people sought to extract grisly profit from repulsive decay or death. And, of course, the railway provides several symbolic passages in *Dombey and Son*, though it does not dominate the novel as the related dump and dirty river do *Our Mutual Friend.*[†]

[†]Topicalities are almost completely lacking in the whole range of Dickens's characteristic twin analogic devices, endowing inanimate objects with animate qualities and the re-

Elaborate analogies of any kind were extremely rare in Victorian fiction (Meredith again excepted). The most extended topical one I have noticed begins chapter 47 of *The Newcomes*:

> All this story is told by one, who, if he was not actually present at the circumstances here narrated, yet had information concerning them, and could supply such a narrative of facts and conversations as is, indeed, not less authentic than the details we have of other histories. How can I tell the feelings of a young lady's mind; the thoughts in a young gentleman's bosom?— As Professor Owen‡ or Professor Agassiz takes a fragment of a bone, and builds an enormous forgotten monster out of it, wallowing in primaeval quagmires, tearing down leaves and branches of plants that flourished thousands of years ago, and perhaps may be coal by this time—so the novelist puts this and that together: from the footprint finds the foot; from the foot, the brute who trod on it; from the brute, the plant he browsed on, the marsh in which he swam—and thus, in his humble way a physiologist too, depicts the habits, size, appearance of the beings whereof he has to treat;— traces this slimy reptile through the mud, and describes his habits filthy and rapacious; prods down this butterfly with a pin, and depicts his beautiful coat and embroidered waistcoat; points out the singular structure of yonder more important animal, the megatherium of his history. (47:2.92–93)

But ordinarily it is in brief, unelaborated analogies and comparisons that topicality manifests itself in the novelists' figurative language. These came from a fairly wide variety of sources, but by all odds the most

---

verse, turning human beings into things. They are equally missing from his exercise of a third device, tagging characters with certain attributes of language, costume, or bearing that identify them on their successive reappearances in the course of serial publication. Only once is an attribute drawn from a novelty of the period. When Pancks first turns up in *Little Dorrit*, Dickens says simply that he was "in a perspiration, and snorted and sniffed and puffed and blew, like a little labouring steam-engine" (1.13:190). But he soon took on a maritime aspect, and thenceforward was regularly presented as a grimy, puffing, bustling steam tugboat. Although Dickens was wrong in asserting that there were "no small steamboats on the river" at the time of the action (the late 1820s), the tugboat image would have been more appropriate to the time the book was written (1855–57), as, indeed, would have been the description of Edmund Sparkler as having "no greater will of his own than a boat has when it is towed by a steam-ship" (2.14:651).

‡ This was Professor Sir Richard Owen, the celebrated comparative anatomist and paleontologist, to whom Dickens referred in his description of Mrs. Podsnap as a "fine woman for Professor Owen, quantity of bone, neck and nostrils like a rocking-horse, hard features . . ." (*Our Mutual Friend*, 1.2:52). Thackeray's allusion is to the feats for which Owen was most celebrated in the public mind, reconstructing the size and form of a giant flightless New Zealand bird from a six-inch fragment of bone brought him by a sailor (1839) and similarly deducing the life habit of an extinct elephant-size sloth from a single skull (1842). In both cases, subsequent discoveries proved him correct.

drawn upon was the railway. When it arrived to enrich the English imagistic vocabulary in the 1830s, the idea of steam as the greatest source and
exemplification of energy noisily expended was already there. Juliet Mc-
Master has recently called attention to the way "the invigorating and
untiring motion of the steam engine is often suggested [in *Pickwick Papers*] in the imagery of heat, explosive pressure under harness, and
movement provided by rhythmic and mechanical means. . . . One of the
recurring jokes is the perpetual-motion machine—starting with the famous cabby's horse, which is surely a kind of prehistoric invention for
producing endless motion by pressure. . . ."[12] In *Ten Thousand a Year*,
Samuel Warren said that "getting up the steam" was "a modern and
significant expression" (37:1047), and when Dickens wrote that the two
Miss Chuzzlewits had "a great amount of steam to dispose of" he credited the phrase to "the figurative language of the day," as if it were a
novelty (*Martin Chuzzlewit*, 4:110). But it was rapidly becoming a cliché,
and the frequency with which steam engines were invoked thereafter
leaves little doubt that the simile "working like a steam engine," as Dick
Swiveller did when he was seen in Sampson Brass's law office, "scratch-
ing on, with a noisy pen, [and] scoring down the figures with evident
delight" (*The Old Curiosity Shop*, 33:328), floated at the top of every Englishman's pool of instantly intelligible tropes.

As time passed, "steam engine" came to refer specifically to a locomotive, which was the form in which the revolutionary machine was
most familiar to middle-class readers, especially women, who had little
firsthand acquaintance with factories and engineering works. But in
a few instances it is industrial engines, not locomotives, that are referred to. In *Lady Audley's Secret*, for example, when George Talboys
read of his wife's alleged death, "He knew that there was a great noise,
as of half a dozen furious steam-engines tearing and grinding in his
ears . . ." (5:25).

In any case, fully one-quarter of all brief topical allusions in metaphorical form were inspired by the railway's presence and the proliferation of its lines: its carefully engineered layout (a conspicuous feature of
contemporary topography, whereas the network of old roads, which had
taken centuries to develop, was absorbed into the landscape), the switch-
working (a completely new mechanical operation), and its running, including the fearsome noise and speed of the engines:[†]

> [The engineman Toodle, imparting moral advice to his assembled children:]
> "If you find yourselves in cuttings or in tunnels, don't you play no secret

---

[†]The dramatic speed with which the railway entered the public consciousness is reflected by the celerity with which poets drew metaphors from it. Tennyson seems to have

games. Keep your whistles going, and let's know where you are. . . . I starts light with Rob only; I comes to a branch; I takes on what I finds there; and a whole train of ideas gets coupled on to him, afore I knows where I am, or where they comes from. What a Junction a man's thoughts is . . . to-be-sure!" (*Dombey and Son*, 38:619)

If the hounds go rather more like a flock of wild geese than like the horses in the chariot of the sun, so do the field, until the diminutive dots, dribbling through the vale, look like the line of a projected railway. (*Ask Mamma*, 52:266)

These great crimes are like great trunk railways. They create many smaller ones: some flow into them; some out of them. (*It Is Never Too Late to Mend*, 15:1.237)

[The "Fathers of the Scrip-Church," i.e., railway contractors and specula-tors, instruct Veneering on how to be a successful financier:] [H]e must leave the valley of the piano on his left, take the level of the mantelpiece, cross by an open cutting at the candelabra, seize the carrying-traffic at the console, and cut up the opposition root and branch at the window curtains. (*Our Mutual Friend*, 3.17:690)

Like those ambitious railways, which ruin a goodly trunk with excess of branches, not to say twigs, he set to work extending, and extending, and sent the sap of the healthy old concern [a London mercantile firm] a-flying to the ends of the earth. (*Foul Play*, 7:70)

---

been first in the field with his famous "Let the great world spin for ever down the ringing grooves of change" ("Locksley Hall" was written in 1837–38, though not published until 1842). Arthur Hugh Clough soon followed, using railway effects and experiences for a variety of figurative purposes:

As, at a railway junction, men
Who came together, taking then
One the train up, one down again,
Meet never—!
("Sic Itur," written 1844, published in *Ambarvalia*, 1849)

As unsuspecting mere a maid
    As, fresh in maidhood's bloomiest bloom [!],
In casual second-class did e'er
    By casual youth her seat assume . . .
("Natura Naturans," written 1846; also in *Ambarvalia*)

I was as one that sleeps on the railway; one, who dreaming
Hears thro' his dream the name of his home shouted out; hears and hears not,—
Faint, and louder again, and less loud, dying in distance;
Dimly conscious, with something of inward debate and choice . . .
(*The Bothie of Tober-na-Vuolich*, 1848)

"We [women] are to run on lines, like the steam-trains, or we come to no station, dash to fragments." (*Diana of the Crossways*, 6:76)

. . . . gradually she was beginning to understand that she was parting company with her original conjectures, but going at so swift a pace in so supple and sure a grasp, that, like the speeding train slipped on new rails by the pointsman, her hurrying sensibility was not shocked, or the shock was imperceptible, when she heard him proposing Mr. Tuckham to her for a husband. . . . (*Beauchamp's Career*, 46:2.217)

"I am sometimes aghast with myself when I think of the small matter which, like the point on a railway, sent me running rapidly on to prosperity,— while the same point, turned wrong, hurried him to ruin." (*John Caldigate*, 15:136)

No little Gradgrind had ever known wonder on the subject, each little Gradgrind having at five years old dissected the Great Bear like a Professor Owen, and driven Charles's Wain like a locomotive engine-driver. (*Hard Times*, 1.3:54)

Mrs. General had no opinions. Her way of forming a mind was to prevent it from forming opinions. She had a little circular set of mental grooves or rails on which she started little trains of other people's opinions, which never overtook one another, and never got anywhere. (*Little Dorrit*, 2.2:503)

. . . Mr. Pancks, whose expressive breathing had been labouring hard since the entrance of the little man, like a locomotive engine with a great load getting up a steep incline. (*Little Dorrit*, 2.13:635)

"Give me the lad who has more steam up than he knows what to do with, and must needs blow off a little in larks. When once he settles down on the rail, it'll send him along as steady as a luggage-train. Did you never hear a locomotive puffing and roaring before it gets under way?" (*Two Years Ago*, 1:24)

[Said of the poet Elsley Vavasour] "One of the Sturm-und-drang party, of course; the express locomotive school, scream-and-go-ahead: and thinks me, with my classicism, a benighted pagan." (*Two Years Ago*, 19:325)

Your high-pressure happiness, your sixty-miles-an-hour enjoyment, is apt to burst up and come to a bad end. Better the quietest parliamentary train, which starts very early in the morning and carries its passengers safe into the terminus when the shades of night come down, than that rabid, rushing express, which does the journey in a quarter of the time, but occasionally topples over a bank, or rides pickaback upon a luggage train, in its fiery impetuosity. (*Aurora Floyd*, 19:182–83)

It is however fruitless to dwell on what was only a glimpse of a wild regret, like the crossing of two express trains along the rails in Sir Willoughby's head. (*The Egoist*, 14:1.161)

. . . there was discernibly to Redworth, under the influence of her phrases, a likeness of the flaming "half-horse," with the animals all smoking in the frost, to a railway-engine. (*Diana of the Crossways*, 11:122)

"Express train" was, of course, a much-used measure of speed; Trollope once speaks of Phineas Finn, the energetic young politician, as an "express train at full speed." The term gained in force by existing alongside its antonym, which had preceded it into the everyday vocabulary: "slow coach," an unflattering personal description that was a byword as early as *Pickwick Papers*, when Serjeant Buzfuz adroitly explicated to the jury in Bardell *versus* Pickwick the true incriminating meaning of the evidential letter from the defendant to the plaintiff, "Dear Mrs. B., I shall not be at home till to-morrow. Slow coach." "And what does this allusion to slow coach mean? For aught I know, it may be a reference to Pickwick himself, who has most unquestionably been a criminally slow coach during the whole of this transaction, but whose speed will now be very unexpectedly accelerated, and whose wheels, gentlemen, as he will find to his cost, will very soon be greased by you!" (34:563). "What are we but coaches?" pontificated Pecksniff some years later. "Some of us are slow coaches—"

"Goodness, Pa!" cried Charity.
"Some of us, I say," resumed her parent with increased emphasis, "are slow coaches; some of us are fast coaches. Our passions are the horses; and rampant animals too!"—
"Really, Pa!" cried both the daughters at once. "How very unpleasant!"
(*Martin Chuzzlewit*, 8:174)

When Pendennis and Fanny Bolton spend an evening at Vauxhall, they run into Pen's Clavering friend Huxter, "dingy shirt-collar," "dubious neck" and all, who has "a lady in pink satin" on his arm. They dance, and Huxter collides with Pen and Fanny. He "broke out into a volley of slang against the unoffending couple. 'Now then, stoopid! Don't keep the ground if you can't dance, old Slow Coach!' the young surgeon roared out (using, at the same time, other expressions far more emphatic) . . ." (*Pendennis*, 46:2.92). Later, after coaches, fast and slow alike, had ceased to coexist with railways, the phrase persisted. As late as 1882–83, in Trollope's *Mr. Scarborough's Family*, Captain Scarborough observed of another character, "That Moody is a slow coach, and will never do anything" (49:474). In a day of express trains, slow coaches were slow indeed, a discrepancy rendered all the wider by the current habit of using *slow* in the additional pejorative sense of "fuddy-duddy," as Lily Dale did in a sentence quoted above: "It's so slow, you know, to use nothing but words out of a dictionary." A "slow coach" of a person was no longer merely dull, plodding, negligent, unambitious—he was an old fogy too. (This was doubtless the origin of the slang word *slow*—detached from *coach*—that was ginger in the mouths of Trollope's sprightly heroines, such as Lily Dale. As a natural consequence, the antonym *fast* came to designate the kind of emancipated modern young lady who was the abomination of Mrs. Lynn Linton and other conservatives.)

Inseparable from the railway in the earlier years was the electric telegraph, whose wires were strung along the right of way and whose instruments were first found in stations:

All the journey, immovable in the air though never left behind; plain to the dark eyes of her [Mrs. Sparsit's] mind, as the electric wires which ruled a colossal strip of music-paper out of the evening sky, were plain to the dark eyes of her body. . . . (*Hard Times*, 2.11:233)

An unquiet fever, generated amidst the fibres of the brain, and finding its way by that physiological telegraph, the spinal marrow, to the remotest stations on the human railway. (*Aurora Floyd*, 21:206)

"Well, Mr. Whitford, the laboratory—ah—where the amount of labour done within the space of a year would not stretch an electric current between this Hall and the railway station: say, four miles, which I presume the distance to be." (*The Egoist*, 24:1.292)

His look was exceptionally jovial now, and the corners of his mouth twitched as the telegraph-needles of a hundred little erotic messages from his heart to his brain. (*The Hand of Ethelberta*, 40:316)

On the London transport scene, the equivalent novelty to the railway was the omnibus, which made its first run just a year before the first train steamed from Liverpool to Manchester. Dickens was the first to seize upon it for analogic purposes: "They [seedy attorneys] have no fixed offices, their legal business being transacted in the parlours of public houses, or the yards of prisons: whither they repair in crowds, and canvass for customers after the manner of omnibus cads" (*Pickwick Papers*, 43:694).

"I understand," said Ralph; "just as some women run into the wrong omnibus, when the right one is straight before them" (*Basil*, 3.7:371). [Collins expanded the simile into one of mock-Homeric proportions two years later, in *Hide and Seek*:] "As the bee comes and goes irregularly from flower to flower; as the butterfly flutters in a zigzag course from one sunny place

on the garden wall to another—or, as an old woman runs from wrong omnibus to wrong omnibus, at the Elephant and Castle, before she can discover the right one; as a countryman blunders up one street, and down another, before he can find the way to his place of destination in London."
(1.2:62–63)

. . . the sallow-complexioned lad walked about in the calm serenity of innocence,—there are honest jockeys in the world,—and took his seat in the
saddle with as even a pulse as if he had been about to ride in an omnibus.
(*Aurora Floyd*, 13:123)

Although ballooning was not strictly a novelty in nineteenth-century
England, it was more widely talked of when it became a popular spectator sport, the main London pleasure gardens serving as launching pads
and aeronauts becoming show-business celebrities. The following are
typical of the many ballooning metaphors in Victorian fiction:

Yes! the bank had stopped. The ancient firm of Smith, Brown, Jones, Robinson, and Co., which had been for some years past expanding from a solid
golden organism into a cobweb-tissue and huge balloon of threadbare paper, had at last worn through and collapsed, dropping its car and human
contents miserably into the Thames mud. (*Yeast*, 14:265)

[Bounderby was] A man with a pervading appearance on him of being inflated like a balloon, and ready to start. (*Hard Times*, 1.4:58)

The world of higher culture—archaeology, art, the theatre—was not
often represented in metaphorical language.

. . . a cipher under each crown [on the panel of the Princesse de Montcontour's brougham] [was] as easy to read as the arrow-headed inscriptions on
one of Mr. Layard's Assyrian chariots. (*The Newcomes*, 40:2.18)

. . . a style of head-dress so admirably adapted to her [Mrs. Hominy's] coun-
tenance, that if the late Mr. Grimaldi had appeared in the lappets of Mrs.
Siddons, a more complete effect could not have been produced. (*Martin
Chuzzlewit*, 22:434)

Not till the music stopped did she [Ethel Newcome] sink down on a seat,
panting, and smiling radiant—as many many hundred years ago I remember to have seen Taglioni, after a conquering *pas seul*. (*The Newcomes*,
41:2.13)

. . . she well knew how being seen at one good place led to another, just as
the umbrella-keepers at the Royal Academy try to lead people into giving
them something in contravention of the rule above their heads, by jingling
a few half-pence before their faces. (*Ask Mamma*, 13:52)

This is the mental picture that Surtees's allusion to "one of Mr. Henson's air carriages" (*Hillingdon Hall*) would have evoked in readers (*Illustrated London News*, 1 April 1843).

A final miscellany demonstrates how widely scattered were the sources in contemporary observation and experience from which the novelists drew their topical analogies and comparisons, and the diverse uses to which they put them:

> Like a gas lamp in the street, with the wind in the pipe, he [Pickwick] had exhibited for a moment an unnatural brilliancy: then sunk so low as to be scarcely discernible: after a short interval he had burst out again, to enlighten for a moment, then flickered with an uncertain, staggering sort of light, and then gone out altogether. (*Pickwick Papers*, 2:86)

> "I remember," Dacier was reminded, "hearing him say, when the House resembled a Chartist riot, 'Let us stand aside and meditate on Life. . . .'" (*Diana of the Crossways*, 30:357)

> He knew perfectly well the Duke would no more think of letting him marry anything below a Duke's daughter, than he would think of sending him off for a trip on one of Mr. Henson's air carriages. (*Hillingdon Hall*, 11:89)[†]

[†]On 27 March 1843, only a month or two before this installment of the novel appeared, an "Aerial Transit Company" bill was introduced in the House of Commons, its

Thus the congregation on Christmas morning is mostly a Tussaud collection of celebrities who have been born in the neighborhood. (*The Return of the Native*, 2.4:95)

. . . a town young man, with a Tussaud complexion and well-pencilled brows half way up his forehead. . . . (*The Hand of Ethelberta*, 3:55)

. . . we run in a crowd to high mass at St. Peter's, or to the illumination on Easter-day, as we run when the bell rings to the Bosjesmen [African bushmen on exhibition] at Cremorne, or the fireworks at Vauxhall. (*The Newcomes*, 39:2.5)

Burton St. Leger was a large place, or rather a small one stretched out into a large one, just as a goldbeater hammers a small piece of the precious metal into a large circumference, or a little moth of a woman distends herself into a hay-stack with crinoline. (*Plain or Ringlets?*, 62:227)

"We must be all on one side like the 'andle of a tin-pot, or like Bridgenorth election." (*Handley Cross*, 21:155)[†]

. . . against the blue sky, sat a Wellington-statue-like equestrian with his cap in the air, waving and shouting for hard life. (*Handley Cross*, 36:280).

. . . his hand coming down upon her shoulder the while like a Nasymth hammer. . . . (*Under the Greenwood Tree*, 1.8:76)[‡]

5.

Gestures and certain social habits conveyed their own message to Victorian readers as much as to the fictional characters to whom they were directed, but, like nuances in verbal discourse, at so far a remove in the time that they are often hard to interpret. Michael Irwin has commented on

the wide range of Victorian gestures [which] involved accoutrements that have now disappeared or become very scarce: hats, gloves, fans, monocles, parasols, snuff-boxes, pocket-watches, beards. . . . Equipment aside, fash-

---

purpose being to permit the formation of a company to "carry out the objects" of "a certain patent, granted to William Samuel Henson, relating to locomotive apparatus and machinery"—in this case, a new and nugatory form of "aerial transit." (*Annual Register 1843*, Chronicle, p. 31.)

  [†]The electors at Bridgenorth (Salop) had chosen a member of the same family, the Whitmores, at every general election from 1832 to 1852. (Gash, *Politics in the Age of Peel*, p. 201.)

  [‡]James Nasmyth, who was still living when the novel was written, had invented a steam hammer in 1839 and patented it in 1842.

ions in gesture have changed. We shake hands less often, bow or curtsey hardly at all. Men no longer shed tears or link arms. In terms of class and social convention Dickens's novels are so remote from our experience that we are liable to misread his finer detail, to overlook or misconstrue carefully recorded snubs, blunders, unorthodoxies. . . . The performance or non-performance of gestures of this kind can convey a great variety of meanings.[13]

As "society" came to be more and more loosely defined and embraced an ever-increasing number of men and women who were not to its manners born, the courtesy books that had provided guidance in social situations ever since Tudor times evolved into a distinctly new genre of etiquette handbooks to meet the demand.[14] In 1837 alone, the *Quarterly Review* took notice of no fewer than eleven such books, all published within the past two years. There the socially ambitious but unpolished members of the middle class, including the new rich, learned the requisite lessons of gentility and decorum, including the bearing to be adopted in their dealings with their inferiors, a delicately maintained balance of distanced reserve and humane consideration. Gentlemen were told when to doff their hats in the streets and what to do with them indoors; ladies learned the subtle conventions governing the leaving of cards (when? where? how many? whose?) and when (and to whom) they were "at home" (or not) when someone called.

Guided by unwritten custom as well, single men and women knew the precise degrees of intimacy permitted between them—the necessity of chaperonage, the mild liberties that formal engagement legitimized, the severe restrictions on bodily contact. A modern reader's interpretation of such nuances of conduct must take into account the date of the report. Much evidence in Trollope's novels, corroborated by the paintings of the time, suggests that kisses and wholehearted embraces between lovers were increasingly lawful in the best circles from the 1860s onward. Compared with the timorous restraint that was the inviolable convention in earlier Victorian fiction, the amount of kissing in which Dick Dewy and Fancy Day indulge in *Under the Greenwood Tree* (1872) constitutes a veritable orgy.

Alongside a gradual relaxation of taboos such as this occurred what was recognized at the time to be a fad that might disappear just as quickly as it appeared. Trollope recorded it in *Phineas Redux* (1873–74):

> Then Mrs. Bonteen took her leave, kissing her dear friend, Madame Goesler, and simply bowing to Phineas.
>
> "What a detestable woman!" said Phineas.
>
> "I know of old that you don't love her" [said Madame Goesler].
>
> "I don't believe that you love her a bit better than I do, and yet you kiss her."

> "Hardly that, Mr. Finn. There has come up a fashion for ladies to pre-
> tend to be very loving, and so they put their faces together. Two hundred
> years ago ladies and gentlemen did the same thing with just as little regard
> for each other [and one hundred years later they would do it again]. Fash-
> ions change, you know."
>   "That was a change for the worse, certainly, Madame Goesler." (37:
> 305–6).

The new effusiveness was perfectly suited to Trollope's purposes as he
developed the character of Lady Eustace beyond *The Eustace Diamonds*.
When she reappeared in *The Prime Minister*, her action was not only
voguish but in harmony with all that readers had previously learned
about her: "Lady Eustace gushed into the room, kissing Mrs. Dick and
afterwards kissing her great friend of the moment, Mrs. Leslie, who followed. She then looked as though she meant to kiss Lord Mongrober,
whom she playfully and almost familiarly addressed. But Lord Mongrober only grunted" (9:1.82).

Trollope was as much an authority on the niceties of the drawing
room as he was on the scaled elitism of London addresses. An anonymous reviewer of *The Golden Lion of Granpere* summed up one reason for
his reputation as a peerless and faithful chronicler of daily life wherever
the people in his superior "world" met and, as we say, interacted:

> Mr. Trollope really knows what we may call the *natural history* of every kind
> of man or woman he seeks to sketch,—by which we mean not so much his
> or her interior thoughts and feelings, but the outward habits in which these
> thoughts and feelings are expressed, the local and professional peculiarities
> of manner and habit in every place and in every trade, nay more, the minu-
> tiae of class demeanor, the value that is attached in particular situations to
> standing up rather than sitting down, to making a statement in one room
> rather than in another; in short, the characteristic dress in which the small
> diplomacies of social life clothe themselves.[15]

These "small diplomacies," an earlier critic (of *Miss Mackenzie* [1865])
said, were "almost an artificial language in themselves, which it almost
takes an art to interpret."[16] Trollope often offered his own interpretation, which could be relied on as being faithful to the mode of the moment. He was the keenest observer of the precarious line, so crucial to
people who elevated ritual decorum over the promptings of the spontaneous spirit, that demarcated correct values and behavior from—that
fearsome word in the Victorian lexicon—"vulgarity." In *The Prime Minister*, the new Duke of Omnium unwarily uses the word in connection
with the elaborate and expensive preparations Lady Glencora is making
for a big house party at Gatherum Castle. Her resentful analysis of the
word and what it stood for, set forth at length in a chapter (19) entitled
simply "Vulgarity," suggests how emotive it could be.

The printed guides to proper conduct, indispensable to our understanding of the everyday dynamics of social intercourse, always represented the norm—if not the norm that was rigorously followed in practice, at least the one that the lawgivers in such matters, presumably echoing the prevailing consensus, deemed desirable. It is against that background of almost prescriptive recommendation that the conduct of characters in novels can be interpreted. Adherence to the rules, like expressed tastes in reading that are conventional to a fault, usually says no more about a character than that he or she is a conformist in that particular situation. But awareness of the dictates applicable to a person of a given social level can carry a modern reader only so far, after which the precise circumstances of the narrative moment in question complicate the issue. "[T]he whole troublesome business of when to sit and when to stand in company, of how to dispose of one's hat or one's hands when addressing a social superior," as Michael Irwin put it, had to be decided on an ad hoc basis. "The modern student can too easily dismiss Joe Gargery's deportment before Miss Havisham as merely imbecilic, or fail to see the full offensiveness of Sir Mulberry Hawk's drawing Kate Nickleby's 'arm through his up to the elbow' within a few minutes of first meeting her. . . . [I]n Dickens, the courtesy offered or neglected acquires meaning in relation to particular personalities or situations." [17] It is the deviations from formulated practice that the Victorian reader would have noticed and interpreted as a member of the same society, just as he would have noticed shadings of expressed attitudes that modern readers, accustomed to a radically different social context, overlook or are mystified by.

But the etiquette books were written for, and read by, only people in the middle classes, and they have little direct pertinence to the gestures and ceremonies common to the urban lower class who figure most prominently in Dickens's novels or the humble country people in George Eliot's or Hardy's. The only printed guidance to social behavior these classes possessed was contained in the moralized tracts sent their way by religious institutions and organizations dedicated to "the reformation of manners," and the rules to be found there concentrated solely (and unrealistically) on the virtues of chastity, abstinence, industry, frugality, and deference to one's betters. A man's tugging his forelock and a maidservant's curtsy were the universal signs of this last prescribed attitude, which shaded into downright subservience. It, and associated gestures, related to a set of unarticulated principles, an unrefined sense of what sort of conduct or response was expected of a man or woman in a given situation, and characters' actions as represented in novels were affected by these communal assumptions. Again, however, it is the deviations from expected practice that are most significant when they occur, and to detect them, in the absence of any formalized body of customary rules applying to such situations, is almost impossible at this distance of time. It is reasonable to suppose, however, that the ritual tugging of the forelock and the quick bob that served as a curtsy were often accompanied by severe inner reservations which might be imaged by a performance of the grinder's salute.

Though the handshake was then, as it is today, a routine gesture of civility upon meeting that was practiced more by men than by women in Victorian times, Dickens, for one, saw it as a more spontaneous act. Several times he depicts the prolonged or repeated shaking of hands in a single encounter, as an expression of joyous excitement or deep rapport. In *Little Dorrit*, for instance, when Pancks reports to Clennam the results of his detective work in ferreting out the Dorrit fortune, Dickens has Clennam "almost incessantly shaking hands with him throughout the narrative" and "exchanging one more hearty shake of the hand" before they finally disengage themselves (1.35:461–62). And in *The Newcomes*, Thackeray explicitly says, as if it were a matter of some significance, that Arthur Pendennis and Colonel Newcome shook hands four times in a single encounter in Warrington's chambers (4:1.44).

The blithely independent Becky Sharp Crawley disregarded, among other conventions of conduct in Regency society, the one that determined whom it was, or was not, proper to shake hands with. A member of superior society did not shake hands with an inferior, as Becky did when she met Briggs, the late Miss Crawley's much put-upon maidservant, outside her London lodgings. After hearing Briggs recount her recent history, Becky "persisted in shaking hands with the retired lady's maid," who had reluctantly extended fingers that "were like so many sausages, cold and lifeless" (40:401). Immediately afterward, returning to Queen's Crawley, where she had once been governess to the late Sir Pitt's daughters, Becky, now the triumphant wife of his son, "insisted upon shaking" the hand of the old lady at the lodge as she opened the gate for the carriage to pass through (41:402–3). In both instances, this wanton disregard of convention was a sign of her exhilaration over her new status as a member of the ancient Crawley family. She had made it into the squirearchy, and the road to Fashion's heavenly city—the Prince Regent's palatial Carlton House—now opened invitingly before her.[†]

[†]Juliet McMaster has called attention to subtler nuances in the Thackerayan handshake: "It is not just a question of whether one does or does not shake hands with a certain person; but there is a whole range of possibilities in a handshake itself, which may include how many of the fingers are offered, whether the hand is gloved or not, whether the gloves are new or merely cleaned, or even dirty. Becky can readjust a whole relationship by offer-

6.

From the language of gesture we return, briefly, to the language of dress. As we saw in Chapter 9, some styles of clothing and hairdo conveyed one message or another about the wearer's social standing, as well, sometimes, as his or her personality. Especially popular ones acted as temporary solvents of social differences, as did the crinoline when it came to be worn by maidservants as well as their mistresses; and the adoption of flamboyant garb by gents was meant to reduce the distance between them and the socially superior swells, as swells also intended it, in turn, to align themselves with dandies. One particular item of clothing, common to both men and women, had the opposite intention and effect, that of distinguishing propriety from vulgarity. Disraeli might well have divided his England into two nations on the basis of who did and who did not wear gloves. The ultra-respectable and rich did, because their position in society excused them from physical toil; therefore their gloves would not be soiled, and wearing them could serve as a sign of status. The poor did not, not only because it would have been impractical (to say nothing of expensive) but because their careworn hands were a token, not to be concealed, of their fixed status as manual workers.

The prejudice involving gloves was first manifest during Colonel Newcome's first long absence in India. That insufferable youth, his nephew Barnes Newcome, sniffed to his father, Sir Brian, on first meeting the Colonel on his return, "His costume struck me with respectful astonishment. He disdains the use of straps [on the bottom of his trousers], and is seemingly unacquainted with gloves." The Colonel himself realized how out-of-date he was: "I must wear gloves, by Jove I must, and my coat *is* old-fashioned" (*The Newcomes*, 6:1.67; 15:1.169). Charles Honeyman's stylish lavender gloves, in the same novel, both widened the temperamental and age difference between the Colonel and himself and completed Thackeray's portrait of him as a "reverend gent." Gloves, not so much worn as carried with a negligent air, as a Micawber might flaunt a quizzing glass or a walking stick, were regulation equipment for dandies and their sedulous imitators, swells and gents. John Chivery flourished them as part of the plumage he adopted in his unrequited court-

---

ing George one finger to shake, transforming his attitude from patronage to deference. Lady Kew shows her estimation of Clive Newcome by offering him two fingers to shake; Sir Brian Newcome similarly condescends to Pendennis, who afterwards regrets that he had not the presence of mind 'to poke one finger against his two'." (*Thackeray: The Major Novels* [Toronto, 1971], pp. 141–42.)

ship of Amy Dorrit, and they completed Turveydrop's sartorial parody of Beau Brummell. The first thing Tittlebat Titmouse planned to do after he came into his fortune and ordered his Stultz coat was to "buy a dozen or two pair of white kid" (*Ten Thousand a Year*, 1:12).

As genuine or factitious status symbols, the message that gloves conveyed to Victorian readers was complicated when, in the 1840s, they became available to a larger market through British manufacturers who introduced cheap so-called Berlin gloves, made not of leather but wool or cotton. Now it was no longer a question only of whether or not a person wore gloves at all, but one of material as well. Their evident cheapness made them unacceptable to all who wished to maintain a fashionable front, and furthermore they were worn by people like the "men in creaking shoes and Berlin gloves" who served at the publisher Bungay's dinner party in *Pendennis*, "carrying on rapid conversations behind the guests, as they moved to and fro with the dishes" (34:1.351). Policeman X, who removed the drunken Altamont from the sidewalk in front of Sir Francis Clavering's house in the same novel, wore one of his "gauntlets of the Berlin woof" and kept the other "stuck in his belt side" (38:1.389). There was particular point, therefore, in one of Thackeray's many definitions of the snob, that he refused "to shake an honest man's hand because it wears a Berlin glove" ("On University Snobs," *Punch*, 13 June 1846; *BS*, 60–61). That "honest men" included freelance waiters and policemen on the beat was, from the snob's viewpoint, reason enough to refrain.

Dickens's lower-class characters silently speak a veritable language of gloves. Time after time gloves are seen on the hands of people who, according to the prevailing rules of etiquette, have no right to wear them. The effect is sometimes farcical, sometimes pathetic; and sometimes there is an element of eccentricity, if not actual disguise, as when, in *Martin Chuzzlewit*, the private detective Nadgett's "mildewed, threadbare, shabby" outfit is completed by a single stained beaver glove (made of heavy woolen cloth), not worn but "dangled by the forefinger as he walked or sat; but even its fellow was a mystery" (27:517). But gloves are most often the sign of a man or woman bent on presenting a respectable image before the world—Tom Pinch, for instance, poverty-stricken in London, whose gloves threaten to fall apart until his "brave little sister" mends their loose stitches (39:683).

Gloves are especially prominent in *Nicholas· Nickleby*. Long ones, as we saw in an earlier connection, were part of Fanny Squeers's extravagant getup as she prepared to bewitch Nicholas. The fat lady in the Kenwigs' back parlor comes to their party "in a low book-muslin dress and short kid gloves" (14:231). (Wearing gloves indoors was a current affectation.) Newman Noggs's fingerless pair are the sole surviving evidence of the gentility that once was his, before drink got the better of him. In one of his routine confrontations with Ralph, his employer, he "took off his fingerless gloves, and spreading them carefully on the palm of his left hand, and flattening them with his right to take the creases out, proceeded to roll them up with an absent air as if he were utterly regardless of all things else, in the deep interest of the ceremonial" (44:657). Gloves were ritualistic objects in more ways than one. When Mrs. Kenwigs is about to be confined, her husband sends out for "a pair of the cheapest white kid gloves—those at fourteenpence—and selecting the strongest, which happened to be the right-hand one, walked downstairs with an air of some pomp and much excitement, and proceeded to muffle the knob of the street-door knocker therein. . . . No genteel lady was ever yet confined—indeed, no genteel confinement can possibly take place—without the accompanying symbol of a muffled knocker" (36:542–43). That Kenwigs chose to spend fourteen pence for a pair of gloves, only one of which was used, and which may or may not have fitted anyone in the household after it served its original purpose, instead of using something freely at hand such as a clean piece of flannel, was a small indication of his aspiration toward gentility.

Mrs. Micawber affects a pair of brown gloves as a reminder that she sacrificed the secure comfort of a middle-class home to marry her feckless husband, and Uriah Heep is seen "slowly fitting his long skeleton fingers into the still longer fingers of a great Guy Fawkes pair of gloves" (*David Copperfield*, 25:436). When Miss Flite visits her friends at Bleak House, she arrays herself "with great satisfaction in a pitiable old scarf and a much-worn and often-mended pair of gloves, which she had brought down in a paper parcel" (*Bleak House*, 35:552). Similarly, when Bounderby's old mother makes her annual trip to Coketown by parliamentary train to look upon her rich son from afar, "loose long-fingered gloves, to which her hands were unused," were among the items—others were a spare shawl, a heavy umbrella, and a little basket—that "bespoke an old woman from the country, in her plain holiday clothes" (*Hard Times*, 1.12:115). Nothing in Dickens's repertory of small social details could more forcefully express the difference between her honest simplicity and her braggart son's deceit, which could take the form of reverse snobbery. "'I never wear gloves,' it was his custom to say. 'I didn't climb up the ladder in *them*. Shouldn't be so high up, if I had'" (1.4:64).

Dickens suggests Mrs. General's inflexible gentility by remarking that "she was never without gloves, and they never creased and always fitted." The importance he attached to that touch is later affirmed by his likening her to "a Ghoule in Gloves" (*Little Dorrit*, 2.5:525; 2.15:671). But they are an even more insisted-upon part of Mrs. Wilfer's act in *Our Mutual Friend*. Unlike most of Dickens's gloved characters, she not only wears them—she brandishes them. They are, in fact, not so much items of apparel as stage properties, to which Dickens calls his reader's attention on at least eight different occasions.

When Pip, in *Great Expectations*, is fully outfitted to assume the life of a young gentleman, he takes leave of Miss Havisham, ringing the bell at Satis House "constrainedly, on account of the stiff long fingers of my gloves," unaccustomed equipment for a blacksmith's apprentice just released from his articles. Later in the novel, Miss Skiffins, Wemmick's intended bride, wears "gloves a little too intensely green," especially as seen against her "too decidedly orange" gown. She doffs them only to wash up after the Sunday tea she sets out during her regular Sunday evening visit to the Walworth mini-fortress, and afterward, when she, Pip, Wemmick, and the aged P. gather round the fire and the aged P. is induced to read from the newspaper, "She retained her green gloves during the evening as an outward and visible sign that there was company" (37:313, 315).

There is similar byplay with gloves in Thackeray's novels, though not with the same insistence as in Dickens's. Fanny Bolton, pathetically trying to climb out of the working class, wears "a shabby little glove" (*Pendennis*, 46:2.84), and a sign of Captain Costigan's temporary solvency is his progression from "a broken black glove" to "a new shoot of clothes, as he called them, and . . . a large pair of white kid gloves" (5:1.46; 6:1.62). In Trollope, men's gloves are frequently mentioned, but they seldom indicate any change of status or aspiration toward a high one; they are simply a routine clothing accessory, appropriate to the rank of Trollopian gentleman.

Conclusion

1.

AT THE END of Chapter 1 we saw that in the early Victorian years, the tendency of mainstream criticism was to resist the encroachment of descriptive realism in fiction, Scott's magisterial example notwithstanding. And as fashionable fiction, now in its deepening twilight, came into still further disrepute, its notorious lavishness of costume and setting cast a shadow over the employment of particulars for specifically contemporary period color. In an essay on "The Historical Romance" in 1845, Archibald Alison applied to post-silver fork fiction the same Enlightenment principle that had governed criticism of that older form of narrative art. "[T]rue novel-writing," he argued, ". . . should aim at the representation of what Sir Joshua Reynolds called 'general or common nature'—that is, nature by its general features, which are common to all ages and countries, not its peculiarities in a particular circle or society. It is by success in delineating that, and *by it alone* [his italics], that lasting fame is to be acquired." With Scott in mind, Alison conceded that "Without doubt every age and race of man have their separate dress and costume, and the mind has its externals as well as the body, which the artist of genius will study with sedulous care, and imitate with scrupulous fidelity"—Carlyle's slashed breeches and steeple hats once more—but, Alison insisted, "the soul is not in the dress; and so it will be found in the delineation of the mind as in the representation of the figure."[1]

Now, however, the ground of argument began to shift; the old conservative refrain was pitched in a new key suited to the time when the novel's popular presence could not longer be dismissed as a temporary phenomenon.[2] Alison's article proved to be the last important attempt to compare "modern" fiction with the historical romance. Fourteen years later, in his book on the current state of fiction which, significantly, employed the newly domesticated words *realism* and *realist*, David Masson began with the familiar concept of human nature as essentially unchanging but diverged from Alison's position. "Human nature comes down the same in its essentials," he admitted; "customs and institutions are also perpetuated from generation to generation; but over this tolerably solid basis there rolls in every generation an assemblage of facts, psychological and political, held in the meantime in vital solution and suspense, as the immediate element in which the generation believes, though soon also to fall down as sediment, a thin additional layer to the stratification foregone."[3]

Masson doubtless would have allowed that his "assemblage of facts" could be expanded beyond the realm of psychological and political abstractions to encompass the small physical and mental accessories of present-day experience. Those accessories that hung in suspension in a novel as its first readers knew it may eventually have turned into sediment, but they did not simply evaporate. They remained an integral part of the book, providing period color as its "modern" setting receded into the past.

Now an already well-known and respected critic entered the discussion. George Henry Lewes was no enemy of realism; he is often credited, in fact, with being one of its first influential advocates. Writing on "The Principles of Success in Literature" in the *Fortnightly Review* (1865), he found no redeeming quality, such as usefulness to historians in the distant future, in novelists' availing themselves of contemporary detail:

> There is, at the present day, a fashion in Literature and in Art generally, which is very deplorable. . . . The fashion is that of coat-and-waistcoat realism, a creeping timidity of invention, moving almost exclusively amid scenes of drawing-room existence, with all the reticences and pettinesses of drawing-room conventions. Artists have become photographers, and have turned the camera upon the vulgarities of life, instead of representing the more impassioned movements of life. . . . Of late years there has been a reaction against conventionalism, which called itself Idealism, in favour of *detailism* which calls itself Realism. As a reaction it has been of service, but it has led to much false criticism, and not a little false art, by an obtrusiveness of Detail and a preference for the Familiar, under the misleading notion of adherence to Nature. . . . The rage for "realism," which is healthy in as far as it insists on truth, has become unhealthy, in as far as it confounds truth with familiarity, and predominance of unessential details. There are other truths besides coats and waistcoats, pots and pans, drawing-rooms and suburban villas. Life has other aims besides those which occupy the conversation of "Society."[4]

This was Lewes's position as a champion of a kind of realism that harmonized rather than conflicted with the "idealism" that had been much in the minds of preceding critics. Early criticism of individual Victorian novelists was tinged with similar reservations. The ephemerality which, Trollope complained much later, was virtually forced upon the novelist was, as Lewes said, inadmissible in any work of art that aspired toward permanence; and inseparable from it, in some critics' minds, was the reformist impulse, which was grounded in the passing affairs of the day in an imperfect world. Two reviews of Dickens in the *Spectator*, perhaps by the same person, associated the two points. In the first, the critic wrote, while *Oliver Twist* was still in process of serialization, "Boz . . . very skillfully avails himself of any temporary interest to give piquancy to his pages. When his matter is not sufficiently attractive in itself, he has no objection to paint up to the flaring tastes of the vulgar great and small; nor does he scruple to avail himself of any current prejudice, whether popular or *feel*osophical, without much regard to critical exactness. . . . These things tell with many readers, but they must detract from the permanence of the writer who freely uses them."[5] Several months later, *Nicholas Nickleby* prompted the same reaction: Dickens's "very faults . . . increase his immediate circulation; for they appeal to the every-day experience and social prejudices of his readers." Witness, for example, his indulgence in the transitory language of the streets, slang, Cockneyisms. "Much the same may be said of his incidental topics introduced to satirize the times: they resemble the passing hits of a pantomime— side-splitting at first, decreasing in effect at each repetition, and vapid or unintelligible by the end of the season."[6]

The issue of built-in obsolescence faded as critics, faced with every year's swelling flood of mediocre fiction, had to admit that, given the inability of literary fame to accommodate all comers, ephemerality was the inevitable doom of most novels; but disapproval of pamphleteering in the guise of imaginative literature persisted. It was, indeed, a leading theme of reviewers who refused to join in the popular acclaim of Dickens as, with his notorious proclivity for attacking institutions or, less often, specific persons who failed to do their jobs or abused their privileged role in society, he became known as the leading reformer among contemporary novelists. In his notably perceptive joint review of *David Copperfield* and *Pendennis* in 1851, Masson wrote:

> The passage on model prisons . . . wherein Mr. Dickens attacks the silent system of prison management, is but one instance out of hundreds in which he has, while pursuing his occupation as a novelist, pronounced strong judgments on disputed social questions. . . . Mr. Dickens seems . . . to act up to his duty as an English citizen, when, by means of pamphlets, public speeches, letters to the newspapers, articles in periodicals, and other such established methods of communicating with his fellow-subjects, he speaks his mind freely on practices or institutions that offend him. . . . Prison-

discipline, the constitution of the ecclesiastical courts, the management of schools, capital punishments; Mr. Dickens's opinions on these, and many other such topics of a practical kind, are to be found explicitly affirmed and argued in his novels.[7]

But, critics insisted, Dickens's indignation was misdirected, or at least belated. The *Spectator* reviewer of *Oliver Twist*, already quoted, rebuked him thus early in his career:

> The earlier workhouse scenes . . . with the hard-hearted indifference of the parochial authorities, the scanty allowance of the paupers, and the brutal insolence of office in the beadle, were intended to chime in with the popular clamour against the New Poor-law: but Boz has combined the severity of the new system with the individual tyranny of the old,—forgetting that responsibility amongst subordinate parish-officers and regularity of management came in with the Commissioners.

This supposed pandering to the popular appetite for scandal behind institutional façades was one of the main charges James Fitzjames Stephen leveled against Dickens in 1857, when his current novel, *Little Dorrit*, represented an unbroken strain of acerb social criticism that had begun with *Hard Times* and was continued, with the volume turned up, in *Bleak House*:

> In every new novel he selects one or two of the popular cries of the day, to serve as seasoning to the dish which he sets before his readers. It may be the Poor Laws, or Imprisonment for Debt, or the Court of Chancery, or the harshness of Mill-owners, or the stupidity of Parliament, or the inefficiency of the Government, or the insolence of District Visitors, or the observance of Sunday, or Mammon-worship, or whatever else you please. He is equally familiar with all these subjects. If there was a popular cry against the management of a hospital, he would no doubt write a novel on a month's warning about the ignorance and temerity with which surgical operations are performed.[8]

Even as *Our Mutual Friend* was beginning to appear (1864), this negative note continued to be heard. Justin McCarthy observed, "It is difficult to name any important subject which has arisen within the last quarter of a century on which [Dickens] has not written something." But, he continued,

> his criticism has generally come too late. The account of the Fleet Prison in "Pickwick" was published in the year in which the Act for the amendment of the Insolvent Laws was passed. The Poor Laws had just been improved when "Oliver Twist" exposed the horrors of the workhouse system. The description of Mr. Bounderby and the hands of Coketown closely followed the last of a series of statutes regulating the management of factories. Jarn-

dyce and Jarndyce might or might not have been true in the time of Lord
Eldon, but it bears about as much relation to the present practice of the
Court of Chancery as to that of the Star Chamber. It is all very well meant,
but very ignorant.[9]

The repeated charge that Dickens was a Johnny-come-lately reformist did not wholly conceal its underlying motivation, which had nothing
to do with literary values. What posed as literary criticism—disapproval
of the use of outdated topicalities—was, in fact, a brief in defense of a
society whose present ameliorated condition (as the critic saw it) Dickens
persistently refused to acknowledge. The grievances of the individual
against corrupt or culpably ineffective instruments of society and politics
may have been justified at some point in the past—so ran the implicit
argument—but they were remedied before Dickens, with belated opportunism, got around to attacking them. Why, then, rake old muck that
had already been disposed of on the midden of history?

Meanwhile, however, reviewers were ceasing to find fault with a
novel's topicality per se: it was only the injection of controversy that
they continued to object to. In 1856 W. C. Roscoe wrote admiringly of
Thackeray's "way of knitting his narrative on at every point to some link
of our every-day experience. His fiction is like a net, every mesh of which
has a connecting knot with actual life. Many novelists have a world of
their own they inhabit. Thackeray thrusts his characters in among the
moving every-day world in which we live." [10]

Such skill proved to be Trollope's fortune—Trollope, Thackeray's
disciple and successor. Typical of numerous reviewers' praise was this,
in an unsigned notice of *Rachel Ray* in the *London Review* (1863):

> . . . he realizes the manners, the habits, and speech of English life in their
> homeliest garb. [His characters] are real beings who play their part in his
> story. We have met them, have spoken and lived with them. We have sat
> with them in our homes, have walked with them over the fields, watched
> with them the setting sun by the churchyard stile, and shared their loves
> and jealousies, their weaknesses, and their virtues. We have seen before
> this cottage interior, with its half-dozen books with gilt leaves arranged in
> shapes on the small round table, where also is deposited the "spangled
> mat of wondrous brightness, made of short white sticks of glass strung to-
> gether," with its shells and china figures on the chimney-piece, the bird-
> cage without a bird, the old sofa, the old arm-chair and carpet, and the old
> round mirror over the fire-place.[11]

Even so, such Dutch-like still lifes did not always redound to Trollope's, or any other novelist's, credit. Actually his critics were about
evenly divided, some maintaining that this dedication to portraying the

everyday scene with fidelity and sympathy constituted his greatest claim to artistry, the rest deploring it as evidence of a commonplace mind and a deficient imagination.

This last argument, being ad hominem, could not easily be countered. But it suggests that reviewers were never entirely won over to fiction which sought to achieve its realistic effects by use of topical materials. In practice, however, opposition on principle to topicalities as an unnecessary and unacceptable component of realism received its resounding empirical answer. Accurate descriptions of coats and waistcoats, pots and pans, and people conversing in London drawing rooms and suburban villas may not have represented the acme of the fictional art, but they were what the reading public wanted and what their suppliers were well disposed to produce for it.

2.

No substantial body of the novelists' expressed views on the subject exists to tell us what influence the running debate on realism had on their craft. In their scattered comments about their art, the question seldom arises. But the wide variation in the incidence of temporal details in their novels implies that the opposing claims of "idealism" and "realism," in this respect, persisted. There was a great difference from novel to novel in the specificity with which each was given an identifiable setting, whether in the immediate present or by the distancing technique that produced what I have called the stereoscopic illusion of the present juxtaposed with the past. At one extreme of the scale lay novels like *The Egoist* and *The Last Chronicle of Barset*, which conspicuously lacked topicalities as well as physical novelties. Even Gaskell's *North and South*, with its timely concentration on the growing schism between the energetic but troubled industrial North and the settled, old-time agrarian South, was noticeably devoid of such details. From the viewpoint that has been maintained throughout these pages, arbitrarily limiting the effect of presentness to the incidence of temporal details, novels like these are examples of what we may call thin realism.

Not many such details were required to establish a novel's bona fides as a "story of today." In applauding *Doctor Thorne* for its up-to-dateness ("the scenery, the personages, the incidents are pure English, and as such might have occurred last year"), a reviewer in *The Leader* went on to say, "indeed, by a casual allusion or two, Mr. Trollope has impressed a sort of contemporary actuality on his scene." [12] In this case, the praise was understated, because Trollope, as we have seen, achieved the sense of "contemporary actuality" by much more than a casual allusion or two. But the principle is sound: a few inconspicuous clues to time, assisted by readers' *desire* to assume a narrative's contemporaneity, were all a novel with realistic pretensions needed. Such was often the case with Wilkie Collins's run-of-the-mine fiction (*The Dead Secret, The New Magdalen, Poor Miss Finch*). If the thematic controversial material in novels of purpose, such as Reade's *Hard Cash* and *A Terrible Temptation,* were deleted, the realistic effect would not be much diminished, for the same reason. Quantitatively, the contribution of isolatable topical allusions to a realistic text might be insignificant, but in qualitative effect it might be as dense as in any novel liberally furnished with time-specific details.

At the other end of the scale reside all of Surtees's novels and Thackeray's three major "modern" ones, whose large incidence of topical allusions and physical particulars makes them, in this sense, examples of dense realism. To decide precisely where, on such a continuum, each Victorian novel with realistic purpose or tendencies lies would be a fatuous and generally futile exercise. Attempting it, however, would reveal that even within the canons of individual authors there is much variation. Among Dickens's novels, *Bleak House* and *Our Mutual Friend* are much more explicit in their use of topicalities to fix the time of action (albeit in the former case there are two not easily distinguishable time planes) than are, say, *The Old Curiosity Shop, Nicholas Nickleby,* and even *Dombey and Son.* In Bulwer-Lytton's medley of novels set more or less in the present, *Pelham, The Caxtons, My Novel,* and *What Will He Do with It?* are more notable for their use of topicalities than are *Ernest Maltravers* and *Alice,* which have remarkably few. Trollope's prodigious output displays a wider range, from the thick stratum of time references in *The Warden, Barchester Towers,* and *The Way We Live Now* to their almost complete absence in such novels as *The Claverings* and *Sir Harry Hotspur of Humblethwaite.* Whereas *Diana of the Crossways* and *Beauchamp's Career* are firmly fixed in their respective time settings, those of *The Adventures of Harry Richmond* and *The Ordeal of Richard Feverel* can be established only by inference, on the premise that any novel not explicitly located in some past years must be a "tale of today." One of the few novelists who were consistent in this regard was Kingsley, all three of whose "modern" novels, *Alton Locke, Yeast,* and *Two Years Ago,* have a relatively high incidence of topical references.

In concentrating, as I have done, on a single aspect of realism in Victorian fiction, the strength it derived from topicalities, I have unavoidably distorted the evidence. Compared with the total contribution made by physical particulars, that made by identifiably temporal details was small indeed. Even in novels with the highest frequency of such details, by far the greater proportion were time-neutral, serving as well for a novel set in Mr. Pickwick's day as for one set in Augustus Mel-motte's. This simply reflects the fact that in any society, even our own, in which we are acutely conscious of onrushing events and the unremitting alteration of our physical surroundings, the familiar—that is, the time-neutral, inherited—aspects of life far outnumber the recognizably new.

Realistic description in any novel does not differentiate between the new and the time-neutral; it is a totally homogenized element in the package the writer hands over to the reader. But it was the strictly temporal ingredient, the "minute and characteristic indicia of the times," that enabled the Victorian novel to strike its roots most deeply into the rich soil of its day.

Appendix A

EDITIONS CITED

IN A BOOK so heavily larded with quotations as this is, the lack of uniform modern editions of Victorian novelists that are at once reliable and generally accessible presents a problem of citation that can be solved only by compromise. "Standard" editions such as the old but still unsuperseded Memorial edition of Meredith and authoritative recent editions of individual titles, as in the Oxford English Novels series and the Clarendon edition of George Eliot, are found mostly in large libraries, and even then, as my experience at my headquarters library has repeatedly proved, such holdings are sometimes incomplete for one reason or another. In these unsatisfactory but unavoidable circumstances, I have had to settle for whatever editions I could have at hand on a long-term basis, giving preference to titles in the Penguin, World's Classics, Everyman's Library, Riverside, and other inexpensive editions that are most likely to be on the shelves of readers of this book. To minimize the potluck effect in the neo-Benthamite interest of the least inconvenience for the greatest number, I have also cited chapters, thus enabling readers to use any edition (with a few exceptions) to which they have access.

Mary Elizabeth Braddon

Aurora Floyd: Virago Press ed., London, 1984
Lady Audley's Secret: Dover reprint, New York, 1974

Charlotte Brontë

Jane Eyre: Clarendon ed., Oxford, 1969
Shirley: Clarendon ed., Oxford, 1979

Emily Brontë

Wuthering Heights: Norton Critical ed., 1963

Edward Bulwer-Lytton

All novels: Saint Botolph ed., Boston, 1897

Wilkie Collins

The Moonstone: World's Classics, 1982
The Woman in White: Riverside ed., 1969
All others: Unnamed New York ed., n.d.

Charles Dickens

Sketches by Boz: New Oxford Illustrated ed., London, 1973
All others: Penguin eds., various dates

Benjamin Disraeli

Coningsby: Capricorn ed., New York, 1961
Vivian Grey: First Novel Library, London, 1968
A Year at Hartlebury: London, 1983
All others: Bradenham ed., London, 1926–27

Emily Eden

The Semi-Attached Couple: Boston, 1947
The Semi-Detached House: Boston, 1948

George Eliot

Adam Bede: Riverside ed., 1968
Daniel Deronda: Clarendon ed., Oxford, 1984
Felix Holt: Clarendon ed., Oxford, 1980
Middlemarch: Riverside ed., 1965
The Mill on the Floss: Riverside ed., 1961
Scenes of Clerical Life: Penguin ed., 1973

Susan Ferrier

The Inheritance: Edinburgh, 1824

John Galt

The Member: Edinburgh, 1975

Elizabeth Gaskell

Cranford: Oxford English Novels, London, 1972
Mary Barton: Norton Library, New York, 1958
North and South: Oxford English Novels, 1973
Ruth: Knutsford ed., London, 1906
Wives and Daughters: Penguin ed., 1969

Thomas Hardy

Far from the Madding Crowd: Riverside ed., 1957
The Mayor of Casterbridge: Norton Critical ed., 1977
The Return of the Native: Norton Critical ed., 1969
All others: New Wessex ed., London, various dates

Charles Kingsley

Alton Locke: New York, 19—
Two Years Ago: London, 1892
Yeast: Eversley ed., London, 1881

Thomas H. Lister

Granby: London, 1826

George Meredith

All novels: Memorial ed., London, 1909–11, where *Emilia in England* bears its
later title, *Sandra Belloni*

Diana Mulock

John Halifax, Gentleman: Everyman, 1955

James Payn

Lost Sir Massingberd: Facsimile reprint, New York, 1976

Margaret Oliphant

Salem Chapel: Facsimile of 1883 ed., New York, 1976

Charles Reade

All novels: "Works of Charles Reade, New Edition," New York, n.d.

Robert Smith Surtees

Ask Mamma: Folio Society ed., Westminster, 1954
Handley Cross: London, 1854
Hawbuck Grange: Folio Society ed., Westminster, 1955
Hillingdon Hall: Folio Society ed., Westminster, 1956
Jorrocks' Jaunts and Jollities: Everyman, 1928
Mr. Facey Romford's Hounds: Surtees Society ed., London, 1982
Mr. Sponge's Sporting Tour: London, 1899
Plain or Ringlets?: London, 1860
Young Tom Hall's Heart-Aches and Horses: Edinburgh, 1926

William Makepeace Thackeray

The History of Pendennis: Everyman, 1959
The Newcomes: Everyman, 1952
Vanity Fair: Riverside ed., 1963
All others: Unnamed ed., New York, 1903

Anthony Trollope

The American Senator: New York, 1940
Ayala's Angel: World's Classics, 1929
Barchester Towers: Riverside ed., 1966
The Belton Estate: World's Classics, 1986
The Bertrams: Tauchnitz ed., Leipzig, 1859
Can You Forgive Her?: Penguin, 1972
The Claverings: World's Classics, 1929
Doctor Thorne: Everyman, 1908
The Duke's Children: Oxford University Press paperback, 1973
The Eustace Diamonds: Penguin, 1969
Framley Parsonage: Shakespeare Head ed., Oxford, 1929
He Knew He Was Right: World's Classics, 1951
Is He Popenjoy?: World's Classics, 1951
John Caldigate: World's Classics, 1946
Lady Anna: World's Classics, 1936
The Last Chronicle of Barset: Penguin, 1967
Marion Fay: Ann Arbor, Michigan, 1982
Miss Mackenzie: World's Classics, 1924
Mr. Scarborough's Family: World's Classics, 1946
Orley Farm: New York, 1950
Phineas Finn: Penguin, 1972
Phineas Redux: Panther paperback, 1973
The Prime Minister: Oxford University Press paperback, 1973
Rachel Ray: New York, 1952
Ralph the Heir: World's Classics, 1939
Sir Harry Hotspur of Humblethwaite: World's Classics, 1928
The Small House at Allington: Shakespeare Head ed., Oxford, 1929
The Struggles of Brown, Jones, and Robinson: Serialized form, *Cornhill Magazine*, 1861–62
The Three Clerks: World's Classics, 1929
The Vicar of Bullhampton: Dover reprint of 1870 ed., New York, 1979
The Warden: Riverside ed., 1966
The Way We Live Now: Indianapolis, 1974

Samuel Warren

Ten Thousand a Year: New York, [1932]

Mrs. Henry Wood

East Lynne: Everyman, 1984

Charlotte Yonge

The Heir of Redclyffe: London, 1964

Appendix B

CHRONOLOGY

MOST SERIALIZED NOVELS appeared in volume form just before or shortly after completing their run. Where this was not the case, the date of book-form publication is given in parentheses.

1824   Ferrier: *The Inheritance*
1826   Lister: *Granby*
1826–27 Disraeli: *Vivian Grey*
1828   Bulwer: *Pelham*

1830   Bulwer: *Paul Clifford*
1831   Disraeli: *The Young Duke*
1831–34 Surtees: *Jorrocks' Jaunts and Jollities. New Sporting Magazine*, July '31–Sept. '34 (1838)
1832   Galt: *The Member*
1834   Disraeli: *A Year at Hartlebury*
[1836   Dickens: *Sketches by Boz*]
1836–37 Dickens: *Pickwick Papers.* Monthly parts, April '36–Nov. '37
1837   Bulwer: *Ernest Maltravers*
1837–39 Dickens: *Oliver Twist. Bentley's Miscellany*, Feb. '37–April '39
1838   Bulwer: *Alice*
1838–39 Surtees: *Handley Cross. New Sporting Magazine*, March '38–Aug. '39 (as *The Gin-and-Water Hunt*). (Enlarged in book form 1843.)
1838–39 Dickens: *Nicholas Nickleby.* Monthly parts, April '38–Oct. '39
1839–41 Warren: *Ten Thousand a Year. Blackwood's Magazine*, Oct. '39–Aug. '41

1840–41 Dickens: *The Old Curiosity Shop. Master Humphrey's Clock* (weekly), 25 April '40–6 Feb. '41
1841   Thackeray: *The History of Samuel Titmarsh and the Great Hoggarty Diamond. Fraser's Magazine*, Sept.–Dec. '41 (1849)
1843–44 Dickens: *Martin Chuzzlewit.* Monthly parts, Jan. '43–July '44
1843–44 Surtees: *Hillingdon Hall. New Sporting Magazine*, Feb. '43–June '44 (22 chapters only). (Enlarged in book form 1845.)
1844   Disraeli: *Coningsby*

1844	Dickens: *The Chimes*
1845	Disraeli: *Sybil*
1846–48	Dickens: *Dombey and Son*. Monthly parts, Oct. '46–April '48
[1846–47	Thackeray: *The Snobs of England*. *Punch*, 28 Feb. '46–27 Feb. '47]
1845–47	Surtees: *Hawbuck Grange*. *Bell's Life in London*, 25 Oct. '46–27 June '47 (as *Sporting Sketches*). (Much altered in book form 1847.)
1847	Brontë (C.): *Jane Eyre*
1847	Brontë (E.): *Wuthering Heights*
1847	Disraeli: *Tancred*
1847–48	Thackeray: *Vanity Fair*. Monthly parts, Jan. '47–July '48
1848	Gaskell: *Mary Barton*
1848–49	Bulwer-Lytton: *The Caxtons*. *Blackwood's Magazine*, April '48–Oct. '49
1848	Kingsley: *Yeast*. *Fraser's Magazine*, July–Dec. '48. (1851)
1848–50	Thackeray: *The History of Pendennis*. Monthly parts, Nov. '48–Dec. '50
1849	Brontë (C.): *Shirley*
1849–51	Surtees: *Mr. Sponge's Sporting Tour*. *New Monthly Magazine*, Jan. '49–April '51
1849–50	Dickens: *David Copperfield*. Monthly parts, May '49–Nov. '50
1850	Kingsley: *Alton Locke*
1850–53	Bulwer-Lytton: *My Novel*. *Blackwood's Magazine*, Sept. '50–Jan. '53
1851–53	Surtees: *Young Tom Hall's Heart-Aches and Horses*. *New Monthly Magazine*, Oct. '51–Jan. '53. (1926)
1851–53	Gaskell: *Cranford*. *Household Words*, 13 Dec. '51–21 May '53
1852	Collins: *Basil*
1852–53	Dickens: *Bleak House*. Monthly parts, March '52–Sept. '53
1853	Gaskell: *Ruth*
1853	Yonge: *The Heir of Redclyffe*
1853–55	Thackeray: *The Newcomes*. Monthly parts, Oct. '53–Aug. '55
1854	Collins: *Hide and Seek*
1854	Dickens: *Hard Times*. *Household Words*, 1 April–12 Aug. '54
1854–55	Gaskell: *North and South*. *Household Words*, 2 Sept. '54–27 Jan. '55
1855	Trollope: *The Warden*
1855–57	Dickens: *Little Dorrit*. Monthly parts, Dec. '55–June '57
1856	Mulock: *John Halifax, Gentleman*
1856	Reade: *It Is Never Too Late To Mend*
1856	Collins: *A Rogue's Life*. *Household Words*, 1–29 March '56. (1879)
1857	Kingsley: *Two Years Ago*
1857	Trollope: *Barchester Towers*
1857	Eliot: *Scenes of Clerical Life*. *Blackwood's Magazine*, Jan.–Nov. '57
1857	Collins: *The Dead Secret*. *Household Words*, 3 Jan.–13 June '57
1857–58	Surtees: *Ask Mamma*. 13 monthly parts, 1857–58
1857–59	Bulwer-Lytton: *What Will He Do with It?*. *Blackwood's Magazine*, June '57–Jan. '59
1858	Trollope: *Doctor Thorne*

1858	Trollope: *The Three Clerks*
1859	Eden: *The Semi-Detached House*
1859	Eliot: *Adam Bede*
1859	Meredith: *The Ordeal of Richard Feverel*
1859	Reade: *Love Me Little, Love Me Long*
1859	Trollope: *The Bertrams*
1859–60	Surtees: *Plain or Ringlets?*. 13 monthly parts, 1859–60
1859–60	Collins: *The Woman in White. All the Year Round*, 26 Nov. '59–25 Aug. '60
1860	Eden: *The Semi-Attached Couple*
1860	Eliot: *The Mill on the Floss*
1860	Meredith: *Evan Harrington. Once a Week*, 11 Feb.–13 Oct. '60
1860	Thackeray: *Lovel the Widower. Cornhill Magazine*, Jan.–June '60
1860–61	Trollope: *Framley Parsonage. Cornhill Magazine*, Jan. '60–April '61
1860–61	Wood: *East Lynne. New Monthly Magazine*, Jan. '60–Sept. '61
1860–61	Dickens: *Great Expectations. All the Year Round*, 1 Dec. '60–3 Aug. '61
1861	Eliot: *Silas Marner*
1861–62	Thackeray: *The Adventures of Philip. Cornhill Magazine*, Jan. '61–Aug. '62
1861–62	Trollope: *Orley Farm*. Monthly parts, March '61–Oct. '62
1861–62	Trollope: *The Struggles of Brown, Jones, and Robinson. Cornhill Magazine*, Aug. '61–March '62. (1870)
1861–62	Braddon: *Lady Audley's Secret. Robin Goodfellow*, July–Sept. '61; completed in *Sixpenny Magazine*, Jan.–Dec. '62
1862–63	Braddon: *Aurora Floyd. Temple Bar*, Jan. '62–Jan. '63
1862–63	Oliphant: *Salem Chapel. Blackwood's Magazine*, Feb. '62–Jan. '63
1862–63	Collins: *No Name. All the Year Round*, 15 March '62–17 Jan. '63
1862–64	Trollope: *The Small House at Allington. Cornhill Magazine*, Sept. '62–April '64
1863	Gaskell: *Sylvia's Lovers*
1863	Trollope: *Rachel Ray*
1863	Reade: *Hard Cash. All the Year Round*, 28 March–26 Dec. '63
1863–64	Gaskell: *Cousin Phillis. Cornhill Magazine*, Nov. '63–Feb. '64
1864	Meredith: *Emilia in England*
1864	Payn: *Lost Sir Massingberd. Chambers's Journal*, 2 Jan.–16 April '64
1864–65	Trollope: *Can You Forgive Her?*. Monthly parts, Jan. '64–Aug. '65
1864–65	Surtees: *Mr. Facey Romford's Hounds*. Monthly parts, May '64–April '65
1864–65	Dickens: *Our Mutual Friend*. Monthly parts, May '64–Nov. '65
1864–66	Gaskell: *Wives and Daughters. Cornhill Magazine*, Aug. '64–Jan. '66
1864–66	Collins: *Armadale. Cornhill Magazine*, Nov. '64–June '66
1865	Trollope: *Miss Mackenzie*
1865–66	Trollope: *The Belton Estate. Fortnightly Review*, 15 May '65–1 Jan. '66
1866	Eliot: *Felix Holt the Radical*

1866–67   Trollope: *The Claverings. Cornhill Magazine*, Feb. '66–May '67
1866–67   Trollope: *The Last Chronicle of Barset*. Weekly parts, 1 Dec. '66–6 July '67
1867–69   Trollope: *Phineas Finn. St. Paul's Magazine*, Oct. '67–May '69
1868   Reade and Boucicault: *Foul Play. Once a Week*, 4 Jan.–20 June '68
1868   Collins: *The Moonstone. All the Year Round*, 4 Jan.–8 Aug. '68
1868–69   Trollope: *He Knew He Was Right*. Weekly parts, 17 Oct. '68–22 May '69
1869–70   Reade: *Put Yourself in His Place. Cornhill Magazine*, March '69–July '70
1869–70   Trollope: *The Vicar of Bullhampton*. Monthly parts, July '69–May '70
1869–70   Collins: *Man and Wife. Cassell's Magazine*, Dec. '69–Sept. '70

1870   Disraeli: *Lothair*
1870   Dickens: *The Mystery of Edwin Drood*. Monthly parts, April–Sept. '70
1870   Trollope: *Sir Harry Hotspur of Humblethwaite. Macmillan's Magazine*, May–Dec. '70
1870–71   Trollope: *Ralph the Heir*. Monthly parts and supplement to *St. Paul's Magazine*, Jan. '70–July '71
1870–71   Meredith: *The Adventures of Harry Richmond. Cornhill Magazine*, Sept. '70–Nov. '71
1871   Hardy: *Desperate Remedies*
1871   Reade: *A Terrible Temptation. Cassell's Magazine*, April–Sept. '71
1871–72   Collins: *Poor Miss Finch. Cassell's Magazine*, Oct. '71–March '72
1871–73   Trollope: *The Eustace Diamonds. Fortnightly Review*, July '71–Feb. '73
1871–72   Eliot: *Middlemarch*, Eight parts, Dec. '71–Dec. '72
1872   Hardy: *Under the Greenwood Tree*
1872–73   Hardy: *A Pair of Blue Eyes. Tinsley's Magazine*, Sept. '72–July '73
1872–73   Collins: *The New Magdalen. Temple Bar*, Oct. '72–July '73
1873–74   Trollope: *Lady Anna. Fortnightly Review*, April '73–April '74
1873–74   Trollope: *Phineas Redux. Graphic*, 19 July '73–10 Jan. '74
1874   Hardy: *Far from the Madding Crowd. Cornhill Magazine*, Jan.–Dec. '74
1874–75   Trollope: *The Way We Live Now*. Monthly parts, Feb. '74–Sept. '75
1874–75   Meredith: *Beauchamp's Career. Fortnightly Review*, Aug. '74–Dec. '75
1874–75   Collins: *The Law and the Lady. Graphic*, 26 Sept. '74–13 March '75
1875–76   Hardy: *The Hand of Ethelberta. Cornhill Magazine*, July '75–May '76
1875–76   Trollope: *The Prime Minister*. Monthly parts, Nov. '75–June '76
1876   Eliot: *Daniel Deronda*. Monthly parts, Feb.–Sept. '76
1876–77   Trollope: *The American Senator. Temple Bar*, May '76–July '77
1877–78   Trollope: *Is He Popenjoy?. All the Year Round*, 13 Oct. '77–13 July '78
1878   Hardy: *The Return of the Native. Belgravia*, Jan.–Dec. '78
1878–79   Trollope: *John Caldigate. Blackwood's Magazine*, April '78–June '79
1879   Trollope: *Cousin Henry. Manchester Weekly Times* supplement, 8 March–24 May '79
1879–80   Meredith: *The Egoist. Glasgow Weekly Herald*, 21 June '79–10 Jan. '80
1879–80   Trollope: *The Duke's Children. All the Year Round*, 4 Oct. '79–24 July '80

1880	Disraeli: *Endymion*
1880	Trollope: *Dr. Wortle's School. Blackwood's Magazine*, May–Dec. '80
1880–81	Hardy: *A Laodicean. Harper's Monthly Magazine* (European edition), Dec. '80–Dec. '81
1881	Trollope: *Ayala's Angel*
1881–82	Trollope: *Marion Fay. Graphic*, 3 Dec. '81–3 June '82
1882	Hardy: *Two on a Tower. Atlantic Monthly*, May–Dec. '82
1882–83	Trollope: *Mr. Scarborough's Family. All the Year Round*, 27 May '82–16 June '83
1884	Trollope: *An Old Man's Love*
1884	Meredith: *Diana of the Crossways. Fortnightly Review*, June–Dec. '84 (26 chapters only)
1886	Hardy: *The Mayor of Casterbridge. Graphic*, 2 Jan.–15 May '86

NOTES

Introduction

1. W. C. Roscoe, "W. M. Thackeray, Artist and Moralist," *National Review* 2 (1856); *Victorian Criticism of the Novel*, ed. Edwin M. Eigner and George J. Worth (Cambridge, 1985), p. 145.

2. *The Stones of Venice* I, *The Works of John Ruskin*, ed. E. T. Cook and Alexander Wedderburn (London, 1902–12), 9:60–61.

Chapter 1: The Glare of the Present

1. Harriet Martineau, "Characteristics of the Genius of Scott," *Miscellanies* (1838; reprint, New York, 1975), 1:54–55. The essay first appeared in *Tait's Edinburgh Magazine* for December 1832 and January 1833.

2. *Four Lectures of Trollope*, ed. Morris L. Parrish (London, 1938), p. 98.

3. See A. Dwight Culler, *The Victorian Mirror of History* (New Haven, 1985), pp. 39–40.

4. Walter E. Houghton, *The Victorian Frame of Mind 1830–1870* (New Haven, 1957), p. 1.

5. "Signs of the Times," *Edinburgh Review* 49 (1829): 441.

6. Hain Friswell, "Circulating Libraries, Their Contents and Their Readers," *London Society* 20 (1871): 523.

7. Neil McKendrick, John Brewer, and J. H. Plumb, *The Birth of a Consumer Society: The Commercialization of Eighteenth-Century England* (London, 1982), p. 66.

8. Culler, *The Victorian Mirror of History*, p. 74.

9. *George Crabbe: The Complete Poetical Works*, ed. Norma Dalrymple-Champneys and Arthur Pollard (Oxford, 1988), 1:181–82.

10. Southey, *Letters from England*, ed. Jack Simmons (London, 1951), p. 342.

11. "Civilization: Signs of the Times," *Westminster Review* 25 (1836): 7.

12. *The Works of Thomas Love Peacock*, ed. H. F. B. Brett-Smith and C. E. Jones (London, 1934), 8:264–65.

13. *Athenaeum*, 27 August 1828, p. 695.

14. Trollope, *The New Zealander*, ed. N. John Hall (Oxford, 1972), pp. 179–80.

15. "Cheap Literature," *British Quarterly Review*, 1 April 1859; *Victorian Fic-

tion: A Collection of Essays from the Period, ed. Ira Bruce Nadel (New York, 1986), pp. 319–20.

16. *Times*, 30 December 1850. The paper reported that Cobden's audience, the culturally elite friends of the Manchester School of Arts, received the remark with "(Laughter)."

17. "The Decline of Art," *Nineteenth Century* 23 (1888): 90.

18. "Our Novels: The Sensational School," *Temple Bar* 29 (1870): 417.

19. Myron F. Brightfield, *Victorian England in Its Novels* (Los Angeles, 1968), 2:282. An invaluable four-volume collection of excerpts from, for the most part, minor fiction, arranged by subject. Hereafter cited as Brightfield.

20. G. M. Young, "The Victorian Noon-Time," *Victorian Essays* (London, 1962), p. 138.

21. *The Poems of Tennyson*, ed. Christopher Ricks (London, 1969), pp. 493, 517.

22. See Jane Marcus, "Bishop Blougram and the Literary Men," *Victorian Studies* 21 (1978): 171–95.

23. Browning to F. O. Ward, 18 February 1845; *New Letters of Robert Browning*, ed. William C. DeVane and Kenneth L. Knickerbocker (New Haven, 1950), pp. 35–36.

24. See the extensive annotations in *Robert Browning: The Poems*, ed. John Pettigrew (New Haven, 1981), 2:1031–37.

25. See William B. Thesing, *The London Muse: Victorian Poetic Responses to the City* (Athens, Ga., 1982), esp. pp. xvi, 37–39.

26. Elizabeth Barrett Browning, *Aurora Leigh and Other Poems*, ed. Cora Kaplan (London, 1978), p. 201.

27. *Poems of William Mackworth Praed* (London, 1864), 1:163, 169, 171.

28. See *The Book of Ballads*, "edited by 'Bon Gaultier'" (1845; reprint, New York, 1986).

29. See *The Bab Ballads*, ed. James Ellis (Cambridge, Mass., 1970), with its expert annotations.

30. David Mayer III, *Harlequin in His Element: The English Pantomime, 1806–1836* (Cambridge, Mass., 1969), pp. 5, 7.

31. See *The Annotated Gilbert and Sullivan*, ed. Ian Bradley (Harmondsworth, 1982), p. 228.

32. "Modern Novelists—Great and Small," *Blackwood's Magazine* 77 (1855): 565.

33. Quoted in *Sir Walter Scott on Novelists and Fiction*, ed. Ioan Williams (London, 1968), p. 1.

34. *Victorian Criticism of the Novel* (cited Introduction, n. 1), pp. 30–41.

35. Quoted in Kathleen Tillotson, *Novels of the Eighteen-Forties* (1954; reprint, Oxford, 1961), p. 13.

36. Clara Reeve, *The Progress of Romance* (1785; reprint, New York, 1930), p. 111.

37. See Matthew Whiting Rosa, *The Silver-Fork School: Novels of Fashion Preceding "Vanity Fair"* (New York, 1936).

38. "The Dandy School," *Examiner*, 18 November 1827, p. 722.

39. Michael Sadleir, *Bulwer: A Panorama. I: Edward and Rosina 1803–1836* (Boston, 1931), p. 115. (The whole description occupies pp. 110–18.)

40. Review of Lady Blessington's novels, *Edinburgh Review* 67 (1838): 357.

41. *Sharpe's London Magazine*, July 1861; *Trollope: The Critical Heritage*, ed. Donald Smalley (London, 1969), p. 129. Hereafter cited as *Trollope: Critical Heritage*.

42. Anthony Trollope, *An Autobiography* (London, 1950), pp. 110–11.

43. J. A. Sutherland, *Victorian Novelists and Publishers* (Chicago, 1976), p. 76.

44. *Quarterly Review* 14 (1815): 192–93.

45. *Athenaeum*, 27 August 1831, p. 554.

46. Quoted in John Butt and Kathleen Tillotson, *Dickens at Work* (1957; reprint, London, 1968), p. 37.

47. John Forster, *The Life of Charles Dickens*, ed. J. W. T. Ley (New York, [1928]), pp. 76–77.

48. [W. F. Pollock], "British Novelists—Richardson, Miss Austen, Scott," *Fraser's Magazine* 61 (1860): 31.

49. Theodore Martin, "Thackeray's Works," *Westminster Review* 59 (1853): 374.

50. *Athenaeum*, 25 September 1841, p. 740.

51. *Victorian Criticism of the Novel* (n. 34 above), p. 42.

52. *Edinburgh Review* 55 (1832): 70.

53. "Recent English Romances," *Edinburgh Review* 65 (1837): 184.

54. *Monthly Chronicle*, March and April 1838; *A Victorian Art of Fiction: Essays on the Novel in British Periodicals 1830–1850*, ed. John Charles Olmsted (New York, 1979), p. 219.

55. *Westminster Review* 28 (1838): 337.

Chapter 2: The Topical Novelists

1. David Masson, *British Novelists and Their Styles* (1859; reprint, Boston, 1889), pp. 269–70.

2. Margaret M. Maison, *The Victorian Vision: Studies in the Religious Novel* (New York, 1961), p. 1.

3. *Four Lectures of Trollope* (cited chap. 1, n. 2), p. 110.

4. See Anthony Steel, *Jorrocks' England* (London, 1932), an impressive demonstration of how rich Surtees's novels are in social-history detail.

5. *The Letters of Mrs. Gaskell*, ed. J. A. V. Chapple and Arthur Pollard (Cambridge, Mass., 1967), pp. 55, 58.

6. Quoted in Sue Lonoff, *Wilkie Collins and His Readers* (New York, 1982), p. 69.

7. "Wilkie Collins," *Fortnightly Review*, n.s. 46 (1889): 598.

8. Quoted in John Coleman, *Charles Reade as I Knew Him* (London, 1904), pp. 263–64.

Chapter 3: Forms and Sources

1. *Quarterly Review* 97 (1855): 377–78.

2. *Spectator*, 18 August 1855; *Thackeray: The Critical Heritage*, ed. Geoffrey Tillotson and Donald Hawes (London, 1968), p. 221. Hereafter cited as *Thackeray: Critical Heritage*.

3. See David M. Bevington, "Seasonal Relevance in *The Pickwick Papers*," *Nineteenth-Century Fiction* 16 (1961): 219–30.

4. See Bernard Darwin, *The Dickens Advertiser* (1930; reprint, New York, n.d.)—a chatty, copiously illustrated canvass of the various kinds of advertisements and the commodities they promoted.

5. "*Hard Times*: The News and the Novel," *Nineteenth-Century Fiction* 32 (1977): 174.

6. See Michael Cotsell, "The Book of Insolvent Fates: Financial Speculation in *Our Mutual Friend*," *Dickens Studies Annual* 13 (1984): 125–42.

7. See Trevor Blount, "The Documentary Symbolism of Chancery in *Bleak House*," *Dickensian* 62 (1966): 47–52, 106–11, 167–74.

8. Butt and Tillotson, *Dickens at Work* (cited chap. 1, n.46), pp. 183–93.

9. See John Wigley, *The Rise and Fall of the Victorian Sunday* (Manchester, 1980).

10. "Dickens and *Punch*," *Dickens Studies* 3 (1967): 6.

11. Michael Slater, introduction to Penguin edition of *Nicholas Nickleby*, pp. 30–31.

12. Jane R. Cohen, *Charles Dickens and His Original Illustrators* (Columbus, Ohio, 1980), p. 158.

13. Kenneth Robinson, *Wilkie Collins: A Biography* (New York, 1952), p. 149; Robert Lee Wolff, *Gains and Losses: Novels of Faith and Doubt in Victorian England* (New York, 1977), p. 162.

14. "Female Novelists," *New Monthly Magazine* 95 (1852): 164.

15. Brightfield, 1:66.

16. Edgar F. Harden, *The Emergence of Thackeray's Serial Fiction* (Athens, Ga., 1979), p. 94.

17. ——Atkins, *The Colonel* (1853); Brightfield, 2:283.

18. Quoted in Elton E. Smith, *Charles Reade* (Boston, 1976), p. 129.

19. Brightfield, 1:66.

20. "The Empire of Novels," *Spectator*, 9 January 1869; *A Victorian Art of Fiction: Essays on the Novel in British Periodicals 1851–1869*, ed. John Charles Olmsted (New York, 1979), pp. 650–51.

21. T. H. Lister, in an omnibus review of Dickens's first three novels, *Edinburgh Review* 68 (1838): 84.

22. *Charles Dickens: The Critical Heritage*, ed. Philip Collins (New York, 1971), p. 437. Hereafter cited as *Dickens: Critical Heritage*.

23. "The License of Modern Novelists," *Edinburgh Review* 106 (1857): 127.

24. See Sheila M. Smith, "Blue Books and Victorian Novelists," *Review of English Studies*, n.s. 21 (1970): 23–40.

25. See Patrick Brantlinger, "Bluebooks, the Social Organism, and the Victorian Novel," *Criticism* 14 (1972): 328–44.

26. "Colliers and Collieries," *Quarterly Review* 70 (1842): 159.

27. See Sheila M. Smith, "Willenhall and Wodgate: Disraeli's Use of Blue Book Evidence," *Review of English Studies*, n.s. 13 (1962): 368–84, and Martin Fido, "The Treatment of Rural Distress in Disraeli's *Sybil*," *Yearbook of English Studies* 5 (1975): 153–63.

28. See Martin Fido, "'From His Own Observation': Sources of Working Class Passages in Disraeli's 'Sybil,'" *Modern Language Review* 72 (1977): 268–84.

29. See Trevor Blount, "The Graveyard Satire of *Bleak House* in the Context of 1850," *Review of English Studies*, n.s. 14 (1963): 370–78; the same author's "Dickens's Slum Satire in *Bleak House*," *Modern Language Review* 60 (1965): 340–51; and K. J. Fielding and A. W. Brice, "*Bleak House* and the Graveyard," *Dickens the Craftsman*, ed. Robert B. Partlow, Jr. (Carbondale, Ill., 1970), pp. 115–39.

30. See Sheila M. Smith, "Propaganda and Hard Facts in Charles Reade's Didactic Novels: A Study of *It Is Never Too Late to Mend* and *Hard Cash*," *Renaissance and Modern Studies* [University of Nottingham] 4 (1960): 135–49.

31. Gertrude Himmelfarb, *The Idea of Poverty* (New York, 1984), p. 312.

32. See Harland S. Nelson, "Dickens's *Our Mutual Friend* and Henry Mayhew's *London Labour and the London Poor*," *Nineteenth-Century Fiction* 20 (1965): 207–22; Harvey Peter Sucksmith, "Dickens and Mayhew: A Further Note," *Nineteenth-Century Fiction* 24 (1969): 345–49; Richard J. Dunn, "Dickens and Mayhew Once More," *Nineteenth-Century Fiction* 25 (1970): 348–53; and Anne Humpherys, "Dickens and Mayhew on the London Poor," *Dickens Studies Annual* 4 (1975): 78–90.

Chapter 4: Events and Movements

1. See Irene Bostrom, "The Novel and Catholic Emancipation," *Studies in Romanticism* 2 (1963): 155–76.

2. See Joseph E. Baker, *The Novel and the Oxford Movement* (1932; reprint, New York, 1962); Wolff, *Gains and Losses* (cited chap. 3, n. 13); and Maison, *The Victorian Vision* (cited chap. 2, n. 2). The latter two are not confined to Tractarian fiction, embracing also some novels produced in the Broad and Low Church and Dissenting interests. Two other books, Valentine Cunningham's *Everywhere Spoken Against; Dissent in the Victorian Novel* (Oxford, 1975), and Elisabeth Jay's *The Religion of the Heart: Anglican Evangelicalism and the Nineteenth-Century Novel* (Oxford, 1979), concentrate on the handling of religious themes by the better-known novelists but also include some material on religious fiction per se.

3. Background details in this passage are from Owen Chadwick, *The Victorian Church* (New York, 1966–70), 1:301–33; James Laver, *Manners and Morals in the Age of Optimism: 1848–1914* (New York, 1966), p. 125; and Francis Sheppard, *London 1808–1870: The Infernal Wen* (Berkeley, 1971), p. 242.

4. The best account of the St. Cross affair is in Robert Bernard Martin, *Enter Rumour: Four Early Victorian Scandals* (London, 1962), chap. 3. See also

G. F. A. Best, "The Road to Hiram's Hospital," *Victorian Studies* 5 (1961): 135–50. On the whistle-blowing Rochester headmaster, see Ralph Arnold, *The Whiston Matter* (London, 1961).

5. John Killham, *Tennyson and "The Princess": Reflections of an Age* (London, 1958), pp. 61–62.

6. Coral Lansbury, *Arcady in Australia: The Evocation of Australia in Nineteenth-Century English Literature* (Melbourne, 1970), pp. 157–58.

7. "Our Novels: The Sensational School" (cited chap. 1, n. 18), p. 417.

8. See W. L. Burn, *The Age of Equipose: A Study of the Mid-Victorian Generation* (New York, 1965), pp. 141–45.

9. C. P. Snow, "Dickens and the Public Service," *Dickens 1970*, ed. Michael Slater (New York, 1970), p. 138.

10. Trollope, *An Autobiography* (cited chap. 1, n. 42), p. 111.

11. Wendy Hinde, *Richard Cobden: A Victorian Outsider* (New Haven, 1987), pp. 248, 251.

12. An excellent three-volume collection of documents relating to Victorian feminism, with informative introductions, is *The Woman Question: Society and Literature in Britain and America, 1837–1883*, ed. Elizabeth K. Helsinger, Robin Lauterbach Sheets, and William Veeder (New York, 1983).

13. For the particulars of this landmark event, see *The Woman Question*, 1:104–25 (chap. 6). A full account of Mrs. Lynn Linton's long crusade against "fast women" is in Nancy Fox Anderson, *Woman Against Women in Victorian England: A Life of Eliza Lynn Linton* (Bloomington, Ind., 1987).

14. See Margaret Hewitt, "Anthony Trollope: Historian and Sociologist," *British Journal of Sociology* 14 (1963): 226–39.

Chapter 5: Lapses of Time

1. This paragraph has been adapted from my essay *"Past and Present*: Topicality as Technique," *Carlyle and His Contemporaries: Essays in Honor of Charles Richard Sanders*, ed. John Clubbe (Durham, N.C., 1976), p. 113.

2. David Cecil, *Early Victorian Novelists* (1934; reprint, London, 1935), p. 149.

3. Humphry House, *The Dickens World* (1941; reprint, London, 1960), p. 27; Tillotson, *Novels of the Eighteen-Forties* (cited chap. 1, n. 35), pp. 91–115.

4. E. S. Dallas, *Times*, 12 April 1859; *George Eliot: The Critical Heritage*, ed. David Carroll (New York, 1971), p. 80. Hereafter cited as *George Eliot: Critical Heritage*.

5. *Cornhill Magazine* 17 (1868): 310.

6. Tillotson, *Novels of the Eighteen-Forties*, pp. 110–11.

7. House, *The Dickens World*, pp. 21–22.

8. The first systematic consideration of this subject, to be followed by many others concentrating on individual topicalities, was that of Butt and Tillotson in *Dickens at Work* (cited chap. 1, n. 46), chap. 7. Susan Shatto's *The Companion to "Bleak House"* (London, 1988) is an exhaustive guide to the novel's allusions.

9. See Elizabeth Wiley, "Four Strange Cases," *Dickensian* 58 (1962): 120–

25, and E. Gaskell, "More About Spontaneous Combustion," *Dickensian* 69 (1973): 25–35.

10. House, *The Dickens World*, pp. 30, 31.

11. Pat Rogers, *Grub Street: Studies in a Subculture* (London, 1972), pp. 94, 98.

12. Patrick Brantlinger, *The Spirit of Reform: British Literature and Politics, 1832–1867* (Cambridge, Mass., 1977), pp. 63–64.

13. See Stanley H. Palmer, *Police and Protest in England and Ireland 1780–1850* (Cambridge, 1988), p. 437.

14. See Harvey Peter Sucksmith, "Sir Leicester Dedlock, Wat Tyler, and the Chartists: The Role of the Ironmaster in *Bleak House*," *Dickens Studies Annual* 4 (1975): 113–31.

15. See Wigley, *The Rise and Fall of the Victorian Sunday* (cited chap. 3, n. 9), from which most of the background facts in this passage have been derived.

16. The story is told in colorful detail in Martin, *Enter Rumour* (cited chap. 4, n. 4), chap. 2, and more recently in Mark Girouard, *The Return to Camelot: Chivalry and the English Gentleman* (New Haven, 1981), pp. 92–110.

17. See Killham, *Tennyson and "The Princess"* (cited chap. 4, n. 5), pp. 272–74.

18. The legend has been retold most recently in Jessica Mitford, *Grace Had an English Heart: The Story of Grace Darling, Heroine and Victorian Superstar* (London, 1988).

19. *Temple Bar* 29 (1870): 412.

20. *Oliver Twist*, ed. Kathleen Tillotson (Oxford, 1966), pp. 65n., 204.

21. *The George Eliot Letters*, ed. Gordon S. Haight (New Haven, 1954–56), 4:395.

22. H. H. Lancaster, "George Eliot's Novels," *North British Review* 45 (1866): 210.

23. See Margaret Harris, "The Topicality of *Beauchamp's Career*," REAL: *The Yearbook of Research in English and American Literature* 4 (1986): 135–94.

24. *History of England*, Everyman edition (1906), 1:270–71.

25. Ibid., 1:297–98.

26. *The Reminiscences and Recollections of Captain Gronow*, abridged by John Raymond (London, 1964), p. 51.

27. *Harriet Martineau's Autobiography* (London, 1877), 1:369.

28. House, *The Dickens World*, p. 27.

29. *Times*, 29 August 1855; *Thackeray: Critical Heritage*, p. 229.

30. Tillotson, *Novels of the Eighteen-Forties*, p. 104.

Chapter 6: New Ways of Riding and Writing

1. Sheppard, *London 1808–1870* (cited chap. 4, n. 3), p. 117.

2. Norman Gash, *Aristocracy and People: Britain 1815–1865* (London, 1979), p. 320.

3. There is a good account of the impact of railroads on the Victorian way of life in O. F. Christie, *The Transition from Aristocracy 1832–1867* (London, 1927), chap. 7, and Brightfield (1:241–51) collects numerous passages in fiction

describing railway travel. For railroads in Dickens, see House, *The Dickens World*, pp. 137–45.

4. *Eclectic and Congregational Review*, November 1865; *Dickens: Critical Heritage*, p. 459.

5. *Master Humphrey's Clock* (New Oxford Illustrated Dickens), 3:79–80.

6. I have taken this from my article, "Varieties of Readers' Response: The Case of *Dombey and Son*," *Yearbook of English Studies* 10 (1980): 86.

7. Brightfield, 4:440.

8. *Quarterly Review* 97 (1855): 356.

9. Details relating to the Victorian postal service are from Howard Robinson, *The British Post Office: A History* (Princeton, 1948). See also Asa Briggs, *Victorian Things* (Chicago, 1989), chap. 9.

10. *The Brownings' Correspondence*, ed. Philip Kelley and Ronald Hudson (Winfield, Kansas, 1984–), 7:93.

11. James Grant, *Sketches in London* (London, 1838), p. 2. (The whole chapter on "Begging Impostors" occupies pp. 1–48.)

12. See R. H. Super, *Trollope in the Post Office* (Ann Arbor, Mich., 1981).

Chapter 7: Consumer Goods

1. "The Dandy School," *Examiner*, 18 November 1827, pp. 721–22.

2. *Westminster Review* 15 (1831): 434–35.

3. John Carey, *Thackeray: Prodigal Genius* (London, 1977), pp. 61–62.

4. Gronow, *Reminiscences* (cited chap. 5, n. 26), pp. 112, 130–31.

5. Errol Sherson, *London's Lost Theatres of the Nineteenth Century* (London, 1925), pp. 121–22.

6. William T. Whitley, *Art in England, 1821–1837* (1930; reprint, New York, 1973), p. 274.

7. Elizabeth Aslin, *The Aesthetic Movement* (New York, 1969), p. 130.

8. Michael Sadleir, *Blessington-D'Orsay* (London, 1933), pp. 341–42, 354.

9. See Allison Adburgham, *Silver Fork Society: Fashionable Life and Literature from 1814 to 1840* (London, 1983), pp. 216–17.

10. Gash, *Aristocracy and People* (cited chap. 6, n. 2), p. 39.

11. Quoted in Adburgham, p. 216.

12. Quoted ibid., p. 221.

13. Brightfield, 3:15.

14. *Fors Clavigera*, vol. 3, letter 26 (February 1873), *Works of John Ruskin* (cited Introduction, n. 2), 27:474.

15. See Robert D. Horn, "Dickens and the Patent Bramah Lock," *Dickensian* 62 (1966): 100–105.

16. Gronow, *Reminiscences*, p. 194.

17. *Diary by E. B. B.: The Unpublished Diary of Elizabeth Barrett Browning, 1831–1832*, ed. Philip Kelley and Ronald Hudson (Athens, Ohio, 1969), pp. 2–3, 311–12.

18. George S. Layard, *Mrs. Lynn Linton: Her Life, Letters, and Opinions* (London, 1901), p. 47.

19. Quoted in William J. Carlton, "In the Blacking Warehouse," *Dickensian* 60 (1964): 11.

20. See Wilfred Partington, "The Blacking Laureate: The Identity of Mr. Slum, a Pioneer in Publicity," *Dickensian* 34 (1938): 199–202.

21. Darwin, *The Dickens Advertiser* (cited chap. 3, n. 4), quotes liberal extracts from Moses' advertisements (pages 140–55).

22. See Sarah Levitt, *Victorians Unbuttoned* (London, 1986), p. 11, and Sheila M. Smith, *The Other Nation* (Oxford, 1980), p. 172.

23. Brightfield, 2:461.

Chapter 8: The Favorite Vice of the Nineteenth Century

1. M. Dorothy George, *Hogarth to Cruikshank: Social Change in Graphic Satire* (New York, 1967), p. 172.

2. Ibid.

3. British Library, Surrey Zoo scrapbook 4.

4. On the gent, see Ellen Moers, *The Dandy: Brummell to Beerbohm* (London, 1960), pp. 215–18, and Mary Cowling, *The Artist as Anthropologist* (Cambridge, 1989), pp. 274–83.

5. Noel Gilroy Annan, *Leslie Stephen* (Cambridge, Mass., 1952), p. 14.

6. Mark Girouard, *The Victorian Country House*, new ed. (New Haven, 1979), p. 36.

7. Brightfield, 4:474.

8. Judith Wilt, *The Readable People of George Meredith* (Princeton, 1975), pp. 138–39.

9. The critical discussion of this point is summarized by Henry Auster, *Local Habitations: Regionalism in the Early Novels of George Eliot* (Cambridge, Mass., 1970), p. 139n.

10. Quoted in Michael Brander, *The Victorian Gentleman* (London, 1975), p. 90.

11. Brightfield, 4:474.

12. *The Letters of Charles Dickens*, ed. Madeline House et al. (Oxford, 1965–), 4:634–35.

13. Brightfield, 4:475.

14. Fred Kaplan, *Dickens: A Biography* (New York, 1988), p. 536.

15. Brightfield, 4:474.

16. Stanley Weintraub, *Victoria: An Intimate Biography* (New York, 1987), p. 470.

17. All in Brightfield, 4:477–78.

18. Weintraub, pp. 470, 509.

Chapter 9: The Way They Looked

1. G. A. Storey, *Sketches from Memory* (London, 1899), pp. 3–4.

2. Maria Edgeworth, *Letters from England 1813–1844*, ed. Christina Colvin (Oxford, 1971), p. 463.

3. Alison Adburgham, *Shops and Shopping* (London, 1964), p. 53; Ruskin to his father, 1 December 1853, *Works of John Ruskin* (cited Introduction, n. 2), 12:xxxv; *Effie in Venice*, ed. Mary Lutyens (London, 1965), p. 316; W. P. Frith, *My Autobiography and Reminiscences* (London, 1887), 2:44.

4. Edward Bulwer, *England and the English*, ed. Standish Meacham (Chicago, 1970), p. 73.

5. Quoted in Adburgham, *Silver Fork Society* (cited chap. 7, n. 9), pp. 130–31.

6. *The Letters of Anthony Trollope*, ed. N. John Hall (Stanford, Calif., 1983), 2:589–90.

7. Moers, *The Dandy* (cited chap. 8, n. 4), p. 215. On pages 218–19, Moers describes Dickens's personal metamorphosis from gent to swell, as his improved circumstances permitted.

8. Quoted in E. W. Bovill, *The England of Nimrod and Surtees 1815–1854* (London, 1959), p. 89.

9. Brightfield, 2:430.

10. C. Willett Cunnington and Phillis Cunnington, *Handbook of English Costume in the Nineteenth Century*, 2d ed. (London, 1966), p. 350.

11. Most of the material on the history of the crinoline in the following passage is from Adburgham, *Shops and Shopping*, pp. 91–93, 133–34, and Duncan Crow, *The Victorian Woman* (London, 1971), pp. 121–22.

12. Levitt, *Victorians Unbuttoned* (cited chap. 7, n. 22), p. 36; Crow, *The Victorian Woman*, p. 124.

13. Angus Easson, *Elizabeth Gaskell* (London, 1979), p. 30.

14. Adburgham, *Shops and Shopping*, p. 133.

15. Cunnington, *Handbook*, p. 480.

16. Elisabeth G. Gitter, "The Power of Women's Hair in the Victorian Imagination," *PMLA* 99 (1984): 936.

17. Quoted in Adburgham, *Shops and Shopping*, p. 175.

18. All in Brightfield, 2:376–77.

19. T. J. Edelstein, "'The Yellow-haired Fiend'—Rossetti and the Sensation Novel," *Library Chronicle of the University of Pennsylvania* 43 (1979): 180–93.

20. See Jeanne Fahnestock, "The Heroine of Irregular Features: Physiognomy and Conventions of Heroine Description," *Victorian Studies* 24 (1981): 325–50.

21. Bagehot, "Charles Dickens," *Literary Studies*, Everyman edition (1911), 2:187. (Originally in *National Review*, 1858.)

22. See Briggs, *Victorian Things* (cited chap. 6, n. 9), chap. 4, "Images of Fame."

23. "Novel-Reading," *Saturday Review* 23 (1867): 196.

Chapter 10: The Sense of Place

1. See George H. Ford, "Light in Darkness: Gas, Oil, and Tallow in Dickens's *Bleak House*," in *From Smollett to James: Studies in the Novel and Other Essays*

Presented to Edgar Johnson, ed. Samuel I. Mintz et al. (Charlottesville, Va., 1981), pp. 183–210, esp. 185–94.

2. Thea Holme, *The Carlyles at Home* (London, 1965), pp. 78, 147.

3. See Mary Burgan, "Heroines at the Piano: Women and Music in Nineteenth-Century Fiction," *Victorian Studies* 30 (1986): 51–76, and Arthur Loesser, *Men, Women, and Pianos: A Social History* (New York, 1954), sec. 3, chap. 10–23.

4. Maurice Willson Disher, *Victorian Song* (London, 1955), p. 149.

5. Quoted in *Human Documents of the Industrial Revolution in Britain*, ed. E. Royston Pike (London, 1955), p. 55.

6. John Prest, *The Industrial Revolution in Coventry* (Oxford, 1960), p. 75.

7. See Owen Knowles, "Veneering and the Age of Veneer," *Dickensian* (1985): 88–96.

8. Quoted in David Rubinstein, *Victorian Homes* (Newton Abbot, 1974), p. 83.

9. See Mrs. C. S. Peel, "Homes and Habits," *Early Victorian England*, ed. G. M. Young (London, 1934), 1:86–87.

10. Hermione Hobhouse, *Thomas Cubitt: Master Builder* (London, 1971), pp. 288, 460–62, 527.

11. Girouard, *The Victorian Country House* (cited chap. 8, n. 6), p. 22.

12. Elizabeth Burton, *The Pageant of Early Victorian England 1837–1861* (New York, 1972), pp. 61–63.

13. *Punch* 28 (1855): 179.

14. Brightfield, 1:418.

15. Quoted in Donald Olsen, *The Growth of Victorian London* (New York, 1976), p. 319.

Chapter 11: The Great Metropolis

1. Olsen, *The Growth of Victorian London* (cited chap. 10, n. 15), p. 311.

2. Masson, *British Novelists and Their Styles* (cited chap. 2, n. 1), pp. 244–45.

3. H. J. Dyos, "Greater and Greater London: Metropolis and Provinces in the Nineteenth and Twentieth Centuries," *Exploring the Urban Past*, ed. David Cannadine and David Reeder (Cambridge, 1985), p. 52.

4. There is a large body of commentary on the idea of the city, which in nineteenth-century British terms, especially in literature, mainly meant London, although Asa Briggs, *Victorian Cities* (1963; new ed. reprinted Harmondsworth, 1968), also deals with several provincial cities. Among the more general and conceptual treatments are John Henry Raleigh, "The Novel and the City," *Victorian Studies* 11 (1968): 291–328; Alexander Welsh, *The City of Dickens* (Oxford, 1971); Raymond Williams, *The Country and the City* (London, 1973); G. Robert Stange, "The Frightened Poets," and George Levine, "From 'Know-not-Where' to 'Nowhere,'" both in *The Victorian City: Images and Reality*, ed. H. J. Dyos and Michael Wolff (London, 1973), 2:475–94 and 495–516; and Thesing, *The London Muse* (cited chap. 1, n. 25). More specific discussions include Christopher Hibbert, "Dickens's London," *Charles Dickens 1812–1870: A Centennial Volume*, ed. E. W. F. Tomlin (New York, 1969), pp. 73–99; Olsen, *The Growth of Victorian*

London (n. 1 above); Philip Collins, "Dickens and London," *The Victorian City*, 2:537–57; Sheppard, *London 1808–1870* (cited chap. 4, n. 3); and F.S. Schwarzbach, *Dickens and the City* (London, 1979). Almost a hundred pages of descriptions of Victorian London are gathered from minor novels in Brightfield, 1:398–492.

5. *The Crown of Wild Olive* I, *Works of John Ruskin* (cited Introduction, n. 2), 18:406.

6. *Spectator*, 3 March 1838; *Dickens: Critical Heritage*, p. 70.

7. *Victorian Novelists and Publishers* (cited chap. 1, n. 43), p. 168.

8. For London urban iconography, see E. D. H. Johnson, "Victorian Artists and the Urban Milieu," and Michael Wolff and Celina Fox, "Pictures from the Magazines," both in *The Victorian City* (n. 4 above), 2:449–74, 559–82; and Bernard Adams, *London Illustrated* (London, 1983).

9. *Times* and *Morning Advertiser* both quoted in *The Victorian City*, 2:560–61.

10. Quoted in Sheppard, *London 1808–1870*, p. 135.

11. Quoted from Eliza Hessel, *True Womanhood*, ed. Joshua Priestley (1859), in *The Victorian City*, 2:551.

12. *Examiner*, 27 October 1839.

13. Olsen, *The Growth of Victorian London*, pp. 176–77.

14. See Philip Collins, *Trollope's London* (H. J. Dyos Memorial Lecture, Victorian Studies Centre, University of Leicester, 1982).

15. *Trollope: Critical Heritage*, p. 511.

16. "Retirement" (1782); *The Poems of William Cowper*, ed. John D. Baird and Charles Ryskamp (Oxford, 1980–), 1:390.

17. A particularly helpful source on the history of Bloomsbury and Belgravia is Hobhouse, *Thomas Cubitt* (cited chap. 10, n. 10). Most of the details in the present passage are drawn from it.

18. Ibid., p. 81.

19. Quoted in Olsen, *The Growth of Victorian London*, p. 129.

20. See Joan Stevens, "*Vanity Fair* and the London Skyline," *Costerus*, n.s. 2 (1974): 13–41.

21. Quoted in Schwarzbach, *Dickens and the City*, p. 195.

22. Quoted in Olsen, p. 296.

23. *Annual Register 1862*, Chronicle, p. 190.

24. See Leonard W. Cowie, "Exeter Hall," *History Today* 18 (1968): 390–97, and Norris Pope, *Dickens and Charity* (New York, 1978), pp. 1–3.

25. *The Letters of Lewis Carroll*, ed. Morton N. Cohen (New York, 1979), 1:205.

26. *Letters of Charles Dickens* (cited chap. 8, n. 12), 1:582.

27. The list of suicides from the Monument is derived from Henry B. Wheatley, *London Past and Present* (London, 1891), 2:559, and Walter Thornbury, *Old and New London* (London, 1873–78), 1:567–68. Further details are in Norris Pope, "A View from the Monument: A Note on *Martin Chuzzlewit*," *Dickens Quarterly* 4 (1987): 153–60.

28. *Annual Register 1842*, Chronicle, p. 139.

29. *George Eliot: Critical Heritage*, p. 108.

30. *A Victorian Art of Fiction*, ed. Olmsted (cited chap. 3, n. 20), p. 412.

31. Details of the spread of the underground railway system are from various publications of London Transport.

Chapter 12: Names in the Cultural News

1. *Spectator*, 6 January 1855; *Trollope: Critical Heritage*, pp. 32–33.

2. See Craig Howes, "Pendennis and the Controversy on the 'Dignity of Literature,'" *Nineteenth-Century Fiction* 41 (1986): 269–98, and Michael Lund, *Reading Thackeray* (Detroit, 1988), chap. 3.

3. The suggestion is Lund's, ibid.

4. *Letters and Private Papers of William Makepeace Thackeray*, ed. Gordon N. Ray (Cambridge, Mass., 1945–46), 1:412.

5. Richard D. Altick, *The English Common Reader* (Chicago, 1957), pp. 368–69.

6. Robinson, *Wilkie Collins* (cited chap. 3, n. 13), pp. 155–56.

7. *Spectator*, 16 April 1846, quoted in Sutherland's edition of *The Book of Snobs*, p. 217.

8. Brightfield, 2:304–5.

9. Ibid., 2:305.

10. Ibid., 2:306.

11. Ibid.

12. Ibid., 2:307.

13. Ibid., 2:304.

14. Harvey Peter Sucksmith, "Dickens Among the Pre-Raphaelites: Mr. Merdle and Holman Hunt's 'The Light of the World,'" *Dickensian* 72 (1976): 159–63.

Chapter 13: Popular Entertainments

1. Details of the various kinds of popular entertainments mentioned in this chapter are from my book, *The Shows of London* (Cambridge, Mass., 1978).

2. David Elliston Allen, *The Naturalist in Britain: A Social History* (Harmondsworth, 1978), pp. 132, 139–40.

3. John Forster, *Life of Charles Dickens* (cited chap. 1, n. 47).

4. See Albert Borowitz, *The Thurtell-Hunt Murder Case* (Baton Rouge, La., 1987).

5. See Jonathan Curling, *Janus Weathercock: The Life of Thomas Griffiths Wainewright* (London, 1938).

6. *Annual Register 1831*, Chronicle, p. 334.

7. James Grant, *Sketches in London* (cited chap. 6, n. 11), p. 37.

8. See also Judith Skelton Grant, "Italians with White Mice in *Middlemarch* and *Little Dorrit*," *English Language Notes* 16 (1979): 232–34, and Marilyn J. Kur-

ata, "Italians with White Mice Again: *Middlemarch* and *The Woman in White*," *English Language Notes* 22 (1985): 45–47.

9. See Ian Ousby, *Bloodhounds of Heaven: The Detective in English Fiction from Godwin to Doyle* (Cambridge, Mass., 1976), and Anthea Trodd, *Domestic Crime in the Victorian Novel* (London, 1989), chap. 2.

10. S. M. Ellis, *William Henry Ainsworth and His Friends* (London, 1911), 2:301.

Chapter 14: The Shady Side

1. David Cecil, *Melbourne* (Indianapolis, 1954), p. 185.

2. The fullest discussion of the dressmaker in Victorian life and literature is in Wanda Fraiken Neff, *Victorian Working Women: An Historical and Literary Study of Women in British Industries and Professions 1832–1850* (New York, 1929), chap. 4.

3. The *Morning Chronicle* articles are reprinted in *The Unknown Mayhew*, ed. Eileen Yeo and E. P. Thompson (New York, 1972), pp. 116–80.

4. See Ashby Bland Crowder, "A Source for Dickens's Sir Mulberry," *Papers on Language and Literature* 12 (1976): 105–9. There is an intimate account of the DeRos affair, by a longtime friend, in *The Greville Memoirs*, ed. Lytton Strachey and Roger Fulford (London, 1938), 3:312, 317, 318–43, 346–54.

5. *The Creevey Diaries*, ed. Sir Herbert Maxwell (London, 1904), 2:78.

6. See William C. DeVane, *A Browning Handbook*, 2d ed. (New York, 1955), pp. 386–89.

7. See Crow, *The Victorian Woman* (cited chap. 9, n. 11), pp. 315–19; James Laver, *Manners and Morals in the Age of Optimism* (New York, 1966), pp. 67–69; S. M. Ellis, *A Mid-Victorian Pepys: The Letters and Memoirs of Sir William Hardman*, rev. ed. (London, 1923), pp. 210–16; Angela Lambert, *Unquiet Souls* (London, 1984), pp. 40–43; Cyril Pearl, *The Girl with the Swansdown Seat* (Indianapolis, 1955), pp. 126–40; and Elizabeth Longford, *A Pilgrimage of Passion: The Life of Wilfrid Scawen Blunt* (London, 1979), esp. pp. 34–41.

8. See Crow, pp. 214–15, Ellis, pp. 191–98, and Pearl, pp. 140–43.

9. See William Roughead, "The Siren and the Sorceress; or, 'Beautiful Forever'," *Rascals Revived* (London, 1940), pp. 95–125; Kellow Chesney, *The Victorian Underworld* (New York, 1972), pp. 239–45; and George C. Boase, "Madame Rachel," *Notes and Queries* ser. 8, vol. 6 (1894): 322–24.

10. See William Llewellyn Parry-Jones, *The Trade in Lunacy: A Study of Private Madhouses in England in the 18th and 19th Centuries* (London, 1972), chap. 8.

11. See Smith, "Propaganda and Hard Facts . . . " (cited chap. 3, n. 30), and Malcolm Elwin, *Charles Reade: A Biography* (London, 1931), pp. 138, 166–67.

12. Quoted in Parry-Jones, p. 230.

13. See C. L. Cline, "Qualifications of the Medical Practitioners of *Middlemarch*," *Nineteenth-Century Literary Perspectives: Essays in Honor of Lionel Stevenson*, ed. Clyde de L. Ryals (Durham, N.C., 1974), pp. 271–81.

14. On Morison, see Darwin, *The Dickens Advertiser* (cited chap. 3, n. 4), pp. 179–90; F. B. Smith, *The People's Health 1830–1910* (New York, 1979), pp. 343–

44; Burton, *The Pageant of Early Victorian England* (cited chap. 10, n. 13), pp. 208–10; *Annual Register 1834*, Chronicle, pp. 305–9; *Annual Register 1836*, Chronicle, pp. 38–45.

15. There is a considerable, though scattered, literature on St. John Long; a monograph might well be devoted to him. See, for example, *The Complete Newgate Calendar*, ed. G. T. Crook (London, 1926), 5:237–41; *The Chronicles of Crime; or, The New Newgate Calendar*, ed. Camden Pelham (London, 1886), 2:217–28; and Eric Jameson, *The Natural History of Quackery* (Springfield, Ill., 1961), pp. 66–74.

16. See John Burnett, *Plenty and Want: A Social History of Diet in England from 1815 to the Present Day* (London, 1966), chap. 5.

Chapter 15: Real People, More or Less

1. [Richard Ford], "Apsley House," *Quarterly Review* 92 (1853): 447.

2. *Works of Thomas Love Peacock* (cited chap. 1, n. 12), 4:13 (separately paged).

3. George Otto Travelyan, *The Life and Letters of Lord Macaulay*, World's Classics edition (1961), 1:174.

4. Robert L. Patten, "Portraits of Pott: Lord Brougham and *The Pickwick Papers*," *Dickensian* 66 (1970): 205–24.

5. Margaret Oliphant, *Annals of a Publishing House: William Blackwood and His Sons* (New York, 1897), 2:224.

6. Henry James, *Partial Portraits* (London, 1888), p. 115.

7. Wolff, *Gains and Losses* (cited chap. 3, n. 13), p. 5.

8. Quoted in Vineta Colby, *Yesterday's Woman* (Princeton, 1974), pp. 64–65.

9. James Grant, *Portraits of Public Characters* (London, 1841), 2:303.

10. Ibid., 2:275–77.

11. Quoted in Colby, *Yesterday's Woman*, p. 54.

12. Whitwell Elwin, *Some XVIII Century Men of Letters*, ed. Warwick Elwin (London, 1902), 1:179.

13. See Rosa, *The Silver Fork School* (cited chap. 1, n. 37), pp. 105–6. This monograph has been valuably supplemented by Adburgham, *Silver Fork Society* (cited chap. 7, n. 9).

14. See Robert Blake, *Disraeli* (London, 1966), pp. 35–37.

15. Adburgham, *Silver Fork Society*, p. 80.

16. The fullest source on Harriot Mellon is the entry for her in *A Biographical Dictionary of Actors, Actresses, [etc.] . . . in London, 1660–1800*, ed. Philip H. Highfill, Jr., et al. (Carbondale, Ill., 1973–), 10:169–81. See also Charles E. Pearce, *The Jolly Duchess: Harriot Mellon, Afterwards Mrs. Coutts and the Duchess of St. Albans* (London, 1915).

17. John Gibson Lockhart, *Memoirs of the Life of Sir Walter Scott, Bart.* (Boston, 1901), 8:54–57. (Chap. 64.)

18. See Anne Mathews, "Ennobled Actresses," *Bentley's Miscellany* 17 (1845): 594–603; 18 (1845): 54–61, 249–55, 601–12.

19. *The Greville Memoirs* (cited chap. 14, n. 4), 5:19–21.

20. Robert A. Colby, *Thackeray's Canvass of Humanity* (Columbus, Ohio, 1979), p. 270, n. 38.

21. Blake, *Disraeli*, p. 215. There is a good summary of Thackeray's use of the Hertford/Steyne figure in Geoffrey and Kathleen Tillotson's Riverside edition of the novel, pp. xxxii–xxxiii.

22. See James D. Merritt, "The Novelist St. Barbe in Disraeli's *Endymion*: Revenge on Whom?," *Nineteenth-Century Fiction* 23 (1968): 85–88.

23. See J. J. Tobias, *Prince of Fences: The Life and Crimes of Ikey Solomons* (London, 1974), pp. 147–50.

24. See Philip Collins, *Dickens and Crime* (1962; reprint, Bloomington, Ind., 1968), pp. 80–81.

25. See ibid., pp. 183–88.

26. See especially J. R. Dinwiddy, "Who's Who in Trollope's Political Novels," *Nineteenth-Century Fiction* 22 (1967): 31–46; A. O. J. Cockshut, *Anthony Trollope: A Critical Study* (New York, 1968), pp. 241–49; and—the fullest discussion—John Halperin, *Trollope and Politics: A Study of the Pallisers and Others* (New York, 1977), pp. 72–83, 271–77.

27. P. D. Edwards, *Anthony Trollope* (Hassocks, Sussex, 1978), p. 141.

28. The most reliable source on Hudson is Martin, *Enter Rumour* (cited chap. 4, n. 4), chap. 4, from which most of the details in the following passage are derived.

29. See Michael Slater, *The Composition and Monthly Publication of "Nicholas Nickleby"* (Menston, Yorkshire, 1973), pp. 30–32.

30. This episode is seen most clearly in the letters and accompanying annotations in *Letters of Charles Dickens* (cited chap. 8, n. 12), 5:674–77.

31. See Lionel Stevenson, "Who Was Mr. Turveydrop?", *Dickensian* 44 (1948): 39–41.

32. See Russell Fraser, "A Charles Dickens Original," *Nineteenth-Century Fiction* 9 (1955): 301–7; Martin Meisel, "Miss Havisham Brought to Book," *PMLA* 81 (1966): 278–85; Harry Stone, "Dickens' Woman in White," *Victorian Newsletter*, no. 33 (1968): 5–8; and Stanley Friedman, "Another Possible Source for Dickens' Miss Havisham," *Victorian Newsletter*, no. 39 (1971): 24–25.

33. See George J. Worth, "The Genesis of Jo the Crossing-Sweeper," *Journal of English and Germanic Philology* 60 (1961): 44–47; Trevor Blount, "Poor Jo, Education, and the Problem of Juvenile Delinquency in Dickens' *Bleak House*," *Modern Philology* 62 (1965): 325–39; and K. J. Fielding and Alec W. Brice, "Charles Dickens on 'The Exclusion of Evidence,'" *Dickensian* 64 (1968): 131–40; 65 (1969): 35–41.

34. See Myron F. Brightfield, *Theodore Hook and His Novels* (Cambridge, Mass., 1928), passim.

35. See Richard D. Altick, "Harold Skimpole Revisited," in *The Life and Times of Leigh Hunt . . .* (Iowa City, Iowa, 1985), pp. 1–15, and Kaplan, *Dickens: A Biography* (cited chap. 8, n. 14), pp. 287, 315–16.

36. See James A. Davies, "Forster and Dickens: The Making of Podsnap," *Dickensian* 70 (1974): 145–58.

37. *The Heart of Charles Dickens, as Revealed in His Letters to Angela Burdett-Coutts*, ed. Edgar Johnson (New York, 1952), p. 166.

38. See Kathleen Tillotson, "Dickens's Count Smorltork," *Times Literary Supplement*, 22 November 1957, p. 712.

39. See Philip Collins, *Dickens and Education* (1963; reprint, London, 1965), pp. 156–59, and K. J. Fielding, "Charles Dickens and the Department of Practical Art," *Modern Language Review* 48 (1953): 270–77.

40. *The Annotated Dickens*, ed. Edward Guiliano and Philip Collins (New York, 1986), 1:896–97.

41. For a detailed comparison of Diana Warwick and Caroline Norton and their respective stories, see Alice Acland, *Caroline Norton* (London, 1948), pp. 168–82.

42. "Mr. D'Israeli's *Tancred*: The Emancipation of the Jews," *Edinburgh Review* 86 (1847): 140.

Chapter 16: Money and Occupations

1. See, for example, Edward Copeland, "Jane Austen and the Consumer Revolution," *The Jane Austen Companion*, ed. J. David Grey et al. (New York, 1986), pp. 77–92.

2. House, *The Dickens World* (cited chap. 5, n. 3), p. 58.

3. Trollope, *London Tradesmen*, ed. Michael Sadleir (London, 1927), p. 86.

4. See my article, "Education, Print, and Paper in *Our Mutual Friend*," *Nineteenth-Century Literary Perspectives* (cited chap. 14, n. 13), pp. 238–41.

Chapter 17: Speculation and Bankruptcy

1. For the background of this subject, see Norman Russell, *The Novelist and Mammon: Literary Responses to the World of Commerce in the Nineteenth Century* (Oxford, 1986), and Barbara Weiss, *The Hell of the English: Bankruptcy and the Victorian Novel* (Lewisburg, Pa., 1986). Both books appeared after the present chapter was drafted; I have taken from them a few additional details not included in that earlier version. See also John R. Reed, "A Friend to Mammon: Speculation in Victorian Literature," *Victorian Studies* 27 (1984): 179–202, and Cotsell, "The Book of Insolvent Fates" (cited chap. 3, n. 6).

2. John McVeagh, *Tradefull Merchants: The Portrayal of the Capitalist in Literature* (London, 1981), pp. 205–6n.

3. "Civilization: Signs of the Times," *Westminster Review* 25 (1836): 15.

4. House, *The Dickens World*, p. 58.

5. See Michael Steig, "*Dombey and Son* and the Railway Panic of 1845," *Dickensian* 67 (1971): 145–48.

6. *Annual Register 1846*, Chronicle, p. 12.

7. This episode was revealed in Rosa, *The Silver-Fork School* (cited chap. 1, n. 37), pp. 121–23.

8. Russell, *The Novelist and Mammon*, p. 86.

9. *Letters of Charles Dickens* (cited chap. 8, n. 12), 5:530.

10. See Sadleir, *Blessington-D'Orsay* (cited chap. 7, n. 8), pp. 343–45.
11. *Letters and Private Papers of W. M. Thackeray* (cited chap. 12, n. 4), 2:532.

Chapter 18: The Free and Independent: I

1. Historical details in this and the following chapter have been derived from Norman Gash, *Politics in the Age of Peel: A Study in the Technique of Parliamentary Representation 1830–1850*, 2d ed. (Hassocks, Sussex, 1977); Michael Brock, *The Great Reform Act* (London, 1973); Cornelius O'Leary, *The Elimination of Corrupt Practices in British Elections 1868–1911* (Oxford, 1962), chap. 1; H. K. Cook, *The Free and Independent Voter* (London, 1949); Charles Seymour, *Electoral Reform in England and Wales* (New Haven, 1915), esp. chaps. 7–8; G. R. Kesteven, *The Triumph of Reform, 1832* (London, 1967); O. F. Christie, *The Transition from Aristocracy 1832–1867* (London, 1927); Joseph Grego, *A History of Parliamentary Elections and Electioneering from the Stuarts to Queen Victoria* (1892; reprint, Detroit, 1974). H. G. Nicholas, *To the Hustings: Election Scenes from English Fiction* (London, 1956) is a useful anthology with a perceptive introduction.
2. *Works of Thomas Love Peacock* (cited chap. 1, n. 12), 2:239.
3. Leonard Cooper, *R. S. Surtees* (London, 1952), p. 68.
4. Trollope, *Autobiography* (cited chap. 1, n. 42), pp. 300–301.
5. On Meredith's experience of practical politics, see J. S. Stone, *George Meredith's Politics as Seen in His Life, Friendships, and Works* (Port Credit, Ontario, 1986), and Harris, "The Topicality of *Beauchamp's Career*" (cited chap. 5, n. 23).

Chapter 19: The Free and Independent: II

1. *The Letters of Sydney Smith*, ed. Nowell C. Smith (Oxford, 1953), 2:522.
2. See Angus Macintyre, *The Liberator: Daniel O'Connell and the Irish Party* (London, 1965), pp. 123–25, 293–95.
3. On Trollope's traumatic experience at Beverley, see Halperin, *Trollope and Politics* (cited chap. 15, n. 26), pp. 112–26, and Rowland H. McMaster, *Trollope and the Law* (London, 1986).
4. Trollope, *Autobiography*, pp. 298–300.
5. Halperin, p. 115.
6. Gash, *Politics in the Age of Peel* (cited chap. 18, n. 1), pp. xxiii, 178.
7. Grego, *History of Parliamentary Elections* (cited chap. 18, n. 1), pp. 270–71.
8. Ibid., p. 292.
9. Gash, p. 149.
10. Nicholas, *To the Hustings* (cited chap. 18, n. 1), p. xii.

Chapter 20: Language

1. The following passage is from my article, "Victorian Readers and the Sense of the Present," *Midway* [University of Chicago] 10 (1970): 104–15.

2. Sidney and Beatrice Webb, *The History of Trade Unionism*, rev. ed. (London, 1920), p. 260n.

3. Richard Ford, review of *Oliver Twist*, *Quarterly Review* 64 (1839): 92.

4. Review of *Nicholas Nickleby*, *Spectator*, 31 March 1838; *Dickens: Critical Heritage*, p. 70.

5. Thomas Cleghorn, "Writings of Charles Dickens," *North British Review* 3 (1845): 83.

6. Richard H. Horne, *A New Spirit of the Age* (London, 1844), 1:56.

7. "Charles Dickens and *David Copperfield*," *Fraser's Magazine* 42 (1850): 699.

8. *North British Review* 15 (1851): 62.

9. *Quarterly Review* 97 (1855): 358.

10. Quoted in Amy Cruse, *The Victorians and Their Reading* (1955; reprint, Boston, 1962), p. 354.

11. *Spectator*, 3 January 1874; *Trollope: Critical Heritage*, pp. 378–79.

12. Juliet McMaster, *Dickens the Designer* (Totowa, N.J., 1978), p. 89.

13. Michael Irwin, *Picturing: Description and Illusion in the Nineteenth-Century Novel* (London, 1979), p. 57.

14. See Michael Curtin, *Propriety and Position: A Study of Victorian Manners* (New York, 1987).

15. *Spectator*, 18 May 1872; David Skilton, *Anthony Trollope and His Contemporaries* (New York, 1972), p. 115.

16. *Spectator*, 4 March 1865; *Trollope: Critical Heritage*, p. 223.

17. Irwin, *Picturing*, p. 57.

Conclusion

1. *Blackwood's Magazine* 58 (1845): 353.

2. There is a good summary of this development in Richard Stang, *The Theory of the Novel in England 1850–1870* (New York, 1959), pt. 4 ("Mid-Victorian Realism: Real Toads in Real Gardens").

3. Masson, *British Novelists and Their Styles* (cited chap. 2, n. 1), pp. 265–66.

4. *Fortnightly Review* 1 (1865): 187, 588, 589.

5. *Spectator*, 24 November 1838; *Dickens: Critical Heritage*, p. 43.

6. *Spectator*, 31 March 1839; *Dickens: Critical Heritage*, p. 70.

7. "*Pendennis* and *Copperfield*: Thackeray and Dickens," *North British Review* 15 (1851): 65–66.

8. "The License of Modern Novelists" (cited chap. 3, n. 23), p. 127.

9. "Modern Novelists: Charles Dickens," *Westminster Review* 82 (1864): 438.

10. "W. M. Thackeray, Artist and Moralist" (cited Introduction, n. 1), p. 125.

11. *Trollope: Critical Heritage*, p. 188.

12. *The Leader*, 28 May 1858, quoted in Skilton, *Anthony Trollope and His Contemporaries* (cited chap. 20, n. 15), p. 10.

INDEX

Boldface page numbers indicate the chief discussion of the subject. *Italic* page numbers indicate the presence of the subject in an illustration or its caption.

Subjects

Aberdeen, Lord, 579n, 620n, 724
Abinger, Lord, 598
Accum, Friedrich Christian, 562
actresses marrying titles and / or wealth, 594–95
Adelaide, Queen, 62n
Adelaide Gallery, 335, 498
adulteration, 80, **562–68**
advertising: of auctions, 666–67, 760; of consumer goods, 441, 549, 555, 636, 683; George Robins's style of, 584–87; in serialized novels, 64–67, 226–38
aesthetic movement, 33
Agassiz, Jean Louis, 782
Agnew, Sir Andrew, 142
agriculture, 363–64
Ainsworth, William Harrison, 74, 132, 520, 531–32, 569
Albert, Prince, 60, 249, 274, *420*, 427n, 430, 573–74
Alison, Archibald, 799
All the Year Round, 70, 386–87
Alvanley, Lord, 221n
Amberley, Lord, 148
anachronisms, 97n, 170, 178–80, 305, 577
Anglesey, Marquis of, 553
animals in zoo, 500
"Anonyma." *See* "Skittles"
Anti-Corn Law League, 232, 685, 703n.
    See also Corn Laws
Apperley, G. L. ("Nimrod"), 290

aquarium craze, 500–501
architecture: of churches, 358–60; of country houses, 361–63; in suburbs, 360
Arnold, Matthew, 12, 394n, 416–17, 551n
artists, allusions to, 480–92
Ashley, Lord, *144*
Astley's Royal Amphitheatre, 475–77, 509–11
atmospheric railway, 187n
Attwood, Thomas, 743n
Auber, Daniel François, 469, 512
auburn hair. *See* red hair
auctions, 664–66. *See also* Robins, George
Austen, Jane, 40–41, 345, 350, 397, 446, 461
Austin, Alfred, 21, 116, 156, 537, 545
Australia, emigration to, 113–17
authors, rights of, 455–57, 659
automatons, 494
Aytoun, William Edmonstoune, 31–32, 238n

Bab Ballads (Gilbert), 32
"Baboon Lady, The," 508–9
Bacon, Francis, 107
Bage, Robert, 34, 50
Bagehot, Walter, 330, 374
bailiffs in possession, 660, 664–65
Balfe, Michael William, 467
Ballantine, Serjeant William, 524–25

Stephen, Leslie, 132, 248
Stephens, Frederic George, 30
Sterne, Laurence, 6
Stevens, Joan, 404n
Stewart, J. I. M., 180
Stone, Elizabeth, 527
Storey, G. A., 275
Storr and Mortimer (jewelers), 215, 218
Stowe, Harriet Beecher, 60n
Stowe House, sale of, 662
Stowell, Lord, 494
Strachan, Lady, 596
Strahan, Paul, and Bates (investment house), 609
Stultz, George (tailor), 239, **275–82**, 285, 287, 290, 582
Sucksmith, Harvey, 491–92
Summerson, Sir John, 414
Sunday observance. *See* Sabbatarianism
Surrey Zoological Gardens, 244, 475, 512
Surtees, Robert Smith, 191–92, 561n; *Ask Mamma*, 55, 77; *Handley Cross*, *311*, *Hillingdon Hall*, 55, *691*, *704*; *Mr. Facey Romford's Hounds*, 54; *Mr. Sponge's Sporting Tour*, 61, 63, *250*; *Plain or Ringlets?*, 55, *158*. Personal references: 54–55, 290–91, 350, 363, 364, 457–58, 564n, 676n, 685
Sussex, Duke of, 248
Sutherland, John, 386–87, 635n
Swan and Edgar (retail merchants), 219–20, 417
sweatshops, 94, 237
swells, 244, *245*, 248, 258, *286*, 287
Swinburne, Algernon Charles, 30, 58, 252n, 259, 327n

Taglioni, Marie, 474
tailors, 282–85
Talbot, William Henry Fox, 335
Tancred, Thomas, 89
Tattersall's horse auction house, 31
taverns. *See* inns
telegraph, 210–13; in metaphors, 787
Tenniel, John, 74, *310*, 768n
Tennyson, Alfred, 26, 29, 30, 241, 252, 350, 356n, 458, 459, 461, 515; in literary allusions, 450, 451–54; topicalities in poems of, 27–28, 783n; "Locksley

Hall," 385–86, 783n; "Maud," 27, 422, 638, 653; *The Princess*, 27, 108, 126, 151, 452
Thackeray, Anne (*The Village on the Cliff*), 489
Thackeray, William Makepeace, 2, 206, 355n, 494, 518, 782n, 803; and anachronisms, 178–79; on art and artists, 485–86; on authors' rights, 457, 659; and blue books, 91–92; brand and trade names, his use of, 215–16, 218–19, 222–23, 228–29, 232, 237; as candidate for Parliament, 729n; carriages in his novels, 366; distancing, 135–36; fortune, loss of, 658, 660; and George Robins, 586–89; and Gore House sale, 662, 664; and historical fiction, 39; as journalist, 53; London localities in, 382–83, 394–95, 399–400, 402–3, 404–5, 407–10; and men's clothing, 278–79, 281–82, 287–90, 303–4; Norton *versus* Melbourne trial, 148–50; nostalgia, 166–67, 170–71, 181–82; on novels with a purpose, 50; and opera, 469–72; originals, his use of, 590; railway travel in novels, 183, 366; rapport with his readers, 160; and red hair, 317–18, 319–20, 325–26, 327; serialization of his novels, 62–63, 67–68; and "seriousness," 762–64; and silver fork fiction, 35, 215; slang, his use of, 771; and smoking, 249, 253–56, 257, 262, 264–65, 266, 268, 269; then-and-now technique, 166–67, 183–85; and Vauxhall Gardens, 431–36; and the Wellington statue, 408, *410*, *411*; and women's dress, 300; *The Newcomes*, 62–63, *109*, *346*, *477*, *661*, *763*; *Our Street*, *663*; *Pendennis*, *435*, *436*, *464*; "Punch's Prize Novelists," 455; "The Snobs of England," 53, 63n, 67–68; *Vanity Fair*, 180, 181–82, *243*, *254*, 337–38, 408, *410*, 433, 457–58, *471*, *588*, *599*
Thames, pollution of, *71*, 417–19, *420*, *421*
Thames Tunnel, 496–97
theatre, allusions to, 475–80
Thelwall, John, 284

Sources of Illustrative Materials